# PC Upgrade and
# Repair Bible,
# 3rd Edition

# PC Upgrade and Repair Bible, 3rd Edition

**Barry Press and Marcia Press**

IDG Books Worldwide, Inc.
An International Data Group Company

Foster City, CA ✦ Chicago, IL ✦ Indianapolis, IN ✦ New York, NY

**PC Upgrade and Repair Bible, 3rd Edition**

Published by
IDG Books Worldwide, Inc.
An International Data Group Company
919 E. Hillsdale Blvd., Suite 400
Foster City, CA 94404
www.idgbooks.com (IDG Books Worldwide Web site)

ISBN: 0-7645-3357-6

Printed in the United States of America

10 9 8 7 6 5 4 3

1P/QY/RR/ZZ/FC

Distributed in the United States by IDG Books Worldwide, Inc.

Distributed by CDG Books Canada Inc. for Canada; by Transworld Publishers Limited in the United Kingdom; by IDG Norge Books for Norway; by IDG Sweden Books for Sweden; by IDG Books Australia Publishing Corporation Pty. Ltd. for Australia and New Zealand; by TransQuest Publishers Pte Ltd. for Singapore, Malaysia, Thailand, Indonesia, and Hong Kong; by Gotop Information Inc. for Taiwan; by ICG Muse, Inc. for Japan; by Intersoft for South Africa; by Eyrolles for France; by International Thomson Publishing for Germany, Austria and Switzerland; by Distribuidora Cuspide for Argentina; by LR International for Brazil; by Galileo Libros for Chile; by Ediciones ZETA S.C.R. Ltda. for Peru; by WS Computer Publishing Corporation, Inc., for the Philippines; by Contemporanea de Ediciones for Venezuela; by Express Computer Distributors for the Caribbean and West Indies; by Micronesia Media Distributor, Inc. for Micronesia; by Chips Computadoras S.A. de C.V. for Mexico; by Editorial Norma de Panama S.A. for Panama; by American Bookshops for Finland.

For general information on IDG Books Worldwide's books in the U.S., please call our Consumer Customer Service department at 800-762-2974. For reseller information, including discounts and premium sales, please call our Reseller Customer Service department at 800-434-3422.

For information on where to purchase IDG Books Worldwide's books outside the U.S., please contact our International Sales department at 317-596-5530 or fax 317-596-5692.

For consumer information on foreign language translations, please contact our Customer Service department at 800-434-3422, fax 317-596-5692, or e-mail rights@idgbooks.com.

For information on licensing foreign or domestic rights, please phone +1-650-655-3109.

For sales inquiries and special prices for bulk quantities, please contact our Sales department at 650-655-3200 or write to the address above.

For information on using IDG Books Worldwide's books in the classroom or for ordering examination copies, please contact our Educational Sales department at 800-434-2086 or fax 317-596-5499.

For press review copies, author interviews, or other publicity information, please contact our Public Relations department at 650-655-3000 or fax 650-655-3299.

For authorization to photocopy items for corporate, personal, or educational use, please contact Copyright Clearance Center, 222 Rosewood Drive, Danvers, MA 01923, or fax 978-750-4470.

**Library of Congress Cataloging-in-Publication Data**

Press, Barry.

PC upgrade and repair bible/Berry Press and Marcia PRESS.—3rd ed.

p. cm.

ISBN 0-7645-3357-6 (alk. paper)

1. Microcomputers—Upgrading. 2. Microcomputing—Repairing.

I. Press, Marica. II. Title.

TK7887.P74 1999                                    99-38351

621.39'16—dc21                                     CIP

is a registered trademark or trademark under exclusive license to IDG Books Worldwide, Inc. from International Data Group, Inc. in the United States and/or other countries.

# ABOUT IDG BOOKS WORLDWIDE

Welcome to the world of IDG Books Worldwide.

IDG Books Worldwide, Inc., is a subsidiary of International Data Group, the world's largest publisher of computer-related information and the leading global provider of information services on information technology. IDG was founded more than 30 years ago by Patrick J. McGovern and now employs more than 9,000 people worldwide. IDG publishes more than 290 computer publications in over 75 countries. More than 90 million people read one or more IDG publications each month.

Launched in 1990, IDG Books Worldwide is today the #1 publisher of best-selling computer books in the United States. We are proud to have received eight awards from the Computer Press Association in recognition of editorial excellence and three from Computer Currents' First Annual Readers' Choice Awards. Our best-selling ...*For Dummies*® series has more than 50 million copies in print with translations in 31 languages. IDG Books Worldwide, through a joint venture with IDG's Hi-Tech Beijing, became the first U.S. publisher to publish a computer book in the People's Republic of China. In record time, IDG Books Worldwide has become the first choice for millions of readers around the world who want to learn how to better manage their businesses.

Our mission is simple: Every one of our books is designed to bring extra value and skill-building instructions to the reader. Our books are written by experts who understand and care about our readers. The knowledge base of our editorial staff comes from years of experience in publishing, education, and journalism — experience we use to produce books to carry us into the new millennium. In short, we care about books, so we attract the best people. We devote special attention to details such as audience, interior design, use of icons, and illustrations. And because we use an efficient process of authoring, editing, and desktop publishing our books electronically, we can spend more time ensuring superior content and less time on the technicalities of making books.

You can count on our commitment to deliver high-quality books at competitive prices on topics you want to read about. At IDG Books Worldwide, we continue in the IDG tradition of delivering quality for more than 30 years. You'll find no better book on a subject than one from IDG Books Worldwide.

John Kilcullen
Chairman and CEO
IDG Books Worldwide, Inc.

Steven Berkowitz
President and Publisher
IDG Books Worldwide, Inc.

**WINNER**

*Eighth Annual
Computer Press
Awards ≥1992*

**WINNER**

*Ninth Annual
Computer Press
Awards ≥1993*

**WINNER**

*Tenth Annual
Computer Press
Awards ≥1994*

**WINNER**

*Eleventh Annual
Computer Press
Awards ≥1995*

IDG is the world's leading IT media, research and exposition company. Founded in 1964, IDG had 1997 revenues of $2.05 billion and has more than 9,000 employees worldwide. IDG offers the widest range of media options that reach IT buyers in 75 countries representing 95% of worldwide IT spending. IDG's diverse product and services portfolio spans six key areas including print publishing, online publishing, expositions and conferences, market research, education and training, and global marketing services. More than 90 million people read one or more of IDG's 290 magazines and newspapers, including IDG's leading global brands — Computerworld, PC World, Network World, Macworld and the Channel World family of publications. IDG Books Worldwide is one of the fastest-growing computer book publishers in the world, with more than 700 titles in 36 languages. The "...For Dummies®" series alone has more than 50 million copies in print. IDG offers online users the largest network of technology-specific Web sites around the world through IDG.net (http://www.idg.net), which comprises more than 225 targeted Web sites in 55 countries worldwide. International Data Corporation (IDC) is the world's largest provider of information technology data, analysis and consulting, with research centers in over 41 countries and more than 400 research analysts worldwide. IDG World Expo is a leading producer of more than 168 globally branded conferences and expositions in 35 countries including E3 (Electronic Entertainment Expo), Macworld Expo, ComNet, Windows World Expo, ICE (Internet Commerce Expo), Agenda, DEMO, and Spotlight. IDG's training subsidiary, ExecuTrain, is the world's largest computer training company, with more than 230 locations worldwide and 785 training courses. IDG Marketing Services helps industry-leading IT companies build international brand recognition by developing global integrated marketing programs via IDG's print, online and exposition products worldwide. Further information about the company can be found at www.idg.com.                                    1/24/99

# Credits

**Acquisitions Editors**
Martine Edwards
Ed Adams

**Development Editor**
Katharine Dvorak

**Technical Editor**
Bill Karow

**Copy Editors**
Robert Campbell
Timothy J. Borek

**Project Coordinator**
Linda Marousek

**Graphics and
Production Specialists**
Dina F Quan
Jude Levinson
Mario Amador
Ramses Ramirez

**Quality Control Specialist**
Chris Weisbart

**Proofreading and Indexing**
York Production Services

**Cover Art**
Peter Kowaleszyn
Murder By Design/Image Poetry

# About the Authors

**Barry Press** has designed leading-edge computer hardware, software, and networks for over 25 years, including a unique cable television modem, campuswide ATM networks, a desktop computer capable of analyzing adverse drug interactions, and an artificial intelligence planning system. He has programmed Windows since Version 1.0 and has taught as an adjunct professor of computer science at the University of Southern California. He is the author of *PC Upgrade and Repair Bible, Professional Edition and Teach Yourself PCs.*

**Marcia Press** worked in public accounting as a tax CPA for what was then one of the Big Eight, moving later to her own practice. She handles the administrative part of the work for the Press' computer books — the tracking, calls, follow-ups, and research — and does the sanity checks on their initial drafts. She's a fan of good wine, gardening, reading, and shopping, and is a serious gourmet cook.

*This book is dedicated to the storytellers for the future, the likes of Isaac Asimov, Arthur Clarke, Robert Heinlein, Larry Niven, and Charles Sheffield.*

*From visions of the future come inspiration to make it so.*

# Preface

The *PC Upgrade and Repair Bible* will tell you about the computer hardware you need to run today's personal computer operating systems and Internet software, and help you to figure out what configuration of hardware is best for your computing needs. The information inside helps you evaluate what you need to run Windows 95 or 98, Windows NT or Windows 2000, or UNIX; it also helps you evaluate what you need to access the Internet.

Tuning your hardware configuration using the ideas in this book will help you get more out of your computer. Windows 95 and 98, Windows NT, and Windows 2000 (the four of which we'll collectively call *Windows*) can do more for you than their predecessors, but they place greater demands on your computer. These operating systems manage the resources of your computer better, and they run 32-bit programs (see the sidebar "32 whats?") more efficiently than Windows 3.1 and Windows for Workgroups 3.11. Similarly, UNIX (be it Linux, FreeBSD, or another version) can be a wonderfully low-cost and stable network platform, but the resources it needs to respond well to an onslaught of network traffic can be large, too.

We have mostly ignored Windows 3.1 and Windows for Workgroups 3.11 in this book. Even though you can still use those versions and programs built for them, the enormous benefits the newer versions of Windows offer are enough that using the old ones is unproductive. Unless we specify Windows 3.1 or Windows for Workgroups 3.11, when we refer to "Windows" in this book, we're talking about Windows 95, 98, NT, or 2000.

Whether you have thousands of machines on a corporate network, a few machines in a small office, or a machine at home shared between work and family, a computer sized for what you do will give you the power you need to get your work done. Using the latest operating systems, you can run more programs at once, access a greater variety of networks, and use new kinds of hardware to the fullest extent. For most users, this increased capability will expand what you do with your computer, which in turn may require more hardware than before. Doing more with your computer makes you more productive, but makes the computer hardware work harder.

## Is This Book for You?

This book provides the information you need to make effective hardware choices, including coverage of system components, upgrades, and new systems. It covers hardware for emerging technologies, including desktop video conferencing, ISDN

(Integrated Services Digital Network) and ADSL (Asymmetric Digital Subscriber Line), and local area networks (LANs) for business and home.

This is a book for people who will be opening up and working on their computers, and for people who want to understand what goes on inside a computer. You'll see what's inside, what the pieces do, how they work, and how they're connected. You'll learn what determines the performance of your computer, what your options are for more performance, and how to add new capabilities to your computer. This book is for you if you want to

+ Evaluate the suitability of upgrading an existing computer

+ Determine the upgrades needed to make an underpowered machine suitable for your specific purposes

+ Specify an effective new configuration of an existing machine to meet your requirements

+ Build a new machine from components that precisely meet your needs

+ Design an approach for integrating personal computers into local area networks, wide area networks, and the Internet

+ Tune your computer system for peak performance

+ Repair or install upgrades into an existing machine

## Yes, if you have good experience using a computer

There's no magic to working on the insides of your computer, but doing so can be complex, and you may encounter odd results that you have to diagnose and correct. If you're comfortable working with DOS, Windows, or UNIX when things go wrong, you've got the most important prerequisite. If in addition to that you can work successfully on small, delicate mechanical parts, this book can teach you how to work inside your computer.

It's not mandatory that you take apart your computer to get the most from this book. If you understand how to use your computer, but want to know what goes on behind the scenes, read this book. We'll show you what's inside and how it works.

If you're a computer novice, though, we recommend that you read another of our books, *Teach Yourself PCs* (IDG Books Worldwide, Inc., 1998), which is written to be a first introduction to computers. After you've worked your way through that book, come back to the *PC Upgrade and Repair Bible* for the how-it-works information.

## Yes, if you know a disk drive from a power supply

If you've worked with computer components before, this book will show you how they relate to each other, how to evaluate each one, and how to combine them to get the most out of your computer. You'll learn how to track down common failures, and what to do to correct problems.

## Yes, if you've built your own computer already

You'll learn about the latest technology advances in this book, helping you predict where you'll be going with your computer in the years to come. You'll learn how to construct networks of computers, how to troubleshoot problems in computers and networks, and how to set up a group of computers to make them easier to maintain.

### Thirty-two whats?

The processor in your computer has a maximum size number it can handle without extra work. In the Intel Pentium, Pentium Pro, and Pentium II processors, that maximum size is 32 bits. (A *bit* is a binary digit -- zero or one -- in the same way that zero to nine are the decimal digits. A 32-bit number is a sequence of 32 binary digits. Converted to decimal numbers, the range of a 32-bit binary value is 2,147,483,648 to –2,147,483,648.)

Windows 3.1 and Windows for Workgroups 3.11 did not exploit the 32-bit capability of these processors well; major parts of their internal operation used 16-bit numbers limited to the range 32,767 to –32,767. This limited the ways in which they could reference memory, leading to artificial constraints that made programming difficult and, in many circumstances, made systems unstable.

# What's In This Book

We've organized this book into six parts, plus four appendixes:

✦ *Part I: Introduction and Issues (Chapters 1–3)*. It seems obvious that not everyone needs the same computer, but it takes some analysis to see the details behind why that's true. You don't necessarily have to settle for a hobbled machine — not with the cheap, screaming-fast ones on the market now — but you get the most value by thinking through what you'll really benefit from. This part of the book looks at the problem from high altitude: What can we tell about what you need before we open up the computer and look inside?

✦ *Part II: Your Workload Determines What Your Computer Does (Chapters 4–5)*. Part II lays out a profile for analyzing how you use your computer to create a baseline for understanding your requirements. There's a set of stereotyped profiles at the end of Part II to make the ideas concrete and provide a basis for looking at real products.

✦ *Part III: Specs, Lies, and Duct Tape (Chapters 6–26)*. To really dig into understanding what you need in a computer, you have to understand what's inside and how it works. You don't need a degree in computer science or electrical engineering for this, just the willingness to look at some interesting concepts and see how they work together to get the job done. Part III contains the details of what the pieces inside your computer are, what they do for you, and what kinds of jobs different options do best. Each of the chapters in Part III looks at a different type of hardware (such as processors, disks, and sound cards), covering the specifics of what the devices are, what you need to consider when choosing them, and what some good representative products are.

✦ *Part IV: Networking Know-How (Chapters 27–30).* Part IV covers the technology and equipment for networks, helping you connect your computers to each other and to the Internet. Most computers in use today are connected to a network, so if you're going to work with PCs effectively, you need to know how to work with a network. You'll see the hardware it takes to put a network together, the devices outside your PC you need to make the network work, and how to configure both the computers and the other devices.

✦ *Part V: Putting It Together (Chapters 31–36).* Once we've worked our way down through the basic building blocks of your computer, we'll work our way back up again. Part V looks at how different component decisions you make affect each other; what you can do to make future growth easier and less expensive; how you can make a group of computers easier to manage; how you might want to access and serve the Internet; and how you can perform benchmarking, diagnosis, and repair of your system. You need not be an expert to understand and apply this material.

✦ *Part VI: Just Do It (Chapters 37–41).* This set of chapters covers how to build workstations (clones) and server computers from individual components. You'll see the step-by-step process of assembling the machine, loading the operating system, and bringing it to life. Part VI closes with a look at your alternatives for certification and what benefits certification can bring.

✦ *Appendixes.* There are four appendixes in this book. Appendix A describes the programs and demonstrations on the CD-ROM. Appendix B is a printed version of the Vendor List you'll find on the CD-ROM. The CD-ROM version is organized as pages you can load into your World Wide Web browser, making it simple to link to a manufacturer's site for support information and software updates. Appendix C is a glossary of terms, with emphasis on telecommunications and networking terms likely to be unfamiliar to most readers. Appendix D describes the test objectives for the A+ certification exam.

Although later chapters build on earlier ones, you don't have to read the book in sequence from cover to cover — you can dive into the parts that most interest you. If you find you're not understanding what's there, go back to the relevant earlier chapters.

# Navigating Through This Book

Every chapter in this book opens with a quick look at what's in the chapter and closes with a summary of the most important points in the chapter. You'll find icons in the margins of the text to draw your attention to specific topics and items of interest. Here are what the icons mean:

**Benchmarking** The Benchmarking icon highlights places in the book with discussion of benchmark results, or with suggestions of how you'll want to conduct your own benchmarks to evaluate your own computers.

**Cross-Reference** The Cross-Reference icon indicates references to more information or more detailed discussion elsewhere in the book.

**Note** The Note icon points out additional important information or an insight related to the topic at hand.

**Tip** The Tip icon highlights things you'll want to do to make sure you get the most out of your computer.

**Caution** The Caution icon n points out a common problem you'll want to know about, along with suggestions for what to do to avoid or fix the problem.

**Future PC** The Future PC icon identifies exciting new developments in personal computer technology that you may want to take into account as you formulate your upgrade strategy.

One notational point: Throughout the book, we talk about both bits and bytes (a *byte* is 8 bits), and about thousands, millions, and billions of those. We'll use the notation in Table 1 consistently. Lowercase "b" stands for "bits," and uppercase "B" stands for "bytes."

| Table 1 Bits/Bytes Measurements Used in This Book | |
| --- | --- |
| **Symbol** | **Definition** |
| Kb | Kilobit — 1,024 bits |
| KB | Kilobyte — 1,024 bytes |
| Mb | Megabit — 1,048,576 bits |
| MB | Megabyte — 1,048,576 bytes |
| Gb | Gigabit — 1,073,741,824 bits |
| GB | Gigabyte — 1,073,741,824 bytes |

# About the Third Edition

Updating this third edition of *PC Upgrade and Repair Bible* to keep its technology coverage current was something of a watershed. When we wrote the first edition, many people were still running computers based on the Intel 486 processor, and upgrades to those systems were an important topic. When we wrote the second edition, the *PC Upgrade and Repair Bible, Professional Edition*, the Pentium and Pentium Pro were thoroughly entrenched; the Intel Pentium II and AMD K6 were just starting to penetrate the market.

By now, writing the third edition, that's all changed. The Intel 486 and its predecessors are largely irrelevant, Pentium processors are found only in older machines (and some laptops), and the Pentium II and K6-2 processors own the industry. We've followed suit in the third edition, removing essentially all coverage of the older chips except where we need the historical perspective to make an explanation clear.

Nor are these changes limited to processors. The lifetime of products in the personal computer industry is often as short as six months, so if you compare the products we highlight in this edition to the ones in the first or second editions, you'll see almost no overlap. Our goal remains to give you an understanding of what the best of the industry has to offer and how to exploit it.

# Keeping Up-To-Date

Books such as the *PC Upgrade and Repair Bible* cycle every 12 to 24 months, making it impossible to remain completely current in the technologies and products we cover. Magazines cycle every 1 to 2 months; while newspapers and Internet Web sites cycle roughly weekly, with news bites popping up the same day. Books offer coverage with good detail on a broad range of topics; magazines provide lightweight coverage on a focused set of topics, and Web sites offer coverage from lightweight to in-depth on a few specific topics. Books are typically the most accurate, because they have a technical review during the publishing cycle, while magazines and popular Web sites are at times dead wrong.

We know that readers of the *PC Upgrade and Repair Bible* need a reliable way to keep up-to-date between revisions, so we and IDG Books Worldwide have launched a reader's Web site: http://www.pcurb.com. On that Web site we're combining current, technically sound information and reviews with cross-references into the in-depth background and technology tutorials you'll find here in the *PC Upgrade and Repair Bible*. You'll find all the hardware resources you need in one place — here's a sample of what you can expect at pcurb.com:

✦ *News* — You can spend all day digging out the key news items you need to keep on top of the latest developments. pcurb.com delivers announcements, analysis, and speculation about new product introductions, new technologies, mergers, and the rest of what drives the pulse of the computer and networks industry.

✦ *Reviews and Comparisons* — The surface analysis and PR-driven features lists in most product reviews and comparisons aren't what you need to make informed buying decisions. pcurb.com delivers sound benchmarking and testing backed by the engineering know how necessary to interpret the results.

✦ *Tutorials and How-to's* — Everyone who uses a computer as more than an anonymous appliance develops the curiosity of what's going on, wanting to understand the technology inside their computers; the how, why, and wherefore of making computers fast, capable, and reliable; and how to upgrade for the best results. pcurb.com explains it all, keeping the content of the *PC Upgrade and Repair Bible* current.

✦ *Tools* — Not only is most of the freely downloadable software available on the Web junk, you're not likely to be able to make smart choices from two-sentence blurbs and feature lists. pcurb.com delivers the recommendations you need, lists the tools we use, explains the key jobs those tools do, and links to the developer's home sites.

✦ *Q&A* — Sometimes you need help with a specific problem, a pointer to ideas more sophisticated than "reformat your hard drive and call me in the morning." pcurb.com's Q&A section will be the mailbag, taking the most interesting of the questions we receive and passing them (and their answers) along to inform and educate.

✦ *Booklist* — There are so many computer books flooding the shelves that it's hard to know what will help. Over time we'll be building and maintaining a booklist with our picks for the titles heavy on meat and light on chaff.

✦ *Online Vendor List* — It can be hard to track down the company you need to talk to trying to solve a problem. You'll find the contact list that's in Appendix B of this book online and linked, so help may be just a few mouse clicks away. We'll be keeping the vendor list current, too, as the industry changes and grows.

We expect to make pcurb.com a one-stop source for everything you need to keep their computers running and in top shape.

You'll be able to write us through pcurb.com, too — write us at barry@pcurb.com or marcia@pcurb.com.

# Acknowledgments

**W**e gratefully acknowledge the assistance of the following people and companies in the development of this book: 3Com Corporation, 3dfx Interactive Incorporated, Actiontec Electronics, Adaptec Incorporated, Adobe Systems Incorporated, Aladdin Systems Incorporated, George Alfs, Altec Lansing Technologies Incorporated, American Megatrends Incorporated, Dave Anderson, American Power Conversion Corporation, ArosNet Internet Services, ATI Technologies, Incorporated, Cheryl Balbach, John Barnah, Belkin Components, Mike Beltrano, Benjamin Group, Dave Berman, Blair Birmingham, Nick Blozan, Frankie Borison, Edward Botello, Danny Brand, Brodeur Porter Novelli, Robert Bruce, Brian Burke, Patrick Burns, California PC Products, Canon U.S.A. Incorporated, Casio Incorporated, Scott Cavanagh, Sonya Chen, Cisco Systems Incorporated, Brian Clair, Compatible Systems Corporation, Computing Technology Industry Association, Chris Craig, Crucial Technology, Monica D'Agostino-Seidel, Caroline DeBie, Adrien deCroy, Earthlink Network Incorporated, Eastman Kodak Company, Eiger Labs Incorporated, Sharon Entenberg, ESC Technologies, Extended Systems Incorporated, Aileen Figueroa, Tina Fletcher, FORE Systems Incorporated, ForeFront Group, Forté Incorporated, Dan Francisco, Amy Frost, Stephanie Furuta, Frank Gabrielle, Rob Galbraith, Gathering of Developers LLP, Jason Gouveia, Craig Grabiner, Granite Digital, John Gray, Chris Hanson, Layne Heiny, Brian Hentschel, Tyson Heyn, Hitachi America Limited, Burton Holmes, Don Horner, Leslie Hough-Falk, Hewlett Packard, Kevin Howard, Mark Huffman, Heather Humphrey, IBM Corporation, id Software, IDG Books Worldwide, Imation, Intel, Iomega Corporation, Ipswitch Incorporated, Heather Jardim, Ron Johnson, Alun Jones, John Junod, Bill "No Comment" Karow, Kathy Keating, Kathryn Kelly, Peggy Kelly, Janice Kiesel, Kingston Technology Company, Debra Kramerage, David Krejci, Lekas Group, Joyce Lekas, Locutus Codeware, Logitech Incorporated, Edam Lozano, Peggy Lohman, Jennifer Lyng, Nico Mak, Khaled Mardam-Bey, Cynthia Marvel, Mike McCollum, Mike McDougall, Robert McKieth, Liz Meagher, Lori Mezoff, Micro House International, Microsoft Corporation, MicroSystems Development Technologies Incorporated, Angel Munoz, Travis Murdock, Doug Myres, NEC Technologies Incorporated, NewWorld.com Incorporated, Nico Mak Computing Incorporated, Kelly Odle, PC Power and Cooling Incorporated, James Peters, Julie Pierre, Pinnacle Systems Incorporated, Larry Polyak, Tara Poole, Power Quest, Jen Press, Kate Press, Qbik Software, Colleen Raley, Robert Raymond, Mike Reeber, The Regents of the University of California, Maureen Robinson, Jim Roche, Tim Roper, Randy Roscoe, Billy Rudock, Eric Ruff, Paulien Ruijssenaars, Joe Runde, Kathleen Ryan, Anthony Sanzio, Seagate Technology, Ted Selker, Jen Seymour, Shandwick International, Jim Shatz-Akin, Solectek Corporation, Ray Soneira, Sonera Technologies, Sony Corporation Of America, Staccato Systems, Bob Starr, Candice Steelman, Steve Sturgeon, David Szabados, Lauren Tascan, Technology Solutions Inc, Argun Tekant, Texas Imperial Software, Toshiba America Information Systems Incorporated,

UMAX Technologies Incorporated, Ray Van Tassle, Rob van Nobelen, Manny Vara, Tjerk Vonck, Voyetra Turtle Beach Incorporated, WACOM Technology Incorporated, Matt Wagner, Walnut Creek CD-ROM, Melanie Watson, White Pine Software Incorporated, Glenn Wilk, Mike Wilson, Yamaha Systems Technology Incorporated, Totally Awesome Computers, and Andrew Zdziarski,

Entries for the Glossary were contributed by 3Com, Adaptec, Seagate, and Kingston Technology.

Thanks to all of you.

# Contents at a Glance

# Contents

• • • • • • • • • • • • • • • • • • • • • • • • • • • • • • • • • • •

## Chapter 13: Hard Disks and Disk Arrays ..................363

## Chapter 14: CD-ROMs, CD-ROM Changers, CD-Rs, and DVD-ROMs ..401

## Part IV: Networking Know-How · 767

### Chapter 27: Network Cabling and Interfaces · 769

## Part VII: Appendixes    1145

# Introduction and Issues

# Getting Ready

**C**omputers have become indispensable for much of the work and play people do. A computer costs hundreds to thousands of dollars, so it's important that your computer work as hard for you as possible. This book helps you make your computer work harder, starting with your answer to the question, "Given what I do with my computer, and possibly given installed hardware and software, how do I decide which hardware will provide me the most value?"

## There Are No Pat Answers

Everyone does something different with their computer, or does similar things in different ways. Those differences lead to different answers to the question of what is the best computer for you.

You can start your analysis of how to get the most value from your hardware by thinking about these issues:

+ For what do you use the computer?

+ What programs do you use, and how?

+ What benefits do you expect from your computer? Will achieving those benefits alter the ways you use the computer?

+ If you upgrade, what will limit the performance of your computer?

+ If you buy new equipment, how much and what kind of equipment do you need? What are the options in choosing that equipment?

+ For both upgrades and new purchases, what are the support and maintenance requirements, and how can your decisions make end-user support easier?

+ Once you select a hardware configuration, what are the growth options during the life of the equipment, and what benefits can those options provide? What choices can you make early on to reduce the cost of future growth?

The following pages expand on each of these questions to explain why they're important and how your answers affect your choices.

## What do you do with your computer?

Different things you do create different amounts of work for your computer. The typist using a DOS version of WordPerfect places relatively small demands on a computer. The game player hosting a network game tournament needs some memory, a decent processor (also called a *central processing unit*, or *CPU*), and high-speed communications. The game player needs screaming fast CPU and video. The publisher assembling books from text, photographs, and graphics needs it all — lots of memory, a fast CPU, high-resolution video, voluminous storage, and good communications if files are transmitted electronically.

Because how you use your computer determines how great a workload you impose on it, we discuss not only what you use the machine for but also what programs you use and in what combinations you use them. These factors will be the beginning of your estimate of how powerful a machine you need. For example, suppose you're still running the computer you bought in the mid 1980s. You might have the DOS version of WordPerfect on a machine with a 386DX processor clocked at 20 MHz, 2 megabytes (MB) of memory, and a 200MB disk. You've never installed Windows on the machine, but your partner says that you'll be fantastically better off with Windows and its what-you-see-is-what-you-get capabilities. She convinces you to move to Windows, but now you ask, "Will I have to upgrade my computer to run Windows?"

With a computer like that, the answer is yes. You'll need more memory, more disk space, and a faster processor. We'll look at how you can get ready for Windows with this machine, and examine the possibility of replacing the main processor board — the *motherboard* — as an alternative to piecemeal upgrades. We'll also talk about whether upgrading this machine makes sense compared to purchasing a new computer.

We want to caution you to be hard-nosed about upgrades, because much of the hype and noise you hear that computers are obsolete six months after you buy them is driven by the notion that people always need the fastest, latest hardware. That's absurd. If your computer does what you want the way you want, nothing forces you to upgrade your hardware or software. You may need upgrades to do new things or to do the same things with new software, but that's an explicit choice you get to make.

## Which operating system do you want, and why?

Upgrades that let you do more with your computer may be more attractive than ones required simply to run new versions of the same programs the same way as before. Upgrades that increase capabilities and productivity create added value, while ones that just maintain existing functionality amount to a surcharge on the cost of the software upgrade.

The hardware upgrades you need also reflect the operating system you decide to run. For example, the current versions of Windows ease most of the resource restrictions that plagued Windows 3.1. Windows now can run more programs at the same time than Windows 3.1 could. If you take advantage of this — say, by keeping your e-mail, word-processing, and fax software open while you run a corporate order-entry application — you will use more memory than before. You may also find that you need higher resolution on your display to keep all those windows visible at once. Greater display resolution may in turn make you want to replace a 14- or 17-inch monitor with a 19-inch one to keep the text legible.

If your computer is on a home or office network, you may find Windows' improved abilities to handle multiple forms of network communication incredibly valuable. While Windows 3.1 had to be coerced into supporting more than one type of network, Windows now does this out of the box. You can talk to your mainframe, NetWare, and Windows network servers while you search the Internet for the latest news. You can let your coworkers pull files off your disks to combine with their own work. As easy as this can be, though, it means your computer is now doing more work. That means memory and processor resources are being used to service the networking load. If you don't have enough of those resources, you'll need to upgrade to keep working at full speed while these features run behind the scenes.

If you're deploying an Internet server, you'll want to choose between UNIX and Windows NT. Both can host a full suite of services, but you'll have to choose among a wide range of choices that affect the hardware you need, the available support, and the cost of software.

Gaining an understanding of your hardware requirements begins by estimating the basic hardware you need to maintain your current capability. We'll show you how to make those estimates and how to achieve a complete understanding of your growth options.

## Should you upgrade your computer?

The starting point for upgrades is always the existing computer. In this book we discuss how to characterize the performance you can expect from that machine and how to identify the components that limit your applications' performance. Knowing that lets you predict whether the machine's performance needs to be improved. You'll see how to identify the "choke points" that limit performance, how to eliminate them, and how to decide which upgrade options make sense. You'll learn how to identify when it's better to replace the entire computer than to make incremental upgrades.

For example, suppose your company's standard user workstation is a Pentium processor running at 166 MHz, hosting Windows 95 in 16MB of memory. You've deployed desktop video conferencing, and you're getting complaints about poor video from many of your users. Can you afford to fix this? You might need faster communications, or you may simply need to drop in a faster video card.

Or, suppose you have a Pentium 200 MHz processor with 8MB of memory, and you want to know if you can take advantage of Outlook, the Microsoft Office electronic mail software. The analyses you'll do with this book will show you that you can, but you'll want to upgrade memory to 16MB or 32MB.

The process of analyzing upgrade options is very much like that of selecting options to include in a new machine. We look at a wide range of computer components from the point of view of what each can do for you, examining the characteristics of each, and looking at how those characteristics affect the performance you can expect. We look at advertised prices to show the relative cost of features and performance. The prices you'll pay for equipment change as technology evolves, so we use the comparisons to illustrate the analysis rather than as the rigid basis for choice.

## What new computer should you buy?

Buying a new computer is very much like a 100 percent upgrade of an old computer, and in fact, new computers are often bought as replacements for older ones. Upgrading a machine constrains the choice of components in order to remain compatible with surviving components, while configuring a new computer opens up all the technology options. The decision of what to buy is therefore more complex for new computers, requiring you to weed through more choices.

For instance, suppose you've narrowed your selection to two vendors who both offer 64MB of memory in the machine you want. If only one of the two delivers the new Rambus memory technology, and that vendor charges more for Rambus, is the extra money worth it? Later we give you the tools to decide by showing you what the different types of memory are, what the characteristics of each are, and how to measure the benefits different memory technologies bring you.

## What about support and maintenance?

Whatever your demands on a computer, you'll want to carefully consider the support available from the suppliers you choose and the options you have for maintenance when something fails. Both UNIX and Windows operating systems are constantly changing, and new versions will at times offer dramatically better performance. Different manufacturers have very different track records for supporting their hardware as operating systems evolve. Some vendors position their products for very specific markets, providing support for some operating systems but not others. We look later at what's required in Windows and UNIX to support hardware fully as well as at the issues of manufacturer support.

There's a wide range of utilities specific to Windows that help automate some of the critically important periodic maintenance items. We look at what problems these tools can solve and what you need to do to be ready for disasters beyond their reach.

## What about future upgrades?

Knowing the relative costs and benefits of upgrade options can help you make new equipment choices that extend the equipment's operating life. Choosing technologies and components that allow low-cost, high-payoff upgrades at a later date requires some thought, but can help you use minor upgrades to put off the next major upgrade for years. This book helps you make technology and component choices so you reap those benefits both by explaining the issues involved and by providing concrete examples. We configure several sample systems and look at what the options and costs are for future increased capability.

For example, systems using a Small Computer Systems Interface (SCSI) card to control the hard disk give you a lot of options. (See Chapter 12 for more about SCSI.) You can connect more disks, CD-ROMs, scanners, and tape drives to a SCSI controller without adding new cards inside the computer. If you'll be hooking in network, modem, video-conferencing, and sound cards later, saving *slots* (the places you put cards in a computer) like this can be critical.

The organization of this book follows the ideas above. We start by discussing ways to understand how you use your computer and how much work you make it do. A look at your operating system (most likely Windows) and what it can do for you lets you expand your understanding of what you need from your computer. We take a computer apart after that, looking at all the pieces inside to understand what they do. We examine the features and characteristics of each element, learning to read manufacturers' descriptions with an eye to making smart decisions. We look at how to decide what components can be upgraded to solve performance problems, and we make comparisons among competing upgrades. We also use the same ideas to decide when a completely new computer is the right idea. Finally, we look at how to evaluate the growth left in a computer and how to get the most out of what you have.

# Basic Techniques

You have to do a few things right if you're going to work on computer hardware effectively. Here they are:

✦ *Control static electricity.* You absolutely have to control static electricity (also called electrostatic discharge, or ESD). Voltages you can't see or feel can kill the chips in your computer.

✦ *Follow careful, well-defined procedures.* You get nowhere ripping hardware (or software) apart and making random changes hoping something will work. You have to have a carefully thought-out sequence in mind. You'll want to change only one thing at a time (and test the result) so you can isolate what causes different results.

✦ *Use the proper tools.* We're as guilty as anyone of using a vise grip as the universal tool, but that's not the right way to go about working on computer hardware. The parts are small and relatively fragile, so you must have the appropriate tools for the job.

## Static electricity

The tens of millions of transistors inside the chips in your computer are fantastically small. While the small size of the transistors makes possible the speed and functionality those chips offer, that same small size reduces the voltage the transistors can withstand. Here's a typical warning about the maximum ratings on chips:

> Warning: Operating the device beyond the "Absolute Maximum Ratings" may cause permanent damage. Exposure to stress beyond the "Operating Conditions" limits specified for the device may affect reliability.

Typical signal and power level operating conditions for chips are from 1.65 to 5 volts. The absolute maximum voltage rating for many chips is 6.5 volts; some are even less. You can't feel static electricity at much below 30 volts, and you can easily generate thousands of volts without intending to. Because you're not likely to feel less than 30 volts, you can destroy a chip without even feeling a tingle. What's worse is that you can weaken one (priming it to fail a little later), damaging it just short of complete failure. Ultimately, your feet scuffing on the ground, clothes rubbing on you, and a multitude of other small things can generate the ammunition that kills a chip.

This is what you must do — at the minimum — to prevent static electricity problems:

✦ *Ground everything, including yourself.* It's not enough to simply touch a piece of metal — static electricity can build back up simply from your moving as you work. The best way to prevent an electrostatic discharge is to not let one build up to begin with. Grounding everything — connecting it to a good ground — takes care of this. A proper antistatic workstation includes not only a grounded workbench, but also a ground mat, a grounded wrist strap (which fastens securely around your wrist), and foot straps. Grounds should connect through an unbroken wire to a secure cold-water ground. (Be sure the pipe into the ground is an unbroken length of metal with no plastic sections.)

If you're going all out, consider grounded tools and a humidifier. Increased water in the air helps static charges bleed off.

✦ *Avoid materials that build up static charges.* Workbench tops should be a conductive, antistatic material. Under no circumstances should you work on a plastic, vinyl, carpeted, cloth-covered, finished, or waxed surface. Parts should be stored in plastic bins or bags made of conductive, antistatic material. Check bins and bags for extraneous material that could cause static buildup.

Floors should be conductive tile. Avoid vinyl, carpet, finished wood, sealed or dusty concrete, and floor wax. You can get carpet spray to minimize static buildup, but it's not really the right answer.

You'll also want to keep static-building material out of your work area. This includes most plastics, nylon, polyethylene, Styrofoam, vinyl notebooks, cellophane, and adhesive tape. Clothing often includes static-building material, so your best bet is to wear a conductive smock.

✦ *Avoid other people.* Onlookers are inevitable, but without their own antistatic protection, they can destroy in a second what you've worked to protect. Keep people without appropriate antistatic protection at least three feet away from the work area so they can't touch anything.

Obviously you can work in a less protected environment, and many service centers are less protected. You increase your risk when you do, though, especially in a dry atmosphere.

## Tools

Almost everything you need to do to a personal computer can be done with just a few simple tools, such as screwdrivers, socket drivers, and pliers. You'll need some more-sophisticated tools if you're making cables. (Of course, if you're making cables you may need to have your head examined. It takes lots of time, saves very little money, if any — it may actually cost more — and is one of the most error-prone assembly jobs. If we had a dollar for every screwed up cable we've had foisted on us . . . .)

✦ *Screwdrivers* — You'll need both blade and Phillips screwdrivers. You'll want a range of sizes from small to medium.

✦ *Socket drivers* — Many of the screws used in personal computers have heads that fit hex drivers, which lets you avoid stripped heads and makes it less likely that you'll drop the screw where it doesn't belong. The most common sizes are $3/16$, $7/32$, and $1/4$ inch.

✦ *Pliers* — The ones we use the most are a pair of very long needle-nose pliers. They won't exert much force, but they'll handle small parts and get into tight places.

✦ *Flashlight* — You'll want one of the compact, halogen bulb flashlights so you can get a lot of light in a small place. One you can make stay put in small places is even better.

✦ *Mirror* — You can't always see what you need to directly. A small mirror on a long handle can solve a lot of problems that would otherwise require you to disassemble more than you need to.

✦ *Multimeter* — Some failures are best diagnosed with a multimeter. We have a portable one from Heath, but you can get them anywhere. You don't need extreme accuracy (which is expensive), but you'll want to look for one that's durable. They have a habit of falling off workbenches and other places.

✦ *Soldering iron* — If you know what you're doing to the point where you want to be able to repair connectors or remove and replace components from circuit cards, you'll need a soldering iron. Not a soldering gun, and not the sort of iron Grandpa used to make tin cans with. You want a grounded, temperature-regulated unit that protects components from overheating and static electricity. If the cost of one of those seems too high, think twice about whether you can afford to be without one.

You'll find most of these tools, if not all, in a compact tool kit for PC service. They're sold by a lot of companies. You don't need the super-spiffy giant size. Look for good quality tools, however — junk is too frustrating to bother with.

As important as these tools are, the most important tools you'll have are your eyes and ears, and some programs you'll keep on disk. You provide the eyes and ears, and we cover some of the programs later in the book.

# Summary

✦ This book will help you decide on the computer configuration or upgrade that is best for you.

✦ The computer that's best for you depends on what you do with it.

✦ The computer you need may be the one you already own after some upgrades.

✦ Understanding what's in computer hardware will give you the tools to choose upgrades or a new computer to meet your needs and budget.

✦ You can simplify support and maintenance, and reduce your future computer costs, by choosing hardware effectively now.

✦　　✦　　✦

# Why Isn't the Same Computer Right for Everyone?

**Y**our computer has at least a dozen or so components
you need to consider when analyzing performance and
capabilities, including the processor, memory, buses (local,
main, and input/output [I/O]), power supply, case, hard disk,
CD-ROM drive, display, network, tape drive, modem, sound,
and printer. Each of these components has a handful of
defining characteristics, with each characteristic having a
range of choices. The result is hundreds of possibilities for
how you configure your computer.

It's important not to underestimate how rapidly computer
technology changes. In the fall of 1995, for instance, 133 MHz
was the fastest clock speed offered in desktop computers sold
by Micron Electronics, with only Pentium processors to be
found. Four months later, the *slowest* desktop machine listed
on Micron's price sheets was 100 MHz; the 133 MHz processor
was found only as a downgrade for their new 150 MHz
machines. Fifteen months later, the 166 MHz Pentium
processor was the minimum configuration on most of their
machines. As we write this in June of 1999, a 400 MHz version
of the Intel Celeron processor is the slowest processor they
sell; the fastest is a 550 MHz Pentium III. In just over three
years, the processor clock speed in Micron desktop systems
has increased by more than three times; the computing power
has increased significantly more than that.

Computer prices are continually falling for machines with equal features and performance, while the low end of the market continually grows in performance and features, so it's important that you don't overvalue change in computer technology. If the machine you have gets your work done, you can expect to use it until that work changes, or until added features in new versions of your software are compelling enough to make you upgrade to a version that does not run well on your machine. When you become dissatisfied with the machine you have, you'll do the necessary upgrades and keep on working.

**Tip** If you haven't already, you'll soon find that different people hold very different opinions—with an intensity that easily approaches that of religious wars—on what's good in computer hardware and what you need. A number of our opinions are expressed in this book, and most of them are based on the idea of computer upgrade and repair by mystic incantation: Remember what has worked well for you in the past and, unless you have a good reason not to, keep doing it.

For example, we're very partial to ATI video boards because they're fast and have proven reliable for us. The same is true for Adaptec SCSI host adapters. Conversely, we won't buy anything from one of the largest competing video board manufacturers, because we know from both experience and insight into the company's operations that their driver software is bug-ridden and not likely to get better soon. The end result has been that we spend less time fixing our computers than some very competent people we know.

We suggest that you adopt the same approach—when you identify a quality manufacturer, stick with them. If it becomes clear to you that a manufacturer's products are not well engineered and manufactured, shun them. Do this for components in complete systems you buy as well as for upgrades.

# Buying into a Moving Target

The wide range of options for configuring computers is one reason manufacturers offer preconfigured systems—predefined system packages meet the needs of most customers, letting the sales staff spend more time with customers having unique requirements. Table 2-1 shows a representative range of complete, new desktop systems available in mid-1999. If the computer industry continues at its current rate, they will be obsolete before the next edition of this book can be published. Laptop and palmtop computers present a whole other set of issues that we talk about later.

We've indicated our minimum recommendations in Table 2-1 in boldface.

### Table 2-1
### Computer Configuration Options In Mid-1999

| Category | Low-End | Midrange | High-End |
|---|---|---|---|
| Case | Desktop | **Mini-tower** or tower | Tower or server |
| CD-ROM access time | 150 to 100 ms | 130 to 100 ms | 90 to 85 ms |
| CD-ROM transfer rate | 3600 to 4800 KBps (32X to 40X) | **6500 KBps (5X DVD)** | **6500 KBps (5X DVD)** |
| Disk access time | 10 ms | 10 ms | 6 ms |
| Disk capacity | 4 to 8GB | **9 to 17GB** | 23GB and up |
| Disk onboard cache (on the drive) | 128 to 256 KB | 256 to 512 KB | 512 to 4096 KB |
| Disk transfer rate | 3.5 MBps | 10 MBps | 10 to 30 MBps |
| Display color depth | **16 bits** | **16 bits** | 24 to 32 bits |
| 3D display frames per second | 15 | **25** | 40 and up |
| Display resolution | 640 × 480 to 800 × 600 | 1024 × 768 | 1280 × 1024 and up |
| Display bus | PCI | **2X AGP** | 4X AGP (late 1999) |
| I/O bus | IDE | IDE or SCSI | Ultra-Wide SCSI |
| Local bus | PCI | PCI | PCI |
| Auxiliary bus | ISA and USB | ISA and USB | ISA and USB |
| Memory error checking correction coding | None | None or parity | Parity or error |
| Memory interface | SDRAM | PC100 SDRAM | Rambus (late 1999) |
| Memory size | 32 MB | **64 to 96 MB** | 128 MB and up |
| Modem | 56 Kbps V.90 | 56 Kbps V.90 | 128 Kbps ISDN or 256+ Kbps xDSL |
| Monitor size | 15-inch | **17- to 19-inch** | 21-inch |
| Network cabling (twisted pair) | 10Base-2 (coax) | 10Base-T | Switched 100Base-T |
| Power supply | 145 watts | **250 to 300 watts** | 350 watts and up |

*Continued*

| | | | |
|---|---|---|---|
| **Table 2-1** *(continued)* | | | |
| *Category* | *Low-End* | *Midrange* | *High-End* |
| Printer interface | Parallel | Parallel | Network |
| Printer resolution and technology | 300 to 1440 dpi color inkjet | 600 to 1200 dpi laser | 600 to 1200 dpi color laser |
| Processor clock and speed | 400 MHz Intel Celeron or AMD K6-2 | 450 MHz Intel Pentium III | 600 MHz and up Pentium III or Xeon |
| Processor cache (L2) | 256 KB | 512 KB | 512 KB and up |
| Scanner resolution | None | 600 dpi | 1200 dpi and up |
| Sound technology | 16-bit stereo | 32-bit wavetable | 32-bit wavetable |
| Tape capacity (uncompressed) | None to 400MB | 4 to 10GB | 10 to 70GB |
| Tape transfer rate (uncompressed) | 0.5 MBps | 0.5 MBps | 0.83 MBps and up |
| Tape | Travan 4 | Travan 5 | Travan 5 or DAT DDS-3 |

Any given configuration is likely to have components from all three columns. How you use a computer and what you do with it, as well as what combinations of technology make sense, will determine the choices you make. For example:

✦ A great machine for graphics designers would combine high-end video with a fast processor and lots of memory, cache, and disk.

✦ A good configuration for economical word processing would combine a low-end machine with a midrange-capacity disk and monitor.

Depending on your objectives, high-end performance may not require the most expensive equipment. For example, video cards with 3D acceleration can provide blazing frame-update rates (the speed at which the game can update the screen), but by avoiding high-end resolution and color depth, they can deliver this performance at midrange cost.

Don't be misled by the term "low-end" at the left of the table into thinking that lesser machines are useless. A machine with a 200 MHz Pentium processor, 16MB of memory, a 640 × 480 VGA display, and a 2GB disk is considered obsolete by the industry, but it's a terrific machine for small- to medium-scale word processing and spreadsheets, and even for some games. You can buy a similar machine today for around $400. It's quick, if not fast, and very capable—indeed, it's significantly faster than the machine on which we originally started writing books. That machine was a 50 MHz 486 with 16 MB memory, 2GB disk space, 1280 × 1024 resolution 17-inch display, modem, scanner, and tape backup. (We wrote much of the first edition of this book on it.)

**Cross-Reference**

You wouldn't build that machine today, because far better components are available in the $1,000 to $1,500 price range. We show you step by step how to build your own first-class 550 MHz desktop machine in Chapters 37 and 38, and how to build your own dual-processor server in Chapters 39 and 40. The server is relatively expensive, but at the start of 1999 you could build the desktop machine for $1,100 (excluding monitor).

You will make your own choices based on your situation. A cramped office or kitchen counter offers little room for a full-size tower case. A two-machine network is simple to work with using 10Base-2 (thinnet) cabling, whereas 10Base-T makes it easier to troubleshoot and to isolate failures. (We talk about cabling options in Chapter 27.) Configuring a machine to your exact specifications requires detailed research and understanding, whereas buying a prepackaged configuration lets you choose based on top-level parameters. Integrating a machine yourself lets you pick exactly the components it will contain, whereas buying from a major vendor may make onsite service available. Buying a complete machine from a vendor eliminates the headaches of putting it together yourself.

The Low-End category of Table 2-1 is above the minimum configuration required to run Windows and UNIX. We don't recommend running desktop computers under Windows NT (or servers under Windows NT or UNIX) on a low-end machine, if for no other reason than that the memory requirements are greater than for Windows 95 and 98. If you need the additional stability, security, and other features of Windows NT, or if you're running a server, you are likely to have work that demands a faster, larger machine. The features shown in the Midrange and High-End columns of Table 2-1 are more representative of what you will want.

However, assuming that the drivers and capabilities you need are in Windows NT, and assuming you have at least a 266 MHz processor with 64MB of RAM, we recommend Windows NT (and expect to recommend Windows 2000) over Windows 95 or 98 because it's more reliable.

# Factoring In 32-bit Windows and UNIX Features

The features and architecture of Windows 95, 98, and NT, and of UNIX, enable you to do more with your computer than you could with older versions of DOS and Windows. The features that make this possible are

✦ Effective elimination of resource constraints

✦ High-performance display drivers, extending to the DirectX subsystem in Windows 95 or 98 and Windows NT or 2000

✦ Faster printing and file access

✦ Better network performance (multiple protocols, dial-up networking, e-mail, and fax)

✦ Preemptive multitasking and multithreading

Windows NT 3.51 addressed many of these issues even before the Windows 95 launch in 1995. As Microsoft moves Windows 95 and NT closer together in future versions, you can expect to see the feature sets converge as well.

The devices you connect to your computer, the software you want to run, and the stability and security you need will be the primary drivers for whether you run Windows or UNIX. Far more devices have Windows 95 and 98 drivers, but Windows NT, 2000, and UNIX are likely to be more stable. More commercial applications are available for Windows NT than for UNIX, but if you're willing to run relatively unsupported software, your total cost to set up a robust Internet server is likely to be less under UNIX. Recent initiatives by Corel and others are making first-class business software available under UNIX, so if you have the ability to handle the more complex support requirements, UNIX may be an option for you.

The relative lack of device drivers in Windows NT (compared to Windows 98) may be solved by the insertion of what Microsoft calls the *Windows Driver Model* (WDM) into Windows 98. WDM allows one set of drivers to be written for both operating systems, so drivers now in Windows 98 should start to appear in Windows 2000.

## Eliminating resource constraints

Windows 3.1 and Windows for Workgroups 3.11 had three critical areas of memory that limited how many programs you could run no matter how much memory your system had. Those three critical areas were

✦ *Conventional DOS memory.* Several key parts of Windows 3.1 insisted on allocating memory in the DOS region below 1MB. If you ran out of conventional DOS memory, the most common result was the dialog box that said you can't start a program because you're out of memory; but all sorts of erratic and unpredictable results were possible, including random crashes, corrupted data transfer operations, and more. Because CD-ROM drivers and many network drivers required space in this region as well, the very machines most likely to be handling complex workloads had the least conventional memory available. Windows 3.1 also had some unfortunate design problems that caused memory in the conventional DOS memory region to be used when other memory would do, making the situation worse.

✦ *The User heap.* "User" is the component in Windows that implements the functions required to support interaction between you and the computer. A *heap* is a collection of memory used to hold data. The heap used by the User component in Windows 3.1 is a 64KB region of memory that holds information about windows, menus, and other elements of the graphical user interface.

The system resources percentage you see in the Help ✪ About dialog of the Window 3.1 Program Manager is the minimum of the percent free values for the User heap, the GDI heap (see below), and overall system memory. If the system resources estimate dropped to 10 percent free, it was likely that either the User or GDI heaps were running out of space. What's worse, at 10 percent free a 64KB heap had less than 7KB of memory available. That little memory could be exhausted between the time you started a program and when you next had a chance to close a program. Because many programs failed to check for heap exhaustion properly, some software bugs could crash your computer if you simply launched a program at the wrong time.

✦ *The Graphics Device Interface (GDI) heap.* GDI is the Windows component that implements icons, fonts, bitmaps, and other things used to draw images. When you run out of space in the Windows 3.1 GDI heap, you see effects like windows not repainting completely or fonts being improperly rendered. The problem is the same one as with the User heap — only the symptoms differ.

The total memory you have in your machine does not affect any of these problems. A 32MB computer can run out of space in these critical resources as readily as one with 4MB. Windows 95 and 98 do not completely solve these resource problems, but Microsoft has enormously improved the design and implementation in these areas over Windows 3.1. The process of correcting the conventional DOS memory allocation problems, using 32-bit technology in the heaps and moving things out of the heaps, has reduced how much of these resources programs use and has made more resources available in Windows 95 or 98. Windows NT and 2000 are even more effective at removing resource constraints.

We (accidentally) demonstrated how effectively Microsoft solved the resource problems in Windows one day while cleaning the keycaps on a keyboard. Pushing the Enter key to clean it happened to cause the machine to start launching multiple copies of Netscape, and by the time we looked up from the keyboard and saw what was happening there were over 50 copies of Netscape open. This was under Windows 95, and it kept running. Windows did notice that we had a resource problem, however, and suggested that we close some of the programs we had running. After we did, Windows 95 continued running perfectly. Had we done the same thing under Windows NT, it would simply have continued getting slower while it kept believing that we knew what we were doing. This is very different than under Windows for Workgroups 3.11 on the same computer, which would often crash when we merely tried to run Word, Excel, and PowerPoint simultaneously.

The biggest impact of these Windows improvements on your hardware requirements is that the total memory installed in your machine becomes much more important. Few users running one application at a time ever filled memory under Windows 3.1 on machines with 8MB or more. Running lots of programs at once works well under Windows now, and will undoubtedly become commonplace. The memory requirements of those programs all add together, making the total memory on the machine important. You'll know you need more memory if, at the points the machine seems to be responding slowly, you see it constantly accessing the disk. That means that Windows is using the disk to simulate the additional memory your programs want. (See the sidebar "Virtual memory: Faking memory with disk" in this chapter.) The machine has gotten slow because disk accesses are thousands of times slower than memory. Windows continues to run when this happens, but it runs slowly.

Experienced Windows users often keep numerous windows open simultaneously for the different programs they are running. Users who like to keep lots of windows open find that there just isn't enough room on a 640 × 480 display to show very much. Upgrading to a higher-resolution display and monitor solves the problem. We write our books using a 21-inch display with 1600 × 1200 resolution, on which we keep Word, Excel, PowerPoint, Outlook (e-mail), Internet Explorer, and several desktop accessories open at the same time without everything getting lost in an incomprehensible clutter. We're more productive that way because we can switch from task to task quickly, and don't have to wait for programs to launch or to restore themselves from being minimized in the taskbar.

## Virtual memory: Faking memory with disk

Simulating memory by moving things on and off the disk, a technology called *virtual memory,* has been in UNIX for a long time. Microsoft introduced virtual memory into Windows in Version 3.0. Depending on what you are doing with each program, some of the memory holding the program may be referenced very rarely. The following figure shows that, although your programs may occupy 8MB, 16MB, or more when they are running, because not all of that memory is used at the same time, your computer may keep some of it on disk until it's really needed. When the total memory required by all programs exceeds what's installed in your computer, Windows identifies the memory that is being used the least and writes it to disk, reading it back only when it's actually needed. (Of course, to read it back in, other memory has to be written out first.) In this way, programs can use more memory than is actually in the computer.

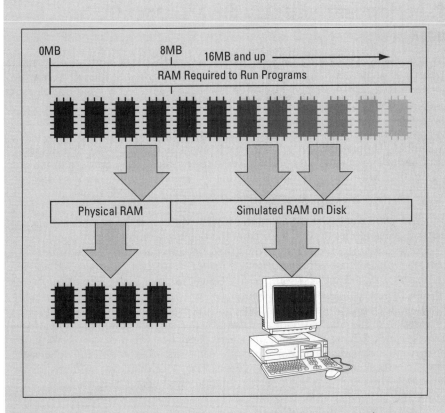

Virtual memory lets your computer run more and bigger programs than your actual memory can support.

The disk space that UNIX or Windows uses to hold this simulated memory is called the *swap file*, and the process of using more memory than you actually have is called *overcommitting memory*. If you overcommit too far, then the time your system spends reading and writing the disk exceeds the time it spends doing useful work. The machine starts thrashing at that point—response gets very slow, and the disk light stays on for extended periods of time. If this is happening to you, you will probably want to consider adding memory to your system.

# High-performance display drivers, OpenGL, and DirectX

Drivers are low-level software programs that talk directly to the hardware, carrying out operations on behalf of the rest of the system. Windows 3.1 video drivers were, for the most part, terrible. They were often unreliable, with many vendors releasing the driver-of-the-day in what seemed like random flailing in the vain hope of pacifying users. Windows 3.1 video performance was highly dependent on the quality of the driver. Installing and tweaking display drivers became a curse (or hobby, depending on your point of view) for thousands of Windows 3.1 users in search of better system stability and display performance. The standard crash debugging ritual always began by substituting the standard Windows VGA display driver — if that made the problem go away, you'd isolated a video driver bug.

Video drivers were the worst problem, but not the only one. Device drivers have been an overall weakness in Windows from the beginning, affecting displays, printing, and networks. One of Microsoft's first steps to cure the device driver problem was to create a core printer device driver (Unidriver) that applied an idea to Windows that Microsoft first shipped in DOS versions of Word. The observation behind Unidriver was that much of what is different among printers are the details of the commands to accomplish functions, not the functions themselves or the implementation of the rest of the print driver. By moving the common code into a module all printer drivers could use, Microsoft simplified the process of building printer drivers and made them more reliable. Windows 95 extended the successful Unidriver idea to 32 bits, and copied it in core drivers for displays, modems, disks, and networks. The result has been better reliability and better performance.

In the display driver arena, Windows provides a generic SuperVGA driver, but requires vendor-specific drivers to activate the features of acceleration chips found on nearly all display boards marketed in the past few years. Many vendors ship drivers with Windows, but some use the delivery of a new version of Windows as an opportunity to phase out boards with low or flat sales.

There's much more to display drivers than the migration to core and 32-bit drivers. UNIX systems have long had the OpenGL programming interface developed by Silicon Graphics and licensed to many companies. OpenGL provides a high-performance, system-independent graphics programming interface capable of supporting sophisticated 3D operations. The OpenGL technology has been included in Windows NT since Version 3.51 and became available for Windows 95 sometime after August of 1995.

Microsoft evaluated OpenGL and decided that, for its purposes, OpenGL should be a high-end programming interface. After a few false starts, Microsoft developed a technology called DirectX that lets games and low-end CAD programs achieve the performance under Windows only previously possible by programming directly to the hardware under DOS. DirectX initially included four components: DirectDraw, DirectSound, DirectPlay, and DirectInput; later versions added Direct3D and

DirectMusic. DirectX Version 6 provides high-performance, device-independent graphics under Windows, including support for high-speed 3D effects such as fog and texturing. DirectX migrated to Windows NT with the release of Windows NT 4.0, and will advance to DirectX 6 on Windows 2000.

Relatively influential 3D software developers, most notably John Carmack of id Software, have decided to write for OpenGL exclusively and to ignore the 3D interface in DirectX. Most game studios seem to have decided that improvements in DirectX 6 make the interface viable, so when you're picking a video card, make sure to get one with both OpenGL and DirectX drivers. Your display and sound cards will require DirectX drivers written by the manufacturers.

## Faster printing and file access

Current versions of Windows implement significant changes to speed printing and file access as well as changes directed at improved systemwide performance. These changes include 32-bit printing, graphics, file, and caching subsystems. In the *Microsoft Windows 95 Resource Kit*, Microsoft states that Windows 95 is as fast as or faster than Windows 3.1 on a 4MB 386DX or better computer, with performance gains increasing as more memory is added.

✦ Printing is faster in terms of how fast your application is ready for you to continue working and in terms of how fast pages are fed to the printer. Applications can enhance printing responsiveness even further by multithreading.

✦ File access is faster due to higher-performance software and better integration of memory usage between disk caching and Windows itself. The Windows 95 file and disk access software extends the architecture first seen in Windows for Workgroups 3.11, 32-bit file and disk access, supporting a wider range of hardware and providing far more reliable operation. Disk access reliability is also enhanced by incorporating a universal driver/minidriver architecture similar to that for printers, displays, and modems.

Independent analyses of Windows performance call the 4MB claims into question, but they do show that performance increases dramatically as memory increases. While Windows 3.1 performance gains flattened in the range of 8MB of memory and made 16MB systems worthwhile only if your specific applications needed it, Windows performance now increases past 16MB, flattening out somewhere between 20 and 32MB. Windows NT performance flattens out even later, with hundreds of megabytes being useful for heavily loaded servers.

**Tip**    The higher performance of the 32-bit subsystems in Windows means that you get more value out of faster hardware. Connecting a fast disk drive to a PCI bus, for instance, provides noticeably better performance than the same disk through the ISA bus, because the software is capable of exploiting the higher-performance disk transfers. Data gets to programs faster, and you wait less.

## Better network performance

You can categorize a network as a *Local Area Network,* which typically means that the connected machines are in an area less than a few kilometers wide, or as a *Wide Area Network,* which includes everything else. Windows for Workgroups 3.11 was the first version of Windows with built-in support for Local Area Networks, but limited its built-in support to Microsoft networks. Third-party solutions were required for Novell networks, for the TCP/IP communication protocol used by the Internet, and for dial-up access to networks. Microsoft provided add-in support for TCP/IP and for dial-up networking some time after the release of Windows for Workgroups 3.11. Even with these improvements, simultaneous access to multiple Local Area Network protocols (such as the Microsoft and Novell protocols) was often difficult to set up properly.

Windows 95 and Windows NT both revamped the networking software in Windows 3.1 from top to bottom. A universal driver/minidriver architecture simplified writing 32-bit network adapter device drivers, making them smaller, faster, and more reliable. A module called the multiprotocol router addressed the problem of supporting more than one network protocol at once, forever eliminating the multiprotocol kludges used in Windows 3.1. New 32-bit client and server software for both Microsoft and Novell networks provided better performance than the 16-bit Windows 3.1 equivalents, and was integrated into the Windows shell to provide simple access to network resources. A 32-bit TCP/IP implementation provided Wide Area Network access, including Internet and local UNIX machines.

✦ Windows users can exploit improvements in network backbones, such as switched Ethernet, which increases the bandwidth to every computer connected via 10Base-T wiring without replacing the cabling or the network adapter. Improved network performance and reliability means you can move more demanding workloads onto network file servers, reducing the per-megabyte cost of storage and simplifying backup procedures.

✦ Individuals, home offices, and small offices can easily create small peer networks (or larger, file-server-based systems) based exclusively on either Windows 95 or NT. Setup and administration is simple, bringing the advantages of shared printers and file systems out of the exclusive realm of larger companies or ones that can afford often-expensive network consultants. Larger networks based on Windows NT retain the familiar concepts and capabilities while scaling up as far as required.

✦ Quality 32-bit Internet software is available that is inexpensive or free and runs with the capabilities — including a very capable e-mail in-box — built into Windows. Examples include the Microsoft Internet Explorer and Outlook Express, John Junod's WS_FTP32 Pro, and Forté's Free Agent. You can find an entire world of resources online, waiting at your convenience. Getting set up on the Internet can still be tricky, but once you get that done, there are few limits to what you can find.

**Tip** You can find Forté's Free Agent online at `http://www.forteinc.com/getfa/getfa.htm`.

It has been said that the power of a computer increases with the speed of the attached network and with the number of computers it is connected to. Windows increases that power both by improving performance and by improving connectivity. The explosive growth of networks in general and the Internet in particular in the last few years is no accident. Information is addictive, and once you get over the hurdles of initial access and discover the power of networks, you'll never want to be without them. Windows makes networks accessible to nearly everyone. If any one feature of Windows 95 or NT changes what you do with your computer, it will be its improved network support.

## Preemptive multitasking and multithreading

With older, 16-bit versions of Windows, your ability to run multiple programs at the same time depended on all those programs working together using a technique called *cooperative multitasking*. Windows itself never stopped a Windows application from running to go do something else. Instead, programs were required to periodically suspend themselves, yielding control to Windows so other programs could run. Poorly designed programs failed to do this during long operations, or failed to do it often enough, resulting in your computer becoming unresponsive or sluggish.

*Preemptive multitasking* is a different technique that Microsoft incorporated into Windows NT and Windows 95 to solve many of the drawbacks of cooperative multitasking. Using preemptive multitasking, Windows forcibly takes control from one application and gives it to another, doing this switch many times every second. Because a badly behaved application can no longer prevent other applications from running, your computer remains responsive at all times. Windows has done this all along for DOS applications running in a Windows window, and now extends the idea to 32-bit applications. Older 16-bit applications do not receive the benefits of preemptive multitasking, because taking the processor away from them at unpredictable times could violate assumptions their programmers made about the behavior of Windows and cause the application to fail.

Eventually, the limitations on preemptively multitasking older, 16-bit applications will cause you to want to upgrade your applications to 32-bit versions. This is not only because the 16-bit applications cannot be multitasked, but also because limitations Microsoft had to impose in Windows 95 for compatibility with those older applications interfere with preemptive multitasking for 32-bit applications. In the process, you will probably find that you will need more memory and disk space, because as companies have converted their applications to 32 bits, they have also added features. Whether you use the new features or not, they take up memory while they run and they take up space on your disk.

Newer 32-bit Windows programs are starting to exploit a variant of preemptive multitasking called *multithreading*. Multithreading means that the program is doing more than one thing at once, and that Windows supports all those things going on within the program by forcibly transferring the processor from one thread to another many times per second. The advantages of multithreading are that writing programs to do several unrelated things (like print in the background while you edit) can be easier, and that it's possible to improve performance by waiting for events to complete while other actions carry on.

All this — preemptive multitasking and multithreading — means your computer does more at once. It means you can get even more out of a faster CPU, more memory, and a faster disk.

## UNIX

The detractors of Windows take great glee in pointing out that many of the things Windows has only implemented in the last few years (32-bit operation, lack of resource constraints, robust Internet access, and multitasking, for instance) have been part of UNIX for years. Those characteristics make UNIX a strong performer for a wide variety of purposes. In practice, though, UNIX has a major market share only in the server market; its application for desktop computers is limited by these factors:

✦ *Limited device support.* Device driver support for UNIX is nowhere near as common as for Windows. When a new device comes on the market requiring a new driver, the manufacturer usually first writes a Windows 98 driver, then a Windows NT driver. Independent programmers are typically left to write UNIX drivers, often without support from the hardware developer.

✦ *Relatively complex administration.* Installing and configuring UNIX is more of a manual process than that for Windows, requiring more knowledge of the operating system internal design. Users without access to support by knowledgeable UNIX system administrators may not be able to make the system do everything they want without investing a lot of time and effort.

Of the nonproprietary versions of UNIX, the two best known are Linux and FreeBSD. Both are available from a variety of companies; we use the Linux version from Red Hat and the FreeBSD version from Walnut Creek CD-ROM. The UNIX community is investing a lot of effort into improving the tools for managing and configuring systems, to the point where it's possible that within a few years a naïve computer user will have the ability to successfully choose UNIX instead of Windows or Macintosh.

# Benchmarking

The best way to figure out what your computer is doing, and what you need to do to make it perform well, is to run tests that isolate a particular characteristic of the machine, stress it, and measure the results. This process is called *benchmarking*. If we make no other point in this book, we want to be very clear on the need for consistent, careful benchmarks. There are a lot of rules of thumb about computers, and a lot of folklore. Much of it is dead wrong; even more of it is wrong outside a very narrow context. By comparing your benchmark results with the result of running the same benchmark on a different machine, or on your machine after you make a change, you compare objective, quantitative data.

Benchmarking is a complex subject, because there's a lot that can go wrong. Here are a few of the most common problems:

✦ *Failure to control conditions.* Suppose you're trying to measure the speed of your processor with a program running under Windows. If you don't control the other programs running — preferably exit them — you can't be sure that you're measuring what you think you are. In Figure 2-1, for example, we've shown a measurement of processor usage on a system with "nothing" happening. As you'd expect, the left side of the graph (the horizontal axis is increasing time) shows essentially zero processor usage. The bump toward the right side is what's interesting — all we had to do to create the bump was move the mouse around vigorously for a while. If you're trying to measure processor usage and this happens (it does!), you're going to get an incorrect and nonrepeatable answer.

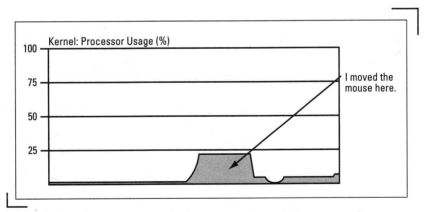

**Figure 2-1:** Failure to control the test conditions can easily render the best benchmark useless.

✦ *Failure to measure what you think you are measuring.* Suppose you're trying to measure disk performance, and your program doesn't take the disk caching — temporary retention of disk data in memory — into account. If the test uses files small enough to fit entirely in the cache, you're going to end up measuring the speed of memory and the caching software, not the disk.

✦ *Failure to measure what you need to measure.* If you're interested in knowing how much plugging a faster processor into your system will speed it up, the obvious thing to do would be to compare the speed of the old processor and that of the new one. If you do, you'll get an answer that wildly overstates how good the results will be when you do the upgrade, because the processor isn't always the limitation — what we'll call the *choke point.* The disk, memory, and video are common choke points as well. Because a choke point limits how fast the processor can go, you'll get results less than a processor speed comparison suggests.

We'll discuss how to do benchmarking, and some tools to do it with, in Chapter 35. In the meantime, the key thing to remember is that you want to be skeptical about most claims about computers that aren't backed up with measured data. Unless you have confidence in the source, you'll want to think some about how the measurements were taken and what they actually measure.

## Summary

✦ No matter what computer you buy, a faster one is coming soon.

✦ The fastest computer isn't the one you need — you need the one that does your work well at a price that fits what you want to invest.

✦ The features and capabilities in UNIX and Windows mean you can get more done than with older software, but you'll stress your computer harder in the process.

✦ Benchmarks are essential to understanding what you need.

✦    ✦    ✦

# Windows System Requirements and Support Options

One of the most often asked questions about Windows is "What are the minimum machine requirements?" As shown in Table 3-1, Microsoft says you need a fairly minimal machine for Windows 98.

| Table 3-1 Stated Minimum Requirements for Windows 98 Are Low | |
| --- | --- |
| **Status** | **Component** |
| Required | 486DX processor or better |
| | 16MB of memory, with more recommended |
| | to improve performance |
| | 120 to 295MB available hard disk space |
| | VGA or higher resolution display |
| | CD-ROM or DVD drive |
| | Mouse or other pointing device |

Windows NT has more capable stated requirements shown in Table 3-2.

| Table 3-2 |
| :---: |
| **Stated Minimum Requirements for Windows NT 4:** |
| **Greater, but Still Low** |

| Status | Component |
| :--- | :--- |
| Required | Pentium processor or better (or a PowerPC, MIPS R4x00, or Alpha processor) |
| | 16MB of memory, with more recommended (32MB for non-Intel compatible processors) |
| | 110MB available hard disk space |
| | VGA or higher resolution graphics card |
| | CD-ROM (or network access in the case of Intel processors) Mouse |

The requirements in Table 3-2 are for Microsoft Windows NT Workstation. NT Server minimum requirements increase only the minimum free disk space. Microsoft also states that system requirements for Windows-based programs may exceed the Windows system requirements themselves.

In reality, the stated requirements are very low. Windows will install and run minimally with these resources, but unless you're an extremely patient person the performance will be unacceptably slow. Many of the features that would make you want Windows in the first place — great networking, multitasking, and multimedia, for example — require additional resources. And, as Microsoft notes, any major application you would want to run requires yet more resources.

The question remains, then, what is the realistic minimum computer you need? We'll see later in the book that the answer really depends on what you want to do with the computer. Before that, though, look at each of Microsoft's recommendations.

## Processor

Microsoft states that Windows 95 can run on almost any 386DX or better processor, while Windows 98 requires at least a 486. The Microsoft Plus! pack recommends a 486 or better processor. They also state that Windows NT requires a Pentium or better processor. Consider those requirements relative to Intel's comparison of "mature" processor performance shown in Figure 3-1, in which you'll see that the slowest 386 processor is only a few hundredths the speed of the 166 MHz Pentium processor (itself out of production), and that the fastest 486 processor is one third the speed of the same Pentium.

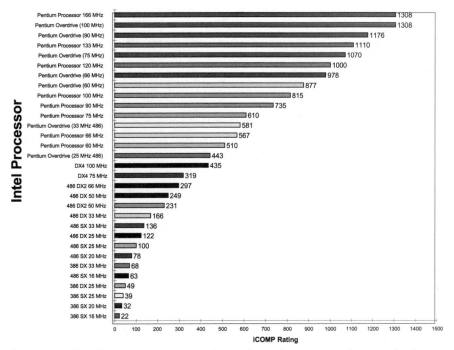

**Figure 3-1:** The slowest 386 processor is nearly 60 times slower than an obsolete Pentium 166 MHz processor.

The figures in the chart are system performance benchmark results. We cover those benchmarks in more detail in Chapter 8. We show you in that chapter that the top of the chart in Figure 3-1 is itself just over one fourth the speed of a Pentium II 450 MHz processor. Realistically, that means that no 386 nor 486 processor will be satisfactory to run Windows 98. Our experiments with a machine using a 386SX-16 processor had dismal results — the machine missed mouse-clicks at times, and although it was stable, it simply wasn't worth waiting for. Performance of a 486 processor at 33 MHz wasn't a lot better. With the price of Pentium machines down under $400, it's not worth using anything less.

Nor do we agree with Microsoft's statement that a Pentium processor is adequate to run Windows NT. While it will run, it will be slow. If your requirements are such that you need the stability or capabilities of Windows NT, you'll want the performance of an Intel Pentium II or AMD K6-2 processor.

We think UNIX systems use nearly as much processing power as do Windows systems. For example, we run a Linux system on a Pentium 133 MHz processor, and while it's no speed demon, it's usable for lightweight work along the lines of what we'd expect to use the same machine for running Windows 98.

## Memory

As Microsoft notes, the minimum memory requirement is for Windows by itself. Table 3-3 shows the minimum memory required for a number of Windows programs.

| Table 3-3 How Far Will the 4MB Minimum Recommended Memory Go? | |
| --- | --- |
| **Program** | **Memory Required** |
| Adobe Illustrator 8.0 | 32MB (64MB recommended) |
| Adobe Photoshop 5.0 | 32MB (64MB recommended) |
| Books That Work 3D Landscape | 4MB |
| Broderbund 3D Home Architect | 8MB |
| CorelDRAW! Version 8.0 | 16MB (32MB recommended) |
| DeLorme Street Atlas USA 6.0 | 8MB |
| id Software Quake II | 16MB (24MB recommended) |
| Microsoft Encarta 99 | 16MB |
| Microsoft Internet Explorer 5.0 | 16MB |
| Microsoft Office for Windows 97 (Standard) | 8MB (more for running multiple programs) |
| Microsoft Visual Basic 6.0 | 16MB (32MB recommended) |
| Microsoft Visual C/C++ 6.0 | 24MB (32MB recommended) |
| Netscape Navigator 4.5 | 16MB |

If anything, the numbers shown in Table 3-3 are low. When quoting system requirements, software manufacturers are not careful to distinguish available memory from total installed memory. These numbers also do not include requirements for most of the optional Windows components, such as the Windows Plus! pack, network server code, disk compression, or additional network protocol support. In practical terms, you'll want at least 4MB to 8MB over the minimum stated memory requirement. Our general memory recommendations are shown in Table 3-4. Specific applications can increase these numbers. (For example, the Windows NT machine we use for image editing with Adobe Photoshop has 192MB; the Windows NT machine we use for developing and printing large, graphics-intensive proposals has 256MB.)

| Table 3-4 | | |
| :--- | :--- | :--- |
| **How Much Memory Do You Need?** | | |
| *Operating System* | *Minimum PCURB Recommendation* | *General PCURB Recommendation* |
| UNIX | 32MB | 64MB |
| Windows 95 | 16MB | 32MB |
| Windows 98 | 32MB | 64MB |
| Windows NT | 64MB | 128MB |

The numbers in Table 3-4 incorporate the observations that memory is relatively inexpensive and that more memory can drastically improve performance on many systems. We'll cover those issues more in later chapters.

## Hard disk

The performance and size of the disk in your computer are critical. If you're still running drives smaller than 1GB, replace them, because they're too small and too slow. It's not difficult to have your Windows 95 directory alone grow to 100MB or more; Microsoft acknowledges that Windows 98 folders can grow to nearly 200MB. Application software has grown in size as well. Our installation of Microsoft Office 97 Professional plus Project 98 is 156MB and doesn't include all the options.

UNIX systems can consume disk space quickly too. We went to install all the software supplied with Red Hat Linux, for example, and found that it wouldn't fit on a 1 gigabyte (GB) drive.

If you upgrade a desktop computer, 2GB is the smallest disk you should consider, and then only for cost-constrained situations. Western Digital terminated production of all drives less than a gigabyte during the summer of 1996. At the end of 1998, Seagate Technology made no drives smaller than 2GB, and made those only for machines targeting the $400 to $500 price point. The ready availability and relatively low cost of high-performance 4GB, 6GB, and 9GB drives makes it impractical to waste time fighting a too-small disk.

## Display

Windows runs at either 640 × 480 or 800 × 600 resolution with a basic Video Graphics Array (VGA) display adapter. No acceleration is necessary to get acceptable performance at those resolutions unless you are playing 3D video games or doing real-time video editing. You can work with a 14-inch monitor at 640 × 480 resolution, but you'll be more productive with a bigger one. We don't recommend anything smaller than a 17-inch monitor now, and suggest 19- or 21-inch units if possible.

You don't need more than minimal video capabilities in a server, because you shouldn't be doing much work directly on a server to begin with. Servers need to be stable and reliable, a quality you enhance by leaving the machine alone to do its work.

# Common Upgrade and Repair Compatibility Pitfalls

Although Microsoft stresses compatibility with existing hardware and software in the development of Windows, there are still pitfalls that you should know about. For example:

✦ Certain display card accelerator chips made by S3 prevent the use of COM4.

✦ Problems have been documented with certain specific versions of the Award BIOS that may or may not have workarounds.

✦ The fact that your PC works well under Windows 3.1 does not guarantee that the hardware is free of problems that may be exposed by Windows 95 and NT. This is particularly true for machines with a great deal of memory, some of which may have been rarely or never used under Windows 3.1.

Microsoft maintains two important documents — the Hardware Compatibility List and the Software Compatibility List. They are available on the Internet on the Microsoft World Wide Web site (the Hardware Compatibility List is at `http://www.microsoft.com/hwtest/hcl/default.htm`; the Software Compatibility List is at `http://www.microsoft.com/windows/thirdparty/compat.htm`). Be sure to check both of those lists for issues relating to the hardware you have or are considering buying, as well as for issues related to the applications you run. You can also check the Microsoft Knowledge Base (`http://support.microsoft.com/support`), which contains a great deal of specific Windows configuration and setup information.

## Shooting yourself in the foot, computer style

A surprisingly common pitfall is trying to take shortcuts on hardware, such as using memory modules at faster than their rated speed or running a processor at a clock speed faster than it is rated for. (You'd do this by setting jumpers on the motherboard to up the processor speed, or by telling the Basic Input/Output System — BIOS — that your memory is faster than it is.) Both are bad ideas.

The problem with running memory too fast is that you can get unreliable operation. Fig. 3-5 shows how the problem can develop. During normal operation, your processor carries out conversations with memory millions of times per second. The figure diagrams one such conversation. At 1, the processor tells the memory the address of the value it wants, and then at 2 commands the memory to read. The memory then starts working, and at 3 completes its operation by returning data to the processor. The processor takes the data at 4.

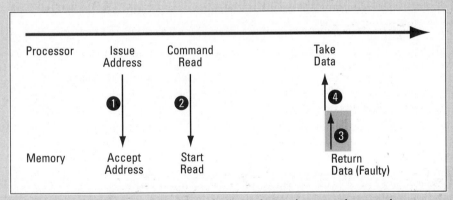

Running memory modules faster than their rated speed can produce random, unpredictable crashes.

Correct operation — not what's in the figure — requires that the memory make the data available prior to the processor taking it. Memories that are too slow create problems because the processor may take the data (at 4) before the memory has retrieved it (at 3). Because the time the memories take varies somewhat, as shown in the shaded area, memories running past their ratings may appear to work. When memories get hot (or when you get unlucky), they can slow down and cause the processor to read garbage. When this happens, your computer crashes.

You need to verify the memory speed required against the documentation for the motherboard. For example, a computer we once built required installing either 60- or 70-nanosecond (ns) memory, depending on the speed at which the processor chip ran. Using 70 ns memory with a processor speed specified for 60 ns memory makes the machine unreliable. Worse, installing a faster processor later as an upgrade could make memories that used to work fail.

*Continued*

*(continued)*

Running any part of a computer faster than specification—called overclocking—can cause random failures. Computer folklore has it that manufacturers label chips for speeds slower than they are capable of running in order to restrict the supply of the faster chips and keep the price up. Although this may be true, chips are most often marked at a particular speed for the obvious reason—running at a faster speed won't work right. Unfortunately for the user trying to save a few bucks, the ways in which a processor fails may not be immediately apparent. Overclocking a processor can cause unreliable operation (for reasons much the same as with trying to run memory too fast), and can cause a processor to overheat. Heat is the enemy of chips and is one of the major causes of failure once a chip has been in service for a while.

These speed and heat problems are due to microscopic chemical variations that occur during the chip manufacturing process. If extreme enough, these variations cause the chip to fail. Lesser variations can limit the speed of the chip, or can cause the chip to consume more power than it is designed for. The power consumed by the processor chip in a personal computer is determined by the computer clock speed, and goes up as the clock speed goes up. Because the power the chip consumes must be dissipated as heat, a chip that consumes too much power generates too much heat. The manufacturer can sell such a chip as a usable device that operates within its specification only by limiting the rated clock speed. You may be able to run the chip at a faster clock speed, but you run the risk of its overheating and ultimately failing.

# Support and Maintenance Service

Computers break and have problems, so one way or another you'll want support and maintenance service. If you have the know-how and the time (and have that time no matter when things go wrong!), you may want to consider doing support yourself or within your company. Otherwise, in making your decisions about what equipment to buy and from whom, you have to consider how you get service and support.

✦ The original manufacturer of your hardware may offer service and support. Most vendors will refer you to the software manufacturers for support on components other than the machine itself. They may also decline to support additions to the machine you make yourself. This is particularly true for the large nationwide computer manufacturers.

✦ Many nationwide vendors offer you the choice of doing repairs yourself according to their instructions (with component exchange by mail), mail-in repairs, or onsite repairs. Local vendors generally offer a choice of walk-in or onsite repair.

✦ Third-party repair companies flourished and then died out in the mid-eighties. The industry trend of outsourcing support operations has once again created third-party companies that, depending on the size of your site and its composition, will contract with you for service and support operations.

What you support yourself and what you support with outside help isn't an all-or-nothing decision. Many companies do in-house computer upgrades, leaving repairs to others. The analysis need not be complex — decide who in your company can do the work you're contemplating keeping in-house, estimate the cost of having them do that work, and compare the estimated costs to bids from outside. Don't forget to account for the value of faster service (whether it's in-house or outside!).

## Summary

✦ The minimum requirements Microsoft states for Windows are unrealistically low.

✦ You can run Windows 98 on a Pentium. You'll want a Pentium II for Windows NT.

✦ You'll end up wanting at least a gigabyte or two of disk, even if you get there via compression.

✦ Check the Microsoft Hardware and Software Compatibility lists.

✦     ✦     ✦

# Your Workload Determines What Your Computer Does

# Choke Points: Where Your Computer Slows Down

**W**hether you balance books or annihilate aliens, the software you run and the things you do determine how much computer power you need. Deciding how to achieve the performance you want in a computer requires that you understand what factors set the speed of a computer. The speed of your computer is determined by the rate it moves information around. The volume of information being moved is set by what you choose to do with the computer. Together, the speed of the computer and the load you impose determine the performance you get. For example:

✦ The volume of data your video subsystem handles every time the processor recomputes the contents of the screen is determined by the resolution and color depth on the screen. The rate for recomputing and repainting the screen (the update or refresh rate) you need is determined by the rate at which the underlying information changes. The rate at which the information changes is in turn determined by what you and your software are doing. Word processors have a low update rate unless you are scrolling the page; videoconferencing and 3D computer-aided design (CAD) fly-throughs require updates many times per second to maintain motion effects. 3D video games require extensive recomputation between updates in addition to the screen updates themselves.

✦ The volume of data the processor needs is determined by the algorithms it runs. The rate at which it needs new data depends on where you look, due to the effects of cache memories. The data requirements are highest inside the processor, less at the external cache, and less yet at the main memory.

In the next chapters, we'll give you an understanding of what makes a computer fast or slow . We start by looking at the computer as a small number of pieces that work together. The central idea behind what you'll learn is that you want to isolate and understand the amount of data being manipulated and the rate at which those manipulations must be done. After we explain what goes on at that level, we take apart each piece and look inside. By the time we're done, at the end of Part IV, you'll understand every part of the computer, why it's designed the way it is, and how to work with manufacturers' literature and magazine reviews to understand what's being offered. In Part V we put the pieces back together so you understand how to specify or build computers that run well as a whole. We do that literally in Part VI, where you'll see how to build both a desktop machine and a server from components.

Computer performance is a balance of the performance of the individual components. In this chapter, we look at what the top-level components are, how they interact, and how they work together to support the software you run. We look at the choices designers have to make in creating products for each component, and at how some choices favor low cost while others favor performance.

# What's Inside Your Computer?

These are the core elements of your computer:

✦ Processor

✦ Memory

✦ Bus

✦ Input/output (I/O) channels

✦ Disk

✦ Display

These basic elements are all that's needed to run programs. A few added pieces, like the keyboard and mouse, give you the ability to interact with those programs, but are not actually required to run programs. Take out the processor, though, and there's no computer. Take out the memory, and there are no programs; the bus, and no components can talk to each other; the disk, and you have no programs to run; the display, and you won't know if your programs ran or not.

The basic operation of a computer is relatively simple. The processor grabs some information from memory (an instruction), and decides what it has been told to do. It grabs more information from memory or disk, changes it if ordered to, and stores it back in memory, on disk, or to the display. It does this basic cycle tens of millions of times every second it's turned on. Only turning it off (or the intervention of power-management programs) pauses the sequence. Every step that fetches an instruction or data and stores a result moves information across the bus, and possibly across the I/O channels.

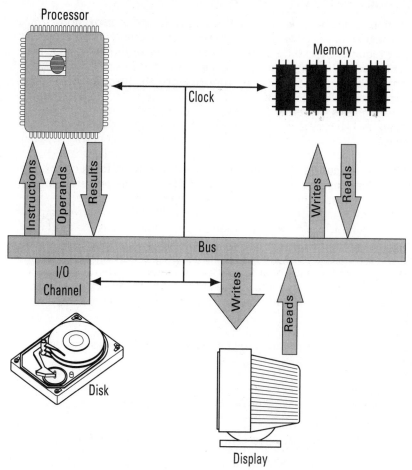

**Figure 4-1:** The speed of the individual components of your computer and the capability of those components to work together efficiently determine the speed of the overall machine.

Figure 4-1 shows the relationship between the core components. Coordinating the operation of it all is a device called the clock, providing the cadence to which the entire assembly marches. The clock times every action by the processor and sets the requirements for operation by all the other components. Every instruction executed by the processor starts on the beginning of a clock cycle. Instructions take one or more clock cycles, and more than one instruction can be executed in a single clock cycle.

## The processor does the work

The execution cycle starts when the processor requests an instruction from memory. The memory receives the request, and one or more clock cycles later returns the requested instruction back across the bus to the processor. The processor decodes the instruction and decides what has to be done to carry it out. If the instruction requires an operand from memory, the processor calculates the address of the operand and commands the memory to fetch the operand. The processor completes gathering the necessary data after some number of clock cycles, computes the result, and if necessary stores it back to memory, disk, or the display.

The instruction execution cycle imposes performance limitations on the computer. If a computer running at a clock speed of 400 MHz can complete an instruction every clock cycle (including reading the instruction and data, computing the result, and storing back to memory), then it will execute 400 million instructions per second, and no more. (Current-generation processors, such as the Intel Pentium II processor, do more than one instruction per clock cycle, so they're faster than this example.) Those instructions are the resources the processor has available to see actions you take with the keyboard, joystick, or mouse; render and present the graphics on the display; move information from disk to memory and back; communicate with your network; run your desktop accessories; keep the current print job going; and do the work you asked.

The actual number of instructions the processor executes per second is determined by a lot of factors, including

✦ How big the instruction is in memory — how many bytes long it is — and how many clock cycles it takes for the memory to deliver the instruction to the processor

✦ How many operands the instruction has, and where they are located

✦ How long it takes the memory or I/O channel (and therefore the disk) to deliver those operands to the processor

✦ How long the processor actually takes to manipulate the operands

✦ How long it takes to put the result where it belongs

✦ The clock rate of the processor

The clock rate is fixed, so counting up how many clock ticks a series of instructions takes tells us how long the series takes. Adding the times the instructions take tells us how long a sequence of instructions (that is, a program) takes to run. The time programs take to run is the measure of performance. Analyzing performance ultimately comes down to counting clock ticks.

# The bus gets information from here to there

The most basic operation a computer does is move information from one place to another — to and from the processor, the memory, the I/O, and the display. Every movement starts in a component and ends in the same or another component. The rate at which things can happen is limited by the rate at which information can be moved across the bus. This rate is typically measured in bytes (8 bits) per second.

Suppose that information moving across the bus comes in chunks of four bytes, which is very common in 32-bit programs written for UNIX or Windows. The simple bus design of the old PC/XT transferred only one byte at a time and took two clock cycles for every byte. The number of information chunks transferred per second over that bus was the clock rate divided by eight (four cycles to fetch the entire 4-byte chunk, with two clock ticks per cycle). The bus clock rate was typically 8 MHz per second, so only one million information chunks could be transferred per second. If an instruction required three chunks to execute (read the instruction, read the operand, and write the result), then only 333,000 instructions per second could be executed.

Computers are not that slow in practice. The example shows that performance in a computer is determined by the rate at which information moves, so any point in the computer that can't move information as quickly as other components becomes a choke point. Understanding and identifying choke points is important because they are what limit the performance of the entire computer.

A bus is a collection of wires, along with an agreement (called a *protocol*) for how all the chips connected to the bus must behave. The wires themselves serve to carry electrical signals among the chips. The signals communicate three kinds of information:

✦ *The command to be carried out.* Computer buses are timed by the clock, with every transaction across the bus taking a number of clock cycles. Every transaction is a bus cycle and carries out a command.

✦ *The address at which the command will be carried out.* Remember that a bus cycle serves to move information from one place to another. One of those two places is implicit in the bus command. The address signals identify the second one. Whether the address specifies the source or destination of the information being moved depends on the bus command.

✦ *The information being moved.* Wires carry information as it moves around the machine. Information is *always* represented as a number, whether its purpose is to be an instruction to start playing a song, a number representing the days until your birthday, or a character in a message from your best friend. Everything is a number, and numbers are what move across buses.

Because bus cycles move information from one place to another, there are two players in every bus cycle, and the cycle itself is very much like a conversation. Let's listen in on one conversation between your processor and memory:

*Processor:* Memory, I'd like the number at address 77349.

*(Pause while the memory works.)*

*Memory:* Here it is. The number stored there was 42.

That conversation represents a read of memory by the processor. The processor can also write to memory:

*Processor:* Memory, store a number at address 77349.

*Processor:* Memory, the number to store is 100250.

*(Pause while the memory works.)*

It's no accident that the memory never states that it has actually received the information. Although there are buses that use that idea (buses in some workstations, for example), the ones in Intel-based UNIX and Windows computers do not. Instead, they rely on the *assumption* that the source will get the data there before the processor reads from the bus. If not, the destination picks up garbage. Your computer crashes at best, but at worst silently corrupts some calculation or stored value.

The device that starts and controls the conversation is called the *bus master*. This will be the processor for most bus cycles (as in both examples above). Other parts of the computer (such as a disk controller, network interface, or display card) can also be bus masters, freeing the processor to do other work while these components transfer their own information. Cycles for the processor are interleaved with bus cycles for other masters, ensuring that all get access to the bus.

In practice, you get at hundreds of millions of bytes per second of data across the bus in current generation computers, not the mere third of a megabyte per second in the PC/XT example above. Computer designers have engineered that speed gain in several ways:

✦ *Transfer more information per bus cycle.* If 32 bits of information (four bytes) need to be transferred, transferring it one byte per bus cycle is inefficient. That's what the original IBM PC did, however, and is what every card in your computer plugged into an 8-bit ISA (Industry Standard Architecture) slot does every time your processor talks to it. The IBM PC/AT extended the ISA bus to transfer 16 bits, doubling the speed of the bus. The Peripheral Component Interconnect (PCI) bus transfers 32 bits in one cycle. Newer display cards transfer 64 and 128 bits between their own private memories and other chips on the card.

✦ *Use fewer clock cycles per bus cycle.* Fewer clock cycles per bus cycle mean that more bus cycles happen per second, so more information gets moved. The number of clock cycles in a bus cycle isn't easy to reduce, however, because it affects how fast other components have to run. For example, suppose a memory read cycle takes three clock cycles (issue read command and address, wait, and pick up data). If we remove the clock cycle where the processor waits, then we reduce the time the memory has from when it gets the address and command to when it has to return the data. We get 50 percent more information across the bus, but we need faster, more expensive memories.

✦ *Run the bus at a faster clock rate.* Having the bus do what it does, only faster, is a pretty direct way to get more performance. The bus on the original IBM PC ran at the same rate as the processor, which was 4.77 MHz. As faster 8088, 8086, and (in the PC/AT) 80286 processors became available, bus speeds tied to the processor increased to 8 MHz, 10 MHz, and faster. Running ISA buses faster than 8 MHz, however, exposed limitations on the cards plugged into the ISA bus. Many of those ISA cards were only capable of performing correctly for bus clock rates up to 8 MHz. Bus masters sometimes could only operate correctly at slower rates than that. Those problems led designers to run the ISA bus clock slower than the processor clock in all current machines.

**Cross-Reference**

Using these tricks and some others, a PCI (Peripheral Component Interconnect) bus can hit burst rates as fast as 133 million bytes per second. That turns out to be enough for communicating with most disks and networks, but not enough for the highest-performance video cards and for communication between the processor and memory. We'll cover how designers accommodate those requirements in the section "PCI" in Chapter 9, "Cache, Memory, and Bus."

## Memory holds information for the processor

If you've ever seen one of the old pigeonhole desks, you've got a picture of how memory is organized in your computer. Figure 4-2 shows the idea—a memory in a PC is a collection of places to store numbers, each with its own address. The meaning of what's stored in each memory location depends on the program that owns the information. The number 42 could be part of an instruction to the processor, part of your address on a network, a count of eggs you own (meaning that you likely have more than enough in the refrigerator), part of a bigger number that's the cost of last night's pizza, one dot in a drawing, the character "B" in "HAPPY BIRTHDAY," or a lot of other things. The memory doesn't care what a number's meaning is, only that it needs to be faithfully stored and retrieved on request.

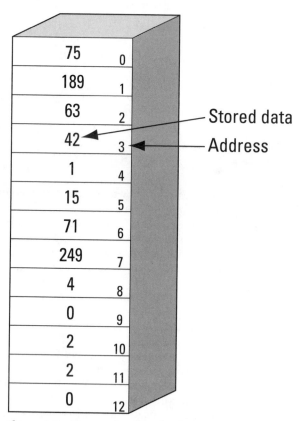

**Figure 4-2:** Memory is a bunch of compartments. Each one stores a number.

In many of these examples the number stored in a memory location is part of something larger, because numbers in the range from 0 to 255 (8-bit [1-byte] values, which are what fit in one memory location) simply aren't enough to do everything. If the computer has to remember that you have thousands of paperclips in inventory, it has to use at least two memory locations — bytes — to store that fact. In 32-bit programs for Windows or UNIX, it's more likely that programs store numbers as 32-bit values, requiring 4 bytes. If the first byte holding your paperclip inventory is at address 102916, then locations 102916 through 102919 hold the entire number. The same idea is true for instructions, which can require one, two, or more bytes to hold. Any time the processor references the first byte of a number or instruction, it will reference all of them.

The fact that the processor is probably going to read all four bytes of a number if it reads any of them is why the idea of making the bus wider works. If the processor isn't going to use the other three bytes following the first one, transferring all four is pointless. Strings — a group of characters in order, one following another — are common exceptions to storing information in 32-bit chunks, but because strings are so often at least several characters long, very little of the effort in retrieving four characters (four bytes) at a time goes to waste.

While buses are multiple bytes wide, memory chips are commonly one or a few bits (four or eight are common) wide, and some number of addresses deep. It takes several memory chips in parallel to form a structure as wide as the bus. Those parallel structures are built into modules. Engineers build up modules from memory chips, and describe the results in several ways:

✦ *Capacity.* A memory module holds a specified number of bytes, with one address corresponding to each byte. The capacity of a memory module is the number of bytes it holds, and is independent of the other characteristics.

✦ *Width.* A memory module built from multiple chips in parallel can be as wide as the engineer wants, with the width being the number of bits (eight to a byte) that the memory accesses at one time. Common widths for memory modules used in current computers are 32, 36, 64, and 72 bits, depending on whether or not your computer checks data transfers from memory for reliability (see the error detection and correction bullet below). Don't confuse the bit width of memory with the number of pins on the module. Common numbers of pins are 30, 72, and 168.

✦ *Access time.* There is a minimum interval the memory requires from the time it's told to read a number to the time when the number is available for the processor to use. Current computers generally expect this interval — the access time — to be no longer than 50, 60, or 70 nanoseconds. (A nanosecond is one billionth of a second.) Times for newer memory technology (made possible by Synchronous DRAM memory architectures) are typically 8 to 12 ns. Smaller access times mean the memory is faster and more expensive, but faster memory does not make your computer run faster. The memory has to be fast enough to keep up with the processor, but because the clock and the processor control speed, not the memory, faster memory than the system can exploit has no value.

✦ *Cycle time.* Another interval, the cycle time, specifies the minimum time from one memory operation to the next.

✦ *Error detection and correction.* Like all the chips in a computer, memories can fail. Chips are vulnerable to soft errors, which are errors that corrupt the value stored in the chip even though the chip itself has not been damaged. (The technology used to put millions of bits into a small memory chip makes them more vulnerable than other, less dense chips.) Computer designers use something called parity checking to detect when errors occur in memories. An extra, ninth bit (called the *parity bit*) accompanies every byte. Inadvertent changes in the bits within the byte (or to the parity bit itself) cause the value in the parity bit to be wrong, which can be detected by the processor when the byte is read. More powerful techniques than parity bits allow errors to be corrected as well as detected, but may require even more extra bits in parallel with the data byte itself.

The performance a memory gives — its *bandwidth* — depends on its width, access time, and cycle time. Greater width and faster times result in greater memory bandwidth. Memory width is relatively easy to come by, because all the engineer has to do is put more chips in parallel. Access time and cycle time can be reduced by building faster chips, but the cost of the memory goes up dramatically.

## The disk holds information the memory can't

Memory costs 50 to 110 times as much as the equivalent in disk capacity. That is why common memory sizes are 32 to 128MB, while fixed, or hard, disks (disks that are permanently sealed in their drives) are now common in the 3 to 16 gigabyte (GB, billions of bytes) range, with drives of 100+GB at the same price points coming in a year or less. This huge difference in size means that you can afford to store far more on disk than in memory. Disks also have the nice characteristic of remembering what you wrote to them after you turn off the power. There is computer memory that can do that too, but it is significantly more expensive than conventional computer memory.

Disks are inexpensive, but their access times are about a hundred thousand times slower than memory, far too slow for processors to use for storing the instructions and data they are working on and still give you good performance. That's why your computer uses disks for storing programs and data when you're not using them, but loads the programs into memory when you're actively working with them.

An I/O channel connects your disks to the computer's bus. (Later in the book we'll use the more common term *I/O bus* instead of I/O channel. We've used *I/O channel* here to be sure there's no confusion between the computer bus and the I/O bus.) The channel interface — often called a *host adapter* — receives requests from the processor, rearranges the request if it needs to, and hands it off to the channel. Your I/O devices — be they hard drives, CD-ROM drives, or tape drives, connect to the I/O channel and receive the processor's requests. I/O channels come in different technologies, such as SCSI or IDE. Drives only work with the corresponding type of I/O channel, so you'll hear terms like SCSI drives or IDE drives. Depending on what I/O channel you have, you may also be able to connect scanners and other devices to the channel.

**Caution**   The two major I/O channel types are IDE (which is quite simple and inexpensive) and SCSI (which can be faster and more flexible, but is more complex). Low-cost I/O channels rely on the processor to help transfer data, reducing overall performance and limiting the achievable transfer rate. Higher-performance I/O channels take on the task of moving the data themselves, working as bus masters to offload the processor and improve the transfer rate. The same techniques that speed the bus — such as making it faster and wider — also speed the I/O channel. Limitations on the transfer rates possible through the bus, such as the very limited transfer rate through an ISA bus, act as choke points to limit the speed of the I/O channel as well.

A disk drive is not only slower than memory, it's also harder to talk to. Instead of having an array of storage locations that are all equally accessible (as memory does), the physical construction of a disk has distinct major structures. The differing characteristics of these structures make a disk much more complicated to use. Figure 4-3 shows the insides of a typical disk, including the spindle, platters, heads, and positioning arms.

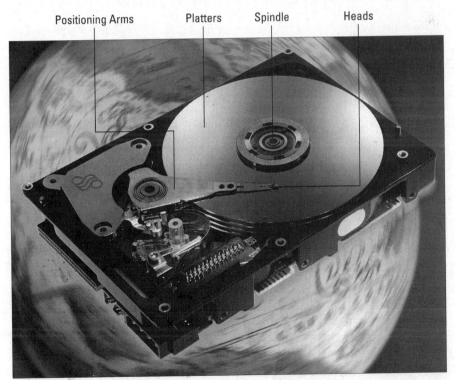

**Figure 4-3:** The many different structures inside a disk make talking to it more complicated.

The disk is built from one or more *platters*, which rotate on the spindle. Both sides of the platter are used. The platters are coated with magnetic material (like on a videotape) so information can be recorded. Information is read and written on the platters by *heads*, which are mounted on arms. The platters spin under the heads, so for a given head position each head traces a circle. The heads move together on the arm, so the set of heads traces a cylinder over the platters. Each circle under a head is called a *track*; each track is divided into chunks called *sectors*. All the bytes in one sector get read or written at once.

A location on a disk is really three numbers:

✦ *Cylinder*—How far in or out on the platters the positioning arm puts the heads.

✦ *Head*—Which surface of which platter. Because there is one head per surface, identifying the head precisely identifies the surface. The combination of a cylinder number and head number uniquely identifies a track.

✦ *Sector*—The chunk of data within a track. The combination of a track number and a sector number uniquely identifies a chunk of data.

Figure 4-4 shows the layout of one platter on a disk. The cylinder, head, and sector numbers combine to uniquely identify one block of data on the disk, called a sector. Sectors on PC disks contain 512 bytes.

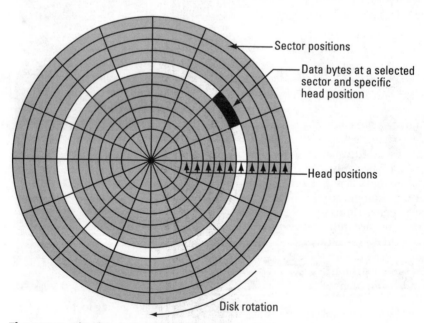

**Figure 4-4:** The data in one pie-shaped cut under one head position is a sector on a disk.

The total capacity of a disk is the number of cylinders times the number of heads times the number of sectors times the sector size, or

```
Total size = cylinders * heads * sectors * 512
```

For example, suppose you have a disk containing 13,456 cylinders, 15 heads per cylinder, and 63 sectors per track. Multiplying those numbers together and then times 512 bytes per sector shows that the disk contains 6,510,551,040 bytes. One megabyte contains 1,048,576 bytes, so dividing shows that the disk contains 6,208.94MB. Your disk is sold as a 6.5GB disk.

Beyond its capacity and expected lifetime, the important characteristics of a disk all relate to performance. The most commonly quoted disk performance characteristics are

✦ *Rotation rate*. Rotation rate is the speed at which the disk platters turn under the heads, measured in revolutions per minute. Rotation rates presently run from 3,600 RPM to 12,000 RPM. Faster rotation rates are better because they reduce one component of the access time and because they increase the data transfer rate the drive can sustain.

✦ *Access time*. Access time is how long it takes from when the processor requests data from the disk until it's available. The position of the heads and platters under the heads makes the access time variable, so specifications are averages. Access times presently run from 14 milliseconds (ms, one thousandth of a second) down to 8 ms. Smaller access times are better.

✦ *Sustained transfer rate*. The data transfer rate a disk can sustain is the rate at which the combination of disk and I/O channel can, over a period of time, maintain a data transfer. The transfer rate is typically limited to the rate at which sectors sweep under the heads, because that determines how much data can actually be transferred onto or off of the platters.

The rotation rate is set by the speed of the motor turning the disk. The faster it turns, the faster sectors fly past the heads. More sectors past the heads means more bytes, so the sustained transfer rate for a disk with a higher rotation rate should be higher. A higher rotation rate also means that, when the sector your processor wants is not right under the head at the time of the request, less time will be required before the sector rotates around to be read. Faster rotation rates improve access times (although rotation rate is not the major factor). Faster rotation rates are more expensive, partly because the electronics needed to handle the higher data rates on and off the disk are more expensive.

Access time is primarily determined by the speed with which the arms can move the heads from one cylinder to another. A head positioning motor moves the arms back and forth. Lower access times require more power and greater accuracy from the head positioning motor, increasing its cost.

Effective sustained transfer rates of from 3MB to 10MB per second are standard today. Rates of 20MB to 30MB per second are possible with excellent equipment. Higher capacity disks sometimes achieve increased capacity by putting more on a single track. For a constant rotation rate, that higher density translates into more data per second sweeping past the head, increasing the sustained transfer rate.

Why are access time and transfer rate important? Access time measures how long it is from the time the processor asks to read the file to the point when the file is actually accessed, while the transfer rate measures how long the transfer will take once it starts. The total time to read a file is the sum of the access time and the transfer time. Knowing that, consider that the executable file alone for Microsoft Word for Windows 2000 is in excess of 8MB; that for Netscape Communicator 4 is nearly 4MB. Supporting files add to these numbers. Not all of the executable file needs to be resident in memory at one time, but it's still a lot to load when the program starts. The enormous functionality of the software translates directly into large program files that have to be read from disk, so the faster the disk does its work, the faster the program starts. Multimedia presents the same issue — relatively large files that need to be retrieved quickly.

## And the display makes it perfectly clear

A display card is memory with some surrounding electronics. Figure 4-5 shows one from that point of view. Your monitor requires three signals, one each for red, green, and blue. These signals are analog signals, like what goes to the speakers in your stereo, not numbers. The digital-to-analog (D/A) converters do the work of changing the numbers the processor puts in the display memory into the signals the monitor needs. Everything else interesting happens in the display memory.

If you look very closely at your monitor, you see thousands of tiny dots. Each one of these dots is called a *pixel*, and is represented by a number in the display memory. Table 4-1 shows the minimum display memory your video board has to have for popular video resolutions. The resolution and number of colors you use directly determine your minimum display memory size. It's interesting to note that at 1280 × 1024 resolution, using only 16 colors, you need 640K of memory on the display card. That size, now inadequate for a video card, is the same as the total amount DOS could once address for programs. If you've ever wondered why a graphical operating system like Windows or UNIX/X Windows needs more power to run than DOS, here's a clear example that you ask more of it!

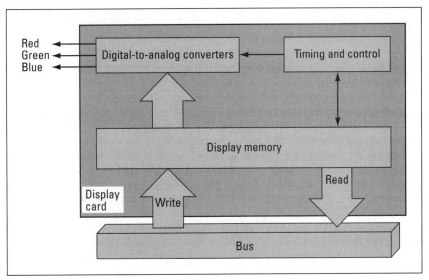

**Figure 4-5:** All the interesting work in a display card centers around the memory.

### Table 4-1
### Resolution, Colors, and Display Memory Size

| Resolution | Colors | Total Pixels | Total Bytes |
|---|---|---|---|
| 320 × 240 | 256 | 76,800 | 75K |
| 640 × 480 | 256 | 307,200 | 300K |
| 640 × 480 | 65,536 (16-bit) | 307,200 | 600K |
| 640 × 480 | 16.7 million (24-bit) | 307,200 | 900K |
| 800 × 600 | 256 | 480,000 | 469K |
| 800 × 600 | 65,536 (16-bit) | 480,000 | 938K |
| 800 × 600 | 16.7 million (24-bit) | 480,000 | 1.38MB |
| 1024 × 768 | 256 | 786,432 | 768K |
| 1024 × 768 | 65,536 (16-bit) | 786,432 | 1.5MB |
| 1024 × 768 | 16.7 million (24-bit) | 786,432 | 2.25MB |
| 1280 × 1024 | 256 | 1,310,720 | 1.25MB |

*continued*

## Table 4-1 (continued)

| Resolution | Colors | Total Pixels | Total Bytes |
|---|---|---|---|
| 1280 × 1024 | 65,536 (16-bit) | 1,310,720 | 2.5MB |
| 1280 × 1024 | 16.7 million (24-bit) | 1,310,720 | 3.75MB |
| 1600 × 1200 | 256 | 1,920,000 | 1.83MB |
| 1600 × 1200 | 65,536 (16-bit) | 1,920,000 | 3.66MB |
| 1600 × 1200 | 16.7 million (24-bit) | 1,920,000 | 5.49MB |
| 1,800 × 1,440 | 256 | 2,592,000 | 2.47MB |
| 1,800 × 1,440 | 65,536 (16-bit) | 2,592,000 | 4.94MB |
| 1,800 × 1,440 | 16.7 million (24-bit) | 2,592,000 | 7.42MB |
| 2,048 × 1,536 | 256 | 3,145,728 | 3.00 MB |
| 2,048 × 1,536 | 65,536 (16-bit) | 3,145,728 | 6.00MB |
| 2,048 × 1,536 | 16.7 million (24-bit) | 3,145,728 | 9.00MB |

As the information to be displayed changes, your processor has to update the contents of the display memory. How much work the processor does to do the update is determined by how much display memory it has to update. For example, when we wrote this chapter for the first edition of the book, we had the display set for 1280 × 1024 resolution and 256 colors. If the screensaver kicked in and we wiggled the mouse, the processor had to redraw every pixel on the screen, which meant (from the table) that the processor had to move 1.25MB of data into the display memory. The processor executes a lot of instructions for every pixel, so in redrawing the screen it executes hundreds of millions of instructions. If all the data the processor needs is in memory, the redraw takes several seconds. If the processor has to bring data back in from disk, the redraw takes tens of seconds.

As computer capabilities go up, so do the computing requirements. When we wrote the first and second editions of this book, we used a display set for 1600 × 1200 resolution at 65,536 colors. That meant that the processor had to move 3.66MB of data to refresh the screen, up from 1.25MB. Our computer had gotten faster in the same time, so the redraw took about the same amount of time although it did much more work.

Display update performance is critically important to game players, particularly those playing action games where the screen changes continuously, and 3D CAD designers doing three-dimensional fly-throughs of their design. Look again at Table 4-1 to see why. Although a few years ago 3D games used a display resolution of 320 × 240 at 256 colors, game designers today assume hardware acceleration in the video board, and it's common to see games running at 640 × 480 in 16-bit color. By the end of 1999, we expect the standard to be 800 × 600 (or higher) resolution and 24- or 32-bit color.

Updating the entire screen at 800 × 600 resolution and 32-bit color requires the processor move 1.88MB out of memory and into display memory for each update, for a total of 3.75MB moved across the bus. If the processor updates the display forty times per second (a good gaming rate), the processor, bus, and memory have to handle about 75MB per second, which is right around the maximum sustained capacity of the PCI bus (remember that the 133MB per second number we stated earlier was a peak number). It's bad design to use the complete capacity of any component, which is why designers have created new buses for video cards and why video cards themselves have onboard accelerators.

Your eye sees motion on the display because it fills in the differences between the successive images (frames) it sees. As long as the frame rate (the rate at which the screen is updated) is high enough, you remain unaware of that process and perceive smooth motion. If the frame rate gets too low, you become aware of successive frames and the motion becomes jerky. Your television updates the screen 30 times per second. Current-technology computer monitors redraw the screen at least 60 to 75 times a second. Many people complain about flicker on the screen at update rates of 60 times per second or less.

What all this means is that the rate at which information flows into the display memory determines how happy you'll be with video performance. Technologies that increase that rate make motion-intensive programs work better, and will make other graphic applications snappier as well. The kinds of approaches engineers are using to get better display performance include

✦ *Get a bigger hammer.* Increasing the performance of the path into the display memory means you get more information in and out. The highest-performance display cards today are ones using the AGP (Accelerated Graphics Port) bus, replacing ones using the PCI bus. The 2X version of AGP can transfer 533MB per second peak; the coming 4X version will double that. Older cards limited to the ISA bus are hopelessly outclassed by these newer boards. The original PC display card data paths were 8 bits wide, while current-generation display cards use 64 and 128-bit data paths. This means that the newer cards move eight or sixteen times as much data into and out of the display memory for every cycle.

✦ *Delegate.* All the performance numbers assume that the processor does all the work. For example, when a line has to go from one place to the other, the processor has to individually draw every dot that makes up the line. The alternative is to put a specialized chip, called an *accelerator,* on the card that can be told to do things the processor needs done. Instead of drawing every pixel in a line, for instance, the processor can simply tell the accelerator to draw the line. Instead of transferring hundreds of thousands of bytes to draw all those dots, the processor transfers a few bytes that give the accelerator the command.

**Cross-Reference** We discuss other tricks for better display performance in Chapter 18, "Video Adapters."

# Why There Are No Simple Fixes

Speeding up the bus so it transfers information in no time at all won't make your computer the fastest one around. Putting a super-wide bus and genius-level accelerator into the display card won't make updates happen in no time at all. Replacing all your disks with far more expensive RAM (as people have done) won't make your programs run instantly.

**Note** The answer to why simple fixes often don't work is *choke points*. Eliminating one choke point—the place that makes the computer slow—doesn't solve all your problems, it just brings another to the surface. Getting your computer to where it's as fast as you want requires that you keep isolating and eliminating choke points. Doing this at a price you can afford requires that you analyze and understand the relationships among components.

## Finding the choke points

Comparing two systems shows how important finding choke points can be. The two systems summarized in Table 4-2 both use processors based on the Intel P6 architecture running Windows 98, and both have 64MB of memory. However, they have radically different video performance.

| Table 4-2 Which System Is Faster? | | |
|---|---|---|
| **Component** | **System A** | **System B** |
| Processor | 266 MHz Pentium II | 266 MHz Celeron |
| Cache Memory | 512K | 0K |
| Memory | 64MB | 64MB |
| Disk Controller | PCI SCSI | PCI IDE |
| Video | PCI (3D accelerator) | AGP (3D accelerator) |

Looking at the components individually shows that the two systems have similarities and unique advantages:

✦ *Processor.* Both systems have a 266 MHz processor and use similar chips inside the processor assembly. There should be no performance differences due to the processor.

✦ *Cache.* Cache memory is very fast memory—three to four times faster than RAM—that remembers instructions and data that have been recently used in the hope they'll be used again soon. If that happens, then the processor gets the value immediately, without any delay. Because the System B processor has no cache, there should be a significant performance difference.

✦ *Memory.* Both systems have the same amount of memory, so if they're running the same software, memory should not be a factor in how fast they run.

✦ *Disk controller.* The PCI I/O channels in the two systems transfer at about the same peak rate. The SCSI channel in System A can overlap operations between two devices, which could reduce total operation time.

✦ *Video.* Both video systems are accelerated. System B uses an AGP display bus, which is faster than PCI. The accelerator chips are identical, and both support 3D acceleration.

Benchmarking

Overall, System A has more cache, while System B has a faster video bus. Which one delivers faster video performance? We ran experiments using drivers intended to provide the fastest possible video performance. The video chips were identical, so we used the same drivers. The experiments showed that System A video was distinctly faster than System B.

The important difference between the two systems turned out to be the processor cache. The instruction sequences for video redraw are repeated over and over, and fit in the System A cache. That means that System A avoids memory access for instruction fetches while running the redraw code, while System B (with no cache) must tie up the bus fetching instructions, slowing updates to the video card. System A has enough cache to hold those sequences, so it avoids those problems.

## Eliminating the choke points

Both System A and System B can be upgraded. Starting with System A and applying what you've read about components and choke points so far, take a look at the options and analyses in Table 4-3. Nothing about the computer is drastically out of balance, so what you'll find are options that improve performance in specific areas. The problem to watch for when upgrading System A is to make sure that you don't upgrade one element past the capabilities of the others.

## Table 4-3
## Upgrade Strategies Vary in Cost and Payoff for System A

| *Upgrade Option* | *Analysis* |
|---|---|
| Pentium II processor at 300–450 MHz | The processor is the source of all the information that shows up on the display, so upgrading to a faster processor from the 266 MHz Pentium II will let the system generate information faster. Some Pentium II motherboards were limited to 300 MHz processor speeds; later ones could handle chips up to 450 MHz. An upgrade to less than a 350 MHz processor probably isn't worth the cost, but if you have one of the later motherboards, the processor upgrade to as high as 450 MHz is relatively painless and inexpensive. Intel's benchmarks suggest that a system with a 450 MHz Pentium II will be around 160 percent faster than one with a 266 MHz Pentium II processor. |
| Add-on or replacement video board | Video boards differ greatly in their performance, particularly their 3D performance. If the 3D acceleration in the system is poor (as was the case for these two systems), replacing the card with a faster one can have dramatic impact. It's possible to get complete replacement boards capable of 2D and 3D acceleration, or to get add-on boards that only accelerate 3D (using the existing board for 2D). The processor and PCI bus can both limit 3D performance to less than the 3D accelerator's maximum frame rate, but with a 266 MHz processor, significant gains can be expected. |
| Motherboard, processor, and video card replacement | Assuming a replacement motherboard can use the same memory as on the existing one, a combination motherboard, processor, and video card replacement can eliminate all the choke points for video performance. Updating to a motherboard capable of supporting a 450 MHz processor, along with the processor itself, gives the system all the processing power currently possible to support the video board. A motherboard upgrade will also likely bring with it an AGP graphics port, so a high-performance 2D+3D accelerator card using AGP can be added. |

Asking the same upgrade question for System B produces the rather different options and analyses in Table 4-4. System B has a significant choke point because it has no cache, so upgrades can be more precisely targeted and provide more payoff for the cost. Once the cache problem is fixed, the existing AGP port makes a video card upgrade (as with System A) a good second candidate.

### Table 4-4
### System B Has More Clear-Cut Upgrade Options

| Upgrade Option | Analysis |
|---|---|
| 300 or 333 MHz Celeron processor with cache | The lack of cache in System B is a result of the 266 MHz Celeron processor, which is a relatively low-cost chip designed for systems at low price points. The 300A version of the Celeron, and the 333 MHz and faster versions, all have cache, so they give up far less performance when compared to the equivalent Pentium II processor. In the case of System B, an upgrade to a 300A processor should give around a 30 percent gain; upgrade to the 400 MHz version should gain over 50 percent. |
| Add-on or replacement video board | As with System A, an upgrade to a faster video card, especially when combined with a processor upgrade, can make a large difference in 3D video performance. The existence of the faster AGP port on the motherboard would tend to favor replacing the existing video board with a 2D+3D AGP unit to avoid a choke point on the PCI bus. |
| Motherboard replacements | The same option for motherboard replacement exists for System B as for System A. In the case of System B, the advantage of a motherboard replacement would be that, instead of a Celeron processor, the system could be upgraded to use a Pentium II or K6 processor, reaching faster clock rates and bringing even more cache onboard. |

In summary, both systems have choke points. Although the choices for upgrade are similar between the two systems, the upgrade costs and performance results will be different. Both systems may perform well for 3D applications with just a video card change, which could cost as little as $70 for a quality board.

For users who don't have severe video performance requirements, both systems we describe may be perfectly adequate—keep in mind that there's no reason to upgrade a computer unless there are specific performance or capacity problems you need to solve. Upgrading just to "tune it up" is likely an expensive and pointless exercise.

# Preventing a modem or network from bringing your computer to its knees

Dropping a modem into your computer is about the easiest upgrade you can make. Windows and UNIX have made creating local area networks (LANs) almost as easy. Every online service and Internet Service Provider, as well as every computer publication you can find, will tell you a modem is the key to the Internet and all the information, entertainment, news, and more available there. LANs are powerful in a different way, giving you the tools to share work and equipment. For the work we do, we literally can't imagine doing it without both the Internet and our LAN.

The untold story of modems and networks, however, is the hidden load they can impose on a computer, slowing an underpowered system to the point of unusability.

## Unseen loads from your modem

If you've ever been subject to frequent interruptions while you work, you'll understand why modems can so dramatically slow a computer. Most of the time, your computer is busy doing what you ask. Whenever the modem needs help, such as to take a received character and store it, the computer has to stop what it's doing, carefully note what was happening so it can go back to work when the interruption is done, start running the program to respond to the modem, read or write the next character for the modem, note what work was accomplished, end the modem service program, find the record of what was happening prior to the interrupt, get set up to resume working, and go back to work. You can get tired just listing it all.

The process UNIX or Windows goes through when the modem needs work done is called *servicing an interrupt*. The interrupt begins when the modem makes an interrupt request (IRQ), and ends when the computer resumes what it had been doing. From a performance viewpoint, interrupting a computer is one of the most expensive things you can do. As you might conclude from the list of everything that has to happen, the operating system has to execute a lot of instructions to service an interrupt. If interrupts happen infrequently, as is the case for the keyboard while you are typing, the number of instructions required for interrupt service isn't a problem. Modems are a very different story, because the rates can be much faster. Table 4-5 shows the problem, and why processing interrupts for a fast modem put a phenomenal load on the processor.

| | Table 4-5 | | |
|---|---|---|---|
| | **Modem Loads on Processors** | | |
| **Modem Speed (bits per second, bps)** | **Time Between Interrupts (in microseconds)** | **Instructions per Second to Service Interrupts** | **Percentage of Processor Used for Interrupt Service** |
| 1,200 | 833.33 | 1,200,000 | 1% |
| 2,400 | 416.67 | 2,400,000 | 2% |
| 4,800 | 208.33 | 4,800,000 | 5% |
| 9,600 | 104.17 | 9,600,000 | 10% |
| 14,400 | 69.44 | 14,400,000 | 14% |
| 19,200 | 52.08 | 19,200,000 | 19% |
| 28,800 | 34.72 | 28,800,000 | 29% |
| 38,400 | 26.04 | 38,400,000 | 38% |
| 57,600 | 17.36 | 57,600,000 | 58% |
| 115,200 | 8.68 | 115,200,000 | 115% |

The calculations in Table 4-5 assume that your computer can execute 100 million instructions per second, and that every interrupt from the modem requires that the processor execute 1,000 instructions to service the interrupt. Real life will vary due to differences in processors and operating systems. Taken simplistically, this table understates how bad the problem can be since it only shows the processing load for one direction. Two-way communication through the modem would (worst case) double this load. Many old computers using the 8250 chip (the device that connects the modem to the processor through the bus) are subject to the particularly severe communications loading as suggested in the table. The older, slower processors incur less interrupt service overhead, so the percentage of the processor used is not as bad as it might appear. As processors have become more sophisticated, the time required to service an interrupt has become greater. As operating systems have become more sophisticated, the work the computer has to do to process the interrupt has become more complex, requiring more instructions to be executed and increasing the time to service the interrupt.

The reason that the 8250 presents such a terrible load is that the processor has to service an interrupt for every character sent or received. Engineers recognized that servicing a modem this way at higher data rates created an enormous load on the processor, and reduced the load to process an interrupt by making it possible for the processor to combine the work of several interrupts that would otherwise be separated in time. The 16550 chip includes a buffer that allows the processor to send or receive between eight and sixteen characters in one interrupt service operation. Assume that the number of instructions is roughly the same for one character as eight (which is true, because the majority of the overhead is in getting to where the processor is ready to do the real work and in resuming the interrupted program). In that case, if we also assume that the average interrupt causes four characters to be handled, the calculations in Table 4-6 result.

| Table 4-6 **Processing Loads is Reduced with the 16550 Chip** | | | |
|---|---|---|---|
| *Modem Speed (bits per second, bps)* | *Time Between Interrupts (in microseconds)* | *Instructions per Second to Service Interrupts* | *Percentage of Processor Used for Interrupt Service* |
| 14,400 | 277.78 | 3,600,000 | 4% |
| 19,200 | 208.33 | 4,800,000 | 5% |
| 28,800 | 138.89 | 7,200,000 | 7% |
| 38,400 | 104.17 | 9,600,000 | 10% |
| 57,600 | 69.44 | 14,400,000 | 14% |
| 115,200 | 34.72 | 28,800,000 | 29% |

The table reflects a significant decrease in processing load. The data in Tables 4-5 and 4-6 represent an imaginary computer. The actual load a modem presents to your processor depends on several factors:

✦ *The sustained data rate.* The calculations in Tables 4-5 and 4-6 assume that the modem transfers data continuously at its maximum rate. If the actual transmissions are *bursty* (that is, if they only happen at times, with intervals of inactivity in between), the processing load is reduced.

✦ *The speed and type of the processor.* For a specific modem data rate, a faster processor (of the same type) uses less of its total capacity servicing interrupts. The Pentium and later processors impose significant overhead for servicing interrupts, so some of the raw speed gain is lost.

✦ *The efficiency of the operating system servicing interrupts.* The cost in instructions to service an interrupt depends on the operating system. DOS imposed an overhead of zero — high-performance communications programs did all the work themselves. Windows 3.1 imposed overhead in its communications device driver. Windows has a more complex, 32-bit communications device driver, but has native support for the 16550 chip. UNIX imposes overheads similar to or a little less than those of Windows.

Some newer modems allow you to connect the modem through the parallel port (that is, LPT2). Combining this with some newer parallel port technologies can significantly reduce the overhead to run your modem.

No matter what modem you have, the software you run will also affect performance. The Microsoft Outlook e-mail program and the Windows TCP/IP software, for instance, let you connect to the Internet and retrieve electronic mail from an e-mail server. Unfortunately, Outlook needs a great deal of memory. If your machine has only 8MB of memory to start with, performance will suffer while Outlook is running. Command-line UNIX e-mail client programs take far less memory and won't incur the same performance hit, but lack the ease of use features. X Windows clients are likely to impose loads as significant as Outlook or other Windows e-mail readers.

### Loads on network servers

Local area networks load your computer in different ways than modems. There is still a processor load to put data onto and take data off the network, but the higher signaling rates of networks caused designers to create more efficient interfaces. A LAN still can affect performance, though, because requests from the network can consume resources — typically processor, memory, and disk resources — to run programs. Requests your computer can handle include access to files, spooling to the printer, or serving Web pages to the Internet. The volume of requests you get and the work that has to be done to service the request determine the load the machine must handle. For example, at the time we used System A (described earlier) for writing, it was also the machine that had the printer and modem for a four-machine network. When one of the other machines printed, System A slowed to a crawl.

If you have a lightweight communications and printing load, or if communications and printing are most of what you do, you can attach a modem and printer directly to your computer without sacrifice. If the load is severe, you'll want to investigate routers and print servers.

# Why You Need to Be a Detective

Deciding the best way to upgrade or configure a computer is a kind of detective work. You take the facts, sift them around, and draw a conclusion. When you're wrong, you dig to find out why. Inevitably, when a computer upgrade doesn't perform the way you expected, it is because some other component of the computer is choking your computer's performance. You can start your investigation with the information in Table 4-7, comparing the performance of different upgrades you might make.

## Table 4-7
## Rules of Thumb to Help Start Your Analysis
## (Courtesy of Intel Corporation)

| Key Subsystem | Initial Configuration | Upgraded Configuration | Performance Improvement |
|---|---|---|---|
| Processor-to-memory bus | 64 bits (conventional memory) | 64 bits (synchronous memory) | 5 to 10 percent |
| Second-level cache | None | 256K Write Back | 26 to 31 percent |
| Graphics | VGA via ISA bus | High-performance AGP or PCI VGA | 43 percent |
| Hard disk | 15 millisecond average access time and 64K cache | 12 millisecond average access time and 256K cache | 11 percent |

The performance improvement estimates in Table 4-7 assume that no choke point limits the gain from the subsystem improvement. Looking at the table naively, it would be easy to conclude that everyone should upgrade their components in order of the greatest percentage of improvement of system performance: first the graphics card, then the cache, and so on. You know from the discussions in this chapter that this view is too simple, that you have to take into account both what you do with the computer and the interactions of the components in the computer. Figure 4-6 shows what's not apparent in Table 4-7 — that deciding what to do to upgrade a computer or configure a new one requires that you investigate what's going on in your computer as it runs your applications, look at its opportunities and choke points, and work forward to a decision.

You'll see drawings like Figure 4-6 elsewhere in this book. The diamonds contain questions — facts you need to gather or decisions you need to make. The labels on the diamonds tell you which path to follow based on the answer to each question. The boxes contain recommendations to consider or tasks you may choose to carry out.

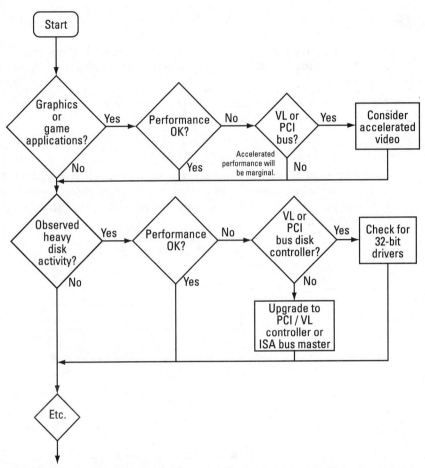

**Figure 4-6:** Analyzing and planning your upgrade or new configuration should proceed along a careful, well-defined process.

# Summary

✦ The speed at which your computer does a task depends on the amount of information the computer has to handle and the rate at which it can process that information.

✦ The core of your computer includes the processor, bus, memory, disk, and display.

✦ You can evaluate the performance of each of the core elements by looking at how much information is handled, and how often.

✦ A choke point is a component — usually one of the core elements — that limits the flow of information through the system. Upgrading a choke point nets you better performance. Upgrading something else nets you very little until you resolve the choke point.

✦    ✦    ✦

# Workloads

When we wrote this chapter for the first edition of this book, we created a graph of the processor speed, disk capacity, and memory size found in then-advertised computers (see Figure 5-1). Looking at the ads for those computers, it was apparent that no matter what your budget was, every manufacturer offered a machine to meet your needs at the price you could afford, independent of what you expected to use it for. There seemed to be a single set of expectations for budget machines, and another for machines for "power users." It seemed odd at the time that no matter what you did, the computer you needed boiled down to a small handful of options, and it seemed odder yet that those options would happen to be what was selling in a specific price range.

Of course, it wasn't at all the case that these machines were being fitted to user requirements. At the time, manufacturers couldn't afford to tailor machines to each customer's individual needs. Instead, they packaged a balance of features into a few combinations of machines, driving what they included by what they could afford to include at a price point. The design process didn't start with identifying what you needed and then working through features to a price; it was the reverse of that. Manufacturers started with a price point, selected a combination of features that seemed to be selling in a market, and promoted the result to that market. The machines targeted at the home were that way because manufacturers determined that home users would at the time spend less than companies, not because the home user necessarily needed a lesser machine.

Redoing that analysis for the third edition, we found that the PC market had changed both in the capabilities of the machines you get for a given price and in that manufacturers had developed the ability to economically let customers specify the exact machine they want. The evidence is in Figure 5-2, where you can see a relatively steady increase in processor speed as the price goes up. Accompanying that steady increase are regular ups and downs in the disk capacity, monitor size, and memory size—you can get most any combination you need.

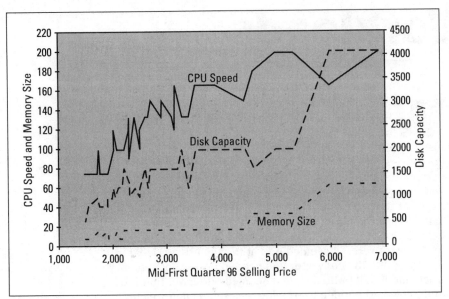

**Figure 5-1:** Features included at various price points for several manufacturers in 1996

If you want to get the machine that best fits your specific needs and budget, though, you have to do the analysis yourself. You have to understand what your needs are and what various components can do to meet them. You need to know that different applications you run stress your machine in different ways:

✦ If you scan and edit pictures all day long, you might be far better off with a 300 MHz processor and 256MB of memory than with a 450 MHz processor and 64MB. The reduced workload on the disk due to the extra memory will speed everything, while a slower processor won't slow the production process terribly.

✦ If you run small, highly detailed numeric simulations, you might need a 500 or 600 MHz Pentium III processor with as little as 32MB of memory. In addition, the tight computational loops in such a simulation probably impose only average stress on disk and video, so cutting down how much you spend on those components in favor of the fastest processor you can get lets you attack your computer's choke point. If you make choices that upgrade cleanly, you can get this payoff without compromising the future value of the machine.

Short of plunking down your money and hoping for the best, how do you decide what to do? The answer is to develop a workload profile—a detailed profile of what you use your computer for and what demands that usage places on the different components of the computer. Your profile will be the basis for making informed decisions about what you need.

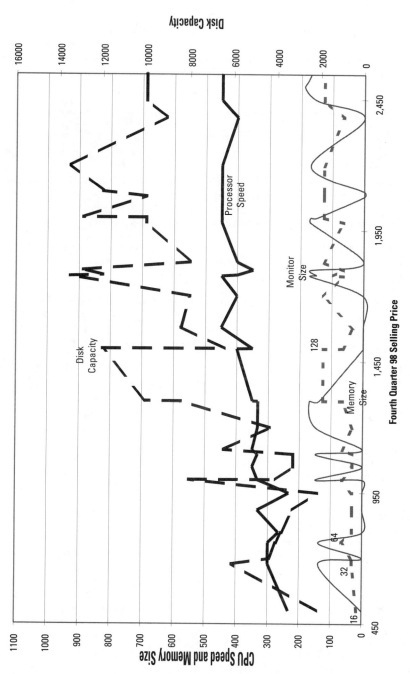

**Figure 5-2:** Features included at various price points for several manufacturers in 1999

Before you get too tied up in what you do now, though, take a look at the accompanying sidebar, which reflects some thoughts of an enormously creative person who has a lot of insight into the future of personal computers, Dr. Ted Selker at IBM's Almaden Research Center in San Jose, California. Dr. Selker's ideas might surprise you.

## Your computer won't just knock your socks off—it'll put them on, too

We had the opportunity in 1996 to talk with Dr. Ted Selker of IBM's Almaden Research Center in San Jose, California, about where personal computers might be heading in several years. We've tried to capture his insights and expectations here. Not only is what he said illuminating, it's as applicable in 1999 as in 1996.

Dr. Selker's underlying message was that the available computer power we now have is going to make computers more personal—enabling them to be more aware of what we are doing and more responsive to the problem of helping us accomplish those tasks.

His first example was of an *agent*—a program that does work independently on your behalf. The prototype he described, developed by a student of his at Stanford, watches what you do playing a game in which you're traveling around in a group of rooms. When you revisit a room, the agent reminds you what happened to you recently in that room.

As simple as that sounds, it's a very powerful idea. By simply watching what you do (and keeping track), your computer can do several things in response:

✦ *Provide context.* You've undoubtedly experienced the problem of being less effective when you're doing several things at once. The problem is that every time you change what you're doing, you have to remember what you were doing and remember the details of what you were going to do next before you can actually do something useful. What you're doing is remembering the context of each task. If your computer can help remember and recall that context, it can help you be more effective.

✦ *Anticipate what you need.* None of us is very effective sitting and waiting for computers to do things, but the delay is often not in the computer itself. Instead, the delay may be in retrieving information from somewhere else. If your computer can figure out what you'll want in advance, it can get it in advance, too. That means the information you need is there when you need it, and you can keep working.

Dr. Selker's group is building on these ideas, and they'll be coming to your PC. He is building software that sits between your Web browser and the Internet, watching what you do and how the Net responds. Using that information, the software shows you on-screen what links are fast, slow, or dead, and automatically builds hot lists of bookmarks so that you can access valuable sites later. More sophisticated versions will figure out what information on the Internet relates to the work you're doing and will retrieve information overnight into a "newspaper" you get in the morning.

The problem these programs will solve is that of having too much information. Corporate intranets and the Internet are making dispersed information widely accessible, and cutting out much of the filtering that refereed journals used to do. That means you have more raw information at your disposal, and it becomes a bigger job to find what's useful.

The Trackpoint "mouse" IBM built into the Thinkpad computers is a second example of how computers are becoming more personal. Starting with the observation that people have difficulty integrating text and graphics visually, Dr. Selker researched the physiology behind that problem as it related to using mice. That research led to algorithms that accommodate the ways in which people's eyes track or fingers shake, making the user's interaction with the computer easier and more effective. The research is what distinguishes the Trackpoint from similar-looking products. The experiments looked at objective data to discover the physiological issues and understand the motor functions underlying the behavior.

This work is further-reaching than just building a better mouse. The Trackpoint is important for the disabled, for example, because it is easy to grip and requires less movement to operate. Someone with an artificial hand, or who uses a mouth stick, may not be able to generate the range of motion a mouse or trackball requires. Tactile feedback from the tip of the Trackpoint can highlight elements on-screen (like dialog box edges) to the blind or partially sighted. Combined with tracking algorithms that adapt to disabilities, voice synthesis, and voiced information about the windowed environment, you have a computer that reaches out to disabled users far more effectively than ever before.

Benefits accrue to users without disabilities as well. A computer can be programmed to determine a user's experience level with computers by observing how he or she manipulates the mouse. The novice moves the mouse more timidly, with less acceleration. The expert flings the mouse around, accelerating it directly to where it belongs next. The more you know about the user, the more you can adapt. You can provide complete or abbreviated menus, basic or advanced help, and training when it's appropriate.

Dr. Selker's third example of how computers are becoming more personal relates to the physical space occupied by PCs. Why should a PC take up a whole desk? Why do we have to change the viewing angle of monitors or lift them on bricks? Why do computer upgrades require the specialized skills they do?

He suggests that computers will eventually look more like what they do, resembling furniture and other well-designed things (file cabinets, desks, and whatnot). In Japan, IBM sells a pocket-size PC with a 4 _ 5 screen, a keyboard, pointing devices, disks, and a battery that fits in your pocket; in most markets you can now get similarly sized Personal Digital Assistants (PDAs) that run a version of Windows. The existence of products like that suggests that you can have a computer packaged into anything you want. Hardware doesn't have to be limited by its intrinsic size any more; it can have a size and shape that fits what you need to have an effective control surface. We've reached the point where the computer designers don't have to design the package any longer — the industrial designers can.

*Continued*

*(continued)*

If computers can be physically less intrusive, they can go more places. The usefulness of a mobile computer is limited by its connections, yet in some areas you can get wireless Internet access at about 14.4 Kbps at a flat rate of $30/month. Those two ideas together (now on the market in the form of the 3Com Palm Pilot 7) mean that we don't have to limit what computers do for us — how personal they can be.

Dr. Selker pointed out the importance of mobile computing and data access by telling of an experience he had in traveling to deliver a presentation. A conversation he had on the airplane, another with his host, and a third with another guest all were relevant to what he had to present. Because he was to deliver the presentation using his Thinkpad laptop computer tied to an overhead projector, he was able to update the presentation up to the point he began to speak. The result was a more relevant, effective presentation.

Dr. Selker's last example is possibly his most compelling — the room-with-a-view IBM demonstrated at the 1996 Summer Olympics in Atlanta. In his vision, your office no longer explicitly has a computer in it. Instead, you have large display panels on the walls and tablets on your desk. The panels display bookshelves and files. When you want to work on something, you pick up a folder from the wall. One of the tablets pulls the corresponding information through an infrared link off your network and becomes the actual open folder on your desk. You can write or type into the open folders, and return them to the bookshelf when you're done. Your computer becomes your office.

# The Workload Profile

The major categories in your workload profile correspond to the pieces you build into a computer:

✦ *Computation.* The processor and supporting electronics

✦ *Memory.* The cache and main memory subsystems

✦ *Storage.* The disk and disk controller

✦ *Display.* The video card and monitor

✦ *Input.* The keyboard, mouse, and other input devices, such as tablet, scanner, joystick, microphone, camera, and MIDI source

✦ *Output.* The printer, plotter, and speakers

✦ *Communications.* The modem and network interface

Each of these categories has a range of defining characteristics, including functionality, capacity, performance, interoperability, maintainability, upgradability, size, weight, power, and mobility. The matrix in Table 5-1 is a way to evaluate each of the equipment categories just named against these defining characteristics. You capture what's important for your computer use by filling in the information in each of the cells in the matrix. In all likelihood, you won't fill out every cell in Table 5-1; you can ignore ones that are unimportant to you. You will assign different levels of importance to the cells depending on what you do. (For example, if you use one computer and never move it around, mobility is unimportant.)

### Table 5-1
### Workload Matrix of Component Characteristics

| Category | Computation | Memory | Storage | Display | Input | Output | Communications |
|---|---|---|---|---|---|---|---|
| Functionality | | | | | | | |
| Capacity | | | | | | | |
| Performance | | | | | | | |
| Interoperability | | | | | | | |
| Maintainability | | | | | | | |
| Upgradability | | | | | | | |
| Size | | | | | | | |
| Weight | | | | | | | |
| Power | | | | | | | |
| Mobility | | | | | | | |

Once you fill in the matrix with descriptions of what's important and how you use the computer, you have a basis for evaluating your current system, upgrades to it, and complete new systems. In the remainder of this chapter, we will analyze the matrix in some detail and look at some sample profiles we've created to stereotype different kinds of computer users. No user is likely to fit one profile exactly, because we've intentionally made the stereotypes somewhat extreme to help highlight the reasons behind the choices we suggest, and because everyone uses computers somewhat differently. In the same way that computer manufacturers can't analyze every customer separately, we can't provide a workload profile for every reader of this book. You need to do your own analysis to make sure the choices are the best ones for you.

## Computation

Look at the processor first. There are no significant differences in end-user functionality running an Intel Pentium, Pentium Pro, Pentium II, or Pentium III processor, or an AMD K6 or K6-2 — they all do the same computations. The important differences are that newer processors are faster and more efficient. The latest processors have added features, such as support for error correcting memory codes in the Pentium Pro; new multimedia instructions in the Pentium and Pentium II processors that make new applications possible; and power management in nearly all processor lines.

### Functionality

A PC processor's critical function is to faithfully run programs written to the Intel instruction set, so the issue you should care about most is compatibility with software. If you run only widely available software, compatibility is less likely to be a concern. Seemingly small issues can matter, however. For example, legitimate differences in floating-point implementations can cause small differences in computed results. Engineering, scientific, and statistical algorithms that are marginally stable from a numerical analysis standpoint may crash if differences in results interact badly with those algorithms.

### Capacity

Capacity relates to the processor in the sense that there is Level 1 and sometimes Level 2 cache memory embedded in the chip. Each of those memories has some maximum capacity to temporarily hold information otherwise found in main memory.

 **Cross-Reference**  See the section "Feeding the Hungry Beast: Cache Memory" in Chapter 7 for more detail on cache memory.

The capacity of the on-board cache determines the *hit rate*, which is the percentage of memory references the processor makes that are handled directly by the cache without reference to memory. Bigger caches increase the hit rate, reducing the memory load.

## How much cache?

Having enough cache memory is crucial to performance, as shown in the following figure. Unlike DOS and UNIX, Windows continues to benefit from additional cache memory at least up to 512KB. This result corresponds to the less formal system evaluation of cache size in Chapter 4, where the system having no cache was noticeably slower.

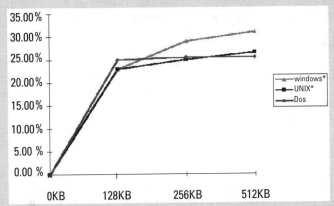

System performance is strongly affected by cache size.
(Courtesy of Intel Corporation.)

The estimates of cache size impact for UNIX only reflect the command-line level of operation and don't reflect what happens when a UNIX machine runs as a network server. Running the X Window graphical user interface or the Apache Web server will increase the value of cache in a system to the level shown for Windows.

## Performance

The processor performance you need is based on the characteristics of your software—the kinds of operations your software does. Do you run massive spreadsheets that take forever to recalculate? Do you run drawing packages that seem to sit there interminably with no disk activity after you make a small change, and then suddenly wake up and redraw the screen? Do you do computer-aided design in programs that show you a 3D view and continuously update the screen? Do you play the latest 3D games, rendering motion in 24- or 32-bit color? All these cases impose a big computational load on the processor and may lead you to choose a faster chip than you otherwise would.

It can be difficult to discover when the performance you see is limited by the processor rather than video, disk, or some other factor. The limiting factor is called a *choke point.* We cover ways to measure processor usage in Chapter 35 when we discuss benchmarking, but you can get some immediate insight into where your system stacks up on processor performance by starting the Windows System Monitor and looking at the Kernel Processor Usage. (In Windows 9x, this is Start ⇨ Programs ⇨ Accessories ⇨ System Tools ⇨ System Monitor. If it's not there, you may need to go into Start ⇨ Settings ⇨ Control Panel ⇨ Add/Remove Programs to install it. See Chapter 35 for equivalent tools for Windows NT and UNIX.)

Processor speed — the most direct measure comparing the performance you'll get from different processors, but not necessarily the most reliable one — is most often measured as the speed of the clock in megahertz (or MHz). Competitors to Intel who believe their chips do more work in a single clock cycle have developed the P-rating system (see "Performance" in Chapter 8) to allow comparisons based on benchmarks rather than simple clock rates.

## Benchmarks

A typical Windows System Monitor display is shown in Figure 5-3, illustrating why a more detailed investigation than System Monitor can provide may be needed. The report of 100 percent processor usage is correct, but a conclusion that the machine's performance is limited by the processor may not be, particularly in light of the fact that it continues at that level when the computer is idle.

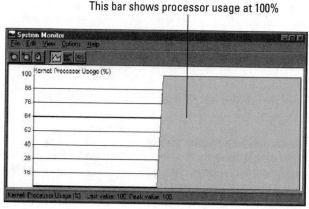

**Figure 5-3:** System Monitor is a great tool, but you can get misleading results if you don't carefully control what's going on when you take measurements with it.

The reason for this misleading report from System Monitor is a programming technique called *background polling* required under Windows 3.1 and earlier versions to allow programs to monitor for external events. In those systems, programs had to continuously check status information within Windows to discover if an event had happened, rather than simply pause and let Windows notify them. This behavior is particularly common in communications programs and some network drivers. UNIX and the 32-bit versions of Windows both provide mechanisms that allow programs to wait (consuming no processor time) rather than poll, but not all programs have been rewritten appropriately. As those older-style programs poll, they consume all the available processor cycles, leading to the sort of System Monitor display in Figure 5-3. The display is misleading, though, because the polling uses only the leftover processor time. As other programs consume processor cycles to do useful work, the polling rate for background operations goes down so that the total remains at one hundred percent.

Because the processor is completely busy when polling is in progress, you can't get a good reading on processor usage until you shut down the program with the background poll operations. Usually you'll just have to shut down programs one at a time until the processor usage display starts giving readings below a steady 100 percent. Figure 5-4 shows a more normal System Monitor display, with variations in processor usage depending on what's happening.

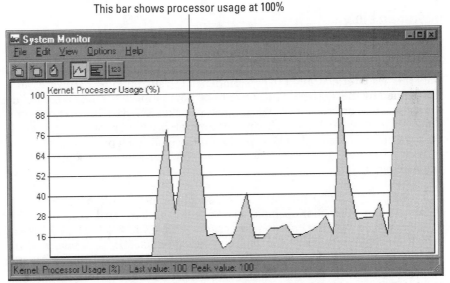

**Figure 5-4:** A more normal Windows System Monitor display shows variations in processor usage depending on what you're doing.

Measurements with System Monitor give you tools to benchmark your system, but it can be difficult to know what to measure and how to interpret the results. For example, Figure 5-5 shows what System Monitor had to say while we copied tens of megabytes over our local area network to two other machines. We interpret the graphs this way:

✦ The rate at which the system could pump data down the network was limited by the processor and the work it had to do to handle the network protocols. This was a 166 MHz Pentium, capable of over a hundred million instructions per second, suggesting that there's a lot of computation involved in network transfers.

✦ None of the network load on the machine was due to the Internet connection (you can see that the Dial-Up Networking Adapter was idle). Nor was any data transferred on the network beyond what we were doing (the Network Server was idle for reads and writes, and the Network Client was idle for reads.)

✦ Disk access corresponded closely to the data going out on the network, so nothing else significant was going on in the machine. This is also borne out by the very low rate for disk writes by the file system.

✦ The disk cache grows as the network transfer progresses, holding the data being read from the disk. The System Monitor display does not show where the bulk of the additional cache memory is being taken from.

## Interoperability

Not all processor chips are physically the same — different processors have different pin configurations, take different voltages, or require different clock signals from the motherboard. The number of pins on the chip, the power to the chip, the bus interface, and the capabilities of the surrounding hardware (all determined by the motherboard) have to be compatible with the chip. Intel defined standard processor socket configurations — Socket 5, 7, and 8 — that helped simplify the processor/motherboard interoperability issues for Pentium and Pentium Pro processors. Intel has packaged the Pentium II processor into a plug-in cartridge, the Slot 1 cartridge, that ensures interoperability with Pentium II motherboards.

Processors designed for the same socket specification can often be directly substituted for others; for example, in a Socket 7 motherboard, you could often directly replace 133 MHz Pentium processors with 150 and 200 MHz equivalents. In Pentium II motherboards, you can replace 233 or 266 MHz processors with faster ones up to the clock limit of the motherboard. Be careful plugging in new processors, even though the old and new one use the same socket or slot specification. Because the newer processors run on lower voltages than older ones, plugging a low-voltage chip into a higher-voltage socket will (at best) not work. At worst, it will ruin the processor, leaving you with an oddly shaped rock to skip over lakes.

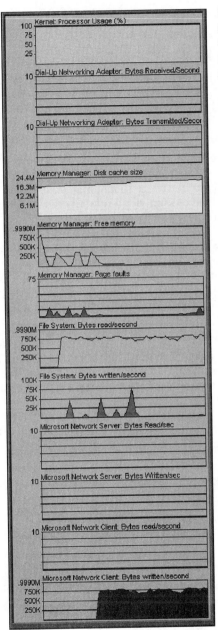

**Figure 5-5:** This System Monitor view shows the activities of key Windows 9*x* components during a copy of tens of megabytes of data to each of two other computers at the same time over a LAN.

## Maintainability

With some apologies to the logistics experts, we've lumped issues of reliability, availability, and maintainability into one group. The issues are these:

✦ *Reliability* is the likelihood that the device will fail, often measured as mean time between failures (MTBF). MTBF is the *average* time a device will go before it fails. It is a statistical measure over a reasonably large number of copies, not a guarantee that the unit you have will perform that way. Yours may fail tomorrow, or it may outlive everything else in the system.

Don't forget that the overall reliability you see on your desktop is a combination of hardware and software reliability. For example, although bad software isn't likely to cause your hardware to fail, buggy display drivers in earlier versions of Windows often caused video-related crashes even though the video card itself was functioning normally.

 We look at some ways to think about MTBF in "Interpreting MTBF" in Chapter 13.

✦ *Availability* is related to the impact a failure has on the system performing its job for you. If you depend on the system for e-mail over the Internet, for instance, a failure in the joystick might not be very important. A failure in the processor, however, would be catastrophic.

✦ *Maintainability* measures the time it takes from the occurrence of a failure to the point when the device is back in service. This includes the time to figure out what's wrong, to get replacements, to install and test the fix, and to repair any collateral damage (such as restoring data from tape in the case of a disk crash).

The point of combining all three of these issues into one characteristic is that they all interact strongly from the standpoint of whether or not you can use your computer.

Using this definition, the processor in your computer is highly maintainable. It's unlikely to fail, being highly reliable, but the machine is useless without it (so it strongly affects system availability). The processor needs no cleaning or other periodic actions, and it's easy to replace if it fails (it's highly maintainable).

## Upgradability

Even if you buy the fastest processor available, you should think about what in your system would affect future processor upgrades. Even if you correctly identify the performance you need now, you may be a candidate for greater performance in the future after adding new applications to what you do, or due to increased demands of upgrades to the software you now use. Processor upgrades can make increased demands on cache size and bus speed.

"Software bloat" and "creeping featuritis" are favorite terms thrown around in the computer media while blasting software developers, but reality is far more mundane:

✦ People continue to buy software based on feature comparisons. Software without the latest rage in features is not competitive and does not sell well. The result is that vendors build in—for everyone—features used by a small minority, because that's what it takes to be competitive.

✦ The quality software vendors do tune their applications for performance, but the sheer size of the application limits how much tuning they can afford to do. Having a programmer hand-tune a stretch of code is very time consuming (and therefore expensive), and is work that may well have to be redone as the software or operating system changes.

The improvements doubling hardware performance every two years or less in the PC will keep on happening for years to come. When you think about upgradability, keep in mind how long you want your computer to serve you and how many times available performance and capacity will double in that time. Projecting too short a service life means you may undervalue the importance of upgrades, while projecting too long a service life may lock you into more expensive hardware than is reasonable. Eventually, the technology changes so much that it becomes less expensive to start over, taking advantage of the combined system pricing you're likely to find.

## Size, weight, and power

The size and weight of the processor chip is insignificant except in portable computers, where smaller is better. The power consumption of the processor is clearly important for mobile computing, but it also affects how much heat the processor dissipates. The total heat the computer dissipates is important in all systems because higher temperatures are bad for reliability, with the constrained spaces in physically smaller systems being very likely to create destructive hot spots unless the manufacturer follows careful thermal and mechanical design practices.

## Mobility

More than size, weight, and power determine your ability to move around with your computer. That rat's nest of cables at the back tied to the monitor, keyboard, mouse, phone line, local area network, scanner, and printer not only make maintenance a nuisance, but they're also a real pain when you want to take the computer with you. The processor has little impact on these issues, but we'll see later that there's a lot you can do with other aspects of your system.

# Memory

The speed and amount of memory in your machine are the primary characteristics you'll want to consider when you specify a computer, but upgrade planning is worthwhile too. There are few options for memory in most of the characteristics in the workload profile.

## Functionality

Your computer's memory does one thing: It stores and retrieves data. Secondary memory functions, such as storing parity data, need to be coordinated with the characteristics of the surrounding hardware. Memory is available that provides error correcting functions independent of the processor and memory control hardware, but because there is not much demand for such a product, it is extremely expensive.

## Capacity

You need to work out carefully how much memory you need. It's unfortunate that software manufacturers are so cavalier about their specification of how much memory their programs require, because in practice it's nearly impossible to be sure if the estimate includes the memory that Windows itself uses or not, and estimates are usually rounded to the next multiple of 4MB. (For instance, if a program actually needs 5MB of memory to operate, the box may say it requires 8MB.) Recalling part of Table 3-3 in Chapter 3, Table 5-2 shows a set of programs you might run at one time in an office.

| Table 5-2 | |
| :--- | :--- |
| **Memory Required to Run Several Popular Programs At Once** | |
| *Program* | *Minimum Memory Required* |
| Adobe Photoshop 5.0 | 32MB (64MB recommended) |
| CorelDRAW! Version 8.0 | 16MB (32MB recommended) |
| Microsoft Encarta 99 | 16MB |
| Microsoft Office for Windows 97 | 8MB (more for multiple programs) |
| Netscape Navigator 4.5 | 16MB |
| *Total* | 88+MB |

While it's definitely the case that you'd be happier with 80MB of memory than 32MB, we can state from experience that this combination of programs runs acceptably at the same time under Windows 9*x* with 32MB. You'll see some disk activity when switching programs, but overall performance will be okay, particularly if you have a reasonably fast hard disk connected through a PCI host adapter. The same set of programs performs much more responsively with 64MB or 128MB, of course; that's the key benefit of more memory.

Windows NT requires more memory for the base code, so the performance of this same combination of programs in 32MB is not good. Sixty four megabytes is (in our estimation) the minimum for the same combination of programs under Windows NT, and we think you'll be much happier with 128MB or more.

You can get a rough estimate of whether you have enough memory by watching for heavy disk activity when you're not actively reading or writing files. You can get an even better estimate under Windows 9*x* by using the System Monitor. (See Chapter 35 for how to make these measurements in Windows NT or UNIX.) The Memory Manager set contains the measurements you'll want to look at, as shown in Figure 5-6. We intentionally had a lot of programs running when we constructed this display, causing memory to be overloaded somewhat. The increased paging activity you see toward the right of each graph reflects the system response when we switched from one program to another that had been paged out as we cycled other programs into and out of memory.

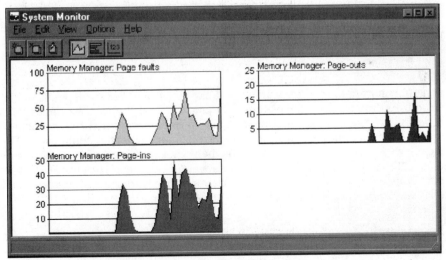

**Figure 5-6:** The memory manager provides measurements to help you see when you're overtaxing memory.

## Using more memory than you have

The process Windows or UNIX goes through when your programs want more memory than you really have is called *paging* (or *swapping*). The range of addresses each program uses, called its *address space*, gets divided by the processor into 4KB blocks called *pages*. The operating system and the processor collectively keep track of how recently each page was used, so that when the total memory allocation requested by programs exceeds what physical memory can hold, the system knows which pages are least recently used and can page them out to the swap file. Each one of these operations is called a *page out*, and contributes to the Page-outs display in Figure 5-7. When a program needs to reference a page that has been paged out, the processor generates a page fault (as in the top left of the figure), and the operating system pages in the data from the swap file. (Page ins are shown in the lower left of the figure.) Disk access is far slower than memory access, however, so if memory is too overcommitted, programs will page excessively (called *thrashing*) and performance heads toward zero.

Increasing memory in a system that thrashes will reduce the paging rate and dramatically improve performance. The benefits in a system that already has little or no paging will be far less evident.

### Performance

The processor and motherboard control the timing of access to memory; either the memory itself is fast enough or it isn't. If the memory is too slow, the computer will be unreliable or may not work at all. Using memory faster than what is required will not make the computer faster, but it won't hurt anything. Some motherboards automatically detect the speed of the memory (or let you state the memory speed), in which case faster memory can give you better performance.

Other memory characteristics affect performance not at the speed level, but in the structures designed into the memory. Common memory types over the past decade have included fast page mode memory, EDO memory, and synchronous memory (see the section "Speed is good" in Chapter 7). In systems that could use it, EDO memory was faster than fast page mode memory. Synchronous memory is faster than EDO and has been the standard for several years now. The choice of which type of memory to use is a cost versus performance trade-off, with direct benefits relatively independent of how you use the computer.

### Interoperability

Memory interoperability is related only to its compatibility with the surrounding electronics. Nothing you do affects this — you simply have to get memory that meets the interface requirements of your processor and motherboard.

## Maintainability

Computer memory is quite reliable. Parity checking or error correcting codes can increase maintainability, while very humid or salty environments can reduce it (due to corrosion of tinned — rather than gold — connector contacts), but these factors are unrelated to how you use the computer.

## Upgradability

Upgradability is a significant concern, because the lifetime of memory modules can be very long and your ability to transfer memory from one motherboard to another can reduce the cost of an upgrade. There are several issues:

✦ *Density.* Pentium processor motherboards commonly provide four or more 72-pin memory sockets, supporting two or more banks of memory. The 72-pin sockets must be populated in pairs with the same type of module. The 168-pin modules can be used singly. If you use all the available memory banks, you have no room for a memory upgrade later without removing some of the existing memory. If instead you use higher-density memory — meaning there is more memory per module — you can install the same amount of memory now and leave room for upgrades later.

✦ *Speed.* Different combinations of motherboard type and processor speed require different minimum memory speeds. Typical memory speeds are 50, 60, and 70 nanoseconds (ns) for 72-pin memory and 10ns for 168-pin memory. Buying memory faster than the motherboard can use has no immediate advantage, but it permits the memory to be migrated later to a newer motherboard that can exploit the added speed.

✦ *Packaging and width.* Your ability to migrate memory to a new motherboard in the future is also affected by the physical packaging of the memory and by whether it provides extra bits for parity / ECC or not. The 72-pin memory module is obsolete. The 168-pin modules were the mainstream technology in 1998 but beginning in 1999 began to be phased out in favor of a newer, incompatible technology (Rambus).

## Size, weight, and power

Other than memory density, there's little you can do or need to be concerned with regarding the size and weight of memory. The power memory consumes is important for laptop computers, but not something you can change. Overall, the power a chip consumes goes up linearly with the frequency of the clock driving the chip, and as the square of the voltage applied to the chip. (Voltage is one of the measures of how strong an electronic signal is — it's analogous to water pressure in a hose.) The standard voltage in computers was 5 V for decades, but as chips have become more complex they have migrated to operation on 3.3 V, 2.0 V, and lower. The change to 3.3 V operation reduces a chip's power consumption to just 44 percent of what it would be at a full 5 V, increasing battery life and reducing heat.

## Mobility

Memory can be packaged to be removable and therefore transportable between machines. Specifically, memory packaged to the PC Card standard consists of a credit card–size device that plugs into sockets on laptop and other computers; the Flash Card standard for digital cameras puts the same idea on a smaller card. Card memory is much slower than SIMM or DIMM memory, but it can be moved from portable devices (such as digital cameras or personal digital assistants) to specialized readers in desktop machines.

# Storage

Storage in your computer means disk drives. What kind of drive, how big, and with what performance are questions having as many answers as for any other component in your system. In Part III, we'll see that you can choose not only from magnetic disks, but CD-ROMs, recordable CD-ROMs (CD-R), DVD-ROM, DVD-RAM, magneto-optical drives, fixed drives, and removable drives. You can choose from IDE and SCSI interfaces, with options to parallel multiple drives in a scheme called Redundant Array of Inexpensive Disks (RAID).

## Functionality

In the simplest terms, disks do nothing more than memory does — they store numbers. Because what is written to disk comes in a wide range of sizes with an even wider range of access patterns, the characteristics of the disk affect your decision about what you need. For example:

✦ *Fixed or removable?* If the sets of data you access are well isolated from one another — if you never use two different sets at the same time — you may be able to take advantage of removable disks. Having one of these devices is like having an enormous floppy disk drive. The drive holds some volume of data, and by changing the specific disk in the drive you can access a nearly unlimited number of files. You can also share data between people or between computers by moving disks around.

✦ *Read/write or read only?* Magnetic disks are read/write devices, but CD-ROMs and DVDs come in both flavors — read only and read/write. If you expect to use CDs only for receiving data, you'll obviously choose a CD-ROM drive, but you will have missed the opportunity to use the same device for backup or for customized data distribution.

## Capacity

The disk capacity you can get has exploded from only a few years ago, and the price per megabyte has plummeted. From 200MB being a large disk in early 1991, drive manufacturers have progressed to the point where (in 1999) a 16GB drive will become standard equipment on new systems, and 4GB drives will be considered small. Drives of 25GB and 50GB are readily available, with 100GB drives in production.

For better or worse, software developers have been quick to exploit the additional capacity and the ability to distribute over 600MB of data on a single CD-ROM, and can be expected to leap on the 4+GB capacity of DVD. The resulting program installations are very large. The directories holding Windows can easily exceed 200MB, and only the most trivial of programs seem to require less than 10MB of disk space these days. Complex programs—such as Microsoft Office or Visual C/C++—can require over 300MB for complete installs. The data files you create with a word processor or presentation graphics program can easily grow to tens of megabytes for substantial projects with embedded graphics. You'll want to look at the file sizes for recent work you've done to be sure you include the requirements for data files in your capacity estimate.

Games can consume every bit as much space as office software—the full installations of id Software's Quake II and of Valve's Half-Life were each 400MB, while a full installation of Black Isle Studios' Baldur's Gate fills 2.5GB!

Don't underestimate how much disk capacity you'll want. The history of one of our older computers illustrates the problem:

✦ When we bought the system in 1990, it had a 200MB disk. We copied over about 45MB of data from the old machine it replaced, and figured we'd have space to burn.

✦ Within two years, we were flat out of space and borrowing space on another machine over a LAN. We added an 850MB drive at that point, and figured we'd have space to burn.

✦ In a little over two more years, we were once again flat out of space and borrowing space on another machine. (There's a pattern here!) We installed a 1GB drive and hoped it would last for a while.

✦ Eight months after installing the third drive, the total available space on the machine—with vigorous pruning to delete useless files—was about 350MB. The machine that replaced that old one started with a 4GB drive and grew shortly to 7GB. Its replacement, a server built in 1996, had 24GB from the beginning. The desktop machines we've built recently have no less than 9GB. We're also careful to use cases and disk controllers with a lot of room for more disks.

Our point is that software upgrades, new software, and data files from doing work accumulate into an astonishing volume of data. Internet World Wide Web users will find this particularly easy to have happen, because the Web browsers (the software you use to access the Web) cache recently used data files to improve performance. You can control the size of the cache, but it's not at all hard to use tens or hundreds of megabytes of disk over several months. If you capture and edit video, plan on 1 to 10 megabytes per second before compression, which means a 60-second clip could fill 600 megabytes.

You may want to factor disk compression into your capacity estimate as well. Windows can compress files before storing them on disk, trading off reduced processing speed for increased storage capacity. The compression isn't the same between Windows 9x and Windows NT, so don't compress if you need to run both systems. You won't compress UNIX disks, either. If you can use disk compression, you can expect to net an effective capacity gain of from 1.6 to 2 times the uncompressed drive size, depending on the sort of files you have. We've never seen the advertised levels of 2:1 compression for an entire disk, but if all you have are text files, it's possible. Typical compression we see runs closer to 1.6:1.

Finally, you have to incorporate the size of the Windows swap file plus any temporary files (including print spooling) into your disk capacity estimate. We recommend you allow two to three times the physical memory in the machine as a minimum swap file, and from four to five times physical memory for all temporary files. Running out of swap file space is a problem that, at best, can cause you to be unable to start new programs, and it can even crash the machine. We regularly see swap files in excess of 120MB on machines with 64MB of memory, and we have run out of swap space with the swap file at over 180MB. At the worst, we've seen swap files in excess of 1GB.

**Tip**

Be sure not to make the partition (the space on the disk allocated for a specific drive letter) containing Windows too small. Some programs (such as Microsoft Office for Windows) insist on putting a lot of components into the Program Files folder in the same partition as Windows. Many programs still put components directly into the Windows folder and the folders under it. The print spooler puts data in the Windows partition as well. If you leave too little space, you'll have problems with software installation and may not be able to print complex or long documents. We recommend that your Windows partition be no less than 1GB; 2GB or more would be good.

The size of a removable disk affects what you can do with it too. A 100MB or 200MB removable drive is too small to be useful to back up several gigabytes of fixed drive because of the cost of the media. If you can organize applications to fit on a single removable cartridge (or can organize projects to fill enough of one to avoid needing too many of them), and if you can arrange not to need more than one cartridge's contents at a time, a removable drive is a great option. Removable drives also offer an effective way to transport large volumes of work from one site to another.

## Performance

For the primary disk drive—the one on which you have the swap file and most of the files you use—you want as much speed as you can get. Having said that, the performance you should target in the disk subsystem needs to be tempered by these factors:

✦ *System limitations.* You won't see any benefit from a disk faster than the controller can support, or from a disk/controller pair faster than the bus and processor can support. Plan on upgrading or replacing any systems still doing disk I/O over the ISA bus, because you'll be doing well to get peak transfer rates as high as 2.5 megabytes per second. Newer disk interfaces can provide speed benefits too, reaching burst transfer rates of 66 MBps and higher.

✦ *Access patterns.* The kind of work you expect to do affects the specific features of the disk and disk controller you will want to get. If your work is primarily multimedia or graphics, performance accessing the large files involved will increase with a faster transfer rate (especially from CD-ROM). If your work is primarily with databases, performance will increase with a faster access time.

✦ *Multitasking.* The combinations of things you do determine the disk subsystem performance you want.

> • If you write CD-ROMs, for example, you'll need to be sure the disk subsystem can deliver data to the CD-ROM writer at a sustained rate at least as great as the drive requires to maintain operation. On most CD-ROM writers, interrupting the data flow will abort the disk writing process.

> • If you choose an IDE CD-ROM, you need to put the CD-ROM on a different port than the hard disk to ensure that access to the relatively slow CD-ROM does not block access to the faster hard disk.

## Interoperability

Conflicts are possible between IDE and SCSI interfaces, and between devices on IDE buses. For example, you generally have to boot from an IDE drive if you have both IDE and SCSI drives in your system. You are usually limited to four IDE devices (two on each of two ports). Planning the connections for the drives you will hook to your storage system, and how you will distribute software on those drives, will help avoid these conflicts.

A key part of planning your storage system is identifying all the storage devices you expect to have — including ones you will add later — and how they will work together in your system. For example, we usually specify SCSI disk and CD-ROM interfaces on our computers, because we typically add more disks, tape drives, scanners, and other peripherals during the system's life. Without the flexibility and connectivity provided by the SCSI interface, we would consume additional card slots for added interface cards, possibly running out of slots and interrupt assignments. You can also use recent technologies such as Universal Serial Bus (USB) to help solve interface limitations.

## Maintainability

Disks and disk controllers are generally quite reliable, but your system can become inoperable or you can lose data if one fails. Backup devices — such as tape — don't disable your system when they fail, but they must be dependable enough to ensure the safety of your data. You will want to investigate the quality reputation of the vendors making your storage components, and to compare the rated MTBF specifications. MTBF is no guarantee how long a device will last, but it is a useful basis for comparison when there are major differences.

You will also want to carefully consider the software required to support your storage subsystem. Nonstandard, proprietary CD-ROMs or disk controllers may not be supported by 32-bit Windows drivers or under UNIX. You take a significant performance hit if you do not use 32-bit drivers in Windows 9x, and you lose features such as the AutoRun capability of CD-ROM titles written for Windows 9x. Windows NT and UNIX simply do not support devices without 32-bit drivers.

Floppy drives, CD-ROMs, DVDs, and other removable disks are not as reliable as sealed electromechanical or purely electronic devices, because they collect dirt from the environment that interferes with their operation. We once cleaned a machine in a veterinarian's office, and found the floppy drive completely packed with dog and cat hair. (He was able to solve his maintenance problem by reducing the traffic past the computer area and regularly vacuuming out the drive.)

## Upgradability

Upgrading storage capacity and performance means adding or replacing disks. Increasing the performance of the disk controller — such as to a bus mastering controller — requires replacing the existing card or adding a new card. You can't connect IDE drives to a SCSI controller, or vice versa. IDE buses support only internal drives, and they severely limit the length of the internal cables. The combination of number of drives possible on a controller and number of controllers in the system limits the number of disks you can install. IDE drives also have capacity limits lower than SCSI ones.

## Size, weight, and power

Disks and tape drives come in two sizes — 3.5 and 5.25 inches. The 3.5-inch devices are typically about one inch tall and can be mounted in a 3.5-inch bay or (with adapter brackets) in a 5.25-inch one. The 5.25-inch devices usually occupy one half-height drive bay (just under 1.75 inches tall).

The number of drive bays open to the front of the case (called *external drive bays*) limits the number of drives with removable media you can mount in the case. A minitower case often has two or three external 5.25-inch bays and one or two 3.5-inch ones. Tower case designs are available that maximize the number of external bays — for example, you can get cases from California PC Products that provide ten external 5.25-inch drive bays (ideal for servers with a lot of CD-ROM drives installed). Another case we used from California PC Products to house a pair of servers (dual motherboards!) provides eighteen 5.25-inch drive bays, 13 of which are external.

## Mobility

The size of the drive you pick has little impact on the mobility of your computer itself, because drives in laptop machines are already selected by the manufacturer. An external drive offers the option to move the drive to another computer, moving the mechanism as well as the media (as with a removable drive). Removable disks are a third alternative, enabling you to move just the media if you have a compatible drive at your destination.

# Display

The most important questions to answer about your display subsystem are: What do you display? How much of it do you want to see? How fast does it have to be updated? If you have never used a large, high-resolution display, you probably underestimate what it can do for you. Table 5-3 shows some of the comparisons. The benefit of higher resolution is seeing more of your work, and more different things you work on. Bigger screens make the higher resolutions easier to see, and can make it possible to use smaller fonts (Small Fonts versus Large Fonts in the Windows Display Properties), in which case you get even more effective space on the screen with a given resolution.

| Table 5-3 Resolution Affects What You Can Comfortably View in Applications | | |
|---|---|---|
| **Application** | **Resolution** | **Expect to See (Small Fonts, Window Maximized)** |
| Word processor | 640 _ 480 | Part of one page |
| | 1,280 _ 1,024 | Two pages, side by side |
| | 1,600 _ 1,200 | Two pages, side by side, with other windows visible |
| Presentation graphics | 640 _ 480 | One slide with fine details difficult to manipulate |
| | 1,280 _ 1,024 | Multiple slides, or all of one slide, with fine details readily visible and easy to manipulate |
| | 1,600 _ 1,200 | Four editable slides tiled left to right and top to bottom. |

*Continued*

| Table 5-3 *(continued)* | | |
| --- | --- | --- |
| *Application* | *Resolution* | *Expect to See (Small Fonts, Window Maximized)* |
| Spreadsheet | 640 _ 480 | 17 lines by 9 columns at default height and width |
| | 1,280 _ 1,024 | 50 lines by 19 columns at default height and width |
| | 1,600 _ 1,200 | 47 lines by 19 columns at default height and width, but using large fonts for better resolution. |

The monitor and video card work collaboratively, setting the parameters of the display system. Display size and resolution are as much of an issue for laptop computers as for desktop machines, only the technology changes. Laptop computers use liquid crystal displays (LCDs) and cannot offer the large screen size or high resolution of the best desktop monitors.

## Functionality

Although functionality issues are secondary to those of what you display, how big you want it, and how often you want it to update, they can make a difference. The functionality issues are these:

✦ *Video card.* All displays offer much the same functionality under Windows or UNIX, with one of the key differences being the quality or availability of the display drivers. Video drivers written specifically for Windows 9*x*, particularly DirectX drivers, offer better performance and better features than ones that have adapted old Windows 3.1 drivers. Windows 9*x*–unique features include resetting the display resolution and color depth without rebooting, font smoothing, full window drag (so you can see what's happening as you move the window), and animated cursors. Many Windows 9*x* features migrated into Windows NT with version 4; more will be in Windows 2000. Display cards such as the ATI All-In-Wonder Pro 128 enhance the basic video card functionality, including a fast 3D accelerator, a TV tuner, video capture, and hardware DVD decoder.

✦ *Monitor.* Most current-generation monitors offer Plug and Play operation using the DDC standard. This feature simplifies setting up the display subsystem to make the video card and monitor work together to the best of each one's capabilities, because the monitor reports its best settings to the video card. Most monitors are wider than they are tall (landscape orientation), but some support portrait orientation (taller than the monitor is wide) or your choice of portrait and landscape orientation. Support for color matching is available in some models to help coordinate the color results you get across your scanner, monitor, and printer.

## Capacity

For purposes of this book, we'll call the capacity of a video card the combination of maximum supported resolution and color depth. Video card capacity is determined by the amount of memory on the card. Similarly, we'll call the capacity of a monitor the combination of the maximum resolution it can support and the vertical dot pitch.

## Performance

The performance of a video card is the combination of several parameters:

✦ *Bus type and transfer rate.* The type of the bus into which the card plugs (AGP [Advanced Graphics Port], PCI, VLB, and so on) and the maximum clock rate on the bus that the card can accept determine the transfer rate possible from the processor. AGP has 1X and 2X versions (1X AGP cards vanished from the market rapidly), with 4X to arrive in 1999. PCI typically runs at a 33 MHz clock rate, although some systems tried to run it at 66 MHz.

✦ *Maximum frame rate.* The maximum vertical refresh rate the card supports affects how bright and flicker-free the image looks. Specifications for frame rate are dependent on the resolution used for the measurement.

✦ *Maximum update rate.* The maximum rate at which an application (in the context of some specific computer) can update the screen. The application may be an office-type application, a multimedia video, or a game. The maximum update rate has to be measured with some standard technique — either a benchmark or your actual workload — to be useful for comparisons. The presence of accelerator hardware on the board and the capability of drivers and software to use that hardware strongly affect the update rate and image quality.

For workload analysis purposes, the performance of the monitor is the maximum vertical and horizontal frequencies it can support. We cover a number of other measurements (such as dot pitch, image distortion, and color purity) in Part III.

## Interoperability

Interoperability for both video cards and monitors is defined by the specific standards they comply with, including PCI, AGP, VESA (Video Electronics Standards Association), Underwriters Laboratories, ISO (International Standards Organization), and others. You should consider not only electrical interoperability, but the physical suitability of the equipment for the area in which you will use it. Those factors include ambient lighting, glare, shock, vibration, and resistance to external electromagnetic fields.

## Maintainability

Video cards are generally subject to the same repair options as any other card in the computer — you replace them when they fail. Weight and size make failed monitors a problem if not covered by a service plan of some sort — the cost of shipping a monitor to the manufacturer likely makes factory repair of an older model uneconomical. Local repair shops may take on only certain brands, and possibly only certain models of those brands. Local repairs may be spotty too. (For example, we once managed to discolor the corners of a display by failing to keep a set of speakers far enough away. The local repair shops we called did not have the tool to repair the problem, so we finally had to buy a degaussing coil from a television repair equipment distributor and fix it ourselves.)

These issues mean you will want to consider the predicted lifetime of the monitor, the length of the manufacturer's warranty, and the local availability of repair services when deciding what your maintainability requirements are.

## Upgradability

Video cards are typically only upgradable with proprietary memory upgrades, but many video cards offer no upgrade options at all. Monitors are not upgradable.

Video card electronics are sometimes built into motherboards. If you are considering buying one of these, make sure that the built-in video can be disabled should you later want to install a separate video card to upgrade the machine. Similarly, if you are evaluating a laptop, make sure that it supports plugging in an external monitor, which can greatly improve the usability of the machine. An external monitor port on a laptop is also the key to connecting to an external projection display system.

## Size, weight, and power

The screen dimension (measured on the diagonal) is the most important size measure for a monitor or laptop display panel. For a desktop machine, the monitor size/weight/power are easy to overlook, but remember that 17, 19, and 21-inch monitors are large and heavy, and they consume a noticeable amount of power. Energy-saving ("green") monitors are now almost universal but require support from the video board and operating system to control the power-saving features. Windows 9x, Windows 2000, and some versions of UNIX support monitor power down; Windows NT 4 does not without third-party software. Some motherboards can control a green monitor by overriding the video card.

When you're comparing screen sizes, keep in mind that the published diagonal measure often isn't the viewable measure — the diagonal measure includes part of the tube that's inside the case. Different monitors will cut off different amounts of the screen, so check this explicitly.

The power consumed by a laptop display can be a major part of the total battery drain, with much of the power taken by the backlights you need to make the display visible. The laptop manufacturer takes the LCD and backlight power drain into account when calculating battery life, but you will want to ask what brightness setting was used in the calculation.

## Mobility

If you need to move a monitor around—such as on a cart supporting a mobile test station—you should think about using a laptop or a display that does not use a cathode ray tube. Sustained shock and vibration will eventually degrade the screen image on a tube.

# Input devices

The amazing number of different kinds of input devices you can attach to a computer is a reflection of the number of different things people do with computers. In addition to the usual keyboard and mouse, you can get joysticks, trackballs, tablets, scanners, gloves, musical (MIDI) keyboards, digital still and video cameras, video capture boards (themselves still and full-motion), bar code and check readers, data acquisition systems, and more. The range of input devices is so broad that it's not possible to cover all the characteristics for every type. Instead, in this book we'll hit some of the ones appropriate to each category.

The analysis you need to do to understand your input workload is to identify what sort of information you need to input, what sort of devices you want to input it with, and what characteristics are important to getting the most out of those devices. You need to consider the skills and limitations of the users of these devices as well as the devices themselves. For example, children are neither as large nor as sophisticated as adults. Some users are more able to reach or manipulate various kinds of controls than others, and some users are more susceptible to repetitive motion injury than others. In any event, you will want to consider the recommendations of ISO and other groups on ergonomics no matter what the individual user requirements are, because those recommendations will help all users work more effectively and avoid strain.

Input devices are often very personal choices, with the keyboard being one of the most personal. Some people like a "clicky" keyboard—one with a lot of tactile feedback. Some like function keys on the left side, some, on the top. Some like the Dvorak layout, which is a different arrangement of the keys from that of the conventional QWERTY layout. Some like the new split keyboards that are reputed to minimize wrist tension and strain. You'll want to experiment with any input device you interact with to make sure it meets your tastes.

Your options for keyboards, mice, and trackballs may be limited if you buy a packaged system from a manufacturer. If you can't get the specific devices you want, remember that all those items are simple, inexpensive upgrades. There's no reason to put up with a keyboard or mouse you don't like.

## Functionality

The main thing to analyze is what you expect the device to do, and what kind of interaction you will have with it. Graphics tablets are popular with artists and designers, for instance, because the interaction is very similar to that of using a pencil. A mouse, in contrast, makes it difficult to draw a straight line freehand and is a very poor input device for artistic work.

## Capacity

The capacity of an input device is the measure of how fast it allows you to input data. Scanners with a page feeder, for example, have much greater capacity than manually fed ones. You should also evaluate capacity in terms of the physical size of the input the device can handle, such as the maximum paper size a scanner can handle.

## Performance

The performance of an input device relates to its accuracy or resolution. Many of the joysticks used with game consoles are arrays of eight switches spaced equally around a circle that detect the direction of movement, giving relatively low resolution. Analog game console sticks are more like the joysticks for personal computers; both measure the degree of movement and direction much more precisely by sampling the actual position of the stick.

The resolution performance of a scanner (and, recently, of a digital camera) is a particularly slippery idea. Scanner vendors have enhanced the resolution of the images they deliver by processing the raw image from the hardware, and report that enhanced resolution in advertising. You want to be careful to determine both the raw and processed resolution when evaluating any imaging device.

## Interoperability

The biggest interoperability issue for input devices is the supporting software. Without device drivers, the nonstandard features of the device (and the entire device, in some cases) are useless. Graphics tablets and scanners illustrate the problem—a graphics tablet can at best emulate a mouse without its own driver. Scanners most often use drivers meeting the TWAIN standard, but the promptness and quality of support vary greatly among vendors.

## Maintainability and upgradability

The likelihood of getting repairs on an input device increases with the cost of the device. Other than cleaning you do yourself, mice are a throwaway item. Keyboards are too — the labor cost to troubleshoot and repair one quickly exceeds the replacement cost. Desktop scanners cost enough to possibly be worth repairing, but service may only be available from the manufacturer.

Few (if any) input devices are upgradable other than by replacement.

### Size, weight, and power

These characteristics need to be appropriate to the application. A bar code reader may need to be mobile. A hand scanner is entirely inappropriate for precision scanning, particularly of larger-format documents. The keyboards on laptops are compromises between portability and the layout of a full-size keyboard.

### Mobility

Some input devices offer wireless operation, either by radio or infrared, or by recording data for later playback. These options offer value beyond the obvious one of not being tied down. For instance, a wireless mouse and keyboard combination can eliminate the clutter of wires on your desk.

## Output devices

Windows output devices include printers, plotters, film recorders, and sound cards (with speakers).

### Functionality

The key decisions are if you need color in a printer or plotter, and how large the maximum size output format should be. Some printers offer the capability to connect directly to your network and to be managed remotely, which can be an asset in the corporate environment. Printers offer a variety of other features, including built-in fonts, PostScript, duplex printing, high-capacity and multiple paper feeders, and envelope feeders. Plotters offer the capability to load multiple pens, enabling you to choose color and line width.

Sound devices offer multiple voices, and wavetables, which are sort of like fonts for sound — a way to more accurately represent different instruments and sounds. The newest sound cards offer 3D surround sound, much like what has been pioneered for home theater.

The software support for output devices is as important as the quality and capability of the device itself. Both sound and printer drivers are variable in quality from one manufacturer to the next, and even among models sold by the same manufacturer. The drivers for our laser printer, for example, have been solid and dependable, yet the ones for a color ink-jet printer from the same manufacturer would crash or lock up frequently when the modem was connected. You'll want to look at the experience of others on the model you're considering if you can. The Internet newsgroups (also called Usenet) are a source of opinion and experience that you can tap for this purpose, but as with most other things on the Internet you'll want to carefully apply your own judgment about what you read.

## Capacity

As with input devices, printer and plotter capacity reflect how fast the unit can put through finished pages or sheets. Printers and plotters are often rated in terms of pages per month as well, reflecting the manufacturer's estimate of how heavily loaded they expect the device to be in normal service. Printer capacity also reflects the amount of memory available to hold text, graphics, and downloaded fonts.

Capacity is also relevant for wavetable sound cards that support downloadable tables. For these cards, the amount of memory on the card determines the size and number of tables that can be held, which in turn determines the number of instruments the board can hold and the fidelity of each.

## Performance

The performance of a printer or plotter specifies the resolution and accuracy of the device. For printers, the issues are:

✦ *Resolution.* Printer resolution is measured in dots per inch and is not always the same vertically and horizontally. Black-and-white printers use patterns of dots to produce grays. The pattern of dots is visible when the printer resolution is 300 dots per inch or less, detracting from image quality. Printers featuring 600 dpi or higher resolution provide much better image quality.

The equivalent measure for plotters is the minimum line width the plotter can produce, which is determined by the pens it carries.

Printers are raster devices like all standard monitors, which means they create images as rows of dots one after another. Drawing a slanted line on a raster device using fixed-intensity dots leads to jagged effects, as shown in Figure 5-7, because a raster has dots only in fixed places. When you draw a line at an angle, it usually crosses the dots in the raster near the edge of the dot rather than right over the center. Because of this, the actual image you see is deformed from the true line, leading to an effect called jaggies. The grayed dots on the left side of Figure 5-7 show the dots that would be active for the line shown. If the resolution of the device is such that you can actually see these dots, the line will appear coarse.

Varying the intensity of the dots (as on the right side of Figure 5-7) lets the printer produce output as good as that from a higher-resolution printer that can't vary dot intensity. Dots centered close to the line show as full-intensity black, while those farther from the line are lighter. Variable intensity technology is built into many laser printers.

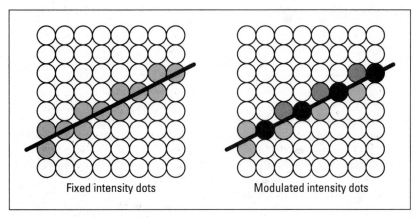

Fixed intensity dots          Modulated intensity dots

**Figure 5-7:** Insufficient resolution in a printer raster can cause lines to appear jagged.

✦ *Accuracy.* A printer or plotter positions a sheet to a known place and marks on it. The accuracy and reproducibility of that positioning, and of the positioning of the marks relative to one another, affect the relative accuracy of the printed result. For example, if you print a three- or four-color separation on a laser printer (in which each color of an image is printed on a separate sheet) and rely on the sheet edges for absolute positioning, any small misalignment of the paper would cause misregistration of the combined result. Any misalignment as the printer or plotter writes on the sheet will similarly affect registration. In practice, it's much more likely that the paper will be misregistered than there will be misalignments within the printed area — that's why color separations are printed with registration marks.

The accuracy with which a printer registers paper position affects the quality of the result when you use preprinted forms. Tractor-feed devices on printers do not always accurately position the top of the form, leading to variation in the placement of the printed text relative to fields on the form.

Sound cards and speakers are subject to the same performance measures you expect to see for a stereo system, such as power, distortion, and frequency response. To date, most buyers do not expect the same quality of sound from their computer as from a quality stereo system, so the more difficult specifications (such as distortion) are not as readily available. Higher-quality computer sound components are starting to be compared with stereo gear, though, so look for those specifications to start being reported.

## Interoperability

Printers and plotters generally interface through a serial or parallel port, with some offering options for infrared and network interfaces. Any unit you buy should conform to the relevant standards (discussed in Part III).

Physical interoperability with the port is the least of the issues to look at, however. The software driving printers and plotters has been a major problem for as long as there have been PCs. You will want to evaluate the track record of a printer vendor for promptness in releasing drivers meeting new standards and for the reported quality of the vendor's drivers. You can't assume that a printer has drivers for your operating system, especially if you're using Windows NT or UNIX instead of Windows 9x. You can check out a vendor by monitoring discussions in Internet newsgroups or on the online services.

Sound cards are subject to the same device-driver issues. Nearly all software supporting sound can work with cards meeting the Creative Labs Sound Blaster standard. You will want to research the quality of support for cards that are not compatible with this standard. Microsoft has enhanced the ability of other sound card vendors to compete with Creative by developing DirectSound and DirectMusic (part of the DirectX drivers), expanding the sound capabilities of Windows.

## Maintainability

The moving parts in printers and plotters, combined with the debris from moving paper, make reliability more difficult to attain for them than for other elements in your computer system. The high reliability some printer vendors have achieved speaks well of their concern for design and suggests that you carefully compare the track record of competing vendors. For example, a Hewlett-Packard LaserJet Series II that we owned failed once (but permanently) after eight years of uninterrupted service. When the Series II failed, we pulled the LaserJet Plus it replaced out of the basement, installed the drivers provided in Windows for a printer well over ten years old, and continued working. As good as the performance we received from the LaserJets was, though, the drivers for the Hewlett-Packard DeskJet 600 series of ink jet printers were not first quality (although the later 800 series is reported to be better).

Sound cards, like other cards in your computer, may not be worth repairing once they're out of warranty, because parts are likely not available and the cost of labor to repair them will exceed the cost of a new card.

## Upgradability

A variety of upgrades are available for printers, including PostScript support, additional fonts, additional memory, other interfaces (including ones for sharing among multiple computers), duplex (two-sided) printing, and paper or envelope feeders.

Sound cards are generally not upgradable, with the exception that some can be upgraded to add wavetable capabilities and to add more memory.

## Size, weight, and power

Printers and plotters can be quite large and heavy, to the point where you need to think about where to put them. They can also be quite noisy. Laser printers consume power to run heaters in the unit, making it worth looking for energy-saving features.

Sound card size, weight, and power consumption are not important factors. Quality sound is difficult to get from small, lightweight speakers, although larger-size speakers are no guarantee of better performance.

## Mobility

The popularity of laptop computers has created a market for portable printers. The small size and light weight of these units require compromises in capability relative to what a full-size printer can offer. Using a printer at your travel destination or faxing the material to the hotel desk using your laptop fax modem are alternatives to a portable printer you may want to consider.

# Communications

You can connect your computer to other local computers; to private, public, and corporate networks; or through the Internet to machines around the world. The range of technologies through which you can communicate from your computer grows all the time, driving the cost of communications down and the speed up. Understanding what equipment you need for communicating starts by understanding what it is you want to communicate with and what you intend to do over the communications link.

Communication between computers is subject to errors because of noise in the communications lines, incompatibilities between the computers, or failures and overloading in one of the computers. Communications links employ rules for intercomputer conversation called *protocols* (see Chapter 30) to detect and compensate for these errors. The type of communications link usually determines the protocol (and therefore the supporting software) you need.

There are two common models for communications between computers: computer-to-terminal connections and network connections. Network connections come in two forms, leading to the three classes of connections shown in Figure 5-8.

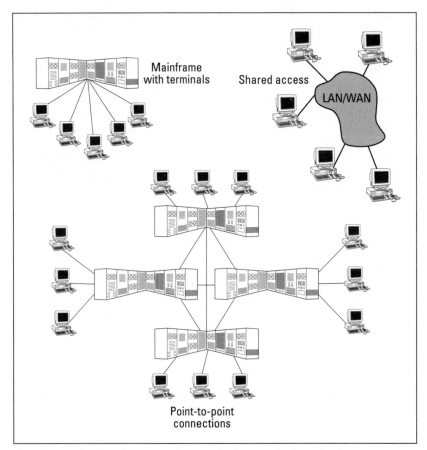

**Figure 5-8:** The development of networks from early time-sharing systems eventually led to the Internet.

✦ *Mainframe with terminals.* Early computer connections were between large (mainframe) computers and attached terminals. The idea of a computer wired to a number of terminals survives today in bulletin board systems (BBSs), which are computers with modems attached. You dial up to one of those modems through your modem, creating a point-to-point connection.

The Network Computer (NC) is the latest revival of centralized, mainframe computing. The NC works as a smart terminal, displaying the results of programs run on a central server. It's useful if you have a fixed, limited set of things to do, but not very useful if your requirements fall outside what an IT shop can put on a server for you.

✦ *Point-to-point connections.* Early networks connected computers together with multiple point-to-point links. Users connected to the computers from terminals. Later versions of this structure used small, specialized computers as dedicated network access ports for terminals.

✦ *Shared access.* The invention of Ethernet made it possible to connect more than one computer to the same wire. That, along with increased capability in personal computers, led to local area networks (LANs) and wide area networks (WANs) as we know them today.

## Functionality

Two factors drive the communications functionality you need: what you want to connect to and what you want to do once you're connected. For example:

✦ *BBSs and online services.* If you plan to use BBSs or the major online services (such as Prodigy, AOL, or CompuServe) exclusively, you need only a modem. The HyperTerminal application in Windows 9*x* is all you need to connect to a BBS, while the online services provide the software they require (it's hard to keep them from flooding your mailbox with free copies).

✦ *Connected pairs of machines.* If you plan to connect a laptop to a desktop machine, or put some other combination of two Windows machines together, you can use a special cable setup for Direct Cable Connection (Windows NT does the same thing using Remote Access Services — RAS). The networking software built into Windows will then enable you to share disk and printer resources across that link.

✦ *Connected groups of local machines.* If you will connect more than two machines locally, or if you're connecting UNIX machines, you need a network. You can use the network software built into Windows and UNIX, or you can add software from third parties.

✦ *Connections to remote networks.* If you will connect to remote networks, you need at least a modem. High-speed connections, including ADSL (Asymmetric Digital Subscriber Line), cable modems, and ISDN (Integrated Services Digital Network) offer greater performance than conventional modems. The performance you need is determined by the operations you will perform once connected.

## Capacity

We'll call the number of physical connections a communications link supports its *capacity*. A modem supports one physical connection (two with ISDN), although technologies are available to bond two modems into a single, faster link. The different forms of Ethernet support connections to many devices on a single wire (using coaxial cable) or connection to one other device on a single wire (using twisted-pair cable). Because networks let you relay information from one computer to another, the number of physical connections is unrelated to the number of computers you can connect to through the network. It's important to understand your physical connection requirements in order to choose the communications technology you need (see Chapter 27).

## Performance

The performance of a communications link is the combination of the rate at which it transmits information and the reliability of the transmissions. A fast modem that introduces lots of errors when faced with a noisy telephone line, for example, may not be what you want in areas with poor-quality lines. Reviews of modems in computer magazines often include tests of their error resistance; check that data carefully if your telephone service isn't top-notch. Don't assume that your telephone lines are good simply because you're in a large city — devices the phone companies insert in lines to increase the number of lines their cables can carry can themselves prevent some of the fastest modem technologies from working.

The technology that communications equipment uses determines the data rate and error rate you will get. The wireless networks, for example, are similar in characteristics to cordless telephones — the technology in lower-cost systems can be subject to noise and interference and have very limited range. More powerful technologies (such as spread spectrum transmission — see the section "Cable television" in Chapter 27) can overcome noise and interference (and increase range), but often come at a higher price.

## Interoperability

The entire point of computer communications is to allow machines to work together, so interoperability is critical. The inflexibility of computers trying to interpret even mildly corrupted messages, combined with the difficulty of sending signals over distances, complicates the problem and has led to the computer and telecommunications industries expending a lot of effort to create standards. Unfortunately, the number of communications standards is bewildering. Looking only at modems, there are standards for telephone systems, for how signals are transmitted over those systems, for how modems negotiate with one another to agree on transmission formats, for how computers talk to modems, and on and on.

In analyzing your communications interoperability workload requirements, you want to identify what sort of circuit you will connect over (voice telephone line, coaxial cable Ethernet, and so on) and what the other equipment on the line is (such as the kind of modem at your Internet service provider). That existing equipment will have a set of standards it follows, which you, in turn, will want to match.

## Maintainability

Communications links fail from hardware problems and (more important) because they have to interact with factors outside of the control of the communication system designer. When that happens, and the link goes down, you'll want tools to identify problems and isolate their source. You can reduce the frequency of service interruptions by choosing equipment that is as resistant to disruption as possible.

The tools built into communications systems to identify problems range from simple loopback tests in modems through sophisticated network-management systems offering centralized facilities to monitor and control a worldwide network. The easiest way to troubleshoot a failed connection attempt to your Internet service provider may be to simply try it again (or at worst, swap out your modem for another). This technique is less effective when your problem is that the online order entry and sales department in Europe has lost access to the servers in Australia.

## Upgradability

The multiple layers of communications standards exist in part to help ensure that individual components can be upgraded without ripple effects throughout the system. You can replace a modem with a faster one and not affect your applications. You can convert an ISA network card to one using PCI and not affect your cabling or software. You can convert from a flat Ethernet topology to a high-speed switched backbone with your network users seeing only the improved performance.

The key to being able to upgrade your communications is to analyze in advance what kinds of upgrades you may need in the future, and then to plan the equipment you buy and the system you construct to enable those upgrades efficiently. The first step is to identify in your workload analysis what your current requirements are and how you think they might change.

## Size, weight, power, and mobility

The size, weight, and power characteristics of communications equipment for desktop machines are not important, but all three factors are crucial for mobile applications. The size of communications equipment can also become a factor for the network infrastructure at the place where the communications links from many users connect to the network backbone.

# Some Sample Workload Profiles

You'll find some examples of workload profiles in this section to help tie all the ideas in this chapter together. The examples are:

✦ The home office/small office user who publishes a newsletter and keeps books

✦ The Internet user who accesses e-mail and the World Wide Web, and the telecommuter who handles order entry for a mail-order sales company

✦ The technical writer and editor who edits, formats, and produces large manuscripts with extensive graphics

✦ An Internet server, used to support access to information through the World Wide Web, electronic mail, and a variety of other Internet services

## Home office/small office

Table 5-4 is a representative matrix for a home office/small office system. This office has three machines on a local area network. The office depends on the computers to run the business (accounts receivable, accounts payable, payroll, and general ledger), as well as for the usual office-automation functions. The individuals using the computers are sophisticated in their ability to apply computers to the business and have some understanding of how the machines work and how to maintain them.

The lettered paragraphs below the table describe the characteristics of the corresponding row and column (for instance, paragraph A describes the Performance requirements in the Computation category).

## Table 5-4
## Home Office/Small Office Workload Matrix

| Category | Computation | Memory | Storage | Display | Input | Output | Communications |
|---|---|---|---|---|---|---|---|
| Functionality | | | F | | G | H | I |
| Capacity | | E | E | | | | |
| Performance | A | | | A | | | |
| Interoperability | | | F | | | | I |
| Maintainability | B | B | B | B | B | B | B |
| Upgradability | C | C | C | C | C | C | C |
| Size | D | D | D | D | D | D | D |
| Weight | | | | | | | |
| Power | | | | | | | |
| Mobility | | | | | | | |

A. Software in the office includes an integrated accounting package and an office suite; a page layout program; tools to drive a scanner and handle scanned images; and the software for an online service. The accounting system supports multiple users simultaneously.

B. The presence of multiple networked machines in the office means that (with the right backup strategy) one machine going down need not shut down the office. The effort required to diagnose and fix a problem is more significant to these users than the absolute reliability of the machines.

C.    The services this office provides to its customers have consistently grown over time. Hiring new personnel will likely occur within a year, implying the need for new systems, additional network capacity, and greater printer capacity.

D.    Although the company is growing, its home office/small office facilities are cramped. Controlling the size of the office equipment is important to forestall the day when the company will have to move to larger, more expensive quarters.

E.    These users each do a variety of tasks in running the business, with little opportunity to completely finish a job without interruption. They benefit by being able to keep all their programs open at the same time, boosting their productivity by reducing the time to switch tasks. Having enough disk storage to keep all their programs and several years of projects handy helps as well.

F.    The need to reference past projects makes quick access to archival storage important.

G.    The graphics these users put in their catalogs and brochures include product photographs as well as drawings, figures, and tables.

H.    The formal color catalogs and brochures are professionally printed from PostScript files produced in the office. Black-and-white catalogs and brochures, along with proposals, reports, and invoices, are printed at the office for distribution.

I.    The office uses a local network for disk and printer sharing. The only external communications requirement is for access to an online service used for product research.

## The Internet and telecommuting

There are many things you can do with the Internet or a private wide area network. Opportunities include research, publishing product data or research results, accessing corporate information databases, home or satellite office-based order and data entry, and hundreds of other activities. It is unrealistic to suggest that one profile could cover all the opportunities. Instead, in this profile (Table 5-5) we try to highlight some of the issues that relate to using computers across many of these possibilities.

## Table 5-5
## Internet and Telecommuting Workload Matrix

| Category | Computation | Memory | Storage | Display | Input | Output | Communications |
|---|---|---|---|---|---|---|---|
| Functionality | | | | | | | G |
| Capacity | | C | D | E | | | G |
| Performance | A | | | | | | G |
| Interoperability | | | | | | | G |
| Maintainability | | | | | | | |
| Upgradability | | | | | | | |
| Size | | | | | | | |
| Weight | | | | | | | |
| Power | B | | B | | | | |
| Mobility | | | | | F | F | G |

A.    Unless there are local applications with greater demands, using a computer to access a network requires only average computer performance. The applications in Table 5-5 are all client applications, in the sense that the machine is communicating with some other machine that actually provides and accepts information (and does the work); the local machine is essentially a very sophisticated terminal. (We show in Part IV, however, that a server can require significant performance, capacity, and everything else.)

B.    Assuming you've made arrangements for access, the Internet or a private network is an ideal way for travelers to get updated information and check for e-mail. The processor for a laptop computer should be a version with reduced power consumption to enhance battery life. The disk should be one that powers down after a period of no access. (All this will be standard on any good laptop.)

C.    In addition to a World Wide Web browser such as Netscape Navigator or Internet Explorer, you're likely to want to run an e-mail application such as Eudora or the e-mail client built into Netscape Communicator or Microsoft Internet Explorer. The Web browsers are extensible with add-on applications such as Adobe's Acrobat reader for the Portable Document Format (PDF) or modules to interpret 3D Web pages using the virtual reality modeling language (VRML). You will want many or all of these applications active at the same time, and that increases the amount of memory you need for good performance.

D.    If you use the computer for nothing but network access, you may not need more than an average amount of storage, and backup may not be terribly important (because you can store critical information on file servers you have access to). If net access is only part of what you do, however, then it will add to the storage you need for everything else, suggesting that you may want to consider somewhat larger capacity.

E.    Standard VGA resolution (640 _ 480) really isn't enough to use the Web effectively, because you can't get enough on the screen. Figure 5-9 shows the difference higher resolution makes; the larger window image has three times the area of the smaller. You'll need a better video card and monitor to create the larger window (ideally you'd run the display at 1280 _ 1024).

F.    A laptop should enable you to connect an external monitor and keyboard for desktop use, possibly through a docking station.

G.    You'll need at least a modem capable of running over a voice-grade telephone line, and you should get as fast a one as the equipment you connect to can support. If you have several people at the same telecommuting site, you may want to look into a local area network with a connection out to the wide area network.

(a)

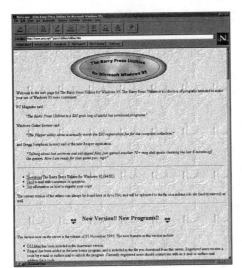

(b)

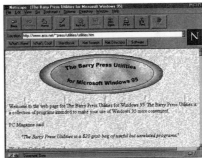

**Figure 5-9:** Higher display resolutions simply make more information available at once.

# Technical writing and editing

By "technical writing and editing" we mean working with relatively large documents that contain some mixture of text, drawings, graphics, and equations. A technical proposal typically fits in this category, as does this book, a thesis, and a product data sheet. You'll probably put those different elements into a document using a wide range of software. We used writing this book as the basis for this profile; the problems and issues any technical writer or editor would encounter doing large-scale work would be similar.

The tools we use include:

✦ Microsoft Word to write the text

✦ Microsoft Excel to develop tables and graphs

✦ Microsoft PowerPoint, Corel Flow, and Adobe Illustrator to draw figures

✦ Adobe Photoshop to run the scanner and process images

The tasks of a technical writer and editor can require surprisingly large resources for good productivity, as reflected in the sample profile for technical writing and editing in Table 5-6.

## Table 5-6
## Technical Writing and Editing Workload Matrix

| Category | Computation | Memory | Storage | Display | Input | Output | Communications |
|---|---|---|---|---|---|---|---|
| Functionality | | | E | | K | M | N |
| Capacity | | C | F | J | | | |
| Performance | A | | G | J | | M | N |
| Interoperability | | | H | | L | M | |
| Maintainability | | | | | | | |
| Upgradability | B | D | I | | | | N |
| Size | | | | | | | |
| Weight | | | | | | | |
| Power | | | | | | | |
| Mobility | | | | | | | |

A.    Working with drawings can create a severe load on the processor very quickly. For example, an obsolete 486 processor at 50 MHz takes nearly 30 seconds merely to resize a fairly simple drawing we worked with. During that time there was no disk activity and no change to the screen, so it was a good assumption that the work was all being done by the processor. The same resize operation with a 166 MHz Pentium takes no more than a second; even the slowest Pentium II processors would cut the Pentium time in half.

B.  Given the importance of processor speed for manipulating drawings and graphics, the ability to upgrade the processor to a faster one will be important if you are constrained in how fast a processor you can get.

C.  Memory is critical to good performance in this environment. Running the set of programs we mentioned on a machine with a marginal amount of memory, we can switch between two programs several times and not really notice the swapping to disk that Windows does. As soon as we add a third program to that set, however, we can no longer limit the swapping—Windows runs out of physical memory to hold the necessary pages in use and has to swap. On a more capable machine, the programs we use for writing plus Internet Explorer, Outlook, and some of the desktop utilities we've written result in a swap file of 128MB under Windows NT 4.0 Server. The swap file will grow even larger if we start scanning and processing images. We have 192MB of memory on that Windows NT machine, which effectively eliminates reads and writes of the swap file while we write.

Running all those programs at the same time shows how effectively Windows 9x and NT solve the resource problem that so often causes Windows 3.1 to crash. With all those programs loaded under Windows 95, we still had 38 percent free system resources. We couldn't even load them all under Windows 3.1.

D.  Our expectations have come down, but we still expect to get at least three years useful life on any machine we acquire, preferably closer to five or six including upgrades. That means the initial complement of memory for the machine needs to fit in the motherboard without using all the memory slots so that we'll have room to upgrade. The question isn't whether we'll need more memory, just when.

E.  In addition to conventional hard disk storage, we need a reliable backup system with removable media to ensure we don't lose any work. We also need a way to archive past projects (so we can retrieve them for reference or update) that is faster to access than tape.

F.  We keep a PowerPoint file containing all the drawings we do for a project, and an Excel file with all the charts and spreadsheets. We do this so that if a problem corrupts the Word file, which still happens at times, we won't lose the auxiliary information. That practice results in lots of large files—by the time we finished the first edition of this book, the directory tree for the project was over 750MB. The files for the second edition (including the CD-ROM material) were over 1GB, showing it's very easy to run through a whole lot of disk storage. We did another project of 100 finished pages where the final document file—one Word file—was well over 150MB, and the supporting directories were in excess of 450MB. Audio and video files will consume storage even more quickly.

G.    The performance of the disk subsystem is important because of the large file sizes and because of the likelihood that you will run applications that want more memory than you have. The faster the machine can swap virtual memory to disk, the better performance you get. Performance of the backup device matters too, because even at rates of 8MB per minute (good for SCSI tapes less than five years ago) a backup of 2 gigabytes takes four hours (and another four to verify). This is overnight-class time, not something you do at the end of the day. You can reduce the time with a backup strategy that writes out only changed files, but it's still time consuming.

H.    Interoperability of removable storage can be important if you use it to send large quantities of data by mail. You have to do this if you want someone else to master a CD-ROM for you, for instance.

I.    One way or another, more storage will be required over the lifetime of the machine. Planning now for the power, space, and connectivity to a controller that additional disk will require, or for removable media to expand storage, will save time and money later.

J.    More on the display is better. Being able to see a full page of text and the supporting spreadsheet, for example, means we can avoid flipping back and forth between programs, so we can work faster. A 1600 _ 1200 display creates a lot of work to update for the processor, so the update performance is important as well.

K.    We type up to ten or twelve hours a day, every day. A keyboard we don't like isn't worth putting up with. The same is true with the mouse. We've never found a trackball we like, but we recognize that's personal opinion.

L.    Devices don't work if the drivers don't work. We never managed to find working 32-bit drivers for the scanner we bought a few years ago; in fact, the only drivers we ever had that worked were the original ones that came with the scanner. The unit is incapable of operation with Windows NT or UNIX for lack of drivers. As good as the images are that we get with that scanner, we wouldn't buy another from that manufacturer, because that manufacturer is demonstrably not committed to long-term, quality product support. We had a similar problem with a video camera from Videolabs we acquired about a year before the release of Windows 98, in that Videolabs chose to orphan the product, failing to provide a Windows 98 version of the device driver. We're not likely to buy any of their other products. You will want to keep track of your own vendor experiences, so that you can favor the ones that serve you well and shun the ones that don't.

The best companies are capable of recognizing and correcting their problems. A company we regard very highly — ATI — is a good example. In the very early days of Windows 3.1, ATI had problems with the stability of their video drivers. They kept after the problem, however, and made public the information they had about what the problems were and what they were doing. By the time Windows 95 shipped, ATI had some of the best hardware in the industry, and rock-solid drivers across their product line. Some other, very high-volume video card manufacturers cannot make that claim. We use ATI video cards exclusively in machines we build.

M.  The printer functionality we need is pretty basic, with the only valuable option to us being PostScript so that we can conveniently print off our UNIX machine. The performance of the printer matters, however, in that we print three to four thousand pages a month and need enough quality in the print to see if scanned images are going to be acceptable. We've had enough problems with print drivers to be very picky about the track record a printer vendor has for timely, quality print drivers.

N.  We have a local area network for cooperative work by people doing research (and for quick backups of critical work to other machines). Ethernet performance is fast enough for that purpose, although in 1999 we converted the network from 10 Mbps Ethernet to 100 Mbps. We used a modem for years to connect to an Internet service provider, and for the volume of traffic it was too slow. The telephone lines in our area are too poor to support 56 Kbps modems. An ISDN line at 128 kilobits per second finally became available from US West in the second quarter of 1997, and after four months of constant problems, it became solid and reliable. A cable modem (at least a megabit per second) would be even better but is not available from our cable operator (TCI).

## Internet server

An Internet server primarily needs to provide superb, high-performance storage and communications, enough memory to support many simultaneous users, and absolute data security (see Table 5-7).

### Table 5-7
### Internet Server Workload Matrix

| Category | Computation | Memory | Storage | Display | Input | Output | Communications |
|---|---|---|---|---|---|---|---|
| Functionality | | | | | | | |
| Capacity | A | B | | | | | C |
| Performance | | B | | | | | C |
| Interoperability | | | | | | | C |
| Maintainability | | B | | | | | |
| Upgradability | | B | | | | | |
| Size | | | | | | | |
| Weight | | | | | | | |
| Power | | | | | | | |
| Mobility | | | | | | | |

A.    It's very common for every incoming Internet connection to a machine to spawn a new process — a new instance of the server software. Even if each instance only takes a few megabytes, the terrific number of connections into a popular Internet server can turn into an enormous memory requirement in order to hold the data for all those server instances. (A *private* Usenet server we use took 80,000 hits a day its first week of operation. Spread over a 14-hour day, that implies an average of nearly 100 concurrent connections, which translates to an average load of 100 active processes, each requiring one or more megabytes of memory.)

B.  The point of the Internet is to make information available. A small World Wide Web site can easily occupy five or ten megabytes; a site with many sound and video files can easily occupy gigabytes. Usenet similarly can fill gigabytes of disk. Losing a file system at best takes the service down until it's repaired and restored. On a corporate intranet, losing a disk or file system could result in the loss of mission critical data.

C.  The connections to the Internet will only get faster. A popular site (say for download of new software releases) can easily draw 1,000 simultaneous connections. If you want the server to be able to keep 33.6 Kbps modems busy, you'll see an aggregate outbound data rate of over 26 Mbps. That's a very heavy communications load; as ISDN and other higher-rate technologies come into widespread use, the loads will go higher yet.

# Summary

✦ You have to do your own analysis to understand what's best for you in your computer.

✦ The key elements you need to consider are the processor, memory, storage, display, input devices, output devices, and communications.

✦ For each element, you should think about functionality, capacity, performance, interoperability, maintainability, upgradability, size, weight, power, and mobility.

✦ The sample workload profiles in this book are extremes to illustrate how you might configure machines for different purposes.

✦    ✦    ✦

# Specs, Lies, and Duct Tape

◆   ◆   ◆   ◆

◆   ◆   ◆   ◆

# Cases, Power Supplies, and Uninterruptible Power Supplies

The case and the power supply for a computer—as basic as they might seem—are crucial parts of the system. The case and power supply might not be as flashy a topic as some of the others we'll cover, but they're vitally important. Poor choices of case and power supply can shorten the life of other components, make a system unreliable, and make upgrades expensive or impossible. Good choices can improve the usability of the system, simplify maintenance, and make the system easier to live with. We've covered desktop and tower cases in this chapter; see Chapter 32 for coverage on laptop computers.

## Cases, Fans, and Cooling

Your computer case has to do a surprising number of things:

✦ Provide mechanical support and protection for the components

✦ Shield the computer (and your TV) from electromagnetic interference (EMI)

✦ Display and control basic system functions such as power-on and reset

✦ Give you access to components for maintenance and repair

✦ Keep everything cool

The case houses the power supply, motherboard, adapter cards, disk drives, and internal cables, providing mechanical support to the components, electromagnetic shielding, and system control. The mechanical relationships among the case, motherboard, and cards are shown in Figure 6-1 and detailed in the following paragraphs. The critical features are that the case and mounts support the motherboard at enough points to prevent flexing, that the motherboard be properly grounded, and that the adapter cards be properly supported and aligned with the connectors on the motherboard.

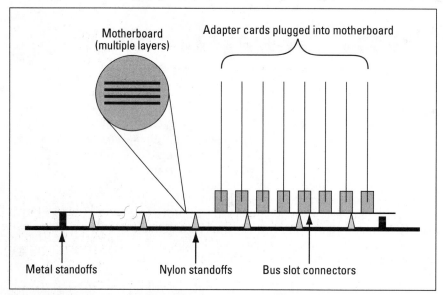

**Figure 6-1:** The case supports the motherboard and cards, and it provides grounding and shielding for the motherboard.

✦ *Printed circuit board.* The motherboard and adapter cards are each composed of a sandwich of layers of fiberglass epoxy and copper conductors. Leads on some components are soldered directly to pads on the outer surface. Holes drilled through the board allow other components and connectors to be soldered. Microscopic cracks from flexing the board can break the conductors or soldered joints, causing a failure. That's why it's important that the case support the motherboard, and why you have to be careful how you push or pull on printed circuit cards.

✦ *Metal and nylon standoffs.* At least two metal standoffs support the motherboard and provide grounding between the motherboard and the case. The case ground helps quiet noise in the system, making signal transmission more reliable. The ATX motherboards we've worked with used all metal standoffs, while the older AT motherboards used a combination of metal and nylon. (See "The ATX form factor" later in this chapter for more on what ATX and AT are.) When you mount an AT motherboard to a case, use as many metal standoffs (versus the nylon ones) as you can to get the best grounding possible.

It's important to have enough metal and nylon standoffs that all parts of the motherboard are well supported, because positive support for the motherboard (particularly around the connectors for the adapter cards and the keyboard) is crucial. Flexing the motherboard or wrenching an adapter connector can create nearly invisible cracks in the printed wiring or the soldered connections that cause the system to operate erratically or to fail altogether. The forces on the connectors when you insert a card are in the tens of pounds, which can easily destroy an improperly supported board.

✦ *Connectors.* Bus slot connectors for the adapter cards are soldered to the motherboard. Each connector contains many small metal fingers that wipe along matching metal pads on the card. Keeping the cards vertical — lined up perpendicular to the motherboard — when you insert and remove them is important to keep the contacts secure and to prevent stressing the connector's attachment to the motherboard.

**Tip**  The connectors have to line up mechanically with the cutouts on the back of the case. The easy way to mount a motherboard so the connectors line up with the chassis is to put all the mounting screws into the motherboard loosely, then put in one or two adapter cards. Screw the adapter cards firmly to the case, which will set the motherboard into the correct alignment, then tighten the motherboard screws.

Disk drives come in 5.25-inch and 3.5-inch sizes (the numbers describe the size of the media a floppy drive of that size uses). The 5.25-inch drives are 5.875 inches wide by 1.625 inches high, while the 3.5-inch drives are 4 inches wide by 1 inch high. The case usually provides spaces (called *bays*) for drives of both 5.25-inch and 3.5-inch sizes. An older 5.25-inch size was twice the height of today's 5.25-inch drives (it's now uncommon except for the largest-capacity hard disks); because the names were set when the taller drives were prevalent, today's standard 5.25-inch drive bays are known as *half-height* bays.

Your computer case will provide some bays that open to the front of the computer and others that are accessible only from the interior of the case. The external bays are for floppy drives, CD-ROMs, removable disks, tapes, and any other devices that use removable media, while internal bays are for hard disks. You can use external bays for hard disks (just put a cover plate over the hole in the case), but you cannot convert an internal bay into an external one.

Figures 6-2 and 6-3 show some of the problems cases can create. The system in Figure 6-2 has run out of external bays for any further expansion, even though it is a full-size tower. It also has too small a space between the upper drive bays and the power supply, making drive removal and insertion difficult, and has run out of spare slots on the motherboard. An upgrade to this system replaced the disks and motherboard. Higher-capacity disks left several internal drive bays free, while the motherboard upgrade moved the memory and sound functions once on adapter cards to the motherboard, freeing adapter card slots.

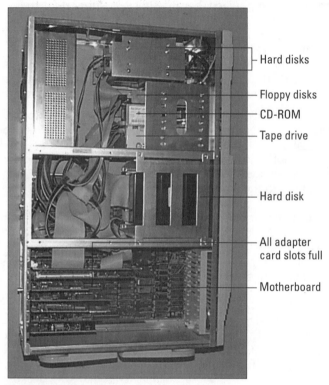

Hard disks

Floppy disks
CD-ROM
Tape drive

Hard disk

All adapter
card slots full

Motherboard

**Figure 6-2:** This system ran out of expansion options due to a lack of internal drive bays.

The system in Figure 6-3 is a minitower case. Although it has blank plates covering external bays of both sizes (5.25-inch and 3.5-inch), there is no room to add an externally accessed device (such as a tape drive) — internal drives occupy the space behind the cover plates. The smaller case is more convenient in an office, but it's very cramped and hard to work on.

In both cases, the lack of space means that cables simply run where they will, without the possibility of a logical cabling plan. The haphazard wiring complicates access and service. The tightly packed interior traps heat. We decided that we wouldn't try to upgrade this system from a Pentium processor to a Pentium II, because the case couldn't provide the clearance away from the motherboard we'd need for the Pentium II processor.

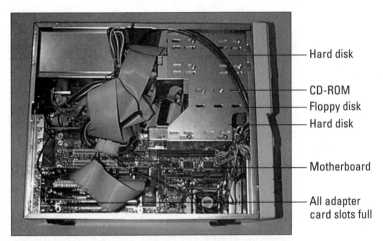

— Hard disk

— CD-ROM
— Floppy disk
— Hard disk

— Motherboard

— All adapter card slots full

**Figure 6-3:** This system is a minitower case, taking up less room in the home or office than a full-size tower, but is very cramped internally and can't be upgraded from a Pentium to a Pentium II processor for lack of room.

**Note** Several manufacturers, including IBM in the PS/2 line sold in the late 1980s, have designed cases to completely eliminate cables. The PS/2 desktop models featured a completely integrated case requiring no internal cables at all. Unfortunately, the integrated case on the PS/2 desktops was so small that adding a tape drive or second hard disk was pretty much impossible. There are no industry standards for highly integrated cases, so you're likely to be unable to buy all the upgrades you want on the open market.

We'll look at arrays of hard disks in Chapter 13. You use disk arrays to create very large, reliable disk archives. Cases for arrays need a very large number of drive bays and contain a lot of cable. The same sort of cases let you put a large number of CD-ROMs online. Such cases are heftier yet let you build an entire server, with redundant power supplies, full-size motherboards, and complete disk arrays. A well-designed case improves array maintainability by allowing drives to be removed one at a time without disassembling the entire case. Even if you're not planning a drive or CD-ROM array, pick a case that has room for the drives you need now plus ones you might add.

## Airflow and heat buildup

Airflow in nearly every desktop computer sold today is created solely by a fan in the power supply. The fan pulls in air from vents located across the case from the power supply, draws it over the motherboard and adapter cards, pulls it through the power supply, and expels it as hot air from the case. This airflow design helps to make sure that hot air does not accumulate around the electronics. Commercial chips are commonly rated for a free-air temperature of 70 degrees Celsius, with some rated as low as 50 degrees. Exceeding the rated temperature can shorten service life, cause the chip to malfunction, or cause immediate permanent failure.

Benchmarking    We measured the power consumption and temperature rise in three different systems to see how effective their fans and cases were at removing heat. Table 6-1 shows the results of those measurements. System A was a full-size tower, system B, a minitower, and system C, a full-size tower with auxiliary fans to improve airflow.

System A runs significantly hotter inside than the other two because it has more disks and adapter cards, and therefore consumes more power. The power the computer consumes turns into heat, so computers that consume more power generate more heat. The airflow from the power supply fans is roughly the same in systems A and B, and it is the only cooling those systems have. The result is that system A runs hotter than system B, so over many years, the reliability of system B should be better than system A. (In Chapter 36, however, we'll see that poor airflow inlet design in the system B case made the machine prone to abnormal failures.) System C should be more reliable than either of the other two, because it runs significantly cooler despite its power consumption being in the middle of the range.

| Table 6-1 Operating Temperature Comparison (in Degrees Fahrenheit) | | | | | |
|---|---|---|---|---|---|
| System | Ambient (F) | Exhaust | Rise | Power Consumption (W) | Degrees per Watt |
| A | 68.0 | 91.6 | 23.6 | 96.0 | 0.2552 |
| B | 71.4 | 87.3 | 15.9 | 46.8 | 0.3590 |
| C | 68.0 | 71.4 | 3.4 | 68.4 | 0.0629 |

The last column in Table 6-1 compares the ability of the three systems to remove heat. The power consumption (in watts) creates heat, which raises the temperature. The more airflow through the case, the fewer degrees of system temperature increase that this heat can create. If you compare system A or B to system C, you'll see why fans and airflow are so critically important to system reliability. System C pulls heat out of the case over four and five times more effectively than systems A and B, respectively.

## Cooling your processor

All processors, be they Pentium, Celeron, Pentium II, Pentium III, or K6 chips, should have cooling fans on the chip. (Some manufacturers save a buck or two cooling processors with large *heat sinks* instead of fans, but if the power supply fan goes out, the chip is cooked. (A heat sink is a finned structure attached to the chip package to remove heat and keep the chip cool.) A processor cooling fan assembly includes both a heat sink and a fan, as shown in Figure 6-4. Heat created by the operation of the chip flows from the chip to the surrounding chip package. Cool air driven past the heat sink by the fan takes heat off the heat sink into the surrounding air. The fins on the heat sink increase the contact between the air and the heat sink, improving the rate of heat transfer. If the fan stops, however, little or no air moves and the rate of heat transfer slows greatly. The chip will get hotter until its maximum ratings are exceeded. At that point it will fail, possibly permanently.

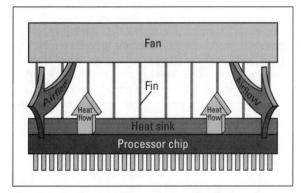

**Figure 6-4:** The fan drives air past the fins on the heat sink, cooling the fins and heating the air.

**Note**  The processor cooling fan gets power either from the motherboard or from a tap on a disk drive power connector. Keyed connectors on the disk drive power tap ensure that the connection is oriented properly. If you get a fan's motherboard power connection backward, the fan will either run backward or not at all, and it will not cool the chip properly.

Although commercial-grade chips are commonly rated for a "free-air temperature" of up to 70° Celsius (158° Fahrenheit, far above the exhaust air temperatures in Table 6-1), the limited airflow created by weak fans in most computers lets heat pockets build up in the case, causing the air temperature in the vicinity of the pocket to go well over the maximum ambient rating.

## Checking your processor fan installation

PC Power & Cooling suggests this way to find out if your processor cooling fan is working right. (Be careful about discharging static electricity; see Chapter 1 for the right techniques.)

**1.** Turn off the computer, open it up, and unplug the processor fan.

**2.** Power up the machine and keep a finger on the fan's heat sink. If the chip and heat sink are in good contact, the heat sink will get very hot—shut down the computer before that happens.

**3.** Shut down the machine, reconnect the fan power, and start up again. Let the chip temperature stabilize by waiting a few minutes, and check the heat sink temperature with your finger again; you'll see that it's a lot cooler.

Don't leave the power on with the fan unplugged for more than a minute or so, or you'll cook the chip.

Figure 6-5 shows one way heat pockets come about. A stack of disk drives and other peripherals is common in most computers. Each drive includes both a drive mechanism and a board of electronics, both of which generate heat that gets trapped in the pockets between drives and boards. Stacking drives one on top of another tends to block the airflow, forcing most of the cooling air to flow around the sources of heat. This allows heat pockets to develop in the stack, as shown in the exploded view of the floppy drive and CD-ROM drive on the right of Figure 6-5. If the air temperature in the pockets exceeds maximum ratings, the drives will fail.

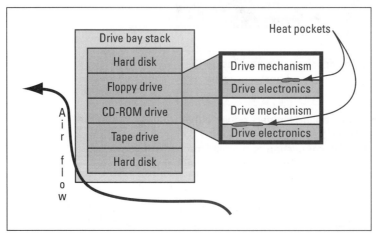

**Figure 6-5:** Trapped air in the case can overheat chips and cause failures.

The example in Figure 6-5 happens all the time. When you stack one drive on top of another, the space between the drives can be blocked from the airflow. Unless the metal drive brackets in the case pull heat out of the drive area, heat builds up and can cause the electronics or drive mechanism to get too hot. The same thing can happen in a group of adapter cards you plug into the motherboard. Each one generates heat, and the tight spaces between cards can impede good airflow.

Figures 6-6 and 6-7 show the normal airflow patterns in desktop and tower cases, respectively. The airflow pattern in a desktop case (Figure 6-6) runs from inlets on the front across the motherboard and cards and out through the power supply. A smaller amount of air comes in from openings at the front of the drive bays and is drawn back to the power supply. The adapter cards benefit from being vertical, because heat rises by convection from between the cards into the air stream.

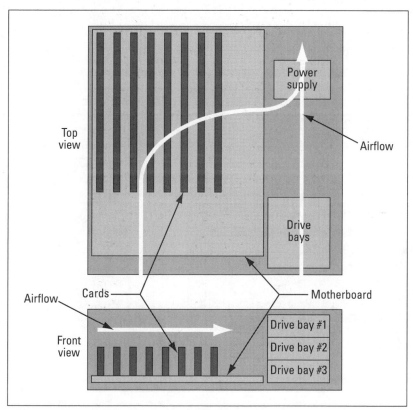

**Figure 6-6:** Desktop cases trap less heat between cards by positioning them vertically, but heat may accumulate around the drive bays unless the metal drive brackets function as heat sinks.

Tower cases (Figure 6-7) are essentially desktop cases turned on end. The airflow pattern in a tower case is therefore similar to a desktop case, running from inlets on the front past the motherboard and cards and out through the power supply. A little air comes in from openings at the front of the drive bays and is drawn back to the power supply, but because the drives are near the top, the heat tends to collect up there rather than being blown out the back. The horizontal positioning of the adapter cards can trap heat too, so the relative position of cards is worth some thought — you should leave gaps between cards to keep hot cards away from each other if possible, and order cards to prevent having two hot cards in adjacent slots.

Open space in any case — and particularly in a tower — helps avoid blocked airflow. Bigger fans or more fans move more air through the case, lowering the internal case temperature, which helps to overcome blockages and heat pockets.

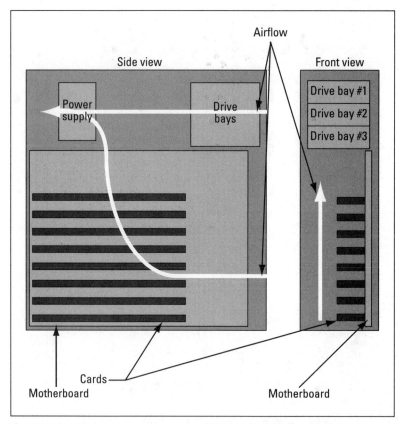

**Figure 6-7:** Tower cases are prone to heat pockets if they are too cramped, so good ventilation is important.

# The ATX form factor

The IBM PC/AT established a motherboard form factor that survived for over a decade. As component technology and systems designs evolved, though, problems with that design became more onerous. Four of the more significant problems are

✦ *Processor positioning.* The processor on an AT motherboard typically sits under the space reserved for some of the adapter cards. The cooling fans for processors now intrude into the space for the cards, preventing full-length cards from being used in those slots. The Pentium II processor cartridge is far bigger than even a Pentium with cooling fan, making the problem even worse.

✦ *Lack of 3.3 V power.* The chips used when the AT motherboard was designed all used 5 V power. The finer geometry now inside chips uses voltages of 3.3 V and below (they can't withstand the higher voltages without conversion), but AT power supplies don't typically provide the lower voltage.

✦ *High-voltage switching within the computer case.* The PC/AT was a desktop unit that positioned the power switch on the side of the case at the back. That's inconvenient for tower cases, leading designers to move the high-voltage power switch to the front of the case. The presence of high voltage within the case can be a service hazard.

✦ *I/O port cabling requirements.* The PC/AT had no I/O ports built onto the motherboard. As the functions built onto motherboards expanded to include serial, parallel, sound, mouse, and Universal Serial Bus (USB) ports, cables had to be built to route the signals from the motherboard to the back of the case. The labor involved led building and installing those cables to become a noticeable fraction of system cost.

These problems in the AT motherboard form factor led to the definition of a new form factor, ATX. The new form factor is incompatible with the older AT layout — you can't use an AT motherboard in an ATX case, nor an ATX motherboard in an AT case, but both types use the same adapter cards. Figure 6-8 shows a rear view of a PC Power & Cooling ATX case. The most striking visual difference between the ATX case and an older AT case is the input/output (I/O) template in the middle-left part of the back panel. The cutouts in the template match connectors rigidly attached to the motherboard, eliminating the rat's nest of ribbon cables AT cases require to hook I/O ports on the motherboard to connectors on the back panel.

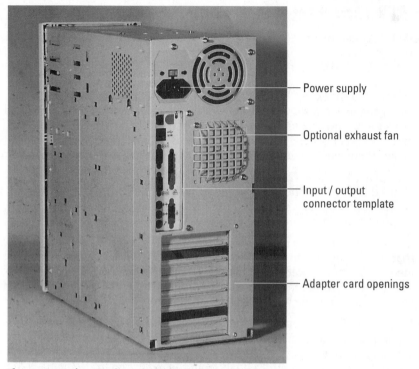

Power supply

Optional exhaust fan

Input / output
connector template

Adapter card openings

**Figure 6-8:** The ATX form factor simplifies internal
cabling and improves component layout.

Here's how the ATX form factor solves the AT motherboard problems:

✦ *Better processor positioning.* The processor in an ATX case is behind the I/O
panel, out of line from the adapter cards. That repositioning allows ATX
motherboards to readily hold the tall Pentium II cartridges. The memory has
been relocated for the same reason.

✦ *3.3 V power.* The power connector on an ATX motherboard is a single
connector with more wires than the two connectors that were standard on
the AT design. The ATX connector includes a 3.3 V supply.

✦ *Elimination of high-voltage switching within the computer case.* The power
supply in an ATX system is more like an instant-on television than older
computer designs. The power connector to an ATX motherboard also includes
a low-voltage signal that gets routed to a power on/off button on the front of
the case. That signal tells the power supply to turn the main supply lines on
or off. As long as power is connected, though, the motherboard receives a
limited 5 V supply to keep standby functions running. (Note: Although you

should also disconnect AT-type supplies too, the standby power makes it even more important to disconnect an ATX supply from wall power whenever you're working inside the case.)

✦ *Built-in I/O port cabling.* The I/O port connectors are built onto the ATX motherboard, terminating in a panel at the back. There's a standard layout for the panel, ensuring cutouts in the case will be in the right places.

The standard ATX I/O template uses a small round (mini-DIN) connector for both the keyboard and mouse instead of the full-size DIN and serial port (respectively) you may be used to. Adapters are available for connectors to older equipment, but some motherboards refuse to accept the older serial mice versus ones designed to the PS/2 specification.

## Proprietary designs

Despite all the competition in the PC industry, proprietary designs remain a favorite tactic of companies hoping to lock you in for expensive upgrades once you've bought their product. For example, the IBM PS/2 MCA bus may or may not have been intended as a proprietary lock-in, but it had that effect. For a long time, you could get MCA cards only from IBM. Disk and tape drives to fit the chassis had to come from IBM for a long time as well.

Lots of other companies do this, too. We had an old computer that required a proprietary card from the manufacturer to expand past 8MB of memory, because the motherboard used a proprietary 32-bit memory bus. There's a long list of these sins; a who's who of the PC industry is full of the guilty. You can rely on paying more if you get caught by one of these, and on being at the mercy of the manufacturer when they decide to stop supporting that model. You may not find out about proprietary models until it's too late, unless you ask about compliance with industry-standard form factors, interfaces, and software standards before you buy. Be sure to ask not only about memory and disk, but also about the motherboard itself (for example, we've seen an AT&T computer that had a proprietary motherboard form factor not available anywhere).

You've been warned.

## Cases and case fans

If you buy a complete computer from a manufacturer, your choices in cases are likely to be whether you want a tower, minitower, or desktop. You might have an option for auxiliary fans available.

If you integrate your own machine, you're in the market for a case and have a wide range of options. A case we've liked for some time now is one from California PC

Products shown in Figures 6-9 and 6-10. The things that make this case a winner are these:

✦ *Gobs of room inside.* We're far more interested in a machine that's easy to work on, reliable, and upgradable than in its being tiny. Your needs may well favor small size, but you'll pay the price in compromises. Having ten external drive bays fits our definition of upgradability, for example, but having one to three does not.

✦ *Airflow to keep the electronics very cool.* We put in two of the three optional fans, so including the fan in the power supply, there are two inlet and two exhaust fans. The combination moves so much air that heat never builds up, and even if one fan fails, there's still enough airflow that the machine will remain cool. Those fans are why the heat comparison in Table 6-1 is so one-sided. There's a filter over the two inlet fans, so dust inside the box is reduced, too.

**Figure 6-9:** This case from California PC Products has room for expansion and great cooling.

✦ *Attention to detail.* For example:

- The construction is heavy sheet metal that provides good support.

- There are four extra card slot brackets at the back to hold those back-of-the-computer connectors that connect to adapter cards with cables and otherwise chew up a real slot.

- You can get a set of casters to make the system easier to move around for maintenance.

- Opening the case requires removing three screws and pulling off one side, leaving everything in the case readily accessible.

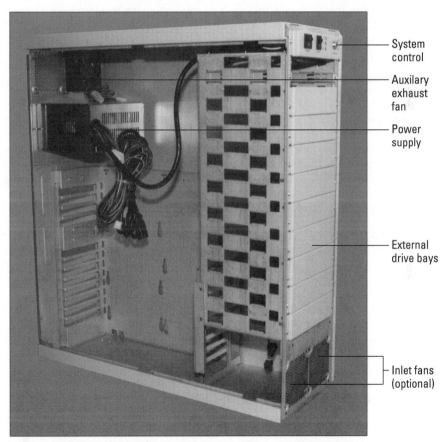

System control

Auxilary exhaust fan

Power supply

External drive bays

Inlet fans (optional)

**Figure 6-10:** The California PC Products case has ten external drive bays, a healthy power supply, and mountings for four auxiliary fans.

Here's what's inside the case:

✦ *Auxiliary exhaust fan.* This fan is standard in the case. It provides additional airflow and ensures that some airflow remains even if the power supply fan fails. An optional fan can be installed next to it.

✦ *Power supply.* This is a compact unit, making access to the drive bays easier. Dual redundant supplies are available, too.

✦ *System control.* The system control panel has the basics — the power on/off switch, reset switch, keylock switch, and indicators for power on and drive activity.

✦ *External drive bays.* There are ten of these, each holding a 5.25-inch form factor drive. The system we built into the case has two floppies, a CD-ROM, a CD-R, a Zip drive, four hard disks, and a tape drive. It's easier to fill drive bays than it seems at first thought.

✦ *Inlet fans (optional).* There's room for two optional fans to push air into the case.

Because properly cooling your computer is so important, you should know about some products from PC Power & Cooling. PC Power & Cooling originally made its name in 1986 after people noticed that the early PC power supplies had fans that were very loud in an office. They developed and sold a line of quality supplies that were very quiet. They still offer a quiet line of power supplies (and redundant ones for critical machines) but have branched out with a number of innovative ideas:

✦ Figure 6-11 shows the K6 version of their CPU-Cool fan. You can get CPU fans everywhere. The advantages of the CPU-Cool fans are that they are thin, and because of ball bearing motors, the entire line is reliable. If your motherboard is arranged so that the CPU sits under where a card would need to be, reduced fan height could be the difference between using the card slot or not.

**Tip**

The CPU-Cool fans come with thermally conductive grease, which lets the fan pull heat out of the chip more effectively. If you use the grease (instead of thermal mounting tape, for instance), be sure to use an extremely thin layer. Too much grease is worse than none at all.

Figure 6-12 shows why you must use a CPU cooling fan. If you don't, it's just a matter of time before you cook the chip.

**Figure 6-11:** These CPU cooling fans are thinner than most, solving clearance problems in a case where the CPU is under one or more adapter cards. (Courtesy of PC Power & Cooling, Inc.)

Figure 6-13 shows the California PC Products Bay Cooler, a frame you can use to mount a 3.5-inch disk drive in a 5.25-inch bay. The Bay Cooler incorporates a pair of small fans, one either side of the drive, to pull in outside air and move it past the drive. If you're using a high-performance drive that generates too much heat for a case with poor airflow, the Bay Cooler could be the difference between a reliable system and the need for a new case.

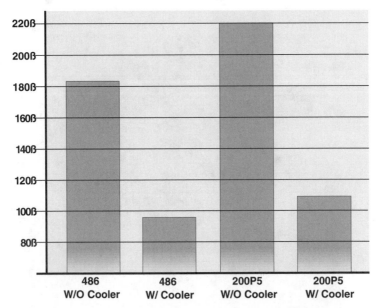

**Figure 6-12:** These measurements by PC Power & Cooling show why you have to use a cooling fan. Intel's maximum temperature specification is 185° F (85°C).

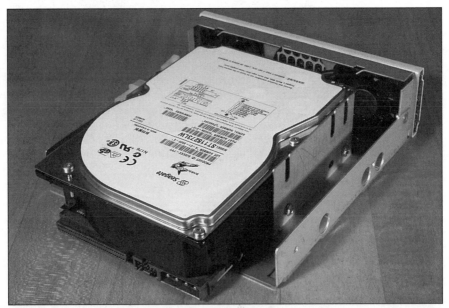

**Figure 6-13:** This fan-cooled disk drive mounting frame moves air over disk drives, eliminating hot spots and keeping the drive cool.

✦ Finally, Figure 6-14 shows a PC Power & Cooling temperature alarm called 110 Alert. Putting one of these devices inside the computer can provide you a warning that the internal temperature is at 110°F and is nearing the danger point. Machines that are on all the time build up dust in the power supply fan and create additional wear on the fan bearings, which can lead to fan failures and overheating. The surrounding temperature can get much higher if the PC is in an office where the building air conditioning shuts down on weekends, which also reduces thermal margins. One of these alarms can warn you of heat problems before your system crashes.

**Figure 6-14:** You can install these over-temperature alarms inside your computer. They all sound an alarm at 110°F. (Courtesy of PC Power & Cooling, Inc.)

# Power Supplies

The power supply converts power coming into your computer from the wall outlet to the forms usable by the electronics in the system. It changes incoming alternating current (AC) at 120 or 240 volts to direct current (DC) at 5 and +/–12 V (the shapes and relative voltage levels are shown in Figure 6-15). A good power supply does more than power conversion—it cleans up the spikes, surges, and sags in the utility power. Motors, copiers, appliances, and other electrical devices create noise in the power at your wall outlet, as do lightning strikes and other effects farther away. If that noise gets through the power supply into the electronics in the computer, it causes trouble ranging from erratic operation to complete shutdown. A high-quality power supply will be more resistant to these problems, giving you more reliable operation from your computer.

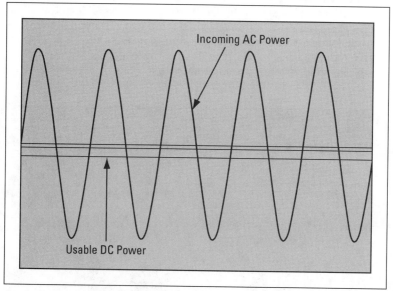

**Figure 6-15:** The power supply converts the alternating current (AC) that your computer receives from the wall outlet to steady direct current (DC) power usable by the electronics.

There are four electrical terms you need to know to understand and compare power supplies—voltage, current, power, and frequency.

✦ *Voltage* is the force pushing electricity through the wire. It's like the water pressure in your garden hose: More voltage is like more water pressure. Voltage is measured in volts (abbreviated V). In North America, common wall-outlet power is at 120 V. European power is commonly 240 V. The vertical axis in Figure 6-15 is voltage, so you can see that the incoming voltage varies over time (the horizontal axis), while what your computer needs is a lower, constant voltage.

✦ *Current* is the amount of electricity flowing through the wire and is like the flow of water through a hose. Current is measured in amperes (or amps, abbreviated A). Common North American utility circuits supply 15 to 20 A.

✦ *Power* is the product of voltage and current (voltage times current), and is measured in watts (abbreviated W). If your computer draws 1 amp at 120 V, it uses 120 W—about the same as a bright indoor light bulb.

✦ *Frequency* is the rate at which the power alternates between positive and negative voltages. Frequency is measured in Hertz (abbreviated Hz); a Hertz is one cycle per second. North American power arrives at 60 Hz; European power is mostly 50 Hz.

A good power supply is easy to describe but very hard to design, because it should meet all of these criteria at the same time:

✦ *Deliver clean, stable power.* The circuits in your computer are terribly sensitive to variations in supply voltage. The power supply has to keep the voltage stable, filtering out the ripples in the incoming AC power and compensating for load variations from the computer circuits. Good power supplies have a wide tolerance for both fast input power variations and for variations that continue over several seconds.

✦ *Convert high-voltage AC to low-voltage DC efficiently.* The voltage your computer needs is at least ten times lower than the power coming into the supply, and it is direct rather than alternating current. Inefficient conversion from utility power to what your computer needs consumes extra power and generates useless heat. Good power supplies are efficient, generating little heat.

✦ *Suppress noise, spikes, and dropouts.* Although your utility power may be dependable and is inevitably controlled well enough to run clocks accurately, it's noisy and full of electrical garbage. Utility power is subject to spikes and dropouts, both short and long as well as big and small. If any of that noise makes it past the power supply into the computer, you're in trouble. Good power supplies filter out the garbage and can ride through complete input power dropouts of at least ten milliseconds (a 20ms hold-up time is reasonable). The hold-up time is important, because an uninterruptible power supply (described later in this chapter) takes a few milliseconds to switch from incoming utility power to battery operation. If the computer power supply can't survive the switch, your computer crashes before the uninterruptible power supply can get going.

✦ *Be small, light, reliable, and free.* As long as we're asking . . . .

You don't have much choice on the input voltage the power supply needs to accept, nor the frequency, nor the output voltages. These are fixed by where you run the computer and what's inside it (although you can convert 120 V to 240 V and vice versa). You do have a choice to specify how much power the supply can give the computer. Revisiting Table 6-1, systems A, B, and C drew from under 50 W to nearly 100 W, with all these numbers going up when the computer is actually doing something. The numbers go up during operation, for example, when the sound card output amplifier draws power to drive the speaker, or when the disk drive head positioner draws power to move the heads. Computers using more memory and larger drives will pull even more power than those three.

Tip You want to leave margin for adding new hardware in the future, and you want to run the power supply at about 50 percent load. In addition to extending power supply life (by letting it run cooler), running below maximum capacity helps extend the power supply's hold-up time during short AC power dropouts. We commonly use power supplies of 300 W capacity for desktop computers. You'll want even more in a server with a lot of memory and disks.

## Redundant power supplies

If the power supply fails, your computer stops immediately. When the power supply fan fails (that's when, not if), the power supply and the rest of your computer gets hot, and the heat may destroy components before the supply itself fails. Either way, you're going to lose time, data, or both. Mission-critical systems — the ones you can't afford to have fail — have to stay running when a power supply fails.

The solution to surviving a power supply failure in a critical computer is to install redundant power supplies. Figure 6-16 shows how redundant power supplies work. You typically buy multiple power supplies plus a power combiner; sometimes you get the whole assembly as an integrated unit, with the complexity in Figure 6-16 hidden by the supply manufacturer. If one of the independent supplies fails, the remaining ones carry the computer load. This automatic compensation gives you time to get a warning from an alarm in the supply and make repairs.

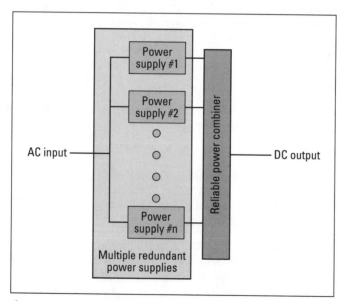

**Figure 6-16:** Redundant power supplies allow your computer to stay running without interruption when a power supply fails.

The key elements for a redundant power supply are these:

✦ *Multiple independent power supplies.* Each power supply converts incoming AC into DC the computer can use. In a scheme with two supplies, each has to be capable of driving the entire computer. If there are three or more, the survivors have to able to drive the computer after one fails.

✦ *Reliable power combiner.* The power combiner collects the outputs of the independent power supplies into a single output for the computer. It hides the effect of a single supply failing.

PC Power & Cooling offers redundant supplies, as well as ones you can repair without taking down the computer. You may be able to get similar units from your case manufacturer.

Data centers supporting mission-critical computers often do more than use uninterruptible power supplies (see the next section) to feed redundant supplies in the individual computers. Because each independent power supply has its own utility power feed, you can split the supplies to be fed by multiple power sources. That way, even if one source goes out, the computer stays running.

## Uninterruptible power supplies

The best power supply won't help much when the AC supply goes out. Admittedly, when you're sitting there in the dark, the work you were doing may not be your first concern, but it's likely to be something you worry about later. Nor is a widespread power failure the only threat. We've seen computers taken out by plugging a vacuum cleaner or coffee pot into the same circuit.

You don't have to put up with losing your work. Once found only in major computer installations or alongside mission-critical systems, an uninterruptible power supply (UPS) is now an inexpensive addition that can easily pay for itself by saving hours of work.

A UPS consists of a power supply, a battery, and a reverse power supply. Figure 6-17 shows how this works. The incoming power supply—similar to what's in your computer—creates the DC the battery needs whenever utility AC power is available. The outgoing power supply does the same thing in reverse: It converts battery DC to AC your computer's power supply can use. In older UPS systems, the power going to your computer's supply always came from the UPS—the source of the DC power the outgoing supply received was either the incoming AC supply (if it was operating) or the battery. Either way, the AC output was stable, with no interruption in output power as the input AC came and went.

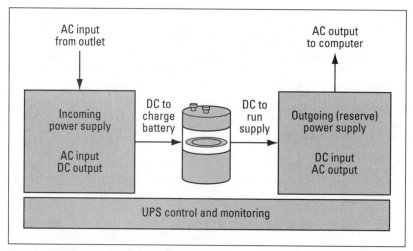

**Figure 6-17:** A UPS can save you hours of work. When you need it, it's too late to go get one.

The output power supply in this form of UPS is expensive because it runs all the time. The need to both charge the battery and run the output supply increases the load on the input supply, so it needs to be larger and more expensive. UPS systems using this "always on" design were expensive.

A newer, less expensive UPS technology introduces a switch inside the UPS to avoid many of these problems. The switch allows the power supplies to turn off until incoming power fails or the battery needs to be charged. This convenience comes at a price: a short gap in the output power that's easily handled if your computer power supply is rated at twice the actual load. Under normal conditions, the switch routes power from the AC input to the AC output. When input power fails, the UPS control starts the outgoing power supply and throws the switch to direct its power to your computer. The result is that the power supplies in the UPS are normally off, so that the UPS stays cooler, the total load on the incoming supply is reduced, and the UPS cost goes down dramatically.

The capacity of the power supplies inside the UPS determine how big a computer (and how many other devices) it can support. The size of the batteries in the UPS determine how long it can provide power during an outage. You can't exceed maximum ratings (so don't buy one that's too small), but the bigger battery in a larger UPS can hold up over extended outages.

We use UPSs from American Power Conversion (APC), including their Back-UPS Pro 650 and Smart-UPS 1400 models (Figure 6-18). Figure 6-19 shows the run times these products support versus system load in watts. The Smart-UPS 1400 is a large, full-featured unit capable of driving large servers (you can get even bigger units for clusters of servers). The Back-UPS 650 is smaller, with fewer features, but with a much lower price.

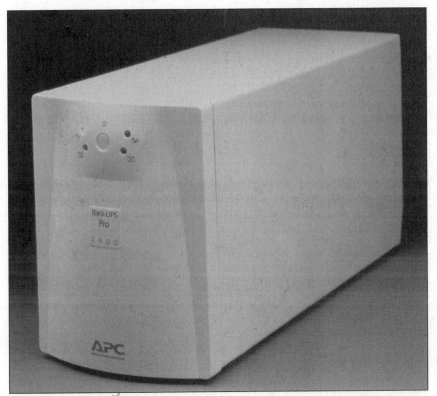

**Figure 6-18:** The APC Smart-UPS 1400 handles loads up to a kilowatt and keeps your server informed about its status.

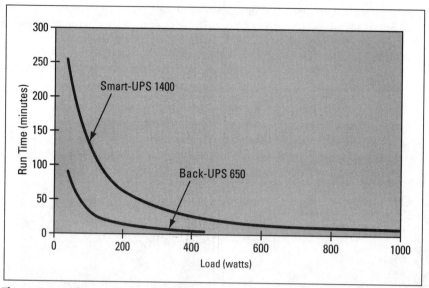

**Figure 6-19:** The run time a UPS gives you after a power failure depends on the size of the UPS battery and the load the computer puts on the UPS.

The run times we get on some of our systems after a power failure are shown in Table 6-2. The APC UPSs on these systems provide enough time to complete an extended operation on the Internet and then safely shut down the computer.

### Table 6-2
### Run Times for the Back-UPS 650 and Smart-UPS 1400 Units

| System | UPS Unit | Power (W) | Run Time (minutes) |
|--------|----------|-----------|--------------------|
| A + B | Smart-UPS 1400 | 143 | 90 |
| C | Back-UPS 650 | 68 | 52 |

The features in a UPS both protect your computers and simplify monitoring the state of the UPS:

✦ *Battery management.* The UPS monitors battery capacity and charge status. It provides alarms for low battery charge and tells you when the battery needs replacement. You can replace the battery while the system is in operation.

✦ *Computer interface and software.* A serial port connection from the UPS to your computer allows software to monitor the state of the UPS and control its operation. More capable software for Windows NT extends the monitoring you can do, providing visibility into the state of the battery charge and remaining run time.

✦ *Under- and over-voltage protection.* In addition to protecting your computer from loss of power, the UPS watches incoming AC power for under- and over-voltage conditions. When the incoming power goes outside specifications, the UPS corrects it to ensure the correct power is provided to the computer.

A UPS can be very inexpensive protection. Units that will keep a small computer running for 15 minutes retail for less than $100.

# Top Support Questions

Every part of your computer has its own frequently asked questions. Here are some of the most common for cases, fans, cooling, power supplies, and uninterruptible power supplies.

## Cases, fans, and cooling

Q: How big a case do I need?

A: Look at the motherboard size — whether it's a baby AT, full-size AT, or ATX. Nearly all motherboards today are ATX. A baby AT or an ATX fits in a minitower, but a full size AT does not. Then look at your drive count, making sure the case has enough bays for all those drives (plus expansion). Finally, look at your office space and at how accessible the case is to work on. If you can, avoid cases that require the motherboard to be behind a drive bay, or that have drive bays that require disassembling half the system to remove the screws on the back side of the drive. If you're building a system with a new motherboard as well as a new case, you'll want to use the ATX form factor.

Q: Can I fit an ATX board in an AT case?

A: No. Essentially all systems being built are now ATX. ATX does have some drawbacks, including the fact that the processor is near the power supply, with hot air blown over the processor. (This was done to create the option of eliminating the processor cooling fan. Don't do that — always use a processor fan.)

Q: Should I have a filtered air inlet?

A: An air filter will help keep dust out. Dust acts as a blanket in your computer to hold in heat. In the worst case, dust can be conductive (condensation from salt air, for instance) and cause electrical problems. An air filter reduces air flow somewhat, so your best option is to use a filter with a small inlet fan. Keep the filter clean, because if it plugs, the system will starve for air and overheat.

Q: When should I use auxiliary cooling fans?

A: Used in isolation, the power supply fan is the key to cooling the entire system. Other fans either are helpers, moving air around inside, or are augmenting the primary power supply flow to move air into or out of the case. Use spot cooling fans for localized heat sources, such as the processor, hot-running cards, or disks. Inlet or outlet fans are worthwhile in very large systems, or in situations where the computer must withstand a high ambient temperature.

Q: Does drive placement affect cooling?

A: Yes. A large stack of drives can create a lot of heat, and they can create heat pockets. You can cool drives using processor cooling fans attached with thermal tape, or you can place fans elsewhere to blow on them. If you have a lot of drives, consider adding exhaust fans. Drive placement counts, too — alternating drives of different physical sizes can help eliminate heat pockets, while putting hot drives on the bottom keeps them away from the reduced circulation at the top of the case.

Q: Do the bearings in fans matter?

A: Yes. Avoid sleeve bearings. They're a few dollars cheaper, but their rated life is only about 5,000 hours versus 50,000 to 100,000 hours for ball bearings. Fans with built-in tachometers (to sense the slowed rotation that happens before the fan fails) are becoming more common for critical applications. There are multiple standards for reading the tachometer, so you'll have to work that issue carefully.

## Power supplies

Q: How do I detect a power supply failure?

A: If the power supply is dead, nothing happens when you turn the computer on. Power supplies have overload protection, though, so a fault elsewhere in the system can look like power supply failure. You can check to see if the power supply is dead by running with nothing but a known-good disk (or known-good motherboard, processor, and speaker, but nothing else) connected. If the disk spins up, or if the motherboard beeps, the power supply is probably working. One common way to shut down a power supply is to insert the small power connector on a 3.5-inch floppy disk drive upside down. It's not too hard to force in, so make sure the little ears on the connector match the body of the connector on the drive.

Q: Can a power supply cause problems without failing?

A: Yes. The power supply has to provide clean, regulated DC output with low noise and ripple. If the filters on the output weaken or fail, the system may operate erratically (or not at all).

Q: Can too much memory or too many drives cause problems?

A: Yes. If the power supply is undersized, excessive variation in one of the outputs — outside the five percent nominal specification limits — can occur in a system with an unusual number of drives (disk, CD-ROM, or tape) or a lot of memory. Too many drives pull excessive +12 volt power; too much memory can pull too much +5 volt power. In economy supplies where one regulator controls both voltages, the opposite voltage can rise to excessive levels (for instance, drawing too much +12 volt power with a lot of drives can cause the +5 volt supply to rise above the +5.25 volt specification limit). You may be able to diagnose this problem by putting a voltmeter on an unused drive connector. You fix it by using a larger-capacity power supply (try to keep actual draw under 30 to 40 percent of rated capacity in extreme systems such as in this example), or by using a higher-quality supply built with independent regulators.

Q: What problems can develop from voltage sags or dropouts?

A: The typical inexpensive power supply saves parts cost by using too little front-end capacitance, or a poorly designed transformer. These shortcuts allow voltage sags as low as 90 to 100 volts to reboot or lock up the computer. A quality supply can hold its outputs steady through a sag down to 85 volts. Power supplies that are working in urban areas with decent quality power may fail on the farm or in a factory where power is more subject to sags. You can test power supply hold-up capability with a variable-output transformer (called a Variac). Slowly reduce the input voltage, noting the point at which the computer fails (back up your data first, just in case). Under the same load, the greater capacity of a higher-wattage supply will extend the hold-up time over complete power dropouts.

Q: Will a higher-wattage power supply damage a system?

A: No, in fact it may solve problems in marginal situations. Nor will the higher-capacity supply pull more power from the wall — it takes just what the computer needs. The higher capacity rating simply means that the supply is capable of more than a lesser unit.

# Uninterruptible power supplies

Q: What equipment should I power from a UPS?

A: Think about what you're willing to lose if the power goes down. Putting your own computer on a UPS protects your local data. Putting your file server on a UPS protects your organization's data. Putting the LAN equipment (hubs and switches, for example) on a UPS protects your ability to connect from one computer to another. Putting your communications gear (for example, routers and modems) on a UPS protects your ability to interact with branch offices and the Internet. Think about asking your Internet service provider if all their equipment — servers, modems, routers, everything — is on a UPS. If it's not and you must have reliable access to the Net, get another provider.

Q: Should I put my laser printer on a UPS?

A: Probably not. Laser printers pull a lot of power to run the heaters that fuse toner to the paper, which means that you'll need a hefty UPS. Those are expensive, while reprinting a lost print job is probably simple and cheap. Unless something about your operation makes a lost print job expensive, it's not worth protecting the laser printer. (You probably should have a good surge protector on it, though.)

Q: Do I care about grounding? Do I have to use grounded outlets and cords?

A: Yes. In addition to the safety a good ground provides in case of a short in the high-voltage parts of power supplies, good grounding is essential for surge and lightning protection and helps eliminate voltage differences among your equipment. If they're large enough, voltage differences can cause erratic operation or even hardware failure, particularly across networks connected with copper wires rather than fiber optics. If you're unsure of the quality of the grounding in your building, you might want to have a professional electrician check it out. If you do that, try to find one trained in the power and ground issues surrounding computers and data communications equipment.

Q: Are the UPSs that are always online better than the ones that switch online when power fails?

A: The reverse is true. Computer power supplies are built to ignore the short power dropout that happens when the UPS takes over the load, and the improvement in UPS reliability you get by leaving the power conversion electronics turned off most of the time is enormous.

Q: Do the lights have to go out before a UPS does any good?

A: No. A power flicker of a few tenths of a second — too short to notice — can reset or lock up a computer. So can a power surge or brownout. Your only indication there was a problem might be hearing the circuits and alarm in the UPS start up.

# Hands-On Upgrades

We've included these "Hands-On Upgrades" sections to fill in the practical details of the most common work you'll do on a computer. Knowing how to work on a computer is different from knowing what's in the computer; that additional knowledge is what you need to work confidently and effectively.

## Disassembling your computer

Once you know what you want to do, the first step in upgrading or repairing the hardware inside your computer is taking the case apart. Even though experience makes disassembly automatic, let's go through it step by step. We used a minitower system in the photographs because its minitower case is hard to work on — if you understand how to work on a case like that, most any other case (including the newer ATX cases) should be familiar territory.

The first thing you do is shut down the computer and disconnect everything from the back. You rarely want to cheat and leave things hooked up, because your chances of breaking something (including you) go up, and because you have to work on the computer in place, not at a good antistatic workstation. Even though the cables that hook up to the back of the computer are generally keyed so they only go into the right kind of connector, you should either label the back of the case and the cables to show what connects to where, or make a good drawing. If you don't, you might get confused when it's time to reassemble.

 If you've never opened a computer before, or if you're not familiar with what you need to do to protect your computer from static electricity while you work on it, read the section "Static electricity" in Chapter 1. Static electricity can do serious damage to your computer without your ever knowing it's a problem.

### Opening the case

Figure 6-20 shows the starting point for disassembly once you've removed all the cables. Once you remove the six screws on the back in the outer cover (see the callout in the photograph), the cover lifts up at the back and slides backward. Be very careful when removing the cover that you don't hook a wire and pull it loose.

After you get the cover off, what you see will look like what's in Figure 6-21 and Figure 6-22. The layout in Figure 6-21 is common to most minitower and tower cases — the motherboard is vertical, mounted to one side, the power supply is at the top in the back, and the external drive bays are at the top in the front. Internal drive bays (if you have any) typically sit under the external bays.

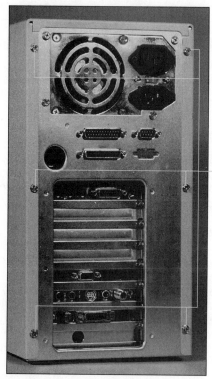

Take out these
six screws to
remove the cover

**Figure 6-20:** The back of System B is typical of
minitowers. Disassembly starts with the six screws
in back (after you disconnect everything).

Figure 6-3 earlier in this chapter shows the interior view from the component side
of the motherboard. That's where you'll do most of the work. The first thing you'll
want to do is to understand what each one of the components you see is. Figure
6-3 shows what you can expect to find; the power supply is the box in the
upper-left corner.

The cabling you see inside the computer tells you a lot. For instance, a flat wide
cable from a disk drive or CD-ROM goes to the IDE or SCSI port, carrying data to
and from the drive, and a small round cable from the CD-ROM is the audio cable to
the sound card.

Beyond what you learn from the cabling inside the case, you can identify what each
adapter card does by looking at its external connectors. Figure 6-22 shows the
detail of the back of the case, marked to show which adapter card does what. We've
also labeled the figure to show the serial, parallel, and keyboard port connectors at
the top right under the power supply — these go directly to the motherboard.

Display    External
Panel    Drive Bays    Motherboard    Power Supply

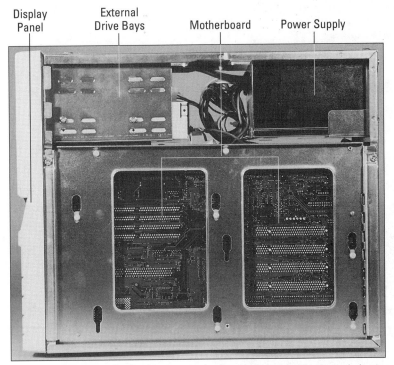

**Figure 6-21:** This interior view from the back of the motherboard shows the major chassis components.

Typical PC connectors have three important properties — type, gender, and number of pins — that let you distinguish one from another.

✦ *Type* is the kind of connector. The ones used for serial, parallel, and video monitor ports are called D subminiature connectors. The one for the keyboard is called a DIN connector and comes in two sizes (regular and mini-DIN).

✦ *Gender* specifies whether the connector has sockets or pins. Serial ports are male subminiature D connectors; parallel ports are female.

✦ *Number of pins* is simply how many connections there are in the connector. Serial ports have 9 or 25 pins. Parallel ports have 25.

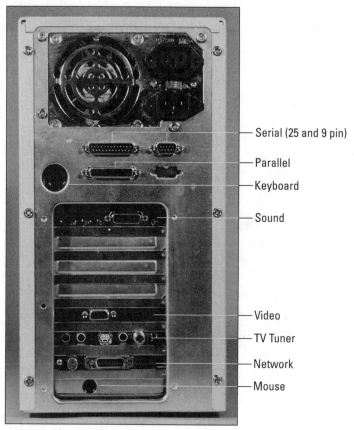

— Serial (25 and 9 pin)
— Parallel
— Keyboard
— Sound
— Video
— TV Tuner
— Network
— Mouse

**Figure 6-22:** This close-up rear view shows what connectors identify some common adapter card types.

Table 6-3 shows the characteristics of some of the more common connectors you'll encounter.

| Table 6-3 Common External PC Connectors | | | |
|---|---|---|---|
| **Connector Purpose** | **Type** | **Gender** | **Number of Pins** |
| 10Base-2 Ethernet | BNC | Female | 1 |
| 10Base-T Ethernet | RJ-45 | Female | 8 |
| AUI Ethernet | D subminiature | Female | 15 (with retainer) |

| Connector Purpose | Type | Gender | Number of Pins |
|---|---|---|---|
| Baseband or composite video | RCA | Female | 1 |
| Game | D subminiature | Female | 15 (2 rows) |
| Keyboard | DIN | Female | 5 |
| Mouse | Mini-DIN | Female | 9 |
| Parallel communications (LPT1:) | D subminiature | Female | 25 |
| Phone (modem) | RJ-11 | Female | 4 |
| Radio frequency (RF) video | F | Female | 1 |
| SCSI | Centronics or SCSI-2 microminiature | Female | 50 or 68 |
| Serial communications (COM1: or mouse) | D subminiature | Male | 9 or 25 |
| Sound | Mini headphone or RCA | Female | 1 |
| SuperVGA monitor | D subminiature | Female | 15 (3 rows) |
| S-Video | Mini-DIN | Female | 7 |
| USB | USB (flat rectangular) | Female | 3 (not readily visible) |

It's easiest to apply Table 6-3 as you disconnect wires, but if you have an unknown connector, the table is a starting point. The connectors in the table are the ones at the computer — the ones at the other end of the cable may be very different. For example, the connector at the printer end of a parallel printer cable looks more like an old-style SCSI connector (they're both Centronics-type connectors; the printer connector has fewer pins). Here's a little more information if some of those connectors seem unfamiliar:

✦ *D subminiature* connectors are most common for cables to external modems, but you'll see them for printer ports, game controller ports, monitor video ports, and Ethernet ports, too. They typically have two or three rows of pins. There's always an odd number of pins so that the connector outline is a trapezoid and only fits one way.

✦ *DIN* connectors are the round ones you typically find on keyboards and some mice. DIN stands for Deutsches Institut für Normung, which in English is the German Institute for Standardization. DIN connectors come in two basic sizes, the normal size you find on older AT keyboards, and the small (mini-DIN) size you find on the PS/2 keyboards and mice now universal on ATX-style motherboards. Little plugs in the connector and the pin layout limit the connector orientation to the correct position. Don't force it.

✦ *RCA* connectors are the unthreaded kind you typically find on the back of your stereo, television, and VCR. Female RCA connectors are about 1/4 inch in diameter, with a relatively large hole in the middle.

✦ *Mini headphone* connectors are the small round connectors found on headphones and on boom boxes and other audio equipment (for connecting the headphones). Typical mini headphone connectors have two or three wires connected through the one pin — if you look closely, you'll see rings of metal on the pin separated by thin rings of insulation.

✦ *RJ-11* and *RJ-45* connectors are the small modular telephone jacks found all over North America since the old boxy four-pin connectors went away.

✦ *F* connectors are the threaded connectors used with coaxial cable for televisions.

✦ *Centronics* connectors are the ones found on printer parallel port connections.

✦ *SCSI-2* connectors are loosely similar to D subminiature connectors, but the pins are much closer together (and look different), the connectors are much smaller, and there are retaining clips at either end of the connector.

✦ *USB* connectors are on essentially all ATX motherboards, and shipped with many AT motherboards in the past few years. The connector is a flat rectangular shape, with the pins not readily visible.

### Taking out adapter cards

Don't remove adapter cards blindly. Any handling you do of electronic components offers the opportunity to break them, so try to determine that you really need to remove the card first.

You'll see in Chapter 7 that there are many kinds of PC buses, each with different kinds of adapter cards. Despite that, removing cards from any PC bus is essentially the same. You remove any attached cables, remove the retaining screw, and pull out the card. Let's look at the process step by step.

1. *Remove cables.* You already disconnected the external cables, but there are ones inside, too. The cables connected to adapter cards inside the computer are usually ribbon cables, which are flat bundles of wires with two or more connectors. Some ribbon cables have handles on the connectors to use in pulling the cable off the card, but most don't. You have to be very careful pulling off ribbon cables, because if you use too much force, the wires at the edge can break inside the cable. You might not be able to see the damage, but the cable won't work right after that. You have to gently wiggle the connector straight off the card. Don't just rotate it off, because you're likely to bend pins on the card and cause problems.

   Be sure to mark the cable in a way that will make sense to you when you go to hook it back up again. Many internal cables have identical connectors but very different functions, and you can damage things by connecting a cable to the wrong place. Be sure to keep track of where pin one (the uniquely marked wire on one edge) is on the cable, and on the adapter board too.

2. *Remove the retaining screw.* The adapter card will have a screw at the top of the bracket that faces the outside of the computer. Figure 6-23 shows the positioning for an ISA card—the bracket extends up from the card, distancing the screw about half an inch from the card itself. If you look at the card immediately above the marked one, you'll see the positioning for a PCI card—the bracket extends down from the card, and the screw is in line with the card. You have to remove the screw before you remove the card. If you pull hard on the card (a bad idea anyhow) before you remove the screw, you can break the card, the motherboard, or both. It's easy to drop the screw inside the computer after you back it all the way out (using hex-head screws and tools helps). If you do, get it back immediately. Forgetting and leaving the screw inside the computer can short wires together when you later turn the power on, damaging the computer. Not all screws inside the computer are the same, so you might want to keep them sorted by purpose in an egg carton.

Retaining Screw                    Adapter Card

**Figure 6-23:** The retaining screw holds the card securely to the case.

3. *Pull out the card.* The final step is to remove the card itself. Be sure you know which slot the card was in so that you can put it back when it's reassembly time. Most cards can go in any slot of the right type, but in some cases the

ordering of cards in slots matters. Ordering requirements can result from a need to cable the card to another card or elsewhere in the computer, or from conflicts with other boards that get solved by one of the conflicting boards being lower on the bus than another.

Hold the card at the top at both ends (see the example in Figure 6-24), and rock it gently along its length until the connector in the motherboard loosens. Be very careful where you grab the card. It's usually safe to put your fingers on empty board space, and on top of chips. Avoid pushing on parts on the board with bendable wires, or on parts that will move out of position, because you probably can't move them back to precisely where they belong, and flexing the wires could break them.

Hold securely onto the circuit board

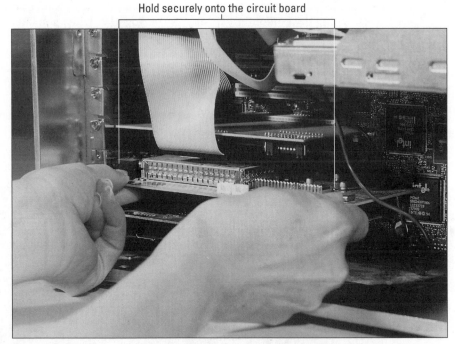

**Figure 6-24:** Be careful where you hold the circuit board and how you ease it out.

Brackets are not all the same on the end of cards — some of them have offsets at the top of the vertical part that cause adjacent brackets to interfere with each other when you remove a card. If yours are like that, you can simply loosen the screws on the adjacent cards. That should create enough play that the card you're working with will come out.

Another thing to be careful about is avoiding pushing or pulling on connectors and other things sticking out through the bracket. Those connectors are usually screwed down to the circuit card, but pressure on them can crack the card or connector.

After you remove the card, put it in an antistatic bag that completely covers the card. If you kept the bags from cards you bought, you'll have some; otherwise, you may need to find a supplier in your area. Antistatic bags are made by 3M and other companies.

## Taking out disks

Disk drives are subject to the same caution as cards — don't take them out unless you have to. The loss from a broken disk drive can be worse than just the replacement cost, though, because you can lose the data it contains. Disk drives belong in antistatic bags after removal, just like any other electronics.

Internally mounted disk drives (floppy drives, hard disks, CD-ROMs, Zips, and the rest) are all essentially the same mechanically, differing only in details of size and connectors. Here's what you need to know:

✦ *Mounting holes.* Disk drives all have mounting holes on the side or bottom. Most have both, as Figure 6-25 shows. The drive mounts to the chassis with screws that go through the chassis bracket and into the drive. You'll want to be careful how much force you put on the mounting screws, because the frame of the disk is usually cast metal. Too much force and you can strip the threads.

Be careful to set aside the drive mounting screws separately (you might consider taping them to the drive frame). There's often a circuit card right behind or above the mounting hole, so if you use too long a screw, you can fracture or short out the card. Both are very hard on the drive.

✦ *Drive form factor.* Drives usually are either 5.25- or 3.5-inch form factor. That measurement is notional, though — a 5.25-inch drive is actually about 6 inches wide, and a 3.5-inch form factor drive is about 4 inches wide. It's common to mount 3.5-inch drives in 5.25-inch drive bays using adapter brackets. The brackets screw to the side of the drive, taking up the extra space. Another set of screws then attach the brackets to the chassis, completing the structure.

✦ *Power connector.* All 5.25-inch drives and some 3.5-inch drives use the same flat four-pin power connector. Some 3.5-inch floppy drives use a smaller connector. The same four power wires connect to the drive, but they're generally a smaller wire to correspond to the smaller connector.

The connector is keyed by bevels in two corners. If you manage to force the connector in reverse against the bevels, you'll misconnect the power lines and probably destroy the drive.

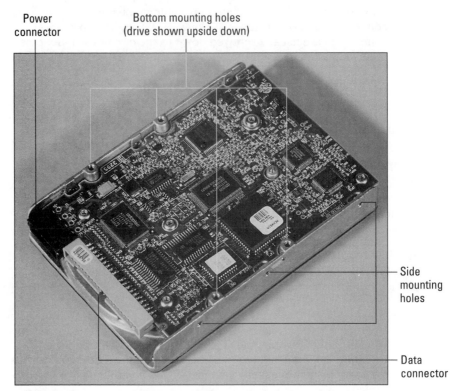

**Figure 6-25:** Horizontal drive mounting usually uses the side holes; vertical mounting uses the bottom holes.

Hold the power connector itself, not the wires, when you insert it or remove it to make sure you don't pull the wires loose. Try to exert force straight along the axis of the wires, not sideways or up and down. You'll probably have to wiggle the connector some to get it to move; try to do that as little as you can to minimize the force the connector exerts on the circuit board.

✦ *Data cable connector.* The same caution about removing flat ribbon cables from adapter cards applies to removing them from drives. Internal damage to cables is hard to see, and bent or broken connector pins are hard to repair.

## Replacing a power supply

Swapping out a failed power supply is one of the more common repairs you'll do on a computer. If you get one that is designed for your computer, so it's a direct replacement, and if you do the swap methodically, it's pretty straightforward. However, inside the power supply (and at the exposed high-voltage switch if you have an older, non-ATX computer) is the one place in your computer where there are dangerous voltages. There's nothing in a power supply that most people can repair. Don't go opening up the power supply or sticking things in it unless you're a trained electronics technician or engineer and you really know what you're doing.

Getting the right supply is both a mechanical and electrical issue. Mechanically, the questions are how big is the supply, and where is the power switch. PC Power & Cooling lists five physical sizes, one each for minitowers, full towers, small desktops, full-size desktops, and ATX cases. Table 6-4 shows the size and power-switch location for these five. If you match the sizes and switch location, chances are the supply will fit.

## Table 6-4
## Common PC Power Supply Dimensions (in inches)

| Application | Height | Width | Depth | Switch |
|---|---|---|---|---|
| Minitower | 3.4 | 5.9 | 5.5 | Remote |
| Full tower | 5.9 | 8.35 | 5.9 | Remote |
| Desktop (small) | 5.9 | 6.5 | 5.9 | Attached |
| Desktop (full) | 5.9 | 8.35 | 5.9 | Attached |
| ATX | 3.4 | 5.9 | 5.5 | Remote |

Electrically, the questions to ask are what the capacity of the supply is, whether the supply generates 3.3 volts for the newer processors, and whether or not the supply has the newer ATX interface. You won't want to put in a supply with a capacity rating (in watts) less than the one you take out. It's okay to put in a supply with a higher rating.

You can identify an ATX supply by the connector for the motherboard. Older supplies have two connectors, each with six attached wires organized into one row of pins. ATX supplies have a single motherboard power connector carrying 20 pins in two rows of ten. A few pre-ATX systems require a 3.3-volt feed from the power supply, which you can identify by the third bundle of wires connected from power supply to motherboard. Most non-ATX Pentium motherboards have on-board regulators that generate 3.3 volts from the 5-volt supply.

ATX power supplies introduce another innovation that should help prevent high-voltage accidents. Instead of having a power switch at the front of the case that switches incoming high-voltage power, the ATX supply receives only a signal through its motherboard connector indicating that the power supply should switch on. That's a low-voltage signal — all high voltage stays confined inside the ATX supply. This design makes it hard to start the power supply with no load connected, eliminating one of the ways to damage a supply.

Once you have the right replacement supply, gather it, the computer, and your tools at your antistatic workstation. Verify that the machine is disconnected from the wall, open the case, and plan out what you'll have to disassemble to remove the old supply. In the minitower system we're looking at in this example, we replaced the old supply with a PC Power & Cooling 300 Watt Slim Turbo Cool unit. We could have done the replacement and only have disassembled the front panel, but instead we removed the adapter cards and the motherboard so that the work would be easier to see in the photographs. Here's the step-by-step process:

1. *Disconnect cables.* Remove all the power connections from the power supply to the motherboard (see Figure 6-26), drives, fans, and anything else it's tied to. If you have a tower case, ignore the relatively fat (and probably black) cable going to the front panel until the next step. You don't really have to track which disk drive power cable went where, because all the drive connectors are the same. Make careful note of where the power cables connect to the motherboard, including which of the two goes where if you have an older AT-style system.

Pull the motherboard power connectors by the nylon body, rotating them away from the keyed connector on the motherboard when they're almost off

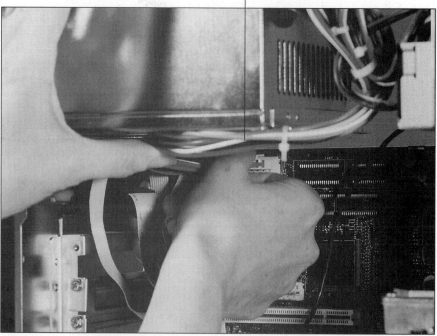

**Figure 6-26:** Hold power connectors by the nylon body, not the wires.

**2.** *Remove front panel and power switch (optional).* That larger cable going from the power supply to the front panel of tower cases is the high-voltage power feed to the on/off switch (see Figure 6-27). Your new power supply will probably have a new switch on the end of its cable to go in the place of the old one. If you have to remove the front panel to get access to all the screws involved, do that now. Watch out for the wires going from the chassis to the motherboard so that you don't pull them off or bend the pins. Unscrew the old switch (and the green ground wire) from the front panel and unthread the cable from within the case.

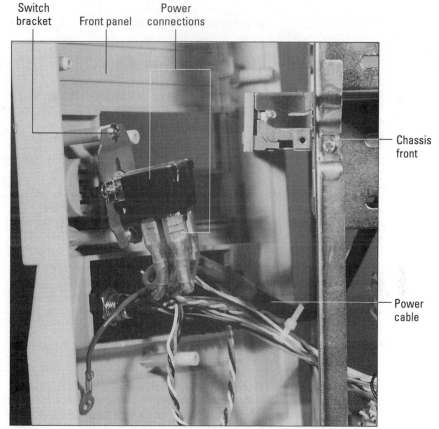

**Figure 6-27:** The power switch attaches to the front panel with a mounting bracket.

**3.** *Remove and set aside the old power supply.* Remove anything else from that case that blocks the exit path of the supply (for instance, disk drives in a desktop case might be in the way). Take out the screws holding the power supply to the chassis (Figure 6-28), lift the supply out, and set it aside. Watch for wires you might have missed disconnecting.

4. *Bolt in the new supply.* This (and the succeeding steps) are simply the reverse of the preceding three steps. Holding the supply in place until you get the first few screws in can be tricky in tower cases; some units have a bracket on the case that will hold one corner of the supply. If your case is like that, first put in the screw diagonally across the face of the supply (that is, top right if the bracket is on the bottom left). Put in all the screws before securely tightening any of them, and don't overtighten. If you can, use the screws that come with the new supply; otherwise, use the ones that were in the old supply. Avoid overly long screws that could contact live terminals inside the power supply and create a hazard.

Mounting screws    Chassis rear    Power supply

**Figure 6-28:** Only remove the power supply screws that go through the chassis. The others hold things together in the power supply itself.

5. *Install the on/off switch and cable, and reattach the front panel.* Typically you can route the new cable the same way as the old one. The switch should screw directly onto the supporting bracket. Be sure to attach the green ground wire securely back where the old one was, making sure that it has good contact with the metal frame of the chassis. As you reattach the front panel, try to keep the cable routed well out of the way of the case and of your hands as you work.

**6.** *Reinstall other components and connect cables.* The last step is to replace anything else you removed and reconnect the power cables. The connectors to the motherboard go in such that the black wires are in the middle, next to each other. Don't forget to reconnect non-obvious things like chip and chassis fans. Check for data cables that might have come loose.

Save only what's cheerfully known as the "smoke test," you're done. Double-check your work, get your hands out of the way, plug it in, and turn it on. If things don't work as you expect, recheck your connections.

## Changing the UPS battery

Like the battery in your car, the rechargeable battery in your UPS eventually wears out and has to be replaced. If you have a UPS that requires return to the factory for replacement, you'll just have to box and ship it. Better UPSs let you change the battery yourself; we'll show you how here with an APC Smart-UPS 1400 (Figure 6-29). There will be directions with your UPS, but except for the mechanical details of how to disassemble the UPS to get at the battery, it's all pretty much like changing the battery in your car.

*Except, of course, that the voltage in your car won't kill you.*

I meant for that to get your attention. You wouldn't stick your hand blindly into a wall socket, right? A UPS is not only the equivalent of a wall socket, it's one that may not be dead just because the UPS is unplugged (keeping the high-voltage power on when there's no wall power is its job!). You want to be very methodical and careful working on a UPS. You can change the battery in some UPSs, like the APC units, while the power is on. That's important if you need to keep a server online, but be sure to keep your hands away from the sockets. Take off all your rings, your wristwatch, and any other metal objects that might accidentally contact something, and don't disassemble more than you need to.

You should treat a UPS with respect, but you needn't be terrified of it. The batteries themselves are relatively low-voltage. Done properly, UPS battery replacement is perfectly safe. (To illustrate the point, APC has a sequence of photographs of a seven-year-old replacing the batteries in a unit supporting an online server. It took her an entire 3 minutes and 13 seconds.)

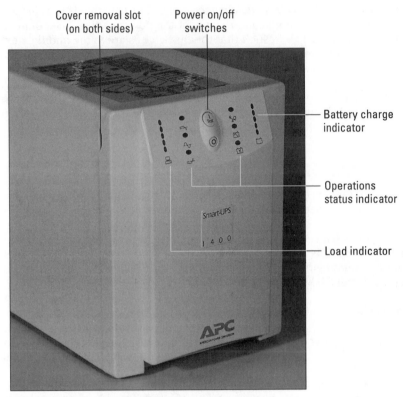

Cover removal slot
(on both sides)

Power on/off
switches

Battery charge
indicator

Operations
status indicator

Load indicator

Smart-UPS

1 4 0 0

APC
AMERICAN POWER CONVERSION

**Figure 6-29:** The Smart-UPS 1400 supports operations
and battery replacement from the front of the unit.

Here are the steps:

1. Get rid of anything metallic on your hands, wrists, and arms, or anything that
   could dangle into the UPS. I'm repeating myself, but this really is important.

2. Clear the work area around the UPS. If the UPS is connected and running
   (check that your UPS supports online battery replacement — don't just
   assume it's okay), clear away any cables or other equipment. If you've moved
   the UPS to your workbench, check for loose tools, wires, and the like. If the
   UPS is not online, make sure it's switched off.

3. Remove the cover over the battery compartment. For the Smart-UPS 1400,
   there's a plastic cover with a metal cover underneath (see Figure 6-30). Once
   you rotate the metal cover down, you'll see the batteries.

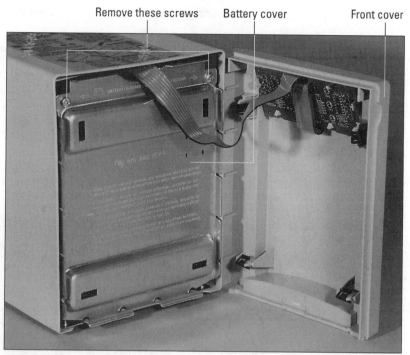

Remove these screws    Battery cover    Front cover

**Figure 6-30:** The only tools you need to change the batteries in a Smart-UPS 1400 are a quarter and a Phillips screwdriver.

**4.** Pull the batteries out as a unit. You'll see a cable in back of the batteries with a large connector on it (see Figure 6-31). Take one half of the connector in either hand, and pull it apart (don't pull on the wires themselves). Lift the batteries out together and set them aside. The batteries contain lead and acid, so don't open their cover.

**5.** Take the new batteries, connect them to the remaining half of the connector in the UPS, slide them into the case, and replace the two covers.

**6.** Dispose of the old battery properly. The best thing you can do is recycle it. APC offers this service, as may local businesses.

Power connector          Batteries

**Figure 6-31:** Once you pull the large connector apart, you can remove the batteries.

# Summary

✦ A well-designed case improves the maintainability, upgradability, reliability, and serviceability of your computer.

✦ Heat is the worst enemy your computer has. Excessive heat reduces the life of every component in the machine.

✦ Extra capacity in the power supply is inexpensive, creates reserve for expansion, and helps the supply run cooler.

✦ An uninterruptible power supply can save you hours of work when the power goes out.

✦     ✦     ✦

# Processor, Memory, and Bus

The first step in understanding the performance you get from a processor and how the processor relates to the bus and to memory is to look closely at what the processor does. Understanding the instruction execution cycle leads to understanding what engineers have done to speed up processors, and to an understanding of why you would choose one processor over another.

## Executing Instructions

If you had an assistant who scrupulously carried out your instructions but had no ability to think independently, you might give that person tasks by writing out detailed lists of instructions. Each instruction would have to be quite simple, and it would have to completely specify what you want done. For example, a list of tasks might include the following instruction:

```
Pick up the green box and put it on the top
shelf.
```

The microprocessor in your computer is very much like this imaginary assistant. It carries out sequences of instructions — programs — accurately but without understanding. Each instruction clearly and precisely specifies an action the processor is to take, leaving nothing undefined.

Here's an instruction that might be executed on an *x*86-architecture machine:

```
c7 05 42 01 15 71 01 00 00 00          mov a,1
```

The instruction does a very simple thing—it takes the number one and stores it in a chunk of memory. The portion of the instruction that you or I would be most likely to understand is the part that says "mov a,1." The same instruction in a form the processor understands (obeying conventions defined by Intel when they created the 386 processor) is the sequence of numbers "c7 05 42 01 15 71 01 00 00 00." Even the "c7" value is a number to the computer. It looks funny because it's not in base 10, it's in base 16 (where the digits are "0" through "9" and "a" through "f").

The machine version of the instruction has the same three components as the readable version, as shown in Table 7-1.

| Table 7-1 Machine Instructions to Processors | | |
| --- | --- | --- |
| **Machine Version** | **Readable Version** | **Description** |
| c7 05 | mov | The operation code (opcode) for the instruction is mov. The mov opcode tells the processor to read a chunk of information from one place and write it to another. The c7 05 code also tells the processor that the chunks of information it should move are four bytes long. |
| 42 01 15 71 | a | The destination for the move operation is a location in memory we've named a. The processor doesn't know or understand that name—instead, it knows that the memory location we want to store into has the address 42 01 15 71. |
| 01 00 00 00 | 1 | The operand for the move—the value we want to store in a—is the number one. That value is stored directly in the instruction in the four bytes 01 00 00 00. |

The processor does a lot of work to execute this simple instruction. Broken down into the micro steps that together store the number one into "a," here's what happens:

1. *Fetch the opcode from memory.* This happens by telling the memory the address of the instruction, commanding a read cycle, waiting, and pulling the memory result off the bus.

2. *Examine the result from the memory* (c7 05). Upon examination, the processor decides that it needs to execute a move of a four-byte operand to a memory location. It also determines from that value that the operand will immediately follow the instruction.

3. *Ask the memory for the four bytes following the instruction* (42 01 15 71). After those bytes are returned, the processor sets itself up to use that value as the address where the result is to be stored.

4. *Ask the memory for the four bytes* (01 00 00 00) *following the result address.* The processor stores those bytes in a temporary operand-holding place inside the processor.

5. *Tell the memory to store the operand in the destination.* After all that setup, the intended action finally happens.

6. *Advance the next instruction pointer (the place where the processor keeps the address of the next instruction).* The next instruction starts at the first byte past the operand fetched in step four. After advancing the pointer, the processor starts the cycle again.

# How Fast Are Instructions Carried Out?

Done in the most straightforward way, the sequence just described takes a long time. The timing diagram in Figure 7-1 shows why by matching up the operations of the processor and memory. Each block in Figure 7-1 is an operation performed by the processor or the memory. Operations by the processor are on the bottom; ones by the memory on the top. You can see from the figure that the price of working straightforwardly is that every time the processor is working, the memory is waiting, and every time the memory is working, the processor is waiting.

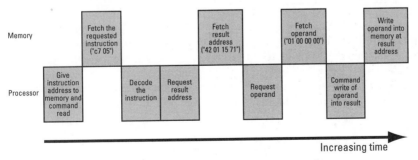

**Figure 7-1:** Simple interactions between the processor and memory mean that one or the other is always waiting for something to do.

Early microprocessors, such as the Intel 8088 used in the original IBM PC, operated just this way. Newer designs do better. Seeing how those newer processors improve execution performance requires that we look at a slightly more complicated program:

```
mov   a,1
mov   b,35
```

This program is almost the same. All we've done is to add a second instruction that stores the value 35 into the memory location named b. The breakdown of the instruction in Table 7-2 is almost identical to that in Table 7-1, differing only in the address of the destination and the value being stored.

### Table 7-2
### A Slightly More Complicated Set of Instructions

| Readable Version | Description |
| --- | --- |
| mov | The operation code (opcode) for the instruction is mov. The mov opcode tells the processor to read a chunk of information from one place and write it to another. The exact numbers used also tell the processor that the chunks of information are four bytes long. |
| b | The destination for the move operation is a location in memory we've named b. The processor doesn't understand the name — instead, it knows that the memory location we want to store into has the address 88 96 40 12. |
| 35 | The operand for the move — the value we want to store in b — is the number 35. That value is stored directly in the instruction. |

The important thing to notice about the new program is that all of the steps the processor carries out to execute the second instruction are independent of what it must do to execute the first instruction. The instructions are so completely independent that the order they are executed in makes no difference. For example, this is the equivalent program, even though the two instructions are in reverse order:

```
mov   b,35
mov   a,1
```

Because the order in which the processor does these instructions doesn't matter, a smart enough processor could choose the order itself. Nor does the processor have to be constrained to execute one of the instructions first — it works out the same if the processor executes both instructions at the same time. This last idea, running multiple instructions at the same time, is at the core of how processors gain speed beyond simply running at faster rates. Computer designers call the idea *superscalar execution*. If we change the timing diagram of Figure 7-1 to add the second instruction in our new program, and use superscalar execution, Figure 7-2 results. The blocks in Figure 7-2 are still operations done by the memory and processor. The processor can now do two things at once, though, so there are two rows of blocks at the bottom to show what the processor does. The arrows in the figure show how commands from the processor turn into operations in the memory.

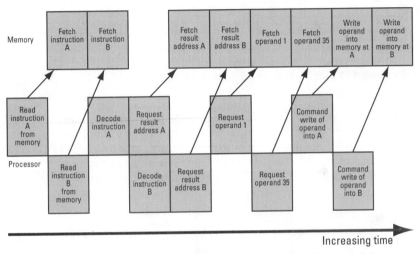

**Figure 7-2:** Superscalar execution allows the processor to do several things at once, making your computer faster.

Figure 7-2 shows a faster computer than the one in Figure 7-1, because there's twice as much work done in almost the same time. Superscalar execution is more complex, however, requiring some very clever work by the processor designers. Figures 7-3 and 7-4 show what happens. In Figure 7-3 (corresponding to the sequence in Figure 7-1), the three sections of a tightly integrated processor work as a single unit to execute instructions. The processor executes one instruction at a time and waits when the memory is working.

Within the processor, the Arithmetic-Logic Unit (ALU) does the computational work. It adds, subtracts, multiplies, and divides numbers, and carries out other operations required by programs. The bus interface communicates with the rest of the computer through the bus, fetching and storing information as directed by the ALU and control sections. The control section decodes instructions and tells the other sections how to carry out the work each instruction requires.

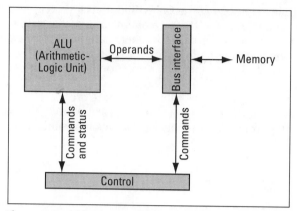

**Figure 7-3:** Older processors had a simpler design that constrained them to running one instruction at a time.

Newer superscalar processors (implementing the parallel execution in Figure 7-2) are designed like the drawing in Figure 7-4. The functions of the processor are broken up into multiple units, each of which operates independently. Several copies of critical units are provided to allow multiple operations at the same time. An execution control unit coordinates the operation of all the units.

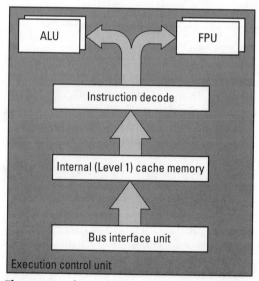

**Figure 7-4:** The multiple, cooperating units in a current-generation processor allow many things to go on at once.

Current-generation processors include these cooperating units:

✦ *Execution control unit.* This unit coordinates the operation of all the rest of the units.

✦ *Arithmetic-Logic Unit (ALU).* There are multiple ALUs. Each one can perform an arithmetic or logical operation independently of all the others, permitting multiple operations to be performed at once.

✦ *Floating Point Unit (FPU).* There may be multiple FPUs. Each FPU can do at least one floating-point operation at a time. A technique called pipelining can permit a single FPU to have multiple operations in progress at one time.

✦ *Instruction decoder.* This unit analyzes instructions to determine the operands and result destinations. It then tells the other independent units what to do to carry out the execution of the instruction. The decoder allows more than one instruction to be in process at once in order to keep all the operation units busy.

✦ *Cache memory.* Cache memory is a relatively small, very fast memory that maintains a copy of instructions and data recently used by the processor. Values found in the cache memory can be retrieved directly, without going over the bus to the regular memory.

✦ *Bus interface unit.* The bus interface unit receives requests by the execution control and instruction decoder for operations that need to be performed over the bus. Operands and instructions are fetched in advance of being needed to keep the decoder and operation unit pipelines busy. Values are buffered and written back to memory over the bus when time is available.

The point of adding all the hardware and complexity in current processors such as the Intel Pentium, Pentium Pro, or Pentium II, or AMD K6 and K6-2, is speed. Adding parallel hardware, increasing the clock rate, and requiring fewer clock cycles to execute each instruction all contribute to increased speed. In the process, however, the demands on the bus and memory for increased performance have increased sharply.

# Feeding the Hungry Beast: Cache Memory

A Pentium II processor clocking at 450 MHz (megahertz, or million cycles per second) can potentially execute at least one new instruction every 2.2ns (nanoseconds, billionths of a second). The memory technology that provides the tens and hundreds of megabytes of memory needed to run programs can return a value 50ns after the processor makes the request. The great difference in these two times — the ability of the processor to execute twenty instructions while waiting for one value from memory — means that without some help these screamingly fast processors will spend all their time waiting for data, doing nothing.

The obvious way to make memory faster is expensive. The dynamic random access memory (DRAM) technology used for the main memory in computers is not the fastest memory technology available. Static RAM (SRAM) memories are today five times faster than DRAMs. SRAMs require six times as many transistors inside the chip for every value they remember, however, and so are much more expensive to make than DRAMs.

The high cost makes SRAM impractical for main memory in PCs — DRAM is the only practical option. Instead, engineers solved the memory access problem with these ideas:

✦ *Exploit the physical design of memory.* The internal structure of DRAM (see Figure 7-7 and the text following it a little later in this chapter) allows designers to shortcut part of the memory access cycle, making 50ns or 60ns memory function much of the time as if it were 25ns or 35ns memory.

✦ *Improve the combined interaction of the processor, bus, and memory.* Changing the basic operation of the bus cycle allows the next memory access to start while the prior one is still wrapping up, increasing the effective rate at which the processor can access the memory. Other memory cycle changes allow the processor tighter control over the memory, speeding operation.

✦ *Don't access the memory so often.* Another way to solve the difference between what the processor wants and what the memory can deliver is to cut back the rate at which the processor wants memory access. The means to do this is a component called *cache memory*, which is a fast memory between the processor and main memory set up to remember what's stored in memory locations the processor is likely to need in the future.

✦ *Organize the memory physically to allow parallel operation.* You can build more than one bank of memory, arranging the memory banks so that they are accessed in rotation. This idea, called *interleaving*, allows separate values to be returned to the processor at the speed of the memory divided by the number of banks. For example, if you have ten banks of memory that can each be accessed every 100ns, then interleaving can provide a memory access as often as every 10ns. Interleaving requires that the order of access to memory — such as always wanting the next higher address location — be known when the memory is designed. Addressing the next sequential location is very common for computer programs, but it is not always the case.

We'll look at cache memory first and then investigate how DRAMs work.

When computer scientists look at the behavior of computer programs, they find that programs do not access all of memory equally often. Instead, locations in memory that the program has accessed recently are far more likely to be accessed again in the near future. Here's why that's so.

Figure 7-5 shows the steps a computer program might carry out to add together all the numbers from 1 to one 100. The important thing about the set of instructions shown in Figure 7-5 is that most of them get executed 100 times, and that each of those 100 times uses the same set of instructions.

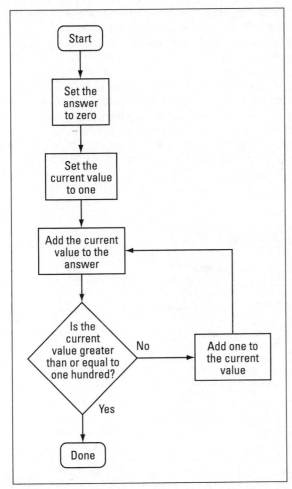

**Figure 7-5:** Looping in programs means that they revisit memory locations frequently.

Suppose the processor could keep track of the three instructions that form the loop:

1. Add the current value to the answer.

2. Is the current value greater than or equal to 100?

**3.** Add one to the current value.

The processor could use a local, cached copy of the instructions for each time around the loop after the first, in which case memory accesses would only be needed the first time through the loop. Only a small amount of storage would be required for this local copy, and if the local copy were fast enough the processor would never wait for memory. That local copy is called *cache memory*, a relatively small, very fast memory between the processor and the main memory. Cache memory remembers the contents of recently used memory locations and provides them to the processor when requested.

The fast SRAM chips used for cache memory currently cycle at 10ns to 15ns, meaning that the cache memory can provide a new value to the processor every 10 to 15 billionths of a second. This isn't fast enough for the fastest processors, however. The answer to that problem is more of a good thing. Memory directly inside the processor chip can be made even faster than these SRAMs — fast enough to keep up with the processor. The result shown in Figure 7-6 is three levels of memory: two cache memories and the main memory.

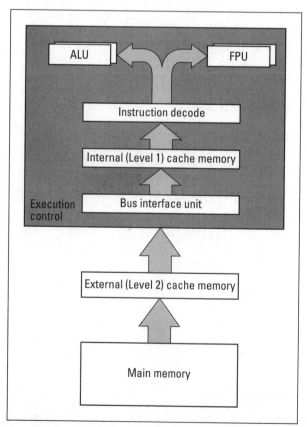

**Figure 7-6:** Multiple levels of cache keep the processor well fed.

✦ *L1 cache.* Cache memory internal to the processor is called level 1 (or L1) cache. It is faster than all other memory, but smaller — typically 8K or 16K. It handles very recently used values, as found in small, tight program loops.

✦ *L2 cache.* Cache memory external to the processor is called level 2 (or L2) cache. It is slower than L1 cache and faster than main memory. L2 cache size ranges from 128K to 1024K, with 256K being typical. It handles values less recently used than L1 cache. Although it's implemented with separate chips, L2 cache is packaged inside the processor cartridge on Intel Pentium II (and some Celeron) processors.

✦ *Main memory.* Main memory is much larger than cache, and much slower. It handles everything not handled by L1 or L2 cache.

Multiple levels of cache memory reduce the demand on main memory created by the fastest processors to the point where affordable 50ns or 60ns DRAMs can be used. Cache memory is so effective that main memory designs offering a 30-percent access time improvement in some cases only improve the performance of well-designed cached systems by 10 or 15 percent.

Cache memory does more than speed up processor access when it reads memory. The cache can record values being written by the processor to memory, delaying writing them until some later time when the memory is not busy. Cache memory that does this is called *write back cache*. This name contrasts its operation to *write through cache*, which is the sort that simply handles read access, forcing the processor to wait while writes complete.

# More Is Better: Faster, More Reliable Memory

Computer memory chips have a very simple, direct function — they remember information you write to them and let you read it back later. Giving them a huge capacity, good speed, and a low price, however, makes memory design so difficult that the newest chip technology almost always shows up first in new memory designs. The original IBM PC used chips holding 16 kilobits (Kb), while chips holding 16 and even 64 megabits (Mb) are used in systems 17 years later. Changes in the way the processor and bus control the memory have at the same time increased the effective speed, although not as dramatically as size has increased.

## Speed is good

The inside of a DRAM chip is organized into a square array of storage locations, as shown in Figure 7-7. The memory breaks the address your processor passes it into two halves, called a row address and a column address. Together, the two half-addresses identify one bit in the memory.

The number of address signals connected to the memory has to match its capacity. Signals are always added to both the row and column addresses at the same time, leading to the progression of memory chip sizes shown in Table 7-3. There has been an exponential growth in memory capacity, as shown in Figure 7-8. (The dates we used to derive the graph reflect when the chip was developed, which is earlier than when the chip enters production.)

| Table 7-3 Increase in Memory Capacity over Time | |
| --- | --- |
| **Address Lines** | **Memory Size** |
| 14 | 16 kilobits |
| 16 | 64 kilobits |
| 18 | 256 kilobits |
| 20 | 1 megabit |
| 22 | 4 megabits |
| 24 | 16 megabits |
| 26 | 64 megabits |
| 28 | 256 megabits |
| 30 | 1,024 megabits |

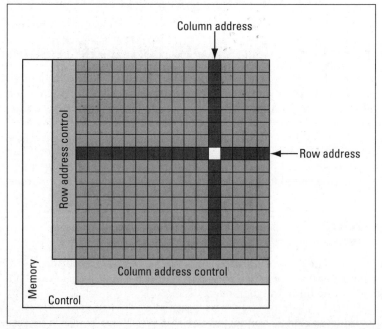

**Figure 7-7:** The memory location your program accesses is at the intersection of a row and column of the square array inside the memory chip.

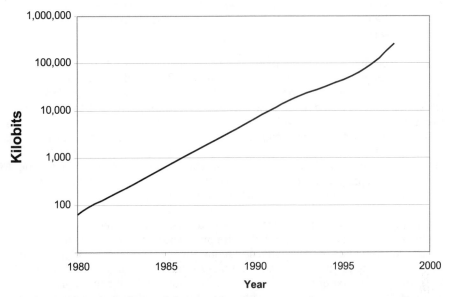

**Figure 7-8:** Exponential growth in per-chip memory capacity powers not only more memory in systems, but also the advanced semiconductor processes underlying faster, more powerful processors.

The actual memory performance you get in a system results from the combination of how fast the chip itself responds and how the chip interacts with the processor and bus. The memory designs now used all exploit the row-and-column structure of Figure 7-7 to speed up both processes. A basic memory read cycle is shown in Figure 7-9, in which the processor puts the desired address on the bus and signals it's there. After some delay, the memory puts the data from that address on the bus so the processor can pick it up.

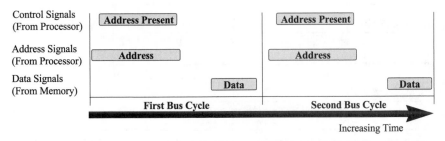

**Figure 7-9:** A basic memory read cycle passes addresses to the memory and data to the processor.

All the designs described in the following paragraphs speed up the basic cycle by reducing the time taken by individual cycle elements or by allowing parts of the cycle to overlap.

The detailed operation of the basic cycle is to set the row address through the row address control, and then to set the column address, wait, and read the data off the bus. One of the first basic memory cycle improvements, called *Fast Page Mode* (FPM), takes advantage of the row/column physical structure of the memory array to remove part of the bus cycle. The entire group of column addresses defining memory cells within a row is called a *page*. There is a necessary delay after setting the row address that only has to be taken when the row address changes. Successive reads at different column addresses within the same page can be done much more quickly. FPM memories make this time savings available to the processor by allowing shortened timing for in-page cycles.

The in-page access requirements for faster access to FPM memory work well with cache memory. It is very likely that if the processor accesses one address it will access the following ones as well, so having the cache quickly read ahead to have the data waiting for the processor increases effective memory performance. Figure 7-10 shows what happens. Suppose the processor needs to access memory at address "30 00 00 04." Using the 64-bit-wide bus on Pentium and later processors, the processor will read the locations at "30 00 00 00" through "30 00 00 07." Anticipating that the processor will need access to the following addresses, the cache then reads another three to seven bus cycles at eight bytes per bus cycle. It's likely that those additional reads are in the same page, so they take only one clock cycle each. Counting cycles, then, the first cycle, which has to set the row address, takes three clock cycles. The subsequent FPM in-page cycles take only one clock each. The total operation of eight bus cycles takes 3+1+1+1+1+1+1+1 = 10 clock cycles and provides 64 bytes to the processor. If all eight bus cycles required three clock cycles (that is, if this wasn't FPM memory), the 64-byte operation would take 24 cycles. Using the faster FPM in-page cycles more than doubled the performance of the memory.

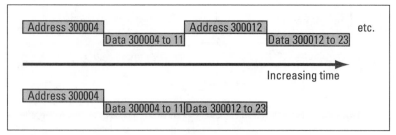

**Figure 7-10:** Cache burst transfers exploit the speed in Fast Page Mode.

After FPM, the next improvement to the basic memory cycle was *Extended Data Out* (EDO) memory. EDO memory improves the idea behind Fast Page Mode by allowing the processor to give the memory the next address in the page at the same time the data from the last cycle is being returned from the memory to the processor. The operation of EDO memory uses the modified bus cycle shown in the bottom of Figure 7-11(the FPM cycle is shown at the top). EDO memory allows the column address to be changing at the end of the bus cycle while the processor reads in the data value, overlapping the data and address operations.

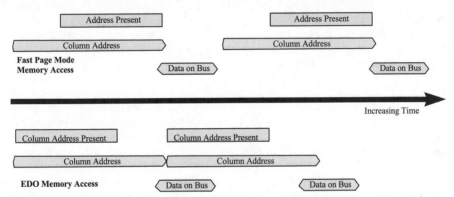

**Figure 7-11:** EDO memory provided over 30 percent faster access to memory than Fast Page Mode.

EDO memory provided over 30 percent faster access to memory than FPM, which was enough of a gain to permit low-end Pentium computers and laptops to perform passably well with no cache. EDO memory is usable along with cache, but the performance gain is only 10 to 15 percent versus Fast Page Mode with the same cache.

The next generation of memory, after EDO, was called synchronous DRAM (SDRAM). SDRAM technology coupled the operation of the memory more tightly to the processor clock, reducing the timing tolerances necessary to coordinate the operation of the processor and memory and increasing performance. Processors will keep needing faster memory access as clocks run up to 500, 600, and 1000 MHz, though, and SDRAM (or it's yet-faster PC100 version) didn't provide enough of a speed gain. PC133 SDRAM is being used as a stopgap measure, but it too will fail to keep up with ever-faster processors.

The next generation memory standard is something called Direct Rambus. The essence of Direct Rambus is a very sophisticated implementation of two ideas — make the memory control more efficient so fewer clock cycles are required, and make memory wider. Because memory is already 8 bytes wide in Pentium and Pentium II systems, expanding the memory bus means expansion to 16 bytes.

Doubling the memory bus width has an enormous effect on performance—a 100 MHz memory bus, as in the 350 to 450 MHz systems, transfers 8 bytes per clock (peak), so the maximum pre-Rambus transfer rate is 8 × 100 = 800 MBps. Doubling the bus width boosts the peak transfer rate to 1.6 GBps.

Directly making memory wider isn't easy, because it requires adding wires to the motherboard, along with pins to the processor and supporting chips. The 64 data line wires in current-generation memory buses are hard enough to handle—it's not practical to expand the bus to 128 bits. What Rambus does instead is wonderfully innovative—it runs a double-width (16 bytes wide) bus inside the memory module, but exposes it to the motherboard as a 2-bytes wide (16-bit) bus running at eight times the speed of the wide internal bus. The end result, one appearing in the fastest PCs during 1999, is a memory bus capable of delivering up to 1.6 GBps to the processor.

The driver behind all these memory technologies is the need to provide faster and faster memory access to increasingly powerful processors. Memory access wasn't much of a problem for the slow 8088 processors in the original IBM PCs, but as processor width went from 8 to 32 bits (with 64-bit processors coming) and processor speeds went from 4.77 MHz to 500 MHz (with 1000 MHz coming), change had to happen. Figure 7-12 shows the lifetime each of the major PC memory technologies has had. The inability of any technology to survive much more than five years is a measure of how fast processor design changes.

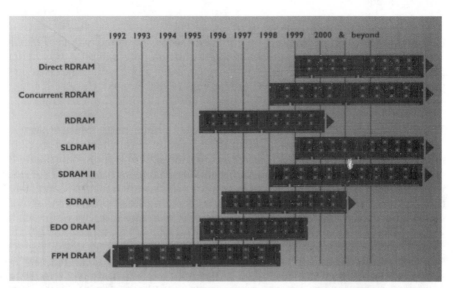

**Figure 7-12:** DRAM technologies rarely survive longer than five years before faster processors demand a next generation of performance. (Courtesy of Kingston Technology Company.)

# Reliable speed is better

The chips that make up your computer are built from transistors. Table 7-4 shows that most of the transistors in your computer are in the main memory. We've ignored nearly all the other components besides the processor and the memory in the table because the number of transistors in those components is far fewer than even in the processor. If the chances of a transistor failing are the same everywhere, then the memory is far more likely to fail than the processor, because it represents over 95 percent of the transistors in the system.

| | Table 7-4 | | |
|---|---|---|---|
| | **Most Transistors Are in Main Memory** | | |
| **Component** | **Approximate Number of Transistors** | **Number of Components in a 64MB System** | **Approximate Number of Transistors in a 64 MB System** |
| 386 processor | 0.3 million | 1 | 0.3 million |
| 486 processor | 1.0 million | 1 | 1.0 million |
| Pentium processor | 3.3 million | 1 | 3.3 million |
| Fourth generation 3D video accelerator | 7.0 million | 1 | 7.0 million |
| Pentium Pro processor (excluding cache) | 5.5 million | 1 | 5.5 million |
| Pentium II processor (excluding cache) | 7.5 million | 1 | 7.5 million |
| 64 million bit memory chip (8MB) | 64.0 million | 8 | 512.0 million |

Although we just assumed all transistors are equally likely to fail, memory in practice is more likely to encounter errors than the processor or any other component. This is because, in addition to permanent failures caused by device breakdown, memories are subject to the values they store being changed by very low-level ionizing radiation that occurs naturally. These changes of stored values are called *soft errors*.

Soft errors used to be a significant problem — an evaluation by Micron Technology states that the 16KB DRAM memory subsystems used in the original IBM PC could be subject to a soft error every 60 or 70 hours of operation. Current DRAM technology is far better. Calculations by Intel reflecting the performance of memories by Micron, NEC, and Toshiba lead to the conclusion that the memory subsystem is not likely to encounter a soft error during the life of the computer. Calculations by IBM (Table 7-5) also suggest that undetected errors are not a problem.

## Table 7-5
## Soft Memory Error Rates

| Memory Size | Usage per Month (Hours) | Probable Soft Error Rate |
|---|---|---|
| 4MB | 100 | One in 39 years |
| 8MB | 300 | One in 8 years |
| 16MB | 600 | One in 3 years |

(Data courtesy of IBM Corporation.)

## Mixing and matching memory

Two very common questions are whether or not you can mix different types and speeds of memory, and whether you can use memory faster than your system requires.

Memory speed is the easier of the two questions. Mixing memory speeds shouldn't be a problem as long as all the memory you install meets the requirements of your processor and motherboard. You may have to set the memory speed in the BIOS (Basic Input/Output System) — be sure to set it for the slowest memory, not the fastest. Check the documentation on your motherboard for specifics. You can always use faster memory than your system requires, but unless you can set up the system to know the faster memory is there (such as through a BIOS setting), you won't see any benefit.

Mixing memory types is a more difficult question. You can mix parity and nonparity memory as long as you turn off parity detection. Some systems allow you to mix Fast Page Mode and EDO memory as long as all the memory in a single bank is the same kind. This is highly variable among systems — some absolutely refuse to run with mixed memory types — so again you'll want to check your motherboard documentation. The conservative approach is to use memory that's all the same.

For example, we once upgraded a machine to a Pentium motherboard carrying a 200 MHz MMX Pentium, a full set of integrated peripherals (including Universal Serial Bus), an AMI BIOS, and six memory sockets. We moved over the existing memory, which included one bank of Fast Page Mode and one bank of EDO. The resulting machine was not stable. We replaced the FPM memory, reconfiguring the system to use EDO in both banks. After that, the machine was rock solid. We moved the combined FPM/EDO configuration into an Intel motherboard, where it worked fine. Short of following manufacturer's recommendations, there's no guaranteed way to tell in advance whether or not a motherboard will handle mixed memory configurations.

The values in the right column of Table 7-5 are the probable number of soft errors the machine will encounter. Some machines will encounter an error sooner than those numbers suggest and others, later. Some machines may encounter an error very much sooner, others, very much later. You can't conclude from these numbers that your machine won't hit a soft error in its first year of operation, just that it's fairly unlikely. You also need to keep in mind that these numbers reflect the probability of a soft error — of a stored number being retrieved improperly because natural ionizing radiation changed the value. Errors due to failed memory — memory that is functioning improperly because of some malfunction in the circuitry — are not considered. (Machine crashes due to software problems also aren't considered in the table. PCs crash far more often than Table 7-5 suggests, implying that soft memory errors aren't the biggest problem users face.)

If you remember back when Windows 3.1 was introduced, you may recall news stories about a rash of memory errors being encountered on machines onto which Windows 3.1 had recently been installed. Several magazine articles recommended removing the Windows 3.1 component that detected those errors. Despite the surprising number of such reports, that experience was entirely consistent with Table 7-5. Here's why:

✦ *The memory test your computer steps through when it starts is nearly useless.* Because a comprehensive memory test is very time consuming, the one in the Power On Self Test (POST) in your BIOS is at best a surface-level test only capable of finding some of the possible failures. It may do no more than identify which banks are populated with apparently working memory.

✦ *Your BIOS may not even be testing all your memory.* Many BIOS (Basic Input/Output System) configurations allow you to specify whether or not memory above 1MB is tested. Your computer may have those tests disabled.

✦ *When you hit a key to speed up the memory test, the BIOS does only a cursory test for presence of the memory.* If you're impatient, you may be skipping even the rudimentary test the BIOS is capable of.

✦ *Memory failures cannot be detected without accessing the affected locations.* Don't do this, but suppose you removed a memory chip from your computer while it was running, and further suppose the computer never accessed the locations stored on that chip after you removed it. If so, no memory error would be detected.

While we have seen the Microsoft HIMEM.SYS device driver shipped with Windows 9*x* detect some memory errors that were not found by the BIOS in the machine, HIMEM.SYS does not do a comprehensive test. Because the tests in the BIOS and HIMEM.SYS, poor as they are, won't detect many failures, the average user does not have an effective memory diagnostic test available. Because of that, the average user cannot possibly verify that the memory is functioning properly. Worse yet, if the computer has more memory than its software uses (as was often true under Windows before version 3.1), a failure could go undetected for years. That combination of problems accounts for many of the problems reported after installing Windows 3.1 — DOS software was relatively unlikely to use the upper reaches of memory on machines with 8MB or more, leaving errors in those parts of memory undetected until Windows 3.1 started to use them.

Memory errors can be detected using a scheme called *parity checking*, which added a ninth bit to every eight-bit byte. Parity checking can detect all instances of one, three, five, or seven simultaneous errors in the byte. It will not notice combinations of two, four, six, or eight errors. Because the most common error is a one-bit error, parity checking provides a useful degree of confidence. When memory was relatively less reliable, parity checking was very common in computers.

As memory became more reliable, it became reasonable to ask if the added confidence you received from incorporating the ninth parity bit in each byte was worth the cost. The simplest answer was that you want to know about any error in the computer, so you care. The counterargument was that not all errors matter — for example, people argued that you probably won't care about errors that cause one dot to be displayed wrong on your display. The argument continued that if Windows' parity-checking software halted the machine, you couldn't save your work, as was sometimes the case with Windows 3.1. If you removed the parity-check error handling component or used memory modules that didn't include parity checking, then you avoided that problem.

Unfortunately, you created two other problems as a result. First, you never found out that there was a problem with memory. Second, if a memory problem corrupted your data, you never found out until the problem became bad enough to crash the software. By then, you probably had corrupted the files on disk, possibly without backup.

The industry is split on whether you need parity checking, largely because of the improvement in reliability of the memory chips. Intel included support for parity checking on the 82420 chip set supporting the 486 processor but omitted it from the 82430 chip set supporting the Pentium. SIS included it in their Pentium support chip set. Cypress includes it in their hyperCache chip set. Intel added back parity checking in a later Pentium chip set.

The reason people omit parity checking is cost. The hardware to generate and check parity costs nearly nothing, but storing the parity check bits increases the cost of memory because you need 9 bits to store a byte, not 8. If you pay by the bit — which is roughly true — then you pay around 12 percent more. In computers sold on price in two-page spreads in the newspaper, 12 percent of the cost of memory can be 10 or 15 dollars more profit.

More interestingly, Intel built an industrial-strength version of parity checking — error correcting codes (ECC) — directly into the Pentium Pro and Pentium II processors. Instead of detecting odd numbers of bit errors, however, the ECC in the Pentium Pro corrects all single-bit errors, detects all double-bit errors within the 64-bit span, and detects certain other errors too.

ECC memory has become widespread in the last few years because the Pentium Pro and most of the Pentium II processors include support for ECC directly in the chip. That feature made the cost of incorporating ECC drop to be the same as that to incorporate simple parity checking — parity checking requires that the memory store one additional bit for every 8-bit byte, while ECC requires an additional 8 bits for every 64 bits. That's no more than what's required for parity checking. Figure 7-13 compares the memory organization required by the two approaches. The ECC approach imposes a greater required structure on the memory organization but needs no more bits of storage. Because the memory structure is determined when the motherboard and memory modules are designed, and because the circuits to support ECC are now built into the processor, there are no additional system costs over that for parity checking.

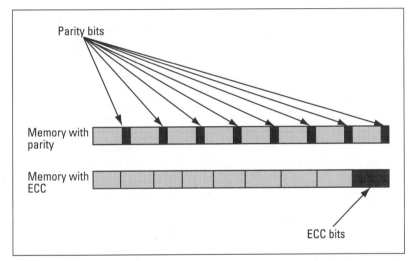

**Figure 7-13:** ECC memory adds no extra cost over parity checking in Pentium Pro and Pentium II systems.

# Simpler Systems from Complicated Sets of Wires

If you're the type that takes apart electronic things to see what's inside, and you've done that for the last 40 years or so, you've noticed a profound change in how electronic systems are built. Forty years ago and more, what you noticed first was the tubes, transformers, and other large components. Inside a box under those components were some other components and a whole lot of wires. Building anything this way took a lot of labor to screw things together, cut wires, and make connections, with a great deal of the labor simply in the process of connecting wires to terminals.

Not too much later, electronics manufacturers switched to using printed circuit boards, which are flat pieces of fiberglass or other stiff, nonconductive material. A printing and etching process places strips of copper (called traces) on the card, with areas at the end of the strips called pads to which the manufacturer attaches components. Printed circuits started out with traces on one side but rapidly evolved to traces on both sides. Later versions laminated more than one card together, providing many layers to hold traces. The reason for adding all these layers to the boards was that the components had become more complex, with more connections, and simple one- and two-layer boards could not provide enough traces.

Every new layer on a printed circuit costs more money to design and build. As the cost to make connections grew, and as the number of connections outstripped even very expensive multilayer boards, designers started looking for ways to reduce the number of connections (and so the number of traces and layers). One very successful way has been to share wires among more than two devices. Figure 7-14 shows the idea, using the problem of connecting a processor to its memories as an example.

The most straightforward design for connecting a processor to its memories uses a separate wire for every connection (this is the drawing on the left in Figure 7-14). Suppose that every memory chip had its own set of wires to connect it to the processor. Using 16Mb (megabit) chips, a 32MB memory array needs 16 chips. Each chip will have in excess of 40 pins, so to connect up every chip with its own wires, you need in excess of 640 wires. If you want to add memory, you need 40 more wires for every chip. You need even more wires to connect to your disk, video, and other components. Because the processor only talks to a few of the memory chips at once, however, most of these wires are doing nothing, while a few do useful work. The wires are functional duplicates of one another, serving the same purpose (such as conveying one of the data signals) except for the fact that they connect to different memory chips.

As connections became relatively more expensive and the cost of circuits built out of transistors became very much cheaper, changes in design to substitute cheap transistors for expensive wires became possible. The idea of a bus grew out of this substitution.

Instead of using point-to-point connections, suppose that every memory chip connects to the same set of wires (so there are 40 wires used with all chips, not 40 for each chip). Since the processor doesn't talk to every memory chip at once, you have to add a few new wires to identify which chips should be active at any instant of time. In an eight-bit ISA bus system, only 62 wires are needed for everything. The drawing on the right side of Figure 7-13 diagrams this scheme, called a *bus*. A wire carrying a data signal, for instance, connects to the processor and equally to all the memory chips. Using the same wire across all the memory chips means that only one can use the wire at a time, but because that's how the processor works in the first place, there's no interference.

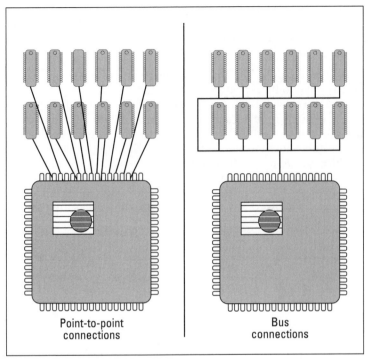

Point-to-point
connections

Bus
connections

**Figure 7-14:** Sharing wires to do more than one thing is the idea behind the buses in all computers today.

## The ISA bus: It's old and slow, but (nearly) everyone has one

Buses have been in personal computers since the first 8080-based designs in the late 1970s. Computers prior to the PC used a variety of buses, with the most common one being called the S-100 bus (after the 100 pins on its connector); the IBM PC introduced the Industry Standard Architecture (ISA) bus. A bus is defined by a specification, which will usually include all these elements to ensure that products built to the specification will fit into and work in a computer built to the same specification:

✦ *The physical specification.* A bus usually includes both a *backplane*, which is the circuit card all the other cards plug into, and those other cards. If the base card has components on it, it's frequently called a *motherboard* rather than a backplane. The plug-in cards have shape and size specified so that they fit into a standard-sized chassis. The physical specification details the connector(s) used between the backplane and the cards, the distance between cards, the maximum heat dissipation, and other mechanical issues.

✦ *The electrical specification.* Every active pin on a bus connector carries either a signal, power, or ground. The electrical specification for the bus defines what signal is on each pin on the connector and the minimum and maximum specifications for each.

✦ *The bus timing and protocol.* The behavior and timing of the signals that control the bus have to be very precisely defined so that everything plays together properly. Figure 7-15 shows the simplified timing and protocol for the ISA bus. If this were the fully detailed drawing, the minimum and maximum times between events would be shown, and the exact signals making up each of the signal groups shown would be identified. The top two lines in the figure show how addresses go on the bus, the middle line shows the timing for read or write commands, and the bottom two show the timing for data being read or written on the bus. The gray areas in the timing diagram represent times when the signals are allowed to be changing; the white areas are times when the signals must remain stable.

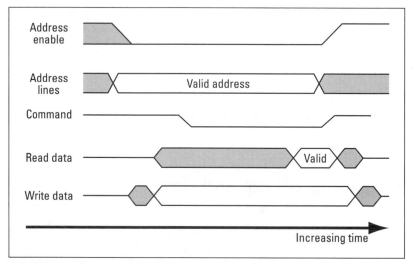

**Figure 7-15:** The operation of the ISA bus is defined by a simple set of signals and rules.

When the processor wants to communicate with memory or an I/O device, it goes through these steps according to the timing of Figure 7-15:

1. Output an address onto the bus ("Address Lines") and assert the "Address Enable" signal so that cards on the bus know that an address is present they should look at.

2. If this will be a memory or I/O write, output the data to be written onto the bus ("Write Data").

3. Output the command to be performed by the cards onto the bus ("Command"). The defined commands include memory read, memory write, I/O read, and I/O write.

4. If this is a memory or I/O read, wait the required amount of time, and after the data is stable pull the data off the bus.

5. Remove the command from the bus.

6. Remove the address enable from the bus.

Amazing as it is that the ISA bus survived for nearly 20 years, there's no longer much of anything good to be said about the ISA bus. It's slow, orders of magnitude slower than the PCI bus (covered later in this chapter). It's not as reliable as PCI, because certain critical signals must be captured at the point they change from high to low or low to high. (More reliable buses allow devices to look for high or low status, not transitions.) It's terribly constraining for software and for system configuration, because it can't address enough memory and doesn't provide enough interrupt control signals. It's difficult to work with, because the vast majority of ISA cards and systems in existence require the user to manually set addresses and interrupts, and to know what addresses and interrupts will work.

The one good thing to be said about the ISA bus is that nearly every PC — Windows or otherwise — has one, and building cards that work in an ISA bus machine is well understood. A manufacturer can sell a card for the ISA bus knowing there's a tremendous number of machines capable of hosting that card. A user can buy an ISA card and know that the chances are good that it can be made to work.

Microsoft and Intel proposed starting a migration away from the ISA bus in their PC 98 Design Guide hardware recommendation, and they made the statement stronger for PC 99 — the ISA bus is going to disappear.

## MCA: The Betamax of personal computers?

It became apparent very soon after IBM introduced the PC that the ISA bus was going to be a terrible problem. Although the personal computers leading up to the PC strained to handle more than 64K of memory, the PC quickly ran up against its original 1MB limit. Increases in processor speed from the original 4.77 MHz to 8 or 10 MHz and higher started to push against the limits of memory speeds. IBM responded in the PC/AT by extending the ISA bus to be sixteen data bits wide rather than eight (making memory access faster), and by expanding the addressing up to 16MB (allowing installation of more memory). Every other PC bus design since then has either replaced or added to that 16-bit ISA bus design.

Expansion to 16 data bits notwithstanding, the ISA bus is too slow even for processors now considered obsolete. At a peak transfer rate of 2.5 to 5MB per second, the ISA bus could only support processors running a few million instructions per second. This was adequate for the 8088 and 80286 processors, but was easily outrun by even the first 80386 machines.

IBM has some of the finest technology and engineering in the world. When IBM engineers looked at the problems posed by the ISA bus, they concluded that they would replace it with a completely new design. That design, the *Micro Channel Architecture (MCA)* bus, debuted with the IBM PS/2 series of computers in the late 1980s. Features of the new design included

✦ *32-bit data path*. The MCA bus supported 8-, 16-, and 32-bit transfers at a clock rate of 10 MHz, for a peak transfer rate of 20MB per second. A later revision of MCA added a feature called data streaming that boosted the peak possible transfer rate to 80MB per second (16 times the best you'll do with the ISA bus).

✦ *32-bit addressing*. The MCA bus provided 32 address lines, capable of addressing 4GB (256 times more then the ISA bus).

✦ *Complete support for bus masters*. Bus mastering allows adapter cards to control their own transfers to and from memory without intervention by the processor, which speeds operation. Implementing bus master cards for the ISA bus (such as the Adaptec AHA-154X series of SCSI adapters) was difficult, with the achievable performance very much dependent on the motherboard and other cards. (For example, the Adaptec 1542 was forced to run at a transfer rate of no more than 5.5 MHz because of limitations in the design of many motherboards.) The MCA bus standard provided comprehensive support for bus masters, including improved handling of contention between multiple masters.

✦ *Automatic configuration*. The MCA bus supported automatic analysis and configuration of the I/O addresses, interrupt request levels, and assigned memory addresses of cards plugged into the bus, and did so years before PCI or ISA "Plug and Play" technology supported this feature.

MCA cards were generally more expensive than ISA cards, and ISA cards could not be plugged into an MCA bus. That incompatibility meant upgrades plugging an existing suite of display or network cards into a new MCA machine were impossible. MCA machines therefore required all new cards, increasing the cost of converting to the new technology.

Despite its technical strengths, MCA did not succeed in the market. Only a few companies licensed the design from IBM, and only IBM sold a significant number of MCA machines.

Even though Windows 95 can run on a 386-based MCA machine (Windows NT requires a 486 or better), MCA constrained what you could do for upgrades. Our experience with an old PS/2 Model 70-121 was probably typical. The machine came standard with a 386DX-20 processor, 2MB of memory, 120MB of disk, and a VGA display, but we had upgraded memory to 5MB and added a network adapter. Performance running Windows 95 was abysmal for three reasons:

1. *Not enough memory.* Our opinion is that 5MB is not enough for Windows 95 on a networked system, and probably not enough for anyone on any system.

2. *Slow disk access.* The disk controller IBM provided in the machine was not supported by 32-bit drivers in Windows 95. All disk access had to go through slower 16-bit code and was deadly slow.

3. *Not enough horsepower.* The 20 MHz 386 processor was almost the slowest processor ever made still capable of running Windows 95.

As an experiment, we installed a memory card adding another 6MB, bringing the total to 11MB. The additional memory made the machine usable, but still terribly slow. Although we never thought we'd gained any speed advantage from the MCA bus in the machine, the computer never failed in the eight years we had it in service. We bought the machine expecting the reliability IBM is known for, and it definitely posted an impressive record.

## EISA: Another nice try

The resistance of the market to MCA did not change the fact that a new, higher-performance bus had to be developed. An industry group — AST, Compaq, Epson, Hewlett-Packard, NEC, Olivetti, Tandy, Wyse, and Zenith — formed to design a bus that had features competitive with MCA while retaining compatibility with the older ISA design. The resulting *Extended Industry Standard Architecture (EISA)* bus included important features such as bus mastering, automated setup, improved interrupt handling, and higher transfer rates.

The issue the EISA bus design had to solve was the problem of how to include pins on the connector for the new signals needed to make the bus capable of 32-bit address and data handling while remaining compatible with older ISA cards. The solution was to make the connector deeper, with a second row of contacts. ISA cards plugged into EISA connectors touched only the first row, while EISA cards reached both the first and second rows. This solution allowed EISA cards to add 90 new pins to the ISA bus connector design.

The advantages of EISA were the features it added:

✦ *Greater transfer rates.* The EISA design supported new data transfer modes capable of 33MB per second operation. That rate is 6 to 15 times faster than the ISA, but still slower than what's required by current generation processors.

✦ *Faster Direct Memory Access.* Direct Memory Access (DMA) uses an additional circuit — the DMA controller — to move blocks of data from one location to another (it's a variant of a bus master). DMA can offload the work of disk data transfers from the processor as well as move from one memory location to another. The EISA design fixed the ISA bus DMA design problems, providing from 2 to 16 times the performance.

✦ *Improved bus mastering support.* The ISA bus supports one bus master in addition to the processor (see Chapter 4) and has problems doing that. EISA moved control of bus mastering away from the processor, provided a structure to ensure competing requirements were properly met. Combined with improved transfer rates, EISA bus masters offered important performance gains for servers and other heavily loaded machines.

✦ *Interrupt sharing.* Even with the addition of seven more interrupts, the 16-bit ISA design restricts the addition of more functionality to systems. The EISA bus kept the same 15 interrupts as the ISA standard but (for interrupts generated by EISA-compliant boards) allowed an interrupt to be shared among more than one device.

EISA provided a reliable, workable solution to the ISA bus performance problems but was expensive. For many computers the benefits of EISA — particularly improved disk performance — were not terribly important in the late 1980s when the bus was introduced. Some surviving EISA systems are still in use, but the EISA bus has been supplanted by the higher-performance PCI bus.

## VESA Local: Yet another bus

Micro Channel and EISA were solutions to the general problem of providing a higher-performance bus for PCs. Each design met the goal of improved performance, but both suffered from increased cost and therefore limited market acceptance. In the early 1990s the Video Electronics Standards Association (VESA) observed that several proprietary designs had boosted video performance by nearly direct connection to the processor bus pins. This approach, called a *local bus*, eliminates many of the capabilities of the more general buses such as ISA, MCA, or EISA but gains simplicity and high speed as a result. VESA chose to create a standard for local bus designs, with the VESA Local (or VL) bus being the result.

The VL bus design was specific to the Intel 486 processor (with some concessions for the 386). The bus clocked at the speed of the processor, providing direct connection to all the processor address and data signals. The VL bus was capable of transfers in excess of 100MB per second, a dramatic and visible performance boost over the rates of the MCA and EISA designs. It required no changes in software to exploit that performance. Because it built on the existing ISA design, it added little to the cost of the system beyond a few extra connectors on the motherboard.

The immediately visible video performance benefits from the VL bus created demand in the market, leading to a large installed base. VL bus systems remained competitive for the life of the 486 processor, with a lifetime extending past the release of Windows 95.

## PCI: The winner of the PC bus wars

Even the VL bus had drawbacks. Being tied closely to the processor meant that the operation of the bus changed when the processor changed (and even as the processor speed increased with new models). The Pentium processor eventually killed the VL bus, because the bus couldn't readily adapt to the bus design on the new processor. Once again, a new bus was required.

Based on the experience of the ISA, MCA, EISA, and VL buses, that new bus needed to meet these goals:

✦ *Provide increased performance.* Target performance was upward of 100MB per second. Support for at least the full 32-bit address and data was required.

✦ *Support multiple bus masters.* Allowing peripheral devices to control high-rate transfers independently offloads the processor, increasing net system performance.

✦ *Enable automatic system configuration.* Incorrectly assigned addresses and interrupts are the cause of far too many system problems. The bus had to establish the underlying structures and mechanisms to allow the computer to assist the user with this problem.

✦ *Be processor independent.* The cost of developing chips to support the bus and products that implement the bus is significant to manufacturers, while the money spent on cards is of importance to users. The bus needed to preserve those investments across generations of processors.

✦ *Retain support for the ISA bus.* The ISA bus had a lot of value for devices that could live within its restrictions, including modems, printer interfaces, and mice. At the time PCI was designed, the number of cards built around the ISA bus far exceeded that for any other bus, including both widely used devices and specialty items such as bar code readers and data acquisition systems.

✦ *Impose low implementation costs.* The PC market is extremely cost sensitive (and getting more so), so it was critical that the bus design not price systems or cards beyond what the market will accept.

The *Peripheral Component Interconnect (PCI)* bus accomplished all this. Although the choice the market would make between the VL bus and PCI was unclear just after both were introduced, the combination of chip sets to implement PCI (which reduced cost) and the Pentium processor (which didn't work with VL) ensured that PCI gained the dominant market share.

The PCI bus is a local bus tied closely to the processor, like the VL bus, but which retains enough independence that it can support the 486, Pentium, Pentium II, and later processor generations equally well. It does this with the three-tier structure shown in Figure 7-16. The fastest operations (including memory) are on the host bus; fast I/O and video are on the PCI bus, and legacy devices are on ISA. Two *bridge* chips connect the three bus sections.

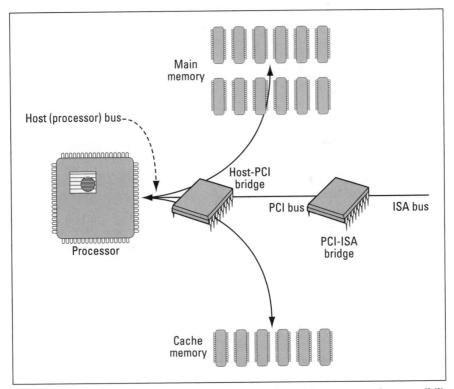

Main memory

Host (processor) bus

Host-PCI bridge

PCI bus                ISA bus

PCI-ISA bridge

Processor

Cache memory

**Figure 7-16:** PCI implements a three-tier structure for performance and compatibility.

Memory and the level 2 cache live on the host bus, connecting through the Host-PCI bridge to the processor. The presence of the Host-PCI bridge chip in this path means that the PCI chip set is involved in support of memory features such as EDO memory and parity checking. Transfers to devices not on the host bus are detected by the Host-PCI bridge chip (sometimes called the *Northbridge*) and passed onto the PCI bus itself. High-speed transfers on the PCI bus, such as to video cards and disk or network controllers, occur at rates up to 133MB per second. The clocking of transfers on the PCI bus is independent of the processor clock, so the design of PCI cards need not be concerned with variations in processor type and speed.

Some of the addresses passed through the Host-PCI bridge chip to the PCI bus are actually destined for cards plugged into the ISA bus. These transactions are detected by the PCI-ISA bridge chip (the *Southbridge*), which passes them off to the ISA bus and the devices there. Other buses besides ISA (such as MCA or EISA) can be bridged into PCI, but ISA is by far the most common.

There's been an addition to PCI in recent years — the Accelerated Graphics Port (AGP) — to permit the processor to achieve very high data rates to one device (the video card). Most AGP devices today run at 533 MBps (called *2X AGP*). Faster 4X devices are on the market as of June 1999 but await the required motherboard support.

# Putting It All Together

The message we want you to get from this chapter — and the entire book — is that all the parts of your computer need to be in balance. If any one component is significantly slower than the rest, it can slow down the entire system. A component significantly faster than the rest of the machine may not be able to deliver the performance it is capable of. Beyond the basic issues of having memory that is of the type and speed required by your processor, the fundamental choices you make in computer configuration — the ones that can be expensive to change later — are these:

✦ *Processor type and speed.* Although you can upgrade the processor in most motherboards, the processor represents a significant percentage of the system cost. As processors have grown faster, low-end processor prices have stayed at $75 and up. The cost to put a faster processor into a new system is typically in the range of $100 to $200, but replacing the chip later could cost twice that.

✦ *Amount and type of cache.* Pentium II, Pentium III, and Celeron processors now include all cache in the processor cartridge, so cache upgrades are not possible. Some other manufacturers' processors still use external cache that may be subject to upgrades.

✦ *Amount, type, and configuration of memory.* Motherboards have only so many slots in which to plug memory modules. If you fill them, adding more memory to the system requires that you remove some of the memory you bought previously.

✦ *Bus type.* The dominance of the PCI bus is complete in current generation computers, particularly when supplanted with an Advanced Graphics Port (AGP) slot for the video card. It's difficult to impossible to buy a computer now without PCI.

Given you make these choices well, most of the other choices you make are less expensive to change. Faster video is a one-card change. Greater disk capacity can be a plug-in operation, or might require you to add an inexpensive controller. Chapter 8, "Processors," covers characterizing your workload, which is the analysis you need to do to refine this basic view.

Upgrading is far less straightforward than new machine configuration, even at this high level of analysis, because of the many different starting combinations possible. Workload analysis is particularly important for upgrades, because until you understand the limiting components in the machine, you can't be sure you'll get the performance you expect from an upgrade. Trial and error is not only time consuming, it can get to be very expensive if you don't have a well-stocked parts bin nearby.

## Summary

✦ Your processor executes instructions at a blindingly quick rate, but each instruction does one literal, simple thing. It takes a lot of instructions to do useful work.

✦ Every instruction requires one or more memory references, so cache memory that can provide high-speed memory access for some references lets the processor run without waiting.

✦ Parity and error correcting codes in memory help your computer detect and correct problems.

✦ The bus ties together the highest speed parts of your computer, so having a fast bus is crucial to great performance. The PCI bus has become the standard on modern computers.

✦ All of your computer components need to be in balance. Adding components that upset the balance gets you less performance than you paid for.

✦    ✦    ✦

# Processors

**B**ecause it contains the processor, bus, and memory, the motherboard is the core of your computer. This core and its vital components warrant a detailed discussion of their functions and relationship; they play a role in many upgrade decisions.

The most important decisions to make about a motherboard involve the processor, cache, bus, and memory you purchase initially. Those decisions define what options you have to upgrade the motherboard in the future. Most everything else you decide about the motherboard concerns secondary performance effects, convenience, or net system cost. The processor is the most visible one of those primary choices, so we'll start there.

You have a phenomenal range of options when you select the processor you want in your computer. You can get chips with a performance range of well over two-to-one (measured by the iCOMP Index 2.0 benchmark we'll discuss in the next section) just in the Intel Pentium II and the related Celeron processor line. You have the freedom to buy new processors from manufacturers including Intel, AMD, Cyrix, and others. You can get upgrade processors or kits from Kingston, Intel, AMD, and more.

## Intel: Pentium, Pentium Pro, Pentium II, Celeron, and Pentium III Processors

Figure 8-1 shows the range of performance and pricing (relative to each other) as of early 1999 for Intel processors from the Pentium through all but the latest members of the product line. The performance measure we used in Figure 8-1 is what Intel calls the iCOMP Index 2.0 rating, a benchmark they suggest for comparing the relative performance you can expect from different processors running 32-bit operating systems and software.

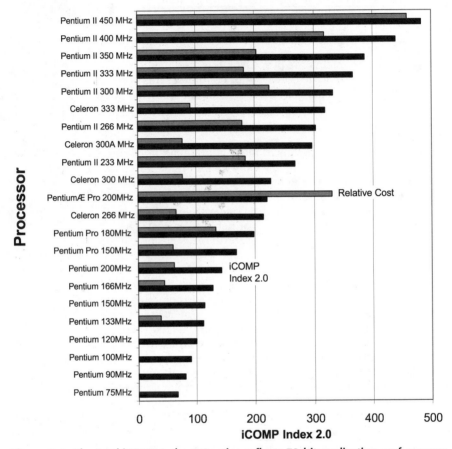

**Figure 8-1:** The Intel iCOMP Index 2.0 rating reflects 32-bit application performance (data courtesy Intel Corporation)

The iCOMP Index 2.0 replaced Intel's original iCOMP rating, a 16-bit evaluation score Intel used to compare 386 through Pentium and Pentium Pro processors. The original iCOMP rating was a composite of five 16-bit benchmarks (SPECint92, SPECfp92, Whetstone, PC Bench 7.0, and Landmark 2.00), while the iCOMP Index 2.0 combines five 32-bit benchmarks (CPUmark 32, Norton SI-32, SPECint 95, SPECfp 95, and the Intel Media Benchmark). The point of blending scores from multiple different benchmarks is to get a view of processor performance that is representative of a mix of things you might use the processor for. The iCOMP Index 2.0 is not directly comparable to the older iCOMP rating.

The increase in performance is consistent as you look from the bottom to the top of Figure 8-1, but the price you'll pay for the processors varies fairly dramatically. Figure 8-2 shows the same data as Figure 8-1 for the Pentium II and Celeron processors, but sorted by increasing price. What you can see more clearly in Figure 8-2 is that Intel has segmented its processor line. You can't see the timing of when the processors were available in Figure 8-2, but in practice Intel has set its product line so that Celeron processors will, at any instant of time, be lower in cost than the comparable Pentium II processors. As time goes on, the fastest Celerons overtake the slower Pentium IIs, which Intel then discontinues. The introduction of new Celerons and obsolescence of older Pentium IIs is what leads to the performance range overlap in Figure 8-2.

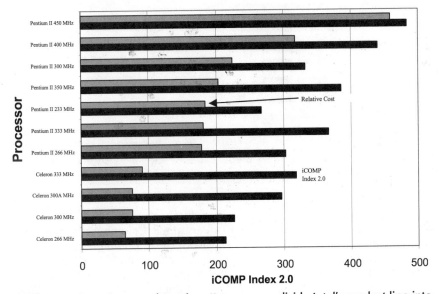

**Figure 8-2:** The Celeron and Pentium II processors divide Intel's product line into low-cost and high-performance segments.

Segmentation is a product strategy change for Intel. Several years ago, the Intel product line had the relative performance and cost values shown in Figure 8-3, with a smooth climb in both performance and cost until you reached the very high end of the product line (at which point you had to pay a premium for performance). The low-cost, entry-level machines available today are so capable, though, that the PC market itself fractured into a price-sensitive segment (under $1000 including monitor) and a specification/performance-driven segment (generally over $1000). In order to compete in the very low cost segment of the market, Intel had to develop processors whose selling price fit into the entry-level machine cost structure. The Celerons are those processors.

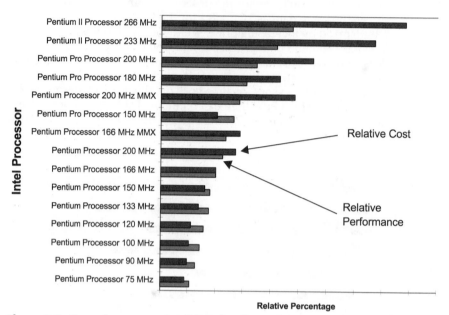

**Figure 8-3:** Several years ago, Intel's product line reflected a consistent increase in performance and price.

If you're putting in a new motherboard — or purchasing an entirely new computer — you're going to end up with a Pentium II, Celeron, or Pentium III processor (or the competitive equivalent). Even the Pentium processors are something you're going to find only on closeout from a liquidator, because (except for certain laptop computer versions) they haven't been manufactured for years. Even the low end of the Pentium II and Celeron lines are vanishing — the 233, 266, and 300 MHz Pentium IIs, and the earlier Celerons are no longer shipped in currently manufactured systems.

The relative prices of processor chips will change as Intel brings new products to market. You can expect that the price of all these processors will continue to decrease over time as new, faster ones come into production. The important things to keep in mind from this comparison when you're deciding what speed processor you should buy are these:

✦ You pay a definite premium for the fastest processors, with the price of newly introduced high-speed chips relatively higher than the speed increase would indicate.

✦ You pay a premium to upgrade a processor for more speed. This is partly because the new, faster processors are in demand, and partly because there's less competitive pressure — alternatives to direct processor upgrades may require replacing the motherboard and possibly the memory, and so they are more expensive than just swapping a chip.

Overall, you need to decide how much performance you need and what you're willing to pay for it. You'll use the processor for several years, and you can expect the demands your software will place on it to go up. What you're willing to pay should balance the immediate cost against the length of time the processor will meet your needs.

## So what's in these things, anyhow?

All the integrated circuits (chips) in your computer are small, flat pieces of silicon surrounded by a package. The structure of what's inside a typical processor package is shown in Figure 8-4 including the protective layer, metal layers, the devices themselves, the silicon substrate, and the package. Here's what each one does:

✦ *Protective layer.* This layer prevents changes in the chip properties due to exposure to the air.

✦ *Metal layers.* Metal lines are printed onto the devices to provide connections. The metal connections are similar to the lines on printed circuit cards, but much smaller and more carefully controlled.

✦ *Devices.* The devices that make the chip do what it does are printed onto the silicon substrate, using carefully controlled impurities to alter the characteristics of the pure silicon.

✦ *Silicon substrate.* The silicon substrate is the bulk of the pure, flat piece of silicon that the chip manufacturer starts with.

✦ *Package.* The package houses and protects the silicon chips. For processors like the Pentium and Pentium Pro, Figure 8-4 is upside down, because in final form the chip is bonded to the underside of the package.

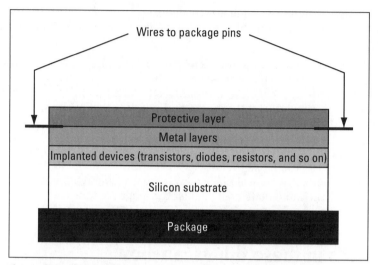

**Figure 8-4:** The inside of a chip is itself a complex assembly.

The chip manufacturer prints the devices and interconnections onto a very pure, flat piece of silicon, creating many chips at the same time on the same wafer of silicon. Individual chips (also called dies), which result from cutting the wafer apart, are bonded to cavities inside the package you actually see.

The photograph of a Pentium III processor chip in Figure 8-5 shows the starting point for package assembly—the photo is of the die for one processor after it's been cut from the wafer, and before the connecting leads are bonded on. The die mounts into the package, after which the leads connect pads on the die to the pins on the package. Once that's all in place, the cover goes on the package chip cavity and the completed chip goes off for testing.

Packaging is a critical part of processor design, because it's hard to extend the highest speed signals inside a chip to outside the package so that they can reach other chips. Extending the high-speed internal data bus to the L2 cache chips is one of the most difficult problems. Any extra lead lengths or stray signals could spell disaster for chips running at hundreds of megahertz. Intel addressed this problem first in the Pentium Pro, for which it put both the processor and cache chips in one package. The Pentium Pro package turned out to be too expensive, though, so for the Pentium II Intel introduced the Slot 1 cartridge, an assembly larger but less expensive than a Pentium Pro package that also houses both the processor and cache chips. (The initial Celeron processors were [electrically] Pentium II chips in cartridges that contained no cache chips.)

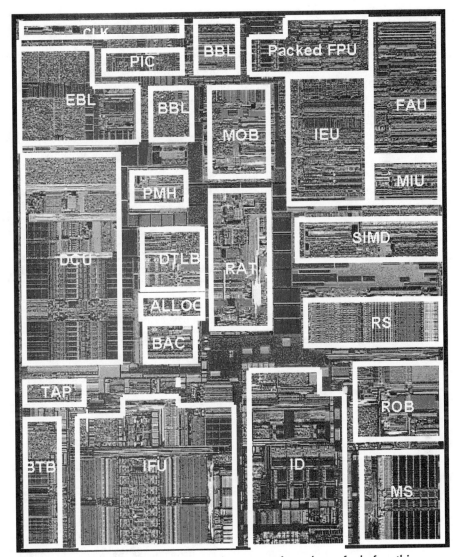

**Figure 8-5:** This Pentium III processor die was cut from the wafer before this photograph was taken. (Courtesy of Intel Corporation.)

# Breaking down the die shot

The 9.5 million transistors in the Pentium III die shot of Figure 8-4 implement a large number of complex functions. Intel's processor designers approach the design task the way all engineers do, by partitioning the overall complex function into smaller, well-defined units. The overlay of rectangles and identifiers on the die shot show how the units of the Pentium III are distributed on the die.

We'll cover the role of many of these functions in the next sections of this chapter — as you read through the material, you might want to flip back to this sidebar to see where the different functions are located.

The bottom-left quadrant implements the front end of the instruction processing pipeline:

| Unit Identifier | Unit Name and Function |
| --- | --- |
| IFU | Instruction Fetch Unit. Instruction fetch logic and a 16KB four-way set-associative level 1 instruction cache reside in this block. Instruction data from the IFU is then forwarded to the ID. |
| BTB | Branch Target Buffer. This block is responsible for dynamic branch prediction based on the history of past branch decisions paths. |
| BAC | Branch Address Calculator. Static branch prediction is performed here to handle the BTB miss case. |
| TAP | Testability Access Port. Various testability and debug mechanisms reside within this block. |

The bottom-right quadrant implements the instruction decode, scheduling, dispatch, and retirement functions:

| Unit Identifier | Unit Name and Function |
| --- | --- |
| ID | Instruction Decoder. This unit is capable of decoding up to three instructions per cycle. |
| MS | Micro-Instruction Sequencer. This holds the microcode ROM and sequencer for more complex instruction flows. The microcode update functionality is also located here. |
| RS | Reservation Station. Micro-instructions and source data are held here for scheduling and dispatch to the execution ports. Dispatch can happen out of order and is dependent on source data availability and an available execution port. |
| ROB | Re-Order Buffer. This supports a 40-entry physical register file that holds temporary write-back results that can complete out of order. These results are then committed to a separate architectural register file during in-order retirement. |

The top-right quadrant implements the execution datapath:

| Unit Identifier | Unit Name and Function |
| --- | --- |
| SIMD | SIMD integer execution unit for MMX instructions. |
| MIU | Memory Interface Unit. This is responsible for data conversion and formatting for floating-point data types. |
| IEU | Integer Execution Unit. This is responsible for ALU functionality of scalar integer instructions. Address calculations for memory referencing instructions are also performed here along with target address calculations for jump-related instructions. |
| FAU | Floating Point Arithmetic Unit. This performs floating point–related calculations for existing scalar instructions along with support for some of the new SIMD-FP instructions. |
| PFAU | Packed Floating Point Arithmetic Unit. This contains arithmetic execution data-path functionality for SIMD-FP specific instructions. |

Finally, the top-left quadrant contains functions including the bus interface, data cache access, and allocation.

| Unit Identifier | Unit Name and Function |
| --- | --- |
| ALLOC | Allocator. Allocation of various resources such as ROB, MOB, and RS entries is performed here prior to micro-instruction dispatch by the RS. |
| RAT | Register Alias Table. During resource allocation the renaming of logical to physical registers is performed here. |
| MOB | Memory Order Buffer. Acts as a separate schedule and dispatch engine for data loads and stores. Also temporarily holds the state of outstanding loads and stores from dispatch until completion. |
| DTLB | Data Translation Look-Aside Buffer. Performs the translation from linear addresses to physical addresses required for support of virtual memory. |
| PMH | Page Miss Handler. Hardware engine for performing a page table walk in the event of a TLB miss. |
| DCU | Data Cache Unit. Contains the non-blocking 16KB four-way set-associative level 1 data cache along with associated fill and write-back buffering. |
| BBL | Back-side Bus Logic. Logic for interface to the back-side bus for accesses to the external unified level 2 processor cache. |
| EBL | External Bus Logic. Logic for interface to the external front-side bus. |
| PIC | Programmable Interrupt Controller. Local interrupt controller logic for multiprocessor interrupt distribution and boot-up communication. |

# Pipelining and superscalar execution

Intel packed over 3 million transistors into the Pentium chip, over 5 million into the Pentium Pro chip (not counting the cache chip also in the package), over 7.5 million into the Pentium II, and 9.5 million into the Pentium III. The Pentium II chips have over twice the number of transistors as the Pentium processor chips, but (as shown in Figure 8-6) they are much smaller, a result of an improved manufacturing process that put more transistors in a smaller area.

4004   8080   8085   8086   8088   80286   386   386SL   486™CPU   Pentium® Processor   Pentium®II Processor

**Figure 8-6:** Die sizes grow with complexity (number of transistors) and shrink as manufacturing processes improve density. (Drawing courtesy of Intel Corporation.)

Early transistor radios needed only tens of transistors to receive radio broadcasts, a completely insignificant number against the millions of transistors in these processors. It's clear just from the numbers that all those transistors are doing more than fetching instructions and adding numbers. The Pentium Pro, Pentium II, Celeron, and Pentium III processors (often called the P6 family) all share a similar architecture, so in this discussion we'll call them the P6 processors.

✦ *Superscalar instruction execution.* Superscalar execution is a way to get more work done at once by having more than one instruction in progress at any one time. The Pentium and P6 processors implement superscalar execution using a "pipeline" in the chip. Figure 8-7 shows how the pipeline in the chip is like firemen delivering buckets of water. When there's just one fireman to do all the work — the equivalent of the top of the figure — it takes at least one clock tick to do each step, and nothing happens in parallel. Firemen get more buckets in motion with a bucket brigade, splitting the job up into multiple tasks that feed forward from one to another. That's what's going on in the bottom of the figure. The pipeline is the equivalent of a bucket brigade, allowing more parallel elements of the processor to work on the job and getting more work done every clock tick.

Each of the "firefighters" in a processor pipeline is called a *stage* in the pipeline. Each stage is different from the others, specialized to the work it has to do. The Pentium processor has five stages in its pipeline, while the P6 processors have 12.

The work the complete pipeline does is the same in the Pentium and Pentium Pro, because they execute the same instructions. This means that having more stages in the Pentium Pro allows each stage to do less work. You can think of it as the stage doing one twelfth of the total instead of one fifth.

Because the stages in the Pentium Pro do less work, they are simpler, which in turn allows Intel's designers to pump them up to run them faster.

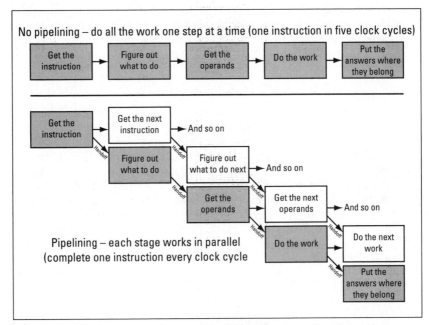

**Figure 8-7:** The pipeline in the Pentium and Pentium Pro lets the processor execute more than one instruction in a single clock cycle.

The Pentium incorporates two pipelines that execute instructions independently. The five stages in the Pentium pipelines are

- Prefetch
- Instruction Decode
- Address Generation
- Execution
- Write Back

These stages correspond to the functions in Figure 8-7. The capability of the two pipelines to execute independently means that under ideal conditions a Pentium can execute two instructions every clock tick. A 200 MHz Pentium can hit a peak instruction issue rate of 400 million instructions per second (MIPS). The P6 processors are capable (ideally) of five instructions per clock tick, so the 450 MHz chip can theoretically issue instructions at 2,250 MIPS.

We're not going to suggest that those numbers are achievable for sustained execution rates, because they're not. Nor are we going to state what the real-life sustained instruction issue rates are for these processors, because the performance you get depends on what you do. Rather than make overly simplified estimates, you should run benchmarks that reflect your real workload or consult composite benchmarks such as the Intel iCOMP Index 2.0.

✦ *Separate code and data caches.* The Pentium and P6 processors all maintain separate physical L1 caches for instructions and data. Splitting the caches creates parallelism, allowing the processor to retrieve instructions and data from the cache at the same time, and prevents the flow of large volumes of data through the cache from flushing out the instructions being executed.

**Cross-Reference**

See "Feeding the Hungry Beast: Cache Memory" in Chapter 7 for more information.

We've redone the drawing of the single pipeline from the bottom of Figure 8-7 as Figure 8-8 to show why the split L1 cache is important. The split cache allows all three operations in the figure (instruction read, operand read, and operand write) to happen in the same clock cycle, enabling the processor to get the full benefit of the pipeline parallelism. At least three cache accesses are possible every clock tick from this five-stage pipeline, one reading an instruction, one reading data, and one writing data. Splitting the L1 cache into an instruction cache and a data cache makes these accesses possible simultaneously, because a cache can do a read and a write at the same time. The split cache provides the increased memory access required to support the pipeline doing multiple things at once without having to wait.

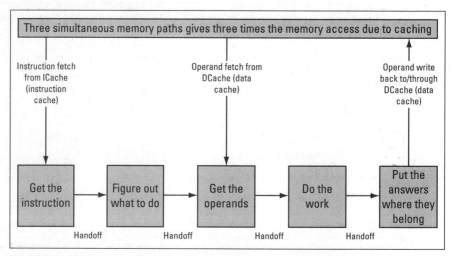

**Figure 8-8:** Splitting the L1 cache into separate instruction (ICache) and data (DCache) caches improves performance by increasing the number of simultaneous accesses to the cache.

✦ *Dynamic Branch Prediction.* If you look at the pipeline in Figure 8-8, you'll see that the processor has to know the address of the instruction that comes third after the one being executed — that is, while the box "do the work" is running, the box "get the instruction" is fetching three instructions ahead.

Suppose the processor comes across an instruction sequence like this:

1. Load the value of COLOR.

2. Test if COLOR equals GREEN.

3. Store a new value in COLOR.

4. If the old value of COLOR was GREEN, the next instruction is number 1. Otherwise, the next instruction is number 5. (An instruction like this one is called a branch.)

At the time the processor is doing the work for the instruction number one in the example, the pipeline is loading instruction number four. The processor next does the work for the instruction at two. At that time, the first pipeline stage ("get the instruction") needs to know what instruction to load. Because the processor won't know what instruction to execute after instruction four until it executes instruction four and makes the branch decision, the pipeline has a problem: The "get the instruction" box doesn't know what to do.

Some older processors solved this problem by doing nothing. In those chips, the pipeline empties out after loading a branch until that instruction executes. In our example, three cycles would pass with no instructions being executed (a *pipeline stall*) while the instruction after number four loads, is looked at, and gets its operands. More complex processor designs do a simple form of branch prediction by assuming that the next instruction is always the one immediately after the branch. If this assumption is true, the processor loses no time. If it's wrong, the processor stalls for a number of cycles while it loads the right instruction.

A more sophisticated approach to branch prediction is to recognize that many branches are there to make the code loop, and so they will be executed over and over. This approach suggests that the most likely next instruction the second time the branch is seen is the instruction that followed the branch last time. The Pentium and P6 processors all use this strategy and improve on it by fetching both the instruction immediately after the branch and the one that followed the branch the last time through the loop.

✦ *Floating Point Execution Pipeline.* The Pentium and P6 processors include a separate pipeline for computations using floating-point numbers (which are numbers that are not integers, such as 3.14159 or 42.000001). The Pentium floating-point pipeline is the same as the pipeline in Figure 8-8 for the first four stages but then has four more floating point–specific stages. Figure 8-9 shows the resulting eight-stage pipeline. Overall, the Pentium floating-point pipeline can execute two floating-point instructions in one clock cycle.

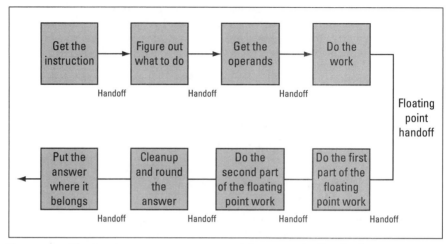

**Figure 8-9:** The Pentium processor uses an eight-stage pipeline for floating-point calculations.

✦ *Enhanced 64-Bit Data Bus.* The Pentium and P6 processors all use a 64-bit data bus, twice the width of the bus on the old 486. These processors transfer twice as much data to and from memory at a time as the 486 did in one cycle. They also cycle the cache faster than the 486, leading to a net access rate five times faster than the 486. Table 8-1 shows the details. The combination of twice the bus width, less than one half the cycle time, and over twice the number of memory cycles per second nets out at the factor of five increase in maximum host bus data rate shown in the table.

✦ *Bus cycle pipelining to increase bus bandwidth.* Bus cycle pipelining, implemented on the Pentium, allows a second cycle to start before the first one is completed, which works well with EDO memory.

| Table 8-1 Comparison of 486 and Pentium Processing Rates | | | |
|---|---|---|---|
| **Processor** | **Maximum Host Bus Data Rate (MBps)** | **Bus Width (Bytes)** | **Millions of Memory Cycles per Second** | **Cycle Time (ns)** |
| Pentium | 528 | 8 | 66 | 16 |
| 486 | 105 | 4 | 26.25 | 39 |

## Dynamic execution

The biggest difference between the Pentium and the P6 processors is increased sophistication of the analysis of the instruction stream and use of the results — a technology Intel calls Dynamic Execution. In the discussion of Dynamic Branch

Prediction in the preceding section, you saw that the uncertainty following a branch instruction could cause the processor pipelines to stall. Other problems cause pipeline stalls too. For example, look at this sequence:

1. Load the value of COLOR.

2. Load the value of SATURATION.

3. Multiply COLOR times SATURATION.

4. Store the multiplication result in COLOR.

The first two instructions can be executed in parallel by the pipelines, but the third instruction has to wait for the first two, and the fourth has to wait for the third. Adding more pipelines to the basic Pentium architecture won't make this sequence faster because of the dependencies among the instructions that cause a conventional pipeline to stall.

The P6 processors are vastly more complex than the Pentium. Intel's engineers devoted a great deal of the additional complexity to solving the pipeline stall problem, because eliminating stalls increases the sustained instruction issue rate. Figure 8-10 shows what they did. The P6 processors break up the linear pipeline structure of the Pentium (refer to the bottom portion of Figure 8-7). The P6 processor execution structure (Figure 8-10) executes instructions a pipeline stage at a time but returns the result to the execution pool between stages. Each stage takes the next instruction it can work on, even if it's out of linear order. This means that the handoff between pipeline stages doesn't have to be in rigid, linear lock step. Instead, each pipeline stage can look into what Intel calls the "instruction pool" for the next instruction it can work on. The control circuits for the instruction pool ensure that necessary dependencies between instructions are observed, but they otherwise allow for out-of-linear-order instruction execution.

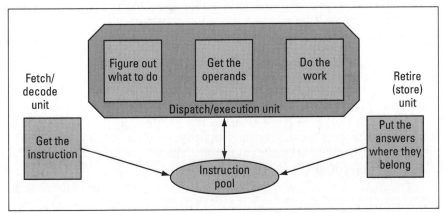

**Figure 8-10:** The key to faster execution in the P6 processors is to keep the high-speed pipeline stages busy.

Extending the preceding example lets us illustrate the advantage of the P6 processors.

1. Load the value of COLOR.

2. Load the value of SATURATION.

3. Multiply COLOR times SATURATION.

4. Store the multiplication result in COLOR.

5. Load the value of CHANNEL.

6. Add one to CHANNEL.

7. Store the updated CHANNEL in SURFCHANNEL.

The advantage the P6 processors have over the Pentium and earlier processors is that even though the instructions at steps three and four may stall, the fetch/decode unit will continue to fill the instruction pool from steps five through seven. At the point the dispatch execution unit stalls at three, the instruction at five will be available. The dispatch execution unit picks up that instruction (and its successors) and keeps working. No cycles are wasted on pipeline stalls, so your program runs faster.

Intel also improved the memory access performance of the P6 processors. Figure 8-11 extends Figure 8-10 to show how—in both the Pentium and the P6—the split L1 cache ties to a bus interface unit, which is an engine that works to get information from the L2 cache or the host bus. New in the P6 processors is a direct interface to the L2 cache from the bus interface unit. This isn't possible in the Pentium because the L2 cache is external to the Pentium package, and there aren't enough pins on the package to add separate connections to the L2 cache. The Pentium Pro includes the L2 cache as a second silicon chip within the package, so it doesn't need additional pins for connection to the cache. The Pentium II includes the L2 cache in the processor cartridge, within which Intel can maintain a controlled environment for propagation of the necessary high-speed signals. The initial Celeron processors omitted the Pentium II L2 cache; later Celerons use a version of the Pentium II cache design.

Parallel access paths to the system bus and the L2 cache give the later processors a huge increase in performance. While the system bus makes a memory or I/O access taking 60ns or more, the processor can continue to pull instructions and data from the L2 cache with an access time of 8ns to 16ns. In the time the system bus makes one cycle, the processor can get nearly eight cycles from the L2 cache. The increased access rate helps the fetch/decode unit, the dispatch execution unit, and the retire unit avoid stalling, boosting performance.

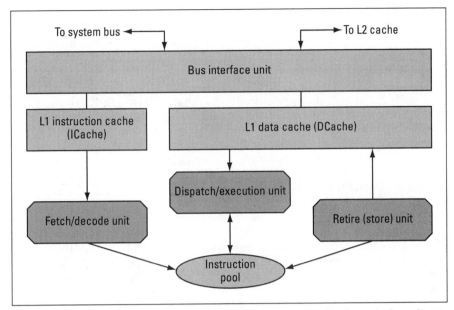

**Figure 8-11:** The decoupled pipeline in the Pentium Pro works through the split L1 cache to the L2 cache and the system bus.

# MMX and SSE (Streaming SIMD Extensions)

One of the questions you want to ask when you're after high-end performance is "what comes next? What's in the labs that is faster yet, and when will it show up?"

Intel started shipping the MMX technology extensions to the current Pentium processor in late 1996. MMX is an addition to the Intel instruction set that improves performance for applications like full-motion video, speech recognition, video conferencing, and image processing, some of the most demanding applications on a Windows PC. Software for those applications using the new MMX instructions registered performance gains of from 1.5 to 4 times the performance of a non-MMX processor.

MMX provides additional instructions that give the processor the capability to process parallel streams of data, such as the values for left and right audio channels, with a single instruction stream. Combining stereo this way doubles the power of the individual instruction; handling more streams (such as red, green, blue, and intensity for color images) delivers more power. The capability for one instruction to handle several data streams is called Single Instruction Multiple Data technology, or SIMD. The MMX SIMD instructions work on integers only, though, and switching between floating-point operation and MMX operation is time consuming.

An extension to MMX known as the Streaming SIMD Extensions (SSE) first appeared in the Pentium III processors. SSE adds to floating-point computations the same capability MMX delivered for integers. Overall, then, Pentium II processors are essentially Pentium Pro processors with the MMX extensions, while Pentium III processors are Pentium Pro processors with MMX and SSE.

MMX and SSE do another wonderful thing. Suppose the range of values you're working on runs from 0 to 255. If you're scaling the value up or down, it's entirely possible that the value could go below 0 or above 255, creating what's called underflow or overflow respectively. If you don't limit the value to the range 0 through 255, the results will be wrong. Without MMX or SSE, you'd have to test for over/underflow and do the correction in software, including a time-consuming jump around the instruction that corrects the error. With MMX or SSE, you just use the new instructions providing range-limited arithmetic. The values get "clamped" at the extremes, and the program continues on as if nothing special had happened.

It's hard to answer the question of how you should react to the continuing march of new PC technology developments. Over any six-month period in the last few years, the increases in performance you could get in a PC, or the drops in price, were nothing short of astounding. You can always get more performance or a lower price by waiting, but you have to balance waiting against the problem of what to use while you wait. If the machine you want is really several years off, it's pretty clear that you should consider the current generation in the meantime. If it's six months off, you have to look at what you can get now versus the premium you'll pay and pain you'll suffer as an early adopter of a brand new product.

## Is the OverDrive worth the cost?

PC processor technology advances so fast that several generations will pass during the life of many PCs. Users expand the workloads they process with their PCs to take advantage of the power in new machines.

The machines in the middle or near the end of their lives become problems as workloads expand, because the older, slower machines often don't have the processor power to support the newer, bigger workloads. Some motherboards support dropping in faster chips, but (depending on the characteristics of the newer chips) many don't. Manufacturers recognized that problem years ago and created versions of the new chips retrofitted to adapt to older motherboards. Intel calls those chips OverDrive processors.

When you go to upgrade the processor in an older machine, you have these overall choices:

✦ *Direct Chip Replacement.* If your motherboard allows it, you can simply install the faster chip in the socket, replacing the old one. You change the motherboard settings for the faster parameters and you're done. If the motherboard supports it, this is your least expensive option.

✦ *OverDrive.* You can drop an OverDrive into your existing motherboard, increasing the processor clock rate in motherboards that aren't otherwise capable of the faster speed. It's quick and simple. Intel never built OverDrive processors that would take a Pentium to a Pentium II but does make OverDrives that will upgrade a Pentium Pro — you can update a 200 MHz Pentium Pro to a Pentium II processor running at 333 MHz.

✦ *Motherboard Replacement.* Your third choice is to replace the entire motherboard with one carrying a faster chip. You need to know what you're doing, and you may have to replace the memory in addition to the motherboard and processor.

Not all motherboards can handle OverDrive processors. You can get more information from your system or motherboard manufacturer, or on the Intel Web site (http://www.intel.com).

Before you jump at any processor upgrade, be sure that the processor really is the choke point for what you want to speed up. For instance, if your bottleneck is really a slow video card, a faster processor won't give you much of a boost. If the system is well balanced, though — if you already know that you have enough memory and the disk and video are what they need to be (such as a PCI SCSI disk controller and a good 3D accelerated AGP video card) — you might be ready for a processor upgrade. If you don't know, some benchmarking might be in order.

## Support chip sets

Early on, the chips surrounding the processor in a PC were there to help it run and to provide the minimal functions necessary for ISA bus support. The chips you found on the motherboard included a clock generator (which was the part of the processor that somehow never fit on the chip itself), a direct memory access (DMA) controller, an interrupt controller, a timer chip, the BIOS chips, and some other small stuff. All those circuits are still required in your computer, but (with the exception of the BIOS) they've been taken over by the chips that support the much faster structures you now use, including the host bus and the PCI bus.

Figure 8-12 shows how things started. Most of the chips on early motherboards had to do with the care and feeding of the processor (like the clock generator), and with helping the processor handle interfaces to the outside world (like the DMA, interrupts, and timer chips). The simplicity of the bus interface — not much more than chips to strengthen the signals from the processor — was possible because the speeds of the processor and memory (on the ISA bus) were reasonably closely matched. That match wasn't an accident, since the ISA bus began as an extension of the bus on the Intel 8088 processor. The placement of added memory, video, disk, and sound functions on the ISA bus further simplified the motherboard design, because all the complexity tended to be on plug-in cards.

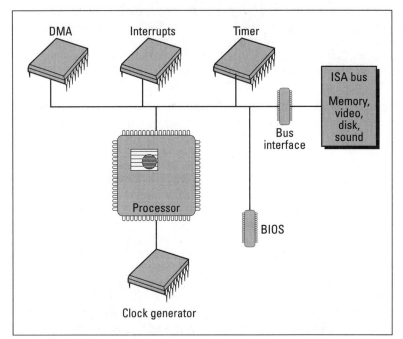

**Figure 8-12:** Most of the chips on early motherboards had to do with the care and feeding of the processor.

Processor speed increased faster than the speed of memory in the evolution of the PC. System and processor designers responded with faster, more complex designs that solved the resulting problems and exploited the additional power possible in larger, faster chips dedicated to specific functions. In the case of the logic that goes on a motherboard, the result was chipsets (Intel calls them PCIsets) (Figure 8-13) that encapsulate nearly all the circuits surrounding the processor and controlling the host and PCI buses.

The PCI bus is enormously more complex to implement than the ISA bus, because the speed gain PCI delivers required sophisticated system and processor designs. Bringing that complexity to market at a low price has required that specialized PCIset chips encapsulate the complete PCI functionality. Elements of the chip set support the processor host bus, the cache and main memory, the PCI bus itself, and integrated peripherals including a PCI IDE disk controller.

Although Intel uses numbers like 82430 for the PCIsets, the computer industry has latched onto the Intel code names, such as Neptune and Triton for the Pentium and Orion or Natomi for the Pentium Pro. Recent P6 processor PCIset code names include Carmel, Whitney, Bannister, Colusa, and Camino. Some of the features moved into the PCIsets include

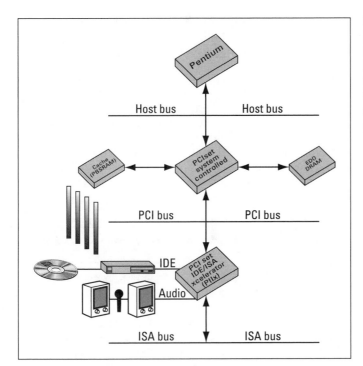

**Figure 8-13:** A PCIset provides the control and support electronics for the processor in a high-performance computer design. (PCISet drawing courtesy Intel Corporation.)

✦ *EDO, SDRAM, ECC, and Rambus support.* The PCIset provides the interface between the processor and main memory. The capabilities in the PCIset determine what memory types your motherboard will handle. The PCIset also determines whether the memory interface supports parity or error correcting codes.

✦ *IDE and Bus-Mastering IDE.* Many PCI chip sets implement a PCI IDE disk interface, enabling support for Fast ATA disks. Some implement a bus-mastering DMA interface, meaning that the processor can go do other work while the transfer takes place. You won't see better disk performance from bus-mastering IDE, but you will see lower processor usage during disk transfers. Because some older disks do not support the option correctly, you should be very careful enabling bus-mastered IDE on an older machine not certified for bus-mastering IDE by the manufacturer. If you built or upgraded the machine yourself, you should conduct extensive read/write disk testing to make sure there are no hidden issues after you enable bus-mastered IDE. (See the sidebar "The importance of testing bus-mastered IDE" that follows.)

✦ *Peripheral support, including audio and USB.* The newest PCIsets add support for audio on the motherboard, eliminating the need for a sound card, and support for the Universal Serial Bus (USB). PCIsets for low-cost machines include built-in video card functions, eliminating yet another separate card.

Table 8-2 summarizes the current Intel PCIsets, including the features you're likely to care about when picking a motherboard. Only a few PCIsets support multiple processors. Most require SDRAM; it's indicative that the PCIset for the next-generation processor, the Pentium III, supports Rambus. The 810, with its support for the Celeron plus on-chip audio and 3D graphics is clearly targeted at the very low cost market segment, because it will make possible complete full-function PCs with very few chips on the motherboard.

## The importance of testing bus-mastered IDE

We can't overstate the importance of carefully testing bus-mastered integrated drive electronics (IDE). A related example showing problems due to elements in the disk subsystem not meeting specifications should make the point. A computer of ours had been running reliably for well over a year when we decided to experiment with changing the BIOS settings for a faster IDE transfer rate. We set the maximum transfer rate based on specifications for the disk and what we read in the BIOS manual, and saved the new setting. Some cursory tests said everything looked OK, with a nice increase in disk performance. About two days later, though, disaster struck: the machine refused to boot because a critical Windows file was corrupt.

As we investigated, we discovered that about 20 percent of the files on the disk were trashed. We reset the disk interface speed and rebuilt the machine from tape backups we had made before we started experimenting. There's no parity checking on the IDE disk interface like there is on a SCSI bus, so marginal timing between the faster operation we'd set into the motherboard and the disk wouldn't be detected when it failed. That means that when Windows wrote to the disk, garbled data due to missing the timing was silently stored on the disk, corrupting the good data that was there. There was no warning that disaster had occurred, and the problem wouldn't come to light until the next time the system read the trashed file.

The lesson here is that the IDE interface is unforgiving because it doesn't incorporate error checking. You can't verify that high performance settings are working right without a lot of careful testing. Worse yet, there have been IDE drives that actually misreported their capabilities, making testing more important.

Table 8-2
**Intel PCIset Overview**

| PCIset | 450NX | 440GX | 820 | 440BX | 440ZX | 440ZX66 | 440LX | 440EX | 810 |
|---|---|---|---|---|---|---|---|---|---|
| Code Name | | | Camino | | | | | | Whitney |
| Processors Supported | Pentium II and III Xeon | Pentium II and III Xeon | Pentium III | Pentium II, III, or Celeron | Pentium II, III, and newer Celeron | Celeron | Pentium II or Celeron | Celeron | Celeron |
| Maximum Number of Processors | 4 | 2 | 2 | 2 | 1 | 1 | 2 | 1 | 1 |
| Host Bus Speed (MHz) | 100 | 100 | 100 or 133 | 66 or 100 | 100 | 66 | 66 | 66 | 66 or 100 |
| Memory Types | EDO | SDRAM | Rambus | SDRAM | SDRAM | SDRAM | EDO or SDRAM | EDO or SDRAM | SDRAM |
| Maximum Number of Memory Banks | 8 | 8 | 3 | 8 | 4 | 4 | 8 | 4 | 4 |
| Maximum System Memory (MB) | 8192 | 8192 | 1024 | 1024 | 256 | 256 | 1024 EDO / 512 SDRAM | 256 | 512 |
| Audio | No | No | No | No | No | No | No | No | Yes |
| AGP | No | 2X | 4X | 2X | 2X | 2X | 2X | 2X | 2X |
| 3D Graphics | No | No | No | No | No | No | No | No | Yes |
| USB | Yes | Yes | Yes | Yes | Yes | Yes | Yes | Yes | Yes |

# AMD

The Intel-compatible processor market is so large that it was impossible for companies to resist building competitors to the Intel chips. AMD licensed designs from Intel for a while but moved on to design and build its own independent designs.

Because Intel is the standard for Windows computers, you have to evaluate competitive alternatives to Intel processors for compatibility with the Intel designs, not just against the usual price/performance issues.

## P6 Competition: The AMD K6 and K6-2

AMD's competitors to the P6 processors — the K6 and K6-2, and the recent K7 — have earned a place as highly credible designs in the Intel-compatible market. Benchmark data from AMD reflected in Figure 8-14 shows the K6 200 MMX processors to be competitive with the Intel products; the later K6-2 processors similarly competed on fairly equal terms with the Pentium II processors. Field experience with the chips showed them to be highly compatible; the only highly notable AMD-specific patches we found on the Internet had to do with some timing loops coded directly into Windows. Those problems are not due to AMD compatibility problems; nor did we find confirmed reports of AMD-caused compatibility issues.

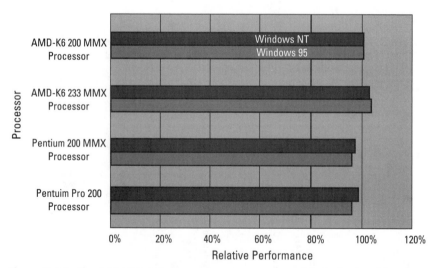

**Figure 8-14:** The AMD K6 delivers performance comparable to the Intel Pentium Pro, establishing the company as a serious competitor.

The K6 and K6-2 processors are interesting P6 competitors because of a number of features AMD designed in:

✦ *Multimedia instructions.* AMD reworked its initial design to implement the Intel MMX technology, and then it added 3DNow! (similar to some of the Intel SSE instructions).

✦ *Pentium socket compatibility.* The K6 and K6-2 plug into many enhanced Pentium processor Socket 7 motherboards (the "Super Socket 7" which, unfortunately, isn't well standardized), so existing motherboards may benefit from an upgrade. You'll want to check with AMD or your motherboard manufacturer to verify electrical and BIOS compatibility before installing one in your system.

✦ *Large L1 cache.* The processors have relatively larger cache; the K6 has a 64KB L1 cache, split into 32KB each for instructions and data.

The internal architecture breaks instructions down into smaller steps, much like the P6 processors. Parallel decoders, branch prediction, a high-performance floating-point unit, and other techniques similar to the P6 processors combine in a six-stage pipeline for excellent performance.

Although Figure 8-14 shows the AMD processors as comparable to the Intel processors, the measurements reflect office automation applications. Their floating-point performance has historically been far worse than the Intel processors. AMD addressed some of its floating-point issues with the 3DNow! instructions, but applications must be tuned to use the new instructions.

## Performance

New and upgrade chips competing with the Pentium and P6 processors are not as obviously easy to choose as was the AMD 486 upgrade, because Intel does not license the Pentium or P6 processor designs to other companies as it did the 486. Competitors have to create their own designs that are indistinguishable to software from the Intel chips. Because we're talking about devices with 3 million to 8 million transistors, this is hard; hard enough that AMD introduced its first processors with Pentium architectural features like superscalar architecture in 1996, well after the first Pentium processor shipped. The initial models offered performance similar to the 75 and 90 MHz Pentium processors. You won't find plug-in competitive replacements for the P6 processors, because Intel holds patents on the interface to the P6 bus for those chips. Intel has licensed the patents to chipset vendors. Cyrix and IBM do have P6 bus patent licenses but have not chosen to market bus-compatible processors.

## Compatibility above all else

The makers of Intel-compatible processors have to provide complete compatibility with the Intel products, because you as a purchaser have to know that your software runs without problems on their chips. If you couldn't be sure of that, no amount of improved performance or reduced cost could make the purchase worthwhile.

Compatibility is paramount. The old Intel 8080 processor, for example, did some odd things with the status flags that characterized the results of arithmetic instructions. Some time after the introduction of the Intel 8080, a competing manufacturer (not AMD) introduced an 8080 "replacement" that was significantly faster. Unfortunately, the manufacturer had "improved" Intel's design to correct the status flag "flaws." Somehow, it didn't seem important to the manufacturer that the change caused a lot of software programmed to work around the supposed flaws not to work. They probably sold some of those chips somewhere after this incompatibility came to light, but not very many. Speed always takes second place to compatible operation, and few chip manufacturers since then have dared to deviate from absolute equivalence to Intel's documented specifications.

With the variety of processors on the market, there's no end of opportunity for confusion about how fast you can expect your system to be using one processor versus another. Intel addressed the issue of comparing performance within the Intel processor line with the iCOMP, iCOMP Index 2.0, and iCOMP Index 3.0 rating systems. Those ratings are unique to Intel, however, not industry-wide standards. If you're considering competitive processors, you need a way to compare.

**Cross-Reference**

AMD uses an independent Windows-based benchmark (the Winstone tests, discussed in the section "The WinBench and Winstone Benchmarks" in Chapter 35,) to measure processor performance. Many other sources (such as hardware reviews on the Internet) use the same benchmarks, so you can take that information and compare it to the prices you'd pay for a variety of upgrades.

Courts have held that manufacturers can replicate Intel's instruction set, but they have imposed difficult conditions for doing so. The competitor can't reverse-engineer what Intel has done, taking apart the Intel product to replicate what it does. Instead, they have to start with a specification of what the product has to do and create a new, independent design. Engineering in compatibility starts very early in the design cycle, well before first chip production. It's difficult and expensive.

AMD's approach to achieve strict compatibility includes the following:

✦ *High-level compatibility model.* Before AMD's engineers design the first circuit in a new processor, they look at the architectural features (like pipelines) they plan to use. The high-level compatibility model allows them to understand how those features will perform against the Intel instruction set. Design doesn't continue until they achieve a mix of features that provide the desired performance.

✦ *Register behavior model and logic model tests.* As designers work out finer and finer details of the design, these models help them verify that the design still meets the specification. Getting errors out of the design early is a big cost saver, so continuous modeling and simulation is essential to getting the product to market.

✦ *Hardware emulation.* This is the final verification before building chips. The actual chip hardware design is run on a computer designed to simulate chip operation. The combination is fast enough to make it practical to run real operating systems and application software, greatly increasing the visibility into the operation of the chip and helping to uncover subtle errors.

✦ *System-level tests.* Once chips come off AMD's line, they go into computers and begin an extensive test sequence to ensure that they run Windows and other PC operating systems and applications; and they also undergo a wide variety of specialized hardware and software tests (including tests by independent laboratories).

## Cost

Assuming you're only looking at products that pass compatibility tests, your choice of processor comes down to the performance you get and the price you pay. At the beginning of 1999, a street-price comparison of a 350 MHz AMD K6-2 to a 350 MHz Intel Pentium II and to a 366 MHz Celeron showed AMD's price to be about 50 percent lower than the Pentium II and 30 percent lower than the Celeron. Comparative Winstone numbers published by AMD show similar performance, although the Intel chips will be faster for applications requiring extensive floating-point calculation. For upgrades where the performance fits your equipment and needs, the AMD products could save you money.

# Cyrix

Cyrix is a small company founded in 1988 to produce Intel-compatible processors. The company develops and markets the processors, relying on partners IBM Micro-electronics and SGS Thomson to manufacture the chips. The company once sold chips to upgrade 386 processors to 486 performance but now focuses on processors for the lowest cost segment of the PC market.

**Note**     The 6X86 processor generates an incredible amount of heat. If you're going to use one, make sure you have an extra-powerful CPU fan, and that there's great airflow within the chassis. If you don't, you're likely to cook something expensive.

The Cyrix processors target the low-cost end of the PC market, but deliver bottom end performance too. Unless your computing requirements are very modest, with price more important than any performance considerations, we'd recommend a system based on the AMD or Intel Celeron chips.

# Multiprocessor Configurations

Building faster processors is not the only way to make a faster computer. Adding multiple processors is a relatively inexpensive way to get more speed. You don't need to add more disks or other peripherals when you add another processor; in fact, in some designs you don't even add a second L2 cache.

In all cases, you need UNIX or Windows NT to support multiprocessing. Windows 9x is exclusively a uniprocessor operating system and will studiously ignore all those other processors.

## Expected performance gains

You don't get four times the performance from a four-processor system. The overhead of coordinating the operation of multiple processors, limitations on main memory, and limitations on your software's capability to keep multiple processors busy reduce the payoff you get. Figure 8-15 shows the idea, although the actual shape of the curve you get will vary depending on the system implementation and the software you run. In all likelihood, you will see performance gains less than shown in the figure.

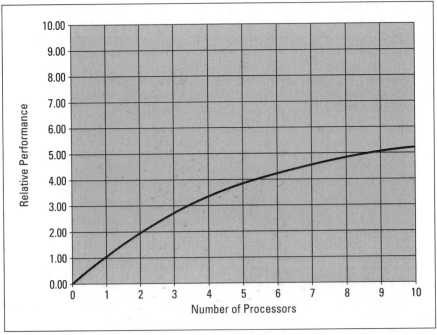

**Figure 8-15:** You don't gain full measure by adding processors to your computer.

The only reliable way you can know the performance gain you get from a particular multiprocessor system is to measure performance running your own workload. The behavior of multiprocessor systems is simply too complex to allow accurate predictions (other than, perhaps, through simulation). For example, consider the following factors:

✦ *Cache implementation and coordination.* Multiprocessor systems with a separate L2 cache for each processor achieve greater memory access bandwidth than unified designs but have to solve the problem of maintaining consistency among multiple copies of a single value that might be multiply stored in the caches. Figure 8-16 shows the problem.

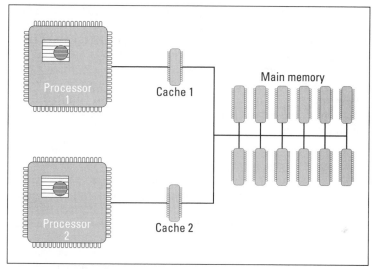

**Figure 8-16:** Cache coherence protocols enable multiprocessor systems to maintain independent caches for each processor and function consistently.

Suppose Processor 1 reads the value of COLOR from main memory, and suppose the value is GREEN. A copy—GREEN—remains in Cache 1. Later, suppose Processor 2 sets COLOR to BLUE. Cache 2 will hold the value BLUE, and main memory will be updated to have BLUE in COLOR as well. The problem is that, unless something specific happens, Cache 1 won't have the news and will store GREEN. This means that if a program runs on Processor 1, it will load the (incorrect) value GREEN from cache and not the (correct) value BLUE.

This problem is called the cache coherence problem. Intel architecture processors implement a protocol for synchronizing the cache contents called "Modified, Exclusive, Shared, Invalid" or MESI. The action of the protocol ensures that, in this example, when Processor 2 changes the value of COLOR,

Cache 1 marks its copy as invalid and throws it away. This process ensures that any later access to COLOR by Processor 1 retrieves the correct value from main memory. If your multiprocessor motherboard doesn't implement MESI properly, you're likely to get random crashes or other mysterious problems.

✦ *Bus performance.* Although the host processor and PCI buses in current-generation Windows computers are fast enough for one processor, loading them with multiple processors can create bottlenecks accessing memory and disk. Designers are looking at ways to create higher-performance buses suitable for the mass PC market. In the meantime, the highest-performance Intel-based multiprocessor designs use multiple buses, such as multiple PCI buses, to meet the demands of these systems.

✦ *Multithreaded software.* Multiple processors won't do you much good if you only have one program running at a time, particularly if the program only does one thing at a time. Server computers, such as the ones used to support access to World Wide Web pages across the Internet, can naturally have a copy of the server program running for each user accessing a page and so can benefit from multiple processors. The computer on your desk, however, may not have much to do other than to run the program you're using, and so unless that program breaks its work into several pieces that can be run in parallel, the second and other processors will sit idle.

The most common example of applications that exploit parallelism is the more powerful image processing programs, which can dispatch processors to crunch on different parts of the image. As word processors evolve, you can expect them to use parallelism to smoothly render and print in the background while you continue to edit. The initial version of Microsoft Word for Windows 95 partially implemented this feature, for instance, but still becomes unresponsive when rendering complex graphics. You can see what the potential of your computer is, though, by opening a second copy of Word and noticing that it operates quickly and smoothly while the first copy prints.

Windows NT has had the capability to let programs run parallel operations from its initial release. Windows 3.1 did not. Because the market for Windows 3.1 programs was far larger than that for Windows NT programs, software developers generally wrote for the larger market and did not implement parallel operations. The widespread adoption of Windows 95 brought to Windows users the capability for programs to divide their work into parallel pieces and vastly increased the market for programs that exploit the processing power you get from a multiprocessor system. Until such software is common, though, you'll want to see if the software you actually run benefits from a multiprocessor before dropping one on your desk.

There's another way you can benefit from multiprocessors besides multithreaded software. If you actively use several programs at once, and if those programs take significant time to do things, a dual-processor system can have a processor completely free to work interactively with you while the other processor does the other work you initiated. In principle, a very fast processor can be shared among several programs transparently; in practice, multiprocessor systems using somewhat slower processors can feel more responsive than the faster uniprocessor. (For instance, a dual-processor system we've used powered by a pair of 300 MHz Pentium IIs feels faster than a uniprocessor powered by a 400 MHz Pentium II.)

## Which processors support multiprocessor systems?

Multiprocessor systems based on Intel's Pentium, Pentium Pro, Pentium II, and Pentium III processors have been available for years. Four processors is the practical limit for what's commonly available, with machines containing eight and more processors now available. AMD will attack the multiprocessor market in 1999 with their K7 processor.

Having had problems when we did otherwise, we're now very careful to use a motherboard and processor from a vendor with a superior engineering track record when integrating a multiprocessor system from components.

 We'll show you how to build a dual-processor server in Chapter 42 using Intel Pentium III processors and an AMI motherboard.

Choosing suppliers is critically important for multiprocessor systems because they're harder to design and test. For example, there were documented problems with very early shipments of the Intel 90 and 100 MHz Pentiums that required the internal cache to be set to a lower-performance mode to ensure proper operation in multiprocessor systems. A white paper from Compaq shows that they became aware of this problem during their engineering testing on some of their server products prior to first shipment and ensured that the work-around was in place on all shipped products. Vendors with lesser technical skills and resources might have missed this.

Nevertheless, you can get quality components that will let you put together a multiprocessor system. The AMI Series 774 (MegaRUM II) motherboard, for example, supports

- ◆ Two Pentium III processors at 450 to 550 MHz (faster processors supporting the 100 MHz front side should be supported too)
- ◆ Six PCI, one 2X AGP, and one ISA slots
- ◆ Up to two gigabytes of interleaved error-correcting memory
- ◆ Onboard Universal Serial Bus, IDE, parallel, serial (2), floppy, and PS/2 mouse ports
- ◆ Onboard dual-channel Ultra2 wide SCSI

# Attached I/O Processors: I₂O

A server computer has a far more stressing I/O load than a desktop machine because the demand for information on the server coming from multiple network sources is greater than you're likely to generate yourself on a desktop. A sustained sequence of I/O transactions (particularly to read or write many small files) requires more seeks and other disk supervision than high-rate reads and writes of relatively large files. Operations on many small files (such as reading Web page files, or reading and writing e-mail or newsgroup messages) are consistent with server operation. Sustained operations (such as file loads and saves, or image and video capture) are typical of high-performance desktop use.

The supervision the processor has to provide keeps it busy. Not only does the supervision workload take processor cycles away from other work, handling interrupts is the most expensive operation the processor does. Constant interruptions slow even the fastest processor to a crawl.

The solution to the problem is to slow some other processor, not the fast, expensive one powering the server. The industry standard way to do that in Intel-architecture computers is *Intelligent I/O* ($I_2O$), an approach to integrating smart I/O devices into standard operating systems. The key benefit of $I_2O$ is that intelligent I/O subsystems allow I/O interrupts, such as those generated by networking and storage transactions, to be handled in the I/O subsystem. $I_2O$ is backed by over 100 companies, so a wide product base should become available over time.

The performance gain from intelligent I/O adapters is substantial. For example, benchmarks by Novell on a specific machine with four conventional LAN adapters show a peak throughput of about 15 MBps at nearly 100 percent CPU utilization. The same measurements with intelligent LAN adapters peak at about 40 MBps and about 60 percent CPU utilization.

Prior to development of $I_2O$, the hard part of implementing intelligent adapters was that no standard existed for how to interface the adapter to the operating system. Host adapters send relatively primitive commands to disks, for example, including seek, read a sector, and write a sector. Intelligent controllers can do more complex operations, such as transferring a file from one disk to another, or transferring a file (or block of data) from the disk to the network. What makes interfacing intelligent adapters hard is that there's been no clean place to intercept high-level commands and route them to the hardware for execution. $I_2O$ creates the necessary break between high-level operations in the device driver and low-level implementation, and it does so in a standard way. The standardization of the interface to the hardware means that manufacturers need only implement one interface whether the operating system is Windows NT, UNIX, OS/2, or Novell. That reduces cost and builds product volume.

The initial version of I$_2$O supports disks and LAN adapters. Planned upgrades to the specification will add support for intelligent tape, clusters, ATM, and other technologies. I$_2$O is relatively new, though, so check to see if the product you want supports the operating system you use, and do careful compatibility testing in your production environment before you rely on the new product.

# Summary

✦ Any new computer you build, or upgrade you do, should be based on the Intel Pentium II, Pentium III, or Celeron processors (or one of the competitive equivalents). Anything less isn't worth the investment.

✦ Upgrading with an OverDrive or other replacement processor is only worth considering if the motherboard won't become a choke point due to cache or bus limitations.

✦ Multiprocessor systems are becoming more and more common on the desktop. You can start by only plugging in one processor and running Windows 9*x*, but you'll need UNIX or Windows NT when you plug in more processors.

✦    ✦    ✦

# Cache, Memory, and Bus

## Cache

The memory caches in your machine include the Level 1 (L1) cache in the processor and the Level 2 (L2) cache, which may be in the processor or on the motherboard. You have no choices for the L1 cache (it's completely dependent on the processor), so in this chapter we focus exclusively on the L2 cache.

If you have a Pentium Pro, Pentium II, Pentium III, or later-generation Celeron Intel processor, the L2 cache is itself built into the processor module.

Intel originated the *Socket 7* specification for Pentium chips faster than 133 MHz. The rest of the computer industry, locked out of the Intel Slot 1 processor interface, extended the Socket 7 specification to *Super Socket 7*, a design capable of supporting the fast, current-generation processors from competitive manufacturers. Super Socket 7 motherboards, including the recent designs supporting the AMD K6 and K6-2, and the Cyrix 6x86MX, most often have no cache, a 256K cache, or a 512K cache. The cache often comes on a module that plugs into the motherboard. The Intel specification for those modules is called COAST (Cache On A STick). COAST modules are about 4.35 inches wide and 1.14 inches high. (Some module vendors, including some major motherboard suppliers, grossly violate the height specification.) Physically, the COAST modules use what's called the CELP (Card Edge Low Profile) size standard.

There are three kinds of cache memory on motherboards: asynchronous, pipeline burst, and synchronous burst. An *asynchronous burst* cache works much like main memory. The processor says go, and some time later the data arrives. The processor has to wait the minimum time to ensure correct data transfer, and it has to pass an address to the cache for every transfer, so this is the slowest (and least expensive) cache technology.

*Pipeline burst* and *synchronous burst* caches receive a clock signal from the processor to allow the processor and memory to run in lock step. The cache contains a counter that, whenever the processor starts a cycle, lets the cache module automatically process four cycles in quick succession (a burst). Figure 9-1 shows the idea. The first, longer cycle in the figure is the one initiated by the processor. The next three are sequenced by the cache module as the processor supplies clock pulses, allowing another cycle every subsequent clock tick. A pipeline burst cache module therefore has a clock pattern of 3-1-1-1. A synchronous burst module may cut the initial cycle time to two clock ticks, permitting a 2-1-1-1 cycle. In many systems, the timing sent to both pipeline and synchronous burst modules will be 3-1-1-1, making their performance the same. In contrast with the burst modules, the asynchronous module read cycle has a 3-2-2-2 pattern.

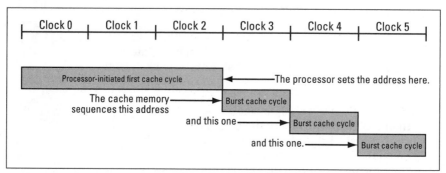

**Figure 9-1:** Synchronous cache memory speeds access by the processor.

## Packing them in

The maximum memory in your system can be affected by the size of the L2 cache. For example, the motherboard in one of our computers requires the following specific cache sizes for different maximum main memory sizes:

| Maximum Main Memory Size | Minimum L2 Cache Size |
|---|---|
| 64MB | 256K |
| 128MB | 512K |
| 256MB | 1024K |

Not all motherboards have this requirement. If you plan to install additional memory over the life of your computer, you'll want to get enough cache for your motherboard to ensure you meet the minimum requirements. The problem occurs in mainstream desktop systems, not just in servers with huge memories.

Part of the reason inadequate cache is more of a problem in Windows 9x and NT is that these operating systems stack things up in memory differently than Windows 3.1 did. Under 3.1, both Windows itself and user applications loaded from the bottom up. That meant that until your programs filled it, the high end of memory was empty. Moreover, the most-often used software—Windows itself, for instance—was in the memory handled by the cache. If you had a machine with only part of the memory cached, the impact would be as small as possible.

Under Windows 9x and NT, though, user applications still load from the bottom of memory up, but Windows itself loads from the top down. In a machine with no cache coverage for the high end of memory, that means that the most often used programs run as slowly as possible.

Some Pentium systems sold by a major system manufacturer came with too little cache, failing to cover all of memory when users upgraded from 8MB to 16MB of main memory. If the machine had cache coverage for all of memory with 8MB installed but not with 16MB, then the machine becomes slower with added memory, not faster as you'd expect. If you had one of those machines, your only solution would be to contact the system or motherboard manufacturer for the necessary update to the motherboard. The integrated cache in the Pentium II, Pentium III, and Celeron processors eliminates this problem; the only limit on memory addressable by a motherboard for those processors should be the limit for the support chipset and the number of memory sockets.

Signals from the cache module to the motherboard identify what kind of cache is installed. During the power-up process, the chip set stores that identification for use by the BIOS to set up the system. Depending on the BIOS, this process may make cache configuration completely automatic.

You can tell what kind of cache is in the system by looking at the cache module (assuming your system has one). A module with three big chips—two identical chips and one smaller chip (all mounted on one side of the module)—is probably a 256K pipeline or synchronous burst cache module. If there are two additional big chips on the other side of the module, you probably have 512K bytes of burst cache. If there are more than nine big chips on the module, you have an asynchronous cache. Assuming any necessary jumpers and BIOS settings are done correctly, most BIOS startup sequences report cache size and type during boot. You may also be able to find the information in the BIOS setup screens.

## Don't believe everything your computer tells you

In 1996, news reports surfaced that some obscure motherboard manufacturers were shipping products with no cache or less than the specified amount but had patched the BIOS to falsely report the expected size. Independent reports confirmed that, as happens in every industry, a few dishonest companies were shipping fraudulent products.

You can check your motherboard cache size easily with the CACHECHK program, which can be found at: `http://www.softseek.com/Utilities/Benchmarking_and_Tune_Up/Review_22226_index.html`. CACHECHK will benchmark cache and memory performance in your computer and report what you've got. If you have doubts about your motherboard vendor, or if your computer performance isn't what you expected, see what CACHECHK has to say.

## Relative size payoffs

Only very low-end desktop and laptop machines ship with no L2 cache. Faster machines use 256K or 512K of cache (pipeline or synchronous burst on the motherboard if the L2 cache isn't included with the processor). Very high-end machines may include as much as 1024K or more of cache.

The payoff from moving to 512K from 256K is less than that from moving to 256K from none. Figure 9-2 shows the diminishing returns as cache size increases. The reason this happens is because Windows and your programs have a "footprint" — the part of the program that actually is executed — that needs to be in memory. You should conclude from the data in Figure 9-2 that the footprint for Windows is larger than for DOS, which follows from the fact that Windows is much larger than DOS and does more. The windowed user interface is part of Windows but not part of the footprint in the UNIX measurement — it's a separate subsystem — so it's reasonable that the UNIX footprint would be smaller as well.

If you're planning to use a motherboard that carries external cache, Figure 9-3 suggests the analysis you might want to go through to select the amount of cache you'll want in a Windows system. Overall, you'll want at least 256K of synchronous (pipeline burst or synchronous burst) cache in anything but a very low-end system. High-performance desktop machines and servers are good candidates for 512K of synchronous cache, and very heavily loaded servers will benefit from 1024K.

Keep in mind that large motherboard caches are not necessarily very expensive. In the first quarter of 1999, for example, a 512K cache from VisionTek cost under $40, less than dinner for two in an average restaurant. The cache will stay with you longer, too.

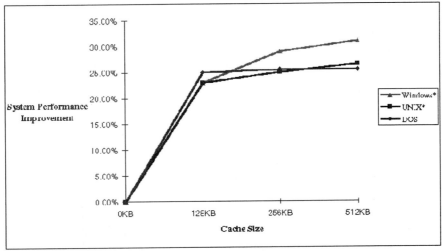

**Figure 9-2:** System performance is strongly affected by cache size. (Courtesy of Intel Corporation.)

## Cache clock speed effects

The cache in Pentium (Socket 7), Pentium Pro, and Pentium II Xeon systems runs at the full system bus speed. Pentium II processors clock the cache at one half the speed of the processor, while cached Celerons, K6-3s, and later Pentium III or Pentium III Xeon processors revert to the prior model and once again run the cache at full speed.

Depending on the software you run, this difference in cache clock rates can affect performance in interesting ways. For example, we've noticed a faster frame rate in some 3D games from a 400 MHz Celeron processor than from an older 400 MHz Pentium II. You'd normally expect the Pentium II to be faster for the equivalent clock rate because it has a larger cache, but in the case we noticed, the critical program code loops could fit in the smaller cache of the Celeron. The small size of those loops meant the program could benefit from the cache clock running at full speed instead of the one-half rate of the Pentium II. Programs whose critical loops can't fit in the smaller cache would run as you expect — faster on the 400 MHz Pentium II.

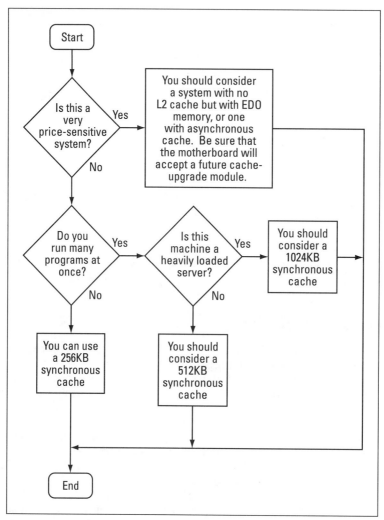

**Figure 9-3:** A 256K cache is okay for most desktop systems. High-performance desktops and servers may need more.

# Buses

There are several categories of buses you need to think about, the most general distinction being between internal and external buses. The I/O buses (SCSI and IDE) arguably overlap the external bus category, but we'll look at them in another chapter.

In our categorization, the *internal buses* are the ones that you need to open the computer to get at, while the *external buses* are the ones that help you connect external devices. Current-technology internal buses include PCI and AGP, while the external buses include PC Card, Universal Serial Bus (USB), and IEEE 1384 (FireWire). You'll still find ISA buses in most computers, but in 1999 you'll start to see computers with no ISA slots. Within a year or two manufacturers will probably have removed ISA completely.

## Internal bus performance

We ran some tests to get numbers that would give you some insight into the difference that a fast bus makes. We hesitate to call the tests benchmarks, because we couldn't control the test conditions well enough to isolate the differences in the tests to just the bus. Nevertheless, the results are quite illuminating.

The tests we ran were to compare the graphics performance of an ISA video board against a PCI video board in the same system. Figure 9-4 compares the two setups. The ISA board was an old Oak Technologies Super VGA, while the PCI board was the ATI Graphics Pro Turbo. We ran the most recent Windows 9*x* drivers as of the time of the tests. The ISA board had no video accelerator chip, so we disabled the accelerator chip on the PCI board to compare one unaccelerated board to another. The measured performance results are only an estimate of the performance of the two buses, because both the drivers and the internal architecture of the graphics boards are different. However, it is reasonable to attribute the difference in measured performance to the bus and video boards.

The result of the tests was that, doing operations representative of a mix of real-world Windows graphics operations, the PCI board was over ten times faster than the ISA board. A more comprehensive study would use boards that were identical except for bus interface, and would look at the impact of processor speed on performance differences. However, for the purpose of defining what you should have in a new computer, the test makes a clear statement — you want all the bus speed you can get. That means you want the Accelerated Graphics Port (AGP) bus for video, and the PCI bus for most other interfaces.

Intel ran tests similar to ours with the results shown in Figure 9-5. In the Intel test, only the bus architecture (and therefore the graphics card) changed. The SVGA graphics cards were versions of ATI's graphics accelerator family. The outcome is similar to our result — around an order of magnitude difference between the ISA card and the PCI card.

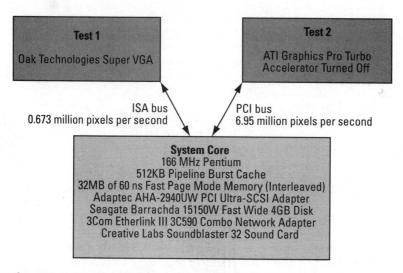

ISA bus
0.673 million pixels per second

PCI bus
6.95 million pixels per second

Figure 9-4: A tenfold video performance gain illustrates why you want the PCI bus in your computer. Get the faster AGP video bus if you can.

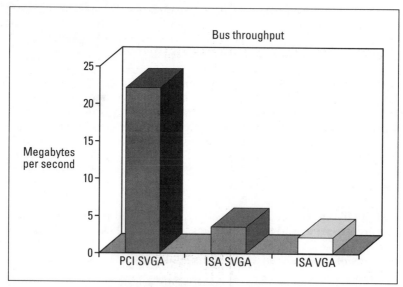

Figure 9-5: A bus throughput benchmark by Intel similar to the tests we ran confirms the PCI performance gains.

Upgrading an ISA bus machine is a performance dead-end, and with the prices of low-end motherboards and memory what they are, quite possibly a bad investment. It's very much like when one of our fathers commented on putting fancy wheels, wide tires, and a loud exhaust on a car, saying "When you're done with that, it's still going to be a Corvair." It was a wonderful car at the time, but he was right. Nothing would make it a race car. An ISA machine is the same way: If there's a specific and very inexpensive upgrade or repair that will keep it working for you for another year or two, you might get your money's worth. Trying to make it compete with systems based on the PCI bus, though, is futile unless you're prepared to replace the motherboard, processor, memory, and one or two key cards.

# PCI

A computer with a Peripheral Component Interconnect (PCI) bus actually has a three-level bus structure like that shown in Figure 9-6. The three-speed, three-level structure lets devices run at the speed that makes the most sense. Very fast buses and devices — ones on the 528MB per second host bus — are difficult to design properly. The high speeds involved require high-speed circuits, short precise traces on printed circuit boards, and careful attention to timing margins. Limiting the number of devices connected to the host bus simplifies system design. Using a predesigned and tested part from a chip manufacturer, such as the Intel PCIsets, simplifies design even further.

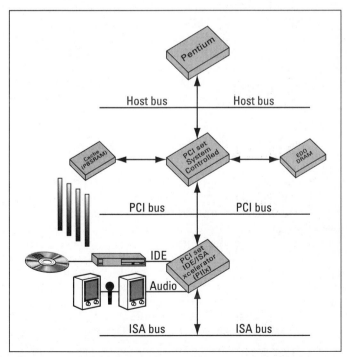

**Figure 9-6:** PCI is the middle level of a three-level bus structure. (Drawing courtesy Intel Corporation.)

✦ *Host bus.* the fastest of the three levels found in a PCI-based computer is the host bus, which is the bus that connects directly to the processor (the "host"). The host bus is always under control of the processor. All I/O transactions, and all memory transactions not handled by the processor's internal L1 cache (and L2 cache in the case of the P6 processors), flow over this bus.

The chip on the other end of the host bus is the system controller, which controls the cache, memory, and bridge to the actual PCI bus. The AGP port ties to the system controller.

The 64-bit-wide Pentium host bus transfers data on the host bus as fast as 528MB per second. Systems based on Rambus memory transfer data as fast as 1.6GB per second.

✦ *PCI bus.* The PCI bus is the middle of the computer in terms of both speed and its position between the host and ISA bus. The PCI bus bridge in the system controller plus the PCI interface chips in individual PCI devices implement the PCI bus protocols. The peak PCI transfer rate is 133MB per second. The PCI bus can be controlled by any of several bus masters, including the processor or an I/O device.

✦ *ISA bus.* The slowest bus of the three is the ISA bus. A bridge chip supports the interface back to the PCI bus. An ISA bus has a typical peak transfer rate of 5MB per second, although 2.5MB per second is a more common effective rate for ISA bus masters.

The PCI bus itself is a compromise between the high speed and difficult restrictions of the host bus and the leisurely speed and casual design of the ISA bus. The signal timing required to achieve 133MB per second transfers limits a single PCI bus to three or four card sockets (which is why any motherboard with more than three or four PCI slots needs to have more than one PCI bus with bridge chips in between).

PCI implementations commonly have a number of features you can enable or disable in the BIOS, including controls enabling buffers (fast holding areas) between the processor and the PCI bus, timings and other limits on burst PCI transfers, and monitoring modes (snooping). The specific settings you have available depend on the chipset on your motherboard. Sadly, the motherboard manuals are never any help at figuring out what the settings do. We'll explain the ones for the motherboards we use in Chapter 37 and Chapter 39.

A BIOS that supports changing PCI settings (like the AMI BIOS) may provide bulk parameter settings that allow you to make wholesale changes affecting compatibility and performance (including the PCI controls). AMI defines setups in their BIOS for both Fail-Safe operation and Optimal operation. Fail-Safe operation is compatible with a wider variety of configurations, but Optimal operation is somewhat faster.

# PC Card

The PC Card (previously PCMCIA, or Personal Computer Memory Card International Association) bus originated as a way to plug in modules to laptop and smaller computers. PC Card devices are roughly the size of a credit card and from 3.3 to 10.5 millimeters thick. The initial PC Card products were add-on memory and plug-in software, but manufacturers were quick to offer a wide range of products:

✦ Read/write and read-only memory

✦ Hard disk drives

✦ Modems (including ISDN and Cellular Data/FAX)

✦ Network adapters (including wireless and adapters combined with modems)

✦ SCSI adapters

✦ Sound adapters

PC Cards plug into a 68-pin host socket. There are three PC Card sizes, with a fourth being debated:

✦ Type I cards (such as memory) are 3.3 mm thick.

✦ Type II cards (usually I/O devices such as modems) are 5 mm thick.

✦ Type III devices (typically data storage or radio devices) are 10.5 mm thick.

✦ Type IV (currently under development) will be an 18 mm slot for large-capacity hard drives.

A PC Card will fit in any slot either its own size or a larger size. For example, a Type II modem will fit into a Type III slot.

A typical PC Card product is the Adaptec AHA-1460 SlimSCSI adapter shown in Figure 9-7. The SlimSCSI provides the functionality of a SCSI adapter that you would plug into an ISA or PCI bus, but with lesser performance because of the 2MB per second limitation of the PC Card bus. As with all PC Card products needing a cable to connect to devices, the SlimSCSI is vulnerable to damage by hitting or bending it at the point where the cable enters the card. The Adaptec card is enclosed in metal and the cable is well reinforced, so the SlimSCSI should be able to take some abuse. You want to look for these features in any PC Card product you buy, because breaking the card while you're traveling can cost you more than just the card.

SCSI interface cable                    PC Card to cable connector

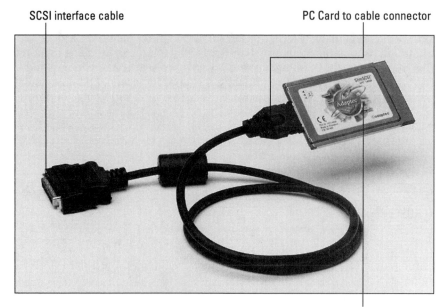

PC Card adapter

**Figure 9-7:** The PC Card bus provides great convenience to mobile users but has a weakness where the cable connects into the card. (Courtesy of Adaptec, Inc.)

The SlimSCSI is useful for connecting CD-ROMs, hard disks, scanners, Zip drives, tape drives, or any other SCSI device to a laptop computer. It supports Windows 9*x* and NT, with installation into Windows 9*x* being particularly painless because the SlimSCSI works with Plug and Play. For example, our laptop computer has a Type II PC Card slot (matching the SlimSCSI) that we had previously set up with the 32-bit Windows 9*x* PC Card drivers. When we pushed a SlimSCSI into the laptop and booted it, Windows promptly noticed the adapter, installed the driver, and was set to go.

You can get a PC Card adapter for your desktop computer (IBM makes one, for instance, as does Eiger Laboratories). Combined with the SlimSCSI, it makes a higher-performance interface to an external Zip drive than the usual parallel port connection and can let you hook up a high-performance external CD-ROM. PC Cards (or Flash Cards with PC Card adapters) are the preferred storage medium for digital cameras, offering several megabytes of memory or tens to hundreds of megabytes of disk.

The next step in plug-in cards, targeted at digital cameras, advanced cellular phones, voice recorders, personal digital assistants, and other devices surrounding your computer, will be the Miniature Card. A Miniature Card measures 38 mm ×

33 mm × 3.5 mm, making it approximately one-fourth the size of PC Cards. Based on current chip technology, it can accommodate up to 64MB of flash, DRAM, or ROM memory.

## Universal serial bus

Connecting things to your computer is a pain. If you stuff your conventional PCI/ISA computer with as many ports as you can — ignoring the network — here's what you can have before you run out of hardware options:

✦ Two serial ports (that is, only two work at the same time)

✦ One mouse port

✦ Three parallel ports

✦ A game (joystick) port

✦ A SCSI port or two

This just isn't enough. For someone who really uses the computer for a lot of things (including games), here's what you might need to connect:

✦ A modem (uses one serial port; we know people with two modems)

✦ The monitoring port for a UPS (another serial port)

✦ A mouse (a serial or mouse port; a bus mouse consumes an interrupt and bus slot you'll wish you had for something else)

✦ A joystick (or two; some require a serial port in addition to the game port)

✦ A laser printer (a parallel port)

✦ A color ink jet printer (a parallel port)

✦ A label printer (a serial port)

If you total all that up, you're out of luck when it comes to serial ports — three or four and a mouse port would just do, but you can't share interrupts on ISA-bus computers, so the ports just aren't there. New devices including chairs, gloves, and joysticks with tactile feedback will make the contention for serial ports worse.

The computer industry is moving quickly to solve the peripheral connection problem, though, and the force that's powering that movement is digital audio, video, photographic, and communications equipment. Through the new connections the Universal Serial Bus (USB) will make possible, you'll connect microphones, speakers, cameras, modems, and telephones not to sound cards and the internal bus, but to a thin cable that snakes from one device to the next. The small USB cable that runs everywhere will replace the mess of cables at the back of your computer. Instead of finding a free bus slot, plugging in a new card, setting switches, and hoping everything still works, you'll just plug the new device into the USB chain. The promise is it will be simple and effective, and that you'll never have to crack open the computer case in the process. Intel believes so strongly in the possibilities that it's built "concept computers" with no internal slots.

Here's what Digital Equipment Corporation (since bought by Compaq) had to say about USB:

*Just how much nirvana are we talking about here? For starters, the 12 Mbps Universal Serial Bus (USB) standard means most of your external peripherals will have an identical connector—poof, no more dedicated ports. And we do mean "most"—from keyboards and mice to modems and PBX interfaces to joysticks, digitizers, and data gloves. For the "Type A" user, always on the move from one thing to another, USB sets you free to go—unplug your printer (work stuff) and zap in a joystick (fun stuff), and after you're feeling sufficiently satiated, you can reconnect and use the printer. No rebooting or reconfiguring needed, required, necessary, or mandatory . . . absolutely none. Get the picture?*

There's a lot of industry horsepower behind USB—the companies listed on the front of the USB specification include Compaq, Digital Equipment Corporation, IBM PC Company, Intel, Microsoft, NEC, and Northern Telecom. The USB devices we use the most ourselves are from 3Com (network interface), Kodak (digital camera), Logitech (mouse), and Microsoft (speakers).

The USB developers recognized the need to keep cost low. Adding a $30 interface to a mouse, for instance, would price the mouse high enough that the USB mice would not sell. For that reason, USB is limited to 12 megabits per second (that's 1.5MB per second) and has a "low-speed" mode that runs at 1.5 megabits per second. While this seems slow in contrast to the 100 megabits per second of IEEE 1394 (FireWire), which targets high-speed devices like disk drives, consider that at the full rate USB is faster than the 10 megabits per second you find on the majority of local area networks today.

USB allows devices to be cabled in a tree-like fashion, not just in a straight line. Figure 9-8 shows a configuration you might use with a desktop computer. The cabling tree idea requires that you not create loops in the cables, but otherwise you can plug anything into anything else that has an empty socket. In Figure 9-8, you could equally well plug the telephone into the monitor or the speaker into the keyboard. Not all USB devices give you connections for other devices, so you may need hubs as well as devices.

If you have enough USB devices that you need to expand your system with a hub, be sure to get a powered hub. Some hubs (unpowered ones) expect to get device power from the computer or other source, but the computer itself is unlikely to be able to supply the necessary power for as many devices as you can use with a hub.

Not enough power will cause erratic operation (or failure to operate). The powered hubs supply their own power and avoid that problem.

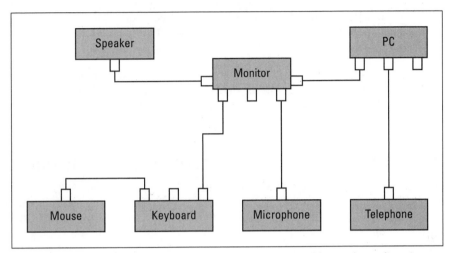

**Figure 9-8:** The USB cabling scheme requires you to avoid loops, but otherwise you can plug things in where it's convenient.

USB moved out of the development labs before 1996 was half over. Intel shipped PCIset chip sets providing the USB controller function needed inside the computer, as well as a separate chip to go in the devices. Logitech demonstrated a USB mouse, Mitel demonstrated a USB telephone, and AMI delivered BIOS code needed to configure systems as they boot. Most computers shipped in the last year or two have USB ports.

The missing component in making USB work was support from the operating system, which arrived with the release of Windows 98 and was further enhanced in Windows 98 Second Edition. If you're running a version of Windows 95, you'll probably need patches and drivers. Support is under development for different versions of UNIX, including FreeBSD and Linux, but is likely to be incomplete because you'll need device drivers in addition to the generic USB support.

**Future PC**  Expect the USB standard to evolve as more people use it and opportunities for improvement become apparent. There's work being done already on USB2, which will raise the maximum data rate to 100 Mbps. USB2 could appear in systems in late 2000.

## IEEE 1394 (FireWire)

Another external bus is the one defined by IEEE specification 1394, popularly called FireWire. Like USB, IEEE 1394 is a serial bus, transmitting one bit at a time over copper wire with multiple devices cabled into a tree. IEEE 1394 is much faster than USB, though, being capable of rates from 100 to 400 Mbps. IEEE 1394 supports far more connected devices than USB, too.

The few products available in early 1999 for IEEE 1394 systems include printers, digital audio, digital movie cameras, digital still cameras, and digital VHS players. The list isn't as long as for USB, but you can expect disk drives, digital television, DVD, satellite systems, scanners, and telephones to be added.

## Plug and Play and other auto-configuration support

Everything in your computer has to have its own unique address. I/O devices often need unique *interrupt request* (IRQ) numbers as well. If two things end up with the same address or interrupt number, you have a conflict and things do not work well (or at all).

The original IBM PC design offered no help solving this problem. IBM apparently assumed that only trained service technicians would ever set up or change the configuration inside the computer, so no automated support for the process was necessary. Moreover, the list of devices they anticipated plugging into the bus was small enough that you could keep it all in your head.

Fat chance. In retrospect, that IBM would make the decision to omit automatic configuration support confirms that at the time IBM saw the PC as an extension of the mainframe. No other characteristic of the PC has caused more anguish and wasted more time, with the possible exception of video drivers and limited system resources in Windows 3.1. Apple managed to avoid most of these issues because their architecture was relatively closed. The wide-open PC design, and the rapid introduction of new products and technologies for the PC, led inevitably to disaster. When you plug in a new device, it's anybody's guess whether things are going to work or not.

To their credit, IBM was among the first to realize that automatic device configuration should be added to the PC. They delivered the technology with the MCA bus in the PS/2 computers. Had the computing world adopted MCA, the current mess would have been avoided. MCA flopped, however, and today there are hundreds of millions of ISA cards plugged into PCs that are chock full of jumpers, switches, and obscure setup procedures. It's amazing anything works at all.

The technical support costs created by configuration problems are huge, so in an effort to reduce those costs and improve the usability of PCs, the industry has responded in two ways:

✦ *PCI Bus.* The PCI bus implements automatic detection and configuration of PCI devices. You can (for the most part) plug in a new PCI card and expect it to automatically be assigned memory, I/O, and interrupt addresses that let it live alongside the other PCI devices you have. PCI has configuration features similar to those of MCA and EISA, in that settings are determined at boot time by the PCI BIOS, without your having to run a hardware setup program.

✦ *Plug and Play.* Because the ISA bus remains useful, and because there are so many of them out there, the PC automatic configuration problem was going to remain unsolved until a technology addressed configuration of devices on the ISA bus. That technology is Plug and Play.

So far, Windows 9*x* is the only operating system available that fully supports Plug and Play. Windows NT 4 and some versions of UNIX have limited support. Windows 2000 should have complete Plug and Play support.

The sequence a fully Plug and Play computer and operating system go through to boot is an interesting combination of compromises needed to let legacy hardware continue to operate:

1. *Identify the installed Plug and Play devices.* When the system first starts up, Plug and Play cards are inactive. They have no addresses assigned, and they respond on the bus only to a special I/O address reserved for Plug and Play operations. The BIOS sets up the display card, keyboard, and boot disk, and it starts Windows running.

2. *Figure out what resources everything needs.* Plug and Play devices, through the special *I/O read data port for ISA Plug and Play enumerator*, report what their requirements are for I/O ports, memory addresses, and interrupt assignments.

3. *Design a system resource configuration.* After the BIOS and operating system get the requirements for all the devices (including preset requirements for legacy devices), they calculate a set of assignments for each card that meets the card requirements and resolves all potential conflicts with other devices. The operating system then tells the cards the assignments it has made, making them live on the bus.

4. *Load the device drivers.* Device drivers are the software components that actually talk to the hardware, providing a consistent interface to other software components. Because the set of Plug and Play devices Windows finds when it starts up can change, it loads drivers dynamically based on what's really there.

In order to know what device drivers to load, the operating system has to know what each device actually is. Plug and Play devices each have a unique identifier that carries information about the device type, manufacturer, and model. The operating system looks the identifier up in a set of information files it maintains. If it locates an appropriate entry, it finds out what files it needs and where to get them. If not, the operating system notifies you that it's found a new device and asks you to provide the necessary software.

## Plug and pray?

Plug and Play requires hardware, BIOS, and operating system support. That means Plug and Play cards, a motherboard with a Plug and Play BIOS, and an operating system such as Windows 9x or Windows 2000 are all required. Here's what happens if you're missing one or another of these components:

✦ *Missing Plug and Play hardware.* It's very likely that your computer will have a mix of Plug and Play and older (legacy) cards. If you have no Plug and Play cards, it's all up to you to do the configuration. If you have all Plug and Play cards, the system should do it for you. If you have a mix, and you have the legacy cards configured properly, the system may get the Plug and Play parts right (but it may not). Plug and Play devices on the ISA bus cooperate with PCI devices.

✦ *Missing Plug and Play BIOS.* If you don't have one of these, Plug and Play simply won't work. In fact, if you buy Plug and Play cards, you will probably have to set them up to a fixed configuration rather than for Plug and Play operation, making the overall process harder. You may be able to get a BIOS upgrade from your system or motherboard manufacturer that adds Plug and Play to an existing system, and if the motherboard has a flash BIOS this is a painless upgrade. If not, you'll have to replace a chip or two on the motherboard.

*Most systems sold in the last several years have Plug and Play BIOS support.*

✦ *Missing Plug and Play Operating System.* If you run a non–Plug and Play operating system, you'll want to set any Plug and Play devices to non–Plug and Play mode so that they start up in a fixed, known configuration. You'll have to set the BIOS for non–Plug and Play operation, too.

For example, we used to run both Windows NT and 9x on a machine with a 3COM 3C509B Ethernet card. The 3C509B is a 16-bit ISA, Plug and Play device. Because Windows NT did not support Plug and Play, we had to go in with the 3Com setup software, force the card to non–Plug and Play mode, and set the card addresses and interrupt. Once we did that, and then set the card up manually in both versions of Windows, things worked well.

If you have all the required components, Plug and Play greatly simplifies setup and maintenance of your computer. Better yet, Plug and Play lets the operating system notice when you dock your laptop at your desk, plug in a CD-ROM or Zip drive, or plug in a PC Card network adapter.

Plug and Play goes further than identifying and configuring cards plugged into your computer. Any device that has two-way communication with the computer can support Plug and Play. The most common peripherals supporting Plug and Play are ones connected to serial or parallel ports. For example, the APC uninterruptible power supplies and many printers are automatically detected by Windows 9x.

Overall, Plug and Play is a good thing. It's not perfect, especially when you still have legacy devices. One of the drawbacks is that Plug and Play resource assignments can change, so any non–Plug and Play–aware software can get confused. If you buy a Plug and Play sound card, its address can change when the machine configuration changes. If you run DOS programs that have setup programs in which you specify the sound card address (many older DOS games do), a change in the addresses Plug and Play assigns could mean you have to go back and set up the program again.

Whether you're upgrading or buying a new machine with an ISA bus, you should be migrating in the Plug and Play direction. You should buy Plug and Play–capable motherboards and cards. Over time, you'll have more Plug and Play devices and fewer legacy ones. When you get to a completely Plug and Play machine, your configuration problems will largely have disappeared. Once you get to a completely PCI-based machine with no ISA slots, your configuration problems should drop to nearly zero.

## Number of slots/shared slots

There are only so many slots on a motherboard, and if you run out, you're stuck. Looking at where the slots go (Table 9-1) shows what can happen. The system we describe is a PCI machine typical of many, and it is completely out of slots. Its motherboard provides four PCI and four 16-bit ISA slots; however, one slot is shared PCI/ISA, so only seven slots are usable.

<table>
<tr><td colspan="2" align="center">Table 9-1<br>**Typical Slot Usage**</td></tr>
<tr><td>*Slot*</td><td>*Usage*</td></tr>
<tr><td>0</td><td>miro video acquisition adapter</td></tr>
<tr><td>1</td><td>Adaptec bus mastering PCI Ultra SCSI controller</td></tr>
<tr><td>2</td><td>3COM bus mastering PCI Ethernet adapter</td></tr>
<tr><td>3</td><td>ATI PCI display adapter</td></tr>
<tr><td>4</td><td>(shared with PCI slot, so unavailable)</td></tr>
<tr><td>5</td><td>Adaptec bus mastering SCSI adapter</td></tr>
<tr><td>6</td><td>3Com V.90 internal modem</td></tr>
<tr><td>7</td><td>Creative Labs SoundBlaster 32</td></tr>
</table>

Running out of slots leaves you with very few options for upgrades. The motherboard on the system provided the usual serial, parallel, IDE, and mouse ports, plus sockets for memory, yet we ran out of slots. Here's how it happened:

✦ *Video capture.* We record and edit digital video on this computer, and to get the best video quality we have a separate video acquisition board. The miro board we use is a PCI device.

✦ *Disk drives.* We elected to use SCSI on this system because we wanted to attach not only three disk drives, but also a tape drive, a CD-ROM, a CD-R recorder, an internal Zip drive, and a scanner. By choosing a SCSI interface for all those devices, we were able to hook them up to a single slot on the motherboard. We use a PCI controller because ISA isn't fast enough to deliver maximum performance from the disk drives, or to support simultaneous I/O to many of the devices at once. (There's also an ISA controller attached so that we can conveniently switch the external scanner on and off.)

✦ *Display.* The motherboard in this system doesn't have an AGP slot, so we use a PCI display adapter for the best performance we can get. Good video display performance is crucial for editing video.

✦ *Modem.* This system used an internal modem. Since we're out of slots, we can avoid using a slot for the modem, connecting instead through a serial port to an external unit. Connecting a modem takes a serial port, whether it's internal or external, so this option gains an available slot without losing any other resources.

✦ *Sound.* The sound card could be ISA or PCI. A PCI sound card can support more simultaneous sounds than ISA, but we were out of PCI slots so we settled for an ISA card.

**Note**    Motherboards like this one have a "shared" slot with both a PCI connector and an ISA connector. If you have one of those, you have to be careful to not overcount the available slots, since the shared slot cannot hold both a PCI card and ISA card at the same time. Some adapters, such as PCI IDE interface cards, are actually designed to plug into the shared slot using both the PCI and IDE connectors. Be sure to get a quality one well supported by Windows, such as from Promise Technology. The one we tried—not from Promise—was literally a "no name" board and never worked. The board diagnostics reported success, but it never talked to the disk properly.

# Memory

The decisions you have to make about memory in your computer are how much, what kind, and from whom.

✦ *How much.* If you run one program at a time under Windows 9*x* (excluding small desk accessories), you'll do well enough with 16MB. If you run more than one program, work on large files, or are impatient, you'll be much happier with 32MB or more. With memory prices under $2 a megabyte in 1999, beefing up memory to 32 or 64MB has become a very attractive upgrade.

If you run Windows NT, you'll want 64 to 128MB or more.

✦ *What kind.* Considering just single inline memory module (SIMM) packages for Pentium or later motherboards, you have to choose between Fast Page mode and EDO memory; between parity (or ECC) and nonparity; between gold and tin contacts; and between 50ns, 60ns, and 70ns access. For dual inline memory module (168-pin DIMM) packages, you mostly choose between conventional or PC100 SDRAM and between ECC or not. There's a small performance loss (about 4–5 percent) using ECC, but you're guaranteed to ride through most memory failures.

Most Pentium processor motherboards accept 72-pin single inline memory module (SIMM) packages. Motherboards for P6-series processors, and for the AMD K6-2, are most likely to use DIMMs.

Figure 9-9 shows how memory chips are mounted on SIMMs or DIMMs. The module itself is a small printed circuit card that acts as a carrier for the memory chips, which can be mounted on both sides. An edge connector on the card fits into a connector on the motherboard.

✦ *From whom.* The semiconductor plants to make the memory chips on your memory modules are phenomenally expensive. The billion-dollar price tag on a fabrication plant for memory chips says that chip manufacturing is not a fly-by-night operation. Memory chip manufacturers tend to be large, established companies that depend on the quality of their products for continued sales.

Making the memory chips isn't the end of the story, though. Some chips pass more stringent tests than others, with the less-capable chips being sold in secondary markets. The timing and signal layout on the modules is crucial too, requiring careful engineering to get right. Moreover, problems with memory happen now and then, and not all companies selling memory have the expertise to provide comprehensive advice when you have questions about what products to use. You want to be sure of the company you choose in case you need to make an exchange under warranty. You also benefit by choosing a memory supplier that does 100 percent testing on all parts before they ship. Thorough memory testing is difficult and time consuming, so you benefit by having this done by the manufacturer.

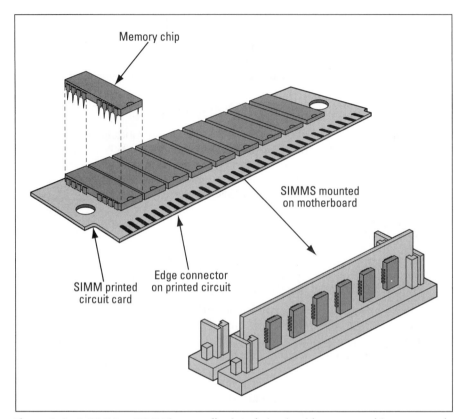

**Figure 9-9:** A SIMM or DIMM is a small printed circuit with memory chips mounted on it. An edge connector matches up with a socket on the motherboard. (Drawing courtesy Kingston Technology Company.)

Although the Celeron processors retained the 66 MHz host bus for speeds exceeding 400 MHz, systems using Pentium II, Pentium III, or K6-2 processors at 350 MHz or more have host buses running at 100 MHz and faster. Not all SDRAM memory on DIMMs is rated for those speeds; you'll want to get modules meeting the PC100 specification for 100 MHz buses. Some systems with 133 MHz and faster buses use PC133 memory; over time we expect the faster systems to migrate to Rambus memory in the Rambus Inline Memory Module (RIMM) package.

Memory modules, SIMMs in particular, have been available that implement *fake parity*. Rather than actually store the parity bit as a ninth bit in each byte of memory, a fake parity memory module regenerates the parity bit when the processor reads from the memory. The use of a parity generator chip instead of the ninth bit in storage makes the module less expensive to build than one properly implementing the parity bit but provides no protection against memory errors.

There's no reason ever to buy fake parity modules. If you don't need the protection parity offers, simply don't buy parity memory.

You want to consider using the memory modules you buy in future motherboard upgrades when you make your choices, so consider things like module type, memory speed, and ECC/parity from the standpoint of upgrades as well as current requirements. If you run a large shop, you may also want to consider the simplified spare parts stocking you would achieve by using the same memory in all your machines (such as PC100 modules).

## Memory speed

SIMM memory is available in 50ns, 60ns, and 70ns versions. DIMMs come in 8ns, 10ns, and 12ns versions, or in a PC100-compliant version. Rambus RIMMs are different than all of these. If you don't get fast enough memory, your computer will be unreliable. Your options are these:

✦ *Let a Serial Presence Detect (SPD) chip define the memory to the motherboard.* Many DIMMs come with a small SPD memory that the motherboard reads to discover the memory specifications.

✦ *Set memory timing in the motherboard.* If your motherboard and BIOS enable you to specify the memory characteristics, you can use whatever memory you like as long as there's a setting for it in the BIOS. Just be sure to tell the BIOS the right thing. Some BIOS/chip set combinations even allow different banks to be different speeds. We recommend finding motherboards that allow this, since they give you the most flexibility.

✦ *Use what the motherboard and processor require.* If the motherboard won't control memory timing, the manual for the motherboard will include a table that shows the memory speed you need depending on the processor clock rate. Don't put in memory slower than the motherboard requires for the processor you're using, and be careful to check motherboard specifications against memory timing when upgrading to a faster processor.

✦ *Use memory faster than required.* You can use memory faster than the processor and motherboard require, but unless you can tell the motherboard what you've done, you won't see any improved performance.

## Choosing between Fast Page Mode, EDO, SDRAM, and Rambus

As shown in Figure 9-10, the evolution of memory modules to DIMM and RIMM technology, using SDRAM and Rambus memory, has simplified the choices you have to make compared to systems using SIMM-based memory. Your decisions for DIMMs, for example, are only whether you need PC100-compliant memory or not, and whether you want ECC support or not.

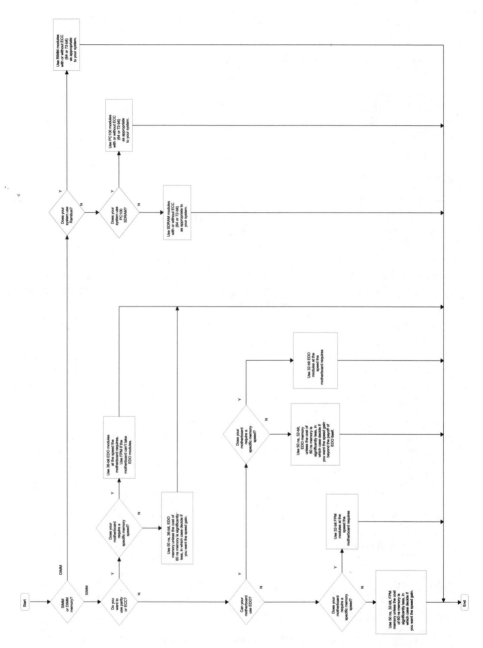

**Figure 9-10:** Your choices of memory characteristics depend on the requirements and capabilities of your motherboard.

Choosing SIMM memory, although nearly obsolete now, isn't as simple as choosing DIMMs or RIMMs. The technology inside FPM and EDO memory — which we looked at in Chapter 7 — is now all that determines which type you pick for these systems, because EDO memory is now not only 15 percent faster than FPM, it's less expensive. Some of the oldest Pentium systems can accept only FPM, so check the specifications for the motherboard on older SIMM-based systems. If you're upgrading a SIMM-based machine that lacks an L2 cache, as some low-budget machines do, be sure to get EDO if the machine can use it. Systems like that can achieve performance nearly as good as that of a system with asynchronous cache when using EDO.

## Interleaving

Many motherboard chip sets support memory interleaving, a technique that lets successive memory accesses go to different banks of memory. In a one-bank configuration (the bottom of Figure 9-11), memory access cycles have to wait until the bank gets ready, so the processor has to wait for an interval between accesses. In a two-bank configuration (the top of the figure), odd addresses go to one bank and even addresses to the other. Because the idle bank can be getting ready for its next access while the other bank delivers data, the combined cycle needs no delay between most cycles.

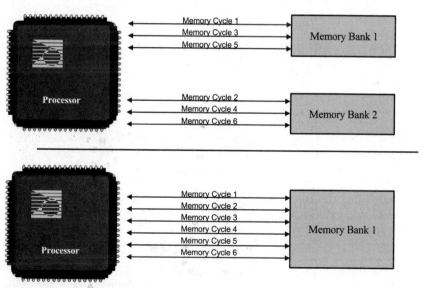

**Figure 9-11:** Interleaved memory increases performance by avoiding the wait while the memory gets ready for the next cycle.

**Note** Remember that, although a single DIMM is one bank (because it provides all 72 bits the bus requires), it takes two SIMMs to form a complete bank. Don't mix SIMMs of different sizes in the same bank. At best, the computer will ignore the memory in the larger SIMM, and at worst, the computer won't boot. Some restricted motherboards may limit the size memory that can be in bank 1 versus bank 2 as well.

Many motherboards only provide sockets for two banks of memory. You have to fill them both to have interleaved memory access, but if you do, no sockets are left for memory upgrades. For example, on older motherboards, if there are only four SIMM sockets to begin with, then two banks fill all four sockets. On newer motherboards, two DIMM sockets implement two banks. Fill the sockets and you have no opportunity to add memory to the motherboard later without removing memory you've already bought.

The cost for a specific amount of total memory is about the same whether you use two banks or one, although the relative costs fluctuate over time as chip technologies are introduced and old ones disappear. If you're sure you'll never need more memory (*really* sure!), or if you have more than two banks on the motherboard, you may want to take advantage of interleaving. The performance gain is only a few percent, however, so if it comes down to interleaving versus having room for expansion (by using modules carrying more memory on each one), we recommend leaving room for expansion.

## Dissimilar metals

At one time, nearly all the contacts on connectors in PCs were plated with gold because of the low-resistance connection you get from gold. As manufacturers replaced gold with tin to reduce cost, people would at times end up with gold in contact with tin rather than gold on gold or tin on tin. Two dissimilar metals in contact generate a weak electrical current that can (potentially) cause corrosion. Corroded contacts are guaranteed to cause erratic operation. If the corrosion is in a memory socket, the memory would operate erratically. After the issue came to light, the December 5, 1995, issue of *PC Magazine* stated:

*Readers have begun to report an insidious problem with their inline memory modules: corrosion caused by incompatibilities between the gold plating on the SIMMs and the sockets on the motherboard. . . . Be sure not to install gold-plated SIMMs into tinned sockets. The combination is corrosive.*

The source of the problem is that manufacturers are continually looking to reduce cost, and so some years back tin replaced gold on the contacts in memory module sockets and on the modules themselves. If you put SIMMs with gold contacts into tin sockets (or vice versa), you have dissimilar metals in contact.

We asked an experienced electronics reliability engineer how serious an issue this is. He pointed out that gold is quite nonreactive, and so the rate at which corrosion would occur would be extremely low. The rate would be greater in areas with high humidity, but still extremely low.

The engineer's opinion differed from that published by the magazine, so we asked several memory and connector companies for their analysis of the issue. All recommended matching the memory module contacts to those on the motherboard, but the reasons had nothing to do with corrosion! According to AMP (a connector company), the underlying chemistry that makes matching the metals important is that tin naturally oxidizes, and when it does, it tends to transfer some debris created by pressure from the harder gold surface to the gold. The debris builds up when one of the surfaces is as hard as gold, leading to increased contact resistance and ultimately to failures.

 **Tip** As much as setting up and configuring a PC might resemble working with Tinkertoys, there's very precise engineering behind much of what's in your computer. If you're going to change your system, try to learn everything you can about what you're doing. If you're unsure, get the opinion of knowledgeable people.

## Flash memory

Your computer requires storage technology that uses "permanent" changes in devices to hold information so that it can retain your programs and data when the power goes off. Disk drives hold data over power cycles because they change the magnetization on the platter surface to correspond to the ones and zeros in the incoming data stream. CD-ROMs use tiny pits in a reflective surface for the same purpose.

The chips that make up main memory in your computer don't use permanent effects to store information. Instead, they depend on the flow of electricity to distinguish between zero and one. When the electricity goes away, the chips lose all the information they once contained. In Figure 9-12, we've used the example of the flow of water past a fork in a river to illustrate what memory chips do. Suppose that you can divert the course of the river down either side of the fork whenever you want. Suppose as well that the water flow causes the diversion to "stick" and that water in the left fork means we've stored a zero, while water in the right fork means we've stored a one. The river is a simple model of how a memory remembers information: Something external (you, in this case) changes the flow, and the river flow itself makes sure it stays that way.

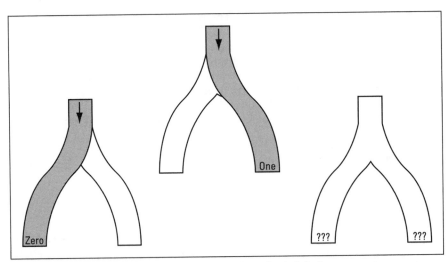

**Figure 9-12:** The river (information) flowing into the left fork represents a zero, while information flowing into the right fork represents a one. Most memory in your computer forgets everything when the power goes off, because the flow of electricity is what stores the information.

The rightmost drawing in Figure 9-12 represents a third option. If the water gets shut off (which is the river's version of you turning off the power to your computer), the river forgets what you told it to do, and so it forgets the information you stored there. When the water flow resumes, it could go randomly down either fork again.

This is very much like how conventional memory chips work, but it's possible to build memory chips that work differently. Figure 9-13 shows another way to do it; instead of the direction of water flow representing a zero or a one, you'll use the presence or absence of water in a basin. We chose to let the absence of water be a one and the presence of water be a zero.

The ability to remember what you were doing when the power goes off is nice, but now you have another problem: It takes time to fill the basin (change a one to a zero), and it's even harder to get rid of the water once it's there (change a zero to a one). The basins are good for storing things, but once stored it's hard to change them.

The basin structure—with exactly the advantages and disadvantages we described—is how Electrically Programmable Read-Only Memory (EPROM) chips work. Transistors in the chip create the basin, and the water is the electricity. EPROM was the way most BIOS settings were stored in computers until relatively recently.

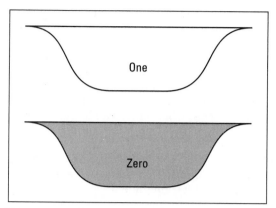

**Figure 9-13:** If you carefully change how you represent information, you can arrange to store it so that it stays around when the power goes off. Here, absence of water is a one, and presence of water is a zero.

If you were really dealing with water and a basin, you could get rid of the water by evaporation under strong sunlight. Real EPROM chips can be erased — set to all ones — by exposure to high-intensity ultraviolet light through a quartz window on the top of the chip. The erasure process takes a while in an EPROM eraser, and you have to remove the chip from the computer first. After it's erased, you then need another device called an EPROM programmer to load in new information. All in all, it's not something most people are equipped to do.

This was unfortunate for a long time, because it meant that the only way to update the BIOS in your computer was to get a new chip from the manufacturer and replace the one already on the motherboard. This was inconvenient and somewhat expensive, so in practice almost nobody did BIOS upgrades. In addition, because a BIOS is software, it was likely to have bugs (or at least behaviors you'd prefer it didn't have!). Both manufacturers and users really wanted a way to conveniently update the BIOS.

Motherboards no longer use EPROMs to hold the BIOS. Instead, they use what's called *flash memory*. Inside, a flash memory is very much like an EPROM with a valve on the side of the basin. Applying the right signal to the flash memory opens the valve and drains the basin, after which a different set of commands can reprogram it. This means that, instead of changing chips on the motherboard to update the BIOS, you simply tell it to erase and reprogram itself. When the manufacturer releases a BIOS update, you go through the erase/reprogramming sequence with the updated file and it's done.

Here's an example. For nearly two years after we built one of our computers, the machine would never warm boot (Ctrl+Alt+Delete) properly. The reset button worked, though, so we never got around to troubleshooting the problem. Eventually, we downloaded an updated BIOS and went through the ten minutes or so of work to update the flash memory. Since then, warm boots on the system work flawlessly. If the machine had used the older EPROM technology, we would have had to order (and pay for) new EPROM chips, gambling that would fix the problem. With a flash BIOS, we could experiment to see whether we had found the problem or not.

Here's another example. Intel released the 440BX PCIset well before the Pentium III processors. Most motherboards built using the 440BX can be upgraded for Pentium III operation with nothing more than a flash BIOS upgrade.

# Power

Computer circuits aren't as straightforward to power as kitchen appliances. You have to give them exactly the right power levels, and you have to keep the power within tight tolerances. Step outside the bounds and the machine might not work.

## Processor voltage

As the number of transistors in chips has gone up, the size of those transistors has gone down and the voltage they can take has gone down. Intel defined three different voltage requirements for Pentium processors: V (Standard), VR (Voltage Regulated), and VRE (Voltage Regulated Extension). Table 9-2 shows you the three voltage specifications, along with a comparison to the more common 5 V level.

| Table 9-2 Comparison of Pentium Voltage Specifications | | |
| --- | --- | --- |
| *Specification* | *Voltage* | *Percentage of 5 V* |
| Conventional | 5 V | 100 |
| V | 3.135 V to 3.465 V | 63 |
| VR | 3.3 V to 3.465 V | 66 |
| VRE | 3.45 V to 3.6 V | 69 |

Because of the smaller geometries in the newer parts, Intel specified the Pentium II processors to operate at even lower voltages. The exact voltage for a processor is dependent on the processor clock rate, as shown in Table 9-3.

### Table 9-3
### Comparison of Pentium II Voltage Specifications

| Processor Clock Rate | Specified Voltage | Voltage Tolerance Range |
|---|---|---|
| 233 to 300 MHz | 2.8 V | 2.73 V to 2.9 V |
| 266 to 333 MHz | 2.0 V | 1.93 V to 2.1 V |
| 350 to 450 MHz | 2.0 V | 1.93 V to 2.07 V |

If you buy a complete system, the manufacturer will have made all the power level settings for you. If you buy a motherboard, you'll have to set it up to match the requirements of the chip you get, although some motherboards like the Intel SE440BX do this automatically. Information on the correct voltage for the processor you have should be available from the processor manufacturer (and possibly from the motherboard manufacturer). Information on how to set the motherboard for a particular voltage specification should be in the motherboard manual.

## Power management

Power management started as a way to extend the battery life in laptop computers, because the less power the computer uses, the longer the battery lasts. Standards for how Windows and the BIOS interact to do this are called Advanced Power Management (APM). Overall, APM reduces system-wide power consumption in one or more of these ways:

✦ *Slow down or stop the processor clock.* Because the power that all the chips in your computer draw depends on how fast the chips are running, slowing down or stopping the processor reduces not only the power consumption by the processor but also the power consumption of the cache and the main memory. You won't notice this happening — Windows knows when the processor is idle and runs the processor at full speed at all other times. The processor goes from stopped to full speed immediately, without a delay.

✦ *Set the display to low power or standby.* Whether you have a desktop or laptop computer, the display consumes a major portion of the total system power. The picture tube and its supporting electronics consume most of the power in a monitor, and the lights for the liquid crystal display (LCD) use most of the power in a laptop display. Screen savers don't affect power consumption directly; the display consumes almost the same power whether the screen is all black or all white.

The difference between low-power and standby modes in a monitor is in how much gets turned off. Standby takes less power but takes a little more time to turn back on. LCD display lights are either on or off, and since they generate more light after they get hot, there will be some difference in the image you see when the lights go back on until they are hot again.

✦ *Spin down the disks.* The motor that rotates the disk spindle and platters consumes most of the power in a disk drive. By keeping the electronics alive but turning off the motor, disk drive manufacturers allow APM to reduce power consumption when the computer is idle. There's an irritating delay to spin the disk back to operating speeds, though, so it's important to strike a balance between power savings and operating convenience.

Power conservation is part of desktop computers as well, providing features like instant-on and making it ecologically reasonable to leave your computer on all the time. Microsoft argues that Windows computers need to be available on-demand—without a boot sequence—to do the work you want. The idea is the PC should always be on and ready, but, like a television, appear off when not in use. When you (or your network!) want service, the computer should wake up immediately, do the work, and then automatically go back to sleep.

**Note**    This isn't a small goal. We've seen a surprising number of manufacturers recommend turning off power management features in the BIOS and in Windows as one of their first steps in troubleshooting erratic problems. Stopping a computer in its tracks in a manner that lets it resume properly later is fiendishly difficult. If you have problems you can't isolate any other way, you might temporarily try turning off power management features yourself. You can always turn them back on if the problem lies elsewhere.

## Summary

✦ The key decisions about your computer—processor, cache, and bus—primarily concern the motherboard. The choice of motherboard drives everything else you do. If you buy a motherboard, insist on a PCI bus with AGP for the video card.

✦ The choice of memory type is now largely driven by the class of processor you have.

✦        ✦        ✦

# The Real World: Motherboard and BIOS

If you open your computer, you'll see a large board on the bottom or side of the case, into which other boards are plugged. That large board is called the *motherboard*, and it is the focus of some of the most significant decisions you make about your computer. Many of the motherboard characteristics you need to consider are prominently featured in computer system advertisements, including processor type, clock speed, cache size, and bus. An equal number of key characteristics are often omitted, such as onboard peripheral support, the range of processor speeds supported, the maximum amount of memory, and the number of memory slots. These latter characteristics strongly affect your ability to upgrade the machine in the future. In this chapter, we'll look at the entire motherboard and what you should consider when you go to buy one, whether in a complete system or by itself.

Figure 10-1 is a typical example, showing the Intel BI440ZX motherboard annotated to identify the major components. The features and layout of your motherboard will vary somewhat, but the ideas are similar and the parts tend to look much the same.

**Figure 10-1:** The motherboard is the core of your computer. (Copyright 1999 Barry and Marcia Press. Used with permission.)

The components in Figure 10-1 are identified in the following list:

✦ *Processor socket.* This motherboard accepts Intel Celeron processors. The ZIF (Zero Insertion Force) socket lets you easily insert and remove the chip. Be careful to seat the processor in the socket firmly before closing the clamp. If you don't, some of the pins may not make contact properly and the machine won't boot.

✦ *ATX power connector.* The ATX power supply output wires terminate in a single relatively large connector that plugs in here. All the power used by the motherboard and adapter cards comes through here.

✦ *DIMM memory sockets.* This motherboard uses SDRAM memory on DIMMs. You can use the faster PC100 SDRAMs (although performance won't change) in case you want to be sure the memory will work later with faster chips and motherboards.

✦ *PCI IDE connectors.* If you use an IDE disk, CD-ROM, or tape drive, these are the connectors you'll plug those cables into.

✦ *Floppy connector.* The floppy disk controller is on the motherboard. You run a standard cable from the floppy disk drive in the case to this connector.

✦ *AGPSet chip.* Although small, the support chip comprises the bulk of the electronics surrounding the processor, including support for the AGP, PCI, and ISA buses, the IDE disk controller, and other functions we'll discuss later in this chapter.

✦ *PCI connectors.* PCI adapter cards plug in here and are secured to the back of the case with a screw. You can use up to three PCI cards if you don't need any ISA cards. (PCI and ISA connectors are discussed later in this chapter.)

✦ *ISA connector.* One ISA card can plug in this 16-bit ISA slot. The presence of only one ISA slot reflects the migration of the computer industry away from ISA toward machines using AGP, PCI, and USB for all connections.

✦ *AGP connector.* If you use one, an AGP video card plugs in here. You get much better graphics performance with AGP. Using the AGP slot, which is good only for video, leaves the PCI slots available for other expansion.

✦ *Sound and game port connectors.* The sound and game ports have commonly been found on sound cards, but more and more are migrating onto the motherboard because of the relatively low cost compared to a separate audio card.

✦ *Serial port connectors.* Serial ports let you plug in modems, some joysticks and game controllers, and other external devices.

✦ *Parallel port connector.* You'll plug your printer into this connector.

✦ *USB connectors.* It's possible to plug keyboards, mice, speakers, cameras, scanners, and other devices into the USB ports. Unlike with the mouse, keyboard, and parallel ports, you don't have to turn off the computer to attach and detach USB devices.

✦ *PS/2 mouse and keyboard connector.* These are standard mini-DIN connectors that match the one at the end of your mouse or keyboard cable. Look for drawings near the connectors to determine which is for the mouse and which is for the keyboard.

✦ *ATX connector panel.* All the external I/O connections, including sound, game, serial, parallel, USB, mouse, and keyboard ports, are directly attached to the motherboard and mounted on the ATX connector panel. This design eliminates the in-case wiring required with older designs.

Also on the motherboard is the BIOS (*basic input/output system*), the program that starts up the computer when you turn on the power. A *flash memory* chip holds the BIOS code, even when the power is off. A special procedure allows you to update the BIOS in the flash with new code.

# The Intel BI440ZX Motherboard

The Intel BI440ZX motherboard illustrates many of the features and capabilities you can expect from a quality product, and it gives good performance even though it's targeted for low-cost systems. We recommend that you choose a motherboard in two steps: Narrow your choice down to products from motherboard manufacturers you trust, and then buy the one that makes the most sense for you in terms of features, price, and performance. We're very narrow-minded about whose motherboards we'll buy; over the last year or two, we've used motherboards from AMI and Intel. You can't get AT form factor boards from those companies any longer, though, so for upgrades we've done on older machines we've tried some boards from other manufacturers.

**Tip**    Be sure to consider the BIOS as well as the hardware itself. From bad experience we've become very picky about the BIOS on the motherboards we'll buy—we like the AMI BIOS for its features and reliability, and we have had good results with Phoenix. One of the problems with AT motherboards still on the market is that they often use a BIOS from some other provider that doesn't have the track record for stability and compatibility with Windows. It's very hard to get support from most motherboard manufacturers, so if the BIOS has problems, you could simply be stuck.

The Intel BI440ZX motherboard has nearly all the features you could want (see Table 10-1), with its only limitation for desktop applications being that it has fewer slots than you might want. The Intel SR440BX motherboard we use to build a desktop computer in Chapter 37, "Building a Desktop—Hardware," has similar features to the Intel BI440ZX but has more slots, supports a faster bus, and uses the faster Pentium II or Pentium III processors.

In the past we've recommended against using motherboards with built-in network, video, or sound functions, because, at the time, the slight cost savings you achieved combined with some performance and reliability problems to make it very likely that you'd soon wish they'd been on replaceable adapter cards. Improved pricing, reliability, and performance over the past few years have made us change that recommendation to the point where we recommend onboard PCI bus sound in all cases, and onboard video when it's done using a high-performance chip with enough video memory.

| Table 10-1 Specifications for the Intel BI440ZX Motherboard | |
|---|---|
| *Characteristic* | *Features and Characteristics* |
| Dimensions | Standard MicroATX form factor (about 9.6 inches square, with a standard mounting hole pattern). |

| Characteristic | Features and Characteristics |
| --- | --- |
| Processors | Celeron processor in a plastic pin grid array (PPGA) package at 300 to 400 MHz. The PPGA package is similar to the older Pentium packages but made from different materials. |
| Cache | L1 and L2 cache are onboard the Celeron chip itself. All supported onboard memory is cached. |
| Memory | 16 to 256MB of SDRAM DIMM memory in two banks. Both 66 and 100 MHz memory can be used, with the memory size and speed detected through the Serial Presence Detect (SPD) chip on the memory module. Intel recommends gold-plated contacts on the memory. |
| Bus | PCI at up to 132MB per second plus a 2X AGP slot. The board provides three PCI slots and one ISA slot. (One PCI slot shares space with the ISA connector, so you can only have two PCI cards if you use the ISA slot.) |
| Onboard disk controller | Two PCI IDE ports (four drives) supporting modes 0–4 plus UltraDMA at 33 MHz. Features include IDE prefetch, large block addressing, support for drives over 504MB, 32-bit data transfer, fast IDE transfer, and IDE block mode. |
| Floppy disk controller | Onboard floppy drive controller with support for 1.2MB, 1.44MB, and 2.88MB drives. The system supports 120MB floppies connected via the IDE port. |
| Serial / parallel | Two serial ports (16550 chip), with support for COM1, COM2, COM3, and COM4 addressing. One parallel port supporting normal, extended (bidirectional), EPP (enhanced asymmetric bidirectional), and ECP (enhanced capabilities, including DMA transfer and symmetric bidirectional support). |
| Input devices | Onboard keyboard and PS/2 mouse port. |
| Power management | Full Advanced Power Management (APM) and Advanced Configuration and Power Interface (ACPI) support. |
| System display and control | Connectors for power on/off, sleep/resume, and reset switches; LEDs for power on and IDE activity; speaker; and infrared interface module. |
| Peripherals management | Automatic BIOS detection of hard disk, floppy controller, serial port, and parallel port conflicts. The BIOS disables the onboard device if it finds a conflict. |
| BIOS upgrades | BIOS in flash memory, with a simple upgrade process that doesn't require opening the case and permits system recovery if the BIOS is corrupted. The BIOS can boot from floppy disk, CD-ROM, and hard disk. |

## The Intel/AMI BIOS

The Intel BI440ZX motherboard includes the Intel/AMI BIOS, a full-featured BIOS with updates to support the features of the Celeron and the 440ZX AGPSet. Features of the BIOS include

✦ Automatic detection of IDE drive parameters. The BIOS supports both onboard and offboard IDE controllers.

✦ User-specified disk drive types. This is necessary in any BIOS you get, because the largest disk explicitly defined has a 152MB capacity. (It's a very old standard.)

✦ Control over the usual keyboard repeat and memory test configurations, plus a handful of other options.

✦ Floppy drive swapping and boot up sequence control. Being able to tell the BIOS to boot the hard disk rather than a floppy is nice protection against accidentally booting a possibly virus-infected floppy that may have been left in the drive. Other BIOSs provide antivirus checking; however, we prefer to use a product such as McAfee VirusScan written specifically for your operating system and regularly updated for continued protection.

✦ Low-level access security through password checking. You can have passwords control nothing, setup parameters only, or complete access to the system.

✦ Full PCI/ISA Plug and Play support, including the capability to set legacy ISA card interrupt number reservations to ensure that the interrupt isn't assigned elsewhere.

✦ Advanced power management support, including configurable power down with both standby and suspend modes.

✦ Detection and support for bootable IDE CD-ROMs.

## Upgrading a flash BIOS

The Intel/AMI BIOS is easy to upgrade. Here's all you have to do:

1. Download the BIOS update file for this specific motherboard from the Intel web site. Intel has pages on their site for all the motherboards they make. We found the pages for the Intel BI440ZX (`http://developer.intel.com/design/motherbd/bi/bi_ds.htm`) by searching the site for the term BI440ZX. Once we were there, we found a link directly to the page for BIOS updates (`http://developer.intel.com/design/motherbd/bi/bi_bios.htm`). The link on that page downloads a file that, when run, extracts and decompresses the BIOS Software License Agreement, the utility for updating the flash BIOS, and the BIOS image itself.

2. Format a bootable floppy (under Windows, use the command **format a:/s**), then put the update files on the floppy by running the command **bios a:** (bios.exe is a file that will be extracted and decompressed in step 1).

3. Boot into the BIOS and write down all the settings. Better yet, use the PrintScrn key to print a copy of every screen.

4. Reboot the system from the floppy disk you made in step 2. The flash update program loads and prompts you from its main menu through commands "Update Flash Memory From a File" and then "Update System BIOS." You'll then select the file with the BIOS image and start the update process.

5. Let the system boot into the BIOS and reset all settings to default, and then program in the settings you saved before the update. Save the configuration changes; once they are complete, turn the power off, wait, and restart the computer.

That's all it takes to update the BIOS. The computer did the grunt work to upgrade the BIOS in its flash memory, with a lot of checks to make sure things were going properly. Here's what it did:

1. Read the floppy disk in drive A: and look for the upgrade data file.

2. Check the size of the file to make sure it wasn't corrupted.

3. Find the flash memory chip.

4. Erase the existing BIOS from the flash memory. A special, protected area of the flash memory, called the boot block, cannot be erased. This is the program that does flash memory reprogramming, so even if something goes wrong during the update process you can always try again. Lesser motherboards with flash BIOS chips that lack a boot block can be unrecoverably corrupted, leading to the motherboard being unusable until the flash memory chip is replaced.

5. Program the new BIOS image into the flash memory.

6. Reset the computer.

Flash memory makes BIOS upgrades simple. Don't buy a system or motherboard without it.

# Choosing a Motherboard

Table 10-2 shows the key decisions you'll make when you decide what motherboard to use.

| Table 10-2 | |
| :-- | :-- |
| **Key Decisions to Make When Choosing a Motherboard** | |
| *Category* | *Key Decisions* |
| Processor | Pentium, Pentium Pro, Pentium II, Pentium III, or AMD K6 / K6-2 / K6-3; possibly another competitive chip or (in unusual circumstances) a 486 upgrade |
| | Speed of the processor |
| L2 cache | Cache Size |
| | Cache Type (Built-in, Asynchronous, Pipeline Burst, or Synchronous Burst) |
| Bus | Type (PCI, VL, ISA, EISA, or MCA; PCI with AGP is the preferred choice) |
| Memory | Amount |
| | Type (Fast Page Mode, EDO, SDRAM, or Rambus) |
| Motherboard and BIOS | Manufacturer |

There are two levels of decisions here. If you buy a complete system from a manufacturer, you can select only some of the items in Table 10-2. You'll then take the rest of what comes in the manufacturer's package. If you build a machine from components, you have more flexibility to choose the rest of the options. For example, suppose you've picked a system manufacturer, and decided you want a 450 MHz Pentium II with AGP and 64MB of memory. At that point, your choices of motherboard and BIOS manufacturer are fixed, and possibly your choice of memory type too. You might have to seek another system manufacturer to get specific equipment you want.

# Top Support Questions

The most common processor, memory, and motherboard questions ask whether certain combinations of components work together — issues you'll see when specifying new computers and upgrading existing ones.

## Processors

Q: Do I have an MMX or SSE processor? Can I upgrade to one?

A: The initial version of the Pentium processor (up to 166 MHz) shipped before Intel introduced MMX, a technology to accelerate multimedia and other applications. Nearly all Intel processors after that (starting with the 200 MHz Pentium processor, and including the Pentium II, Celeron, and Pentium III but excluding the Pentium Pro) include MMX. The Pentium processors with MMX technology required special voltage support from the motherboard. The processor receives two supplies from the Socket 7 on the motherboard, one for the I/O pins on the processor, and one for the circuits internal to the chip. The pre-MMX Pentium processors use around 3.3 volts for both purposes, but an MMX Pentium processor requires that the internal circuits receive 2.8 volts, reduced from the usual supply. Your motherboard must explicitly support the reduced internal voltage requirements of the MMX Pentium processor for you to directly upgrade your processor by plugging in an MMX technology chip.

If your motherboard can't accept a direct MMX upgrade, you could consider using one of the MMX OverDrive processors. The OverDrive versions have internal voltage regulators that perform the 3.3 to 2.8 volt conversion.

The Pentium III chips were the first processors to implement the SSE extensions.

Q: I have an old 486-based computer I want to keep. Will a 486 accelerator chip work in my system?

A: Most 486-based systems can be upgraded with something like Kingston's 133 MHz Turbo Chip. To use the Turbo Chip, your motherboard needs a 486 SX/DX motherboard with a CPU socket capable of operating at 5 volts. (The 486 DLC/SLC motherboards cannot be upgraded with the Turbo Chip.) If your system has a soldered-on 486 CPU, the Turbo Chip is installable in the math coprocessor socket.

Q: Some of my friends speed up their systems with something they call "overclocking." It seems like a good idea, because I get more speed for free. Should I do it to my computer?

A: We introduced overclocking in the sidebar "Shooting yourself in the foot, computer style" in Chapter 3, so it should be no surprise that we don't recommend overclocking. Running the processor, memory, or other component past its rated speed can cause unreliable operation, can shorten the life of the component, and can cause overheating. Putting large fans and heat sinks on chips doesn't eliminate the risks inherent in overclocking, because no amount of additional cooling can make circuits run faster than their maximum design capabilities. If you exceed those design limits, your computer will crash.

## Memory

Q: Can I mix memory types and sizes?

A: Some motherboards will accept mixed memory configurations, and some won't. Your motherboard or system manufacturer is your best source to answer the question. It's always safe to use a single memory type and speed in all memory banks, but be sure the type and speed you use is supported by the motherboard and that the BIOS is configured properly. If you use SIMM memories, be sure that both SIMMs in a bank are the same.

Q: Can I mix tin and gold contacts?

A: It's best not to. You won't encounter problems immediately, but you're asking for trouble in the long run.

# Motherboards

Q: I get no video when I power up my computer, just a series of beeps. What's wrong?

A: The BIOS checks for a series of errors early on in the boot process, including video card missing or failed, memory refresh failure, memory missing or failed, timer failure, processor failure, BIOS ROM failure, CMOS failure, cache failure, and others. These failures are generally so severe that any of them will cause the computer to be incapable of generating and displaying an error message. The beeps are coded to indicate what's wrong, but since the beep codes are not standardized, you may have to check with your motherboard or BIOS manufacturer.

Q: Why won't my serial ports work?

A: There are no industry standards for the cable from an AT motherboard to the serial port connector on the back of the case. That means that, unless you have cables specifically designed for your motherboard, the port may not work. The ATX motherboards eliminate the cabling problem because the connectors are directly attached to the motherboard. See the next question for another cause, too.

Q: The BIOS or operating system reports an I/O conflict, or some of my I/O doesn't work. Why?

A: You may have more than one device in your system configured for the same I/O address or IRQ. For example, if your motherboard is set up to provide COM1 and COM2, plugging in a modem configured for COM1 will create a conflict unless you have a motherboard that can automatically disable or readdress a conflicting motherboard device. That automatic change could cause a previously working port to disappear when you plug in a new adapter card. You can get conflicts on DMA channels as well as addresses and IRQs. For example, DMA channels are used by sound cards (many use two). If you switch your parallel port to ECP (Enhanced Capabilities Port), it gets assigned a DMA channel too, which might conflict with the assignment for the sound card.

Q: I upgraded my motherboard and now the keyboard doesn't work. I tried the keyboard on another machine, and it's okay. What's wrong?

A: Most likely you reversed the 5-pin power and keylock connection from the chassis to the motherboard. If you do that, the motherboard ends up always thinking you want the keyboard locked, making it look like the keyboard doesn't work.

Q: Does it matter which ISA or PCI slot I put a card into?

A: Usually not, but there are a few exceptions.

✦ A very few cards need to be installed in a shared ISA/PCI slot so that they can plug into both connectors.

✦ Plug and Play sometimes mishandles interrupt assignments on the PCI bus, so if a board doesn't install right, try changing the order of the PCI cards on the motherboard to cause the software to try different combinations of assignments.

✦ Some cards use ribbon cables to wire over to connectors that mount on the back of the case in the space for another slot, requiring you to leave that slot empty.

✦ The BIOS initializes PCI cards from one end to the other in order. If you have multiple SCSI host adapters with disks on them, the order of the cards affects which drive will be seen as drive C:.

Q: What are all those tiny rectangular things soldered on the motherboard?

A: The very small ones are mostly resistors and capacitors. The number of capacitors matters a lot, particularly on the faster motherboards, because they filter noise out of the power lines on the motherboard. If you don't have enough of them (over a hundred isn't a lot), the residual noise can cause your machine to run erratically or crash. In the second quarter of 1997, news reports surfaced that some lesser quality motherboard manufacturers were using fewer capacitors than recommended by Intel, or were substituting poor-quality electrolytic capacitors for high-quality tantalum ones. Poor-quality capacitors are a particularly nasty issue, because the machine will run properly until the capacitors age. Once they do, though, the noise level increases on the power lines and the machine becomes unreliable. There's not much the average buyer can do to avoid these problems other than to be sure to buy motherboards from established, reputable manufacturers.

Q: Why does it take so long for my system to boot?

A: There are two components to system boot time: the time the BIOS takes, and the time the operating system takes. Some of the functions that the BIOS performs during system boot are the Power On Self Test (POST), scan for add-in cards with BIOS extensions, configuration of PCI add-in cards, assignment of system resources to devices that are needed to boot the system, and the isolation of ISA Plug and Play cards. The BIOS also checks for and configures IDE devices connected to the onboard IDE interfaces. System boot times can vary with different add-in hardware combinations. You can minimize the BIOS boot time by using the BIOS Setup utility to disable entries that correspond to unused IDE devices.

Q: Will an ATX motherboard board work in my existing non-ATX system?

A: No. The ATX form factor has a different size, shape, and electrical interface to the power supply than previous motherboard products. ATX has different requirements for mounting, cooling, and peripheral connections.

Q: Will my existing ISA and PCI boards work in an ATX motherboard??

A: Yes. The ATX specification has no special requirements for ISA or PCI cards.

Q: What is the 3.3-volt connector for on some AT motherboards?

A: The PCI Bus has 5V, +12V and –12V supplied to it on most motherboards, but commonly the 3.3 V supply to the PCI bus required by the PCI specification is not implemented. If you use PCI adapter cards requiring 3.3 volts on the PCI bus, you will need a special power supply or voltage regulator to connect to the motherboard 3.3 V connector. You may also find a 3.3 V connector on motherboards for larger servers to help supply the needs of the processors and massive amounts of memory.

Q: What is the latest BIOS upgrade for my motherboard?

A: The only straightforward way to find out about newer BIOS versions is to check the manufacturer's Web site, if they have one, or call their technical support line. The BIOS generally reports its version when the computer starts up. It's not always a good idea to change BIOS versions, though — if your computer is performing well and is stable, you might be better off leaving things alone.

Q: How can I ensure that I have the best settings in my BIOS?

A: Most often, the "optimal" default settings, if the BIOS offers a command to change settings in bulk, are your best compromise between performance and compatibility. Loading these values should let your system perform well. You can enable other chip set features, but be sure to test thoroughly to make sure you don't get surprised by hidden compatibility problems.

Q: How can I use the built-in PS/2 mouse feature on my motherboard?

A: Unless you have an ATX motherboard, you'll probably need a cable from your motherboard manufacturer to run from the motherboard to the back panel of the computer. Once you wire that up and plug in a PS/2-compatible mouse, your operating system should recognize it. If not, you'll need to configure for the specific I/O port and IRQ setting used by your board. If you have an ATX motherboard, you should be able to simply plug in the PS/2 mouse. (Some systems ship with the BIOS setting for the PS/2 port disabled, so if the mouse port doesn't work, check that.)

Q: Will two processors increase performance in Windows 3.x/9x and DOS?

A: No. The operating system has to support recognizing and managing multiple processors, and neither Windows 3.x/9x nor DOS support multiprocessor systems. You can run those operating systems on multiprocessors, but only one processor will be used. Windows NT and many versions of UNIX support multiprocessors.

Q: I can't see which pin is pin 1 on the USB cable for my AT motherboard. Does it matter if I get it wrong?

A: Very much so. One motherboard support technician we spoke to, for example, commented that getting the cable backward is likely to "blow up the board." We don't literally expect a motherboard to explode, but it's not likely you'll use it for computing after making that mistake. The pin 1 mark can be hard to see. If you're unsure about pin 1 on your cable, keep looking.

# Hands-On Upgrades

Motherboard-related upgrades range from simple to complex. Adding memory to a motherboard is among the simplest; replacing a motherboard is as hard as it gets. Let's look at both.

## Adding memory to a motherboard

The computer industry standardization on 72-pin SIMM and 168-pin DIMM modules simplifies memory upgrades to the point where they're simple and straightforward. Once you disassemble your computer to the point where you can get at the memory sockets (refer back to Chapter 6, for how to do basic disassembly), you'll see something like Figure 10-2. The photograph shows both SIMM and DIMM sockets for memory. You can't populate all the SIMM and DIMM sockets on this motherboard at the same time; other motherboards supporting both SIMM and DIMM memory are likely to have similar restrictions, so check the manual before you order parts.

Both types of sockets are built to make sure you can only insert modules one way, and to ensure a reliable mechanical fit. If you look at the DIMM sockets in Figure 10-2, you'll see that the rows of pins are not symmetric — there's a gap in the pins on the left not present on the right. The orientation mechanism for SIMMs is more subtle, as shown in Figure 10-3, where you can see a sloped key at the end of the socket. That key is only present on one end of the socket and mates with a notch on the SIMM itself. Make sure you get the key and notch lined up at the same end; forcing the module in with it backward will at best damage the memory module or the socket.

DIMM socket
(2 total)

SIMM socket
(4 total)

**Figure 10-2:** Memory sockets on your motherboard will be labeled
Bank 1, Bank 2, and so on. Populate the lowest numbered banks first.

## Installing SIMMs

You can also see the mechanical catch that secures the module in Figures 10-2 and
10-3. The SIMM catch is the metallic arm in the corner of the long white socket. You
can see it just above the key in Figure 10-3. (The DIMM catch is the gray lever
extending up over the socket in Figure 10-2.) You must release the catches before
removing modules. The catches snap in place when you insert the module properly
and completely. You should never have to force either the catch or the module to
get a proper fit.

The order in which you insert SIMMs into the motherboard matters, because you
have to insert them at a slant and then rotate them into position. Figure 10-4 shows
the problem. In the photograph, we've positioned a module into a socket but not
rotated it to the vertical position so that it snaps into the catches. Before we rotate
it to vertical position, it interferes with the space over the socket to its right, which
means that if a module were already in the rightmost socket, we couldn't insert the
module shown. From the point of view of the photograph, the right sequence is to
insert modules from left to right. We're only populating one bank of memory in this
series of photographs, so the two rightmost sockets in Figure 10-4 are the ones we'll
use. The key to knowing that is the lettering on the motherboard right below the
sockets that says "Bank 2" on the left and "Bank 1" on the right. For Pentium and
Pentium Pro processor motherboards, you fill both sockets of a bank with identical
modules, filling lower-numbered banks first.

Catch    Key

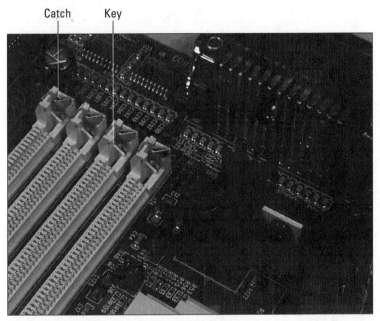

**Figure 10-3:** SIMM sockets all provide a key and catch mechanism to ensure correct, secure mounting.

SIMM edge in socket

**Figure 10-4:** SIMMs install by settling them into the pins of the socket, and then rotating them vertical into the catches.

Figure 10-5 shows the finished installation, with both banks of memory snapped into Bank 1. A later upgrade to put memory into Bank 2 would require first removing the modules in Bank 1, then installing from left to right.

SIMMs locked in socket

**Figure 10-5:** A complete installation into Bank 1 uses identical modules in both sockets.

Once you insert the new memory, you'll have to check that the settings in the BIOS are correct. Parameters you may have to set include total memory (although newer BIOS revisions are likely to figure this out for themselves), type of memory (also subject to automatic detection), and memory speed.

## Installing DIMMs

Upgrading a motherboard with DIMMs is simpler than a SIMM upgrade, because one DIMM forms a complete bank. Most motherboards using DIMMs let you put the modules in any DIMM socket in any order, so (once you get the right memory) the installation is little more than plugging the module into a socket. You insert DIMMs vertically into the socket, without any of the rotation needed for SIMMs. Vertical insertion means that you can insert modules in any order, because you won't have one module interfering with access to another module socket.

Figure 10-6 shows how to insert DIMMs into a motherboard. Orient the module so that the key matches the slot in the socket, and then push the module down evenly until the latches at the side click in. Open the latches if you need to remove the module—when you do, the module lifts out of the socket and can be pulled out.

Empty DIMM Socket   DIMM Memory Strip

**Figure 10-6:** This back view of a DIMM shows the module installed alongside an empty socket. (Copyright 1999 Barry and Marcia Press. Used with permission.)

## Replacing a motherboard

Replacing a motherboard is complex not only because of the mechanical operations involved, but also because of the requirement to configure switches and jumpers on the motherboard and to reconnect the surrounding electronics.

The first step is to remove the old motherboard. Start by removing all the adapter cards and cables attached to the old motherboard, marking everything to indicate what it was connected to. You'll want to detach cables from the adapter cards before removing them; keep the adapter cards in antistatic bags while they're out of the machine.

Figure 10-7 shows how the motherboard comes out of a minitower case. A metal plate the size of the motherboard screws to the rest of the chassis; removing the two attachment screws shown in the figure allows the plate (and motherboard) to pivot down and away from the chassis. We've never seen two cases that were exactly alike, though, so spend some time looking at yours to understand how it comes apart before diving in.

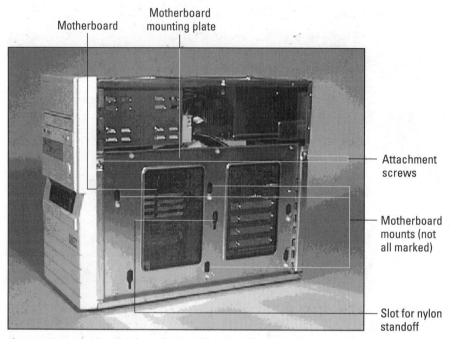

Motherboard

Motherboard
mounting plate

Attachment
screws

Motherboard
mounts (not
all marked)

Slot for nylon
standoff

**Figure 10-7:** The motherboard mounting plate in this system unscrews from the chassis, making motherboard removal simpler.

The detail in Figure 10-8 became visible after removing the plate and motherboard. Motherboards have a standard mounting hole pattern mirrored by the chassis. You'll find two forms of attachment from the motherboard to the chassis, threaded metal standoffs and nylon standoffs. Metal standoffs screw or clip into the chassis and are secured to the motherboard with screws. Nylon standoffs snap into the motherboard and slide into enlarged slots in the chassis. (You can see the shape of the enlarged slot in Figure 10-7.) ATX motherboards most commonly use only clip-in metal standoffs with screws attaching the motherboard; the combination of metal and nylon is prevalent on AT boards.

You may or may not choose to remove the nylon standoffs from the old motherboard. They're generally difficult to remove (gently squeeze the leaves on top with a pliers), so unless you need them for the new motherboard, it's not worth the trouble.

Installing the new motherboard is definitely more complex than removing the old one. Here are the steps:

   **1.** Set the switches and jumpers to correspond to the processor you will use. This is completely motherboard dependent.

Keyboard connector

AT-style power connectors

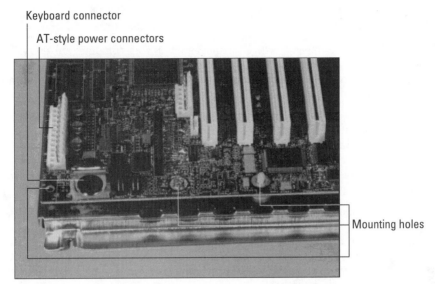

Mounting holes

**Figure 10-8:** Holes on the motherboard line up with holes in the mounting plate. Use metal screws and standoffs or plastic spacers.

**Cross-Reference**    Chapter 37 and Chapter 39 show how to configure the Intel SR440BX and AMI MegaRUM II motherboards.

2. Mount the motherboard into the case. Use metal standoffs and screws everywhere there are threaded or clip-in holes in the case that line up with plated-metal holes on the motherboard. The metal standoffs provide grounding, reducing noise in the motherboard signal paths. Using screws on holes without metal pads risks shorting signals on the motherboard, preventing correct operation and risking damage. (See the sidebar "Folklore and good mechanical practice.")

Use nylon standoffs everywhere else there are holes that line up in the chassis and motherboard. The more you use, the better the motherboard is supported and the less the risk of flexing.

3. Don't tighten the screws on the motherboard completely — leave them loose enough for the board to move somewhat.

4. If the motherboard was on a plate, such as in Figure 10-8, mount the plate back in the chassis.

5. Temporarily insert an adapter card at each end of the motherboard bus, and then screw the cards to the case to establish precise alignment between the motherboard and chassis. Tighten the screws anchoring the motherboard to the chassis, and then remove the adapter cards again.

## Folklore and good mechanical practice

A single conductor never forms an electrical circuit. Signals in your computer are always referenced to ground, or zero volts. It's critically important that all parts of the computer be firmly tied to the same zero-volt reference to avoid introducing noise into signals as they traverse the circuit boards.

The chassis of your computer is a primary ground reference. The system of metal pads on the motherboard and metal mounts under those pads is designed to make sure the ground traces on the motherboard are robustly connected to the chassis. It's no accident that ATX motherboards use far more metal mounts for the motherboard than did AT boards—the increase in signal frequencies and reduction in voltage levels that occurred at the same time ATX was designed make good grounding much more important than in the past.

You're likely to find other writers saying that you should use insulating washers between the metal mounts and the motherboard to avoid creating shorts. (Even the author of a computer book we did the technical edit for chose to ignore our vehement protests.) We can't emphasize strongly enough—that's very bad advice. Preventing connections from the motherboard grounds to the chassis tends to isolate the motherboard from the rest of the system and can cause random crashes.

There's a real problem underlying that bad advice, however. Many people are careless about positioning the motherboard on the metal mounts, or they are careless about the size of the head on the screws attaching the motherboard to the mount. Worse yet, some motherboard manufacturers have been sloppy designing the metal pads for the mounts, allowing inadequate clearance around the hole. If any part of the screw or metal mount extends past the metal pad on the motherboard, there's the chance that a signal or power wire will short out, creating failures in the system. The right way to solve the problem isn't to put in insulating washers, it's to position the motherboard carefully on the mounts and to use a screw with the proper size head.

Don't underestimate how serious this issue is. Your computer is likely to appear to work right even if there are no ground connections from motherboard to chassis. Noise effects are erratic, and it's unpredictable when or how badly grounding will affect operation.

6. Reattach the power supply connectors. For AT and baby AT motherboards, the power connectors go such that the black wires are at the middle, where the two connectors abut each other.

7. With the exception of the wide ribbon cables, reattach the cables that used to attach to the old motherboard. Here are the most common possibilities:

   • *Speaker.* The speaker connection is four pins wide, but only the outer two are used. It doesn't really matter which way you orient the connector. You may find a key in the connector on the speaker wires but all four pins present on the motherboard; in that case, simply remove the key from the connector.

   • *Turbo switch and LED.* Older case front panels provide switches to control a high/low speed setting for the motherboard, and indicators that show which setting is active. This is a holdover required at one time by old software unable to function correctly at the processor's full speed. Recent motherboards omit the switch connection and may omit the indicator. Your BIOS may provide the speed control function in response to keyboard commands; check the manual in the unlikely case you need to slow the processor down.

The orientation of the switch connection is immaterial; the LED connection has to be oriented properly. (See the sidebar "Getting the LEDs connected right.") If the turbo LED is connected backward, it won't work. Nothing bad happens — the light simply stays dark.

- *Reset switch.* The reset switch is a two-position connector. It doesn't matter which way you orient the connector.

- *Keylock / Power LED.* There's a combined five-position connector for the keylock and the power LED (although we've seen some chassis lately in which the connector is split into two, one with three positions and one with two). The pinouts are standard but not reversible. If you get the connector backward, the power LED won't work.

- *Hard drive activity.* If the motherboard has an integrated disk controller, such as for PCI IDE ports, there will be a connector for a disk activity LED. Not only does getting the connector turned the right way matter, but many motherboards provide a four-position connector, although most cases provide a two-position one. You'll use two pins at one end of the four; check your motherboard documentation for which ones. There are four ways to put on the two-position connector (two places, with two orientations each). Only one will work, but as with the turbo LED, the only bad result from installing the connector incorrectly should be that the LED doesn't work.

8. Mount the memory in the motherboard. If the memory sockets are behind something when the motherboard is installed, you may need to do this before you mount the motherboard in the case. We prefer to install the memory after putting in the motherboard so that it doesn't get hit as you work on the motherboard.

9. Mount the processor in the socket. The pattern of pins on the bottom of the chip or cartridge is not symmetric — there is only one way it will fit. If you bend pins, you can ruin the processor, so be sure you get it right. Mounted properly, with the lever on the socket all the way up, a chip should drop into the socket without any force. It takes a little pressure to snap a cartridge into the slot — you have to make sure that the cartridge snaps into the retaining clips on the side.

You may have to mount the processor on the motherboard before mounting the motherboard in the case. This would be true if it's hard to reach the processor socket after installing the motherboard. As with memory, we prefer to install the processor after the motherboard so that the major mechanical operations are complete.

If there's not already one attached, put a cooling fan on the processor and connect it to power. Some fans connect to the larger power connectors used for disk drives, while others connect to a small three-pin connector on the motherboard. The motherboard version is becoming increasingly common in newer machines so that the system can monitor the fan rotation rate and watch for failures.

10. Connect the remaining power and data cables, such as ones to the floppy disk and disk drives. If you have a system using an AT board, wire up the serial and parallel ports. Be sure to get pin 1 oriented properly on all data cables, and don't forget the power connections for auxiliary case fans.

11. Insert the adapter cards, hook up the keyboard and mouse, power up the system, and check the BIOS settings. If you're conservative, you may want to insert only the video card before powering up and checking basic operation.

That last step, putting in cards and powering up, is where things are likely to go wrong. If the machine doesn't come up, recheck cable connections and the placement of the processor in the socket. If that doesn't work, disconnect disks and remove adapter cards until just the video is left, and build from there.

## Getting the LEDs connected right

Cases seem to show no consistency in marking the wires that connect to the LEDs on the front panel, using a variety of wire colors and coding schemes. This is really unfortunate, because LEDs only work on one orientation — if you get them backward, they won't light.

LEDs connect between power and ground, with a resistor on the power side to limit current through the LED. The computer turns the LED on and off by connecting or disconnecting the LED from ground. Knowing this helps you figure out how to wire up the LEDs, because most often the wires will have one black lead and one colored one. The black lead will be the wire that goes to ground. For example, suppose the LED wire pairs are black/red, black/blue, black/white, or what have you. The black wire in each pair is likely the one that goes to ground.

Once you sort out the colors, read the motherboard manual to figure out what goes where. For example, one manual we looked at shows the Power LED connections with pin 1 as "Red wire, LED power" and pin 3 as "GND, black wire." That's straightforward. Less simple are the connections for the Hard Drive LED, which show pins 1 and 4 as "Pull_Up_330," pin 2 as a key, and pin 3 as "HD Active." A pull-up is a resistor connected to power, so the correct connection is the black wire to pin 3 and the colored wire to pin 4.

## Upgrading a processor

We have a real Frankenstein's monster of a machine. It started life as an actual IBM PC/AT with a 6 MHz Intel 286 processor. We've upgraded it every few years, first to a 386-based motherboard, then to a Micronics M4PI 486 PCI motherboard we took out of another machine during an upgrade. We use the machine as a print server on our network, but it had gotten slow and was due for another performance boost. Because it had a PCI motherboard, we decided to look at the payoff of a processor upgrade rather than a complete motherboard overhaul. We chose to replace its Intel 486DX2/66 with a Kingston TurboChip 133. You might do this sort of upgrade for a machine you use for similar light work, or for a machine you use with Linux or FreeBSD (which can have lesser hardware requirements than Windows). You might use the Kingston TurboChip 233 to upgrade slower Pentium processor machines.

Figure 10-9 shows the interior of the system around the processor. Because the Micronics motherboard included a Zero Insertion Force (ZIF) socket that made it easy to remove the old chip, the upgrade was far simpler than we'd expected. Total time was about five minutes — all that was required was to open the case, remove the old chip, plug in the new one, and close things back up. No jumpers, no switches, no cables, and no BIOS changes. (Other motherboards will have different configurations and may be more complicated to upgrade.)

486DX2/66 processor     ZIF socket release lever

**Figure 10-9:** Prior to upgrade, this 486DX2/66 processor ran in the Micronics M4PI PCI motherboard.

Figure 10-10 shows the result after plugging in the TurboChip 133. The fan you see in the picture (replacing the heat sink on the 486DX2/66) draws its power from the motherboard through the processor socket, so there's no cable to connect over to the power supply.

TurboChip
133 processor

**Figure 10-10:** The upgrade to a Kingston TurboChip 133 processor resulted in a significant performance boost.

We used benchmarks to measure the performance improvement. Kingston ships a version of the Landmark benchmark with the upgrade, which reported the results in Table 10-3.

| Table 10-3 The Landmark Benchmark Reports a Doubling of Processor Performance | | | |
| --- | --- | --- | --- |
| *System Component* | *TurboChip 133* | *486DX2/66* | *Improvement* |
| Processor | 452 | 226 | 100% |
| Floating point unit | 1130 | 568 | 99% |
| Video | 1908 | 1908 | 0% |

That's a stunning improvement for an upgrade that (in the second quarter of 1999) retails for $70 to $90 U.S. If it really doubles the performance you get at that price, it's a no-brainer when you've got a motherboard able to deliver enough bus performance.

Because we know that choke points limit the effect of upgrades, it's worth looking deeper to measure system-level performance. We did this upgrade in early 1997, so we ran the WinBench 96 benchmark suite under Windows 95 on the machine before and after the upgrade. Beyond the M4PI motherboard, the machine has 16MB of memory, a 256KB L2 cache, an Orchid ProDesigner II video card, an Adaptec AHA-2940 SCSI host adapter, and a Fujitsu disk. The WinBench 96 (version 1.0) results before and after the upgrade are in Table 10-4.

| Table 10-4 | | | |
| --- | --- | --- | --- |
| **A WinBench 96 Measurement Reports More Conservative Improvements from the Upgrade** | | | |
| *Benchmark* | *TurboChip 133* | *486DX2/66* | *Improvement* |
| CPUMark 16 | 123 | 84.2 | 46% |
| CPUMark 32 | 130 | 94.7 | 37% |
| Disk WinMark 96 | 477 | 414 | 15% |
| Graphics Winmark 96 | 2.12 | 1.87 | 13% |

While not as dramatic as the Landmark measurement would lead you to believe, the WinBench scores reflect solid processor speed gains. The video and disk scores aren't terribly better than before the upgrade, but the processor gain will definitely help print server performance. If you're running data base or CAD software, you might not see much benefit. If you're one of the holdouts still running DOS or Windows 3.1 with a combination of word processor, spreadsheet, and e-mail, you'll like the results.

# Summary

✦ The key decisions about your computer — processor, cache, and bus — primarily concern the motherboard. The choice of motherboard drives everything else you do. If you buy a motherboard, get both the PCI and AGP buses.

✦ A motherboard including features such as a PCI IDE interface and a flash BIOS can save you money and time.

✦ Memory upgrades are simple and, if your system is starved for memory, very effective.

✦ Motherboard upgrades can be difficult but may be the key to better performance at a reasonable cost.

✦    ✦    ✦

# I/O and Peripherals

**F**or purposes of this book, we call any device other than the processor and memory that's attached to the bus a *peripheral*. Peripherals can attach to the AGP, PCI, or ISA bus but are not attached directly to the processor. Peripherals themselves either attach directly to the internal bus, as in the case of a modem, or attach to an I/O bus, as in the case of a disk drive. Some intermediary electronics, generally called an I/O channel, bridge the internal bus to the I/O bus. Specific I/O channels are often called *controllers* or *host adapters*. Here are some examples of I/O channels:

- ✦ A card that connects a SCSI disk, CD-ROM, tape, or scanner to a PCI bus.

- ✦ A credit card–sized device that connects a small computer system interface (SCSI — pronounced *scuzzy*) scanner to a PC Card (once called PCMCIA, or Personal Computer Memory Card International Association) bus.

- ✦ The electronics that connect Universal Serial Bus (USB) mice, joysticks, monitors, and other devices to the PCI bus.

- ✦ A card that connects an IDE disk, CD-ROM, or tape to an ISA bus. A similar I/O channel is often built into the motherboard and connected to the PCI bus.

- ✦ An infrared port that connects a laptop computer to a digital camera.

As with the processor, bus, and memory, the issues for I/O channels center around performance and functionality. These factors are more complex for I/O channels than for the processor, memory, and internal bus, because the kinds of devices that can be attached are more varied and their interfaces are less regular. While there are only a few different types of chips (and therefore interfaces) in the Intel-compatible processor series, every kind of peripheral device has its own sets of interfaces.

The issues for I/O channels are

✦ What is the *function* of the connected peripheral device, and what are the commands that control that function?

✦ What are the *standards* that the device conforms to, and what are the features and limitations of those standards?

✦ What are the *performance capabilities* of each element of the I/O chain, from controller through device, and where are the limitations?

✦ What is the *impact on the system as a whole* of the peripheral's functionality and performance?

We've covered what's inside I/O channels and peripherals, what determines their characteristics in your system, and how overall system performance depends on them in this chapter. The most dramatic system-level effects of increased performance in peripheral devices are from faster disk and network transfers.

# Bigger and Faster Disks Do More

Disk drives provide large-scale storage for the computer, and they provide the only storage for user information while the power is off. Although common specifications evaluate disks in gross terms by capacity in gigabytes and access time in milliseconds, the performance of different disks of the same capacity and access time in different systems is likely to be very different. The reason is that both disk capacity and performance are affected by the disk controller, the processor and bus, the operating system software, and even the cables to the disk.

Starting at the disk itself, the first factors in disk performance are the number of sectors the disk has per track and the rate at which the disk spins. Sectors normally contain 512 data bytes each, so the more sectors that fly past the heads in one second, the more data that can be transferred. Tracks on the inside of the disk, nearer the spindle, may have fewer sectors than those on the outside, sometimes by as many as a factor of two. Because the disk rotation rate is constant, varying the number of sectors on a track will cause differences in the transfer rate the disk supports between the inner and outer tracks. The actual number of sectors per track will generally be hidden from the computer by the disk drive electronics, but the difference in transfer rate will be measurable.

The disk rotation rate has a direct impact on transfer rates, because the sustained transfer rate for a disk will be the track capacity times the rotation rate. If the disk contains 63 sectors per track, then one track stores 31.5K. Table 11-1 shows the sustained data transfer rate a disk like that (and some others) can support based on its rotation rate. Because the number of sectors per track varies (whether the controller reports it as a constant or not), these numbers are a snapshot of some drive characteristic. Part of what makes benchmarking interesting is discovering which characteristic that is (see the sidebar "A lesson in benchmarking" in this chapter).

| | Table 11-1 Disk Geometry and Rotation Rate | | |
|---|---|---|---|
| **Rotation Rate (RPM)** | **Sectors per Track (Average)** | **Track Capacity (Kilobytes)** | **Sustained Transfer Rate (MB per second)** |
| 3,600 | 63 | 31.50 | 1.85 |
| 3,600 | 68 | 34.00 | 1.99 |
| 4,500 | 63 | 31.50 | 2.31 |
| 5,400 | 63 | 31.50 | 2.77 |
| 5,400 | 96 | 48.00 | 4.22 |
| 5,400 | 133 | 66.50 | 5.84 |
| 7,200 | 63 | 31.50 | 3.69 |
| 7,200 | 146 | 73.00 | 8.55 |
| 10,000 | 170 | 85.14 | 13.85 |

The sustained transfer rate is critically important to the performance of your computer. Operating systems often do long reads and writes to the swap file, as well as long reads to load programs. (See the sidebar "Virtual memory: Faking memory with disk" in Chapter 2 for a refresher on swap files.) Faster swap file operations mean you can overcommit memory more before the performance drop becomes objectionable. Faster program loads mean better responsiveness to what you ask the computer to do.

## Onboard disk cache improves I/O performance

Table 11-1 raises more questions than it answers, in that it shows that some of the high rotational rate—7,200 RPM—disks now available cannot sustain a transfer rate greater than 3.69MB per second. (Actually, on the outer tracks the disks can sustain a rate greater than this, but not by more than a factor of two.) You'll see in Chapter 12 that IDE and SCSI disk interfaces are much faster than 3.69MB per second, supporting speeds of 20 to 40MB per second. The question is, why are the disk and disk interface speeds so different? Why would the disk controllers be so much faster than what the disks can sustain?

The answer is threefold. First, the disks themselves incorporate cache memory and small onboard microprocessors that together permit very fast transfers between the computer and the cache along with slower transfers between the cache and the disk platters. Onboard disk caches range from 32KB upward to 4,096KB and more, equivalent to as many as 16,384 sectors. Second, because the cache can operate at the speed of the controller, the processor can read a burst of data from the disk, or dump data to the disk, and continue running programs. While the processor goes off and does other useful work, the cache works with the much slower disk to complete the job. Third, if the disk interface is much faster than the sustained disk rate, there will be time available on the bus for more than one drive. (For example, an 80 MBps disk interface could support four 20 MBps disk drives with only minimal contention.)

The role of cache in a disk is different than that of the cache between the processor and memory — the disk cache mediates between devices of wildly different speeds, while the memory cache reduces the demand on the slower device to levels it can handle. The onboard disk cache also has a role different than the disk cache implemented in DOS, UNIX, and Windows. The operating system disk cache has the same role as a memory cache — if the data needed by the processor is in that cache, then the processor never communicates with the disk at all.

Allowing the processor to resume work while the disk cache buffers the transfer is terribly important. Suppose that the processor has 32KB of data to write to the disk (a small spreadsheet or the text part of a Web page, for example). At a burst transfer rate of 3MB per second (ATA Mode 0), the processor requires about 10.5 milliseconds to hand the data over to the disk (plus the overhead of working with the disk controller; that overhead is significant — we'll get to it soon). A 450 MHz processor may execute more than five million instructions in that time. If the processor handles the data transfer, most of those millions of instructions go to service the disk. If instead the controller and cache support transfers at 10MB per second (FAST SCSI), the transfer is complete in a little over three milliseconds, and the processor will have executed only about 1.5 million instructions. The remaining millions of instructions go to doing other things you want done. The numbers are all proportional — if the controller and disk cache can support 20MB per second for the burst (FAST wide SCSI, or narrow Ultra SCSI), then the transfer can complete in about 1.5 milliseconds, and the operation only consumes 750,000 instructions.

Because of these relationships, increasing the transfer rate to the disk can free up the processor significantly. Newer disk interface specifications such as ATA-2 and SCSI-2 incorporate faster transfer rates for this reason. Bus mastering and direct memory access (DMA) further reduce the processor load, because they only require processor intervention to start and finish a block transfer, not to move individual words. Nevertheless, putting a faster controller and a disk that supports it in your system may or may not speed up your system. One of the reasons why may be the disk cache.

**Benchmarking**    Figure 11-1 shows the results of repetitively reading one sector on three different disks. We've used this data from some relatively old and slow disks — the Conner brand no longer exists — to highlight the interesting behavior of the Maxtor disk. All three disks were in the same computer, connected to the same SCSI controller. We used the SCSIBench program from the Adaptec EZ-SCSI 4.0 software to take the measurements. Table 11-2 shows the calculated disk characteristics corresponding to these measurements. These characteristics (reported by SCSIBench) suggest significantly better performance may be available from the Toshiba and Conner drives than the Maxtor.

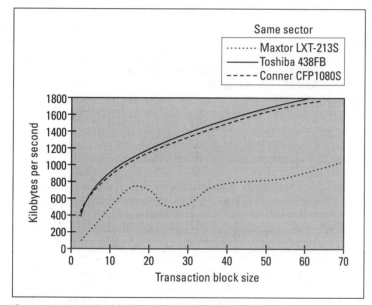

**Figure 11-1:** A disabled cache on the Maxtor drive causes significantly lower performance.

## Table 11-2
## Benchmark Comparisons of Disk Performance

| Drive | Cylinders | Heads | Sectors / Track | RPM | Rate (MBps) |
|-------|-----------|-------|-----------------|-----|-------------|
| Maxtor LXT-213S | 1,698 | 4 | 42 | 3,551 | 1.243 |
| Toshiba 438FB | 1,692 | 15 | 68 | 3,600 | 2.029 |
| Conner CFP1080S | 3,658 | 6 | 96 | 5,400 | 4.325 |

The speed gain from disk cache is clearly apparent in Figure 11-1 once you know that the caches are enabled for reads and writes on the Toshiba and Conner drives, but not on the Maxtor. All three drives are running with their factory settings — the Maxtor as it came when Northgate Computer Systems originally sold us the computer in late 1990, and the others as they came out of the box when I added them to that system. The SCSIBench "Same Sector" test is designed to discover the maximum performance the path through the controller to the disk (but exclusive of the rotating components) can provide. Because the disk cache is turned on in the Toshiba and Conner drives, repeated requests from the processor for the same sector are always satisfied out of the cache. The Maxtor drive can't do that, so it has to wait for the disk to rotate to the right sector and perform the read for every request.

As Figure 11-1 shows, you can't assume that the manufacturer of your computer always sets it up for best performance. If you have SCSI drives, you can use the Adaptec SCSI Explorer to check the drive cache settings, and to enable the caches if they're off. Read and write caching are different settings, so be sure to check them both. If you benchmark drive performance before and after you make changes, you'll gain a good understanding of the effect of the caches in your system. Be sure to use a benchmark that tests a mix of disk activity.

**Cross-Reference**    Details on choosing a benchmark are in Chapter 35.

Another interesting effect shown in Figure 11-1 is apparent when you look at the maximum calculated transfer rate for the disks in Table 11-2. The Toshiba and Conner drives benchmark at roughly equal performance in this test, but according to the table, the Conner should have about twice the performance. This means that some other component in the system is limiting performance. The disks were connected through an ISA bus controller, so the most likely candidate for the choke point is the slow ISA bus. Uncovering choke points like this is difficult to do reliably without benchmarks but is invaluable to understanding how to upgrade effectively. In the case of that specific computer, knowing the ISA bus is the choke point makes it clear that the disk is going as fast it can given the constraint of the motherboard. In addition to showing that the added speed of the Conner disk was wasted, the measurement suggests that exchanging the processor for a faster one won't do much except for computations that stress the processor alone, because the processor will otherwise be starved for disk access. The only way to use faster disks in that system would be to upgrade the motherboard to one with a PCI bus, eliminating the ISA bottleneck.

Measurements like the ones in Figure 11-1 are the basis for our decision to state in this book that the ISA bus has a 2.5MB per second peak effective transfer rate, even though in theory the ISA bus should be good for 5 to 8MB per second. You'll find those higher numbers in a lot of other sources, and theoretically they're right. In practice, the lower estimate is more accurate.

## A lesson in benchmarking

As you look at more benchmark results, and as you conduct benchmark tests yourself, you'll see numbers that don't make sense. One of the most interesting aspects of doing benchmarks well is discovering why things didn't turn out as you expected.

We ran the Adaptec SCSIBench program against a Seagate Barracuda ST15150W drive, using an Adaptec AHA-2940UW PCI bus mastering controller on a machine with a 166 MHz Intel Pentium processor. The Adaptec controller with the Seagate drive is a very fast combination; the sustained transfer rate we saw for sequential 64K blocks was just under 7MB per second. What made the benchmark very interesting was the fact that the next to last row in Table 11-1 corresponds to specifications for this drive, so I expected nearly 9MB per second. That prediction is different than what we measured, so the right question is to ask why there is such a difference.

The answer is the fact we looked at earlier in the chapter — disk drives don't really have a constant number of sectors per track. The physical length of the track gets longer as the track gets closer to the outside edge of the disk (this is because the circumference of a circle gets bigger as the radius goes up), so designers can pack more sectors into the longer tracks without increasing the data density per inch of track. The minimum sectors per track on the Seagate drive is 96, and the maximum is the value in the table — 146. The transfer rate the benchmark achieves depends on where on the disk it goes to run the test. The rate of nearly 7MB per second corresponds to a position at a track having slightly fewer than the average number of sectors per track (that average is 121, which gives a calculated sustained transfer rate of 7.26 MB per second). If the benchmark had used tracks at the very inside of the disk, the rate would have been under 6MB per second. If it had operated at the very outside of the disk, the rate would have been nearly 9MB per second (as expected). All three rates are characteristic of the same disk — it just depends on where you measure.

The design of the operating system and how it organizes files on disk interacts with the physical characteristics of the disk. Returning to our example of the processor writing a file to disk, suppose that the processor has not 32KB to write, but 320KB, and suppose that the disk cache is larger, but nevertheless only 256KB. In that case, although the first part of the data transfers quickly from processor to cache, the processor must still wait for the cache to empty before transferring the remainder. Even if free space in the cache can be written as soon as it's available, the processor must work at slower disk speeds rather than fast memory or I/O channel speeds for the second half of the transfer. The processor will make no progress completing the operation until the disk actually starts accepting data from the cache.

The operating system determines the size of the blocks read from and written to the disk. The FAT (File Access Table) file system used by Windows sets the disk transfer block size to correspond to what DOS has called cluster size. Like many file systems, FAT does not allocate disk space precisely to fit the files that programs write. Instead, FAT allocates disk space in units called *clusters*. The size of a cluster varies according to the type and size of the disk. Tables 11-3 and 11-4 show the cluster sizes of the floppy and fixed disks FAT can support. Floppy disk cluster sizes are generally small and not a significant factor in system performance. Fixed disk (FAT16) cluster sizes can become quite large, with major impacts on system performance.

### Table 11-3
### FAT Floppy Disk Cluster Sizes

| Disk Size (KB) | Cluster Size |
|---|---|
| 2,880 | 1,024KB |
| 1,440 | 512KB |
| 720 | 1,024KB |
| 1,200 | 512KB |
| 360 | 1,024KB |

With the exception of the 2.88MB disks, the smaller cluster sizes correspond to the higher-density floppy disks.

### Table 11-4
### FAT16 Fixed Disk Cluster Sizes

| Disk / Partition Size (MB) | Cluster Size |
|---|---|
| 0 to 15 | 4KB |
| 16 to 127 | 2KB |
| 128 to 255 | 4KB |
| 256 to 511 | 8KB |
| 512 to 1,023 | 16KB |
| 1,024 to 2,048 | 32KB |

A revision to FAT released for Windows 95 in 1996 increased the size of individual FAT entries from 16 bits (FAT16) to 32 bits (FAT32), increasing the maximum possible cluster number and therefore allowing more clusters on a drive. The change to FAT32 permits support for drives larger than 2 gigabytes (GB) and enables smaller cluster sizes on large drives.

Table 11-5 shows the FAT32 options for a 2GB partition we converted from FAT16 on one of our computers. As you can see, FAT32 allows smaller clusters on large drives, reducing wasted space.

| | Table 11-5 FAT32 Clusters Reduce Wasted Space | | | |
|---|---|---|---|---|
| Cluster Size | Overhang (Bytes) | Efficiency | FAT Size | Total Waste |
| 512 | 4,272,505 | 99.7% | 33,283,072 | 37,555,577 |
| 1,024 | 9,106,297 | 99.4% | 16,706,560 | 25,812,857 |
| 2,048 | 19,815,289 | 98.8% | 8,370,176 | 28,185,465 |
| 4,096 | 42,865,529 | 97.4% | 4,189,184 | 47,054,713 |
| 8,192 | 92,230,521 | 94.6% | 2,096,128 | 94,326,649 |
| 1,6384 | 199,668,601 | 89.0% | 1,048,576 | 200,717,177 |
| 3,2768 | 435,581,817 | 78.8% | 524,288 | 436,106,105 |

The columns in Table 11-5 have these meanings:

✦ *Cluster Size.* The size of the minimum allocation unit on the disk.

✦ *Overhang.* The total amount of space wasted on the disk due to the difference between what files actually require and what Windows has to allocate due to the cluster size. Overhang is sometimes called slack space.

✦ *Efficiency.* The percentage of the disk space being used that's occupied by files (versus being overhang).

✦ *FAT Size.* The number of bytes required to store the file allocation table. The FAT is stored on disk and gets bigger with smaller cluster sizes, so it represents overhead space in addition to the overhang.

✦ *Total Waste.* The sum of the overhang and the FAT size.

We converted the partition, which contained about 1.6GB of data, to FAT32 using 4,096-byte partitions. In the process, we recovered over 370MB of space that had been lost in overhang as wasted space at the end of files. These calculations show how FAT32 is a big improvement that is crucially important as drive sizes go past 1GB to 2, 4, 9, and 23GB. FAT32 also permits partitions to grow past the 2GB FAT16 limit, letting you organize disks of over 2GB using fewer partitions and therefore fewer drive letters.

The smaller clusters enabled by FAT32 require more memory to hold the file allocation table itself, however (see the FAT Size column in Table 11-5), so reducing the cluster size is not without cost. The right balance for a given machine depends on the disk size, the file sizes commonly stored on the disk, the amount of memory in the machine, and the speed of the disk. You'll want to convert your large Windows 95 drives to FAT32. Before the release of Windows 98, you had to use tools such as PartitionMagic to do the conversion without having to reformat the drive (be sure to back up before you do the conversion). Windows 98 includes a tool to perform FAT32 conversions.

If the onboard disk cache size is at least as large as the cluster size, the processor can finish disk operations for many files in one high-speed operation. An onboard disk cache larger than the cluster size increases performance for multiple-cluster operations such as reading a program, sound, or video file. Because the cluster size gets larger for larger disk capacities, having a bigger cache is more important on bigger disks.

Disk compression reduces the effective cluster size for files but does not help a small cache perform well. Compressed files benefit from reduced overhang due to reduced cluster size (to 512 bytes) but are not what's actually transferred to and from the disk. Instead, compressed files are all stored in a single hidden file, called the host file, and it's the host file on the host partition that is actually read from and written to the disk. The host file is a single, large file that avoids the penalty of unused space at the end of many large clusters, but it is still stored in and accessed using the cluster size of the host drive. If that drive is over 1GB, the cluster size is 32K (prior to FAT32), so 32K is the minimum useful cache size.

**Tip**    The only hope to improve performance for a drive with a too-small cache is to reduce the cluster size for the drive hosting the compressed file, either by dividing the drive into multiple, smaller partitions or by converting to a different file system technology. For example, if you reduce the size of a FAT16 partition to less than a gigabyte, you can reduce the cluster size to 16KB, and if you make it less than 512MB, you reduce it to 8KB.

Windows 2000 includes support for FAT32, enabling machines that dual-boot on FAT32 partitions. Windows NT also offers the NT File System (NTFS), which adds security and other functionality and uses reasonably small clusters. UNIX has its own file system versions but is typically capable of mounting and reading FAT16 partitions on dual-boot machines.

# Cables: Your computer's plumbing

Inevitably, you've seen and been plagued by all the cables hanging off the back of your computer. If you've opened up your computer, you likely have seen the flat, wide cables going from the adapter cards to the disks. As simple as they appear, cables can greatly affect the performance and reliability of your computer.

The reason for this is the speed at which the computer and peripherals are sending signals across those wires. When the signals start to go fast enough, they no longer stop at the end of the wire; they bounce. Figure 11-2 shows the idea. The slower signal has no problem at the end of the wire, but the faster signal bounces and starts going the wrong way. When it reflects back to where the next signals in line happen to be, they collide. That interference with later signals coming down the wire causes noise and errors. (See the sidebar "The terminator" for information on how this problem is dealt with.)

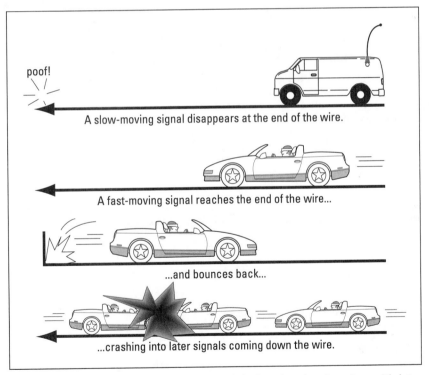

**Figure 11-2:** When signals bounce at the end of a wire, they interfere with later signals coming down the wire.

## The terminator

Devices called terminators keep signals from bouncing in wires and cables. The actual electrical effect on the wire is that a wave (the signal) traveling down the wire hits the end and is reflected when the electrical properties at the end do not match the properties the wave encountered moving down the wire. Matching the electrical properties of the terminator at the end of the wire to those of the wire itself prevents reflections and keeps the signals free from reflected noise. The bus on your motherboard uses terminators, as does a SCSI I/O bus if you have one. There's more detail on SCSI termination in Chapter 12.

The IDE I/O bus does not use terminators. The consequence of that, higher levels of reflected noise, is why you need to keep IDE cables as short as possible, why you are not likely to see IDE devices external to your computer, and why you wouldn't want an external IDE device if you could get it. We'll see in Chapter 11 that in some cases IDE cables need to be kept as short as seven inches. Violating this requirement can cause corrupted data or erratic system crashes.

Long, parallel runs of wire in cables cause another form of noise as well, shown in Figure 11-3. Magnetic interaction between adjacent wires induces a small echo as the signal passes, creating noise that interferes with the signals in the adjacent wires. In Figure 11-3, the wire in the middle carries a signal. Its magnetic field (the wavy lines) induces smaller signals in the adjacent wires, which look like noise to the real signals on those wires.

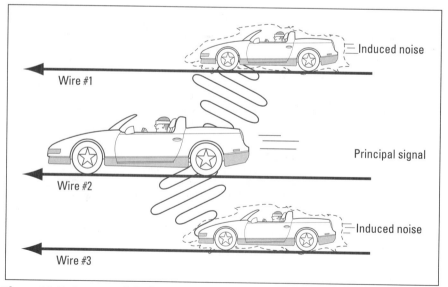

**Figure 11-3:** Long parallel wire runs cause noise in adjacent wires.

Every electronic signal is referenced to a "zero" signal in the system called *ground*. The way designers cut down induced noise between wires in flat ribbon cables is to interpose ground wires between the active wires, such as in Figure 11-4. The ground wire acts as a shield, cleaning up the signals and making faster operation possible.

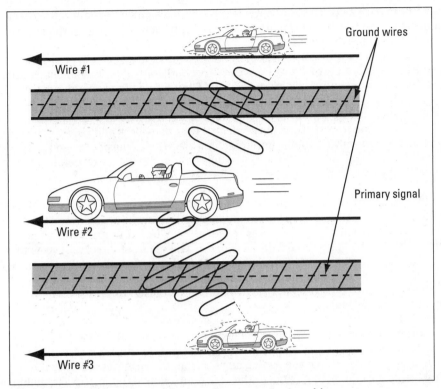

**Figure 11-4:** Interposed ground wires clean up noise in cables.

Different bus designs — with different permissible speeds — address the problems of induced noise in cables in different ways. Very high speed signals on motherboards may be routed with ground lines completely surrounding them. The SCSI I/O bus pairs every signal with a ground, creating exactly the interposed structure of Figure 11-4. Both these approaches work well. On the other hand, IDE cables have too few grounds for complete isolation and are not terminated. The evidence that poor grounding, shielding, and termination is a problem in IDE is that the ATA-2 specification says cables should be at most 18 inches long, while SCSI cables can be 6 meters long without taking special measures. (Insufficient ground pins are also a problem in the Macintosh Plus SCSI connector, which is nonstandard.)

# Disk controllers: Ringmasters of the circus

Up through the time of the IBM PC/AT, disk controllers plugged into the computer bus had a much more complex job than they do now. Disks at that time passed the analog signal from the heads to the controller over the flat ribbon cables when data was being read, and received analog signals from the controller when data was being written. The conversion between the analog signals the disk actually reads and writes and the digital signals the computer uses was the job of the controller, not the job of the disk drive.

In retrospect, that partitioning between drive and controller was a mistake that didn't matter for the 10MB disk of the PC/XT but was a big problem for larger, faster drives. Many of the 20MB disk systems shipped in the PC/AT had reliability problems caused not by failure of the drive or controller, but by electrical mismatches due to variations between specific controllers and drives. The problem was that synchronizing timing and matching electrical levels between the two became more difficult due to the faster data rate of the bigger drive; the analog interface provided no mechanism to solve the problem.

As IBM struggled with the PC/AT drives, advances in chip technology combined with increasing sales volumes in the PC market to make it possible to fit more onto the drive electronics board. The response, initially from Compaq, was to move most of the disk controller onboard the disk drive. The result of the change was to move the digital-to-analog conversion function out to the drive, making the interface over the ribbon cable a more reliable digital one. The only functions remaining in the card plugged into the computer bus were those required to bridge the computer bus out to the I/O bus.

The internal connection between the head disk assembly (HDA) and the drive electronics carries analog signals in all disk designs. In the older disk interface design used in the PC/AT, the analog signals from the HDA passed over the relatively long connecting cable to the disk controller. Matching up the timing and electrical levels between the disk and the controller became critical. All disk designs since then connect the analog signal path from the HDA to the onboard electronics that convert the signal to data and implement an IDE or SCSI controller interface to the computer. The signals on the I/O bus connecting cable are all digital, with better provisions for synchronizing the disk with the controller. More reliable operation at faster data rates is the result.

The controller's job of bridging between the fast computer bus (ISA, PCI) and the generally slower digital interface to the disk is still a lot of work. Figure 11-5 shows the job of the controller. The complete disk transfer process starts when a program wants to read or write data to the disk. The program communicates with a device driver (another program), which in turn communicates with the disk controller. The controller talks to the disk drive electronics, which operate the disk mechanism. Here's the process step by step:

1. The complete cycle of a disk transfer begins in the device driver. The driver interprets what the program wants into commands the disk and disk controller can understand, and gives those commands to the controller. This doesn't take very long.

2. The controller receives what the processor has commanded over the bus, coordinates it with what the disk might currently be doing, and passes the command to the disk. The command processing doesn't take much time, either.

3. It takes a (relatively) enormous amount of time to actually transfer data off a disk platter, with most of the time spent waiting for the heads to move and the disk to rotate. This is why adding cache into the disk electronics is so effective — it permits the disk to read ahead, anticipating what the processor will want, or to buffer writes, allowing the processor to go on with its work. In either case, if the cache can meet the processor request, most of the disk cycle time is eliminated.

4. When the disk then indicates that it's ready (seek and rotation are done), the controller transfers data and informs the processor. This takes relatively little time.

5. The device driver completes the operation by handling the results from the controller and informing the program of what happened (including passing back data on a read operation). This takes little time.

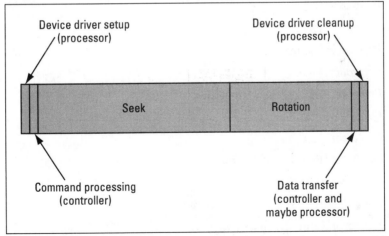

**Figure 11-5:** Getting data on and off a disk is a complicated process, with the controller in the middle of it all.

The commands the device driver sends to the controller can be simple, such as for an IDE controller, or complex, as for a SCSI controller. A typical IDE command is to set the head address to some number; a SCSI command may be as complicated as to queue up a set of commands to read entire series of sectors off the disk and notify the processor when the entire sequence is complete.

# Coordinating I/O Addresses and Interrupts

If you keep in mind that all a bus really does is to transfer numbers from one place to another, getting information back and forth to a disk really seems like a miracle. The tricky part is the way in which the bus lets the processor send numbers to the controller that are interpreted sometimes as commands and sometimes as data. That careful interpretation has to happen in the other direction — controller to processor — too. If we were to listen in on the conversation between the processor and controller over the bus (assuming the controller is not a bus master), we would hear a dialog like this:

> *Processor:* I'm interested in talking to disk number zero.
>
> *Controller:* Fine.
>
> *Processor:* Cylinder 53.
>
> *Controller:* Fine.
>
> *Processor:* Head 4.
>
> *Controller:* Fine.
>
> *Processor:* Sector 42.
>
> *Controller:* Fine.
>
> *Processor:* And I want to read four sectors.
>
> *Controller:* Fine.
>
> *Processor:* Start now.
>
> *Controller:* Fine. (Controllers are really not much at conversation.)
>
>     *– Time Passes –*
>
> *Controller:* Here's the first chunk of data.
>
> *Processor:* Got it. Keep going.
>
>     *– Time Passes –*
>
> *Controller:* Here's the second chunk of data.
>
> *Processor:* Got it. Keep going.
>
>     *(and so on)*

The controller keeps handing data over to the processor until all four sectors are done, and then it goes back to waiting for something to do.

Looking closer at the conversation, there are actually five kinds of information passed between processor and controller. Table 11-6 breaks down the preceding conversation into those five kinds of information: commands, status, data (two-way), and interrupts.

| Table 11-6 Five Kinds of Information Communicated by the Processor to the Controller | | | | |
|---|---|---|---|---|
| Command (Processor to Controller) | Status (Controller to Processor) | Data (Processor to Controller) | Data (Controller to Processor) | Interrupt (Controller to Processor) |
| Set disk ID | | 0 | | |
| | OK | | | |
| Set cylinder address | | 35 | | |
| | OK | | | |
| Set head address | | 4 | | |
| | OK | | | |
| Set sector address | | 42 | | |
| | OK | | | |
| Set number of sectors | | 4 | | |
| | OK | | | |
| Go | | | | |
| | OK | | | |
| | | | | Wake up |
| What do you want? | | | | |
| | Here's data | | | |

*continued*

| Table 8-1 *(continued)* | | | | |
| --- | --- | --- | --- | --- |
| **Command (Processor to Controller)** | **Status (Controller to Processor)** | **Data (Processor to Controller)** | **Data (Controller to Processor)** | **Interrupt (Controller to Processor)** |
| | | | (Chunk of data) | |
| OK | | | | |
| | | | | Wake up |
| What do you want? | | | | |
| | | Here's data | | |
| | | | (Chunk of data) | |
| OK | | | | |

Those five kinds of information are enough to create a structure allowing the processor to communicate unambiguously with the controller. The implementation of that structure used for disk controllers and many other peripheral devices is shown in Figure 11-6. The essential components of the interface in Figure 11-6 are two registers — places to store numbers — and an interrupt request wire. The registers can be read and written by the processor and by the controller. One of the registers is for transferring commands and status, while the other is for transferring data. The two registers are distinguished on the bus by different addresses. The interrupt request wire connects the controller to the processor's interrupt processing hardware, providing a way to signal that the controller needs service.

✦ *Command and Status Register (CSR).* Carries commands to the controller when written by the processor and status from the controller when read by the processor. A unique I/O address identifies the CSR, much as a unique address identifies a memory location.

✦ *Data Register.* Transfers data between the processor and the controller. Data for the controller is written by the processor, while data for the processor is written by the controller. A unique I/O address also identifies the data register, often at the next address after that of the CSR.

✦ *Interrupt Request (IRQ) signal.* Lets the controller tell the processor that intervention is needed. A unique IRQ has to be assigned to the controller on an ISA bus. The PCI bus has provisions for devices to share IRQs, with the processor doing the work to discover which specific device needs help.

The categories in Table 11-6 correspond directly to operations on the interface in Figure 11-6, as shown in Table 11-7. The actions shown in the table are the model for implementing all the I/O operations necessary for the computer to support an operating system.

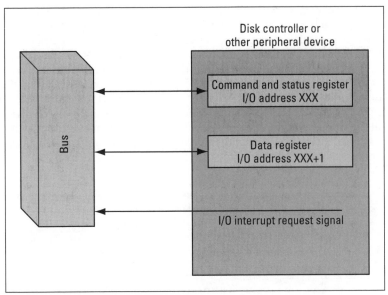

**Figure 11-6:** Two I/O registers and an interrupt line are enough for basic communication between a peripheral device and the processor.

## Table 11-7
## Implementing I/O Operations

| I/O Operation | Implementing Action |
|---|---|
| Command (processor to controller) | Processor writes numbers corresponding to the command sequence to the CSR. Controller detects the write operation and reads the numbers as the processor writes them. |
| Status (controller to processor) | Controller writes numbers corresponding to its current status to the CSR at the time the processor reads the register. |
| Data (processor to controller) | Processor writes numbers (the data) to the data register. Controller detects the write operation and reads the numbers as the processor writes them. |
| Data (controller to processor) | Controller writes numbers (the data) to the data register and interrupts the processor. The processor responds to the interrupt and reads the data from the data register. |
| Interrupt (controller to processor) | Controller activates the IRQ. Processor stops what it's doing, clears the IRQ, and does whatever work is necessary. |

The key to making all this work is having unique register addresses and interrupt signals for every device. Because real devices often have many registers (not two), because there are many devices in even the simplest PC, and because there are only a limited number of addresses and interrupts, it's easy to have conflicts. IBM recognized this problem and the need to coordinate products from the many companies it expected to build cards for the PC when it defined the ISA bus, defining a set of recommendations for how I/O register addresses and interrupts would be assigned. Table 11-8 shows the recommendations for addresses. IBM really tried to anticipate all the things that might need I/O addresses, but real life turned out to be a lot more complex. Table 11-9 shows the corresponding recommendations for interrupt numbers. Numbers in the tables are in base 16 (hexadecimal).

### Table 11-8
### IBM's Recommended I/O Address Assignments

| I/O Addresses Low | High | Recommended Assignment |
|---|---|---|
| 0 | 1F | Direct Memory Access (DMA) controller number one. A DMA controller picks up blocks of data from one place in memory and copies them to another location. The processor is free to do other work while the DMA controller does this operation. Your sound card, for instance, uses a DMA channel to transfer data out to the card without bothering the processor frequently (which improves overall performance). |
| 20 | 3F | Programmable Interrupt Controller (PIC) number one. A PIC is the device used by the processor to receive signals from peripherals that they need service. It remembers the request until serviced by the processor, and it gives the processor a mechanism to handle the most important requests before less important ones. |
| 40 | 5F | System timers. The timers help the processor keep track of the passage of time by generating a periodic interrupt, and they are used for other housekeeping purposes as well. |
| 60 | 6F | Keyboard and built-in speaker. |
| 70 | 7F | Real-time clock (RTC). The RTC maintains the current date and time and is kept alive by a battery while the computer is off. This is how your computer finds out the current date and time when it starts. |
| 80 | 9F | Other registers supporting both DMA controllers. |
| A0 | BF | PIC number two. |
| C0 | DF | DMA controller number two. |
| E0 | EF | Unassigned except on certain IBM PS/2 models. |

| I/O Addresses Low | High | Recommended Assignment |
|---|---|---|
| F0 | FF | Math coprocessor. The math coprocessor handles basic add/subtract/multiply/divide calculations on floating-point numbers (like 3.14159) as well as certain mathematical functions. If the coprocessor is not present (it was a separate chip for the 386 and SX versions of the 486, for example), software has to do those functions and is much slower. |
| 100 | 1EF | Unassigned except for the IBM PS/2 (MCA bus). |
| 1F0 | 1FF | Fixed disk controller, including IDE. The PC/XT used a different set of addresses. |
| 200 | 20F | Game I/O (joystick). |
| 210 | 26F | Unassigned. PC/XT computers could accept an expansion unit to provide additional bus slots, but current-generation computers no longer use this technology. A few addresses in this range were reserved for controlling the expansion unit. |
| 270 | 27F | Second parallel (printer) port (LPT2:). |
| 280 | 2DF | Unassigned. A now-obsolete IBM video card (the Enhanced Graphics Adapter — EGA) had an alternate set of addresses in this range. |
| 2E0 | 2EF | Data acquisition card. |
| 2F0 | 2FF | Serial port two (COM2:). |
| 300 | 35F | Unassigned. The PC/XT fixed disk controller was in this range, as were some mainframe communications products. Addresses were identified for experimental, prototype cards as well. |
| 360 | 36F | Network adapter. |
| 370 | 37F | First parallel (printer) port (LPT1:). |
| 380 | 3AF | Unassigned. Some specialized communications cards were in this range. |
| 3B0 | 3BF | Monochrome Display Adapter (MDA). The MDA provided a character-only video display at lower cost than graphics cards could be implemented when the PC was introduced. It's now obsolete. |
| 3C0 | 3CF | Enhanced Graphics Adapter (EGA). It is now obsolete, but the addresses are supported by many Video Graphics Array (VGA) cards. |
| 3D0 | 3DF | Color Graphics Adapter (CGA). It is now obsolete, but the addresses are supported by many Video Graphics Array (VGA) cards. |
| 3E0 | 3EF | Unassigned. |
| 3F0 | 3F7 | Floppy disk controller. |
| 3F8 | 3FF | Serial port one (COM1:). |
| 400 | FFFF | Not available in the original PC, or on ISA buses. EISA allocates addresses in this range on a per-bus slot basis. The MCA bus also allocates certain addresses in the range. |

The most interesting thing about Table 11-8 is what's *not* there, such as now-common devices like sound cards, SCSI controllers, video cards, and mice. Table 11-9 shows the assignments IBM planned for the PC/AT along with common devices that also use the IRQs. There are very few unassigned IRQs to handle all the cards that can be plugged into an ISA bus. The problem is made worse by the restrictions individual cards create in the IRQs they can handle.

| | **Table 11-9** | |
| | **IRQ Assignments and Uses** | |
| **IRQ Number** | **Recommended Assignment** | **Other Common Use** |
|---|---|---|
| 0 | System timer | |
| 1 | Keyboard controller | |
| 2 | Second PIC cascade. The occurrence of this interrupt tells the processor that an interrupt has been recorded by the second PIC, and that it can go interrogate the second PIC to find out what interrupt actually happened. IRQ 2 cannot be generated by a device—the signal line on the ISA bus called IRQ 2 actually is routed to IRQ 9. | |
| 3 | Serial port two (COM2:) | Network card, mouse |
| 4 | Serial port one (COM1:) | Network card, mouse |
| 5 | Parallel (printer) port two (LPT2:) | Sound card, mouse. This was the fixed disk interrupt prior to IDE and SCSI. |
| 6 | Floppy disk controller | |
| 7 | Parallel (printer) port one (LPT1:) | Sound card |
| 8 | Real-time clock (RTC) | |
| 9 | Unassigned. This is the actual assignment forced by the motherboard for devices generating IRQ 2. | Video card frame sync |
| 10 | Unassigned | |
| 11 | Unassigned | |
| 12 | Unassigned | PS/2 (motherboard) mouse |
| 13 | Math Coprocessor | |
| 14 | Unassigned | Primary IDE |
| 15 | Unassigned | Secondary IDE |

You can get Windows 9*x* to show you the actual I/O address usage for your system. A particularly useful summary report is available by clicking the Print button while "Computer" is selected in the Windows Device Manager. Figure 11-7 shows the initial Device Manager display for one system, while Table 11-10 shows the I/O addresses reported by Device Manager for that machine. Table 11-11 shows the IRQ assignments. If you compare these two tables to Tables 11-8 and 11-9, you see that neither the addresses nor the interrupts used for the sound card, the mouse, the SCSI controller, and the network card were in the original IBM plan.

**Figure 11-7:** The Windows 9*x* Device Manager tells you how I/O addresses and IRQs are assigned in your computer.

## Table 11-10
## I/O Addresses System Usage Example

| I/O Addresses | Actual System A Usage |
| --- | --- |
| 0000h–000Fh | Direct memory access controller |
| 0020h–0021h | Programmable interrupt controller |
| 0040h–0043h | System timer |
| 0060h–0060h | Keyboard |
| 0061h–0061h | System speaker |
| 0064h–0064h | Keyboard |
| 0070h–0071h | System CMOS/real-time clock |
| 0081h–008Fh | Direct memory access controller |
| 00A0h–00A1h | Programmable interrupt controller |

*continued*

| Table 11-10 *(continued)* | |
|---|---|
| **I/O Addresses** | **Actual System A Usage** |
| 00C0h–00DFh | Direct memory access controller |
| 00F0h–00FFh | Numeric data processor |
| 0200h–0207h | Gameport joystick |
| 0220h–022Fh | Sound card |
| 023Ch–023Fh | Mouse |
| 0278h–027Ah | Printer port (LPT2) |
| 02F8h–02FFh | Communications port (COM2) |
| 0330h–0333h | SCSI host adapter |
| 0340h–034Fh | Network interface card |
| 0380h–038Fh | Sound card |
| 03B0h–03BBh | Video card |
| 03BCh–03BEh | Printer port (LPT1) |
| 03C0h–03DFh | Video card |
| 03F2h–03F5h | Standard floppy disk controller |
| 03F8h–03FFh | Communications port (COM1) |

As much as you might want to, you can't share interrupts between two devices on the ISA bus. Nor can you share interrupts with one device on PCI and the other on ISA. The reason is that the ISA bus loses track of the fact that multiple devices want service, which can lead to failure to see the second interrupt.

| Table 11-11 **IRQs System Usage Example** | |
|---|---|
| **IRQ** | **Actual System A Usage** |
| 00 | System timer |
| 01 | Keyboard |
| 02 | Programmable interrupt controller |
| 03 | Communications port (COM2) |
| 04 | Communications port (COM1) |
| 05 | Microsoft InPort adapter mouse |
| 06 | Standard floppy disk controller |

| IRQ | Actual System A Usage |
|-----|----------------------|
| 07 | Sound card |
| 08 | System CMOS/real-time clock |
| 11 | SCSI host adapter |
| 13 | Numeric data processor |
| 15 | Network interface card |

Plug and Play has helped solve the problem of finding I/O addresses and interrupts for ISA. Plug and Play requires that the BIOS, cards, and operating system all support each other. Windows 9x provides the operating system support, but in older machines you're unlikely to have a Plug and Play BIOS, and you may well have a number of cards that do not support Plug and Play either. You'll need to configure cards manually for those older systems.

## Controlling other peripherals

You can connect many devices to an I/O channel besides a disk, including CD-ROMs, tape drives, scanners, printers, joysticks, and mice. Every one of these devices follows the same pattern to talk to the controller as a disk—they send command/status, data, and interrupts. The following table illustrates the command/status transactions these devices use. The data corresponds to what the transaction needs. Most devices also have a reset command (not shown in the table) that sets the device to its power-up state.

| Device Type | Command/Status | Transaction |
|-------------|----------------|-------------|
| CD-ROM | Command | Open / close door |
| | | Lock / unlock door |
| | | Position head |
| | | Read |
| | | Write (recorders only) |
| | | Play audio |
| | Status | Get current position |
| | | Query door status |
| Tape | Command | Eject |
| | | Lock / unlock |
| | | Rewind |

*continued*

*(continued)*

| Device Type | Command/Status | Transaction |
|---|---|---|
| | | Skip forward / backward |
| | | Read |
| | | Write |
| | Status | At beginning / end of tape |
| | | Get error count |
| Scanner | Command | Set resolution, scan mode, scan area |
| | | Set color mask |
| | | Set position |
| | | Read |
| | Status | Get resolution, mode, set area, mask, and position. |
| Printer | Command | Eject paper |
| | | Select feeder (and other options) |
| | | Write |
| | Status | Paper out |
| | | Paper jam |
| | | On / off line |
| Joystick | Command | None (yet) |
| | Status | Get position |
| | | Get button up / down |
| Mice | Command | None (yet) |
| | Status | Get position |
| | | Get button up / down |

Connecting input devices like joysticks, mice, or trackballs to I/O channels — which is important for new technologies such as USB — opens new possibilities for these devices to provide feedback. Joysticks, for example, now offer variable stiffness and active force to respond to differing game conditions. Mice and trackballs could incorporate small LCD readouts that report the current function of each button based on the cursor position on the screen.

# Summary

✦ Sustained transfer rate, access time, and cache size are the key disk drive parameters. Rotation rate completely determines the maximum sustained transfer rate.

✦ More disk cache is usually better, but you may need to benchmark to be sure. Disk cache is not always enabled by default.

✦ The cluster size on your disk partitions affects wasted space and the interaction between the processor and the disk cache. Use NTFS or FAT32 if you can.

✦ Poor cables can cause unreliable data transfer. IDE cables are not terminated, so longer cable lengths are very susceptible to noise. IDE cables should be kept under 18 inches if possible.

✦ You have to have unique I/O addresses and interrupt numbers for everything in your system.

✦     ✦     ✦

# I/O Buses

**A**fter you've set the foundation for your computer with the right combination of motherboard, cache, bus, and memory, it's time to turn to the I/O bus and decide how you'll connect your disks, CD-ROM, tape drive, and other devices. With the exception of choosing a motherboard, your I/O bus choice has the greatest *long-term* impact of any component upon how you can upgrade the machine. You have two choices:

+ *Integrated Drive Electronics (IDE)*. IDE is generally less expensive than the alternative, and for many users it will deliver the same performance. It's less capable of expansion, though, and on a computer with heavy disk loads, it will offer lower performance.

+ *Small Computer Systems Interface (SCSI)*. SCSI is $100 to $200 more expensive to begin with, and SCSI devices are usually somewhat more expensive. The highest-performance SCSI drives are faster than IDE, and larger. If you have demanding disk I/O requirements, you'll want SCSI.

Years ago, the IBM PC/XT and PC/AT designs used a disk controller plugged into the ISA bus and a separate disk cabled to the controller. The controller did all the work, sending carefully timed analog signals to and from the heads on the disk. In a major public relations fiasco, IBM discovered after it shipped a lot of PC/AT computers that although the disk and controller worked well individually, a small number of systems failed due to mismatches between their specific disk and controller. In response to this problem, the entire industry moved the controller onto the disk itself, ensuring a close match between controller and disk. A new component, the disk interface (sometimes called a host adapter), provided the connection between the computer bus and the I/O bus (the cable running to the disks). The result was two successful designs for the disk interface — one in which the interface did the minimal work possible, and one in which the interface added considerable value.

The low-end interface, doing minimal work between computer bus and I/O bus, is what we know as *Integrated Drive Electronics* or *IDE*. More recent versions are called Fast ATA and Enhanced IDE; we'll use IDE for all of them unless we need to distinguish among specific versions. The high-end interface, including a dedicated processor to control the disk on behalf of the computer, is what we know as SCSI. This chapter is a detailed look at both IDE and SCSI, including examination of first-class products in each category.

# Integrated Drive Electronics (IDE)

IDE is a low-cost approach to an I/O bus. The processor does more of the work with IDE than with SCSI, reducing the complexity needed on the IDE adapter card and therefore reducing its cost. IDE supports two drives per bus, with one drive on the bus set as the master drive and one as the slave drive. There can be two IDE buses in a system (each with a master and a slave), for a maximum of four IDE drives.

An IDE disk interface is as simple as an I/O channel can be, as shown in Figure 12-1. There's a disk controller (on the drive) with a minimal set of interface electronics to extend the computer bus out to the controller. The interface design is specific to the bus and the controller, meaning that specialized interfaces are required to connect IDE to each type of bus.

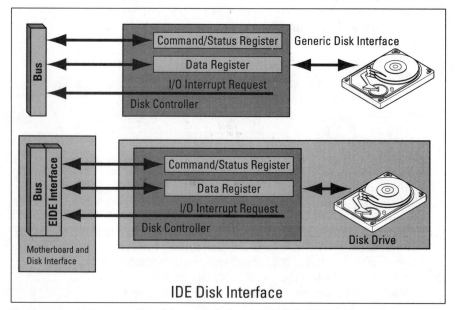

**Figure 12-1:** IDE moves the disk controller onto the disk drive, using a simple interface to connect the controller through to the bus.

Usually, you have to set jumpers on the drives to indicate master/slave status. If you have one drive, it's the master. If you have two on the same bus, one is the master and the other is the slave. Not all combinations of drives from different manufacturers work together as master and slave, even if they individually work in the computer as a master.

**Note**  IDE drives typically offer jumper setups on the drive to configure it as the only one on the port (a master), as a master in a dual-drive configuration, or as a slave in a dual-drive configuration. It's become common to find the jumper settings drawn on a sticker on the top of the drive, and many manufacturers put configuration and jumper information (including drawings specific to each model of drive) on Internet Web sites. Appendix B provides technical support telephone numbers and Web addresses for many vendors.

**Tip**  The simplicity of the interface means that IDE is cheap to build, which accounts for its popularity. IDE only supported disk drives at first, requiring changes and enhancements to add CD-ROM and tape capability to IDE. A CD-ROM or tape controller behaves nothing like a controller for a hard disk, so compromises were needed to allow all those kinds of devices to coexist.

## Improvements to the original IDE interface

The original name for IDE was AT Attachment, or ATA. ATA and its successors ATA-2 and Ultra ATA are the specifications for IDE drives and controllers. The name AT Attachment reflects the origins of the technology. When the drive electronics moved from the disk controller in the 16-bit ISA bus (first found in the IBM PC/AT) to the drive itself, the remaining set of interface electronics became the "AT Attachment." The ATA specification described a way to connect up to two hard disks to your computer, with a limitation of 504MB per disk. The ATA-2 specification, which loosely corresponds to Enhanced IDE, was the industry's response to the shortcomings of ATA, adding these features:

✦ *More storage.* You can address more than 504MB. Some implementations impose a 2.1GB limit; others can handle drives larger than that.

✦ *Faster data transfer.* ATA-2 defines ways for the computer to transfer data to and from the disk faster than ATA and adds ways for the drive to tell the computer what it's capable of. You get better performance and (most of the time) easier setup.

✦ *More drives.* You get two ports on an ATA-2 controller, called the primary and secondary ports. Each port can handle two drives (as in the ATA specification), so you can attach four drives instead of two.

✦ *Attaching other kinds of peripherals.* ATA-2 includes the ATA Packet Interface (ATAPI), which supports CD-ROMs and tape drives.

Not everything you buy that's called Enhanced IDE actually supports the complete ATA-2 specification, an unfortunate distinction which has been a source of confusion and wasted time. For instance, some companies have sold "Enhanced IDE" adapter cards that only add support for larger drives. If you buy a card like that and expect it to support a CD-ROM, you're in trouble. To make ATA-2 work properly, you need the right capabilities in the disks, adapter card, BIOS, and operating system. (If Windows has drivers for your adapter — or for the support built into your motherboard — you're in good shape on the operating system front.)

Some disks offer other features beyond ATA-2. For example, some drives include Self-Monitoring, Analysis, and Reporting Technology (SMART), which makes information about pending drive failures available to the system so that you can take action before the failure actually occurs. Newer disks are also likely to support UltraDMA/33 and UltraDMA/66, higher-speed versions of the ATA-2 DMA specification.

Several things have to cooperate with each other to make each of the ATA-2 features work. The simplest feature is faster data transfer, for which the BIOS and the disk have to cooperate. The most complex is CD-ROMs and tapes, for which support is required by all four components. Here are the details of what's involved in each feature:

✦ *High capacity.* Drive, BIOS, and operating system

✦ *Fast data transfers.* Drive and BIOS

✦ *Dual host adapters.* Host adapter, BIOS, and operating system

✦ *Non–hard disk peripherals.* Peripheral, host adapter, BIOS, and operating system

## More storage

Early IDE products were limited to 504MB because of a limitation in the interface between DOS and the BIOS. (You may see the 504 value as 528MB instead — it depends on whether you count a megabyte as 1,000,000 bytes or 1,048,576 bytes. Because we use the latter number in this book, the limitation is at 504MB.) When DOS requests a disk operation through the BIOS, it passes as parameters the cylinder, head, and sector it wants. (Chapter 11 covers what these are.) Unfortunately, the maximum values for those parameters are too low. There can be no more than 1,024 cylinders and 63 sectors, and drives commonly have no more than 16 heads. Sectors are 512 bytes, and if you multiply all those numbers together, you get 504MB. There was no way to pass a larger address, largely because of the 1,024-cylinder limit.

Taking no for an answer sells no computers, so it was inevitable that this problem had a solution. The straightforward answer is for the BIOS to fool DOS. The maximum head number is actually 64, so there's a lot of room there if we can make use of it.

Here's what we can do. Suppose the BIOS reports to DOS (and Windows) that the disk has four times as many heads as it really does, and one quarter as many cylinders. Table 12-1 shows what happens to the maximum drive capacity when we do that — it jumps to 2GB. The last line in Table 12-1 shows what happens if we use the largest value DOS can possibly pass for the number of heads (256): you get a drive with 8GB capacity.

### Table 12-1
### The Effect of a Translating BIOS on Drive Size Limits

| BIOS Mode | Cylinder Limit | Head Limit | Sector Limit | Drive Limit |
|---|---|---|---|---|
| Standard | 1,024 | 16 | 63 | 504MB |
| Translating | 1,024 | 64 | 63 | 2GB |
| Translating | 1,024 | 256 | 63 | 8GB |

For example, suppose the drive really has 2,048 cylinders, 16 heads, and 63 sectors. The BIOS fakes out Windows — translating real life into something the old DOS interface can handle — and reports that the drive has 512 cylinders, 64 heads, and 63 sectors. The total number of sectors is the same, but they're laid out differently so that they fit into the allowed values. (See the sidebar "Reversible lies" for the details on how the BIOS does these computations.)

The BIOS has a little more work to do than lying to Windows: It has to recreate the truth to tell the drive, because the drive isn't party to the crime. If it didn't translate the results for the drive, the drive would receive addresses it didn't know how to handle. For example, suppose Windows — believing what the BIOS told it — innocently asks for the sector at cylinder 400, head 39, and sector 12. If the BIOS didn't intervene, the drive would go off and look for that address, report that it didn't have a head 39, and fail the operation. Instead, the BIOS undoes the translation, converting the address from Windows to the (equivalent) disk address. In our example, it might convert cylinder 400, head 39, and sector 12 to cylinder 1602, head 7, and sector 12. (Again, see the sidebar "Reversible lies" for the details of why the conversion results in those numbers, and how it is that the BIOS can unerringly undo the lie it told Windows.)

Different BIOS implementations may do the translation differently; don't assume it always works exactly this way. If you try to move a disk from one system to another with a BIOS that translates differently, the files on the disk may appear corrupted (although they'd be fine on the old system). If the new system writes to the disk using the different translation, it may destroy information on the disk.

**Note**    Your BIOS may have limits on the maximum number of heads it will handle for an ATA-2 disk, and if it does, the maximum drive size will be less than the 8GB that is possible. A 2.1GB limit is fairly common, particularly in BIOS versions older than 1996. Western Digital notes that, of systems with a BIOS version dated from 1992 through February 1996, nearly half will lock up when faced with a drive bigger than 2.1GB. Most of the remainder will simply ignore the space that they can't address properly on the drive.

## Reversible lies

Take the address from Windows — say cylinder 400, head 39, and sector 12, and convert it to binary. If you do, you get this:

|            | *Decimal* | *Binary*   |
|------------|-----------|------------|
| Cylinder   | 400       | 110010000  |
| Head       | 39        | 100111     |
| Sector     | 12        | 1100       |

The BIOS strings all these values together, like this:

| *Cylinder*  | *Head*  | *Sector* |
|-------------|---------|----------|
| 110010000   | 100111  | 1100     |

To convert to the address the disk drive expects, the BIOS simply moves the first two digits of the value for the head (10) to the low end of the of the cylinder:

| *Cylinder*   | *Head*  | *Sector* |
|--------------|---------|----------|
| 11001000010  | 0111    | 1100     |

Turning those numbers back into decimal (so we can read them better) gives these values as what the drive sees:

|            | *Binary*     | *Decimal* |
|------------|--------------|-----------|
| Cylinder   | 11001000010  | 1602      |
| Head       | 0111         | 7         |
| Sector     | 1100         | 12        |

BIOS translation isn't the ultimate answer, in part because differing BIOS implementations have imposed artificial capacity limits. The simpler answer, taking a cue from what SCSI disks have always done, is to use what the ATA-2 specification calls Large Block Addressing (LBA). The idea behind LBA is that the first sector on the drive is numbered zero, then one, on up to the maximum sector number on the drive. No distinction exists between sectors on one cylinder or head versus another—the sectors each simply have unique numbers assigned. Table 12-2 shows how this works for a disk that has 2,048 cylinders, 16 heads, and 63 sectors. The formula for computing the large block address reflected in the table is to multiply the cylinder number by the maximum number of heads, add the head number, multiply by the maximum number of sectors, and add the sector number. Using this formula, we get the sequential numbering we want for sectors with no gaps.

### Table 12-2
### Large Block Addressing Assigns a Single, Unique Number to Each Sector

| Cylinder | Head | Sector | Large Block Address |
|----------|------|--------|---------------------|
| 0 | 0 | 1 | 1 |
| 0 | 0 | 2 | 2 |
| 0 | 0 | 63 | 63 |
| 0 | 1 | 1 | 64 |
| 0 | 2 | 1 | 127 |
| 1 | 0 | 1 | 1,009 |
| 1 | 1 | 1 | 1,072 |
| 1023 | 15 | 63 | 1,032,192 |
| 2047 | 15 | 63 | 2,064,384 |

A BIOS that handles LBA will use the entire range of values Windows can pass as a disk address, and so should be able to handle a disk as large as 8GB.

Even if your BIOS offers both LBA and translation, don't assume you can freely switch between the two. The way the BIOS transforms disk addresses may change, and if it does, the data won't be where Windows thinks it is. You can lose data. This can also happen if you switch between standard (untranslated) operation and translation, and it can happen if you move a disk from a machine with one brand (or version) of BIOS to another. Unless you know exactly what you're doing and can verify that the change had no bad effects, you should never switch from one form of ATA-2 addressing to another unless you do it in the following way:

1. Back up the drive twice (this isn't paranoia; it's being smart), and verify the backups against the files on the drive.

**2.** Change the BIOS as you please, such as to LBA from untranslated addressing.

**3.** Boot from a floppy disk and reformat the drive.

**4.** Restore a backup to the disk.

It's horribly inconvenient to do this on your boot drive (the C: drive) using Windows-based backups, because you usually can't read the backup until you have Windows running. Sadly, the freshly formatted drive you created in step 3 has nothing on it, not even Windows (or CD-ROM drivers), so if it was your boot drive, you have no easy way to read in your backup. A far better approach is to use LBA whenever you install an ATA-2 drive and avoid the problem from the beginning. (If you must change the BIOS setting, try setting the drive up as something other than the boot drive, and have Windows on the boot drive. This way, you can back up the drive and format it without losing your ability to run Windows or to run your backup software.)

You should be aware that some older drives don't support LBA, which could force you to use translation.

### Faster data transfer

An IDE adapter communicates with the disk in much the same way your processor communicates with memory — it says what it wants and assumes that a specific amount of time later the result will be ready for it to pick up. The most common interaction between the processor and the disk is what's called Programmed I/O, or PIO, in which every transfer between the disk and the processor requires the processor to execute an input (or output) instruction.

The ATA specification defines three (relatively slow) required speeds — commonly called *modes* — for transfers between the processor and the disk. ATA-2 added several faster speeds in order to keep up with the increased transfer rates supported by newer disk drives. Table 12-3 shows the data transfer rates in each specification. When you see a reference to "Mode 3," it means PIO Mode 3, with a peak transfer rate of 11.1MB per second. The direct memory access (DMA) modes are not faster than the PIO modes, except for UltraDMA/33 and UltraDMA/66, but impose less load on the processor, freeing it to do other work. The various ATA specifications provides transfer rates nearly as fast as Fast SCSI, but not nearly as fast as the newer Ultra SCSI products (which run at up to 80MB per second).

| Table 12-3 | | |
| **ATA-2 Transfer Rate Specifications for Each Mode** | | |
| *Mode* | *Specification* | *Transfer Rate (MBps)* |
| PIO Mode 0 | ATA | 3.3 |
| PIO Mode 1 | ATA | 5.2 |

| Mode | Specification | Transfer Rate (MBps) |
|------|---------------|----------------------|
| PIO Mode 2 | ATA | 8.3 |
| PIO Mode 3 | ATA-2 | 11.1 |
| PIO Mode 4 | ATA-2 | 16.6 |
| DMA Mode 1 | ATA-2 | 13.3 |
| DMA Mode 2 | ATA-2 | 16.6 |
| UltraDMA/33 | Ultra ATA | 33.3 |
| UlatrDMA/66 | Ultra ATA | 66.6 |

Remember that these rates are for transfers between the computer and the disk electronics but are independent of the actual sustained transfer rate the drive can support.

ATA-2 added an Identify Drive command that allows your computer to ask the drive for its characteristics, including the fastest data transfer mode it supports. This is how the automatic drive speed detection functions in some BIOSes works — the BIOS simply asks the drive what it can do.

As we saw in Chapter 11, the rate at which the drive can sustain data transfers is set by the rotation rate of the drive. Figure 12-2 shows the relationship between disk rotation rate (in RPM) and computer performance running a mix of applications. The same computer ran all the tests, with the only difference being the disk. The figure shows performance for five different disks of increasing rotation rate, and it displays good correlation between the two curves. The fastest drive in the group tested was good for a sustained transfer rate of nearly 6MB per second. The scale on the left of the graph is the disk RPM; we have not shown a calibration for the relative performance curve.

In comparison, a fast, wide SCSI Seagate drive that we tested can sustain a transfer rate onto or off the disk of over 7MB per second; the Ultra2 wide SCSI Seagate Cheetah running at 10,000 RPM can sustain 14 to 21MB per second. The fastest IDE drives are not as fast as that, but if you only have one drive, if you're only running one thing at a time, or if your programs don't access the disk more than average, IDE will give you passable performance and save you money. IDE versions prior to Ultra ATA/33 and Ultra ATA/66 don't do parity checking on the connection between the computer and the disk. That's not what you want for mission-critical data — use SCSI on servers.

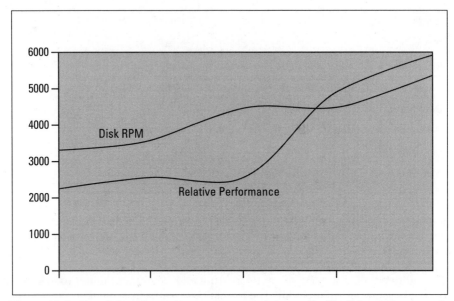

**Figure 12-2:** The disk performance you see correlates well with disk rotation speed.

## More drives

One of the big problems with IDE was that you had one connector available, to which you could attach two drives. If you needed more, you were severely out of luck. IDE CD-ROM drives (and now IDE tape drives) have made this problem much worse—you can't attach a disk, CD-ROM, and tape to the same IDE port.

Once again, the fix was to patch the design, but not by allowing more drives to be attached to the port. Instead, ATA-2 gives you one more port, so you get two more drives. Choose them wisely. You'll want to be aware that on some machines an IDE port has to run at the speed of the slowest device, so it may be to your advantage to use both ports even if you only have two disks.

We don't recommend IDE for anything but low to mid-range machines where the user won't be expanding the machine much. The products are less expensive than SCSI, but unless your requirements are forever going to stay within some severe limitations (including number and type of devices, and the inability to attach external devices), it's an expensive choice in the long run. Besides, with the terrific software supporting SCSI in both Windows 9x and Windows NT, we've had fewer problems setting up SCSI machines. (Don't underestimate this; with multiple devices, SCSI is easier to set up than IDE!)

## CD-ROMs and tapes

CD-ROMs using IDE interfaces provide a lower-cost alternative to SCSI CD-ROMs and are responsible for much of the growth in sales of CD-ROM drives. All DVD-ROM drives are IDE at this time. Another patch to the ATA/ATA-2 design was required to make these (and IDE tape drives) work, though, because the interactions between your computer and an IDE disk are different from what a CD-ROM or tape requires. This patch is the ATA Packet Interface (ATAPI) specification.

The first problem with adding CD-ROMs and tapes to IDE was that IDE retains the old interface from the IBM PC/AT, which was designed exclusively for disks. The interface is very rigid, including commands to set the disk cylinder, head, and sector; to read and write at the set address; and other disk-unique commands. CD-ROMs and tapes take complete commands in messages called packets (hence ATA Packet Interface) and take different commands (imagine rewinding a disk!). Without the ATAPI patch, there was no way to bridge the gap.

The ATAPI designers took the expedient approach to designing the specification. They patterned it after what was already implemented and proved in SCSI controllers, CD-ROMs, and tapes.

The other problem with adding CD-ROMs and tapes is that the IDE interface allows only one device to be active at a time on a port, and all devices on the port usually have to run at the speed of the slowest one. This means that if you hook a CD-ROM onto the primary IDE port with your disk drive, the disk can't read or write while the CD-ROM is reading. Also, if the CD-ROM can't transfer data as fast as the disk, the disk will probably have to run at the slower speed. (Some systems can split the master and slave PIO or DMA modes, and some can't.) This isn't a problem the ATAPI designers could solve—you have to work around it. When you place a CD-ROM or tape drive on an IDE interface, your best bet is to use the secondary port, keeping the disk drives themselves on the primary port. This ensures that the CD-ROM or tape drive can't interfere with the operation of the disk drives, and that the disk drives run at the fastest possible speed.

# Fixing a machine with a broken IDE BIOS

If your machine has an older BIOS, it may not support IDE, or it may have disk capacity limitations at either 504MB or 2GB. If you want to add an IDE port to a machine with none, or if you want to use an IDE disk larger than your machine supports, you have two options:

✦ *BIOS upgrade.* Your system vendor or motherboard manufacturer may have a BIOS update to add IDE support and/or fix the IDE size limitation problem. This is easy with a flash BIOS and more difficult otherwise. You can also get an IDE BIOS update from AMI on a card you plug into the ISA bus.

✦ *Software.* You can install software (such as OnTrack Disk Manager version seven or later) to work around the BIOS problem. You gain access to the full capacity of the drive (up to 8GB) and can use Disk Manager with both Windows 9*x* and Windows NT.

You need to watch out for specific BIOS problems as well. For example, the Award 4.50G BIOS dated earlier than 12/13/94 has a problem doing translations for drives with more than 1,024 cylinders. If you have one of these, you must use LBA and not large address translation.

## Troubleshooting other IDE problems

There's no shortage of obscure things that can go wrong with IDE. Here are a few of the most common:

✦ *You're getting corrupted data from the disk.* The most likely way to corrupt data on an IDE disk is to set the BIOS to a faster mode than the drive can handle. Some older drives misreport their fastest mode, so you can get in trouble even though everything seems to be according to specification.

You can check for the BIOS setting being too fast simply by slowing it down — say to the slowest setting — and then fixing the drive contents. If the problem goes away, you need to either leave it at the slower setting or discover what setting is supported reliably.

**Note**

You can also get corrupted data on an IDE disk by using cables that are too long. The specification requires cables to be *less than 18 inches.* If you're using both ports of a dual-channel IDE interface that uses the CMD640x PCI-to-IDE chip, you have to keep the cable less than seven inches, because the chip effectively joins the two cables together (so the lengths of the cables plus the lengths of the wires on the motherboard add together).

✦ *You're getting compatibility mode for the drive under Windows 95, or Windows NT won't work.* If you're running software such as Disk Manager, you probably don't have a version supporting Windows 9*x* or NT. An update to Version 7 or later of Disk Manager, or a Windows 9*x*–compatible version of another program, should fix the problem.

✦ *Your IDE CD-ROM isn't visible.* You may have connected the drive to the secondary IDE port but not enabled that port in the BIOS. Also, many IDE CD-ROMs are shipped set up to be the slave drive, so if it's the only drive (and therefore the master drive), you need to change the drive configuration jumpers.

## IDE on the PCI bus

The ISA bus itself is not fast enough to support the faster IDE modes, which is one of the reasons for introducing PCI IDE interfaces. The close tie of the IDE interface to the structure of the ISA bus, however, means that it's not possible to simply drop the ISA part of the interface in favor of a PCI version. Designers had to keep both.

The version of IDE your BIOS knows about, for example, is inherently an ISA interface. If your motherboard includes a PCI IDE interface, the motherboard solves the problem of providing both ISA and PCI interfaces to your IDE devices. If you use an IDE card — rather than an interface built into the motherboard — the card has to provide both these interfaces.

The ATA-2 and Ultra ATA specifications added DMA modes, making it possible to have IDE drives do bus mastering like the better SCSI controllers. Microsoft released a service pack for Windows 9x in 1996 that provides drivers to make use of DMA for PCI controllers, but unfortunately testing has shown that some early IDE drives designed to support DMA have bugs that can cause data corruption using the new driver. There is no simple test you can do to guarantee that your disk will work correctly, so if you're unsure, you should contact the disk drive manufacturer.

# Small Computer Systems Interface (SCSI)

There's a lot of history behind SCSI, history that contributes to SCSI being a flexible, well-engineered, reliable I/O bus. SCSI has its roots in the Shugart Associates System Interface (SASI) design of the early 1980s. Unlike IDE, SCSI is a general-purpose I/O bus capable of connecting a variety of devices in high-performance, useful ways. Devices supported by SCSI implementations include:

✦ *Disks.* Although SCSI is not a disk-centered interface, most devices hooked to SCSI buses are in fact disk drives.

✦ *CD-ROMs.* The SCSI bus is a packet bus, which means that SCSI controllers send complete command sequences to the device. SCSI also features a "generic" command set, including commands like "read" and "write" that work for most attached devices. The packet design and generic commands make it simple to connect different types of devices to the bus, such as CD-ROMs.

✦ *Tapes, modems, scanners, disk arrays, printers, other computers.* SCSI supports all these things, without patching the SCSI specification to allow for one or the other of them.

SCSI is a formal standard widely supported by lots of manufacturers. The original SCSI standard was set in 1986 and updated in 1994 (ANSI X3.131-1994). The standard is evolving to a next generation, but rather than patching shortcomings of the current standard, SCSI developers are working on refinements that will allow the standard to be easily adapted to new technologies as they evolve. For example, the next-generation SCSI standard is a candidate for the design baseline as fiber optics replace the parallel wires in current designs.

The most fundamental engineering difference between IDE and SCSI is that SCSI puts a significant amount of intelligence into the interface between the computer bus and the SCSI bus. That interface, called a host adapter in SCSI terms, has its own onboard processor that receives commands from the computer and carries out entire sequences of actions on the SCSI bus to implement those actions. The host adapter can also keep track of multiple outstanding (incomplete) requests it has made to devices, so you can have several things happening on the SCSI bus at once. IDE cannot do this, which (along with the relatively common bus mastering capabilities of SCSI host adapters) is why SCSI usually outperforms IDE in an environment where the computer is doing many different things at the same time or splits the I/O load across multiple drives.

The other critical difference between SCSI and IDE is that the electrical interface along the SCSI bus — the properties of the cable connecting the host adapter and all the devices — has been carefully engineered for reliable high-frequency performance. Instead of the almost-haphazard arrangement of signals in the IDE data cable, the SCSI cable design puts ground lines between data lines to reduce magnetic coupling between the signals. A SCSI bus is terminated (refer to Chapter 11) to minimize signal reflection from the end of the cable that could cause transmission errors over the bus. The quality of the engineering that went into SCSI data transmission over the cable is shown by the fact that ordinary SCSI cables can be six meters long, while IDE cables are limited to 18 inches under the best of circumstances. You'll pay somewhat more for SCSI, but you get better engineering for the money. It's no accident that servers from major computer vendors use SCSI almost exclusively. When reliability and data integrity are paramount, you go for quality engineering.

There's more. Conventional SCSI buses (like the one on the Adaptec AHA-2940 host adapter) enable you to attach eight devices including the host adapter. Wide (two-byte) SCSI buses (as on the Adaptec AHA-2940W and AHA-2940UW host adapters) allow 16 devices including the host adapter. One SCSI bus of either type supports almost twice as many disks as two IDE ports.

The SCSI bus has two approaches to coordinate timing between the host adapter and a device — asynchronous and synchronous timing. Asynchronous timing works with a full, two-way handshake — the sender sets a signal to say "here's the data," followed by the receiver setting a signal to say "I got it." This paired handshake happens for every transfer down the cable.

The other timing approach is synchronous timing. In synchronous mode, the sender doesn't wait to receive the acknowledgment from the receiver. The acknowledgment has to arrive eventually, but the sender can keep sending at up to the maximum rate in the meantime. Eliminating the wait for the acknowledgment allows more data to be transmitted per second, especially on long cables for which the signal propagation time from one end of the cable to the other can be significantly greater.

That's not to say that SCSI can't have problems. For example, a number of manufacturers have exploited the robustness of the SCSI design and delivered sloppy implementations that create problems when pushed to higher rates. It's also common for SCSI buses to have termination problems if people don't understand the rules for how to terminate the SCSI cable correctly. If you insist on components from quality vendors (such as the Adaptec host adapters in this chapter and Seagate disks in the next chapter), and if you connect it all together with well-engineered cables (such as those from Granite Digital), you'll avoid all these problems.

Without question, the most common SCSI problem is faulty termination. Here's what you need to know about termination:

✦ *You have to terminate the ends of the cable (both ends!) and only the ends.* See Figure 12-3. If all your SCSI devices are inside the computer, you'll have a terminator on the host adapter and one on the device at the other end of the cable. If all your devices are outside the computer, it's the same thing—a terminator on the host adapter and one in the device at the end of the cable.

If you have devices both inside and outside the computer, you need to remember that electrically they are connected to the same cable. That means that you terminate the device at both ends of the cable, and not the host adapter.

The host adapter can help you with termination. All the ones being made by Adaptec, for instance, automatically sense whether or not they are at the end of the cable and apply or remove termination automatically. As long as you take care of the device terminators, you're set. Automatic termination is a timesaver if you use the external connector to attach a tape drive or removable disk. You just plug in and go, without needing to worry about whether or not the machine needs a special terminator plug.

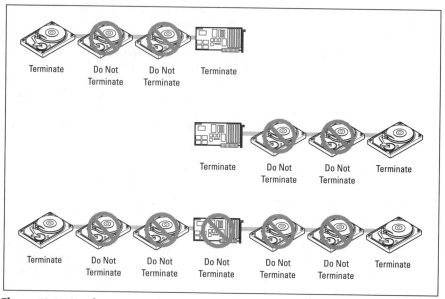

**Figure 12-3:** You have to get the termination right for reliable SCSI operation.

✦ *There are active and passive terminations.* Active works better and is essential for FAST-20 SCSI. See the following section for more information.

✦ *The terminators need to be powered.* This is more of a problem for Macintosh computers than Windows machines, because Apple failed to follow the SCSI standard completely, but it is still a source of confusion. SCSI terminators require a connection to a power source to work. If no power (or not enough power) is fed to the terminators, they don't work, meaning they don't suppress reflections on the cable. In that case, your system may work erratically or fail altogether.

## Active and passive SCSI termination

The reason for termination is to eliminate reflection from the ends of cables. Reflection can corrupt your data or cause unreliable operation, so this is hardly some irrelevant engineering nit. What's worse is that the faster the signals on the bus, the more severe the reflections are. As speeds on the SCSI bus go up to FAST-20 and UltraSCSI rates, you want to be more careful about how you handle terminations.

You can get two kinds of terminators: active and passive. The internals of both kinds of terminators are shown in Figure 12-4, with passive termination on the left and active termination on the right.

The squiggly components in the drawings are resistors, which affect the flow of electricity through the wire. In the passive terminator, a pair of resistors for each separate SCSI signal connects the signal to both power and ground. The two-resistor network has the effect of making the end of the cable look more like a pillow to oncoming signals that reach the end, rather than a mirror. In the process, the resistors tend to push the voltage at the end of the wire toward a point between the power level (about 5 V) and ground (0 V). The circuits on the disk or host adapter are strong enough to override the resistor network, but it takes a little time.

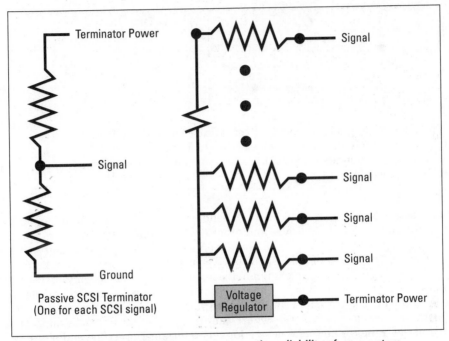

**Figure 12-4:** Active SCSI termination increases the reliability of your system.

Figure 12-5 shows what happens at the end of the cable when a SCSI signal transitions from zero (low voltage) to one (high voltage). On the passive termination curve in Figure 12-5, the signal starts up quickly but then dips down as the reflections from the end of the cable interact with the signal. The reflections eventually die down, and the signal rises to its ultimate value.

As shown on the right side of Figure 12-4, the internals of an active SCSI terminator are different. Instead of the pair of resistors for each signal running between power and ground, an active terminator has one resistor per signal that runs to a regulated voltage source. This design looks like a more effective pillow at the end of the wire, as is shown in the active termination curve in Figure 12-5, where the signal starts its rise a little later, has far less interference from reflections, and reaches a nice high value sooner. The payoff in your system is cleaner signals on your SCSI bus and more reliable system operation.

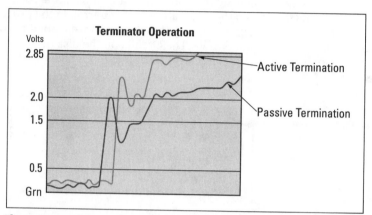

**Figure 12-5:** This graph shows the effect of active termination. When the signal switches, the SCSI bus voltage rises to the specified level sooner, without transients that could corrupt your data. (Graph courtesy of Granite Digital.)

Host adapters like those from Adaptec handle their end of the termination and power issue for you. Disk drives and other devices usually have jumpers you need to set and (on older drives) small components called resistor packs that you need to remove. Those older SCSI devices have passive terminators—the resistor packs—that you remove to eliminate termination at that device. If you're going to go with passive termination, you take out the resistor packs on all the devices except the ones at the cable ends. If you're going to use active termination, you can remove the resistor packs everywhere and then plug in the active terminator at the end of the cable (or jumper a device for active termination at the end of the cable).

**Caution**

Although termination has commonly been available from devices themselves, the trend is to termination on the cable itself. Fast SCSI and Ultra SCSI commonly use termination capabilities integrated into the disk drive. The integration of low-voltage differential signaling technology into Ultra2 SCSI disk drives precludes supporting termination directly within the disk drive, so a terminator is required on the Ultra2 cable itself.

## SCSI-1, SCSI-2, SCSI-3, and UltraSCSI

SCSI-1 was the first standardized version. The 1994 update, SCSI-2, defined additional connectors based on newer technology, added an option—FAST SCSI—to exploit newer, faster devices, defined a wider extension of the bus to improve maximum data rates, and improved the SCSI command structure. The latest standard version is Ultra and Ultra2 SCSI. All of these changes in SCSI are compatible with the older SCSI-1 specification, applying the same sort of technology enhancements to the I/O bus that are happening at the same time to internal computer buses.

SCSI introduces some terms you need to understand:

✦ *FAST SCSI.* The SCSI-1 specification (now obsolete for disks, but used for scanners, tape, and CD-ROM) required that signals go onto the bus at a rate no higher than 5 MHz. SCSI-2 introduced a faster timing specification, allowing operation at rates as high as 10 MHz. SCSI-1 used a one-byte-wide data path and so was limited to 5MB per second. Using FAST timing, a SCSI-2 bus can transfer 10MB per second on the one-byte-wide data path and 20MB per second on a double-wide path.

✦ *FAST-20 SCSI (also called Ultra SCSI).* In addition to the FAST SCSI 10 MHz rate, the SCSI-2 specification defines an even faster transfer rate for the SCSI bus called FAST-20 SCSI (commonly called Ultra SCSI). This rate sends data down the path at 20 MHz per second, so you can get a transfer rate as fast as 40MB per second on a wide FAST-20 bus (Ultra Wide SCSI).

✦ *Wide SCSI.* The two-byte wide SCSI bus data path is called Wide SCSI. You'll find wide SCSI implemented with a 68-pin connector. The wide SCSI specification permits versions even wider than two bytes, but the wide products you can buy are all two bytes wide.

Wide SCSI and FAST-20 wide SCSI extend the addressing on the SCSI bus as well. Instead of a host adapter and seven devices, you can attach the host adapter and 15 devices.

✦ *FAST-WIDE SCSI.* You can combine different SCSI characteristics. FAST-WIDE SCSI products run at 10 MHz on a two-byte wide bus. FAST-20 wide SCSI products (Ultra wide SCSI) run at 20 MHz on the two-byte wide bus for a total of 40MB per second.

✦ *Ultra and Ultra2 SCSI.* Describes the latest published ANSI SCSI standard, X3T10/1071D revision 6. The specifications are also known as FAST-40 and FAST-80 SCSI, respectively. Ultra2 SCSI on a two-byte-wide bus transfers data at 80MB per second.

✦ *Ultra 3 and Ultra160/m SCSI.* The latest versions of SCSI to come to market double the performance of Ultra2 SCSI data transfers by clocking data on both the leading and trailing edge of the clock pulse. That change boosts the speed of the bus to 160MB per second. You'll want to support the host adapter with a 64-bit, 66 MHz PCI bus on your motherboard running at 532MB per second.

All the versions of SCSI are downward compatible, so you can mix all versions of SCSI on the same cable. The host adapter sorts it all out, and the messages between the host adapter and the devices communicate the results so that each device gets the service it needs. You can connect devices faster than the host adapter — they'll simply run at the fastest speed the adapter supports. Similarly, you can use a host adapter faster than your devices — each device runs at the fastest speed it can.

## Integrating SCSI

The SCSI standard defines what happens between the host adapter and its attached devices, not between the computer and the host adapter. IDE — by virtue of its simple host adapter patterned after a direct computer-to-controller interface — has a better-defined interface to the computer. Figure 12-6 shows the range of the two specifications, showing that the SCSI specification does not control the low-level communication between the processor and host adapter. Because of this, integrating SCSI into the operating system used to be harder than integrating IDE. The differences in standardization are these:

✦ *Host adapter–to–device interface.* IDE and SCSI both standardize this interface (although differently).

✦ *Processor–to–host adapter interface.* IDE standardizes this interface, but SCSI does not.

✦ *BIOS-to-device interface.* IDE and SCSI both standardize this interface. The IDE BIOS code is generally built into the motherboard, while the SCSI BIOS code is generally built onto the SCSI host adapter. The SCSI BIOS code has the specifics of the processor-to-host adapter interface built in, hiding the details from the rest of your software.

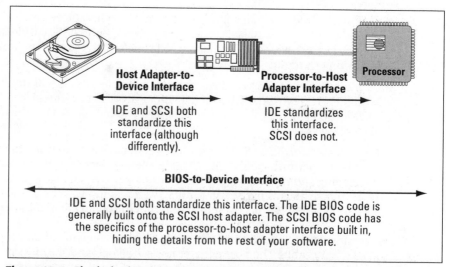

**Figure 12-6:** The lack of standardization at the interface between the processor and the host adapter used to make integrating SCSI into a computer harder than IDE.

✦ *BIOS support.* When your computer starts to boot, the BIOS provides the driver to start loading the operating system from the disk. The interface to IDE devices is simple and (ignoring the translation issues described previously) has been unchanged for quite some time. As a result, nearly all BIOS manufacturers include support for accessing IDE drives in the BIOS on the motherboard.

SCSI host adapters are not standardized at the interface between the computer and the host adapter, so their manufacturers have had to include BIOS extensions on the host adapter to allow the computer to boot. The IDE BIOS components on the motherboard don't know about the SCSI extensions, which is why you configure the BIOS settings to show no disks installed for a computer using SCSI disks. The BIOS settings are for IDE disks only — SCSI disks describe themselves to the system and need no additional settings.

✦ *Operating system support.* MS-DOS uses the BIOS interface to the disk. Windows 9*x* is capable of (and Windows NT requires) faster operation using 32-bit drivers that replace the functions of the BIOS. The extensive support built into Windows ensures that most SCSI host adapters will run at peak performance. Before you buy, you can verify compatibility with the manufacturer or check the Hardware Compatibility List on the Microsoft Internet site.

Every SCSI device — including the host adapter — has an address, or ID. Addresses must be unique on a single cable — you can have a device at address zero on two separate host adapters, but not on the same one. Table 12-4 shows the addressing we set up on two of our systems. In a SCSI-only system, the disk at ID zero is usually the boot drive. Drive letters are assigned sequentially to disk drives in order of increasing ID. System B in the table identifies the Seagate drive as C, the Quantum as D, and the Micropolis as E. A second partition on the Seagate becomes F.

## Table 12-4
## Unique SCSI IDs Assigned to Each Device on Two Systems

| SCSI ID | System A Device | System C Device |
|---------|-----------------|-----------------|
| 0 | Maxtor disk | Seagate disk |
| 1 | Toshiba disk | Quantum disk |
| 2 | NEC CD-ROM | Toshiba CD-ROM |
| 3 | Archive tape drive | [none] |
| 4 | [none] | Micropolis disk |
| 5 | Conner disk | [none] |
| 6 | Epson scanner | [none] |
| 7 | Adaptec SCSI host adapter | Adaptec SCSI host adapter |

It's not necessary to use every SCSI ID, nor is it necessary to use them in any particular order. (For instance, System A has nothing at ID four, and System B has nothing at IDs three, five, and six.) Besides the fact that you should put your boot disk at ID zero, the only other restriction is that some adapters expect IDs zero and one to be nonremovable disks. Because of that, you might consider putting your CD-ROM drive at address two or higher.

**Tip**

If you combine IDE and SCSI in the same system, the boot drive will be the master disk on the primary IDE port. You usually can't boot from a SCSI drive in a mixed configuration.

## Setting the SCSI ID

Unless all your SCSI devices and your host adapter implement SCSI Plug and Play, you must set the ID on each device. You do this with jumpers or switches on the device. Jumper positions are commonly labeled something like JID0, JID1, and JID2 (or JID0 through JID3 for wide SCSI). Here is the most common correspondence between the ID numbers and jumper settings. (Ignore ID 3 if you're not using a wide SCSI device.)

| ID | JID0 | JID1 | JID2 | JID3 |
|----|------|------|------|------|
| 0  | Open | Open | Open | Open |
| 1  | Jump | Open | Open | Open |
| 2  | Open | Jump | Open | Open |
| 3  | Jump | Jump | Open | Open |
| 4  | Open | Open | Jump | Open |
| 5  | Jump | Open | Jump | Open |
| 6  | Open | Jump | Jump | Open |
| 7  | Jump | Jump | Jump | Open |
| 8  | Open | Open | Open | Jump |
| 9  | Jump | Open | Open | Jump |
| 10 | Open | Jump | Open | Jump |
| 11 | Jump | Jump | Open | Jump |
| 12 | Open | Open | Jump | Jump |
| 13 | Jump | Open | Jump | Jump |
| 14 | Open | Jump | Jump | Jump |
| 15 | Jump | Jump | Jump | Jump |

If your device uses switches instead of jumpers, you'll have to check the manual to see which direction is which for the switch. (You should double-check the manual for a device with jumpers too, just to be sure.)

Devices that use jumpers are often shipped with only two jumpers for JID0 through JID2. This is because the host adapter is nearly always at ID 7, which is the place you'd need the third jumper. You won't put a device there, so you only need two jumpers.

SCSI Plug and Play is a recent technology that — once all devices implement it — will eliminate even this chore. A SCSI Plug and Play host adapter interrogates all the devices on the bus, checks what their default ID assignment would be, and changes some of the assignments if it finds conflicts. You could set every device in the system (except the boot drive) to ID 1 and SCSI Plug and Play would set up your system to work.

## Comparing ATA and SCSI

Overall, ATA is less flexible than SCSI and is limited in performance and connectivity. Table 12-5 shows the key differences.

### Table 12-5
### Comparison of Key ATA and SCSI Characteristics

| Characteristic | ATA | SCSI |
|---|---|---|
| Devices per channel | 2 | 7 (narrow), 15 (wide) |
| Maximum disk capacity | Many implementations have limits at 504MB, 2GB, or 8GB. | 2TB (terabytes) |
| Peak bus transfer rate | 66.6MB per second with UltraDMA/66 | 80MB per second with Ultra2 wide; 160MB per second with Ultra3 or Ultra160/m |
| Maximum cable length | 18 inches (some systems restricted to 7 inches) | 1.5 meters; more with special provisions |
| External device support | No | Yes |
| Termination | No | Yes |
| Parity or ECC on bus | Only for UltraATA | Yes |
| Multiple devices with overlapped activity on same bus | No | Yes |

Overall, ATA uses less sophisticated engineering than SCSI, trading performance for lower costs. Here are some of the details.

✦ The IDE interface supports two disk drives. The ATA-2 interface supports four disk, CD-ROM, or tape drives. The SCSI interface supports multiple devices, including modems, scanners, printers, CD-ROMs, tape drives, and disk drives. You can put 7 devices on a narrow SCSI channel, and 15 on a wide one.

✦ The IDE interface is limited to 504MB hard disk capacity as a result of the MS-DOS BIOS interface used to access IDE drives. ATA-2 extensions to the BIOS are required to solve that problem. The SCSI interface is limited at 2TB (terabytes) per drive. (See the sidebar "Breaking the 8.4GB disk capacity barrier.")

✦ A PCI IDE interface offers up to 66 MBps peak host transfer rates. The SCSI interface offers up to 80 MBps peak host throughput. Ultra 3 / Ultra160/m SCSI boost the bus speed to 160MB per second.

✦ The IDE interface uses a badly designed interface cable between the adapter and the drives, restricting cable lengths severely. IDE is incapable of reliable connection to external drives and offers no option for parity protection on transfers to internal ones. (Ultra ATA/33 addresses the parity shortcomings, and Ultra ATA/66 improves the cabling somewhat. Neither add terminators, and neither extends the maximum cable length.)

The SCSI interface uses a carefully designed, terminated cable capable of reliable operation over extended distances. Even the fastest SCSI rates permit cable lengths as long as 1.5 meters. A variant of SCSI has been defined to allow operation over yet longer cables, but it's uncommon. SCSI buses implement parity error checking on all transactions.

✦ The IDE interface does not allow more than one device to be active on a single cable at a time, and some IDE interface chips (such as the CMD640) don't allow more than one device to be active between both cables. That last restriction means that your computer can't be transferring data from the CD-ROM and the disk at the same time, degrading disk performance because the system has to wait. The SCSI interface can have all attached devices active at once, which particularly improves performance when you're doing several things at once. (Most benchmarks do one thing at a time and so don't report this SCSI performance advantage.)

The only advantages to IDE are that it's cheap and you don't have to worry about terminators when you add or remove devices. If you will only ever have one disk and one CD-ROM (and they're on separate channels), IDE performance can match SCSI. Figure 12-7 shows a sequence for choosing between SCSI and IDE reflecting that perspective. Overall, unless the lower price for IDE is the most important factor, we recommend SCSI.

The fact that you can combine SCSI and IDE means that a compromise between the two is possible. You can use IDE for low-cost disk storage and add an inexpensive SCSI adapter for a scanner, tape drive, or other peripherals.

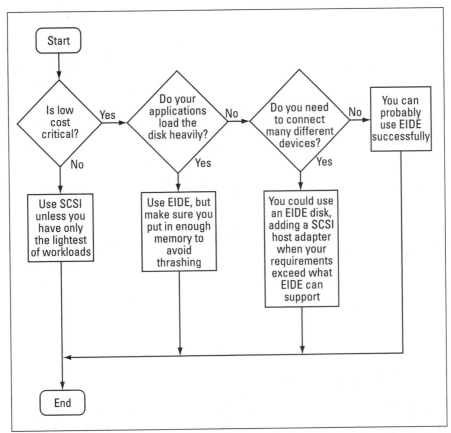

**Figure 12-7:** SCSI is the I/O bus of choice unless cost is more important than performance and flexibility.

## Breaking the 8.4GB disk capacity barrier

Currently, 16,383 cylinders is the absolute upper limit for BIOS support of ATA drives. When combined with the normal 16 heads and 63 sectors per track (16,383 × 16 × 63 × 512 bytes per sector = 8,455,200,768 bytes), this produces a limit of about 8.4GB for capacity reporting using Cylinders, Heads, and Sectors (CHS). That limit means that the normal way of computing drive capacity (Cylinders × Heads × Sectors × 512 bytes/sector) is unusable for drives larger than 8.4GB.

*continued*

*(continued)*

For drives larger than 8.4GB, calculations must use the total number of addressable sectors on the drive times 512 bytes per sector. For example, the label on the Seagate 9.1GB model ST39140A drive shows 17,803,440 addressable sectors (17,803,440 total sectors × 512 bytes per sector = 9,115,361,280 bytes).

If you set up the drive with the "User" option in the BIOS, then even with LBA enabled the drive capacity will be limited to 8.4GB because you have to enter the drive geometry using CHS numbers. If your BIOS supports large drives, use the "Auto" option with LBA enabled to get the full capacity of the drive. Some system BIOSes have a separate HDD detect utility that normally uses the standard CHS method, and they do not function correctly with large drives. Using "Auto" lets the system use the total addressable sectors on the drive to compute drive capacity.

Even so, the total capacity of the drive may or may not be displayed correctly by the BIOS. You can verify the true capacity seen by the BIOS and the operating system using FDISK, SCANDISK, or CHKDSK.

The BIOS on most Adaptec SCSI host adapters provides *Extended INT 13h* support, letting systems using those adapters break the 8.4GB barrier for recognized capacity so long as the operating system supports the INT 13 extensions.

# Future I/O Channels

As drive speeds increase, I/O channels will evolve to a serial data connection between the host adapter and the attached devices using copper or fiber optics. In previous editions of this book, we noted that the most likely serial connection technology was Fibre Channel, or FC. Today, the situation is different, because SCSI has eclipsed Fibre Channel's basic 100MB per second speed, moving upward to 160MB per second with Ultra 3 or Ultra160/m. Other new technologies — Future I/O and Next Generation I/O — surpass Fibre Channel in system-level performance.

However the market selects between Fibre Channel, Future I/O, or Next Generation I/O, the next step past SCSI for I/O buses is serial for two reasons — it's simpler to build very high speed electronics for serial data channels, and high-speed parallel channels are subject to changes in timing as the signals propagate down the wires. Although signals might start out on the wire at the same time, *skew* can cause them to arrive at slightly different times. Skew isn't much of a problem at slower speeds but becomes critical at 100MB per second and faster.

Table 12-6 shows the tradeoffs between fiber optics and copper wire for high-speed connections. You simply can't send data quickly and inexpensively over significant distances on a copper cable, but fiber-optic components capable of 1 Gbps over several kilometers are commonly available. Achieving comparable rates on copper requires multiple conductors and remains very difficult over long distances.

**Table 12-6**
**Fiber Optics versus Copper Cable for Data Transmission**

| Characteristic | Copper Cable | Fiber Optics |
|---|---|---|
| Distance limitations | Less than 30 meters without special transmission technology | Up to 2,000 meters |
| Relative cable cost | Favored for short distances | Favored for long distances |
| Electronics cost | Low | Medium to high |
| Installation cost | Low | Medium to high |
| Total cost | Lower under 30 meters | Lower over 30 meters |
| Noise sensitivity | High (depending on cable design) | Very low |
| Ground loop immunity | Low | Very high |

# IDE and SCSI Products

You're likely to find a PCI IDE interface on your motherboard. If you do, it's the best choice if you're going to use IDE. If you don't have one, you can purchase a PCI IDE card from vendors such as Data Technology Corporation or Promise Technology Incorporated. Before you do that upgrade, though, consider that your machine is probably so old that you'd get much better results by replacing the motherboard (or the entire machine).

IDE motherboard interfaces are so widespread that there's not much of a market for add-in products any longer, so we've not bothered to cover them in this section.

SCSI interfaces (add-in and motherboard) are less common than IDE. SCSI is almost never found on desktop system motherboards, being the nearly exclusive province of server designs. We've covered the add-in SCSI cards we recommend (by Adaptec) in this chapter, plus an AMI motherboard with built-in SCSI support. In addition to Adaptec, you can find SCSI adapters from Advansys, Buslogic, Compaq, DPT, HP, IBM, Mylex, Promise Technology, and SIIG.

## Adaptec AHA-2940U, AHA-2940UW Pro, and AHA-2940U2W

The AHA-2940 series of PCI SCSI host adapters is one of the best known, best performing, and reliable options for SCSI support. The line has evolved from the original AHA-2940 and currently includes these cards:

✦ *AHA-2940U.* This is the FAST-20 version of the original AHA-2940. It supports FAST-20 SCSI, with transfers to SCSI devices at up to 20MB per second.

✦ *AHA-2940UW Pro.* This is the one to get (unless you'll be using Ultra2 drives), because over time it will continue to support the newest SCSI disks. It supports FAST-20 WIDE SCSI, so it can transfer at up to 40MB per second when hooked up to the right device.

✦ *AHA-2940U2W.* If you want maximum SCSI performance, use Ultra2 SCSI. The AHA-2940U2W includes an onboard port for Low Voltage Differential Signaling (LVDS) SCSI drives required in the Ultra2 SCSI specification.

The wide 2940 series cards allow you to mix normal and wide SCSI devices on the same cable. All three cards allow a mix of device speeds. Table 12-7 shows the combinations of what you can put on the SCSI bus for each model. The simplest answer is to choose the AHA-2940U2W because it supports all SCSI standards, but depending on your needs you may find the other models sufficient at a lower price.

## Table 12-7
### Device Compatibility Comparison for the AHA-2940 Family of PCI SCSI Adapters

| SCSI Profile | AHA-2940U | AHA-2940UW Pro | AHA-2940U2W |
|---|---|---|---|
| SCSI | X | X | X |
| FAST SCSI | X | X | X |
| FAST-20 SCSI | X | X | X |
| WIDE SCSI | | X | X |
| FAST-WIDE SCSI | | X | X |
| FAST-20 WIDE SCSI | | X | X |
| FAST-40 WIDE SCSI | | | X |

The AHA-3950 is very similar to the AHA-2940U2W but provides two fully independent SCSI channels to increase total system I/O capacity. The AHA-3950 can support the 64-bit version of PCI if your motherboard offers that feature, but it is backward compatible with original 32-bit PCI.

Figure 12-8 shows the AHA-2940UW Pro. Besides the PCI bus connector, ports on the card include

External Connector            50-pin narrow SCSI connector

68-pin wide SCSI connector                    Activity LED connector

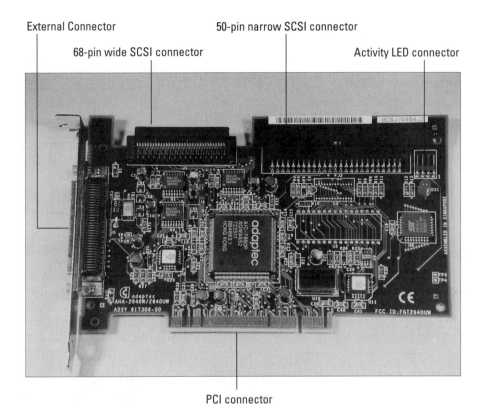

PCI connector

**Figure 12-8:** The Adaptec AHA-2940UW Pro PCI SCSI adapter offers significantly better performance than is possible with an ISA card.

✦ *Activity LED.* This connector hooks up to the "disk activity" light emitting diode (LED) on the computer front panel. It turns on the LED any time there is activity on the SCSI bus, so you'll end up seeing not only disk activity but also anything happening on any other device attached to the host adapter, such as a CD-ROM, scanner, or tape drive.

✦ *Internal SCSI bus connectors.* Depending on the model card you have, there will be one to three internal bus connectors. Differences between the connectors include narrow versus wide SCSI bus support and conventional versus Ultra2 LVDS support.

✦ *External SCSI bus connector.* This is the place where you attach the cable for scanners, portable SCSI tapes and disks, and any other external SCSI devices. The card provides its own terminators and automatically detects if they are needed or not.

The AHA-2940 host adapters are the standard against which you have to measure any other SCSI host adapter. Features of the series include:

✦ *Bus mastering operation on the PCI bus.* Bus mastering improves performance and frees the processor to do other work.

✦ *Simple installation.* Adaptec offers a kit version of the card that includes an internal SCSI cable and their EZ-SCSI software. The kit gives you all the pieces you need to bring SCSI up in your system. If you've bought drives that support the SCSI Plug and Play specification (in addition to ISA Plug and Play), the card can detect and resolve ID conflicts for you as well. You don't have to fiddle around with jumpers or switches on the drives.

✦ *Simultaneous synchronous and asynchronous SCSI device support.* Not all SCSI devices support the faster synchronous transfers. The AHA-2940 series detects what the device can do and deals with it based on that.

✦ *Disconnect/reconnect and scatter-gather.* Disconnect/reconnect enables drives to go off on their own and work while the computer and host adapter tell some other device what to do, and then reconnect and finish the operation. Scatter-gather enables the processor to transfer data from several places in memory to and from the disk, eliminating the need to first move everything into a contiguous block of memory. The two are sophisticated features that — when exploited by the device driver in Windows — increase the performance you get.

Adaptec has put a lot of years and a lot of thought into making SCSI easy to get running, and it paid off. Suppose you've just assembled a system yourself using one of their host adapters. Assuming you have a bootable DOS floppy disk with the FDISK and FORMAT programs on it, here's all you have to do to get Windows installed and running, including setting up your CD-ROM drive:

1. Boot the floppy disk. Use FDISK to partition the SCSI drive and reboot from the floppy.

2. Use FORMAT /S to apply a DOS format to the hard disk and make it bootable. Remove the floppy.

3. Reboot and place the EZ-SCSI floppy in the drive. Run the DOSINST batch file. Follow the prompts, including CD-ROM driver support.

4. Reboot. Your CD-ROM will now be available. Put the Windows CD-ROM in the drive and run SETUP.

It's that easy. No fooling around finding drivers or configuring them yourself. Just go. If you have a Windows 98 boot floppy, it's even easier, because Adaptec worked with Microsoft to make sure the necessary drivers were on the floppy. You'll just boot the floppy, choose CD-ROM support from the boot menu, and then start Windows setup on the CD-ROM.

The EZ-SCSI software gives you some excellent tools to understand and evaluate your SCSI system. EZ-SCSI also includes the SCSI Explorer, which lets you find out an incredible variety of things about the SCSI devices you have. Figure 12-9 shows what it looks like.

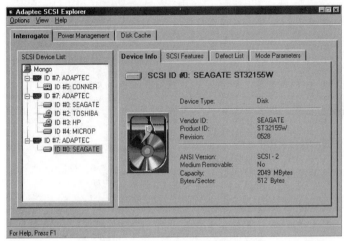

**Figure 12-9:** The SCSI Explorer lets you see the low-level details of what your SCSI devices are capable of.

## Symbios Ultra2 Wide LVDS SCSI Host Adapter on AMI MegaRUM II motherboard

As the mandatory electronics on motherboards have shrunk into physically small support chipsets, manufacturers have added new functionality to better serve users (and, incidentally, to boost their share of the total system cost). Some of the most popular additions for motherboards used in servers are high-performance SCSI ports. Integrating the ports onto the motherboard provides the same speed, reliability, and simplicity benefits to servers that onboard IDE ports do for lower-performance desktop machines. Figure 12-10 shows a typical example, a pair of Ultra2 Wide LVDS SCSI ports supported by a Symbios chip set, on an AMI MegaRUM II motherboard.

Each Ultra2 wide port supports up to 15 devices, so you can attach as many as 30 disks or other devices to the MegaRUM II board. If you used the commonly available 9GB drives, that would be 270GB on a single computer. Use the newer (but still competitively priced) 23GB drives and you'd have a system with 690GB online!

**Figure 12-10:** Two Ultra2 wide SCSI ports on the AMI MegaRUM II motherboard provide high-speed support for large disk farms.

The specifications for the Symbios Ultra2 wide ports are shown in Table 12-8:

| Table 12-8 | |
|---|---|
| **AMI MegaRUM II SCSI Interface Specifications** | |
| *Characteristic* | *Specification* |
| Ports | Dual channel using Symbios 896 Ultra2 PCI bus master SCSI controller |
| Throughput | Up to 80MB per second |
| Interfaces | Two 68-pin connectors for wide internal drives (LVDS or single ended) |

## Granite Digital cables and terminators

If you're serious about having the most reliable SCSI system you can—especially if you're running one of the faster SCSI variants—you should use the cables and terminators from Granite Digital. Here's what you'll want to consider:

✦ *Cables.* Granite Digital makes both internal and external SCSI cables. They design them to minimize coupling between signals, reducing noise and improving system reliability. You order them by specifying the mix of devices you need, and in what order. For example, you might specify a FAST-20 WIDE SCSI cable for a small system to have a 68-pin female connector for an active terminator, four 68-pin male connectors for devices, and a 68-pin female connector for the host adapter.

If you must make your own SCSI cables, you should know that the minimum spacing between connectors is four to six inches (12 inches for Ultra SCSI). When you specify a cable to Granite, they'll make sure the small details like this are covered.

✦ *Terminators.* The SCSIVue Active Terminator plugs into the end of the SCSI cable. In addition to active termination on all the signal lines, the SCSIVue provides LEDs to show you whether you have terminator power, whether any device on the bus is selected, and in what state the bus is. Those lights, along with the instructions Granite Digital provides, can help diagnose many of the common SCSI problems.

Between quality cables and active termination, you can eliminate most of the problems you're likely to see before they happen. This can save you a lot of time.

# Top Support Questions

There are more questions in this section concerning SCSI systems than IDE, but you shouldn't conclude that SCSI systems are more difficult to configure and integrate than IDE ones. In our experience, the problems people have with SCSI are due to lack of knowledge and experience—people who understand the basic principles and requirements of SCSI (mainly termination and unique device IDs) find SCSI simple and reliable. Unless cost is the determining factor, we build SCSI systems for performance and reliability.

## SCSI

Q: My SCSI host adapter is recognized by the motherboard during boot, but some of the devices don't show up (or they don't work). What's wrong?

A: Most likely the termination is wrong, or you have conflicting SCSI IDs. If no devices show up, or they work erratically, check the termination. You should have one device terminated at each physical end of the bus, and none in the middle. If you happen to have a wide controller and only narrow devices, try switching the controller from automatic to manual termination. Some autoterminating controllers don't handle that case correctly. If you're sure the termination is correct, remove all devices but the one at the end, and see if it works (the host adapter BIOS or a hardware diagnostic may be more useful for this level of test than your operating system, because less hardware has to work). If the problems clear up, try adding devices back one by one, checking the ID and termination on each before you add it back. If none of that works, try replacing the SCSI cable.

Q: Can I mix SCSI and IDE in one computer?

A: Yes. Primary partitions on disks on the IDE controller will receive DOS or Windows drive letters before letters for SCSI disks, meaning you'd have to boot from the IDE drive, but otherwise it works. If you have no disks on the IDE controller (only CD-ROM, for example), you can boot from a SCSI disk.

Q: Can I have more than one SCSI controller?

A: Yes, but this can present problems on old, non–Plug and Play ISA machines because of potential I/O and interrupt conflicts. Multiple controllers work fine for PCI and for Plug and Play systems. It works to have different models of a SCSI host adapter, too. You might want to use multiple controllers if you need a lot of devices, or to speed disk access on systems implementing RAID — Redundant Array of Inexpensive Disks — file systems in software (see the next chapter for details on RAID).

Q: Can I let two machines access the same disks on a SCSI bus?

A: Technically, yes. If you assign them different SCSI IDs, most host adapters allow multiple adapters on the same bus. There's little or no software support for doing this, though — be sure you line up software support before you plan on making this part of your systems.

Q: Can I replace a SCSI adapter from one manufacturer with one from another and read the data from the disk?

A: SCSI is standard, but how data is translated onto the drive is not. Host adapter manufacturers each use their own translation scheme. It's possible the drive will have to be reformatted once it is connected to the new host adapter.

Q: When should I disable the BIOS on the adapter?

A: The BIOS can be disabled when the adapter is not operating a SCSI hard disk drive. Your system should work with the BIOS enabled under most situations, but because the BIOS is only needed to boot from a SCSI drive, disabling it may eliminate some conflicts.

Q: Does it matter what ID the host adapter has?

A: Generally the host adapter should have the highest ID to give it the highest arbitration priority on the bus. This means the host adapter should be ID 7 on a narrow bus and 15 on a wide bus.

Q: The adapter recognizes the drive on bootup but gives "Drive not ready." Why?

A: Make sure that the drive is jumpered for spin up on power up. You may also enable the Send Start Unit command on some host adapters.

Q: When I boot up, I get the message "HDD controller failure." Why?

A: This usually happens when you are only using a SCSI hard disk drive in your system but have the motherboard BIOS set up to expect an IDE disk as well. You need to enter the CMOS SETUP in your system and ensure that "Hard Disk" is marked as "not installed" or "none."

Q: Can I put narrow SCSI devices on a wide SCSI bus?

A: Yes, and there are several ways to do this. You can get a cable that supports mixed narrow and wide configurations, such as are available from Granite Digital, or you can get a converter that adapts a wide connection to narrow. For example, the Adaptec ACK-68P-50P-IU and the Granite Digital 6006 are internal converters that convert a 68-pin ribbon cable connector to a 50-pin connector. Be careful that you don't use a narrow device as the termination on a SCSI bus, though, because it won't terminate the wide bus lines.

Q: My ISA SCSI host adapter isn't being recognized in my PCI motherboard. What's wrong?

A: All SCSI host adapters need an I/O address and an interrupt. Assuming your ISA host adapter is assigned a free I/O address, the most likely problem is that the IRQ isn't working. This can happen if there's a conflict with another board, but it can also happen when the PCI motherboard and BIOS don't assign the interrupt over to the ISA bus. Check the settings in your BIOS for the interrupt the ISA card is using, and if necessary force the interrupt over to the ISA bus.

## IDE / ATA / ATA-2

Q: I added a second disk to my IDE system and now neither disk works.
What happened?

A: Most likely you connected the disk to the same port and cable as the existing
disk, and both are jumpered to be the master drive. Check the jumpers on both
disks, ensuring one is set as master and one as slave.

Q: I added an IDE disk and checked the jumpers, but it doesn't show up. Why?

A: After you connect the disk, you have to set it up in the BIOS, and you may have
to partition and format it. See the hands-on section in the next chapter on how to
add an ATA-2 disk.

Q: Should I connect a CD-ROM to the primary or secondary IDE port?

A: You can connect the drive to either port, as long as you observe the limit of two
devices per port. You're likely to see reduced performance connecting the CD-ROM
to the same port as a disk drive.

Q: Can I mix UltraDMA/66 with other speed devices?

A: You can, but you'll lose the speed advantages. If an UltraDMA/66 device detects
another, slower device on the same port, it slows down to the speed of the slower
device. This is true whether the UltraDMA/66 device is master or slave.

# Hands-On Upgrades

You might add a SCSI host5 adapter to an ATA system to support a ZIP drive or
scanner, or simply to add in a faster, larger drive. This section shows you how.

## Adding a SCSI Host Adapter to an ATA-2 system

Suppose you decide to add a SCSI tape, removable disk, or scanner to your IDE-
based system. Your first step is going to be to add a SCSI host adapter, so let's look
at how to do that.

1. *Pick a host adapter.* What host adapter you choose depends on what you plan
   to do and what slots you have in your system. If you have a PCI slot free, I
   suggest getting a PCI host adapter so that, should you later add a disk or
   other high-speed device, you'll have the performance you want. If you're slot-
   limited, your alternatives are an ISA adapter or a PC Card adapter. Neither will
   be as fast.

**2.** *Think about the I/O address and IRQ.* Before you add any card to your system, think about what I/O addresses and interrupt request lines it needs. If it's a PCI or ISA Plug and Play card, this should be automatic, so you can skip this step. If it's an older ISA card, you've got work to do.

Read the manual for the card to find out what its default I/O addresses and IRQ are, and figure out if they are available in your system. If you're running Windows, the Device Manager makes this easy. Figure 12-11 shows the Windows 95 Device Manager; if you select the "Computer" entry at the top of the listed components and then click "Properties," you'll get the display shown in Figures 12-12 and 12-13, which show you all the I/O addresses and interrupt levels known to be assigned. (You can see Direct Memory Access and Memory assignments too, using other selections in the window shown in the latter two figures.)

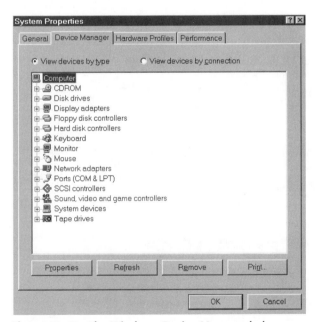

**Figure 12-11:** The Windows Device Manager helps you track I/O address and IRQ assignments.

There's a limitation on how far you can rely on what the Device Manager tells you — you only see I/O addresses and IRQs claimed by 32-bit device drivers. If you have real-mode (16-bit) drivers loaded, or if the driver doesn't reliably report all the resources the device uses, you'll get bogus information.

In Figure 12-12, you can see that all the I/O addresses from 0000 to 0061 are in use. You can check the rest of the addresses by scrolling the window down. You get similar information from Figure 12-13 — Interrupts 00 through 08 are all assigned and in use. In both windows, you identify free addresses and interrupts by the fact that they don't show up.

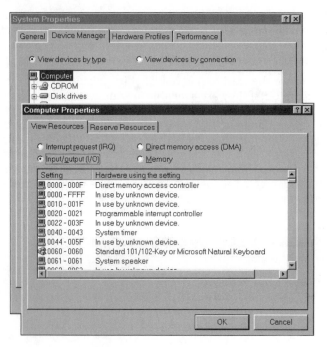

**Figure 12-12:** The I/O address display shows all addresses known to be used by 32-bit device drivers.

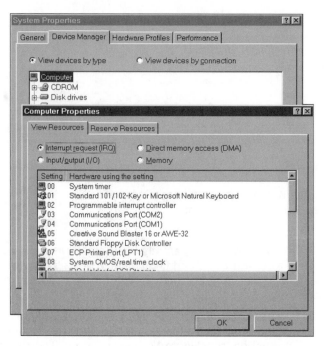

**Figure 12-13:** The I/O IRQ display shows all interrupt levels known to be used by 32-bit device drivers.

Suppose, for example, that the default I/O address on your non–Plug and Play ISA SCSI host adapter is 330, and the IRQ is 12. Look in the Device Manager, and see if those settings are available. If so, you can proceed to the next step. If not, you'll have to follow the directions in the manual for changing the settings. (Unfortunately, not all boards with a built-in BIOS support operation at alternate addresses. If yours is one of those, try changing the settings on the conflicting board in your computer.)

3. *Install the card.* Figure 12-8 shows an Adaptec AHA-2940UW Pro PCI SCSI host adapter. Once you firmly seat the card in its socket, you'll start to attach cables. Internal cables go on the 50-pin or 68-pin connectors (or both); an external cable can go on the external connector. (If you use an external SCSI cable, you can only use one of the two internal connectors.) You can connect an LED from the front of your computer's case to the Activity LED connector so that you'll see when any device on the SCSI bus is active. The Adaptec card has four pins for LED connection, even though most activity LED connectors have two pins. Connect to either of the two outer pairs of pins, trying the reverse orientation on the pins if the LED doesn't light.

4. *Boot the system.* After the motherboard BIOS comes up, you should see messages from the SCSI adapter BIOS. If you do, and the messages don't report problems, the card is probably working properly in your system. The next step is to add drives, which we'll look at in the Hands On section in the next chapter.

## Setting the SCSI ID and disk jumpers

There are a bunch of jumpers on most SCSI drives, and it's important to get them right to get the best results in your system. We'll use the Toshiba XM-3801 15X CD-ROM to illustrate how to set up a drive. Figure 12-14 shows the jumpers for the drive.

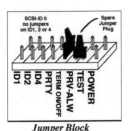

*Jumper Block*

**Figure 12-14:** You set all the important system-level characteristics of a SCSI drive though its jumper block. (Drawing courtesy of Toshiba America Information Systems.)

1. *SCSI ID.* This drive is a narrow SCSI device, so there are three jumpers (ID1, ID2, and ID4) to set the ID. Figure 12-15 shows the options. A rectangular block in the figure means the jumper is installed, while two vertical dots mean the jumper is not present.

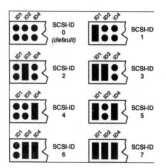

**Figure 12-15:** The SCSI ID selects the device address on the SCSI bus. (Drawing courtesy of Toshiba America Information Systems.)

Most SCSI adapters expect to boot from the device at ID 0; some SCSI adapters expect devices at ID 0 and ID 1 to be nonremovable disks. ID 7 (15 for wide SCSI) is preferred for the host adapter itself. Because of that, you'll typically want to use an ID between 2 and 6 inclusive for a CD-ROM. The default shipped from Toshiba is ID 0, so you'll want to add some jumpers. Any ID that's not otherwise used on the same host adapter is fine. Push the jumper onto both pins of the jumper position (vertical in Figure 12-15). Don't assume you can store jumpers in a horizontal position as suggested in Figure 12-15 unless the manufacturer states that is acceptable.

2. *Parity.* The SCSI bus includes a parity check signal to ensure reliable data transfer across the bus. Recent SCSI devices automatically generate parity signals when sending on the bus but allow you to control whether or not the device should check parity when receiving on the bus. Unless you have a device that can't generate parity, you should always jumper your SCSI devices to check parity.

3. *Termination.* All SCSI devices provide a way to control whether or not internal terminators in the device are enabled. Many older drives supply terminators as two or three removable resistor packs near the SCSI connector, requiring you to physically pry out the resistor packs to disable termination. (There's a pin 1 on the resistor packs. If you go to reinstall terminators, make sure you use the packs you previously removed, and make sure you orient pin 1 properly.) More recent drives, including the Toshiba XM-3801, let you enable and disable the terminators with a jumper. The Toshiba enables the terminators with the jumper installed and disables them with the jumper removed. (Ultra2 SCSI disk drives never include terminators — you have to separately terminate the end of the LVDS Ultra2 cable.)

4. *Media Eject.* You can choose to prevent or allow disks to be ejected from the drive using the eject button. Leave the jumper off to make the button work; insert the jumper to disable the button.

5. *Test.* Test jumpers on drives can do a wide variety of odd things. What they do is generally not documented, so test jumpers should generally be left alone. In

the case of the Toshiba XM-3801, setting the right configuration of the ID, Parity, and Test jumpers lets the drive perform as a simple stand-alone audio CD player.

6. *Terminator Power.* SCSI terminators can be powered from the host adapter, from a device, or from a combination of those. Applying the terminator power jumper allows the drive to supply terminator power to the SCSI bus. Most drives supply power by default; some high-speed SCSI host adapters work better with terminator power supplied only by the host adapter. If your SCSI bus is performing erratically (and you know the terminators are installed correctly), check the terminator power configuration.

SCSI systems offer more flexibility and simpler device integration than IDE. If you keep the requirements for termination and unique device IDs in mind, you should have few or no problems.

# Summary

✦ Most users will do fine with IDE, but there may be integration problems.

✦ CD-ROM and tape devices can slow down IDE disks.

✦ SCSI is more expandable than IDE, offers larger drives, and (in some cases) provides higher performance.

✦ IDE is less expensive than SCSI.

✦　　✦　　✦

# Hard Disks and Disk Arrays

**M**any technologies go into building the high-performance disk drives we use. They include the magnetic effects that pack data onto the platters, the design and construction of the heads themselves, the precision with which the platters themselves are built, and the electronics that turn small signals from the disk heads into data for your computer.

As interesting as they are, however, these don't matter from the standpoint of choosing the disk products you'll put in your computer. What you really care about is capacity, performance, reliability, and price. The large volume of disks manufactured and sold to the personal computer market ensures that you can base your buying decisions on actual field experience, not projections, so the underlying technology is less important than what's being delivered in users' machines.

Capacity is reasonably straightforward: It's how many gigabytes the disk holds. You have to be careful to look at the capacity of the drive after it's been formatted (which is what most drive manufacturers specify). The formatting operation eats up space for sector addresses, space between sectors, and the like, and that's space you can't get at or use. Disk manufacturers most commonly specify capacity as the formatted capacity of the drive, but divide by 1,000,000,000 to convert to gigabytes, not 1,073,741,824 (1024 × 1024 × 1024) as do Windows and UNIX. A 9.1GB drive sold by the manufacturer will report as 8.48GB when you look at it through the operating system.

## What should you expect from disk drive technology?

Where disk drive technology really matters to you is how it has an impact on what you'll be able to buy next year and several years from now, and how much you'll pay for those drives. The industry has adopted magnetoresistive heads and new signal processing–intensive drive electronics, leading to the areal density and corresponding product capacities shown in Figure 13-1. The most interesting things in Figure 13-1, though, are the two data points that show what IBM has demonstrated in their labs. IBM demonstrated areal density of one gigabit per square inch in 1989, and three gigabits per square inch in 1995. Their projection in 1997 was that they'd ship products at that density sometime in the 1998 to 2000 time frame, which meant you could expect about 30GB in a 3.5-inch disk no later than the turn of the century. Seagate shipped 23GB drives in late 1996 using a 5.25-inch size, and 50GB drives in early 1999. The 23GB drive density was about 1 gigabits per square inch, while the new 50GB drive density is up at 3.25 gigabits per square inch. In early 1999, Hitachi shipped a laptop drive with an areal density of 6.1 gigabits per square inch, and Seagate demonstrated a drive operating at 16.7 gigabits per square inch.

Disk drives work by writing small magnetic changes onto the surface of the disk platter. Until IBM pioneered magnetoresistive heads, most disks used a tiny coil in the head to both generate a magnetic field (to write data) and to sense magnetization changes on the platter (to read data). The magnetoresistive head uses a different sensor to read back from the platter, one in which the resistance to electrical current changes when the magnetization on the platter changes. These heads allow the bits to be packed closer on the platter, increasing disk capacity.

Magnetoresistive heads aren't the end of disk drive progress. In 1997, Terastor announced disks using Near Field Recording, a technology that may deliver 20GB on one side of a 3.5 inch platter. Near Field Recording achieves that density with a laser and a lens that reduces the laser beam spot size, creating a very small bit cell size. In 1998, Quinta announced a hybrid of optical and conventional technology with the possibility of delivering hundreds of gigabytes in a 3.5-inch form factor.

# Disk Drive Performance

The most important factor in disk drive performance is throughput on and off the disk, as measured in the system while running your workload. That's not possible for manufacturers to measure, so they specify a number of parameters that you can use to estimate what you can expect from a drive:

✦ *Sustained throughput.* For reasonably large transfers, such as loading programs from disk or reading/writing the swap file, the performance you'll get is the sustained throughput onto or off the disk itself. As we saw in Chapter 4, the rotation rate of the disk and the number of sectors per track determine the sustained throughput.

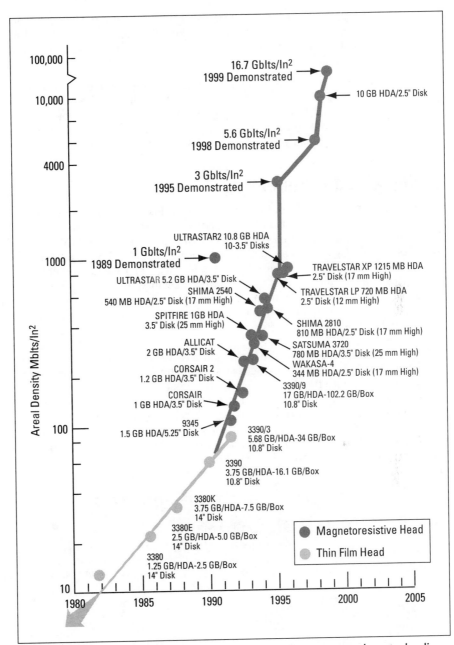

**Figure 13-1:** The areal density of disks has increased at a spectacular rate, leading to the fast, cheap drives we now use.

✦ *Seek and rotational latency.* For short transfers, the performance you get is determined by the time it takes to move the head to the right cylinder and for the right sector to rotate under the heads. A faster rotation rate reduces the rotational latency.

✦ *Cache buffer size.* As we saw in Chapter 4, the cache buffer on the drive can strongly affect the performance you get. Predicting the effect of different cache sizes is hard, though; you're better off relying on benchmarks for this comparison if you can. If not, you can assume that in general a bigger cache is better, as long as you remember that this is not always true in every case.

## Sustained transfer rate

The sustained throughput in bytes per second is the number of bytes in a sector times the number of sectors per track times the track rotations per second. Disk manufacturers sometimes don't specify the sustained throughput of the disk explicitly, but you can calculate it from other specifications (such as rotation rate times sectors per track times 512 bytes per sector). Disk manufacturers put more sectors on the outer tracks of the platter (because they're larger and have more space), so there's no one number for sectors per track. You can use the minimum number, the maximum, or the average. As long as you compare rates you compute consistently, it doesn't matter.

For example, suppose you're looking at a drive that rotates at 5,400 RPM and has from 95 to 177 sectors per track. There are almost always 512 bytes per sector, so you can compute the drive's sustained transfer rate as shown in Table 13-1. We've calculated the track capacity in the table on the basis of sectors per track and then used the rotation rate and the track capacity to get sustained transfer rate. The drive in this example gives you sustained performance (for a single transfer, ignoring latency) from over 4MB to nearly 8MB per second, with an average rate of nearly 6MB per second.

### Table 13-1
### Sustained Transfer Rate as a Factor of Rotation Rate, Sectors per Track, and Track Capacity

| Rotation Rate (RPM) | Sectors per Track | Track Capacity (KB) | Sustained Transfer Rate (MB per second) |
|---|---|---|---|
| 5,400 | 95 | 47.50 | 4.17 |
| 5,400 | 136 | 68.00 | 5.98 |
| 5,400 | 177 | 88.50 | 7.78 |

This isn't too bad an estimate. The numbers in the table are from a Quantum Fireball, and when we ran the Adaptec EZ-SCSI benchmark (SCSIBench) on the drive, we recorded a sustained transfer rate for large blocks of about 5MB per second. The benchmark doesn't report what tracks it uses for the test, so we can't compute the expected performance with better accuracy. Assuming the track the benchmark used is somewhere toward the middle of the drive, the measurement correlates well with the calculations in Table 13-1.

## Seek and rotational latency

For small transfers, we saw earlier that the time to get the heads positioned over the right sector is much larger than the time to actually transfer the data. As the drawing in Figure 13-2 shows, the positioning time can be enormously longer than the actual transfer time. The average seek time is commonly specified by the disk manufacturer and depends on the physical design of the heads and the actuator mechanism that mounts and moves the heads. The lighter (and by implication smaller) the heads and mechanism, the faster they can start and stop moving, and the smaller the seek time will be.

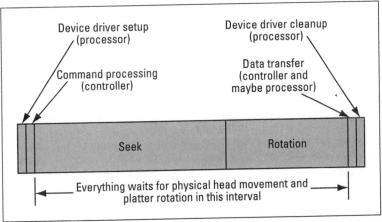

**Figure 13-2:** The time to transfer small data blocks is essentially the time to position the heads over the data.

The rotational latency isn't always specified, but because we know the rotation rate we can calculate the delay. If we assume that on the average the disk is positioned one half of a revolution away from the data we want, then the average rotational latency is one half of the rotation time. For our example 5,400 RPM drive, the rotation time is about 11ms (calculated as the reciprocal of the rotation rate), so the average rotational latency is about 5.5ms. The average seek time is specified to be 11ms, so the total average access time — the time it takes from when the drive gets the command to read to when it starts delivering data — is the sum of the two, or 16.5ms.

That is an extremely interesting number, because it enables us to predict the random access performance of the drive. The 16.5ms access implies that we can do about 60 random transfers per second (there are about 60 16.5ms intervals in one second). If we're transferring single sectors (so we get 512 bytes per transfer), that's a transfer rate of only 30KB per second — pretty awful. Even though Windows transfers a cluster at a time, which would be at least 4KB on a drive like this, a database program might only use one sector in the cluster. If that's true, the additional data transferred is wasted, and the 30KB per second represents usable data transfer.

This analysis shows why the operating system disk cache is so critical, and why the value of a disk cache goes up as the size of the reads your programs do goes down. Operating systems dynamically size the disk cache in memory based on disk activity and on how much memory your programs need. If programs need all the available memory, the cache can get too small, and performance can drop precipitously. You have to have more memory than just what your programs are specified to require if there's going to be room for the cache — that's part of why more memory can provide a significant performance boost to machines with limited memory.

# Disk Drive Reliability

If you go looking at disk drive data sheets, you'll see that manufacturers commonly boast mean time between failures (MTBF) of 500,000 to 1,000,000 hours. If you leave the drive powered up and running all the time, this is between 57 and 114 years. No one is likely to use the same disk that long, so it's worth asking why anyone worries about disk failures.

The answer is that MTBF is really only a measure of the probability that a device will fail. You can use it to estimate how likely it is that the device will run for a specified amount of time without failure, but it's not an obvious computation. Figure 13-3 shows the probability a device will survive a stated length of time for different MTBF values. For example, the probability that a disk with an MTBF of 800,000 hours will go five years without a failure is nearly 95 percent. Said differently, if you have a large number of these drives, after five years you can expect one drive in twenty to have failed. In practice, you'll probably do better than this shows, because these calculations assume the drive is powered on 24 hours a day.

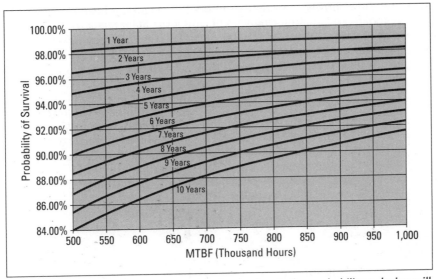

**Figure 13-3:** The MTBF specification lets you estimate the probability a device will last a specified lifetime.

If you conclude from this analysis that eventually you're going to see a hard disk failure, you're undoubtedly right. (Yes, now might be a good time to go back up your computer if you can't remember when you did it last. Check that your restores work too.) Disk failure is one of the worst computer failures from a lost-time standpoint, because in addition to the time it takes you to diagnose the problem and replace the drive, you have to find the backups, restore them, and worry about the data that wasn't backed up.

Disk drive manufacturers are keenly aware of the cost of disk failure and are working to reduce the impact of a failure. Notice we didn't say they're working to reduce the chances of failure, we said the impact of a failure. The drives as-is are reliable enough that it's not worth the cost of trying to reduce the failure rate. The top disk manufacturers (Seagate Technology, IBM, Western Digital, and Quantum) developed the Self-Monitoring, Analysis, and Reporting Technology (SMART). SMART monitors critical drive performance parameters in the disk's controller. When one of the parameters degrades past a threshold, the drive reports out to your computer that a failure may be pending. That report is your warning to back up data carefully and replace the drive.

Figure 13-4 shows how a drive that monitors the height the head flies above the platter responds to variations in flying height. If the height gets too high, the signal the head generates weakens and the error rate off the drive skyrockets. If the head gets too low, it hits the surface and damages the drive. The dotted lines in the figure represent the alert thresholds, at which the drive reports it has a problem.

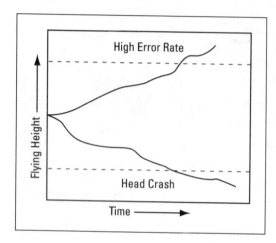

**Figure 13-4:** Measuring variations in head flying height helps predict disk failures. (Drawing courtesy of IBM.)

Other typical characteristics SMART watches include:

✦ Data throughput of the drive

✦ Time for the drive to spin up to operating speed

✦ The number of sectors declared defective during operation (and remapped to other, good sectors)

✦ The frequency with which errors occur while the heads are seeking a new position

The specific drive parameters and the trigger thresholds depend on the drive and manufacturer, who will choose them to give the best warning possible of impending doom. SMART is not infallible — disk failures can occur on a SMART drive without warning, because there are both predictable and unpredictable failures. Predictable failures (today) are preceded by gradual degradation of some parameter before the failure. Unpredictable failures can be due to internal chip failures (which can themselves be caused by power surges). Predictability is more common for mechanical failures in the drive. According to Seagate, 60 percent of drive failures are for mechanical reasons, so in practice SMART gives good coverage of coming trouble.

# Redundant Array of Inexpensive Disks (RAID)

Reliability and performance are the keys to a quality file and Internet server. You want to know that the gigabytes of data you're responsible for are completely safe, and that your tens, hundreds, or thousands of users can get the data they want, when they want it, without waiting for their turn at the disk. These are not simple problems to solve:

- ✦ Disk drives are vulnerable to failure. When they do fail, data written since the last backup is lost.

- ✦ Disks have limitations on how fast they can go, with those limitations becoming more severe for the less expensive disks.

- ✦ I/O buses have limitations on speed as well, and if you attempt to solve that problem with multiple host adapters, you then confront the problem of deciding how to spread files across the adapters to balance the load.

Suppose you want to connect 100 users to a file server, and suppose that at any one time as many as 20 of them may be reading or writing files. Transfer rates of 100KB per second from a single machine across a network are easy to achieve, so the combined data rate at the file server could easily exceed 2MB per second. Aggregate disk performance of 2MB per second is within the limits of most machines.

Now suppose you have not 100 users, but 1,000, or suppose that your users keep all their software on the file server along with their data files. For either reason, we'll assume that the load is now ten times greater, or 20MB per second. You can get that kind of rate into a network server, but it's difficult to sustain that transfer rate with a single disk. Worse yet, you probably only back up files overnight, so if a disk fails, you could lose an entire day's work of all 1,000 users. If an hour's work costs only $25, that failure could easily cost a quarter of a million dollars. The cost could be far higher if you lose a customer because you couldn't perform.

You can get the server performance you need and at the same time avoid losing data from disk failure. Better yet, you can do it at reasonable cost using a technology called Redundant Array of Inexpensive Disks (RAID), invented at the University of California at Berkeley by D.A. Patterson, G. Gibson, and R.H. Katz. (The industry is starting to use the phrase Redundant Array of Independent Disks, so you'll probably see both.) RAID uses conventional disks with specialized host adapters to change how data goes onto your disk.

## What RAID does

The idea behind RAID is to take the conventional disks in personal computers — usually SCSI — and gang them together in parallel. The resulting assembly can give you the low cost of disks manufactured in high volume plus good reliability and a multiplier on the performance of individual disks. Figure 13-5 shows how this works. The host adapter (frequently called a controller in RAID systems) sits between one high-rate data stream (on the computer side) and several lower-rate streams (on the disk side). When the computer writes to the disk, the host adapter takes high-rate data and breaks it into multiple synchronized streams, one for each disk, in a process called striping. Reads by the computer cause the host adapter to take a data stream from each disk, multiplex the set of streams into one stream, and send that resulting stream on to the computer. In the example of Figure 13-5, the one high-speed stream splits into four separate disk data streams at one-fourth the rate of the combined stream.

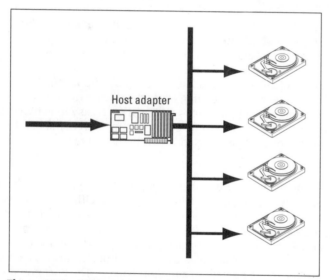

**Figure 13-5:** RAID arrays can give you vast amounts of storage and the reliability you'd want to stake your job on.

Continuing the example in Figure 13-5, if the rate into the host adapter is 20MB per second, each of the four disks will see a stream at 5 megabytes per second. Buffers (that is, a block of memory) on the host adapter match burst transmissions from the computer to the more constant transfer rates of the disks and isolates the computer from delays while the disk heads move and the platters rotate into position.

A RAID controller can do more than just broker between a fast computer and several slower disks — it can also insert error correction codes. In an eight-disk

RAID system, for example, you can add a ninth disk to hold nothing but error correction information. In a system built that way, you can remove any of the nine disks and lose no data. If you remove a data disk, the host adapter reconstructs the missing data from the error correction codes. If you remove the code disk, the system notices that it has lost the code data and continues operating. When you replace the failed disk, most RAID controllers can reconstruct the contents of the disk from the surviving ones. Until that process is complete, however, your data is vulnerable to a second failure (so you should be prepared to react to a disk failure promptly).

Do not confuse the data reliability RAID offers with the need for backup. RAID cannot protect you, for example, from a catastrophic software (or user) error that destroys your file systems or deletes important files. You need removable backup media as well as reliable storage.

## Oops: When RAID wasn't enough

We want to make the point very strongly that RAID won't protect you from your own mistakes. One of the most capable Information Technology professionals we know told us this story:

> A Windows NT RAID array reported that one of its SCSI drives had failed and was off-line. He tried running CHKDSK to verify that the file system was still valid, but CHKDSK was unable to run. The program asked if he wanted to run CHKDSK during bootup.

> Answering YES turned out to be a fatal mistake. When he replaced the damaged disk with a spare, he had forgotten to check the SCSI terminator on the drive. The resulting termination problems meant that on reboot WIndows NT could only detect some of the drives. CHKDSK nevertheless began to run, and had unfortunately been scheduled with the /F option (fix damaged files) when he agreed to schedule it to run during bootup. Because the RAID array was missing disks, CHKDSK attempted to salvage recoverable files from a fraction of the complete array. The net effect was to delete 30% of the information on the array.

> He then turned off the server and reconfigured the replacement drive without the SCSI terminator. When NT rebooted it began CHKDSK again. The program saw file fragments, orphaned files, and corrupted indexes. As it attempted to salvage any recoverable files, it scrambled the remaining directories, losing all the data on the file system.

There are many lessons in this episode, but the one we want to highlight is that it took two serious mistakes before the array lost data—allowing CHKDSK to run, and misconfiguring the replacement drive. Both were human error beyond the scope of RAID to prevent.

# RAID levels

There are six different levels of RAID functionality. The simplest RAID system, RAID level 0, merely stripes the data onto multiple disks for better performance. There is no overhead for redundant data storage, and no protection against failure. The highest level is RAID 5, which provides both striping for performance and redundancy for failure protection.

## RAID Level 0

Figure 13-6 shows how RAID level 0 works. Suppose your computer sends a sequence of data to a RAID 0 host adapter connected to two disks. The host adapter will interleave the data to the two drives, sending odd blocks to one drive and even to the other. The block size is up to the host adapter, and can be a byte, a sector, or some other size.

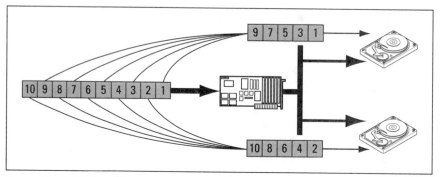

**Figure 13-6:** RAID 0 offers better performance than conventional disk setups but does not enhance reliability.

Because the data rate to any specific disk is a fraction of the aggregate, you get better performance from RAID 0 than from a single conventional disk. There is no error correction or redundant data written to the array, however, so RAID 0 cannot survive a disk failure. You would use RAID 0 only in situations where you needed the performance but not the enhanced data reliability. Be certain about the reliability issue, however. Suppose you have a RAID 0 array of four 9GB drives that's full, and you lose one of the drives. You haven't lost 9GB of data—you've lost 36GB, because your data was spread across all four drives and you have no way to reconstruct the files.

If you use a host adapter with a single I/O bus, you may not get a performance boost equal to the number of drives, unless it's a very fast adapter, due to contention between the drives for access to the bus. For example, three of the Seagate Barracuda ST15150W drives can sustain a transfer rate greater (in sum) than the 20MB per second the wide SCSI bus they connect to can support. This effect becomes more limiting as the number of drives on the bus increases. A RAID host adapter with multiple I/O buses — especially with multiple onboard processors to control those buses — will give better performance. Overall, you can expect better performance from RAID 0 than from most of the other levels, because none of the transfer time is consumed by error correcting or redundant data. The performance of RAID 0 is usually better for long reads and writes than short random requests because the rotation of the individual disks isn't synchronized. When the processor starts a read operation, for example, data can't start to arrive from the controller until all the disks rotate to the proper sector. The access time is therefore not the average, but the worst case position of all the disks in the array. You can partially mask the effect with a larger cache memory on the RAID controller.

Subject to the I/O bus limits, you can add drives to a RAID 0 system to boost performance. In Figure 13-6, for example, there could be three, four, or more drives attached to the host adapter. Multiple I/O buses off the adapter increase the maximum number of drives as well as the achievable performance.

RAID 0 was not part of the original RAID specification by Patterson *et al.* but instead was created by the industry to meet user needs. You can get a similar effect to that of RAID 0 by having multiple host adapters and disks, but (unless you have software such as Windows NT that simulates RAID in the operating system) you will have to manually work the problem of allocating files across the drives to boost performance. RAID 0 does that job for you automatically. The price you pay is the added cost of the RAID host adapter. You might use RAID 0 for a system you use for video capture to increase the sustained data rate to the disk.

## RAID Level 1

In the same way that RAID 0 focuses solely on performance with no concession to reliability, RAID 1 focuses on reliable data storage with no concession to performance. (Note that you get protection against hardware failure, not user error.) RAID 1, also called disk mirroring, uses disks in pairs with both disks of a pair storing the identical data. Figure 13-7 shows how this variation works. Suppose your computer sends a sequence of data to the RAID 1 host adapter connected to two disks. The host adapter will write all the data to each of the two drives. The identical data is stored on both drives, so if one fails, the data is still available. The operation completes when both drives have written the data, so the write can take longer than for one disk alone because of delays for unsynchronized rotation and for I/O bus contention.

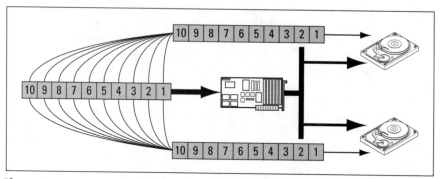

**Figure 13-7:** RAID 1 offers better reliability than RAID 0 or conventional disk setups but does not increase performance.

Depending on how the operating system works and how the host adapter is set up, RAID 1 can be faster on reads than conventional systems because it can read data from either disk. This means that if the operating system makes multiple read requests at the same time, the host adapter can have two reads in process at the same time. This allows the seek and rotational latencies of the drives to overlap each other, delivering two operations worth of data after a single latency delay. Use care when selecting a host adapter for a RAID 1 system; not all host adapters can process two or more requests at once. You'll have to check with your host adapter vendor to see if the specific product you're looking at has this capability.

RAID 1 is commonly done in software. The operating system defines a pair of disks as being mirrors and does all operations to both at the same time. You can do this entirely in software with Windows NT, using a pair of disks on one or two host adapters. The load on the processor, memory, and bus is higher, but otherwise the two approaches are very similar. Whether you implement mirroring in hardware or software, you pay twice for the disk capacity you need. You will pay more for a RAID 1 host adapter than a standard one but get better overall performance compared to software RAID 1 due to the reduced load on the computer. You might choose RAID 1 for a small file server.

## RAID Level 2

RAID 2 is the first RAID version we'll look at that uses error coding to improve data reliability. RAID 2 adds one or more disks to hold the same sort of error correction code often used for memory with Pentium Pro, Pentium II, Celeron, and Pentium III processors. Figure 13-8 shows how the data flows in a RAID 2 system. When your computer sends a sequence of data to a RAID 2 host adapter connected to two data disks and an ECC disk, the host adapter interleaves the data to the two data drives. Odd blocks go to one drive, and even blocks, to the other. The host adapter computes the error correction code (see Chapter 7) for the data written to the data drives and writes it to the ECC drive. On the surface, RAID 2 is a good combination of increased performance and improved reliability.

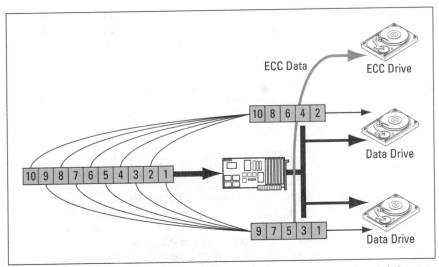

**Figure 13-8:** RAID 2 offers better reliability than RAID 0 or conventional disk setups and has a smaller storage overhead compared to RAID 1.

In practice, however, no one uses RAID 2 for several reasons:

✦ The drives have to be rotationally synchronized, because the data writes all happen at the same time. If they were not synchronized, then the system would have to wait for several rotational latency periods, making things very slow.

✦ There is more storage overhead with RAID 2 for the error correction code than with other versions, so the total system cost is greater. We'll see when we look at RAID 3, 4, and 5 that simpler codes allow recovery from single disk failures, so there's no advantage to the more complex code. Moreover, because disks themselves incorporate the RAID 2 error correcting code internally, the likelihood of a partial, undetected disk failure is very low.

✦ RAID 2 performance on small data blocks will not be any better than on a conventional disk, because the transfer time will be dominated by the seek and rotational delays.

## RAID Level 3

RAID 3 is the same as RAID 2, except that it uses a simpler code—parity instead of ECC. The sidebar "Using parity to recover lost data in RAID systems" shows how the additional knowledge that a drive has failed allows parity coding to reconstruct the contents of the lost drive. (Data reconstruction requires full error correction coding when the location of the failure is not known.) Striping and parity coding is on a byte basis for RAID 3, with the writes done in one operation. The single write operation implies that synchronized rotation is required for good performance.

RAID 3 retains the small-transfer performance limitations of RAID 2, performing well for larger transfers. The storage overhead for the parity data is less than for RAID 2, and it goes down as the number of data drives in the array goes up (which is also true for RAID 2, but to a lesser extent).

You need at least three drives for RAID 3 through 5. RAID 3 is a good choice for large file servers, although you would get better performance from RAID 4, described in the following section.

## Using parity to recover lost data in RAID systems

The following table shows how parity would be stored if the data streams go to two drives. Parity is enough to recover from a failed drive, because the host adapter will know which drive has failed. This is crucially different than the case for main memory, where the identity of a failed chip may not be known until after you run diagnostics. Parity coding written to additional drives in RAID 3 takes less space than full error correction coding but gives the same benefits.

| Data Drive 0 Value | Data Drive 1 Value | Parity Value |
| --- | --- | --- |
| 0 | 0 | 1 |
| 0 | 1 | 0 |
| 1 | 0 | 0 |
| 1 | 1 | 1 |

The following table shows how you rebuild the lost data on a failed drive. If you compare the preceding table to the one that follows, you'll see that they're the same, but in a different order. All the cases are covered, however, and the reconstructed values here precisely corresponds to the preceding cases. You can extend this idea indefinitely, adding as many data drives as you want. Only one parity bit is required for a one-bit slice across the data drives, so you can recover from one failed drive. As long as you replace the failed drive and reconstruct the data before another failure, you're covered.

| Known Value | Parity Value | Reconstructed Value |
| --- | --- | --- |
| 0 | 1 | 0 |
| 0 | 0 | 1 |
| 1 | 0 | 0 |
| 1 | 1 | 1 |

Because knowing which drive failed provides all the information the host adapter needs, a RAID 3 system gives you all the security of a RAID 2 system at less storage overhead.

## RAID Level 4

RAID 4 is nearly the same as RAID 3, but instead of striping across disks at the byte level, it operates at the sector level. This makes RAID 4 like RAID 2 (Figure 13-8) except that it uses parity rather than ECC, and it interleaves sectors. RAID 4 therefore has good data reliability and storage efficiency, as do RAID 2 and 3, and retains fast writes for large data blocks. RAID 4 does not require synchronized spindles, because it's easy to buffer sectors and write them out independently to all the drives. Multiple independent writes mean the I/O operations are processed in parallel, which in turn means that small writes can be faster. Unsynchronized rotation can slow reads for small data blocks.

## RAID Level 5

RAID 5 is the same as RAID 4, except that instead of dedicating a single disk to storing parity, the parity data stream is striped across all the disks along with the rest of the streams. Figure 13-9 shows how this works. Suppose your computer sends a sequence of data to a RAID 5 host adapter connected to four disks. The host adapter interleaves the data to the drives, ensuring that no one drive ever holds two blocks of a group protected by a parity block. The host adapter inserts the new parity information in the data stream that it sends to the disks mixed in with the original data. As long as there is at least one more disk than there are original data streams, the loss of a disk can only take out one data stream, and so parity is enough to regenerate the lost data.

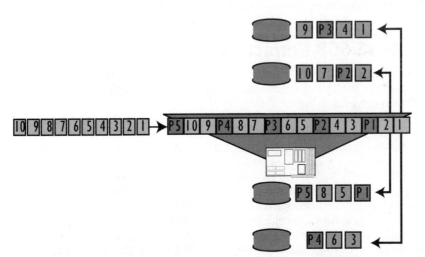

**Figure 13-9:** RAID 5 offers data reliability, handles small and large blocks, and does not require spindle synchronization.

RAID 5 is a good choice for database servers doing many small operations.

Other RAID levels are defined by specific companies, as well as combinations of levels. RAID 0/1, for example, is striping (as with RAID 0) that is mirrored on a duplicate set of disks (as with RAID 1). This combination gives you the speed of RAID 0 with the data reliability of RAID 1 but carries the high storage overhead of RAID 1 too.

The time needed to recreate your file system depends on the RAID level you use and the performance of your host adapter. You'll want to check the performance of the host adapters you're considering before you buy.

# Hard Disk, RAID, and Storage Management Products

In addition to several disk drives, we've covered a host adapter and some useful software in this section. We'll look at some Ultra2 SCSI and UltraDMA/66 IDE disks, a RAID host adapter, and some software to make the job of dealing with disk partitions easier.

We've used disk drives from Seagate Technology as product examples in this chapter. You can also get competitive disk drives from IBM, Maxtor, Quantum, and Western Digital; we use the Seagate drives because over time we've had fewer problems with them than others we've tried.

## Seagate 13.6GB Barracuda ATA

For a long time, drives over 2GB were exclusively SCSI. ATA drives now are far larger than 2GB, with the 13.6GB Seagate Barracuda ATA being typical of current value-priced drives.

This is a drive you'd expect to find in many desktop systems. Performance specifications for the drive is shown in Table 13-2.

The development of high-capacity ATA drives extends the reach of lower-cost systems using the PCI IDE interface on the motherboard, keeping pace with the needs of newer applications such as video record, playback, and editing; audio; multimedia; 3D graphics; and electronic publishing. The important question is always how a drive will perform in a real system — ideally, yours — so at one time we ran benchmarks to compare performance of IDE and SCSI drives that were identical except for the I/O bus technology. The only differences in the tests were the controllers on the drives and the host adapters.

## Table 13-2
## Specifications for the Seagate Technology 13.6GB Barracuda ATA Drive (Model ST313620A)

| Characteristic | Performance |
|---|---|
| Interface | Ultra ATA/66 |
| Formatted capacity | 13.6GB |
| Platters | 2 |
| Surfaces | 4 |
| Average sustained transfer rate | >15 MBps |
| Bytes per sector | 512 |
| Areal density | 4.8Gb per square inch |
| Average seek time (read) | 8.6ms |
| Track-to-track seek time (read) | Not specified |
| Rotation rate | 7,200 RPM |
| Cache size | 512 KB |
| MTBF | Not specified (3 year warranty, 5 year service life) |
| Buffer-to-host peak data rate | 40.38 MBps |

The test results showed that the speed of the two drives was essentially the same under Windows 9x running a mix of disk operations representative of common business applications. The access time and the sustained transfer rate, both of which are set by the performance of the disk assembly rather than the platters, determine the achievable disk performance. The disk itself was the same for the two versions of the drive, so you would expect those characteristics to be the same.

At the same time, the test we ran did not show any speed advantage for the SCSI version, either. This is because the benchmark runs one test and one program at a time, so in that test the capability of the SCSI bus to handle multiple commands at once buys nothing.

## Seagate 9.1 and 18.2GB Barracuda

The Seagate Technology Barracuda drives (see Figure 13-10) are high-performance, high-end drives. They use an Ultra2 SCSI interface; models are also available for Fibre Channel. We looked at the performance and characteristics of the ST39173LW, which is a 9.1GB Ultra2 version. (18.2GB versions are available.)

**Figure 13-10:** The Seagate Barracuda provides high-performance SCSI storage with a high MTBF. (Photo courtesy Seagate Technology.)

Figure 13-11 shows the layout of a typical SCSI drive.

✦ The SCSI I/O connector is the standard 68-pin version for wide SCSI.

✦ J5 lets you set the SCSI ID and provides the connection to a spindle synchronization cable and the connection for an activity LED tied directly to the drive.

✦ J4 lets you set the parity checking option (on the SCSI bus), the motor start option, and the motor start delay. J4 also lets you enable or disable the terminators on the drive.

✦ J01 lets you select how termination power is handled (from the drive, from the SCSI bus, to the SCSI bus, and to the SCSI bus and the drive).

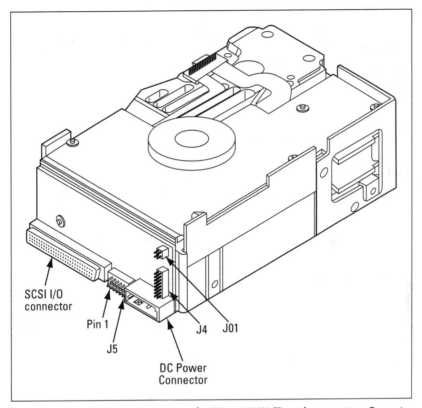

**Figure 13-11:** The Seagate Barracuda ST39173LW (Drawing courtesy Seagate Technology.)

This is a more complete set of options for a SCSI drive than you'll find on lesser drives. The key performance specifications for the ST39173LW are shown in Table 13-3. The fast rotation rate and access time of the drive, combined with the relatively large cache, boosts performance considerably. The MTBF is better than many others, suggesting that this is a drive appropriate for critical applications.

According to our price-checking research, the Barracuda cost per megabyte is 1.6 times that of the Medalist UltraATA, but the specifications are significantly better. For example, if you calculate the average sustained transfer rate for the Barracuda (it's 237 sectors × 512 bytes per sector / 1,048,576 bytes per MB × 7,200 RPM / 60 seconds per minute), it's over 14MB per second—about 6MB per second faster than the Medalist. The cache is substantially bigger, the seek times, faster, and the MTBF, longer.

## Table 13-3
## Specifications for the Seagate Technology Barracuda ST39173LW Drive

| Characteristic | Performance |
| --- | --- |
| Formatted capacity | 9.105MB |
| Platters | 5 |
| Surfaces | 10 |
| Tracks per surface | 7,501 |
| Sectors per track | 237 (average) |
| Bytes per sector | 512 |
| Areal density | 1.485Gb per square inch |
| Average seek time (read) | 7.1ms |
| Track-to-track seek time (read) | 0.8ms |
| Full-stroke seek time (read) | 16ms |
| Rotation rate | 7,200 RPM |
| Cache size | 1MB (4MB optional) |
| MTBF | 1,000,000 hours |
| Buffer-to-host peak data rate | 80 MBps |

## Seagate 50GB Barracuda

If you really need as much storage in as small a space as possible, you'll want to take a look at the Seagate Barracuda 50 (Figure 13-12). This SCSI drive stores 50GB in a single 3.5-inch package. If you look at the figure, you'll see one of the ways Seagate does it. You'll find an amazing 11 platters in that package.

The other way Seagate reaches 50GB is to put a phenomenal number of sectors in each track—an average of about 370. The Barracuda 50 specifications are listed in Table 13-4.

**Figure 13-12:** The Seagate Barracuda 50 packs the most storage available in a 3.5-inch package. (Photo courtesy Seagate Technology.)

## Table 13-4
## Specifications for the Seagate Technology Barracuda 50 Drive

| Characteristic | Performance |
| --- | --- |
| Formatted capacity | 50.1GB |
| Platters | 11 |
| Surfaces | 22 |
| Tracks per surface | 12,024 |
| Sustained transfer rate | 14.9 to 25.7MB per second |
| Bytes per sector | 512 |

*Continued*

| Table 13-4 *(continued)* | |
|---|---|
| *Characteristic* | *Performance* |
| Areal density | 3.252Gb per square inch |
| Average seek time (read) | 7.4ms |
| Track-to-track seek time (read) | 0.6ms |
| Full-stroke seek time | 16ms |
| Rotation rate | 7,200 RPM |
| Cache size | 1MB (4 and 8MB optional) |
| MTBF | 1,000,000 hours |
| Buffer-to-host peak data rate (Ultra2 SCSI) | 80 MBps |

## Seagate Cheetah 18LP

We saw earlier that the key to high-sustained disk transfer rates for a single disk is a high rotation rate and many sectors per track. The Seagate Cheetah (Figure 13-13) is designed specifically for high rotation rate, as shown in Table 13-5.

**Figure 13-13:** The Seagate Cheetah has a 10,000 RPM rotation rate, giving it great sustained transfer rates and fast access times. (Photo courtesy Seagate Technology.)

## Table 13-5
## Specifications for the Seagate Technology Cheetah 18LP Drive

| Characteristic | Performance |
| --- | --- |
| Formatted capacity | 18.2GB |
| Platters | 6 |
| Surfaces | 12 |
| Tracks per surface | 9,772 |
| Average sustained transfer rate | 18.3 to 28MB per second |
| Bytes per sector | 512 |
| Areal density | 1.64Gb per square inch |
| Average seek time (read) | 5.2ms |
| Track-to-track seek time (read) | 0.6ms |
| Full-stroke seek time | 12ms |
| Rotation rate | 10,000 RPM |
| Cache size | 1MB |
| MTBF | 1,000,000 hours |
| Buffer-to-host peak data rate (Ultra2 SCSI) | 80MB per second |

Seagate notes that the Cheetah generates more heat than conventional drives because of the more powerful motor required to achieve the 10,000 RPM rotation rate. More case fans help, but the best approach is to make sure the drive is mounted in a metal bracket providing a robust path for heat to be conducted away from the drive. With good airflow, the drive should remain cool and reliable.

High-RPM drives such as the Cheetah provide fast access times as well as high transfer rates. That means that, in addition to good support for video recording and editing, these drives will improve the performance of transaction-driven network servers. Examples of network services that will benefit include client/server transaction processors, and Internet web, commerce, and news servers.

# Adaptec AAC-364 PCI to Ultra2 SCSI RAID Array Controller

There are several ways to add RAID storage to your computer. At the very high end, you can buy a complete RAID subsystem, including controller, disks, power supplies, and cabinet. Subsystem-level products often look like a disk to your SCSI host adapter and are relatively expensive. In return for the cost, however, you get an integrated product that you — more or less — just plug in and run. At the low end, your operating system itself may support RAID file systems spanning multiple disks (as does Windows NT).

For mid-range RAID performance — high compared to a conventional disk, but less than high-end dedicated RAID arrays — you might want to look at products like the Adaptec AAC-364 PCI to Ultra2 SCSI RAID Array Controller. With the AAC-364, you can plug in up to 60 disks, ideally spread evenly over the card's 4 Ultra2 SCSI channels (there's a limit of 15 disks per channel). The AAC-364 supports RAID levels 0, 1, 0/1, and 5, giving you the option of striping without error correction, mirroring, striping with mirroring, or striping with interleaved parity error correction. The aggregate sustained transfer rate for the AAC-364 is in excess of 200MB per second when connected to a 64-bit PCI bus. The peak transfer rate for the AAC-364 is 320MB per second, reflecting the capability to run all four Ultra2 wide SCSI buses in parallel.

You may need to check your motherboard before integrating the AAC-364. The AAC-364 uses a PCI bridge, a device that links the motherboard PCI bus to another PCI bus on the adapter. If you have an older motherboard that doesn't support PCI bridging, the AAC-364 won't work.

If you run your server unattended, you have several options with the AAC-364 to increase storage reliability:

✦ *Dynamic sector repair.* The AAC-364 adapter can detect sector failures as they occur, and it can remap the sector to a spare one on the same disk. Following the remap, the adapter reconstructs the lost data.

✦ *Hot-spare standby.* You can put additional disk drives in your server and configure them as online spares. If an operational drive fails, the AAC-364 will automatically swap in one of the spares and reconstruct the content of the lost drive.

✦ *Array management.* You can monitor the status of your array remotely, with alerts coded by severity. Given the combination of automatic fault tolerance through dynamic sector repair and hot-spare standby, you can be sure that you can get to the remote server in time to repair it before failures interrupt online operations.

The AAC-364 knows how to work with drives using SMART reporting, so you get the earliest possible warning of trouble.

# PowerQuest PartitionMagic and ServerMagic

Your disk acts as a single area in which you can store things. You can understand this most easily by remembering large block addressing (LBA), which we discussed as one of the ways IDE drives are addressed and the only way SCSI disks are addressed. Under LBA, the host adapter sends addresses to the drive starting at zero and ending at the number of the last sector on the drive.

Your computer may not look at the drive as a single space, however. Windows and UNIX require that you create structures called partitions to define how the space on the drive is split up. You can create a single partition containing all the space on the drive, or you can subdivide the space into multiple partitions. Using the FAT16 file system, Windows 9x cannot define a partition bigger than 2GB. With FAT32 (available in later versions of Windows 95 and in Windows 98), you can have partitions of several terabytes (thousands of gigabytes). Windows NT — using the NT File System (NTFS) — can have huge partitions too.

The size of the partition determines the size of clusters — the minimum allocation unit — for the FAT file system. The issue doesn't affect the NT File System (NTFS) or the FAT32 file system, because they're not subject to the same restrictions as FAT16. With FAT16, partitions up to 128MB use 2KB clusters, partitions from 128MB and 256MB use 4KB clusters, and so on. By the time you get over a gigabyte partition size, the clusters are 16KB each. As we saw in Chapter 11, this can waste a lot of disk space. You have three options to get back the wasted space:

1. Repartition the disk into several smaller partitions.

2. Compress the disk with DriveSpace or another compression technology.

3. Recreate the partition with FAT32.

We dislike using multiple partitions to reduce the cluster size, because fragmenting the size of the partitions makes us choose arbitrarily which partition we put a file or program in, and changes in what we do later can make us want to move things. Moving programs in Windows can be very hard due to references to the program locations in the Registry or other places. There are tools to assist with moving programs, but they're not problem-free. We don't recommend moving programs. It's usually easier to uninstall and reinstall.

Compression has its drawbacks too, the worst of which are that it takes up memory if you have to boot Windows 9x to DOS, and that the compression schemes are incompatible among Windows 9x, Windows NT, and UNIX. If you boot one machine to either Windows 9x or NT, the two operating systems can't both see the compressed volumes. Our preferred Windows 9x solution is to use as few partitions as possible, and to use FAT32. Microsoft hasn't released software that allows Windows 95 to read the Windows NT file system, NTFS, and won't release FAT32 support for Windows NT until the release of Windows 2000. If you need to dual-boot on the same machine, you have to use the lowest common denominator, FAT16. (File system compatibility isn't a problem for connections across networks, because the file system type isn't of concern to the remote machine.)

Unless you have Windows NT up and running (so you can run the Disk Administrator), you've probably used a program called FDISK from the DOS command prompt to create, change, list, and delete partitions on a disk. FDISK is a Spartan program designed for experienced users. It does a specific job, with few options. Among the worst failings of FDISK is that you can't change the size of a partition without destroying the data in the partition in the process. Repartitioning a disk with FDISK is a pain at best (if you make and test full system backups) and can be a disaster if you blunder ahead without understanding the warnings you get. Unless you're running Windows 98, you can't convert a FAT16 partition to FAT32 without encountering the same problems.

The alternative you'll want if you do anything with partitions is a program called PartitionMagic from PowerQuest, or the NT version ServerMagic. These programs do everything FDISK does and more. The key thing that makes PartitionMagic and ServerMagic worth having even if you never use them for anything else is the capability to change partition sizes and to change from FAT16 to FAT32 (and back) without destroying files you have stored in the partition. Figure 13-14 shows the opening screen from PartitionMagic, showing the drives physically on the computer, the partitions on the selected drive, and the characteristics of those partitions.

> **Tip**    You can find a demo of PartitionMagic at `http://www.powerquest.com/partitionmagic/pmdemo.html`.

If you're completely adept with DOS FDISK and FORMAT and have time to burn, you can get the same results with it that you get with PartitionMagic. Personally, though, we'd rather get useful work done.

## PowerQuest Drive Copy

Being a programmer, Barry is prone to smacking himself on the forehead every so often and exclaiming "Rats" (or words to that effect). He particularly does that when he realizes that someone's written a program he should have taken on to solve a nagging problem.

He smacked his forehead rather hard and walked around with a major headache for a long time after he saw PowerQuest's Drive Copy, because it's a simple program that solves one of the nastiest upgrade problems. Drive Copy lets you copy the entire contents of one disk to another. It handles both IDE and SCSI drives, and it copies DOS, Windows 9*x*, and Windows NT partitions. (It can copy NetWare and UNIX partitions but doesn't support them comprehensively.) It copies hidden files, the complete directory structure, and long file names. It expands partitions on the fly. Instead of a lengthy backup and restore process, you simply copy the old, smaller drive to the new one. Painless and reliable.

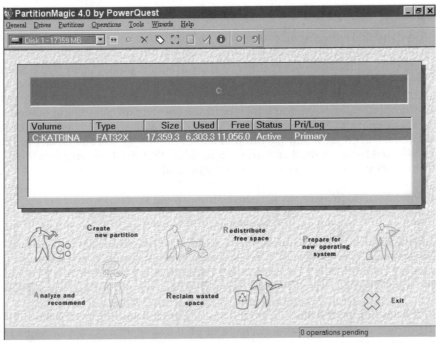

**Figure 13-14:** PartitionMagic shows you the drives and partitions on your machine and lets you change things around easily.

Drive Copy wipes out any data you had on the new drive (the one that gets the copy of the old drive). Here's all you have to do to bring up a new drive:

1. *Reconfigure the disks.* For example, if you have one IDE drive and are adding another, you change the old one to be the slave and add in the new one to be the master on the same port. Don't forget to check the BIOS settings.

2. *Boot.* You'll need a boot disk to start the computer, booting to DOS with few or no drivers loaded.

3. *Run Drive Copy.* Operation is mostly automatic. You just sit and watch.

4. *Reboot and test.* Don't forget this step to make sure everything worked right. The best way to test is to disconnect the old drive and verify the new one works the same as the old one did.

# Top Support Questions

Disks seem to generate more confusion than any other single part of a computer. That's probably because a lot of things come together on the disk drive: the BIOS, the operating system, the bus, the host adapter, other drives, the case, and the power supply. That leaves room for a lot of things to go wrong.

## Adding ATA and SCSI drives

Q: How should I set up my IDE drive?

A: The settings the BIOS offers differs among systems, but typically you'll want to set the BIOS CMOS Hard Disk type to "Auto Configured" and IDE Translation Mode to "Auto Detected." Once you do that, you should be able to boot and have the BIOS recognize the drive. You'll then partition the disk using FDISK or something like PartitionMagic. If you're installing a new drive, you should delete any existing partitions and create a new partition to make sure things start clean and properly coordinated between BIOS and drive. Remember that deleting partitions deletes all the data they contain beyond recovery by normal means.

Q: What can I do to make my IDE drive (from an old system) work with my new motherboard?

A: Many older PC BIOSes supported only CHS (Cylinder-Head-Sector) mode for IDE disk drives, even if the IDE drive itself was capable of supporting a more advanced translation mode. When a more advanced IDE drive is connected to a motherboard with a BIOS capable of supporting the more advanced mode, the drive will tell the system which translation modes it is capable of supporting. Unfortunately, the drive does not tell the BIOS which mode was being used when the drive was originally formatted, just what it's capable of. If a mismatch occurs between the old mode and what the newer BIOS picks, the disk drive may exhibit problems when used (including what looks like scrambled or missing data). There are two possible solutions:

1. Force the new system to use CHS Translation Mode. To do this, set up the BIOS Hard Disk type to "Auto Detected" and the IDE Translation Mode to "CHS." If your data is now present without corruption, you should be okay; otherwise, you'll need step 2.

2. Put the drive back with the old motherboard, back it up, connect it to the new motherboard, and reformat the disk drive to use a more advanced translation mode. All data on the hard drive will be lost (which is the point of the backup — be sure to verify the backup before you reformat). After you reconnect the drive to the new motherboard, here are the steps:

   a. Set up the BIOS Hard Disk type to "Auto Detected" and IDE Translation Mode to "CHS."

   b. From a DOS-bootable floppy, use the DOS FDISK utility (or PartitionMagic) to delete any existing partitions on the hard drive.

   c. Reset the system, enter the BIOS Setup menu, and change the entry for the Hard Disk type to "Auto Configured" and IDE Translation Mode to "Auto Detected."

   d. Use the DOS FDISK utility or PartitionMagic to create a new partition(s).

Q: I installed a new 6GB IDE drive, and it shows up as 2GB. Can't I use an IDE drive over 2GB with my motherboard?

A: Older motherboards may not support IDE hard drives larger than 504MB; even recent motherboards may not support drives larger than 2 or 8GB. Connecting a drive larger than is supported to one of these systems may result in one of several symptoms, depending on your hard drive configuration. In some cases — such as where only a single IDE drive is being used, or where the drive is configured as a slave in a master/slave pair — the hard drive will not be recognized by the BIOS or by your operating system's partitioning utility. If the hard drive is a master in a master/slave configuration, the system may freeze during boot. Many hard drive manufacturers supply a utility (such as Microhouse EZ-Drive and Ontrack Disk Manager) that allows the full capacity of the hard drive to be accessed in these situations.

More recent motherboards should support IDE hard drives larger than 2GB, although some will have problems with drives larger than 8GB. If you are using an operating system with an advanced file system (such as Windows 9x and FAT32, Windows NT and NTFS, OS/2 and HPFS, or UNIX), you can partition/format and use the entire drive as one device. Under MS-DOS or Windows using the FAT16 file system, you can create drive partitions up to 2GB in size. FAT16 cannot support individual partitions greater than 2GB, so it requires hard drives larger than 2GB to be divided into multiple partitions of 2GB or less.

Q: My hard disk is using MS-DOS compatibility mode under Windows 9x. What is the problem?

A: Assuming you're not loading a disk driver in your config.sys file that Windows 95 doesn't recognize, you may encounter DOS Compatibility Mode on IDE hard disks with more than 1,024 cylinders in some older computers that don't use Large Block Addressing (LBA) translation. Compatibility mode results from invalid drive geometry translation in the system ROM BIOS that prevents the protected-mode IDE device driver from being loaded. You're going to need an updated BIOS for your motherboard; alternatively, you can try a utility like EZ-Drive or Disk Manager. Viruses can also cause Windows 9x to use compatibility mode, so be sure to scan your disk after booting from a floppy you absolutely know to be uninfected.

Q: How should I set up my system BIOS when I'm using only SCSI drives?

A: SCSI drives connected to a SCSI host adapter are recognized by the host adapter BIOS, not the motherboard BIOS. Configure the motherboard to show there are no disk drives installed on systems not using IDE devices.

Q: My system hangs or stops and then issues error messages during boot when it should be looking for hard drives. Why?

A: You may have configured the motherboard BIOS to look for disk drives in a system configured with only SCSI drives. The motherboard is looking for IDE drives and not finding them, leading to the hang or the errors.

Q: Can I use IDE and SCSI drives on the same system?

A: Yes. Configure the motherboard BIOS for just the IDE drives. Your system will boot from the primary partition on the first IDE drive, and both the IDE and SCSI drives should be visible.

## Disk partitions

Q: How are drive letters assigned to new partitions or new drives?

A: The Windows and DOS operating systems assign drive letters (UNIX uses a completely different scheme to identify drives and the space on them). DOS assigns drive letters to all primary partitions, and then to all logical drives in extended partitions. For example, suppose you have two drives set up as in Table 13-6. The first primary partition on the first physical drive is C; the first primary partition on the second physical drive is D. Next, the logical drives are labeled, covering first the logical drives on the first physical drive (E, F) and then the logical drives on the second physical drive (G, H). Your CD-ROM and any removable drive are assigned the next available drive letters after your hard drive partitions.

| Table 13-6<br>The DOS Drive Letter Assignment Sequence Isn't Always<br>What You Want | | |
|---|---|---|
| | **Drive 1** | **Drive 2** |
| Primary partition (C) | Primary partition (D) | |
| Extended partition | Extended partition | |
| | Logical drive 1 (E) | Logical drive 1 (G) |
| | Logical drive 2 (F) | Logical drive 2 (H) |

Windows 9x follows the DOS scheme for drive letters. Windows NT follows the DOS scheme by default but in some cases lets you use the Disk Administrator tool to change the letter assigned to specific drives.

Q: What will happen to my CD-ROM drive letter if I create a new partition or add a new drive?

A: If you consume the drive letter previously assigned to the CD-ROM drive, the CD-ROM gets assigned the next available drive letter after your hard drive partitions. You can prevent the CD-ROM drive letter from changing in the future by assigning it a higher drive letter to begin with (such as M: or N:), creating some unused letters between the last hard disk and the first CD-ROM.

Q: Can I install Windows 9x on the same disk as Windows NT?

A: You cannot install Windows 9x in the same folder (directory) as holds Windows NT, but you can install it to the same disk in a different partition or different folder. You'll have to install to a different partition if you have Windows NT in an NTFS partition, and if the NTFS partition is drive C, you'll have to convert it to FAT because the Windows 9x boot code doesn't understand NTFS.

## RAID

Q: How do I decide if I need RAID?

A: A RAID array can give you any or all of three things: greater storage capacity in a single partition, faster transfer rates, and more reliable data storage. Hardware RAID controllers are relatively inexpensive; software implementations of RAID are supported by Windows NT and some versions of UNIX. The minimum requirement for RAID is simply enough disk drives to support the RAID level you decide to use; a hardware controller offers improved performance but isn't mandatory.

Q: What RAID level should I use?

A: If you're strictly after improved transfer rates, go with RAID level 0 to stripe your data across multiple disks. The data transfer rate increase is proportional to the number of disks in the RAID array. If you're only after reliable storage, use RAID level 1. If you're after performance and reliability, choose RAID level 3 or level 5. Level 3 is best for large transfers; level 5 is good for transactions and is an excellent overall choice.

# Hands-On Upgrades

The key to upgrading your computer by adding disk drives is planning — thinking through the physical, electrical, performance, and software issues before you order parts and pick up your tools.

## Adding a SCSI Drive

Our experience is that it's far easier to add a drive to a SCSI system than IDE — get a few things right, and it's going to work. You have a lot of flexibility with SCSI, though, so let's work through the options and issues.

✦ *Physical.* The most basic decision is whether the drive will be internal or external to your computer. External drives are subject to getting banged around, but under some circumstances they can be moved from one computer to another. You may be constrained in connections to your host adapter — the Adaptec wide controllers, for example, provide internal 50- and 68-pin connectors and an external 68-pin connector, but you can only use two of the three. That means that if you've used two cables internally, one for narrow devices and one for wide ones, you can't use the external connector.

If the drive will be internal, think about both cooling and cabling. If you have the option, leave air space around the drive, and choose a drive bay where it will be in the air flow. (For instance, some cases have drive bays low near the air inlet. Putting the drive there should give it the best cooling possible. If you're concerned about heat, consider sticking a CPU cooling fan on the drive. Try to mount the drive so that there's solid metal contact between the drive bay and the drive so that heat has a good path away from the drive.

Figure 13-15 shows a Seagate ST34501W Cheetah internal SCSI drive installed in a 3.5-inch form factor mounting bracket. We used the lower position on the mounting bracket to ensure good airflow over the top of the drive. You can see in Figure 13-16 that the drive is positioned in the case just under the power supply, so the lower mounting position keeps the drive away from heat coming from there. We also positioned the drive as far into the bracket as possible, so that the bracket conducts heat away from the drive to keep the disk assembly and electronics cool. Don't ever use a nonmetallic mounting bracket on a disk drive, because you'll lose the cooling from conducted heat through the bracket. Be sure to set the drive termination options before installing the drive in the bracket — you set those using a jumper block that's covered up once you attach the drive to the bracket.

You can also see the 68-pin SCSI connector, drive options jumper block, and power connector at the back of the drive in Figure 13-15. Make sure you position the drive so that those connections are easy to get to.

Figure 13-16 shows the drive and bracket assembly mounted into the chassis. You can see there's good clearance between the drive and power supply, and that the drive is well up into the airflow in the case. Look also at the final connector position — you'll see that the connectors are easy to access for simplified cable installation and system maintenance.

**Figure 13-15:** Position drives in mounting brackets so that they'll get good air flow and heat conduction.

**Figure 13-16:** Choose positions within mounting brackets to get the best service access within the chassis.

✦ *Electrical.* You have to get power and the data cable to the drive. If you don't plan both the sequence in which drives sit on the cable and the routing of the power feed, you'll end up with a rat's nest that makes working on the computer difficult. Once you work out the order in which drives will connect to the cable (which is just the physical order and is independent from their SCSI ID), make sure that only the drive at the physical end of the cable is terminated. You want active termination if you can arrange it, so if you have a device that provides active termination, try to use it at the end of the cable. If you're using Ultra2 SCSI with LVDS (Low Voltage Differential Signaling), keep in mind that the drives won't provide termination — make sure to use a termination block at the end of the cable.

If you put connectors on the cable yourself, make sure they obey minimum spacing requirements (connectors should be at least a foot apart). Whether you make cables yourself or buy them, you have to make sure you have the right ones. Internal narrow SCSI uses a 50-pin connector with two parallel rows of pins, similar to the ones for IDE and floppy drives. A narrow SCSI cable often isn't keyed, so be careful to get pin 1 oriented properly.

Internal wide and Ultra SCSI both use a 68-pin connector with very fine pitch pins, but the cable for Ultra SCSI is a flexible bundle with pairs of wires physically separated from each other. The connector is keyed by the shape of the connector shell so that you won't get it backward.

External SCSI connectors are either the large Centronics type or the fine-pitch external SCSI-2 type. If your devices use the fine-pitch connectors, make sure you get a cable with the right number of pins.

Finally, check the IDs of all devices on the bus before you set the ID for the new device to ensure you choose a free identifier. Under Windows, you can do this with the SCSI Explorer in Adaptec's EZ-SCSI, or you can check them individually in the Device Manager. (You'll have to check the devices themselves under UNIX unless your system has a tool to report IDs). The simple way to get device IDs in Windows 9*x* and Windows NT 4 and later is this:

1. Open Device Manager.

2. Select Computer at the top of the list, and choose "View devices by connection."

3. Open "Plug and Play BIOS" and then "PCI bus."

4. Select your SCSI adapter and look at the devices under it. (Some SCSI adapters using PCI bridges may list the bridge directly, with the SCSI host adapter channel under that.)

5. For each device, examine its properties. The dialog box you get will show the device ID.

✦ *Performance.* If you have one SCSI host adapter with one channel, you're limited in choices. If you have two or more channels on the adapter, or more than one adapter, group slow devices together away from the fast ones.

You can choose which disk is the boot device by making it ID 0. If the new disk will be your boot drive, you'll have to copy the content of the old drive over using Drive Copy or some other method. Think about the remaining space on your boot drive when making this decision. If you're running out of space on your old boot drive, consider moving it to the larger new drive.

✦ *Software.* Once you get the disk installed and recognized by the host adapter (check that by going into the adapter BIOS), you need to partition and format the drive. With DOS and Windows, you use FDISK and FORMAT for that. Other operating systems have different requirements.

You may want to move programs from one drive to another to take advantage of the additional drive. If you do, you have to update any record the operating system maintains about the location of the program you move. One way is to uninstall the program and reinstall on the new drive; another way is to use utilities written for that purpose (as are provided with PartitionMagic).

## Adding an IDE Drive

Much of the planning you want to do before adding an IDE drive is similar to that for SCSI drives. The physical installation is the same as the typical setup shown in previous Figures 13-15 and 13-16 . You're more constrained in your system options with IDE drives, so there are some different choices to make.

✦ *Physical.* An IDE drive has to be internal. You have at most two IDE ports, with at most two drives on each one. Because the cable length is severely limited, the drives need to be reasonably close to the motherboard or host adapter connector. (We once built a machine in a full-size tower case with a motherboard whose IDE ports were in the middle of the motherboard. That positioning combined with the 18-inch cable limit meant that we couldn't put IDE drives in the upper bays of the case.)

The same cooling and airflow issues apply for IDE as for SCSI.

✦ *Electrical.* You have to get the master/slave settings right on the drives. It doesn't matter which connector the master or the slave uses on the cable, but if you have only one drive on a cable, use the end connector. Each IDE port you use must have a master and may have a slave. You can have a master on both ports and slave on none, on either, or on both (see Table 13-7).

| | Table 13-7 ATA Master/Slave Combination Requirements | |
|---|---|---|
| | *Primary* | *Secondary* |
| Master | OK | OK |
| Slave | Requires primary master | Requires secondary master |

✦ *Performance.* You have options on how to arrange your drives across the IDE ports. If you have only two hard disks, make each one a master, putting one on each of the two IDE ports. If you have a hard disk and a CD-ROM, make the hard disk the master on the primary IDE port and the CD-ROM the master on the secondary port. If you have two hard disks and a CD-ROM, put both hard disks on the primary port, isolating the CD-ROM on the secondary port. (SCSI devices in the same computer don't affect how you allocate drives on the IDE ports.)

The general strategy is to group faster devices together and away from slower ones. The idea behind splitting two hard drives (if that's all you're connecting) is that it gives the operating system the option to deal with the two independently.

Assuming it's a hard disk, the master drive on the primary IDE port will be drive C and therefore will be the boot disk.

✦ *Software.* Once you get the disk installed, you need to tell the BIOS about it. You'll mostly want to use the automatic detection and configuration settings of the BIOS to set that up. See the top support questions given earlier for reasons why you might override the BIOS settings. Once the drive is recognized by the BIOS, you partition and format the drive.

# Summary

✦ Seek and access times, and sustained data transfer rate, are the most important determiners of disk performance in your system.

✦ RAID systems can give you greatly increased performance and reliability at reasonable cost.

✦ Be sure to get enough disk space. Your requirements will always increase over time.

✦    ✦    ✦

# CD-ROMs, CD-ROM Changers, CD-Rs, and DVD-ROMs

CD-ROMs originated for two reasons: The industry needed a high-capacity, removable medium for multimedia and software distribution, and the consumer electronics industry had developed an inexpensive, high-capacity digital technology for distributing music. Put together, the result was a small, inexpensive, and rugged way to hold about 650MB of data. DVD extended the CD-ROM technology to provide far more capacity and greater data transfer rates.

This chapter covers how CD-ROMs and DVDs work, how you can use CD-ROM and DVD drives in your computer system, and how you can make your own CD-ROMs. We'll look at the newest technology and discuss what you can expect from a quality CD-ROM or DVD drive.

## What Is a CD-ROM?

A CD-ROM most resembles the vinyl long-play records still dear to the hearts of audio fanatics. On a record, a single spiral in the vinyl winds from the outside to the inside, with the contents encoded in the deflections along the course of the groove. On a CD-ROM, a single spiral encased in plastic winds from the inside to the outside, with the contents encoded by the presence or absence of tiny optical pits. A record stores sound as analog levels—much the same as what arrives at your ear. A CD-ROM stores its data as numbers, so it requires conversion to analog before you can see it or hear it. Figure 14-1 shows a few tenths of a second of what's stored on a CD-ROM (and an audio CD, for that matter)—the analog waveform you hear has been sampled by the computer at fixed, precise intervals, and a number has been assigned corresponding to the amplitude of the stored waveform. Each of the small discontinuities in the waveform is a point where the computer has measured the amplitude of the waveform and recorded the number for that value. The measurements happen at a fixed rate, so you see a jagged point in the waveform at regular intervals. The sequence of numbers from the start of the sound (or song, picture, or video) is stored in a file. Because the sampling rate can be large, the file holding the numbers can be large as well.

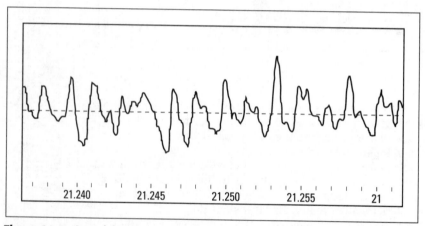

**Figure 14-1:** Sound, images, and video are analog waveforms. Recording them in a computer requires that we sample the waveform and store the digital samples.

For example, an audio CD holds numbers sampled about 44,000 times per second. Each sample is two numbers (one per stereo channel), and each number is 16 bits. If you multiply it out, you get a data rate of 176KB per second. On a CD holding 660MB, that's a little over one hour of recording time. Your computer can record through the sound card at a variety of rates less than this, but files can get large quickly even at the lowest rates.

Video files get large even faster than sound files. If you record broadcast-quality video natively—without compression or other transformations that would reduce the data rate—you have to store over 23MB per second. This translates into less than 28 seconds of video on a single CD-ROM. The huge amount of data required for both sound and video is why compression is so important for computers and networks handling multimedia.

**Cross-Reference** We explain how different forms of compression work in Chapter 18.

Recording long sequences of numbers is exactly what CDs were built to do. After we look at how the disc is recorded, we'll look at the mechanism in the CD player itself and what challenges the designers have had to face.

Figure 14-2 shows what's inside the CD itself. In cross-section, the CD is a layer of reflective aluminum with lacquer on top and protective plastic underneath. The zeros and ones (transformed in a way that makes the recording more reliable) get turned into flats and pits on the surface of the reflective layer when the CD is mastered. The layers include

✦ *Spiral data track.* The information on the CD-ROM is recorded in a continuous spiral, as on the old vinyl long-play records. The spiral starts at the inside edge of the recorded area and continues out to the outer edge of the disc.

✦ *Top surface.* The top of the CD-ROM is lacquer over the aluminum layer. The CD-ROM label is painted on top of the lacquer.

✦ *Reflective aluminum.* A reflective aluminum surface carries the flats and pits that physically encode the information. The flats and pits, by reflecting light differently, enable the CD-ROM drive to read back the information.

✦ *Plastic coating.* The back side of the disc is covered by a plastic coating that protects the aluminum layer.

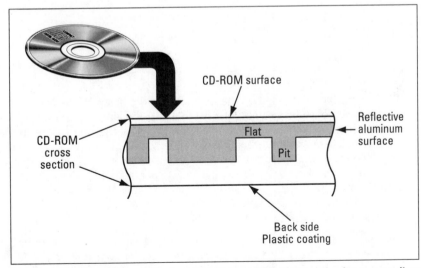

**Figure 14-2:** The data spiral on a CD-ROM is nearly three miles long, encoding zeros and ones along the path as small flats and pits.

The CD mastering process is similar to the vinyl record-making process. A mirror image of the disc, with all the pits and flats, is used to stamp out the plastic bottom of the disc with an accurate impression of the entire spiral. Aluminum is then deposited on the plastic and covered with lacquer, resulting in the finished disc. The accuracy required in the process is far greater than vinyl records needed: Adjacent turns of the spiral along the disc are only 1.6 micrometers apart, which means that there are nearly 16,000 of them every inch.

## Coding data onto a CD-ROM

The flats and pits on a CD-ROM do not directly correspond to the ones and zeros that eventually make it into your computer. Instead, the data stream is coded in a particular way before recording, with the coding reversed when you read back the disc to recover the original data pattern. The conversion from your data to what's recorded changes every 8 bits of your data into 14 bits that get recorded, allowing the drive to compensate for limitations of the physical device. The following table shows how that transformation works for part of the 256 possible 8-bit values. For example, if a byte value of three needs to be recorded, the 8-bit value would be 00000011. After that byte gets remapped for recording, the result is 10001000100000.

| Value | 8-bit Representation | 14-bit Representation |
|-------|---------------------|----------------------|
| 0 | 00000000 | 01001000100000 |
| 1 | 00000001 | 10000100000000 |
| 2 | 00000010 | 10010000100000 |
| 3 | 00000011 | 10001000100000 |
| 4 | 00000100 | 01000100000000 |

The pattern of pits and flats used on the CD to record the bits is interesting. A one is indicated by a change from a pit to a flat (or a flat to a pit). The length of the subsequent pit or flat (after the transition) indicates how many zeros follow the one before the next one occurs. If you look back at the preceding table, you'll see that there is never a pattern in the 14-bit representation where two ones occur together, which is necessary because you can't put two transitions back to back. The actual 14-bit code is more restrictive yet; a one will always be followed by at least two zeros. This pattern limits the minimum size of the pits and flats and in turn allows designers to make decisions about the wavelength of the laser in the drive and about the lenses used with the laser.

When the 14-bit codes are read back from the CD, the drive converts back to the 8-bit code the computer expects to see and (after passing the data through some powerful error correcting circuits) sends the data out onto the I/O bus.

Mastering a CD is straightforward, if not easy. You feed data to the laser head at a constant rate, turn the master disc at a constant rate, and sweep the laser head from the inside to the outside at a constant rate. The laser burns pits into the master as required. The end result is a precise, even spiral of pits and flats.

Reading a CD from beginning to end — without pauses or other interruptions — is straightforward too. The read laser head sweeps the same way the record head did when making the master, allowing light to reflect back off the aluminum surface plated onto the CD, as in Figure 14-3. Light reflected from a flat on the CD bounces back cleanly, sending most of the light back to a photodetector in the drive. Light reflected from a pit on the CD is scattered by the shape of the pit, sending most of the light away from the photodetector. A sensor converts the change in intensity of the reflected laser beam as the beam sweeps from a pit to flat into the pattern of ones and zeros for the 14-bit representation.

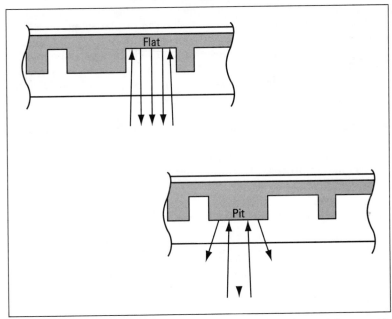

**Figure 14-3:** The presence and absence of reflected light, and the transition between them, indicate the pattern recorded on the CD to the drive.

As with magnetic disks, there's more room per revolution of the disc to pack in data as you go further out from the center. In the same way that magnetic disks pack in more sectors at the outside, so do CDs pack in more pits and flats, and therefore more data as well.

The similarities between CD and magnetic disk don't stop there. If you look at the pattern

00000010001000000001001000010000001001000100000

you can't necessarily tell where one bit pattern stops and the next one ends. If, instead, we give you the same information like this,

00000 01000100000000 10010000100000 01001000100000

you can tell that the sequence starts with the last part of a bit, followed by the bits for the sequence 420.

The information that gives you the bit boundaries, and that divides the information on a disc into sectors, is called *framing*. The framing information on a CD doesn't address the data as cylinder-head-sector (as on a magnetic disk), because the spiral arrangement of the data means that there aren't distinct cylinders, and because there's only one head. The sector placement on a CD is a little more complicated than that on a regular disk. The smallest unit above the byte is called a frame, containing 24 bytes. Frames are in turn grouped into blocks, which contain 98 frames (2,353 bytes). A CD-ROM actually carries only 2,048 data bytes per frame—the remainder goes to added error correction, synchronization, and addressing bytes.

When your computer asks the CD-ROM to read a specific frame, the sequence of events is similar to that for a read from a magnetic disk. The head has to move to the right place and pick off the data. Because the data is arranged in a spiral, though, this is a difficult process. The controller in the CD-ROM uses the following sequence:

1. Position the head as close as possible to where the frame should be.

2. Wait for the CD to turn enough for pits and flats to spiral under the laser beam, and start tracking outward along the spiral.

3. Wait for synchronization with a frame, and read the frame address.

4. Adjust position based on how far the frame the head found is ahead or behind the one you wanted.

CD audio drives rarely change position to a specific place—they do it only when you say to go to a specific track, which is almost never on the computer time scale of millions of operations every second. In an application like that, a few tenths of a second longer to find the right place is far less important than making the drive reliable and inexpensive. Because computer CD-ROM drives were built from the CD audio technology, it was inevitable that the first-generation drives were slow to seek from one place to another.

The sustained transfer rate off a first-generation CD-ROM drive was also driven by the capabilities of the CD audio equipment, which meant that the drive transfers about 1.2 megabits per second (153.6KB per second). Video compression technology gets pretty lousy below about 1.5 megabits per second; this fact provided much of the impetus for the second, "double speed" generation of CD-ROMs.

Over time, CD-ROM manufacturers boosted performance to four, eight, sixteen, twenty-four, thirty-two, and now forty times the basic audio CD rate by spinning the disc faster, and they built better drive mechanisms to hold or reduce the seek times. Table 14-1 shows what that means. Manufacturers have boosted the data transfer rates up to 6MB per second from the 150KB per second of the original CD-ROM drives. The sustained transfer rates from CD-ROM are now as high as from some economy hard disk drives.

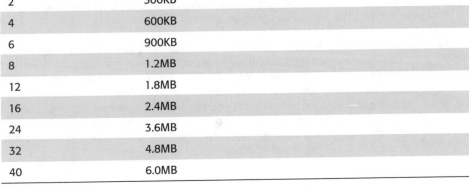

| Table 14-1 | |
|---|---|
| **Increases in CD-ROM Speed Increase the Data Transfer Rate** | |
| *Speed Multiplier* | *Data Transfer Rate (per second)* |
| 1 | 150KB |
| 2 | 300KB |
| 4 | 600KB |
| 6 | 900KB |
| 8 | 1.2MB |
| 12 | 1.8MB |
| 16 | 2.4MB |
| 24 | 3.6MB |
| 32 | 4.8MB |
| 40 | 6.0MB |

**Benchmarking**  You need to be careful when choosing a CD-ROM drive, however, to look at more than just the transfer rate. The faster the disc spins, the more difficult it becomes to position the head to a particular frame. The early 8X CD-ROMs to hit the market, for example, had seek times greatly inferior to the 6X drives then on the market, resulting in poorer performance overall. Similarly, the size of the buffers and the way the drive manages them strongly affects overall performance. If possible, you should find or perform benchmarks on a CD-ROM drive before you buy it. Otherwise, get a drive from a manufacturer with a good record for reliable design and construction.

There have been reliability problems reading discs on some faster CD-ROM drives. The major component of the problem is vibration created as slightly out-of-balance discs spin at high speeds, creating vibration in the laser that affects the signal read off the disc. The problem started to be reported with 8X or faster CD-ROM drives and has continued with faster units. The vibration problem is more severe even than issues of tolerance in the manufacture of the CD-ROMs. The vibration dampening built into the disc carrier and drive mechanism is crucial—better-designed drives isolate the laser and pickup from vibration, producing a cleaner and more reliable signal (all the more reason to buy from quality manufacturers).

**Tip**

If your current CD-ROM works reliably, ask yourself if you'll really benefit from a super-fast CD-ROM drive before deciding to upgrade. Multimedia files don't require the fastest drives. If your 8X or faster CD-ROM is working reliably, consider keeping it.

CD-ROM drives initially came with either SCSI or proprietary interfaces into your computer. Proprietary interfaces let the manufacturer cut corners (and therefore price) but usually died for lack of support. SCSI has been complemented by ATA-2 CD-ROM interfaces using the ATAPI interface specification. A SCSI CD-ROM will generally cost a little more than one with an IDE interface. You can get good performance with either one—your choice will most likely be driven by whether you have available IDE ports and whether you have a SCSI host adapter. Hooking a CD-ROM onto the same ATA-2 port as a hard disk causes problems in many systems though, such as loss of hard disk performance. (See Chapter 13.) If you can, keep the CD-ROM on the secondary port away from the hard disks.

**Caution**

CD-ROM drivers for ATA-2 drives are built into Windows 9*x*, but if the drive is on the secondary port, you may have to set up the driver manually. You can do this with the Add New Hardware Wizard in the control panel. Windows 9*x* supports only primary and secondary ports. (Vendors of other devices, such as sound cards, may have drivers for tertiary ports you can use.) The primary port must be at I/O address 1F0 and interrupt 14. The secondary port must be at I/O 170 and interrupt 15. Other assignments are not supported; you have to reconfigure the hardware to these settings if they're set differently.

# Bootable CD-ROM

Until early 1995, there was no way to boot your computer from the CD-ROM drive, which meant that if you built a new machine (or replaced the disk in an old one), you had to boot from a floppy, install drivers, and build up the disk contents from there.

The El Torito Bootable CD-ROM Format Specification—standardized in January 1995—changed that. (No, we haven't been able to dig out why the specification is called *El Torito,* which is also the name of a chain of Mexican restaurants. We're willing to bet they're short a few napkins with some very detailed drawings on the back.) If you have a bootable CD-ROM, you can load the drive, start the machine, and have it come up from the operating system on the CD-ROM. If you're building up from an empty hard disk, a bootable CD-ROM will let you boot Windows and start the install without shuffling floppies or worrying about drivers. This works for the Windows NT CD-ROMs and for many UNIX CD-ROMs (including FreeBSD and some versions of Linux).

**Tip**

If you write your own bootable CD-ROM, you have the opportunity to store an archive of your data that you know can be loaded onto an empty computer. Creating a bootable archive CD-ROM means you can create and test a disaster recovery disc, knowing that it has everything you need to reconstruct your operation.

In addition to a CD-ROM written to the El Torito standard, you need a computer with a BIOS supporting bootable CD-ROMs. Some motherboards provide this for ATA-2 CD-ROMs. The Adaptec AHA-2940 SCSI host adapter series also provides the necessary SCSI BIOS support.

## CD-ROM Changers

If your experience with computers goes back to floppy disk–only machines, you remember what a nuisance it was to have to shuffle floppies to get the programs and data you needed in the right drive. If you use many CD-ROMs, you've run into the same problem: The CD-ROM you want is often not the one in the drive, so you shuffle. If you need two at once, you're in trouble. If you use CD-ROMs from a network server, you're almost guaranteed to have a problem.

The problem isn't (usually) that a CD-ROM holds too little information; it's that different programs and data are on different discs, and you have no good way to consolidate them.

One solution comes from the same source as CD-ROM itself — consumer audio technology. Multiple-disc audio changers have been available for years, and the mechanisms finally migrated into CD-ROM products. Versions holding four to seven discs are available, some using cartridges and some carrying the CD-ROMs directly on trays. Products are available with both SCSI and EIDE interfaces. Windows support is not universal, though, so you'll want to check on the specifics for any drive you're considering. Changer performance typically peaks at 16X speeds, much less than the fastest single-disc units.

The disadvantage of CD-ROM changers is that — despite their holding multiple discs — there's still only one drive, and so only one disc can be read at a time. The time to switch between discs is several seconds, so this isn't something you want to do frequently. The problem is particularly severe in network environments, in which several users may want constant access to different discs.

If the number of titles in a changer isn't enough for what you need, you can also get a CD-ROM jukebox — a device holding tens or hundreds of discs. You still only have one disc online at a time, but you can choose from an enormous number of them. In combination with a CD writer, a CD-ROM jukebox can provide you a relatively inexpensive solution to online archival storage.

# Recordable CD-ROMs

Recordable CD-ROMs (CD-R) have become inexpensive, flexible options for offline data storage. If you need archival copies of files — say, of work you've done and can't afford to lose, of critical audit data, or of customer original material — CD-R is for you. CD-R works on the same pit and flat principles as CD-ROM. The difference is that a CD-R disc uses a different material for the reflective surface that can be burned by a laser to form pits, and a CD-R drive includes a more powerful laser to burn the disc. (For details on CD-R, take a look at the *Recordable CD Bible*, published by IDG Books Worldwide, 1998.)

Software tools to write CD-R have become very flexible and simple to use. When you're adding a CD-R drive to a system, keep in mind that CD-R is very picky about delays while you're writing the disc. Any interruption in the data flow to the drive and you've ruined the disc you were recording, because (with some limited exceptions) you can't restart the process. If you're using the CD-R for network backup, you particularly need to be concerned about this issue — contention and slowdowns across the network are beyond your control. Your best choice is to collect the files you'll write to the CD-R on a hard disk in the computer with the CD-R drive, and then write the CD-R. Even in this case, contention with other I/O in the computer can still interfere with the process.

Using a very fast disk, host adapter, and processor is one way you can reduce the number of discs you scrap, because those upgrades reduce the contention for the disk and I/O bus. You might want to consider a completely separate host adapter and hard disk to support the CD-R drive. Figure 14-4 shows how this design works:

✦ *Recording bus and drive.* A separate recording I/O bus keeps system I/O traffic away from the recording devices. The hard drive on the recording bus stores an image of the data to be written on the CD-R. The drive needs to be at least as big as the CD-R image, so it should have at least 660MB free. The disk needs to be a distinct physical drive so it can be on a different SCSI bus from the rest of the system.

✦ *CD-R drive on recording bus.* The CD-R drive requires that data be available as fast as it's written to ensure the process never stops. Feeding it from the disk on the same SCSI bus — with no contention from other computer activities — helps ensure a steady supply of data.

✦ *Main system bus* . The main SCSI bus connects to the hard disk for your system. Isolating the CD-R image and drive from this bus ensures that activity on the main SCSI bus cannot prevent the CD-R drive from getting the data it needs.

One of the most reliable ways to create a CD-R is to first write a master image on a hard disk and then write the image to the CD-R. If the disk with the image and the CD-R drive are on the separate recording I/O bus, it's more likely that the disc write can progress without interference from whatever else the computer is doing. The upper device chain in Figure 14-4 is the host adapter, disk, and CD-R drive dedicated to the CD-R mastering process.

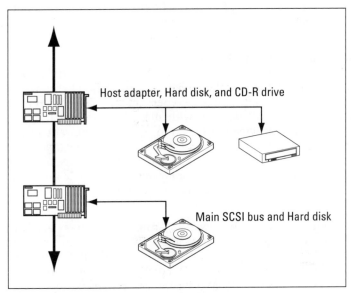

Host adapter, Hard disk, and CD-R drive

Main SCSI bus and Hard disk

**Figure 14-4:** Isolating a CD-R drive and its supporting hard disk on a separate SCSI bus ensures a steady flow of data.

If you can, you should look for an AV-rated hard disk to use for mastering. The AV rating means that the drive is not susceptible to the periodic thermal recalibration that normal hard disks do to adjust the head position to the current operating temperature. Large memory buffers found in recent CD-R designs help mask data flow problems too.

It's not necessarily enough to have the CD-R on its own SCSI bus. For example, the first disc we tried to burn several years ago with that configuration (on a 166 MHz Pentium system using a Yamaha CDR-100 at 4X speed) failed due to data underrun. Here are a few things you want to check before you start recording:

✦ *SCSI disconnect.* Be sure the CD-R is set up to enable disconnect in the BIOS of your SCSI host adapter. That ensures that bus resets due to the hard disk or other devices don't abort an ongoing operation in the CD-R.

✦ *Write a master image.* There are two ways to record a CD: on the fly, which records from the files as they sit in your file system, and from an image master. You'll get better I/O to the CD-R drive if your system doesn't have to search here and there on your disk for the data to record, so recording from a master image is less likely to fail due to buffer underrun.

✦ *Speed test.* Your CD-R software should offer a test to see if it can successfully master the disc before actually recording. The test is there for a reason: You can't assume everything is going to work right. It's worth the time to let it run the test on the actual data you intend to record, because a smaller test may not expose a data rate problem that emerges later in the process.

✦ *Defragment the source disk.* Check to be sure that the file system on the hard disk you retrieve files from (or on the disk to which you write the master image if you use a master) is completely defragmented. Don't assume that because Windows says it's only one or two percent fragmented that all is well. You can get those kinds of percentages with all kinds of holes in the free space on the disk. (Force the defragmenter to run to see this.) You want a clean, defragmented file system with all the free space collected together before you begin mastering to ensure that the disk spends as little time seeking and reading data as possible. Defragment the disk before you write the master image on it. It's faster than if you write the image and then defragment, and you get the same results.

✦ *Disable auto insert notification (Windows 9x).* Your system may pause at the point that Windows 95 polls the CD-ROM to see if you've put in a new disc. You can disable this by turning off auto insert notification in the Properties page of the Device Manager for the CD-ROM device. At a minimum, be sure there's actually a disc in the CD-ROM drive. Some systems pause for several seconds periodically when there's not.

✦ *Reboot.* We've found that trying to write a CD-R after using the machine for a long while is bad practice. Sooner or later, Windows is going to come along and want to clean up the swap file. When it does, the CD-R becomes a shiny coaster for your coffee mug. Defragment the disk, reboot, and immediately write the CD-R to avoid that problem.

✦ *Leave the computer alone.* Anything you do with the computer while it's recording can divert it from the critical task of passing data to the CD-ROM. The current generation machines are often fast enough to let you do things while writing a CD-R, but overall if you turn off the screen saver, System Agent, and your e-mail client, and avoid doing anything with the machine (including accessing it over the network), you're less likely to scrap a disc. Several manufacturers caution against vibration around the CD-R drive too, so postpone the victory dance until you're done.

Over time, you'll discover the things you can get away with and the things that are fatal while recording CD-Rs. Before we shifted to sending manuscripts over the Internet, we wrote CD-R discs of our manuscripts that we sent to IDG (this book's publisher). We used early CD-R equipment for that work, writing the discs on a Yamaha CDE-100 using Adaptec Easy-CD Pro, with the recorder connected to an Adaptec AHA-1542CP ISA bus mastering SCSI host adapter. The preceding list of tips were what it took to go from guaranteed buffer underrun and ruined disc to reliable, underrun-free recording every time. We later changed the configuration to one where the recorder was on one channel of an Adaptec AHA-3940UW PCI host adapter. The increased data rate through the PCI adapter, in conjunction with the preceding tips, completely eliminated scrapped discs (even if we did minor things with the computer at the same time).

**Caution**

If you plan to copy from one CD to another, try to put the CD-ROM drive on a different SCSI bus from the CD-R. A number of CD-ROM drives tend to stay on the SCSI bus longer than you'd like, which can interfere with the flow of data to the CD-R and scrap the disc. Splitting the two drives apart solves that problem. It's also mandatory that the source CD-ROM drive be faster than the CD-R so that it never falls behind the recording process.

**Caution**

If you buy a 4X CD-R, you need to be careful to follow the manufacturer's recommendations for blank discs. More than one type of recordable CD is available, and while the 2X drives are relatively insensitive to the differences, the reduced time the laser has on a pit in a 4X drive requires that you use the kind the drive was designed for. As a minimum, be sure the blank discs you get have the 4X logo. If you end up with discs not certified for 4X operation in your recorder, you can back down to a 2X rate and use them.

The other key component of your CD-R toolkit is recording software. It lets you select the files you'll write to the CD-R, form the master image, and write the disc. Figure 14-5 shows one of the control dialogs from the program. This dialog lets you select the form of filenames the CD-R will hold, from fully standards-compliant names stored according to the ISO 9660 standard through a 128-character version of Windows long filenames stored using the "Joliet" standard. ISO 9660 is the basic standard defining the structure of CD-ROMs, including how files and filenames are stored, and will be readable by the greatest number of non-Windows systems.

Other dialogs let you control where the CD-ROM image is written on disc, the rest of the details of the CD-ROM format, disc serial numbers, copyrights, and other data, and the files written to the CD-R.

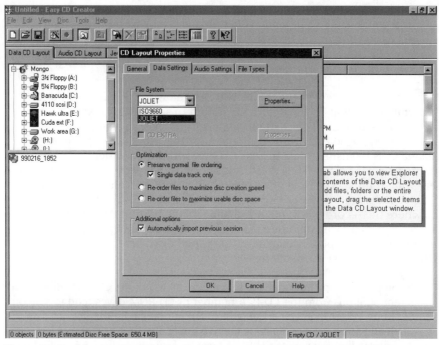

**Figure 14-5:** Adaptec Easy-CD Creator gives you the tools to create a CD-R.

**Future PC**

Next after CD-R was CD-Rewritable (CD-RW), a variant in which you can bulk erase the content of the disc and reuse the media. The CD-RW is a read/write optical disc, a removable-media device holding 660MB. This is over 2.5 times what Iomega's latest ZIP drives hold (see Chapter 15, "Removable Disks"), but less than the 1 or 2GB capacity of the Iomega Jaz. The CD-RW has the advantage that its media cost less than those for the magnetic competition, but the disadvantage that its transfer rates are not as fast as a magnetic drive. There are also some media problems—not all CD-RW drives can use all CD-RW media, and not all CD-ROMs can read CD-RW discs.

Next after CD-RW will be DVD Recordable and DVD Erasable, or DVD-R and DVD-E. We expected to see these drives in late 1997, but problems with competing technical standards delayed product introductions until late 1998. As of mid-1999 the drives are still expensive, so it may be some time until the market for DVD-R and DVD-E really develops.

# DVD

With hard disk sizes many times larger than a CD-ROM — and people filling those disks with great abandon — it's not surprising that interest developed in creating a higher-capacity CD-ROM. The new format is called DVD, which used to stand for Digital Versatile Disc (or a number of other variants), but the "official" name is now simply DVD. The content driving DVD is multimedia, and video in particular — consider that the DVD of the movie *Starship Troopers* has 4.16GB of files! Table 14-2 shows why — you just can't fit a lot of high-quality video on a CD-ROM, and if you add a high-quality stereo sound track, the situation gets worse. MPEG 2 data streams can run at a variety of data rates, so in Table 14-2 we've included data for 4 and 10Mb per second.

| Table 14-2<br>**Data Storable on a Conventional CD-ROM** | | |
|---|---|---|
| *Content* | *Mbps* | *Minutes (CD-ROM)* |
| CD-quality stereo | 1.3781 | 62.36 |
| Radio-quality mono | 0.0861 | 997.73 |
| Uncompressed video (CCIT-601 standard digital video is a little slower, at 167 megabits per second). | 184.3200 | 0.47 |
| MPEG 1 compressed video | 1.5000 | 57.29 |
| MPEG 2 compressed video | 4<br>21.48 | 10<br>8.59 |

Both the consumer entertainment and computer industries wanted a new, higher-capacity format. The consumer entertainment companies wanted to deliver over two hours of video disc–quality movie on a single, small disc. The computer companies wanted to do that too — for training videos and games — and also wanted to store greater volumes of computer data. The result was DVD.

Compared to CD-ROM, DVD is simply all-around better. DVD-ROM holds up to twenty-five times more data than CD-ROM (see Table 14-3) and over four times more on recordable DVD. It uses high-quality MPEG 2 video compression, resulting in near studio-quality pictures. It stores higher-quality sound with multiple channels. Its plastic disc is the same size as CD-ROM and should be as durable. DVD drives can read CD-ROMs, letting you use either format in a DVD-equipped computer.

| Table 14-3 DVD Capacities Far Exceed CD-ROM | | |
|---|---|---|
| **Sides** | **Layers** | |
| | **1** | **2** |
| 1 | 4.7GB | 8.5GB |
| 2 | 9.4GB | 17GB |

The only real downside to DVD has been that—as was true with CD-ROM—it took a while for manufacturers to drive the cost down. DVD drives for computers initially shipped at between $500 and $1,000 but came down in cost as manufacturers designed for lower cost and achieved higher manufacturing volumes with later product generations. In early 1999, we found first-generation drives as low as US $60, second-generation drives at US $90, and third-generation drives at US $120. Given pricing like that, we no longer build computers using CD-ROM drives—we build in DVDs so that as the industry transitions to the newer format the computer will be compatible. You can expect there to be few DVD titles available at first, growing as drives penetrate the market.

DVD uses a combination of improvements to outperform CD-ROM:

✦ *Smaller pits and flats.* Figure 14-6 shows that the geometry of the pits and flats, as well as the spacing between turns of the spiral, is smaller on a DVD. The pits are less than one-half the length of those on a CD-ROM, and the spacing along the spiral allows twice as many turns.

✦ *Shorter wavelength laser.* The laser in a DVD uses a higher-frequency beam, resulting in a shorter wavelength that is better able to see the smaller pits and flats. The lens for the laser is also improved, creating a more tightly focused beam.

✦ *Two-layer format.* Figure 14-7 shows how a single-sided DVD disc can deliver two sides worth of content. The key is a partially reflective, partially transmitting layer at the bottom of the disc, and a laser that can focus on either the bottom or top data layer.

Although CD-ROM recording format standards define how files and filenames (and audio tracks) are stored, there are no standards for how video and other specialized files are compressed and stored on CD-ROM. For this reason, you find CD-ROMs with QuickTime Video for Windows, and MPEG video. If you don't happen to have the magic decoder software, you can't play the disc.

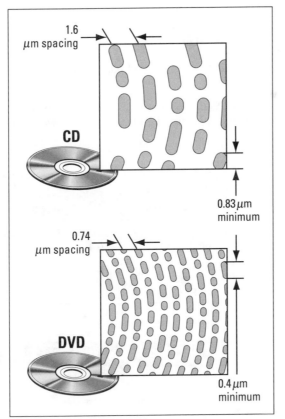

**Figure 14-6:** Compared to CD, DVD uses smaller pits and a more closely spaced track. The result is a significant increase in data density. (Drawing courtesy Sony Electronics Incorporated.)

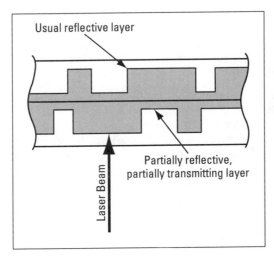

**Figure 14-7:** The partially transmitting layer near the bottom of a DVD allows the laser to read either of two surfaces, doubling the capacity of the disc while allowing it to be read from one side.

DVD designers learned from the CD-ROM file format confusion and specified MPEG 2 video compression. MPEG 2 video uses data rates of between four and ten megabits per second, much faster than MPEG 1.

**Cross-Reference**    There are more details on video compression in Chapter 18.

Table 14-4 shows that all sizes of DVD hold over two hours of video (plus the audio tracks) at 4Mb per second, and that two-sided DVDs hold over two hours at 10Mb per second.

| Table 14-4 | | | | |
|---|---|---|---|---|
| **DVD Video Capacity in Hours versus MPEG 2 Data Rate** | | | | |
| | **Single-Sided Capacity** | | **Double-Sided Capacity** | |
| **Data Rate (Mbps)** | **4.7** | **8.4** | **9.4** | **17.0** |
| 4 | 2.67 | 4.78 | 5.35 | 9.67 |
| 10 | 1.07 | 1.91 | 2.14 | 3.87 |

## Blue lasers: More capacity on the horizon

In the same way that a shorter wavelength red laser diode lets DVD use smaller pits and flats, even shorter wavelength laser diodes would allow even denser structures and increased capacity. The target for designers is a blue laser diode, with a wavelength as little as 60 percent that of the red diodes used in CD-ROMs. Designers expect a fourfold increase in capacity.

Unfortunately, blue laser diodes have been terribly hard to make. In most of the materials researchers have tried, it takes a lot of power to generate the shorter wavelength light. Only some of the power turns into light, though; the rest turns into heat. Too much heat is deadly to semiconductors, and they soon degrade.

What this means is that to create a blue laser diode you'll find in a product, manufacturers have to solve the heat problem. There are two ways: Find another material that uses less power and generates less heat, or find a way to extract the heat before it can damage the device. The wide variety of approaches they're now trying suggests that it's not clear how to do either one, although in early 1999 there are indications that a workable device could be near production.

# CD-ROM and DVD Products

As with disk drives, the choice you made for your I/O bus — IDE or SCSI — determines the kind of CD-ROM you buy. SCSI CD-ROMs will cost slightly more than

IDE ones but don't take the performance hit from combining them on the same bus with a disk drive.

**Tip**    DVD-ROMs were, until mid-1999, only made for IDE. DVD-RAM is available in SCSI. If you incorporate an IDE DVD-ROM into your SCSI system (so there's nothing else on the motherboard IDE ports), set up the DVD as the master on the primary port. Be sure to check the BIOS to make sure the port is enabled.

## CD-ROM

CD-ROMs are made by Plextor, Panasonic, Teac, Sony, Toshiba, and others. The Toshiba XM-6401B CD-ROM drive (Figure 14-8) is a 40X unit with a SCSI-2 interface. An external version differs only in its packaging. The XM-6401B front panel, visible in Figure 14-8, is representative of nearly all CD-ROM drives. The front panel includes the CD-ROM loading tray (which slides out for you to insert and remove discs), the eject button (which controls the loading tray), an activity light (to indicate when the computer is accessing the drive), and a jack for headphones (with volume control). The drive can be mounted either vertically or horizontally, with holders built into the loading tray to retain the disc in the vertical position.

**Figure 14-8:** The Toshiba XM-6401B SCSI CD-ROM provides top CD-ROM performance along with all the features you expect. (Photo courtesy Toshiba.)

The drive is capable of handling the standard CD-ROM formats, including Kodak Photo CDs. Its performance characteristics — shown in Table 14-5 — show a transfer rate of 40X, with very good seek performance. The 256K buffer allows read-ahead by the drive, improving net transfer rate. The sidebar "Keeping the data flowing at a constant rate" explains why you'll see a range of rotation rates, even though this is described as a 40X drive.

| Table 14-5 XM-6401B CD-ROM Drive Specifications | |
|---|---|
| *Characteristic* | *XM-6401B Performance* |
| Rotation rate | 3,000 to 8,500 RPM |
| Sustained transfer rate | 2.595 to 6,000MB per second |
| Burst transfer rate | 10MB per second |
| Average access time | 80ms |
| MTBF | 100,000 hours at 20% |

The XM-6401B has an MTBF less than what we saw for hard disks. This reflects that the drive mechanism cannot be sealed to keep dust and dirt out. If you leave the machine on eight hours a day, the drive has an 86 percent likelihood of surviving five years without failing. Of course, you care far less that a CD-ROM drive fails (versus a magnetic disk), because a failed CD-ROM drive doesn't take any data with it.

**Note**    Not all CD-ROMs read the CD-R discs equally well. If you look at the reflective surface on a CD-R, it's a green or golden color rather than the silvery color of mass-produced discs. The signal reflected back from the CD-R is not as strong, leaving less margin for the drive to work with. There's no commonly published specification you can use to estimate how well a drive will read CD-Rs, but in practice we've found that some drives do this better than others. Old 4X drives (and slower) have little chance of reading a CD-R.

**Tip**    Some SCSI host adapters assume that SCSI IDs zero and one are reserved for non-removable disks. It's a good general practice to use an ID of two or greater for CD-ROM drives to ensure you don't have problems due to the system failing to notice you changed the disc.

## Keeping the data flowing at a constant rate

Older CD-ROM drives use the Constant Linear Velocity (CLV) approach to reading the disc, in which the rotation rate varies based on the distance of the head from the center in a way that keeps the rate of travel along the data track constant. Because the length of one rotation's worth of the data spiral gets longer as the head moves from the inside to the outside of the disc, the distance traveled along the spiral per rotation gets longer. The size and spacing of the pits and flats remain constant, however, so more pits and flats occur per rotation toward the outside of the disc. If the rotation rate (in RPM) stayed constant, the increased data content toward the outside would mean that less data flowed at the inside of the disc and more at the outside. Slowing the rotation rate at the outside of the disc keeps the data rate constant.

Newer CD-ROM drive designs abandoned CLV for Constant Angular Velocity (CAV), in which the rotation rate is independent of the head position. CAV is the same approach used in hard disk drives. CD-ROMs do still vary the rotation rate, however, to help adapt to the transfer rate required by the computer. The reason for the rate changes is that seeking to the correct block is time consuming for a CD-ROM, and if the computer can't take data at full rate, the drive spinning at full rate will move past the point the computer is reading. When that happens, the drive has to seek back to the current read point, a slow operation. By slowing the rotation rate to match the computer, the drive avoids the seek and gives better performance. The drive avoids having to reposition the head backward, saving tens of milliseconds.

## CD-ROM changers

NEC, Nakamichi, and Panasonic are among the companies that offer CD-ROM changers. The Panasonic SQ-TC512N five-disc changer — with an IDE interface — sells for under $90, making it worth consideration in systems needing the unique characteristics of a changer. Specifications for the unit are shown in Table 14-6.

| Table 14-6 |
|---|
| **Panasonic SQ-TC512N CD-ROM Changer Specifications** |

| *Characteristic* | *Performance* |
|---|---|
| Transfer rate (sustained) | 1800KB per second |
| Access time | 130ms (typical) |
| Buffer size | 128K |
| MTBF | 100,000 hours at 10% |
| Disc formats | SD Book |
| | Red Book |
| | Yellow Book |
| | Photo CD |
| | CD-Extra |
| | CD-I |
| | CD Plus |
| | CD-R |
| | CD-ROM XA |
| | Video CD |

## What are all those CD-ROM disc formats, anyhow?

The more you look into how computers are built, the more specifications you find. That's because manufacturers need precise definitions of what to expect to build products that work with each other. There is a large pile of standards just for CD-ROM. Here are some of the more important:

✦ *Red Book* — The Red Book defines the physical format of audio CDs. This is also called CD Digital Audio, or CD-DA.

✦ *Yellow Book* — The Yellow Book defines the physical format for data CDs, so its purpose is similar to that of the Red Book. It's possible to mix audio and data on the same CD.

*continued*

*(continued)*

✦ *Green Book* — The Green Book defines the physical format for CD Interactive, or CD-I, a format used in a game player from Philips. However, having a CD-I compatible drive doesn't mean you can do anything with a CD-I disc on your PC. In general you can't without some added hardware and software in the computer.

✦ *Orange Book* — The Orange Book defines the physical format for recordable CDs. There are two kinds — magneto-optical and write-once. The CD-R is a write-once device. (Magneto-optical drives have remained expensive and are not widespread.)

✦ *CD-ROM XA* — This stands for CD-ROM eXtended Architecture and is a combination of Yellow Book and Green Book. CD-ROM XA has generally superseded the Yellow Book.

✦ *CD Plus* — Also called CD Extra, this is a specific combination of audio and data on the CD.

✦ *ISO 9660* — Once called the High Sierra format, ISO 9660 defines the file and directory layouts on a CD. Extensions such as Joliet and Romeo have been defined to handle Windows 95 and NT long filenames but are not yet formal standards.

Some of the other standards you'll see referenced include single and multisession Kodak Photo CD and Video CD.

The only time you'll really need to worry about any CD standards is when new ones emerge, because the product you're looking at may or may not support the newer standard. Otherwise, the drive and software manufacturers tend to support them all to avoid being at a competitive disadvantage.

## CD-R

CD-R drives — once nearly all SCSI, but now common in IDE and SCSI — are sold by a number of companies, including Hewlett-Packard, Pinnacle, Yamaha, Sony, Smart and Friendly, and Philips. The Yamaha CDR400TIPC (a 6X read / 4X write unit) and Sony Spressa series are among the best. The CDR400 has packet write capability (which lets you add data to the recording incrementally, and helps prevent data underruns). Figure 14-9 shows what the Yamaha drive looks like — much like a conventional CD-ROM with some additional indicators on the front to tell you what's going on as it records.

Table 14-7 shows the specifications for the CDR400TIPC. Notice particularly that their access times and MTBF are nowhere near as good as what you would expect from a good CD-ROM drive, so you'll want to buy a CD-ROM drive to put in your system too rather than using the CD-R drive for both purposes.

**Figure 14-9:** The Yamaha CDR400TIPCis a combined 6X CD-ROM reader and 4X writer. (Photo courtesy Yamaha Systems Technology.)

| Table 14-7 | | |
| --- | --- | --- |
| **Yamaha CDR400TIPC Specifications** | | |
| *Characteristic* | *CDR400t Performance* | |
| Sustained transfer rate | 900KBps (6X read) 600KBps (4X write) | |
| Burst transfer rate | 3.4 to 4.2MBps (async) | |
| Access time | 250ms | |
| Buffer size | 2MB | |
| MTBF | | |

CD-Rewritable (CD-RW) drives finally arrived in the market in mid-1997. CD-RW drives such as the Yamaha CRW4416S support both CD-R and CD-RW, depending on the type of media you use. The CRW4416S offers 16X read, 4X write, and 4X rewrite performance. You can read CD-Rs in most CD-ROM drives, but because CD-RW is a later addition to the specification, you may not be able to read the discs in conventional drives.

## DVD

DVD products arrived in the PC market in 1997 and became reasonably widespread in 1998. As we said earlier, the combination of price, CD-ROM compatibility, and capability to handle both DVD video and data discs as they become widespread make DVD an obvious choice for any new machines you buy or old machines you upgrade.

In early 1999, DVD technology had reached the third generation of products, with the fourth generation due out before the end of the year. Table 14-8 shows the specifications for a third-generation drive, the Toshiba SD-M1202, shown in Figure 14-10.

| Table 14-8 Specifications for the Toshiba SD-M1202 DVD-ROM | |
|---|---|
| *Characteristic* | *Specification* |
| Data transfer rate | 2,704-6,536KB per second (sustained, DVD) 2,069-4,800KB per second (sustained, CD-ROM) |
| DVD capacity | 4.7, 8.5, 9.4, 17GB |
| ATAPI burst transfer rate | 16.7MB per second (DMA Mode 1, PIO Mode 4) |
| Average access time (ms) | 135ms (DVD) 95ms (CD-ROM) |
| Host interface | ATAPI |
| Buffer size | 256KB |
| Disc formats | DVD ROM DVD Video DVD-R (read only) SD Book Red Book Yellow Book CD-ROM XA CD-I CD-I Ready CD Plus |
| MTBF | 100,000 power-on hours |

DVD offers you an option besides very large data capacity — a computer DVD drive is capable of playing DVD movies on your computer. You'll need DVD video player software and (except on very fast computers) a hardware DVD decoder.

✦ *DVD video player software.* DVD discs record video in a specialized format. You'll need DVD video player software to interpret the control files and create the on-screen menus.

**Figure 14-10:** The Toshiba SD-M1202 is a third-generation DVD-ROM that connects to your system through the IDE ports. (Photo courtesy Toshiba.)

✦ *Hardware MPEG-2 decoder.* The DVD video itself is encoded on disc in the MPEG-2 format. You'll need at least a 266 MHz Pentium II processor to do the decode in software. Use a faster processor or hardware decoder if possible. You can get hardware decoders as separate cards (such as the Sigma Designs REALMagic), or built into some video cards (such as the ATI Rage Fury using the Rage 128 chip).

We're not including DVD-R or DVD-RAM products in this version of the book, because as of early 1999 we don't think the standards and technology have matured to the point where the products are ready for widespread application.

# Choosing a DVD or CD-ROM

It's hard for us to imagine any but the most bare-bones computer without a CD-ROM. It makes software installation easier and opens up great gaming, multimedia, and information options that just aren't possible from software distributed on floppy disks. With the price of a first-class DVD-ROM at US $120 in early 1999 (and IDE CD-ROM at US $42), DVD or CD-ROM are an inexpensive upgrade to most any machine.

Here's our recommendation for how to pick a CD-ROM drive. We started with some recommendations from Toshiba for picking a CD-ROM drive and modified them to reflect the newer DVD technology. We suggest you look at specifications in the following order, keeping in mind that price is an overriding factor:

1. Pick a DVD drive so long as you can accommodate an ATAPI drive in your system. If not, pick a SCSI CD-ROM drive if it fits your system and budget; otherwise choose an ATAPI unit. The capability of a SCSI host adapter to do multiple operations simultaneously means the drive won't bog down the rest of your system.

2. Pick a drive with the highest speed rating you can. The faster drive ships data to your system sooner, boosting performance. (This is contrary to many reports — see the sidebar CD-ROM and DVD drive fraud?).

3. Pick the drive with the lowest access time. Every time the drive switches from one file to another or starts up from a stop, you pay the access time delay.

4. Pick the drive with the highest minimum speed.

## CD-ROM and DVD drive fraud?

A number of reports in the media of measurements made on high-speed CD-ROMs stated that the drives perform far under the 16X, 24X, or faster advertised rates, and suggested that manufacturers are duping buyers. The measurements in those reports showed performance of 8X to 12X at the inside of the disc, reaching advertised numbers only at the outside edge.

A balanced view is somewhat more complex. It's absolutely true that the high-speed drives vary the transfer rate, with the minimum rate being at the inside of the disc. A 12X rotation rate (6,320 RPM) is as fast as CD-ROMs are likely to be spun at the disc inner edge. If the drive actually maintained a constant rotation rate while the head moves to the outside, a 12X drive would read at nearly 80X at the outside edge. In practice, the drive rotation rate slows as the head moves to the outside, and the fastest you're likely to see at the outside edge is 40X.

The open question is where the drive is most likely to be reading at the time you care about speed. If the title you're reading is a relatively small set of files (say 100MB), they'll all be at the inside of the disc, and you'll see transfer rates at the low end. This is typical of software distribution discs where you might read the CD-ROM once onto a hard disk. If the title is a set of programs plus multimedia files (typical of a reference work you leave in the drive), you can expect the programs (which you load infrequently) to be at the inside and the multimedia files to be at the outside. That means that the files you access most often would be the ones that read at the highest rate.

The result is that high-speed CD-ROMs and DVDs aren't single-speed drives — their performance is characterized by a range of speeds. Manufacturers whose advertising and specifications have the objective of communicating accurate, useful information will recognize this and give you the complete range.

**Caution** You'll want to think about choke points if you add a DVD or CD-ROM expecting to get great video and sound from multimedia applications. If you have a slow video card, a slow bus, or a slow processor, your computer may not be able to keep up. This can cause video frames to be dropped — making the picture look jerky — and often causes the video and sound to not be properly synchronized. You specifically need to worry about your disk and bus if you intend to use a CD-R or CD-RW. Your best bet is a bus mastering PCI SCSI host adapter, such as the Adaptec AHA-2940 series, or a PCI IDE port for ATAPI drives.

Consider a CD-ROM changer if you have a set of CD-ROM discs, such as Microsoft's Bookshelf or Parsons Technology's It's Legal, that you use all the time. A changer allows several such titles to be online at once. If you put the changer on the network file server, you can share across the entire office. You'll want to look carefully at the licensing terms for any given title before providing it to multiple users, however, to make sure you're allowed to do this.

# Top Support Questions

CD-ROMs tend to stay working for years once you get them set up properly, which is why you'll see mostly configuration questions in this section. DVD should behave the same way. CD-Rs are a little more delicate than CD-ROMs — changes in the rest of the computer can adversely impact the transfer rate and latency to the CD-R, leading to buffer underruns and scrapped discs.

## DVD and CD-ROM

Q: Do I need special drivers to make my DVD or CD-ROM work?

A: Frequently not. FreeBSD UNIX, Windows 95, and Windows NT natively support both SCSI and IDE (ATAPI) CD-ROMs. FreeBSD and Windows NT will boot their installation CD-ROMs on systems supporting the El Torito bootable CD-ROM format. You will need drivers and the mscdex.exe program to operate the CD-ROM under DOS. If the device isn't seen under Windows, try the Add New Hardware applet in the control panel; under UNIX, try *MAKEDEV* (or the lower-level *mknod*).

You do need special software (and maybe hardware) to make your DVD drive play movies. See the discussion earlier in the chapter.

Q: Can I use my CD-ROM with the CD-ROM port on my sound card?

A: It depends. Otherwise-identical sound cards are shipped with proprietary CD-ROM interfaces, IDE interfaces, and SCSI interfaces, so you have to check the specifics of the card and drive. Even if the two are compatible, you're better off connecting all but the slowest CD-ROMs to a port on the PCI bus.

Q: How do I set up my BIOS to handle my CD-ROM?

A: There's nothing you need to do to set up for a SCSI CD-ROM, other than perhaps to disable booting from the CD-ROM in case you prefer to leave a bootable disc in the drive. For IDE CD-ROMs, you don't have to configure cylinders, heads, and sectors in the BIOS for a CD-ROM. Some BIOSes need to be told about the drive, though, requiring that you select a CD-ROM setting for the specific port and master/slave status.

Q: My system frequently locks up when I access the CD-ROM. What's wrong?

A: This can happen with Windows 95 when the DOS drivers for the CD-ROM are left in the config.sys file. Try commenting out the DOS driver (for instance, sbide.sys, taisatap.sys, nec_ide.sys) in the config.sys file. We've also seen SCSI systems lock up in some cases where the Windows SCSI drivers had to be updated.

Q: I added an IDE CD-ROM to my Windows 95 system, and it's not recognized. What's wrong?

A: First, make sure your IDE controller itself is recognized by Windows 95 and isn't in compatibility mode. The CD-ROM connected to it can't be seen until that's true. If the controller is seen and the drive isn't, try detecting new hardware (Start ⇨ Settings ⇨ Control Panel ⇨ Add New Hardware). If that doesn't work, try reinstalling Windows on top of itself. The reinstallation should preserve most of your settings, and the more comprehensive detection should finally see the drive. Your motherboard may also have what Intel calls a PIIX-4 IDE interface, which requires a patch for Windows 95 or an upgrade to Windows 98.

Q: How long will CD-ROMs last?

A: Properly made CD-ROMs will last for a very long time, but poorly made CD-ROMs or CD-Rs can have a very short lifetime. Key manufacturing issues include the purity of the materials making up the disc, proper control of tolerances, and the integrity of the seal at the edges of the disc. There's not much you can do to check the materials. Imation suggests looking at the data side of the disc (the side without the label) with a very bright light (the sun or an overhead projector) behind the disc. Be careful not to look directly at the light. If you see a large number of pinholes — bright points of light coming through the disc — or you see the label through the metal, the disc is doomed. Look at the label too — it should be smooth and free of defects. If not, substances in the air and environment might attack the metal layer. Exposing discs to high temperature can accelerate aging and cause failure too.

Q: My system pauses for a long time at boot after seeing my CD-ROM (or CD-R). Can I stop it from doing that?

A: Your motherboard BIOS (or SCSI host adapter BIOS) may be looking for a bootable CD-ROM in the drive, taking a while to decide that there's no disc there. You can keep a disc in the drive, or you can change the BIOS settings to disable booting from CD-ROM.

Q: My CD-ROM drive doesn't work. How can I find out what's wrong?

A: CD-ROM drives normally spin up the disc when it's inserted, so you can find out if the drive is even minimally alive by inserting a CD-ROM, noting which way the label is turned before you close the drive. Wait a while, and then eject the disc. If the label hasn't turned, it's likely the drive itself isn't working. If the label has moved, your problem could be operating system, BIOS, cabling, or the drive. You could run a set of diagnostics, or simply try a different drive.

## CD-R (hardware and software)

Q: My mastering software sees my CD-R drive, but my operating system doesn't. What's going on?

A: CD-R drives used to tell Windows the drive was a Write Once Read Many (WORM) drive, not a CD-ROM. You may be able get software from the drive manufacturer or from your host adapter manufacturer (for instance, Adaptec's cdr4up.exe) that fixes the problem, letting the "WORM" drive be used as a CD-ROM.

Q: My operating system gave a drive letter to my CD-R, but I can't put a disc in and read it. What's going on?

A: This is a different symptom of the preceding problem—your drive is reporting it's a WORM drive, and the operating system is confused. The problem where you get a drive letter but the device won't work as a CD-ROM can be caused by multiple drivers trying to work with the drive. Under Windows 9x, the drivers are going to be in \windows\system\iosubsys. Typical ones include cdr4vsd.vxd and c4324hlp.vxd. You may also want to try updates from your CD-R or host adapter manufacturer. One of my computers had this problem, for example, which I fixed with a combination of an update to Adaptec EZ-SCSI 4.01b and their cdr4up.exe patch.

Q: I followed your tips earlier in this chapter to avoid CD-R buffer underruns, but I keep getting them. What can I do?

A: You may have a very slow hard drive, or one with bad sectors that cause the machine to pause trying to reread them. Try a surface scan (such as with SCANDISK in Windows). See what happens if you master on a different hard disk. You can also try a different recorder with a bigger buffer—the Yamaha CDR400t, for example, has a 2MB buffer, which is good for over three seconds of delay by the computer.

# Hands-On Upgrades

Adding a CD-ROM, CD-R, or DVD drive is a great training exercise for new technicians. There are enough things that can go wrong to be somewhat challenging, but few of the mistakes you can make are catastrophic. (Just be sure you don't exceed the distance limitation on IDE cables!)

## Adding a CD-ROM, CD-R, or DVD

Adding a CD-ROM, CD-R, or DVD drive is mechanically the same as adding a disk. See the Hands-On section in Chapter 13 and the photos in Chapters 39 and 42.

Once you install the drive and boot up, it's likely that Windows 9x, Windows NT, and UNIX will all see the drive and configure themselves. If not, you may have to add the device manually. If you need to access your CD-ROM under DOS, though, you 're going to need drivers. The Windows 98 emergency boot disk has drivers for most setups, but you're not guaranteed to be exempt from the problem if you're running Windows 95, Windows NT, or UNIX. Take a look at this example:

1. You install Windows 95 and carefully make an emergency startup disk.

2. Some time later, for whatever reason, one of your hard disks dies. You check for loose cables, a dead power supply, or a power failure. You go into the BIOS and check that the settings are right. Nothing helps — no matter what, you get "Boot disk failure" or "Operating system not found" messages, or the system simply hangs looking for the disk.

3. Suppressing panic, you reach for that emergency startup disk and boot it. You discover that the user has done a really competent job of reformatting the hard drive, or that the drive is dead, so you replace it.

4. Now that you have a working drive, you reach for the rack of tapes, planning to reinstall Windows, reinstall the backup software (you do make backups, right?), and reload. You pause, though, remembering that your backup software only runs under Windows, so you'll have to install that first.

5. You slap the Windows 95 CD-ROM in the drive and tell DOS to give you a directory of the CD-ROM. DOS replies "Invalid drive." You realize where your CD-ROM drivers are — out on the CD-ROM you can't get to. Not good.

We recommend that Windows 95 users upgrade to Windows 98, but if you're not in a position to do that, let's fix your emergency disk before you end up in trouble. Making your CD-ROM work under DOS requires drivers in the config.sys file and a load of MSCDEX in your autoexec.bat file. Here are the typical lines from config.sys for an Adaptec AHA-2940 host adapter:

```
device=aspi8dos.sys
device=aspicd.sys /d:aspicd0
```

In addition, you'll need this line in autoexec.bat:

```
mscdex /d:aspicd0
```

If you had an IDE CD-ROM tied in through a Creative Labs SoundBlaster 16, you'd see a line like these in config.sys:

```
device=sbide.sys /p:1E8,11 /d:CD00
```

and the corresponding line in autoexec.bat:

```
mscdex /d:CD00
```

Collectively, these lines load the real mode support software it takes to access the CD-ROM. The components loaded in config.sys are device drivers, the software responsible for actually going out and talking to the hardware. MSCDEX, which loosely stands for "Microsoft CD-ROM Extensions" is the software that tells DOS how to look at files out on the CD-ROM, which are organized somewhat differently than the files on your hard disk. Be sure to add the real mode device drivers to your emergency startup disk, creating the necessary config.sys and autoexec.bat files if they do not exist. If you don't know what they should look like, check with your CD-ROM or host adapter vendor. Be sure to test the emergency disk by booting it and checking for CD-ROM access.

Windows NT avoids the problem by including a wide variety of hardware drivers on the setup floppy disks. Even if you install Windows NT directly from CD-ROM, be sure to build a set of setup floppies so that you have an emergency recovery capability.

Emergency recovery for UNIX systems is system dependent. FreeBSD will install from floppy disk, CD-ROM, or over a network but doesn't offer an emergency recovery floppy disk capability. The Linux boot disk can read many common CD-ROM setups. No matter what operating system you use, remember that there's no substitute for good backups.

## Recording a CD-R

Let's work step by step through recording a CD-R. In this example, we'll take a set of files from hard disk and write them on CD-ROM using Adaptec's Easy-CD Creator under Windows 98.

We make master images before burning the CD-R, so the first thing to do is to decide where to put the CD master image. You might need up to 660MB of space, so take a look at what you have available. An easy way to do that is to use the "My Computer" view of your computer in details mode. Figure 14-11 shows what that looked like on the computer we used for this example:

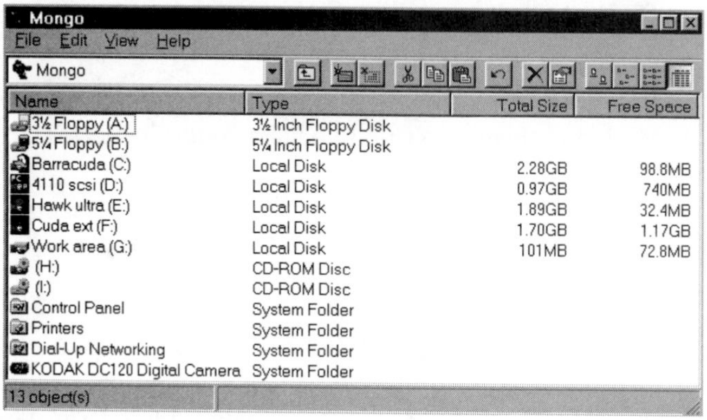

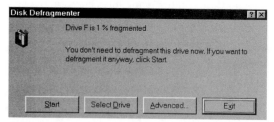

**Figure 14-11:** The details view in Windows Explorer shows you the space on all your drives.

We could use either drive D: (740MB free) or F: (1.17GB free) for the master image file. We'll use F: because we know it's a much faster drive. Once you pick the drive, defragment it. You can use Windows DEFRAG (Start ⇨ Accessories ⇨ System Tools ⇨ Disk Defragmenter). Select the right drive, and choose OK. Don't be fooled if DEFRAG claims it doesn't need to defragment the drive (see the dialog box in Figure 14-12) — it doesn't look at the fragmentation of free space on the drive. Choose start to force DEFRAG to run.

**Figure 14-12:** Don't let DEFRAG fool you — force it to run.

Once DEFRAG is done, start your CD-R mastering software, and create a new project. With Easy-CD Creator, you use the main window shown in Figure 14-13 to drag and drop files into your CD layout.

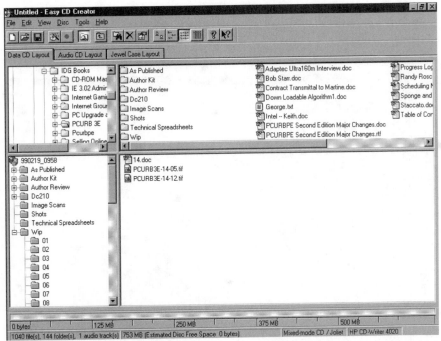

**Figure 14-13:** CD-ROM mastering software supports data, audio, and mixed-mode discs.

Your options are these:

✦ *CD-ROM.* You drag data files onto CD-ROM using the "Data CD Layout" tab (shown visible in the figure). You can put as many files in the recording as fit, and you can support long filenames in both file and folder names.

✦ *CD-DA.* You can record audio tracks onto CDs using the Audio CD Layout tab. You use wave audio files on your hard disk as source material; subject to copyright restrictions, you can pull wave files from other data CDs, audio CDs, or other sources.

✦ *Mixed-mode CD.* You can record both data and audio tracks on a single CD-ROM by dragging in data files with the Data CD Layout tab and audio files with the Audio CD Layout tab. This option is how game titles record both game files and background music. You can use the same technique for training video and other multimedia work.

✦ *CD from an image.* If you build an image file on hard disk using the File ⇨ Create Disc Image command, you then write one or more copies of the image to a blank CD with the File ⇨ Create CD from Disc Image command.

✦ *CD Copy*. You can read one CD-ROM (or individual tracks on a CD-ROM) and copy it to a CD-R, using tools included with Easy-CD Creator called CD Copier Deluxe and CD Spin Doctor (Figure 14-14).

**Figure 14-14:** CD Spin Doctor lets you edit CDs you own into custom CD-Rs with just the tracks you want.

You pick the data files to write by dragging them from the Explorer pane in the upper half of the Easy-CD Creator window to the lower pane under the Data CD Layout tab. We did that for a number of files for this book, leading to what you see in Figure 14-13.

You don't have to put files in the same folder on the CD-ROM as they are in on your disk—you can reorganize them to be in completely new places, or to remove part of the directory structure you don't need. We've left the files in the same folder as they came from in Figure 14-13, but we could equally well put them in the root folder, in folders organized by subject, or anywhere else on the CD.

The order of the files in the window is normally the physical order they'll be written to the CD-ROM. You can change that by setting file priority—right-click the file and then choose Change Priority. The resulting File Priority dialog box (Figure 14-15) lets you set the file for Normal Priority, Faster Access, Fastest Access, or other priority levels you can create.

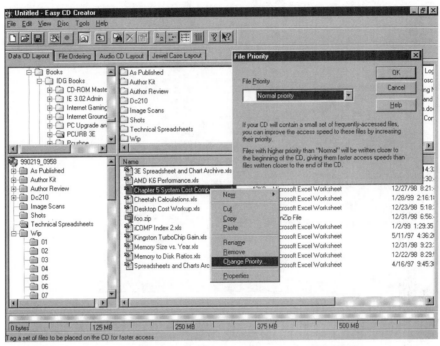

**Figure 14-15:** Elevate the priority for files you expect to access often.

If you're using the ISO 9660 standard, you may have to rename files on your CD image (right-click the file, then choose Rename — See Figure 14-16 for the results). The ISO 9660 level 1 standard is very restrictive, requiring DOS-style filenames and limiting the characters that can appear more restrictively than what DOS allows. CD-ROMs written to ISO 9660 can be read on essentially all systems. The Joliet format supports Windows long filenames but may not be readable on UNIX, Macintosh, or other systems.

You can drag entire directories into the CD-ROM layout. If you do, remember that files in the folders that are invisible in Explorer may be included in the CD-ROM layout. That means, for example, even if you have Explorer set to not display some file types (such as .dll and .vxd) using its View ➪ Options ➪ Hide Files of These Types choice, those files may end up on the CD. Check the files listed in the CD-ROM layout carefully and delete the ones you don't want to include. (You can also use the File ➪ CD Layout Properties command, File Types tab, to exclude hidden files, system files, and files with specific extensions.)

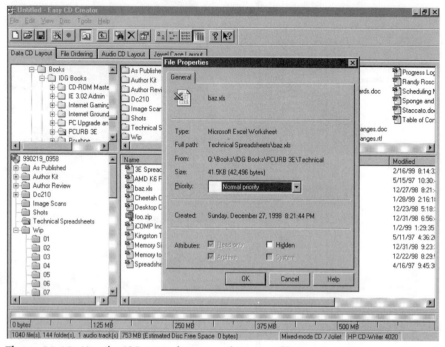

**Figure 14-16:** Use the ISO 9660 format and rename files to short file names if you need to read the disc on multiple kinds of systems.

The Volume Info tab lets you fill in the rest of the information defining the CD-R. Here's what you can supply:

✦ *Volume Label.* The name of the disc. This is what shows up in the Windows Explorer for the disc; it's equivalent to the disk label on a hard disk.

✦ *Publisher's Name.* The publisher of the disc.

✦ *Prepared By.* The name of author of the content of the disc.

✦ *Copyright.* You can protect the work with a copyright notice. Easy-CD Creator lets you fill in the copyright notice directly in this field.

✦ *Abstract.* This field may contain up to 128 characters describing the disc contents.

✦ *Bibliography.* This field stores up to 128 characters of bibliographic information (such as an ISBN number).

Figure 14-17 shows the result after we filled in those fields for the example disc.

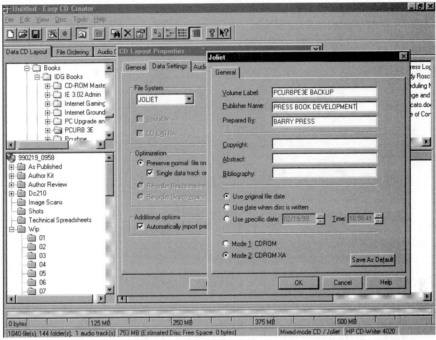

**Figure 14-17:** Fill in properties for the file system to specify details of the CD-ROM.

That's all there is to setup. Run the File ➪ Create Disc Image command, and Easy-CD Creator writes the image to disc. You might have to deal with a few issues as it works:

✦ *Auto-insert notification*. If you're running under Windows, your CD-ROM can report to the system when you insert a new CD into the drive. That can interrupt data flow to the recorder, so the software warns you that there's the potential for trouble. This isn't an issue for creating the master file, and on some systems it isn't a problem writing to CD-R. If it's an issue on yours, simply turn off auto-insert notification in the CD-ROM's properties in the Device Manager (Figure 14-18).

✦ *Invalid filenames*. If you've used the ISO 9660 format, you may get a warning that some of your filenames are invalid. That's because you can have filenames on your disc that aren't valid under those restrictions. You'll want to fix the filename (and any references to it) or use a less-restrictive format.

The master image file is large, and it will be somewhat larger than the total data you will write to the CD-R. (That's why you defragment the disk first — there's less data on the hard drive and so less work to do that way.) Once you've created the file, Run File ➪ Create CD from Disc Image to write the disc.

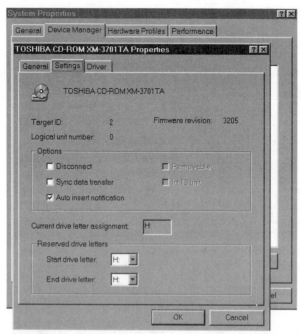

**Figure 14-18:** Turn off auto-insert notification in the Device Manager to prevent blocking access to the CD-R drive.

## Multisession discs, CD-ROM, and CD-ROM XA

There's a lot of confusion about what multisession discs are and how to make them. Multisession discs are recorded according to the Orange Book Part II standard and (technically) can be written in either the CD-ROM or CD-ROM XA format. A multisession CD-ROM drive should always look at the *last* session on a disc, no matter its format. Unfortunately, some manufacturers assumed that CD-ROM XA (the first way multisession CDs were actually made — Kodak Photo CDs) was the only way, and they developed products that could only handle XA multisession discs. When one of these products sees a non-XA disc, it assumes that the disc is single-session. The result is that it reads a multisession disc as if it were a single-session disc, and you see only the data in the first session.

This isn't a problem with newer equipment, but you should check if you have older drives (or simply be sure to use the XA format).

# Summary

✦ You want a DVD, or at least a CD-ROM.

✦ Use a CD-ROM changer to make multiple titles available at once, but remember that it takes time to go from one disc to another.

✦ Use a CD-R drive to make archival copies of relatively large sets of files and to publish your finished work. Be careful how you set up the hardware to ensure you can write the discs successfully.

✦ A CD-R drive may not be a good substitute for a CD-ROM — you may be better off with both.

✦        ✦        ✦

# Removable Disks

**R**emovable disks have a long history in personal computers, from early 160KB floppy disks to the latest in multigigabyte removable media. You'll continue to see removable disk storage in nearly every computer you encounter because of the convenience and universal compatibility they offer.

## Floppy Disks

The floppy disk drive in your computer uses one of the oldest storage technologies in computing. Floppy drives are commodity items, built in huge quantities with little to distinguish one from another. The 3.5-inch, 1.44MB drive is a universal standard, with 5.25-inch drives used only for backward compatibility. You can get dual drives that package a 3.5-inch and 5.25-inch drive in the same space, but unless you specifically need the 5.25-inch capability, even that's not worth doing. A higher-capacity 2.88MB floppy format was developed by Toshiba and used by IBM, but it never sold in enough volume to matter.

A floppy drive is a two-headed device, one head for each side of the disk. (Older drives used only one head, and with the early two-headed drives, the heads sometimes smacked together and damaged the disk.) Figure 15-1 shows the layout. The cross-section view shows the structure of a floppy disk drive with a disk inserted. The heads are in direct sliding contact with the disk (which is why your computer turns off the drive motor when not accessing the disk: it avoids excessive wear). The disk is a flexible plastic with a magnetic coating on both sides. Small gaps in the heads confine the magnetic image to the current track. Separate gaps on each head assembly trailing the read/write head trim down the magnetic image, keeping adjacent tracks from interfering with each other.

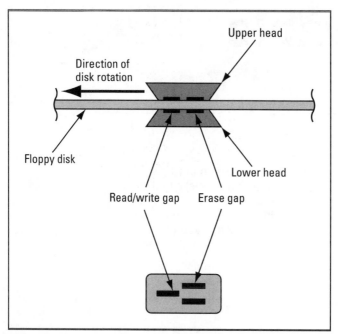

**Figure 15-1:** Floppy disk technology hasn't changed much in years, because newer versions haven't offered compelling advantages in the market.

One of the key limitations on 5.25-inch floppy drive capacity was the capability of the drive to accurately position the head over the tracks. The 5.25-inch floppy format uses a hole in the center of the flexible plastic disk to position the disk on the drive spindle. Over time, wear and deformation of the hole cause the disk to be misaligned on the spindle, resulting in an off-center path for the head. The manufacturers of the disks and drives, knowing of the possibility, make the tracks spaced fairly far apart on the disk so that, even if a disk is misaligned, the head does not read the wrong track. The large track spacing limits the capacity of the disk; a 5.25-inch floppy uses only 48 tracks per inch on each of the two sides.

The key difference between 5.25- and 3.5-inch floppy formats is the metal positioner in the middle of the 3.5-inch disk. Unlike the 5.25-inch disk's hole, the metal positioner in the 3.5-inch disk seats accurately on the disk spindle every time, reducing the minimum track spacing required so that you get 135 tracks per inch on each of the two sides. You can compare the two sizes by realizing that the greater capacity of the 3.5-inch floppy (1.44MB) requires only 15 millimeters (mm) along the radial axis of the disk, while the larger 5.25-inch floppy requires over 42mm to store less data (1.2MB).

## The problem reading Apple floppy disks

There are two reasons why the early Apple floppy disks (Apple II, for example) cannot be read on an IBM-compatible computer. First, the drives used a constant linear velocity recording scheme (similar to what we saw in Chapter 14 for CD-ROMs) to pack more data on the outer tracks. IBM-compatible floppy disks spin at a constant speed (constant angular velocity) and so don't get the data at the right rate. The other problem is that the coding used to write data on the disk on some Apple floppies is completely different from that used by IBM-compatible computers, so even if the data came in at the right rate, the floppy disk controller chip could not understand what it was seeing.

If you've transferred data between Macintosh and IBM-compatible computers, you know that most Macs are able to read IBM-compatible floppies. This is because the Mac incorporates the circuits to read the more-common IBM formats. In addition, newer Macs use the same standard floppy disk drives as the IBM-compatible computers (to reduce costs), so the rotation problem is avoided as well.

Despite the improvements in head alignment that the 3.5-inch drives offer, you will at times come across 3.5-inch floppies that can't be read in some machines even though other seemingly identical machines can read them. The cause of this problem is usually head position misalignment between the machine that wrote the floppy and the one that is trying to read it. If the heads on both machines are slightly misaligned in different directions, one machine will not be able to read tracks that the other machine has created.

The most direct approach to fixing the problem is to format the disk on the computer you want to read the data and then rewrite the contents to the disk. If this doesn't work or if your floppy commonly gets data errors reading original copies of software you've purchased, the drive is probably severely misaligned and should be replaced. Floppy drives are inexpensive enough that they're not worth repairing.

# The LS-120 Floppy Disk Drive

Compaq, 3M, Optics Research, and Matsushita-Kotobuki Electronics Industries, Ltd., have developed a new floppy disk drive — called LS-120 — that packs 120MB onto a disk the same size as the conventional 3.5-inch floppy. The drive accepts the older 3.5-inch floppy types as well as the new media, so it's backward compatible. The drives now sell for under US $80, which is price-competitive with other removable-media drives in this capacity range. The disks sell for around $10 in 3-packs, which is high for casual floppy disk use but competitive with other drives in the same capacity range. Because the drive also handles conventional 3.5-inch disks, you have the choice of using whichever capacity disk is most appropriate for each data storage job.

Table 15-1 shows how impressively the LS-120 compares against a conventional floppy. The drive has an IDE interface, so an update to the BIOS is probably necessary for older machines if you want the drive to work as a bootable floppy (replacing the floppy drive you now have). Drivers in Windows should suffice to run the disk drive in all other situations. The EIDE interface, combined with the faster rotation rate of the LS-120 compared to conventional floppy disk drives, allows conventional 3.5-inch disks to be read at three times the speed you're used to. That means you will see performance improvements even when you are not using the new high-capacity disks. The drive has a sustained transfer rate of 565 kilobytes per second, and an average access time of 70 milliseconds.

### Table 15-1
### Comparison of LS-120 with Conventional Floppy Disks

| Specification | LS-120 | Conventional High-Density Floppy |
|---|---|---|
| Formatted capacity | 120MB | 1.44MB |
| Maximum sustained transfer rate | 565 kilobytes per second | 62 kilobytes per second |
| Average seek time | 70 milliseconds | 84 milliseconds |
| Track density | 2,490 tracks per inch | 135 tracks per inch |
| Number of tracks | 1,736 on each of two sides | 80 on each of two sides |
| Rotation rate | 720 RPM | 300 RPM |

The drive uses an optical track permanently written onto the disk and a laser servo that reads the track to accurately position the heads. The laser servo, along with improvements to the head and media, enables the drive to put 1,736 tracks on each of two sides of the 3.5-inch media (which is over 21 times more than conventional floppies). Figure 15-2 compares the track densities.

The LS-120 product concept and the optical positioning technology is similar to the technology used a few years ago in what were called floptical drives. Floptical drives, which held 21MB and could also read and write normal 3.5-inch floppy disks, never sold well. This may have been because no high-volume computer manufacturer included flopticals in their product line; the only manufacturer commonly associated with flopticals was Silicon Graphics in their workstations. It may equally have been that the device lacked easily accessible drivers for common operating systems (such as DOS and Windows).

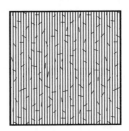

Standard High-Density Tracks
192x magnification

Standard LS-120 Tracks
192x magnification

**Figure 15-2:** The increased track density of the LS-120 technology supports 120MB per disk. (Drawing courtesy Imation.)

For all of the technology in the LS-120, the history of the floptical drive suggests that it remains to be seen whether the LS-120 will be a success in the market. The history of PCs is full of great proprietary technology that went nowhere. MCA comes to mind, as do some innovative computers by Sinclair. Widespread availability and low price will be mandatory to success. If you look at the Iomega Zip drives later in this chapter, you'll see another product with similar capacity that is also a contender for universal adoption. It's possible that neither the LS-120 or the Zip will be the dominant drive — the old 3.5-inch floppy may continue to be used along with CD-ROM and DVD.

# Magneto-Optical Disks

Using an optical servo track written and read by a laser isn't the only successful combination of optical and magnetic technology to be developed. The other major approach focuses on the need to make the area on the disk dedicated to a specific bit of information exceedingly small and exploits the fact that it's easier to focus a laser beam tightly than to confine a magnetic field. Figure 15-3 shows how this works. The basis for this technology — called magneto-optical disk — is that there are magnetic materials that (unlike the materials on all other magnetic disks) are quite difficult to magnetize in their normal state. The key to their usefulness is that they become easy to magnetize when heated above a critical temperature.

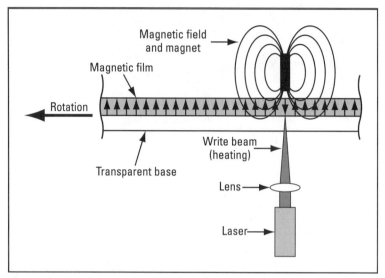

**Figure 15-3:** A magneto-optical disk is written optically and read magnetically. The combination of properties results in a durable structure not susceptible to accidental demagnetization under most circumstances.

The other part of the technology is a laser powerful enough (when focused) to heat the material past the critical temperature. Because the point where the laser hits the disk is a very small point, the density of bits and tracks on the disk can be very high. Because the disk is very difficult to magnetize without the laser, it is resistant to data loss while you carry it around or store it. These two properties together make magneto-optical disks attractive for archival storage.

✦ The magnetic film on the disk in a magneto-optical disk starts out all magnetized in one direction (up in the drawing) and is not susceptible to changing its direction due to the magnetic field alone. Suppose the upward magnetization represents a zero (so the disk stores all zeros to begin with).

✦ At the points where the laser hits the magnetic film, the film gets hot and changes its magnetic properties to the point that it can be switched downward by the magnetic field. The size of the region that switches downward is determined by where the laser strikes, so it can be quite small. The points where the field in the disk switches now represent ones, and we have a way to store both zeros and ones on the disk.

✦ The magnetic field doesn't switch back and forth quickly, so it's not practical to write both zeros and ones as the disk turns. Therefore, to rewrite a track, it has to first be completely erased (heating all points along the track) to write all zeros. Then the laser writes the new data by selectively writing ones in the right places.

Most products using magneto-optical technology have been very expensive, ranging into the thousands of dollars for removable disks of up to a few gigabytes capacity, which means that CD-R is the more popular choice for high-capacity archival storage. Standard magneto-optical disk capacities include disks holding 650MB, 1.3GB, and 2.6GB.

# Removable Disk Products

Removable disk technology occupies an interesting niche in the PC market. Before the introduction of the Jaz drive—current models of which holds two gigabytes of data—low-cost removable disks did not offer much unique benefit. They couldn't hold as much data as tape, and they weren't as fast as conventional magnetic disks. However, the most recent generation of removable media—the Iomega Jaz and Zip drives—have changed the playing field somewhat.

The greatest value of removable disks is that you can take relatively large amounts of data with you in a single cartridge, and you can access that data far more quickly and conveniently than you can with a tape. The scarcity of installed drives means that you'll want to take your drive with you as well unless you know there's one where you're going. This means that most people will want an external rather than internal drive.

Removable disks are also useful for backing up your system. Good backup practice requires that you back up to a removable medium (or to another computer located somewhere else), and the speed and convenient file access of removable disks make them very desirable for this job. However, the relatively high cost of the drive and media (compared to tape, for instance) makes a backup to removable disk impractical in all but very specialized applications.

## Iomega Zip drive

The Iomega Zip drive is one of the most common removable disks available. It stores 250MB on a single removable disk. Versions are available for SCSI, USB, or parallel (printer) port interfaces. The external model can have the SCSI or parallel port interface (the USB version is separate), whereas the internal version has a SCSI. Table 15-2 shows the key specifications the drives offer.

If you choose the external version of the Zip drive, you have to decide whether to choose the USB, SCSI, or parallel port version. Because the most common reason to want the external version is so you can take it with you, the USB or parallel port interface (although slower) makes the most sense; nearly every computer has a parallel port, many have USB, but relatively few have SCSI.

| Table 15-2 Iomega Zip Drive Specifications | |
|---|---|
| **Characteristic** | **Specification** |
| Average seek time | 29 milliseconds |
| Buffer size | 32K |
| Available interfaces | External — Parallel, SCSI, USB<br>Internal — SCSI |
| Sustained data transfer rate | SCSI: 0.79–1.4MB per second<br>Parallel Port: 333 kilobytes per second |
| Disk drop height tolerance | 8 feet / 1000G |
| MTBF | 100,000 hours |

**Tip**

If you choose the SCSI Zip drive, you may be able to use it as a boot drive. You need a SCSI host adapter that allows you to specify the boot device as one with a SCSI ID other than zero, such as the Adaptec AHA-2940 series. Older Zip drives supported SCSI IDs of five or six, so if you set the host adapter to the ID for the drive and insert a disk formatted with system files, you should be up and running. Newer Zip drives support IDs 0 to 7, so you can set the ID to 0 and make no changes to the host adapter. Because the files needed to install Windows 98 all fit on the 250MB Zip disk (but no longer on the 100MB version), this is an easy way to install Windows onto machines that don't have a CD-ROM.

## Iomega Jaz drive

The Iomega Jaz drive (Figure 15-4) is the high-capacity version of the Zip drive. Like the Zip drive, it uses a removable disk cartridge, and is available in both internal and external versions. The Jaz drive differs from the Zip in that it holds ten times as much data, and transfers data ten times faster (burst). Table 15-3 shows the Jaz drive's specifications. The drive MTBF (Mean Time Between Failures) is competitive with hard disks, and far better than that of most removable disks. The disk itself can't take an impact as severe as the Zip drive, reflecting the closer tolerances required to pack in the additional data. The Jaz drive is available only with a SCSI interface; a parallel port simply can't keep up with the transfer rate. You can use one of the parallel port SCSI adapters (devices that look like a SCSI bus to the disk but plug into the computer's parallel port), but performance will be much slower.

**Figure 15-4:** The Jaz drive is the high-capacity version of the Iomega Zip drive, holding 1 or 2GB of data. (Courtesy of Iomega Corporation.)

## Table 15-3
## Jaz Drive Specifications

| *Characteristic* | *Specification* |
|---|---|
| Storage capacity | 2 or 1GB |
| Average seek time | 10ms read, 12ms write |
| Sustained transfer rate | 8.7MB per second maximum<br>57.4MB per second average<br>4.9MB per second minimum |
| Rotational speed | 5,400 RPM |
| Average stop/start time | 10 seconds |
| Buffer size | 256KB |
| Disk drop height | 3 feet |
| Interface | Ultra SCSI |

## The printer passthrough

If you use the parallel port interface with an external Zip drive, you usually interpose the drive between your computer and the cable leading to your printer. Because you can write anything to a disk, there has to be some way for the print software to signal whether the data being sent is for the disk or the printer. This is the same problem faced by copy protection key locks (often called dongles) that attach to the parallel port.

There are two generic ways to specify which device the data is for:

✦ *In-band signaling.* If the software can create a sequence that isn't permissible to one of the devices on the port, that sequence can be used to signal a switch to the other device. For example, suppose that a printer can never receive two zero characters in a row. If, by default, all data is passed through to the printer, then the passthrough can detect two zeros in sequence and switch the interface over to the disk drive when it encounters them. The command sequence going to the drive would end with a command to revert the interface back to the printer.

✦ *Out-of-band signaling.* A signal wire, not one of the data lines, can be used to direct data between the disk and the printer. The standard PC printer port doesn't provide a signal specifically for this purpose, though, so a passthrough using this approach has to "misuse" one of the standard signals.

Both approaches have problems. There is no data sequence that is guaranteed never to be sent to a printer, because many printers use all the possible data values to send graphics from the computer. There's similarly no guarantee that a slight misuse of one of the signal lines won't be misinterpreted by the printer. The actual techniques used by the Zip drive (and other parallel port attachment products) minimize this problem, but don't be surprised if things don't always work right. The safest alternative is to have two parallel ports — one for the printer and one for the Zip drive — or to use a USB drive.

Some situations require that no data be left in unattended computers — that all permanent storage (like disks) be locked up when not in use. The Jaz drive is an ideal solution for computers in those environments, because you can use an internal Jaz drive instead of a conventional hard disk. When you're done for the day, you eject the disk, power down, and lock up. Both the computer and your data are completely secure. With two gigabytes capacity and the ability to change disks for different projects, one drive may be all you need.

# Small-Scale Backup

Any technology that replaces the 1.44MB floppy drive will have to offer a lot of capacity, good speed, and competitive costs. Most important, it will have to be shipped by a lot of manufacturers, so that no matter where you go, you can be assured that you'll find a drive that can read your disk. Today, the contenders for that role are the LS-120 laser servo disk and the Zip drive. They're all much more expensive than floppy disks, and none has shipped enough that you can be assured of finding one. For the moment, high-capacity removable storage remains a product you buy only if you have a specialized requirement.

Backups of the work an individual user does are important, but their limited volume suggests that either floppies or other removable disk would be the right choice. Table 15-4 shows the comparison, assuming you were to back up 10MB, among the LS-120 drive, the Zip 250MB drive, and a conventional floppy disk. On cost alone, the floppy disk is the clear winner.

## Table 15-4
## Comparison of Removable Disk Backup Alternatives

| Characteristic | LS-120 | Zip 250 | Zip 100 | 1.44MB Floppy |
|---|---|---|---|---|
| Drive cost (February 1999) | $80 | $160 | $60 | Included with computer |
| Media cost (February 1999) | $10 | $15 | $7 | Free to less than $1 |
| Media capacity | 120MB | 250MB | 100MB | 1.44MB |
| Maximum sustained data rate | 565 KBps | 1,400 KBps | 1,400 KBps | 62 KBps |
| Estimated backup time (10MB) | Less than 1 minute | Less than 1 minute | Less than 1 minute | Less than 5 minutes |
| Number of media | 1 | 1 | 1 | 7 |
| Total media cost | $10 | $15 | $7 | $0 to 5 |
| Total solution cost | $90 | $175 | $67 | $0 to 5 |

The situation isn't as straightforward as a cost comparison, of course. For example:

✦ *Compression*. Data compression will reduce the number of floppies required, but not all the way down to one disk. The net effect is to reduce the total backup time.

✦ *Price changes*. The prices in Table 15-4 will change, of course, but the price will probably change most significantly for the Zip 250, which is a relatively new product. The floppy disk is a mature product sold in high volume, so the prices for the drive and the media are relatively stable.

✦ *Actually doing backups*. Making backups is like painting the outside of your house. It's a really good idea that no one wants to do. Cleaning the fireplace is more popular. What this means, of course, is that almost nobody does backups. A backup solution that does the job automatically, with no action on the user's part, is what you want.

# Data Transport

Many times you'll need to archive projects or to transport large files from one place to another. Both requirements can be met with removable disks, CD-R, or tape, so the trade-offs are worth looking at. Table 15-5 shows the comparison, with drive and media costs normalized to the lowest entry in each row. The decision you make depends on what's most important to you: drive cost, media cost, capacity, speed, or protecting your data. Removable disks can offer low costs with moderate capacity; CD-R offers moderate capacity at high drive cost and low media cost; and tape offers moderate to high capacity, relatively low speed, and low to high media cost. CD-R is likely to be the only widely sharable medium of the three.

**Note**    The vulnerability of all magnetic media except the magneto-optical disks to erasure or corruption by nearby magnets means that if you use a removable disk or tape for archival storage, you have to take special care to keep the media in a cool, dry place free of magnetic fields. If you intend to store disks for very long at all, you even have to avoid the residual magnetic fields that can occur in metal file cabinets and desks.

The relative permanence of CD-R, combined with the nearly universal availability of CD-ROM drives to read the disk, makes CD-R the choice for this application.

| Table 15-5 | | | |
| --- | --- | --- | --- |
| **Alternatives for Home Office/Small Office Removable Data Storage** | | | |
| *Characteristic* | *Removable* | *CD-R* | *Tape* |
| Relative drive cost (normalized to lowest in the row) | 1 to 4 | 2.8 to 3.3 | 1.3 to 5 |
| Relative media cost (normalized to lowest in the row) | 7 to 15 | 1 | 5 to 35 |
| Capacity (uncompressed) | 100MB to 2GB | 660MB | 400MB to 4GB |
| Sustained transfer rate | 565 KBps to 5 MBps | 1 to 1.2 MBps | 62 to 300 KBps |
| File access time | Seconds | Seconds | Minutes |
| Data vulnerability | Low to High | Low | High |

# Top Support Questions

In most ways, removable drives have the same issues as fixed drives. The most common questions center around interfaces and software.

Q: Should I use a parallel port or SCSI removable drive?

A: It depends on whether you value portability of the drive or performance more. You'll get better transfer rates to and from the drive through a SCSI interface, because a parallel port simply hasn't the speed SCSI does. SCSI adapters are nowhere near as common as parallel ports, though — you can hook a parallel port drive to most any computer. (There's no speed gain by using a SCSI drive through a parallel port SCSI adapter, because the parallel port remains a bottleneck.)

Q: Do I have to use the SCSI adapter that came with my removable drive?

A: Usually not. You need to verify that the software for the removable drive is compatible with the host adapter and operating system you use and whether your host adapter supports the ASPI (Advanced SCSI Programming Interface) standard. Adapters with built-in Windows 95 or NT drivers meet this requirement. Removable drive support for UNIX is variable; check with the drive manufacturer relative to the specific version of UNIX you use.

Q: Can I boot from a removable drive?

A: Sometimes. You're not going to be able to boot from a parallel port drive, but (depending on the combination of host adapter and removable drive) it may work for SCSI drives. The most straightforward way to experiment is to disconnect your SCSI boot drive (this won't work at all if you usually boot from IDE) and change the removable drive ID to be 0. Some host adapters let you specify that drive IDs other than zero are the boot device.

Q: Do I have to use the software that came with my drive?

A: You may be able to omit using the manufacturer's software if your operating system recognizes the drive and knows that the drive contains removable media (this isn't likely with parallel port drives). Even if your system meets these requirements, you may be unable to format disks without the manufacturer's software.

Q: My computer hangs or otherwise malfunctions when I use the parallel port pass-through to connect to my printer. What's wrong?

A: Your printer may use two-way communication between itself and the computer (this is common for recent printers, including many ink jet and laser printers). The two-way communications may conflict with the operation of the removable drive, causing problems. You have two possible options: Disable bidirectional communications (which may or may not work), and use separate parallel ports.

Q: Can I share a removable drive across a network?

A: Most operating systems supporting removable drives allow sharing across a network. The remote computer may not end up configured to know the network drive is removable, though, and may appear to hang while it waits for data when there's no disk in the drive.

# Hands-On Upgrades

Adding a second floppy drive to a computer isn't the most common upgrade any longer because the 5.25-inch drives are obsolete. If you need to copy floppies regularly, or if you still need to deal with the older format, a second drive is worth having.

## Adding a second floppy drive

Some situations make a second floppy disk drive really useful. Examples include small-scale disk duplication (there are machines designed to duplicate large numbers of floppy disks), and computers that need to handle multiple disk sizes. It's pretty straightforward to add a second floppy disk to your computer. Here's how:

1. *Mechanical installation.* Mount the drive in your computer. Mounting a drive into a bay of the same size requires only that you carefully adjust the drive position to fit the front panel before tightening the screws. If you're putting a 3.5-inch drive into a 5.25-inch drive bay, you're going to need an adapter kit. You should be able to get the adapter kit at the same place that sold you the drive. Figure 15-5 shows a 3.5-inch floppy drive and the pieces of a mounting kit before assembly. Figure 15-6 shows the assembled result. The brackets on either side of the drive attach to the mounting frame of the case.

2. *Cabling.* You connect two cables to the floppy disk, one for power and one for data. The power cable connector is either the same large one used for fixed disks (common on 5.25-inch floppies) or a smaller one used on 3.5-inch drives. It's relatively common to put the small power connectors on upside down, so check what you're doing rather than forcing it into place. You may find you don't have spare power connectors from the power supply. If so, get a Y-cable (Figure 15-7) to split the power going to some other device.

   The data connectors on a floppy drive are either the card edge type (on 5.25-inch drives) or the kind made from parallel rows of pins (on 3.5-inch drives). A floppy disk data cable (see Figure 15-8) will have multiple drive connectors to support connecting both the A: and B: drives. Many have four connectors, supporting connection to two drives with either kind of connector. The normal configuration makes the drive at the physical end of the cable the A: drive, and the one connected inboard of the twist the B: drive. Many BIOSes allow you to swap the A: and B: designation in case the physical connections to do that are inconvenient.

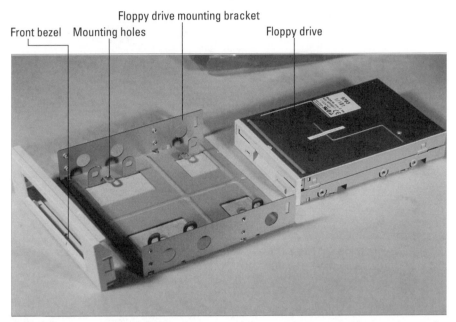

**Figure 15-5:** The adapter bracket fits a 3.5-inch floppy drive into the drive bay and the case front panel.

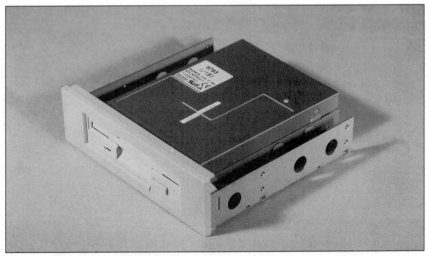

**Figure 15-6:** The completed mounting assembly mounts using the threaded screw holes on the side of the bracket.

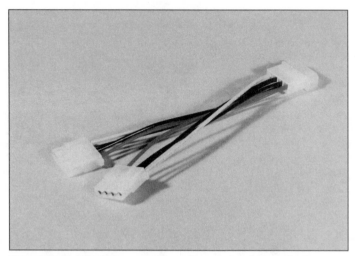

**Figure 15-7:** The Y power cable splits one feed from the power supply to drive two devices.

Drive A: Connectors      Drive B: Connectors

5.25 inch drive connector      5.25 inch drive connector

3.5 inch drive connector    Cable twist    3.5 inch drive connector

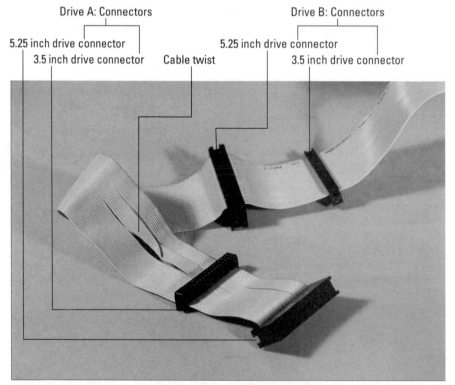

**Figure 15-8:** The floppy disk data cable uses a reversed cable segment to switch drive identification.

Don't connect two floppy drives on the same side of the twist in the cable. It won't work.

3. *BIOS setup.* The last step is to change the BIOS settings to let it know you've installed a second drive. You'll tell the BIOS the type of drive, and whether you want to swap the drive letters. That's all there is — boot the machine, and the new drive should be visible.

## Can you use that old floppy drive?

You can, but it's less clear that you should. The electrical and physical interfaces of the first PC floppy drives are compatible with the computer you build today. That means that, if you want, you can blow the dust off the fifteen-year-old drive on your shelf and bolt it into a new machine.

Whether you should or not is a different question. The alignment of the heads and accuracy of the motor speed can drift due to wear and jarring. As they do, the drive becomes less compatible with other drives, less able to read and write disks that can be handled in other machines. With the price of floppy drives as low as it is (under US $15 for a Samsung 3.5-inch drive in the first quarter of 1999), it's hard to make a case that an old drive is worth the time you'll spend dealing with its failings. You won't get to choose when the problem happens, either. If you're lucky, it won't be when a customer cares.

## Using a removable drive for standard configurations

Not every PC is a personal computer — some are standard workstations that many different people use. You find impersonal computers in university and school laboratories, telephone call centers, cyber-cafés, software test laboratories, copy centers with rental computers, trade shows, and training centers.

The problem with impersonal computers is that, for whatever reason, they get changed. Often, their software configuration gets changed to the point where the computer no longer works.

Maintaining a set of impersonal computers doesn't have to be hard. You don't have to live your life chained to the machine, endlessly reformatting and rebuilding the disk. Here's another way to do it. Make absolutely sure the hardware configurations of the machines are identical, and equip them all with a large removable drive as the boot drive. (An Iomega Jaz would work.) Then, build up your standard software configuration on a disk and save it as the standard. Use a machine with two drives and utility software like PowerQuest Drive Copy to manufacture copies of the boot disk. Each new user gets a fresh copy of the standard disk, leaving her free to work without concern for anything the prior user did.

Be sure you have licenses for every duplicate copy of your software you make this way.

# Summary

✦ There are several removable disk technologies, each with its own combination of features.

✦ Laser servo technology may finally offer reasonably priced 120MB floppy disks.

✦ Magneto-optical technology offers high capacity and good resistance to accidental erasure, but is very expensive (except for the MD Data drive).

✦ The Zip and Jaz drives are the most common, widely sold removable disks, but they are not common enough for the drives to be universally available.

✦ You need to consider CD-R and tape in addition to removable disks when evaluating your removable storage requirements.

✦    ✦    ✦

# Tape

**M**ost of the tape drives in use with PCs today are the quarter-inch mini–data cartridge type, built to standards defined by Quarter-Inch Cartridge Drive Standards, Incorporated (QIC, an industry trade association). QIC says there are over 15 million QIC tape drives installed. There have been a number of earlier tape formats and standards, such as the DC-6000 data cartridges, but because of the price and capacity advantages of the mini–data cartridge, the earlier tapes are dying out. This chapter covers Travan tapes and drives, based on QIC standards, and the DAT (*Digital Audio Tape)* tapes and drives.

**In This Chapter**

Quarter-inch tape

Tracks, blocks, Travan, and DAT

Backup strategies

Size counts

## The QIC Standards

QIC has created a large number of standards, the most important of which for the PC user are QIC-40, QIC-80, QIC-117, and QIC-3010/3080/3095.

+ *QIC-40.* The standard defining how to record on low-density mini–data cartridge tapes. It includes the specifications for how the tape drive interfaces through the floppy disk controller, so the more expensive SCSI interface is not required. The standard supports 40MB (uncompressed) on a tape.

+ *QIC-80.* Defines how to record on high-density mini–data cartridge tapes. QIC-80 also interfaces through the floppy disk controller (although manufacturers have defined higher-speed interface cards as well). QIC-80 writes 80MB (uncompressed) onto a tape.

+ *QIC-117.* Specifies a set of commands for controlling a tape drive. (See Chapter 11 to learn how processors send commands to devices.) The standard command set (predated by standard commands for SCSI tape drives) is the first part of making it possible for any tape backup program to read any tape. (QIC-113, a standard format for how to organize information on tape, is the other part. The Windows 95 backup program uses QIC-113; other tape backup software can be expected to converge to being able to handle that standard at a minimum as a lowest common denominator.)

✦ *QIC-3010, QIC-3080, QIC-3095, and QIC-3220.* Higher-capacity formats, offering from 425MB to 10GB capacity.

The consistency these standards have provided has been important. Prior to the QIC standards, companies defined their own proprietary formats. Tapes were generally not interchangeable, and it was an entirely hit-or-miss proposition whether the backup software you bought would support the drive you had.

# How Tape Works

If you know how the old eight-track tape players worked, you have some idea how QIC tape works. The drive writes data on multiple tracks (see Figure 16-1), using a serpentine arrangement so the end of one track immediately ties to the start of the next. On a 740-foot tape with 72 tracks, this provides over 53,000 feet of recordable tracks. In addition to the quarter-inch-wide format in Figure 16-1, the specifications define a QIC-Wide format using wider tape (slightly over three-tenths of an inch wide) to increase the number of tracks.

In the normal QIC format, a quarter-inch magnetic tape records tracks in both directions. It starts out reading track zero. At the end of the tape, it reverses and starts reading track one. The process continues, ping-ponging back and forth, until all tracks are read. Depending on the tape standard, there may be from 36 (QIC-40) to 72 (QIC-3095) tracks on a single tape. Newer designs push densities up to 144 tracks.

Data is written on tape similarly to the way it is written to a disk. Reversals in the magnetic direction recorded on the tape are interpreted by the drive electronics into bits sent back to the computer. The recording technology (shown in Figure 16-2) reverses the direction of magnetization for "one" bits, and leaves it unchanged for "zero" bits. The result is that the image recorded on the tape consists of a series of bit cells, each defining the opportunity for a transition.

✦ *Bit cells.* Each of the boxes, called a *bit cell,* is the space allocated to one bit. A transition occurs in the middle of a bit cell for a one bit. The absence of a transition signals a zero bit.

✦ *Transitions.* Transitions in magnetic polarization indicate one bits.

✦ *Non-transitions.* Cells with no transitions in magnetic polarization indicate zero bits.

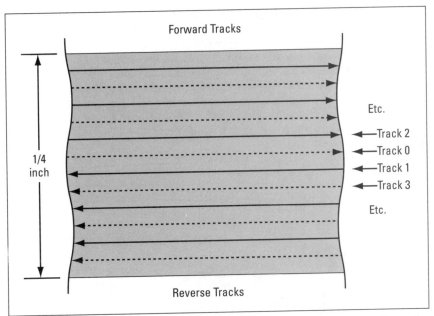

**Figure 16-1:** The serpentine arrangement of data tracks on a QIC tape allows the drive to reverse directions at the end of the track and immediately begin working again.

Too long a run of zero bits causes a lack of transitions on the tape. If the tape stretched or other physical problems occur, the drive loses the accurate timing that allows it to know where the bit cells are. Coding imposed on the data stream from the computer (similar in concept to the coding we discuss in Chapter 14) ensures that only a limited number of zero bits can occur together, eliminating this source of error.

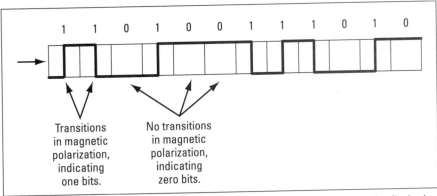

**Figure 16-2:** Magnetic recording on tape is designed to accommodate the limitations of the physical medium.

Although your computer can frequently supply long, uninterrupted streams of data, it's neither possible nor practical to ensure that the data flow never stops. Because of this, the bits written to tape can't be written as a continuous stream for the entire length of a track. Instead (as in Figure 16-3), the data written to tape are divided into units called segments (QIC-80) or frames (QIC-3095), with a gap of erased tape between each segment. In the QIC-80 format, each segment contains 32 sectors, 29 for data and 3 for error correction codes. Data sectors carry 1K. The QIC-3095 format puts 52 data blocks of 512 bytes in a frame, followed by 12 error correction blocks. Gaps between frames (and segments) allow the tape motion to be stopped and started.

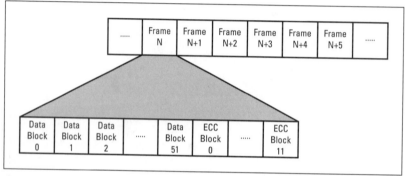

**Figure 16-3:** The format of data on tape allows data to be read and written incrementally rather than all at once.

The gaps between segments (frames) allow space for the tape motion to start and stop. This enables the tape drive to respond to the computer's requests to read and write, even if the time between requests is too long to allow continuous operation. It takes a relatively long time to stop, reverse, and restart the tape, so you get much better sustained data rate performance when your computer can keep the tape streaming. Pauses in the data stream happen most often when the processor is busy and can't read or write data fast enough.

As the extensive error correction space allocation in frames (9 to 18 percent or more) suggests, tape operations are subject to problems. The error correction codes are very strong, with the capability to

✦ Correct errors in up to three blocks detected to have been corrupted

✦ Correct errors in one sector detected to have been corrupted and in a second sector that has been corrupted but escaped error detection

✦ Correct errors in a single corrupted sector that has escaped error detection

The error detection codes — separate from the error correction codes — are themselves quite powerful, making the chances that a data error can escape undetected very small. The end result is that even though the tape medium itself is prone to error, the probability of an error being allowed to escape to the computer is very small. For example, the QIC-80 specification requires that the drive deliver a corrected error rate of no more than one error in 1014 bits, or one bit wrong in over 11GB. Some formats, including QIC-3095, provide for simultaneous read-after-write checking, eliminating the time required after writing the tape to verify it and increasing the reliability of the operation.

The end result is that, for Travan and DAT tape technology, your concerns are really speed and capacity, not reliability.

# Travan

The early inexpensive quarter-inch formats, QIC-40 and QIC-80, quickly became inadequate to contain the volume of data commonly being stored on disks. The growth in tape capacity did not keep up with the 30 to 60 percent cumulative growth rate of disk technology, so if things had stayed the same, no one would have continued to use tape in personal computers. Fortunately, things did not stay the same.

In late 1994, 3M (now Imation) and several equipment manufacturers introduced a new tape technology they called Travan. Key to the technology was a change in the interface between the drive and the tape cartridge, allowing more precise control. Table 16-1 shows the specifications for the five announced Travan mini-cartridges. Under data density you'll see the abbreviation *ftpi*. This stands for "flux transitions per inch," which means how many one bits will fit in an inch. We saw in Figure 16-3 that the magnetic orientation flips — a flux transition — in bit cells containing a one bit. The number of flips per inch is the ftpi number. If the ones and zeros are randomly distributed, then on average there are twice as many bits per inch as flux transitions. That means there are around 160,000 bits per inch on a TR-5 tape, or (multiplying the numbers) a total of nearly 106 billion recordable bits. That large number divides down to over 11GB of recordable space, which after deducting space for interblock gaps, error correction, and other system overhead works out to the 10GB capacity of the tape.

All the capacities shown in Table 16-1 are uncompressed. Manufacturers typically state that you can get a 2-to-1 gain with compression. Our experience is more like 1.4 to 1.6 to 1, but the compression you get is highly dependent on what's on your disk. The section later in this chapter "Lossless Data Compression" explains what compression is and how it works to increase the capacity of your tape.

## Table 16-1
### Travan Tape Specifications

| Characteristic | TR-1 | TR-2 | TR-3 | TR-4 | TR-5 |
|---|---|---|---|---|---|
| Capacity (uncompressed) | 400MB | 800MB | 1.6GB | 4GB | 10GB |
| Min. data rate | 62.5 KBps | 62.5 KBps | 125 KBps | 567 KBps | 1.0 MBps |
| Max. data rate | 62.5 KBps | 125 KBps | 250 KBps | 567 KBps | 2.0 MBps |
| Tape length | 750 feet | 750 feet | 750 feet | 750 feet | 750 feet |
| Tape width | 0.315 inch | 0.315 inch | 0.315 inch | 0.315 inch | 0.315 inch |
| Tracks | 36 | 50 | 50 | 72 | 108 |
| Data density | 14,700 ftpi | 22,125 ftpi | 44,250 ftpi | 50,800 ftpi | 79,800 |
| Interface | Floppy | Floppy | Floppy | SCSI/EIDE | SCSI/EIDE |

# Digital Audio Tape

While Travan is common in individual computers and small offices, servers and large installations often use a more robust technology — Digital Audio Tape (DAT). DAT drives use the Digital Data Storage (DDS) format developed by Hewlett-Packard and Sony to use DAT drives for storing computer data. DAT is now standardized by the Digital Data Storage (DDS) Manufacturers Group. The most common DDS formats are DDS, DDS-2, and DDS-3. Summary specifications for DDS formats from the DDS Manufacturers Group are shown in Table 16-2.

## Table 16-2
### Newer DDS Tape Formats Provide Growth in Capacity and Performance

| Characteristic | DDS | DDS-DC | DDS-2 | DDS-3 | DDS-4 | DDS-5 |
|---|---|---|---|---|---|---|
| Date | 1989 | 1991 | 1993 | 1997 | 1999 | 2001 |
| Capacity | 1.3GB | 2.0GB | 4.0GB | 12.0GB | 20.0GB | 40.0GB |
| Transfer rate (min) | 183 KBps | 183 KBps | 360 KBps | 750 KBps | 1 MBps | 3 MBps |
| (max) | | | 720 KBps | 1.5 MBps | 3 MBps | 6 MBps |

A physical cartridge coding standard called the Media Recognition System uses stripes on the beginning of the tape and a series of recognition holes to let a drive distinguish between DAT tapes meeting the DDS standard and ones designed for consumer audio, so your tape drive can automatically figure out what kind of tape you've inserted.

DAT drives record differently than QIC and Travan tape — instead of packing many tracks longitudinally along the length of the tape, the recording is done like a VCR, with the data striped at an angle across the tape. Figure 16-4 shows how this happens. The side view shows the tape path running diagonally across the head. As the head spins at relatively high speed, the recording gap wipes across the tape leaving a diagonal stripe. By the time the gap spins around for the next swipe, the tape has wound around the head (top view) to position a fresh section of tape in its path.

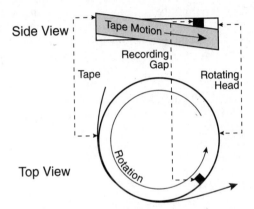

**Figure 16-4:** DAT records stripes on the tape in the same way as a VCR.

DAT drives have several advantages over Travan. Of the two, they're the drive of choice for high-reliability server operations, because they report when the error rate on the tape is getting too high. You can use that notification as a warning to clean the drive and, if you still have problems, to discard the tape (which is probably worn past its useful life). DAT drives may perform hardware compression, removing the load from the processor. A DAT drive can do verification on the fly as data is written, eliminating the need for a separate verification pass and cutting the backup time in half.

(The Travan 5 drives support hardware compression and read-while-write verification, but they don't have the raw capacity of DDS-4.)

# Lossless Data Compression

Data compression is one of those seemingly impossible things, violating all the rules about getting something for nothing. Data goes in the compressor, and less data comes out. You feed the reduced data into a decompressor, and your original data comes back unchanged.

Compression is wonderful for tape. Not only does more data fit on a single tape, but the rate at which data goes onto the tape increases, because fewer bytes actually need to be transmitted to the tape and written. If you get as much as 2-to-1 compression on a TR-4 tape, then the maximum data rate goes up to 1,134K per second at the same time the tape capacity goes up to 8GB.

There's not much downside to compression onto tape, either. The price you pay for compression is that your processor has a lot of work to do to perform the compression operation. However, with a reasonably fast processor, the output of the compressor keeps up with the tape, so all you see is the reduced time to back up your data. All the work the processor is doing is invisible. Things are even better if your drive does the compression in hardware, because then there's no additional processor load.

So how does compression work, and why is the amount of compression you get hard to predict? Let's look at a simple form of compression. Suppose we have a file containing 50 copies of the letter A like this:

```
AAAAAAAAAAAAAAAAAAAAAAAAAAAAAAAAAAAAAAAAAAAAAAAAAA
```

If we want, we could equally well represent the file this way:

```
50A
```

The new representation makes some assumptions, such as that we will write a repetition count followed by the letter we want to repeat. The string 50A then means that, to expand the compressed line back to its original form, we would write 50 copies of the letter A. Doing this, we've reduced a 50-character string down to 3, so we have a compression ratio of 50 to 3, or better than 16 to 1.

Of course, it's not very useful if all we can do is compress files with copies of the same letter in them. We can extend this simple compression method by allowing copy counts and characters to occur one after another, so if we had the string

```
AAAAAAAAAABBBBB
```

which is ten letter A's followed by five B's, we could compress it to

```
10A5B
```

In this example, we've compressed 15 characters into five, for a 3-to-1 compression ratio.

Compression like what we've shown is commonly called run-length encoding, because the numbers represent the length of each run of repeated characters. As the examples show, we don't always get the same compression ratio; it's dependent on the amount of redundancy in the information we're compressing. In fact, compression doesn't always make files smaller. Look at this example:

```
Thequickbrownfoxjumpedoverthelazydog
```

If we encode that string using run-length encoding, a terrible thing happens:

```
1T1h1e1q1u1i1c1k1b1r1o1w1n1f1o1x1j1u1m1p1e1d1o1v1e1r1t1h1e1l1a1
z1y1d1o1g
```

The string has doubled in length. This happens because the string is not compressible with this type of coding; there are no repeated characters. The run-length encoding we're using requires a repeat count, so for every character we have to have at least one count. The pairs of repeat counts (always one) and characters themselves double the total length at the output of the compressor.

Run-length encoding works well for images represented as pixels, such as on a video screen, because in the left-to-right pixel scan you often find long repetitions of the same color. (The compression approaches we're looking at here faithfully recreate the original data and so are called *lossless compression.*

**Cross-Reference**

In Chapter 18, we'll talk about another approach, *lossy compression,* which recreates something merely very close to the original data. Lossy compression isn't useful for compressing programs or spreadsheets, but it works very well for sound, image, and video — information in which small variations from the original aren't perceptible.)

Better compression than run-length encoding is possible, because we can incorporate what we know about the structure of the files we're compressing into the process. Let's return to the sample data that we couldn't compress, inserting spaces between words:

```
The quick brown fox jumped over the lazy dog
```

Suppose also that we have a dictionary stored with the compressor and decompressor, and that the dictionary looks like Table 16-3. Using the dictionary, we can represent entire words with short numbers. For example, we can represent the word "incorporate" with the number 17. Words that aren't in the dictionary don't yet have a number assigned but could be added at the end.

### Table 16-3
### This Dictionary Table Lets Numbers Represent Words

| Word | Index |
|------|-------|
| about | 1 |
| be | 2 |
| because | 3 |
| belonged | 4 |
| between | 5 |
| brown | 6 |
| can | 7 |
| compress | 8 |
| compressing | 9 |
| couldn't | 10 |
| data | 11 |
| dog | 12 |
| encoding | 13 |
| files | 14 |
| fox | 15 |
| how | 16 |
| incorporate | 17 |
| inserting | 18 |
| into | 19 |
| jumped | 20 |
| know | 21 |
| lazy | 22 |
| let's | 23 |
| of | 24 |
| over | 25 |
| process | 26 |
| quick | 27 |
| return | 28 |
| run-length | 29 |

| Word | Index |
|------|-------|
| sample | 30 |
| smarter | 31 |
| spaces | 32 |
| structure | 33 |
| than | 34 |
| the | 35 |
| they | 36 |
| to | 37 |
| we | 38 |
| we're | 39 |
| what | 40 |
| where | 41 |
| words | 42 |
| yet | 43 |

We can now write the sample sentence using only the short numbers:

```
35 27 6 15 20 25 35 22 12
```

Including the spaces between words, the compression ratio for this approach is 45 to 25, or 1.8 to 1, which is much better than the 2-to-1 expansion run-length encoding gave us.

The hard part in dictionary-based compression is having identical dictionaries for the compressor and decompressor to use that are guaranteed to contain the strings you want. Nearly all PC compression software, including WinZip (on the CD-ROM) and software that compresses for output to tape, solves this problem by building the dictionary on the fly as it compresses the data. That means that the first time a word is seen by the program, it both goes in the dictionary and is output by the compressor. Every time the word occurs thereafter, just the dictionary index gets sent.

Different compression software gives different results. For dictionary-based compression, the difference is often in how the software creates the dictionary — how big it lets the dictionary get, and how much of the input data it works over before resetting the dictionary. Looking at more data at once for redundant strings makes more compression opportunities available but takes more computation to process and can be slower.

# Picking Your Tape

The tape characteristics you need depend on what you plan to do with the tape. Saying you plan to back up your data to tape isn't enough. You need to consider how much you need to back up, how often, how automatic the process needs to be, and how often you expect to retrieve data from your backups. You also need to consider the software you'll use with the tape. For example, UNIX systems commonly let a tape drive look like a big, slow disk drive, making retrieval of files much simpler than with conventional backup software, and making tape more convenient for transmitting data from one place to another.

## How much will you back up?

How much you back up depends not only on how big the files you change or create are, but also what files you actually write to tape. You might choose to write more than just the new data. There are three major types of backups you might do:

✦ *Full backup* writes everything to tape, regardless of whether you've ever written it to tape before or not. More data gets written to tape with a full backup than with the other two approaches, but in return you get the security of knowing that you hold everything in your hand. Because everything is written to tape, you know that, should you need something back from the tape, it's there. You can't be surprised by finding out when it's too late that you're missing a critical file.

✦ *Incremental backup* is based on your full backup. You do a full backup to establish a baseline, after which you write to tape everything that's new or different since the last tape was written. To know not only that you have all your files, but also that you have the latest copy of every file, you have to have the original full backup you did plus every incremental tape you wrote since then. A restore from a combined full plus incremental backup is likely to leave files on disk you'd deleted before the restore.

✦ *Differential backup* is based on a full backup too but uses a different strategy than incremental backup. It writes to tape everything since the full backup. Instead of needing a sequence of tapes as does an incremental backup (the full backup plus every incremental backup since then), you only need the full backup plus the most recent differential backup to know you have the most recent version of everything. A restore from a combined full plus differential backup, like an incremental restore, is likely to leave files on disk you'd deleted before the restore.

Incremental and differential backups require careful tape management, because if you lose track of which tapes go with which other ones, or if you lose a tape, you're in trouble. The reason people use incremental or differential backups is that they can drastically reduce the amount of data they have to write to tape, saving a lot of time.

If you have a single machine with a limited amount of data — say, 1 to 2GB — you're probably better off simply backing up everything each time. You can easily and inexpensively do that to one tape, so you can even schedule the backup to run automatically. You'll never have to worry this way about whether you have what you need on tape.

If you have more data — say in the 3GB to 5GB range — you can still back it all up to one tape, but the drive costs more and the backup takes longer. The Seagate Hornet 8, for example, can back up as much as 4GB (uncompressed) to tape, but it will take over two hours, plus another two hours to verify the tape. If you leave the computer on overnight, you can conveniently schedule backups then. That's too long to wait while you're working, though, so if overnight backups aren't an option, you'll have to turn to a faster drive or to incremental or differential backups.

If you run a server, either for a LAN or for the Internet, you probably want to provide continuous (24-hour) operation. If so, you need to minimize the time you spend backing up so that you get the best performance possible out of your server. Incremental backups are a good choice in this situation.

If you run a server with a very large file system — tens to hundreds of gigabytes — you need more horsepower yet in your backup equipment. Many servers use DLT (Digital Linear Tape) or AIT (Advanced Intelligent Tape) tape systems. For the largest file systems, you'll want to look into hierarchical storage management (HSM), a technology that invisibly moves files among disk, optical, and tape storage while managing the location of everything for you. You may also want to look into jukeboxes, devices that (like the jukeboxes of the 1950s) move disks or tapes automatically from a filed location to a station where they can be read and written when required.

## How often will you back up?

The frequency with which you back up depends on how often you generate new or changed files, and on how difficult it would be to recover if you lost those files. The more work you do, and the harder it is to reconstruct your work, the more often you'll want to back up.

Backup strategies for file servers particularly need to take backup frequency into account. If you have a server handling files for hundreds of people, the cost of even a lost hour's worth of work can be enormous. The obvious answer is to back up all the time, but it's not really practical, and starting one incremental backup when the previous one finishes still can leave significant intervals between writing a file and backing it up. Instead, you can use a RAID disk array for redundancy. If you size the performance of the array to include the transfer rate needed to support backups during normal operation, you can run incremental backups to tape several times a day without risking your data or having an impact on the performance your users see.

# Products

The products in this chapter are the kinds of products you'd use in a desktop computer or a small to medium-sized server. Specifically, we'll look at Travan quarter-inch tapes, exemplified by the Seagate Hornet 8 drives, at the latest in DDS DAT drives, and at the high-speed, high-capacity AIT drives (see the sidebar "Space, The Final Frontier"). The products you would use to back up massive corporate file systems are highly varied and need to be integrated with your storage and network architecture. For example, you can get hierarchical storage systems for Windows NT that combine RAID disks, optical jukeboxes, and tape libraries, enabling you to securely store thousands of gigabytes online without a massive labor investment to handle the backup chores.

## Seagate Hornet Travan

The Seagate Hornet 8 uses the Travan TR-4 tape, providing 4GB capacity uncompressed and up to 8GB capacity compressed. The Hornet 20 uses the TR-5 Travan technology, storing 10GB per tape uncompressed and up to 20GB compressed. Figure 16-5 shows what the drives look like. Table 16-4 gives the key specifications.

## Space, the final frontier

Travan TR-5 and DAT DDS-4 are the latest versions, but they're not the biggest, fastest drives you can get. If you need more space and more speed from your tape, look at drives using the Sony Advanced Intelligent Tape (AIT) technology. For example, the Seagate Sidewinder 50 drive holds 25GB uncompressed on a single tape and transfers at 6 MBps. (Early field reports on the new compression technology in the Sidewinder 50 document compressed capacity up to 65GB.) Competitive drives (using other technology) include DLT, holding up to 20GB uncompressed and transferring at 1.5 MBps. A 35GB drive, the Sidewinder 70, is now available.

At the point you store that much data on one tape, finding what you're looking for becomes a serious issue. AIT technology includes a small flash-like memory, giving the drive fast access to directory information without rewinding to the start of the tape. Manufacturers using AIT claim access to data on the tape can be 50 percent faster than without the memory.

**Figure 16-5:** The Seagate Hornet drives offer a cost-effective backup solution for low to medium desktop file storage. (Courtesy Seagate Technology.)

| | Table 16-4 **Hornet Specifications** | |
|---|---|---|
| **Characteristic** | **Hornet 8** | **Hornet 20** |
| Format | QIC-3095 | QIC-3220 |
| Capacity | 4GB (uncompressed) up to 8GB (compressed 2:1)) | 10GB (uncompressed) up to 20GB (compressed 2:1) |
| Interface | ATAPI or SCSI | ATAPI or SCSI |
| Typical speed | 25–45MB per minute, depending computer and compression | 50–100MB per minute depending computer and compression |
| Form factor | 5.25 or 3.5 inch half-height | 5.25 or 3.5 inch half-height |
| Reliability | 330,000 hour MTBF, less than 1 × 1015 bit error rate | 330,000 hour MTBF, less than 1 × 1015 bit error rate |

The MTBF specification includes the assumption that the tape is moving only 20 percent of the time. This reflects the expectation that you're not going to do backups continuously; you do them once or twice a day at the most.

We installed a Hornet 8 in one of our computers. The initial physical installation went well, but because we had run out of 50-pin connectors on the Granite Digital cable connected to the SCSI wide port on an Adaptec AHA-2940UW, we had to connect the tape drive with a conventional cable to the narrow SCSI port on the host adapter. Doing that had two ramifications illustrating the importance of thinking through your I/O and upgrade plans:

✦ *Termination.* We didn't have a second narrow SCSI Granite Digital cable (which would provide active termination from the cable), so we had to rely on the terminations in the drive itself. Fortunately, the Hornet 8 features active terminators within the drive, making it particularly suited for faster SCSI systems.

✦ *External SCSI port.* Because we used both internal ports on the AHA-2940UW, we could no longer use the external port on the adapter. That meant we had to disconnect our scanner and move it to another machine.

We can't overstate the importance of choosing products from companies that have competent technical support. A unit from another major tape drive manufacturer never did work in the same computer — either in DOS or Windows — and we were never able to resolve the problem. That company's technical support staff never had anything to offer besides useless drivel, like saying we'd have to reinstall Windows to solve the problem, even though the drive was also inoperative from DOS. There's a critical message in that: Remember who builds good products and gives good support, and who doesn't.

The drive performs well, with the results shown in Table 16-5. Filling a TR-4 Travan tape, we can back up 5.8GB at once with compression turned on. The transfer rate we measured is near the upper end of the drive specification, something we've not always seen in older tape drives using other technologies. We had the backup software configured to compress for fastest backups, not to minimize space on the tape. The 5.8GB we get on that tape is enough to back up a few machines on a small local area network overnight. We can trade off speed for better compression, though, and increase the compression ratio. We've had the same backup software do 1.6-to-1 compression on that computer at its highest compression setting, which lets us store 6.4GB on the tape. You'll need to have your data compress as well as 2 to 1 to realize the 8GB tape capacity. We've never seen that happen.

If you're going to use software compression writing to tape, we suggest that you schedule backups at a time when little else is happening. Trying to use the computer while the backup runs can cause the processor to fall behind the tape, breaking the streaming data flow and drastically slowing the process.

| Table 16-5 | |
|---|---|
| **Travan TR-4 Performance** | |
| *Backup Characteristic* | *Measured Performance* |
| Backup volume | 3.3GB |
| Average data transfer rate | 37.56MB per minute |
| Backup time | 87 minutes |
| Compression ratio | 1.47 to 1 |

## Seagate Scorpion DAT

The Seagate Scorpion tape drives (Figure 16-6) are DDS format DAT drives. The usual external and 3.5-inch internal versions are available. Table 16-6 shows the drive specifications. The Scorpion 8, a DDS-2 drive, has capacity comparable to the TR-4 Travan drives. The Scorpion 24 has capacity comparable to Travan TR-5 units, while the Scorpion 96 autoloader exceeds anything available in Travan technology.

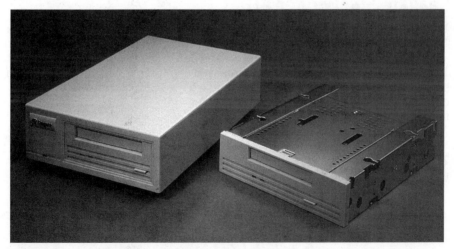

**Figure 16-6:** The Seagate Scorpion drives are DDS-format DAT drives. (Courtesy Seagate Technology.)

## Table 16-6
## Scorpion DAT Specifications

| Characteristic | Scorpion 8 | Scorpion 24 | Scorpion 96 |
|---|---|---|---|
| Capacity (uncompressed) (compressed) | 4GB 8GB | 12GB 24GB | 48GB 96GB |
| Backup performance | 30 to 66MB per minute | 66 to 132MB per minute | 66 to 132MB per minute |
| Tape drive interface | SCSI-2 | SCSI-2 | SCSI-2 |
| Format compatibility | DDS-2, DDS-DC, DDS, R-DAT | DDS-3, DDS-2, DDS-DC, DDS, R-DAT | DDS-3, DDS-2, DDS-DC, DDS, R-DAT |
| MTBF reliability (hours MTBF @ 20% tape motion) | 265,000 (Internal) 150,000 (External) | 265,000 (Internal) 150,000 (External) | 135,000 (Internal) 80,000 (External) |

## Seagate Sidewinder AIT

The Seagate Sidewinder tape drives (Figure 16-7) are AIT 3.5-inch form factor units. The internal version of the drive fits a 3.5-inch drive bay (or a 5.25-inch bay with an adapter bracket and faceplate). External and autoloader versions are also available. The Sidewinder 50 holds 25GB uncompressed and up to 50GB compressed on a single tape. The Sidewinder 70 extends capacity to 35/70GB (uncompressed/ compressed) by using a longer tape. The Sidewinder 200 autoloader mounts 4 AIT tapes for access by the 50GB drive, with a total capacity of to 100/200GB (uncompressed/compressed).

Table 16-7 shows the drive specifications. A 3MB per second uncompressed backup rate means you can back up 1GB in less than six minutes.

## Table 16-7
## Sidewinder AIT Specifications

| Characteristic | Sidewinder 50 | Sidewinder 70 | Sidewinder 200 |
|---|---|---|---|
| Capacity (uncompressed / compressed) | 25/50 | 35/70 | 100/200 |
| Backup performance MB per second (uncompressed / compressed) | 3.0 / 6.0 | 3.0 / 6.0 | 3.0 / 6.0 |

| Characteristic | Sidewinder 50 | Sidewinder 70 | Sidewinder 200 |
| --- | --- | --- | --- |
| Tape drive interface | Fast-Wide SCSI-2 | Fast-Wide SCSI-2 | Fast-Wide SCSI-2 |
| Internal buffer | 4MB | 4MB | 4MB |
| MTBF reliability (hours MTBF @ 20% tape motion) | 200,000 | 200,000 | 185,000 |

**Figure 16-7:** The Seagate Sidewinder drives are AIT-format drives. (Courtesy Seagate Technology.)

# Backup Practices

It's easy for even casual users to generate a significant amount of changed data in a day, so we recommend you run backups at least every night. Automatic backup is worthwhile because it lets an office run backups overnight when they won't interfere with anything else going on. If the backups are going to be automatic and unattended, all the data has to fit on one tape. A nightly full backup is probably out of the question without a drive the capacity of the larger DAT or AIT units, which are much more expensive than the Travan tapes. Instead of a full backup, you can use a cycle of incremental or differential backups between regularly scheduled full backups. The full backups will have to be done during the day so that the tape can be changed when it fills.

If you're restricted to a combination of full and incremental/differential backups, you could use a simple backup plan in which you do full backups on Fridays with incremental backups in between. Be sure to alternate the full backups across at least two sets of tapes so that you're never overwriting the previous full set. Here's the basic plan:

1. *Friday (cycle 1).* Write a full backup to a tape labeled FRIDAY-1.

2. *Monday.* Write an incremental backup to a tape labeled MONDAY.

3. *Tuesday.* Write an incremental backup to a tape labeled TUESDAY.

4. *Wednesday.* Write an incremental backup to a tape labeled WEDNESDAY.

5. *Thursday.* Write an incremental backup to a tape labeled THURSDAY.

6. *Friday (cycle 2).* Write a full backup to a tape labeled FRIDAY-2.

7. *Monday.* Write an incremental backup to a tape labeled MONDAY.

8. *Tuesday.* Write an incremental backup to a tape labeled TUESDAY.

9. *Wednesday.* Write an incremental backup to a tape labeled WEDNESDAY.

10. *Thursday.* Write an incremental backup to a tape labeled THURSDAY.

11. *Friday (cycle 1).* Write a full backup to a tape labeled FRIDAY-1.

12. *Monday.* Write an incremental backup to a tape labeled MONDAY.

13. Continue with this pattern.

The idea is that you write full backups on Fridays and incremental backups during the week. This plan takes five tapes plus however many a full backup takes, but your data on tape are never at risk. You'll want to periodically use another tape for a full backup that you store offsite, ensuring a measure of protection in the event of catastrophe.

This is a minimum scheme for business applications, because the backup sets are overwritten every two weeks. That means that if you accidentally delete an important file, you have only two weeks to detect the loss and restore the file. Go any longer and the file is probably gone forever. A more comprehensive strategy would use four sets of full backup tapes in cycle and would retire one set a month to archival storage (replacing it with a new set). The retired sets could be brought out of storage after a year or more, providing comprehensive data loss protection.

You might want to tailor your backup strategies to limit the data they lose in a catastrophic failure. For example, in addition to a strategy like the one just described, it's possible to configure the backup software to write out just the critical data and write a tape during lunch. A critical data-specific backup combined with the incremental strategy ensures that data loss can never exceed half a day, and still restricts the backup operation to times when the computer is relatively unused. Writing a critical data tape is easier if you confine the information you're working on to a single folder (possibly with subfolders under the top level). The noon tape contains that folder and everything below it. Using a critical data folder ensures that you don't accidentally omit something important from the backup.

Here's a snapshot of the folder tree we used to implement this idea writing this book:

```
IDG Books
   PCURB 3E
   Proposal and Startup
           Development
                   Author's Kit
           Correspondence
                   Machine Construction
           Chapters Not Started—Material
                   Benchmark Data
           Questions
           Chapters For Rework
           Transmitted Chapters
           Work In Progress
                   Chapter 11
                   Chapter 12
                   Chapter 13
                   Chapter 14
                   Chapter 15
                   Etc.
```

Besides keeping different kinds of material well organized, the tree cleanly separates the material that needs frequent backups. The Work In Progress folder contains all the material we're actively working on, so if we back up that folder, we've captured all the day's efforts. At the point we wrote this section, the Work In Progress folder contained 241MB of data. The larger tree, PCURB 3E, contained 854MB. Backing up just the Work In Progress directory shortens the time to do the backup to 28 percent of what the larger folder would require, 2.1 percent of what the drive I have the book on requires, and 1.7 percent of the overall computer's files. The complete backups we do nightly catch everything, so even if we change a file outside the critical folder, we're still protected.

Here's a reasonable question: Why do we use a full backup on the critical data rather than a differential or incremental backup on some larger scope? The answer is that the full backup ensures that we don't have to go searching for files on other tapes, and the amount of data isn't that large.

# Top Support Questions

A lot of different questions come up relating to tape drives, reflecting the need for the hardware, drivers, and software to all work together. Beyond these questions, many of the problems you'll see related to the less-standardized support available for proprietary, floppy-based, and ATAPI tape drives; our experience is that SCSI tape drives are often easier to integrate and use.

## QIC

Q: My floppy-based (QIC) tape drive gives me "Tape not formatted or unreadable by drive" errors, is constantly stopping and starting, or gives me "DMA specified for this device may be incorrect" errors. What's wrong?

A: Experiment with turning off the "High Speed Burst Transfers," "Concurrent Hard Disk Access," and/or "Concurrent Video Update" options in the Windows Device Manager for your drive. Incompatibility with overlapped operations or an inability of your motherboard to handle the fastest DMA transfers can cause these errors.

**Tip**

Better yet, replace the drive with a newer Travan unit. The floppy-based drives are old, slow, and not really worth continuing to fight with. You'll get more capacity on tape along with faster and more reliable backups, and you should only have to spend a few hundred dollars. If your data is important to you, it's a good investment.

## SCSI tapes

Q: During any tape operation, I get messages reporting controller or other hardware errors. The hardware checks out OK. What should I check?

A: Examples of this situation in Seagate Backup Exec for Windows 95 is that it reports either of the following error messages: "Tape Controller is not Responding 07-1F-21-01-0002" OR "ASPI Manager has reported an Error 07-1F-21-01-0002." This can happen if the driver causes a SCSI bus reset when the hard drive or CD-ROM is idle for more than 10 seconds. The reset can cause the tape drive to abort the present operation, leading to the error. Because the problem is due to an interaction between the disk or CD-ROM and your tape drive, the reset only happens in multiple SCSI device setups. You can fix the problem by allowing the tape drive to "disconnect" from the SCSI bus while it's working on a command. You enable disconnection in your SCSI controllers BIOS, changing the setting for the SCSI ID used by the tape drive.

## DAT

Q: When can I remove my DAT or Travan tape from the drive?

A: Don't take the tape out unless the tape drive status lights tell you it's OK. On a DAT drive, you'll typically find a drive status light and a tape status light. Wait for the drive status light to go out and stay out before removing the tape. On a Travan drive, there's typically only one light; wait for that light to go out and stay out before removing the tape. Don't remove a tape from a DAT drive by grasping the tape — use the eject button on the drive.

Q: How long does a DDS tape last?

A: The high-speed rotation of the DAT head past the tape wears the oxide and eventually leads to errors. Overall, you can expect about 2,000 passes over a section of tape. The drive makes as many as 6 passes over the tape in a single backup run, though, so practically speaking you can expect the tape to last for 100 backup or restore cycles. That means that if you use a tape weekly in your standard backup cycle, it will last for two years.

Q: Can I use regular DAT audio tapes in my DDS drive?

A: DDS tapes are engineered specifically for data storage and are higher quality than audio tapes. DDS drives will attempt to read audio DAT tapes, but will not write to them. You're better off with DDS media.

Q: Can my DDS drive record music?

A: Not the way a DAT drive will, because there are no connections on DDS drives for microphones or headphones. You can record digital audio files from your computer onto tape, but they're simply files.

Q: Do I need to clean my DAT drive?

A: Yes, following the manufacturer's instructions. If you back up a full tape nightly, you'll probably want to clean the drive weekly.

Q: Can I use newer DDS tapes in my drive than it was originally built to use?

A: No. DDS-1 drives can only read and write DDS-1 tapes. DDS-2 drives can only read and write DDS-1 and DDS-2 tapes, not DDS-3. This is because the magnetic oxide coatings on newer tapes require write currents and read amplifier settings not possible in the older drives. Typically, if you put a DDS-2 tape in a DDS-1 drive, or a DDS-3 tape in a DDS-2 or DDS-1 drive, it will be ejected immediately.

Q: How long is it safe to store tapes?

A: Manufacturers claim a data retention life of 30 years when the tape is properly stored in a dry, cool, nonmagnetic place. We'd never rely on a tape that long — plan on reading out and rewriting the tape at least every five years.

## Backup software

Q: What's the Registry, and why do I care about backing it up?

A: Operating systems and application software need to store information about configurations and preferences you've defined. That information includes how to set up your hardware configuration, how your desktop should appear, where to find application files, and more. UNIX reads and writes that data from a relatively large number of files, the identity of which can be somewhat hard to track down. Windows used to store the data in the system.ini and windows.ini files (along with a flock of application-specific files) but now stores it in a structure called the *Registry*. If you lose the Registry, you'll have to rebuild your entire Windows and application software installation up from bare metal, or restore from a backup.

# Hands-On Upgrades

Both floppy-based tape drives and SCSI units are easy to add to your system. IDE drives are somewhat less common, and require you to think through what device is on what IDE port.

## Adding a tape drive

Let's look at adding a SCSI-2 DAT tape drive to an existing system. The mechanical procedure is the same as for disks and CD-ROMs — you attach brackets if you're mounting a 3.5-inch drive in a 5.25-inch bay, then screw the assembly into the chassis.

Before you mount the drive, though, you'll want to work through the settings for the switches and jumpers on the drive. Figure 16-8 shows the switches on the bottom of a Seagate Scorpion 8 DAT drive, the Model STD28000-N. Here's what each switch does:

✦ *S1-S3 — SCSI ID.* Pick an unused SCSI ID and program it into these three switches. The default is ID 0, but usually you'd want to reserve 0 and 1 for hard disks.

✦ *S4 — MRS Mode.* The drive is capable of detecting physically coded DDS cartridges using the Media Recognition System (MRS). If you turn S4 on, the drive disables MRS and will read or write cartridges regardless of the presence of MRS coding. If S4 is off, the drive will read any cartridge but will only write to MRS-coded ones. Typically you'd leave MRS enabled.

✦ *S5 — SCSI Parity Checking.* You can have the drive parity-check data from the SCSI bus by turning on S5. You'll want to do that for the greatest data integrity protection.

3.5 inch to 5.25 inch
mounting bracket  DAT tape drive   Configuration switches   Configuration switch legend

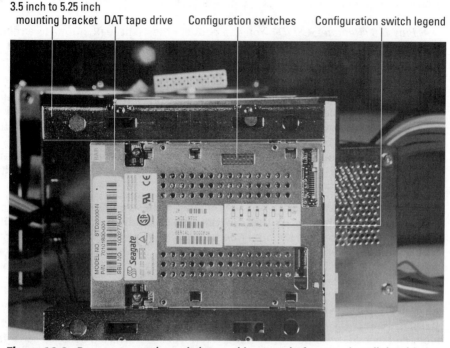

**Figure 16-8:** Be sure to set the switches and jumpers before you install the drive.

✦ *S6—Data Compression.* S6, confusingly called *DDS Pass-Through Mode* by Seagate, controls the default for whether hardware-assisted data compression is enabled or disabled on the drive. Turning S6 off enables data compression. Regardless of the S6 setting, software can override the data compression setting by a command over the SCSI bus.

✦ *S8—POST.* You can direct the drive to perform a Power-On Self Test (POST) when it receives power by turning on S8. The test takes about five seconds, which is less than the corresponding processor boot time before it initializes the SCSI adapters, so the drive should be ready to respond to commands by then. Enabling POST is a good idea to be sure the drive is capable of operation when you need it.

Switch S7 is for factory use and should be left at the factory setting (off for this drive). It's common for drives to have factory-only switches that enable manufacturing tests. The functions those switches enable generally aren't useful under normal circumstances.

After you set the switches, check the jumpers. Here's what you have to work with:

✦ *Pins 1–6 (Remote SCSI ID).* You can connect these three positions to a remote SCSI ID switch (such as if you're putting the drive in an external case that you'll move from one computer to another). If you're using S1–S3 to control the ID, leave these three positions open.

✦ *Pins 11–12 (Termination).* The drive will provide active termination for the end of the SCSI cable if you jumper these two pins. If the drive isn't at the end of the cable, remove the jumper. Because you get active termination, it's better to use this drive at the end of the cable than another device with passive terminators. Don't try to use the drive to terminate a wide SCSI cable, though, because it only connects to the narrow part of the bus — you'd end up with the wide part unterminated.

✦ *Pins 15–16 (Terminator Power).* If you jumper these pins, the drive will supply power to terminators in other devices. The host adapter usually does that, so jumpering these pins shouldn't be necessary. If you do enable terminator power and happen to connect the SCSI cable backward, you'll likely blow a fuse inside the drive. If that happens, the drive won't supply terminator power until it's repaired.

Leave the other pins (7–8, 9–10, and 13–14) unconnected. Mount the drive in the chassis, connect the data and power cables, and power up the computer. Watch the boot sequence for your SCSI adapter (if it reports the devices it sees) to see if the tape drive shows up. If it doesn't, check the data and power cables, the terminators, and the SCSI IDs.

Once the adapter recognizes the drive, check that you've enabled disconnection for the tape and let the operating system boot. The operating system may not inherently recognize the drive (Windows 95, for example, doesn't report SCSI tape drives in the Device Manager until you install drivers, which themselves usually come with the backup software). Install the software compatible with your operating system that came with the drive. Under UNIX, you may have to make up a device node in the /dev directory.

**Cross-Reference**    We show you how to make up a device node in Chapter 40.

Once you've installed the software, do a test backup, and verify the backup against the files on disk. Until you do that, you have no assurance that things are really working right.

The final step is to create standard backup jobs (such as ones for full and incremental backups), save them, and schedule them if you'll be using automatic backups. Be sure to do a test backup and verify the results to make sure the standard jobs are working right!

# Summary

✦ The QIC standards help ensure that your hardware, software, and Windows will all work together properly.

✦ The Travan and DAT technologies pack more data onto a quarter-inch tape drive than do QIC tapes, with uncompressed capacity up to 12GB.

✦ The results from data compression depend on your software and on what's on your disk. You can expect somewhere between 1.4-to-1 and 2-to-1 compression. Compression can speed the rate data flows to your tape by reducing the number of bytes actually written.

✦ A backup strategy that fits the capacity and performance of your tape drive to the size, criticality, and volatility of your data is the key to keeping your data safe.

✦    ✦    ✦

# Video

**Y**our monitor and video display board are a pair, much like a disk and its controller. The capabilities of the monitor must match the needs of the display modes requested by your software. To understand how the monitor and video board work together and contribute to the performance of your computer, we'll start at the monitor and work inward through the functions of the video board.

## A Computer Monitor Is Not the Same as a Television

Although much of what a computer monitor does appears similar to what a television does, the capabilities of a computer are much more complex. A television that meets the North American standard, for example, displays roughly 525 × 700 pixels, with a viewable area smaller than those numbers. The European Phase Alternating Line (PAL) standard is a little different at 625 × 833 pixels but close to the same size. The most basic computer monitor meeting the Video Graphics Array (VGA) standard displays no fewer than 640 × 480 pixels — all viewable — with high-end monitors capable of resolutions of 1,600 × 1,200 pixels and more. It is for this reason that products that display television in a window on the computer screen are fairly inexpensive and work well, but products that display computer images on televisions are limited to basic VGA resolutions and often smear the images.

The image you see on your monitor is created by your programs and operating system. If you look closely at the screen, you'll see a pattern of tiny colored dots that, when each is lit up at the right brightness, forms the picture you see. These dots are *pixels* (picture elements). The chain of electronics that delivers this image to you runs from the face of the cathode ray tube (CRT) back through the monitor electronics, to the video display card, and on back into the rest of the computer. Figure 17-1 shows the major elements in the monitor, including the tube itself and its electronics. A single electron beam sweeps across the tube in a left-to-right, top-to-bottom pattern. The CRT deflection coil, driven by the horizontal and vertical deflection amplifiers, moves the beam in its pattern. The video amplifiers switch the beam on and off to control which of the dots on the face of the screen are illuminated, and how brightly. The video input stages in the monitor electronics get synchronization timing from the VGA signals and use it to control the horizontal and vertical deflection amplifiers.

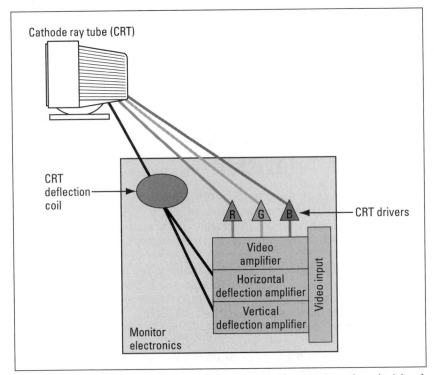

**Figure 17-1:** A computer monitor is similar to the video section of a television but has higher-performance characteristics suited for high-resolution information display.

## Painting pictures on the screen

Figure 17-2 shows in more detail the process of drawing a picture by sweeping the dots on the screen. One complete traverse of the screen starts at position ❶ and moves to the right. At the end of the line ❷ the beam rapidly moves down and to the left. The beam is turned off, moving to ❸ and the start of the next line. The sweep of the second line takes the beam to the right, ending at ❹. This process continues with the beam moving downward until the pattern finishes at ❺. The beam then turns off and moves back to ❶ to repeat the process.

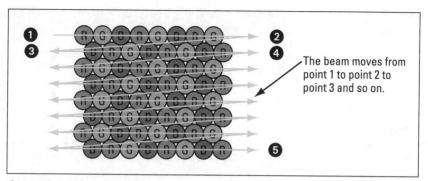

**Figure 17-2:** The picture on your screen is an array of red, green, and blue dots. The beam sweeps left to right and top to bottom to illuminate each dot in turn.

The pattern of brightness that the beam delivers while sweeping over the dots determines the picture you see. For example, a completely blue screen results if the beam is off for the red and green dots but on for the blue ones. The brightness of the blue dots is controlled by the brightness of the beam when it's over each of the dots. More complex pictures are simply combinations of red, green, and blue dots at the right brightness. Your eye sees the composition of the individual dots as a complete image.

## It's all in the numbers

Each complete pass from the top to the bottom of the screen is called a *frame*, and the number of complete frames per second is the *frame rate*. The Video Electronics Standards Association (VESA) commonly recommends a frame rate of 75 frames per second (a recent update suggests 85 frames per second; televisions refresh at 30 complete frames per second). Their recommended frame rate ensures that your eye will not see the successive frames being drawn, which appears as flicker. Part of the performance your monitor electronics have to deliver is measured in terms of maximum vertical and horizontal frequencies. These are critical parameters in the design of the vertical and horizontal deflection amplifiers shown in Figure 17-1. The performance you need from your monitor depends on the display resolution (horizontal and vertical sizes, in pixels) and on the frame rate. Knowing these two parameters allows you to compute the requirements for your monitor. (Refer to the sidebar "Computing monitor line rates" to determine your monitor's requirements.)

Let's look at the vertical and horizontal frequency specifications for an excellent monitor, the 21-inch Hitachi SuperScan 814 (Model CM814U). We write our books on an earlier model from the 21-inch SuperScan series, and its size and clarity make the job much easier. The 814 offers a maximum horizontal frequency of 125 kHz, and a maximum vertical frequency of 160 Hz. The individual dots on the screen are so close together that you can't see them separately. All the VESA recommended specifications shown in the table in the sidebar "Computing monitor line rates" are supported. The 1,600 × 1,200 resolution provides added workspace that's wonderful when you're doing complex work or running many different programs at once.

## Computing monitor line rates

The resolution of your screen combines with the frame rate to determine the performance your monitor must deliver. The following table shows the computed line rates for a variety of common Windows screen resolutions at the VESA-recommended 85 frames per second. The frame rate has to be no higher than the monitor's maximum vertical frequency. The number of lines drawn on the screen (the line rate, which is the vertical size times the frame rate) has to be no higher than the maximum horizontal frequency. The computed line rate is less than what the monitor must actually deliver, because all displays draw a few lines above and below the actual image, increasing the total line count. The increase incorporated by VESA for overscan is generally an additional four percent.

| Horizontal Size (Pixels) | Vertical Size (Pixels) | VESA Frame Rate (Hz) | Computed Line Rate (Hz) | 104% Vertical Overscan (Hz) |
|---|---|---|---|---|
| 640 | 480 | 85 | 40,800 | 42,432 |
| 800 | 600 | 85 | 51,000 | 53,040 |
| 1,024 | 768 | 85 | 65,280 | 67,891 |
| 1,280 | 1,024 | 85 | 87,040 | 90,522 |
| 1,600 | 1,200 | 85 | 102,000 | 106,080 |

For example, at 640 × 480 resolution in the table, the line rate is 480 pixels times the 85 Hz frame rate, or 40.8 kHz. Incorporating vertical overscan at 104 percent, the monitor needs to support a line rate of 42.4 kHz.

Interlacing, the same technique that reduces the horizontal frequency requirements in a television, can be used to reduce the performance required from computer monitors as well. Unlike the row-by-row scan shown in Figure 17-2, an interlaced display scans every other line and then goes back to the top and scans the lines it skipped. Each half-scan is called a field, with one frame consisting of two sequential fields. Interlacing cuts the frame rate in half, so it reduces the frequencies the monitor must support. This makes the deflection amplifiers less expensive but causes flicker perceptible to many people.

Is the cost of a monitor like this — around US $1,400 in early 1999, and close to US $1,000 for other 21-inch models in the SuperScan line — worth it? The difference our 21-inch monitor made for us — replacing a good-quality 17-inch monitor — was far more dramatic than we expected. If you do a lot of things at once, if your vision is less than perfect and you can really benefit from a larger image, or if you regularly give demonstrations on your monitor, then in our opinion a monitor of this size and quality is a sound investment that will serve you well for many years. The size and sharpness of this screen means we can run 1,600 × 1,200 resolution and retain excellent readability. The 600 × 1,200 display provides over six times the number of pixels as a conventional VGA display at 640 × 480. We regularly keep seven major applications open at once (Word, Excel, Outlook, and Powerpoint from Microsoft Office, Adobe Photoshop and Illustrator, and Microsoft Internet Explorer), along with a number of accessory programs, so the additional screen space we get from using a very high display resolution means we can work with all those windows at the same time without losing track of what's going on. That capability lets us work faster and more efficiently.

**Tip**   The ability to keep many windows open and visible at the same time is a big productivity boost. For example, we can leave a spreadsheet open on the left side of the screen and write about its results into a document on the right side. Or we can see two full-size pages of text side by side without switching programs (four if we squint a little). If a 21-inch monitor is too expensive or to too big for your work area, look at the 20- and 19-inch monitors now available. You can get a 20-inch monitor for under $580, and a 19-inch unit for under $360.

**Note**   Cost issues aside, you have to consider where to put a large monitor. They are much heavier than smaller ones (the Hitachi weighs 61 pounds!), and are deeper from front to back. Large monitors also have relatively short cables to attach to your computer in order to avoid distorting the much higher-frequency signals they receive from the video board in the higher-resolution modes. You can attach a cable extender to one of these monitors, but unless you get very high quality, low capacitance cables, the distortion an extender introduces into the signals creates ghosts on the screen. The best option is to ensure that the connector on the back of the display card is close enough to the monitor without an extension.

Two other critical specifications for a monitor are the horizontal and vertical dot pitch. As Figure 17-3 shows, these numbers specify the spacing between the adjacent groups of red/green/blue dots. *Dot pitch* measures the detail the tube in the monitor can render. Finer dot pitch is better but increases cost. The horizontal and vertical dot-pitch specifications for a given monitor are not necessarily the same; there is often some confusion when only a single specification is given. The vertical pitch should be specified in that case (but we've seen instances where only the horizontal value was given).

Table 17-1 shows the required maximum dot pitch for a variety of screen resolutions and sizes. You can determine the maximum display resolution a monitor can support by using this table (assuming the display electronics also meet minimum requirements). The screen size is in inches, the resolution, in pixels, and the pitch, in millimeters (reflecting the complete schizophrenia the industry has about consistent units of measurement). The aspect ratio is the horizontal size (in pixels) divided by the vertical size (also in pixels). The aspect ratio for most common display modes is 1.33, with the only standard exception being the 1,280 × 1,024 mode (which has an aspect ratio of 1.25).

Dot pitch measures how closely the RGB triads are packed. Here, I show the vertical dot pitch measurements as the distance between the gaps on top of stacked blue dots. You could equally measure the distance between vertically-stacked red centers, etc.

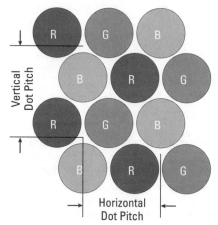

The same idea as for vertical pitch applies horizontally, except that packing the triads evenly requires that colors be offset in adjacent triads. I've measured here between corresponding gaps preceding green dots

**Figure 17-3:** Dot pitch measures the detail the tube in the monitor can render. Finer dot pitch is better but increases cost.

## Table 17-1
### Maximum Dot Pitch for Varying Monitor Screen Size and Display Resolution

| Display Resolution Horizontal/Vertical | 14 H/V | 15 H/V | 17 H/V | 19 H/V | 20 H/V | 21 H/V |
|---|---|---|---|---|---|---|
| 640/480 | 0.44/0.44 | 0.48/0.48 | 0.54/0.54 | 0.60/0.60 | 0.64/0.64 | 0.67/0.67 |
| 800/600 | 0.36/0.36 | 0.38/0.38 | 0.43/0.43 | 0.48/0.48 | 0.51/0.51 | 0.53/0.53 |
| 1,024/768 | 0.28/0.28 | 0.30/0.30 | 0.34/0.34 | 0.38/0.38 | 0.40/0.40 | 0.42/0.42 |
| 1,152/864 | 0.25/0.25 | 0.26/0.26 | 0.30/0.30 | 0.34/0.34 | 0.35/0.35 | 0.37/0.37 |
| 1,280/1,024 | 0.22/0.21 | 0.24/0.22 | 0.27/0.25 | 0.30/0.28 | 0.32/0.30 | 0.33/0.31 |
| 1,600/1,200 | 0.18/0.18 | 0.19/0.19 | 0.22/0.22 | 0.24/0.24 | 0.25/0.25 | 0.27/0.27 |
| 2,048/1,536 | 0.14/0.14 | 0.15/0.15 | 0.17/0.17 | 0.19/0.19 | 0.20/0.20 | 0.21/0.21 |

For a constant screen size, the required pitch becomes finer (smaller numbers) as the screen resolution increases, reflecting the need to cram more pixels into a smaller space. The allowed pitch becomes larger for a constant resolution as the screen size increases, because there is more space in which to draw the pixels. Table 17-1 shows why a 0.28 mm dot pitch was for a long time the standard in the industry—it is the coarsest dot pitch that will support the 1,024 × 768 resolution on a 14-inch monitor. Current monitors now often boast dot pitch of 0.25 mm or smaller, permitting a 20-inch unit to display 1,600 × 1,200 resolution.

 **Tip**

The Hitachi 21-inch monitor provides a 0.22 mm vertical dot pitch (0.16 mm vertically) and will support 1,856 × 1,392 display resolution. Lesser-performance 21-inch monitors may have 0.28 mm dot pitch or larger, which limits them to 1,280 × 1,024 resolution and below. We've seen 21-inch monitor specification sheets that acknowledged the inadequate resolution provided by a 0.28 dot pitch tube and then boasted that the monitor electronics would deliver 1,600 × 1,200 resolution. You wouldn't want to own one of those.

If you have a choice, don't buy a monitor from a specification sheet—see it perform before you buy it. Even better is to choose a few competitors and then compare them side by side.

# The Video Board Converts a Torrent of Data into Signals for the Monitor

The monitor plugs into the VGA connector on the back of the video display board. Figure 17-4 adds some detail to the video board top-level block diagram from Chapter 4 ("Choke Points—Where Your Computer Slows Down") to show more of the components that determine capabilities and performance.

Because the brightness of the beam must be critically synchronized to the position of the beam on the screen, the display board timing controls the scan frequencies of the monitor as well as the operation of the board. All the signal timing is controlled by the dot clock, which is a signal within the video board that pulses once every time the beam on the screen passes a set of three dots (one each red, green, and blue). The set of three dots is a pixel. For example, if the display is set to 640 × 480 resolution, the dot clock pulses 640 times as the beam traverses once from left to right on the screen over the visible part of the image. The dot clock continues to pulse as the beam makes its fast retrace from right to left, and then it repeats the cycle for the next line. Ignoring overscan and retrace, the dot clock frequency is the resolution of the screen times the number of frames per second. For a display at 1,280 × 1,024 at 75 Hz, the dot clock runs at slightly over 98 MHz.

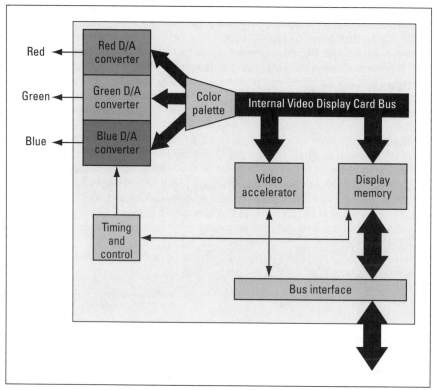

**Figure 17-4:** A video board lives or dies by how fast it moves data around.

## Merely fast memory isn't good enough for video

An analog to digital (A/D) converter is a device that outputs a signal corresponding to the number fed to the converter. If the converter receives a zero value, it outputs a zero signal. If it receives a large number, it outputs a large signal. There are three A/D converters on a video board, one each for the red, green, and blue signals sent to the monitor. The dot clock times the arrival of pixel data from the display memory at the A/D converters, sending a new pixel value for each clock pulse. Suppose the display is in a 256-color mode, so one byte encodes one pixel. In the previous example of a 98 MHz dot clock (1,280 × 1,024 at 75 Hz), the display memory must provide data to the D/A converters at 94MB per second (don't be confused — 1MB = 1,048,576 bytes, 1 MHz = 1,000,000 Hz). If you run 24-bit color, the memory must feed the D/A converters at 281 MHz. Table 17-2 shows the bus data rates for some other video modes.

As we saw in Chapter 7, "Processor, Memory, and Bus," the bus data rates shown in Table 17-2 are faster than the buses found in Windows computers. Achieving this constant, extremely fast flow of data to the D/A converters across the internal video board bus led designers to many of the same techniques used in main buses, including making the bus wider to get more out of each bus cycle and using optimized bus cycles to speed access. The completely predictable pattern in which the pixels are read from the memory (left to right, top to bottom on the display) also allows fast bus cycles that take advantage of the memory architecture. It's not marketing hype that video cards have gone to a 64- or 128-bit internal bus — making the bus wider reduces the bus cycle rate for the worst case in Table 17-2 (the last line) to a little over 47 MHz for a 128-bit bus. Comparing that rate to the 33 MHz speed of the PCI bus clock (or the 66 MHz rate for the 64-bit PCI clock) suggests that the added width was required to keep the electronics reliable at low consumer product prices. The high resolutions and frame rates common in systems today generate amazingly high data rates between display memory and the D/A converters, demanding improved architectures rather than a brute force faster clock.

## Table 17-2
## Data Rates between Display Memory and D/A Converters

| Horizontal Size (Pixels) | Vertical Size (Pixels) | Color Depth (Bytes) | Frame Rate (Hz) | Data Rate to D/A Converters (MBps) | Dot Clock (MHz) | 64-bit Bus Clock (MHz) | 128-bit Bus Clock (MHz) |
|---|---|---|---|---|---|---|---|
| 640 | 480 | 1 | 75 | 21.97 | 21.97 | 2.75 | 1.37 |
| 640 | 480 | 2 | 75 | 43.95 | 21.97 | 5.49 | 2.75 |
| 640 | 480 | 3 | 75 | 65.92 | 21.97 | 8.24 | 4.12 |
| 640 | 480 | 1 | 85 | 24.90 | 24.90 | 3.11 | 1.56 |
| 640 | 480 | 2 | 85 | 49.80 | 24.90 | 6.23 | 3.11 |
| 640 | 480 | 3 | 85 | 74.71 | 24.90 | 9.34 | 4.67 |
| 800 | 600 | 1 | 75 | 34.33 | 34.33 | 4.29 | 2.15 |
| 800 | 600 | 2 | 75 | 68.66 | 34.33 | 8.58 | 4.29 |
| 800 | 600 | 3 | 75 | 103.00 | 34.33 | 12.87 | 6.44 |
| 800 | 600 | 1 | 85 | 38.91 | 38.91 | 4.86 | 2.43 |
| 800 | 600 | 2 | 85 | 77.82 | 38.91 | 9.73 | 4.86 |
| 800 | 600 | 3 | 85 | 116.73 | 38.91 | 14.59 | 7.30 |
| 1,024 | 768 | 1 | 75 | 56.25 | 56.25 | 7.03 | 3.52 |
| 1,024 | 768 | 2 | 75 | 112.50 | 56.25 | 14.06 | 7.03 |

*continued*

## Table 17-2 (continued)

| Horizontal Size (Pixels) | Vertical Size (Pixels) | Color Depth (Bytes) | Frame Rate (Hz) | Data Rate to D/A Converters (MBps) | Dot Clock (MHz) | 64-bit Bus Clock (MHz) | 128-bit Bus Clock (MHz) |
|---|---|---|---|---|---|---|---|
| 1,024 | 768 | 3 | 75 | 168.75 | 56.25 | 21.09 | 10.55 |
| 1,024 | 768 | 1 | 85 | 63.75 | 63.75 | 7.97 | 3.98 |
| 1,024 | 768 | 2 | 85 | 127.50 | 63.75 | 15.94 | 7.97 |
| 1,024 | 768 | 3 | 85 | 191.25 | 63.75 | 23.91 | 11.95 |
| 1,280 | 1,024 | 1 | 75 | 93.75 | 93.75 | 11.72 | 5.86 |
| 1,280 | 1,024 | 2 | 75 | 187.50 | 93.75 | 23.44 | 11.72 |
| 1,280 | 1,024 | 3 | 75 | 281.25 | 93.75 | 35.16 | 17.58 |
| 1,280 | 1,024 | 1 | 85 | 106.25 | 106.25 | 13.28 | 6.64 |
| 1,280 | 1,024 | 2 | 85 | 212.50 | 106.25 | 26.56 | 13.28 |
| 1,280 | 1,024 | 3 | 85 | 318.75 | 106.25 | 39.84 | 19.92 |
| 1,600 | 1,200 | 1 | 75 | 137.33 | 137.33 | 17.17 | 8.58 |
| 1,600 | 1,200 | 2 | 75 | 274.66 | 137.33 | 34.33 | 17.17 |
| 1,600 | 1,200 | 3 | 75 | 411.99 | 137.33 | 51.50 | 25.75 |
| 1,600 | 1,200 | 1 | 85 | 155.64 | 155.64 | 19.45 | 9.73 |
| 1,600 | 1,200 | 2 | 85 | 311.28 | 155.64 | 38.91 | 19.45 |
| 1,600 | 1,200 | 3 | 85 | 466.92 | 155.64 | 58.36 | 29.18 |
| 1,800 | 1,440 | 1 | 75 | 185.39 | 185.39 | 23.17 | 11.59 |
| 1,800 | 1,440 | 2 | 75 | 370.79 | 185.39 | 46.35 | 23.17 |
| 1,800 | 1,440 | 3 | 75 | 556.18 | 185.39 | 69.52 | 34.76 |
| 1,800 | 1,440 | 1 | 85 | 210.11 | 210.11 | 26.26 | 13.13 |
| 1,800 | 1,440 | 2 | 85 | 420.23 | 210.11 | 52.53 | 26.26 |
| 1,800 | 1,440 | 3 | 85 | 630.34 | 210.11 | 78.79 | 39.40 |
| 2,048 | 1,536 | 1 | 75 | 225.00 | 225.00 | 28.13 | 14.06 |
| 2,048 | 1,536 | 2 | 75 | 450.00 | 225.00 | 56.25 | 28.13 |
| 2,048 | 1,536 | 3 | 75 | 675.00 | 225.00 | 84.38 | 42.19 |
| 2,048 | 1,536 | 1 | 85 | 255.00 | 255.00 | 31.88 | 15.94 |
| 2,048 | 1,536 | 2 | 85 | 510.00 | 255.00 | 63.75 | 31.88 |
| 2,048 | 1,536 | 3 | 85 | 765.00 | 255.00 | 95.63 | 47.81 |

## Sixteen million is a whole lot of colors

Three different pixel formats are shown in Table 17-2 — one, two, and three bytes — corresponding to the three most common Windows color settings. (A 4-byte, 32-bit format is also available.) One-byte pixels can specify 256 colors. Two-byte pixels — called High Color — can specify 65,536 colors. Three-byte pixels — called True Color — can specify 16,777,216 colors.

> When you're using 24 bits of color, most people can't see the difference between two adjacent colors. It also becomes hard to name them.
>
> Microsoft Beta Tester T-Shirt

Each of the three D/A converters (one each for red, green, and blue) accepts one byte at a time, so some work is needed to be able to feed all three pixel formats to the converters. Figure 17-5 shows the options. In 24-bit display modes, one of the three bytes in a pixel goes to each of the three converters. In 16-bit modes, the 16-bit value is split into fields (usually five bits for red, six for green, and five for blue). The fields are extracted from the value and sent to the corresponding D/A converter. The only difference between the two modes is the number of bits used to store the color values.

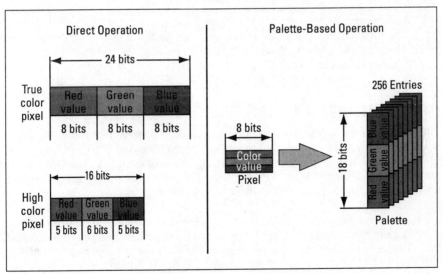

**Figure 17-5:** Windows supports three different pixel formats. More bytes per pixel give you more colors but require more work from your computer.

The 256-color mode is different from the other two, using 8 bits to store each pixel. If the video card divided that one byte into fields as with High Color — say with 3, 3, and 2 bits per color — the card could not provide good rendition. Instead, the 8-bit value gets used as an index into a color palette with 256 entries, each holding a wider value that can be sent to the D/A converters. Every pixel is therefore one byte, and as bytes are read from the display memory, they go through the color palette shown in Figure 17-5. Each of the 256 possible values in the byte corresponds to one entry in the palette. Each entry in the palette contains a value for red, green, and blue, each of which are fed to the corresponding D/A converter. The overall structure permits programs to choose a set of 256 possible on-screen colors from a much wider range of colors.

The limited number of simultaneous colors in the 256-color mode creates a problem. Graphics programs that need a lot of colors to accurately represent pictures on-screen can easily use all the colors in the palette. If two different programs are on-screen at the same time and both want their own palette values, there won't be enough colors available. Windows solves this problem by assigning the palette to the foreground application, repainting the windows for the background applications as best it can using the available palette. This is why in 256-color display modes you get the odd-looking screen repaints that change colors when you switch applications — Windows has written a new set of color values to the palette and is redrawing the screen to make things look as good as it can.

**Tip**

A common bug in Windows programs is mishandling the notification from Windows that the palette has changed, leaving the image on the screen in the wrong colors. You can try minimizing and restoring the windows to get the program to correct the display.

## After you. No, please after you . . . .

The pattern of what gets painted on your screen is stored in video memory, which is a block of memory on the display board. Video memory has to solve a very difficult problem — in addition to providing a torrent of data to the D/A converters, it has to provide high-speed access for the processor accessing the video memory from the bus. Figure 17-6 shows where the problem is:

✦ *Video bus.* The interface between the video memory and the video bus transfers data to the D/A converters. It operates at a constant data rate determined by the video mode set by the processor. The data rate can be almost 800MB per second, which on a 128-bit bus means nearly 50 million bus cycles per second.

✦ *Computer bus.* The interface between the video memory and the computer's bus stores and modifies the data representing the image. It operates at the speed of the memory bus, which could be from 10 to 66 million bus cycles (and up to 528 million bytes) per second.

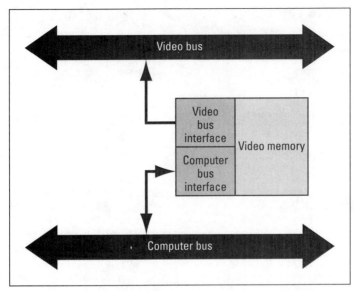

**Figure 17-6:** If the memory transfer to the video bus blocks access to video memory by the processor, the processor has to wait.

Video memory access 50 million times per second works out to a memory cycle on average every 20 nanoseconds. That rate is faster than the main memory in some older computers.

As shown in Table 17-3 (and interpolating to common memory sizes), the memory has to be between 0.5 (one-half) MB and 9MB to hold the complete image, with any additional space needed by the video device driver software adding to this requirement. The total memory requirements are such that a 2MB video memory can support no more than 256 colors at 1,280 × 1,024 resolution (or up to High Color mode at 1,024 × 768), whereas a 4MB board can only support High Color mode at 1,600 × 1,200 resolution. (You'll find accelerated 3D cards with as much as 32MB of memory—the extra memory is to store textures, something we'll cover in the next chapter.)

| Table 17-3 | | | |
|---|---|---|---|
| **Video Memory Size Grows Quickly** | | | |
| *Horizontal Size* | *Vertical Size* | *Bytes per Pixel* | *Memory Size (MB)* |
| 640 | 480 | 1 | 0.29 |
| 640 | 480 | 2 | 0.59 |

*continued*

| Table 17-3 (continued) | | | |
|---|---|---|---|
| Horizontal Size | Vertical Size | Bytes per Pixel | Memory Size (MB) |
| 640 | 480 | 3 | 0.88 |
| 800 | 600 | 1 | 0.46 |
| 800 | 600 | 2 | 0.92 |
| 800 | 600 | 3 | 1.37 |
| 1,024 | 768 | 1 | 0.75 |
| 1,024 | 768 | 2 | 1.50 |
| 1,024 | 768 | 3 | 2.25 |
| 1,280 | 1,024 | 1 | 1.25 |
| 1,280 | 1,024 | 2 | 2.50 |
| 1,280 | 1,024 | 3 | 3.75 |
| 1,600 | 1,200 | 1 | 1.83 |
| 1,600 | 1,200 | 2 | 3.66 |
| 1,600 | 1,200 | 3 | 5.49 |
| 1,800 | 1,440 | 1 | 2.47 |
| 1,800 | 1,440 | 2 | 4.94 |
| 1,800 | 1,440 | 3 | 7.42 |
| 2,048 | 1,536 | 1 | 3.00 |
| 2,048 | 1,536 | 2 | 6.00 |
| 2,048 | 1,536 | 3 | 9.00 |

This is a lot of memory if you have to buy chips as fast as those that implement the cache for your processor. Because of the low video board prices the market demands, cache memory chips are too expensive to provide the amount of memory required. Instead, designers are constrained to using the same basic DRAM technology for video memory as does the main memory in the computer, technology which can be three or four times slower than is needed.

## Making video faster at a great price

The problem video designers face, then, is how to get speeds as fast as those of cache memory with relatively slow technology. There are four common solutions:

✦ *Exploit the consistent access pattern from the video bus.* The pattern the monitor sweeps, called a *raster*, is consistent in its left-to-right, top-to-bottom path (refer to Figure 17-2). Because a fixed location in video memory corresponds to each pixel on the monitor screen, the raster pattern causes a consistent pattern of addresses to be read from the video memory. These addresses increase in the same pattern as the raster. The fixed pattern allows designers to implement patterns of reads and memory bank interleaving using simple, inexpensive hardware. The net result of the two techniques is to decrease the access time.

✦ *Create a dual-port memory interface.* The two memory interfaces shown in Figure 17-6 can be designed to provide a separate connection, called a port, for each bus. The two ports can be interlocked to work cooperatively, reducing the chances that the processor has to wait for video memory accesses. DRAM memory with this sort of dual-port interface is called *VRAM* (Video RAM) and is frequently found in higher-performance boards.

✦ *Use faster memory, integrating other speed boosts into the memory design.* For example, Micron builds a Synchronous Graphics RAM (SGRAM). Within a single package the device incorporates multiple interleaved banks of memory, Fast Page mode access bursts, and other overlapped operations to speed bus cycles. The fastest version of the chip is capable of providing four bytes of data every 10 nanoseconds.

✦ *Reduce the load the processor imposes on video memory.* Many of the accesses to video memory the processor makes can be eliminated by adding a specialized graphics processor — called an *accelerator* — on the video board. The accelerator still accesses the memory but can do it in a way that is timed to coordinate with the accesses the video bus requires.

Windows does specific operations over and over to draw the images you see on the screen. Two of the most common operations are to fill an area on the screen with a color and to move a rectangle of pixels from one place on the screen to another. Figure 17-7 shows what these operations do:

✦ *Polygon fill.* When Windows draws the star on the screen, it fills it in by coloring all the pixels on lines within the outline of the star. The same process fills in all other objects, including window backgrounds, buttons, and other fundamental objects within Windows itself. Depending on the size of the shape being filled, thousands of pixels may be set, with many calculations required to determine which pixels are inside the outline of the object.

✦ *Block transfer.* When Windows moves a window from one place on the screen to another, or when it scrolls the contents of a window, it has to copy pixels from one place in video memory to another. The movement operation requires that the pixels involved be read from video memory at the old location and written at the new. The operation becomes more complex if the two rectangles overlap.

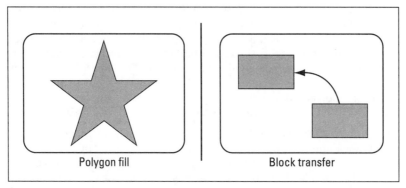

**Figure 17-7:** Windows creates the images on the screen by using a few operations over and over.

Other common two-dimensional (2D) operations include drawing lines and moving the mouse cursor around. A video accelerator implements some or all of the common Windows drawing functions. The 3D accelerators have much more complicated primitive operations. Because a video accelerator is designed specifically for its purpose and is not a general-purpose processor, it can be faster at its dedicated tasks than the computer's processor can be. At the same time that the accelerator takes much of the drawing load off the processor, it takes a significant load off the computer bus. The combination of faster video computation, reduced processor load, and reduced bus load significantly increases computer performance.

Any video operation that is done frequently is a candidate for incorporation into an accelerator on the video card. Functions in addition to the straightforward ones used by Windows include

✦ *Multimedia support.* Live multimedia video and stored compressed video overlaid on the screen show up in a variety of applications, including training sequences and games. A video accelerator can improve performance for these operations by combining the video sequence with the relatively static display on the screen and by handling the conversion of colors from values stored in the video to ones compatible with the screen image, or by performing the entire video decompression operation.

✦ *3D support.* Three-dimensional rendering in CAD software requires common operations like surface rendering and hidden surface elimination to create pictures that appear three-dimensional on the screen. These operations consume a lot of processor time, and (for games or virtual reality fly-bys) the large areas of the display that are updated many times every second create lots of traffic into the video memory. Moving the critical operations into a video accelerator eliminates these bottlenecks.

The computer's processor, memory, and bus all benefit from accelerators. Instead of directly reading and writing pixels, many of the operations Windows needs performed are sent to the accelerator as high-level commands. The accelerator then carries out the detailed work, keeping the high-rate memory accesses confined to the video board.

# For the Historically Inclined

Monitors and displays have not always been as complex as they are now, nor as capable of the performance they now deliver, nor priced as attractively as they are now. Barry spent many hours programming in front of a 2,048 × 2,048 resolution 21-inch color monitor in the late '80s. The available space on the display was magnificent, but the monitor was not as sharp as our current Hitachi and cost tens of thousands of dollars.

How displays have evolved to their present state parallels the progress of personal computing. Prior to the IBM PC, most personal computer displays were character based. That means that the information written from the processor to the video memory was characters, not pixels, and the conversion from characters to pixels was done by the board itself. Figure 17-8 shows what happens on a character-based video board.

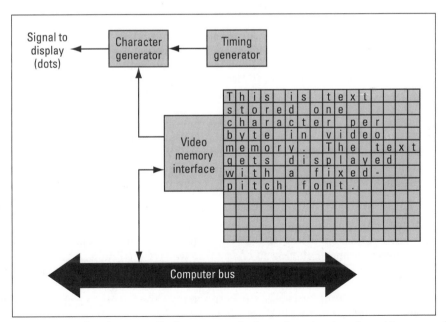

**Figure 17-8:** The character display was nearly the only technology found in reasonably priced computer terminals and personal computer displays until some time after the introduction of the IBM PC.

The key elements in Figure 7-7 are the timing generator, the character generator, and the memory interface. Those three operate in lock step to create the pattern of dots on the screen that make up the display image.

✦ *Timing generator.* The timing generator sequences characters out of the video memory into the character generator. Each line of characters is rescanned once for every line of dots making up the line of characters (often seven because the character matrix was frequently seven dots wide by nine dots tall). Individual accesses to memory were infrequent enough that access by the computer and the character generator could be synchronized to never interfere.

✦ *Character generator.* The character generator turns character codes (as stored in the video memory) into sequences of dots (pixels) sent to the display. The character generator is essentially a font stored on the video board.

✦ *Memory interface.* The interface between the video memory and the computer's bus stores and modifies the characters stored in the video memory. A typical character display was 80 × 25 characters resolution. Characters were displayed in one color.

Character displays used a fixed-pitch font to simplify the design of the timing generator and to make the places where characters went on the screen easy to determine. Fixed pitch fonts (like Courier New in Windows) shown on displays use a constant-size matrix of pixels to hold each character, but the dot pattern within the matrix depends only on the font design.

Character displays were the basis for most of the terminals used with large-scale computers and were commonly attached to early personal computers as well. A terminal communicated with the attached computer not through a memory attached to the bus, but by sending characters over a cable. A mechanism was required to distinguish characters to be displayed from ones used to control the terminal itself, leading to the development of terminal control protocols. One of the most common terminals — and therefore protocols — was the Digital Equipment Corporation (DEC) VT100 (and the clones that implemented the same interface). The model of a display terminal connected to some other computer survives in Windows as HyperTerm, an application that (among other things) lets your PC look like a VT100 to a remote computer connected through your modem.

The original IBM PC shipped with a character display. The video adapter was called the Monochrome Display Adapter (MDA). It implemented a display of 80 × 25 characters in one color, using a 9 × 14 character matrix that provided a very high quality character image. It allowed characters to have attributes, which meant that they could be brighter than normal, underlined, blinking, and reverse (black on white versus white on black) video. Monitors generally used white, amber, or green phosphors on the front surface of the cathode ray tube to turn the electron beam into light. The adapter provided a printer port as well.

The MDA was the only video adapter available for the IBM PC when it was introduced, and it seemed a good match for the character-oriented business software — including word processors like WordStar — available on microcomputers at the time. Newer programs, particularly spreadsheets like Lotus 1-2-3, soon made the lack of graphics on the card a liability, because the volumes of data people entered into spreadsheets lead naturally to the desire to graph that data. Two solutions were available to early spreadsheet users:

✦ *IBM Color Graphics Adapter (CGA).* The CGA corrected the problem of having no graphics in the MDA, and it added limited color capability. The CGA implemented the modes shown in Table 17-4, which included distinct modes for text and graphics. The graphics resolution was low enough that it could not support high-quality text — even the text mode reduced the 9 × 14 character matrix of the MDA to one of 8 × 8 dots. You had to buy a new monitor when you replaced an MDA with a CGA. Many people used both an MDA and CGA at the same time in a two-monitor setup — Lotus 1-2-3, for example, would show you the text of your spreadsheet on the MDA while showing you your graph on the CGA.

✦ *Hercules Graphics Card (HGC).* The HGC retained the high-quality monochrome text display of the MDA and added monochrome graphics to support business applications. It was arguably the most visible entry in the start of the third-party IBM PC hardware market. The HGC made every pixel on the entire 720 × 350 screen of the monochrome adapter accessible — over 80 percent as many pixels as on a standard 640 × 480 display you might use today.

### Table 17-4
### CGA Provided Limited Graphics and Color Capability

| Display Mode | Graphics Resolution | Text Resolution | Number of Colors |
|---|---|---|---|
| High-resolution text | — | 80 × 25 | 16 |
| Low-resolution text | — | 40 × 25 | 16 |
| High-resolution graphics | 640 × 200 | 80 × 25 | 2 |
| Medium-resolution graphics | 320 × 200 | 40 × 25 | 4 |
| Low-resolution graphics | 160 × 200 | -- | 16 |

For comparison, 60 of the images the CGA could display will fit on a high-end display today at 1,600 × 1,200 resolution. You can get a million times more colors, too.

The CGA suffered from low resolution and too few colors — the hardware forced images on the screen to look like cartoons. It also had a problem with contention

for access to the video memory between the display generator and the bus —
access by the processor other than when the beam on the cathode ray tube
was retracing from bottom to top produced white noise (snow) on the screen.

IBM responded to the problems of the CGA with the Enhanced Graphics Adapter
(EGA). The EGA solved many of the shortcomings of the CGA, adding colors
and better screen resolution and thus higher-quality text and graphics to the
capabilities of the CGA, although the screen resolution and number of colors
were still limited. This left fertile ground for third-party vendors. Table 17-5 shows
the EGA's capabilities. The 640 × 350 resolution made an 8 × 14 character matrix
possible, which was nearly as good as the MDA.

### Table 17-5
### EGA Colors and Resolution

| Display Mode | Graphics Resolution | Text Resolution | Number of Colors |
|---|---|---|---|
| EGA-resolution text or graphics | 640 × 350 | 80 × 25 (or 80 × 43 with an 8 × 8 character matrix) | Any 16 out of 64 choices |

The EGA sold well because it had good software support, but it was relatively
expensive. IBM sold the EGA piecemeal — first you bought the board and monitor
and then you bought an add-on memory board and add-on memory chips to get the
full resolution and number of colors.

The high cost of EGA combined with still-limited performance to create a market for
better video. IBM offered the Professional Graphics Controller but made it both
expensive and sufficiently incompatible that little software could use it (even
though it offered acceleration functions like clipping and 3D rotation just now
coming to market at reasonable price points). There were never any Windows
drivers for it. Other vendors created proprietary solutions as well, with their
own software driver and compatibility problems.

The solution to the problem was one of the most enduring standards ever for
personal computers, the Video Graphics Array (VGA) that IBM introduced with
the PS/2 computers in 1987. The VGA changed the key characteristics of the
video subsystem:

✦ *Analog signal interface to the monitor.* The monitors for the MDA, HGC, CGA,
and EGA all received digital signals from the display card. This means that the
signal was zeros and ones. For the MDA, for example, a one meant to turn on
the dot, while a zero meant to leave it black. A second signal in parallel told

the monitor to make a dot particularly bright, allowing for boldface effects. The increased capabilities of the succeeding generations of video cards meant, however, that the monitors for MDA, CGA, and EGA were incompatible. The VGA standard changed the digital signal interface to an analog one, where the magnitude of the signal indicates the brightness of the beam at any instant of time.

✦ *Increased resolution and number of colors.* The VGA standard increased the graphics resolution to 640 × 480 with 16 colors. Super VGA extensions to the standard have made 256 colors common.

The change to the analog monitor interface was required to enable the greater number of colors the VGA supports (262,144 possible colors in the palette, with 16 or 256 colors on-screen at once).

Figure 17-9 shows the difference between the two, using the EGA as the example of a digital monitor interface.

✦ *EGA.* The connecting cable contains two-bit digital signals for red, green, and blue. Separate horizontal and vertical signals provide timing information for the monitor electronics.

✦ *VGA.* The connecting cable contains analog drive signals for red, green, and blue intensity (with paired returns — grounds — to reduce noise). Separate horizontal and vertical synchronization provide timing information for the monitor electronics.

At the same time that the VGA standard was making it possible to use software with any manufacturer's advanced video board, Microsoft Windows and X Window for UNIX were making it possible to write software that doesn't care what the interface to the board is. Before these windowing systems, software developers had to incorporate low-level device drivers into their programs that encoded how to use the capabilities of video boards. The VGA standard gave developers a relatively fixed target that had the features and capabilities they needed. With the device-independent graphics interface, developers could write to one software interface with good confidence that their programs would work on current and future hardware. Video card manufacturers now build unique interfaces into their video cards and, by writing a device driver for the card, give applications the benefit of all the features of the hardware. Video cards are now more diverse than when VGA was the standard everyone implemented carefully, yet the video problems software developers have to cope with are less than ever.

The analog interface also freed the monitor from being so closely tied to the timing of the video card, leading to monitors that can synchronize with a variety of display resolutions, and that can accept any number of display colors.

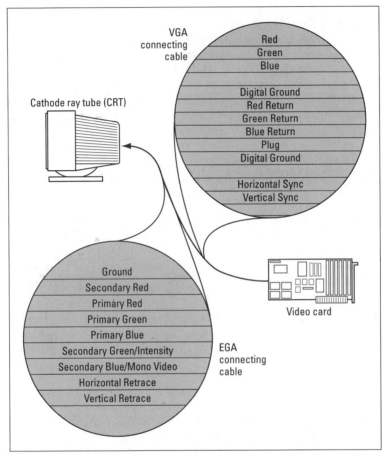

**Figure 17-9:** The VGA connecting cable uses analog drive signals for red, green, and blue, permitting many more colors to be displayed.

# Summary

✦ Monitors create images from sequences of dots (pixels) output by the video board.

✦ Higher resolution — more pixels — means closer dot spacing on the monitor, and more work for the video board.

✦ You get more possible colors by using more bytes per pixel, which takes more memory and creates more work for the video board.

✦ The data rates required on the video board to feed the monitor may be higher than found in the rest of your computer.

✦        ✦        ✦

# Video Adapters

In Chapter 17, "Video," we looked at how an image is formed on the screen of your monitor, what your video card does, how the video card stores the image, and what kind of performance is required from a video card. In this chapter, we'll look more closely at how programs draw through Windows onto the screen, how video accelerators work, and what video compression is all about.

This chapter is more Windows intensive than the rest of the book, because manufacturers have put less effort into supporting their accelerated video cards under UNIX. If you're looking for top video performance under UNIX, start with the list of video cards your version of UNIX supports. The most likely software support is X Window and OpenGL, so look for those too.

## The Windows Graphics Device Interface

The *Graphics Device Interface* (GDI) and *DirectDraw/Direct3D* (part of DirectX) are the Windows subsystems programs use to draw images. Both work through drivers to draw on the screen, printer, plotter, or other imaging devices. The key thing GDI and DirectX do is to make the programs themselves reasonably independent of the actual hardware. Under DOS, programs had to incorporate their own device drivers. Whenever a new generation of hardware arrived, your high-performance software either received new drivers or became obsolete. With GDI and DirectX, a set of drivers for the hardware updates all your applications.

Windows does another critical thing through these subsystems. It defines the set of operations a program can do to the display. Because the set of operations is limited, it's possible to build hardware that makes just those operations faster and know that you've covered all the functions you need to make Windows programs fast.

The drawing operations GDI supports are

✦ Set a particular pixel to a given color.

✦ Draw a line including characteristics of width, pattern, color, and endpoint style.

✦ Draw an arc.

✦ Draw an ellipse (which includes circles).

✦ Draw a rectangle, rounded rectangle, or polygon.

✦ Draw filled versions of closed figures, with the fill being a solid color or a pattern.

✦ Draw text in a specified font, color, and size.

✦ Move a rectangle on the screen from one place to another, making the rectangle smaller or larger on the way if required.

✦ Clip any of the drawing or movement operations to a specified region, disallowing changes outside the clipping region.

If you look at the drawing commands offered by the simpler drawing programs, such as Paintbrush, which is included with Windows, you'll see that those commands generally mirror the functions offered directly by GDI. The more complex drawing programs, such as CorelDRAW, include more complex operations, such as fountain fills and sophisticated curve shapes. (We'll see later that DirectX adds primitives derived from the capabilities of modern 3D accelerators.)

One of the most common operations Windows does on your video screen is to move rectangles from one part of the screen to another, an operation called a Bit Block Transfer or BitBLT. (The operation is pronounced *Bit Blit*, or just *blit*, and the verb is *to blit*.) You can see Windows doing blits when you scroll a window. If you scroll toward the bottom of the file, the image on the screen moves toward the top of the window. Well-written programs move the image they've already drawn upward, drawing new information into the part of the window exposed by the blit. Because the rectangles being moved typically include a lot of pixels, there's a lot of data being moved. Speeding the blit operation makes scrolls faster.

A blit done in hardware is faster than the equivalent transfer in a program because it performs only one operation. It doesn't have to fetch instructions, decode them, and execute them. Similarly, polygon fills in hardware can be faster because they have faster access to video memory and (again) don't have to execute program code.

Blits do even more than this in Windows, because the movement can be to or from main memory as well as video memory. Fonts, for example, are collections of small bitmaps. Drawing text amounts to drawing sequences of small bitmaps — one per character — with each bitmap being blitted from main memory to the right place in video memory. Faster blits mean faster text draws.

# What a Video Accelerator Does

An accelerator simplifies the work of GDI, as shown in Figure 18-1, resulting in faster video operations. For every operation required by a program, GDI decides if the hardware can carry out the operation directly, and if so, tells the device driver to let the hardware do the drawing. If not, GDI simulates the operation in software. For each operation the simulation layer has to carry out, it goes through the same process, letting GDI decide if any of those simpler operations can be done entirely in hardware. GDI ends up making those decisions through this sequence:

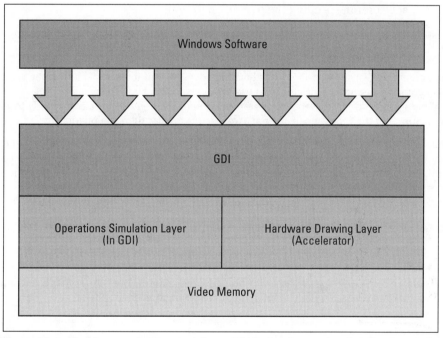

**Figure 18-1:** A video accelerator speeds up GDI by implementing the draw operations in hardware.

✦ *Software interface into GDI.* Windows programs draw on the screen by making calls to GDI. The operations that programs ask for may or may not be supported directly by the hardware.

✦ *GDI operations in software.* If there's no accelerator, or if there are GDI operations that aren't done in hardware by the accelerator, GDI simulates those operations in software. For example, if the accelerator doesn't draw dashed lines, GDI simulates the operation by drawing a sequence of shorter lines. If the accelerator doesn't draw lines at all, GDI simulates the operation by drawing a sequence of dots.

✦ *GDI operations in hardware.* The video accelerator can implement operations directly in hardware. One of the most common and most effective techniques is to do BitBLT operations in hardware, because the reads and writes of memory for a scrolling operation never have to go out on the computer bus. The operations are entirely self-contained on the video card, eliminating any waits for other components in the computer.

✦ *GDI operations mixed in hardware and software.* Though the operation requested by the program may have to be implemented in software by GDI, the individual actions GDI uses may be supported in hardware. For example, if the hardware doesn't do polygon fills, GDI breaks the operation down into a sequence of horizontal line draws. The line draws may be supported by the accelerator, speeding the overall operation.

## Pictures — the Windows Metafile format

The operations GDI supports are directly reflected in the Windows Metafile Format, which is the basis for the structure of files with the WMF extension and of objects of type "picture" you find in the clipboard. Because metafiles contain the sequence of commands to draw the picture, not the image itself, they are frequently smaller than the picture they create.

Look again at the picture from Chapter 16 that shows how magnetic transitions encode data on magnetic tape. The picture is entirely composed of graphic elements that correspond to specific GDI operations: text, lines, and polygons. The heavier black line indicating the encoded data and the thin black lines from the text to the graphic are GDI lines. The gray boxes indicating cells are polygons, as are the arrowheads. The words are all GDI text.

We took the drawing out of PowerPoint (where we drew it) and stored it two ways: as a Windows metafile, and as a bitmap. The metafile was 11K; the bitmap, written the same size as we drew it, at 300 dots per inch resolution, and then compressed, was 112K. The metafile is more useful than the bitmap, too, because Windows can render a drawing from the metafile to be any size we ask with no loss of resolution. The bitmap has a set resolution and suffers a loss of quality if we make it larger or smaller.

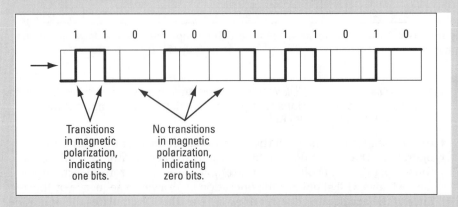

The size of a drawing can be far smaller using the Windows Metafile format than is required to hold all the dots in the video image.

To see how a hardware accelerator can help, look at the process GDI uses to draw text on the screen. Figure 18-2 illustrates the overall process, while Figure 18-3 shows the work GDI goes through to create the text on your screen. The row of characters at the top of Figure 18-2 represents the small bitmaps GDI stores in memory for a font. Each character has its own individual bitmap; there's a different set of bitmaps for each different size of each different font. Italic and bold fonts have their own sets of bitmaps too. For TrueType fonts, GDI creates the bitmaps from character outlines that it can scale to the right size when it renders the bitmap.

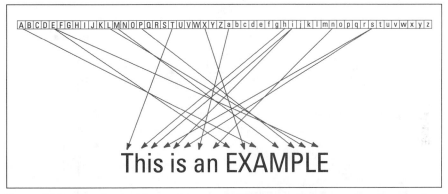

**Figure 18-2:** Drawing text is a sequence of BitBLT operations, one per character in the text string.

When GDI draws text on the screen, it first creates the font bitmaps it needs and then loops for each character it needs to draw. Each trip through the loop copies the bitmap for the character at hand from the font in main memory to the right place on the screen. Each arrow in the Figure 18-2 corresponds to one trip through the GDI loop. Each individual character draw operation is a BitBLT of the small font bitmap from main memory to video memory. If the hardware accelerator has a BitBLT function, the processor can simply give the accelerator a sequence of commands and let it do all the work. Each character requires one BitBLT operation.

The leverage the accelerator has is that every character has hundreds of pixels in it, and the processor has to loop to deal with them all in order to copy them to the screen. Even when the processor can handle multiple pixels at a time in a single pass through the bitmap copy loop, it still takes hundreds or even thousands of instructions to move a character to the screen. Large characters take many more pixels and so create more work for the processor. Commanding the accelerator to copy the bitmap takes the same number of instructions by the processor no matter how big the character, and the processor can do other work while the accelerator carries out the command.

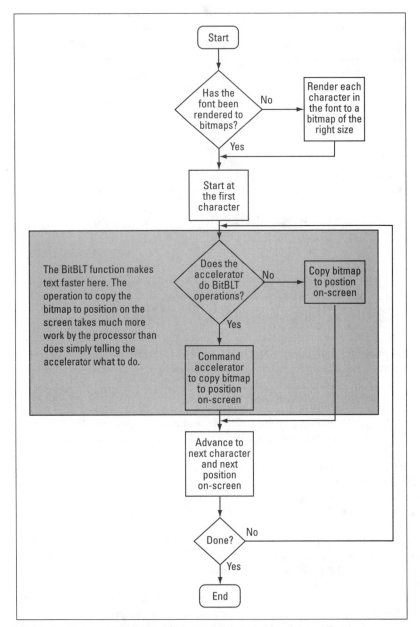

**Figure 18-3:** The BitBLT accelerator turns hundreds of operations per character into a single command.

The shaded area in Figure 18-3 shows where the BitBLT function makes text faster. The operation to copy the bitmap to a position on the screen takes much more work by the processor than does a simple instruction to the accelerator.

Filled polygons take even more work on the processor's part, and the speed increase is even greater from an accelerator. The fill operation proceeds line by line down the screen, finding the ends of the lines within the polygon. The processor can then draw the line in the right color and move down to the next line. The computations to figure out where the line ends are can be complex for oddly shaped polygons, so off-loading the work onto the accelerator speeds things up.

# Three Dimensions on Your Screen

Three-dimensional games, visualization, and virtual reality systems put you in a simulated first- or third-person world where you can move around in a highly detailed environment. These programs work by maintaining a "wire-frame" structure giving shape to the objects in the world (walls, floors, and ceilings), and by painting the surfaces of the objects with colored patterns called *textures*. Figure 18-4 is a three-dimensional view of a room. Figure 18-5 is the wire-frame view of the textured representation in Figure 18-4. Everything you see in Figure 18-4 is textures painted on floors, walls, and ceilings defined by the wire frame.

**Figure 18-4:** Three-dimensional visualizations map walls and surfaces to perspective views and render textures onto the walls to create a realistic image.

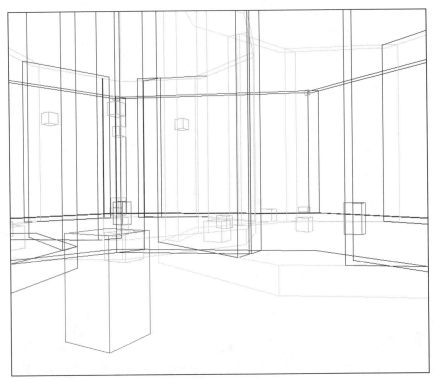

**Figure 18-5:** The 3D spaces you traverse are "wire-frame" structures whose surfaces are covered by textures.

Texture mapping is more complicated than simply copying a patterned bitmap to the screen, because it requires dealing with the perspective effects in the wire frame and with visibility of objects due to solid surfaces being in front of one another. A rectangular pattern bitmap has to be distorted to fit perspective changes. You can see this in Figure 18-4 on the walls that are not perpendicular to your point of view. Surfaces like that have to recede along perspective lines toward a vanishing point, requiring that the texture map be distorted to be shorter and shorter as your eye moves back toward the vanishing point.

The calculations to do texture mapping (and to decide which parts of what surfaces are visible) are computationally expensive — they require a lot of work by the processor. That's the basic reason why real-time 3D rendering requires a fast processor for good performance. Higher-resolution screen formats require significantly more computation (640 × 400 resolution takes four times the computation of 320 × 200), which is why the higher resolutions are only becoming common with the advent of faster processors like the Pentium II and III along with high-performance 3D accelerators. Updating the screen to move the wire frames and texture maps on the screen at a fast frame rate requires a high-capacity path to the video card, too, which is why you want an AGP bus motherboard and video card for the best 3D video performance.

Another key 3D rendering operation is polygon drawing, which is the most common technique to represent moving objects. Textures drawn on the polygons give the object a realistic look while retaining the advantages of fast 3D views. Polygon drawing is similar to the process of covering wire frames with texture maps but is somewhat more restrictive to get good performance. A mesh covering a 3D surface can be fitted entirely with triangles, which reduces the complexity of the software (or hardware) needed to render the object onto the screen. You can make objects arbitrarily detailed this way by making the triangles smaller.

Because the two most important operations for high-speed 3D graphics are texture mapping and polygon rendering, you usually measure 3D software and hardware performance in textured pixels (*texels*) per second and filled polygons per second. Some of the most highly-tuned 3D software is in games; those that report rendering performance measures sometimes make excellent 3D video benchmarks.

## Who's in front, what can you see, and where's the light?

Part of what's hard in 3D graphics is making the results look realistic. I found a good quote on the Internet that expresses that goal:

> *"When do graphics not look like graphics? When we get it right."*
> —*Brian Marshall*

The first thing you have to do is get relationships between objects right in the third dimension—into and out of the screen. The following figure shows the problem and one way of solving it. There are two situations on the left side of the figure, with a blow-up of one on the right.

When two objects overlap, we have to know which is in front in order to know which object's pixels will show on the display. The solution shown in the preceding figure, used by essentially all current-generation accelerated 3D cards, is to maintain another array of memory called a Z-buffer in parallel with the display memory. Each location in the Z-buffer tracks the distance along the Z axis (into and out of the screen) for the pixel currently drawn there, so it's a simple test to see if a new pixel being written is obscured or not.

A Z-buffer requires additional memory, and the greater the resolution we keep for the Z-values, the more memory we need. If we're rendering at 640 × 400 resolution and maintaining Z-values with 16-bit numbers (two bytes), we need one half a megabyte of memory for the Z-buffer alone and have nothing to spare if we want higher resolution. Rendering at 1,600 × 1,200 with 24 bits in the Z-buffer requires nearly 5.5MB just for the buffer.

*continued*

*(continued)*

Suppose we have two objects (the star and the sun below). In a two-dimensional world, they can't be in front of or behind each other, so I don't have to worry about overlaps.

In a three-dimensional world, though, one object can be in front of another. The usual behavior of light rays – that they don't go through opaque objects – means that we see the one in front and not the one in back, as in the drawing below.

Let's look a little closer at an area where the two figures overlap. Using boxes to represent overly large pixels, I've numbered each pixel with its "distance" from an imaginary background, letting zero be the background, three be the star, and five the sun. If I maintain a map of these distances for every pixel in addition to the usual video memory, I can always know whether to paint a pixel or not – if the pixel I'm painting has a smaller distance (or Z) value, it's in back and should not be painted.

I can implement this idea in hardware with a block of memory I'll call a Z-buffer. Every time I write a pixel, I also write its Z-value. Pixels with larger Z-values get written and the Z-buffer updated with the correct distance. All other pixels get ignored.

A Z-buffer makes deciding what's in front simple but requires doubling the amount of video memory.

There are other ways to solve the hidden surface problem, but they all trade memory in the display for work by the processor. The general approach is to sort the vertices of the polygons along the Z axis. We then paint the ones furthest into the screen (furthest away) before the nearer ones, so the end result is that the nearer objects overlap the ones further away. The approach has problems handling surfaces inclined in the Z axis, in that the distance a pixel is from the background can change as it gets further away from the vertex. Solving those problems requires yet more processing power.

If we sort in the Z axis more cleverly, we can eliminate some work for the processor. If a surface is completely hidden by other ones, or if it faces away from the observer's viewpoint, there's no reason to draw it in the first place. Eliminating the drawing operation means we don't have to fill the polygon with a texture map, reducing the work the processor has to do.

Yet more work is required to create a realistic image. For example, in the real world light sources usually come from points, so the lighting on a surface is not even. It's biased toward the point source. Surfaces have varying reflective properties that affect the texture maps we would use. A shiny metal curve will reflect a point source to the observer at one place with what's called a specular reflection. The mathematics that make all this work has been known for some time. It's only recently that processors and video graphics cards have offered enough performance at a reasonable price to make compelling 3D visualization possible.

# What a 3D Accelerator Does

A lot of work is required to create a 3D image. Overall, the sequence is like what's shown in Figure 18-6, with each step moving the program's model of what exists closer to dots on your screen. As the sequence progresses, there are more objects to do computations for, increasing the load on the processor. A 3D hardware accelerator takes over operations on the right side of the pipeline, freeing the processor for the work on the left. Simple accelerators will do only the polygon rendering and texture mapping. More capable accelerators will scoop up functions in prior blocks of the figure, such as by permitting the "Compute Vertices" block to pass floating-point coordinates into the next stage, reducing the workload on the processor.

✦ *Geometry processing.* The program maintains locations in "world" coordinates to make relating different objects simpler. The computation is often done in the processor, and done with floating-point arithmetic.

✦ *Transition and rendering.* The program maps 3D coordinates to the 2D view and applies textures. This work is often done in hardware.

The details of each step in Figure 18-6 are

✦ *Compute vertices.* The processor computes the position of each vertex of each object in the overall coordinate system.

✦ *Clip edges.* Objects may extend past the edges of the visible area. The overhang has to be eliminated, so the processor clips the edges of objects against the drawing region boundaries, one polygon of an object at a time.

✦ *Eliminate hidden surfaces.* You don't want the display to include hidden surfaces. The processor has to identify visible surfaces and eliminate back-facing surfaces.

✦ *Compute projections.* The display is only 2D, as if a glass surface is interposed between your eye and a 3D scene. Simulating this in the computer requires that we compute 3D to 2D projections of the vertices of each polygon.

✦ *Paint surfaces.* Once we have a set of 2D polygons, we can paint the surface of each one with a shaded texture map.

Figure 18-7 shows you how the geometry elements of these steps relate. On the left of the figure, an object in model space defines the properties of the object itself. Conversions to the overall coordinate system define how the parts of the model fit into the world being simulated in the program. Edge clipping, hidden surface removal, and projections let the program convert the parts of the object into a projection you'd see if your eye were as shown in the middle of the figure (and shown in more detail on the right of the figure).

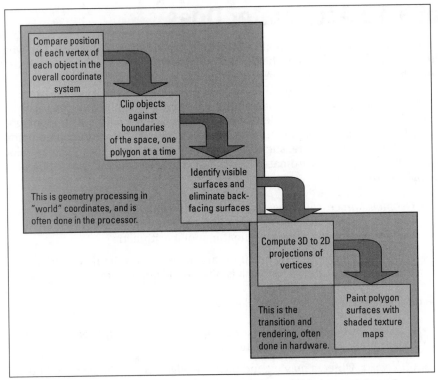

**Figure 18-6:** The 3D viewing and rendering pipeline transforms a program's model of what exists into the image you see.

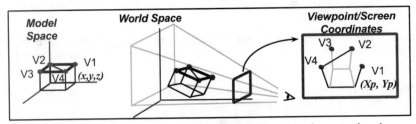

**Figure 18-7:** Each transformation in the 3D pipeline gets closer to the view you see on-screen. (drawing courtesy Intel Corporation.)

The ATI Rage 128 accelerator is designed to provide low-cost, high-performance 3D graphics. The chip does the following 3D operations:

✦ *Floating-point setup.* Triangle setup — the first stage in the pipeline of Figure 18-6 — is handled entirely in the Rage 128. This offloads the processor, supporting triangle draw rates of millions of triangles per second.

✦ *Drawing primitives.* Points, lines, triangles, quadrilaterals, and BitBLTs.

✦ *Z-buffer.* Hidden surface removal through Z-buffer processing using the ideas in the sidebar "Who's in front, what can you see, and where's the light?" The Rage 128 supports a 32-bit Z-buffer, improving the resolution for depth computations.

✦ *Shaded polygons.* Lighting effects using interpolation along and between polygon edges.

✦ *Texture maps.* Perspective-corrected texture map drawing onto polygons, with the capability to designate parts of the texture map as being transparent to simplify effects such as windows in vehicles. On-chip filtering improves image quality as the textures are transformed for display.

✦ *Resolution and color.* Support for full 32-bit color operation at resolutions up to 1,920 × 1,200 pixels.

✦ *Intel Accelerated Graphics Port (AGP) support.* The performance of the latest-generation video boards requires more bandwidth than even the PCI bus can provide. Intel defined the AGP with a mode providing a dedicated bandwidth of over 500 MBps, far more than the shared 133 MBps of the PCI bus.

Future PC

Functions in the Rage 128 speed MPEG decompression to cover a wide range of Windows accelerations requirements (2D, 3D, and motion video) in one chip. With the appropriate control software, boards using the Rage 128 provide a complete DVD decoder in hardware. Other vendors, including S3, are developing competitive technology. The combination of fast 3D video, OpenGL or the Microsoft Direct3D software drivers, and new software written to one of those standards has taken 3D video to a new level of performance. The applicability of cards with all these capabilities to multimedia, presentation graphics, and video conferencing should help ensure they sell well, creating a market that will spur software developers to make use of the new capabilities. It's possible that within a few years all video accelerators will include this complete feature set as part of the basic package.

# Video Compression and Acceleration

Digital video data rates can become high enough to stress your computer's performance and take up a significant amount of storage, as shown in Table 18-1. The most interesting point about the data in Table 18-1 is that it's possible to compress video at well over 100 : 1 and still get useful images on playback.

| Table 18-1 Digital Video Requires Compression to Be Useful in a PC Environment | | |
| --- | --- | --- |
| Content | Mbps | Minutes per One CD-ROM |
| Uncompressed video (CCIT-601 standard digital video is a little slower, at 167 megabits per second) | 184.3200 | 0.47 |
| MPEG 1 compressed video | 1.5000 | 57.29 |
| MPEG 2 compressed video (MPEG 2 supports variable data rates) | 4.00 8.00 | 21.48 10.74 |

Two major video compression technologies are used in personal computers today: vector quantization (VQ) and Motion Picture Experts Group (MPEG) compression. The two use significantly different approaches to compression and have very different liabilities and applications. VQ is used in Cinepak and in Intel's Indeo-3 compression products. The MPEG 1 and MPEG 2 standards define MPEG. Two later sections in this chapter describe some of the internals of VQ and MPEG. The key things you need to know about compression when you're buying video cards are

✦ *Requirement.* Video compression is required for stored video in PC systems. Uncompressed video is simply too large to be stored and processed reasonably.

✦ *Processing load.* VQ and MPEG are roughly equally expensive in terms of the processing to compress video. Both require hardware assistance to compress full-screen video in real time using most processors (the Pentium III using its new multimedia instructions can do MPEG encoding in real time). VQ requires far less processing to decompress; you get faster MPEG decoding with a hardware accelerator than without, and you may need acceleration for full-screen video.

✦ *Applications.* VQ is commonly found in some video conferencing systems (see Chapter 27) and in video compressed with Cinepak. MPEG may be found in a wide range of multimedia titles and is the standard for video stored on DVD. Over time, it's likely that MPEG will dominate the PC video compression market.

## Vector Quantization

Vector quantization is a compression technique applicable to speech, images, video, and a variety of other signals. It relies on having a predefined table, called a codebook, available to both the compressor and decompressor, although file and transmission formats that include the codebook as part of the compressed information have been defined. VQ is not well standardized in general, but specific company-standardized implementations do exist.

A VQ-based video compression system has the components shown in Figure 18-8. It's most common to get an analog signal out of the camera (the better the camera, the better your results), so the first step in compression is to digitize the signal. There are several ways to decode and represent the color signal, so the video acquisition block may have to convert from the representation decoded out of the camera to the one your VQ compressor expects to see. Once the raw digital signal is formed, it goes to the compressor, where it's transformed into the lower-rate video signal. The high-rate signal is somewhere between 150 and 200 megabits per second, depending on format. The output from the compressor can be most anything the specific compression format wants to see, from 64 kilobits (videoconferencing quality) up to tens of megabits (broadcast television quality) per second.

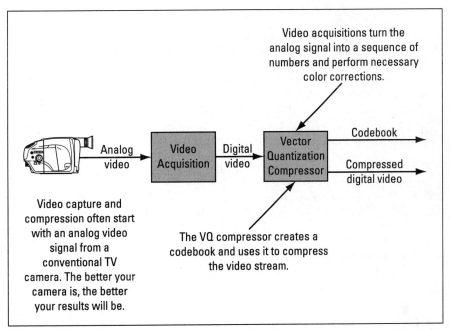

**Figure 18-8:** VQ compression is capable of compressing video down to 1.5 megabits (Mb) per second with reasonable quality.

The VQ decompression system is roughly the inverse. A decompressor outputs digital video from the codebook and the compressed digital video stream. Hardware very similar to a video display card (or the video card itself, for that matter) turns the digital video stream back into analog video for a television or monitor.

A combined VQ compression/decompression pipeline offers two unique properties:

✦ *Fixed rate*. The data rate out of the compressor (and later into the decompressor) is fixed once the codebook is chosen. If you're sending compressed video over a communications link, the fact that the output is a fixed number of bits per video frame means that it's much easier to recover from bit errors during transmission. Other compression schemes, such as MPEG, wavelets, or fractals, need a variable number of bits per video frame, and so finding the boundaries of a new frame after a bit error is difficult. The resulting loss of information before those other techniques find the next boundary can degrade the received image.

✦ *Simple decompression*. Although the computation required to do VQ compression is comparable to MPEG, the workload for decompression is far less. The VQ compression process is asymmetric. VQ decompression can handle high-quality, full-screen video completely in software on a processor like the Pentium, something beyond the reach of MPEG without hardware assistance on anything but a fast Pentium II or Pentium III processor.

VQ is among the simplest compression schemes available. Figure 18-9 shows how it works for single images (we'll get to video in a moment). Rectangular groups of pixels in the image, called vectors, are stored in the codebook and processed in the image. For each vector in the image, we find the closest approximation in the codebook and output its number instead of the full vector. Because the index number takes fewer bytes than the vector it represents, the image is compressed. Because the size of an index number and the size of the vector it replaces is fixed, the compression is constant (which is why you get a constant output rate).

In Figure 18-9 we've blown up a small patch of an image so that you can see the individual pixels (the square blocks inside the black outlines we've drawn over the image). The black outlines represent vectors — in this case, two-by-two groups of pixels. The first step in VQ compression is to develop the codebook, which is simply a collection of vectors. We've suggested the contents of a sample codebook on the right of Figure 18-10. Each vector in the codebook is assigned an index, which in our example ranges from 0 to 16383.

To compress the image in Figure 18-8, we start with vector number zero and find the entry in the codebook that most resembles that vector. Suppose that codebook entry turns out to be the one we've shown as number 16382. If so, we output the index 16382 and repeat the process for vector number 1. If we're using 24-bit True Color in the source image, for instance, one vector takes three bytes per pixel times four pixels per vector, or 12 bytes. The codebook index only takes two bytes, so we've compressed the vector by six to one.

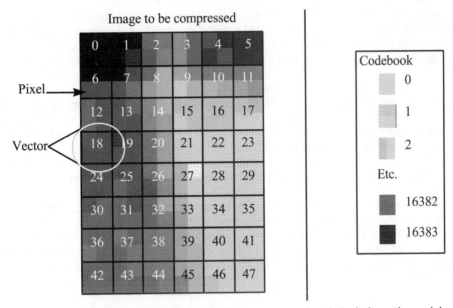

**Figure 18-9:** VQ compression works by finding a rectangle of pixels from the codebook that best matches each rectangle in the video frame and sending the codebook index.

Reconstructing your original image (decompressing it) is the inverse process. For each codebook index, take the corresponding vector from the codebook and place it in the proper position in the output image. The decompression operation is a blit from the codebook to display memory for each index. The simplicity of the blit operation means that decompression is easy and takes relatively little processing power. The value of fast decompression is that you can invest once in a good compressor, publish the compressed result, and decompress on a reasonably fast computer with no special hardware.

The degree of compression you get from VQ depends on the size of each pixel, the size of the vectors, and the number of vectors in the codebook. Holding everything else constant, bigger pixels result in greater compression, larger vectors give greater compression, and a smaller codebook gives greater compression. The quality of the reconstructed image goes down as the compression goes up (as is true for all image compression schemes).

In a sense, video is a sequence of still images, so if you compress the sequence of images one after the other, you've compressed the video sequence. Using the compression example in Figure 18-9, you could VQ compress video at six to one in just this way. Six to one isn't good enough, though. You need 100 to one or better. Video doesn't change much from frame to frame. If that fact could be exploited to avoid compressing the parts that haven't changed, the compression rate would go up.

There are two ways to handle interframe compression. One is motion compensation, which is used with MPEG (we discuss that in the next section). The other, which is unique to VQ, is to extend the vectors to multiple frames. Instead of a two-by-two vector in one frame, we can take the same two-by-two vector in two frames, creating an eight-pixel vector. (You're not restricted to two-by-two vector sizes; it's just the example we're using.) This one change alone (everything else staying the same) boosts our example to twelve-to-one compression.

The art to VQ is in creating codebooks, in making compression fast, and in getting the best quality result for a given degree of compression. Done well, eight-to-one compression is possible for still frame images with essentially no loss in image quality. We've seen VQ-compressed full-screen color television signals that retained passable image quality down at the 1.5Mb rate associated with MPEG 1 compression.

## MPEG

As with VQ, MPEG is based on still image compression with features added to exploit the interframe redundancy in video. The MPEG still image compression technology is completely different from that of VQ, using what's called the Discrete Cosine Transform, or DCT. The DCT is based on the idea that a time-varying signal — the sequence of pixels in a line, for instance — can be represented by the sum of a number of signals at different frequencies. Figure 18-10 sketches the idea. The upper graph is a time-varying signal we made by adding two single-frequency signals together. We did a frequency analysis on the composite signal, producing the lower graph. The two blips in the signal occur at the points corresponding to the two signals we added together, and they show that one of the two signals was significantly stronger than the other.

Here's the idea behind intraframe compression in MPEG. Because you can reconstruct the time-varying signal (the image) from the frequencies, you can send the frequencies (and their amplitudes) instead of the image itself. You can compress the image by omitting some of the high-frequency information, and by compressing the representation of the frequency and amplitude data.

Figure 18-11 shows the intraframe compression process. The DCT algorithm compresses blocks in the image (rather than the entire image at once) to simplify the computations. After conversion of the image to DCT coefficients, quantization limits the number of bits, exploiting the fact that the eye is more sensitive to the effect of the low-frequency coefficients than the high-frequency ones.

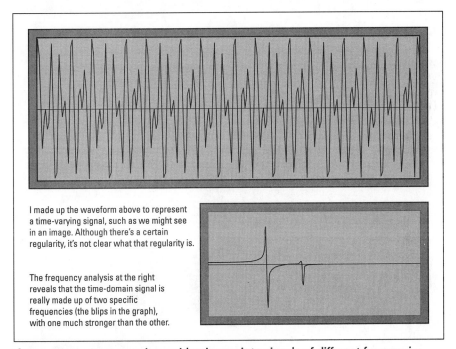

**Figure 18-10:** Decomposing a video image into signals of different frequencies that can reconstruct the original waveform is the point of the Discrete Cosine Transform used in MPEG compression.

Manipulating the quantization process allows greater or lesser quality in the compressed image and in the process requires more or fewer bits in the output data stream. A straightforward lossless data compression over the quantized output stream (see Chapter 16) completes the process.

It's possible that a block in a frame can't be found in a preceding or succeeding frame. If so, the block is individually DCT-coded and transmitted in the output sequence.

The complexity of the MPEG compressed bit stream causes the decompression operation itself to be complex, and so it imposes a significant load on the processor. The processing is feasible for small pixel resolutions, but if you're decompressing a bit stream for full-screen video resolution, the computations may exceed the available processor performance. There are specialized chips — accelerators — to speed up the decompression operations. You can get MPEG-accelerated video boards that will let a lesser processor do full-screen video at full-speed frame rates.

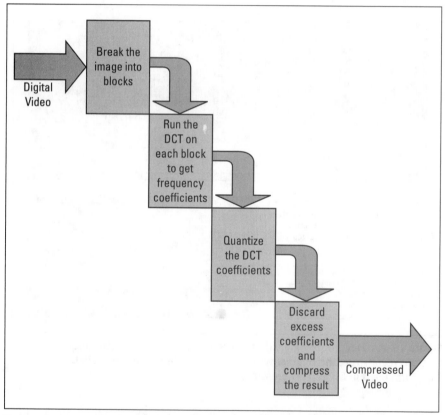

**Figure 18-11:** Intraframe MPEG compression is a complex, multistep process that depends on discarding high-frequency image information and compressing the result.

P-frames – interframes – code the differences from the previous frame, so they depend on the preceding frames. The differences are presented as motion of a coded block from the preceding I-frame or P-frame, so the motion coding process requires finding the best match block in the prior frame and describing how it has moved in the x and y directions. The arrows show the successive relations from I-frame to successive P-frames.

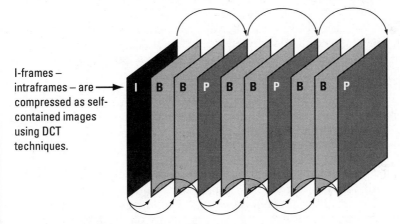

I-frames – intraframes – are compressed as self-contained images using DCT techniques.

B-frames – bi-directional frames – code the differences from preceding or succeeding frames. The differences are presented as motion of a coded block from the referenced frame. These arrows show the possible B-frame dependencies. The precise I-/B-/P- frame sequence is determined by the encoder, and need not be the IBBPBBPBBP sequence shown here.

**Figure 18-12:** The frame structure in an MPEG file defines how motion estimation relates successive video frames.

# Television in a Window

We have to admit that when we first saw a board for a computer that would let us turn part of a computer screen into a television, we didn't believe it. Fun's fun, but we felt that we were better off working without television programs in the corner of the screen. In the same way that we didn't need to turn our computer into a several-thousand dollar boom box that plays CDs, we didn't need to turn it into an expensive television.

In both cases, we learned that we didn't think through the potential of these products and the range of capabilities they provide. CD audio from your computer is used for the music tracks in games, reducing the load on the processor while delivering better sound. On-screen television combines well with video capture — digitizing, compressing, and storing video to your disk — to let you create the source content that takes your presentations to a higher level. You can do better than pictures and sound in presentations now — you can include video using the equipment on your desktop.

You may not be able to create the special effects for the next Hollywood blockbuster on your PC. What you can do with PC video capabilities isn't that good (yet). But you can videotape special events, product demonstrations, or training sequences, and you can store them in your computer (particularly once recordable DVD is well established, because DVD-RAM holds 6/8GB on one disk). With these capabilities, you can do a better job of selling your product, training users, and explaining maintenance and repair, right on the computer screen. Better yet, with some software development the same products will be able to do videoconferencing. That's a lot of opportunity.

The challenging part of TV tuner products is getting the video image from the video capture card onto your screen. The frames, lines, and dots that make up the television picture are at different rates and different resolutions than your computer screen. More is needed to get the picture on the screen than a few wires. The first TV tuner cards did this by overlaying the analog video signal from the television image on top of the computer display signal (see Figure 18-13). The television picture remained an analog signal at all times, so the card couldn't do much else but be a television.

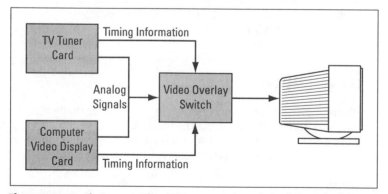

**Figure 18-13:** First-generation TV tuner cards switched the television video on top of the computer video to produce the television inset window functionality, but they couldn't do much else.

The products now on the market do the overlay work digitally. They send the television signal out to the video board as a digital pixel stream (Figure 18-14). The video board updates the video memory with the pixels from the television board (it works as a relatively large rectangular blit happening 30 times a second). The usual output and digital-to-analog conversion circuits on the video board create the combined signal sent to the monitor. If you write the digital video to disk (ideally after compressing it), you have video capture.

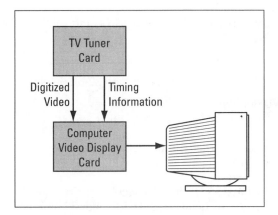

**Figure 18-14:** Newer TV tuner cards send the television image to the video card digitally. In addition to greater flexibility in terms of the on-screen display, the digitization function allows the board to work as a video capture system.

The data rate from the TV tuner card to the video card is relatively high. Some manufacturers allow the high-rate data to flow across the PCI or AGP bus (as with versions of the ATI All-in-Wonder 128 board). The bandwidth that data flow requires becomes unavailable for other operations, slowing your computer. To deal with the video bandwidth problem, some manufacturers have developed products that keep that data off the computer bus. At this writing there's no standard for that interface. At present, when you're looking for TV tuner capability, you may have to buy the tuner and video card to work with each other.

# Products

Choosing a video board is dependent on what you want from your computer and on which manufacturers you have confidence in. Even though video drivers come with Windows, you may still be dependent on the board manufacturer. (For instance, one of the video boards we use is capable of 1,600 × 1,200 resolution and is supported in that mode by the Windows NT 4.0 drivers shipped by Microsoft. The Microsoft Windows 95 drivers supported only 1,280 × 1,024 resolution — the manufacturer's enhanced drivers were required to realize the full capability of the board.)

It's terribly hard for one video board to implement all possible features and capabilities at a reasonable price. Because of that fact, you have to evaluate the features you want from your video board and select the product that comes the closest to your requirements. Typical features you can choose from include

✦ 2D acceleration

✦ 3D acceleration

✦ Maximum sustained bus transfer rate

✦ Resolution (640 × 480, 800 × 600, 1,024 × 768, 1,280 × 1,024, and 1,600 × 1,200 are the most common sizes)

✦ Maximum frame rate

✦ Supported color formats (usually 8-bit, 16-bit, 24-bit, and 32-bit pixels)

✦ MPEG acceleration and DVD decode

✦ TV tuner

✦ Video still frame and motion capture (see Chapter 24, "Digital Still Cameras, Video Capture, and Video Conferencing")

A high-resolution card will typically have a very fast 3D accelerator, a large video memory, and support for resolutions up to 1,600 × 1,200 with 24 or 32-bit color. A general-purpose card will have a 2D or 3D accelerator too but may top out no higher than 1,280 × 1,024 resolution. Full-featured cards will add support for MPEG and DVD decoding, video capture, and/or television output. The availability of the other functions in the preceding list varies among products.

Don't assume that a low-cost video board means low performance. The competition in the PC video market is so great that manufacturers have had to build custom chips to be able to sell their products at competitive prices. These chips end up in most of their products, so the fundamental performance and core feature set are similar across the product line. The differences among cards are typically in the components surrounding the video chip, such as the size and speed of the video memory or the speed and resolution of the digital-to-analog converters.

**Tip**    For anything but the lowest resolution and simplest features, you'll want a PCI bus video card (and preferably AGP). Without a fast bus, the video card will starve for data and you'll be disappointed at the performance you get.

## ATI Rage Fury

The ATI Rage Fury (Figure 18-15), first shipped in early 1999 and updated to the Rage Fury Pro later in the year, delivers 32-bit 3D performance faster than competing boards on the market at the time including the STB Velocity 4400 (which uses the nVidia TNT chip) or the STB BlackMagic 3D shown later in this chapter (using the 3Dfx VooDoo2 chip). The feature complement for the 32MB, 1,600 × 1,200–capable board is shown in Table 18-2.

**Figure 18-15:** The ATI Rage Fury provides accelerated video at up to 1,920 × 1,200 resolution.

## Table 18-2
### ATI Rage Fury Specifications

| Characteristic | Specification | |
| --- | --- | --- |
| Acceleration | 3D (Rage 128 chip) | |
| Video memory | 32MB SDRAM | |
| Bus interface | AGP | |
| Supported 2D resolutions and colors | Up to 1,920 × 1,200 | 32-bit pixels |
| Supported 3D resolutions and colors | Up to 1,920 × 1,200<br>1,920 × 1,440 | 32-bit pixels<br>16-bit pixels |
| Maximum frame rate | 640 × 480<br>800 × 600<br>1,024 × 768<br>1,152 × 864<br>1,280 × 1,024<br>1,600 × 1,200<br>1,920 × 1,200 | 200 Hz<br>200 Hz<br>180 Hz<br>160 Hz<br>125 Hz<br>85 Hz<br>76 Hz |

*continued*

| Table 18-2 *(continued)* | |
| --- | --- |
| **Characteristic** | **Specification** |
| 3D rendering | Quake II frame rates in excess of 60 frames per second at 640 × 480, 32-bit color, using a 400 MHz Pentium II |
| MPEG acceleration | Full hardware DVD decode support |
| Other | Plug and Play and DDC monitor support Windows 9x and NT drivers, including DirectX 6 and OpenGL |

The Streaming SIMD Extensions (SSE) instructions Intel added to the Pentium III processor boost the performance you'll get from a board like the Rage Fury. In tests we ran, we measured 10 to 20 percent performance gain for 640 × 480 and 800 × 600 resolutions by updating the video drivers to SSE versions, and gains of up to 250 percent for games using SSE throughout.

In addition to fast 3D acceleration (including in 32-bit color), the Rage Fury works well in 2D situations where you have to have as much information on-screen as possible, such as when you're using computer aided design tools or when you have several applications open at the same time. The 1,600 × 1,200 pixel resolution is 2½ times the standard VGA 640 × 480 resolution in each direction. That's a total of over six times the screen area to hold information. If you were happy at 640 × 480, that means you can have Word, Excel, PowerPoint, Exchange, Schedule+, and Access all open at the same time, each at the resolution you're used to, with none overlapping another. The 2D accelerator boosts speed to the point where performance at that resolution in the 16-bit or better modes is quite good. After you get used to the opportunities the high resolution of the board makes possible, you'll hate going back to something smaller.

Television output from the Rage Fury lets you conduct computer-based presentations to large audiences without the expense of a dedicated projection system, or play games on a big screen TV. The television output of the Rage Fury supports up to 800 × 600 resolution (the TV imposes the limit). Hardware in the television output chip handles the technical problems inherent in television display of computer images (including scaling and flicker removal), avoiding the completely illegible text and low-definition graphics you get with stand-alone VGA encoders.

# ATI All-in-Wonder 128

The ATI All-in-Wonder 128 extends the 3D acceleration and DVD capabilities of the Rage Fury with a stereo TV tuner, video capture, and real-time video compression. Its features are shown in Table 18-3. The board is shown in Figure 18-16. The board is available in both PCI and AGP versions, making upgrades possible for PCI-only systems that can't host the AGP-only Rage Fury.

## Table 18-3
## ATI All-in-Wonder 128 Specifications

| Characteristic | Specification | |
|---|---|---|
| Acceleration | 3D (Rage 128 chip) | |
| Video memory | 16 / 32MB SDRAM | |
| Bus interface | AGP or PCI | |
| Supported 2D resolutions and colors | Up to 1,920 × 1,200 | 32-bit pixels |
| Supported 3D resolutions and colors | Up to 1,920 × 1,200 | 32-bit pixels |
| | 1,920 × 1,440 | 16-bit pixels |
| Maximum frame rate | 640 × 480 | 200 Hz |
| | 800 × 600 | 200 Hz |
| | 1,024 × 768 | 180 Hz |
| | 1,152 × 864 | 160 Hz |
| | 1,280 × 1,024 | 125 Hz |
| | 1,600 × 1,200 | 85 Hz |
| | 1,920 × 1,200 | 76 Hz |
| 3D rendering | Quake II frame rates in excess of 60 frames per second at 640 × 480, 32-bit color, using a 400 MHz Pentium II | |
| MPEG acceleration | Full hardware DVD decode support | |
| Other | Stereo TV tuner | |
| | Video capture from external source or TV tuner | |
| | Plug and Play and DDC monitor support | |
| | Windows 9x and NT drivers, including DirectX 6 and OpenGL | |
| | Software support for VCR-like programmed record, WebTV for Windows 98, and NetMeeting video conferencing | |

**Figure 18-16:** The ATI All-in-Wonder 128 (Courtesy of ATI Technologies Inc.)

The All-in-Wonder 128 TV tuner is more than a television. It permits video capture to still images and video clips. You can record from a camera at your computer, from a portable video camera, or from video sources including a recorder or your cable system.

## STB BlackMagic 3D

The STB BlackMagic 3D (Figure 18-17) is designed to add 3D acceleration to existing computers with video cards not up to the demands of high performance games. The board uses a 3Dfx VooDoo2 chip, providing fast 3D acceleration in 16-bit color. Specifications for the BlackMagic 3D are shown in Table 18-4.

**Figure 18-17:** The STB BlackMagic 3D adds 3D acceleration to a system, operating alongside the conventional video board. (Photo courtesy STB Systems, Inc.)

## Table 18-4
## STB BlackMagic 3D Specifications

| Characteristic | Specification |
|---|---|
| Acceleration | 3D using 3Dfx VooDoo2 chip |
| Video memory | 12MB EDO DRAM<br>(4MB frame buffer, 8MB texture buffer) |
| Supported resolutions and colors | Up to 800 × 600, 16-bit color<br>(more with two-board configuration) |
| Maximum frame rate | 640 × 480        120 Hz Frame Rate<br>800 × 600        120 Hz Frame Rate |
| MPEG acceleration | None |
| Other | OpenGL and GLide (3Dfx proprietary)<br>software support |

The BlackMagic 3D exists for one focused reason — to deliver the maximum frame rate for 3D action games. The board won't help you do word processing, crunch spreadsheets, or work with the Web. It's for getting the maximum performance out of 3D games like Quake and Quake II, Unreal, Half-Life, and Shogo. Nor should you expect the BlackMagic 3D to help with 3D animations in tools like 3D Studio Max, because it only implements a subset of OpenGL, not the full specification, and because it doesn't accelerate the video image you normally see on-screen.

That last statement can be confusing without knowing how the BlackMagic 3D connects into your system. The board doesn't replace your existing video card; it complements it. You connect the output from your video card that would normally go to the monitor over to the BlackMagic 3D (using a supplied cable), and then connect the monitor to the BlackMagic 3D. For normal Windows or UNIX operation, the BlackMagic 3D is passive while your existing 2D card does the work. When you switch to a 3D game, though, the BlackMagic 3D kicks in and steals the monitor connection away, replacing the image you used to see with a complete new one the board creates. None of the images on the 2D board carry through. The BlackMagic 3D doesn't accelerate what the 2D board does; it replaces it when you're running in 3D.

The BlackMagic 3D has another limitation that could become significant as game technology evolves. Until late 1998, the 3D games on the market primarily rendered using 16-bit color, which is the maximum supported by the VooDoo2 and VooDoo3 chip sets. Unreal (published in late 1998) and Quake III: Arena changed that, rendering in 24- or 32-bit color for better appearance. The chip designers at 3Dfx (which now owns STB) decided to favor maximum speed over color rendition, limiting their chips to 16-bit color.

## ATI TV Wonder Tuner

The ATI TV Wonder Tuner accessory is a separate card that plugs into both the PCI bus and the video card. It's compatible with the VESA feature connector on many video cards, and with the ATI video cards featuring the "ATI Multimedia Channel," a proprietary interface into the video card. Connectors on the board include video in (such as for cable), S-video and composite video in (such as from a video recorder), audio out, and audio in. The ribbon cable connector at the top ties the card into the video board.

The ATI TV Tuner does more than video display and capture. It tracks the closed-caption signal from television programs, searching for hot words you specify, and zooms in on key parts of the picture. Combined with software for on-screen display (Figure 18-18), it offers you simple control over a lot of capability. You can see the capabilities of this card in the tabs on the dialog box: display on the screen, still-frame capture, TV channel display, video capture, and closed-caption text processing.

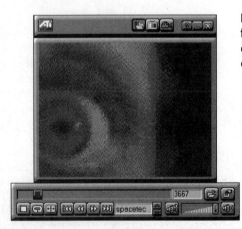

**Figure 18-18:** Software is the critical link for a computer TV tuner, giving you control over the hardware functions. You can do only what the software lets you.

# Choosing a Video Adapter

The basic decisions for video are clear. You want at least a 2D accelerator and 4MB of video memory (which will get you 1,600 × 1,200 resolution at 16-bit color). The video card should use the fastest bus in your computer, be it PCI or AGP. If you're playing games, get a good 3D accelerator. In 1999, boards meeting that specification would use the Rage 128, Riva TNT, or VooDoo3 chips. You can get an excellent, high-performance 3D accelerated video adapter for no more than $150.

A 3D accelerator affects the balance of what you need in your computer in an interesting way. The processing demands for 3D rendering are so high that they require a fast processor for good performance, and the benefit is greater the faster the processor. This is good example of balance and choke points. The choke point for unaccelerated 3D is the processor because of the computations rendering requires. Cranking up the processor speed is one approach, but it can cause the machine to be out of balance. You'd end up buying a faster processor than the rest of what you do demands, and if you're buying a complete machine, you're likely to get more disk and memory than you may need too. That's because the vendor assumes the fast processor is for a power user, not a casual user who wants good game play. Using a 3D accelerator lets the rest of the machine stay in balance—processor, memory, and disk—while giving the performance you want.

# The Top Ten Support Questions

Video cards generate a lot of calls to technical support centers. Most of the time, the problems are due to buggy or incompatible software.

## Video cards

Q: Where can I get updated drivers for my video card?

A: The most direct way to get updated video drivers for Windows is on the Internet from the card manufacturer's World Wide Web site. Manufacturers often don't provide drivers for UNIX systems; contact your UNIX vendor or, if you use a UNIX system with the XFree86 X Window system, look at http://www.xfree86.org.

Q: My system won't display resolutions above 640 × 480, even though my video board should do more. Why?

A: Windows maintains a database of monitor characteristics to help avoid conflicts between what the video board outputs and what the monitor can display. If you haven't set up your monitor type in Windows, the video driver may restrict you to the minimum 640 × 480 resolution. Change the monitor type to reflect your hardware (which with monitors no more than a few years old should likely be Plug and Play Monitor).

Q: The screen flickers when I run high-resolution applications. Why?

A: Some video boards default to relatively low refresh rates for the protection of older monitors that do not support the higher refresh rates. Vertical refresh rates less than 70 Hz may cause you to see flicker. In addition to checking that Windows or UNIX know what monitor you have (so they know the allowable refresh rates), you may need to set the monitor's capabilities into the video board directly using setup software shipped with your video board.

Q: My computer monitor loses sync when I connect a television to the TV output on my video board. Why?

A: The television output on your video card is designed to send the same horizontal and vertical frequencies to both the monitor and the television. The horizontal output frequency is different for television, so the board is shifting its outputs to adapt. If your monitor can't synchronize to the different frequency, the image will lose sync. You'll have to either turn off the monitor when the television is connected or replace the monitor with one capable of a wider range of frequencies.

Q: Where can I look for UNIX video drivers?

A: LINUX: `http://www.xfree86.org`
   SCO: `http://www.sco.com`
   SunSoft, Incorporated: `http://access1.sun.com/solaris/#x86`

## TV tuner

Q: I don't get audio (or video) from my TV tuner. Why?

A: Your TV tuner card needs more connections than just plugging it into the bus. You have to supply a video source, and you have to cable the audio output into your sound card. Once you do that, you have to check the software. Be sure the TV tuner is using the right source (composite video or antenna/cable, for instance), and that your sound card mixer has the input for the tuner (usually "line in") turned on.

Q: When I try to view channels 2 through 6 the image quality is very poor. Channels 7 and higher receive the signal properly. Why?

A: You may not be providing a strong enough or good enough signal to the tuner. Signals that work for your television may be insufficient for your computer TV tuner. Adding an in-line amplifier may help correct the problem. Keep in mind that even good coaxial television cable weakens the signal every foot it travels, so try to keep the cable short.

Q: How long can S-Video or RCA cables be?

A: S-Video or RCA cable lengths up to 20 feet are workable, and the signal quality should be okay, but remember that the longer the cable, the more signal degradation. High-quality cable and connectors can minimize loss. Use S-Video cables if you can, because the overall image quality is better.

# Hands-On Upgrades

There are lots of ways to go wrong upgrading your video card, some hardware and some software. If you follow the sequence I show you here, you should be able to avoid getting into trouble.

Because many video cards use their own specialized drivers, the first thing to do when you're upgrading a video card is to undo anything that's tied to your existing card. In Windows, that means you'll want to change your video driver to the Standard VGA driver, which should work with both your old and new cards. We've also seen driver updates that failed if the prior ones weren't uninstalled, so check that in the Add/Remove Programs applet in the Windows control panel.

While you're at it, note what display resolution and color depth you're using, and what the refresh rate is. You may be able to get the refresh rate from the monitor. Having the monitor manual handy (you may need the specifications in it) is a good idea too.

Once you change the driver, here are the steps to upgrade an existing video board (don't forget your antistatic strap):

1. Turn off the computer and disconnect the monitor.

2. Open the computer and remove the existing video board. If you don't have a video board — if it's integrated on the motherboard — follow the manufacturer's procedure to disable the onboard video. Some machines let you disable onboard video in the BIOS, while others require that you change switches or jumpers.

3. Put the new video board in an empty slot and screw in its bracket.

4. Connect the monitor to the new board. If your board includes television output or video capture connectors, hook them up as described in the manufacturer's documentation.

That's all there is to the hardware swap. The software may be a little more complicated:

1. *Set up the adapter hardware.* Some video cards have flash memory onboard into which you can set the parameters for your monitor. Windows drivers for these cards typically check the flash memory, so you want to set the card up in DOS before you start up Windows. If your card has a DOS installation routine, run it and look for monitor configuration. If your monitor has predefined settings in the setup program use them; otherwise, define a custom setup using the specifications from the monitor manual.

2. *Boot Windows.* If you're running Windows 9*x* and have installed a PCI or AGP display card, Plug and Play should detect the card and offer to install a driver. If the wrong card is detected (for example, very new ATI cards are sometimes detected as the VGA Wonder), *do not* restart Windows when offered the choice. Instead, install the drivers supplied by the manufacturer for the card, then reboot. You will need some Windows patches to make an AGP card work completely in Windows 95.

   If you have Windows NT 4, you'll have to install the drivers manually.

3. *Configure the display settings.* Go into Display Properties (the Display applet in the control panel), and choose the Settings tab. Pick your resolution, color depth, and font size there.

4. *Load any additional video accessories.* Your adapter may come with additional software, including MPEG file players, TV tuner control and display software, or video capture software. Install them now.

5. *Adjust your application software.* Some programs store their window locations and allow you to set preferences based on resolution and color depth. If you've upgraded your settings along with the new board, you'll need to check application preferences.

Software quirks ("It's a feature!") can make integrating a new video card with your monitor hard. Our Hitachi CM2110 monitor, for instance, is capable of 1,600 × 1,200 resolution, and the data base for Windows NT is set up that way. It works. Windows 9*x,* unfortunately, only thinks the monitor can do 1,280 × 1,024. We worked around that by lying to Windows, telling it I have a CM2111. There's a problem doing that, which is that the CM2111 supports a higher vertical refresh rate than the CM2110. If I let Windows 9*x* choose rates automatically, the display is unreadable at 1,600 × 1,200. Instead, we force the maximum refresh rate to a lower value acceptable to the monitor, and the combination works.

You can troubleshoot most video problems yourself by assuming the core of what's wrong is software. Start with the Standard VGA drivers and see what works. Build up the capabilities you use slowly, testing against the applications that have problems. (Example: We've had no end of problems with the Disney kid's software, the worst of which was when the video in the Disney Toy Story Animated Story Book insisted on displaying upside down. We tracked it down to an incompatibility between the Disney software and the video drivers.)

# Summary

✦ Hardware accelerators that take over the work of software can improve video performance.

✦ Realistic 3D displays on your screen require enormous numbers of computations, leading to other opportunities for accelerators to improve performance.

✦ Video compression makes huge data streams manageable. MPEG video compression technology dominates the market but may require hardware acceleration for good full-screen performance.

✦ Video cards and accessories need to be matched due to a lack of standards.

✦     ✦     ✦

# Monitors

## CHAPTER 19

I t's easy to state what you want in a monitor. You want it to be sharp, with bright, clear color. You want what you see to fill the screen, free of geometric distortions. You want it to deliver all the capabilities of your video card.

Getting what you want is more complex. We saw in Chapter 17, "Video," that the dot pitch and the horizontal and vertical frequencies of your monitor determine the limits of the display modes you can get on the screen. Sharpness, color balance, distortion measurements, and the rest of the characteristics are harder to specify or measure. Some require specialized test equipment or software to put up test displays. Often you can find information on those technical characteristics in product reviews, and sometimes in manufacturer data.

## Specifications and measurements

Let's look at the technical characteristics that define your monitor's performance: focus and convergence; color balance, tracking, purity, and saturation; ghosting; and geometry. The equipment to measure these properties isn't common, but later in this section we discuss products such as DisplayMate from Sonera Technologies, software that can help you evaluate the performance you're getting from a monitor.

### Focus and convergence

As we noted in Chapter 17, a monitor uses triangles of three color dots filling the screen (or lines grouped in tri-color sets in the case of monitors using the Sony Trinitron tube). How the beams inside the picture tube illuminate those dots determines how well the monitor can generate crisp edges on what it draws, rather than blobs with colored halos at the edges. Figure 19-1 shows how this works. The phosphors on the cathode ray tube (CRT) surface — the red, green, and blue dots — are in groups of three called triads. Each triad has one corresponding hole in the shadow mask. The hole keeps the beam from an electron gun from illuminating the wrong color phosphors.

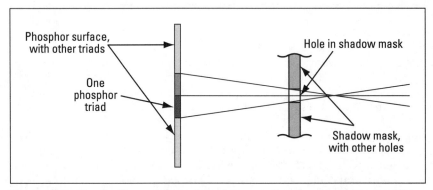

**Figure 19-1:** The shadow mask is a layer between the phosphor triads and the electron guns that causes the three electron beams to land on the phosphors in a distinct triangle so that each beam illuminates only the right color dot.

There are three separate electron beams: one for red, one for green, and one for blue. All three go through the same hole in the shadow mask for the same triad; but, because the electron guns are offset in a triangle around the centerline of the CRT, the pattern of the beams through the shadow mask—the "shadow"—is itself a triangle. If the beams from the electron guns are precisely focused, they project dots onto the phosphor layer no bigger than the dots themselves and don't overlap onto adjacent triads. Lining up the individual beams through the shadow mask is called *convergence*. If the aim of the electron beams onto the phosphors, through the shadow mask, is precise, then each beam illuminates only its own color dot. Misconvergence shows up as miscolored edges on lines and in areas.

You see poor focus on the screen as a fuzziness because adjacent triads get some illumination from the beam and light up. A poorly focused monitor can't form a one-pixel edge.

Misconvergence and poor focus most often show up at the corners and edges of the screen, or in the center if the corners and edges are right. Figure 19-2 shows why this happens. The extensive bend required in the electron beam to reach the sides and corners of the tube tends to distort the beam, which in turn requires the electronics to adapt to correct the distortion. If the electronics do this badly, they distort the beam in the center and force you to compromise by setting the controls for a place between the center and the outside. As a result, neither area ends up in focus or well converged on the monitor.

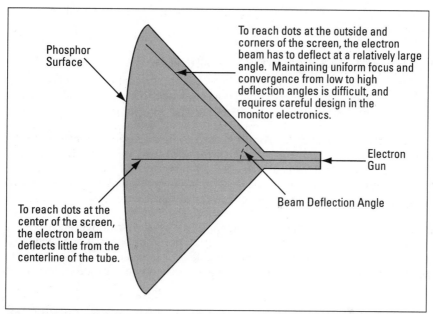

Phosphor Surface

To reach dots at the outside and corners of the screen, the electron beam has to deflect at a relatively large angle. Maintaining uniform focus and convergence from low to high deflection angles is difficult, and requires careful design in the monitor electronics.

Electron Gun

Beam Deflection Angle

To reach dots at the center of the screen, the electron beam deflects little from the centerline of the tube.

**Figure 19-2:** The greater deflection angles required in shorter CRTs help big monitors fit on your desk, but they make the job of the electronics designer harder.

Another cause of poor image quality can be poor design of the shadow mask. The electron beam carries a certain amount of power, some of which is absorbed by the shadow mask. The shadow mask heats up as a result, which can cause it to distort if it's not well constructed. This means you'll want to look at a monitor's performance after it's been on for a while as well as when it's cold, and also when you have the brightness and contrast cranked up (which increases the heat load on the shadow mask).

**Tip**    The brightness and contrast your monitor delivers is the result of a balancing act with the sharpness of focus and accuracy of convergence. A brighter image is the result of more power in the electron beam, which is harder for the electronics to control. This means that you should check focus and convergence with the brightness at its maximum useful setting. This doesn't mean all the way up; it means at the brightest point you'd actually set it to. For many monitors, that's the point just before the black areas start to turn gray, with the contrast adjusted to its maximum useful point. That's as difficult as it's going to get for the monitor, so if it handles well at that adjustment, it should be okay at lower levels as well.

Another important element to check on the monitor is its antiglare treatment, because different monitors have different antiglare treatments. Some use coatings on the face of the CRT, some use lenses, and some roughen the face of the CRT.

Most antiglare approaches degrade the sharp focus a little, so you'll want to see how the manufacturer balanced these elements.

## Color balance, tracking, purity, and saturation

Your eye is sensitive to color relationships. Skin tones that are off-color draw your eye. A monitor needs to achieve good color balance to look right. It has to maintain the correct intensity relationship between red, green, and blue.

The characteristics of the electronics in the monitor are such that the color balance tends to vary with brightness. Having the monitor balance on a bright image doesn't mean that it will remain balanced on dark ones. The electronics may not maintain good color tracking as the brightness varies. Check for balance both on bright areas and in dark grays because of this limitation.

Your video card may have adjustments for color balance, but overall you want the monitor to get the balance and tracking right. Color balance on the video card is most useful for adjustments to get screen and printer colors to correspond. If the monitor is off-balance, you may not have the necessary range of adjustments available.

Color purity means that the colors on the screen are uniform everywhere, with no patches of odd color. The most common causes of purity problems are unwanted magnetic fields deflecting the beams on their way to the shadow mask, through the shadow mask, and to the phosphors. This can happen two ways: A device outside the monitor can create a magnetic field that reaches into the tube, or the shadow mask can become partially magnetized.

### Incident static magnetic fields

A surprising number of things can create static magnetic fields, including power transformers, telephones, speakers, and (of course) magnets. Don't forget that magnets and power transformers can be inside other objects. Their magnetic fields can extend through an unshielded or poorly shielded equipment case and into your monitor. If they do, one of two consequences can happen: you get local discolorations, or you get a ripple in the image on the screen.

If the problem is a static magnetic field, such as from a magnet or a speaker (which contains a magnet), it can slowly magnetize the shadow mask (see Figure 19-3). The problem is that the permanent magnet must provide a strong, stable magnetic field for the voice coils to push against. If the speaker isn't shielded or is shielded poorly, that magnetic field reaches outside the speaker. If the speaker is placed too close to your monitor, it can reach into the CRT. When that happens, it starts to magnetize the shadow mask. Magnetization of the shadow mask can distort the color and the focus in the affected parts of the tube.

A device called a degaussing coil inside the monitor is wound around the tube and activated every time you turn on the monitor. This device tries to neutralize residual magnetization of the shadow mask by these constant fields, but it's only so strong and can do only so much. Over time, the shadow mask can acquire a local magnetic field that discolors the display in that region. We've also had the combination of a field from speakers and the action of the degaussing coil combine to leave no residual field, so that when we removed the speakers, discolorations appeared in the corners of the display that had been near the speakers.

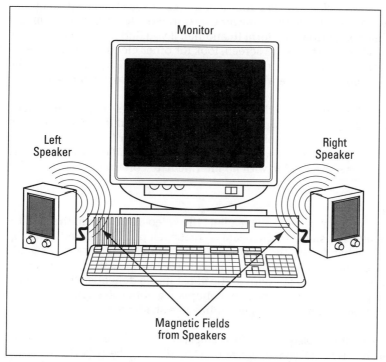

**Figure 19-3:** Magnets in speakers can leave discolored corners on your monitor.

Your options are to use well-shielded speakers, or to keep the speakers well away from the front of the CRT. The safe distance depends on the speaker and on the shielding in the monitor itself. Moving the speakers to the back of the monitor helps, as well as spacing them laterally away from the monitor case.

**Tip** You can check a monitor for color-purity problems by looking at a pure white screen. (For instance, set the document background color to white, open an empty document in Word, and use the View ⇨ Full Screen command. More comprehensive tests are available in DisplayMate, covered later in this chapter.) If you see patches of faint color, the monitor may need to be degaussed with a strong degaussing coil. Degaussing is an operation involving passing a strong alternating magnetic field past the entire screen. Over tens of seconds, you slowly move the coil far away from the tube, and then turn it off. You can get degaussing coils at electronics supply stores. Follow the directions carefully, because you can make things worse if you use the coil improperly.

### Incident dynamic fields

Varying magnetic fields too near your monitor can cause the image to be wavy. A common source of such fields is power transformers: devices that use magnetic fields to shift power from one form to another. If you find one part of the display vibrating back and forth on the screen, look for other electronic components (wall transformers, uninterruptible power supplies, boom boxes, and so forth) that are close to the monitor and see what happens when you move them away.

Good color saturation means that colors are neither too strong, with similar colors being indistinguishable, nor washed out and faded. The difference is the same as when you run the color control back and forth on a color television. At one end, colors wash out to black and white, while at the other end colors are sharply defined like those on a poster, with no intermediate color tones.

## Ghosting

As the electron beam sweeps along a line, the video amplifiers in the monitor have to pass an intensity signal to the beam so that each pixel is painted at the right intensity. If the bandwidth the video passes is too small, the intensity signal can't change fast enough. When this happens, you get ghosts — shadows and streaking of the on-screen image. The strength of the ghost image depends on how intense the original image is. A small change may not create a noticeable ghost, but a black-to-white vertical edge can create highly noticeable shadows.

**Note**    The relevant capability of the video amplifier is called the maximum video bandwidth, and is typically in the range of 50 to 150 megahertz (MHz). An acceptable maximum video bandwidth is implied by a manufacturer specification that the monitor will handle the resolution you want. To be sure that it does meet your requirements, look at a maximum-resolution display with alternating black and white bars. If you see ghosting (and the monitor cable hasn't been extended), the video bandwidth is inadequate and you should find another monitor.

## Geometry

For the image you see on-screen to look right, it has to be geometrically correct, straight, even, and flat. Figure 19-4 shows the distortions monitors are prone to creating. Each can be corrected with the right electronics and adjustments on the front of the monitor. However, if your monitor doesn't provide the right adjustments, you're limited to whatever performance it can give you.

Monitor test software like DisplayMate is useful for adjusting geometric distortions, because it displays test patterns that allow you to see and remove these errors.

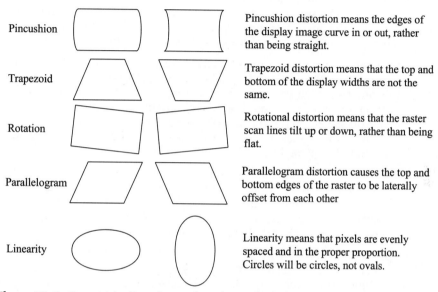

Pincushion

Pincushion distortion means the edges of the display image curve in or out, rather than being straight.

Trapezoid

Trapezoid distortion means that the top and bottom of the display widths are not the same.

Rotation

Rotational distortion means that the raster scan lines tilt up or down, rather than being flat.

Parallelogram

Parallelogram distortion causes the top and bottom edges of the raster to be laterally offset from each other

Linearity

Linearity means that pixels are evenly spaced and in the proper proportion. Circles will be circles, not ovals.

**Figure 19-4:** Geometric distortion makes shapes look different from what the program intended.

# Controls

There's no apparent consensus on what controls you really need on a monitor. There are monitors with nothing but contrast and brightness controls, and others with a complete set of controls letting you adjust everything. You'll find controls with simple, clear layouts, and ones that would leave a genius hard pressed to figure out how to use them. A great image is more important than great controls, but the controls may be what you need to get the image you want.

The control options for monitors include

✦ *Horizontal size and position.* This control adjusts the width of the raster on the screen and lets you center the image laterally. You'll find that both the horizontal and vertical characteristics of the image change as you change display resolution and refresh rate, so you need these controls to compensate. Some display cards let you make similar adjustments, but in my experience it's often easier to do the adjustment at the monitor.

A good monitor will store control settings independently for each resolution, so you don't have to keep readjusting the controls.

✦ *Vertical size and position.* These controls are similar to the ones for horizontal size and position, letting you set the height and top-to-bottom position. They should be stored along with the horizontal settings.

✦ *Pincushion.* A pincushion control lets you vary the bulge or tuck at the side of the raster. The setting applies to all resolutions and refresh rates. Be sure that you have the horizontal and vertical settings right before you adjust pincushion. Otherwise, you're almost guaranteed to get the setting wrong.

Be careful how you decide if the edges are straight. The bezel of the monitor surrounding the tube is not always itself straight, so it may not work well for this process. What you use can be as simple as a folded piece of paper (to get a straight edge). Make sure that it's reasonably straight. Also be sure that the image displayed on the screen completely fills the screen (a maximized window works, because you can use the window frame as the reference line that should be straight).

✦ *Tilt, rotation, and trapezoid.* These controls work in the same way as the pincushion control, but they relate to other distortions. The same caution applies about getting the horizontal and vertical settings right first. You're also likely to notice that the four settings interact some, so you may have to adjust them several times before you get it right.

✦ *Color temperature.* If you've ever played with a light dimmer, you've probably noticed that as the light gets dimmer, it gets redder, and as it gets brighter, it gets bluer. This change in color, which affects the perceived color of objects illuminated by the light, corresponds to a change in the temperature of the filament in the light, or what's called the color temperature. Color temperature is measured in degrees Kelvin (relative to absolute zero), with lower temperatures giving redder colors. Monitors with color temperature adjustments provide settings for several standard temperatures, such as 9300 and 6500 degrees Kelvin, and may provide a user-defined setting. The color temperature interacts some with color balance (which you normally adjust on the video card, if at all), because the effect is to alter the balance between red and blue.

The color temperature can be very important if you're doing critical color matching to make sure that the results you get on the screen correspond to what you scan and what you print. Otherwise, it's a matter of personal preference.

✦ *Brightness and contrast.* While most of the other controls on a monitor correspond to those a service technician sets on a television, the brightness and contrast are exactly the same as you're used to. The two controls interact somewhat and have limited range on some monitors. It's common to adjust the contrast at around 80 percent of the full range (or more), with brightness just below the point where the raster outside the image appears, but many people find this setting too harsh. The setting you use is personal preference, influenced by the lighting and other characteristics of where you work.

Glare off the screen and directly in your eyes can make the image hard to look at no matter how you adjust brightness and contrast. Try to avoid the situations illustrated in Figures 19-5a and 19-5b to keep glare to a minimum. Light shining directly on the screen or in your eyes reduces contrast and can make working very uncomfortable. Figure 19-5c shows more desirable arrangements.

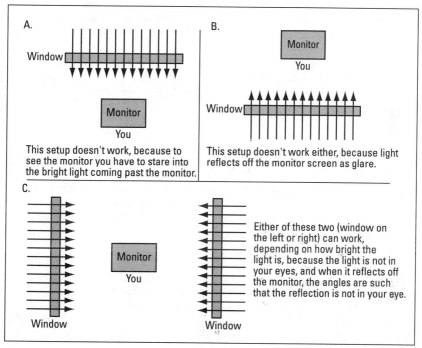

**Figure 19-5:** Placing the monitor to minimize glare.

✦ *Degauss.* In the same way that magnetic fields from speakers and transformers can leave the shadow mask with residual magnetism, so can other weaker fields. Most monitors have a coil wound around the tube near the front, called a degaussing coil, used to remove these effects. When you turn the monitor on, a strong alternating current in the coil produces a strong alternating magnetic field that penetrates the tube and slightly magnetizes the shadow mask, first one way and then the other. Over several seconds, the monitor reduces the current, reducing the field strength as it alternates back and forth. By the time the field reaches zero, the process leaves the shadow mask completely demagnetized.

There's a limit to the strength of the degaussing coil, partly due to the relatively large current flowing through it. That current generates a lot of heat, too much of which will destroy the coil. For this reason, if your monitor has a manual control to energize the coil, you don't want to use it too often. Waiting several minutes between activations should be long enough. If the built-in degaussing coil can't clear the problem after a few tries, you probably need to use a stronger coil as we discussed earlier.

 **Tip**   For the same reason you keep magnets away from monitors, keep them away from floppy disks and tapes. Keep floppies and tapes away from monitors as well because of the degaussing field.

Another useful control feature is the capability for the monitor to display the current horizontal and vertical frequencies. Most current monitor designs will blank when they see an invalid signal. Many units will also blank when they see a signal they can't handle. You want that feature to make sure a misconfigured video card can't damage the monitor.

## Multimedia

It's become fashionable to build speakers into monitors and offer them at higher prices as multimedia products. The same strategy seems to apply to power controllers (devices you put under the monitor that have switches to control the power for different peripherals) and keyboards.

We don't recommend buying these products. It simply isn't a good idea. Packaging the speaker into the monitor ensures that its magnetic field is as close to the display tube as possible. Even if the manufacturer shields it well, you're starting out with a difficult problem. Speakers in monitors tend to use smaller magnets, smaller amplifiers, and limited bass. All those compromises reduce sound quality. Speakers in power controllers and keyboards suffer from limited size, making it hard to get good sound as well.

You can also get speakers that are designed to hang from either side of your monitor. Mounting them there ensures they're right where they can cause the most trouble, up near the shadow mask and as close as possible to the tube. If you need such an arrangement to maximize desk space, make sure you choose units that move the low-frequency drivers into a subwoofer you can put somewhere else. If you can't do that, it's better to space your speakers somewhat away from and toward the back of the monitor.

# Flat panel displays

A flat panel display is the desktop version of the display you find in laptop computers. The design has the advantages of requiring less space and less power than a CRT. There are several ways to build a flat panel display:

✦ *Light-emitting diodes.* If the display is far enough away, you can use light-emitting diodes (LEDs) as individual pixels, stacking lots of them in either direction to get the resolution you want. The pixels are relatively large, however, so it's difficult to get good resolution. It takes a relatively long time for the diode to turn on, and so an LED display isn't appropriate for handling fast-moving information.

✦ *Plasma display panels.* The pixels in a plasma display panel (PDP) are similar in operation to the old neon lights electronic equipment used before LEDs came along. A PDP can be built to be very rugged and reliable, can do color, and can be manufactured at relatively low cost in high volume. It takes much more power than other flat panel technologies, and it is hard to see in bright sunlight.

✦ *Electroluminescent displays.* These displays work somewhat like LEDs. They can be very compact and can be written much faster than LEDs — fast enough for video. An electroluminescent (EL) display has good readability in sunlight. They are relatively expensive and consume a fair amount of power. It's not clear when color EL displays will be available.

✦ *Liquid crystal displays.* These are the most common form of flat panel display. Liquid crystal display (LCD) panels are now built mostly using the active-matrix technology, with three transistors at each pixel. Figure 19-6 shows how this works. When the active matrix transistors are off, the liquid crystal material blocks the transmission of the incident light at the back of the cell (upper drawing). Each transistor in the cell (one per color) can be turned on independently. When a transistor is turned on, it reorients the liquid crystal material and allows white light to pass. A colored filter in front of the transistor blocks all but one color, creating the usual red-green-blue triad making up one pixel (lower drawing).

The LCD panel itself requires very low power, but significant power is required for the backlight. LCDs are the lowest-cost flat panel technology at this time and offer high contrast and color operation. Their operation is affected by very low temperatures, to the point where their operation slows down and ultimately stops.

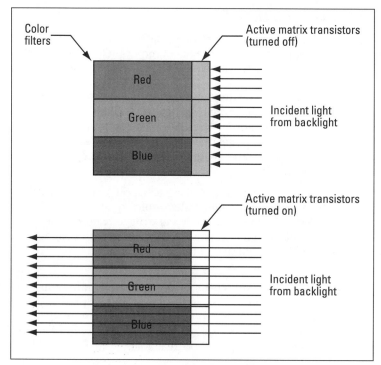

**Figure 19-6:** An active matrix LCD gives good color and contrast at reasonable cost but is hard to manufacture.

An LCD at 1,280 × 1,024 resolution contains nearly 4,000,000 transistors, more than in a Pentium processor, spread out over a large area. The manufacturing problems this creates make it hard to build LCD panels free from bad pixels and other defects, a problem that gets worse as the size of the panel increases.

The LCD requires a backlight for operation, and the mean time between failures (MTBF) of the backlight is around 20,000 hours. Backlights are not generally replaceable by users. If you use a flat panel display for long periods, it's quite likely you'll have to have the light replaced.

**Future PC**

The limited reliability, small size, and relatively high cost of an LCD have to become competitive with CRT-based monitors before flat panels will take a significant share of the desktop display market. Companies now manufacture desktop flat panel monitors capable of resolutions up to 1,600 × 1,200, but you'll pay around $800 for a 15-inch 1,024 × 768 unit, and nearly $3,000 for an 18-inch 1,280 × 1,024 unit. Over time we expect the size to increase and prices to come down, but over time the price and performance of CRT-based monitors will increase too. Whether desktop LCDs can compete with CRT-based monitors remains to be seen.

# Display data channel

The Display Data Channel (DDC) is a way for your computer to get information about your monitor and its capabilities. DDC-compatible monitors can feed that information to a DDC-capable video card, which in turn forwards the information to your operating system. Windows knows how to use DDC (setup your monitor as Plug and Play compatible); UNIX may not. Plug and Play software can detect and configure your monitor automatically, simplifying setup.

There are three levels of DDC implementation, as shown in Figure 19-7a through 19-7c. All three let the monitor send data in a specific format to the computer, making it possible for Plug and Play software to detect what the monitor is and configure the video card appropriately. The DDC2AB version also lets the computer send commands to the monitor, allowing software to set the monitor controls just as you would from the front panel controls.

Making DDC work requires that your video card be capable of receiving the data. The ATI video cards in Chapter 18, "Video Adapters," all provide this capability. So do the Hitachi monitors we discuss in this chapter. Look for DDC when you upgrade, so that eventually you migrate to a fully DDC-capable, Plug and Play system.

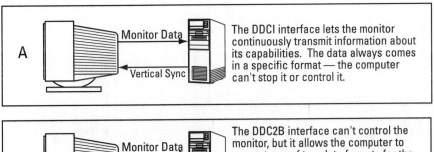

A — Monitor Data / Vertical Sync

The DDCI interface lets the monitor continuously transmit information about its capabilities. The data always comes in a specific format — the computer can't stop it or control it.

B — Monitor Data / Data Clock

The DDC2B interface can't control the monitor, but it allows the computer to request one of two data formats for the information continuously transmitted by the monitor. The data clock signal adds this capability, and allows the computer to control the data transmission from the monitor.

C — Monitor Data / Data Clock

The DDC2AB interface creates a two-way control interface between the monitor and the computer, allowing the computer to request specific information and to send commands to the monitor.

**Figure 19-7:** The three levels of DDC implementation

# Products

We did a price comparison of 14-inch through 21-inch inch monitors available for sale in early 1999, and we plotted the results in Figure 19-8 (we've plotted LCD monitors a little later in this section). Actual prices will change, but the relationships remain relatively the same over several years. The variables we looked at were dot pitch and screen size. The range of important specifications is much broader than these two, but generally the other specifications were in line with those two. We don't recommend dot pitches greater than 0.28 millimeters, so the figure includes data for 0.28 down to 0.22 millimeters.

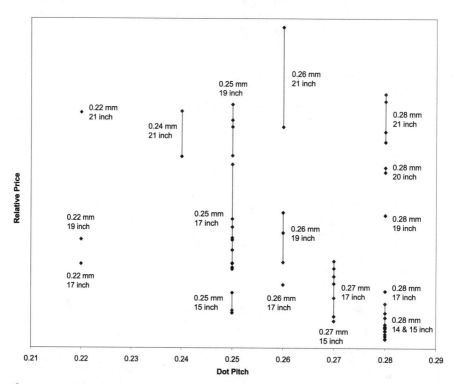

**Figure 19-8:** Monitors come in a wide range of specifications. You can get a better monitor by carefully shopping around and comparing.

There are some important conclusions to draw from the figure. The easiest one to see is that it's worth spending time shopping and comparing units. (To help you see that, consider that the actual price range for the data we collected was $88 to

$1,413). The figure shows that you can find a 15-inch monitor with 0.25mm dot pitch for the same price as units with a 0.28mm dot pitch. You'd want to compare the other specifications, and see the units if you can, but the difference in dot pitch is suggestive of a better product. When you go shopping, take along a test disk with DisplayMate on it so you can really wring out the ones you're interested in.

Another conclusion you might draw is that larger monitors aren't necessarily much more expensive. Look at the isolated point in the lower left of the figure. That point represents the Hitachi SuperScan Elite 641. We bought one in early 1999 for just over $400, and we can tell you from direct experience that it's an excellent monitor. Even though it's only a 17-inch unit, we run it at 1600 × 1200 resolution, getting a sharp, readable image. When you consider that you might pay $300 for a 0.28mm monitor capable of only 1,280 × 1,024, you'll realize that there are some real values to be found if you look hard enough.

The other two data points in the figure at 0.22mm dot pitch are the reason we've included the Hitachi monitors in the following paragraphs. The middle point is the SuperScan 751; the higher one is the SuperScan 812. The entire line is priced no higher than competitive units with dramatically inferior specifications.

There's one more interesting point we found — monitor prices in our data were almost without exception more expensive from companies selling complete systems. You could usually save money by buying a system without a monitor and then buying the monitor separately on the Internet. Monitor upgrades were also expensive from those companies — the pricing differences suggested that on upgrade you paid the difference in retail prices between the one they offered and the one you want.

We've not considered the radiation emitted from monitors in these comparisons, because nearly all current models comply with the low-radiation ergonomic standards. It's unclear what the effects of the low-level radiation from the monitor CRT are, but if you're concerned, you should verify compliance with the appropriate standards.

Many more desktop LCD products are available in early 1999 than when we wrote the first two editions of this book. Figure 19-9 illustrates the characteristics of what you can get, using the style of Figure 19-8 but replacing dot pitch on the horizontal axis with diagonal size. We've annotated the points with maximum resolution rather than size and dot pitch, too.

We plotted relative price in the figure to emphasize price structures rather than actual numbers, but don't underestimate how much a desktop LCD can cost. You'll pay nearly $700 for the least expensive unit we found, but over $7,700 for the most expensive.

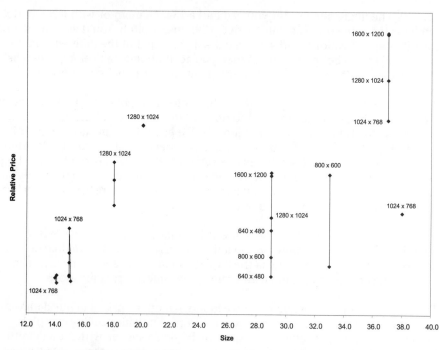

**Figure 19-9:** Desktop LCD monitors are available in a wide range of sizes, but it will be a while before prices come down.

## Hitachi SuperScan

Large, high-resolution monitors, such as the Hitachi SuperScan series (Figure 19-10), are what you want for complex or exacting work on your computer and, given their pricing in the market, are arguable for any application. We've used a predecessor to the current generation, a SuperScan Pro 21-inch monitor, that's easily the equal of any monitor we've ever used: mainframe, minicomputer, workstation, or PC.

Table 19-1 shows the specifications for three different SuperScan monitors. Note particularly the maximum resolution of 1,600 × 1,200, the horizontal dot pitch of only 0.22mm, and the maximum video bandwidth of 130 to 160 MHz. These specifications mean that the monitor will have a great image even at the highest resolution. Visual comparisons against large monitors with poorer dot pitch and other specifications will show you how important these specifications are. The 19- and 21-inch monitors are a little large and heavy, so they may not fit in highly restricted workspaces. The prices of 19-, 20-, and 21-inch monitors in this class have dropped to the point where they're worth serious consideration for high-end business and home use; at no more than $400, the 17-inch version is pretty much a no-brainer.

**Figure 19-10:** The Hitachi SuperScan monitors deliver a large, crisp image for exacting work. (Courtesy of ATI Technologies, Inc.)

## Table 19-1
## The Hitachi SuperScan Specifications Illustrate What You Want in a High-Quality Large Monitor

| Characteristic | SuperScan Elite 641 (17") | SuperScan 751 (19") | SuperScan 812 (21") |
|---|---|---|---|
| Active display area (horizontal × vertical, in millimeters) | 325 × 245 | 367 × 276 | 406 × 305 |
| Viewable image size (in inches) | 15.9 | 18.0 | 20.0 |
| Dot pitch (V × H, in mm) | 0.13 × 0.22 | 0.14 × 0.22 | 0.16 × 0.22 |
| Maximum horizontal frequency (kHz) | 95 | 93.75 | 107 |
| Maximum vertical frequency (Hz) | 130 | 160 | 160 |
| Maximum resolution | 1,600 × 1,200 | 1,600 × 1,200 | 1,600 × 1,200 |

*continued*

| Table 19-1 *(continued)* | | | |
|---|---|---|---|
| *Characteristic* | *SuperScan Elite 641 (17")* | *SuperScan 751 (19")* | *SuperScan 812 (21")* |
| Maximum video bandwidth (MHz) | 150 | 200 | 230 |
| Color temperature (degrees Kelvin) | 9,300, 6,500, User Defined | 9,300, 6,500, User Defined | 9,300, 6,500, User Defined |
| Dimensions (width × height × depth, in inches) | 16.2 × 15.8 × 16.3 | 17.6 × 17.9 × 18.1 | 19.2 × 19.0 × 18.5 |
| Weight (pounds) | 37.4 | 53 | 61 |

The SuperScan series includes other models, the 753 and the 814, with even more advanced specifications than the 751 and 812. Table 19-2 shows the key differences for those two. The payoff is that the more advanced models can support a higher frame rate at the highest resolutions.

| Table 19-2 More SuperScan Advanced Models Give You Higher Frame Rates | | | | |
|---|---|---|---|---|
| | *19 inch* | | *21 inch* | |
| | *753* | *751* | *814* | *812* |
| Maximum horizontal frequency (kHz) | 107 | 93.75 | 125 | 107 |
| Maximum vertical frequency (Hz) | 160 | 160 | 160 | 160 |
| Maximum video bandwidth (MHz) | 230 | 200 | 270 | 230 |
| Maximum 1,600 × 1,200 frame rate (Hz) | 85 | 75 | 100 | 85 |

The screen shot in Figure 19-11 shows the payoff from a screen supporting 1,600 × 1,200 resolution. We set Windows for large fonts, and all the elements are still visible in the figure at the same time. At 1,024 × 768 resolution, even with small fonts, we'd get Word on the screen (showing less of the text) and little else.

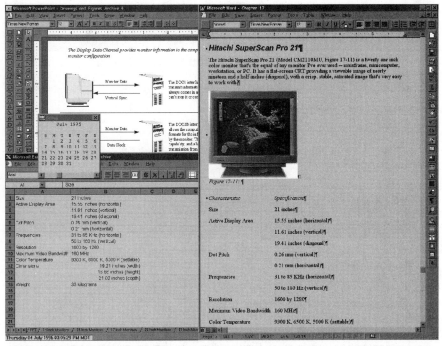

**Figure 19-11:** Very high resolution, such as the 1,600 × 1,200 screen shot here, lets you have more on the screen at the same time, so you can work more effectively.

## NEC MultiSync LCD

As LCD technology evolves to better address the needs of desktop computer users, manufacturers are delivering more capable desktop LCD products to the market. There are two classes of desktop LCD today — smaller ones intended to replace desktop monitors, and larger ones intended for presentations. The NEC MultiSync LCD series (see Table 19-3) targets the desktop monitor market, while their MultiSync X series is much larger and targeted at presentations. If you can get past the high price (over $4,000 in early 1999) and limited resolution, you get a monitor that emits almost no magnetic fields, uses little power, takes very little space (you can mount it on a wall!), and can be rotated 90 degrees from the usual landscape orientation to a vertical portrait setup.

| | Table 19-3 NEC MultiSync LCD Specifications | | | |
| --- | --- | --- | --- | --- |
| Characteristic | LCD400 | LCD1510 | LCD1810 | LCD2010 |
| Screen size (inches) | 14.1 | 15.0 | 18.1 | 20.1 |
| Viewing angle (degrees) | 160 | 160 | 160 | 160 |
| Maximum resolution | 1,024 × 768 | 1,024 × 768 | 1,280 × 1,024 | 1,280 × 1,024 |
| Refresh rate at maximum resolution (Hz) | 75 | 75 | 60 | 60 |
| Maximum horizontal frequency (kHz) | 60 | 60 | 60 | 80 |

## DisplayMate

It's difficult to compare monitors without the right tools to help you isolate different performance characteristics. The most widely used program for display work at the time of this writing is DisplayMate, from Sonera Technologies.

**Tip**    Demonstration versions of DisplayMate can be found at: `http://www.displaymate.com`.

One of the key functions of DisplayMate is to provide test patterns you can use to evaluate specific performance characteristics. Figure 19-12 shows the display pattern to check that circles are displayed as true, round drawings. The pattern gives you sets of circles in the corners as well as in the center, so that if there's geometric distortion at the edges of the screen, you'll be sure to see it.

DisplayMate is available in several versions:

✦ *DisplayMate for Windows* and *DisplayMate for Windows Video Edition*. These versions support any Windows display from VGA upward and operate at any color depth. These versions run from a floppy disk, so their well suited for monitor evaluation in stores to help you compare performance. The Windows version includes online help screens and expert advice, making it appropriate for individual and corporate support use. The multimedia edition adds support for video projectors and televisions, including intensity control and overscan handling.

**Figure 19-12:** Test patterns in DisplayMate help you isolate and correct problems in a monitor, and to compare performance of monitors.

✦ *DisplayMate for DOS* and *Displaymate Professional for DOS.* These versions are designed for technical and manufacturing areas. They add support for accurate measurement of screen distortion and timing, and include a script facility to support manufacturing-line product quality tests, video board and BIOS tests, and a report generator. DisplayMate Professional for DOS supports VESA-compatible graphics cards in any mode. An extensive manual discusses monitor technology as well as the use of the program.

# Choosing a Monitor

We recommend buying a monitor 17 inches or larger, with a dot pitch no larger than 0.28 millimeters. A monitor of that size or larger lets most people run Windows at resolutions of 1,024 × 768 or more, and the added screen space you get from the higher resolution lets you work more effectively.

You can find monitors with worse dot pitch, such as the 0.31 millimeter dot-pitch 20-inch unit we once saw advertised as a "corporate grade" unit. If you do the side-by-side comparison with higher-quality monitors, you'll quickly see the loss of sharpness and understand why working with one of these units can be uncomfortable. There are a lot of makes and models to choose from, so there's a lot of competition in the market. If you shop and compare carefully, you can find a sharp 17-inch or larger unit you like at a good price. If you can afford a larger monitor, look at them. A comparison will show you quickly how valuable resolution up to 1,600 × 1,200 can be in Windows. Some office applications, such as Computer Aided Design (CAD) and other detailed graphics work, may make a larger monitor worth the added cost.

# Top Support Questions

Q: Can't I just buy a monitor from its size and dot pitch specifications?

A: You shouldn't. You'll see things looking at monitors with test patterns that don't show up in the specifications. As important as dot pitch (or maybe more) are color registration or convergence, beam size and focus, and video bandwidth.

Q: I see Moiré patterns — regular geometric interference — on my monitor. What can I do?

A: A Moiré pattern arises when pixels are not perfectly aligned with the phosphor dots on the screen, hitting some on-center and some off. A Moiré pattern is the result of limitations in display technology — you'd need a far smaller dot pitch to eliminate the pattern. For example, a 17 inch diagonal display with a resolution of 1,024 × 768 requires a dot pitch of 0.12mm to eliminate the pattern. You can try several things to reduce the visibility of the Moiré pattern on your monitor: turn on the Moiré pattern reduction feature of your monitor, if you have one; change the image size slightly on the monitor to alter the overlap pattern; change the resolution on your video card; use as bright an image as you can; and use as many colors on-screen as possible (avoid 16 and 256-color modes).

Q: My monitor flickers. What can I do?

A: You see flicker on your monitor when the refresh rate isn't high enough. Flicker is generally worse with interlaced display modes, so be sure your video card is set up for non-interlaced operation. Similarly, you can minimize flicker by setting the video card for the highest vertical refresh rate the monitor will handle at the resolution you use. You'll be able to use a higher vertical refresh rate at lower resolutions. To see why, look back at the table in Chapter 17, "Video," in the sidebar "Computing monitor line rates," keeping in mind that your monitor has a maximum line rate.

You can't exceed that, so for higher resolutions you may have to accept a reduced frame (vertical refresh) rate.

Q: I can't keep people from pointing at my screen and leaving fingerprints. How can I clean them off?

A: Unless your monitor manufacturer says differently, clean your monitor with ordinary glass cleaner and paper towel. Don't let liquid drip into the monitor (you can wet the paper towel and then clean the screen). Be very careful of the anti-glare coating if your monitor uses one, since it can scratch or rub off. You might want to use a special monitor cleaning kit, taking advantage of its anti-static cleaner and soft lint-free cloths.

Q: Do I care about an energy-saving monitor?

A: We think you should have an energy-saving monitor (and set up to use it) for two reasons. First, although the difference in power cost to you whether the monitor is on or not while its idle is small, the difference in power usage over hundreds of millions of monitors is huge. A typical 17-inch monitor uses over 100 watts more power when on than when in standby; so if 100 million monitors switch to standby, that's a savings of 10,000 megawatts — several large power stations. You also care because having the monitor go into standby lets it cool off, reducing aging and extending its life.

Q: I put in a great new monitor, but I can't get more resolution than before. What's wrong?

A: Assuming your video card is capable of higher resolution, the issue is probably that the video card (or your operating system) doesn't know what the monitor is capable of and is trying to protect you from damaging a less-capable monitor. See the steps in the next section to configure for the new monitor.

# Hands-On Upgrades

It's not always enough to plug in a big new monitor and expect everything to automatically readjust. You may have to reconfigure your video card, and you will undoubtedly have to reconfigure settings in your operating system.

## Configuring for a new monitor

You have three things to do installing a new monitor — handle physical placement and installation, configure the video card, and configure your operating system and applications.

## Physical setup

Aside from being careful taking the monitor out of the box—they can be heavy, and the warranty on your back expired a long time ago—there's a lot more to placement than plopping the monitor down on your desk. We showed you in Figure 19-5 how to place the monitor to minimize glare. The essential thing is to place the monitor so that the brightest light skims along the face of the monitor rather than bouncing off it, and so you're not staring into a light source behind the monitor. It's better to be able to site the monitor to avoid these problems than to have to work around them. You may be able to help the situation with glare filters and shades on the monitor, or with shades over windows. The tilt of the screen matters too, because a change in tilt may alter the reflections off the screen to where they're not in your eyes.

Check the video cable length when placing the monitor. The higher performance the unit, the shorter the cable is likely to be, and since it has to reach the back of your computer, you can end up restricted in where the monitor can go. Try as hard as you can to avoid using a video cable extender, because you'll reduce the image sharpness and create ghosts on the screen. (If there's just no choice, get a very high-quality, low-capacitance cable. These can be hard to find; we've found them at Cables N Mor, http://www.cablesnmor.com.) The end of the video cable is a 15-pin male subminiature D connector. There are usually screws on the connector that secure it to the video card.

The power cable can plug in near the computer. Ideally, you'll plug them both into the same uninterruptible power supply; at least, plug them both into the same surge protector. Be sure to hook up the monitor with the power off, because connecting or disconnecting most computer components with the power on will damage them.

## Video card setup

Once you have everything hooked up, your next step depends on your video card. If your card has no requirement for configuration to define the monitor capabilities, you can simply skip to the next section on operating system and application settings. Many of the recent video cards we've seen are like that, probably because most monitors now support the DDC standards.

If your video card needs to have a monitor configuration set, boot the computer to DOS (or a UNIX command line; you'll be dependent on your UNIX vendor for support for the operations described here). If you haven't installed the DOS-level configuration software for your video board, do that now, and start the program. The text that follows is what you see running that program for the older ATI video boards that still require monitor configuration—the program you run is called INSTALL.EXE.

```
PCI mach64              Version 2.2        Copyright (c) 1996
                        +------------------------------------+
+---------------------+ _Quick Setup will automatically     _
_Main Menu            _ _initialize your card for the best  _
+--------------------- _ _possible configuration.           _
_System Information   _ _                                   _
_Quick Setup          _ _You do, however, have the choice   _
_Utilities Installation_ _of selecting the monitor type,    _
_Diagnostics          _ _from the list of available monitors_
_Advanced Setup       _ _                                   _
+---------------------+ _If the monitor you are currently    _
                         _using is not in the monitor list,  _
                         _you may want to Customize for best  _
                         _possible screen size\position.     _
                                                             _
                         _Any system conflicts or suggestions_
                         _will be made known to you here.    _
                                                             _
                         _Press <Enter> for Quick Setup.     _
                                                             _
                                                             _
                                                             _
                        +------------------------------------+
    <  _Home End > to Select  < Enter > to Proceed < Esc > to Exit
```

The five options in the INSTALL main menu are on the left; the text on the right describes what the option will do (we had Quick Setup highlighted on the left when we captured the preceding text you see). System Information gives you video-related data about your system. Quick Setup lets you configure the board for your monitor. Utilities installation copies software to your hard disk. Diagnostics checks out the video board. Advanced Setup lets you configure the boot-up mode of the video board.

The option we want is Quick Setup, so we can program the board to know the capabilities of your monitor. Here's what you get after you select Quick Setup:

```
PCI mach64              Version 2.2         Copyright (c) 1996

    +------------------------+
    _ Main Menu             _
    +------------------------
    _ System Information    _      +------------------------+
    _ Quick Setup           _      _ Monitor Selection Menu _
    _ Utilities Installation _     +------------------------
    _ Diagnostics           _      _ Factory Default        _
    _ Advanced Setup        _      _ Apple...               _
    +------------------------+     _ IBM...                 _
                                   _ MIT...                 _
                                   _ NEC...                 _
                                   _ VESA-Std...            _
```

```
                                       _ Generic...                    _
                                       +-----------------------+

     +-------------------------------------------------------------+
     _Supported Modes:[Some modes were removed due to Hardware/space
     limitation]_
     _640x480 60Hz N.I.(-/-), 800x600 60Hz N.I. (+/+), 1024x768 60Hz
     N.I. (-/-),_
     _1280x1024 43Hz I.(+/+)
                                                                     _
     _                                                               _
     _
     +-------------------------------------------------------------+
     < F10 > to Preview Modes < Enter > to Accept  < Esc > to Return
```

The Monitor Selection menu pops up on the right. If the configuration program has
settings for your monitor built-in, or if the monitor manufacturer shipped a VESA-
standard configuration file for the monitor, this is easy. You simply select the
manufacturer, pick the monitor, and you're done. Most likely neither is true, so
you'll scroll the menu down to the "Custom" setting, and choose that. When you do,
you get this screen:

```
     PCI mach64              Version 2.2           Copyright (c) 1996

          +-----------------------+
          _ Main Menu            _
          +-----------------------_          ++------------------+---+
          _ System Information   _          __ Select Applicable _nu _
          _ Quick Setup          _          +_     Resolutions    _---_
          _ Utilities Installation _         _+-------------------_   _
          _ Diagnostics          _          __ 640x480 ...         _   _
          _ Advanced Setup       _          __ 800x600 ...         _   _
          +-----------------------+          __ 1024x768 ...        _   _
                                             __ 1280x1024 ...       _   _
                                             __ 1600x1200 ...       _   _
                                             __ Other ...           _   _
                                             ++------------------+---+

     +-------------------------------------------------------------+
     _Select the resolution(s) which you wish to set up your monitor
     for. It is _
     _recommended that you go through each one of the available
     options and      _
     _configure for the most stable and flicker-free display.       _
     _Following your selection, you will be asked to choose from a
     list of other_
     _monitor parameters that will define your monitor's
     specifications._
     +-------------------------------------------------------------+
      < _ _Home End > to Select < Enter > to Proceed < Esc > to Exit
```

What you're going to do from this screen is to define the maximum vertical
frequency the monitor supports for each video resolution you're interested in. You
do that by choosing each resolution in turn, which leads you to this screen:

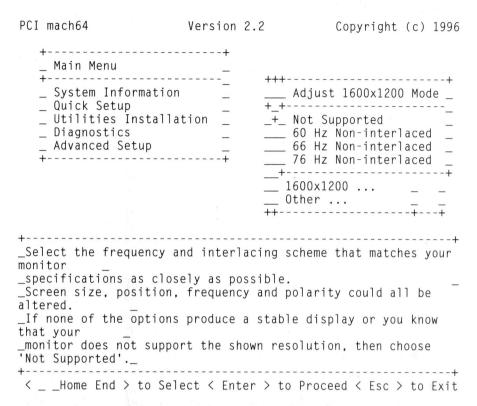

```
PCI mach64            Version 2.2         Copyright (c) 1996

     +-------------------------+
     _ Main Menu            _
     +-------------------------_
     _ System Information   _          +++-----------------------+
     _ Quick Setup         _          ___ Adjust 1600x1200 Mode _
     _ Utilities Installation _        +_+----------------------
     _ Diagnostics         _          _+_ Not Supported       _
     _ Advanced Setup      _          ___ 60 Hz Non-interlaced _
     +-------------------------+       ___ 66 Hz Non-interlaced _
                                       ___ 76 Hz Non-interlaced _
                                       __+----------------------+
                                       __ 1600x1200 ...      _  _
                                       __ Other ...          _  _
                                       ++------------------+---+

     +----------------------------------------------------------+
     _Select the frequency and interlacing scheme that matches your
     monitor       _
     _specifications as closely as possible.                _
     _Screen size, position, frequency and polarity could all be
     altered.       _
     _If none of the options produce a stable display or you know
     that your       _
     _monitor does not support the shown resolution, then choose
     'Not Supported'._
     +----------------------------------------------------------+
     < _ _Home End > to Select < Enter > to Proceed < Esc > to Exit
```

You pick your monitor's best capability from the list based on the specifications. Use noninterlaced modes if you can. For example, in the case of the Sylvania P700S monitor we've used, the user's guide shows the frequencies we list as "User's Guide Vertical Refresh Rate" in Table 19-4 for each of the resolutions shown. We added another column to the table showing the refresh rate we actually could make work. Those rates are higher than the specified rates.

| Table 19-4 Supported Vertical Refresh Frequencies for the Sylvania P700S | | |
|---|---|---|
| **Resolution** | **User's Guide Vertical Refresh Rate (Hz)** | **Workable Vertical Refresh Rate (Hz)** |
| 640 × 480 | 72.81 | 90 |
| 800 × 600 | 75 | 85 |
| 1,024 × 768 | 75.029 | 85 |
| 1,152 × 864 | N/A | 70 |
| 1,280 × 1,024 | 59.747 | 60 |

Current-generation monitors that adapt to the input frequency usually protect themselves when you send them signals they can't handle. The Sylvania simply turns a normally green indicator orange and keeps the screen blank. The Hitachi Elite 641 blacks the screen and displays an on-screen message. We exploited that capability to find the workable refresh rates in the table, choosing higher rates until the monitor refused to handle the test image supplied by the ATI software. If your monitor doesn't permit that, you'll have to live within the published specifications.

You may have to adjust the image size and position on either the video card or the monitor (or both) to get each resolution to display the way you want. Once you have everything set, save the settings and let the software reboot.

## Operating system and application settings

All that's left is to tell your operating system about the new monitor type (if it cares, as Windows does). Figure 19-13 shows the Settings tab of the Windows 95 Display control panel applet (Start ⇨ Settings ⇨ Control Panel ⇨ Display). The equivalent dialog boxes are a little different for Windows 98, Windows NT 4, and Windows 2000. If you push the Advanced Properties button at the bottom, then choose the Monitor tab and push the Change button, you'll get the dialog box in Figure 19-14.

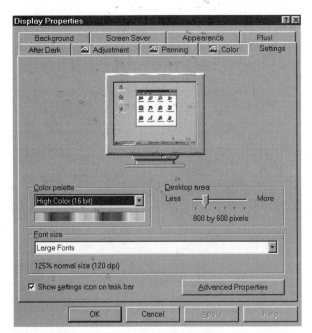

**Figure 19-13:** The Display control panel applet is where you'll tell Windows about your new monitor and choose a new resolution.

If your monitor manufacturer and model are available in the dialog box shown in Figure 19-154 you can go ahead and choose them. If not, and if your video board and monitor both support DDC Plug and Play, choose the settings shown in the figure. That may not work. For instance, the Sylvania P700S wasn't known to an old version of Windows we tried, although it's known to Windows 98. We tried Plug and Play on the older version of Windows and found that Windows believed the monitor capable of 1,600 × 1,200 resolution. It isn't, but as long as we remembered that problem and only set Windows for a maximum of 1,280 × 1,024, everything worked right.

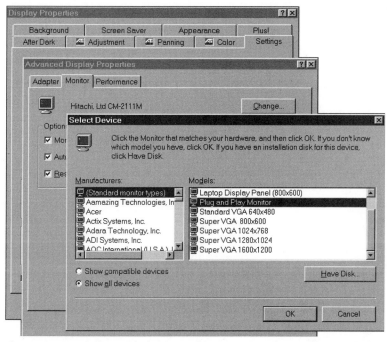

**Figure 19-14:** If Plug and Play is working, you can choose this monitor setting and have Windows automatically figure out how to work with your monitor.

If Plug and Play doesn't work for you, pick from the other models shown in Figure 19-14 under standard monitor types. One of them should do what you need.

# Summary

✦ Monitors should be compared side-by-side using technical software like DisplayMate.

✦ A monitor with a comprehensive set of controls can be made to perform better than the same monitor with few controls.

✦ Most users will do well with a good-quality 17-inch monitor. Some types of work benefit from larger monitors and therefore benefit from the added cost.

✦    ✦    ✦

# Keyboards

**K**eyboards are an integral part of computers. Most of the input you give your computer comes through the keyboard. Despite being simple devices in concept, good keyboards are relatively complex to build.

## Switches and Tactile Feedback

The basic component inside a keyboard is a switch, over 100 of them in each keyboard. Under every keycap is a switch that signals your computer in two ways: once when you push the key and again when you release it.

Keyboard switches are subject to a wide range of force, so their design is not as straightforward as you might think. One of the most severe problems is that people really hammer their keyboards at times yet expect them to survive for years. Figure 20-1 shows two keyboard switch designs. The one on the left in the figure has an obvious design flaw: letting the force directly close the contacts. This design subjects the electrical parts to damage, resulting eventually in unreliable operation. Better designs (such as the one on the right in the figure) direct the force only to mechanical parts, allowing the switch designer to control what happens to the contacts. No matter how hard you pound on the keyboard, the force on the contacts is only that of the springs that support them. The key impact force is absorbed by the base plate, not the contacts.

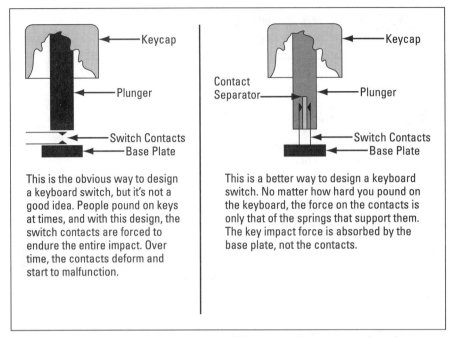

This is the obvious way to design a keyboard switch, but it's not a good idea. People pound on keys at times, and with this design, the switch contacts are forced to endure the entire impact. Over time, the contacts deform and start to malfunction.

This is a better way to design a keyboard switch. No matter how hard you pound on the keyboard, the force on the contacts is only that of the springs that support them. The key impact force is absorbed by the base plate, not the contacts.

**Figure 20-1:** Keyboard switches get a lot of abuse. Good ones keep that abuse away from the key contacts.

Keyboard switches need more than reliable contacts. People sometimes are prone to dropping in paper clips and food; spilling coffee, wine, soda, and other sticky stuff; and generally abusing the electronics terribly. The first line of defense in a good keyboard is a shield (Figure 20-2) to keep debris and liquids out of the mechanism. The figure shows how a shield not only can cover the circuit board that mounts the switches, it can also come up under the keycap to protect against liquid spills. The debris and liquid shield completely covers the circuit board holding the switches and extends up under the keycaps. Anything falling into the keyboard gets caught by the shield and is kept out of the switches and electronics.

**Tip**  If you do spill, the resulting stickyness can make the keyboard unusable. You can shut down the computer, disconnect the keyboard, and then wash it out with clean water. Let it dry *completely*, and then try it out. If you're lucky, everything will work as before.

Don't ever disconnect or reconnect a keyboard with the power on. It's not dangerous to you, but it could be lethal to your computer. We rebuilt a computer that had been the victim of half a dozen disconnect/reconnect cycles in reasonably close succession. The owner reported the machine had been operational until the keyboard became erratic after being unplugged. After several cycles it had started showing keyboard errors on boot, then it showed more severe boot errors, and then it went completely dead. Our testing showed the motherboard was completely inoperative. Because it was an older machine, the parts necessary to restore operation included a motherboard, processor, and memory. Total parts bill: $325. (In all fairness, though, it was much faster after we were done.)

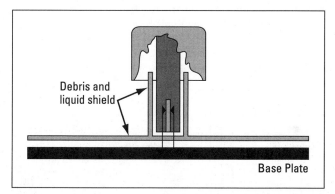

**Figure 20-2:** Reliable keyboard operation requires keeping dirt, debris, and liquids out of the switches and electronics. A good keyboard uses a shield to do that.

People are often picky about the feel of their keyboards. Some like a distinct click and tactile feedback, while others like soft resistance and a quiet keyboard. Springs and cams in the switches determine what the keyboard will feel like, and they are not something you can adjust. Try out any keyboard you're interested in before you buy it to make sure it is one you're willing to live with.

## Keyboard controllers and key matrices

Your keyboard has a simple interface into the computer: Each key press and key release results in a transmission from the keyboard that sends a code stating what happened. The switches themselves can't do that. They can only open or close a single connection.

The following figure shows how a small microprocessor in the keyboard (called the *keyboard controller*) translates switch closings into the codes your computer expects to see. Every key switch uniquely connects a pair of wires that are part of a horizontal/vertical grid. The keyboard controller finds out which switches are pushed down (closed) by looking at pairs of scan lines. It starts on the top horizontal scan line, and looks at each vertical scan line. Every connection is noted. The controller then moves to the second horizontal line, and again checks every vertical scan. It repeats this process until it has looked at all combinations of horizontal and vertical scan lines. The code representing the most recently pressed key gets reported to the computer when the key is pushed.

*continued*

*(continued)*

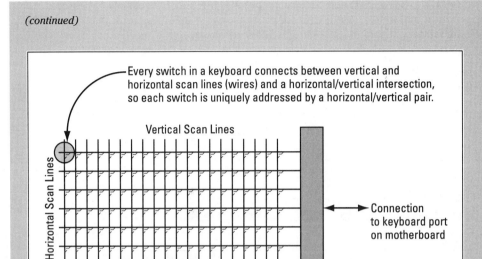

Every switch in a keyboard connects between vertical and horizontal scan lines (wires) and a horizontal/vertical intersection, so each switch is uniquely addressed by a horizontal/vertical pair.

Vertical Scan Lines

Horizontal Scan Lines

Connection to keyboard port on motherboard

Keyboard Controller

The keyboard controller polls the scan lines looking for key pushes and reports them to the computer.

The keyboard controller has another critical job, which is to eliminate bounce from the key switch contacts coming together or opening up. The key contacts are springs, and like any other springs, will bounce a little when they strike or move away from another surface. This bouncing looks like multiple connections and disconnections at the speeds computers run, but it occurs in far less time than a person could actually move the key. The controller uses timing to decide if a contact opening or closing is something you did or a bounce. If it happens a few milliseconds after the last one, it's a bounce; otherwise, it's you.

The keyboard controller's other job is to turn on the light-emitting diodes (LEDs) on the keyboard—the ones for Num Lock, Caps Lock, and Scroll Lock—in response to messages sent by the computer.

There are other ways to build keyboards than with switches. One way is to include conductive membranes separated by an insulator with holes in it. Membrane keyboards are used to withstand corrosive atmospheres and avoid generating sparks, but they are less common in conventional systems.

# Keyboard Layouts

Most keyboards use the standard QWERTY (or Sholes) key layout, meaning that the alphabetic keys are arranged in the following pattern:

```
QWERT     YUIOP
ASDFG     HJKL
ZXCVB     NM
```

The QWERTY keyboard layout was devised by Christopher Sholes early in the development of manual typewriters, and had the objective of moving common pairs of keys away from each other, which reduced jamming in those early mechanical keyboards. (It's commonly reported that Sholes intended the QWERTY layout design to slow typists down to prevent jamming, but some studies indicate that QWERTY is at least as fast as other designs.)

The most common alternative keyboard layout is the Dvorak keyboard, designed by University of Washington professor August Dvorak and William Dealey in 1936. The Dvorak layout uses the following pattern:

```
 PY       FGCRL
AOEUI     DHTNS
 QJKX     BMWVZ
```

The idea behind Dvorak's keyboard is that it's more efficient to put the most-used letters on the home row (the one where your fingers rest when you're not typing), to set up the key patterns so that your strongest fingers do most of the work, and to divide the letters so that the workload is balanced between your left and right hands. Dvorak International reports that in QWERTY, 31 percent of typing is done on the home row, compared to 70 percent for Dvorak. The Dvorak layout has 35 percent more right-hand reaches, 63 percent more same-row reaches, 45 percent more alternate-hand reaches, and 37 percent less finger travel. Other studies seem to show a smaller difference. Dvorak International further notes that Sholes himself devised another layout after mechanisms improved, but it never caught on.

# Ergonomics and Repetitive Stress

If you type at all quickly, you can easily perform thousands of repetitive motions in a single hour of typing. Many sources, including the United States National Institute of Occupational Safety and Health, state that such work can contribute to repetitive strain injury. Most authorities recommend the following preventative measures:

✦ *Equipment placement.* It's crucial that your equipment is designed and arranged so that you can maintain good posture, with all parts of your body in the proper position.

✦ *Take breaks.* Periodically changing what you are doing to something other than working at your computer is important. Short, relatively frequent breaks are worthwhile, particularly if you can stretch a little at the time. The point isn't that you have to stop working; rather, it's to recommend that you do other things besides work at your computer from time to time in order to give your body a restful change of position.

✦ *Know what to look for.* If you do develop a problem, you're much better off dealing with it before it becomes severe. Specific symptoms may arise in a number of ways, including tingling in the fingers; fatigue, numbness, and aching in the wrist and hand; and eventually severe pain in the wrist and hand. In a larger sense, though, if working at your computer leaves you sore and uncomfortable, you need to attend to the discomfort before it becomes serious.

Not all experts agree that typing causes repetitive strain injury. However, a large majority of authorities assert that long-term or frequent use of a keyboard can cause problems. This is a medical issue, so if you experience pain or unusual discomfort from typing at a computer, you should consult a medical authority for information, diagnosis, and treatment.

Prevention is your best response to repetitive stress injury. Avoid the problem in the first place. Setting up your workplace so you maintain good posture is your first step. Here's what to do:

✦ *Table and chair height.* The relative height of your keyboard and chair should be adjusted so that, with your hands on the keyboard, your arms and legs are horizontal, and your back is vertical.

✦ *Wrist angle.* The table and seat height should combine so that your hands rest on the keyboard with your wrists straight, not angled either up or down. If the keyboard is too high, you'll have to bend your hands up; if too low, you'll have to bend them down. Both positions are bad.

The recent generation of "split" keyboards enables keeping your wrists straight by angling the rows of keys so that you don't have to cant your hands outward to line up with straight rows of keys. Many of these units also have a support that will raise the front of the keyboard to eliminate any requirement to angle your hands upward. Whether you use a support like that depends on your workstation. Your goal is to keep your wrists comfortably straight.

✦ *Elbow angle.* You can adjust either the table or chair height to get your arms parallel to the floor. Whichever you do, your position needs to be relaxed and comfortable. At the same time, you're better off sitting straight with good back support, and with your feet flat on the floor.

There's no consensus on the best furniture and equipment, or on the value of split keyboards, wrist rests, and other products. There's a lot of information available on this topic on the Internet. Search using keywords like "repetitive stress keyboard," or go directly to sites focusing on the problem. One excellent starting point is "The Typing Injury FAQ" (Frequently Asked Questions) by Dan Wallach, at `http://www.jpgaq.com`. This paper addresses a wide range of issues and provides pointers to many other resources on the Internet.

The second key step in preventing a problem is to give yourself the opportunity to recover. Many sources suggest you break up your typing with frequent rest breaks, taking at least a one-minute break every 20 minutes or 5 to 15 minutes every hour. You can have your computer remind you to take breaks using software such as WorkPace (Niche Software, Ltd.), which combines education on exercises and stretching with monitoring and reminders to take breaks.

# Products

A large variety of products and accessories are designed to facilitate ease of input from your fingers to your computer. In addition to alternative keyboard physical layouts, software is available that is intended to simplify or accelerate your rate of typing. Few of these have achieved widespread acceptance, perhaps because it's difficult to tailor them for the wide range of things any one person may do with a computer. Even an accessory as generic as the macro recorder — a program that could turn a keystroke into an entire sequence of key and mouse operations — was so unused that Microsoft removed it from Windows 95.

One important issue regarding computer keyboards is making them usable by people with impaired mobility. Typing on the usual grid of closely spaced keys is difficult without reasonably precise accuracy, and more difficult yet for people who need to use a typing stick. The close proximity of the keycaps and the ease with which you can hit the wrong key (or multiple keys) increase the error rate, requiring yet more keystrokes to correct.

The following sections discuss some keyboard products that are intended to reduce the strain on hands, wrists, and body, as well as some products that are available to help the disabled communicate with and through their computers.

## Adaptive Computer Systems Visual Keyboard

One of the key operations a computer can perform to help a motion-disabled person is to anticipate what the user is doing and help complete the action. The Adaptive Computer Systems Visual Keyboard is a software program to help people who cannot type with a conventional keyboard to use Windows. It isn't a normal keyboard; it is Windows software you can use in conjunction with the accessibility features in Windows to create the following assists:

✦ *Launch and resize.* Reshapes Microsoft Windows application windows to fit on the screen along with the Visual Keyboard.

✦ *Word prediction.* Completes words when enough of the word is seen.

✦ *Abbreviation expansion.* Converts specified abbreviations into complete words and phrases.

You can re-layout the keyboard to match the arrangement you find best.

## IBM KeyGuard

IBM offers a product called KeyGuard for use on its Enhanced and Space Saving keyboards supplied with IBM computer systems including the PS/2, PS/ValuePoint, EduQuest, and others. The KeyGuard is a molded plastic overlay that fits over the keyboard, with holes over the keys and solid material between them. The plastic between keys helps direct keystrokes to individual keys and away from the spaces in between, reducing the error rate.

## Maltron

Conventional keyboards are sized to fit adult hands, and arranged for two-handed operation. The result is a relatively wide spread of keys in front of the user. For example, the distance between the outer edges of the left-most and right-most keys on a Microsoft Natural keyboard is $19^1/_2$ inches; the same distance on a Northgate OmniKey Ultra is 19 inches.

That distance creates problems for motion-impaired users. It can be difficult to reach the keys with your hands, and impossible with a mouth stick. Maltron (http://www.maltron.co.uk) makes a keyboard for these users with the key layout optimized for distance, not two-handed typing. Using conventional keycaps—not larger or smaller ones—the span of the keys from left to right on the keyboard is slightly over nine inches, a far shorter distance to reach.

Used in combination with software like the Adaptive Computer Systems Visual Keyboard, the Maltron keyboard lets you build solutions for people that reduce the workload greatly and can make the difference between using a computer or not.

## Microsoft Natural Keyboard

In the past few years, split keyboard designs—ones that divide and rotate outward the groups of keys for each hand—have become available from nearly every keyboard manufacturer. One of the first to sell in large quantities was the Microsoft Natural Keyboard (Figure 20-3), which in turn spawned a number of similar units. Microsoft states that the Natural Keyboard is designed to promote a better, more comfortable posture for typing. The keyboard also provides a support you can use to raise the front of the keyboard, allowing the keys to slope away from you, permitting your wrists to remain straighter.

In designing the Natural Keyboard, Microsoft added three new keys for use with Windows and provided enhanced software to help control the keyboard. The new keys are two Windows logo keys and an application key. The Windows logo keys give you quick access to Windows functions such as the Start menu, the Run dialog box, and the Explorer. The application key is available for use in applications; for example, you can use it to control macro functions.

The enhanced drivers that Microsoft packages with the Natural Keyboard provide features such as control over the keyboard Num Lock, Caps Lock, and Scroll Lock status when Windows starts and the ability to enable sounds for each keystroke.

**Figure 20-3:** The Microsoft Natural Keyboard splits the keypad, rotates the keys, and slopes the keyboard to promote straight wrists and relaxed shoulders. (Photo courtesy Microsoft Corporation.)

## Logitech Cordless Desktop Keyboard and Mouse

If you've done much with desktop computers, you know that the cables coming out of the back of the computer can make neatness impossible. If you've tried to use a desktop computer from a distance, say when it's connected to a big-screen television, you know how restrictive it can be to have the keyboard and mouse tethered to the computer.

If those are problems that bother you, the Logitech Cordless Desktop Keyboard and Mouse is the answer you've been waiting for (Figure 20-4). A small receiver plugs into the keyboard and mouse connectors at the back of your computer. The receiver can be six feet from the keyboard and mouse, using radio waves in between. If you need the extra separation, or extra convenience, there's no substitute for cordless.

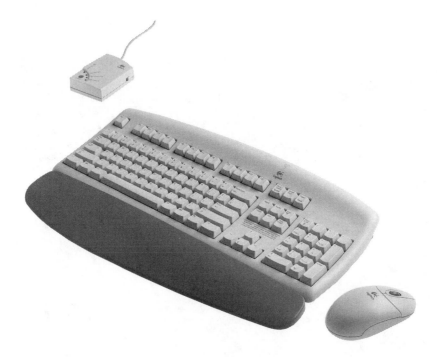

**Figure 20-4:** The Logitech Cordless Desktop Keyboard and Mouse lets you move away from your computer, taking full advantage of your big-screen television. (Courtesy of Logitech)

# Hands-On Upgrades

You can make Windows 9x handle your keyboard with the Dvorak layout using the control panel keyboard applet. Here are the steps:

1. Open the keyboard applet. You get to it by opening the control panel with Start ➪ Settings ➪ Control Panel, and then double-clicking the Keyboard applet icon.

2. Choose the Language tab. This gets you to the dialog box shown in Figure 20-5. The list box shows the languages you have installed (the left text on the line), and for each the keyboard layout (on the right). You can see in Figure 20-5 that we have US English installed and that we use the conventional Sholes layout on a 101-key keyboard. (Actually, Barry uses the Microsoft Natural Keyboard and Marcia, a conventional one; we used the conventional one in this dialog.)

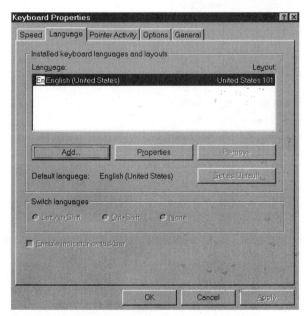

**Figure 20-5:** The Language tab in the keyboard control panel applet lets you switch keyboard layouts in Windows 9x.

3. Select the line you want to change in the list box (you'll have more than one if you switch keyboard layouts or have multiple languages installed), and push the Properties button. You'll see the smaller dialog shown in Figure 20-7, which lets you pick a specific keyboard layout.

4. Once you pick a layout from the list (we've shown the list dropped down in Figure 20-6), you'll see the usual OK and Cancel buttons. Push OK and you'll have changed the layout.

5. If you want to switch between Sholes and Dvorak layouts (an opportunity ripe for confusion!), you can pick Add in step 3 instead of Properties. You'll select the language you want, and a new line will show up in the list. You then go through steps 3 and 4 on the new line. If you do have multiple setups, you can enable a keystroke (Left Alt+Shift or Ctrl+Shift) to switch between them.

The control panel Language applet does the same thing in Windows NT.

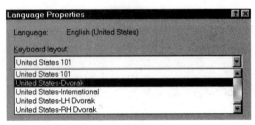

**Figure 20-6:** The LH and RH Dvorak layouts are intended for typists using a single hand or wand.

# Summary

✦ Look for both solid construction and a feel you like in a keyboard.

✦ Good posture and straight wrists are important to minimize repetitive stress. Get qualified medical help early for repetitive stress problems.

✦ Keyboards designed for the motion-impaired can improve the ability to use and communicate through the computer.

✦        ✦        ✦

# Sound Cards, Speakers, and Microphones

**A**s we explain in Chapter 14 (and as shown in Figure 21-1), sound stored on disk is really a sequence of numbers that represent the amplitude of a sound wave. The numbers are sampled at regular, precise intervals, and by playing them back at the same rate, the computer can use them to reconstruct the waveform.

This chapter looks a little more closely at what sound is and how computers create and reproduce sounds.

Sound is vibration—alternating greater and lesser air pressure—traveling through the air that is received at your ears and heard by your brain. Many people can hear sounds as low as 16 to 20 Hertz (although you can feel lower-frequency sounds than that if they're strong enough). Some people can hear sounds as high in frequency as 20 kHz.

Sound waves have shape too, as illustrated in the waveforms in Figure 21-2. This fact makes creating sound systems more complicated. The top-left waveform in Figure 21-2 is a *sine* wave, a smoothly varying signal of a single frequency. The frequency analysis at the top right verifies this—there's one frequency peak in the graph. A sound system that reproduces that one frequency can accurately reproduce the sine wave. The lower-left waveform in Figure 21-2 is called a *triangle* or *sawtooth* wave. The lowest, or fundamental frequency of the sawtooth wave in the figure is the same as that of the sine wave, but the frequency analysis at the bottom right of the figure shows many frequencies have to be added together to reproduce the specific shape of the sawtooth wave. If a sound system rolls off the high frequencies, the wave shape distorts. If the sound system cuts off all the frequencies above the fundamental frequency, the waveform becomes a sine wave like the one in the top-left box of Figure 21-2.

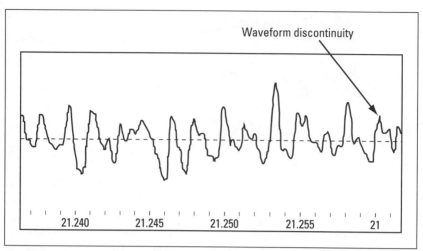

**Figure 21-1:** Sound, images, and video are analog waveforms. Recording them in a computer requires that we sample the waveform and store the digital samples.

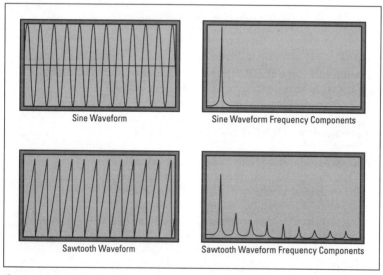

**Figure 21-2:** Accurately reproducing a waveform may involve frequencies far higher than the fundamental frequency you hear.

The need for high-frequency sound components to form complex signals is why sound systems sound better when they support extended frequency responses. The added frequencies enable them to better reconstruct the complex waveforms that make up the sounds you listen to.

The shape of the amplitude of a note is most of what distinguishes the sound one instrument makes from another. (Timbre, which is the tone quality, is the other characteristics that distinguish instruments.) Figure 21-3 shows the leading part of a note is called its *attack*, followed by the *decay*, the *sustain*, and the *release*. An acoustic guitar, for example, has a sharp attack, quick decay, and medium length sustain. A flute or clarinet has a slow attack, slow decay, and long sustain.

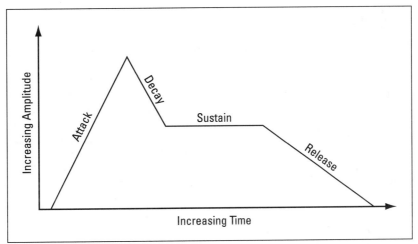

**Figure 21-3:** Attack, decay, sustain, and release are what differentiate the sound of one instrument from another.

Hardware and software that manipulate attack, decay, sustain, and release creates musical instrument sounds the way the original PC sound cards did (such as the ones manufactured over a decade ago by AdLib). Figure 21-4 shows how this works. One or more *waveform generators*, providing the raw pitch and timbre, couple into *envelope shapers* that provide the attack/decay/sustain/release amplitude profile. All the separate signals then get added together in the *summer*, forming a single instrument. That single instrument is called a voice. If you need to play multiple instruments at one time (multiple voices), you need more than one of the complete channels in Figure 21-4. Each distinct instrument in an FM synthesizer uses a collection of generators, shapers, and a summer to create the output voice. FM synthesizers typically have 4 to 32 voices.

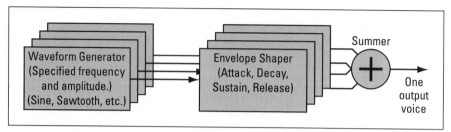

**Figure 21-4:** FM synthesis uses relatively simple hardware and creates passable music effects.

# Analog Audio

Figure 21-5 shows how sound generation is implemented in most computers. Software running on a processor receives a request to make a sound, retrieves the necessary data, and sends commands to the sound card. A small processor on the sound card receives the command and data, coordinates the operation of specialized chips (including digital-to-analog converters similar to those in your video card) to create sound waveforms. Those waveforms then pass through filters (to eliminate noise and other effects) and amplifiers (to boost the signal strength) and show up at the output jacks on the card. You connect those jacks to your computer speakers or stereo system, which add more amplification, let you control the bass and treble, and hand off to your speakers. The speakers in turn translate the electrical signal into a corresponding sound pressure wave, which is what you hear.

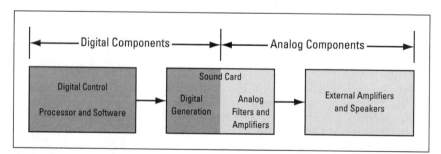

**Figure 21-5:** Generating sound in your computer combines digital and analog components.

Some recent computers alter this scheme a little using the Universal Serial Bus (USB, see the section Universal Serial Bus in Chapter 9, "Cache, Memory, and Bus"). Computers using USB to send sound to speakers can operate without a sound card, moving all the sound card functions out to the speakers.

The analog components in a sound card, external amplifier, and speaker operate much the same way as a traditional stereo sound system. Because of this similarity, the specifications for computer sound system analog components are similar to those for stereos. Here are some of the more important characteristics:

✦ *Output power.* This is a measure of how strongly the amplifier can drive an output device, such as a speaker. Power is measured into a load, which in the case of a speaker is typically rated at four ohms (the measure of resistance). Just as with stereo equipment, the output power has more to do with how things sound than how loud you can crank it up. Signals with sharp attacks (drums, gunshots, explosions) need a lot of power to move the speaker quickly even at moderate volume, so larger output power specifications are better.

✦ *Frequency response.* This is the measure of the range of frequencies the components are capable of handling. Not all the sounds you'll put through the card actually use the full range, though, and no amount of quality in the sound system can compensate for frequencies that just aren't there in the first place. (More about this in the "Sampling rates" section of this chapter.) A broader range of frequencies is better.

✦ *Total harmonic distortion.* Frequencies that are multiples of a base frequency are called *harmonics*. The sounds you hear are full of harmonics because, as shown in Figure 21-2, harmonics are part of what gives each signal its distinctive shape. Amplifiers create harmonics that aren't part of the original signal through an effect called *harmonic distortion*. The transistor amplifiers you find in modern stereos and in sound cards produce odd harmonics, which can be objectionable to listen to. The sum of all the harmonic distortion your amplifier produces is called its total harmonic distortion, or THD. Smaller THD numbers are better.

Keep in mind that when you're talking computer sound cards, you're not talking about connoisseur-grade stereo. You're talking about a card you'll use for presentations, accents in the user interface (the beeps, blurps, and other noises Windows makes when it wants your attention), background music, and games. You won't get the same quality as in an exquisite stereo, and you probably don't need that level of quality unless you're a professional musician creating music with your computer.

# Digital Audio

So far in this chapter, you've seen two ways to create sound from your computer — playing back a sampled audio waveform, and synthesizing waveforms from a sequence of timbre/attack/decay/sustain/release commands. These two ways are both used in your computer. Sampled waveforms are what's in *wave files* (which have the extension .WAV), while command sequences form the content of MIDI files (which have the extension .MID). This section covers waveform audio; the next (Musical Instrument Digital Interface) covers MIDI.

Most sounds begin as audio in the real world. The fundamental process for creating digital waveform audio from those sounds is shown in Figure 21-6. The audio source gets conditioned, filtered, and sampled in an analog-to-digital (A/D) converter. A sampling clock strictly times the action of the converter so that measurements are taken at fixed intervals. The sampling clock has to run at twice the frequency of the highest frequency component of the input signal (see the section "Sampling rates: the magic number is two" to learn why), so to sample music with a maximum frequency response of 22 kHz, the clock has to run at 44 kHz.

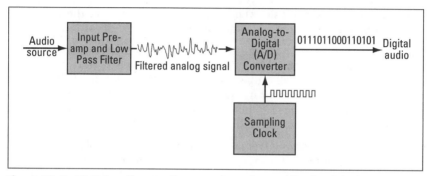

**Figure 21-6:** Digital audio sampling measures the amplitude of the input signal at fixed intervals set by a clock.

Each element in the figure has a specific function:

✦ The *input pre-amp* conditions the signal to the amplitude the A/D converter wants to see, isolating it from the characteristics of the audio source.

✦ The *low-pass filter* removes frequencies over one half of the sampling clock rate, ensuring that the digital samples will be ones that accurately reconstruct the input signal.

✦ The *A/D converter* measures the amplitude of the input audio signal each time it is clocked. Each measurement produces an 8-bit or 16-bit number corresponding to the measurement. If you have a stereo card, there are two input pre-amps, two low-pass filters, and two A/D converters.

✦ The *sampling clock* triggers the A/D converter at regular intervals. The faster the clock runs, the faster the A/D converter samples and the higher the maximum frequency you can digitize.

Every time the A/D converter samples the waveform, it outputs 8 or 16 bits of data to your processor (which typically writes it to a file). If you're recording stereo, there are two converters, each outputting at that rate. This is why wave sound files can get so large—there's a lot of data there. Table 21-1 shows how extreme the volume of data can get. Recording stereo at 44 kHz (equivalent to what's on an audio CD) takes over a gigabyte for an hour's worth of material.

**Table 21-1**

**The Relationship between Sampling Rate, Data Rate, Frequency, and Disk Space Used for Uncompressed Waveform Audio**

| Sampling Rate (kHz) | Maximum Frequency (kHz) | Stereo 16-Bit Data Rate (Kbps) | Recorded Seconds per Megabyte | Recorded MB per Hour |
|---|---|---|---|---|
| 8.00 | 4.00 | 32.00 | 32.00 | 113 |
| 11.03 | 5.51 | 44.10 | 23.22 | 155 |
| 22.05 | 11.03 | 88.20 | 11.61 | 310 |
| 44.10 | 22.05 | 176.40 | 5.80 | 620 |

In Chapter 14 we showed that a CD holds around 660MB, which permits audio CDs to commonly hold around 74 minutes of material. Compression can be used in waveform audio files and on an audio CD, so the sizes predicted by Table 21-1 are really upper bounds.

## Sampling rates: the magic number is two

The reason Table 21-1 shows a maximum frequency of one half the sampling rate is that you can't sample any slower and still reconstruct the input waveform accurately. A mathematical result called the Nyquist sampling theorem shows that a signal can be perfectly reconstructed only if it is sampled at twice the frequency of the highest frequency component of the signal.

Figure 21-7 suggests why this is true. We've drawn two waveforms in the figure, one at twice the frequency of the other. We then drew in points to represent where we might sample if we did the measurements at the same frequency as the faster signal. What you see in the figure is that the measurements follow the variations of the slower signal but detect no variation at all in the faster one.

There are two frequencies involved in sampling an audio signal, that of the signal, and that of the sampling clock. The reason for the twice-rate sampling requirement is that sampling effectively adds and subtracts the two frequencies, and forms new frequencies as a result. If you have a signal with components from 0 to 20 kHz that you sample at 40 kHz, new frequencies appear in the range of 20 through 60 kHz. These new frequencies, called *aliases*, are easy to filter out because they're all above the ones we care about. If you sampled at a lower rate, say 30 kHz, the aliases would be in the range from 10 to 50 kHz, and you'd be unable to filter out the ones between 10 and 20 kHz because they overlap the original signal.

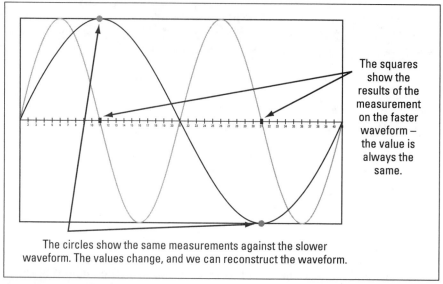

The squares show the results of the measurement on the faster waveform — the value is always the same.

The circles show the same measurements against the slower waveform. The values change, and we can reconstruct the waveform.

**Figure 21-7:** Mathematical analysis shows that you have to sample twice as fast as the highest-frequency component to be able to reconstruct a waveform accurately.

Many people believe that because the frequencies you can hear are limited means sampling rates as high as 44.1 kHz are excessive. It's true that telephones reproduce signals no higher than 4 kHz. The lowest A on a piano is 27.5 Hz, while the highest A is 3.25 kHz. A sound system limited to 4 kHz (a telephone, for instance) sounds nowhere near as good as one that can extend up to 20 kHz, though, because of the harmonics needed to reproduce the sound of instruments accurately, to reproduce the specific wave shapes instruments generate instead of a smooth sine wave. We've shown in Figure 21-8 how you can start to square up a smooth signal (a sine wave) by adding in odd harmonics. The added frequency range in better sound systems reproduces higher frequencies, so the system faithfully delivers the recorded signal. In Figure 21-8, we've added a fundamental frequency and its third harmonic — the signal at three times the frequency — together to approximate a square wave. We added the third harmonic in at one-third the amplitude of the fundamental. If you add them in the same amplitude, the small dips you see in the result would reach to the zero line in the middle.

A sound card implements wave audio hardware (and that for the reverse audio output process) on a card that fits in your computer. Figure 21-9 shows the wave audio components on the card. There are two parallel channels everywhere for stereo, although they share a common sampling clock and bus interface. The ISA bus has been the most common sound card interface but is being replaced by PCI. The low-pass filter on the output side, before the amplifier, removes frequencies higher than one half the sample rate (similar to those on the input side), ensuring that you get a clean signal out of the digital-to-analog converters.

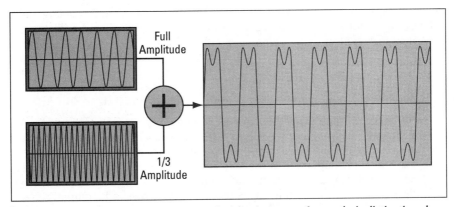

**Figure 21-8:** Adding higher-frequency signals gives waveforms their distinctive shape.

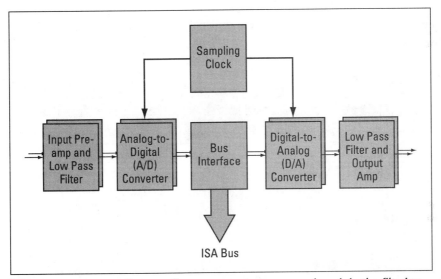

**Figure 21-9:** The waveform audio components on a sound card do the filtering and sampling to convert analog signals to digital and back to analog again.

Some sound cards let you run the wave audio input and output sections at the same time, in what's called *full-duplex operation*. This is important for videoconferencing applications (see Chapter 27), because it lets you both speak and listen in the conversation at the same time. You'll want full-duplex support for gaming too, because as multiplayer Internet gaming starts to support audio, you'll want to talk and listen at the same time. Much of the fun in multiplayer games is the conversation among players—multiplayer games don't work anywhere near as well in private.

Another set of characteristics — adding to the ones just given for analog audio — defines the performance of the wave audio section of your sound card:

✦ *Sampling rate*. This is the clock rate at which the converters can operate. It's harder to build quality A/D converters than D/A converters, so the A/D devices are commonly the limiting factor in the design. A good typical sound card can sample at rates in the range from 5 kHz to 44.1 kHz.

✦ *Bus interface*. The usual interface elements apply to a sound card, including I/O addresses, an interrupt level, and direct memory access channels. Table 21-2 shows some of the more common options for these settings. (MIDI and wavetable are explained in the next section.) The setting options in the table are *de facto* standards established by the Creative Labs SoundBlaster and its descendants. Other sound cards that have their own — incompatible — interface setups are available. PCI sound cards have a different set of addresses and interrupts but emulate the old interface to support old programs.

Sound cards typically provide bass and treble controls, mixers, input selects, and volume controls. Software in Windows allows you to set these controls on-screen.

### Table 21-2
### Creative Labs SoundBlaster Interface Specifications, Often Imitated by Other Companies

| Characteristic | Common Sound Card Options |
| --- | --- |
| I/O address | 220, 240, 260, or 280 (Wave)<br>300, 330, or 388 (MIDI)<br>620, A20, or E20 (Wavetable)<br>200 (Joystick) |
| Interrupt | 2, 5, 7, or 10 |
| Direct memory access channel | 0, 1, or 3 (8-bit)<br>5, 6, or 7 (16-bit) |

## Audio compression

Look again at the signals in Figure 21-8. We took 41 samples per complete waveform cycle in the waveform on the right, a total of 256 samples. For each sample, we recorded the amplitude of the waveform. Looking at the figure makes it apparent that there's a maximum range to the samples, which in the case of Figure 21-8 was from 9,428 to –9,428. Analog-to-digital (A/D) converters have a maximum analog amplitude they can handle, corresponding to the largest digital values they can output. Suppose that the converters for Figure 21-8 could handle the range from 10,000 to –10,000. In that case, the actual values we sampled nearly filled the range.

Because audio takes a lot of space to record, we might want to find a way to compress what goes on disk. One way to compress the recording is to use fewer bits to store each sample value. We can do that by recording smaller numbers — in example from Figure 21-8, that means using numbers smaller than +/–10,000. The smaller the numbers, the more compressed the recording.

One way to create smaller values is to record not the actual values, but the differences between successive values. If we do that, the range of numbers we have to record gets smaller. We calculated what happens to the samples from Figure 21-8, and determined that the differences range from 5,512 to –5,512. It takes 15 bits to represent the range +/– 10,000, but only 14 for the range +/– 6,000. By recording the difference between two adjacent samples rather than the raw magnitude, we saved one bit every sample.

Of course, if the savings in this example were the best we could do, it would be pointless — we've only saved around six percent from the uncompressed recording because the difference between successive values is just too great. One of the most successful audio compression algorithms, called Adaptive Digital Pulse Code Modulation (ADPCM), solves this problem in an interesting way. ADPCM compression commonly transforms 16-bit samples down to 4-bit differences, achieving 4-to-1 compression, by using prediction. The ADPCM compression process guesses where the next point will be and outputs the difference between the prediction and the actual value. The prediction is generally close enough that far fewer bits are needed to encode the error, so the data stream ends up being highly compressed.

Figure 21-10 shows how predictive compression works (somewhat simplified from the actual method for ADPCM). The thick line is a small section of the curve in Figure 21-8. When it is blown up like this, you can see that the curve is really a sequence of straight lines between sample points. If we take one line segment and extend it to the time for the next sample point, we get the prediction line at the top of the figure. That line extends upward and to the right to intersect the time for the next sample at the predicted value. The actual value (shown as the continuation of the curve) is somewhat less, so we output the difference between the actual and predicted values to the compressed data stream. The better the prediction, the smaller the differences and the fewer bits we need per sample in the compressed data stream.

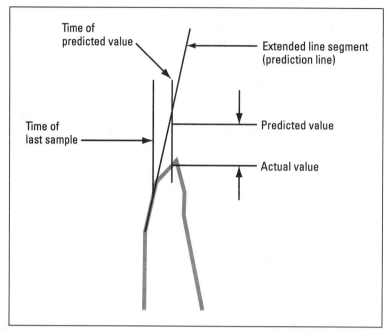

**Figure 21-10:** Prediction lets an ADPCM audio compressor output only the error in the prediction, taking far fewer bits.

# Musical Instrument Digital Interface

The wider range of sounds possible with wave audio allowed sound cards such as the Creative Labs SoundBlaster to replace older synthesized audio designs (such as the AdLib cards) in the market. The newer cards didn't eliminate synthesizers, though — they're alive and well in PC sound cards supporting the Musical Instrument Digital Interface (MIDI, pronounced *mih-dee*), which is a standardized way of telling a synthesizer what you want it to do.

Although it can't create all the sounds that wave audio can, MIDI has the key advantage that it takes far less data to represent things with MIDI than with wave audio. We saw in Table 21-1 that wave audio can take around 10MB per minute. A typical MIDI sequence may consume only 10K per minute, and for things MIDI does well, it can sound as good as wave audio.

The real application of MIDI is in recording, editing, and playing music. A MIDI file is a sequence of commands — mostly notes — that you send to a synthesizer. Because the file contains commands, not the music itself, you can edit it, speed it up, slow it down, change the pitch and key of the music, and change the instruments playing.

A MIDI file plays against a set of instruments. Each instrument being played is assigned a channel number, commonly in the range of 1 to 128. The MIDI file contains interleaved messages for each instrument ("play this note this loud until I tell you to stop"), along with systemwide messages to set tempo and other variables.

Two of the key measures for MIDI synthesizers are *polyphony* (the number of notes the synthesizer can play at once) and *timbres* (the number of different sounds or instruments it can play at once). The SoundBlaster AWE32, for example, can play 32 notes at once and 16 different instruments. The AWE64 could do more but required help from the processor. Synthesizers running entirely in software, possible since Intel developed the MMX technology, often support as many as 200 voices at once.

## General MIDI, I presume?

The instruments that the composer or artist expects to be on each of the MIDI channels need to be the ones the synthesizer presents. If not, the music is going to sound as bad as if you scrambled the arrangements among the sections of an orchestra. If the composer expects a violin on channel one and the synthesizer presents a trumpet, it's going to be no better than comical. Worse yet, the synthesizer may well have a perfectly good violin available on a different channel.

The setup that defines what instruments are available is called a *patch map*. A standard called the General MIDI Specification defines in a patch map what instruments are assigned what numbers, from 1 to 128. A MIDI sequence — a file you play — can then define what instruments it wants on each channel, making the assumption the General MIDI patch map is available. Table 21-3 shows what's in the General MIDI patch map. There are 16 different instrument categories (piano, brass, reed, and so on). Each category of instrument has eight specific instruments defined. These patches are used with channels 1 to 9 and 11 to 16 in a General MIDI synthesizer. Channel 10 is reserved for percussion, which has its own patch map.

Different synthesizers create the sounds specified by General MIDI in different ways, and so can sound very different. Among FM synthesizers, the differences are in the number of waveform generators, the control the processor can exert over the generators, and the shape of the waveform envelope (Figure 21-3). The same synthesizer can be programmed with different parameters to produce varying sounds.

## Wavetable audio

The accuracy of the sounds from an FM synthesizer is limited, just as the kinds of sounds a synthesizer can make are limited. Waveform audio is more accurate, so it was inevitable that the two would be combined. That combination is called *wavetable audio*.

## Table 21-3
## The General MIDI Patch Map

| No. | Name | No. | Name | No. | Name | No. | Name |
|---|---|---|---|---|---|---|---|
| | *Piano* | | *Bass* | | *Reed* | | *Synth FX* |
| 1 | Acoustic Grand piano | 33 | Acoustic Bass | 65 | Soprano sax | 97 | FX 1 (rain) |
| 2 | Bright acoustic piano | 34 | Electric bass (finger) | 66 | Alto sax | 98 | FX 2 (soundtrack) |
| 3 | Electric grand piano | 35 | Electric bass (pick) | 67 | Tenor sax | 99 | FX 3 (crystal) |
| 4 | Honky-Tonk piano | 36 | Fretless bass | 68 | Baritone sax | 100 | FX 4 (atmosphere) |
| 5 | Electric piano 1 | 37 | Slap bass 1 | 69 | Oboe | 101 | FX 5 (brightness) |
| 6 | Electric piano 2 | 38 | Slap bass 2 | 70 | English horn | 102 | FX 6 (goblins) |
| 7 | Harpsichord | 39 | Synth bass 1 | 71 | Bassoon | 103 | FX 7 (echoes) |
| 8 | Clavinet | 40 | Synth bass 2 | 72 | Clarinet | 104 | FX 8 (sci-fi) |
| | **Chromatic Percussion** | | **Strings & Orchestra** | | **Pipe** | | **Ethnic** |
| 9 | Celesta | 41 | Violin | 73 | Piccolo | 105 | Sitar |
| 10 | Glockenspiel | 42 | Viola | 74 | Flute | 106 | Banjo |
| 11 | Music box | 43 | Cello | 75 | Recorder | 107 | Shamisen |
| 12 | Vibraphone | 44 | Contrabass | 76 | Pan flute | 108 | Koto |
| 13 | Marimba | 45 | Tremolo strings | 77 | Bottle blow | 109 | Kalimba |
| 14 | Xylophone | 46 | Pizzicato strings | 78 | Shakuhachi | 110 | Bag pipe |
| 15 | Tubular bell | 47 | Orchestral harp | 79 | Whistle | 111 | Fiddle |
| 16 | Dulcimer | 48 | Timpani | 80 | Ocarina | 112 | Shanai |
| | Organ | | Ensemble | | Synth lead | | Percussive |
| 17 | Drawbar organ | 49 | String ensemble 1 | 81 | Lead 1 (square) | 113 | Tinkle bell |
| 18 | Percussive organ | 50 | String ensemble 2 | 82 | Lead 2 (sawtooth) | 114 | Agogo |

| No. | Name | No. | Name | No. | Name | No. | Name |
|-----|------|-----|------|-----|------|-----|------|
| | *Piano* | | *Bass* | | *Reed* | | *Synth FX* |
| | **Organ** | | **Ensemble** | | **Synth Lead** | | **Percussive** |
| 19 | Rock organ | 51 | Synth strings 1 | 83 | Lead 3 (calliope) | 115 | Steel drums |
| 20 | Church organ | 52 | Synth strings 2 | 84 | Lead 4 (chiff) | 116 | Woodblock |
| 21 | Reed organ | 53 | Choir aahs | 85 | Lead 5 (charang) | 117 | Taiko Drum |
| 22 | Accordion | 54 | Voice oohs | 86 | Lead 6 (voice) | 118 | Melodic tom |
| 23 | Harmonica | 55 | Synth voice | 87 | Lead 7 (fifths) | 119 | Synth drum |
| 24 | Tango accordion | 56 | Orchestra hit | 88 | Lead 8 (bass & lead) | 120 | Reverse cymbal |
| | **Guitar** | | **Brass** | | **Synth Pad** | | **SFX** |
| 25 | Acoustic guitar (nylon) | 57 | Trumpet | 89 | Pad 1 (new age) | 121 | Guitar fret noise |
| 26 | Acoustic guitar (steel) | 58 | Trombone | 90 | Pad 2 (warm) | 122 | Breath noise |
| 27 | Electric guitar (jazz) | 59 | Tuba | 91 | Pad 3 (polysynth) | 123 | Seashore |
| 28 | Electric Guitar (clean) | 60 | Muted Trumpet | 92 | Pad 4 (choir) | 124 | Bird tweet |
| 29 | Electric guitar (muted) | 61 | French horn | 93 | Pad 5 (bowed) | 125 | Telephone ring |
| 30 | Overdriven guitar | 62 | Brass section | 94 | Pad 6 (metallic) | 126 | Helicopter |
| 31 | Distortion guitar | 63 | Synth brass 1 | 95 | Pad 7 (halo) | 127 | Applause |
| 32 | Guitar harmonics | 64 | Synth brass 2 | 96 | Pad 8 (sweep) | 128 | Gunshot |

**Tip**

The basic idea behind wavetable audio is to record all the notes an instrument can make as waveform audio, and store those recordings in memory in the synthesizer. When the MIDI sequence commands a particular note, the synthesizer finds the right wave audio clip in memory and plays it.

Although wavetable audio is a great idea, it's much harder to implement in practice than you might think. Here are some of the stumbling blocks:

✦ *Note duration.* It's not practical to separately record every possible length note that a composer might use. Instead, the attack/decay and sustain parts of the note can be recorded separately, and the sustain recording can be looped until the right duration is achieved.

✦ *Effects.* Effects like vibrato can be applied during the sustain portion of the note by varying the amplitude of the signal after initial generation. Other effects, such as the differences in sound between a piano played softly and one played forcefully, can be handled by recording different wavetable entries or by low-pass filtering that is dependent on amplitude.

✦ *Pitch shifting.* It's possible to generate other notes within a limited range around the recorded sample by changing the playback rate to be different than the recording rate. A slower playback rate lowers the pitch, while a faster one raises it.

The techniques that a vendor builds into a wavetable audio card to store instrument notes are generally invisible to the user. The closest you'll get is when you want to create your own instrument setups and load them to memory on the card, in which case you'll need software that takes waveform audio samples and lets you create your own wavetable audio setups.

# CD Audio and Line Interfaces

Most sound cards offer two other capabilities. They can accept analog audio signals from your CD-ROM or DVD drive, letting you play audio tracks through your computer's speakers, and they can both accept and output "line" audio signals (the sort that you get at the tape in and tape out jacks on your stereo preamplifier).

A device called a *mixer* goes in front of the waveform audio input electronics on your sound card, as shown in Figure 21-11. Each of the individual sources routes to the mixer, which contains volume controls for each channel plus a master volume control on the output channel. The mixer itself is controlled by the processor in your computer, from which it receives messages to set the volume for each channel and the master control. The processor can also mute any or all of the channels, so you can suppress noise that may occur on channels you're not using.

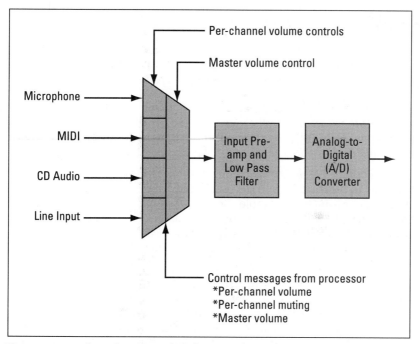

**Figure 21-11:** The mixer controls volume and muting independently on each of the input channels.

The mixer gives you more than volume control on multiple inputs; it lets you do more with your sound card. For instance:

✦ *Recording sound outputs.* You can record the MIDI output from your sound card and music from an audio CD in your CD-ROM drive. (It's important to be careful about copyrights when you record CD audio.) The MIDI input is what we used to create the sample files we mentioned previously that show the difference between FM synthesis and wavetable audio. We simply selected the MIDI input with the mixer, started some recording software, and started the MIDI output.

✦ *Combining sounds.* Suppose you want to build up multiple tracks in a sound file. You can record one, and then play it and record additional sound on top of it. Or suppose you want to record a voice and sound track to go with a presentation. You can do that by pulling in CD audio or MIDI for the music and adding the voice-over from the microphone input. Your sound card likely has a line-out output, and if you want to record wave audio sounds mixed with others, you can cable the line-out connector back into the line-in port.

# USB Speakers

Computers using USB—a digital connection—between the computer and the speakers don't require a sound card, because most of the functions of the sound card are moved to the speakers in a USB setup. Here's what happens:

✦ *Wave audio.* Digital audio streams from WAV files or from effects embedded directly into programs don't require anything but USB speakers. The digital stream goes from the processor out the USB port to the speakers, where it gets converted to analog audio and played.

✦ *MIDI and wavetable audio.* Most computers have used a sound board to convert MIDI files to the digital audio sequences ultimately required by speakers, with modern boards using wavetable audio for the conversion. All processors since the Intel 200 MHz Pentium MMX processor have been capable of doing the MIDI synthesis operation in software, which is how MIDI works on a USB speaker-based system without a sound card. MIDI commands go into the synthesizer software, which in turn outputs wave audio to the speakers.

✦ *CD-ROM or DVD audio.* Playing CDs on a CD-ROM or DVD drive is the one potential weakness of a USB speaker system with no sound card, because some CD-ROMs and DVD drives can't output a digital sound data stream. For those drives with only an analog output port, you'll need a sound card to play CD and DVD audio. USB speaker-based computers with a sound card can play back CD and DVD audio by using the input side of the card to digitize the analog signal from the drive.

The sound card manufacturers recognize the threat to their products from USB speakers, and they have responded in several ways. Some have added other, non–sound card products to their line; others have added new technology to their sound cards (such as 3D sound effects) to create value not yet supported by USB.

# Speakers

Choosing speakers for your computer is as easy—and as difficult—as choosing speakers for your home or car stereo. The speakers that come packaged with computer systems are generally small, tinny, and abysmal—not worth using even with the cheapest transistor radio. If sound quality matters to you, you'll want better speakers than come with most computers.

If you have an auxiliary or tape input on your stereo, you can find out what a good set of speakers can do for you by wiring your sound card over to your stereo. (You don't want to connect speakers from your stereo directly to the sound card, because it doesn't have the power to drive them properly.) You'll need a male mini–phone connector on the computer end, and male RCA phono jacks on the stereo end. If you get a cable set up for stereo, you'll hear both channels through the stereo. Be careful to make sure the stereo volume is all the way down when you power things up, in case the output level from your sound card is higher than your stereo expects.

What you're going to hear is that there's more, tighter bass; clearer, cleaner treble; and overall much more appealing sound. This will be true for playing audio CDs, for multimedia titles and presentations, and for games. Live with the difference for a while, and then reconnect your old computer speakers. If you're appalled by the difference, you're in the market for new speakers.

It's important to evaluate speakers both ways — how much better the new ones sound, and how much worse the old ones sound after you've spent some time with the new ones. You hear differences one way you don't with the other, so you need to do both to get a complete evaluation.

The kind of speakers you want will depend somewhat on what you do. Action games sound better with strong bass. You may want a more full-range speaker for music, but can do well with a good budget speaker for the voice tracks in a self-paced training presentation.

If you decide to choose a set of computer speakers, there are some differences between computer speakers and stereo speakers you need to think about:

✦ *Tone and volume controls.* It's inconvenient to go in and adjust the tone or volume using software, and the sound characteristics of different programs vary enough that you'll end up adjusting them fairly often. Controls located on the front of the speakers make this easy.

✦ *Magnetic shielding.* Most speakers depend on strong electromagnetic fields to provide a reference for the moving cone that actually generates sound. Strong magnets help create better sound but can lead to problems (see Chapter 19, "Monitors") with distorted images or colors on your monitor. Good computer speakers are shielded to compensate for that sensitivity of monitors.

✦ *Power amplifiers.* Every sound system needs a power amplifier strong enough to drive the speakers. There's one built into your stereo, but not into your sound card. (More precisely, the one in your sound card is usually too weak to do the whole job.) You need amplified speakers to couple into your computer and provide good sound. If you use speakers designed for a stereo, you'll need a separate amplifier between the computer and the speakers.

Be careful about amplifier power ratings — they're not all the same. The ones to look for are Root Mean Square (RMS) Power, which is the average power to a single speaker, and Total Power, which is the RMS power times the number of speakers. You should ignore Peak Power ratings (the instantaneous maximum the amplifier puts out), because they don't accurately reflect much about the capability of the amplifier.

✦ *3D sound.* Several technologies are competing in the PC world to deliver sound that surrounds the listener. Surround technologies include analog mixed signal approaches (such as the Sound Retrieval System from SRS Labs), and the multichannel AC-3 from Dolby Laboratories. SRS develops the 3D effect with two speakers; AC-3 requires five (as shown in Figure 21-12). The 3D sound technologies for games are the Aureal A3D and Creative Labs' Environmental Audio. Both work best with headphones, cooperating with the game software to more accurately "place" sounds in the space you hear.

It's not yet clear what impact 3D sound will have on your computer. Dolby AC-3 is the standard for DVD CD-ROMs, offering better dynamic range (softest to loudest sounds) than other approaches. Whether or not people decide they want to invest in the extra equipment to hear the surround-sound elements from their PCs will depend on the availability of compelling PC software, and on whether suggestions that PCs and large-screen televisions are merging turn out to be true.

Implementing Dolby AC-3 (or any other sound system using more than two channels) will require changes in how speakers connect to your computer. It's unlikely that we'll see more analog connections — it is more likely that all five channels will be delivered over a Universal Serial Bus or FireWire (see Chapter 9, "Cache, Memory, and Bus").

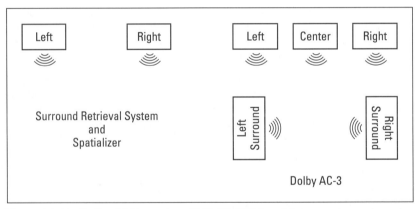

**Figure 21-12:** Dolby AC-3, used on DVD CD-ROMs, adds more channels and speakers for the next step in three-dimensional sound.

# Microphones

Unless you're doing high-quality professional sound recording, your application for a microphone is likely to be one of these:

✦ *Voice annotation.* You can record sound files and attach them within documents in many applications, including Microsoft Word and Excel.

✦ *Voice recognition.* Software listening to your microphone can match what you say to a vocabulary, giving your computer some capability to react to what you say.

✦ *Internet phone.* You can create a two-way voice connection across the Internet, allowing conversation with people connected to the Net and using compatible software.

✦ *Videoconferencing.* You can do the same thing for sound with video (see Chapter 24) as for network phone connections.

You can choose the microphone you use to make these applications easier, although for the most part you're looking for one that stays out of the way and delivers clear sound. Let's look at each one of these applications.

## Voice annotation

Windows includes a simple application called Sound Recorder that lets you record from a microphone (or any other source on your sound card). Using Sound Recorder or functions built into your software, you can record your comments and embed them into a document. For example, to record a voice note in Microsoft Excel you follow these steps:

1. Select the cell you want to annotate.

2. Choose the Insert Note menu item, and click the Record button.

3. Use the record button and other controls in the Record dialog box to start and stop recording.

4. Choose OK; then add the note to the sheet.

You can also import existing sound files into your spreadsheet. From then on, each time you move your mouse cursor on the annotated cell, the annotation plays, reminding you (or your colleagues) of what you had in mind.

Voice annotation is really a mixed blessing. In Excel, the annotation plays automatically, so you don't have to fumble through a series of menus and other windows. It's disruptive to play sounds in offices, though, particularly the "open floor plan" sort of cubicles. It also gets irritating to hear the same comment over and over (even if it was yours), so after a while you'll want to delete the sound.

You won't want to keep reaching for a microphone every time you create an annotation. Combined with the problems of noise in an office, you might want to consider the same sort of headset telephone operators use—one combining a headphone with a small microphone.

# Voice recognition

Even after decades of intense research, voice recognition is terribly difficult for computers to do well. Figure 21-13 shows the different levels of interpretation voice recognition can require. Once you have digital audio coming from the sound card, voice and speech recognition become a software-intensive process that tries to make choices to classify what the computer recorded. Phonemes — the first classification applied in many recognition systems — are the basic sound units in spoken language, covering voicing, articulation, accent, and others. A recognition system simplifies the voice recognition problem by turning raw sound into phonemes, reducing the volume of data and number of choices higher layers in the processor have to examine. As the recognition process continues, it abstracts basic structures to more complex ones — words, phrases, and understood concepts.

You'd want voice recognition for a variety of reasons, not all of which require all the levels of functions in Figure 21-13. The simpler the problem, the more restricted the vocabulary can be and the better your chances of getting accurate recognition.

A microphone suited for voice recognition is essential for accurate results. A voice recognition microphone will focus on the speaker, keeping out background noise and the voices of other speakers. A directional microphone, one on a headset, or even a throat microphone are candidates to consider.

Software now available, including Dragon Naturally Speaking and IBM ViaVoice, can recognize speech in real time with accuracy of about 90 percent or better. You'll have to decide if that's good enough — remember that 90 percent accuracy means on average one word out of every ten will be wrong and need to be corrected. You'll also find that dictation is very different than writing; not everyone's thinking is organized in ways that end up creating coherent results while dictating. From our experiments with recognition software, we decided it's not ready for the kind of writing we do.

We're not making a universal condemnation of voice recognition here, and in fact the answer to the accuracy problem may be at hand. Intel added instructions to the Streaming SIMD Extensions (SSE) instructions in the Pentium III processors, instructions that resulted in better than a 35 percent performance gain for Dragon Naturally Speaking in benchmarks we ran on a 450 MHz Pentium III. That increased performance allows software developers to let their programs work harder to decide what you've said, improving accuracy. When you combine SSE with processor clock speeds headed toward 1 GHz, it's likely that voice recognition software will become very accurate within a few years.

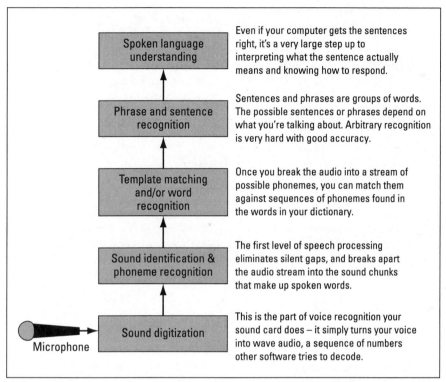

**Figure 21-13:** Voice and speech recognition is very difficult for computers because there are many levels of interpretation that computers must perform accurately to give you a useful result.

## Internet phone

In the last few years, people have written software that lets you send two-way audio between two computers connected by a network. When that idea landed on the Internet, people saw a way to avoid long-distance telephone charges, paying only the local access fees and the costs for an Internet service provider. The sound quality and reliability of connections isn't as good as with the best telephone systems, but the technology does work, and it is improving. More than a few major long distance carriers are busy working to convert their voice networks to Internet-style operation.

The hard part in running telephones over a computer network is that telephones need a continuous, uninterrupted stream of data in order to give you continuous speech. The telephone system sends frequencies up to about 4 kHz. If we take 8-bit samples at the necessary 8 kHz rate (see "Sampling rates—the magic number is two" earlier in this chapter) and don't compress the data, we need to send 64 Kbps both ways to maintain a conversation. If we pause the transmission slightly, say due to congestion in the network somewhere along the way, there's a gap in the sound as the supply of wave audio values runs dry.

## It's hard to do recognition well

We once tested some voice recognition software being developed by a major software manufacturer for integration into other products. The software did word recognition using menu commands in individual Windows applications along with some built-in phrases as the range of what it would recognize.

The end result for us during testing was that the software wasn't accurate enough to be useful, correctly identifying only 50 to 80 percent of the words we spoke. This isn't good enough to replace keyboards, mice, and other input forms, because the effort to deal with the errors is much greater than the value of the words it gets right. (Other recognition software is much more accurate than this.)

The episode that really tells us how hard recognition can be occurred with that software. One of the commands it was always supposed to recognize was "Close window," which was supposed to do the obvious thing—close the active window. We spent about half an hour training the software to know voice and speech patterns, and then tried to see if the computer would recognize the phrase. After about ten times with no results, and completely exasperated by then, we said "Close the @#$% window."

Of course, that worked.

You can't get 64 Kbps of data through a conventional modem. You either need to compress the data down to rates of 20 to 53 Kbps or less (see "Audio compression" earlier in this chapter), or you need an ISDN, ADSL, or cable modem connection capable of 64 Kbps to several megabits per second. Internet phone software compressing down to 4 Kbps exists; we've seen systems capable of delivering understandable speech at data rates as low as 1.2 Kbps per second. Getting the data rate down as low as possible—well below the modem rate—is important because the throughput you get between two points over the Internet is often abysmally low. The fewer bits you need, the shorter the dropout when you get too slow a data rate across the Internet. You trade more continuous sound for lower voice quality.

Given the compromises required to make Internet phone work at all, you'll want to give it every chance you can for success. That means a good quality microphone that eliminates extraneous noise.

## Videoconferencing

Videoconferencing (see Chapter 24) has much the same problem as an Internet phone—you have too much data to cram down a modem without an incredible amount of compression—but it's even worse because you have to handle the video as well as the voice. Microphones for videoconferencing are often different than for other voice applications; you commonly want to move around, and so being constrained by a wire or microphone you hold is inconvenient. Consider a wireless unit, or one that sits on a stand and has some range. You'll have to control the noise environment in that case, but because you want to control clutter and motion in the image behind you as well (so you'll be eliminating extra people from the room), this may be less of a problem.

# Products

It's not difficult to set up good sound for your computer. Perhaps more difficult than getting good sound is achieving compatibility with the rest of your hardware and with your software, although as programs have migrated to using the Windows sound interfaces instead of directly accessing the hardware this problem has become less troublesome. DOS games can still be a problem, because they have sound card drivers built in, often don't have support for every card made, and don't always support "compatible" hardware.

## Turtle Beach Montego II Quadzilla

The Turtle Beach Montego II Quadzilla sound card (Figure 21-14) is a two-slot PCI board supporting hardware sound acceleration, 320-voice wavetable MIDI synthesis, A3D positional audio, and full-duplex operation. The Montego II Quadzilla emulates the Creative Labs SoundBlaster Pro hardware for DOS programs accessing the hardware directly.

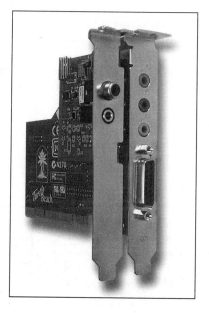

**Figure 21-14:** The Turtle Beach Montego II Quadzilla sound card delivers 3D positional audio plus accelerated digital sound. (Courtesy of Voyetra Turtle Beach, Inc.)

The card offers capabilities new to the market in the last few years, including 3D positional audio, hardware-accelerated digital mixing, support for four speakers, and S/PDIF digital output. Table 21-4 lists the card specifications. The Montego II Quadzilla incorporates the positional audio technology from Aureal, so it delivers 3D sound for a long list of games. The hardware-accelerated digital mixing is perhaps more interesting, though, in that it permits software to simultaneously output many different sounds without burdening the processor with the calculations necessary to mix the sounds for playback. That task is taken by the sound card, freeing the processor for other work.

## Table 21-4
## Turtle Beach Montego II Specifications

| Characteristic | Specification |
| --- | --- |
| **Digital Audio** | |
| Sample size | 18-bit |
| Sample rate | Up to 48 kHz |
| Digital channels | Full duplex operation. Capable of simultaneously mixing up to 96 wave audio streams |
| A3D 2.0 interactive sound | Hardware-based A3D positional audio, including wave tracing with wall reflections and occlusions (64 sources) |
| **Wavetable Audio** | |
| Wavetable processor | 320-voice wavetable synthesis (64 hardware + 256 hardware accelerated software) |
| Sound samples | 4MB stored in system RAM |
| Digital effects | Reverberation and chorus |
| **Analog Audio** | |
| Signal to noise | Better than 97 dB |
| Total harmonic distortion | Better than −93dB (0.005%) |
| Hardware stereo crosstalk | 100 Hz (−89dB); 1kHz (−90 dB); 10 kHz (−87 dB) |
| Frequency response | 20 Hz — 20 kHz (+/−1 dB) |
| Audio inputs/ outputs | Mono microphone input, stereo line input, stereo line output, stereo aux input on internal header, CD input on internal header, Modem audio in/out on internal header. Paired output board provides S/PDIF digital output and analog output for a rear pair of speakers. |

## Labtec C-316 Headset/Boom Microphone

In office environments where you want to limit the noise you create around you, look for products similar to the Labtec C-316 Headset/Boom Microphone (Figure 21-15). The characteristics that make the C-316 a good choice are that it plugs directly into your sound card, has only one headphone so that you can readily hear people around you, and has an integrated noise-canceling boom microphone for effective voice or videoconferencing.

**Figure 21-15:** The Labtec C-316 Headset/Boom Microphone helps you control noise in office environments. (Photo courtesy Labtec.)

## Altec Lansing ACS-48 Speakers

The Altec Lansing ACS-48 speakers are high-quality, general-purpose desktop units. They're analog speakers, not USB, but their performance reflects their manufacturer's heritage of quality stereo equipment — to this point they are the best-sounding PC desktop speakers we've found. There are three units in the assembly (see Figure 21-16), a subwoofer and two higher-frequency satellite speakers. They offer simple controls — a combined power/volume control setup on top of one of the satellite speakers, but the sound quality is good enough that we've never cared about the absence of tone controls. At the end of the first quarter of 1999, the ACS-48 speakers were widely available on the Internet for around $100, making them a great value.

**Figure 21-16:** The Altec Lansing ACS-48 speakers offer good sound at a moderate price. (Photo courtesy Altec Lansing.)

The specifications for the speakers are shown in Table 21-5. The low-frequency response is higher than the usual 20 Hz for hi-fi stereo speakers, but it sounds clean and powerful.

| Table 21-5 Altec Lansing ACS-48 Speakers Specifications | |
|---|---|
| **Characteristic** | **Specification** |
| Transducers | Subwoofer: One 6-inch long-throw woofer <br> Satellite: One 3-inch shielded full-range driver <br> One 3/4-inch high-frequency tweeter |
| Power output | Subwoofer: 40 Watts at 0.8% THD <br> Satellite: 20 Watts / channel RMS at 0.8% THD |
| Frequency response | 35 Hz – 20 kHz |
| Amplifier input impedance | > 10K Ohms |
| Signal to noise ratio | > 65dB |

## Microsoft Digital Sound System 80

If your system supports the Universal Serial Bus, USB speakers offer you two advantages — you may not need a sound card, and you may get less noise in the sound you hear. We've experimented with several sets of USB speakers, and found the sound from the Microsoft Digital Sound System 80 to be good (see Figure 21-17). What's exceptional about the speakers is the price — late in the first quarter of 1999, they were selling for less than $100 on the Internet and had a $50 rebate coupon attached. We've seen no speakers the equal of these for $50, and if you add in money you can save by not buying a sound card, the speakers are almost free.

**Figure 21-17:** The Microsoft Digital Sound System 80 delivers good USB sound performance at an amazing price. (Photo courtesy Microsoft.)

As with the Altec Lansing ACS-48 speakers, the Digital Sound System 80 is a three-piece unit with a subwoofer and two satellite units. They're more noticeable than the Altec units — the subwoofer looks something like an art deco steam engine. Connections on the subwoofer include power, USB, the two satellite speakers, and an analog input you can connect to a sound card or to a stereo source.

| Table 21-6 Microsoft Digital Sound System 80 Specifications | |
|---|---|
| **Characteristic** | **Specification** |
| Transducers | Subwoofer: 13.3cm (5.25 in) active woofer, 15.2cm (6 in) passive radiator |
| Satellite: | 7.62cm (3 in) full range, magnetically shielded |
| Power output (per IEC 268.3) Satellite: | Subwoofer: 44 watts 16 watts per satellite |
| Frequency response | 40 Hz to 20 kHz |
| Amplifier analog input impedance | 100K Ohms |
| Input ports | USB, stereo analog (line) |

Software included with the Digital Sound System 80 offers a surround sound option, but not A3D or Environmental Audio 3D positional sound. You'll need a 3D sound card to get that feature. You'll need Windows 98 or Windows 2000 for USB sound support. If you haven't upgraded to one of those operating systems, you'll have to use the analog input with a sound card, foregoing USB.

# Picking a Sound System

The issues you need to think through regarding sound cards, speakers, and microphones center around what kinds of sounds you expect to handle, how much you care about the quality of sound reproduction you get, and how many people you want to hear what you're doing.

✦ *Kinds of sounds.* The simple beeps and honks that punctuate the user interface in Windows are simply attention-getters. They quickly become part of the background — sounds you would notice more by their absence. Any combination of sound card and speaker that works reliably will do.

Although adequate sound cards are almost universal, games and presentations work much better with speakers better than the paper cup–sized ones sold as a package with many computers. The kinds of sounds you'll handle are different based on the applications you run. Games tend to stress impulsive sounds (good bass and high end), while for presentations you'd want to have speakers that deliver clear, understandable speech (which requires good mid-range with good power handling). Never buy speakers whose performance matters to you without hearing them first, preferably driven by the sound card you expect to use.

✦ *Sound quality.* Beyond the minimum threshold that keeps sound from being annoying, the sound quality you want really depends on how closely you're going to listen to it. Background noise has the minimum requirement.

Presentations, telephony, and videoconferencing require good intelligibility, but not necessarily good fidelity. Casual music requires good fidelity. Critical listening to music requires you abandon the computer and move to your high-quality stereo — sound boards aren't as good as a quality stereo.

Multimedia information, such as training sequences, falls into the same category as presentations — it needs to be intelligible to everyone listening.

✦ *Privacy and groups.* You don't want to impose your sounds on others in close office environments. It quickly gets irritating. You definitely want everyone to hear if you're doing presentations.

Remember that sound is relatively easy to upgrade. Sound cards are relatively inexpensive and simply plug in. Speakers can be unplugged and swapped out, as can microphones. Business users may want to consider headsets plugged into the sound cards rather than speakers. Small, lightweight headsets can be plugged into telephones and computers, switching between the two to answer the phone. The sound quality from headsets can be surprisingly good for inexpensive equipment, in part driven by technology developments for portable radio, tape, and CD players. If you have a voice modem (see Chapter 23), you can plug a computer headset into your sound card and let the voice modem software couple the headset audio into the telephone line.

# Top Support Questions

Many computers have CD-ROMs plugged in via their sound cards. Look in Chapter 14 ("CD-ROMs, CD-ROM Changers, CD-Rs and DVD") for those issues.

## Sound cards

Q: My pre-Win9x or UNIX operating system doesn't support Plug and Play, but I have a Plug and Play sound card. Can I use the card?

A: Maybe. If the card comes with software that lets you configure the card out of Plug and Play mode to a fixed set of addresses and interrupts, you're in business. Figure out a workable setting (make sure the settings are unused by other devices), use the software to set up the board, and configure the operating system. If you don't have software that does that, see if you can get a Plug and Play Configuration Manager for your operating system. A Configuration Manager is, essentially, add-on software that will set up your Plug and Play devices, adding the essential parts of Plug and Play.

Q: Where can I find a Plug and Play Configuration Manager for Windows NT 4?

A: Look on the CD in the \drvlib\pnpisa\x86, \drvlib\pnpisa\alpha, \drvlib\pnpisa\mips, or \drvlib\pnpisa\ppc as appropriate to the processor in your NT machine. In there, you'll find a file pnpisa.inf. Right-click that with NT running, and choose Install. Reboot when prompted, and log in with administrative privileges. You should see a New Hardware Found dialog for PnP devices on your computer.

Q: Some WAV files are distorted when I play them, but not all. Why?

A: Sixteen-bit sound cards have two DMA channels assigned, one capable of 8-bit transfers and another one capable of 16-bit transfers. The 16-bit DMA channels on some motherboards don't work properly with all sound cards. Diagnostic software that comes with your sound card may help you test for this problem. If you find your motherboard has the problem, you can reconfigure Windows to use only the lower number (8-bit) DMA channel. Check with your UNIX vendor for fixes to the problem.

Q: Should I use the IDE port on my sound card?

A: It depends on what's on your motherboard. Although addresses are defined by Creative Labs and others for a third and fourth IDE port, few BIOSes support more than two. If there are already two on your motherboard, and especially if the motherboard IDE ports are on the PCI bus, just disable the port on the sound card (to avoid conflicts). If you don't have any IDE ports, or just one, it's OK to use the one on the sound card. It will give you the same performance as any other IDE port on an ISA bus, but not performance suitable for the fastest drives.

Q: I've recorded some WAV files, but now I need to edit them to clean up the beginning and end. What can I use?

A: A shareware copy of GoldWave can be downloaded from `http://www.goldwave.com/release.html`. GoldWave is a highly capable sound file editor that should do everything you need.

## Speakers and microphones

Q: I only hear sound out of one speaker. What's happening and what can I do?

A: You can troubleshoot this by isolating the problem to the sound card/computer, cable, or speakers. You can test your speakers on an alternate source, such as a WalkMan, portable stereo, or other audio source. If the test works (and you used the same cable), the problem is probably in the computer or sound card set up. If the test fails, try a different cable. If that works, the cable is the problem; otherwise there may be a problem with the speakers. Check the cabling between speakers, and make sure the balance control is set properly. If your speakers have independent power sources, make sure both are working (don't forget that batteries fail).

Q: Why does the volume control on my speakers not work?

A: Your speakers require either an external power supply or batteries to power the amplifier, which is what implements the volume control. Make sure that you have fresh batteries or the appropriate power supply and that the power switch is turned on.

Q: Why does the red light on my speakers not turn on when I turn on the power switch?

A: Verify that you have *fresh* batteries, or that you're using a power supply for the speakers and that it's powered on. If the speakers plug in, make sure there's power at the wall outlet.

Q: Can I use any speakers with any subwoofer?

A: No, because some speaker/subwoofer combinations have nonstandard connections. What you can do, though, is to cable the speakers as if there are two independent sets of speakers (the speakers themselves and the subwoofer). You do that by connecting a "Y" adapter to your sound card. Plug the tail of the Y into the computer and speakers into the branches. (Alternatively, some subwoofers work when plugged into the line-out jack on the sound card, eliminating the need to split the speaker-out jack connection.)

Q: I need to set up my computer for videoconferencing, but the noise is too distracting to my office mates. What can I do?

A: The best answer is the same solution as for noisy speakerphones — get a headset. You can get headsets that plug into your sound card speaker and microphone jacks directly, giving you good sound quality, keeping background noise out of your conversation, and keeping peace in your office.

Q: There's a microphone jack on the front of my speakers. Do I have to use it?

A: No. The microphone jack is strictly for convenience, as is the headphone jack you may have on your speakers. A headphone jack on your speakers usually mutes the speaker itself when you plug in the headphones, so if you have both microphone and headphone jacks, you can conveniently choose whether you'll use the speakers or a more quiet headset/microphone combination.

Q: I haven't used my microphone in a while, and it's stopped working. I checked all the connections, and they're OK. What happened?

A: Some microphones have small batteries inside that can drain over time. If you have one of these, you may need to take the microphone apart and replace the battery.

# Hands-On Upgrades

A little preparation can make installing or upgrading your sound card far easier.

If you already have an ISA sound card installed, record its settings while its still installed and working. Doing that ensures you know a workable configuration for the I/O addresses, interrupts, and DMA channels.

If you're running Windows 9x or Windows NT 4 (or later), remove the existing card from your configuration after you collect that data (use the Device Manager in Windows 9x). Install the Windows NT 4 Plug and Play ISA support (in \drvlib\pnpisa on the CD-ROM) if you're going to need it, and shut down the computer. The patch isn't necessary for Windows 2000, which incorporates Plug and Play. Then, remove the old card (or disable the function on the motherboard if that's where it is).

Install the new card. Here are the steps.

1. Make sure you have the cables you need. The CD-ROM end of the audio cable from the sound card to your CD-ROM isn't standard, so make sure you have what the CD-ROM needs. The sound card end is more standard, but check that too.

   (There are subtle things that can go wrong on the sound card end of the audio cable. For instance, the Intel Advanced/EV motherboard, otherwise called an Endeavor motherboard, has the Vibra 16 chip from Creative Labs built in. There's an audio connector on the motherboard that looks like the standard one on Creative Labs sound cards. Trouble is, Intel mirror-reversed the connections, and a standard cable won't work. If you're very careful with a small, sharp knife, you can extract the pins from the cable connector and reverse them to make it work.)

2. Find an empty slot, and install the card. Wire up the cables (don't ignore setup for the IDE port if you have one on the card — see Chapter 14 ("CD-ROMs, CD-ROM Changers, CD-Rs, and DVD").

3. Start your computer. Follow your sound card manufacturer's directions for installing software.

# Summary

✦ Computers produce sound using wave audio, FM synthesis, and wavetable synthesis.

✦ Wave audio can reproduce any sound. FM and wavetable synthesis mostly reproduce music.

✦ Wavetable synthesis sounds much better than FM synthesis.

✦ Drivers and compatibility are as important in a sound card as the sound itself.

✦ Computer speakers have important differences relative to conventional stereo speakers, including shielding and built-in amplifiers.

✦    ✦    ✦

# Mouse/Trackball/ Joystick/Tablet

◆  ◆  ◆  ◆

**In This Chapter**

Mice and how
they work

Trackballs,
joysticks, tablets, and
specialized
controllers

◆  ◆  ◆  ◆

Years ago, a personal computer had a display, a
keyboard, and a printer. The display gave you 25 by 80
characters, so moving the cursor from character to character
by pushing keys was reasonable. Life was simple enough that
you didn't need a pointing device.

Life changed to put a lot more on the screen, and to put it
on-screen using graphics that give you up to 1,600 × 1,200
resolution. It was impractical to point at things on a high-
resolution graphics screen by moving a pointer with the
keyboard, so new technology was required. Pioneering work
by Doug Englebart at Stanford Research Institute in 1963
created what we now call the mouse (along with the On-Line
System and some incredibly innovative ideas) and enabled the
pointing motions we all use in the graphical Windows (and
UNIX X Window) interface. Development by Microsoft and
other companies made the mouse the most common pointing
device on personal computers, and almost as essential as a
keyboard. Competitive devices such as trackballs and touch-
sensitive pads have flourished, but they are nowhere as
prevalent as mice.

## Mice

The insides of a mouse — shown in Figure 22-1 — contain two
kinds of input electronics. One part of the mouse detects
movement and reports it, while the other part detects button
activity and reports that. Switches (the buttons) are no
problem; the trick is to convert movement into electrical
signals the computer can understand. A few mice use optical
sensors and a special mouse pad, but nearly all PC mice use
the mechanical ball described here.

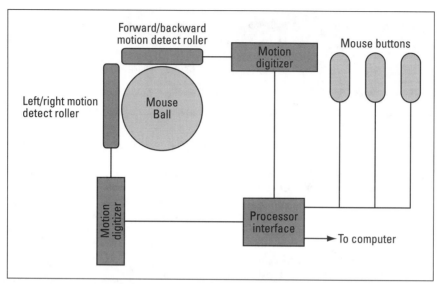

**Figure 22-1:** Your mouse is really two independent devices — one that reports motion and one that reports button actions.

Movement of the mouse is limited to combinations of forward/backward and left/right motion. Most mice use a rubberized ball that, when it rolls, causes two rollers to turn. The rollers are carefully mounted perpendicular to each other so that they each detect one of those two directions. Movements of the rollers are coupled into motion digitizers that sense rotation. The motion digitizers report that rotation to the processor interface, which creates and sends messages to your computer.

## Your word processor is a 30-year-old idea

For all of the power and features in the best word processors we have today, many of the features they implement are 30 years old. In addition to inventing (and patenting) the mouse, Doug Englebart created something called the On-Line System (NLS) while at Stanford Research Institute. The primitive terminals of the day couldn't support the interactions Englebart designed for NLS, so he invented a completely new terminal. In addition to the mouse, his terminal included a redesigned keyboard and a five-paddle device that you played chords on to type letters (think of a five-key, one-handed piano). Using the mouse with one hand and playing chords with the other, an experienced user could control the system and edit text surprisingly quickly. The combination of mouse and chords allowed operation without continually moving from keyboard to mouse and back, a problem we haven't eliminated in today's systems.

Unlike today's PC software that, until Windows 9x (and X Window under UNIX) rarely used the second mouse button, Englebart's mouse had three buttons that were all used by NLS, as were all the combinations of mouse buttons. His software allowed a seemingly infinite set of views into your documents, foreshadowing outline views in today's word processors. Running on a Digital Equipment Corporation mainframe (a PDP-10), NLS included spell checkers, text styles, group collaboration, and much more. In fact, it included so many features that — like many of today's word processors — it required some intensive training and practice to use competently.

Like many other people, we have word processors that we like and ones that we detest. NLS was one of the ones we really liked. NLS never made the transition from the Digital Equipment Corporation mainframes Englebart used to PCs, though, so only its concepts remain alive.

## Mickeys, balls, and other mouse jargon

The motion reports that a mouse sends your computer don't contain absolute position information; the mouse has no idea where it is on your desk. Instead, the mouse reports that it's moved a specified distance, measured in units called *mickeys*. One mickey is the least movement that the roller and digitizer can detect. In the first Microsoft mice, one mickey was about one one-hundredth of an inch. The newer ones improved this resolution down to about one two-hundredth, and later to one four-hundredth of an inch. Every time the mouse sends a message to the computer, it reports the number of mickeys it has moved since the last message. Mickeys are reported independently from each of the two digitizers and are used by your computer to update the mouse cursor position on-screen.

Mouse buttons are simply reported to the processor as being up or down. Mice typically have from one to three buttons, in part because Windows internally has provisions for left, middle, and right buttons.

**Tip**    Mice, being mechanical devices, are prone to picking up dirt and debris off your desk. When this happens, the garbage from your desk often gets wound around the rollers and stops them from rolling. That leads to "bumps" in the mouse movement or to situations where the mouse simply stops moving in one direction.

If that happens to you, you'll need to clean the insides of the mouse. There's usually a panel that rotates and lifts off the bottom of the mouse, allowing you to remove the ball. Once you do, you can gently rotate the rollers and remove the dirt and lint. Don't use oil or grease in the mouse — it'll just attract more dirt.

## Mouse cursors

A key part of your mouse isn't hardware at all — it's the cursor the computer draws on the screen to show you where you're pointing. There's no direct connection between your mouse and the cursor position. Instead, Windows uses the movement reports from the mouse to update the horizontal and vertical position where it thinks the cursor should appear, erases the old drawing of the cursor, and draws the cursor again at the new position.

The mouse cursor also gets erased and redrawn by Windows every time a program draws on the screen near the mouse. (You can see this effect by starting a video clip — an AVI, MPG, or MOV file — in Windows and then moving the mouse cursor over the video playback window. You'll see it flicker on and off or possibly disappear entirely until the video stops.)

The process of erasing and redrawing the mouse cursor creates work for the processor, so at one time some video board manufacturers built-in hardware assists for cursors called sprites. Sprites also are useful for moving characters and flying objects around in video games, so in principle this was a good idea. In practice, though, the sprites often caused software problems, and because there was no standard programming interface to control the sprites, game programmers ignored them. Very few video boards offer sprites today.

## Feeding your mouse

A serial port on a PC conforms to the Electronic Industries Association RS-232C standard, which defines both the electrical properties of signals at the port and the way in which those signals are used. The RS-232C port of your PC uses voltages to indicate logical states: A one bit is signaled by −3 V to −15 V on a pin, while a zero is signaled by +3 V to +15 V. Plus and minus 12 V are typical.

None of the pins in an RS-232C port were intended to deliver power. When Microsoft developed the serial mouse, though, they noticed that the typical output line in an RS-232C port could supply a little bit of power — around five hundredths of a watt. By using very low power electronics (and very little electronics at all), they could keep power consumption below that limit and run the mouse completely off the port.

That observation, and the engineering behind it, has been a big part of making mice a part of every computer. Eliminating the mouse card that had to go inside the computer reduced cost and, perhaps more important, simplified installation. No screws to remove, no slots to find, no conflicts to solve. Plug it in and go.

Since then, electronics have become smaller, doing more in the same space and requiring less power. You can get cordless mice and keyboards today, such as the Logitech Wireless Desktop mouse and keyboard set that uses radio to communicate with your computer rather than the wire you're used to. By combining wireless links with gyroscopes or tilt sensors, companies have built "air mice" — mice that you simply hold in your hand wherever you happen to be. An air mouse is, for some people, a key element of a workable computer-based presentation system.

# Trackballs

One of the most common alternatives to a mouse is a trackball, which is basically a mouse turned upside down. You rotate the ball directly while the body stays put. Trackballs solve three problems inherent to mice:

✦ *Space.* Only the ball moves in a trackball, not the body. By comparison, mice take space to operate (and even then, you can end up picking up the mouse and moving back on the desk when you run out of room). In some situations — a computer built into a rack of equipment, or most of the airline seats you'll find — you don't have that kind of space.

✦ *Staying put.* You can attach a trackball securely to a computer or shelf so it stays in one place. By comparison, a mouse won't stay where you left it if it's being bounced around. Airline seats are like that, but so are boats, cars, and most any other moving platform.

✦ *Fine control.* The buttons on a trackball aren't physically coupled to the ball as they are by the body of a mouse. People tend to move a mouse a pixel or two when they push one of the buttons. If you're doing drawings or other very fine work, that motion can destroy the precision you need. You won't have that problem with a trackball.

Unfortunately, trackballs have problems of their own, the most prominent of which is that your hand is always moving relative to the buttons, and you may have to stretch quite a bit to reach the button you want. If you need to hold the button down while you rotate the ball, this can turn into the computer equivalent of patting your stomach while you rub your head. (More than a few trackball manufacturers have added buttons to their products that latch down when pushed, telling the computer they're down until you push them again.) Some people never get comfortable with a trackball, finding the movements awkward, while others are fanatic about them.

# Joysticks

While a mouse and a trackball are roughly the same thing, joysticks are completely different (see Figure 22-2). In analog joysticks, the handle is pivoted at the bottom on the shafts of a pair of variable resistors. When you move the handle, the shafts rotate and change the value of the resistors. The computer measures this resistance change periodically and calculates the position represented by the resistor. The left/right resistor position determines the X coordinate; and the forward/backward resistor, the Y coordinate.

The process by which your computer measures the value of the two resistors uses very inexpensive hardware, but it's very slow. Imagine a bucket full of water with a hole in it. The bucket and water, plus your eye to see when the bucket is empty and a stopwatch to time how long it takes, represent the equipment the computer uses to do the measurement. The hole corresponds to the variable resistor.

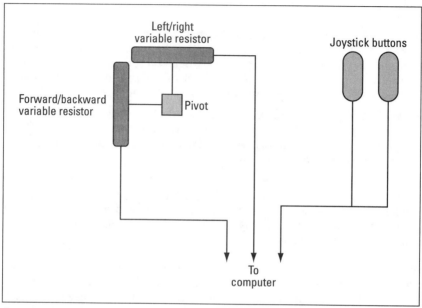

**Figure 22-2:** A joystick attaches variable resistors to a pivot, letting the computer measure the angle of deflection in two directions.

Your computer fills the bucket and times how long it takes to empty out all the water. (Of course, this happens electronically — not with a real bucket.) Longer times correspond to smaller holes (greater values of resistance). The computer interface to the joystick is called a game port; it is commonly combined on a sound card with the wires needed to connect to an external MIDI keyboard. (There's actually provision for two joysticks in the game port — see the sidebar "You only get so many options.")

The problem with this approach, which is used in nearly every joystick made, is that getting an accurate, repeatable measurement takes a relatively long time, and during that interval the processor can't do anything else. That means that the processor isn't updating the screen, isn't playing sound, and isn't calculating. It's waiting for the bucket to empty. The time is short in human terms, but long for your computer. Ultimately, the smoothness of movement suffers in highly interactive software. Joysticks have other problems too, foremost of which is that it can be tiring to keep your hand and arm elevated on the stick. Their responsiveness is very different from mice and trackballs as well, and not suited to all tasks. (For example, word processing with a joystick is nearly impossible, but locating points on a map — or flying an airplane — is natural.)

## You only get so many options

The game port interface design allows two variable resistors and two switches on a joystick. There are provisions for two complete joystick interfaces in a single game port, however, so that two players can compete with each other at the same time.

In practice, what has happened is not that users attach two joysticks, but that they attach a more complex joystick that uses both sets of controls. The Logitech Wingman Extreme, for example, has, in addition to the two variable resistors for the stick, four buttons plus a "hat" switch with four positions. Designers took the two independent joystick connections in the game port and wired them all to the one joystick, allowing a more complex interface.

If you're one of the people who want to hook up two joysticks, however, you can't use one of these enhanced models. One complex stick consumes the capabilities of the entire game port. You'll have to use a basic, two-button joystick and a "Y" cable that splits out the wires to two physically independent sockets.

Joystick technology has evolved a lot in the last few years. Digital joysticks, still connected to the game port at first, replaced the variable resistors with digital optical position encoders, allowing your computer to simply be told the stick position. Digital joysticks are quick and accurate, leading to smoother game play and better responsiveness. Force-feedback joysticks exploited the fact that the digital interface can send information from the computer as well as to it, adding motors that are commanded by the computer to push against your hand through the stick. USB joysticks improved the digital interface, moving the connection from the game port to the USB connection.

# Tablets

Yet another pointing device is the tablet, a flat surface on which you can write, draw, and trace. Tablets come in a range of sizes, from card-sized through units several feet on a side. You can get ones with a corded or cordless stylus, and ones with buttons and other controls.

The real advantage of a tablet is that it lets you use the drawing motions you're used to — the fine arc around the heel of your palm and the stroke with your elbow and shoulder. These motions are completely impossible with a trackball or joystick, and unnatural and ineffective with a mouse. A tablet is the closest computer approximation to a sketchpad and so is commonly found in the hands of artists.

While mice typically have resolutions of 400 points per inch or less, most tablets have a resolution of at least 1,000 lines per inch. A 5-inch-wide tablet provides at least 5,000 lines of resolution and, for some tablets, gives you as many as 12,700 lines. This is far beyond PC monitor display screen capabilities and similar to the resolution of a printer for the entire page.

Not all software handles tablets equally well, so you'll want to check and see whether the tablet has drivers for the software you plan to use. You should check what functions the software and driver support. Many tablets come bundled with drawing software. If you choose one of those, check to see whether the software does the things you need.

Some of the companies that make tablets (such as Wacom) also build their digitizers into transparent surfaces you can use as a touch screen. When the user touches the screen, it sends a set of coordinates to the computer that your program can correlate to areas of the screen.

# Specialized Controllers

The common thread among all the input devices we've looked at — keyboards, mice, trackballs, joysticks, and tablets — is that you use different gestures or actions to carry out the different tasks you do, and that no one device is the best one for all of them. Just as you don't (or shouldn't!) use a screwdriver and hammer as your only tools, you won't want to use just a keyboard and mouse as your only input devices.

The advantage you get from the right controller is that you can do what you want to do easier and faster. Nothing is more frustrating, for instance, than having to remember just which of 20 or 30 keys on the keyboard you need to push to get the effect you want. Specialized devices make your work easier by making combinations of movements more natural, so you work more effectively.

# Products

We've included more products in this chapter than usual because there are so many kinds of input devices. No matter what products you choose, however, you have to carefully consider the software that interfaces to the device — its driver — as well as the device itself.

**Tip**

We're fanatic about driver quality. Creating drivers is some of the most difficult programming people do, and many companies have demonstrated their inability to get them right. When you can, it's the safe alternative to buy a product that's completely compatible with the Microsoft mouse and uses the Microsoft driver. If you can't do that, make sure of the quality of the drivers from the manufacturer you choose. We very much doubt you'll be happy about saving a few dollars after you discover that the source of your crashes has been a buggy driver.

# Microsoft Intellimouse

We consider the Microsoft mouse, in any of its serial, PS/2, or USB versions, the standard of comparison, primarily because of the stability of the Microsoft mouse drivers and the durability of the unit (see Figure 22-3). The Microsoft mouse had always been a two-button unit until 1996, when Microsoft announced the Intellimouse—a new design that added the wheel you see between the two buttons in Figure 22-3. The wheel combines with changes in Windows 98 and Windows 2000 to simplify scrolling and zooming in documents, reducing the number of times you have to move your hand from mouse to keyboard. Later designs build on the Intellimouse—the Intellimouse Pro offers an arched shape for better ergonomics, while the Intellimouse Explorer adds optical tracking and other features.

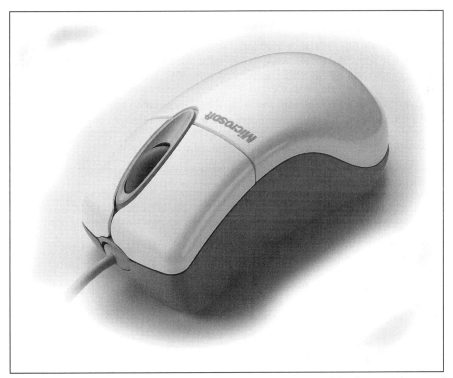

**Figure 22-3:** The Microsoft Intellimouse combines a comfortable shape with rugged construction and quality drivers. (Photo courtesy Microsoft Corporation.)

The interface you choose for your mouse depends on your system and the other equipment you expect to use. The Universal Serial Bus is now commonplace, augmenting the more traditional choices you have:

✦ *Serial ports.* So many devices want to connect through a serial port — UPS, modem, game controllers, sound controllers, and countless others — that consuming one for the mouse might not be a good idea. Even though you can have four serial ports (COM1 through COM4), you can't use them all at once in most machines. (See Chapter 23, "Modems.")

✦ *PS/2 mouse port.* This is essentially a serial port, but at a different I/O address and with a different IRQ. If you have a PS/2 port on your motherboard, it's a good choice since that way you don't use up a serial port (and you can't use the PS/2 port for anything else).

✦ *USB mouse.* Like the PS/2 mouse port, a USB mouse port leaves the serial port free for other uses. If you use a USB mouse, make sure the BIOS in your computer offers *Legacy USB Support,* which means that it can make the USB mouse look like a conventional serial mouse for programs that don't know how to handle USB directly (for instance, DOS or the BIOS itself).

Mice often come with software to tie various functions to the mouse. The Microsoft Intellipoint software, for instance, lets you do things like:

✦ Bring up the Explorer when you push both buttons

✦ Highlight the mouse cursor when you press and release the Ctrl key on the keyboard

✦ Use the mouse pointed in other than the usual direction (that is, with the cord and buttons pointing away from you)

✦ Move the cursor to the default button in dialog boxes, and a variety of other effects

Programming the mouse buttons is quite useful, but you have to exercise some restraint. Not all commands are useful all the time, and if you get too complex, it's hard to remember what you have set up.

## Logitech USB Gaming Mouse

Some years back Logitech discontinued a three-button mouse that had a reasonably fanatic group of users. Among those users were gamers who found the third button wildly useful for controlling game functions. The outcry from gamers who could no longer get the old mouse became so strong that Logitech reintroduced the product, but with a twist — it's a USB mouse with a special adapter that lets you plug it into a conventional PS/2 mouse port (see Figure 22-4). You can use the Gaming Mouse with an older, non-USB system, and keep using it when you upgrade.

**Figure 22-4:** The Logitech USB Gaming Mouse works with both PS/2 and USB computers. (Photo courtesy Logitech.)

Hard-core gamers have found another reason, beyond convenience, to move to USB mice — fast reaction game response. Your computer gets updates from a USB mouse nearly twice as often as from a PS/2 mouse, leading to smoother, more responsive play at expert levels.

## Logitech Wingman Force joystick

Despite their more common use with games, joysticks have value in business for controlling movement over maps and for input to environments such as flight simulations. The Logitech Wingman Force joystick (see Figure 22-5) delivers optical encoder technology to reduce processor overhead, adds more controls, connects with USB, and enhances game play with force feedback.

**Figure 22-5:** The Logitech Wingman Force joystick offers force feedback and a USB digital interface. (Photo courtesy Logitech.)

Game joysticks have evolved to add buttons and controls on the body of the stick to reduce the need to keep a hand on the keyboard. Controls on the Wingman Force include a trigger, control hat, and buttons on the stick itself, along with buttons and a throttle slider on the base. Force feedback adds tactile effects to games, letting the software create effects that simulate the texture of surfaces, the click of a golf ball hit, the resistance of a hard turn in a car or plane, or the kick of a weapon.

**Tip**    Something you want to look for in a joystick is sturdiness. You need to consider the internal mechanism as well as what you see externally; people exert a surprising amount of force on the trigger button and stick pivots. Because you can't always tell about a stick's internal construction by inspection, you should consider looking for experiences of other users. One source is the Internet newsgroups, which you can search with the Dogpile search engine at `http://www.dogpile.com`.

## Wacom Intuos graphics tablet system

Wacom has long been the best-known manufacturer of graphics tablets. The company has extended the range of what you can do with a tablet with their Intuos graphics tablet system that combines 2,540 lines per inch resolution, a pressure-sensitive battery-free pen, a cordless mouse, an optional airbrush tool, and a tool identification system that lets you store your preferences in the tools themselves.

Buttons on the barrel of the stylus let you select objects in your software or choose special drawing functions. Wacom's stylus has an "eraser" on the top, letting you use the pad even more as you would a pencil and paper. The eraser has the same pressure-sensitive capability as the tip, so you can use it for shading, feathering, and other artistic effects (see Figure 22-6).

**Figure 22-6:** The Wacom Intuos Graphics Tablet System is as close to pencil and paper as you'll get. (Photo courtesy Wacom Technology Corporation.)

Wacom has a new tablet that's a combined color LCD display and tablet. It's new and expensive as of early 1999, but as prices come down the fact that you can finally see your drawing under your pencil could revolutionize the tablet market.

The software you use with a tablet is critical to getting the results you want. Beyond good drivers, you need software that interprets what you're doing with the tablet and creates the effects you want. Wacom packages Corel Print & Photo House with some of its tablets. More advanced software supporting the Wacom tablets includes Adobe PhotoShop, Fractal Design Painter, and Autodesk AutoCAD.

## Microsoft SideWinder Force Feedback Wheel and SideWinder Freestyle Pro USB game pad

Games bring perhaps the most unique environments to PCs, so it's predictable that games would lead to the development of specialized controllers. Two of the most popular game-specific controllers are steering wheels (and pedals) for driving games and game pads for fighting and other games imported from dedicated game consoles such as the Sony Playstation.

A number of companies make both wheels and game pads; of the ones we've tested, the ones we've found to be the most reliable are the ones by Microsoft. Figure 22-7 shows the Microsoft SideWinder Force Feedback Wheel. You mount the wheel to the top of a table, in front of your monitor, and put the pedals on the floor. The wheel connects to the game port on your sound card. Once you install the software and set up the game software, the wheel controls your race car the way you'd expect — turn left to go left, turn right to go right. Press the right pedal to accelerate, the left to brake.

Dedicated game consoles, such as the Sony Playstation or Sega Dreamcast, use a specialized controller, called a game pad, for input. Game pads typically have a directional button capable of sensing input in one of eight directions plus a generous complement of buttons. Individual games assign specific functions to the buttons.

Even though the controls on a game pad don't extend controls you use commonly in the real world, as does a racing wheel, they've become ingrained in the user interface of many role playing and fighting games, and they seem most natural to players accustomed to that interface. The Microsoft SideWinder Freestyle Pro USB Game Pad (Figure 22-8) provides that standard interface and ties it in to the DirectX software most games now use. The end result is that ports of console games to the PC, along with PC titles themselves, can deliver the same enjoyable experience as on a dedicated console.

The SideWinder Freestyle Pro USB incorporates tilt sensors that detect movement of the game pad left and right along with forward and back. The software maps those motions into the left/right and forward/back axes you'd normally get from a joystick, making the motions accessible to software. The result is very natural for driving games (the controller ships with Motocross Madness), so natural that relatively young children can make sense of the game and have a great time.

**Figure 22-7:** The Microsoft SideWinder Force Feedback Wheel combines force feedback with the motions you expect for driving. (Photo courtesy Microsoft.)

**Figure 22-8:** The Microsoft SideWinder Freestyle Pro USB Game Pad duplicates the familiar game console interface on PCs. (Photo courtesy Microsoft.)

# Picking Input Devices

With the exception of the importance of rock-solid drivers, the most important thing to keep in mind about input devices is that there is an enormous number of them, each suited to some things more than others. This means that you can use a single one for everything, or you can have specialized controllers each suited for a specific task.

A mouse is the most common input device, applicable to nearly everything you do with your computer. A lot of people choose trackballs instead of mice, so you'll want to check that alternative for a general-purpose pointing device. If you're doing artistic or drawing work, you're probably familiar with tablets and will definitely want to consider one. It's simply faster and easier to draw with one.

There are support issues surrounding the choice of devices in an office. You can't afford to waste all the time you save from one of these devices fooling around with software and hardware configurations, or with balky drivers. Instead, you'll want to maintain a reasonably standard set — a preferred mouse and tablet, for example.

If you're mobile and not using the point device built into your laptop, you'll probably want a trackball, both because it takes less space and because it will stay stationary. (See Chapter 32, "Making Choices That Fit the Road Warrior.") Some airlines won't let you use externally attached equipment in flight, so consider where you'll use the device carefully.

# Top Support Questions

Most of the problems you'll see with pointing devices are a result of underlying problems with serial ports or driver software. Using dedicated PS/2 mouse ports or USB connections, and staying with the drivers that come with your operating system (rather than those from third parties) can help eliminate most of these problems.

## Mouse

Q: I installed a modem and my mouse stopped working (or vice versa). What happened?

A: Most likely, you have a serial mouse and you installed the other serial device on a port with a conflicting interrupt. For example, if you have a mouse on COM1 and modem on COM3, they both share interrupt 4; a mouse on COM2 and modem on COM4 would share interrupt 3. You can't share the interrupt over both ports at the same time, because the electrical characteristics of the ISA bus are such that interrupts can get lost when multiple devices trigger the same interrupt. You can check to see if this is what happened by removing the non-mouse device and seeing if the mouse works again. If so, you need to configure the device for a complementary port (for instance, for COM2 or COM4 if the mouse is on COM1). Alternatively, you can install a bus or PS/2 mouse, giving you more flexibility for configuring the mouse interrupt.

Q: I installed a Plug and Play card and my PS/2 mouse quit working. Why?

A: In some machines, the BIOS, not the operating system, assigns interrupts and I/O addresses to Plug and Play cards. In those cases, the BIOS may assign another device to the PS/2 mouse interrupt (IRQ 12), effectively disabling the mouse. Disable support for Plug and Play in the BIOS (so that the operating system makes the assignments) and see what happens.

Q: My serial mouse isn't detected by Plug and Play. Why?

A: Check if you're using an adapter to connect a 9-pin serial mouse connector to a 25-pin serial port. If so, it's possible that some lines in the 9-pin connector required by Plug and Play aren't being bridged to the 25-pin connector. Try using a 9-pin port, a different connector that you know bridges all 9 signals, or a manual installation of your mouse via Add New Hardware.

Q: My mouse doesn't respond to double-clicks. Why?

A: If you can, try another mouse. If that works, the original mouse is probably defective. If the second mouse doesn't work either, check the speed setting for double-clicks. If it's set too high, it may be looking for the second click faster than you can push the button. Slow down the double-click setting and see what happens.

Q: My mouse jumps across the screen, or moves in bursts. Why?

A: Check if your mouse is connected to a serial port using the 16550 chip. If so, verify that the 16550 hardware functions are disabled for that port — that the chip is functioning as an older 8250 chip. Your BIOS may label the setting you need as turning on and off the FIFO (First In First Out hardware buffer).

Q: My mouse stops going in one direction sometimes. If I move it away and then back, it continues past the sticking point. Why?

A: You probably have dirt in the mouse (on the rollers) or on the mouse ball. Remove the ball and check carefully for dirt, cleaning out any you find.

## Tablet

Q: In my system with a tablet and mouse, the mouse has gone berserk, moving erratically and leaping across the screen. What's wrong?

A: If you have a tablet installed, check that the stylus hasn't accidentally come near the surface of the tablet, creating unintentional mouse motion inputs to your system.

# Hands-On Upgrades

Installing a new controller is a matter of plugging it in and installing the software. The hard part is figuring out where to connect it.

As I've noted, serial ports are scarce resources. Unfortunately, tablets (all the Wacom units, for instance) tend to connect through a serial port, as do many wheels and other specialized controllers. If you already have a serial mouse and a modem, you've got some decisions to make, because you don't have a free serial port. Here are your choices:

✦ *Move the mouse to a PS/2 port.* A PS/2 mouse port uses different addresses and interrupts than serial ports, so moving the mouse to the PS/2 port from a serial port frees the serial port for use. Not all serial mice are PS/2 compatible, so even if you have a PS/2 mouse port, you still might have an expense for a new mouse. If you don't have a PS/2 mouse port, you'll either need an adapter card that provides one or a new motherboard that includes one.

✦ *Get a USB mouse.* USB solves so many connection problems that it's inevitable almost all serial port devices will migrate to the newer interface. If you must, you can even get a device that adds serial ports to your computer via a USB connection.

✦ *Move the modem to COM3 or COM4.* You can share the interrupt between the modem and tablet as long as you never use both the tablet and modem at the same time.

✦ *Get a serial port adapter using alternate addresses and interrupts.* The STB Systems STB 4-COM (http://www.stb.com), for example, lets you add four serial ports, with a lot of flexibility in how you assign I/O addresses and interrupts. The device supports interrupt sharing among the serial ports, so you're not likely to run out of interrupts due to the card. Their DSP/550 gives you two serial ports with some interrupt flexibility — it can let you add COM3 and COM4 ports that don't share interrupts with COM1 or COM2. Keep in mind that many video cards conflict with the COM4 I/O port address, so you may not be able to use COM4 unless you reassign the address.

✦ *Use an external modem and a switch box.* If you can't live with one of the first two choices, you can connect both an external modem and the tablet to the same physical serial port, using a switch box to choose which is active. You'll also have to activate and deactivate the tablet software, since tablet drivers commonly hook in as a mouse device and therefore both check for the tablet working at boot time and try to interpret any input from that port.

✦ *Get a parallel port modem.* Although tablets that connect to the parallel port are uncommon, you can get parallel port modems (such as the parallel port–based US Robotics DataBurst external ISDN modem).

The only zero-cost option is to move the modem to COM3 or COM4, sharing the interrupt. This is very inconvenient, though, and can lead to lockups if you do the wrong thing at the wrong time. A switch box choice is equally inconvenient. Using the PS/2 mouse port on your motherboard, if you have one, might be zero-cost if your mouse is already PS/2 compatible, or might cost you the price of a mouse. All the other choices offer good convenience but have some cost and (in the case of nonstandard addresses and interrupts) can be tedious to set up.

In the case of Windows, you set up nonstandard ports by manually setting the resources. Under FreeBSD, you'll have to rebuild the kernel specifying a device line in the configuration file that identifies the parameters for your additional or non-standard serial ports. Check the MAN page for sio for details.

## Summary

✦ Mice and trackballs are electromechanical devices that translate movement into inputs to your computer.

✦ Input devices like joysticks, tablets, and other specialized controllers adapt different movements to computer input, making specialized control easier.

✦ Drivers and software are critical to getting value from any input device you choose.

✦     ✦     ✦

# Modems

**I**t may seem simple, but communications and networks are some of the most complex things computers do. Barry has written a lot of communications software and built communications hardware, and even though he knows intellectually why all that complexity is there, intuitively it seems harder than it should be. In any event, there's a lot to talk about.

You look at modems in this chapter — the devices that send your data down telephone lines in one form or another. In Chapter 27, "Network Cabling and Interfaces," you look at the devices that ship your data around over local and wide area networks. Finally, in Chapter 30, "Accessing and Serving the Internet," you look at how things operate over the Internet, how you get connected, and how you can put up an Internet server.

## Whistling into the Phone

Modems are the first bit of magic in computer communications and networks. What makes them interesting (and difficult to design) is that doing what a modem does — pushing tens of thousands of bits per second down miles of wire with really awful characteristics — can't be done the obvious way. The modem's job is to overcome the limitations of that wire and of the telephone system.

### Signals and very long wires

Let's look at why the obvious approach to sending data down the long wires of a telephone network doesn't work in most cases, and then we'll move from there to the different modulation schemes used in modems.

The obvious approach to sending your data is to do what most of the signals in your computer do: Use one voltage level for a one bit and another for a zero. On your motherboard, for example, a one is either five or a little over three volts, and a zero is zero volts. On your computer's motherboard, signals like that go up and down hundreds of millions of times per second, and (with careful design) it all works well. On a telephone line, factors computer designers can't eliminate intervene to make this impossible.

The first thing that distinguishes the wires on your computer's motherboard from a telephone wire is simply their lengths. Wires on your motherboard are measured in inches, whereas telephone wires are measured in tens of thousands of feet. Wires have a property called *capacitance*, which amounts to the ability to hold electricity. A short wire has almost no capacitance, whereas a very long wire has significant amounts. Capacitance is a problem because you have to fill the wire up with electricity before the change will show up at the other end.

We showed you an analogy between signals in a computer and water in a lake in Chapter 9 ("Cache, Memory, and Bus"), letting a full lake represent a one bit, and an empty lake represent a zero bit. If you think of a river as corresponding to a wire, the same analogy holds — let a full river represent a one, and a dry one represent a zero. The capacity of the river (its width times depth times length) is like the capacitance of the wire: The bigger the river, the more water it takes to fill, and so the longer it takes to go from empty to full. If you have a big lake feeding the river, you can reduce the fill time. In terms of computer signals, the bigger lake feeding the river corresponds to more powerful chips to drive the signal down the wire. There's a limit to how hard chips can drive signals down tens of thousands of feet of wire, though, which limits how fast direct transmission of signals can go.

The second thing that distinguishes the wires on your computer's motherboard from a telephone wire is noise. Wires pick up noise from magnetic fields, sparks, lightning, and almost any other electrical activity. (This is why proper grounding and shielding on an I/O bus turned out to be such a major difference between IDE and SCSI interfaces in Chapter 11, "I/O Buses.") Computer designers are very careful about keeping wires away from each other to minimize noise. Telephone wires don't have that luxury. Telephone wires are often strung along the same poles as power lines for thousands of feet, guaranteeing they'll pick up noise. They're out in the weather too, subject to corroding connections, fields from lightning strikes, and other effects making the circuit as bad as it can be.

The third thing that distinguishes the wires on your computer's motherboard from a telephone wire is that there's a telephone switch at the other end of a telephone line. That's a more complex problem than you might think; telephone switches are designed to carry many voice conversations from one place to another, not computer network data. Computer data transmission is more of an afterthought (more on this when we discuss ISDN—Integrated Services Digital Network—and ADSL—Asymmetric Digital Subscriber Line—later in this chapter). To communicate over the telephone network, your computer has to look like a telephone to the switch. That's very constraining on what the modem can do.

Here are three of the most difficult problems telephone switches introduce for modems:

✦ *Analog operation.* Telephones are analog devices like your stereo, not digital devices like your computer. For your computer to look like a telephone, it has to convert its signals to analog waveforms and back again.

✦ *Frequency response.* Telephones are designed to send voices back and forth, not symphonic music. What that means in practice is the frequency response of a telephone circuit is very limited. The lower frequency cutoff is about 150 Hz; the upper is less than 4 kHz.

✦ *Full-duplex operation.* If you look at the wiring to your telephone, you'll notice a very interesting thing—there are only two wires, even though you can talk in both directions at once. That requires the telephone switch (and your telephone) to transmit and receive on those wires simultaneously. That's similar to putting a live microphone in front of the speaker it connects to; you're asking for a nasty feedback howl. A circuit in your telephone (and a similar one in the switch) called a *hybrid* suppresses the feedback by subtracting some of the transmitted signal from the received signal.

Figure 23-1 shows a typical telephone line frequency response. We generated the raw data for the graph by calling the U.S. Robotics bulletin board (847-982-5092) with a Sportster Voice 33.6 FAXmodem and running the USRSTATS service. You can't do this over the Internet, because the service has to have a direct connection—it gathers the frequency response information by querying the modem at the U.S. Robotics end. The data comes back to you as a graph displayed in characters. (Use the MS LineDraw font in your terminal program to see it correctly.) We've converted the data to a smooth line representative of the actual response.

The response changes from call to call because you're likely to get a different connection through the switch each time, and the condition of each line depends on its physical characteristics. The response you see in Figure 23-1 is one of the better connections we received in several tries. What's important about the graph is how it shows the frequency response of the circuit between our modem and the U.S. Robotics site rolling off at the higher end. The loss of high-frequency response reduces the data rate your modem can support, because it restricts the bandwidth of the modulated waveform the receiving modem can hear.

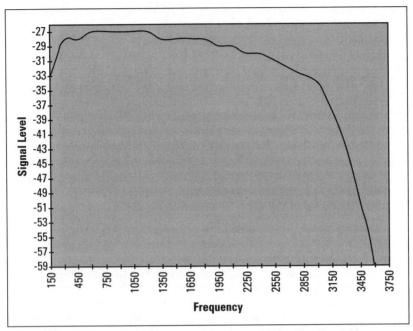

**Figure 23-1:** Your telephone line frequency response rolls off quickly as frequencies approach 4 kHz, which limits the achievable data rate.

## Modulation

The word *modem* is really an acronym, formed as a contraction of MOdulation and DEModulation. It's been used so commonly, though, that it's often no longer capitalized as most acronyms are. It's just a word now. The first thing that happens to your data as it goes down a telephone line is *modulation* — changing your data into a signal that can be shipped over long wires. (Demodulation is the job of undoing modulation — recovering your data from the incoming modulated signal.) The fundamental job your modem has is to convert the data stream into sounds that can be transported within practical limits imposed by the telephone system (as in Figure 23-1). The method the modem uses — its modulation technique — has to be standardized between the sending and receiving modems so that what's transmitted can be reconstructed at the other end. Modem standards are currently set by the International Telecommunications Union/Telecommunication Standardization Sector (ITU-T, or more commonly ITU), but in the past they have been set by the Consultative Committee for International Telegraph and Telephone (CCITT) and the old Bell System.

The earliest common standard for modems was the implementation in the Bell 103 modem, which supported data rates of 300 bps. The Bell 103 modem type was common while the laws and regulations concerning attaching non-Bell System equipment to the telephone network were changing in the United States. So rather than the direct electrical connection we're familiar with today, the modems used acoustic couplers — "ear muffs" that wrapped around a standard telephone handset to couple the modem tones and shut out surrounding noise.

## The Bell 103 — frequency shift keying

The Bell 103 modem converted bits to sound using a modulation technique called *frequency shift keying* (FSK). Figure 23-2 shows how this worked. Each transmitter (one in the modem that originates the call and one in the modem that answers) needs to transmit either ones or zeros. FSK modulation assigns a frequency to each state, so you need four tones. The figure shows those four tones. The originating modem creates a tone at either 1,070 or 1,270 Hz. The answering modem listens at both frequencies at once, and depending on which it hears, it outputs either a zero or a one. The originating modem chooses the tone to send 300 times per second, using the tone corresponding to the bit it has to send.

The answering modem does the same thing for the bits it has to send, but at different frequencies: It uses 2,025 and 2,225 Hz for zeros and ones.

The separation between the tones used by the originating modem and the receiving modem is what allows a Bell 103 modem to transmit and receive at the same time. Filters in the receiver pass in the band it wants to hear and attenuate in the one it's transmitting on.

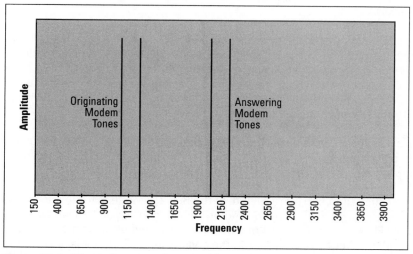

**Figure 23-2:** The Bell 103 modem used frequency shift keying to send three hundred bits per second in both directions over a voice-grade line.

The Bell 103 standard isn't a very efficient modulation in terms of the bit rate it achieves in the available frequency spectrum. It gets a total of 600 bits per second through nearly 4 kHz of bandwidth. The reason it's so inefficient is that the receivers in the modems — the demodulators — need several complete cycles of a tone (at least three) to lock on to a change. The need to lock on to the tone means that the bit rate is one-third of the lowest frequency, which is where the 300 bit per second rate comes from.

## The Bell 212 — phase shift keying

Frequency shift keying isn't the only way to convert bits to sound. All that a modulation technique requires is some detectable difference in the received signal. A far more efficient way to send data is using an idea called *phase shift keying* (PSK). Figure 23-3 shows what phase shift means. The two waveforms in Figure 23-3 have the same frequency and amplitude; they differ only in the time at which they cross the zero axis. That difference is called a *phase difference*. In the figure, the waveforms are 180 degrees out of phase with each other, evenly dividing the full 360 degrees of a circle.

We can send data down a wire by changing (modulating) the phase of a signal, leaving the frequency and amplitude constant. Suppose we assign the bit value zero to the phase represented by the solid line in Figure 23-3, and one to the phase represented by the dotted line. We start sending bits (suppose a one bit is the first one out), sending a tone of a single frequency and phase. When we encounter a zero, we change the timing of the tone so that we flip the phase 180 degrees. The demodulator can detect this timing difference and change the output bit to a zero. We continue with the zero phase until we see a one again, at which time we flip the phase again.

Phase differences amount to rotations around a circle, so it's convenient to draw phase shift modulation with a diagram such as in Figure 23-4, which is called a *constellation*. The constellation shows how the phase circle is divided up by points, which represent the different phases of the constant-frequency tone the modem sends. The specific constellation in Figure 23-4 is for *binary phase shift keying* (BPSK), which simply means that there are two points.

Because a sequence of two successive bits that are the same requires a full circle, you get one bit per cycle of the underlying tone (called the carrier). Each of those transitions in the signal (even if the phase doesn't change) is a *baud*.

You're not limited to one bit per baud. In the Bell 212 modem, for instance, the phase circle gets divided up by four points, which allows you to send two bits per baud (see Figure 23-5). This sort of modulation is called *quadrature phase shift keying* (QPSK) after the four points in the constellation. The labels next to the points indicate the bit pair each phase signals. (Actually, the labels in Figure 23-5 reflect the specific phase relationships for ITU-T Recommendation V.22.) Transitions are possible from any point to any of the four points, so you can send any combination of bits at all. The Bell 212 modem sent data at 600 baud, and because it sent two bits per baud, it achieved a 1,200 bits per second data rate.

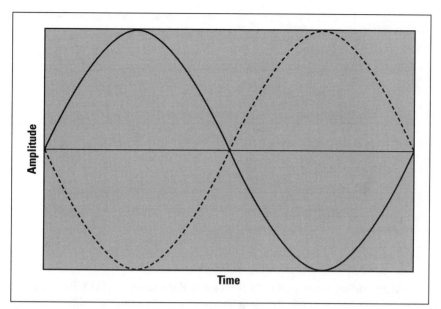

**Figure 23-3:** Signals can differ in timing as well as in frequency and amplitude.

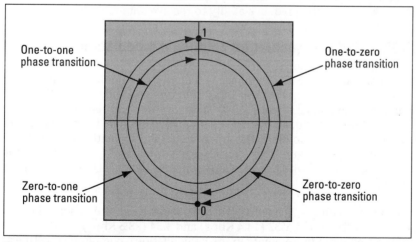

**Figure 23-4:** A phase constellation shows the details of how a phase shift keying modulation scheme is designed.

Keep the distinction between the bit rate and the baud rate clear. The bit rate is the performance your computer sees, in bits per second. The baud rate is the rate at which the signaling changes state on the telephone line.

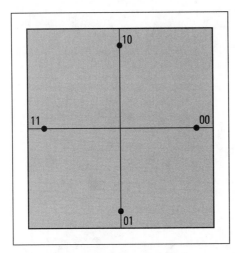

**Figure 23-5:** A QPSK constellation sends two bits for every baud.

You can keep adding more points in the circle. For example, ITU-T Recommendation V.27 uses what's called 8PSK, dividing the phase shift circle into eight sectors and realizing a 4,800 bps data rate in each direction. The increased discrimination needed to resolve more closely spaced points depends on sending higher-frequency information through the telephone line, and after a while the noise and distortion swamp out the modem's ability to receive data reliably.

## V.29, V.32, and V.34 — quadrature amplitude modulation

The next step in modulation is to observe that you don't have to keep the signal amplitude constant; you can vary phase and amplitude simultaneously. Figure 23-6 shows the constellation for 16-QAM (for *quadrature amplitude modulation*). Think of what happens in Figures 23-4 and 23-5 as an arrow from the center to the circle of points as it rotates around, and you'll see that while in those figures the length of the arrow (which corresponds to the amplitude of the signal the modem sends) is constant, it changes in Figure 23-6. This change allows more points to be resolved out of the constellation, which means more bits per baud; 16QAM, for instance, sends four bits per baud.

ITU-T Recommendation V.29 used 16-QAM at a 2,400 baud rate to send data at 9,600 bits per second. The ITU-T V.32 (14.4 Kbps) and V.34 (28.8 Kbps) recommendations use QAM as well (with more points in the constellation), combining it with error correction coding. When used in communications circuits, error correction coding is called *forward error correction* (FEC). FEC sends redundant bits along with your data bits that, when processed at the receiving end, reduce the chances that the demodulator chooses the wrong point in the constellation. The performance gains from forward error correction outweigh the additional bits per second they require to be transmitted, increasing the actual data rate performance you see across the telephone line. (We'll see shortly that your modem adds more error correction than the FEC that is done in the modulator and demodulator to ensure the integrity of your data.)

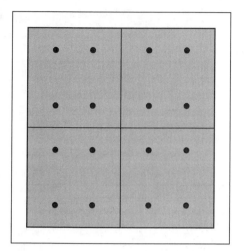

**Figure 23-6:** The 16-QAM constellation combines phase rotations and amplitude changes to send four bits per baud.

## A short summary of modem specifications

There are more than enough different modem specifications to keep anyone confused. Table 23-1 summarizes many of them. At this point, the V.34 specification is dominant, with the future of ISDN in question because of egregious mishandling by the telephone companies. Many of the specifications incorporate slower, fallback operation to handle poor line conditions.

| Table 23-1 Modem Standards | | | |
|---|---|---|---|
| *Specification* | *Operation* | *Circuit* | *Maximum Rate (bps)* |
| Bell 103 | Full duplex | Two-wire switched | 300 |
| V.21 | Full duplex | Two-wire switched | 300 |
| Bell 202 | Half duplex | Two-wire switched Conditioned leased | 1,200 1,800 |
| Bell 201 | Half duplex | Two-wire switched | 2,400 |
| V.26ter | Full duplex | Two-wire switched | 2,400 |
| Bell 212 | Full duplex | Two-wire switched | 1,200 |
| V.22bis | Full duplex | Two-wire switched | 2,400 |
| V.27 | Full duplex Half duplex | Four-wire leased Two-wire switched | 4,800 4,800 |

*continued*

### Table 23-1 *(continued)*

| Site title | Description | | |
|---|---|---|---|
| V.29 (includes Group 3 fax) | Full duplex | Four-wire leased | 9,600 |
| | Half duplex | Two-wire switched | 9,600 |
| V.32bis | Full duplex | Two-wire switched | 14,400 |
| V.FC (nonstandard) | Full duplex | Two-wire switched | 28,800 |
| V.34 | Full duplex | Two-wire switched | 33,600 |
| V.90 | Full duplex | Two-wire switched | 56,000 to subscriber; 33.3 return (subscriber limited to 53,000) |

## V.90

In late September 1996, both Rockwell Semiconductor Systems and U.S. Robotics announced that they had developed technology for 56 Kbps modems that operate on conventional analog telephone lines. The two versions were incompatible, but some time later ITU standard V.90 emerged to standardize operation of 56 Kbps downstream/33.3 Kbps upstream modems. Modems implementing the V.90 standard have almost completely supplanted older models using the V.34 standard.

The 56 Kbps modems are not problem free, largely because some telephone lines and switches can't support the technology. The modem industry estimates that perhaps 80 percent of telephone lines in North America can operate with the new technology. A V.90 modem falls back to V.34 operation when the lines can't support the faster standard, so there's no liability to buying one of the newer units.

In addition to bad telephone lines, the issues with V.90 modems are these:

✦ *One analog hop.* The 56 Kbps modem technology abandons the quadrature amplitude modulation of the V.34 modems, transmitting each eight-bit symbol as a voltage level down the line. The coder-decoder (CODEC) at the telephone switch turns that voltage into digital signals, which go to the modem at the other end. That modem has to be digitally connected to the telephone switch. If it's not, the modems revert to normal 33.6 Kbps analog operation.

✦ *No CODEC conversions.* The CODECs in North America are different than those elsewhere in the world. Because the digital version of the 56 Kbps signal can't survive the translations between different CODECs, you likely won't be able to make international calls at 56 Kbps.

✦ *Asymmetric data rate.* The upstream data rate (the rate out of your computer) is limited to about 33 Kbps. It's the rate *into* your computer that's 56 Kbps. Asymmetric operation works for Web access, but not if you're running a server or trying to upload files to another site.

✦ *Data rate limitation.* In the United States, the Federal Communications Commission has limited the signal power levels 56 Kbps modems can use in order to prevent signal crossover to adjacent lines in wiring bundles. The limited signal power restricts the modems to operation at 53 Kbps or slower.

In our case, the telephone lines where we live simply aren't good enough for V.90 operation—in one series of tests we ran, we were able to connect using V.90 once in weeks of trying. That connection ran at 33.3 Kbps, no faster than a V.34 modem can go. (In all fairness, though, V.34 modems don't connect at 33.6 Kbps where we live, either—a 28.8 Kbps connection is as good as it gets.)

Even if you don't get the full 53 Kbps rate from a V.90 modem, there is a subtle benefit that you'll want if you play games over the Internet, which is that games will be more responsive with modems that have less transmission latency. Table 23-2 shows the performance we measured for several modem technologies.

| Table 23-2 | |
| --- | --- |
| **Modem Latency Comparison** | |
| **Modem Equipment** | **Representative Ping (ms)** |
| V.34 (analog) | 180 |
| V.90 (digital) | 120 |
| ISDN | 30 to 80 |
| ADSL | 12 |

The "Ping" values in Table 23-2 are the time it took for a low-level message to leave our computer, go through the modems, reach the nearest Internet computer to us, and return. The round-trip times are higher inside games. For fast action games, a difference in faster response time can be the difference between winning and losing. Table 23-2 shows that a V.90 modem connected digitally will have response times 60ms faster than an analog connection, and that it will deliver that faster response even if it's running no faster than 33.3 Kbps.

# Serial Ports

The other connection on your modem is the one to your computer. It's called a *serial port* because, although it gets data from the computer eight bits at a time, it transfers bits serially—one bit at a time. The serial port leads to a connector on the back of your computer if you're using an external modem, but it's buried in the circuits on the card if you're using an internal one.

## The RS-232C standard

The serial port on the back of your computer follows the Electronic Industries Association (EIA) specification RS-232C, providing a number of signals:

✦ *Send and receive data.* All the bits that actually go out the connector go on a single wire (plus a ground). There's another one for data from the modem back to the computer.

✦ *Control transmission.* Two wires control when your computer is allowed to send data to the modem: one to say the computer wants to send, and the other to reply that it's okay to do so.

✦ *Control reception.* Two more wires control when the modem can send data to the computer. The idea is the same as transmission control: One wire says the modem wants to transfer, and the other says it's okay to do so.

✦ *Monitor the connection.* One more wire lets the modem tell the computer when it has established a connection with a modem at the other end.

A few more signals are defined in the RS-232C specification, but they're rarely used.

There are two kinds of serial port connectors you'll find on the back of your computer. The one originally defined in the RS-232C standard has 25 pins in two rows. Because only nine of those pins are used (except in very rare circumstances), it's possible to reduce the 25-pin connector to a 9-pin one. IBM did this initially for the PC/AT, and most vendors have followed this design because it saves space. (For instance, you can put a parallel printer port and a 9-pin serial port on one adapter card, but there isn't room for the parallel port connector and a 25-pin serial port in that space.) You can get adapters between the 25-pin and 9-pin connectors in case you need to connect equipment that uses different forms. The 9-pin version has been around for long enough that 25-pin serial ports are relatively rare now on PCs.

## Matching serial data transmission rates

Things get interesting if the bit rate between the computer and the modem is not the same as that between the two modems (and, in fact, it usually isn't). Figure 23-7 shows the differences. The computer-to-modem serial port speed is most often faster than the modem-to-modem transmission rate.

If the rates are in fact different, several possibilities can occur:

✦ *Serial port faster than modem.* If the serial port sends data faster than the modem transmission rate, the data sent by the computer can overrun the modem. If the modem compresses the data before it sends it, and compresses it tightly enough, the computer can continue to send at the higher rate without problems.

Otherwise, the modem has to tell the computer to stop sending temporarily while the modem empties its buffers. This operation is called *flow control* and can be done with hardware (using the control lines in the serial port), or with software (using special characters to tell the computer when to stop and when to resume). It takes coordination with the software doing the transmissions over the modem to make software flow control work, so that actual characters being transmitted are not confused with the flow control characters.

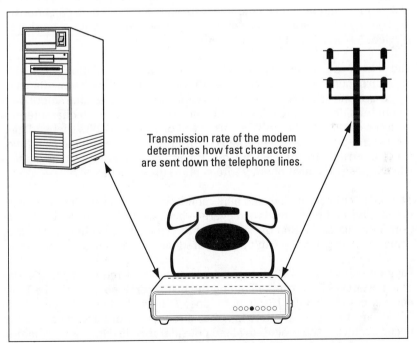

Transmission rate of the modem determines how fast characters are sent down the telephone lines.

**Figure 23-7:** The rate at which your computer communicates with your modem can be different from the rate at which the two modems communicate.

✦ *Serial port same speed as modem.* If no compression is going on in the modems, overruns can't happen if the computer and modem run at the same speed. You sacrifice performance by turning off compression (especially for Internet Web pages, in which the text compresses well).

✦ *Serial port slower than modem.* You can get overruns at the receiving end if the serial port is slower than the modem, because the transmitting computer may have its own serial port set faster. That means characters can arrive from the modem faster than the computer takes them, and because the computer generally can't tell the modem to stop the character stream, you get an overrun.

It's not a problem if the computer doesn't send characters as fast as the modem can take them — all modems have provisions to fill in when there's a gap in the character stream.

## The 16550 chip

The section "Preventing a modem or network from bringing your computer to its knees" in Chapter 4, "Choke Points: Where Your Computer Slows Down," shows that sending and receiving characters through a fast modem can impose a terrible load on the processor because of the relatively large amount of work it takes to service the interrupts the modem creates.

The chip in your computer that's the focus of all this attention is called a Universal Asynchronous Receiver Transmitter, or UART. A UART, which mediates between the processor and the rest of the modem, sends and receives characters on the computer side, and single bits on the modem side. For each character it receives from the computer, the UART sends seven or eight data bits (depending on how it has been set up) plus two or three control bits (see the sidebar that follows). The UART interrupts the processor when it has a character received from the modem or when it needs the next character to send to the modem.

The UART chip originally used in personal computers was identified as 8250. The processing load it creates is so severe — because the computer has to service the port immediately so that overruns or underruns don't occur — that serial ports using the chip generally can't be operated faster than 9,600 bits per second.

Faster modems — 14.4 kilobits per second and up — required faster serial ports. The newer UART chip implementing the faster serial port is called a 16550. (There's another chip called the 16450, but it doesn't have the benefits of the 16550.) The 16550 can stack 16 characters in either direction before overruns or underruns occur. That cuts the processing load considerably, making serial communications far more efficient. You should buy motherboards, serial port cards, or internal modems using the 16550.

## How many characters per second?

Knowing that your modem transmits at 28,800 or 53,000 bits per second isn't very useful; your computer doesn't send single bits. The interesting number is how many characters per second you get, and even though there are eight bits in a character, you can't send the 3,600 or 6,625 characters per second that simple division would suggest. The reason you don't get that rate is that your modem sends more than just your data bits—it sends additional bits to indicate the start and stop of each character. These bits are, predictably, named the start and stop bits. Current personal computer modems all use one start and one stop bit. That means that every character requires sending ten bits, so if your 53,000 bits per second modem (that's the most you get from a 56K modem) keeps the telephone line completely full, you'll send 5,300 characters per second.

Even if your modem works perfectly, you still may not transfer data at the full rate. The computers at both ends of the connection have to send and receive fast enough as well—because the modems fill in unused time on the communications line, it's possible for computers to send data as slowly as 100 characters per second (or less) through modems that are actually communicating at 2,880 characters per second.

Mice using a serial interface don't do well connected through the buffers on a 16550 UART. You can generally turn off the buffers in the BIOS on a motherboard providing a 16550 serial port. If your mouse won't work, or if it works erratically, check if the buffers are turned on for the port the mouse is hooked to. (These buffers are commonly called FIFOs, for First In First Out—which is the policy the buffer uses to hold and release characters.)

# Murphy Was a Modem Designer

The noise on telephone lines and the multiple ways your computer and software can mishandle communications make data transmission highly error-prone. The forward error correction used in the newer modems helps, but it's really there as part of the design to put higher rates down the wire. The modems themselves can and do make errors receiving data, especially on poor telephone lines. Modem designers added error correction to their products to give you the reliability you need without having to worry about setting up complex software.

The data rates your modem gives you are rarely as high as you would like them to be. When modems ran at 300 bits (thirty characters) per second, you sat waiting for text to arrive because a full page of text is thousands of characters. When modems ran at thousands of bits per second (hundreds of characters), you sat waiting because the programs you wanted to download were tens and hundreds of thousands of characters. Now that modems run at tens of thousands of bits per second (thousands of characters), you sit waiting because the graphics you want are tens of thousands of characters, the sound clips you want are hundreds of thousands of characters, and the video clips are millions of characters. The volume of data you want through your telephone line continues to go up to fill the capacity of the modem. Modem designers added data compression to their products to give you greater throughput than the data transmission technology can support by itself.

## Error correction

When the noise on the telephone line becomes too large compared to the signal, the demodulator starts to make mistakes. In a modem using QAM, noise moves the signals off the center of the points in the constellation. If the signal moves far enough — when the noise level is too high — it becomes closer to some point besides the correct one, resulting in a demodulation error. If too many demodulation errors occur, the forward error correction codes can't recover, and the errors make it into the data stream.

As Figure 23-8 shows, however, there's more to a modem than the modulator and demodulator. Error correction operating above the modulator/demodulator level detects garbled characters, allowing the receiver to notify the transmitter that retransmission is needed. Compression (the next section) slims down the data stream using lossless techniques, allowing faithful reconstruction at the other end.

Data-level error correction for modems is most commonly specified by ITU-T Recommendation V.42. (Compression is ITU-T Recommendation V.42*bis*; which isn't the same thing.) Some modems support a standard called Microcom Network Protocol (MNP) created by Microcom; ITU-T V.42 includes one of the MNP methods, so a V.42 modem should be able to create an error-correcting connection to an MNP modem.

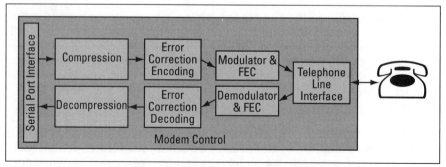

**Figure 23-8:** Error correction coding and compression increase the reliability and throughput of your modem.

Unlike forward error correction, which transmits enough redundant information to permit reconstruction of a limited number of errors in the data stream, data-level error correction focuses on detection of errors followed by retransmission of the bad data. To do this, your modem divides the data stream arbitrarily into blocks of characters. Each block is prefixed by a start-of-block indicator and followed by an error detection word. The transmitting modem computes the error detection word from the data in the block, using an equation that guarantees that the probability of an undetected error is very small. The receiving modem repeats the computation of the error detection word using the received data, so if the two error detection words differ, the modem knows there's been a problem. If so, it tells the transmitter to resend the block.

There's overhead in data-level error correction because of the extra information that's transmitted—notably the start of block indicator and the error detection word. The number of overhead bytes sent is roughly constant for varying data block sizes, so if the data blocks are large, the overhead is relatively small. If the data block size is small, the overhead is large. It's not an obvious decision to use large data blocks, however, because when a retransmission is required, the entire block has to be sent. Larger blocks suffer from a greater retransmission overhead in exchange for their smaller initial overhead.

Bulletin board systems (BBSs, which are becoming less common as the Internet expands) use protocols in your communications software to ensure reliable transmission of files between their computer and yours. If there are error correcting modems at both ends—such as ones using V.42—the modems handle the issue, and you don't want to use an error correcting protocol in software. Using a simpler protocol increases your effective transmission rate because the characters the protocol would use for error detection and correction can instead be used for data. Moreover, you're better with a large block size in the software protocol, because it reduces the overhead. The modem's error correction operates with a block size independent of your communications software, so there's no downside to using a large block size in the communications software.

## Data compression

Besides error correction, the other added function in Figure 23-8 is data compression. Most modems use the compression methods specified in ITU-T Recommendation V.42bis, which provides lossless compression (see Chapter 16, "Tape") on the data stream going through the modem. Compression in the modem applies to everything you send—files, Web pages, electronic mail, or images. The sending modem compresses the outgoing data before transmission, and the receiving modem decompresses it back to its original form before sending it to your computer through the serial port. Compression and decompression are "outside" error correction (before coding on transmit and after correction on receive) so that they operate only on clean, uncorrupted data.

As with all other compression, the degree of compression you get through your modem depends on what it is you're compressing. Text files and otherwise uncompressed graphics will compress well, whereas files that are already compressed (such as with WinZip, found at `http://www.winzip.com/ddchome.htm`) will not compress noticeably. You can see the effects of compression in programs that report the effective transmission rate (such as WS_FTP32) — with a high-performance server, you'll see a higher reported transmission rate for text files than for ZIP files.

You want to set a higher serial port rate between the processor and modem than the speed over the telephone line. This lets you feed the compressor on the modem to keep the line full, and it lets you extract incoming data from the modem without overruns.

It's not sufficient to simply have a compressing, error correcting modem — you have to enable those features in software. The modem control panel applet in Windows lets you do this if Windows has the setup strings for your modem. Windows 95 gets those for most modems through the autodetection process; you may have to set up the strings for Windows NT.

# Extending the Modem

Because communication is so valuable in your computer, it's no surprise that facsimile transmission (fax) and other extensions to pure data transmission have migrated to your computer and its modem.

## Fax

A stand-alone fax machine is really a very complex device (see Figure 23-9). It includes a scanner, a compressing modem, and a printer. The scanner converts the image into a bitmap (an array of pixels, just like we looked at in Chapter 17, "Video"). The compressor uses a fax-specific algorithm (called Group 3 compression) to reduce the size of the data to be transmitted. The modem sends and receives the data stream. The decompressor reconstructs the bitmap from the compressed data stream, and the printer gives you the hard copy fax.

Most of the operations that a stand-alone fax machine performs can be duplicated by your computer. Working from the right side of Figure 23-9, your modem does the necessary data communications and (with a little tweaking by the modem designers) does Group 3 fax compression as well as the usual V.42bis. Your printer handles the problem of creating hard copy. The only issue would seem to be the scanner, which isn't as common as the rest of the components.

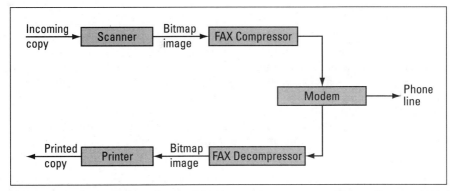

**Figure 23-9:** A stand-alone fax machine is a scanner, compressing modem, and printer.

However, a scanner may not always be needed. The scanner's job is to create the image you want to send. In a stand-alone scanner, that image comes from a paper copy of the fax. In your computer, the material you want to send is usually in the computer already, so printing it so you can scan it makes no sense. Instead, fax software sets itself up to look like a printer. Instead of creating paper, it sends the resulting image to the modem.

Computer fax modems fall into two classes, called (of course) Class 1 and Class 2. Both are specified by the Electronics Industries Association (EIA). (Strictly speaking, the two fax classes are Class 1 and Class 2.0. Class 2 is an older, nonstandard specification compared to Class 2.0.) Class 1 was the initial version and places most of the load to handle the fax process on your computer. Class 2 defines additional modem commands and transfers much of the work into the modem. It's not obvious, though, that you want a Class 2 modem. Recent software, including the Windows Messaging component in Windows 95, can send data to another computer through a fax connection using a Class 1 modem. If that's important to you, go for the Class 1 products. Otherwise, there are some minor advantages to Class 2, but probably not enough to sway your choice of products. (The U.S. Robotics Sportster Voice 33.6 FAXModem discussed later in this chapter can do either Class 1 or Class 2.)

**Tip** Another fax-related modem interface, Communications Application Specification (CAS), was developed by Intel and Digital Communications Associates (DCA). The interface was intended to further offload the fax work from the processor. The standard was never widely adopted, however, and is not well supported under Windows. Avoid it.

## Voice modems

There's yet more value in combining computers and modems (which is what CTI— Computer Telephony Integration—is all about). If you think about what an answering machine does, and if you extend that thinking to what voice mail and voice response systems do, you'll quickly realize that the missing element is— essentially—a wave audio sound card in your modem. Figure 23-10 shows the idea. The digital-to-analog and analog-to-digital converters needed for wave audio sound (see Chapter 21, "Sound Cards, Speakers, and Microphones") handle digital data at the serial interface and sound at the telephone line interface.

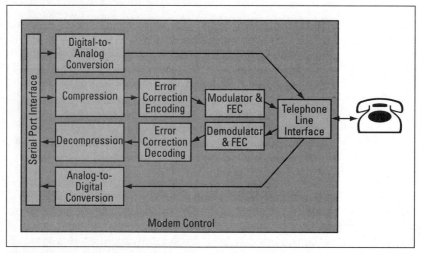

**Figure 23-10:** Adding wave audio to a modem lets it record messages and play prerecorded greetings.

You can do a lot with a voice modem that's not possible with a conventional fax modem. For example, you can set it up to answer the phone and take messages (like an answering machine). You can add a voice menu for callers that lets them select which mailbox they want access to. You can use the voice menu to let callers select documents for fax-back service. You can also tie the modem to your pager so that you're signaled when a fax or voice message is waiting for you.

## Simultaneous voice and data

The limitation of a voice modem is that you have to pick what you want to do— either voice or data, but not both at the same time. Sometimes that's not what you really want; you want to talk to someone at the same time your computer exchanges data with theirs. For example:

✦ *Collaboration and training.* With the right software, you can work on a project with someone else at the other end of your modem, talking with that person while you both work over a document, spreadsheet, or drawing.

✦ *Training and help.* Combined voice and data let a trainer show the student the moves while explaining what's going on, while watching what the student does to look for problems. Computer help desks can use the data capability to look for problems and download patches and fixes.

✦ *Multiuser games.* There's no comparison between multiuser games when you can hear your partner/opponent and ones when you cannot. The screams, taunts, and shouts between players in the same room on a local area network make deathmatch Quake literally playable for hours and hours on end. A modem link that transports a voice circuit along with the game data extends the reach of that environment to remote players.

✦ *Interactive shopping.* You can expect an entirely new technology from direct telephone sales companies based on simultaneous voice and data modems. While you talk to a representative, you can be seeing pictures and video of the items you're investigating and ordering, allowing the representative to point out features and make sure you get what you're looking for.

The modem technology that could have made these applications possible is Digital Simultaneous Voice and Data (DSVD). A DSVD modem is almost the reverse of the voice modem in Figure 23-11 — it compresses analog voice signals into relatively low rate data that it pipes down the telephone line along with the computer's data stream. DSVD modems compress voice into as little as ten kilobits per second using lossy compression techniques (Chapter 18, "Video Adapters"), leaving as much as 19.2 Kbps for data. We've used voice equipment that provided recognizable voice transmission in as few as 1.2 Kbps, so there's still room for improvement in the data-to-voice ratio.

The disadvantage of DSVD technology is that it requires a direct connection between modems, not a network. You have to call your partner, not connect over the Internet. That requirement proved fatal for DSVD technology — with the tremendous rise in use of the Internet, virtually no one uses DSVD modems.

Voice compression technology also goes into Internet telephone software, but instead of sharing the overall data transmission path at a low level in the modem, Internet telephones open a high-level network connection and share the data capacity at that level. Because of this, an Internet phone doesn't require a long-distance connection between the two parties that is likely with a DSVD modem, but it has all the same capabilities.

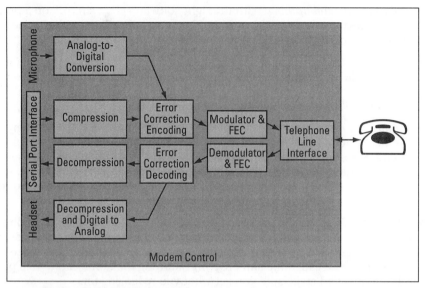

**Figure 23-11:** Digital compression of analog voice lets both voice and data be transmitted over the same circuit.

# Cellular Telephones and Modems

Wherever you find telephones, you're going to find modems. That includes cellular telephones, but the differences between cellular telephones and conventional telephones change what you can do. Alternative modems that adapt to the characteristics of the cellular network are going to perform better than regular modems when using cellular equipment.

## What makes cellular telephones different?

The first thing is to understand that cellular telephones (analog or digital) are very different from conventional ones. Simplistically, they're not telephones — they're radios masquerading as telephones. Figure 23-12 shows what a cellular network is. The basic unit of the network is the cell, which is the region around a base station. Nearly all the calls within a cell are handled by its base station, whose job is to connect the call into the public-switched telephone network and to control the cellular telephone.

In the widely deployed AMPS (Advanced Mobile Phone System) cellular network — an analog system — the network itself is a packed region of cells. Transmitters in adjacent cells use different frequencies (channels) to avoid interfering with each other. As cellular telephones move from one cell to another, they are handed off from one base station to the next, enabling you to move around the area. The capability of a cell to support conversations from more than one telephone at a time happens because the base station controls the operation of the telephone, commanding the channel and power level the telephone will use.

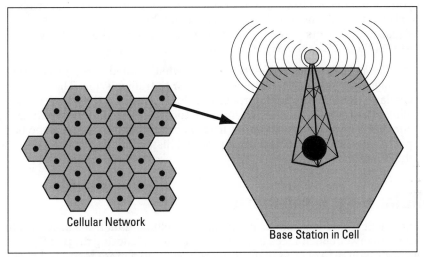

**Figure 23-12:** A cellular telephone network is a collection of cells, each with a base station at its center.

If you've used a cellular telephone, you know that this doesn't always work well; you may have experienced noise, cross-connected calls, dropped calls, and calls in which voice dropped out in one direction. This isn't too terrible for voice calls, because people are remarkably adaptable. Modems and data networks are nowhere near as forgiving, however; the best you can expect from these problems is a reduced data rate. It's far more likely that you'll simply lose your connection.

In practice, some characteristics of the cellular telephone system that you barely notice compound the problems cellular modems face:

✦ *Blank and Burst.* Signaling from the base station to the modem is required to let the base station direct the modem to switch to another base station, to change channels, and to change its output power. The base station mutes the audio transmission for a short interval (blanking) to send the control information (burst). During that interval, the modem receives no signal from the telephone.

✦ *Compression.* Cellular networks compress the voice signal to pack more capacity into a limited set of resources. Some compression methods used in cellular systems limit the response of the connection, which in turn limits the speed at which the modem can run.

✦ *Network maintenance.* The cellular network engineers and technicians have to periodically tweak the system to ensure that signal levels are consistent as you get handed off from one base station to another. If the signal levels are not balanced, the changes affect the agreements the modems have made to equalize the effects of the connection, which requires that both modems retrain themselves to adapt to the new level.

✦ *Pre-emphasis.* Cellular connections apply what's called *pre-emphasis* to boost the high-frequency parts of the signal prior to transmission. The effect is similar to what Dolby audio processing does, and is for the same reason — it allows the receiver to filter out much of the noise you'd otherwise hear in the channel. The audio signal output from a conventional modem can be boosted past allowable thresholds by this process, distorting the signal received at the other end.

## Cellular data transmission

The end result of all these effects is that analog cellular data transmission is hard, and under many circumstances it may not be reliable. Ignoring dropped connections, you're likely to see much more noise and a more restricted channel over a cellular connection. That means that a conventional modem would see a much higher bit error rate, requiring the error correction protocol to do more retransmissions. In a high error rate environment, large error correction blocks are a disadvantage because every error requires a large amount of data be resent. For this reason, the V.42 error correction protocol isn't well suited to cellular connections. Instead, an error correction protocol designed for the cellular environment called MNP-10EC has been developed by Microcom. MNP-10EC not only reduces the error correction block size, but it allows the size to be changed dynamically to adapt to the conditions experienced over the connection. MNP-10EC has the disadvantage that it requires the modems on both ends of the connection to support the protocol, so you can't be assured that buying an MNP-10EC modem will improve the performance you get. You need to check with the provider of the modem you're calling. Another cellular protocol is Enhanced Throughput Cellular (ETC) from AT&T.

A third option used by some cellular modem suppliers is TX-CEL, developed by Celeritas. It improves cellular data throughput from a different perspective: It changes the characteristics of the waveform output by the modem to compensate for many of the characteristics of the cellular connection. Because it operates at the modulation level, TX-CEL can improve performance even when implemented at only one end of the connection. Your equipment can combine MNP-10EC (or ETC) and TX-CEL for protocol-level error correction as well as improvement in the transmission characteristics.

Overall, you can expect connections from 2.4 to 14.4 Kbps, depending on your equipment and the quality of the signal where you are. Some cellular providers have set up data-specific circuits you access by prefixing the call with *DATA — check with your carrier. You're likely to pay for airtime based strictly on the number of minutes you're connected.

One of the key things you want to be sure to do is to get a modem specifically adapted to your cellular telephone. Not all cellular telephones are equally well supported by cellular modems. The range of prices for the cable or adapter to connect a cellular modem is very wide. I've seen adapters costing $400 and more. If you want cellular data capability, look into compatibility and prices of both the telephone and modem before you buy either.

## Cellular digital packet data

The shortcomings of data transmission over analog cellular circuits have led to the development of an improved technology called *Cellular Digital Packet Data* (CDPD). CDPD is an overlay on the analog cellular network — an additional set of equipment that uses the analog facilities in a different way. CDPD uses inactive voice channels, passing small chunks of data at rates up to 19.2 Kbps. Each chunk is encrypted and coded for error correction, addressing two of the most significant problems with conventional analog cellular connections.

As yet, there are implementation issues facing CDPD. The overlay equipment is available in major cities, but not widely elsewhere. The equipment has to be installed at each cell site, not just in a city, so the costs and construction effort is considerable. Worse, agreements are not generally in place to allow the equivalent of roaming in other cellular systems, so you aren't assured that you can use the service outside your home area.

## Digital cellular

Cellular telephone networks have evolved in the last few years, changing over to use digital transmission. If you can set up your computer to connect through your digital cell phone, you'll avoid most of the problems inherent in the analog cellular system, and you should get faster data rates.

# High-Rate Telephone Connections

The explosive growth of the Internet has created a demand for faster Internet connections. Three technologies are competing to deliver broadband access: ISDN, ADSL, and cable modems. We'll cover the first two here, and cable modems in Chapter 27, "Network Cabling and Interfaces."

## ISDN

Most of the problems with sending data over telephone lines stem from the need to look like a telephone — to live within the restricted frequency range telephone switches accept. The alternative is to remain digital in the first place — to not try to look like a telephone. This is the idea behind the Integrated Services Digital Network, or ISDN, and its successors.

ISDN comes in two flavors — the Basic Rate Interface (BRI) and the Primary Rate Interface (PRI). A BRI circuit runs at 144,000 bits per second. A PRI circuit runs at 1.544 or 2.048 million bits per second. We'll only look at BRI in this chapter; PRI is relevant to high-rate network interconnections, such as you'd use to connect a large network or Internet service provider to the Internet. In the meantime, we'll use the terms ISDN and BRI interchangeably. An ISDN circuit is required to transmit at those rates for lines up to 18,000 feet (3.4 miles, or 5.5 kilometers) from the telephone company's switch.

One ISDN line contains three data channels. Two of them are called B (for Bearer) channels. The other is called the D (for Delta) channel. B channels run at 64,000 bits per second. The D channel runs at 16,000 bits per second. Adding the three together results in the 144,000 bits per second total. The 64,000 bits per second number comes from the fact that each B channel is capable of carrying a single telephone call — voice data sampled 8,000 times per second (for a 4,000 cycle per second frequency response) using eight-bit samples results in a 64,000 bits per second data rate.

The D channel carries signaling information, such as the number you dialed. Collectively one ISDN line can therefore carry two independent voice calls. Of course, if all you wanted was voice, you wouldn't bother with the higher cost and complexity of ISDN. The payoff from ISDN is that you can get at the digital transmission capacity directly. Under most circumstances, the full capacity of the two B channels is available to you for sending data. Rather than being limited to 28.8 kilobits per second, you get 64,000 or 128,000 bits per second, because the overhead of having to send your data as audio tones is gone.

Using the higher 128,000 bits per second rate for data transmission requires that your equipment support *bonding*, which is a technology to combine the two B channels into a single transport. Some telephone switches have to reserve some of the B channel capacity for signaling, reducing their capacity to 56,000 bits per second each. If your telephone company can offer 64K Clear Channel Capability, that means that the switch handles signaling over the D channel and the entire B channel capacity is available for data.

Sadly, bringing up ISDN service isn't as straightforward as getting a conventional telephone line.

✦ *Availability.* Even though it's existed for many years, ISDN simply isn't available everywhere, and it can be hard to get even in areas where it *is* available. It's as if the telephone companies don't really want to sell it to you. For example, U S WEST has a convenient Web page at `http://www.uswest.com/com/customers/interprise/isdn/isdn_slavailability.html` through which you can conveniently find out that ISDN isn't available where you live.

Even if the telephone switch that delivers your service provides ISDN, you either have to be within 18,000 feet of the office or have to meet requirements for loop extension.

✦ *Compatibility and interoperability.* One of the sleazy little secrets of the American telephone companies is that for quite some time ISDN service was not interoperable among all telephone switches. If you wanted to call an Internet service provider that was served from a different switch than yours, for example, you weren't guaranteed that the call would work. It depended on what the switches were and what software they were running. Fortunately, the telephone companies and equipment manufacturers have created what's called National ISDN, which solves this problem. If you have to make a choice of what kind of ISDN to take, choose National ISDN if possible.

Even with National ISDN, you should verify with the telephone company that you can call the destinations you have in mind.

✦ *Service Profile ID and service configuration.* In addition to a dial number (of which an ISDN line will often have two, roughly equivalent to "telephone numbers"), an ISDN line will usually have a *Service Profile ID* (SPID). The form of the SPID you get depends on what company (often AT&T or Northern Telecom) made the switch you're connected to. Getting your ISDN service configured to support the devices you'll be connecting is not simple. Some vendors (such as Ascend) make the necessary information available for you to give to your telephone company.

Your other problem with ISDN is that you need someone to call. Both ends of the connection have to be running ISDN. You can place a conventional analog call over ISDN, but you don't get any better performance than with a conventional analog line. Unless your Internet service provider or private data network has a dial-up ISDN capability, ISDN won't do you any good. Most medium to large ISPs now support ISDN dial-up lines, because better, more manageable equipment at their end happens to provide ISDN service automatically.

Installing ISDN equipment is more involved than plugging in a wire. There are two kinds of interfaces and two kinds of equipment (see Figure 23-13). The equipment you need depends on what you get from your telephone company.

✦ *Network Termination 1 (NT1).* This unit recovers the signal from the incoming wire and turns it into a signal more readily used at your premises. It's also responsible for taking your data and placing it out on the wire. The premises side of the NT1 is called an S/T interface.

✦ *Terminal Equipment 1 (TE1).* This is the equipment that converts the S/T interface into something your computers can use, such as a port onto your local area network. (A Terminal Equipment 2 device converts the S/T interface signal into an interface suitable for analog telephones and fax machines.)

✦ *Terminal Adapter.* This is an ISDN interface that supports other kinds of equipment besides a local area network. Less expensive ISDN interfaces to your computer connect via a serial port or other interface, rather than an Ethernet, but may not be able to deliver the full ISDN 128,000 bits per second data rate.

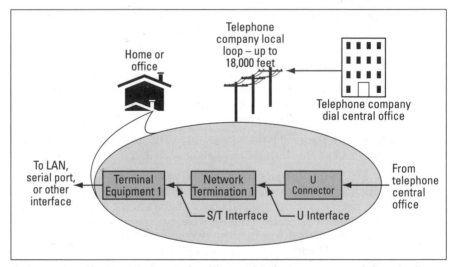

**Figure 23-13:** The U connector is the demarcation between you and the telephone company. You must provide the network termination and terminal equipment, but you may be able to buy or rent it from the telephone company.

Most ISDN equipment combines the NT1 and TE1 functions into a single product, accepting a U interface from the telephone company. Others require separate devices for NT1 and TE1. You can connect several TE1 devices into a single NT1, so you'll want to decide if you need multiple terminals in your ISDN setup when you decide whether or not to go with a combined product. Your safest alternative is to ask your service provider what ISDN equipment they have confirmed compatibility with. There are enough options and variations on ISDN that not all equipment talks to each other; it's not as simple as plugging in an analog modem.

In its most basic application, ISDN amounts to a faster modem. It gets bits from your computer to somewhere else faster. Most of the places you'll call through ISDN are network access points, though, and you're using ISDN as a wide-area extension of your local network capability.

We'll discuss networks further in Chapters 27, 28, and 30 ("Network Cabling and Interfaces"), Chapter 28 ("Peripheral Network Equipment"), and Chapter 30 ("Accessing and Serving the Internet").

## ADSL

ISDN isn't the only way to send digital data down a copper telephone line. Technology to directly send digital data on telephone lines is more generically called Digital Subscriber Line (DSL), with the variants often called xDSL. In addition to ISDN sometimes being called IDSL, Table 23-3 shows some of what you might find:

| Table 23-3 Common xDSL Technologies | |
|---|---|
| **Technology** | **Characteristics** |
| ADSL (Asymmetric Digital Subscriber Line | 1.5 Mbps to 9 Mbps to the subscriber; from 16 Kbps to 640 Kbps return. A recent variant is DSL Lite or G.Lite, which is slower but easier to install. G.Lite runs at 1.544 Mbps to 6 Mpbs to the subscriber and 128 Kbps to 384 Kbps return. |
| HDSL (High data rate Digital Subscriber Line) | Symmetric operation at T1 or E1 speeds. Typically requires two or three subscriber lines. |
| RADSL (Rate Adaptive Digital Subscriber Line) | Data rates of 128 Kbps to 7.168 Mbps to the subscriber, and 30 Kbps to 1.088 Mbps return. |
| SDSL (Single Line Digital Subscriber Line) | Symmetric T1 or E1 operating over a single telephone line. |
| VADSL (Very high speed ADSL) | Subset of VDSL. |
| VDSL (Very high data rate Digital Subscriber Line) | 12.9 to 52.8 Mbps over wire lengths from 4,500 feet to 1,000 feet, respectively. |

The industry is still shaking out the standards and the economics. Don't assume you can simply go buy equipment and hook it up without careful coordination with your telephone company and service provider.

ADSL works by forcing very high frequencies down the telephone line, frequencies well above what you can hear. The high frequency two-way data transmission shares the telephone wires with your regular telephone service, letting you make telephone calls and send data at the same time. Conventional ADSL technology requires that a device called a splitter be installed where the telephone line enters the building so that the ADSL signals can be separated from the telephone voice signal. If you look at the ADSL entry in Table 23-3, though, you'll see mention of another technology—G.Lite—that modifies ADSL to eliminate the need for a splitter. No splitter means no service call to the home or office, so installation costs are less. G.lite is slower than ADSL, but for many people the loss in speed won't be noticeable compared to the gain in speed when you replace a slow modem.

ADSL has another interesting characteristic—computers on an ADSL line are always connected to the Internet. Being always connected means other computers on the Internet can see your computer, even if you're not actively doing anything. You need to be aware of computer security if you're going to use ADSL, the always-on version of ISDN, or a cable modem. One of the key security problems if you're running Windows is file sharing; if you're running Windows 95 or Windows 98, you have to make sure that the Internet protocols (TCP/IP) aren't tied into file sharing.

We'll cover how to break the connection between TCP/IP and file sharing in Chapter 27 ("Network Cabling and Interfaces") when we look at how to install and configure a network adapter card.

# Choosing a Modem

We should probably admit to some bias here—we don't understand why anyone would have a computer that wasn't in some way connected to a network (and preferably to the Internet). There are bound to be other people in the world who share work or personal interests you have, and a network connection is one of the easiest ways to find them. You need not be a computer fanatic to get your computer connected, and it need not be computers themselves you're interested in. We think everyone needs a modem.

The minimum modem you should install is a V.90 one capable of operation up to 56 Kbps. Modems meeting the 56 Kbps V.90 standard also work for connections using the V.34 standard at rates up to 33.6 Kbps. You're likely to get fax capabilities in a V.90 modem, too. A V.90-compatible modem will connect with all the major online services and Internet service providers. It's more likely you'll find a service with modems that don't support 56 Kbps on their end than one that a V.90 modem can't connect to.

# Choosing an internal or external modem

There's not a lot of basis on which to choose between internal and external modems for desktop computers. (We'll look at PC Card modems for laptops in Chapter 31, "Making Choices That Fit the Road Warrior.") Here are the factors that should influence your choice of an internal versus external modem:

✦ *Internal bus slots.* An internal modem requires an ISA bus slot, whereas an external modem connects to a serial or USB port. If you get a USB modem, or if the serial port for your external modem is provided directly off your motherboard (as is often the case), the external modem won't consume a bus slot. There's no difference in the I/O port or interrupt usage, though — unless you use USB — you have a serial port on a conventional modem whether you use an internal or external unit.

✦ *UART.* As we saw earlier in the chapter, an 8250 UART serial port will not support a fast modem well. Upgrades are inexpensive if your 8250 chips are in sockets; otherwise forget it. If you can upgrade, an external modem will work fine. If not, consider disabling the old serial port and using an internal modem that supplies the 16550 you need. (Fortunately, most computers now in use are new enough to use 16550 chips for the serial ports.)

✦ *Status lights.* Some people find the status lights on the front of an external modem very useful. Among other things, they show you when data is being sent or received. Windows 9*x* displays an icon in the taskbar to show data transfer, but it doesn't have the immediacy or information content of lights on an external modem.

✦ *Speakerphone.* You really need an external unit if you plan on using your modem as a speakerphone. Internal units can provide headset connections, but a real hands-off speakerphone means that the microphone and speaker are reasonably near you.

✦ *Cost.* Because an external modem has to include a case, power supply, connectors, and lights, it has components an internal modem need not have. That means it costs more.

# Choosing a conventional or DSVD modem

If you can afford to dedicate a computer to voice mail (such as one that's been replaced by a newer computer), a voice modem can let you implement voice mail and fax-back relatively inexpensively, as can the Microsoft Phone, which incorporates parts of a voice modem and includes voice mail handling software. You're better off dedicating a computer for voice mail and fax processing (versus hosting it on the computer you use), because your customers expect telephone systems to always work, but computers you're actively using are going to crash now and then. (Yes, we'd like to think computers are stable and reliable. In practice, they're not. Doing "normal" things, we generally have to reboot Windows 98 computers a few times a week and Windows NT computers once every several weeks. Doing more adventurous things, such as running prerelease (beta) versions of software or installing new hardware, we can end up rebooting several times an hour or more.)

DSVD promised to do more than voice modems, but unless DSVD capabilities come for free in the modem you want, ask yourself what you'll do with the technology. Unlike a voice modem, DSVD modems require both ends of the connection to support DSVD before the additional features come into play. Few companies offer DSVD-enabled telephone support, and without that support there's not much you can use for a DSVD modem. If you're making decisions for a company, consider that few users have DSVD modems, so it's unlikely to benefit many users if you migrate your company's product support infrastructure to a DSVD-based approach.

## Choosing a V.90, ISDN, or ADSL modem

If your home or small office uses a remote network a lot, and if you can get service from your telephone company, you may want to consider ISDN or ADSL. You'll pay more for the faster data rate, so investigate the costs carefully including equipment, installation, telephone company service costs, and your network provider's costs. Depending on where you live and what equipment you use, you can expect to spend from $400 to several thousand dollars just to get your first data transmission, and you may spend a significant amount on monthly fees.

It's still not clear what and who the winners in the high-speed network access sweepstakes will be. The limited availability, high costs, and complexity of making ISDN or ADSL work have kept the issue a race rather than a runaway. Cable modems (Chapter 27, "Network Cabling and Interfaces") can be ten times faster than ISDN (on a par with ADSL), but the cable companies have been so slow in rolling out service that it's likely to be 2001 or later before most people can get access.

**Tip**    Because of these problems, you need to evaluate any communications technology on the basis of what it will do for you now and whether its cost can be supported based on those capabilities. Whether you're considering a 56 Kbps modem, ISDN, ADSL, or some other technology, evaluate it in terms of the data rates you can get, where you can connect to, and how the combined setup meets your communications requirements. Don't get caught in the trap of waiting for tomorrow's communication technology.

The fact that you connect to the Internet or a private network means you need a modem, but not necessarily that you need anything fancier than a 56 Kbps unit. You have to evaluate what you do with the network and whether the other end of your connection can support anything faster. If you're simply transmitting and receiving electronic mail, or casually browsing the Web on the Internet, 56 Kbps may be all you need. If you're shipping large files back and forth, such as to and from a remote file system, you will want to consider faster access.

## Evaluating your modem against the network

Another factor to consider is whether or not your communications link is the choke point. In many cases, the limitation is the network or server and not your computer or your communications link. For example:

✦ *Server overload.* When a new version of Quake or Internet Explorer is put on the Internet, it creates an immediate, enormous demand on the server that stores the files and ships them out onto the network. If the server can't keep up with the demand, or if the communications link into the server can't keep up, there's nothing you can do at your end to make things better.

✦ *Network overload.* Even if the specific server you're working with has the performance and communications link necessary to give you what you want at a high rate, the network connections between you and that server may be overloaded to the point where you still see poor performance. For example, I've played multiplayer Quake over the Internet at times when the response was as good as on a local machine, and at times when the remote players couldn't move responsively at all. The computers and communications links at both ends were the same; all that changed was the performance of the intermediate network connections.

Even if the servers and network you're tied into can support you well, you can then decide if the improved performance is worth the cost. Table 23-4 shows how different connection speeds determine how long operations take for different kinds of data. Generally, things you do regularly that take more than a minute or so can present a problem. The table shows that large sound and video files exceed that threshold, as do large software files. If you're transferring large video or software files regularly, you'll probably want to consider faster communications links.

### Table 23-4
### Transmission Times for Various Connection Speeds

| Application | Relative Size | KB | Transmission Time at Data Rate (Seconds) | | | | | | | |
|---|---|---|---|---|---|---|---|---|---|---|
| | | | **33.6** | **53.0** | **64** | **128** | **256** | **512** | **1,024** | **2,048** |
| Text and | Small | 2 | 0.6 | 0.4 | 0.3 | 0.2 | 0.1 | 0.0 | 0.0 | 0.0 |
| e-mail | Large | 100 | 30.5 | 19.3 | 16.0 | 8.0 | 4.0 | 2.0 | 1.0 | 0.5 |
| Graphics | Small | 10 | 3.0 | 1.9 | 1.6 | 0.8 | 0.4 | 0.2 | 0.1 | 0.1 |
| | Large | 200 | 61.0 | 38.6 | 32.0 | 16.0 | 8.0 | 4.0 | 2.0 | 1.0 |

*continued*

| | | | Transmission Time at Data Rate (Seconds) | | | | | | | |
| Application | Relative Size | KB | 33.6 | 53.0 | 64 | 128 | 256 | 512 | 1,024 | 2,048 |
|---|---|---|---|---|---|---|---|---|---|---|
| Sound | Small | 10 | 3.0 | 1.9 | 1.6 | 0.8 | 0.4 | 0.2 | 0.1 | 0.1 |
| | Large | 500 | 152.4 | 96.6 | 80.0 | 40.0 | 20.0 | 10.0 | 5.0 | 2.5 |
| Video | Small | 10 | 3.0 | 1.9 | 1.6 | 0.8 | 0.4 | 0.2 | 0.1 | 0.1 |
| | Large | 10,000 | 3,047.6 | 1,932.1 | 1,600.0 | 800.0 | 400.0 | 200.0 | 100.0 | 50.0 |
| Software & data files | Small | 20 | 6.1 | 3.9 | 3.2 | 1.6 | 0.8 | 0.4 | 0.2 | 0.1 |
| | Large | 20,000 | 6,095.2 | 3,864.2 | 3,200.0 | ,600.0 | 800.0 | 400.0 | 200.0 | 100.0 |

Table 23-4 *(continued)*

High-speed equipment costs are dependent on how big an operation you're supporting. Equipment like the U.S. Robotics Courier I-modem looks like a modem to your computer but runs at ISDN rates. If you need to connect more than one computer with the I-modem, you have to route through your computer (via Windows NT or—under Windows 9*x*—with the WinGate software found at http://www.wingate.net). If you want your local area network itself to be connected over the modem, you need a more expensive device.

# Products

Regardless of the media—conventional telephone line, cellular telephone, or high-speed line—there's a device involved in connecting your computer across a wide-area connection. There are often many details involved in setting up communications and networks properly, so you should give some thought to the manufacturer's support for standards like Windows' Plug and Play. You should also know that some phone companies, particularly in rural areas, use compression to pack more calls on a wire. This limits the frequency response the modem sees, and it can be so bad that it limits your modem to 9.6 Kbps no matter how you set its options. In such cases, an upgrade may not buy you more performance.

## U.S. Robotics 56K V.90 Faxmodem

The U.S. Robotics 56K V.90 Faxmodem (shown in Figure 23-14 in both internal and external models) provides V.90 data capability plus Group 3 fax. The modem can interoperate with all ITU-T standard modems from 300 bps to 56 Kbps. Faxing is supported at 14.4 and 9.6 Kbps.

Essentially all the medium and large Internet service providers have upgraded their equipment to support the V.90 56 Kbps standard, so upgrading to a modem like the 56K V.90 Faxmodem should be all you need to boost your connection speed if your telephone lines can support the standard. (If you have a V.34 modem but never see 33.6 Kbps connections, though, you might not have adequate phone service.)

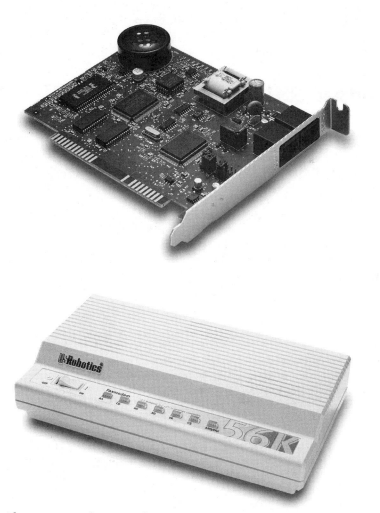

**Figure 23-14:** The U.S. Robotics 56K V.90 Faxmodem provides data, fax, and voice modem capabilities. (Photos courtesy 3Com Corporation.)

Although the 56 Kbps V.90 technology is probably the end of the line for analog modems, with ISDN, ADSL, cable, and other high-speed technologies taking over the market, 53 Kbps isn't the fastest rate you can get with these products. If you run Windows 98, and if your ISP supports analog multilink bonding (much the same technology as required to use both ISDN B channels), you can install two modems and two phone lines to get 106 Kbps downstream and 66 Kbps upstream. Expect to pay twice the usual fee to your ISP, though, because to their equipment you'll look like two dial-up users.

You can get external modems that connect via USB, too, including ones from 3Com, Askey, Aztech, Compaq, Multi-Tech, Netcomm, and Shark. You'll want to be running Windows 98 or 2000 to use one of these modems, simply because the USB support in Windows 95 and Windows NT 4 is inadequate.

## 3Com Sportster ISDN Terminal Adapter and ISDN LAN Modem

The 3Com Sportster ISDN Terminal Adapter and ISDN LAN Modem provide ISDN connections for one or several computers, respectively. If you're only connecting a single computer to an ISDN line, you should pick an internal ISDN modem, because external modems with serial port interfaces are likely to be limited to the 115 Kbps limit of PC serial ports. If you're using both B channels, you need a 128 Kbps interface to run at the full rate, and an even faster interface if your ISP supports compression on the ISDN line. The Sportster ISDN Terminal Adapter is an internal ISDN modem that plugs into an ISA slot in your PC and looks like a fast modem to your software. You can plug a single telephone into the modem too, for voice service, but you'll need an optional cable if you expect the attached telephone or fax machine to ring.

The Sportster ISDN Terminal Adapter includes tools to help you troubleshoot ISDN connection problems, including protocol monitors, diagnostics, and problem logging.

The 3Com ISDN LAN Modem is representative of what you'd want to connect a small local area network (LAN) of up to 25 computers to the Internet through an ISDN line. We'll go into more detail on how that works in Chapter 28 ("Peripheral Network Equipment"); the ISDN LAN Modem is a simplified version of some of the equipment we'll see in that chapter. What makes the ISDN LAN Modem useful is that it connects to your LAN and lets each computer on the LAN have direct access to the Internet without going through one of the local computers. Each connected computer sees the Internet as an extension of your LAN, not as a modem on a serial port.

# Top Support Questions

## Modems

Q: My modem and that of my ISP are capable of 56 (or 33.6) Kbps connections. Why don't I get connections at that rate from my equipment?

A: According to 3Com, very few people can reach a consistent 33.6 Kbps (V.34 modem), or 56 Kbps (V.90 modem) connection. Speeds of 33.6 Kbps or faster require perfect line conditions along the entire length of the connection. These modems are capable of pushing the limits of analog phone lines, commonly offering connect speeds of 21,600, 24,000, and even 26,400 bps or higher. Variations in line quality are typically the cause of low connection rates, which is why you can sometimes get a bad connection, hang up and call again, and do better. If you rarely connect at rates above 19,200 bps, check that your computer's serial port is set for 38.4 Kbps or higher, and try dialing another number (ideally, to another modem distant from the first to see if the problem is at your end or the other one).

Q: How can I test for V.90 connection capability on my phone line?

A: Go to `http://www.3com.com/56k/need4_56k/linetest.html` and follow the directions there with any V.34 or V.90 modem.

Q: What are the requirements for a 56 Kbps connection?

A: There are three primary requirements: 1) A digital connection at your ISP, which must be an ISDN PRI, an ISDN BRI, or a "trunk-side" T1. Ask your ISP/online service if they support 56 Kbps to verify this requirement (and check if they have upgraded to V.90 support). 2) 56 Kbps support at both ends. In order to achieve 56 Kbps speeds, both ends of the connection must support 56 Kbps. In other words, you must have an 56 Kbps modem on your end and your ISP/Online Service must have an 56 Kbps device on their end. 3) At most one analog section, which will be the lines from your modem to the telephone company equipment. If the phone company has analog sections between elements of its equipment, you're not likely to make 56 Kbps work.

# ISDN

Q: Can an ISDN modem be used on my current analog line until I get an ISDN line?

A: No.

Q: What do I have to ask the phone company for when getting an ISDN line?

A: Generally, you will need National ISDN 2B+1D BRI service where both B-channels are CSV/D (circuit switched alternating voice and data) and the D channel is for signaling only. Also, no special services such as "hunt groups" or multiway calling should be activated.

Q: When I dial to an analog number, I get: Fast Busy, constant ring, or No Carrier. Why?

A: This is by far the exception rather than the rule, but it happens because of improper handling of the digital call attempts by the telephone company serving the called line. This is usually caused by the telephone company on the far end not properly rejecting the digital call. They are supposed to reject digital calls placed to analog locations, but they don't always do so. "No Carrier" can also be caused by invalid SPIDs or the line being out.

Q: When I connect to my Internet service provider, I hear multiple beeping sounds from my ISDN modem, and the connection rate seems to change from 64K to 128K and back again. What is happening?

A: ISPs commonly allocate ISDN subscribers one 64K channel. If your ISP has this policy, then even though both sides are capable of supporting connections at 128K, the server will reject your request. You'll need to have your ISP enable the second channel, but be aware that usage fees may go up for your ISP and your telephone service.

Q: I can't connect to my ISDN ISP. Why?

A: Most likely, the Internet service provider does not support V.120 or V.110. The ISP is probably using a device that "talks" SYNC PPP. You need to configure your ISDN modem to talk SYNC PPP as well. Check the manual for your modem; on the U.S. Robotics I-Modem, for instance, you can add *V2=5 at the end of your initialization string in your dialer.

Q: When hooked to an internal ISDN modem, my phone doesn't ring when inbound calls come in. Why?

A: An internal ISDN modem may not supply the normal ring voltage found on an analog phone line to the analog device port (RJ11). This ring voltage is what activates the ringer on a phone, or causes a fax machine to answer a call. The internal modem will instead ring on the modem card itself through its speaker, and the kind of ring and volume is adjustable. External ISDN modems are more likely to supply this ring voltage to the analog device port, so a fax would answer, and a regular phone would ring. Incoming calls not ringing can also be caused by incorrect information in the Directory Number field.

# Hands-On Upgrades

Modem installations can be simple, or they can be the stuff of nightmares. Most of the problems you'll see relate to the serial port between your computer and the modem and to conflicts among multiple serial ports.

# Adding a modem

Even though a modem's interface to your system is no more than a serial port, adding a modem to your system can range from trivial to fiendishly difficult. The trivial version is that you plug in a Plug and Play modem, boot up Windows 9*x*, the hardware is recognized, and you're done. We've actually seen that happen (although sometimes we've had to download a new information file from the modem vendor so Windows recognized what the new modem was).

One of the ways things can go wrong happens when you have a Plug and Play system with serial ports on the motherboard and are upgrading from an older non–Plug and Play internal modem to one that supports Plug and Play. The problem happens when, with that combination of hardware, you have relied on the BIOS to automatically disable motherboard serial ports. What happened with the old modem was that the BIOS saw the serial port on the modem, figured out that there was a conflict with a port on the motherboard, and turned off the motherboard port.

Plug and Play gets in the way of this scheme. When the BIOS initializes and goes looking for conflicting serial ports, the modem won't have been initialized by Plug and Play, so the BIOS sees no conflict and enables the ports. That consumes (most likely) the COM1 and COM2 ports, along with interrupts 3 and 4. Plug and Play then sees the modem and goes looking for resources to assign. COM4 may well conflict with I/O addresses on your video board, and (depending on your modem) there may be no interrupts left to assign. The end result is that the modem doesn't get configured.

There are several ways to work around this problem. One is to go into the BIOS and forcibly turn off one or both serial ports on the motherboard. Don't assign them to COM3 or COM4, because that will still consume interrupts and may still give Plug and Play trouble. Once you do the configuration, Plug and Play should see the modem and configure it.

Another way to work around the problem, probably more reliable than the first, is to disable Plug and Play in the modem, forcibly configuring it onto the serial port you want. Once you decide if it's going to be COM1, 2, 3, or 4, set that port ID into the modem and restart. If the operating system doesn't then recognize the modem, use the information in Table 23-5 to set the modem I/O address and interrupt in your operating system.

### Table 23-5
### Use These Values to Forcibly Configure the Serial Port of your Modem into Your Operating System

| Port | I/O Addresses | Interrupt |
|------|---------------|-----------|
| COM1 | 03F8–03FF | 4 |
| COM2 | 02F8–02FF | 3 |
| COM3 | 03E8–03EF | 4 |
| COM4 | 02E8–02EF | 3 |

More than likely, there are jumpers or switches on your modem to set the port configuration. The U.S. Robotics Sportster x2, for instance, has jumpers. The diagram on the left shows where the jumpers are on the board; the ones on the right show the configurations of the COM jumpers for each of COM1 through COM4. You can select any of interrupts 2, 3, 4, 5, or 7 for the port by moving the IRQ jumper.

If you remove all the jumpers (address and interrupt), the modem reverts to the Plug and Play mode.

## How fast is your modem connection?

There's a lot of information available from your modem about your connect speed. For example, if you turn on extended result codes from a U.S. Robotics Courier V.Everything (using the command AT &A3), you'll see results like this when you connect:

```
CONNECT 26400/ARQ/V34/LAPM/V42BIS
```

This string means that the modem achieved a 26.4 Kbps connection, that error control is enabled, that the connection is using V.34 modulation, that the link uses LAPM error control, and that V.42*bis* compression is active.

There's some other good information available. Once you disconnect a call, the V.Everything lets you enter the ATI6 command to report on the technical details of the call. Here's a sample:

```
ATI6

USRobotics Courier V.Everything Link Diagnostics

Chars sent          50   Chars Received      11112
Chars lost           0
Octets sent         50   Octets Received      4579
Blocks sent         40   Blocks Received       232
```

```
Blocks resent             0

Retrains Requested        0    Retrains Granted        0
Line Reversals            0    Blers                   3
Link Timeouts             0    Link Naks               0

Data Compression          V42BIS 2048/32
Equalization              Long
Fallback                  Enabled
Protocol                  LAPM SREJ 128/15
Speed                     28800/26400
Last Call                 00:01:28

Disconnect Reason is DISC Received
```

The upper block lets you know how much data was sent and received. The second block of values contains data on link errors. In the preceding example, 3 of the blocks (groups of characters) sent by the modem during the call were received with errors (and therefore retransmitted since ARQ was active). A few BLERS (block errors) are OK, but more than a very few indicates poor line quality.

The last block of values tells you the features used in the call (compression, equalization, ability to slow down in the presence of errors, link protocol, speed, and call duration). Notice that the speed data gives you the transmit and receive speeds independently (and that they need not be the same).

The other technical data screen in the V.Everything is under the ATI11 command (as in the example that follows). The values are the technical details of the modulation used and the telephone line parameters. The x2 status (last line) in the example is commonly due to poor line frequency response; other possibilities will tell you that x2 worked, that there were multiple CODECs in the line, or any other condition that might prevent x2 from working.

```
ATI11

USRobotics Courier V.Everything Link Diagnostics

Modulation                V.34+
Carrier Freq     ( Hz )    1829/1829
Symbol Rate                3200/3200
Trellis Code               64S-4D/64S-4D
Nonlinear Encoding         ON/ON
Precoding                  ON/ON
Shaping                    OFF/ON
Preemphasis Index          8/8
Recv/Xmit Level (-dBm)     25.5/11.6
SNR             ( dB )     6553.5
Near Echo Loss  ( dB )     0.0
Far Echo Loss   ( dB )     35.7
Roundtrip Delay (msec)     33
```

```
Timing Offset   ( ppm)   -672
Carrier Offset  ( ppm)   207
RX Upshifts              1
RX Downshifts            0
TX Speedshifts           2
x2 Status                Unspecified negotiation failure
```

## It still does nothing (ISDN)

Despite the fact that ISDN is decades old, and despite the fact that there may be some very capable and dedicated people at your local telephone company, reality is that the telephone companies couldn't have screwed up ISDN more thoroughly if they subcontracted it out to the cable TV companies. The early reports on ADSL are no more promising.

Skeptical? Consider our own ISDN experience.

The first indication that U S WEST might actually be extending its ISDN service offerings to our area came when we discovered that ISDN had become available in a part of the state populated mostly by fence posts and cow flops. It seemed like an odd business strategy to us, but a few months later the U S WEST Web site proudly announced that ISDN single line service was now available out of the central office serving us. We ordered National ISDN for voice and data, with no extra services.

The only way to find out how long the wait to install would be was to schedule the install, which resulted in an estimate of 16 days. The U S WEST representative explained that that didn't really mean it would be installed, but given we'd placed the order they'd check the lines and we'd find out when the install would happen. Nothing happened for over a week. We called and were told that there was a problem, so the line wouldn't be installed as scheduled. Nothing happened for several days. We called a few days later, and discovered the lone qualified representative was out of the office for several weeks—his backup would handle the call. He wasn't there, so we called again after the weekend. Five calls later, he can't even find the order in their computers. Some time later he said there are no lines available and he'd check status. He then called to say an engineer had been assigned to reroute pairs, and we should know what was happening within three weeks from placing the order. A few days later two installers showed up unannounced to install the line.

Once the line came up, we programmed the modem, dialed our ISP, and the connection worked. Sort of. Only one of the two B channels worked, and the U.S. Robotics I-Modem we were using at the time said the SPID on the other one is wrong. After a protracted conversation with U S WEST ISDN service to convince them the modem had the SPIDs programmed correctly, they checked their equipment and returned to the phone denying we have ISDN service. (Prophetically true.) Some more digging turned up that they'd misprogrammed the central office. A little keyboarding on their part and both lines work.

The next morning, our analog line went down. We checked out the building wiring, verified there was no service coming into the building, and called U S WEST service. Two days later, a technician arrived, determined that the ISDN installers left a wire a little long, fixed the problem, and left. Within two hours, the ISDN line went down. The simple-minded conclusion we made was that the two events were related. We were much too optimistic.

Another two days later, the ISDN repair technician arrived. His progress was slow, because his test equipment had just been upgraded and turned out not to work. Eventually he found out that the ISDN card in the U S WEST equipment feeding our line had been removed and replaced with an analog card. Replacing it with an ISDN card restored service. For a while. Two days later, the line went dead. We'd memorized the service number by then and called U S WEST ISDN service. Nothing happened. Three days later, we called again and were told that a technician looked at the equipment, found the ISDN card still installed, and left (ignoring the small point that nothing was working). Another service technician looked at the problem later, replaced the ISDN card, and left. The line remained down. Later that day, the line started bouncing up and down. We talked to a service representative again and made a terrible mistake, letting slip that the line had been up for five minutes. Unbeknownst to us, she canceled all the service orders logged. In celebration, the line went down.

The disaster continued. By the time U S WEST made repairs, the line had been down for 12 out of 15 days. Even after service came up, it was prone to data errors that took U S WEST several months to clear up.

## These *are* professionals

Despite that grim performance, it was evident throughout that all the U S WEST people we spoke to were trying very hard and were completely embarrassed by what was happening. It was six or seven months after installation that the line became reliable, from which we drew several conclusions:

✦ *Adequate training, planning, coordination, and follow through weren't in place.* When a lot of intelligent, motivated people can't do the job they're supposed to do, there aren't a lot of conclusions possible other than it simply can't be done with the tools and information at hand. The individuals didn't fail here, the group of people—the company—did.

✦ *Don't depend on new digital service working reliably until some time after it does.* This experience may have been extreme, but it's not unique. Starting up a new digital line—ISDN, T1, or anything else—isn't the same as bringing in a conventional analog line. You can't assume it will just work.

✦ *There's a lot of information available from your equipment.* While my line was down, I used two tools (the U.S. Robotics I-Modem and my NetProbe program described later in this chapter) to help understand what was going on. The information those tools gave me helped me give good information to U S WEST as they worked through the problem, and it helped me understand when what they did worked or not.

✦ *You don't have to sit by idly.* At one point, a U S WEST manager told me that whenever a problem remains open for 24 hours, the right thing to do is to call service and ask to escalate the problem to a manager. Doing that ensures coordination mistakes get spotted and corrected. You have to know the trouble ticket number to do that, so be sure to get it when you call in the first time.

## Using the modem lights

Your first line of attack troubleshooting ISDN problems is to use the information provided by your modem. Use the tools provided in software or external lights on the modem. For example, the lights on the front of an external U.S. Robotics Courier I-Modem have a lot of information to offer. Here's what they are:

✦ *B1 and B2.* The B1 and B2 lights tell you the status of each of the ISDN B channels. The possibilities are:

- *Fast blink (4 per second).* A digital call is connected at 64 or 56 Kbps.

- *Slow blink (1 per second).* An analog modem or fax call is connected.

- *Solid on.* A voice call is connected (B1 only).

- *Off.* There is no connection.

✦ *AA.* The AA light tells you the auto-answer status for the modem. Auto-answer is on if the light is on; there's an incoming call if the light is blinking, and auto-answer is off if the light is off.

✦ *CD.* The CD light gives you carrier detect status, much like a conventional modem. The light is on if a carrier from the remote device is detected. This means that there's a connection for digital service, and it has the usual meaning for analog connections.

✦ *NS.* The NS light (Network Status) is probably your best line troubleshooting tool. If it's green (and stays that way), the line is ready and there's an operational connection into the network. If not, here's what you might see:

- *Slow green blink (1 per second).* The S/T ISDN interface is working properly, but the line isn't ready yet.

- *Slow red blink (1 per second).* The line is connected to the network, but one of the SPIDs in the modem doesn't match what the network expects.

- *Slow amber blink (1 per second)*. The modem is looking for the S/T interface.

- *Fast amber blink*. The modem is looking for the U interface.

- *Solid red*. The modem can't find the U interface.

- *Off*. The modem doesn't have control of the line.

✦ *RD*. The RD light indicates the modem is receiving data from a remote device.

✦ *SD*. The SD light indicates the modem is sending data to a remote device.

✦ *DTR*. The DTR light (Data Terminal Ready) indicates the computer is willing to accept data from the modem.

✦ *MR*. The MR light (Modem Ready) indicates that the modem is powered on. If the light is flashing, the modem is retraining with a remote device or is in test mode.

✦ *RTS*. The RTS light (Request to Send) indicates that the computer wants to send data to the modem.

✦ *CTS*. The CTS light (Clear to Send) indicates that the modem is sending a signal to the computer telling it to send data.

✦ *SYNC*. The SYNC light (Synchronous status) indicates that the modem is sending data synchronously (versus asynchronously as is common). If the light is blinking, dial security has been activated.

✦ *ARQ/FAX*. The ARQ/FAX light indicates that error correction is active when it's on solid. If it flashes, the modem is retransmitting data. If it blinks steadily, the modem is in FAX mode. If it's off, error correction is disabled and the modem is not in FAX mode.

The most useful of these lights for pinpointing network outages is NS. If it's anything but green within a few seconds of powering on the modem, you've got a problem. While our line was down, the light would sometimes cycle to solid green, then drop to amber, red, and off within a few seconds. Until it went on solid and stayed that way for an extended time, the line wasn't working.

The NS light was also the tool we used to tell that the line hadn't had the SPIDs set up properly after installation. We double-checked that we'd programmed them correctly, leaving an error by U S WEST as the only cause for the blinking red NS light. (As it happens, our SPIDs are the line telephone number with 1111 as the last four digits. One of them had been programmed into the central office switch without the trailing four ones. Once U S WEST fixed that, the modem showed the SPIDs were right.)

## NetProbe

Even if you have an ISDN line, you need to know that the line is carrying data reliably and without interruption.

Figure 23-15 shows how one of the programs Barry wrote, NetProbe, can help you see what your connection is doing.

**Tip**    You can find a copy of NetProbe at `http://www.aros.net/~press/utilities/utilities.htm`.

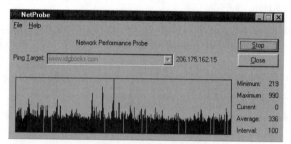

**Figure 23-15:** NetProbe shows what performance you're getting over a network, whether your connection is stable, and how often you're dropping packets.

NetProbe benchmarks the performance of an IP network, measuring the time it takes for a packet to go to a remote host and return. Because the display shows the history of those times, you can get an idea of how consistently your network is delivering packets. In Figure 23-15, you can see two places where the black band is interrupted by a white line. Those points in the display represent times when the network simply lost the packet sent by NetProbe.

The graph gets scaled automatically — the maximum value on the graph will be the same as the maximum shown on the right (unless you've set a clipping value, as described later). Each vertical line in the graph represents one measurement, with the height of the line corresponding to the round-trip travel time. The graph scrolls from right to left every time NetProbe takes a measurement, so the most current measurements are on the right. In Figure 23-15, the empty space on the left represents time for which NetProbe has no measurements.

Here's what else is in the window:

✦ *Ping Target.* You tell NetProbe where on the network it's supposed to send its ping message by filling in the Ping Target. You can enter a computer name (such as `www.idgbooks.com`) or the IP address of the computer (such as

206.175.162.15). The target computer must have an IP address, and the computer you're on must support IP.

✦ *Resolved Address.* The field to the right of the ping target is the resolved address. In Figure 23-15, it's filled in with 206.175.162.15. An error message shows up if NetProbe can't resolve the computer name you give as a ping target to an IP address.

✦ *Stop/Ping button.* This is the "default" push button, pressed when you press Enter. It says "Ping" when no measurement is in process, and "Stop" when one is. You hit the button to start/stop measurements.

✦ *Close button.* Push this button to exit NetProbe (you can also press Esc, or you can click the X icon in the upper-right corner of the window).

✦ *Minimum.* The number to the right will be the minimum measured ping time shown in the window, measured in milliseconds. The number only appears when a measurement is in process.

✦ *Maximum.* The number to the right will be the maximum measured ping time shown in the window, measured in milliseconds. The number only appears when a measurement is in process.

✦ *Current.* The number to the right will be the current measured ping time, in milliseconds. The value will be zero for failed measurements. The number only appears when a measurement is in process.

✦ *Average.* The number to the right will be the average of all non-zero measurements shown in the window, in milliseconds. The number only appears when a measurement is in process.

You can customize NetProbe's operation with the File ➪ Settings command, which brings up the dialog box in Figure 23-16:

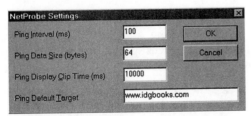

**Figure 23-16:** The NetProbe Settings dialog box lets you control defaults for the program.

The settings have these functions:

✦ *Ping Interval.* This is the time in milliseconds between measurements. It's the interval from the completion of one measurement to the start of the next, so an interval of 1,000 milliseconds will give you slightly fewer than one ping per second. NetProbe enforces a lower limit of 100 milliseconds on the ping interval.

✦ *Ping Data Size.* This is the size, in bytes, of the message NetProbe sends. The transmission time is (partly) dependent on the data length, so if you're trying to infer performance of an application that sends large messages, you may want to boost this value.

✦ *Ping Display Clip Time.* This is the maximum time value (in milliseconds) NetProbe will display in the graph. The maximum, current, and average values displayed on the right are unaffected by the clip value; its purpose is to prevent sporadic, large ping times from eliminating all the detail from the remainder of the measurements. If the maximum value is less than the clip time, the display is unaffected.

✦ *Ping Default Target.* This is the default computer name NetProbe will offer to measure against when it starts. The default you'll find in the settings dialog is the last target you actually pinged.

# Summary

✦ You should have a modem.

✦ The telephone system is the key constraint on how modems work and what they can do.

✦ A 33.6 Kbps modem meeting ITU-T Recommendations V.34, V.42, and V.42bis is the least you should have; we recommend a 56 Kbps modem meeting the V.90 standard. Fax capability is usually included at no additional cost. Choose your modem carefully; reviews consistently show that modems from the top vendors outperform other modems on noisy lines.

✦ Cellular modems are useful if you need the mobility, but otherwise plan on using a wired modem.

✦ If you need the speed and can get service, investigate ISDN and ADSL. There's no point in waiting for the communications market to settle out.

✦    ✦    ✦

# Digital Still Cameras, Video Capture, and Video Conferencing

In the same way that sound cards let you capture audio, you can get cards and other devices that let you capture still images and video. The volume of data you create that way can be immense, so designers have made some compromises to live within the limits of what a personal computer can do. Those limits are becoming less and less restrictive, though, putting the images and video you work on your PC on par with what you expect to do with a camera and camcorder.

The improvements in digital still cameras have been particularly dramatic. When we wrote the first edition of this book starting in early 1996, we used a 35mm Canon film camera for all the pictures we took because the available digital cameras couldn't produce publication-quality images. For this third edition, we used Kodak DC260 and DC265 digital cameras for all the new photographs we took, and shipped the resulting files to IDG Books Worldwide, our publisher. The quality of the pictures is good enough that we no longer bother with film.

# Turning Images into Files

Let's start with a simple problem—taking a photograph and getting it into your computer. For a long time, your only option was to literally take a photograph, have the film processed, and scan the picture (see Chapter 25, "Scanners"). That process has the disadvantage that it's slow—unless you use something like a Polaroid instant camera that develops the print while you wait, you have to go somewhere to get the processing done. Even then, you have to go to where your computer and scanner are before you have the digital result.

## Image capture

There's another way. Building the same kind of electronic sensors that made high-performance, inexpensive video cameras possible into a still camera—substituting the sensor for the film—creates a camera that records the electronic image directly. You can see the image in the viewfinder or download it to a computer for viewing, printing, and further processing.

Figure 24-1 shows what's in an electronic still camera. The biggest difference between an electronic camera and a traditional camera is that, rather than focusing light through a shutter on a strip of film, the electronic camera focuses the image on a *charge-coupled device* (CCD) array. The body of the camera is filled with electronics and batteries, and an LCD display (like in a laptop computer) serves as the viewfinder. There's no shutter, because the CCD array is constantly feeding a video image back to the viewfinder.

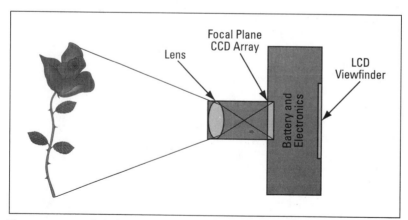

**Figure 24-1:** A digital still camera substitutes an electronic sensor for film, recording the picture directly in memory.

Because there's no film, the camera has to do something else with your picture when you push the button. What it does is store it in a memory.

## Image resolution and memory

In Chapter 17, "Video," we pointed out that the amount of memory an image requires depends on its horizontal and vertical resolution, in pixels, and on the size of each pixel (which determines the number of possible colors for each pixel). Using 24-bit pixels (over 16 million colors), an image of 300 × 200 pixels requires less than 190K of memory. An uncompressed image of 1,600 × 1,200 pixels (still in 24-bit color) requires nearly five and one half megabytes.

The number of pixels in the image, and therefore the amount of memory an image occupies, is a critical issue for digital cameras. To see why, consider what happens when you want to print your photograph on your 300 dpi (dots per inch) color printer, filling the entire page with the picture. Suppose we try to print a 320 × 240 image onto a page. If the printable area on the page is 10 × 7.5 inches, then along the 320-pixel dimension we have about 30 pixels per inch — a tenth of what the printer can do. Figure 24-2 illustrates the problem, showing what happens to the image resolution when we take what may be a very small number of pixels and replicate them to make the picture fill the larger number of pixels the printer wants.

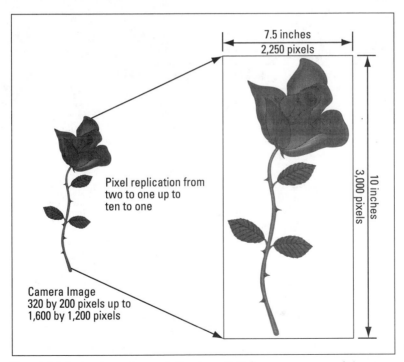

**Figure 24-2:** Inadequate resolution in a digital camera can result in poor results when you print your pictures.

Figure 24-3 is a digital photograph we took to illustrate what can happen. The image on the left in the figure is the complete picture with a resolution of 320 × 240 pixels. We took a section of the image — the horse's eye — and blew it up on the right side to show the effects of pixel replication. The image on the left is small but reasonably sharp, while the image on the right is large and unacceptable. This is the same effect that happens when you blow up the image to fit on a printed page. No matter how high the printer resolution, it can't make up for lack of detail in the source image.

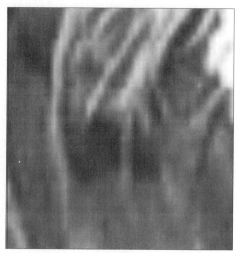

**Figure 24-3:** Blowing up a digital photograph replicates the pixels, which can become objectionably large and blocky.

The low-quality results from pixel replication mean that you may not be satisfied with the results from a low-resolution digital camera. Film can be as sharp as thousands of grains per inch (which corresponds to pixels per inch), so if you use a standard medium-format camera you can get very high resolution.

That's not to say that digital photography can't give you high-quality results. Mid-range digital cameras (such as the Kodak DC260 and DC265 we used for this edition) are available with resolutions up to 1,600 × 1,200, which approaches what you can get with 35 mm film. High-end digital cameras built into top-flight film camera bodies offer resolution up to 3,060 × 2,036 using the complete suite of lenses and attachments available for a professional film camera body. Cameras with 2 to 2.5 megapixels are now entering the market, extending what you can do with the technology.

Let's work some of the numbers. A camera giving you 320 × 240 resolution with 24-bit pixels uses 225K. If the camera contains a megabyte of memory, that's no more than four images. It's going to be hard to find a use for a camera like that. There are two ways to solve the problem:

✦ *Image compression.* The same lossy image compression ideas we discuss in Chapter 18, "Video Adapters," as the basis for MPEG video compression are applied in JPEG (Joint Photographic Experts Group) compression for still frame pictures. JPEG compression can boost the capacity of a 1MB memory to about 160 images, each 320 × 240 resolution (24-bit color).

There's a loss of image quality at higher compression levels, though, so many cameras give you the option to trade off fewer pictures in memory for better quality. Some reject lossy compression altogether, using lossless compression or no compression instead.

✦ *More storage.* This is the "bigger hammer" idea. If the product selling price can go up, you can go so far as to put a disk drive in the camera. (Yes, these really are fixed-purpose computers.) Some cameras include a port to allow you to insert a PC Card disk for added capacity.

The need to put a disk in the camera is no joke. If you're capturing pictures at 1,600 × 1,200 resolution, each uncompressed picture is over five and a half megabytes; with high-quality compression, the images can still be half a megabyte. At 3,060 × 2,036 resolution, an uncompressed image occupies 18 megabytes.

## A darkroom on your desk

You have to transfer the pictures from your camera to your computer before you can do much with them. Low-end digital cameras today use a serial port (as if you had one to spare). Better cameras use the Universal Serial Bus (USB). Software specific to your camera controls the process, pulling images from the camera and storing them as files on your disk. Once you have files in a standard format, any image processing program can crop, recolor, and otherwise reprocess the pictures for you, and can send the results to your printer.

Let's do some calculations to analyze what resolution you want in a digital camera. Table 24-1 summarizes the lowest specifications we found examining the Kodak digital cameras. The image size and minimum resolution are from the Kodak data; the horizontal and vertical resolutions are values we calculated.

### Table 24-1
### Recommended Camera Resolution Specifications

| Image Size | Minimum Resolution (pixels per inch) | Total Pixels (millions of pixels) | Horizontal Resolution (pixels per inch) | Vertical Resolution (pixels per inch) |
|---|---|---|---|---|
| 8 × 10 | 1,536 × 1,024 | 1.6 | 153.6 | 128.0 |
| 5 × 7 | 1,152 × 864 | 1.0 | 164.6 | 172.8 |

What's interesting is that the resolution required for photo-realistic prints, according to Kodak (who should know!), is a lot less than possible with ink jet or color laser printers. We calculated another table (Table 24-2) to show how many pixels would be required to create images at full printer resolution.

### Table 24-2
### Calculated Printer Resolution Specifications

| Print Image | | Camera Image | | | |
|---|---|---|---|---|---|
| Height | Width | Height | Width | Total Pixels (millions) | Pixels per Inch |
| 4 | 6 | 1,200 | 1,800 | 2.16 | 300 |
| 8 | 10 | 2,400 | 3,000 | 7.20 | 300 |
| 11 | 14 | 3,300 | 4,200 | 13.86 | 300 |
| 16 | 20 | 4,800 | 6,000 | 28.80 | 300 |
| 4 | 6 | 2,400 | 3,600 | 8.64 | 600 |
| 8 | 10 | 4,800 | 6,000 | 28.80 | 600 |
| 11 | 14 | 6,600 | 8,400 | 55.44 | 600 |
| 16 | 20 | 9,600 | 12,000 | 115.20 | 600 |

The 300 pixels per inch specification corresponds to the 300 dots per inch print a common ink jet printer can do; 600 dots per inch is possible with a color laser printer. (You can get ink jet printers capable of 1,440 dots per inch on special paper.) Comparing Tables 24-1 and 24-2 shows that you'd need a professional-quality digital camera with a 6 megapixel image to approach printing an image at 8 × 10 with no pixel replication. If we take Kodak's recommendations as accurate, then we conclude that pixel replication of up to 2:1 on an ink jet or 4:1 on a color laser printer is acceptable.

There's one more conclusion to draw from Table 24-1. Knowing that computer monitors typically deliver 90 dots per inch or more (corresponding to 0.28mm pitch or finer), it's apparent that even the least expensive digital camera should have enough resolution for pictures destined for Web pages.

Ultimately, digital cameras are still cameras, so the issues that are important for film cameras are equally important for digital ones. You still care about the focal length, resolution, contrast, and speed of the lens. You still have to have enough light to form a picture, so the effective "film speed" matters. You'll still use a flash in low-light situations, so the synchronization and control of the flash unit (and the time it takes to recharge) are important. You have to worry about parallax between the lens and the viewfinder, and you may want features like macro focus and a self timer. These are cameras; only the "film" is different.

## I'll have onions with that battery, please

A lot of electronics are packed into digital cameras, all of which want to eat power from the batteries about as fast as you would chow down a carton of onion rings. Because the batteries have to fit in the camera (and the camera in your hand), there's a limit to how much power the electronics can use. Too much power drain, and the batteries have a very short life—you'll go through them like fast food.

Camera designers have to do extreme things to bring power consumption under control. For example:

✦ *Stop the processor.* When nothing's happening, the processor can stop. When it does that, it essentially stops drawing power, reducing the load on the batteries. When you cause something to happen, the processor starts up and does the work you need done.

✦ *Use low-power displays.* It's unusual to find anything but an LCD display on a camera. LCDs are low-power displays, so they help reduce power consumption.

✦ *Use flash memory.* The usual DRAM memory draws power all the time and needs additional electronics to keep it active. Many cameras use flash memory instead (see Chapter 9, "Cache, Memory, and Bus"), which lets the camera turn off the power to the memory when it's not being accessed.

It's a testament to the ingenuity of camera designers (and to improvements in battery technology over the past several years) that their products can run as long as they do on a handful of small batteries. The rate of improvement in battery technology has slowed, though, so it's going to be a major challenge to continue to make significant improvements in how many pictures you get from a set of batteries (or from one charging). We use only high-energy lithium photo batteries or rechargeable Nickel Metal Hydride (NiMh) batteries in digital cameras.

## Video capture

If there's any one thing you might want to do with your computer that has the potential to overwhelm what the computer can do, it's capturing and editing digital video. Video capture has a lot of value, but you'll have to decide what you want it for and what compromises you're willing to make.

### Data rates

The problem with digital video is that there's so much of it. We mentioned earlier that naively recording broadcast-quality video transfers over 23MB per second onto disk. Here's where that calculation comes from. A full video frame occurs 30 times per second and contains (approximately) 512 pixels by 512 lines, for $30 \times 512 \times 512$ = 7.8 million pixels per second. If we record 3 bytes per pixel (24-bit color), that's 180 million bits per second, or about 23MB per second.

Tip Even though disk drives like the Seagate Ultra2 SCSI Cheetah and Barracuda series can now sustain rates of around 23 MBps, most personal computers don't handle that kind of data rate onto or off of the disk. Nor can a video capture card handle data at that rate if it's connected to an ISA or USB bus with limits of a few megabytes per second—you're going to want to use PCI and/or FireWire to handle that rate.

## Decimation, frame rates, and compression

Because 23MB is still too fast, you're going to have to make some compromises for video capture on a PC. As always, you have choices:

✦ *Black and white or limited color.* It's fairly straightforward to transform 24-bit color down to 16 bits with little perceptible difference. If you dispense with color altogether, you find that 256-level grayscale is useful for applications like video conferencing and cuts the pixel size to one byte. You can also use 256-color video, which similarly requires only one pixel.

✦ *Smaller frames.* It's not necessary to capture each and every pixel if you're willing to live with smaller images. If you ignore every other one—called *pixel decimation*—you can capture frames that are about 320 × 240 pixels. That single change cuts the data rate by four—instead of 23MB per second, you only need to handle 5.75MB. Many computers today can sustain that rate.

✦ *Slower frame rates.* You don't have to capture every frame, either. If you're willing to take every other one—*frame decimation*—you're down to 15 frames per second.

If you combine all three of these ideas—one-byte pixels, pixel decimation, and frame decimation—you can cut the data rate by a factor of 24, so the data rate you have to store to disk goes down to just under a megabyte per second. Most any personal computer using a Pentium or faster processor can do this today. If we need to reduce the data flow further, we can cut the frame size by another factor of four, and the frame rate by another factor of two. The resulting factor of eight cuts the data rate to a mere 125K per second (which you can almost do with pencil and paper).

The other way to cut the data rate, of course, is with compression. The problem with that idea is that lossless compression doesn't do enough to be useful, and lossy compression is highly mathematically intensive. Just a few years ago lossy video compression was beyond the capability of PCs to do in software as you captured video. Today, the new Streaming SIMD Extension (SSE) instructions in the Pentium III processors, combined with 450 MHz and faster clock rates, makes software video compression a reality. If you have a Pentium or Pentium II class processor, though, you have only two choices—either do the compression in hardware (which has become inexpensive), or limit the data rates to what software can handle (which limits image quality).

## Video stills, clips, or conferencing?

The upshot of all this is that you can have any two of the three — low data rate, good video quality, and low cost. You can't (yet) have all three. For this reason, there are three things you can expect to do when recording video on a PC:

✦ *Still capture.* It's fairly easy to capture a single frame and pull it into your computer. Low-cost devices exist that do this well. It's a limited application, though — what you get is one (or several) still images. You can't play them back as video, and recording enough frames this way to turn into video is impractical.

✦ *Quality recording.* You can record high-quality video on a computer, but the equipment is still relatively expensive. You can get lower-cost equipment that delivers reasonable quality, but typically the highest-quality compression is still expensive.

✦ *Video conferencing.* There is a market for relatively poor-quality video, because there can be a lot of value in video conferencing. In most cases, video conferencing is limited by the speed of the communications line rather than computer performance.

Ignoring the hype about television over the Internet, the success of voice telephony on the Internet suggests that video conferencing is something that will build the way all the successes on the Internet have — people will find something useful and latch onto it. (See the sidebar "New ideas on the Internet.") Two elements have come together to make this possible:

✦ *Freely available video-conferencing software.* CU-SeeMe, developed and copyrighted by Cornell University, is a free video-conferencing program available to anyone with a Macintosh or Windows computer and a connection to the Internet. Using CU-SeeMe, you can videoconference with anyone else using the program anywhere on the Internet. You can create conferences among several people using an intermediary computer on the Internet called a reflector. (For more information about CU-SeeMe Pro, a commercial version of CU-SeeMe, see the Products section later in this chapter.)

✦ *Inexpensive video capture hardware.* You can get a simple black-and-white camera capable of 320 × 240 resolution for about US $100. Combined with your sound card, microphone, speakers, and Internet connection, you're ready to go. (You should note, though, that not all video cards work with CU-SeeMe. Cornell University maintains a Web server at `http://cu-seeme.cornell.edu`. You can find compatibility information at `http://cu-seeme.cornell.edu/PC.CU-SeeMeCurrent.html`. There are also some important configuration issues; see `http://cu-seeme.cornell.edu/PC.faq.html`.)

## New ideas on the Internet

We're very skeptical of corporate pronouncements of the "next great thing on the Internet." Push technology, a scheme to shovel data onto your computer companies think you should have was but a most recent one, albeit one that received an unconscionable level of hype. In real life, few if any important developments on the Internet have resulted from one company (or a few of them) promoting an idea. Instead, the Internet has demonstrated time and time again that the next great thing will be a great idea that someone makes available and a lot of people pick up on because it has value to them.

The Web is a perfect example of this, as more recently is the Linux operating system. Tim Berners-Lee invented the World Wide Web, writing the first Web clients and server while working at CERN (the European Particle Physics Laboratory) in late 1990. People discovered that the Web was a useful way to make information accessible, and thanks to a great deal of work on Mosaic (the browser most people used in the early days of the Web) at the National Center for Supercomputing Applications (NCSA) at the University of Illinois in Urbana-Champaign, the software evolved into a highly viable product.

Some time after that, parts of the original Mosaic development team broke off and founded Mosaic Communications Corporation (now Netscape Communications Corporation) to develop and market the Netscape browser. Contrary to what many people seem to think, Netscape did not invent the Web. Microsoft later developed Internet Explorer, resulting in the two products shooting it out to dominate the Web browser market. The key point, though, is that the Web wasn't invented by Netscape or Microsoft. It's something that grew from a grassroots start because it had a great deal of value.

We think you'll see Internet video conferencing do the same thing as more high-speed Internet connections are installed and the user base for CU-SeeMe grows. Video conferencing is going to matter to a broad base of users because of the time and money it saves them.

The modem-based video conferencing you'll do on the Internet today (or any other network limited by analog modems) is going to be limited to relatively small images and less-than-smooth-motion video. Nevertheless, it works, it's useful, and as faster network access (such as ISDN, ADSL, and cable modems) becomes widespread, these limitations will be removed. You'll need an Internet connection at 28.8 Kbps or faster for both audio and video to work with CU-SeeMe, and you'll probably have to do some tweaking before it works right. A commercial version exists (see http://www.wpine.com), which follows the notion that useful products on the Internet migrate from freeware to supported, enhanced products.

If you have reliable access to the Internet at ISDN or faster rates, desktop video conferencing becomes a valuable business tool. You get reasonably smooth motion video, acceptable sound, whiteboard support, and immediate access. Problems that once required a trip for a face-to-face meeting can sometimes be solved with a video conference, saving you time and money. The free accessibility of desktop video conferencing, in sharp distinction to expensive video-conferencing rooms, extends the reach of the technology down to the worker levels of the company.

# Products

Although still photography, video capture, and video conferencing are still in their infancy as personal computer applications, they're among the applications with the most growth potential. There are products today that deliver these capabilities, and, depending on your requirements, deliver solid value for getting your work done. Following are the ones we think are most promising.

## White Pine Software CU-SeeMe Pro

CU-SeeMe Pro is a supported, augmented version of the Cornell University CU-SeeMe desktop videoconferencing software for real-time person-to-person or group conferencing. You can use CU-SeeMe Pro over the Internet (or other TCP/IP network), with the capability for full-color video, audio, chat, and whiteboard (multiparticipant graphical collaboration) communications. You can participate in conferences, broadcasts, or chats. Communications over a 28.8 Kbps modem, ISDN link, or better are supported, although even the 56 Kbps modems are marginal performers for good video. For audio-only telephony use, CU-SeeMe works effectively over a 14.4 Kbps modem. Person-to-person, group conferencing, and large-audience broadcasting over TCP/IP networks are all possible. CU-SeeMe Pro is partly compatible with the Cornell University version; users of the Cornell University version may not be able to receive video from the White Pine version, but audio works in both directions and the enhanced version can receive video from the Cornell University version.

CU-SeeMe achieves low bandwidth Internet connections through compression in software, reducing the data rate you have to transmit. It does not require hardware compression/decompression boards. There are versions of CU-SeeMe Pro for Windows NT, Windows 9x, and Macintosh. You can have up to eight video windows, or an unlimited number of audio and talk windows. In addition to caller ID, the software features multiuser whiteboard support for collaboration during conferences.

White Pine suggests that to receive with CU-SeeMe Pro you have at least these components:

✦ *Processor.* Pentium 133 MHz or faster, with 166 MHz recommended (not much of a limitation)

✦ *Video.* 256-color (8-bit) video with 640 × 480 or higher resolution

✦ *Sound.* At least 16-bit sound

✦ *Memory.* At least 32MB of memory

To transmit, White Pine recommends you add:

✦ *Sound.* A microphone input on your sound card

✦ *Video.* A video camera with serial port digitizer, or a video camera with standard NTSC output (like a camcorder) and a video capture board

The biggest issue in any of this, of course, is the camera—all the rest you'll find in an entry-level machine. You'll want to check for compatibility rather than assuming a given video camera setup is compatible.

## Kodak DVC325 video camera

The best choice we've found for video conferencing is the color Kodak DVC325 digital video camera. The camera (Figure 24-4) plugs into a USB port to send 640 × 480 pixel still images or digital video up to 320 × 240 resolution in 24-bit color to your computer.

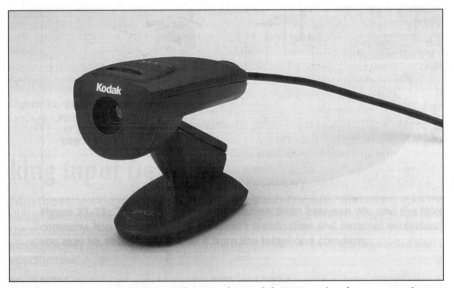

**Figure 24-4:** At under $130 in mid-1999, the Kodak DVC325 is a low-cost option for desktop video conferencing. (Photo courtesy Kodak.)

The DVC325 is the successor to the DVC300 and DVC323, two of the first cameras to exploit the higher speed of the USB port to provide higher frame rates and better color. There's hardware compression in the camera, although it's a format proprietary to Kodak. Table 24-3 shows comparable specifications for the DVC-325. Table 24-4 breaks down the frame rates the camera delivers at varying settings.

### Table 24-3
### Kodak DVC-325 Specifications

| Characteristic | Specification |
| --- | --- |
| Resolution Video: | Photo:   640 × 480, 24-bit color<br>160 × 120<br>176 × 244<br>320 × 240<br>352 × 288 (all in 24-bit color) |
| Imaging sensor | Color CCD |
| Focus | Manual, 5 inches to infinity |
| Exposure control | Automatic white balance and exposure control with software option to adjust manually |
| Frame rate | See Table 24-2. |

### Table 24-4
### Kodak DVC-325 Video Frame Rates

| Horizontal View Mode | Max. Frames per Second (fps) at Selectable Image Quality Levels | | |
| --- | --- | --- | --- |
| | Good | Better | Best |
| Telephoto (20°) | 30 | 20 | 10 |
| Normal (30°) | 30 | 20 | 10 |
| Wide angle (42°) | 28 | 20 | 12 |

If you have a USB-capable system, the USB interface on the DVC-325 is a definite asset — it doesn't consume a parallel port, and it doesn't use a bus slot. The camera includes Microsoft Netmeeting video-conferencing software.

## US Robotics Bigpicture

Another video telephone and video-conferencing option is the US Robotics Bigpicture (Figure 24-5). The Video Kit version includes a color camera, a PCI video acquisition card, and a "video modem," which is a U.S. Robotics 33.6 Kbps analog FAX modem enhanced to support the H.323, V.80, and G.723 standards. The Bigpicture modem supports the 56 Kbps V.90 modem standard. (Other versions include just the video modem and capture card, or just the video modem and the camera.) You can do video capture for editing with the Bigpicture board too.

**Figure 24-5:** The US Robotics Bigpicture integrates a capable video camera with PCI video capture and a specialized video modem.

Table 24-5 shows specifications for the Bigpicture. The camera in the Video Kit version is NTSC-compatible, meaning that (in North America, at least) it outputs video signals compatible with your VCR and television. The NTSC interface between the camera and the video acquisition card also means that you can record video from your VCR using the card if you want. You can capture still photographs with the Bigpicture camera.

## Table 24-5
## US Robotics Bigpicture Specifications

| Characteristic | Specification |
| --- | --- |
| Resolution | 160 × 120, 320 × 240, and 640 × 480 |
| Imaging sensor | Color |
| Field of view | 51 × 39 degrees |
| Focus | Manual, zero to infinity |
| Exposure control | Automatic, including white balance, background level, contrast |
| Frame rate | 24-bit color at up to 30 frames per second |

The videophone capabilities of the Bigpicture are for point-to-point calls — essentially, you call with your computer rather than a telephone, and you get voice and video instead of just voice. The H.323 standards-based videophone (using included software) should interface with any other H.323 system, and because of the video and voice compression included in the standard, gives you good images and sound. The direct connection, modem to modem, means you're not subject to the problems surrounding connection through the Internet, but also means that one of you are paying the (potentially long-distance) phone bill, and you'll be tying up a telephone line for the duration of the call.

The Bigpicture works over the Internet, too, using CU-SeeMe or White Pine's CU-SeeMe Pro. The video modem needs a direct audio connection to the camera microphone for videophone operation, so if you alternate between videophone and Internet videoconferencing, you'll want to set up one of these connections:

✦ *Split the signal.* You could use a splitter cable, dividing the signal from the microphone in the camera to both the microphone input on your sound card and the microphone input on the video modem.

✦ *Chain the cards.* You could connect the line out signal from your sound card to the microphone input on the video modem. You may have to turn down the volume on the line out signal. Using this connection, any audio from the sound card (including wave audio, MIDI, and the microphone signal) is available to the modem.

✦ *Use two microphones.* External microphones are relatively inexpensive, so your third alternative is to simply use two microphones, connecting one to the sound card (for Internet video conferencing) and one to the video modem (for videophone calls).

As with other video cameras, the maximum resolution of the Bigpicture camera may give you a fairly small image on a high-resolution display. If that's a problem, temporarily switch the screen resolution to a lower setting.

## Kodak DCS Professional digital cameras

The Kodak Professional digital cameras (Figure 24-6 shows the DCS620) are high-end digital still cameras, using professional Canon or Nikon camera bodies, that are designed to be complete replacements for film-based photography. Using a CCD sensor array of up to 6 million pixels, these cameras can give you high-quality pictures at resolutions from 1,524 × 1,012 to 3,060 × 2,036 pixels, all in 36-bit color. The files for these images are large, so the cameras include a PC Card slot capable of handling disk drives holding over a gigabyte to store images before you download to your computer. You retain the ability to shoot pictures in quick succession, with some models able to shoot as fast as 12 pictures in one second. Standard Canon and Nikon features including autofocus, exposure modes, metering modes, flash, and self-timing all work in the Kodak digital cameras.

**Figure 24-6:** The Kodak DCS Professional digital cameras create high-resolution digital pictures, storing them on an internal disk drive. (Photo courtesy Eastman Kodak.)

Figure 24-7 shows how good the pictures from the DCS cameras can be. Except for conversion to black and white, what you see is exactly as we received the file and has not been retouched for publication. If you look carefully, you'll see a level of resolution, sharpness, and tonal gradation competitive with that of film cameras.

The specifications for the DCS series (Table 24-6) back up the quality of Figure 24-7.

**Figure 24-7:** We received this photo as a file and, except for converting it to black and white, have not retouched it for publication. (Photo courtesy Rob Galbraith.)

## Table 24-6
## DCS Series Specifications

| Characteristic | EOS·DCS 1 | DCS620 | DCS460 |
|---|---|---|---|
| Resolution | 3,060 × 2,036 | 1,728 × 1,152 | 3,060 × 2,036 |
| Imaging sensor | 6 million pixel area CCD | 2 million pixel area CCD | 6 million pixel area CCD |
| Color depth | 36-bit | 36-bit | 36-bit |
| Image file size | 18MB | 6MB | 18MB |
| Lens | Any Canon EOS 1N compatible | Any Nikon compatible | Any Nikon compatible |
| Focus | Depends on lens | Depends on lens | Depends on lens |
| Aperture | Depends on lens | Depends on lens | Depends on lens |
| Strobe | Any Canon EOS 1N compatible | Any Nikon compatible | Any Nikon compatible |
| Shutter speed | Any available on camera | Any available on camera | Any available on camera |
| ISO rating | 80 | 200 to 1,600 color | 100 |
| Computer interface | SCSI-2 | IEEE 1394 (FireWire) | SCSI-2 |
| Battery life | 300 pictures per charge | 300 pictures per charge | 250 pictures per charge |

## Kodak DC200 Plus, DC260, and DC265 cameras

The Kodak DC200 Plus, DC260, and DC265 zoom digital cameras (Figure 24-8) are, relative to the Kodak professional cameras described earlier, mid-range digital cameras that can give you high-quality images at resolutions for your computer screen or high-quality printouts. The DC200 Plus takes pictures at a resolution of 1152 × 864 pixels in 24-bit color, storing them in a 4MB removable picture card. The DC260 supports resolutions up to 1280 × 960 with 24-bit color, has 8MB of memory, and lets you plug in Compact Flash memory cards to extend its memory. We used a DC260 and DC265 for all the new photographs in this third edition of the *PC Upgrade and Repair Bible*, getting results like Figure 24-9.

The DC265 is an enhanced version of the DC260, adding more storage on the picture card (16MB) and faster processing internally. The DC265 eliminates the AC power adapter, replacing it with a more useful set of rechargeable batteries and AC-powered charger. The optional expansion pack adds another set of rechargeable batteries, a Compact Flash card reader for very high speed picture transfers, an additional Compact Flash card, and photo album processing software.

**Figure 24-8:** The Kodak DC200 Plus and DC260 cameras are mid-range digital cameras with good resolution and a zoom lens. (Photo courtesy Eastman Kodak.)

You can choose from three levels of compression with both the DC200 Plus and DC260. The best image quality level on the DC200 Plus stores seven pictures in 2MB and is nearly lossless. Mid-level compression stores 13 pictures, while maximum compression stores 60 pictures. You trade off image quality for the capability to store more pictures. The DC260 offers three levels of compression too, storing images in an 8MB flash card. The good, better, and best compression settings on the DC260 store 11, 20, and 32 pictures. You can select lower resolution settings on the DC260 if you need capacity more than detail, or you can use larger flash cards. Both the DC260 and the DC200 Plus have a zoom lens, letting you reach out and frame the picture exactly the way you want. Specifications of the DC200 Plus and DC260 are shown in Table 24-7.

**Figure 24-9:** The Kodak DC260 and DC265 cameras are capable of professional-quality results for under $1,000. (Copyright 1999 Barry and Marcia Press. Used with permission.)

## miroVIDEO DC30 *plus* Video Capture and Editing

High-quality video capture and editing requires more and better hardware than the cameras you'll use for video conferencing. You need a quality video source, a well-engineered video capture card, a fast disk subsystem, and a processor fast enough to keep it all running.

The miroVIDEO DC30 *plus* video capture and editing system (Figure 24-10) gives you the complete video capture electronics and editing software — Adobe Premiere — you need to capture, edit, and add special effects, mix in audio and narration, and output a finished product back to video tape. You can convert video from the system's hardware motion JPEG format to Windows-standard AVI for use directly on computers or as part of multimedia CD-ROMs.

### Table 24-7
### Kodak Digital Camera Specifications

| Characteristic | DC260 Specification | DC200 Plus Specification |
| --- | --- | --- |
| Resolution | 1,548 × 1,032, 24-bit color | 1,152 × 864, 24-bit color |
| Lens | 38mm to 115mm (3X power optical zoom and 2X digital zoom) | 39mm. 37mm threads accept optional lenses |
| Focus | Auto-focus, range 12″ to infinity | Focus free, range 27″ to infinity |
| Aperture | Wide: f/3.0–f/14 Telephoto: f/4.7–f/22 | Wide: f/2.5–f/16 Telephoto: f/3.8–f/24 |
| Shutter speed | 1/400 to 1/4 seconds | 1/500–16 seconds |
| ISO rating | 100 | 160 |
| Computer interface | Audio, infrared, RS-422/232C serial port, USB, and composite video, PC Card | RS-422/232C serial port |

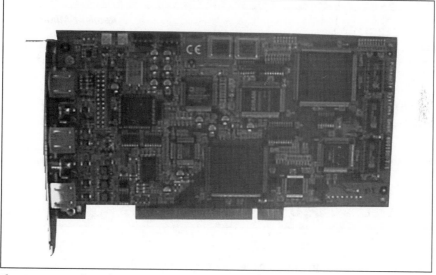

**Figure 24-10:** The Miro DC30 Video Capture and Editing System. (Photo courtesy Pinnacle Systems, Inc.)

The combination of the DC30 *plus*, Adobe Premiere, and a fast computer is more powerful than you might expect. You can digitize from composite or S-Video sources, record clips to disk, and then combine and edit clips to create a complete sequence. When you're done, you can output to a file, for use on computers, or to video for rerecording back to tape. In one package you have everything you need to digitize, edit, and rerecord training videos, presentations, or other content. Chips on the DC30 *plus* do compression in hardware, speeding the job of producing finished video.

Don't make the mistake of using an underpowered computer for video editing. We initially used a machine powered by a pair of 200 MHz Pentium Pro processors and a Seagate Cheetah disk through an Adaptec AHA-2940UW controller. Benchmarks in the miro software showed that the system could sustain video capture at rates over 5 MBps, fast enough to record very high quality video. Current-generation machines are faster, but take this recommendation seriously and don't expect to get much editing done with an older, underpowered machine. Table 24-8 shows the minimum manufacturer's system requirements, along with what we recommend for serious work.

### Table 24-8
### Minimum miro DC30 and Adobe Premiere Hardware Recommendations

| Characteristic | miro DC30 plus | Adobe Premiere | Realistic Minimum Specification |
|---|---|---|---|
| Processor | Pentium | Pentium | Pentium II 233 MHz |
| Operating system | Windows 9x | Windows 9x | Windows NT |
| Memory | 32MB | 32MB | 128MB or more |
| Hard disk | 1 to 7MB per second | 60MB for installation | 4GB Ultra2 SCSI |
| Video adapter | 16-bit DirectX | 8-bit | 24-bit DirectX |
| Monitor | | | 21 inch |
| Other | | | Sound with headphones, CD-R, or tape |

Here's why our recommendations are so much higher than those of miro and Adobe:

✦ *Processor.* At a 3 MBps data rate for initial capture (320 × 240 × 24 bits × 15 frames per second, compressed a little over 15 percent), you'll consume 180 MBps of disk every minute. That means you'll be handling large files even if you're only doing short clips. When you go to splice clips together, move from one end of the clip to the other, or apply special effects, you're creating a lot of work for the processor. We found the response on a dual processor 200 MHz Pentium Pro good, although not spectacular. We'd not want to wait around for the 386 Adobe once recommended.

We compared operation of Adobe Premiere with one 200 MHz Pentium Pro to that with two, and it's clear that if you have the option you should consider a machine with two processors (although we'd recommend a 400 MHz machine rather than one with two 200 MHz processors). Having two processors under Windows NT lets one work on capturing or presenting the video while the other one manages the disk. The ability to split the processor workload results in faster, smoother response that makes the work easier. Figure 24-11 illustrates how the two processors split the load, using the workload of playing a video clip for an example. You can see that CPU 0 is very busy (it's actually putting video on the screen), while CPU 1 is less busy (it's getting data from the disk). The total of the two at times exceeds 100 percent, meaning that the workload exceeded what a single 200 MHz Pentium Pro can deliver. Maintaining smooth video on a lesser machine would require a smaller on-screen image or a lower frame rate.

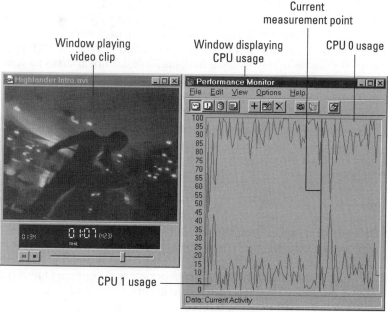

**Figure 24-11:** High-performance video can consume enormous amounts of processing power.

The reason we'd recommend a 400 MHz processor rather than a pair of 200 MHz ones is that, when it comes time to output the video in compressed format, the compression is being done in software, and by a single processor. The faster the processor, the faster the output conversion.

✦ *Operating system.* The ability of Windows NT to handle multiple processors, along with its better stability and better multitasking of disk operations, means that it's a more suitable platform for digital video editing. There are no drivers for UNIX.

✦ *Memory.* The same problem that makes a fast processor worthwhile — slinging around large quantities of data — makes it useful to have a lot of memory for disk cache and program operations. We consider 64MB a workable minimum for Windows NT 4, so bumping that figure to 128MB gives the software room to work.

✦ *Hard disk.* At 180MB per minute, you'd fill a 500MB disk in less than three minutes. What's worse is that you eventually need to store multiple copies of your work, because you'll have both the raw capture files and your finished output. Working with about five minutes of clips, we quickly filled a 1GB partition containing nothing more than Windows, part of Microsoft Office, Adobe Photoshop, and Adobe Premiere. To us, that means that 4GB is comfortable for a few small video editing projects, but you'll want much more if you do a lot of video work.

If you do serious video editing, you might want to go beyond the performance of a fast Ultra2 SCSI disk and controller to the performance of a RAID disk subsystem. If you accept our recommendation of Windows NT, you can implement one simply by attaching multiple, identical disks to your machine and configuring them in Windows NT for software RAID. Whether you use software or hardware RAID, choose RAID 0 (striping) or 5 (striped parity) for higher performance handling video.

✦ *Video adapter and monitor.* The miro DC30 provides a real-time video overlay for real-time monitoring as you record or playback. The Adobe Premiere software uses DirectX access to the video card for playback. These techniques require a PCI video adapter to work, and you'll be handicapped in your work without those features. The video card radically impacts the processing workload, too. Figure 24-12 is a similar situation to that in Figure 24-11, except it's under Windows 95 rather than NT, is running on a 166 MHz Pentium processor with 64MB of memory, and (most important) is running on a far better video board. The measurement in Figure 24-11 is with a generic board we were testing; the one in Figure 24-12 is against an ATI Graphics Pro Turbo, and (accounting for a processor power difference of nearly two to one) shows around a ten to one reduction in processor load.

You're going to want a high-resolution display to work, too. The different control windows in Adobe Premiere each consume screen space, and if your screen doesn't have high enough resolution, you'll have to overlap them. I'll show you examples of why that's important in the "Video Editing Basics" Hands-On Upgrades section in this chapter.

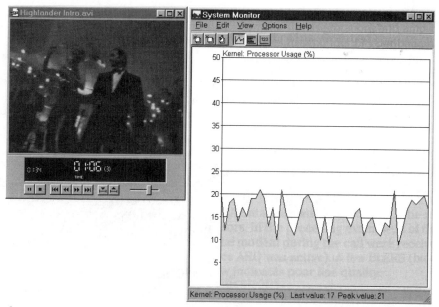

**Figure 24-12:** Good video hardware reduces the processing workload.

# Choosing a Digital Camera

In the summer of 1996, digital cameras with usable resolution were relatively expensive. By spring 1999, prices came down for equivalent performance, and available resolution went up. You can use a camera with 320 × 240 resolution for images you might put on Web pages, in on-screen slide presentations, or in reports where the image stays small enough to avoid pixel blockiness when printed. The later Kodak cameras can give you close to 2 million pixels of resolution at prices under $1,000; with photo-quality paper for inkjet printers, you can get 8 × 10 prints of comparable quality to what you'd do with a conventional camera and film.

Video conferencing-quality digital video is reasonably priced, although high-quality digital video capture remains expensive. New chips capable of real-time, broadcast-quality MPEG-2 compression went on the market in 1998 at prices of a few hundred dollars for the chip, so you can expect consumer-priced quality video compression products to come on the market in 1999 or 2000.

# Top Support Questions

An unfortunate number of the common questions for both still and video digital cameras center on problems connecting the camera to your computer. The easiest connections today use USB, so if you're buying a camera, see if your computer and camera can communicate that way.

## Digital cameras

Q: I don't seem to be able to hold many pictures in my camera. What can I do?

A: Most digital cameras can store images with varying degrees of compression. Table 24-9, for example, shows the options for the Kodak DC-120 along with the Kodak recommendation for maximum print size. The fourth column in the table shows how many pictures you can hold in the camera at once using the built-in 2MB memory.

### Table 24-9
### The Higher Compression Setting for the Kodak DC-120 Takes an Order of Magnitude Less Storage (Data Courtesy Eastman Kodak.)

| Image Quality Setting | Approximate Image Storage Size in Camera (KB) | Maximum Printed Size | Number of Images in 2MB |
|---|---|---|---|
| Uncompressed | 800 | Any print size | 2 |
| Best | 210 | 7.5 × 10 inches | 9 |
| Better | 120 | 4 × 6 inches | 17 |
| Good | 80 | 2.25 × 3 inches | 25 |

Your other option (so you can use higher resolutions and still get more pictures without downloading to the computer) is, for cameras that support it, to carry Compact Flash or PCMCIA memory cards. When one fills, you exchange it for another one. When they're all full, though, you have to download.

Q: Does the camera always have to be connected to a computer?

A: No. The camera only needs to be connected to a computer to download pictures. However, some cameras let you optionally control the camera and take pictures with computer on-screen controls. Using that feature requires a computer connection.

Q: Will pictures be lost if the camera's batteries go dead?

A: No. The memory in the camera is either disk, flash, or another form of nonvolatile memory. Your pictures remain stored in the camera until they are downloaded.

Q: Why is there a delay from the time I press the shutter button to the time the picture is actually taken?

A: A time delay may be caused by two things — power saving mode, and autofocus. If the camera has gone into power save, it takes a few seconds to wake up. In addition, the camera needs time to perform automatic focus measurements and set the lens.

Q: It takes too long to download pictures from my camera. How can I make it faster?

A: Assuming you're using the fastest serial port speed that works with your computer and camera, consider downloading through your laptop computer's PCMCIA slot or adding a PCMCIA adapter (such as is made by Eiger) to your desktop computer. The transfers from the camera memory card through the PCMCIA port are at speeds up to 2 MBps (16 Mbps), which is at least ten times faster than through the serial port. You'll get much faster downloads — up to a factor of 10 times faster — with a USB-capable camera and computer.

## Digital video cameras

Q: Does the camera always have to be connected to a computer?

A: Most likely yes. Digital video cameras rarely have enough internal storage to operate independent of your computer.

Q: How does the camera connect to my computer?

A: Digital video cameras are available that connect through the parallel port, a USB port, or an IEEE 1384 (FireWire) port. USB is likely to be the best choice for the next year or so, because IEEE 1384 has been slow to reach the market.

# Hands-On Upgrades

The jobs you do with digital and film cameras are similar, so you're right to expect that the way you use the two would be the same. Let's walk through what you do to get from taking a picture through having a print.

## From subject to image: digital darkroom

If you're using conventional film photography (and assuming you already have your camera), here's what you do:

✦ *Select your film.* Film comes in a variety of kinds, including color or black and white, fine/coarse grain, sensitivity, and number of exposures.

✦ *Pick your lens.* Depending on what you're doing, you'll want a lens focal length ranging from telephoto through normal to wide angle or macro. The sensitivity of the lens (f-stop) will vary depending on the length.

✦ *Set up the lighting and subject.* Whether you use a light meter or automatic exposure control, you need to set up the light, subject, and camera to get the picture you want with perfect exposure.

✦ *Shoot.* You then take the picture, being careful to not move the camera for the longer exposures. You might brace yourself against a wall, or use a tripod.

✦ *Develop.* When you're done shooting, you process the film. This involves running the film through controlled-temperature baths of complex organic chemicals in a controlled-temperature environment.

✦ *Print.* Finally, you'll select the images you want, apply whatever corrections it takes to compensate for problems when you took the picture, and print.

The makers of digital still cameras have worked at making the process for using their cameras as similar to that for film cameras as they can. Here's what you do:

✦ *Select your resolution and storage.* You can't affect the speed of the sensor in a digital camera, but your choice of compression affects resolution, and your choice of storage capacity affects how many exposures you can make.

✦ *Pick your lens.* Your camera may have a zoom lens, or it may have interchangeable lenses. If so, you'll pick focal length just like you do for film cameras. If you're trying to do high-resolution close-ups, be sure to have a lot of light, and use the macro setting on the lens if you have one.

✦ *Set up the lighting and subject.* What you'll do here is no different than with film, other than needing to adjust to the different speed and contrast characteristics of the digital sensor. Set up the light, subject, and camera to get the picture you want with perfect exposure.

✦ *Shoot.* You'll notice that the response of the camera when you push the shutter button is slightly delayed, allowing time for autofocus actions. There might be a delay for the camera to "wake up" — the limited power available from the batteries to run the electronics means that the camera has to be as aggressive as possible about limiting power consumption.

Some cameras can take a short burst of photos at once, but once you're done you'll notice that the camera takes a few seconds to recover after you take the picture. During this time the camera is compressing the image and storing it in nonvolatile memory. You can't take another picture until the process completes.

✦ *Download.* The digital equivalent of developing a picture is downloading it to your computer. You'll need a TWAIN driver for the camera if you're using the serial interface; if you're accessing the PCMCIA card directly, the pictures should look like files stored on a disk.

✦ *Print.* Instead of light and gelatin filters, you use an image processing program (such as Adobe Photoshop or Ulead Photoimpact) to manipulate and print your images.

Because of the efforts of the digital camera manufacturers to make the operation familiar, you don't have to learn a whole new procedure—you just have to adapt what you already know.

## Video-editing basics

Composing and editing video is somewhat different than handling digital still images. We've used Adobe Premiere as the basis for the following example, but other video editing software does similar things. Here's what you'll do:

✦ *Plan, set up, and shoot.* This is relatively standard—you figure out what the end content is going to be, set up the different scenes you need, and shoot. All the usual ideas (such as storyboards, rehearsal, and lighting) apply.

✦ *Capture the raw video and audio.* You need to get the video into your computer. You can record directly, with an IEEE 1384 camera, or with a conventional camera and a video acquisition card, or you may record onto tape that you then play back into the video acquisition card. You're better off putting each separate scene into a different file—you end up with smaller files (which are easier to handle) and have more flexibility to cut and splice scenes.

You can also dub external audio—music, narration, or other content—into your project. You'll want to record wave audio files of the raw material to use while editing.

**Tip**

We recommend making archive backups of all your clips for a given sequence once you've recorded them, so that they're not lost if you happen to make a mistake while editing. Your usual backup system (we use tape) is convenient for this if you don't have enough disk space to store copies of your raw video.

✦ *Start a new project and import raw clips.* Figure 24-13 shows a screen shot from Adobe Premiere in the middle of an editing session. We have the project window in the lower-left corner, and we have loaded up two raw clips into the project. The two clip preview windows (lower half of the figure) show frames from each clip, while the output preview lets you view the current finished product.

The image in Figure 24-13 is a screen shot at 1,600 × 1,200 resolution; as shot, the window you see completely filled the screen. It was quite readable on a 21-inch Hitachi monitor. If we'd had to use a lower resolution, we'd not have been able to tile the windows as you see. Instead, we'd have had to have them all overlap one another, making the work much slower and more tedious.

Output Preview          Output Construction          Clip Preview

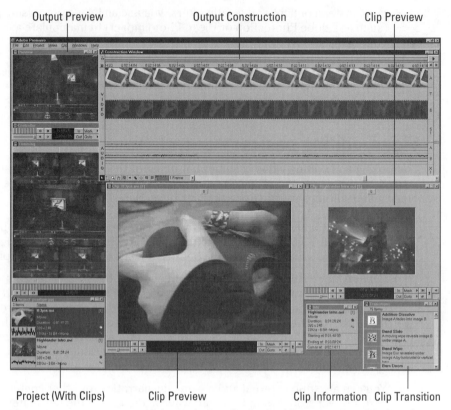

Project (With Clips)      Clip Preview          Clip Information  Clip Transition

**Figure 24-13:** You want a high-resolution display and large monitor for digital video editing.

✦ *Cut, splice, overlay, and filter to create the composite output.* You create your composite output sequence in the output construction windows shown in Figure 24-13 (at the top). You can load multiple clips in the window, position them relative to each other, and use a variety of effects to splice one into another.

✦ *Output to file or video tape.* When you're finished editing, you'll output either to a file playable on a computer or back on to video tape through a capable video acquisition card (the miro DC30 *plus* will do this). If you're capturing and recording video tape, be sure to use the S-Video inputs and outputs to retain as much image quality as you can.

# Summary

✦ Digital still cameras let you get at your images faster, and without a scanner, but they may not provide the resolution you need. The LCD viewfinders on some models may be difficult to use outdoors in sunlight.

✦ If you're willing to pay what high-end digital still cameras cost, and you're a good photographer, you can get professional-quality photographs with a digital camera.

✦ Data rates for raw, full-screen television video are greater than most computers can handle, requiring decimation, reduced frame rates, and/or compression to handle in a PC.

✦ Desktop video conferencing over your local area network or the Internet can provide great communications at very low cost.

✦ You won't do the next blockbuster film on one, but high-end personal computers have become useful workstations for quality digital video editing.

✦    ✦    ✦

# Scanners

## CHAPTER 25

**S**canners do a specific, direct thing—they convert a printed image into an image in your computer. The image comes in as a bitmap—a rectangular array of pixels—from the scanner itself, so it doesn't matter if you're scanning pictures, text, or a combination of the two. The essential characteristics of a scanner that define what kind of work you do with it are these:

◆ *Mechanism.* Scanners pass your image by a sensor. The mechanism that creates that movement can be one of several types, affecting the precision of the results you get and the price you'll pay for the scanner.

◆ *Color or black and white.* You can get either color or black-and-white scanners. Black and white will be less expensive, but a color scanner is more versatile (and may solve some problems on black-and-white copy).

◆ *Resolution.* As with a digital camera, a scanner turns your image into a bitmap. The number of pixels per inch in the bitmap—the resolution of the scanner—determines the quality of what you'll see on your screen or printer and affects the accuracy of converting scanned text into characters.

◆ *Interface.* Scanners come with a variety of electronic interfaces, ranging from serial ports and SCSI to USB. The interface you use determines how fast the image can get into your computer, and whether or not you have a suitable port on your computer.

◆ *Software.* More so than many other devices, scanners require application software to really be useful, to let you acquire, edit, crop, publish, and convert images to text.

Let's take at look at each one of these.

## In This Chapter

Scanner mechanisms, color, resolution, interfaces, and software

Hand, roller-driven, and flatbed scanners

Raw and interpolated resolution

Optical character recognition

# Mechanisms

Most digital still cameras use a rectangular sensor array so that they can capture the entire picture at one time. Scanners are different — they use a line sensor in conjunction with a mechanism that sequentially moves the sensor relative to the paper to capture the entire image. The mechanism works one of three ways:

✦ *Hand scanners.* You hold the scanner in your hand, moving it across the paper.

✦ *Roller-driven scanners.* The scanner sensor stays stationary while a set of rollers moves the paper past it.

✦ *Flatbed scanners.* The paper stays stationary while the scanner slides the sensor along it.

## Hand scanners

Some of the least expensive scanners are ones where you roll the scan head along the paper. Hand scanners are usually only a few inches wide, so if you want to scan an entire page, you have to scan it in strips and paste the strips together. The scanner senses movement along the paper with a roller, using that input to tell how fast and how far you're moving the head (which in turn lets the scanner software know when to capture the next line of the image).

The scan-in-strips idea is problematic. It's hard to line up the strips exactly adjacent to each other, to keep the scanner tracking straight on the page, and to keep the strips exactly parallel. These problems make it impossible to simply paste strips one to another — you have to correct the errors in software. Some of the scanners come with software just for this purpose, but it takes time to do and isn't going to create a result as precise as if you had scanned the whole image at once.

## Roller-driven scanners

Another approach to scanning is to mount the sensor in a fixed place in the body of the scanner and then pass the paper through a set of drive rollers and past the sensor. The entire page gets scanned in one pass this way, eliminating most of the problems of hand scanners.

However, there are problems with roller-driven scanners. You can't put everything between the rollers (like books), and variations in thickness or other problems with the feed process can cause the paper to move unevenly past the sensor. If the paper doesn't move evenly, you'll end up with a distortion in that area of the scan.

## Flatbed scanners

The third way to scan documents is to hold the paper stationary on the scanner and move the sensor (inside the scanner) past the paper. As long as the sensor mount and drive mechanism are designed well, this approach results in precise, accurate scans. The ability to close a door over the document retains a closed light environment during the scan, allowing the device to control exposure to what the sensor needs.

If you're feeding stacks of paper into the scanner to scan successive pages, you'll want to consider a document feeder. These are most often accessories for flatbed scanners, usually holding 10 to 50 pages and supporting automatic scanning once you start the operation. (High-end production scanners can hold far more than this and can scan far faster than the rates of the units discussed in this chapter.)

# Color or Black and White

You can get scanners that produce either color or black-and-white images. The sensors are color independent, reacting merely to light intensity, so if we shine a white light on the image, the sensor will give us a black-and-white scan.

It's a little harder for color — the red, green, and blue intensities need to be sampled and recorded independently. That means the color of the light the sensor sees to be red, green, or blue (but not combinations of them) needs to be controlled. Designers use one of two strategies to do this:

✦ *Filters*. A color filter in front of the sensor restricts the light from the image to just that in one of the red, green, or blue spectra. The sensor blindly reports light intensity, unaware that we've limited what it can see.

✦ *Lights*. Instead of shining white light on the image and filtering it down, we can use lights that only emit the right spectra, choosing which color is on at any given time.

Because the scanner has to alternate the filters or lights, the designer has to make a choice — alternate during one pass over the image, or make multiple passes (one per color). Scanners operate at relatively high resolution, which means that this isn't a completely simple decision:

✦ *One pass*. If the scanner designer chooses to scan all three colors in one pass, it's easier to ensure the images on all three color channels are tightly aligned, but the scanner has to be able to turn the lights on and off quickly. The sensor then has to unload its data three times as quickly, because there's three times as much of it. If that's not possible, the scanner has to move along the image more slowly.

All hand scanners and roller-driven scanners are one-pass models — it's not reasonable to try to control the registration of the paper between passes closely enough to make multiple passes. A flatbed scanner can do multiple passes because all the moving parts are inside the scanner body, where tolerances can be carefully controlled.

✦ *Multipass.* The other way to scan is to turn on one color light, make a complete scan, go back to the beginning, turn on a second color, scan, and so on. This eliminates the complexity of having to change colors rapidly and so is more compatible with the idea of using colored filters. It's very important to precisely align the three scans so that when they're combined on your screen the images have sharp edges. Misalignment among passes shows up much like misconvergence on a color monitor.

## Number of colors

For a fixed resolution on the scanner, there's three times more data required for color than for black and white. It's common for scanners to use 8 bits per pixel per color, so a black-and-white scan commonly reads up to 256 shades of gray. A color scanner will most likely use 24 or more bits per pixel (8 or more bits per color for each of three colors). That means the color scanner can resolve to one of over 16 million colors, catching more subtle nuances in the image than the black-and-white one can.

This last point—that a color scanner can produce a better result than a black-and-white scanner—is true even if you're scanning black-and-white copy, but not because it can resolve over 16 million colors. After all, if the copy is truly grayscale (and the scanner is calibrated properly), each of the three color channels should see the same intensity at every point of the image. Getting the same result from three channels instead of one adds no new information and doesn't improve the scan.

Tip

The reason a color scanner can be advantageous for black-and-white copy is because it can be used to drop out colors. Suppose, for example, that you have copy that's become discolored. Many scanners can be set to scan with only one color, so if you choose a color that causes the discoloration to not show up, you'll clean up the image in the process of scanning.

## Color matching

The first time you scan a color image, you're likely to be in for a nasty shock—the piece of paper in your hand isn't likely to look at all like what you get on-screen, and neither one is likely to look like what comes out of your color printer. About that time you're going to understand exactly what that odd phrase "color matching" is all about.

From a hardware perspective, it's not at all surprising that you get differing results—in fact, it's nothing short of a miracle if you get matching colors without doing anything to make that happen. All your devices have independent calibrations, use different color technologies, and in some cases even represent colors using systems different from the red-green-blue system we've talked about (see the sidebar "RGB, CMY, and some other alphabet soup"). Most products don't include options supporting color matching—largely because there's been no industry standard for how to do this. Windows 95 introduced Image Color Matching (ICM), and as hardware and software products have adopted that standard, there has been some improvement in coordination among products. Until then, you'll have to check out the capabilities of each hardware and software product and see if it does what you need.

## RGB, CMY, and some other alphabet soup

It's not practical for scanners, monitors, printers, or other devices to directly sample every possible color—there's just too many of them. Even your eyes don't (the red-green-blue, or RGB, color model is patterned after the response of your eyes to color). Instead, all these devices use combinations of a few colors, just as children do with finger paints.

So the question really is, why is there more than one color model?

The most obvious reason is that there are two sorts of color mixing—transmitted light and reflected light. These basic mixing approaches are called additive and subtractive mixing, respectively. See-through filters and color monitors use additive mixing, which corresponds well to the RGB model. When a color monitor has to create yellow, it turns on both the blue and green pixels. The light from both combines to form yellow.

Now, imagine a red filter with a light shining on it. If you're on the opposite side of the filter, you'll see red light transmitted through the filter. This is the same thing that filters in a color LCD screen do. If you stand on the other side of the filter, though, you'll see not the transmitted light—you'll get the reflected light. The green and blue light that didn't get transmitted through the filter gets reflected, and that's what you see. Those colors combine to form yellow, so if you look at light reflected off a red filter, you'll see yellow. (This doesn't work if you put white paper behind the filter, because the red then reflects back through the filter and becomes visible.)

This effect—that a red filter reflects yellow light—happens because the reflected light from the filter uses a subtractive mixing color model. Subtractive mixing is also what happens with images printed on paper. The primary colors for a subtractive model aren't red, green, and blue; they're cyan, magenta, and yellow (CMY).

Of course, life isn't that simple. It's hard to get good, saturated colors with only cyan, magenta, and yellow, so printers use a fourth color—black. The resulting color model is called CMYK. It creates better colors, but not ones as good as spot color models (such as the Pantone Matching System) that mix more than four colors.

Video has its own color models, because some camera technologies work better with other color sets than RGB, and because different video compression technologies work better in some color models than others.

Your end goal is that, in fact, what you scan is what you see on the screen, and that both of those match what comes off the printer. Each component will likely have its own color adjustments in software. Scanner adjustments can often be done in the scanner software that reads in the image, and if not, they can be done in the image processing software you use. Display color correction generally requires enhanced drivers from the manufacturer. UNIX drivers and the drivers packaged with Windows itself usually don't have correction capabilities, so check the manufacturer's Web site. Printer color correction is usually in the printer driver but may also be accommodated by your image-processing software.

# Resolution

We sometimes think that scanners are a lot like used cars, because there's a very peculiar sort of specification that's become common for them, and you have to be careful that you know what you're getting. Specifically, scanner manufacturers report one or both of two different resolutions:

✦ *Raw.* This is the actual resolution produced by the scanner sensor, in dots per inch. Like monitors and printers, scanners have both vertical and horizontal resolutions, and the two numbers don't have to be the same.

✦ *Interpolated.* This is the specification that may or may not give you what you paid for. Many scanners process the scanned image (often in your computer) to compute more pixels than you actually read off the scanner. They do it by assuming that the change between one pixel and the next is linear.

Take a look at Figures 25-1 and 25-2. In Figure 25-1, the actual image changes smoothly, and so calculating the interpolated pixels based on the linear assumption works well—the added pixels correspond well to what's in the image.

In Figure 25-2, the assumption is a poor one, because the real image has sharp edges the interpolator doesn't know about. Because the interpolator's assumption is bad, the "increased resolution" from the scanner does you no good because the calculated data is bogus. Your scanned image doesn't faithfully reproduce the actual image at the enhanced resolution. *Caveat (scanner) emptor.*

At the minimum, you'll want to be sure to find out the raw resolution of the scanners you're looking at. If you can't find out, find another scanner.

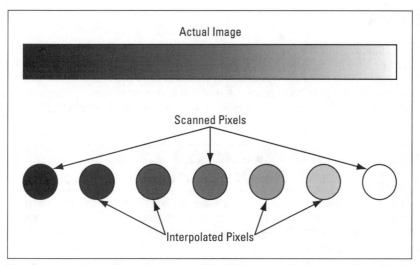

**Figure 25-1:** If your image has smooth intensity or color changes, the added pixels from interpolation can increase the apparent resolution of the scan.

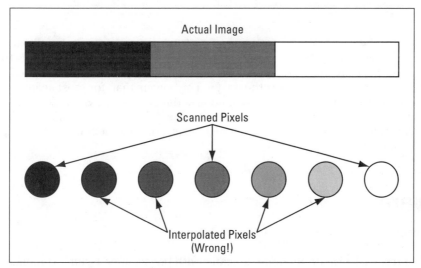

**Figure 25-2:** If your image has sharp images, the interpolator may be fooled into blurring them in the added pixels.

# Interfaces

Scanners typically interface into your computer through a serial port, parallel port, SCSI port, or USB port. Table 25-1 shows that the SCSI port is worth having if you'll be doing large, high-resolution scans, but that will only be true if the scanner processes fast enough to take advantage of the faster interface. (We've assumed in the table that a SCSI scanner has at most a narrow, fast SCSI interface.)

| Table 25-1 Typical Speeds of Scanner Interfaces | | |
|---|---|---|
| *Interface* | *Typical Speed* | *Minimum Time for 4MB Scan (seconds)* |
| Serial | 115,200 Kbps | 291 |
| Parallel | 2 Mbps | 16 |
| SCSI | 5 Mbps | 6.4 |
| USB (slow) | 1.5 Mbps | 213 |
| USB (fast) | 12 Mbps | 2.7 |

In real life, however, scanners (other than professional ones) don't do full-page scans in 6 seconds, so they're not keeping the fast bus busy. Times in the 15- to 30-second range are more common, with the time being primarily determined by the rate the sensor traverses the image. This means that, for most scanners, a parallel port interface is fast enough, but a serial port is not. We prefer USB or SCSI scanners because they are easier to set up and less prone to configuration problems than ones using serial or parallel ports. For most people, USB is the ideal scanner interface.

# Software

You need two kinds of software to use a scanner:

✦ *Driver.* A device driver communicates with the scanner, issuing commands and reading back data. Most scanners now use a control interface called TWAIN, which serves as a standard way for any image-processing program to acquire data from an image source. TWAIN decouples specific knowledge of how to drive the scanner out of the image-processing software, making the application programs device independent.

✦ *Image processing.* Beyond the device driver, you need a program to (at least) initiate the scan, receive the image, and store it to disk. Programs like that come with every scanner we've seen. If you want to do anything other than look at (and possibly print) the image, you'll need a more sophisticated program that can adjust colors, crop, and otherwise manipulate the image (Kai's Power Tools or Adobe PhotoShop, for instance). Once you have the image you want, you can incorporate it into most other Windows or X Window (the UNIX graphical user interface) programs.

In addition, you may want software that can convert scanned text images to text. That conversion process, called *optical character recognition (OCR)*, matches pieces of the image with guidelines for what each character looks like, and outputs a "typed" document. The good OCR programs are not only accurate, they can help you deal with pages that have combinations of text and graphics, can accommodate text wrapped in columns throughout the page, and can output the page in your word processor's format with the necessary control codes included to make the text look like what you scanned.

Scanner resolution interacts with OCR accuracy and processing time. The OCR programs are generally at least as fast as a scanner—they take less time to turn the page into text than the scanner took to capture the image in the first place—so there's no real loss in using higher scanner resolution. We conducted some experiments with Caere's WordScan Plus, for example, and noticed that recognition accuracy improved significantly when we simply boosted the scanner resolution from 300 to 400 dots per inch.

# Products

People do a wide variety of things with scanned images, so it's predictable that there's a wide variety of scanners available.

## UMAX Astra 2000U

The UMAX Astra 2000U2000U (Figure 25-3) is a one pass color flatbed scanner with a USB interface offering 36-bit color and 600 × 1200 dpi resolution. Features and characteristics are in Table 25-2. You can scan sizes from business cards up to standard letter. The unit takes 41 seconds to scan a 4 × 6 inch color image at 300 dpi, so it's really for relatively light duty. (Versions are available with parallel port and SCSI interfaces, too.) In the second half of 1999, we found it advertised on the Internet for US $109, so it's relatively inexpensive. The scanner includes Adobe PhotoDeluxe and Caere OmniPage LE OCR software, plus a utility for simplified page copying. You can get an optional transparency adapter that lets you scan slides, overheads, and transparencies.

### Table 25-2
### UMAX Astra 2000U Features and Specifications

| Characteristic | Specification |
|---|---|
| Maximum image size | 8.5 × 11.7 inches |
| Typical scan time | 36 seconds for a 4 × 5 inch color image at 300 dpi |
| Color depth | 36- and 24-bit color, 12- and 8-bit grayscale, 1-bit halftone, and 1-bit line. |
| Raw resolution | 600 × 1,200 dpi |
| Interpolated resolution | 9600 x 9600 |
| Interface | USB |
| Software | TWAIN driver, Adobe PhotoDeluxe, Caere OmniPage LE OCR, and others |
| Operating System | Windows 9x |

## HP ScanJet 6250C Professional Color Scanner

The HP ScanJet 6250C Professional Color Scanner (Figure 25-3) is a 36-bit color flatbed scanner with an attached sheet feeder. Controls on the scanner let you select a part of the page to scan, eliminating the need to crop separately after the scan is done, and speeding scan times. Software included with the scanner — in addition to the usual Caere OCR and Adobe PhotoDeluxe — includes tools to convert line drawings to scalable files printable at any resolution and software to fax your scanned images. An adapter to scan 35mm slides is included.

The scanner comes with a USB or SCSI interface. Table 25-3 shows the key features.

### Table 25-3
### HP ScanJet 6250C Professional Color Scanner Specifications

| Characteristic | Specification |
|---|---|
| Maximum image size | 8.5 × 11.7 inches; 8.5 × 14 inches with automatic document feeder |
| Typical scan time | 6, 4.5, and 3 milliseconds per line in color |
| Color depth | 36-bit color |

| Characteristic | Specification |
|---|---|
| Raw resolution | 1,200 dpi |
| Interpolated resolution | Unlimited |
| Interface | USB or SCSI |
| Software | TWAIN driver, image acquisition and editing, OCR, and faxing, and network sharing |

**Figure 25-3:** The HP ScanJet 6250C Professional Color Scanner is a 36-bit sheet-fed color flatbed scanner bundled with software for image acquisition, editing, line drawing conversion, OCR, and faxing. (Photo courtesy HP.)

# Choosing a Scanner

More than the network or video equipment we looked at in the last few chapters, what you need in a scanner very much depends on the specific work you do — there are scanners specifically targeted at the "fun" user, at OCR, and at higher-quality graphics capture. Keep in mind as well that the quality of what you get is very much dependent on what you scan — you can't create quality that's not there in the source document.

You'll probably want to avoid scanners built into keyboards and computers themselves. The reliability of the mechanisms in a scanner isn't as good as that of the computers and keyboards themselves, so it's likely that the scanner will break before the rest of the unit. When it does, you take the entire unit out of commission, meaning you're without a computer or keyboard while it gets fixed. Not a great idea.

Shopping carefully for a scanner, looking at both software and hardware included in the bundle, can save a lot of money — some scanners come packaged with very competent software such as Kai's Power Tools or Adobe PhotoDeluxe, software that costs hundreds of dollars when bought separately.

**Tip**    Keep in mind that graphics-processing programs use a lot of memory. In addition to having enough memory in your system for good performance (64MB is probably the minimum you'd want if you use the scanner a lot), you want to make sure that there's a lot of free disk space on the drive with your swap file.

In most offices, you'll want a capable general-purpose color scanner rather than one specialized to a certain task. If your scanning workload is large enough, you could consider letting one or another of the scanners be more specialized. Most small offices don't have the volume of scan work to justify multiple scanners, however, and many don't have the volume to justify a document feeder. Keep track of how much time you spend tending the scanner, though, and if it starts to become noticeable, consider a feeder. It doesn't take many saved hours of labor (scarce in many offices) to pay back the added cost.

# Top Support Questions

## Scanners

Q: What is a driver and what kind of driver do I need for my scanner?

A: A driver is a software interface that (in this case) mediates between your application software and the scanner. Most scanners use interface software written to the TWAIN standard. Another, less common standard you might see is ISIS; some old software may also look for a DOS device driver. You almost always get scanner drivers from the scanner manufacturer.

Q: Can I connect the scanner to my computer's parallel port which is used for the printer?

A: Maybe. Some scanners specifically require an 8-bit bidirectional parallel port. This may exclude standard, EPP, and ECP parallel ports. If your system has the parallel port on the motherboard, check in your CMOS setup to see if the mode can be changed from its current setting to bidirectional. If you use LPT2 for your scanner port, be aware that it requires IRQ 5, which is the default for many sound cards as well. You could end up with a conflict resolvable only by moving the sound card resources.

Q: What resolution should I scan images at?

A: For printing, double the resolution of the printer. For example, if you have a 300 dpi printer, scan at 600 dpi (if you can). This allows the image processing software to downsample to the printer resolution with as few artifacts as possible. For on-screen display, scan at the screen resolution (typically 120 dpi for high-resolution screens).

Q: Can any SCSI scanner be used with any SCSI host adapter?

A: No. Most SCSI cards run under Windows use the ASPI (Advanced SCSP Programming Interface) standard; however, not all scanners do. Your chances are better with a recent model scanner. Check with the scanner manufacturer regarding compatibility with third-party SCSI cards and, when connecting the scanner, be sure you get the termination configured properly.

# Hands-On Upgrades

Scanners used to be tricky to install, and (without a high performance machine) slow and difficult to use. The phenomenal increase in computer performance over the past few years, combined with the simplicity of USB hardware installations, should be all it takes to overcome the fear factor and get a lot of value from a scanner. To make the point, this section covers how to install a USB scanner and how to use optical character recognition software with your scanner to convert scanned images to text.

## USB Scanner Installation

Here's the short version of how to install a USB scanner like the UMAX Astra 2000U: plug it in to the USB port, plug in the power, and install the software. It's really as easy as that.

Nevertheless, let's look at a little more detail.

Figure 25-4 shows the back panel of the Astra 2000U, including the USB and power connectors. The USB connector is the square connector on the left (under the label USB); the power connector is the round one on the right.

**Figure 25-4:** The USB connector on the left of the back panel of the Astra 2000U accepts the USB data cable to connect the scanner to your computer.

Figure 25-5, in turn, shows the interface cable connectors. Although both are USB connectors, the shapes at either end are different — the square connector goes in the back of the scanner, while the flat, rectangular one goes in the back of your computer.

After you connect the USB cable, plug in the power block. That completes hardware setup. Software setup is even easier — insert the CD-ROM into the drive and follow the prompts. You'll probably want to accept all the options. If setup doesn't start automatically, find setup.exe on the CD-ROM and run it. We recommend you use Windows 98 Second Edition with the USB scanner — the USB support is better developed and more robust.

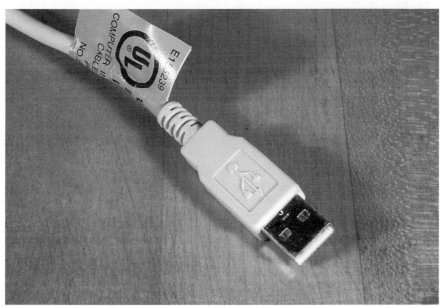

**Figure 25-5:** The USB cable has a square (top) and flat (bottom) connector, corresponding to the USB connectors on the scanner and computer respectively.

# Optical Character Recognition

A scanner converts images into raster images, sequences of dots that taken together look like the original image. That's directly useful if you merely wanted a copy of the image, but not so useful if what you wanted was editable text.

Optical Character Recognition (OCR) programs do the work required to convert the dots back into text. Doing the conversion requires that the program distinguish pictures from text; figure out which groups of dots form each character; and account for differences in font face, size, spacing, and orientation. Figure 25-6 shows some of the problems developers of OCR software have to solve.

✦ *What's a character?* Your eye easily recognizes that the symbol at the top of the images in Figure 25-4 is a logo, not a character. You know that because it's too different from any character in any common font. Similarly, you know that the characters I, D, and G are characters because (although you may or may not recognize the font), they are similar enough to known characters in common Latin fonts.

**Figure 25-6:** Optical character recognition has to solve problems of finding characters in the image and decoding what each one is.

✦ *Where are the characters?* Not all characters in all fonts are connected sets of dots. For example, if you look at the dots at the right of the D and left of the G, disregarding the other parts of those characters, you can easily imagine the pattern to be an X.

✦ *What's the font?* The letters in Figure 25-4 are all uppercase and are all in a single font. Real-world text is commonly in mixed case, mixed sizes, and mixed fonts (not to mention italic, underline, and bold). The number of variations the program must search goes up dramatically with the number of options in the text.

✦ *Defects in the scanned image.* Compare the images at the left and right of Figure 25-4. We scanned the left image at 100 dpi, and the right one at 400 dpi. You can clearly see the difference in the edges of the characters and lines, even though in the original image the letters are a full 0.25 inch high. If we'd scanned smaller text, the dots you see in the left-hand image would be a significant fraction of the character, making it harder to decide what the pattern is. If the image isn't of good quality to begin with (this was an engraved business card), you may get dropouts in the text, which can confuse the OCR software.

There isn't much you can do about the source image you're running the OCR software over. If you have a choice (such as how the text is printed before being faxed to you), ask for a fixed-pitch font (such as Courier), and use relatively large characters (12 or 14 point text). You might want to try having all characters bolded to eliminate thin lines in the characters.

Once you have the image, try these techniques:

✦ *Scan in color, then drop out dirt and light colors with an image processing program.* Your OCR software can only be so sophisticated, and in general it's going to have more problems with multicolored, low-contrast images. If you can use an image processing program (such as Adobe PhotoShop) on the image first, you can convert the image to pure black and white, dropping out background noise and graphics.

✦ *Tell the OCR software where the text is.* Most OCR software lets you define the regions where text is found, and whether or not the text is wrapped in newspaper-like columns. Defining the text areas lets the program ignore graphics and other noise on the page.

✦ *Scan at the highest physical resolution you can.* Figure 25-4 shows the effect of low-resolution scans. Using the highest resolution the scanner optics can deliver helps the software find the edges of characters and pick out small features in them.

You can always type in source material — OCR is something you do to save time. You'll want to test and fine-tune your OCR tools before you need them; otherwise, the time it takes to get set up could well be longer than the time to simply type the material (and longer than you have!).

# Summary

✦ You'll prefer the results of a roller-driven or flatbed scanner to a hand scanner.

✦ Interpolated resolution isn't the same as raw optical resolution — don't get fooled by inflated specifications.

✦ You can use OCR to create editable text from a printed page.

✦ Choose your scanner on the basis of the work you expect to do.

✦    ✦    ✦

# Printers and All-in-One Units

The paperless society hasn't happened, despite radio, television, and computers. You'll ultimately need to get some part of what you do with your computer onto paper. That means you'll need a printer.

## Getting the Ink (Only) Where It Belongs

Computer printers for personal computers started out as adapted typewriters (see the sidebar "Not your parents' Selectric anymore"). Instead of being driven by a keyboard (although some had them), they received instructions from the computer. Operation notwithstanding, they remained typewriters inside.

The point of a printer isn't to be a typewriter, of course; it's to get ink on paper in just the right amount and in just the right place. The same technology that created the microprocessors that drive your computer created smaller microprocessors that could be built into printers. When that happened, designers discovered that they could abandon the typewriter-based approach and build printers based on the job that needed to be done. When they started looking at how to do high-quality graphics along with text, they noticed that copiers and monitors (that is, raster-based devices) were a better starting point. The result was the range of printing technology we can choose from today, including laser and ink jet printers.

### Ink jet printers

Ink jet printers are really high-tech versions of the older dot matrix printers. An ink jet printer cartridge (see the side view in Figure 26-1) has an ink reservoir and some circuitry—the interface circuit and impulse drivers, and the nozzles—down at the bottom:

✦ *Ink reservoir.* The reservoir has to ensure a continuous, uninterrupted supply of ink to the drivers and nozzles. It has to prevent sloshing and foaming as the head moves. The ink composition is very important—it has to flow smoothly out of the reservoir, not clog the tiny holes in the impulse drivers and nozzles, have enough surface tension to avoid smearing as it is ejected from the nozzle, dry soon enough to maintain the image, and avoid wicking out on the paper fibers (which would make the image fuzzy).

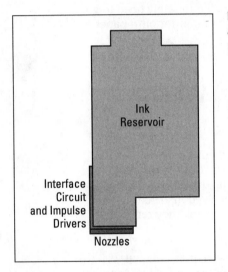

**Figure 26-1:** An ink jet cartridge contains all the high-precision parts of an ink jet printer in a disposable unit.

✦ *Interface circuit and impulse drivers.* The printer electronics command the driver behind each nozzle independently, so a high-resolution printer contains a lot of separate circuits. Each is terminated at a connecting point on the side of the cartridge that lines up with a corresponding pin on the print head. The interface circuit (a flexible printed circuit) routes these signals down to the impulse drivers and nozzles at the bottom of the cartridge.

When activated, the impulse drivers force a small drop of ink through the nozzle (one below each driver) and onto the paper that's in contact with the head. There are two ways impulse drivers work—some companies use a small piezoelectric crystal (one that expands when hit with an electrical impulse); others use a small ball of vapor produced by heating a pocket of ink. Figure 26-2 shows the effect of the driver—forcing a small, precisely measured drop of ink down through the nozzle and onto the paper.

## Not your parents' Selectric anymore

Engineers adapted electric typewriters—then one of the few electrical printing devices—to create the early personal computer printers. Mainframe printers had long used faster, larger-scale approaches but weren't in the price range required for PC printers. Typewriters were basically mechanical devices, driven by motors, levers, and cams, that could be controlled by electrical signals. Adapting them for computer interfaces simply required that the incoming characters "typed" by the computer be translated within the printer to the equivalent action on the (now removed) keyboard. All of the electric typewriter mechanisms—the banks of typewriter keys, the daisy wheels, and the golf balls—applied directly, letting these printers create high-quality, proportionally spaced text.

High-quality electric typewriters were relatively expensive, though, and the fact that a computer can "type" far faster than people meant that a quality mechanism was mandatory. To create printers at a lower price point, engineers developed the "dot matrix" printer, in which printing was accomplished by a print head that moved back and forth sideways across the paper. The head typically had from 9 to 24 independent pins stacked vertically that could fire toward the paper, creating a dot where they pushed the ribbon against the paper.

Dot matrix printers solved a problem with typewriters, which was that changing fonts required mechanically changing the type ball or wheel. In a dot matrix printer, the font is determined by the order in which the pins fire as the head sweeps across the page, which means that the font is really just a data table stored in the printer's microprocessor (or downloaded from your computer). The limitation to this approach was that the pins can only be so small, after which you can't generate enough force to whack the ribbon against the paper without damaging the pins.

The matrix pin size limitation forced printer designers to look at other approaches. One was to adapt copiers, substituting a laser writing on a photosensitive drum for an optical imaging lens system that had the same purpose. The other was to transform the dot matrix into the ink jet printer, in which the ink transports itself against the paper, allowing microscopic dots and higher resolution.

The operation of the drivers and nozzles is shown by comparing the leftmost nozzle in Figure 26-2 with the one next to it. In the leftmost nozzle, the driver isn't activated, so the surface tension of the ink keeps it confined to the nozzle. In the next nozzle, the driver has activated, ejecting the ink out of the nozzle and onto the paper.

✦ *Nozzles.* The nozzles establish the precise position of the dots relative to one another and form the physical interface between the print cartridge and the paper.

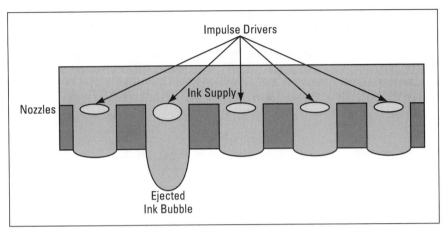

**Figure 26-2:** The impulse drivers create small bubbles, forcing drops of ink out from the nozzles.

The print head positions the cartridge laterally along the paper. The nozzle spacing positions the dots the printer puts on the paper perpendicularly to the head movement, while the printer electronics time the signals sent to the cartridge with the head motion to position the dots laterally. The net result is that ink jet printers — the modern version of the old dot matrix technology — can today achieve resolution of 1,440 dots per inch in both directions, a resolution competitive with laser printers.

It's relatively straightforward to create a color ink jet printer — you simply have three or four heads (using the CMY or CMYK color model; see Chapter 25, "Scanners," for information on color models) and carefully track the relative position of the heads among one another. Color ink jet printers often use one or two cartridges to do this, with cyan, magenta, and yellow in one and (optionally) black in the other. Some color ink jets use four separate cartridges, one per color.

When there are multiple cartridges, a calibration process is required to make sure they are physically lined up. Typically, the printer will output a set of test patterns, requiring you to select the specific pattern that has the best alignment.

You can recycle ink jet cartridges. Details for Canon cartridges are on the Web at `http://www.usa.canon.com/contacts/usedcart.html`. Recycling details for Hewlett-Packard cartridges are at `http://www.hp.com/ijbu`.

## Laser printers

Laser printers use fine, dry ink particles (called toner) to create an image on paper. This is the same process used in copiers. The key laser printer components are shown in Figure 26-3. The process starts at the point between the charging roller and the photoconductor drum. The charging roller imposes an electrical charge on the drum, which causes it to repel the toner particles. The drum rotates under the laser (which sweeps back and forth in lines), and everywhere the laser illuminates the drum, the charge dissipates. Those points will attract toner from the toner roller — the laser effectively draws black and gray areas on the drum. The drum continues to turn, bringing the patterned toner image into contact with the paper. The transfer roller attracts the toner to the paper, where it sticks. The combination of the fuser roller and the backup roller heat the toner, bonding it to the paper and making a permanent image.

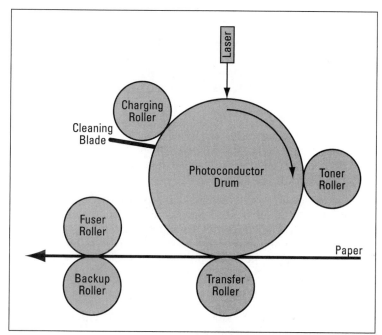

**Figure 26-3:** The laser writes onto the photoconductor drum where the image should be dark, allowing the drum to pick up black toner particles.

The laser is under the control of the raster processor in the printer, which has the responsibility of turning the codes sent from your computer into a bitmap of the image to appear on the page. This is a similar process to what GDI does (see Chapter 18, "Video Adapters") when it converts commands from your software into a raster on the screen.

The same arithmetic — counting pixels — that causes your video card to need a lot of memory causes your printer to need memory as well. The raster processor generally can't keep up with the photoconductor drum as it rotates, and the drum can't stop in the middle of a page (because the image would end up distorted). That means that the entire image has to be in memory when the drum starts to rotate to print the page. If we assume quarter-inch margins and multiply out the number of pixels on a page at 600 dots per inch (a typical laser printer resolution), we find that we have nearly 32 million dots on an 8.5 × 11-inch page. If each pixel takes one bit in memory, we need nearly 4MB to hold the entire page (more if we're storing fonts as well).

Printers that enhance the apparent resolution of the image by controlling the darkness of each dot may require even more memory—if the printer can store four levels of intensity per dot, it needs nearly 8MB. Many printers are starting to compress the raster image in memory, decompressing it on the fly as the laser scans the page. Using lossless compression, this technique can reduce memory requirements by a factor of 1.5 or 2 to 1 or more.

You can get laser toner in different colors besides black (even for a black-and-white printer). Color laser printers use four sets of toner to create the image, typically making four passes around the photoconductor drum (one for each color) before imprinting the image on the paper. Because the image has to be rasterized separately for each color, the printer's memory requirements go up drastically. It's not unusual to require 32MB in a color laser printer (which, along with the more complex mechanism and lower sales volume, is why they're expensive).

## Solid ink printers

Solid ink printers work a lot like a child with a crayon—there's a solid stick of colored material that gets transferred to the paper. The method a child uses (rubbing the crayon on the paper) isn't precise and fine enough for a computer printer, though, so instead a solid ink printer melts the crayon to create an ink fluid and delivers the ink to the paper much like an ink jet printer. The ink hardens on the paper, leaving a sharp image. Separate crayons provide the cyan, magenta, yellow, and black colors.

Printers using solid ink technology produce printed results competitive with color laser printers, at about the same up-front cost.

## Thermal wax transfer printers

A thermal wax transfer printer, unlike all the other printer types we've looked at, uses a ribbon; in that sense it is much like a dot matrix printer. Heating elements replace the impact pins, though; when one of the very fine elements heats, it melts the colored wax on the ribbon and transfers a dot onto the paper. When you reach the end of the ribbon it has to be replaced, even though most of the wax remains on the ribbon. This is because (unlike an ink ribbon) the wax is either there or not, and you can't be sure that the dot you want to leave on the second ribbon pass isn't already used up.

# The cost of printing

Table 26-1 helps you compare the cost to print a page using different color printer technologies. In the table, the base page cost is what you pay for feeding a sheet of paper through the printer. For laser, ink jet, and solid ink printers, it's the cost of the paper itself. For wax transfer, it includes the cost of the wax ribbon, because it's used up whether you printed anything on the page or not. The relative density factor measures how much it costs per page depending on how densely the ink appears on the page (multiply the factor times the page density as a percentage). Laser and ink jet have about the same density cost, solid ink is more expensive, and wax transfer incurs no added expense (you paid it all when you fed the sheet to begin with).

| Color Technology | Laser | | Ink Jet | | Solid Ink | | Wax Transfer | |
|---|---|---|---|---|---|---|---|---|
| | Min | Max | Min | Max | Min | Max | Min | Max |
| Base page cost ($) | 0.007 | 0.007 | 0.007 | 0.007 | 0.007 | 0.007 | 0.232 | 4.927 |
| Relative density factor | 0.085 | 0.280 | 0.185 | 0.494 | 0.000 | 0.407 | 0.000 | 0.000 |

**Table 26-1**
**Cost of Different Color Printer Technologies**

Figure 26-4 gives you the same information as Table 26-1 (excluding wax transfer) but casts the costs as cost per page for different print densities. The printer acquisition cost is not included in the per-page costs. The minimum density factor for solid ink is zero because Tektronix offers black ink (only) for the Phaser 840 for free.

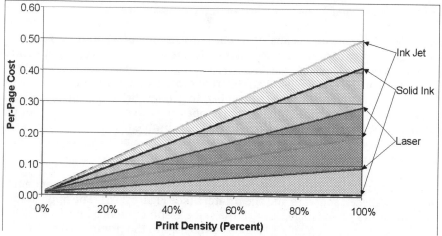

**Figure 26-4:** Evaluate per-page color print cost against your printing needs.

# Telling the Printer What You Want: Page Description Languages

Now that you have the means to put images where you want them on paper, you need a way for your computer to tell the printer what to do. Let's think back to how typewriters worked to get an idea of what you need to do with your printer:

✦ *Characters.* For the most part, what you did with a typewriter was print characters. The typewriter automatically moved from one character to the next, spacing them apart so the resulting text looked right.

✦ *Positioning.* You defined where you wanted the characters on the page by moving the paper around in the typewriter. You could scroll the paper up and down and move the print head back and forth.

✦ *Margins.* You set margins with stops on the body of the typewriter that limited the travel of the carriage. By coordinating the stops with how you registered the paper in the carriage, you established the margins where you wanted them on both the left and right sides of the paper.

✦ *Font.* Daisy wheel and golf ball typewriters let you change the font you typed by changing the print element. You had to reach into the typewriter, remove the old one, and put in the new one.

Early personal computer printers did basically these same four things based on codes sent from the computer. Characters were sent as-is, while the other functions were indicated by special codes. The codes for printers from different manufacturers were incompatible with each other, and each program had a different set of printer drivers with those codes embedded. Worse, only printers with tractor feeds (mechanisms that engaged the holes in tear-off strips at the edge of the paper) could reliably move the paper backward as well as forward, so most printers required that programs send commands in order from top to bottom of the page.

As software became more capable — word processors, presentation graphics, and page layout programs in particular — the mess surrounding printer control sequences became impractical. WordPerfect had a different set of drivers than Microsoft Word, both of which had different drivers than Harvard Graphics, and so on. If you bought a new printer, you had to get new drivers from each of your software vendors. If a vendor hadn't developed the driver yet, or chose not to, you had a problem. The software vendors had a problem as well, because each of them had to invest a lot of money in creating and maintaining their printer driver libraries.

Windows simplified this problem, because it provided a printer-independent interface between software and the printers (see Figure 26-5). The applications program draws on the page through the same graphics device interface (GDI) it uses to draw on the screen. GDI sends commands to the printer driver, which translates into the language the printer understands and (with the help of the communications port driver) sends the result to the printer.

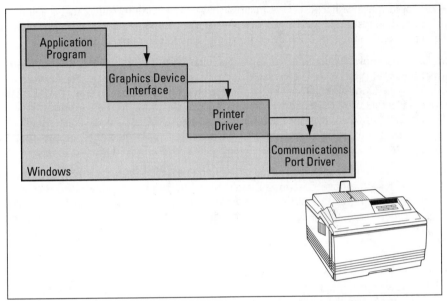

**Figure 26-5:** The print interface Windows programs see is nearly the same as for drawing on the screen.

The complexity of the things programs can do with GDI creates a problem for printer designers. If they let the computer itself compose the entire page bitmap, then there's a big processing load on the computer (even for simple text), and the massive volume of data to be sent to the printer for every page makes printing slow. If you're printing over a network, the volume of data bogs down everyone's communications. Alternatively, if designers have the printer raster image processor do the work (as in laser printers), they need some good way to convey all the richness and complexity from GDI into the raster image processor.

For the most part, printers use the second approach — there's a correspondingly rich language (called a *page description language*) the printer driver uses to communicate what's required to the printer. Two page description languages dominate the industry: PostScript (developed by Adobe) and PCL (developed by Hewlett-Packard). PostScript was originally developed for use with the Macintosh computers but has migrated to PC systems. (See the sidebar "You can get there from here" for how this can have unexpected benefits.) Both work and (with the most current versions of PCL) have roughly equivalent capabilities — you'd only explicitly choose one versus the other if compatibility at the page description language level was important for communicating with an outside service bureau, or if you're doing complex graphics fill operations that are supported only in PostScript.

## You can get there from here

PostScript is very widely used in the publishing industry, in part because of the widespread use of Apple Macintosh computers in publishing. That commonality can be valuable in more ways than just printing. For example, PostScript played a major part in getting figures for an earlier edition of this book from our computers to the printing presses.

Although IDG Books Worldwide, Inc., specified that figures should be in Adobe Illustrator format, we drew them with Microsoft PowerPoint—it was easier for us, because we knew PowerPoint well, and didn't know or have Illustrator. Our plan was to transfer the pictures individually into CorelDRAW! and export in Adobe Illustrator format. Unfortunately, this didn't work—along the way from PowerPoint to CorelDRAW! and Adobe Illustrator, the files became very large, embedded bitmaps dropped out, and elements of the drawings became distorted.

Fortunately, Adobe Illustrator is capable of reading PostScript files as a drawing representation—it can take the page description you'd normally send to a printer and recreate the drawing. Printing the figures out of PowerPoint to files normally destined for a PostScript printer and then reading the files back into Adobe Illustrator brought the figures into the IDG Books production department's Macintosh computers nearly perfectly.

Until a few years ago, PostScript printers had one other extremely valuable advantage. At the time, the common approach to distributing files over the Internet that could be printed on almost any computer was to post a PostScript printer file—you downloaded the file and copied it to your PostScript printer. If you didn't have a PostScript printer, either you found a PostScript emulator on the Internet (such as GhostScript) or you were severely out of luck. Since then, however, Adobe has created and promoted Acrobat and its Portable Document Format (PDF). Most Internet sites have started distributing print files in the Acrobat format, wildly simplifying the entire problem and allowing the documents using PDF to be compatible with any Windows- or Macintosh-supported printer.

**Tip**     The Acrobat reader is distributed free on the Internet by Adobe at `http://www.adobe.com/prodindex/acrobat/readstep.html`.

# Drivers, Monitoring, and Control

Notwithstanding the fact that many printer manufacturers have standardized on PCL or PostScript, you still need drivers specific to the printer you have. This is because (in addition to the fact that small differences in PCL or PostScript implementation can be catastrophic) the print drivers allow you to control options and features in the printers, and the controls for them are not the least bit standardized. The result is that you have to think about three things when evaluating the software supporting your printer: its drivers, its monitoring capabilities, and its control functions.

## Drivers

Most Windows print drivers are based on a core print driver, developed by Microsoft, that handles things like rendering fonts, choosing the port the printer is connected to, and otherwise performing the chores needed to send your page to the printer. The printer manufacturer builds tables that tell the core driver how to accomplish the necessary functions, and adds functions related to color matching, paper handling, and maintenance.

Not all printer drivers are created equal — some of them work. Nor is past quality always an indicator of future performance. You're entirely dependent on the printer manufacturer for drivers (they generally supply even the ones packaged with Windows), so if the manufacturer is shipping junk for drivers, you're stuck. Make sure you understand the return policy for a printer when you buy it, and plan to thoroughly wring out the printer before the return policy expires. If the driver doesn't support what you need to do, the best printer in the world is no better than an unwieldy doorstop.

## Monitoring

Printer monitoring lets you see what remote printers are doing. Even though you typically connect a printer to a computer, having a printer remote from your own computer over a network means you'll want some help in keeping track of what it's doing from your desktop. That way, you don't have to continually go and look at the printer. Monitoring a network printer is part of what you can expect from good printer software support. You can expect good network printer management software to help you do things like:

✦ *Status and resource monitoring.* You should be able to find out if the printer is jammed or offline; if it needs paper, toner, or other supplies; and what job it's currently working on.

✦ *Configuration.* Your printer management software should identify all the options attached to the printer, and how each is configured. You should be able to remotely change the configuration, download fonts, and enable or disable options.

✦ *Statistics.* Heavy-use printers are generally rated, like copiers, for a number of pages before they should have preventative maintenance to ensure top image quality and jam-free paper handling. Your printer network management software should collect statistics from the printer to let you track when you need to schedule service.

✦ *Access control.* You may choose to limit access to some of the printers on your network (for example, a color printer—supplies for color printers may cost ten times as much as for black-and-white printers; see the estimates of color consumables costs in Table 26-1). Your printer network management software should provide convenient tools to track and manage access control.

## Control

You'll want to be able to control how your applications print, no matter if the printer is local or remote. You should be able to control any aspect of the printer, including at least:

✦ *Print density.* You can control the overall darkness of the print. If you do a whole lot of large drafts before printing a final copy (other than on a wax transfer color printer), turning down the print density can reduce your costs (refer back to Table 26-1; a similar effect applies to black-and-white printers). You can reset to best quality when you're ready for the final copy.

✦ *Color or grayscale.* Color printers usually let you specify that the print should be grayscale only, turning off the color inks. This saves costs on all but wax transfer color printers, and if you'll be copying your printouts in black and white anyway, it's pointless to make color prints.

✦ *Duplex.* Some printers offer the option to print on both sides of the paper, either by feeding the paper in twice or directly using a more involved paper feed path. Either way, you should be able to turn the duplex print on and off to fit your immediate needs, and you should be able to specify whether you flip the page over on the long edge (like a book) or the short edge (like a tablet).

✦ *Graphics resolution.* Printers can't always reproduce as many colors or grayscale tones as are in your images. In that case, the printer simulates the shade by a process called *halftoning,* which involves using a grid of mixed colors of dots that, viewed from a distance, blend to simulate the color you want. The resolution of the halftoning process is often controllable from the device driver and can be set to relatively low resolution to conserve memory or speed print times. In high-resolution printers, the halftone patterning should be unnoticeable when the driver does fine-grained processing.

Some printers offer more basic resolution control, allowing you to use less than the maximum resolution on the printer, which you might want to use if you're after a quick print and don't care what the graphics look like.

✦ *Paper size.* Most printers can accommodate a range of paper sizes, from envelopes through legal and European sizes. You should be able to specify the paper you've loaded to the driver; better is for the printer to automatically tell your computer. You should also be able to specify which way the print is oriented on the page (portrait is with the long way vertical, while landscape is with the long way horizontal). For printers with unprintable areas (due to the paper feed mechanism, for example), you should be able to control the size of this area.

✦ *Paper source*. If your printer has several paper trays or has a manual feeder in addition to the paper tray, you should be able to specify from where you want paper to feed.

✦ *Fonts*. If your printer has built-in fonts or allows you to insert cartridges containing fonts, you'll need a way to control whether or not Windows uses those fonts. You might not want to use them, overriding with TrueType fonts, for example, to make sure things look the same from one printer to another.

✦ *Other options*. You should be able to control all the other features and specifications of your printer, such as informing Windows how much memory is installed or if an optional paper tray is installed.

# Combining Printing, Fax, and Copying

In a way, scanners, printers, fax machines, and copiers are all different ways to shuffle the same set of components. If you have an imaging device, a modem, and a printer, you can do all four functions.

If you buy all four devices separately, you've duplicated hardware and cost — you've bought three scanners and three printers. You can attach a scanner, a modem, and a printer separately to your computer and use software to get all four functions. This works and is a good solution for many situations. But it requires that you be involved in copy and fax functions, for the most part, involvement that can interrupt what you're doing.

Instead of doing a lot of busy work, you have the option of choosing a combination piece of hardware, one that includes all these components. We'll call these products all-in-one machines for lack of a better term. (Some companies call them multifunction devices, for instance — the terminology isn't much better, is it?) All-in-one machines are basically fax machines (which is the most complex function) that you can access as components from your computer when you need to, and that you can leave running independently as a fax and copier.

The advantage of an all-in-one machine is that you can leave it running unattended for fax and copier applications, even if your computer is turned off. Incoming faxes don't interrupt what you're doing with your computer (but are accessible from the computer for printing, OCR, and retransmission). You won't want to do heavy-duty copying with one, but it's sufficient for small jobs. Memory in the device buffers between faxes and printing, so no matter what goes on, you don't have to wait to get control back at your computer, and a print job won't cause you to lose an incoming fax.

The biggest problem with all-in-one machines is resolution and performance — neither the scanner nor the printer offer the image quality or speed you can get in more expensive separate units. Also, if a part of the machine breaks, you might be completely out of commission until repairs are done. If you can live with those limitations, though, one of these can save you money.

# Products

Printers come with a variety of interfaces, including serial ports (that's right — another thing to connect to those two solitary ports), parallel ports, SCSI, and network. Most printers connect to a parallel port by default, with options for serial, network, or SCSI connections. Network interfaces are commonly 10Base-T (prevalent in companies of the size that would be using network printers), so if you need a thinnet interface, check that the product explicitly supports it. You also need to check that the network printer supports the network software on your network, be it Windows 9*x,* Windows NT, Novell NetWare, or something else. SCSI interfaces aren't common — network interfaces can be almost as fast, and are more flexible — so check hardware and software compatibility carefully.

Something else to consider carefully is the resolution of the printer you get. The difference in grayscale (or color) tones between 300 dots per inch and 600 dots per inch is very noticeable. At 300, you'll see the dots making up the filled area very clearly; at 600, this effect is far less noticeable. Printers that can control intensity at the dot level effectively increase the dot resolution as well, because they can use that capability rather than create the tones from a halftone screen.

## Canon BJC-6000 color ink jet printer

For many applications, a color ink jet printer is the best way to get color printing capability. Ink jets tend to be slower than laser printers, and in some cases they offer lower resolution, but they are far less expensive. At resolutions up to 1440 × 720 dots per inch, the Canon BJC-6000 color ink jet printer (Figure 26-6) is a high-resolution printer. Its use of both black and color cartridges ensures strong colors and lets you replace only the black cartridge if you do mostly black-and-white work. Because the cartridges are about the same price but the black one holds three times the ink as the color one does for each color, it's less expensive to use the separate black cartridge.

Both color and black-and-white print speed is good for the unit, delivering up to eight pages per minute for black and white text and five pages per minute for color. The printer specifications (Table 26-2) show equivalent quality to that of a good black-and-white laser printer, and you get color.

**Figure 26-6:** The Canon BJC-6000 is a high-resolution color ink jet printer. (Photo courtesy Epson.)

| Table 26-2 Canon BJC-6000 Specifications | |
| --- | --- |
| *Characteristic* | *Specification* |
| Resolution | 1,440 × 720 dpi (dots per inch) |
| Print speed | Black: 8 ppm<br>Color: 5 ppm |
| Sheet feeder capacity | 130 sheets/15 envelopes |
| Paper types | Plain, bond, photo-quality film and paper, transparencies, self-adhesive sheets, ink jet cards, banner paper, labels, envelopes, and iron-on transfers |
| Cartridges | Separate black and color, with individual color tanks for separate replacement. Black life: 700 pages at 5%. Color life: 500 pages at 15% coverage (5% each cyan, magenta, yellow) |
| Interface | Bidirectional parallel |
| Page description language | Windows 95/98 and Windows NT 4.0 |

## HP LaserJet 2100 Series laser printers

The HP LaserJet 2100 series black-and-white laser printer (Figure 26-7) is unusual in the mid-price range ($600 to $700 on the Internet in the first quarter of 1999) in that it offers 1,200 × 1,200 dots per inch print resolution. Combined with its high rated workload and relatively large paper bins, it has the horsepower to handle jobs usually reserved for more expensive "departmental" printers. You'll get 16 pages per minute (if your computer can keep up) and very good print quality. If you have the LaserJet 2100TN with an included network print server, you'll find that the HP JetDirect management software lets local or network users check the status and configuration of the printer, get job statistics, and change printer settings.

Complex pages printed at 1,200 dpi with the LaserJet 2100 may require more than the standard 4MB memory that comes with some versions of the printer (Table 26-3).

**Figure 26-7:** The HP LaserJet 2100 series offers 1200 × 1200 dots per inch print resolution. (Photo courtesy HP.)

| Table 26-3 HP LaserJet 2100 Black-and-White Laser Printer Specifications | |
|---|---|
| *Characteristic* | *Specification* |
| Resolution | 1200 × 1200 dots per inch with resolution enhancement technology (RET) |
| Memory | 4 or 8MB, expandable to 42–50MB depending on model |

| Characteristic | Specification |
|---|---|
| Print speed | 10 pages per minute at 1600 dpi |
| Duty cycle | 15,000 pages per month |
| Paper capacity | 350-sheet and 10-envelope input trays<br>150-sheet output tray (many options) |
| Paper types | Plain paper, envelopes, transparencies, card stock,<br>postcards, labels and recycled paper |
| Cartridges | 5,000 pages at 5% coverage |
| Interface | Bidirectional parallel, infrared; some models include<br>network interfaces |
| Page description language | PCL 6; option for PostScript Level 2 |

# HP Color LaserJet 4500 printer

The HP Color LaserJet 4500 printer (Figure 26-8) is, of all the printers we've ever used, the one we like the best, because it's sharp, does great color, holds a lot of paper up to legal size, prints on both sides without shuffling paper, and talks to all our computers over our LAN. If we had to choose one printer for a small to medium-sized office, the Color LaserJet 4500 would be it.

The Color LaserJet 4500 printer offers high-capacity color printing; with the network support in the 4500N version and 4500DN versions, it's a great choice for an office with everyone on the LAN. You'll get sharp 600 × 600 dots per inch resolution color images, with one black and three separate color toner cartridges to make sure you only replace the supplies you need. HP JetDirect networked remote printer management software on the network printer versions lets local or network users check the status and configuration of the printer, get job statistics, and change printer settings.

The standard configuration handles paper from #10 envelopes up through legal size and has 32MB of memory (Table 26-4). The network version has 64MB memory and a network print server (so any client machine on the LAN can print without tying up a computer as a server). The duplex network machine adds a duplex unit (to print on both sides of the page) and a large paper drawer to increase paper capacity. Prints come out dry (not wet as with an ink jet) and relatively quickly as compared to an ink jet. The network interface supports TCP/IP, NetWare, and other protocols, and it can switch protocols automatically. The printer automatically powers down after a delay (typically one hour), waking back up when it receives data to print.

**Figure 26-8:** The HP Color LaserJet 4500 printer offers high-capacity color printing with excellent network support. (Photo courtesy HP.)

| Table 26-4 HP Color LaserJet 4500 Printer Specs | |
|---|---|
| *Characteristic* | *Specification* |
| Resolution | 600 × 600 dots per inch |
| Color matching | Windows 9x ICM, sRGB color management, and automatic color calibration. Pantone palettes available from the HP Web site |
| Memory | 32 or 64MB, expandable to 208MB |
| Print speed (600 dpi) | 4 pages per minute color<br>16 pages per minute monochrome |
| Duty cycle | 35,000 pages per month |
| Paper capacity | 250 and 150 sheet trays. Optional 500 sheet feeder |
| Paper types | Copier, bond, recycled, gloss, and multipurpose papers, transparencies, envelopes, and laser-qualified labels |
| Cartridges | Four separate (CMYK) |
| Interface | Parallel (ECP port) and network (10/100Base-T) |
| Page description language | PCL 5C and PostScript Level 2 |

Remote status and management is one of the more exceptional characteristics of the Color LaserJet 4500. HP's software to let Windows print to and manage the printer is called JetDirect; Figure 26-9 shows some of the capabilities of the software. The window in the back is the JetAdmin utility, giving you a view of the JetDirect printers on your network. The dialog box in front shows the detailed properties view for the printer, including notification that the printer requires replacement of the drum kit.

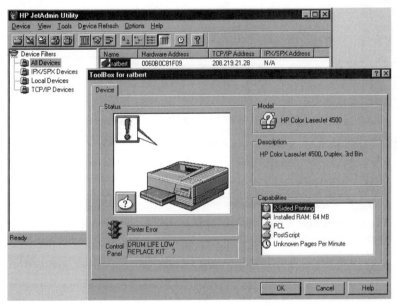

**Figure 26-9:** HP's JetDirect remote printer management software gives you complete status of the Color LaserJet 4500's operation.

Monitoring and administration of the Color LaserJet 4500 isn't limited to using JetDirect or to computers running Windows. HP has embedded a Web page server inside the printer, as shown in Figure 26-10, so any computer with a Web browser that can connect to the printer can show and update current status, configuration, and other settings. The Internet Printing Install Wizard button on the left of the screen even makes it trivial to install the software necessary for Windows NT computers to print to the displayed printer.

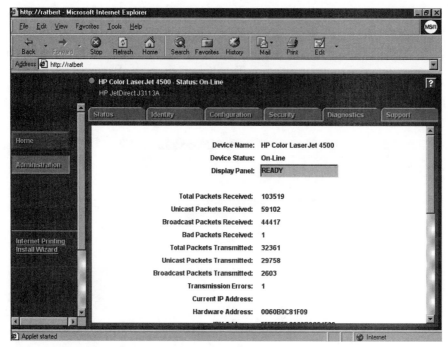

**Figure 26-10:** HP's JetDirect remote printer management software gives you complete status of the Color LaserJet 4500's operation.

## Canon MultiPASS C5500

The Canon MultiPASS C5500 (Figure 26-11) is a combination photo-realistic color ink jet printer, plain paper fax machine (with connectivity to your computer), plain paper copier that works without your computer, and monochrome scanner. It prints at 720 × 360 dots per inch resolution—unlike most other printers, the MultiPASS C5500 print resolution is asymmetrical—the vertical and horizontal resolutions are not the same. The lower resolution—360 dots per inch—isn't bad, but you'll be able to see the halftoning in grayscale or dithered color areas.

**Figure 26-11:** The Canon MultiPASS C5500 is a combination color ink jet printer, plain paper fax machine, plain paper copier, and monochrome scanner. (Photo courtesy Canon.)

As a stand-alone fax machine, the MultiPASS C5500 will send and receive manually or through your computer. It has the usual fax features such as stored frequently dialed numbers, automatic incoming call switching between the fax and a telephone, and 42 pages of memory to ensure that incoming faxes don't interfere with printing from your computer.

The MultiPASS C5500 works as a copier and scanner, including a 30-page automatic document feeder. The copier works at 360 dots per inch in both directions; the scanner works at 300 dots per inch optical, 600 dots per inch with enhancement. The specifications for the MultiPASS C5500 are given in Table 26-5.

### Table 26-5
### Canon MultiPASS C5500 Specifications

| *Characteristic* | *Specification* |
|---|---|
| Resolution | 720 × 360 dots per inch |
| Print speed | Color: 2 pages per minute<br>Black and white: 6.5 pages per minute |
| Paper capacity | 100 sheets letter/legal<br>50 sheets transparencies<br>10 envelopes |
| Paper types | Plain, coated, and transparencies<br>Film, fabric sheet, and T-shirt transfers<br>Banners, photo paper, and greeting cards |
| Interface | IEEE 1284 bidirectional parallel |
| Fax compatibility | G3 |
| Modem speed | 14.4 to 2.4 Kbps |
| Fax resolution | 203 × 196 dots per inch, or 203 × 98 dots per inch |
| Fax memory | 42 pages |
| Automatic document feeder | 30 pages |
| Copy resolution | 360 × 360 dots per inch (smoothed) |
| Scanner resolution | 300 dots per inch optical, 600 dots per inch enhanced |
| Scanner interface | TWAIN |
| Scanning speed | 9 to 78 seconds per page monochrome,<br>39 to 234 seconds per page color |

Laser printer–based all-in-one machines are available too, such as the Canon MultiPASS L6000 and the HP LaserJet 1100A Laser Printer, Copier, and Scanner. You'll get better print and scan quality from the laser units in return for a slightly higher price and monochrome-only operation.

## Choosing a Printer

The basic issues in picking a printer are how much you print, whether you need color, what print quality you need, and what price range you're in. Ignoring specialized applications like phototypesetting, high-volume label printing, or form printers, Figure 26-12 summarizes the decision process you might want to consider in picking a printer technology. The essence of what's in Figure 26-12 is that because the print quality is quite good in ink jet printers (although somewhat less than better laser units), you should consider cost, the volume of printing you want to do, and whether you need features such as color or a network connection in addition to resolution.

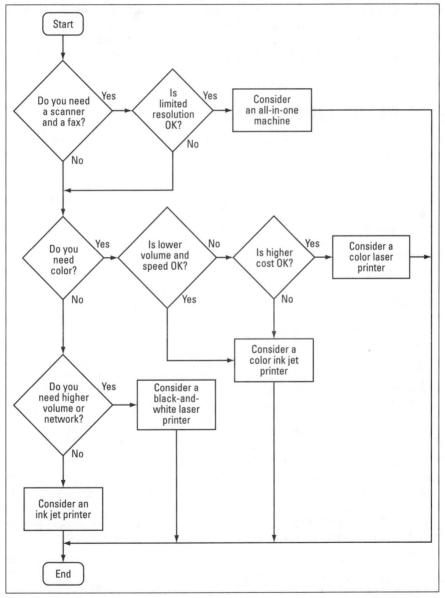

**Figure 26-12:** In addition to resolution, when selecting a printer technology, you should consider cost, the volume of printing you want to do, and whether you need features such as color or a network connection.

If you send and receive faxes, you might want to consider a stand-alone fax machine (instead of an all-in-one machine) along with one or more fax modems. The printer in an all-in-one machine may be too slow to really be of value other than, perhaps, as a color supplement to a network laser printer. The scanners in all-in-one machines are too low-resolution for publication work—they're good enough for OCR and presentations, but not for quality publication. The addition of one or two fax modems into the configuration allows you to do computer-based fax transmission and reception when you really need to do that, while the stand-alone fax machine allows you to be independent of the computers for all fax services.

# Top Support Questions

Q: My printer only handles PostScript. How can I print from DOS or UNIX applications?

A: Some PostScript printers only accept data formatted with the PostScript page description language. Programs that output unformatted data directly to the printer port don't work with these printers without some help. Under Windows, you can capture the printer port and run your program in a DOS box—the Windows printer driver will intervene and do the formatting you need. Under UNIX, you need a program that accepts text and outputs PostScript, such as *a2ps*, source code, which is available at `ftp://ftp.uu.net/usenet/comp.sources.misc/volume10/a2ps3.Z` or from the page at `http://www-stud.enst.fr/~demaille/a2ps.html`.

Q: How do I print from my DOS applications to my printer?

A: Windows gives you a setting in the properties dialog for the printer that lets you capture a DOS printer port and direct its output to the printer. In the Details tab for the printer properties, click Capture Printer Port and then pick an output port and direct it to the printer you want.

Q: Do I have to use special ink jet paper?

A: It used to be the case that the output from ink jet printers would wick into conventional paper, diffusing the image and producing inferior results. The inks have improved since then, and you can now use most any good copy paper. Papers are available for ink jet printers that look much like copy paper and, depending on the cost difference where you are, may be worth trying. For the best output of graphics, though, you'll want to try one of the very high-gloss papers sold for ink jet use.

Q: Can I make transparencies with my printer?

A: Most ink jet and laser printers can make transparencies directly rather than requiring you to print on paper and then make the transparency with a copier. Ink jet printers are likely to require special transparency material to avoid smearing, and to require that you let the copies dry completely before handling. Laser printers should print directly on the same material you'd run through a copier, although there are materials specific for lasers. Don't forget that you can get material with a light color tint to reduce the glare from the projection screen.

Q: The printed output on my ink jet printer looks out of focus. What's wrong?

A: Ink jet printers that use multiple cartridges (such as multi-color and black, or individual colors and black) are susceptible to the cartridges being out of alignment with each other. When that happens, the image looks like a color television that's out of convergence—one or more of the colors may be offset from the others. Your printer should provide an alignment procedure you can use to make the necessary adjustments.

Q: My computer slows down terribly when I'm printing. What can I do?

A: There's two potential causes for this—the software you're using may keep the computer busy generating the printed output, or the work of sending the output to the printer may create a significant load on the printer. (Some color laser printers also print more slowly in color than in black and white.) In the case of Microsoft Word, for example, rendering images for print can make the program completely nonresponsive. You can check if that's the problem by printing from a different instance of the program—open two copies of the program, start one printing, and switch to the other. If the second copy responds well (but the first one doing the printing doesn't), the problem is the software and—short of using a second copy—there's not much you can do. If there's no difference in response, you can try changing printer setup (see the next section on adding a printer).

# Hands-On Upgrades

## Adding a printer

Adding a printer under FreeBSD UNIX consists primarily of making sure the serial or parallel port you'll use is known to the system, and then telling the spooler about your printer. Here's the overall set of steps for FreeBSD; details will differ from one UNIX system to another.

✦ *Connection setup*. If you're connecting via a serial port, you have to make sure the printer and port are using the same rate and data format, and that you've made provision for flow control. You'll set the printer parameters on the printer itself; the port parameters get set in the next step. If you're using a parallel port, there's little or nothing to configure on the printer.

✦ *Port setup*. Make sure the UNIX kernel knows about the device you've connected to. If the generic kernel doesn't include support for the device, you'll have to make an entry in the configuration file and rebuild the kernel. You then check for the necessary entry in the /dev directory; entries would typically be /dev/ttyd0, /dev/ttyd1, or /dev/lpt0. (Note that the hardware serial devices are sio0, sio1, and so on, but the /dev devices are /dev/ttyd0 or /dev/cuaa0, and so on.) You may need to run a program to enable interrupt handling if you plan on using that feature. In FreeBSD, the program to do that is lptcontrol.

✦ *Testing functionality.* Next, check to see if the printer works. For parallel port printers, try the command:

```
lptest >/dev/lpt0
```

You should change lpt0 in the command to correspond to the port you're using. If you have a serial port printer, you have to edit a line into the file /etc/remote that names the port, baud rate, and parity. A typical line might look like this:

```
printer:dv=/dev/ttyd2:br#19200:pa=none
```

You can then run the command:

```
tip:dv=/dev/ttyd2:br#19200:pa=none
```

tip opens a connection to the printer; if it doesn't work, try using cuaa instead of ttyd. Then, send data to the printer with the command:

```
~$lptest
```

If something prints, you're connected. If not, check the kernel and /etc/ remote settings.

✦ *Configuring the spooler.* LPD is the UNIX print spooler. It takes configuration from the file /etc/printcap. Here's a typical printcap entry:

```
lp:\
:lp=/dev/lpt0:sd=/var/spool/output/lpd:lf=/var/log/lpd-errs:
```

The entry names the printer (lp on the first line) and sets several variables (the constructs of the form var=*xxx*:). The specific variables are lp, which defines the device to use; sd, which defines the spool directory for this printer (be sure to create the directory explicitly); and lf, which defines the log file for the printer. If you have a serial printer, you'll also set br and pa. Other variables let you set up the modes for the device and define filters, which are programs that (in this case) transform the printer output before it actually goes out the port. You can find more information in the *FreeBSD Handbook* in the section on "Printing."

This detailed process of editing configuration files until the system does what you want is typical of most elements of UNIX. Furthermore, the printer you set up this way under UNIX doesn't inherently provide the printer-independent graphics and font handling capabilities of Windows. You can do graphics and fonts to a PostScript printer with a program that's PostScript aware, but each program will need to be configured separately.

Under Windows, things are somewhat simpler. You open the Printers folder (Start ⇨ Settings ⇨ Control Panel ⇨ Printers) and run the Add New Printer icon. Answer the questions the installation wizard asks and you're done.

# Summary

✦ Nearly all printing requirements can be met with ink jet or laser printers, which are most of the units sold.

✦ Specialized color or large format printing requirements may drive you to other print technologies.

✦ Printer drivers and software are at least as important as the printer itself.

✦ In some situations, an all-in-one machine can save you several hundred dollars in duplicated equipment.

✦  ✦  ✦

# Networking Know-How

# Network Cabling and Interfaces

✦   ✦   ✦   ✦

**In This Chapter**

Baseband or broadband, point to point or shared, circuit or packet

Coaxial cable, twisted pair, fiber, and wireless

Ethernet, token ring, FDDI, wireless, and ATM

Cable modems

✦   ✦   ✦   ✦

**W**hen networking replaced point-to-point connections between pairs of computers, the need for more capable connections created a range of new technologies. The overall characteristics of your network are defined by a relatively small set of issues:

+ *Baseband or broadband.* The signals between computers can be either baseband, meaning that digital information is directly impressed onto the transmission medium, or broadband, meaning that the information is modulated onto a carrier signal. (The definition of broadband is subject to confusion because the term is also used to refer to any communications technology running at ISDN BRI rates and above. In this book, we'll use narrowband and wideband to distinguish network speeds, using wideband to refer to communications links at 1 Mbps and above.)

+ *Point-to-point or shared-media.* The connections in your computer network may use one physical pathway per computer, or they may share a pathway among several computers.

+ *Full or half duplex.* Half-duplex connections permit transmission in only one direction at a time. Full-duplex connections support simultaneous transmissions in both directions.

+ *Circuit or packet switching.* A defined relationship (circuit switching) can be set up to route the data stream from one computer to another (even through many other computers), or the switching computers can take the chunks of data containing addresses and route them as required (packet switching).

✦ *Access methods.* If the medium supports multiple computers over the same physical pathway, a mechanism will exist to tell the computers when it's okay to transmit.

✦ *Cabling.* The physical connection can be coaxial cable, twisted pairs, fiber-optic lines, infrared light, radio waves, or anything else that will carry digital information.

# Network Characteristics

If you're going to network your computers together, you have to decide what technologies to use. You should base that decision on what the competing choices do well and what they do poorly. We'll start by looking at some of the most important characteristics in networks, and then we'll look at specific technologies and how they relate to those characteristics.

## Baseband or broadband

The modem modulation technologies we described in Chapter 23, "Modems," are examples of broadband transmission. The digital information is impressed on a carrier signal, which in turn moves the information across the medium. In the case of a modem, the carrier is sound. Here are some other possibilities:

✦ *Fiber optics.* The carrier is a light wave. The modulation is often variations in the intensity of the beam.

✦ *Infrared.* The carrier is a light wave, as with fiber optics, but the medium is open air. The modulation is commonly a variation in the intensity of the light wave.

✦ *Wireless.* The carrier is a radio wave. The modulation can be variations in amplitude, frequency, or phase.

✦ *Power lines.* You can send signals back over the power lines you plug your computer into. A low-frequency radio wave could be the carrier, likely using frequency or phase modulation.

✦ *Tin can and string.* As silly as it sounds, you could make this work at low data rates. You could let a standing vibration on the string be the "carrier," pulling more or less on the string to vary the frequency (which would be the modulation). The point isn't that this is realistic, but that what might not come to mind today might be the transmission technology of tomorrow.

Several of these media support baseband transmission—sending the signal over the medium without a carrier. Fiber optics and infrared can be used like Morse code—they can simply turn the signal completely on or off. Wireless connections can send pulses, varying the time between pulses to send zeros or ones.

No one scheme — baseband or broadband — or one modulation is best all the time. Some are less expensive to implement (copper), some are good for high rates and long distances (fiber optics), and some are very easy to deploy (infrared).

## Point-to-point or shared-media

Depending on the communications technology, you can hook one device at each end of a connection (typical of fiber optics) or many along the length (easy with copper or wireless).

Point-to-point connections can still look like shared media. For example, twisted-pair Ethernet connects ports on a *hub* to computers (or routers or other devices). There is one device on each end of the wire, and nothing in the middle. Because of the way the hub works, though, all the separate connections appear to be a single wire.

In Chapter 28, "Peripheral Network Equipment," we show that this isn't always an advantage. High-performance networks can replace hubs with switches, giving each computer higher potential data rates on the network.

Point-to-point connections have the advantage that when a problem occurs with one computer's connection, the others generally stay operational. Shared media connections have the advantage that they don't require all the wiring to be collected at a central point. One connection can be strung from unit to unit and return only one cable to a more central place.

## Full or half duplex

Connections can allow transmission one way at a time (half duplex) or both ways simultaneously (full duplex). With the exception of telephone lines, full-duplex operations generally require two independent half-duplex connections — one in each direction. (Telephone lines use a special transformer called a hybrid to prevent echoes and allow transmission both ways over two wires.)

Copper Ethernets either operate half duplex (only one transmitter at a time) or use independent pairs of wires, one in each direction.

## Circuit or packet switching

After you have a connection, your data can go to a fixed place (circuit switching) or to a place determined by address information you provide with the data. For example, when you make a telephone call, the telephone network uses the number you dial to set up a circuit. All the subsequent information (voice or data) goes to the place at the other end of that circuit. None of the information you send changes the end point.

A packet-switched connection is different. Every data block contains the address of its destination, and each data block can go to a different place. (Data blocks are more commonly called cells, frames, or packets in networks. We discuss these terms more closely in the next chapter.)

Circuit switching has the advantage that (after you create the circuit) it requires no overhead to cause the information to go to the right place. You can have more than one circuit at a time in some systems (letting you send data to several places), but circuits take time to set up and tear down. Packet switching eliminates the time penalty for creating and destroying circuits and makes it simpler to have many end points, but it exacts a penalty for having to put an address on everything.

Circuit switching is used in telephone systems and in computer networks where the destinations don't change frequently. Packet switching is used in most computer networks.

## Access methods

A shared-access medium requires a way for the transmissions of one computer to be kept separate from those of the rest. There are five common ways of doing that:

✦ *Carrier sense multiple access/collision detect (CSMA/CD)*. As in Ethernet, a computer waits for silence on the wire. When it hears no other transmissions, the computer transmits its own data. When a collision occurs, each computer waits a random time and tries again.

✦ *Token passing*. The computers sharing the medium can cooperate, telling each other when it's okay to transmit. They do this by passing a marker among all the computers sharing the medium, called a token, and following the rule that only the computer with the token is allowed to transmit. Special provisions are needed to let computers enter and leave the network, and to detect when a computer holding the token has failed to pass it along.

✦ *Time division multiple access (TDMA)*. Each computer sharing the medium can be assigned a time slot (in a rotation) according to a clock shared by all the computers. So long as a computer stays in its slot, it can transmit freely. Computers listen to all time slots except their own.

✦ *Frequency division multiple access (FDMA)*. Broadband systems are frequently capable of supporting multiple transmission carriers on different frequencies. If the frequencies are separated far enough, filters can eliminate all but the one you're interested in.

✦ *Code division multiple access (CDMA)*. In the same way that pairs of people can talk separately in a crowded room, listening only to each other, computers can shut out other conversations on the same wire. They do this by coding their data at the transmitter in a way known only to the receiver, mixing it up with a high-speed series of random numbers. The receiver applies the same code again to extract the data. Receivers without the right code see only noise except for the signal they're supposed to see—the one for which they do have the right code.

Each of these access methods has its advantages and disadvantages. CSMA/CD requires only loose coordination between individual computers and readily takes advantage of having fewer machines on the wire. It's more effective in baseband systems (such as Ethernet) than in broadband ones. However, it's vulnerable to one computer failing and taking out communications for all the computers on the same wire, and it tends to suffer when the traffic on the wire climbs to a significant percentage of the raw capacity.

Token passing is efficient and enables you to use nearly all of the raw capacity of the medium. The common implementations of token passing (token ring) use two counter-rotating rings interconnecting all the computers, so if one goes down you still haven't lost connectivity. The latency between when a computer transmits and when it gets to transmit again can be significant in a large, heavily loaded token ring network, and if a computer crashes while it holds the token, there can be a delay before the network recovers. Token passing is used in both baseband and broadband networks.

TDMA is common in telephone networks, being used to combine circuits into a high-capacity connection. TDMA is also common in wireless systems, because it allows many users on a channel at relatively low equipment cost. It guarantees a circuit a specified data rate but limits flexibility in changing the rate. The time division structure has to be specified in advance, so there are likely to be upper limits to how much of the total channel capacity a given circuit can have. Synchronizing the timing among all the computers is critical, because a mistimed transmitter can step on someone else's interval, while a mistimed receiver can get the wrong data.

FDMA is common in wireless systems, because it simplifies distinguishing one signal from the others. It's also used as a way to increase the data rate over fiber-optic links. The electronics supporting the link can't run as fast as the fiber is capable of transporting, so rather than try to force them to run faster (making them much more expensive), it's easier to send several optical carriers down the fiber at different frequencies. (This is called *wavelength division multiplexing* when applied to fiber optics.) Filters at the receiving end split out the beams and send each one to its own set of electronics.

Finally, CDMA is uniquely suited to noisy transmission channels. The properties that let it ignore other conversations also let it ignore noise and give it a degree of privacy (we pointedly said privacy and not security) not inherent in the other technologies. The best CDMA implementations can carry as much or more traffic in a channel as other technologies; most CDMA systems carry somewhat less.

# Network Cable Types

In addition to networks having overall characteristics, every network implementation has a specific medium it uses to transmit signals. Three of these are common, with one having the possibility of becoming widespread. Collectively, we'll call the network medium its cable (or cable type), ignoring the fact that wireless transmissions don't have a physical cable.

## Baseband copper cable

Ethernet was among the earliest networks. The initial version of Ethernet used a thick coaxial cable about 0.4 inches in diameter. Later copper-based versions used a thinner coaxial cable and twisted copper pairs.

### Thicknet

In a thicknet, cable runs between devices called *transceivers,* which in turn have cables that connect to the associated computer. Figure 27-1 shows how this works. Cables can tee off one another using devices called repeaters, as long as there are no circles in the connections and as long as the maximum distance limitations (500 meters, or 1,640 feet, leading to the name 10Base-5 for the cable technology) are met.

The transceiver cable (or *attachment unit interface,* AUI) connects between the transceiver and the Ethernet interface on the computer. The transceiver (also called a *media access unit* or MAU) is equipped with a male 15-pin connector with locking posts, and the computer's Ethernet interface is equipped with a female 15-pin connector. A sliding latch (the corresponding attachment for the locking posts) is on the computer Ethernet interface. The transceiver has an identical female 15-pin connector on one end, and a male 15-pin connector on the other. The cable connects between the computer and the transceiver, using the locking pins and sliding latch to ensure the connectors remain tightly secured. The transceiver cable carries three data signals between the Ethernet interface and MAU: transmit data, receive data, and detect collision. Each signal is sent over a pair of wires. Another pair of wires carries 12 volt DC power from the Ethernet interface to the MAU. The standard transceiver cable is relatively thick (approximately 1 cm or 0.4 inch diameter), and may be up to 50 meters (164 feet) long.

The transmission characteristics of the cable require that transceivers be attached only at specific places on the cable. Thick Ethernet cable invariably has bands marked on the insulation to indicate allowed attachment points. There are two kinds of transceivers: those that require the cable to be cut and coaxial connectors to be added, and those that can clamp onto the cable (often called a vampire tap). Reliability problems are common unless vampire taps are installed very carefully.

Thick Ethernet isn't used much anymore. The cable is quite stiff, making it hard to route physically, and a failure on a segment will take down the entire network for all the computers attached to that segment. The separate transceivers and AUI cable increase cost as well. Thicknet is limited to 10 Mbps.

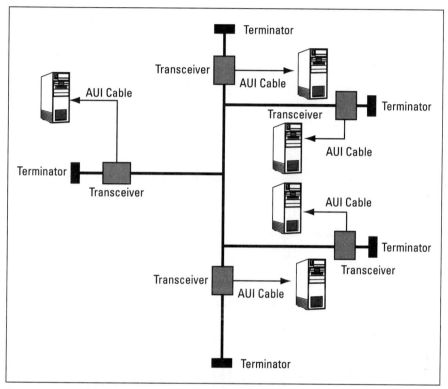

**Figure 27-1:** Thick Ethernet attaches transceivers to the cable and runs AUI cables from the transceiver to a connector on the attached computer.

## Thinnet

The first variant of thicknet Ethernet — thinnet, shown in Figure 27-2 (also called 10Base-2 and cheapernet) — simply changed the type of coaxial cable used in the network from the 0.4-inch, stiff type to a 0.2-inch, flexible cable. The cable connector changed at the same time from a relatively large, screw-on type "N" connector to a smaller, twist-lock "BNC" connector. Because thinnet is less expensive than thicknet, and because the transmission characteristics of the thinner cable are not as good as the thicker type, thinnet restricts the way in which computers are connected:

✦ *No external transceiver or AUI cable.* The thinnet transceiver is built into the adapter card. A tee coaxial connector mounts on the back of the board, and the cable attaches to both sides of the tee. If one side of the tee has no cable attached, a terminator attaches directly to the tee.

✦ *No spur directly connected segments.* No branches off the thinnet cable are allowed — even to connect a computer to the associated tee connector. The cable must run to the tee connector directly on the adapter card. Thinnet repeaters that will let you join multiple segments exist.

✦ *Reduced maximum transmission length.* The maximum segment length is 185 meters (607 feet). You can attach up to 30 computers to a segment. There are no special spacing requirements (as with thicknet), but the minimum spacing is 0.5 meters (1.6 feet).

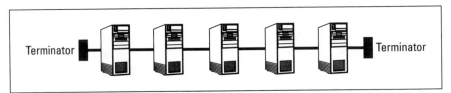

**Figure 27-2:** Thinnet attaches the cable directly to the back of the computer, allowing no spur cable segments. The transceiver is built into the adapter card in the computer.

As with thicknet, if you open the cable at any point, the entire network segment goes down. You can remove a computer from a thinnet segment, but you have to do it by removing the tee connector from the back of the computer.

**Note**
It's very common to use a short spur segment from the tee connector to the back of the computer, and it's a very bad idea. The spur causes signal reflections, degrading the signal on the network and causing errors. The error rate goes up as the load on the network goes up, and as the number of spurs (and their length) goes up.

As with thicknet, one misbehaved computer (or connector or terminator) can take down the entire thinnet segment. Thinnet is easy to install and less expensive than 10Base-T (twisted pairs), but if you have a network of more than a handful of computers all close to each other, it can be a nightmare to keep running. Thinnet is limited to 10 Mbps.

## Twisted pair

By far the dominant Ethernet cabling technology is twisted pair, or 10Base-T. (A faster version — 100Base-T — is also widely used.) Unlike coaxial cable–based Ethernet, 10Base-T attaches only one computer to each wire segment (see Figure 27-3). Each segment contains two twisted pairs of wire: one pair for transmitting and one for receiving. The wires have an RJ-45 modular connector (slightly larger than the usual RJ-11 connector on most telephones) at each end. One end connects to the computer, while the other connects to a device called a *hub*. The hub functions similarly to a repeater in coaxial Ethernet wiring, with the exception that it provides connections for four, eight, or more computers.

There are two kinds of cable used to make up twisted-pair connections: unshielded twisted pair (UTP) and shielded twisted pair (STP). The two differ in that STP has shielding wrapped around the conductors to minimize noise and interference. STP consequently has better transmission characteristics than UTP.

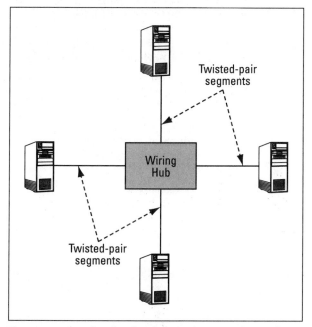

**Figure 27-3:** Twisted-pair Ethernet (10Base-T) attaches one computer per cable. If any one wire goes down, all the rest of the computers are unaffected.

In addition to only having one computer connected per cable, twisted-pair wiring has one other fundamental difference versus coaxial cable — it provides separate wires for transmitting and receiving. Coaxial cable uses the same wire for both and so is restricted to half-duplex operation; only one computer can transmit at a time. Twisted pair can operate full duplex, so it's possible for a computer to transmit and receive simultaneously. With more complicated versions of the hub (called Ethernet switches — see Chapter 28, "Peripheral Network Equipment"), many computers can transmit at the same time, increasing the performance of the network.

Tip Twisted-pair connections can be up to 100 meters (328 feet) long. If you allow ten meters for connections within a wiring closet and from the wall to the computer, the in-wall wiring can be up to 90 meters. In addition to the division between shielded and unshielded wire, there are three categories of twisted-pair wiring called categories 3, 4, and 5. Category 3 is the usual voice-grade wiring that is commonly prewired in buildings. Category 5 uses higher-quality cables and connectors. If you ever plan to upgrade from 10Base-T to 100Base-T, you'll want to start with category 5.

If you have the tools to attach the modular connectors, you can make twisted-pair cables yourself. If not, you'll have to order them in the right length. Either way, if you make a cable that reverses the transmit and receives pairs between the connectors, you can connect two computers directly, without a wiring hub.

Twisted-pair interfaces monitor the link status, and most provide a light to indicate that the link is up. You have to check the lights at both ends, though, because link status is based on the receive side only.

## Fiber optics

Fiber-optic networks use a wide variety of equipment. Most use configurations similar to twisted pair, in which a fiber cable interconnects two pieces of equipment. Two fibers are used in each cable: one for transmitting and one for receiving. Depending on the equipment you have, fiber-optic connections may be up to 100 to 600 kilometers long.

There are two kinds of fiber: single-mode and multimode. Single-mode fiber is more expensive but more able to transmit optical signals across long distances. Type SC connectors are common for single-mode fiber; type ST is common on multimode fiber. Attaching connectors to the ends of fibers is difficult, so it's more common to buy premade connector ends and to splice the fiber strands themselves using a machine designed for that purpose.

## Wireless transmission

Wireless networks use radio or light waves to communicate between stations. The frequencies for radio-based networks vary based on national licensing. Systems in the United States often use bands designated by the Federal Communications Commission for "unlicensed" operation, meaning that, after the manufacturer has qualified the equipment, the operator doesn't need special training or licensing. Optical systems often use infrared frequencies (light waves just below the visible spectrum). Some of the key characteristics are:

✦ *Range.* Radio systems have ranges up to tens of miles. Infrared systems are typically limited to a few hundred feet.

✦ *Blockage.* Radio waves penetrate walls and floors with varying degrees of success. Light waves require a direct line of sight between the transmitter and receiver.

✦ *Data rate.* Radio systems don't always carry the usual 10 Mbps Ethernet rate, particularly at longer ranges. Many radio systems are limited to 2 Mbps. Short-range infrared systems tend to operate at speeds of 10 to 100 Kbps. (Some can operate as fast as 1 Mbps.) Laser-based infrared systems can operate at 10 Mbps and higher.

Wireless networks can operate with point-to-point topologies, like the twisted-pair networks, or with shared access (like the coaxial-cable networks).

## Cable television systems

In addition to ADSL service from the local telephone company, the best opportunity for home users to get a high-rate network connection in the range of 1 to 10 Mbps is through their local cable television systems. Early deployments of the technology have had mixed results, with the biggest issues being reliability and performance. Cable operators will also have to overcome their reputation for poor quality and abysmal customer service.

A cable television network runs coaxial cable (or a combination of fiber optics and coaxial cable) past residences, using splitters to tap the signal for each home passed. Although the vast majority of cable networks are built for one-way transmission of television signals only, some have been upgraded to handle two-way transmission and to have extra capacity that can be used for data transmission. Private networks have also been built using the same technologies. Figure 27-4 shows the key components. All signals start or end at the *headend,* a facility maintained by the cable operator. Fiber-optic or coaxial-cable trunks feed the signals to neighborhood nodes, from which lines run past individual homes and buildings. The neighborhood lines are amplified periodically to maintain signal levels. Splitters tap the signals and provide feeds to the drop cables that run to individual structures.

The hard part for cable networks is two-way communication. All the signals from all the homes and buildings on the cable have to be summed together, adding not only the individual signals but also the noise. It's like holding a megaphone to your ear: Everything gets collected. What's worse is that cable networks use frequency division to separate upstream signals (from you to the headend) from downstream ones (from the headend to you), and the frequency band they reserve for upstream communication is small and very noisy. Cable modems (discussed later in the chapter) can overcome these problems, but it's difficult. When cable modems are finally widely deployed, you can expect from 1 to 20 Mbps downstream, and from hundreds of kilobits per second to several megabits per second upstream.

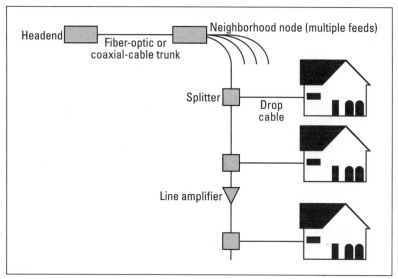

**Figure 27-4:** A cable television network uses coaxial cable from the headend, splitting the signal for each drop. Upgraded networks use fiber optics from the headend out to the neighborhood.

# Network Technologies

After you have a medium running from one place to another, you need to put a network on top of it. There are many different approaches, the most common of which is Ethernet. Most of the other network technologies have been developed to address one or another limitation of Ethernet—speed, distance, or the need for a cable. Table 27-1 summarizes the key characteristics of the three most common network technologies—Ethernet, token ring, and Fiber Distributed Data Interface (FDDI).

### Table 27-1
### Characteristics of Common Network Technologies

| Characteristic | Ethernet | Token Ring | FDDI |
|---|---|---|---|
| Data rate | 10 or 100 Mbps | 4 or 16 Mbps | 100 Mbps |
| Maximum distance between stations | 185 m (607 feet) for thinnet; up to 2.8 km (1.7 miles) for optical fiber | 300 m (984 ft) for 4 Mbps 100 m (330 ft) for 16/4 Mbps | 2 km (1.2 miles) (multimode fiber) 20 km (12.4 miles (single-mode fiber) |
| Logical topology | Bus | Single ring | Dual ring |

| Characteristic | Ethernet | Token Ring | FDDI |
|---|---|---|---|
| Physical topology | Star, bus | Ring, star | Ring, star |
| Media | Optical fiber, twisted pair, coaxial cable | Twisted pair, optical fiber | Optical fiber |
| Access method | CSMA/CD | Token | Token |

# Ethernet

Ethernet is the most common local area network because it's simple to set up, inexpensive, and reasonably fast. Ethernet is a baseband technology, most often at 10 or 100 Mbps. Gigabit (1 Gbps) Ethernet is starting to be used. Ethernet is designed for shared media. Point-to-point wiring (such as twisted pair) connects the wiring segments together electrically in most cases, creating a shared medium through the wiring hub. Similarly, Ethernet expects a half-duplex medium, although specialized wiring (such as twisted pair) and hubs (such as some Ethernet switches) can operate full duplex.

Ethernets use carrier sense with collision detection to support multiple access. When any given transmitter has something to send, it listens on the network to try to verify that no other device is currently transmitting. If the network appears idle, it starts to send. Because transmitters can be relatively far apart, however, it's possible for two transmitters to sense that the network is idle and both start to transmit at roughly the same time. Ethernet transceivers detect this occurrence and schedule a retransmission. The time for the retransmission is based on a random number to help the two colliding stations avoid further contention.

Ethernet is designed to run as a *packet-switched* network. The shared medium amounts to a "cloud" that interconnects all nodes on the network equally. Every packet on the network arrives at every receiver. Addresses in each packet define the destination.

**Tip**  Keep in mind that an unencrypted shared medium (such as Ethernet) is inherently not secure. Every packet arrives at every transceiver, and a transceiver programmed to listen to all addresses indiscriminately hears them all. This is useful for building network analyzers, but it means that (with the right software) the traffic from the executive suite to marketing is equally visible to anyone else connected to the network.

Another downside of Ethernet is its limitation to 10 or 100 Mbps on a single segment. As fast as that seems, when you start to connect tens or hundreds of computers to that single segment, network performance accessing the file servers quickly becomes intolerable. In the next chapter (Chapter 28, "Peripheral Network Equipment"), we discuss how to build multilayer networks that use inexpensive Ethernet to connect to computers but still retain excellent performance.

## Gigabit Ethernet

As you connect more computers to your network, your requirement for network bandwidth at the core of your network goes up. The next jump in Ethernet speed after Fast Ethernet is Gigabit Ethernet, products that will support full-duplex Ethernet operation on your existing unshielded twisted pair wiring at 1,000 Mbps. Fast Ethernet is 10 times faster than conventional Ethernet, entered the market at a price point 2–3 times that of 10 Mbps products, but ramped down to be almost the same as 10 Mbps prices since then. Gigabit Ethernet should do the same thing—expect 10 times the performance at an initial price 2–3 times that of Fast Ethernet.

Here are the variants of Gigabit Ethernet you can expect:

| Designation | Media | Distance |
| --- | --- | --- |
| 1000Base-SX | Multimode optical fiber (850 nm) | 500 m |
| 1000Base-LX | Multimode and single-mode optical fiber (1,300 nm) | 500 m to 2 km |
| 1000Base-CX | Short-haul copper ("twinax" shielded twisted pair) | 25 m |
| 1000Base-T | Long-haul copper over unshielded twisted pair | 25 to 100 m |

The compatibility with existing wiring will simplify deployment, although distance limitations may become a factor. Expect to see Gigabit Ethernet deployed first to connect servers to networks, and to interconnect switches as the network backbone. As higher-performance applications emerge (such as video editing), expect to see Gigabit Ethernet migrate out toward individual computers.

The need for Gigabit Ethernet isn't speculation. A high-performance server can, today, generate sustained network traffic in the range of 300 Mbps and up. A highly loaded backbone with several servers will therefore benefit today from the performance boost.

## Token Ring

Token ring networks are similar to 10Base-T networks in that they are commonly wired in a star configuration using a twisted-pair medium. The initial version of token ring developed by IBM ran at 4 Mbps; newer versions run at 16 Mbps. Like Ethernet, token ring is a baseband technology.

Although physically hosted on a shared medium, token ring creates a logical ring sequencing all the computers on the segment. A computer has to wait to transmit until it receives the token — the message on the network. The token can be an actual message, or it can be a message indicating that the prior station had nothing to send. Messages are handed from computer to computer in the order specified by the ring until they arrive at the destination. The destination computer marks the message as received and sends it off to the originator. When the originator sees the receipt, it transmits a token (empty) message to the next computer in the sequence. Because only the computer with the token is allowed to transmit, token ring networks do not encounter collisions. Because a token ring network is physically a collection of point-to-point connections joined at a hub (called a *media access unit,* or MAU, in token ring terms), the failure of one computer won't take down the entire network.

Because only one station transmits at a time, token ring operates as a half-duplex system. It's a packet-switched network, requiring every transmission to carry the destination address.

## Fiber Distributed Data Interface

*Fiber Distributed Data Interface* (FDDI) and the related *Copper Distributed Data Interface* (CDDI) were developed to provide a higher-rate alternative to Ethernet networks. FDDI is the more common version and is usually wired as a physical dual-fiber ring with each station wired to exactly two other stations (Figure 27-5). Each ring transmits at 100 Mbps. The rings operate in opposite directions, with one as the primary ring and one as the backup. If the primary ring fails, traffic wraps around on the backup ring, ensuring that all stations except the failed one remain operational while repairs are made. CDDI is essentially the same thing, except that category 5 copper cable is used instead of fiber.

FDDI and CDDI networks use token passing to regulate access to the network. Stations can transmit as much as they want until they complete operations or until a timer expires. The transmission is passed from node to node until it reaches the destination, which in turn marks it and passes it along to the sender.

FDDI and CDDI are baseband systems. The rings are a sequence of point-to-point connections operating in half duplex. Addressing accompanies every transmission, so this is a packet-switched technology.

In practice, FDDI is becoming obsolete. 100Base-T is much less expensive, and it provides essentially the same capacity for short distances, while ATM (explained in the following section) provides superior capacity for long distances.

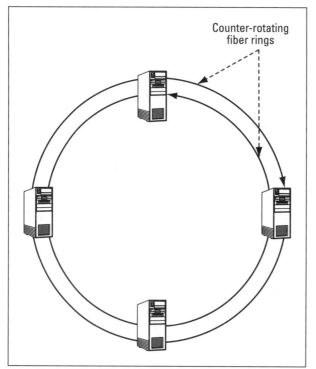

**Figure 27-5:** FDDI networks are characterized by dual counter-rotating fiber rings, each running at 100 Mbps.

## Asynchronous Transfer Mode

The next key network technology is *Asynchronous Transfer Mode,* or ATM. ATM is very different from the networks we've looked at up to now. It is circuit switched and runs at rates from 45 Mbps up to 622 Mbps (with growth to faster speeds likely). The circuit-switched nature of ATM derives from its telephone-related heritage. ATM is the growth technology for telephone network backbones and data networks. Although the physical data rate on a connection is fixed, the transmitted rate can vary from zero up to the connection rate.

ATM can run over a variety of media, from twisted pair and coaxial cable to multimode and single-mode fiber. ATM physical connections are all point-to-point. The distinguishing characteristic of ATM is that data transmissions are broken up into 53-byte units called *cells.* Five of the bytes in a cell are reserved for addressing and network control, leaving 48 bytes for user data.

An ATM network consists of a number of ATM devices connected to an ATM switch (Figure 27-6). The *User-to-Network Interface* (UNI) is different from the *Network-to-*

*Network Interface* (NNI), reflecting the need for switches to communicate among themselves to establish circuits and otherwise keep the network running.

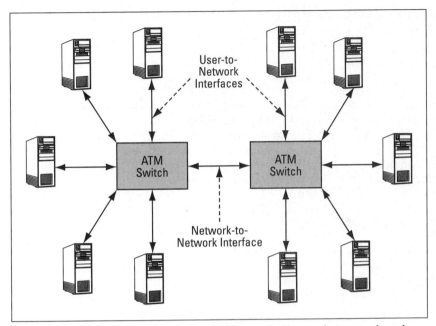

**Figure 27-6:** ATM defines an interface from user devices to the network and between network switches.

Although ATM is circuit-switched, multiple circuits can be active across a connection, so every cell carries an address. The address is relative to the next switch in line, though; as the cell traverses the switch, a new address applicable to the next switch is substituted. Circuit paths consist of sequences of paths across switches. The routing actions required within ATM switches are therefore very simple and can be carried out directly in hardware. The capability to route in hardware means that ATM can handle data switching very quickly (as you might expect with data arriving at rates up to 622 Mbps).

Because ATM can be carried over many different media, it can run either baseband or broadband. It has no inherent collision detection or access control—requiring point-to-point connections—and uses full-duplex connections.

**Cross-Reference**

Unless you have workstations requiring low-latency, high-speed connections to the network, the cost of ATM probably isn't warranted. It's cheaper to use a 100 Mbps Ethernet through an Ethernet switch. You're more likely to see ATM as a part of your backbone and wide area network (see Chapter 28).

# Wireless

Optical wireless networks operate either at baseband — turning the infrared light on and off — or on a modulated carrier (broadband). Although baseband radio networks are possible, all available products are broadband systems, modulating a carrier in one or another way.

Optical wireless and many radio wireless networks use a central node, called a *base station*, which corresponds to a wiring hub in a 10Base-T network. Transmissions between computers on the wireless network all go through the base station and are retransmitted after reception if the destination is also on the wireless network. (Base stations are commonly attached to a wired network as well, giving the mobile units access to the wider network.) Networks organized with a base station generally transmit out of the base station on one frequency and receive on another; the computers reverse the frequency assignments. Radio networks without a base station let all units transmit on the same frequency.

In either scheme, wireless networks require a method for collision detection. The carrier sense/collision detect approach used in Ethernet doesn't work well on wireless networks because of the time delay between the start of the transmission and the receiver's notice of the carrier. The relatively long latency while the receiver locks up the signal creates too long a window in which a second transmitter might start operations and step on the transmissions of the first one. That's why many wireless networks use a token passing scheme, positively identifying the next station allowed to transmit.

Some radio networks use spread-spectrum technology to isolate transmissions from one another. (See the sidebar "Sharing frequencies with spread spectrum" later in this chapter.)

The advantages that wireless networks have over wired ones are mobility and not having to run wires (not as silly as it sounds). In addition to allowing you to move around — useful if you're taking inventory in a warehouse, for instance — a wireless connection can solve the problem of linking networks that have physical barriers between them. Point-to-point wireless links can solve the problem of how to cross roads and railways between building networks, or of how to cross parts of a town without the expense of a leased telephone line. Multidrop wireless networks can simplify linking stations on several floors of the same building when it's impractical to run wires between the networks. Wireless networks are generally more expensive than their wired equivalents, so you will want to use them only where mobility or access are issues.

# Cable television

In a sense, cable television data networks look like wireless radio networks using a base station. The base station resides in the cable operator's headend, and transceivers (usually called cable modems) sit at each connected site. Radio frequency signals traverse the cable between either end.

Because the cable confines the signals—so that they don't radiate into free space—a wider spectrum is available for signals. Most North American cable television systems start the transmission band from headend to user at 54 MHz, which is channel two. The upper limit is typically somewhere between 200 and 750 MHz. Each television channel occupies 6 MHz of this spectrum. (You can guess at the bandwidth of your system by taking the number of channels, multiplying by 6 MHz, and adding 54 MHz—see Table 27-2 for some examples.)

| Table 27-2 The Number of Channels Your Cable System Can Carry Depends on the Upper Frequency Limit | |
| --- | --- |
| **Number of Channels** | **System Upper Limit (MHz)** |
| 13 | 132 |
| 34 | 258 |
| 70 | 474 |
| 116 | 750 |

Newer cable television systems—using fiber optics for the trunks out from the headend—have greater bandwidth and better performance than older, more restricted systems. You can't assume that you are on a fiber-optic/coaxial-cable hybrid network system, though, because despite all the hype in print, the actual number of cable systems with fiber out to all the neighborhood nodes is rather small. That's unfortunate, because cable modems won't be popular and feasible until 1) there's spare bandwidth on the network to carry data traffic, 2) two-way operation between you and the headend is installed, and 3) the noise levels on the path from you to the headend are low enough for reliable service.

That last point — the amount of noise on the return path between you and the headend — is crucial. Radio systems need a strong signal-to-noise ratio to operate reliably. The return spectrum on a cable system starts at 5 MHz, extending up to somewhere between 25 and 40 MHz (depending on the system). The first 10 MHz (5 to 15) are extremely noisy; the region from 15 MHz on up is merely noisy. (In the United States, Citizen's Band radio operates at 27 MHz and is picked up as noise by a cable system return path. The lower part of the return band is much worse due to noise from power supplies and other equipment.) Manufacturers have used a variety of approaches to countering the noise problem.

✦ *Low-rate modulation.* The quadrature phase shift keying (QPSK) modulation technology used by older voice line modems applies to radio as well (at higher frequencies) and requires a weaker signal-to-noise ratio than more efficient technology such as quadrature amplitude modulation. This means that, for a given data rate and signal strength, QPSK can withstand more noise. The total data you can pass on the return path is limited, though, because the return path bandwidth is constrained.

✦ *Narrow channelization and noise avoidance.* The first generations of cable modems channelized their data traffic into 6 MHz bands, which made it easy to fit them into the frequency plans of cable television systems. Some modems now use smaller channels on the return path — some as small as 600 kHz, fitting eight of them plus guard bands into the usual 6 MHz channel. Because noise on cable television systems is often narrowband, interfering with only part of a 6 MHz channel, narrow channelization allows the modems to simply change frequencies and avoid temporarily noisy sections of the return path.

✦ *Spread spectrum.* A different form of transmission, *spread spectrum,* is inherently noise resistant. There are two forms of spread spectrum: frequency hopping and direct sequence. A frequency hopper divides the overall allocated spectrum into many small bands, transmitting for only a brief moment in one before hopping to the next. The hops are made in a predetermined sequence. Frequency hoppers are noise-resistant in the same way that systems using narrow channelization are: They can either avoid the noisy subbands or dwell there for so short a time that error correction codes can overcome the noise.

The second form of spread spectrum, *direct sequence,* enables all the transmitted signals to use the entire allocated band at once. The greater the ratio of the available channel bandwidth to the data rate, the more noise resistant direct sequence spread spectrum will be. (See the following sidebar for more details.)

## Sharing frequencies with spread spectrum

There's an interesting operation computers do on numbers called "exclusive or" or XOR. The XOR operation is interesting because if you do it twice, you get back your original number. For instance, if we compute

```
11001010 XOR 11111111
```

we get 00110101. All the bits in the initial number have flipped. If we repeat the operation on the result and do

```
00110101 XOR 11111111
```

we get 11001010 again. Now, suppose we take two digital signals: one a real data stream and one a much faster stream of random numbers. If we XOR the two streams together, we pretty much get garbage out, but we can throw away the garbage and get back the data stream if we repeat the XOR using the exact same random number sequence.

In a nutshell, that's what direct sequence spread spectrum does. It combines your data with a fast random number stream in the modulator and extracts it back out from the random numbers in the demodulator. Of course, if you followed that as well as we did the first time someone waved the idea at us, you've got a blank look and you're thinking "So what?" (or worse) about now.

Here's why this is really good. The frequency spectrum a signal takes up is proportional to how fast the data goes. Double the data rate, and (everything else being the same) you double the spectrum. If we keep the power level the same, then the power at any specific frequency is less, because the total power is being divided over a greater range of frequencies. In the transmitter, having the modulator mix the data with the random numbers widens the spectrum of the transmitted result (because we use a fast random number stream).

Now, watch what happens in the receiver. We mix the random numbers back in with the received signal, and two things happen: First, the actual signal gets contracted back from its wideband spectrum to the narrower one needed for the actual (slower) data rate. Second, the random number mix spreads out any noise signals that the receiver happened to pick up. Unless they contain just the right random number sequence (which they don't), the mixing operation works just like spreading data in the transmitter. The power of the data signal gets collected back into a narrow range, and the power of the noise gets spread out into a wide range. Signal power goes up and noise power goes down.

The best part of this is that lots of us can talk in the channel at the same time. Your transmitter and receiver use a different random number sequence than ours. Because we use a different sequence, my receiver doesn't despread your transmission; it stays spread out, so it remains low-power noise. We simply don't hear you.

To your computer system, a cable modem is most likely to look like a local area network. You'll either have a card you plug in like a network adapter or an external box that connects to your local area network. You'll access the modem through local area network software and protocols such as the *Internet Protocol* (IP).

The performance you'll see from a cable modem is very much dependent on which modem you have. In the forward direction, most modems use a single 6 MHz channel and transmit at from 4 to 25 Mbps. Multiple subscribers will get data through that one channel. If the modem uses time division multiplexing (see TDMA in the section "Access methods" in this chapter) to divide the channel among all those users, there will be an upper limit to the burst rate you see that may well be below the channel capacity. If the modem uses packet addressing to divide the forward channel, you can get burst rates (and average rates on a nearly empty network) close to the channel limit.

Return path data rates may be less than the forward path rate (an asymmetric network) or may be the same. Most cable modems — specifically, ones not using CDMA and spread spectrum — use time division or token passing to synchronize access to the return path from all the attached users. You can expect 4 to 10 Mbps in a single return path 6 MHz channel.

With performance like that, it's surprising that there is still any demand for ISDN, which is around ten times slower. The reason is that, as hard as it is to get ISDN, it's even harder to get cable data service.

# Products

It's hard to draw the line between which products to cover in this chapter and which to reserve for the next one (see Chapter 28, "Peripheral Network Equipment"). We've chosen to cover the things that go directly in your computer — such as local area network adapter cards — in this chapter, and all the rest in the next.

You will find no discussion here of specific cable modem products. That's because — despite the Cable Television Laboratories DOCSIS standard — your only choice (if you have one at all) is to take what your cable operator offers.

## 3Com Fast Etherlink 10/100 Adapters

Ethernet adapters are one of the products that we're picky about. Networks are difficult enough to set up and keep running reliably; you don't need extra excitement on that front. We've always found the 3Com series to be fast and dependable, and we have the scars to prove that less expensive isn't always better. We've since thrown away a network card, for instance, that was a solid piece of hardware, but for which the vendor never fixed an admittedly buggy driver that caused the computer to lock up. In contrast, the Etherlink series has given us good performance and rock-solid reliable operation.

If you're using category 5 twisted-pair wiring, you could use the 3C905B Fast Etherlink 10/100 adapter (Figure 27-7). It auto-senses whether your network is running at 10 or 100 Mbps and configures itself accordingly. That means that you can install these adapters in your 10MB network and later — when you upgrade your hubs to handle more traffic — know that the attached computers will automatically take advantage of the increased performance. You won't have to open boxes or reconfigure operating system software.

The Fast Etherlink 10/100 adapters have specifications typical of first-class network interfaces, as shown in Table 27-3. The TX version uses two wiring pairs in category 5 unshielded twisted-pair cable. The T4 version uses four wiring pairs (eight wires) in category 3, 4, or 5 unshielded twisted pair. If you expect to install hubs or Ethernet switches capable of full-duplex operation (see Chapter 28), you have to use the TX model.

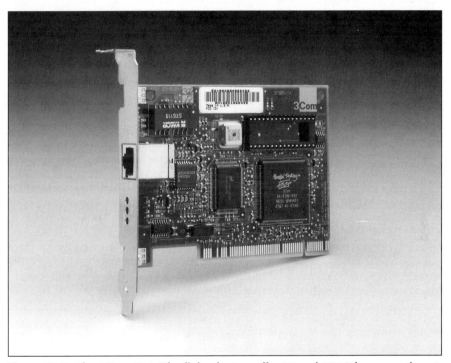

**Figure 27-7:** The 3Com Fast Etherlink adapters offer 10 and 100 Mbps operation at near 10MB prices. (Photo courtesy 3Com.)

If you don't run twisted pair, you may want to consider combo cards. The 3C905B-COMBO, for example, is a combo model with connectors on the back for 10Base-T (but not 100Base-T), thinnet, and anything you can adapt through an AUI connector. See the Black Box catalog for possibilities.

| Table 27-3 | |
|---|---|
| **3Com Fast Etherlink 10/100 Adapter Specifications** | |
| *Characteristic* | *Specification* |
| Cable type support | 100Base-TX model: 10Base-T or 100Base-TX (category 5 unshielded twisted pair) 100Base-T4 model: 10Base-T or 100Base-T4 (category 3, 4, or 5 unshielded twisted pair) |
| Bus interface | PCI, with or without bus mastering |
| Network management | Simple Network Management Protocol (SNMP—see Chapter 33), Remote Wakeup (Wake on LAN), and Desktop Management Initiative (DMI) |
| Operating system driver support | Windows 9x, Windows NT, UNIX, Novell, and OS/2 |
| Transmit/receive buffer | 4 to 64K, depending on model |

## Adaptec ANA-62044 Four-Port NIC

The Adaptec ANA-62044 four-port adapter (Figure 27-8) is a quick way to unclog overloaded small to medium-sized networks. The adapter supports four independent twisted-pair Ethernets at 10 or 100 Mbps each from a single PCI board, so it can replace a four-port hub (using crossover twisted-pair wiring), splitting it into four independent Ethernets each capable of independent operation, or can split the networks created by several hubs. You can also use it to connect your server over four fast paths to an Ethernet switch, making sure it has all the network access it can use. The ANA-62044 is a 64-bit wide PCI device, providing added throughput with motherboards supporting the enhanced PCI bus (see Table 27-4).

Installing one of these adapters probably means you need to route traffic among all four segments as well as to the computer in which you install the card, so you'll probably want to be running Windows NT (there are no drivers for UNIX, and Windows 9x doesn't natively do routing.)

The full-duplex capabilities of the board mean that you'll run at a peak rate of 80 Mbps on 10Base-T (four circuits at 20 Mbps each, which in turn is the 10 Mbps rate running full duplex). You'll run at 800 Mbps peak rate over 100Base-TX cabling.

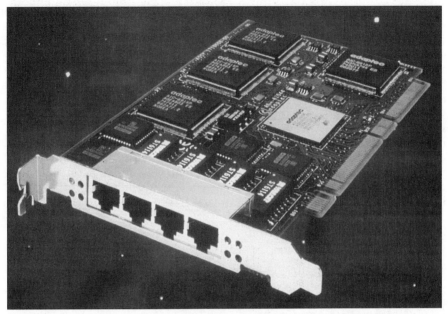

**Figure 27-8:** The Adaptec ANA-62044 four-port adapter lets you connect four independent 100 Mbps Ethernet segments to a file server. (Photo courtesy Adaptec.)

## Table 27-4
### Adaptec ANA-62044 Specifications

| Characteristic | Specification |
| --- | --- |
| Cable type support | 10Base-T (category 3, 4, or 5 unshielded twisted pair), full duplex<br>100Base-TX (category 5 unshielded twisted pair or category 1 shielded twisted pair), full duplex |
| Bus interface | 64-bit PCI bus master |
| Operating system driver support | Windows NT and Novell |
| Transmit/receive buffer | 4K each transmit and receive on each of four channels |

## ActionTec ActionLink telephone line LAN NIC

The rapid increase in homes with several PCs, and in homes using the Internet, has created a demand for home networks. Many home computer users don't have the ability or inclination to install twisted pair or coaxial cable, though, leading to the need for home network products that simplify installation.

The best answer so far is a technology promoted by the Home Phoneline Networking Alliance (HPNA) that lets you run up to a megabit per second over the telephone wiring in your home. You can connect two or more PCs using an ActionLink card in each. As with a modem, if you plug in the ActionLink where there's currently a telephone, you wire the card to the wall and then plug the phone into the card. Once the system's up and running, you won't notice it. The telephone will still work as it always has, even when your network is busy working.

Figure 27-9 shows the ActionLink card. If you look carefully at the photo, you'll see the usual PCI connector on a card, a very few small components, and one enormous chip. That chip, made by AMD, makes the card look like a conventional PCI NIC to your computer and implements the electronics to meet the HPNA standards over the telephone wires. Using the ActionLink, you'll send and receive at 1 Mbps between your computers.

**Figure 27-9:** The ActionTec ActionLink telephone line network cards let you use your phone lines as a LAN and retain use of the phone. (Photo courtesy ActionTec.)

The ActionLink cards (and the software drivers), combined with Windows, are all you need to network your computers together. It takes a little more software to let all your networked computers share your Internet connection—ActionTec ships software called DynaNAT with the cards that handle that chore, or you can use Internet Connection Sharing (ICS) in Windows 98 Second Edition. We found ICS worked smoothly with the ActionLink—once we'd set up the computer that runs ICS, adding more computers to the network was as simple as installing the ActionLink card. All the details of network addresses were automatic.

# Choosing Your Network Technologies

The first question, of course, is whether you have more than one computer in the same location. If not, a local area network won't buy you much.

Ignoring that, all local area network equipment decisions really boil down to how many computers you have, what your bandwidth requirements are, and whether you have mobile users. With the exception of home networks that can use the 1 Mbps phone line technology, we recommend twisted pair for nearly all applications. Fiber optics or wireless to the desktop is more expensive than most applications warrant, although one notable exception for fiber is that it provides complete electrical signal isolation between the connected computers. This can be important for noise and lightning immunity, or for special security requirements.

Having a network connected doesn't necessarily mean you've created everything you need. You need to think through the issues of where users keep files, how they're backed up, and what kind of security you need. See Chapter 30, "Accessing and Serving the Internet," for how to create high-performance, high-capacity networks, and how to approach security. Chapter 16, "Tape", looked at tape backup technologies you might want to consider.

The recommendations in this section really deal with what you might do in a small-to-medium office. In a large office, you'll want to use 10/100 Mbps adapters without question, and you should choose the hubs you use as part of your backbone network architecture. Take a look at Chapter 30 for some ideas, and be prepared to monitor traffic in your network and make adjustments.

The twisted-pair connections for 10Base-T, 100Base-TX, or 100Base-T4 are more reliable than 10Base-2, but if you have more than two computers, twisted pair means you need a hub. That means that 100 Mbps speeds are inexpensive for two computers but not for three or more. Figure 27-10 summarizes an approach for small office users. The basic lessons to draw from the figure are:

✦ *Avoid obsolescence when it's inexpensive to do so.* Because you can get 10/100 Mbps adapter cards for minimal added cost, you should go for that technology.

✦ *Use a 100 Mbps connection (back to back, with no hub) for two computers.* If you only have two computers, you can use a crossover cable directly between the two adapters and get 100 Mbps speed for nearly zero cost beyond the adapters.

✦ *Use twisted pair if the computers are somewhat distant.* If the computers aren't within arm's reach of each other, you'll want the reliability of 10Base-T rather than 10Base-2 coaxial cable. A 100 Mbps hub is prohibitively expensive, so go for a 10Base-T unit.

It's a good idea to have all your adapters be the same model if you can. This prevents your having to worry about varying software configurations, and it reduces the number of technical support departments you'll have to call if you end up needing help.

If you have a local area network and use an Internet (or other network) connection extensively enough to have a connection at ISDN speeds or faster, you'll want to tie that connection to your local area network. That strategy simplifies the problem of letting all the computers access the network on an equal basis. Otherwise, you'll need to route the machines that don't have the wide area network connection through the one that does, which complicates your software setup problems.

Table 27-5 shows another view of how to choose network cards and technology.

| Table 27-5 Your Computer Bus and Network Speed Interact at the Network Adapter Card | | |
|---|---|---|
| *Wiring Type* | *Bus Type* | *Card Technology and Advantages* |
| Unshielded twisted pair (UTP) | PCI | 100Base-TX or 100Base-T4 provides top network performance. A PCI network adapter has the bus bandwidth to sustain full-rate network transfer. A PCI network card on a 10 Mbps network provides slightly better transfer rate than an ISA card, but not dramatically so. |
| | ISA | You can connect a 100Base-TX or 100Base-T4 ISA network adapter to an ISA bus, but the bus won't support sustained full-rate network transfers. An ISA network card is well matched for a 10 Mbps network. |
| Coax or mixed UTP and coax | PCI | Use PCI Combo cards offering both 10Base-T and 10Base-2 connections. The availability of both connection types on the card means you don't have to be concerned about the card type when you move a PC to a different place in your network. |
| | ISA | Use ISA Combo cards. |

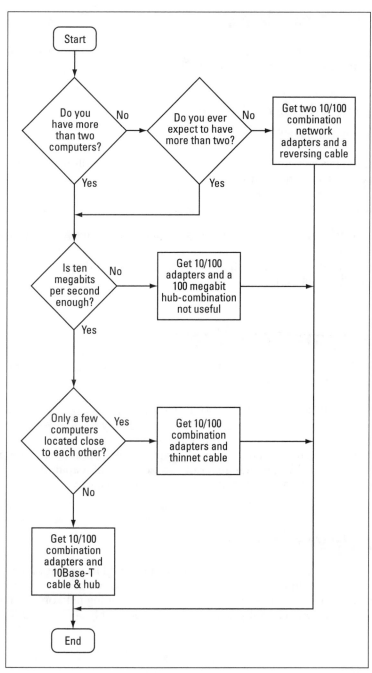

**Figure 27-10:** If you have only two computers, you can have a really fast network for very little cost.

# Top Support Questions

The cabling and other network devices are nearly invisible to most users, so the common problems are related to the network interface cards.

## PCI Network Interface Cards

Q: Do I have to configure my PCI adapter for my computer?

A: Usually not. PCI is a self-configuring bus architecture, so you should not need to do anything except install the board in your system.

Q: Which PCI slot is best for my network adapter?

A: PCI adapters will work in any PCI slot in the system; some will work in slave-only slots. Check the motherboard user's guide for information on which slots support bus-master data transfers. Older motherboards with 3 PCI slots seem to have slave-only slots more often than others.

# ISA Network Interface Cards

Q: I installed a Plug and Play ISA network adapter in my computer, but neither the diagnostic and configuration program nor the driver can find it. What's wrong?

A: Your computer's BIOS is issuing a series of I/O instructions that causes the adapter to think it's going to be activated as a Plug and Play device. Your manufacturer should provide software that can turn off the Plug and Play features, leaving the board as a conventional adapter. This problem is common with Windows NT 4 and UNIX, which generally don't have PnP capability. Windows 9x and Windows 2000 can configure PnP cards properly.

# Hands-On Upgrades

A network is one of the most powerful upgrades you can add to a computer, because it lets you share information, disks, printers, and other resources. Many users are put off by the new ideas and terminology surrounding networks, but if you work methodically and carefully, a network upgrade is only slightly harder than any other.

# Adding a Network Card

Bringing your computer up on your network requires that you add a network interface card (NIC). Let's start with Windows 9*x*. These directions apply not only for traditional NICs, but for phone line network cards like the ActionTec ActionLink.

If you're not using a PCI or Plug and Play ISA card, you'll need to identify free I/O ports and a free interrupt, and configure the card accordingly. You may need to identify a free block of memory in high memory too, depending on the requirements of your NIC. The Device Manager (Start ⇨ Programs ⇨ Settings ⇨ Control Panel ⇨ System ⇨ Device Manager) can help you do that, particularly if you look at the properties of the "Computer" entry at the top of the window displaying your devices.

Insert the card, and power up your computer. In the best case, Windows will see the card, assign (or identify) its resources, and request to load programs from your CD-ROM; you'll then be on the LAN. If Windows doesn't automatically see the card, try letting it detect new hardware (Start ⇨ Programs ⇨ Settings ⇨ Control Panel ⇨ Add New Hardware), letting Windows scan itself. If that doesn't work, try the same sequence, but rather than having Windows scan automatically, choose your hardware manually. If Windows doesn't have a driver for your network card, use the Have Disk option part way into the manual process for adding hardware, and point Windows at the drivers on the disk from the card manufacturer.

Even if Windows sees the card, it may detect a conflict with another device in your system. If that happens, use the Device Manager to look at the properties of the device, and switch to the Resources tab to see where the conflict is. You may have to set the device resources manually.

Here's an example. We put a Plug and Play ISA network card into a completely Plug and Play system (all PCI cards except a Plug and Play ISA sound card). Windows detected the new network card and loaded software for it, but the network didn't work. Checking the Device Manager, we found a conflict for IRQ 3 between the network card and the COM2 port. Plug and Play should have avoided that conflict but didn't. We checked in the Device Manager, found that IRQ 9 was unused, and went into the configuration software for the NIC. We changed the setup there, leaving the card in Plug and Play mode but changing the interrupt listed on the same screen to IRQ 9. We then rebooted the computer and found the conflict solved. (An important underlying lesson here is that there's a certain degree of pragmatism that helps in fixing computers. Rather than spend days trying to find out why Plug and Play failed to move the NIC interrupt off IRQ 3, we simply fixed the problem.)

Once you have the card set up so that Windows thinks it's operating correctly, check what software it's loaded (Start ⇨ Programs ⇨ Settings ⇨ Control Panel ⇨ Network). Figure 27-11 shows some of the options you might see. Here's what they are:

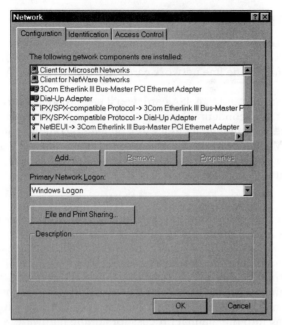

**Figure 27-11:** Use the Network applet to choose the network capabilities you want on your system.

✦ *Client for Microsoft Networks.* This is the top-level software that enables access to and from other computers running the Microsoft protocols.

✦ *Client for NetWare Networks.* This is the top-level software that enables access to other computers acting as Novell file servers. Even if you don't have a Novell server locally, you might need the Novell client for dial-up access to a remote computer.

✦ *3Com Etherlink III Bus-Master PCI Ethernet Adapter.* This is the NIC on the machine; the name you see will vary if you have a different card.

✦ *Dial-Up Adapter.* This allows network access out through a directly attached modem. Even if your network provides Internet access through a router, you may want a directly attached modem because some private services aren't available on the Internet. If you use a directly connected modem, you'll need this component.

✦ *IPX/SPX-compatible Protocol ⇨ 3Com Etherlink III Bus-Master PCI Ethernet Adapter.* This component provides the capability to run the Novell protocols. You would use this component as part of the software to reach a Novell file server.

✦ *IPX/SPX-compatible Protocol ➪ Dial-Up Adapter.* You can bind a protocol to more than one network device, such as if you have multiple NICs or a NIC and a modem.

✦ *NetBEUI ➪ 3Com Etherlink III Bus-Master PCI Ethernet Adapter.* NetBEUI is the protocol underlying the Microsoft network services. Binding it to the NIC enables those protocols over the LAN. NetBEUI isn't routable under normal circumstances, so there's little point in binding it to the dial-up adapter unless you'll be dialing directly into another Windows machine.

✦ *TCP/IP ➪ 3Com Etherlink III Bus-Master PCI Ethernet Adapter* and *TCP/IP ➪ Dial-Up Adapter.* TCP/IP is the Internet standard protocol suite, so you'll need TCP/IP bound to every network device over which you'll access the Internet. It's possible to have Internet connections both over a LAN and through a modem at the same time. You can also run TCP/IP on a network not attached to the Internet.

✦ *File and printer sharing for Microsoft Networks.* You need to include this component if you want to let other computers access files or printers on your computer.

✦ *File and printer sharing for NetWare Networks.* Include this component if you want this computer to act as a Novell-compatible file and print server. Be very careful using this component, because — introduced carelessly into a working LAN — it can redirect default logins from other file servers to itself, disabling other people's computers.

FreeBSD network card support is built into the kernel and is specific by address and interrupt. You'll want to use the manufacturer's utility software to take the card out of Plug and Play mode, and to specify the I/O address and interrupt.

If you're using TCP/IP, you'll need to set up six values:

✦ *Host name.* This is the name of the computer, such as *Mongo, Callisto,* or *Computer1.* Windows doesn't want the domain name included with the host name; FreeBSD does.

✦ *Domain name.* This is the name associated with the network you're on, such as *aros.net* or *IDGBooks.com.*

✦ *IP Address.* This is the numeric address of this specific machine (or specific interface on the machine if you have more than one network device). An example is 206.80.51.140.

✦ *Netmask.* This is the numeric value that distinguishes the network portion of the IP address from the host number. An example is 255.255.255.0. You'll get the IP address and netmask from your network administrator or Internet service provider. Dial-up Internet connections frequently supply the IP address and netmask to your computer each time you connect, sparing you the need to set them statically.

✦ *Gateway.* Your computer needs to know the IP address of the computer to which it should forward messages for machines not directly known in the network. This would typically be your outbound router on a LAN. The gateway is handled automatically for dial-up connections.

✦ *Domain Name Server (DNS).* This is the IP address of the machine used to translate computer names to addresses.

# Summary

✦ In most cases, you probably want twisted-pair wiring and 10/100 Mbps adapters (the fast adapters require PCI or another fast bus). Home networks that can live with 1 Mbps speed can use existing telephone wiring.

✦ You can use a 10 Mbps twisted-pair hub now and upgrade painlessly later (after costs drop).

✦ Wireless and fiber-optic connections to the desktop are for specialized applications. The cost premium is too high for general use.

✦ Cable modems might be great if you can get one, but it is currently very difficult to do so.

✦    ✦    ✦

# Peripheral Network Equipment

**O**nce you've put network and communications equipment into your computer, and once you've set up your network cabling, it's time to connect it into a network. You've got two levels of issue to think about — how to build your local area network, and how to hook up into wide area networks. We'll look at local area network equipment and structures in this chapter. Later, in Chapter 30 we'll look at wide area networks in general and the Internet in particular.

## Local Area Network Design

Network design involves a lot of different (and sometimes conflicting) considerations, including:

✦ *Capacity.* The rate at which information can be sent over the network. You care not only about the rate between pairs of computers, but also about the aggregate rate among many pairs of computers.

✦ *Latency and jitter.* The transit time across the network from one computer to another is the *latency.* The variability in the arrival times of packets, the differences in the arrival time intervals (assuming constant transmission intervals) is the *jitter.* Both latency and jitter affect interactive work. Excessive latency or jitter in a video-conferencing application, for example, can result in choppy audio or video.

✦ *Reliability.* How dependable your network is. This is more complex than whether the electronics are working properly, because an overloaded network can drop packets and fail to complete transmissions. You'll also want to think about the environment surrounding your systems, such as uninterruptible power and dependable backup.

✦ *Security.* How vulnerable your data and systems are to accidental or malicious damage (or theft).

✦ *Scalability.* Networks grow, and you'll want to be able to accommodate growth without having to rip all your equipment out and start over. You'll need to think about connecting more users, more sites, more storage, and more capacity.

You'll no doubt consider other factors specific to your situation as you design networks. Rather than attempt to give you a step-by-step recipe for assembling a local area network (and fail to cover your actual situation), we'll start by describing a very simple network, touching on the most important concepts, and then move on to a discussion of larger networks.

## Small networks

The simplest network is two computers connected back-to-back. Figure 28-1 shows two possibilities — you can connect them with a half-duplex system, such as 10Base-2 (thinnet), or with a full-duplex one like many implementations of 10Base-T. We've chosen two 10-megabit network technologies for this example to keep things as comparable as possible.

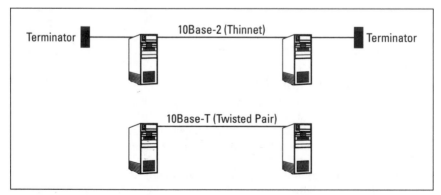

**Figure 28-1:** The differences in performance due to contention are apparent in these two setups.

Suppose you start transmitting two large files, one from each of the machines to the other, so that overall the network is doing full-duplex operations. On the 10Base-2, the cable only does half-duplex transmission, so either one computer or the other (but not both) is transmitting. If both want to transmit (as is likely if both have large files to send), one waits or a collision occurs. The net effect is that the total bits per second you can transmit over the 10Base-2 network is substantially less than the 10 megabits per second raw rate of the cable—it's 10 megabits less the time for a lot of things:

✦ Time spent waiting to see if it's okay to transmit

✦ Time spent waiting to retransmit after a collision

✦ Time lost because a transmission was garbled because of collision

✦ Time lost retransmitting data that didn't get to the destination

✦ Time spent waiting for the destination to reply that it received the transmission

The wasted time goes up as you attach more computers to the network, because it is likely that more than one computer will want to transmit at any one time. The wasted time also goes up as the length of the cable (and therefore the end-to-end signal propagation time) increases, because it is more likely that two computers at either end of the cable may start to transmit within the time window required for propagation along the length of the cable.

In practice, it's certain that you'll get less than a 10 megabits per second raw data rate, but the actual rate you achieve depends on how many other computers are on the network, how active they are, how long the cable is, and how good the cable connections are. It's pretty safe to assume you'll get an average of as much as 2 megabits per second through, but more than that—while likely—isn't assured.

Compare that result to the situation for the full-duplex 10Base-T network. (This requires cards that can do full duplex plus a crossover cable to set up the connection shown in Figure 28-1.) Because the network itself supports full duplex, and because there are only two computers, no collisions are possible—when either computer wants to transmit, it may do so. The result is that you get data through the network as fast as the two computers can push it across.

## Adding to a small network

If you add one more computer to the network in Figure 28-1, the network looks like the one in Figure 28-2. The 10Base-2 setup is largely unchanged—you add another tee connector and the third computer. Operation on the half-duplex 10Base-2 network is unchanged. Each computer, when it has something to send, waits for an opportunity and transmits on the cable.

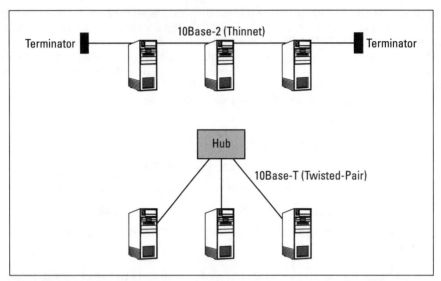

**Figure 28-2:** Adding a third computer to a small network requires only connecting to the cable for 10Base-2 but requires breaking the network into separate physical segments for 10Base-T.

The 10Base-T network is different, though, because you have to add a hub to provide a way to connect the third machine. Each of the three computers is now on a different physical wire. The hub connects the three electrically, but if one computer's network adapter fails, the physical isolation prevents the others from being affected by the problem. A similar failure on the 10Base-2 network would take down the entire network.

Once you convert the two-computer, 10Base-T network to the three-computer, 10Base-T network using a simple hub, you lose full-duplex operation. Every physical wiring segment is electrically connected, so signals on one get sent to all the rest. The network is now half duplex and has the same contention issues as on the 10Base-2 network.

## Medium-sized networks

You can extend the networks in Figure 28-2 by adding more computers. (We'll drop further discussion of the 10Base-2 network here. With multiple computers and connections, the configuration quickly becomes too hard to maintain.) As you add computers, you will probably want to use at least one of them as a *server*, a computer used to provide network resources. The network in Figure 28-2 with a server might look something like the one in Figure 28-3.

The computers where most users work are called *client computers* (using the computer industry's common client/server terminology). The client computers often have their own disk drives, files, and printers. Servers are used to provide larger shared resources to groups of people.

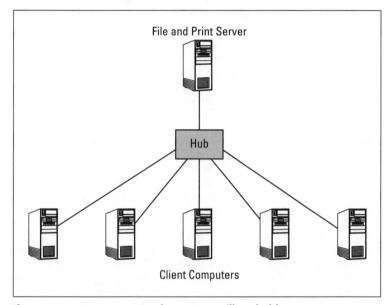

File and Print Server

Hub

Client Computers

**Figure 28-3:** As your network grows, you'll probably want to create a file and print server to make resources broadly available and to improve performance.

You could easily keep adding computers (clients or servers) to the network through a single hub up to about 24 units, which is about the limit for a single hub device, or to as many units as you like if you cascade hubs. Suppose you add a lot of computers, setting up the network as one server supporting 23 clients. On a 10Base-T network, if all 23 clients start to load or store a reasonably large file at the same time against the server, then each one can expect to get one twenty-third of the effective network data rate. That rate will be somewhere between 20 and 70 percent of the raw 10 megabits per second signaling rate on the twisted-pair wires, so the transfer rate between each client and the server will be between 10 and 38 kilobytes per second.

The performance in this example is about 100 times lower than what the same computers would achieve accessing local disks. Admittedly, it's unlikely that all 23 clients would start an operation at the same time. Nevertheless, even if only one in four of the clients accesses the server at any given time, performance is still far lower than on the local disk. Even if the server has enough power to keep up, the reduced transfer rate caused by contention and sharing the network bandwidth in this network architecture causes these problems:

✦ *Server-resident software.* It's very convenient to buy network licenses for programs and keep one copy of commonly used programs on the server. Each client loads the program as required from the server. This makes patches and updates simpler and eliminates having to buy enough disk to store all the programs on all the computers (when you have thousands of computers, a hundred dollars here and there really adds up). Suppose your computer has to load all 5.2MB of Word for Windows 97 to start the program. (It doesn't do this in practice — only part of the program loads.) If you get 100KB per second across your network, Winword takes 52 seconds to start. People don't like waiting that long.

✦ *Loading and saving large files.* It's common to create very large files working with graphics or CAD drawings. Storing a 50MB file across a slow network is not a good use of time for anyone. This isn't a contrived example — we've seen a real-world network on which, due to a combination of network and server limitations, large computer-aided design files take from one and one-half to three *hours* to load onto a fast client computer.

✦ *Multimedia.* This is a variant of the large file problem, with the difference that some multimedia files are read by the processor as the playback runs, not read all at once (reading tens of megabytes of video all at once does not enhance performance). If the network can't deliver the file fast enough — 180 or 200MB per second, as a minimum — or creates excessive delay between some packets due to contention with other users, you'll see jerky playback or hear dropouts in the sound.

✦ *Audio and videoconferencing.* In a way, this is the same issue as for multimedia, except that some of the tricks software developers can play for multimedia files (like buffering a lot of data in advance) are impossible with conferencing. Too much buffering creates what sounds or looks like an excessively long round-trip delay, making the system unpleasant to use.

The next problem in a medium-sized network is that you may want to connect more computers than will attach to one hub, or computers that are farther away from the hub than the 100-meter limit. Figure 28-4 shows the problem you might encounter, say, with separate networks in Engineering and Marketing. If the computers are out of range — spanning the farthest one in Engineering from the farthest in marketing — you can't cable them all to one hub. Moreover, if both the Engineering and Marketing hubs are nearly full, you can't combine them on one hub, either.

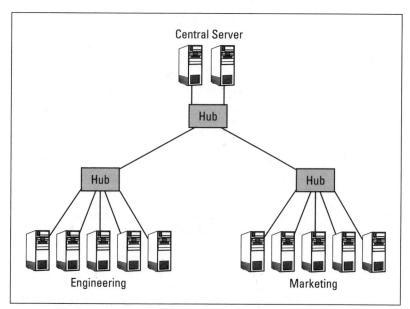

**Figure 28-4:** A hierarchy of hubs lets you connect more computers and provides some extension to the reach of the network.

One answer, shown in Figure 28-4, is to start constructing a hierarchy of hubs, using a hub to interconnect the individual ones in the departments. Extending this idea indefinitely solves the problem of having enough ports (you can have more than two levels of hubs), although there will remain practical limits to how far you can extend the network. We've shown the two servers collected at the same central point as the new hub. This isn't mandatory, but it may be convenient to simplify maintenance.

Another answer to the distance problem is to use a device called a *repeater,* which is (roughly) a hub with only two ports. Putting a repeater in the middle of a connection allows both sides to be extended to the full 100-meter limit. This is fine for specific problems but isn't a general solution to the problem of networking hundreds or thousands of clients in a campus full of buildings.

The other problem that remains unsolved is network capacity—the data rate each computer can achieve over the network. The problem here is that all the computers are sharing one single network, so only one can communicate at once. The obvious answer is to divide things into multiple interconnected networks, and there are devices to do that.

# Interconnected and large networks

One of the ways to reduce network traffic is to make the hubs a little bit smarter. You could do this by building a device that has two (or more) network segments connected to it — like a hub — but instead of a mere electrical connection, you could put a processor and some memory between the segments to pass messages back and forth.

## Bridges

The device you could build this way, shown in Figure 28-5, is called a *bridge*. You need the memory (in addition to the processor) for buffering, because the bridge typically needs to finish pulling a message off one network interface before it can send it on the other. If the processor does no filtering, passing everything it hears on one segment over onto the other one (and vice versa), the network will work the same as it used to. You can have dissimilar network media on the two Ethernet interfaces (10Base-T and 10Base-2, for instance), which means a bridge can join physically incompatible networks.

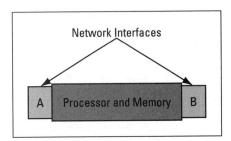

**Figure 28-5:** A bridge (in its simplest form) lets you join dissimilar Ethernets.

You can improve the programming in the bridge so that it notices what network addresses it sees on each segment, because every Ethernet packet includes both its source and destination address. If the bridge software records the source address of every packet and remembers the network interface it's associated with, it will soon build a table that lets it know the identity of every device connected to each segment.

Once the bridge knows what physical addresses are where, it can start being smart. Suppose the bridge receives a packet on Interface A in Figure 28-5 that's destined for an address on the same segment to which A is tied. That means the bridge doesn't need to forward the packet on Interface B — it's pointless, because that's not where the destination is. The bridge can drop the packet "on the floor," secure in the knowledge that despite its doing so the packet will reach its destination.

Look what happened in the process: You reduced the traffic on Segment B. If the bridge does the same thing for traffic on Segment B, you reduce the traffic on Segment A. Overall, you're identifying traffic local to a segment and declining to let it out of the local network. This corresponds fairly well to how things work in practice in many offices. People tend to have offices near the other people they work with, and so it's logical that most of their network traffic would be local. If you keep the server local (unlike the network in Figure 28-4), you can keep the server network traffic localized.

This makes a strategy for increasing network capacity possible: Divide the network into segments based on traffic distribution, and use intelligent bridges to connect the segments with a backbone (see Figure 28-6). Each department has its own local hub-based network. Only traffic for destinations unknown in the local department make it through the hubs into the backbone. If there are enough computers, individual departments may need their own hierarchical hub setups (or even their own bridges).

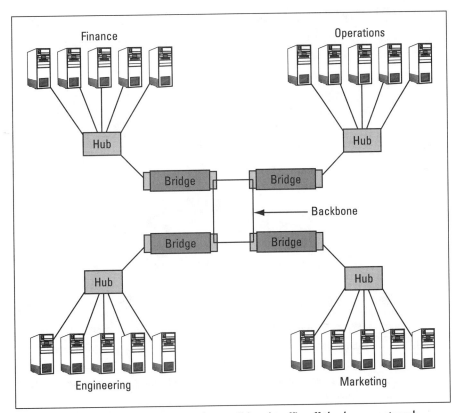

**Figure 28-6:** Intelligent bridges can keep all local traffic off the larger network, increasing capacity.

Although bridges work well for many applications, they have a few disadvantages:

✦ *Local capacity.* A bridge does little or nothing for network capacity in a local area. If the traffic local to Engineering (Figure 28-6) overloads the network in that area, the only answer to improving performance with bridges is to further split up the network. The problem becomes that, sooner or later, there are no more sensible divisions to make—the traffic is simply too interconnected. When that happens, there are no more gains to be had from localizing traffic.

✦ *Backbone capacity.* As the nonlocal traffic among departments grows, you're eventually going to overload the capacity of the backbone. You can try creating intermediate backbones (Figure 28-7), but this approach eventually fails in the same way as for local traffic—there's some volume of nonlocal traffic you can't subdivide.

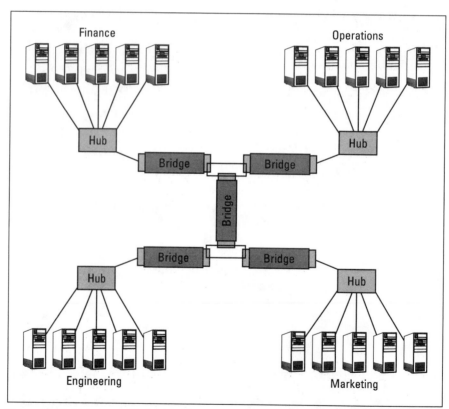

**Figure 28-7:** You can split the backbone to divide the traffic, but eventually you'll run out of capacity.

✦ *Security.* Bridges provide no access control—any machine can send any message to any point in the network.

✦ *Wide area network access.* You're not likely to connect to the Internet (or other wide area networks) through a bridge, and even if you manage to find a way to do so, you're going to want to think hard about the security issue before you do it.

## Ethernet switches

Let's solve the local problems and some of the backbone capacity problems. Recall the half-duplex, one-at-a-time operation of Ethernet. It's the shared media that cause the raw capacity to be divided among all the connected computers. Bridges increase capacity by reducing the number of computers sharing a segment.

To address the local capacity problem, you could build another kind of device along the lines of Figure 28-8. The idea is to have a set of network interfaces, similar to what is used in a bridge, but instead of a single path from the input segment to all output segments, you use what's called a *switching fabric*. The switching fabric is capable of connecting any one interface to any other, without involving the rest. Better yet, it can do many such connections at once, meaning (for example) that packets can go from A to D at the same time as other packets go from B to E, C to G, and H to F. An eight-port hub connecting half-duplex 10Base-T segments can transfer no more than 10 megabits per second; our device can transfer up to 40 megabits per second because it can support four paths independently. If it worked full duplex, it could transfer up to 80 megabits per second.

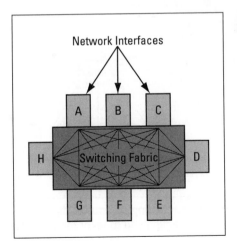

**Figure 28-8:** An Ethernet switch partitions your network into separate segments, keeping traffic confined to appropriate places.

Devices like the one in Figure 28-8 are called *Ethernet switches*. They let each interface act like an independent segment, but at the same time they interconnect them all. Ethernet switches are available with a very large number of ports and can be cascaded in a hierarchy just like hubs. There are two basic options for using them (see Figure 28-9). One is to attach clusters of computers through hubs into the switch; the other is to attach computers directly to the switch. Every port on the switch is an independent 10 (or 100) megabit per second segment, so computers attached through a hub divide that capacity among themselves, while a computer attached directly receives the entire capacity for itself. Some switches don't support attaching hubs, just single devices. These are called *node switches,* while the kinds that allow attached hubs are *segment switches.*

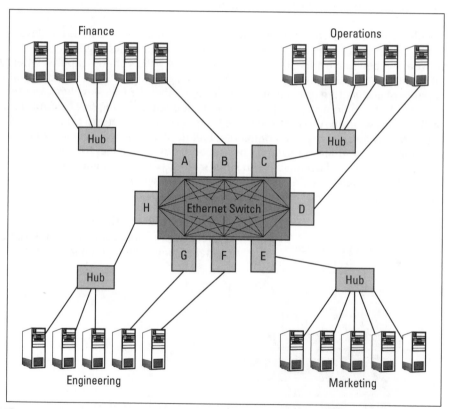

**Figure 28-9:** An Ethernet switch creates options for attaching computers directly to the backbone as well as in clusters through hubs, enabling you to tailor the capacity available to any computer.

In a large office, you might have several Ethernet switches in a single department to divide the network into enough segments to provide the capacity you want. If you do, you'll want to connect the switches together with a backbone, much as in Figure 28-6 connecting the bridges. The backbone will eventually run out of capacity, so you need to beef it up.

The most straightforward way to get more backbone capacity is to use a faster network technology. If you interconnect the switches with an FDDI ring, for instance, you not only get a 100 megabit per second rate on the fiber, you also get the ability to connect switches that are physically quite distant. This solution lets local area networks span several buildings. Switches closer to one another may be interconnected with a 100-megabit Ethernet switch.

If your network gets large enough, or your backbone-level traffic is great enough, even the FDDI or Fast Ethernet backbone networks will get congested. You could migrate to Gigabit Ethernet, or you could use the two other switching technologies in the next two sections: routers and ATM switches. With ATM switches, you can resolve the congestion problem caused by large, high-capacity networks. You can use another switching technology — Asynchronous Transfer Mode — to create arbitrarily high-capacity networks. Routers are the next logical step after bridges and Ethernet switches, though, so the discussion of ATM comes after the one on routers.

### Routers

Even with technologies like Ethernet switches to join network segments, there comes a point when it's not practical (or desirable) to keep connecting networks together this way. You probably don't want to connect to a network that is not under your control without some safeguards, and the tables that your bridges and switches have to maintain to know what physical addresses are associated with what network interfaces will get unmanageably large.

To understand how networks solve these problems, you need some more networking background. Specifically, you need to understand the conceptual *layers* with which networks are built. Each layer serves a different function. Figure 28-10 shows three layers from a larger structure called the Open Systems Interconnect (OSI) Reference Model. The layers shown in Figure 28-10 are the bottom three of seven layers in the full OSI model:

> ✦ *Physical layer.* The actual conversion of data to signals on the network cable, and recovery back to data at the other end, is handled by the physical layer. In a 10Base-2 Ethernet, this means driving signals onto the wire and detecting collisions. In FDDI, this means driving signals onto the fiber ring.

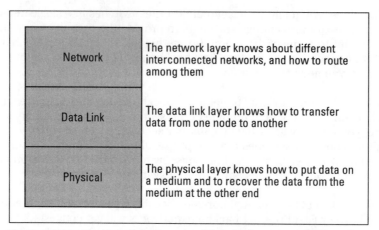

**Figure 28-10:** The OSI Reference Model provides a way to structure network hardware and software to make interconnections easier.

✦ *Data link layer.* The identification of stations on the medium, and the low-level control of transmissions between stations, is the responsibility of the data link layer. In an Ethernet network, the data link layer defines unique identifiers for each station, defines the way in which stations find out each other's addresses, and defines the mechanisms for handling collisions.

✦ *Network layer.* Tracking interconnected networks and the routes among them and transferring network packets along the way to the right network, are the task of the network layer. The network layer operates independently from the media technologies below it.

These three layers of the model are just that — a model. Real networks correspond roughly to the model but have differences and compromises in order to make things run efficiently and economically.

The transmission media form the physical layer. The key characteristic distinguishing the network layer from the data link layer for our purposes here is that the network layer is independent of the underlying media characteristics. Devices operating at the data link layer, such as bridges and Ethernet switches, exploit the physical characteristics of Ethernet (and the similarities among 10Base-2, twisted-pair, and fiber-optic versions of Ethernet) to do their work. Devices operating at the network layer, called *routers,* transfer network data from one port to the next independent of the type of network connected to the interfaces.

Because networks operate at both media-dependent and media-independent levels, it follows that your computer has both physical and logical (that is, network) addresses. The physical address on an Ethernet is a unique number wired into your Ethernet card by its manufacturer — the one for one of our computers, for example, is 00-20-AF-F8-29-B4.

The network address is more complicated. Figure 28-11 shows how two computers connected back to back communicate. A protocol stack implements the network layers on each computer. Each layer in the stack interoperates as a peer with the same layer on the other computer, so (for example) the network layer on Computer A in Figure 28-11 communicates peer to peer with the network layer on Computer B. The two network layers don't connect directly, though — they have to send messages back and forth through the data link layer. A (different) peer relationship exists between the network layers, which themselves communicate by sending messages back and forth using the physical layer. It's the physical layers that are actually connected, so they have a real connection and do communicate directly.

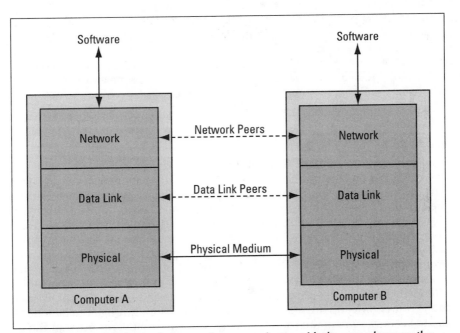

**Figure 28-11:** Each layer in the network communicates with the same layer on the other end of the connection, operating through the layers below it in the protocol stack.

## Physical addresses and network addresses

Because the network layer is independent of the specific data link and physical layers, it can't use the physical device address used by the data link and physical layers. The network layer still needs an address for every node on the network, though, so it has to have its own address. The network address is completely independent of the physical address—if I change Ethernet cards, for instance, I change the computer's physical address but not the network address.

The form of a network address depends on what software you're running at the network layer. If you run the Internet Protocol (IP), you probably have an IP address consisting of four numbers (like 206.164.111.239). If you run Novell's IPX protocol, your network address will look quite different (for example, 00000000:0020AFF829B4).

You can run more than one network protocol at a time, in which case you'll have several different network addresses that all refer to the same machine. If you have more than one network interface (a network card and a modem connected to the Internet, for example), you can have more than one network address for each protocol. For example, 206.164.111.239 might be a network address temporarily assigned to your computer by your Internet service provider, while you might use 192.168.0.1 for your local area network (valid for local area networks that are not directly connected to the Internet). That would be true if you were using Windows 95 on the machine with the modem, or Windows NT and had not enabled routing. If you were using Windows NT to route the local network through to the Internet, you'd have to have IP addresses assigned by your Internet service provider.

In order to connect two different networks without merging them physically, you need a device that joins networks at the network layer, not the data link layer. That device is a *router*. It contains network-layer software that connects as a peer to the network software in your computer, receives messages, decides which port leads to the message's destination, and sends the message down to the data link layer in the right protocol stack. Figure 28-12 shows these relationships. Suppose software on your computer needs to send a message to a computer on the Internet. Your software passes the message to the network layer on your computer (IP—Internet Protocol—in this case), which figures out which of the data links on your computer leads to the Internet. The message gets handed off to the data link layer for that interface, passed to the physical layer, and sent down the wire. The physical layer in the router picks up the message and percolates it up through the data link layer to the network layer in the router. That software in turn figures out that the next data link to receive the message is the one leading to the Internet, and it sends the message down the protocol stack and on its way.

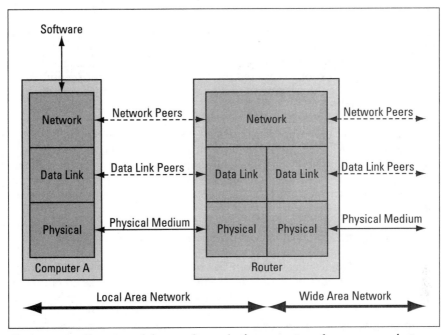

**Figure 28-12:** The network layer software in the router transfers messages between the otherwise incompatible data link and physical layers, allowing you to disconnect your local area networks like the Internet.

The magic is that the network layer in the router allows the data link and physical layers to need peer relationships only with compatible hardware and software at the other end of a connection. The data link layer and physical hardware in your computer — an Ethernet card — don't know and don't care that the ultimate connection is out to the Internet, or that that connection is through a modem and not the Ethernet. Similarly, the modem data link layer and hardware don't know and don't care what your local area network looks like. The network layer in the router is the only software that has knowledge of the characteristics of both links.

This really is serious magic, because it means that, no matter what kind of network you want to attach to your local area network, the right router (meaning one with the right data link and physical interfaces) can do the job without any change in your local network. Better yet, the same magic that lets you splice into the Internet is also the answer to providing backbone networks with as much capacity as you need. Which, as you might suspect from the title of the next section, leads us to Asynchronous Transfer Mode (ATM) and ATM switches.

## ATM switches

Let's revisit the preceding campus network design (Figure 28-9). In that design, a combination of hubs and Ethernet switches serviced local areas. An FDDI ring or fast Ethernet segment connected the switches together. The weakness of that design is that the backbone is limited to about 100 megabits per second and is shared among all the Ethernet switches in the network. It's impractical to simply add lots of parallel backbones.

Here's a scenario to illustrate a situation in which the shared backbone fails. Suppose you're designing a campus network for a relatively large university, and suppose that most of the students live in campus housing that's to be connected to the network, as are all the offices and laboratories. Finally, suppose that about 10,000 total computers will be attached to the network, spanning an area several miles square.

This real-world scenario neatly ruins the shared backbone design:

✦ *Traffic locality.* Students will want to connect to computers in offices and laboratories from their residences, which means that those computers will be accessed both from the physically local area and from clear across campus. It's impractical to think that student housing can be arranged to cope with inadequacies of the network, and the sheer number of connections is guaranteed to overwhelm a backbone running at 100 Mbps or so. The load is even worse when you consider that the campus is likely to have a high-rate Internet connection, all of the traffic for which has to funnel to one or a few points.

✦ *Connection distance.* The physical size of the campus effectively precludes designs using cascaded Ethernet switches to get more capacity.

A large Ethernet switch would be an appealing answer, because a switch with a large number of full-duplex 100 megabit ports sitting in the middle of the network would give us a peak aggregate backbone bandwidth roughly equal to the number of ports times 100 megabits. It won't work in our scenario because of the distance problem. (Actually, the way that bridges and switches route traffic around the network is a problem as well, but it's secondary to the distance problems.)

It's a fair conclusion that what you need for a backbone, then, is a large switch (or matrix of switches). There are a few other features the ideal switch should have:

✦ *High-rate ports.* One hundred megabits per second (full duplex) is the slowest rate worth considering for a big network — slower means you need too many ports on the switch and cables across long distances.

✦ *Fiber-optic ports.* The ports on the switch should be fiber optic so that (within a reasonable size city) you don't have to worry about the length of the run between devices.

✦ *Standards.* The switch should use widely accepted, public standards for the fiber links and for the network protocols.

✦ *Scalability.* The switch technology should be scalable from relatively small devices with a few ports up to telephone office–sized units with hundreds or thousands of ports and the internal capacity to carry traffic simultaneously among all those ports.

✦ *Cost.* The cost of a switch (and of interfaces for connecting devices) has to be affordable in the context of the networks it's being applied to.

This list is a pretty good characterization of what ATM switches can do for you. Let's look at how they work, and then we'll take on integrating them into our campus scenario.

### Cell switching

Any time designers need to make something happen really quickly in a computer, they start moving functions out of software and into hardware. This works because hardware doesn't have to execute programs to get the work done — it just does it. If you want to create a very high speed switch, then, it follows that you'll want to move the switching functions out of software (as in bridges and routers) and into hardware.

The problem in doing this is that the functions performed by the software in bridges and routers are complex, and any time you do something complex in hardware, it gets expensive. Instead of directly attacking the issue of making complex hardware inexpensive, ATM designers took the approach of defining a network technology that could directly be built in reasonably priced, very high speed hardware. Here's what they came up with:

✦ *Multiple data streams on each pipe.* The basic ATM technology assumes that you'll want to carry multiple data streams on each high-speed connection, and that each data stream can route to a different destination.

✦ *Small payloads.* ATM assumes that you'll want to transmit voice and video as well as data, which means that there have to be distinct limits on the latency between chunks of data you receive (otherwise, you'll have dropouts in the audio and frozen frames in the video). Making the data chunks (which ATM calls cells) small helps achieve this by allowing relatively small granularity in switching between data streams.

✦ *Circuit switching with simple decisions.* ATM switches let you set up virtual circuits, which means that you can request the switch to create a connection between you and some other place. Once that happens, a simple circuit identifier in each cell tells the switch everything it needs to know to pass the cell along its way. The complexities of network addresses and routing are taken care of when the circuit is set up.

An ATM cell is 53 bytes long. Of these, 48 bytes are for your data and the other 5 bytes are overhead for the network. In those 5 bytes are the information about how to reconstruct your data stream at the other end and where the next switch in line should send the cell. As the cell transits the switch, the switch rewrites the destination with the right information for the next switch in line (having been given that information when the circuit was set up).

The end result of all this is that what the switch has to do in high-speed hardware with each incoming cell is very simple (to describe, at least) — it transfers it from the input port to the output port, rewrites the destination address, and sends it out the door. This lets entry-level ATM switches have about 16 ports, each running at 155 megabits per second. The switching fabric within the switch is commonly at least 2.4 gigabits per second. Large switches have more ports and higher-capacity switching fabrics. Some have ports running at 622 megabits per second. No matter how you keep score, this is very fast.

### SONET and other non-Shakespearean issues

You may have noticed in the preceding section that we never explicitly mentioned a physical medium for ATM. The reason for that is , like Ethernet, ATM can run over a wide variety of media. Some of the more common alternatives are:

✦ *TAXI (Transparent Asynchronous Transmitter/Receiver Interface).* One of the first ATM fiber-optic interfaces used multimode fiber and the TAXI fiber-optic interface (originally developed for FDDI). The interface runs at 100 megabits per second.

✦ *DS3 coaxial cable.* A T3 (45 megabits per second) circuit on paired coaxial cable was also common in early ATM products.

✦ *SONET (Synchronous Optical Network) OC-3 and OC-12.* The standard for very high speed fiber-optic connections is SONET (or the nearly identical SDH in Europe and other parts of the world). A SONET OC-3 link operates at 155 megabits per second, while an OC-12 link operates at 622 megabits per second. SONET includes extensive monitoring facilities and provides extremely low transmission error rates over very long distances using single-mode fiber.

✦ *Unshielded twisted-pair (UTP).* UTP transmission technology similar to that for fast Ethernet provides 100 megabits per second but is limited to distances far shorter than optical fiber.

ATM is being used for data transmission on cable television networks, and on some ADSL systems, because of its ability to handle a wide variety of data types, from voice and video to data. ATM transmission has been demonstrated over wireless networks, although wireless technology presents unique problems for ATM because

ATM fundamentally assumes transmission error rates better than are common on wireless nets. If you're designing a network, don't combine ATM and wireless links indiscriminately.

Twisted-pair is often the least expensive option for ATM cabling, but for the long-distance backbone application in our scenario, you'll want to use SONET over single-mode fiber to take advantage of its faster data rate and very long-distance capability.

### Integrating ATM as your network backbone technology

ATM switches as the backbone of a network offer great capacity and flexibility. They don't connect directly to Ethernets or Ethernet switches, though, so you'll have to use a router between the ATM switch and the Ethernet. (Strictly speaking, that's not quite true — some ATM switches have built-in routers and can connect to all the sorts of interfaces that routers do.)

If you interpose routers between the Ethernet and ATM switches, you can construct the sort of network shown in Figure 28-13. The Ethernet switches (or hubs if traffic permits) connect to the computers with Ethernet and to the routers with fast Ethernet or fiber-optic Ethernet as required by distances. If network traffic permits, you might be able to combine several Ethernet switches on a single FDDI ring connecting to the router (technically, that makes the switches bridge/routers, or *brouters,* but at this level of discussion the distinction isn't terribly important). You use routers as required (again, by distance and network capacity), connecting the routers to the switches with FDDI and to the ATM switches with SONET fibers. If the overall network capacity requirements are higher than a single ATM switch can handle (or you need more ports than a single switch provides), you can cross-connect multiple switches in a mesh.

If you look at this design for a while, you'll see that you can expand this network to add as many computers as you want — the network design offers essentially unlimited aggregate capacity. Better yet, you can expand it incrementally, adding Ethernet switches, routers, ATM, and fiber runs as demand (or the number of attached computers) grows.

It's also relatively simple to attach a network like this to the Internet. You may want to dedicate an ATM link and router to the Internet feed if the feed is large enough, in order to keep the network traffic from swamping localized parts of your network. This isn't always a small problem. Microsoft, for example, had eight T3 connections in place for the launch of Internet Explorer 3 — a total of over 350 megabits of capacity onto and off the Internet. They were absolutely full for several days, creating major problems in accessing other computers at Microsoft and loading down the Internet worldwide. No matter how you keep score, that's an impressive accomplishment.

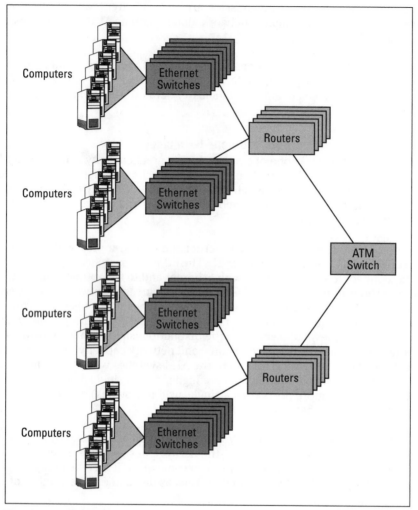

**Figure 28-13:** ATM switches can provide the high-capacity backbone a very large local area network demands.

# Products

Networks aren't a "one size fits all" proposition, because each one exists in a different environment, and because each one grows and evolves to meet different requirements. There's no one best network technology, and no one best network device. That means that network designers need a toolbox — a set of products that they can combine in different ways to meet the needs of different situations.

There's a lot more to good network design than we have space to cover in this book, so rather than cover the ground broadly, the product selection here is a representative set from quality, industry-leading companies.

## 3Com OfficeConnect Hubs

As you start to expand your 10Base-T network up from two computers, or to migrate your 10Base-2 network over to 10Base-T, you'll need hubs to join computers together. The 3Com OfficeConnect series, including hubs, is designed for small offices (or in homes — don't overlook how many homes with personal computers have more than one) and can be stacked to grow into larger configurations. Figure 28-14 shows what the OfficeConnect Hub 8/TPC looks like. It's an eight-port 10Base-T hub and includes a 10Base-2 port to let you integrate your older network cabling. That feature means you can migrate to 10Base-T gradually, not all at once in a spasm of network mania. You can use the 10Base-2 port to daisy-chain several hubs together, or you can convert the eighth 10Base-T port for that purpose.

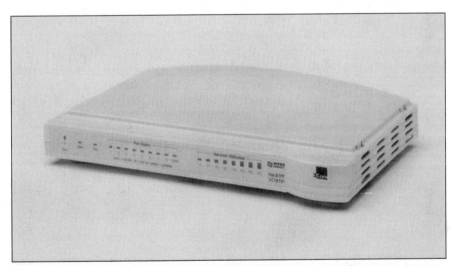

**Figure 28-14:** The 3Com OfficeConnect Hub 8/TPC gives you eight 10Base-T ports plus a 10Base-2 BNC connector to attach existing 10Base-2 equipment in an inexpensive configuration for small offices. (Photograph courtesy of 3Com.)

There's a wealth of information about your network displayed on the front of the hub. From left to right in Figure 28-14 are an alert LED to highlight network overload or an isolated port, a power-on LED, a collision LED to give you a sense of how efficiently the network is running, port status LEDs for all eight 10Base-T ports and the 10Base-2 port, and a row of indicators that gauge how busy your network is (ranging from 1 to 80 percent).

The OfficeConnect series includes many other choices, including hubs that can be remotely interrogated and managed, ones that handle 100Base-T connections, and ones that provide ISDN interfaces.

## 3Com LinkBuilder BNC/AUI repeater

Sometimes you don't want to insert a hub; you simply want to lengthen a cable run beyond normal limits or connect different Ethernet media. The 3Com LinkBuilder repeater (shown in Figure 28-15 and part of the larger LinkBuilder product line) lets you do this. You can get versions of the repeater with two AUI ports, a 10Base-2 and an AUI port, or ST fiber and AUI ports.

The repeater with two AUI ports is the most versatile, because you can get a full range of transceivers from 3Com that adapt the AUI ports to other media. The transceiver types you can get include thick and thin coaxial cable, shielded and unshielded twisted-pair, and ST connector fiber optics.

Don't go wild with repeaters — they don't provide logical isolation between segments, so failures at one end are seen at the other. Repeaters solve two specific problems (limited cable length and dissimilar Ethernet media) and should be applied with care. A network with too many repeaters is going to be a maintenance nightmare because failures will be seen everywhere and will be hard to isolate.

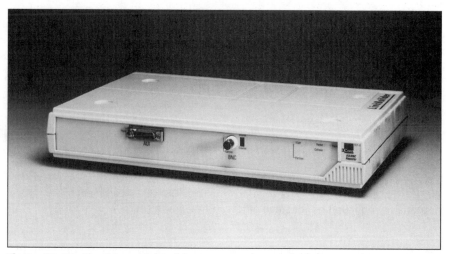

**Figure 28-15:** The 3Com LinkBuilder repeaters let you lengthen a cable run beyond normal limits or attach different Ethernet media together. The photograph shows a BNC/AUI repeater. (Photograph courtesy of 3Com.)

## Compatible Systems MicroRouter 900i

The need to connect a local area network over a dial-up line to an Internet service provider is common enough to warrant specialized, low-cost router solutions such as the Compatible Systems MicroRouter 900i (Figure 28-16). The MicroRouter 900i provides one local area network port (10Base-2, AUI, or 10Base-T) and one RS-232C modem port. It routes TCP/IP (only) between your network and the Internet using the nearly universal Point-to-Point Protocol (PPP) over the modem connection. The modem port runs at speeds up to 115 Kbps (this can be a limitation — see the sidebar "Serial ports and ISDN").

**Figure 28-16:** The Compatible Systems MicroRouter 900i connects a local area network over a dial-up line to an Internet service provider. (Photo courtesy Compatible Systems.)

**Note**   The direct advantage the MicroRouter 900i provides over a proxy solution (such as WinGate found at http://www.wingate.net or Internet Connection Sharing included with Windows 98 Second Edition) is that each machine on the network has its own direct connection through the router to the Internet, without the need to configure software for a proxy. Some Internet Web sites and other services don't work through proxies — you can avoid that problem with the MicroRouter 900i. The MicroRouter 900i is also an alternative to using a Windows NT computer as a router, removing the network processing load from what is probably a server and transferring it to a dedicated, lower-cost device.

## Serial ports and ISDN

If you read the reviews of ISDN modems, you'll see reports that external ISDN modems don't have the speed of internal ones. There's no difference in the ISDN line, of course, so it's reasonable to look for what the choke point is.

It turns out that the problem is the serial connection between the modem and the computer or router. Current-generation computers only support serial port connections at rates up to 115 Kbps, which means that, ignoring compression or any other factor, most computers can't talk to an external ISDN modem fast enough to handle the full line rate. If your modem negotiates compression with your ISP, the situation is worse yet.

This means that, to get full performance from your ISDN connection, you need to do one of four things:

✦ *Use an internal modem.* The serial ports in internal modems typically aren't limited to the 115 Kbps rate. If you can set the port to speeds at 200Kbps, you're going to be able to keep the pipe full. (Of course, the workload on your computer handling interrupts that fast is horrific — you're likely to notice the performance hit on all but the fastest machines.

✦ *Use an external modem with a parallel port interface.* You can get data through a properly designed parallel port interface much faster than through conventional serial ports. The US Robotics DataBurst ISDN modem does this, for example, and commonly rates among the fastest modems available.

✦ *Use an external modem interfaced to a router with a fast serial port.* The serial port problem is usually in the computer or router, not in the modem. If you hook up through a LAN to a router with a fast serial port, you'll keep the modem full, provide all your computers first-class access to the net, and reduce the workload on the connected computers.

✦ *Use a combined router and modem.* There are now a lot of products, such as the 3Com OfficeConnect Remote Access 500 series, that combine a router (or gateway) and ISDN modem in one package. That gives the device the advantages of high-speed internal serial ports and gives you the advantage of the modem workload being offloaded from your computer.

There are other, less obvious benefits from using a router to connect even a small network to the Internet. Compared to a proxy, the router has enormous advantages:

✦ *Better reliability, with no captive computer required.* Using a router frees you from having your Internet access dependent on a specific computer. The software you run on personal computers isn't perfectly reliable, and if ill-behaved software takes down the proxy computer, you've lost your Internet tie until it comes back up again. The router is dedicated to one purpose and is highly reliable.

✦ *Automatic redial.* Internet connections go down at inconvenient times. A router will redial your ISP automatically, restoring the connection without manual intervention.

✦ *Better security.* You can set up filters in the router to disallow different kinds of connections to your network. The resulting security isn't bulletproof (see Chapter 30), but it's far better than what you get with simple proxy gateways.

✦ *Better performance.* A router is likely to increase the performance of communications to the Internet unless you use a fast computer for the proxy. Competition for the processor and I/O tends to slow down the proxy software, increasing network access latency (which is particularly important for both interactive games and videoconferencing).

The MicroRouter 900i is simple to set up. Working with technical support at our ISP, we set one up in about 15 minutes. The steps involved were these:

1. *Assign static IP addresses.* Every computer on your network will require its own fixed IP address. (If that's not practical, you can use a program like WinGate or a gateway access device like the 3Com OfficeConnect 535, in which case you only need one externally known IP address for your entire network.) Your Internet service provider assigns these to you. You change the IP address and subnet mask assignments for your LAN cards to match what the provider tells you. You can tell your TCP/IP software the address of the provider's Domain Name Server at the same time.

   Some routers support Network Address Translation (NAT) and Dynamic Host Configuration Protocol (DHCP). Together, these two features let you assign IP addresses on your LAN automatically, greatly simplifying your LAN setup.

2. *Connect the router.* The MicroRouter 900i has one port for an external modem and another for your LAN. You simply plug them in.

3. *Install and run the configuration software.* Compatible Systems provides a Windows utility (CompatiView) that simplifies configuring your router. If you're running the IPX protocol on your LAN as well as IP, CompatiView can find the router for you automatically.

4. *Set up the IP addresses, subnet mask, and login method.* The router has two IP addresses assigned by your provider, one for the modem port and one on your LAN. You configure the router with those addresses (and with the LAN subnet mask). You then configure the login account name and password (using a simple script language if neither of the standard protocols is suitable).

For installations with simple requirements, you're done — you've added high-performance, reliable Internet access to your network. A ping to a server at your provider should cause the router to automatically dial the modem, link up to your provider, and connect. It's that easy. Don't forget to change the router security password there's a factory default, and you should assume that anyone trying to hack your network would try that first!

## 3Com Office Connect Remote Access Router

We've become strongly convinced that, for sites connecting to the Internet with ISDN, the best approach is to use an integrated ISDN or ADSL modem and router. Not only does the integrated pair reduce your computer's workload, the integration of the modem and router eliminates problems of making the two work together and eliminates the requirement for ISDN software support in your operating system.

The 3Com 500-series Office Connect Remote Access Routers (Figure 28-17) are examples of what you can expect from integrated modem/router units. Versions of the 500 series offer combinations of protocols, ports, and capabilities, as shown in Table 28-1. (The OfficeConnect Remote 811 ADSL Router does the same thing, but for ADSL.)

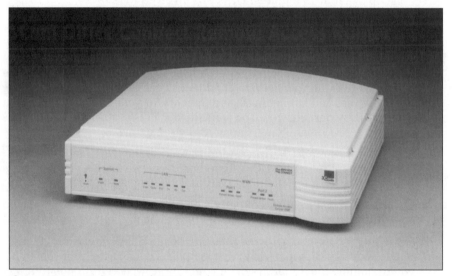

**Figure 28-17:** An integrated ISDN modem and router gives you top performance with simplified system integration.

The 535 is an interesting variant of the remote access router — it lets you use any IP address on your LAN you want, gatewaying the outbound traffic through using its single assigned IP address. You won't be able to have computers out on the Internet connect in to yours, but outgoing traffic will work smoothly. The single-IP gateway eliminates the need to get a static IP address from your Internet service provider for each computer on your network, and since some ISPs don't offer that service, it can be the difference between a computer being on the Net or not.

**Table 28-1**
**Combined ISDN Modems and Routers Offer Varying**
**Feature Sets to Fit Your Application**

| | Remote Access Router Model | | | |
|---|---|---|---|---|
| *Characteristic* | *510* | *520* | *530* | *535* |
| Ports | 10Base-T BRI | 10Base-T BRI Analog | 10Base-T BRI Analog WAN | 10Base-T BRI Analog WAN |
| Protocols | ---------------- IP and IPX routing, PPP, Multilink PPP ---------------- | | | IPX to IP |
| WAN support | | | X.21, V.24, V.35 | X.21, V.24, V.35 |
| Line speed | ------------------------- 64 and 128 Kbps ISDN ------------------------- | | | |
| | | | --- 19.2 Kbps to T1 WAN --- | |
| Functionality | Router | Router | Router | Gateway |

## Cisco 7000 series routers

In a wide variety of situations, you'll want to apply a router. Most of them are of the industrial-strength sort, with the need to handle multiple incompatible protocols and to network among dissimilar data link layer protocol stacks. The Cisco 7000 series (the 7500 is shown in Figure 28-18) is a top-of-the-line solution to those problems, offering broad protocol support, a wide range of physical interfaces, and high performance.

The Cisco 7000 family is designed to cover a wide range of internetworking requirements. Table 28-2 shows the range of physical interfaces the 7000 family supports. You can get direct ATM interface capability using the family's ATM Interface Processor (AIP), letting you interface the router directly to ATM switches. You connect high-speed telecommunications interfaces (T1 or T3 lines, for instance) through Channel Service Units/Data Service Units (CSU/DSUs) into the High-Speed Serial Interface (HSSI) port.

Building a large-scale network requiring a router of the class of the Cisco 7000 series is a difficult problem requiring you to make far more decisions than I can cover here, although you'll look at some of the issues in Chapter 30. The point of (briefly) showing you what these routers can do is to make you aware of the power of what's available, and to illustrate the options you'll want to consider before you start working on your network design.

**Figure 28-18:** The Cisco 7500 is a heavy-duty router. Estimates are that Cisco routers carry over 80 percent of the Internet backbone traffic. (Photograph courtesy of Cisco.)

| Table 28-2 Cisco 7000 Family Maximum Network Interfaces | | | | | |
|---|---|---|---|---|---|
| **Interface** | **Cisco 7000** | **Cisco 7010** | **Cisco 7505** | **Cisco 7507** | **Cisco 7513** |
| Ethernet (10Mb) | 30 | 18 | 24 | 30 | 66 |
| Fast Ethernet (100Mb) | 10 | 6 | 8 | 10 | 22 |
| Token ring | 20 | 12 | 16 | 20 | 44 |
| FDDI | 5 | 3 | 4 | 5 | 11 |
| Serial | 40 | 24 | 32 | 40 | 88 |
| HSSI | 5 | 3 | 4 | 5 | 11 |
| ATM | 5 | 3 | 4 | 5 | 11 |
| IBM channel | 5 | 3 | 4 | 5 | 11 |
| Channelized T1/E1 | 256/256 channels | 144/180 channels | 256/256 channels | 256/256 channels | 256/256 channels |

# 3Com SuperStack II Switch 1000 and Office Connect Switch 140

For many networks, an Ethernet switch such as the 3Com SuperStack II Switch 1000 (Figure 28-19) is the single most significant thing you can change to improve performance. As we explained earlier in this chapter, an Ethernet switch decouples what were formerly shared Ethernet segments, allowing computers on each segment to access your network in parallel and increasing the aggregate bandwidth of your network. The SuperStack II Switch 1000 gives you up to 24 switched 10Base-T ports and up to two 100Base-T ports, allowing you to connect switches together (or to a router) over a fast backbone while you deliver full 10 megabit per second performance to desktops.

3Com offers a range of LinkSwitches, starting with the 12-port SuperStack II Switch 1000. You can get LinkSwitches configured to interface to ATM or FDDI backbones (which may allow you to eliminate the need for a router, depending on your network), and ones providing only fast Ethernet ports. The configuration you'd use depends completely on your network design.

**Figure 28-19:** An Ethernet switch gives you far more capacity over your existing LAN wiring. (Photograph courtesy of 3Com.)

If you have a smaller network but still have large bandwidth requirements, you have options too. The 3Com Office Connect Switch models 140 and 280 (Figure 28-20) provide four 10Base-T ports and one 100Base-TX port or eight 10Base-T ports and two 100Base-TX ports, respectively. You can connect a mix of hubs and computers (see the sidebar "Node and segment switches") to the 10Base-T ports, keeping the 100Base-TX port for connection to your backbone or to a high-performance server.

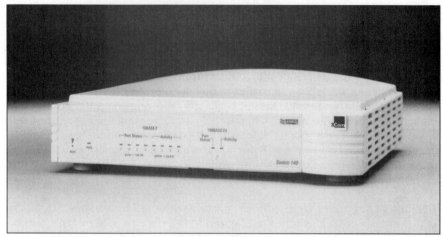

**Figure 28-20:** Small Ethernet switches can increase network capacity in home and small office LANs. (Photograph courtesy of 3Com.)

Here's an example of how a switch can benefit your network. Suppose you have the network shown in Figure 28-21.

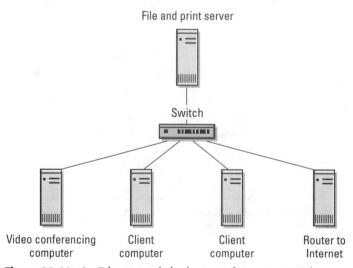

File and print server

Switch

Video conferencing computer

Client computer

Client computer

Router to Internet

**Figure 28-21:** An Ethernet switch gives you far more capacity over your existing LAN wiring.

## Fore Systems ForeRunner ATM switches

When you run out of backbone capacity, you'll want to consider migrating to an ATM solution using switches such as the ForeRunner series (Figure 28-22) from Fore Systems. Comparable in market position to the Cisco routers, the Fore switches are solid, reliable units with an installed base greater than all others. The ASX-200BX offers 24 ATM ports, while the larger ASX-1000 supports up to 96. Both switches support T1, E1, T3, TAXI, twisted-pair, OC-3, and OC-12 interfaces, meaning you can connect them to almost anything. The switches provide fault-tolerant internal operation and allow you to connect them to each other with multiple links to guard against failure of an individual connection.

**Figure 28-22:** The ForeRunner ASX-1000 ATM switch can give you a high-capacity backbone for your local area network. (Photograph courtesy of Fore Systems.)

For computers with the need for low-latency, high-rate connections directly into the core of your network, you can use ATM adapters from Fore (and others, including Adaptec) in the computers and direct ATM connections into the switches.

## Solectek MP series bridge

There will be times when what you need isn't blazing speed or thousands of computers worth of connectivity, it's a wire from here to over there, and the space in between is somewhere you can't go. When that happens, you have two options: You can run wide area network connections through telephone company facilities (expensive), or you can use a wireless local area network bridge like the Solectek MP series bridge. The wireless bridge divides into an inside network unit and an outside radio unit to give you 5.5 to 11 megabit per second network connectivity between points up to 25 miles apart (or up to 13 miles in urban environments). No FCC license is required because the devices operate in an unlicensed band. (Requirements may be different outside the United States.)

**Cross-Reference**

The MP series bridges transport whatever protocols you have on your Ethernet, and support remote monitoring and analysis using the standard Simple Network Management Protocol (SNMP; see Chapter 33). A token ring version is available.

# Top Support Questions

Unless you're a network administrator working with a medium to large-scale network, most of the issues you'll see in your network will center around the wiring and your hubs.

Q: My hub indicates it has partitioned off the BNC part of my network. What does this mean?

A: The BNC port (a barrel connector most likely in the back of the hub) is the connection to your 10Base-2 network. The hub partitioning off the BNC port means that the port has been shut off. If you are not using the BNC port (that is, there's nothing connected to it), then this is normal. The hub may partition off the port if it receives excessive continuous collisions, however, to prevent propagating collisions through the other ports. If you are using the BNC port and have a partition indication, check your cabling and terminators.

Q: My hub indicates it has partitioned off one or more of my 10Base-T or 100Base-T ports. What does this mean?

A: In addition to partitioning off a port that's generating excessive collisions, the hub will partition off ports that appear to be circularly connected. Check your wiring to be sure that you've not connected a set of hubs or switches in a circle.

Q: What type of cabling does the BNC port require?

A: The BNC port typically requires 10Base-2 Coax Cable (RG-58) and 50 ohm T-connectors and terminators.

Q: Does a hub require any software or setup?

A: Unmanaged Ethernet hubs require no setup or software. Managed hubs (such as those supporting SNMP) require configuration into your network management system.

Q: Can I connect a 10Base-T hubs to a 100Base-TX or -T4 hub?

A: You can't connect the two directly unless the 100Base-T hub has a 10Base-T port or has a port that automatically senses 10Base-T/100Base-T operation.

Q: I wired two hubs together, but it doesn't work. How can I expand my network?

A: The ports on a hub are wired expecting to connect to a NIC on your computer, so wiring two hub ports together has the same problem as trying to wire two NICs together. You could use a reversed twisted-pair cable to connect the two, but usually one port on the hub will have a switch that lets you reverse one port internal to the hub. That switch is sometime labeled MDI/MDIX. If you throw the switch on one hub (not both, or you'll still have the same problem), it reverses the wiring and lets you connect that hub to a port on another hub.

# Summary

✦ In designing local area networks, you have to consider individual and aggregate network capacity requirements.

✦ Network performance is not uniform — it will vary across physical regions of your network.

✦ As your requirements go up, you gain capacity by subdividing your shared media segments into independent ones.

✦ The switched backbone architecture scales to very large networks easily.

✦　　✦　　✦

# Hands-On Networking

The component that distinguishes a LAN interconnected with other LANs or the Internet is a router. Router setup can be confusing until you've done it many times, so we've devoted this chapter to giving you the overview you need to understand the process. We've covered setup for a Cisco router you'd use in medium to large-scale networks and also setup for a small LAN with a 3Com router/ISDN modem.

## The Essential Guide to Cisco Router Setup and Operation

If you're going to connect a LAN to the Internet or create an intranet spread over several locations, you're going to end up installing and configuring a router. In this chapter, we'll cover the key information you need to design and set up an IP network, using the command line forms for Cisco routers as examples to illustrate what you need to do. Once we cover the end-to-end basics for the Cisco routers, we'll look at some simpler examples — how to set up a small LAN that's not connected to the Internet, and how to add a small router to that LAN to link it to the Internet through an ISDN LAN. We've used the 3Com Remote 510U as the router in the last part — it's a compact unit that integrates a router and an ISDN modem.

You saw the differences among hubs, bridges, switches, and routers in the last chapter (Chapter 28,). Three key concepts from that chapter are:

♦ *Packet.* A packet is a small unit of data which is transmitted across the network. In IP networks, the packet contains enough information to reach its destination and be processed properly.

✦ *Host.* A host is any network-aware device that is connected to the network. This includes computers, printers, fileservers, and (in certain places like MIT) toasters.

✦ *Network.* In its simplest form, a network is a collection of hosts that can communicate with each other over a local communications medium. It's not necessary to have a router to have a network — in fact, the minimum requirement is simply to have two interconnected computers. Collections of networks are themselves networks, often referred to as *internets.* The largest example of an internet is the Internet.

## What is a router?

In the last chapter, we defined a router as a device that joins networks at the network layer, not the data link layer. An equivalent definition focusing on the operational characteristics of a router is that a router is a device that allows two networks to communicate with each other by sending only the appropriate traffic across the network.

You can see this use of a router looking at the small network in Figure 29-1. Network A has hosts "1, 2, and 3"; Network B has hosts "4, 5, and 6." The two networks are connected via routers — data which needs to go from Network A to Network B must traverse the routers.

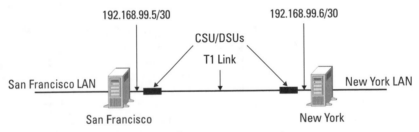

**Figure 29-1:** An example network

When host 1 wishes to communicate with host 2, the router does not send the packets across to Network B, preventing unnecessary traffic from barging in on network B and on any links between Networks A and B. When host 1 wishes to communicate with host 4, however, the router forwards the data across to Network B, where host 4 can receive it.

It's operation at the network layer that lets routers choose what data to forward between connected networks. Data link layer devices, such as bridges, perform functions similar to routers but are less intelligent — they simply redistribute packets across the link without checking the destination more than to suppress transmissions from known physical addresses. If the routers in example A were instead bridges, then the first packet that host 1 sent to host 2 would be sent by the bridge over the slow and expensive WAN link, wasting network bandwidth.

In their simplest application, routers choose to forward or not to forward packets based upon the address of the receiver — does that address belong in Network A, or Network B? Many routers are capable of making other decisions about the data, such as "should I allow this packet to go through at all, or should I throw it away?" This kind of decision making gives a router the capability to act as a screening router or a packet filter. Some of the information routers use for security decisions are:

✦ The address of the sender of the data

✦ The address of the recipient of the data

✦ The program from which the data originated

✦ The program for which the data is destined

✦ The part of the router into which the data first entered, or out which the data would exit

## Why do I need a router?

You need a router to deal with several situations:

✦ *Slow WAN links.* In most wide area networks, the communication links joining the remote ends of the network are slow in comparison to the speeds of the networks that they connect. It's common to find two 10 Mbps office Ethernets that are joined by a 1.544 Mbps T1 phone line. The in-office network is nearly seven times faster than the T1 link, so traffic flowing across those networks could easily overwhelm the relatively limited capacity of the T1 line. At the same time it interfaces the dissimilar communications links, the router helps to limit WAN traffic by keeping all local network traffic from going across the expensive WAN links.

✦ *Maintaining autonomy and security.* If two companies want to share data between their computers, they may choose to link their networks together. Even if this connection is over fast local area network links, it's in the best interest of both companies to restrict the other company's access to the internal network. This issue involves both routing and filtering, and crops up within companies as well as between them. It may be desirable, for instance, to separate traffic within Accounting from that of Engineering.

A more general case of the autonomy and security issue is that of connecting a network to the global Internet, in which both routing and filtering are both advisable and necessary.

✦ *Isolating a network segment.* You'll often find it useful to isolate one segment of a network from others. This can happen because the data on that segment is sensitive (as just described) or dangerous (the research group is experimenting with new networking protocols that could crash unprepared computers), or simply because a group uses a great deal of bandwidth in internal communications that you want to isolate from the wider company. You can also restrict traffic for bandwidth isolation with intelligent bridges and switches (as in Chapter 28), but segregating some forms of broadcast traffic (such as video broadcasts) typically requires more intelligence than a switch possesses.

# TCP/IP Networking

Although the Cisco routers (and many others) can handle multiple protocols, such as IP, IPX, SNA, and others, it's IP (commonly called TCP/IP) that underlies the Internet.

## TCP/IP addressing

IP routing uses a 32-bit address to uniquely identify a host on a network. (This will change when IP version 6 is deployed, but is the standard on the Internet today.) An IP address is written in "dotted quad" or "dotted decimal" notation in which the address is split into four numbers separated by "dots," each having values between 0 and 255, as in "192.168.32.1." This IP address represents the decimal number 3194556361, or the hexadecimal C0A82001. The dotted-quad notation is much more memorable and readable than an unbroken string of eight hexadecimal numbers, which is why most IP addresses you see will be in dotted quad notation.

## Gateways

Host computers in IP networks are generally not required to know how to reach every destination directly. This is important, because as of the third quarter of 1997 the full Internet routing table incorporates nearly 45,000 individual entries and consumes many megabytes of memory on backbone routers. Computers avoid having to have all those entries by being configured with a "default gateway" — when the computer does not know how to contact the host it wishes to reach (such as when it's not on the local network), it sends the message to the default gateway and allows the gateway to route the information properly.

## Subnets

In order to determine the size of a network, IP uses the concept of a *subnet* or *subnet mask*. The term subnet arose because the mask partitions the IP address to create smaller ("sub") networks out of a larger network.

The subnet mask of a network allows hosts on that network to make the distinction between "local" and "nonlocal," where a local host is one to which packets may be sent directly. Recall the network diagram in Figure 29-1 — hosts 2 and 3 are both local to host 1, but hosts 4, 5, and 6 are not. Host 1 may send information directly to host 2 without needing to go through an intermediate node. Host 1 knows that host 2 is local and that host 4 is not from its own address and its subnet mask. The protocol software uses the subnet mask as a bit mask on the address of the host. In IP parlance, the subnet mask tells the computer which bits of its address are the *network* bits, and which bits are the *host* bits. Any address whose network bits are the same as the originating host is local; otherwise, the address is nonlocal.

Suppose we assign the addresses in Table 29-1 to the computers in Figure 29-1:

**Table 29-1**
**Example Network Addresses (Binary Shown below Decimal Forms)**

| Host | IP Address | Subnet Mask |
|---|---|---|
| 1 | 192.168.32.3 | 255.255.255.0 |
| | 11000000 10101000 00100000 00000011 | 11111111 11111111 11111111 00000000 |
| 2 | 192.168.32.4 | 255.255.255.0 |
| | 11000000 10101000 00100000 00000100 | 11111111 11111111 11111111 00000000 |
| 4 | 192.168.33.5 | 255.255.255.0 |
| | 11000000 10101000 00100001 00000101 | 11111111 11111111 11111111 00000000 |

If we write host 1's address in binary with its subnet mask beneath it, we can see the partition between the network bits and the host bits:

```
/--------------network------------\ /---host--\
11000000 10101000 00100000 00000011  IP Address
11111111 11111111 11111111 00000000  Subnet Mask
```

Using the 255.255.255.0 subnet mask, the first 24 bits of the address are the network, and the remaining 8 bits are the host address. That means that 192.168.32 (or 11000000 10101000 00100000) is the network address, and 3 (or 00000011) is the host bits.

A subnet has a starting and ending address, being the first and last addresses in the interval spanned by the host bits. The first address in a network, where the host portion is all zeros, is known as the *network number*. The network number must not be used as the address of a host on the network — it instead identifies the network itself. You compute the network number by taking the logical AND of the host address and its subnet mask:

✦ 192.168.32.0 is the network number of host 1.

✦ 192.168.33.0 is the network number of host 2.

Similarly, you compute the last address in a subnet by setting all of the host bits to 1. This last address is called the *broadcast address*. A packet addressed to the broadcast address is received by all computers in that network.

✦ 192.168.32.255 is the last address in the network 192.168.32.0.

In the example of Table 29-1, host 2 has the same network number as host 1 because it differs only within the last 8 bits (outside the subnet mask), but host 4 has a different network number, as you can tell from computing the network number in the preceding example.

```
/--------------network------------\ /---host--\
11000000 10101000 00100000 00000011  Host 1
11000000 10101000 00100001 00000101  Host 4
```

Here's how to compute network numbers and sizes by looking at the subnet mask:

1. The decimal value 255 as one of the quads of a netmask means that portion of the netmask is all ones, since 255 in decimal is 11111111 in binary. The quads in the netmask correlate directly with the quads in the address, so the value 255 in a quad in the netmask means the entire quad in the address is part of the network address. Similarly, a zero quad in the netmask means that that entire quad in the address is part of the host address.

For example, for the address/mask pair:

```
10.1.1.1    Address
```

```
255.255.0.0  Netmask
```

The network number is 10.1.0.0.

2. Any value other than 255 or 0 in a netmask quad means that part of that quad is network address and part is host address. For these more complicated netmasks, start by identifying what's easy to determine. In the following example:

```
192.168.1.23     Address
255.255.255.240  Netmask
```

the first three quads — 192.168.1 — are part of the network address.

3. There will only be one quad in the netmask that is other than 255 or 0, because all the ones and all the zeros in the netmask have to be contiguous, which means that only one quad can have both ones and zeros. If you're working with the rightmost quad, you subtract that quad from 256 to compute the number of host addresses. For the subnet mask of 255.255.255.240, for example, there are 16 host addresses in this network.

If the netmask partitions at a quad other than the leftmost, you have to multiply times a power of two after you subtract to account for the quads containing zero in the rightmost part of the netmask. If there is one zero quad, multiply by 256; if two zero quads, multiply by 65,536; and if three zero quads, multiply by 16,777,216. For example, if you have a subnet mask of 255.255.224.0, you compute the number of hosts as (256 − 224) × 256, which is 8,192.

4. The easiest way to compute the number of bits in the netmask and the host address is to simply convert each quad of the netmask to binary. Table 29-2 shows you the conversions for values you'll see in netmask quads. Using Table 29-2, the netmask 255.255.252.0 converts to 11111111 11111111 11111100 00000000. The binary value makes it easy to see that there are 22 bits in the network number and 10 in the host address.

## Table 29-2
## Decimal to Binary Conversions for Netmask Quad Values

| Decimal | Binary |
| --- | --- |
| 255 | 11111111 |
| 254 | 11111110 |
| 252 | 11111100 |
| 248 | 11111000 |
| 240 | 11110000 |

*continued*

| Table 29-2 *(continued)* | |
|---|---|
| **Decimal** | **Binary** |
| 224 | 11100000 |
| 192 | 11000000 |
| 128 | 10000000 |
| 0 | 00000000 |

The subnet 255.255.255.254 is peculiar, in that it only has a network address and a broadcast address. That subnet is only used for routing, because it leaves no space for hosts.

5. To compute the network number from the address, you can round the address down to the nearest multiple of the number of hosts. In the case of the subnet mask 255.255.255.240 there are 16 host addresses, so you round down to the nearest multiple of 16. The IP address 192.168.99.23 with a subnet mask of 255.255.255.240 rounds to 192.168.99.16, which is the network number for that subnet.

It is common (especially in Internet routing) to see blocks of addresses referred to by the number of ones in the subnet mask. Instead of writing out 255.255.255.0, you could write "/24" (pronounced *slash twenty-four*) at the end of the IP address. Similarly, the subnet 255.255.0.0 is "/16," and 255.255.255.240 is "/28." Table 29-3 shows the subnet masks for network blocks commonly used on the Internet, along with the number of bits in the network address and the permitted number of hosts in the subnet.

| Table 29-3 **Common Network Blocks** | | |
|---|---|---|
| **Bits** | **Netmask** | **Number of Hosts** |
| 29 | 255.255.255.248 | 8 |
| 28 | 255.255.255.240 | 16 |
| 27 | 255.255.255.224 | 32 |
| 26 | 255.255.255.192 | 64 |
| 25 | 255.255.255.128 | 128 |
| 24 | 255.255.255.0 | 256 |
| 23 | 255.255.254.0 | 512 |

| Bits | Netmask | Number of Hosts |
|------|---------|-----------------|
| 22 | 255.255.252.0 | 1,024 |
| 16 | 255.255.0.0 | 65,536 |
| 8 | 255.0.0.0 | 16,777,216 |

# IP address classes and routing

Early in the development of the Internet, attached networks were organized into classes in a now obsolete routing scheme called *classful routing* that defined classes A, B, C, D, and E. Classful routing segmented the IP routing space into those five classes, which in turn defined the size of individual netblocks and (in some cases) the use of those addresses. A "Class C" netblock, for example, is now generally a synonym for a "/24" subnet, or a block of 256 IP addresses.

The available IP address space under classful routing was defined this way:

✦ *Class A networks.* A class A network is a /8 — a network with 8 bits for the network portion and the remaining 24 bits for the host portion. There are only 128 class A networks, so they are generally either reserved or allocated to very large organizations that had prominent roles in the development of the Internet.

Class A addresses range from 0.x.x.x to 127.x.x.x.

✦ *Class B networks.* Class B networks are /16 allocations, blocks with 16 bits in the host field and 16 bits in the network field. These blocks are more widely allocated but are still generally found at large institutions and very commonly at schools.

Class B addresses range from 128.0.x.x to 191.255.x.x.

✦ *Class C networks.* A class C network is a /24, which is one of the most commonly encountered size of blocks because the relatively small number of hosts in a class C (256) is quite easily managed. Class C addresses are frequently found in the commercial sector.

Class C addresses range from 192.0.0.x to 223.255.255.x.

✦ *Class D addresses.* Class D addresses are reserved for use in multicasting, a form of "directed broadcasting" under IP.

Class D addresses range from 224.x.x.x to 239.x.x.x.

✦ *Class E addresses.* Class E addresses are reserved for future use.

Class E addresses range from 240.0.0.0 to 247.255.255.255.

Classful routing permitted large blocks of address space to be routed easily to a destination without needing to individually route, multiple blocks of (say) 256 addresses — you could route one block which contained all of the addresses.

Classful routing has been obviated by Classless Inter-Domain Routing, or CIDR (pronounced "cider"). CIDR promotes route aggregation — under classful routing, if an organization needed 1,024 IP addresses, it was still necessary to route it four "Class C" addresses. Under CIDR, it became possible to simply route it a "/22," (four class C addresses) as one network block. Most modern routers support CIDR.

# Interface Configuration

The interfaces on a router are its gateways to the networks it joins. The traffic for which a router makes decisions comes into the router over an interface and leaves the router over an interface (possibly the same one). You have to tell the router parameters about the interface in order for it to function properly.

Different interface types, of course, require different bits of information to describe, but all interfaces (Ethernet and serial interfaces alike) enable the router to communicate only with other hosts in the same network as defined by their addresses and netmasks. Communication to distant networks still happens a hop at a time between hosts on the same network.

Interfaces on Cisco routers are specified by their interface names and numbers. A router that has two Ethernet ports, for example, has interfaces "Ethernet0" and "Ethernet1."

You configure an interface on a Cisco router from the command line by obtaining permission to write to the configuration, obtained by the `enable` command, and then entering configuration mode. Here's the command line sequence:

```
router>enable
Password: <does not echo>
router#config t
Enter configuration commands, one per line. End with CNTL/Z.
router(config)#
```

The prompt `router>` indicates the lesser privilege level; after you gain permission to write the configuration, the prompt changes to `router#`. Once you command configuration mode, the prompt further changes to `router(config)#`.

## Ethernet interfaces

Cisco routers, as well as routers from most other vendors, support two different types of Ethernet interfaces: 10 Mbps and 100 Mbps. There are few distinctions between the names (Ethernet and FastEthernet) except for certain configuration directives that are rarely needed. Ethernet interfaces are the simplest interfaces to configure on a Cisco router — simply give them an IP address and bring them up:

```
router(config)# interface Ethernet0
router(config-if)# ip address 192.168.1.1 255.255.255.0
router(config-if)# no shutdown
```

This configures the router to have an IP address of 192.168.1.1 on its Ethernet0 interface, and gives it a subnet mask for that network of 255.255.255.0.

## Serial interfaces

Serial interfaces, generally used for wide area connections, are more complicated than Ethernet interfaces because of the wider variety of protocols in serial communications. Cisco serial interfaces have several defaults that are important to recognize — interfaces default to using HDLC encapsulation, a Cisco-specific serial line protocol. This default works perfectly when used in conjunction with other Cisco routers, but in a multivendor routing environment you may need to change the interface over to the more-common PPP — Point to Point Protocol — settings.

For example, let's set up the serial interfaces for two Cisco routers (named "San Francisco" and "New York") connected by a leased, point-to-point T1 (Figure 29-2). Both routers have a CSU/DSU attached to their first serial interface, Serial0. In this example, the address block "192.168.99.4" with a subnet mask of 255.255.255.252 (this is a block of four addresses with two usable host addresses) is available for assigning to the interfaces. Here's the setup (we've omitted the router prompts from here on to simplify the examples):

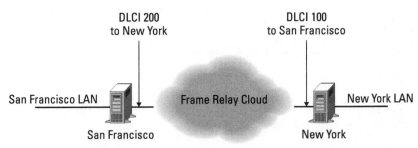

**Figure 29-2:** Two routers are connected by a T1 line, using one IP address for each serial interface.

San Francisco:

```
int serial 0
description T1 to New York router. Circuit ID 101-1
no shutdown
encapsulation hdlc
ip address 192.168.99.5 255.255.255.252
```

New York is nearly identical:

```
int serial0
description T1 to San Francisco router. Circuit ID 101-1
```

```
no shutdown
encapsulation hdlc
ip address 192.168.99.6 255.255.255.252
```

The two routers are now connected. On San Francisco, communicating with the address 192.168.99.6 will reach the router in New York; in New York, communicating with 192.168.99.5 will reach San Francisco.

Instead, suppose you're setting up the same configuration as the last example but no netblock is available to use for addresses on the serial interface. You can use a technique called *ip unnumbered*, which causes the router to borrow the address of another interface for use in the serial link. Using IP unnumbered requires a *routing* statement in the router. Here's how to do it:

San Francisco:

```
int Ethernet0
ip address 192.168.1.1 255.255.255.0
int serial 0
no shutdown
encapsulation hdlc
ip unnumbered Ethernet 0
ip route 192.168.2.1 255.255.255.255 ser0
```

New York:

```
int Ethernet0
ip address 192.168.2.1 255.255.255.0

int serial 0
no shutdown
encapsulation hdlc
ip unnumbered Ethernet 0
ip route 192.168.1.1 255.255.255.255 ser0
```

The statement `ip unnumbered Ethernet 0` causes the router to recognize packets on its serial interface that are destined for the address of its Ethernet interface, that is, to "borrow" its address. Because the two routers' serial interfaces are not on the same network, however, it is necessary to explicitly route the IP address of the remote router to go out the serial interface. This is handled by the `ip route` statement.

More complicated than a direct T1 connection is a Frame Relay leased line. Frame Relay is commonly used to connect networks with multipoint or point-to-point links because of their flexibility and cost advantages. We'll cover point-to-point Frame Relay connections here.

Similar to how a dial-up or leased-line connection establishes a physical circuit, Frame Relay uses a *virtual circuit* between two communicating points on the frame "cloud." The telephone company running the Frame Relay network creates the virtual circuit and assigns you Data Link Connection Identifiers, or DLCIs, to identify the routers.

The best way to assign Frame Relay interfaces is to use Cisco's subinterface capability, because it allows separate bandwidth and link-state monitoring via SNMP and the command line, plus more powerful configuration options. Non-Cisco routers frequently provide a method called *mapping* that lets you assign an IP address for routing to a DLCI.

Frame Relay uses a protocol called Link Management Interface (LMI). The most common LMI is "ansi" or "annex-d." You should coordinate the version of LMI with your Frame Relay service provider, and should use the same LMI type on both sides of the link.

Here's an example. Suppose that, instead of using the T1 line in the previous examples, New York and San Francisco are connected through a Frame Relay link (Figure 29-3). The telephone company has pointed DLCI 100 of New York's Frame Relay cloud to San Francisco, and DLCI 200 of San Francisco to New York. The DLCI assignments are only on a per-router basis, so both routers could see DLCI 100 as the pointer to the remote router had the Frame Relay carrier configured it that way.

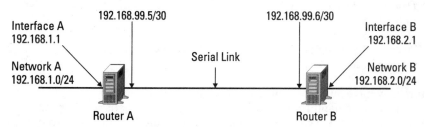

**Figure 29-3:** Two routers connected by Frame Relay.

New York: Configure the serial interface like those just described, giving it no interface and specifying it as a Frame Relay interface.

```
int serial 0
no ip address
description Frame-Relay link
encapsulation frame-relay
frame-relay lmi-type ansi
From here, we need to configure the subinterface
int ser0.1 point-to-point
description Link to San Francisco
ip address 192.168.99.5 255.255.255.252
frame-relay interface-dlci 100 broadcast ietf
```

You'd configure San Francisco similarly, but with the New York IP address and DLCI 200 instead of 100. This establishes the link between the two routers on their serial subinterfaces.

# Routing

A router needs routing information to make decisions about forwarding packets between networks. Some of that routing information is implicit in the router's own configuration — if the router has an Ethernet interface with an address of 192.168.1.1 and a netmask of 255.255.255.0, the router already knows how to reach all of the hosts in the 192.168.1.0/24 network. In many cases (such as a WAN link), the implicit routing information is not enough, so you have to tell the router how to reach other networks.

There are several ways a router gets routing information:

✦ *Implicitly.* It's connected to that network, so it knows the network number and hosts.

✦ *Via static routes.* The information is manually programmed into the router.

✦ *Via a routing protocol.* The information arrives through communication with other routers.

✦ *Default route.* If one is configured, all otherwise undefined routes revert to the default route.

On a Cisco router, you can list the information contained in the router's *routing table* by using the `show ip route` command.

Routers may have multiple sources of routing information. For example, a router may have both a default route and a network route that leads to a certain network. In that case, the router will use the most specific route. For example, to reach a destination, a route that encompasses 65,536 addresses will be ignored in favor of a route that encompasses only 256 addresses.

If there are multiple, equally specific routes to the same destination, the router picks the route with the highest precedence. Precedence is determined by the manner in which the route was learned: Static routes may specify a precedence, while information learned from routing protocols is given a precedence based on the protocol. Within a protocol, multiple route arbitration is handled by the use of the "metric," which is that protocol's idea of which route is best. The way in which the metric is determined is specific to the routing protocol. Static routes do not have a metric.

# Static routes

Static routing is the simplest method of handling routing. In a statically routed network, all routers are manually configured with the routing information that is necessary for their functioning. In many simple networks and for end routers, this may be all of the routing information that a router needs in order to behave properly. For example, consider the network in Figure 29-4.

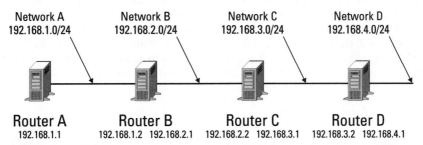

**Figure 29-4:** Static routes tell routers how to reach one another over unchanging communications links.

Network A is 192.168.1.0/24 with router A on 192.168.1.1. Network B is 192.168.2.0/24 with router B on 192.168.2.1. Routers A and B are connected via a point to point link, using the netblock 192.168.99.4/30. Router A's interface is 192.168.99.5, and Router B's interface is 192.168.99.6. Router A needs to know how to reach network B, while Router B needs to know how to reach network A. Here's how to configure both routers to understand their network topology using static routes:

Router A:

```
ip route 192.168.2.0 255.255.255.0 192.168.99.6
```

Router B:

```
ip route 192.168.1.0 255.255.255.0 192.168.99.5
```

From the point of view of Router A, 192.168.99.6 is the address of the Router B serial interface, to which Router A is connected via the point to point link. The route statement given to Router A has the effect of letting it know that to reach the network 192.168.2.0/24, it should send all of its packets to Router B. The command to Router B mirrors this structure, providing the information to route to Router A.

# Routing protocols

Routing protocols allow routers to exchange information among themselves about ways in which to reach networks. There are several routing protocols, each with its own benefit. Routing protocols make life easier on the network administrator and increase network flexibility.

Consider the sample network in Figure 29-5. If you managed this network using only static routes, you would have to configure much more routing information on Routers B, C, and D than seems necessary — Router D would need three static routes, Router C, two, and Router B, one. With a routing protocol, Router A could inform Router B that it was attached to Network A, Router B could inform Router C that it was attached to Network B and knew a path to Network A, and so on. Letting the routers tell each other what they know eliminates the need for tedious static route configuration in all of the routers.

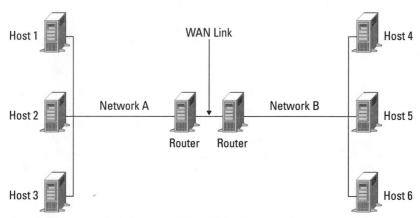

**Figure 29-5:** An example network benefiting from routing protocols

## Routing Information Protocol

The Routing Information Protocol (RIP) is the simplest of routing protocols in use on routers today. RIP implements a vector-distance algorithm in which each intervening router adds one to the route desirability metric. Under RIP, the metric is a count of the number of hops it takes to reach the destination.

The advantages of RIP are that it's easy to use and very widely supported — every router and many hosts support RIP. Disadvantages of RIP include:

✦ *Security.* There's no authentication for information passed via the protocol.

✦ *Recovery performance.* RIP is based on a 30-second route update interval, so it's slow to adapt to changes in the network status.

✦ *Simplistic routing decisions.* RIP has no understanding of route preference other than number of hops. You can't use it to do load balancing or other traffic management. Worse, RIP can only handle one route to a destination, so it does not permit load-balancing across multiple links.

✦ *Limited flexibility.* The original RIP (not RIP-2, a newer and less widely supported version of RIP) can only handle host and network routes, not subnet routes. A network consisting of many subnets of smaller blocks of addresses cannot successfully use RIP. RIP only handles classful routing of full network addresses, not CIDR routing.

✦ *Limited scale.* RIP is limited to 15 hops in the network, rendering it unsuitable for large-scale routing needs.

RIP is ideal for small-scale routing in localized networks but lacks the power required to directly handle the Internet.

### Configuring for RIP

In Cisco's RIP implementation, the `network` statement tells the router the blocks of IP addresses for which it should accept and send routing requests. The sequence that follows configures RIP to accept and send four different IP blocks.

```
router rip
network 192.168.1.0
network 192.168.2.0
network 192.168.3.0
network 192.168.4.0
```

You may not want to accept routing updates from everywhere. For instance, you may want to accept routes from your Internet service provider but not allow machines on your internal network to affect your gateway to the Internet. Suppressing updates from the Ethernet interface on the router simply requires that you add these commands — the passive-interface keyword instructs the router to ignore the specified interface.

```
router rip
passive-interface Ethernet 0
```

### Open Shortest Path First

Open Shortest Path First (OSPF) is a newer routing protocol than RIP. OSPF is more robust and powerful than RIP but is correspondingly more complicated to configure. OSPF uses a link-state protocol instead of RIP's vector distance protocol, which means that OSPF maintains an internal table that reflects the state of all links between the routers with which it is exchanging routing information. Because of that, OSPF is capable of understanding more complicated routing topologies involving multiple paths to a destination, responds more quickly to a routing change, and uses less bandwidth to transmit its routing information (it merely needs to transmit link-state changes when a link between routers goes up or down).

The advantages of OSPF are:

✦ *Security.* Allows authentication

✦ *Compatibility.* Supported by most major router vendors

✦ *Robustness.* Allows complicated, redundant network topologies

✦ *Effectiveness.* More efficient than RIP

✦ *Large scale.* There are no arbitrary limits on hops

✦ *Capability.* Handles CIDR and subnet routes properly, with support for more advanced route preference management

The disadvantages of OSPF are:

✦ *Complexity.* More complicated than RIP

✦ *Interoperability.* Not supported by most host platforms, only routers

### Configuring with OSPF

Your network needs to have an autonomous system number, or AS, to configure a router with OSPF. The AS defines the management area under which your routers are controlled. If you are participating in global Internet routing (which generally means your site has multiple Internet connections through different providers), you'll have to coordinate an AS. If not, you should choose an AS from the reserved AS range of 64512 though 65535. (The examples that follow use 65534 as a sample AS.)

1. Begin configuring OSPF on a Cisco router by defining the router (the protocol) and its AS identity:

```
router ospf 65534
```

2. Then, as with RIP, enter the networks that are under the control of this routing protocol. Let's assume that your network is using a large block of addresses: 192.168.0.0/16, chopping the block up into small segments as in Figure 29-5.

3. Tell the router about this network with a statement different from how you configure an interface, because it uses a wildcard mask and not a netmask. A wildcard mask specifies which bits may change and still be covered by the statement; you can think of the network that you specified as the first address in the range, while you compute the last address in the range obtained by adding the wildcard mask to the network. The statement

```
network 192.168.0.0 0.0.255.255
```

specifies that the router will accept routing information for any address (inclusive) between 192.168.0.0 and 192.168.255.255.

**4.** On our sample network, we simply want to inform the other routers on our network about the addresses to which we are directly connected, so we use the `redistribute connected` command:

```
redistribute connected
```

The router will already redistribute OSPF routing information to its peers, so the network is now complete.

### OSPF authentication

Routing updates from the wrong place, containing bad information, can cause bizarre routing problems. Adding authentication to an OSPF network is often the simplest way to maintain routing integrity. You do this by configuring two things: the OSPF router, and the interfaces. The router controls the state of authentication (used or not), while the interfaces control the authentication password. In this configuration, we introduce a new term, the `area` command. OSPF can have multiple "areas" of routing; area 0.0.0.0 (or just 0) is the backbone area and is the default.

```
router ospf 65534
area 0.0.0.0 authentication
```

This uses plain text authentication. It is also possible to use MD5 message-digest authentication for encrypted authentication:

```
area 0.0.0.0 authentication message-digest
int serial0
ip ospf authentication-key <password>
```

Authentication passwords on a Cisco are on a per-interface basis. Two routers speaking OSPF to each other over the same communications fabric must have the same password set. If you have five routers on an a fiber ring routing together, they need the same password. That password could be different than the password shared by one of those routers and its peer at the other end of a T1 line. All interfaces that participate in OSPF routing should be configured with an authentication key to prevent unauthorized updates.

Instead of having one monolithic routing clump, you can use OSPF to split your network into separate *areas*. Routers inside of an area know only about the routes within that area, which keeps things simpler. For instance, suppose an ISP has a complicated remote point of presence (POP) in another city, with multiple routers using OSPF at the POP. By defining the POP as a routing area from the "backbone" at the ISP, you would shield those routers from the bulk of the routing traffic. Addresses outside the area would be routed over their default gateway up to the backbone.

## Other routing protocols

The other widely supported nonproprietary routing protocol is the Border Gateway Protocol, BGP. BGP (specifically BGP4) is used almost exclusively on the backbone of the global Internet. BGP has proved very successful for handling very large routing tables because of its support for CIDR and its relatively low-bandwidth updates — much like OSPF, BGP only transmits updates to the routing table as they occur. BGP is used primarily as a routing protocol between autonomous systems (which are networks under one management hierarchy) but can be used within a network. The configuration of BGP in an internal network can become more complex than OSPF.

Many manufacturers support proprietary routing protocols in their routers. If you don't need to support legacy networking protocols, avoid using them. Sticking with an open standard such as RIP, OSPF, or BGP4 lets your network support products produced by other vendors. Using vendor-specific protocols typically simplifies configuration, but that won't matter much when your network suddenly requires that you set up one or several routers to redistribute proprietary routing information into a different protocol supported by a different vendor.

Here are a few other routing protocols you may encounter:

✦ *EGP.* EGP is the Exterior Gateway Protocol. Completely obsolete, EGP is the predecessor to BGP.

✦ *EIGRP.* EIGRP is a proprietary routing protocol in Cisco routers. EIGRP is a distance vector protocol with much more link information than RIP, incorporating bandwidth, delay, utilization, and reliability statistics into its distance calculations. It is a better solution for routing than RIP in many cases, but it lacks RIP's easy portability. For larger networks, EIGRP is a much more suitable routing protocol than RIP.

## Choosing a routing protocol

Choosing a routing protocol can be difficult and always depends on the situation. For small networks with only a few distinct network blocks, static routes are a good solution. Static routing is stable and predictable, is not susceptible to possible route leaks from other routers or from misconfigured machines, and requires that no routing information ever be transmitted across communications links.

For small to medium-sized networks that operate with distinct blocks of address space (that is, networks that do not route subnets, or larger blocks of address space that fall outside of traditional classful divisions), RIP may be the choice. The ease of configuring RIP makes it simple to debug and set up on all the routers. RIP is a good choice in environments where hosts on the network need routing information, because it is so widely supported. RIP or static routes may be the only choice if your network includes older routers or routers that do not support more modern routing protocols such as OSPF. IPX routing, primarily used in Novell networks, uses RIP.

Medium to large-sized networks without complicated Internet connections frequently benefit from OSPF. The benefits of OSPF become more and more important as a network grows in size and complexity — networks using "real" Internet IP addresses are increasingly required to support subnetting and CIDR in order to make efficient use of their IP address space. You'll want redundant network connections if reliability is important in your network; under OSPF, you can use those connections to gain extra bandwidth by load balancing. OSPF's authentication capability is a benefit for networks that may have unfamiliar hosts or untrusted computers, and for protection from misconfigured routers.

OSPF may not be usable in situations where large numbers of older or non-OSPF supporting routers are present.

Large networks with complicated and redundant Internet connections, or networks with multiple, multihomed Internet connections, benefit from using BGP on the gateways to the Internet, where it is essentially the required routing protocol. (Most connections to the Internet do not require the use of BGP; a simple default route to your provider will suffice.)

# Security

Connecting computers together raises security issues more complex than those of isolated computers, issues spanning the range from ensuring that payroll computers are not accessible from outside of the Accounting department to protecting a corporate intranet from the global Internet. No matter what the situation, security is primarily about ensuring that only those events occur which should occur. Defining the events which are allowed to occur are an important part of the *security policy*.

## Security policy

Network security begins with a security policy, not with implementation. While an in-depth discussion of network security is beyond the scope of this book, certain aspects of the security policy are critical to the configuration of the router. Your security policy defines the overall policy toward security and can reflect one of two general views:

✦ *Permissive*. Everything is permitted except that which is expressly denied.

or

✦ *Restrictive*. Everything is denied except that which is expressly permitted.

The restrictive view of security is the common view in a firewalled environment where access is severely restricted, but it is not necessarily the correct view for a router deep inside a corporate intranet. Which of these policies applies in your case depends, of course, on what your router is doing.

The most relevant portions of a security policy for configuring a router will answer these questions:

✦ What are hosts allowed access to?

✦ What are other routers allowed to do?

✦ What important conditions need to be logged or trapped?

For example, a part of your security policy may state that:

✦ No traffic with invalid source addresses is permitted.

✦ All traffic between internal hosts is allowed.

✦ Internal routers should only listen to other internal routers for routing information.

✦ Only specific computers may Telnet to internal routers for configuration; Telnet attempts by other people should be logged.

## Screening routers versus firewalls

A router capable of screening (filtering) packets is a very powerful tool in network security, both internally and externally. However, there are some things that routers do not do well and for which a firewall is more suitable.

Packet filters are less intelligent. They make their decisions based upon the source and destination addresses, the source and destination port numbers, protocol, and certain IP or TCP flags set on the packet. This kind of filtering is quite applicable to allowing certain services through, but it fails in the face of other protocols such as FTP or when your requirements are more subtle than wholesale restrictions. A packet filter is good for implementing a highly restrictive security policy ("only outbound Web service and inbound e-mail is permitted"), or a highly open security policy ("everything but remote file sharing is permitted"), but for more complicated security policies, you'll want a firewall.

## Securing a router

If you're using a router in a security-sensitive location, it is important to secure the router as well. Securing the router is most easily achieved by disabling all services on the router that are not necessary to its operation. Don't forget to secure physical access to the router too.

By default, Cisco routers come with certain TCP and UDP debugging services, called the small servers, enabled. These are services like *echo*, which echoes back all received characters to the sender, *chargen*, which generates a continuous stream of characters, and others. Some of these services can be used in a denial-of-service attack, or to try to find more information about your network. To disable them, go into configuration mode and type these commands:

```
no service udp-small-servers
no service tcp-small-servers
```

SNMP can be used to remotely obtain information about your router. In a sensitive location, SNMP should be disabled or very heavily restricted. To disable SNMP, run this command:

```
no snmp-server
```

You should always assign a password to the Telnet ports of the router to prevent unauthorized remote access. Do that with these commands:

```
line vty 0 4
password <your Telnet password>
```

The `line vty 0 4` tells the router that this configuration applies to virtual terminals (the Telnet ports) 0 through 4 — all of them. You can also specify a password on the console and auxiliary ports by specifying `line con 0` or `line aux 0` respectively.

To set the enable password on your router, use the `enable secret` command:

```
enable secret <your enable password>
```

The keyword `secret` forces the router to encrypt the password after you have typed it in.

## Access lists

You control packet filtering on routers using access lists. On Cisco routers, there are two different types of access lists for IP, *standard* access lists and *extended* access lists. (There are other types of access lists for other protocols.) Standard access lists specify only an action, a host or network, and wildcard bits. Standard access lists are numbered from 1 to 99.

```
access-list 34 permit 192.168.0.0 0.0.255.255
access-list 34 deny 0.0.0.0 255.255.255.255
```

This access list permits any address between 192.168.0.0 and 192.168.255.255 and denies everything else.

You can use standard access lists to control routing updates, effectively saying "accept routing updates for 192.168.x.x" and for permitting access to services such as SNMP ("allow SNMP from 192.168.1.39"). Standard access lists are less effective for specifying more complicated security policies, which leads to extended access lists.

Extended access lists allow the specification of both source and destination addresses, source and destination ports, packet type, and flags set on the packet (for example, the SYN flag, which initiates a TCP connection). Extended access lists are suitable for implementing security policies such as "no packets with invalid source addresses are permitted."

For example, Network A in Figure 29-5 has hosts with addresses in the range 192.168.1.1–192.168.1.255. The security policy indicates that only these addresses are allowed to come out of Network A. This policy is a good way to ensure that local network configuration problems (an incorrectly configured machine on the network, for instance) don't spread out of their local network. Network A requires two sets of access lists for this policy, one to control inbound packets and one to control outbound packets.

The format of extended access lists is this:

```
access-list # action   [proto] source source-mask
    [port] dest dest-mask
    [port] [flags] [optional logging]
```

The access list supports these parameters:

✦ *action* is either permit or deny.

✦ *proto* is an optional protocol specifier (commonly ip, tcp, or udp). The default is IP if left unspecified.

✦ *source* is a source host or network.

✦ *source-mask* is the wildcard mask that applies to the source.

✦ *port* is an optional port or set of port range specifiers (TCP/UDP only).

✦ *dest* is the destination host or network.

✦ *dest-mask* is the wildcard mask that applies to the destination.

✦ *flags* are optional flags for established (an already established connection), precedence, or TOS (type of service) specifiers.

✦ *log* tells the router to log any packet that matches this rule.

To implement the address restriction policy for outbound packets, you'd create this extended access list:

```
access-list 101 permit ip 192.168.1.0 0.0.0.255 any
access-list 101 deny ip any any
```

which means permit packets from any source address within the 192.168.1.x range, and to deny anything else. The `any` used in the first access list says to permit packets from these sources to anywhere.

Inbound packets, by the logic just described, may come from any address *except* 192.168.1.x, because those addresses are all used internally. That reasoning leads to this access list:

```
access-list 102 deny ip 192.168.1.0 0.0.0.255 any
access-list 102 permit ip any any
```

## Filtering packets

A router applies an access list to an interface to filter packets. The filter can apply to either inbound packets (those entering the router) or outbound packets. The filter is applied in the interface configuration using the `ip access-group` statement.

For example, to apply the preceding access lists to the Ethernet interface of a router:

```
int ether0
ip access-group 101 in
ip access-group 102 out
```

These commands apply access list 101 (the list that allows only valid addresses to be used on the network) to all incoming packets on the Ethernet port, and access list 102 (the list that disallows other people from pretending to use our addresses) to packets that the router wants to send out the Ethernet port. You can apply access lists to all types of interfaces, including Frame Relay subinterfaces.

## Filtering routing

In some cases, you'll want to have a router accept routing updates for an entire network, such as 192.168.0.0/16, but only accept routing updates for a small portion of that network over a specific interface. To implement this restriction, use the `distribute-list` command with a standard access list. For example, our router wishes to participate in routing all packets in the 192.168.0.0 network but only needs to accept updates for 192.168.0.0 through 192.168.7.255 on its Ethernet interface. Here are the commands:

```
access-list 11 permit 192.168.0.0 0.0.7.255
router rip
network 192.168.0.0
distribute-list 11 in Ethernet0
```

This instructs the RIP router to apply standard access list 11 to RIP inputs from Ethernet0. Standard access list 11 permits only updates in the range 192.168.0.0 — 192.168.7.255.

This same filtering can be applied to routing updates sent by the router by specifying *out* instead of *in*:

```
distribute-list 11 out Ethernet0
```

## Security logging issues

Specifying the log keyword in an access list tells the router to log any packets matching that list to the console and, if defined, to the syslog host (a machine on the network with a syslogd daemon, a program that records messages on the syslog port). Think it through when specifying the log keyword. On a busy router, logging all packets flowing through, it could slow down the router dramatically and flood your logging host with unnecessary messages. Instead, use the log keyword only in places where packets that match the rule are unexpected. (Unexpected packets should occur rarely, so the load to log them should be small.) In general, an access list's permit lines are poor choices for logging — the deny lines are better candidates.

# Planning, Testing, and Upgrading a Network

It's not too hard to see that you need to plan the physical aspects of your network, yet how well you plan the logical aspects of your network is what will determine how much sleep you get. Proper allocation of addresses and creation of a maintainable and expandable hierarchy of routing and addressing are mandatory if you want an efficient and scalable network.

The problem you have to solve is how to map network addresses — the logical topology — onto the physical network. You need to assign every computer in your network an address, and you need to group addresses into blocks to give your routers something to work with. If address groups are random, or fail to reflect the usage patterns of your network, you're going to have to administer the network at very low levels — possibly at the level of individual hosts. Doing that is going to be tedious, boring, and error prone.

You have options, though. Here are two of the key ideas to keep in mind:

1. *Group like entities.* The people and work your network supports have different interests and responsibilities, which means that what they want to do on the network and what the security policy authorizes them to do will be different. You need to understand and map out those differences. In many cases, the organizational differences will correspond to location differences as well — Engineering will be separated from Marketing and Accounting; the West Coast production plant is distinct from the East Coast service and repair plant.

How simple or difficult your routing tables are to manage depends on how physically coherent your IP address assignments are. If all the addresses in an area are from the same network block, the table is small and easy to handle. If addresses are scattered over the physical landscape, you'll need larger tables to reflect the exceptions in the address space to the physical grouping.

Similarly, how simple or difficult your access lists and filters are to manage depends on how organizationally coherent your IP address assignments are. If everyone in Accounting is in the same address block (and all others are excluded), controlling access to sensitive information within that group is easy. If the computers authorized access are scattered into many network blocks, you'll need large, error-prone access lists and filter tables to implement the same policy.

2. *Plan for growth.* IP addresses come in restricted-size blocks, ones that are powers of two. This fact makes growing a subnet past its limit awkward—adding to a subnet with 31 computers, for example, requires that you assign a block of 64 addresses for the larger, 32-computer group. That leaves 30 addresses unused (at least temporarily). You can solve this problem two ways:

   • *Build smaller groupings of computers.* Smaller subnets waste slightly more address space because proportionately more is consumed by the network and broadcast address, but they allow for a closer approximation of the number of computers in the group by the size of the subnet.

   • *Use large, monolithic groupings of computers.* A large, undifferentiated group of computers in a single network block avoids wasting IP address space but may not be feasible with the network's physical topology. You don't have to break up a large IP block simply to make more bandwidth available, though—a switched network is probably a better solution, offering a greater increase in bandwidth. The cost of a switched network may be less, too.

   Whichever approach you use, be sure to build room for growth in your network plan. If you have address space to spare, leave gaps between assigned address space so that, if you have to, you can increase the size of a block routed to a certain department.

No network plan can avoid the problem of computers moving from one department or place to another. If those computers are servers, or if access is based upon their address matching up with access lists or filters, it will be tempting to add a host route for those specific computers to the new network. Avoid the temptation—renumbering one computer is generally a much easier task than dealing with the complicated routing mess that *will* result from an overabundance of small routes in your routers. If you have a lot of computers, consider using automated IP address management, such as Dynamic Host Configuration Protocol (DHCP) or bootp servers, to simplify network configuration and reconfiguration.

## Testing a network

Router configurations in a medium or large-scale network are complex and potentially fragile constructs. Even with the best planning, you need to do disciplined testing of every new configuration to ensure you won't encounter problems later.

Back up the old configuration of your router first, before you make configuration changes to your network. On Cisco routers, you have two configuration backup options:

✦ *Text dump the configuration to the Telnet or console screen.* If you turn on the text or screen capture facility of your terminal or Telnet program and then display the router configuration, you'll create a record in a file of the information you need to recreate should you have problems. To dump the configuration to the screen, type:

```
write terminal
```

The show config command is equivalent to the write terminal command. The show run command lets you view the configuration actually running in memory.

Although it takes little or no effort to do backups this way, text dumps have the disadvantage that you have to type them back in manually, which is slow and error prone.

✦ *Dump the configuration via TFTP to a different computer.* This is a better way of saving the configuration, because it can be immediately restored over the network. It retains the advantage of the text dump approach, though, because you can read the text file dumped to the TFTP server.

You'll need a server running TFTP (Trivial File Transfer Protocol) on your network to dump the router configuration. TFTP frequently requires that the files it writes are publicly writable/readable (check the guide for your TFTP daemon to be sure). To dump the configuration, type:

```
write network
```

The router will prompt you for the name of the host on to which you wish to dump the configuration, and some other parameters relating to the dump.

You can restore a previously backed up configuration by using the copy command to copy from the network to the router configuration:

```
copy tftp startup-config
```

This command writes the file it receives via TFTP to the startup configuration. At the next router reboot (initiated by typing **reload**), the router will run with the restored configuration.

If there's any way you can — even if you have to buy spare equipment — test network changes on a spare router so that you can find problems in private, not in public where your users are going to lose service. If this isn't possible, make changes at night or during off-peak hours so that you have several hours to find and debug problems before users are impacted.

Testing things like OS upgrades on a spare router can save you from disaster — sometimes configuration commands (or worse, entire routing setups) change between IOS versions. Cisco generally tries to minimize this, but sometimes the commands you used on the old version of your IOS, especially if they're very weird, won't work. Developing changed configurations with a spare router reduces down time too, because you can load your existing configuration into the spare, update it, and then swap the spare router into the network replacing the old router (which then becomes the spare). Your old configuration is always immediately available if the new one doesn't work.

If you're modifying or upgrading a remote router, especially if you're making changes that could take the router out of service, have someone place a modem online on the auxiliary port of the router and test the connection. That modem is a network-independent back door into the router — if it loses its network connection, you can still get in and fix the problem. The auxiliary connection is mandatory if you're changing the IP address of the router — you're going to lose your Telnet connection, and you don't know for sure if the new one will come up properly. You should think about security before Telnetting into a remote router, too — if the password traverses an insecure network in plain text form, anyone intercepting your network traffic would have free access into your router. You can't be sure you've solved the problem by changing the password from your remote terminal, because the password change traffic can be intercepted as readily as the login commands. If you *must* log into a router over an insecure network, have someone local to the router change the password when you're done.

## Software upgrades

Upgrading the software on a router is not as fearsome as it sometimes seems. The actual operation is simple, but the time pressure while you reboot or are offline makes it seem more difficult than it is.

As with any upgrade, make a backup of your current configuration before upgrading your router. You'll do this using one of the techniques just described, preferably TFTP, resulting in an off-router backup you can restore to a different physical router if the original one fails. In addition to the configuration backup, it's very important to have a backup of the operating system (IOS for Cisco routers) in case the upgrade fails and you have to back out the changes you made.

You'll follow a procedure quite similar to that for backing up the configuration in order to back up the router operating system. If you have a TFTP server, you should back up to that; if not, you can back up the IOS to additional flash memory installed in the router. Start the operating system backup with the command:

```
copy flash tftp
```

The router will take you through the prompts necessary to accomplish this operation. Afterward, you can proceed with the software upgrade, copying the new software from your TFTP server to the router with this command:

```
copy tftp flash
```

New releases of the software for Cisco routers come out quite regularly. Like all new software releases, router updates incorporate bug fixes, feature enhancements, and new bugs. New releases frequently require more memory than previous releases to support new features, so before upgrading you'll want to scrutinize carefully the memory and hardware requirements for the new release. Remember that in a traffic- or routing-heavy environment the minimum specified memory won't ensure that your router has adequate buffer and routing table space.

## Hardware upgrades

Beyond the value of being able to get yourself back to your prior operating state, you'll want to begin hardware upgrades with a backup of the configuration of the existing router. The reason for this is that an offline copy of the configuration of the old router makes it simpler to start up the new router. This is because you'll build up the new router configuration manually from the complete configuration snapshot – we don't mean to imply you can just upload the old configuration to the new hardware and be done.

Several problems make a manual configuration desirable, the first of which is that the syntax of the operating software may change between releases and between routers. That means that the configuration that ran perfectly on your old router may not be quite compatible or adequate for the new hardware. Second, your old router configuration isn't likely to take advantage of special features of the new hardware. As a result, unless the upgrade is part of the same product line and running the same major version of the software, you'll probably want to build a new configuration for the router instead of blindly copying over the old config file.

## Memory upgrades

Adding memory to most Cisco routers is nearly painless. The routers typically use standard 72-pin *parity* SIMMs and are field-upgradable by inserting a new SIMM into the memory socket or sockets. Be sure to check on the Cisco Web site to find out what size and speed strips you need. Cisco includes a list of suggested alternative (lower cost) memory suppliers on their Web page and suggests using only their own memory or memory from the approved list of suppliers — they have checked the items on the approved list to ensure that they will function properly in the router. You should know that using other memory may void the warranty on your router. For the latest list of approved memory sources for your router, contact the Cisco Technical Assistance Center for a list of vendors and part numbers.

As with your computer, you'll want to know what the choke points are before you dive in and upgrade a router. Cisco provides processor and memory monitors built into its routers. These displays can be shown using the show proc (show processor) command.

```
show proc cpu
```

The processor CPU utilization will display information like this:

```
CPU utilization for five seconds: 31%/11%; one minute: 21%;
five minutes: 19%
PID  Runtime(ms)  Invoked  uSecs  5Sec  1Min  5Min  TTY
Process
1  3022868  5642397  535  0.08%  0.01%  0.00%  0  OSPF Router
2  56873352  581991  97723  0.00%  0.35%  0.43%  0  Check heaps
3  2080  4751  437  0.00%  0.00%  0.00%  0  Pool Manager
4  529800  136098438  3  0.00%  0.00%  0.00%  0  Timers
...
```

The important fields for looking at processor utilization are the summary display in the first line. The one-minute and five-minute averages tend to be the most accurate, because the five-second utilization is affected by your commands themselves. In general, a router will start to slow its packet forwarding speeds at processor utilization above 50 percent, but this may depend on your network. The best way to check this is to look at the router's effect on round-trip ping times on unloaded links. If the ping times begin to degrade seriously at higher processor usage, you should think about upgrading.

Each line in the remainder of the display corresponds to a process running in the router and has these fields that are important for performance analysis:

✦ *Five second, one minute, and five minute percentages.* These values help you to know what is taking up the majority of your processing power.

✦ *TTY.* This shows the port from which the process was initiated.

✦ *Process.* The Process field gives you the name of the process, which helps to convey what it's doing. In the preceding display example, "OSPF Router" is the actual routing code; "Check heaps" looks at memory structures for problems; "Pool Manager" allocates memory; and "Timers" causes periodic events to be run.

Sometimes, you'll get more payoff from a configuration or topological change than an increase in raw power. For example, RIP routing is frequently much less efficient than OSPF or other more advanced routing protocols that do not send frequent updates. Because of that, migrating your core routers away from RIP may reduce your CPU utilization dramatically. Moreover, if your router is low on memory, you're likely to get more from a memory upgrade, because in many circumstances the router will use the additional memory to cache more information and reduce processing time spent recreating the data.

### When to add more memory

You can see several statistics about memory usage in a Cisco router. To see the amount of memory (main, shared, and flash) in your router, issue the command:

```
show version
```

The router responds with a line like this:

```
cisco XXXX processor (revision X) with aaaaaK/bbbbbK bytes
of memory.
```

The first number (aaaaa) is the amount of main memory your router has; the second number is the amount of shared memory. To see the amount of memory that your router is actively using, use the show proc mem command (described in more detail in the text that follows). At the end of the output, that command displays one or more lines indicating the amount of nonvolatile memory in the router (used to store configurations and Cisco operating system images):

```
128K bytes of non-volatile configuration memory.
4096K bytes of processor board System flash (Read/Write)
4096K bytes of processor board Boot flash (Read/Write)
```

### Flash memory

To see the contents of the flash memory that stores the IOS images, use the command:

```
show flash
```

The router will display the files that are stored in flash, their size, and a total indicating how much space is used and how much space is available.

Flash memory is used primarily to store the operating system images from which the router boots. The most important consideration with flash memory is, "Will the operating system fit in the amount of memory I have available?" Each new release of the Cisco IOS tends to grow larger than the previous release, so you need to ensure that you have enough free space to hold the new image before you start an upgrade.

## Main memory

Main memory on a Cisco router is used for holding routing information, doing most normal tasks, and buffering and caching in some lower-end routers. (High-end routers have separate cache memories instead.) If a Cisco router runs out of memory, it is in desperate trouble — in many cases, the router will panic and reboot. Routers do not have hard drives to which they can store extra information, so when they run out of memory, they have no options. (Perhaps more important, the router can cache information more effectively when it has memory to spare, improving performance.)

The point is that you're better off keeping routers well supplied with memory. In routers where performance and stability are important, this means at least one megabyte of free memory. (Routers doing light duty at network endpoints can certainly get along with less). Internet-connected routers that download the entire Internet routing table (46,000 routes and counting) should have more free memory than in these guidelines so that they can deal with unexpected fluctuations in the size of the routing tables.

Check the amount of memory your router is using with the command:

```
show processor memory
```

This command (abbreviated show proc mem) shows the memory utilization of the processor. At the top of its display, it shows summary statistics:

```
Total: 57046640, Used: 26773764, Free: 30272876
```

This output is from a Cisco router with 64 megabytes of main memory — note that the router has already allocated 9.6 megabytes of memory for use internally. When the amount of free memory overall dips too low, the router may begin to deliver poor performance. "Too low" depends entirely on the environment and the router, but maintaining 10 percent free memory is advisable in any situation. Note that the router may still need more memory, even if it displays enough free memory. This is because the router will stop caching and buffering some information in order to free up memory. Maintaining a few hundred kilobytes of free memory is a good plan in any router that needs to handle high-speed connections (128 Kbps and above), or any router performing payload compression.

The show processor memory command also displays the memory used by each process in the router. The output looks like:

```
PID TTY  Allocated      Freed    Holding    Getbufs    Retbufs
Process
```

PID is the process ID. TTY is the interactive port, valid only for sessions involving user interaction. The Allocated column indicates the amount of memory allocated to the process over its lifetime. The Freed column indicates the amount of memory the process has freed. The Holding column is the most relevant column, indicating the amount of memory the process is currently using. The Getbufs and Retbufs columns indicate the number of buffers that have been allocated/returned to/by the process (buffers come out of a separate chunk of memory). The Process column indicates the name of the process.

The Holding column lets you determine which processes are currently using the most memory. The Allocated and Freed columns are useful for determining historically the amount of memory that has been used by a process; bursty activity may be reflected better in these columns than the currently allocated column.

Most modern Cisco routers use 72-pin parity SIMMs for their main memory (see the sidebar, "Memory Upgrades" earlier in this chapter), which makes installing new memory virtually painless. Flash memory comes on separate flash memory SIMMs. Before installing more memory, especially flash memory, make a full backup of your router configuration and operating system image. From there, upgrading memory is frequently a matter of opening the case, inserting the memory, and closing the case again. As with all static-sensitive equipment, be sure to use a static-protective wristband or other protective device when in contact with the insides of your router.

# Logging and Monitoring

Sophisticated routers give you a wide range of options you can use to log and monitor what goes on over your network. Most routers provide at least one mechanism for monitoring nearly all aspects of the operation of their operation, so you need to think through the question of what to log.

Overall, you'll want to log any event that is important to you. Some events you might care about are:

✦ *Link failures.* If a WAN or LAN link goes down, you'll want to know that it happened (so that you can fix it or work around it) and have a time-stamped log so that you can see if there's a pattern to the failure.

✦ *Congestion.* Excessive congestion can be a very serious problem in slow links. You'll want to know when it happens and from where so that you can both notify users and plan how to fix it.

✦ *CPU utilization trends.* The amount of spare processor power that is available to your router is very useful for making decisions about upgrading, but it's inconvenient to be tied to a console probing with the `show proc cpu` command. Logging the processor load lets you gather the information painlessly.

✦ *Bandwidth utilization trends.* Like processor usage trend data, historical information about the amount of bandwidth used/available on your networks helps in both long- and short-term planning.

✦ *Access list violations.* Access list violations warn you of an unexpected or undesired event on your network. It may be an attacker attempting to subvert your network, or it may be a sign of an external or internal misconfiguration that should be corrected. Either way, you want to know about the problem as soon as possible.

✦ *Router reloads/reboots.* An unexpected router reboot may signify a hardware problem in the router, that it's exceeded its memory capacity, or that there's a bug in its software. The reboot could equally be a sign that the router power source or UPS has problems. Routers are capable of very extended uptimes — it's common to see a router that's been running continuously for months or longer — so you should treat reboots as serious events.

Depending on your network, there may be other conditions or trends that you wish to monitor. Routers traditionally provide one or more ways to obtain status information (the Cisco routers we're looking at provide several), so it's very likely that the router provides a way to accomplish what you need.

✦ *Syslog.* Syslog is a traditional UNIX method of recording information, but syslog "daemons" that receive and record this information are available for a variety of platforms, including Microsoft Windows 95 and Windows NT. Syslog records messages sent over the network to a text file or database; the messages are one-way transmissions from the router that have no guarantee of arriving at their destination; therefore, syslog is a method best used on a reliable local area network or over uncongested links.

✦ *Telnet or other interactive monitoring.* Many routers provide an administrative interface via the Telnet protocol normally used to connect from one computer to another in TCP/IP networks. The variety of information and interfaces provided via Telnet includes highly graphical text user interfaces (an example is the Ascend command line interface), sophisticated command line interfaces (Cisco), or very simple interfaces to internal data structures.

Cisco routers are well known for their Telnet user interface, from which all aspects of the router may be controlled, and many aspects monitored.

✦ *Proprietary interfaces.* Some router vendors provide client programs that allow configuration or monitoring of their products. Typically, these interfaces are graphical and run on a smaller variety of platforms; most support Microsoft Windows, and many support some platforms using the X Window System under a UNIX-style operating system. These interfaces are frequently quite good, but their proprietary nature makes them difficult to use in multivendor environments. The RouterView software from Compatible Systems is a good example of a proprietary interface, providing good summary-level data and convenient access to even very detailed router configuration capabilities.

✦ *SNMP.* SNMP, the Simple Network Monitoring Protocol, provides facilities for both reading and writing data to and from your router. Nearly all routers intended for use in corporate networks support SNMP to some degree (to the extent of supporting the basic SNMP MIB or MIB-II — a generic Management Information Base). SNMP is excellent for recording trend data, and many SNMP monitoring programs support these operations with ease. SNMP may also be used to receive alerts from the router, called "traps," about important events or network status changes. SNMP monitoring programs range from free software that will run on a PC or in Java, to complex integrated network management systems that cost thousands of dollars.

## Syslog

All but the simplest routers are capable of noting many status changes or important events via syslog to a remote host. Changes you can expect to record via syslog include router reboots, link state changes, access list violations, BGP and OSPF router events, remote command executions, and others. For example, here's part of a syslog we recorded while configuring a 3Com OfficeConnect NETBuilder 142 (we've edited some information out for reasons of privacy and security of the associated network):

```
#8  root  "Login Successful"
#9  root  "SETD !2 -PORT NORMalBandwidth = 56"
#10 root  "SETD !3 -PORT NORMalBandwidth = 56"
#11 root  "SETD !2 -PORT CONTrol = enable"
#12 root  "SETD !3 -PORT CONTrol = enable"
#13 PPM2   "DOD INITIATING CALL ON PATH 2.1, PORT 2"
```

In lines 9 and 10, we've set up the two ports on the ISDN line to use 56 Kbps rates rather than 64 Kbps clear channel to solve a problem at the interface between the telephone company at the router end and the competitive provider serving the Internet service provider at the other end of the connection. We then enabled the ports in lines 11 and 12 (each B channel on the ISDN line looks link a separate port on this router). Finally, the router responds by dialing out (line 13).

In Cisco routers, the `logging` configuration option controls how logging is handled. You have several options:

✦ *logging <ip address>* tells the system to log to this IP address. The computer at that address should be running a syslog daemon.

✦ *logging trap <level>* sends syslog messages for this level of messages and above. The level you select determines how much information gets dumped.

✦ *logging facility <facility>* sends syslog messages with this syslog facility.

✦ *logging on* activates logging.

✦ *logging buffered* logs to an internal buffer that can be reviewed with the `show logging` command.

The level of messages describes the severity of the messages that the router will report to its logging host. By telling a router to log messages of a certain level, it will record all messages at that level and above. You don't need to specify multiple levels in order to receive important messages.

The logging facility is the manner in which the router reports its log messages. Typically, syslog supports several "facilities" for logging, including *auth, authpriv, mail,* and *news,* plus seven "local" logging facilities (numbered local1, local2, and so on). It is often convenient to pick an unused local logging facility and instruct your router to log to that facility to segregate router messages from standard system messages.

## Monitoring via Telnet

You can watch the current state of many aspects of a Cisco router via the Telnet interface, including a live display of the messages it is sending via syslog, packet traces, debugging information, and configuration information. Some of this information, such as interface state and statistics, is available via nonprivileged access on the router; other information, including configuration and debugging information, may only be accessed in the "enable" state. The show command can display a huge variety of configuration and status information. For a list, type **show ?** at the router prompt. Here are some of the commands you can use to watch what's happening and what they report:

```
show interface [optional interface name]
```

The show interface command, when used alone, displays the interface statistics for all interfaces. If you supply the name of a particular interface, it displays the statistics for only that interface. The first line of the output shows the interface status. For example, you might get this result:

```
Serial0 is up, line protocol is up
```

The first up is for the physical line; for a serial line, this indicates that the router is receiving a signal from the CSU/DSU attached to the interface and that the serial line is "live" in some fashion. The second up shows the status of the line protocol, which represents the status of the link management on the interface.

The show interface display (abbreviated show int) also displays a five-minute average of the bandwidth used through the interface in bits and packets per second, the number of collisions and errors of various types on the interface, and more.

```
show ip route
```

This command shows the contents of the IP routing table. You can add parameters to narrow down the output: a hostname or IP address, a routing protocol from which to list the routes, or the keyword summary for look at the state of the routing table.

```
show ip [router type] [optional keywords]
```

The `show ip [router type]` command displays the status of the BGP, EIGRP, or OSPF routers, which also lets you look at the state of neighboring or peer routers in your network.

## Monitoring via Simple Network Management Protocol

The Simple Network Management Protocol (SNMP) examines and controls the operation of network devices. SNMP operates between devices and managers; a router is a device. Information is passed back and forth with SNMP through Management Information Blocks (MIBs).

Router SNMP monitoring capabilities fall in to two general categories: queries and traps. You can *poll* a router via SNMP to discover information; the router may on its own initiative send a *trap* to an SNMP monitoring station or host to alert the station to an important event.

SNMP uses *communities* to control access. Only members of the proper community have SNMP access to the router. Under SNMP v1 (the first version of SNMP), the community string functions as the only form of authentication for SNMP — it acts as a password. Only computers that know the SNMP community string are granted access. Many products use a default community string of `public` in their SNMP configuration, so be sure to change the community string to something else, especially if you grant the public community read/write access.

You control SNMP on Cisco routers via the `snmp-server` command. With this command, you can activate or deactivate the server and set configuration options.

```
snmp-server community <string> [parameters]
```

The `community` command lets you create a community and define its access privileges. The community may be *ro* (a read-only community), *rw* (a community that can both read and write), or restricted to a view of the router provided by a specific MIB. (You do this last with the `view` command.) You can further control SNMP access to the router by specifying the number of a standard IP access list that has permit lines for the hosts that are allowed access. For example, we could define a server as:

```
access-list 5 permit 192.168.1.5 0.0.0.0
snmp-server community monitoring ro 5
```

This server allows read-only access to an SNMP monitor using the community string `monitoring`. You can access the monitor to examine the router from the host 192.168.1.5, but not from other locations.

```
snmp-server host <hostname> <community> [list of traps to send]
```

The `host` command defines where you want the router to send SNMP trap notifications. The community should match the community string for the SNMP monitor running on that host. The list of traps that may be sent to this host allows you to define the events you want to see. You can get a full list of the traps your router defines by typing a question mark (**?**) from within the snmp-server host configuration command.

```
contact <contact information for network manager>
```

The `contact` command lets you give the router additional information to be reported to authorized monitoring hosts. The contact information lets you include identifying information about the router itself, so you can more readily figure out what router has the problem.

## A simple beginning-to-end walkthrough

Hook the console port of the router up to a serial port of a computer or terminal, using the appropriate connector in the box. Turn on the router. At this point, you should be able to see text flow across the screen when you turn the router on. If you don't, you have a problem with the physical connection to the router. Ask yourself:

✦ Is it plugged in?

✦ Are you using the right serial port?

✦ Do you have your terminal set to 9600-8-N-1?

✦ Is it a bad day and you should give up and go home?

The first thing that a new router will ask, is:

```
Notice: NVRAM invalid, possibly due to write erase.
Would you like to enter the initial configuration dialog?
[yes]:
```

Hit Enter, or type **yes**. This will take you into the Cisco configuration dialog, which will walk you through the setup.

Before you start this, you'll need the following information:

✦ The IP address of the serial interface

This is the address used by the router on the serial WAN link (for instance, a T1). Because only two machines on this small network will be talking (their interface and our interface), it's best to pick a small network — namely, one with two available IP addresses, or a block of four: a /31, or a subnet with a mask of 255.255.255.252.

✦ The netblock allocated to the user

✦ If user provided, passwords for router:

- The Telnet login password
- The "enable" password for administrative control

✦ The Circuit ID of line from telephone company

✦ If Frame Relay, the DLCI on their side of the frame link

Continue with the configuration. The interface summary doesn't matter (say no).

```
Enter host name [Router]:
```

This prompt doesn't really matter much. It's a cosmetic and SNMP issue. Don't worry about it — we'll use **gw**.

```
Enter enable secret:
```

The enable secret is the enable password you picked before. Enter it here. This will be the password required to configure the router in the future.

```
Enter enable password:
```

The enable password isn't used, because we have an enable secret. Make something up that's garbage.

```
Enter virtual terminal password:
```

The virtual terminal password is the password needed to Telnet in to the router. Make it something good, but not impossible.

```
Configure SNMP Network Management? [yes]: no
```

SNMP should be off unless required.

```
Configure bridging: [no]: no
```

This is a router. Use routers to route, not bridge.

```
Configure IP? [yes]: yes
Configure IGRP routing? [yes]: no
Configure RIP routing? [no]: no
Configuring interface Ethernet0:
Is this interface in use? [yes]: yes
Configure IP on this interface? [yes]: yes
IP address for this interface: xxx.yyy.zzz.aaa
Number of bits in subnet field [0]: (whatever)
```

The number of bits in the subnet field is Cisco's attempt to be clever. It failed. If you say 0, it will give you a /24 (255.255.255.0). If you say 1, it will give you a /25 (255.255.255.128). Yadda. Yadda. Yadda.

It's a good idea to use the first available IP address in their netblock for the Ethernet address unless strong circumstances dictate otherwise (for instance, you're replacing an old router that wasn't configured that way). There's nothing legal about this; it's just a matter of keeping the same conventions on all routers you administer. That way the gateway address is the lowest address for everyone.

```
Configuring interface Serial0:
Is this interface in use? [yes]: yes
Configure IP on this interface? [yes]: yes
Configure IP unnumbered on this interface? [no]: no
IP address for this interface: 207.173.19.??
Number of bits in subnet field [0]: 6
Configuring interface Serial1:
Is this interface in use? [yes]: no
```

The router will now spit out a configuration script it likes. Accept it.

```
Use this configuration? [yes/no]: yes
```

Now, we need to go set up a few more things. You'll have to reenable yourself with the enable password you specified before.

```
gw>enable
Password: (enter enable password here)
gw#
```

The # prompt is the enable prompt. Enter the configuration mode, by typing:

```
gw#config t
```

The config t means to configure from the terminal. Now add a few inconvenience features for security:

```
no service tcp-small-servers
no service udp-small-servers
```

This turns off things like echo, chargen, and discard, and removes the possibility of certain DOS attacks such as udp storms. Type **exit** to return to the main router configuration.

Now we need to configure some routing. This is kind of strange; we'll explain it in a second.

```
gw(config)#ip route 0.0.0.0 0.0.0.0 ser0.1
gw(config)#ip route 207.173.19.0 255.255.255.0 ser0.1
```

Now if the netblock assigned to the user is less than a full /24 (a class C, 255.255.255.0), you'll need to add a route for the rest of the network so that the Cisco doesn't get confused. No, we don't understand the reason for this — it should be caught by the default route, but for some Cisco-ish reason, it is not and needs to be added manually.

```
gw(config)#ip route (netblock address).0 255.255.255.0 ser0.1
```

This is the same reason that we added a route for 207.173.19.0.

Last, you should create an antispoofing filter. The antispoofing filter is based upon two ideas:

✦ The user should never receive packets from the Internet that appear to come from their internal network.

✦ The user should never send packets to the Internet that do not appear to come from their internal network.

From the configure prompt, define the inbound filter using 101. It's an extended access list.

```
access-list 101 deny ip (NETWORK) (WILDMASK) any
access-list 101 deny ip host (INTERFACE) any
access-list 101 permit ip any any
```

For example, suppose a test router has a netblock of 192.168.3.1 / 24 (255.255.255.0) and serial interface of 207.173.19.3:

```
access-list 101 deny ip 192.168.3.0 0.0.0.255 any
access-list 101 deny ip host 207.173.19.3 any
```

Note the wildcard mask. This is different from a subnet mask — it's backward. It specifies the number of addresses to add to the network to get the matched range; any address that falls between NETWORK and NETWORK+WILDMASK will be matched. A class C network has 255 usable addresses, so put **255**. A /29 has seven usable addresses, so put **7**, and so on.

Now define the outbound filter, using 102:

```
access-list 102 permit ip (NETWORK) (WILDMASK) any
access-list 102 permit ip host (INTERFACE) any
access-list 102 deny ip any any
```

This second filter permits source addresses from within the local network but denies all others — thus, the only packets that may be transmitted to the Internet will appear to come from within the LAN — exactly as it should be. Again, the example:

```
access-list 102 permit ip 192.168.3.0 0.0.0.255 any
access-list 102 permit ip host 207.173.19.3 any
access-list 102 deny ip any any
```

Now we need to apply these lists to the interface:

```
int ser0.1
ip access-group 101 in
ip access-group 102 out
```

Now write the configuration changes:

```
exit (gets back to the main configuration)
exit (exits configuration)
write
```

# Home Office and Small Business LANs

Let's shift from the complex environment of an Internet-capable router to the simple one you'll find setting up a LAN in a home or small business. We'll assume you're going to use 10Base-T wiring and network interface cards (NICs).

## Setting up the LAN

Here's the parts list (go back to Chapter 27 if you need details):

✦ *10Base-T Hub.* You need at least one hub to connect all the computers together. We commonly use the 3Com OfficeConnect Hub 8/TPC (which provides eight 10Base-T ports plus a ninth 10Base-2 port), but if you don't have a requirement for linking in a legacy thinnet, you could use the Hub 8/TPO.

✦ *Network interface card.* You need one of these for each computer. We use PCI NICs like the 3Com whenever we have spare slots, but an ISA card works if you have no choice. There's not much of a price premium to giving yourself a 100 Mbps option (such as with the 3Com Fast Etherlink 10/100 Adapters).

✦ *Cable.* For nearly all purposes, you can use Category 5 Unshielded Twisted Pair (UTP), which works at both 10 and 100 Mbps. If you're running the wiring in walls, ceilings, or plenums, be sure to check your local wiring codes and get cable rated for the application. You can get bulk cable and attach the connectors yourself, or you can buy the cable prewired.

That's all you need. One way to get the entire setup in one step is with "networking kits" — 3Com, for example, offers the OfficeConnect Networking Kit, which includes a hub, three ISA NICs, and three 50-foot cables.

Once you have all the parts, install NICs in at least two computers, cable the NICs to the hub, and start up the operating system. If Windows automatically detects the NICs, you're nearly done. If not, you'll have to work a little harder. You can try to let Windows scan for them using the Add New Hardware applet in the Control Panel. If that doesn't work, use Add New Hardware, but answer no when you're asked if you want Windows to scan for new hardware. Then choose Network Adapters and select the one you have from the next screen. If your adapter isn't shown in the list, choose Have Disk and use the drivers that came with the card.

Once you have the drivers installed, you're likely to have to reboot, after which you need to do some software configuration. Here are the steps for Windows 95:

1. Check if the right protocols are installed. To do that, find the Network Neighborhood icon on your desktop. Right-click that and choose Properties (this is equivalent to Start ➪ Settings ➪ Control Panel ➪ Network). There's a tab at the top that says Configuration that contains a list of the installed networking components. If you're simply going to use the Microsoft networking components, you'll want at least these:

   • Client for Microsoft Networks

   • Your NIC (on one of our computers, for example, this line says 3Com Etherlink III Bus-Master PCI Ethernet Adapter)

   • The NetBEUI protocol

2. Add File and Print Sharing so that the computers will be able to look at each other's files. Do this by selecting Client for Microsoft Networks, and then clicking File and Print Sharing. Turn on at least file sharing; turn on print sharing on the machine with the printer attached if you want to share printers over your network.

3. Choose the Identification tab (at the top of the window), and enter a name for the computer plus a name for the group of computers (the workgroup). The computer name should be unique among all your computers on your network; the workgroup should be the same for all computers on a small network. (For example, we use PRESS for the workgroup; some of our computers are named Callisto, Joxer, Llamah, Mongo, and Ratbert.) In case the name isn't enough, you can enter any string you want for the computer description — you'll see it on the other computers.

4. Choose the Access Control tab (also at the top of the window). If you have an NT server to provide authorizations, you can choose user-level access control; for small networks, you can simply choose share-level access control. The difference is that user-level control lets you specify centrally what resources each user on your systems can get at; share-level control simply associates passwords with resources.

5. Click OK — you'll have to reboot. Repeat the process on the other machine.

6. Open Windows Explorer, and for each drive you want to be shared, right-click the drive icon and choose Sharing. Turn on Shared As, and select the access options you want. We keep the share name the same as the drive letter to minimize confusion.

**Tip** Don't forget that you can share floppies and CD-ROMs! That can be very useful when one machine has the resource and the other doesn't.

Here are the equivalent steps for Windows NT 4:

1. Check if the right protocols are installed. To do that, find the Network Neighborhood icon on your desktop. Right-click that, and choose Properties (this is equivalent to Start ➪ Settings ➪ Control Panel ➪ Network). A tab at the top that says Protocols contains a list of the installed protocol components. If you're simply going to use the Microsoft networking components, you'll want the NetBEUI protocol.

2. Check under the Services tab to see if what services are installed. You'll likely want Computer Browser and Workstation, and possibly Server.

3. Choose the Identification tab (at the top of the Window). If what's shown isn't what you want for the computer name and workgroup, choose the Change button and make the changes you want. For a small network, you'll want the computer to be a member of a workgroup rather than a domain.

4. Access controls in Windows NT are different than in Windows 95, so now click OK and reboot. Repeat the process on the other machine.

5. Open Windows Explorer, and for each drive you want to be shared, right-click the drive icon and choose Sharing. Turn on Shared As, and set the share name and description.

6. Click Permissions, and set access controls in the dialog you get. Giving Everyone the rights for Full Control is equivalent to no restrictions. You can also set No Access, Read Access, and Change. You can set these permissions by account as well as class of user. OK your way out of the dialog when you're done.

7. Finally, you have to enable the Guest account. If you don't do this, you'll be asked to enter a password for the $IPC resource on the remote machine, and nothing you do will work. Enable the account by starting the User Manager (Start ➪ Programs ➪ Administrative Tools (Common) ➪ User Manager), and double-click the entry for Guest. If you see in the dialog you get that the account is disabled, clear that flag and OK your way out.

   *Important:* Enabling the Guest account lets people access this computer anonymously from other computers, which weakens the security built into Windows NT. If your computer is connected to the Internet, make sure you find out what your site security protections are, and what you should do to properly configure your computer.

FreeBSD UNIX setup is more difficult; we'll cover it in Chapter 40. Whichever operating system you're using, if you plan to connect to the Internet or to a Novell file server, you'll need to install the TCP/IP and IPX protocols, respectively.

At this point, you should be able to open Windows Explorer on one of the machines, drill down into the Network Neighborhood, and find the other machine. Continue working your way down and you'll see the shared drives and their files.

Sharing a printer on the net is similar — open the Printers folder, right-click the printer, and select sharing. When that's done, create a new printer on the remote machine, and follow the dialogs for a network printer. Browse to find it on the other machine and finish the setup.

Once you have two machines communicating, adding more is just a matter of repeating the steps on the next machine.

## Setting up the router

Let's do a quick setup on a combined router and ISDN modem, typical of what you'll have to do to link your office LAN to the Internet. We'll use the 3Com OfficeConnect Remote 510U in the example. One of the nice features of the Remote 510U is the configuration software 3Com supplies with the device. Using the Transcend Quick Configuration Manager, we completed basic setup of a Remote 510U in less than five minutes.

You hook up the Remote 510U with four cables:

✦ *ISDN.* The line from the telephone company U interface termination plugs directly into the back of the Remote 510U. An NT1 interface is built into the unit.

✦ *LAN.* The Remote 510U includes both thinnet and 10Base-T interfaces. You connect the right one into your coaxial cable or hub, respectively.

✦ *Console.* Although you can Telnet into the router once you've configured the IP address for the LAN interface, you'll need to do that initial configuration using the console port. A cable supplied with the Remote 510U connects from the console port to a serial port on one of your computers. You have to use the console port to use the Transcend Quick Configuration Manager.

✦ *Power.* One of those external wall transformers powers the Remote 510U. It's nice in that the unit itself is smaller and cooler, but by the time you stack several devices using them, you'll be wondering why power strips don't come with more widely spaced sockets.

You're going to need some information from your Internet service provider and from your telephone company to do the configuration. Specifically, you need to know:

✦ *IP addresses.* Every computer on your network will need its own IP address. Your ISP will assign you a block of addresses; make sure you get at least three more addresses than you have computers (the network address, the broadcast address, and an address for the LAN side of the router). You'll also need a WAN-side address for the Remote 510U, which won't be part of the LAN address block.

✦ *IP netmask.* As we've discussed, your IP address block has an associated netmask to define the subnet.

✦ *ISDN SPIDs.* In North America, ISDN circuits have one or two SPIDs associated with the service. You need these two numbers (and the associated dial numbers) for your ISDN service.

Once you wire the Remote 510U and load the configuration software, you start setup by starting the software. Figure 29-6 shows what you get. The buttons in the toolbar at the top of the screen are for more advanced functions — the quick setup functions are in the main menu in the center of the figure.

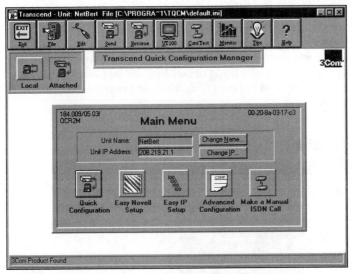

**Figure 29-6:** The 3Com Transcend Quick Configuration Manager makes basic ISDN setup of a Remote 510U simple.

Start configuration with the Quick Configuration button. When you click it, you'll get the dialog in Figure 29-7, where you can set up the basic ISDN and IP characteristics of the unit. (The numbers and addresses in the figures in this section have been changed from their real values to retain network security.) The IP address and netmask are the ones for your LAN, not the WAN port. The SPIDs and directory numbers are provided by your ISDN supplier, as is the network (switch) type. When you have the parameters set, click Send to download to the router.

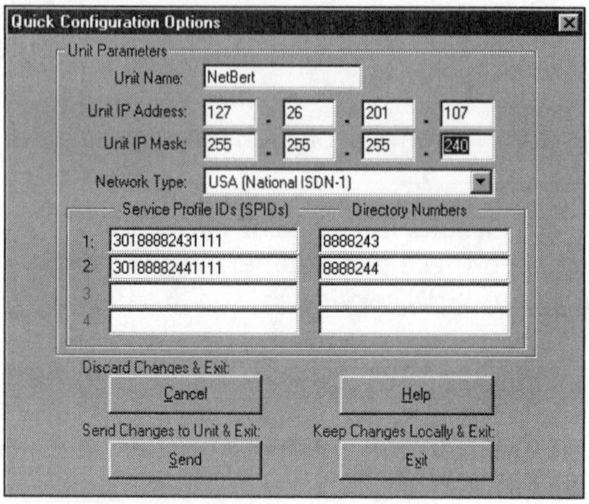

**Figure 29-7:** Use this dialog box to set up the basic ISDN and IP characteristics of a unit.

If you then click Easy IP Setup, you get the partially hidden dialog in Figure 29-8. Click Internet to get the dialog in the front of Figure 29-8. Enter the telephone number of your ISP and the type of ISDN call (64 Kbps or 56 Kbps, for instance). When you enter IP addresses, remember that the LAN port IP address and netmask are for your LAN netblock, not the WAN.

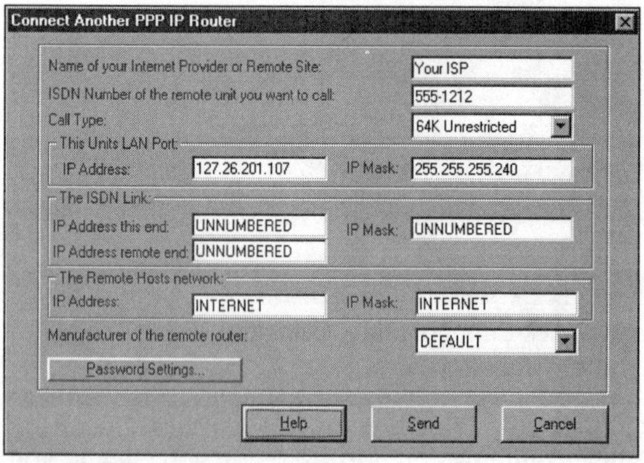

**Figure 29-8:** Use Easy IP Setup to configure the rest of the router addresses.

You'll probably have to set up passwords and an authentication protocol if you're on a dial-up line, so click Password Settings to get the dialog in Figure 29-9. In this example, you're only dialing out, so fill in the "When I log on to others" block. We've shown a password for PAP only, which works with our ISP.

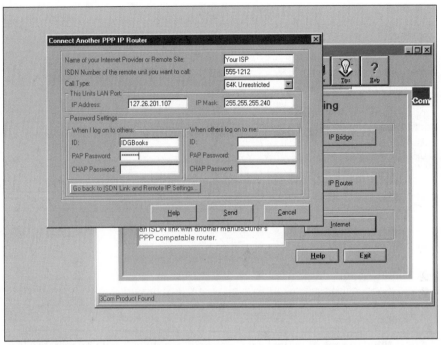

**Figure 29-9:** The choice of PAP or CHAP for authentication depends on what your ISP requires.

When you complete this, send the data to the router. You should then be able to Telnet into the router (you'll need to give it the default password that's in the router manual). Change the password immediately — using the default password while the router is connected to the Internet is a security risk.

If you haven't plugged in the ISDN line, do that now and try to ping a host at your ISP. The router should dial out, connect, and establish network connectivity. If it doesn't, use a Telnet window (or the VT100 button at the top of the configuration manager) and issue the Configure Port command to get the menu of interfaces. Select the first ISDN line, and use the Examine command. When you do, you'll get a screen like this:

```
V05.03f  NetBert                ISDN Port 1 Stats
Nat ISDN1 Ok
------------------------------------------------------------------
------------------
Status    : Connected (Outgoing)    Number    : 5551212
B Channel : B1: 64K Unrestricted    Last Clear :
        RX COUNTERS                         TX COUNTERS
```

```
Octets           : 12907          Octets           :
13046
Frames           : 38             Frames           :
36
        RX ERRORS                         TX ERRORS
Missed Frames    : 0              Discarded Frames : 0
CRC Errors       : 0              Underrun Errors  : 0
Overflows        : 0
Frames Too Long  : 0
Alignment Errors : 0
Abort Sequences  : 0
DPLL Errors      : 0


CLear—Clear Statistics
------------------------------------------------------------
----------------

^G—Main menu

^L—Prev menu
------------------------------------------------------------
----------------
( co po ex ) Enter command :
```

The first thing to look at is the Last Clear field, which will tell you why the last call was terminated. If that looks okay, check the transmit and receive errors, and go back into the configuration manager to check passwords.

You create more powerful capabilities by networking your computers, and even more power by connecting your LAN to the Internet. The power you gain is worth the investment of time to understand how to build and interconnect those networks.

# Summary

✦ A small, disconnected, private LAN has far fewer issues and requirements than one connected to the Internet.

✦ There's a much larger learning curve for sophisticated network equipment.

✦ Choose small office/home office equipment that provides simplified setup and configuration tools.

✦  ✦  ✦

# Accessing and Serving the Internet

It takes more than network plumbing to access or serve the Internet. We'll cover more software than hardware in this chapter, but by the time we're done, we'll have covered what goes over the network pipes, what you can do with the Internet, and how it all fits together. Using that as a basis, we'll be able to cover the hardware resources you need to do the things you want.

## The Internet Protocols

In Chapter 28 we showed you that networks have at the lower three layers protocols for physical data exchange, data link control, and network control and routing. For the Internet, the network layer is the Internet Protocol, or IP. Most of the time, you'll hear IP mentioned as part of TCP/IP, which stands for Transmission Control Protocol/Internet Protocol. The reason for that is that very little software actually talks to IP directly. Instead, there are protocols above IP that solve some of the other problems of communicating across computer networks. TCP is one of those upper-layer protocols.

# Transmission Control Protocol

The first problems IP has that we need to solve come from IP's function: to route information from there and back. IP doesn't guarantee that your messages will actually arrive at the destination, doesn't guarantee that they'll arrive in the order you sent, and doesn't give you any indication of whether the network has the capacity to transmit as much data as you want. Every one of these problems stems from the nature of the underlying network:

✦ *Unreliable delivery.* Neither IP nor the Internet itself guarantees that the data you send through your modem will get anywhere. Your Internet connection could get dropped, the modem could garble the data, a communications link could be full to capacity, the computer at the other end could mishandle the message, or a thousand other things could go wrong. Any one of them can cause your message to get lost.

✦ *Out-of-order delivery.* IP and the Internet don't make any promises about the order in which messages get delivered. Because it takes a lot of messages across the Internet to do anything useful, they can arrive in a sequence very different from the one in which they were transmitted. Most programs send messages and replies in a tightly defined sequence, so out of order delivery would be very confusing. It would be like getting the check in a restaurant before you've even seen the menu.

✦ *Capacity limits.* Getting your message sent through your modem provides no assurance that it's actually going anywhere. For instance, suppose your message arrives at a router, but its destination circuit is already full of traffic. Your message can get dumped if the router doesn't have enough memory to hold the incoming messages until they can get a turn on the output circuit.

Every one of these problems is solvable—and most of the time, programs communicating on the Internet want them to be solved. It's not efficient to require every program that communicates over the Internet to include code to solve the problems independently—that would mean many, many different implementations, would increase software costs, and would make interoperability among programs unlikely.

Instead, a protocol layer on top of IP—TCP—provides these services to programs. A program hands data off to TCP for transmission and having done so can assume that the data will make it to the other end intact and in order. If TCP can't do that, it explicitly notifies the program. If there are no error notifications, the program can assume TCP did its job.

The implementation of how TCP does what it does requires that programmers handle a mind-numbing set of details, but the ideas behind TCP are pretty straightforward:

✦ *Put sequence numbers in messages.* Every message TCP sends out onto the network gets a sequence number. By looking at the sequence numbers of messages as they come in, the TCP receiver can tell whether it has the next message yet, or whether it has to wait for the network to deliver some out-of-order messages.

✦ *Tell the sender when messages arrive.* The TCP receiver sends a message (an acknowledgment) back to the sender when messages arrive correctly and in sequence, telling the sender the sequence number of the highest correctly received message.

✦ *Retransmit failed messages.* The TCP sender keeps a timer for every message it sends. If the receiver doesn't acknowledge the message within a certain interval of time, the sender retransmits the message. This process keeps up until TCP has tried a specified number of retransmissions, after which it reports an uncorrectable failure to your program.

✦ *Retransmit garbled messages.* Even if your message gets to its destination, it might have been corrupted in transmission. TCP uses error detection codes it wraps around your message to know when this has happened. When the TCP receiver detects a garbled message, it explicitly sends a message back to the sender requesting retransmission. (If you're keeping score, you'll notice that the data transmission equipment — such as your modem — does error correction too. See the sidebar "How much error correction is too much?" for a look at how the different error-correction functions interact.)

**Note**

Only the garbled (or lost) messages are sent again. If other messages in the sequence after the bad one arrive properly (even if that happens before the bad one finally gets there), they don't need retransmission.

✦ *Limit the number of outstanding messages.* The TCP sender limits the number of messages it sends before receiving an acknowledgment, which has the effect of limiting the average data rate you need on the connection between you and the destination. More than one message can be outstanding, however, so that the sender doesn't have to wait for the round-trip delay for an acknowledgment to arrive (which greatly increases the amount of data you can get through the connection).

Don't assume that when someone refers to TCP/IP (including in this book) that the reference is exclusively to TCP and IP — it's common usage to call the *complete set of Internet protocols* TCP/IP.

The reliable transport services of TCP come at a price. In particular, the need to wait for acknowledgment messages limits the data rate you can put into the communications channel. This limitation (along with all the other work TCP does) creates an additional processing load at both ends of the channel.

## How much error correction is too much?

Your connection over the Internet has many layers of software and hardware preserving the integrity of your data. The modem hardware uses forward error correction (FEC — see Chapter 23,), sending redundant information that lets the receiving hardware repair damage to the data. Software in the modem (typically using V.42 or one of the MNP protocols) detects corrupted transmission blocks and requests retransmission until it gets the message across properly. TCP does error detection and message retransmission as well.

The high-speed circuits that connect pieces of the Internet together have FEC too. Because there's FEC all along the line, it's likely that your data will be in good shape when it gets to its destination.

Suppose, however, that the FEC fails somewhere along the line — that one of the communications circuits takes a hit that creates too many bit errors for FEC to handle. TCP can handle that situation by retransmitting the affected message, which means that the link-level retransmission in the modem isn't really necessary.

That's an opportunity. The modem has to transmit extra data along with the data you send in order to do link-level error correction. If we turn off link-level error correction in the modem, those bytes won't get sent, and the modem can send your data instead. Your data rate across the telephone line goes up.

Of course, if the decision were that simple, we'd all have turned off link-level error control, and modem manufacturers wouldn't include it in their products. The problem is that the data-compression algorithms (V.42bis in Chapter 21) get very confused when they see corrupted data — you really don't want compression turned on with link-level error correction turned off. If you decide to gain back the bytes link-level error correction was using, you're going to lose the advantages of compression.

We're still not done — you may not care about turning off data compression. If most of what you do with the Internet is use the Web or download files, the large data files you receive are already compressed. Pictures in Web pages are usually in the Graphics Interchange Format (GIF) or JPEG; video is commonly in Audio-Video Interleave (AVI) or MPEG formats (see Chapter 18, and Chapter 24, for more about JPEG). Programs are almost always compressed, either in the ZIP format or as self-extracting compressed archives. Music files are often in the MPEG-based MP3 format. The prevalence of these compressed file formats on the Web means that, with the exception of sound files in the WAV format, almost everything you receive besides the text itself is already compressed and doesn't benefit from compression in the modem. The text itself is a relatively small fraction of the total, so overall the loss from turning off compression may not be so bad.

The end of this story is that, if you're interested, you should experiment. You can control error correction in your modem (through the Windows Modems control panel applet, for example). The results you get will depend on how good your telephone line is, which varies widely. As with so many computer situations, you'll want to run some controlled benchmarks so that you can compare performance with and without link-level error correction.

# User Datagram Protocol

Some applications, such as Internet phone and videoconferencing, or many multiplayer Internet games, can't afford the overhead TCP imposes. The volume of data they send and the need to ensure a data flow uninterrupted by waits for message acknowledgments make TCP unworkable.

Take Internet videoconferencing (such as with a Kodak DVC323 camera and CU-SeeMe) as an example. If your data does get damaged in transit, the worst that's likely to happen is that you'll see a glitch in the video or hear noise in the audio. Slowing the data transmission — one consequence of what TCP does to provide reliable delivery — reduces the frame rate and creates gaps in the sound. Because your eyes and ears handle noise better than gaps, you're better off with more data, even if it contains a few errors.

The situation is about the same for multiplayer games across the Internet. The rapid, timely flow of data between computers is more important than getting every bit right — the programs mostly send updates to the same data over and over, so even if you drop a message, it won't matter.

The Internet protocols solve this problem by replacing TCP with the User Datagram Protocol (UDP), which does none of the corrective things TCP does. UDP does not provide in-order delivery, acknowledgments, retransmissions, or flow control. It's relatively basic. In exchange for that, UDP gets more data sent for a given link capacity and imposes less workload on the processor.

# Point-to-Point Protocol

There's one more fundamental protocol we need to cover — the Point-to-Point Protocol (PPP), which is what you'll use to connect to the Internet over a modem. Because connecting with TCP/IP over a modem involves a number of special issues, there's a protocol devoted to solving the problem. The issues PPP solves are these:

✦ *Single-point connectivity.* You know what's at the other end of the modem — the other modem. It's the only device out there, and there aren't more coming. That means that protocol capabilities to handle multiple devices on a shared medium aren't needed.

✦ *Security and authentication.* Unlike a local area network on which access to the network (if not the servers) is freely available, dial-up connections have to be protected from unauthorized access. (Actually, PPP doesn't specifically handle security and authentication, but it supports protocols that do, and it supports less formal interactions to type in user names and passwords.)

✦ *Network address acquisition.* Because of the way the Internet allocates network addresses, there simply aren't enough IP addresses to give one to everyone who wants one. In the case of dial-up connections, it's common to tell the computer making the connection what its address will be for the duration of the session. The same interaction tells the computer the address of a Domain Name Server (see the next section).

An older protocol, Serial Line Internet Protocol (SLIP), is still in use in some places. PPP is more capable and has almost completely replaced SLIP.

## Domain Name Service

When we have an Internet pipe set up, we need a few more things. One of the most important is a way to translate computer names people deal with (for example, `www.godgames.com`) to the numbers computers want to see (such as `208.249.19.168`). The Internet function that does this for you is called the Domain Name Service. Computers providing that service are called Domain Name Servers. Both phrases are abbreviated DNS.

Internet domains are a hierarchical structure based on the words you find separated by dots in computer names. The last word in the computer name (for example, `com`) is the least specific part of the domain name. Table 30-1 shows some of the root terms for domains.

### Table 30-1
### Domain Name Roots

| Root | Usage | Root | Usage |
|------|-------|------|-------|
| ac | Ascension Island | br | Brazil |
| ae | United Arab Emirates | bs | Bahamas |
| af | Afghanistan | bt | Bhutan |
| al | Albania | ca | Canada |
| am | Armenia | ch | Switzerland |
| ar | Argentina | cl | Chile |
| as | American Samoa | cn | China |
| at | Austria | co | Columbia |
| au | Australia | com | Commercial sites |
| aw | Aruba | cr | Costa Rica |
| be | Belgium | cx | Christmas Island |
| bg | Bulgaria | cy | Cyprus |
| bh | Bahrain | cz | Czech Republic |
| bm | Bermuda | de | Germany |
| bn | Brunei Darussalam | dk | Denmark |

| Root | Usage | Root | Usage |
|------|-------|------|-------|
| do | Dominican Republic | lc | Saint Lucia |
| ec | Ecuador | li | Liechtenstein |
| edu | Universities and other educational sites | lk | Sri Lanka |
| ee | Estonia | lt | Lithuania |
| eg | Egypt | lu | Luxembourg |
| es | Spain | lv | Latvia |
| fi | Finland | mc | Monaco |
| fo | Faroe Islands | md | Moldova |
| fr | France | mm | Myanmar |
| ge | Georgia | mo | Macau |
| gf | French Guiana | mt | Malta |
| gl | Greenland | mu | Mauritius |
| gov | United States Government | mx | Mexico |
| gr | Greece | my | Malaysia |
| gt | Guatemala | net | Network providers |
| hk | Hong Kong | ni | Nicaragua |
| hr | Croatia | nl | Netherlands |
| hu | Hungary | no | Norway |
| id | Indonesia | nu | Niue |
| ie | Ireland | nz | New Zealand |
| il | Israel | org | Organizations |
| in | India | pe | Peru |
| is | Iceland | ph | Philippines |
| it | Italy | pk | Pakistan |
| jm | Jamaica | pl | Poland |
| jp | Japan | pt | Portugal |
| kr | Republic of Korea | ro | Romania |
| kw | Kuwait | ru | Russian Federation |
| lb | Lebanon | se | Sweden |

*continued*

### Table 30-1 (continued)

| Root | Usage | Root | Usage |
|------|-------|------|-------|
| sg | Singapore | tt | Trinidad and Tobago |
| si | Slovenia | tw | Taiwan |
| sk | Slovak Republic | uk | United Kingdom |
| su | Former USSR | us | United States |
| th | Thailand | uy | Uruguay |
| tj | Tajikistan | ve | Venezuela |
| tm | Turkmenistan | yu | Yugoslavia |
| to | Tonga | za | South Africa |
| tr | Turkey | zw | Zimbabwe |

As of May 1999, some other top-level domains were under consideration, including .firm, .shop, .web, .arts, .rec, .info, and .nom.

The word immediately to the left of the root is the domain name (for example, *idsoftware* in www.idsoftware.com). Domain names are chosen by their owners (for example, id Software). There are really no controls on who can register a name, but a given name can be registered by only one person or organization (so it's unique on the Internet). The lack of controls has spawned some interesting disputes after someone unrelated to a company registers the name the company would most likely want (for example, disputes followed registration of mtv.com and gateway.com because the companies you instinctively think of weren't who registered the names).

Finally, the rest of the words in the computer name are subdomains, with the leftmost word being the computer itself. In the name www.idsoftware.com, www is the computer name. Similarly, in the name clyde.isp.net, clyde is the computer name. The complete name less the computer name (*isp.net*) is commonly called the *domain name*, but in fact all the subsets (*isp.net* and *net* in this case) are domain names as well.

## WinSock

All these protocols and services require software to implement. On Windows machines, the Internet software up through TCP and UDP is embedded in the files WINSOCK.DLL and WSOCK32.DLL. These files are *dynamic link libraries* (DLLs), code modules that can be accessed by any program you run. They come as part of Windows; other companies offer alternative versions.

As with most things surrounding the Internet, there are standards defining WinSock. Unfortunately, a number of services (most notably CompuServe) at one time chose to implement not only their own versions of WinSock, but their own *proprietary* versions of WinSock. Replacing the proprietary WinSock with a version that is merely compliant with the standard can render the service's software inoperative.

You don't have to put up with sloppy practice like that. Great software for all the services on the Internet — that works properly with standard WinSock implementations — is available.

# Application-Level Internet Protocols

Even when we get past IP and all its immediate family, we find that we've still done no useful work. We still need a few more protocols (hang in there — we've reached paydirt). Most Internet application programs are tied to one or a few specific protocols, because each program's purpose is to deliver the service the protocol encapsulates. We'll take a quick look at how programs talk to each other on the Internet, and then we'll look at the most common services on the Internet.

## Clients and servers

An Internet service is very much like a telephone call. You start the program (pick up the phone), choose which computer will handle your request (dial the number), and wait for it to do your work (your friend picks up the phone).

The trick is that there has to be something there to answer the phone — to respond to your request for service. That something is a program, called a *daemon*, that sits in the computer you connect to, waiting for a message to arrive. The computer that runs this program is called a *server* (in this case, your computer is called a *client*). Daemons typically only respond for a specific service, so a fully loaded server will run multiple daemons.

The way the server knows which daemon gets your incoming message is by the protocol your message uses. Every protocol has a unique identifier. The daemons register themselves with the IP-level software on the server; each specifies which protocol it handles.

## Ping

The simplest client/server pair is a service called Ping, which lets you find out whether another computer is reachable on the Internet and, if so, how long the round trip to that computer and back takes. The Ping daemon is really built into IP itself — it's not a separate daemon. A typical invocation of Ping (from a Windows DOS window through an analog modem) looks like this:

```
Pinging idgbooks.com [206.175.162.15] with 32 bytes of data:

Reply from 206.175.162.15: bytes=32 time=206ms TTL=244
Reply from 206.175.162.15: bytes=32 time=225ms TTL=244
Reply from 206.175.162.15: bytes=32 time=190ms TTL=244
Reply from 206.175.162.15: bytes=32 time=223ms TTL=244
```

This output shows several things:

✦ *Multiple names for one address.* A single machine can have many names, all of which resolve to the same Internet address. In the example just given, the name idgbooks.com resolves to the Internet address 206.175.162.15.

✦ *Round-trip response time.* The parts of the replies that say things like "time=206ms" show you how long it took from the time your machine sent out the Ping message until a reply came back (1ms is one millisecond, or one thousandth of a second). The variability in the times you see reflects that networks don't always respond identically. Differing amounts of traffic on the communication lines or differing loads on the server are common causes.

You'll see very different response times depending on the access equipment you use. For example, we've measured typical responses for 64-byte pings to a nearby server of 180ms with a V.34 analog modem, 120ms with a V.90 modem, 80ms with a router and separate ISDN modem, 40ms with an integrated router and ISDN modem, and under 10ms with ADSL.

✦ *Routing hop count.* The part of the replies that says "TTL=244" tells you about the route the message took from here to there. The acronym TTL stands for Time to Live, which is a measure of how many reroutings from one point to another the packet has to go before IP declares it undeliverable. The number following TTL is the hop count, which is a number that usually starts at 255 and counts down by one every time the message gets rerouted.

Ping is one of your most important tools in troubleshooting Internet problems. It shows you whether the Domain Name Server is working, whether the computer you're trying to talk to is reachable, and how long it takes to get there. It does this at a very low level — only the most basic Internet functions have to be up and running.

## World Wide Web

The Internet service you're the most likely to use (if not electronic mail) is the World Wide Web (WWW). Your computer runs client software called a Web browser (such as the Microsoft Internet Explorer). Your messages are transported across the Internet using the Hypertext Transfer Protocol (HTTP). The server computer runs a software daemon called a Web server.

The combination of a Web browser, HTTP, and a Web server is more complex than many other protocols, because it does much more than move a type of information from one place to another. Additional functions the combination supports include:

✦ *Page formatting*. Messages sent from the Web server to your Web browser are coded in the Hypertext Markup Language (HTML), which defines an embedded structure and a set of codes that tell the Web browser what the image it displays on your screen should look like.

✦ *Hypertext links*. Links from one page in your Web browser to another are identified by special codes in the message from the Web server. When you click a link, the Web browser sends a request to the right Web server (possibly one you've not communicated with previously) to send it the page data.

✦ *Image, movie, and sound links*. Web pages can contain images as well as text, so a page in HTML can contain codes that specify from where to retrieve the image.

✦ *Forms*. Web pages can contain forms that let you fill in information and send it out to the Web server. HTML specifies how forms are defined for display on your screen. Elements of HTTP define how that information gets to the Web server and is processed.

Even a single Web page may draw information from more than one Web server. The Web uses a standard specification for addressing servers and information on those servers. A standard Web address is called a Uniform Resource Locator (URL). URLs (such as `http://www.aros.net/~press/utilities/utilities.htm`) have three parts:

✦ *Protocol*. The protocol used to access the referenced information need not be HTTP. It is in the example just given but can equally be other protocols such as FTP (for example, `ftp://ftp.aros.net/pub/users/press/bput95s.zip`). In addition to HTTP and FTP, prefixes are defined in URLs for Gopher, electronic mail, newsgroups, and Telnet (see the sections that follow). The first part of the URL defines what protocol to use and is separated from the rest of the URL by the `://` characters.

Recent versions of both Microsoft Internet Explorer and Netscape Navigator let you omit the `http://` element from a URL, supplying it for you. If your URL requires another protocol, you have to provide it.

✦ *Server*. The second part of the URL is the name of the server computer holding the information or services you want. This is `www.aros.net` and `ftp.aros.net` in the two immediately previous examples. The computer name may be suffixed with a port number to tell TCP how to find the daemon on the server. The default port for HTTP is eighty, so `www.aros.net` is equivalent in a URL to `www.aros.net:80`. The server computer name is the only part of a URL you have to supply with current Web browsers.

✦ *File or service location.* A forward slash separates the server computer name from the rest of the URL. Both the forward slash and anything after it are optional, depending on what's being addressed. In an HTTP URL, the file or service location points to a file on the server that is either sent back to you by the server or run as a program on the server. In the latter case, the program creates output dynamically and returns it to you.

## File Transfer Protocol

It's common to want to retrieve files onto your computer from another, or to send files from your computer to another. The File Transfer Protocol (FTP) is the Internet standard protocol to do that. As with other Internet application protocols, FTP operates between a client and a server. The FTP client is the program that initiates the FTP connection; the FTP server is the daemon that receives the connection. You can send files either way across an FTP connection, regardless of which of the two computers is the client and which is the server.

**Tip**    Excellent Windows FTP client and FTP server programs—WS_FTP Limited Edition and WFTPD, respectively—can be found at `http://www.wftpd.com/products.htm`.

Because it is specific to the problem of transferring files from one computer to another, the primitive operations in FTP reflect the things you need to do:

✦ *Authenticate access.* This being an imperfect world, it's often necessary to impose restrictions on who is allowed to connect to the FTP server. FTP implements a username and password authentication scheme and refuses the connection without a valid login. It's common on many FTP servers to allow the username "anonymous" to log in with any password whatsoever; it's conventional to use your electronic mail address for the password. Files kept in an anonymous login area are available to anyone with Internet access — this is the basis on which much of the software downloaded across the Internet is accessed.

✦ *Navigate the remote file system.* In the same way that you need mechanisms such as the DOS Change Directory (CD) command or the Windows Explorer to move around as you use your computer, you need the capability to find files on the remote computer. FTP defines commands and responses between client and server that report the current directory (folder in Windows 9*x* terms), change to a different directory, and list the contents of the current directory.

✦ *Set the file type.* As it happens, some computer systems (such as UNIX) distinguish between pure text files and files that contain other information. Such computers alter the characters at the end of each line in a text file when sending and receiving. (Windows doesn't do this.) This becomes a problem when you go to send a binary file (such as a program), because every time a UNIX computer sees an end-of-line character in the binary file, it converts it to a pair of characters (carriage return and line feed). This is okay for text, but it completely corrupts programs, word processor files, spreadsheets, sound files, and most everything else. FTP lets you control whether files are transferred as text or binary, giving the remote system the information it needs to do its job properly.

✦ *Send or receive files.* This is, of course, the point of the protocol. FTP can transmit files from the client or the server, and it can send one or many files at the same time.

Early versions of the FTP client—starting over twenty-five years ago—on a number of different computer systems provided a command-line interface. The same FTP client interface is standard in UNIX and still available in Windows—open a DOS window on a computer connected to the Internet and type FTP. It's much less convenient than, and lacks many of the features of, the graphical Windows interface provided by WS_FTP32, but it's there. The commands you can enter into the command-line version are very directly related to the primitives in the FTP protocol (such as open a connection to a server, enter username and password, change directory, set the file type, send or receive files, and close the connection). The responses from the server appear directly on-screen, interleaved with your commands.

## Simple Mail Transfer Protocol and Post Office Protocol

The Internet protocol for exchanging electronic mail is the Simple Mail Transfer Protocol (SMTP). As far as we know, there's no Complex Mail Transfer Protocol, but SMTP is quite complex enough. It's almost an Internet tradition to prefix Simple to the name of protocols with cavalier disregard for the truth of the resulting phrase. One of the most complex Internet protocols is called the Simple Network Management Protocol—see Chapter 33,

SMTP itself allows you to exchange text mail messages with users on computers on the Internet. Addresses you can mail to are typically like max@acme.com—there's the username, an at-sign, and the name of the user's mail server computer.

Because electronic mail can be sent to you at any time, it's best to have it come to a computer that's always on the Net (such as one at your Internet service provider). After electronic mail for you reaches your mail server computer, it's common for you to retrieve it to your own computer using the Post Office Protocol (POP3— there've been several versions).

SMTP includes primitives for the things involved with sending mail:

✦ *Validate recipient address.* The server verifies that the addressee on the message exists.

✦ *Deliver to a user's mailbox.* One computer connects to another and exchanges mail between the two.

✦ *Read receipt.* You can request receipts when the recipient opens the message you sent.

Some SMTP mail servers support forwarding — you can receive mail on one system and (transparently to the sender) forward it to a completely different address on another system. For example, a message sent to `max@acme.com` could be relayed by the acme.com mail server to `sam@whizbang.ca`.

The worst thing about raw SMTP is that it accepts only text messages, not binary files. People commonly want to mail files, however, and to send text that includes fonts, colors, and other formatting (which itself is typically stored as binary additions to the standard mail text). Two approaches to handling this requirement are common: UUE and MIME.

✦ *User-user encoding (UUE).* It's possible to recast the binary data stream you want to send differently. For example, you could take every six bits (creating numbers in the range from zero to sixty-three) and remap the resulting numbers onto the printable characters. This expands the data stream, producing eight bits from every six, but it results in a new data stream that contains nothing but text characters acceptable to SMTP. This was the original way of sending binary data through SMTP on the Internet — encode the data, mail the text, and decode at the other end. Current-generation electronic mail client programs, such as Windows Messaging that's included with Windows, support this transformation automatically.

✦ *Multimedia Internet Mail Extensions (MIME).* Internet software such as Web browsers actively knows what sort of data is stored in different kinds of files — that EXE files are executables, ZIP files are compressed archives, WAV files are sound clips, and so on. The MIME coding standard for electronic mail allows the properties of files to be sent along with the files themselves. Technically, MIME uses the same approach as does UUE, expanding a smaller number of bits to a larger number that transforms strictly to printable characters.

Not all Internet mail clients know how to decode UUE or MIME text in a message automatically. If you have one that doesn't and receive binary data in a message, the tipoff will be a bunch of gibberish in the text. (Take a look at the sidebar "What does encoded data look like?")

## What does encoded data look like?

Data that's been encoded for transmission via SMTP looks nothing like what it did before encoding (although what a binary file looks like depends completely on what program you look at it with). We've taken our autoexec.bat file and converted it to UUE coding to show the difference. Here's the original file:

```
@echo off
PATH C:\WINDOWS;C:\WINDOWS\COMMAND;
c:\windows\oldmsdos;c:\win32app;
c:\wintools;c:\config;c:\bin
set BLASTER=A220 I5 D1 H5 P330 T6 E620
set ColorDir= DIRS COM EXE BAT BTM:Bright Yellow On Blue
set dircmd=/o:gen /l /p

SET MSINPUT=C:\MSINPUT

set temp=f:\temp
set tmp=%temp%
set tz=MST6MDT
set winpmt=[Windows 95] $d $t $p$_$n:$z$g
prompt $d $t $p$_$n:$z$g

SET ATI_NOEE_M64=C:\MACH64\EEDATA.EE_
C:\MACH64\CUSTOM.COM

rem-By Windows Setup-C:\WINDOWS\COMMAND\MSCDEX.EXE /D:ASPICD0
/M:12 /L:H
```

This is a purely text file, but it converts to UUE just as well as a binary one (and makes it easier to show what's happened). Here's the resulting UUE file:

```
begin 644 AUTOEXEC.BAT
MO&5C:&\@;V9F#0H-"E!!5$@@0SI<5TE.1$]74SM#.EQ724Y$3U=3\34U!
M3D0[8SI<=VEN9&]W<UQO;&1M<V1O<SMC.EQW:6XS,F%P<#MC.EQW:6YT;V]L
M<SMC.EQC;VYF:6<[8SI<8FEN#0IS970@0D-!4U1%4CU!,C(P($DU($0Q($@U
M(%`S,S`@5#8@138R,`T*<V5T($-O;&]R1&ER/2!$25)3($-/32!%6$4@0D%4
M($)433I"<FEG:'0@665L;&]W($]N($)L=64-"G-E="!D:7)C;60]+V\Z9V5N
M("]L("]P#0H-"E-%5"!-4TE.4%54/4,Z7$U324Y054-"@T*<V5T('1E;7`]
M9CI<=&5M<`T*<V5T('1M<#TE=&5M<"4-"G-E="!T>CU-4U0V341400T*<V5T
M('=I;G!M=#U;5VEN9&]W<R`Y-5T@)&0@)'0@)'`D7R1N.B1Z)&<-"G!R;VUP
M="`D9"`D="`D<"1?)&XZ)'HD9PT*#0I314,\04314].3T5%7TTV-#U#.EQ-
M04-(-C1<145$051!+D5%7PT*0SI<34%#2#8T7$-54U1/32Y#3TT-"@T*<F5M
M+4)Y(%=I;F1O=W,@4V5T=7`M0SI<5TE.1$]74UQ#3TU-04Y$7$U30T1%6"Y%
M6$4@+T0Z05-024-$,"`O33HQ,B`O3#I(#0H-"@``
`
end
```

*(continued)*

On inspection, there's nothing in common between the two. That's because of the transformation of every six bits into the original file to eight in the UUE file. All the information a program needs to reconstruct the original is there, however.

MIME files are different in detail. They have a similar header giving the filename followed by gibberish (like what's in the example). If your electronic mail client doesn't do the decode automatically, you can recover the original file using a program like Aladdin Systems StuffIt Expander from the CD-ROM with this book. What you'll have to do is to save the gibberish (only) including the begin and end lines to a file, and then use StuffIt Expander to do the conversion.

Some Internet mail systems limit the maximum size of a mail message you can send. We've seen limits as low as one and four megabytes; you'll undoubtedly encounter others. This isn't much of a problem for small text messages, but it's easy to create messages containing coded binary files that are that large. Part of the problem is that the six-to-eight coding process expands the file by 33 percent. If you compress your files with WinZip before sending them, you can reduce the net expansion. The effects you'll see if you exceed the maximum size limit are unpredictable — the most benign thing we've seen is for the mail server to send back a message saying it won't deliver the mail. We've had messages silently disappear without notice, had the mail server crash at one end or the other, and had our mail client crash. Just keep in mind the most important rule of the Internet:

### *The Internet is not perfectly reliable.*

That doesn't mean the Internet's not useful, and it doesn't mean you can't depend on it. It means you have to assume that things will go wrong. It means you have to have planned how you will detect when things fail and what to do about it.

## Telnet

In the same way that you can connect a terminal program to your modem, you can connect the equivalent program to the Internet and log into remote computers (or at least the ones you have an account on). The client program that lets you do that is Telnet; the server (usually) is the Telnet daemon. If we log into our Internet service provider, for example, here's a typical example of what we get in the Telnet window:

```
FreeBSD/i386 (ttyp1)

login: xxxxx
Password:
```

```
Last login: Fri Apr 23 18:47:49 from xxxxx
Copyright (c) 1980, 1983, 1986, 1988, 1990, 1991, 1993, 1994
The Regents of the University of California. All rights
reserved.

FreeBSD 3.1-RELEASE (SHELL) #2: Mon Mar 29 15:13:12 MST 1999

4/14/99—Just a reminder that bots are prohibited on this
machine. Any other unattended processes must be approved.

----
Welcome. All access may be logged for auditing and security
purposes.
See /etc/rotd for more information.

For the user-friendly menu, type 'menu'. For help at any time,
type 'help'.
>
```

This is typical of what you get logging in to most UNIX computers. Telnet provides a completely character-oriented terminal—the line at the bottom is a command prompt to a UNIX command shell (analogous to command.com in Windows 9*x*). It's also possible to connect to UNIX computers with a graphical interface called X Window. Telnet doesn't do that—you need more complex software. Telnet ships with Windows—simply run "telnet" from Start ⇨ Run.

## Network News Transfer Protocol

The Network News Transfer Protocol (NNTP) is the mechanism underneath a worldwide Internet bulletin board covering nearly any subject you can think of— the USENET newsgroups. For example, if you're a Quake player, you'll find no fewer than five relevant newsgroups:

```
alt.games.quake
rec.games.computer.quake.announce
rec.games.computer.quake.misc
rec.games.computer.quake.playing
rec.games.computer.quake.servers
```

If you're interested in barbequed food, you might look at

```
alt.food.barbeque
```

There are both moderated and unmoderated newsgroups. The protocol arranges to distribute postings worldwide; in many ways the newsgroups are the broadest, fastest medium for spreading information yet devised. (Newsgroups spread viruses in file attachments, too. You should have your machine protected by good virus software, such as from Network Associates at http://www.nai.com.)

You need a newsreader to access the newsgroups. Microsoft's Outlook Express is included with Windows; UNIX systems include a variety of readers. You'll also need access to a news server — see your Internet service provider for that.

Finally, there are two characteristics of newsgroups you need to know:

✦ *Content.* The same widespread, often-uncensored characteristics of newsgroups that make them valuable also make them a conduit for information that may be unacceptable or offensive to some people. You may want to supervise minors' access to the newsgroups.

✦ *Significance and accuracy.* Don't expect the messages in a newsgroup all to be polite, accurate, or interesting. Indeed, in most newsgroups, the bulk of the messages (and people) are not. Reading all the traffic in even a small number of active newsgroups can take hours, and you might not find what you're looking for when you're finished. If you're looking for a specific topic, you might want to try a search engine, such as at http://www.altavista.com, or a multiple search engine such as at http://www.dogpile.com. Both let you search newsgroups rather than the Web. (Another great newsgroup search site is http://www.dejanews.com.) When you find a newsgroup and topic that's interesting, you can look directly, or you can bring up your newsreader and go look in depth.

## Archie

Although anonymous FTP provides access to downloadable software and files all over the Internet, it can be hard to find the files you want. The Web contains a number of catalogs for software, and there's a number of good FTP archive sites (see http://www.cdrom.com, possibly the largest such site in the world, and http://www.tucows.com). Dogpile can do FTP archive searches, but it's hard to know what to search for.

Prior to the explosion of the Web onto the Internet, it was even harder to find software. If you knew the name of the file you wanted, however, there was a way — a protocol (and software) known as Archie.

Archie works this way: Several Archie servers are located throughout the world. Periodically, each Archie server asks all the anonymous FTP servers it can find to give it the list of files they contain, and logs the results of the request in a database. When you connect to an Archie server with Archie client software (you can get one for Windows 9*x* at http://www.tucows.com/perl/tucowsSearch?word= archie&key=all&platform=win95 or you can search Tucows for the operating system you use), you specify the file you want, Archie searches its database and returns to you a list of anonymous FTP servers having the file you want. You then connect with an FTP program and pull down the file. The process in not as straightforward as using one of the Web catalogs, but you may find files that aren't available through a catalog.

## Network Time Protocol and other time servers

One of the facts of life is that clocks are usually wrong to some degree. A fallout of that fact is that the clock in your computer is probably wrong. Worse, some motherboards are simply incapable of keeping time accurately (for instance, we've had a computer for years that would gain more than a minute a day if we let it. It's not worth pulling out the motherboard and sending it back to the manufacturer to repair it, and Internet software such as we describe here keeps the clock on track).

Very accurate clocks do exist, however, and there are servers on the Internet that are slaved to them. An Internet protocol, the Network Time Protocol (NTP), lets your computer get the current time from one of those servers, as do a number of other forms of time servers.

## Internet Relay Chat

As useful as electronic mail is, it's not interactive. You can carry on "conversations" in extended time, but it's not the same as spontaneous conversation. Nor is the telephone always the answer; it's expensive to carry on extended group discussions at multiple sites using long-distance conference calls.

In the same way that Citizen's Band radio allowed people access to low-cost party lines, computer chat has grown to provide the same capability. The Internet version of chat is a service called Internet Relay Chat (IRC).

Internet Relay Chat works like this. You connect to an IRC server using IRC client software. When you connect, you choose one or more channels you want to "talk" in. You can search for channels with names containing a string you specify, but it's somewhat hit-or-miss whether you'll find the one you want. The last time we looked, the IRC server on our Internet service provider handled over 17,200 channels. Newsgroups covering your interests are sometimes a way to find out about IRC channels, as are search engines such as DejaNews, AltaVista, and Dogpile.

# Network Access Hardware

The most obvious thing you'll need for the Internet, besides your computer itself, is a modem. You don't want to underestimate how fast a modem to get. I characterize a 14.4 Kbps modem as low-speed, 28.8 Kbps as medium, and anything above 28.8 Kbps as fast; Table 30-2 describes the minimum speeds you'll want if you are going to use the services I described earlier. Keep in mind that the Internet is migrating toward capabilities (such as videoconferencing and real-time audio) that use even more speed; the modem speed you'll want will continue to grow. Within a few years, it's reasonable to expect that the slowest acceptable modem will have changed from today's 28.8 Kbps unit to either the new 56 Kbps modems, ISDN, or cable modems.

## Table 30-2
## You'll Want at Least a 33.6 Kbps Modem If You Use the Internet Much, Faster If You Can Get It

| Protocol | Required Bandwidth |
| --- | --- |
| Archie (anonymous FTP file locator) | Low. You send Archie a small command and receive back a size-limited response. |
| FTP (file transfer) | Medium to high. Downloaded files are commonly in the kilobytes to megabytes range. It may take longer to download a file than your network connection stays alive. The registered version of WS_FTP Limited Edition (WS_FTP Pro) solves this problem by allowing you to resume an interrupted download. |
| HTTP (World Wide Web) | Medium to high. Images, movies, and sound clips on Web pages can range from kilobytes to megabytes, requiring absurd amounts of time to download on a slow connection. Some pages with extensive graphics offer a "text only" version to address this issue. |
| IRC (chat) | Low to medium. Messages in an IRC channel are all text. You'd only need more than low bandwidth if you're trying to participate in several very active channels at once. |
| NNTP (newsgroups) | Medium to high. It's common to find hundreds or thousands of new messages in a single active newsgroup. Some newsgroups contain messages with embedded files (similar to embedding files in electronic mail messages; Free Agent can decode these for you). Those messages, like files, can take a long time to receive. |
| NTP (time reference) | Low. The messages are small, and the protocol takes care of network delays to ensure reasonable accuracy. |
| Ping | Low. Ping helps you evaluate network performance by measuring round-trip transit times. |
| SMTP (electronic mail) | Low to high. Simple messages take very little time to transmit or receive. Messages with file attachments can be worse than FTP; the data expands when converted to text for SMTP transmission. |
| Telnet (network terminal) | Low. Telnet is strictly a character-oriented display, rarely sending more than one screenful of text at time. |

# PCs and network computers

Some computer hardware manufacturers invested a lot of money into the development of what they call *network computers* (NCs) — low-cost machines that let you connect to the Internet (or a corporate network), send electronic mail, and access the Web. Because programs can be downloaded to the network computer and run, NC proponents claimed that you'd be able to do almost anything you can do now with a PC, and at less cost.

If your users only run a specific application — say at the departure gate for an airline — a return to the days of mainframe and terminal-based computing could well reduce support costs. Such a transition would certainly increase the control that information-technology departments can exert over users. What's wrong with the arguments promoting this model for general-purpose applications, however, is this:

✦ *Available network bandwidth.* The Network Computer idea assumes you'll download and run all the software you need. It seems to cheerfully ignore the fact that the Internet doesn't have mountains of available capacity; neither do a lot of corporate networks. The whole assumption ignores the reality that the Internet can be very sluggish as it is, and that some observers suggest more serious trouble could be coming.

✦ *Compatibility problems.* Worse, it's unlikely that the network applications the NC runs will be completely compatible with PC applications. That means headaches for people who want to work at home or with laptops on the road. With the advent of very high-rate, fiber-optic networks, we've been told many times that the right way to design networks and distributed computing systems is to assume that communications capacity is free and unlimited, which would solve this problem. So far, neither is true.

✦ *Fat versus thin browsers (and other programs).* The software you run on your computer to access the Web — your Web browser — isn't a small, simple program. Nor is it getting smaller. A stripped-down box without the resources to run that complex software (which is what WebTV is) will either lack the features used across the Web or be slow.

✦ *Resource-intensive applications.* Nor are the common office programs, the word processors, spreadsheets, presentation graphics, and electronic mail programs small. If you try to run several applications at one time, you're going to need a lot of memory, which drives up cost.

✦ *Available software.* Unlike personal computers, which have an incredibly large base of available software (and of creative software developers), the NC has no base at all and will have no leverage to draw from the Windows software market. You'll have to write its programs yourself, choose from a limited selection of immature programs written by hardware manufacturers or a few software developers, or do without. Much of the projected cost savings from NCs (if the savings are real at all) evaporate at this point.

The Java language is promoted as a "write once, run anywhere" platform independent way to free developers and users from ties to specific operating systems. To date, Java's record for cross-platform independence is very poor. Whether the language can mature into that idealistic role is very important for the future of the NC, and very unclear from a technical and standards perspective.

✦ *Historical perspective.* This isn't the first time this idea has rolled around, it's just the latest time. Character terminals attached to mainframes, graphics terminals attached to minicomputers, and diskless workstations (PCs without a disk) all preceded the Network Computer. All were so limited compared to a capable personal computer that they died out except for a limited set of applications where you need to do a single, well-defined function.

✦ *Fading cost advantage.* PCs are now on the market for as little as $300 (without monitor). It's hard to imagine an NC costing much less, because on the inside an NC is really not much different than a personal computer.

Over time, the Network Computer is likely to have no more impact on personal computers than its predecessors — it should be fine for workstations in telemarketing centers or any other well-defined, limited work. It's not likely to have much impact on the mainstream of personal computers.

## What it really takes to run your Web browser

Independent of the success or failure of Network Computers in the market, you shouldn't underestimate the resources it takes to run a Web browser. The CD-ROM installation files for Microsoft Internet Explorer 5 are over sixty-five megabytes but include many extras. The Internet Explorer 5 download file for UNIX is fifteen megabytes, as is the one for Netscape Communicator 4.51. Those files aren't full of graphics, either — they're full of code that takes space and horsepower to run.

We did a small experiment to look at the memory required to run both of those programs, using tools in Windows NT to report the total allocated memory. Table 30-3 shows our results on a dual-processor system with 128MB memory. The numbers you measure may well be different; they'll probably be smaller if you have less memory. The inescapable conclusion from the table is that the functions built into Web browsers are large, complex, and demanding of computer power to run quickly.

| Table 30-3 Don't Underestimate How Much Memory Windows Wants for Web Browsers (Microsoft Word Included for Comparison) | |
| --- | --- |
| *Program* | *Memory Usage (MB)* |
| Microsoft Internet Explorer 5.0 | 9.9 |
| Netscape Navigator 4.51 | 11.3 |
| Microsoft Word for Windows 2000 | 6.1 |

# Servers

In the same way that the functions at the client and server ends of an Internet connection are different, the software and the load on the computer are different. Unlike a desktop machine, for which the load is simply what you generate yourself, a server handles a load for every connected user. The total load on a server is the sum of the load each user generates. You may only see a few users on a server you use locally to your office, but a popular Internet Web site can see very heavy loads.

## Services, software, and loads

The reason an Internet server can be so heavily loaded is simply that there are millions of people out on the Internet. If you catch their attention (which is the point of putting a public server out there, after all), you can attract hundreds of simultaneous connections, putting a tremendous load on your server.

Here are some rule-of-thumb estimates of how much work a server will have to do on the Internet. The actual workload you'll see on your server depends on the software you run, which is why we've identified the software in these estimates (data courtesy of ArosNet; these estimates are based on running the FreeBSD 2.1.5 version of UNIX). Running multiple services on the same machine can create requirements that are worse than additive due to conflicting requirements among the server programs. Here are the estimates:

✦ *World Wide Web (HTTP; FTP for downloads)*. A Pentium processor at 133 MHz with 64 megabytes of memory and SCSI disks can support about 130,000 hits per day on the Web server (using the Apache software in this case), and 6,000 connections per day for electronic mail retrieval. More memory is better.

✦ *Newsgroups (NNTP)*. You'll want one to two megabytes of memory for each newsreader you expect to service at one time, plus 15 to 40MB of memory for the master news server process (this data is based on using the INN server program). The number of newsgroups you handle and the rate of your newsgroup feed drives these parameters too; a full-up news feed ships you about one gigabyte per day. If you're planning on a heavily loaded news server, expect to use a striping RAID disk subsystem, at least 64 megabytes of memory, and 9GB to 20GB of disk. News servers aren't terribly processor-intensive, so even a Pentium processor at 133 MHz is enough.

✦ *Electronic Mail (SMTP)*. Each concurrent outbound mail connection requires about a megabyte; incoming mail doesn't require too much memory until someone sends in a very large file (which on a percentage basis is uncommon, but it does happen — we've received images as large as 20MB by electronic mail). A low-end Pentium processor can handle at least 40,000 outbound messages. Disk space requirements are fairly low (unless your users don't pick up their mail regularly).

✦ *Internet Relay Chat (IRC)*. Even the slowest Pentium with 64 megabytes of memory can handle an average of 560 connections at a time, and a peak of about 950. No one connection requires a lot of resources, but to be an IRC server you have to allow incoming connections from all over the world, which can lead to very large numbers of connections. Disk space isn't an issue.

An IRC server requires some kernel tuning to operate properly. BSD UNIX systems (such as FreeBSD) use a static number of network buffers, and it's necessary to turn this value *WAY* up. Way, way, way up. On some systems that have a set limit on the number of network connections a program can use (Linux, for instance), it's necessary to boost that number as well — your server process needs to have one open socket for every connection, plus a few out to the Net. The default Linux configuration can't handle it. In line with the large number of Internet connections, expect to need a reasonable amount of network capacity.

If you have serious plans to set up an Internet server, you'll want to dig into the subject of high-speed connections (and security) more thoroughly than we can cover in this book.  We suggest you go find a copy of *Getting Connected — The Internet at 56K and Up* by Kevin Dowd. It's published by O'Reilly & Associates. The ISBN number is 1-56592-154-2.

Depending on how popular a site you have (the Microsoft, Netscape, and Walnut Creek CD-ROM sites come to mind; so do the Web search engines or the id Software site when they release a new version or new game), you may generate a bigger load than one computer can handle. The Internet is open for business worldwide, twenty-four hours a day, seven days a week, so you may want to consider multiple servers to ensure that your site's always available. Sites needing absolute reliability should consider multiple independent connections to the Internet using independent physical connections to different service providers. You'll also want to go back to Chapter 6, and Chapter 13, to look at the ways you can keep your servers running and your data protected.

## Modems and terminal servers

If you run a server, you may need to support dial-up users. This happens if you're an Internet service provider, if you have dial-up toll-free access for travelers in your office, or if you choose to restrict remote access to your servers to those whose telephone numbers are on file (and with whom your modems can establish a dial-back connection).

If you do decide to support dial-up users, you have to solve several problems:

✦ *Number of ports*. Unless you do something special, you get only two serial ports on a personal computer, which means you get only two modems.

✦ *Packaging.* You'll need a place to put all the modems you use. Even if we ignore the serial-port constraint, it's impractical to expect to put more than a few modems in slots in a PC. The usual external modem is designed to sit on a desk; although you can get rack-mount shelves you could put them on, the resulting installation ends up cluttered and creates a rat's nest of cables.

✦ *Security and authentication.* You'll want to authenticate the users who dial in, and provide security in the system to protect yourself from unauthorized callers.

(Beyond these issues, you'll need to monitor the modems and telephone lines to make sure they're all working and take corrective action when some of your equipment — or the telephone company's — fails.)

If you're only running a small handful of modems, you might want to use the DigiBoard from Digi International to connect them into a PC. The DigiBoard is supported under Windows NT, providing you with a comprehensive solution (although not one that supports V.90).

You can extend the DigiBoard approach to hundreds of modems. As your operation expands, however, this becomes problematic — you still need a good way to mount the modems. As the number of lines goes up, the load on the computer gets to the point where it has no resources to do anything else but service the modems. At that point, you've turned the PC into a *terminal server* — a device that exists solely to link callers on modems into a network.

A PC makes a fairly expensive terminal server, because to do the job, you don't need video, lots of memory, or a disk — you need a little memory, a processor, a network connection, and a bunch of serial ports. Not surprisingly, you can buy terminal-server products tailored just that way. Because they're stripped down and tuned to do just what it takes for that one job, they do it more efficiently and provide features you'll need (like rack-mount support for lots of modems) that more general solutions don't have.

Don't overlook putting your modems and terminal servers (and your Internet connection equipment) on uninterruptible power supplies, just as you would your servers. A running server isn't very useful if you can't get at it.

## Security

There are a lot of reasons why you should consider security for your computers and your network. A few of them are:

✦ *Competitive information.* You don't want to make everything you know public to your competitors. You may have a lot of that information on your computers tied to the Internet, however, so you'll want enough security in place to ensure that information remains yours alone.

✦ *Private information.* It's likely you also have information on your computers that's simply private to individuals or the company. If you don't want it spread all over, you need security between you and the Internet (and probably internally as well).

✦ *Charging for access.* Some firms make services available for a fee over the Internet. With the release of products like Microsoft's Merchant Server, the number of companies doing this is going to increase. Without security, you could end up finding your site hacked apart, rendering services (or customer data) to anyone with the know-how to go get it.

✦ *Protection from malicious damage.* Not all people trying to penetrate your site are simply after information they're not authorized to get. Some are out to take down your site, such as the people who launched an attack at the PANIX Internet service provider in late summer of 1996.

✦ *Protection from inadvertent damage.* Of course, we all do stupid things now and then. The appropriate internal and network security controls can help protect your site from accidents.

Here's the first rule of computer security, however, which takes priority over all others:

### *If you don't have physical security, you don't have any security.*

The point is, if you don't control who can get at the computer, you can't control what can be done to that computer. Windows 9*x,* Windows NT, UNIX, and other systems are vulnerable to attacks if someone can get at the system — to boot a floppy, remove the hard disk to another system, or otherwise circumvent whatever controls are in place. We've never seen an exception to this rule — give us uncontrolled physical access to your computer, and you've given us your data.

Beyond that, let's focus on keeping the people coming in from the Internet away from places they don't belong.

The way you do this is to put in what's called a firewall between you and the Internet. You can use a capable router as a simple firewall, or can put in a dedicated computer for the purpose. What the firewall does (see Figure 30-1) is filter traffic coming in from the Internet, letting past only the ones that meet the criteria you set. This filtering can happen in two ways — you can filter incoming packets by source address and requested service, and you can let programs on the firewall (called proxies) look like servers to the outside world while they screen messages before passing them to the actual servers behind the firewall.

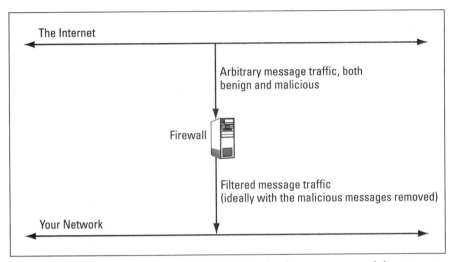

**Figure 30-1:** A firewall provides a layer of protection between you and the Internet.

Most of all, you need a coherently thought-out security policy, careful implementation of that policy, regular monitoring and review of network operations, and periodic independent review. Your policy can have a range of objectives:

✦ *No security.* You might decide that you don't care whether someone penetrates and takes over your site. Perhaps the information on the site is completely public; perhaps you might judge the cost of rebuilding the site if it's destroyed to be less than the cost of providing useful security.

✦ *Minimal security.* Some companies are a likely target just because of who they are (Microsoft is a popular target, for example). Companies (and individuals) that do not believe they are targets may choose to implement just enough security to be an annoyance to potential intruders. If you can be enough of an annoyance, they may go somewhere else.

✦ *Industrial-strength security.* You may need to be as secure as you can while remaining connected to the Internet. Sites like this would include those that do electronic commerce over the Internet; you'll want to protect the records of your customers' accounts and your own order-entry system from electronic theft.

✦ *Disconnected systems.* The most secure systems are those that are not connected to a network. Assuming you have physical security, intruders can't attack if they can't connect.

You may not have to pay a fortune to implement a security policy and plan that meet your needs. For example, with some thought you can implement the two-layer firewall strategy (shown in Figure 30-2) at relatively low cost. The firewall screens incoming service requests heading for the public server, allowing only those for services you've approved (such as your Web server and an FTP server). All incoming service requests are denied if they're headed for your secured network. There are potential holes in even this approach, so if you don't have real-world Internet security experience, get some—the question is always *when* your network will get penetrated, not *whether*.

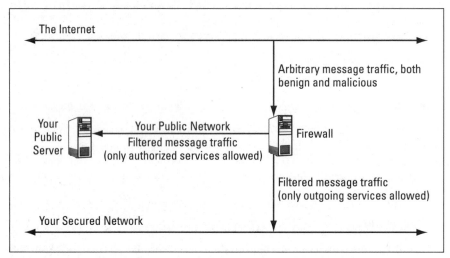

**Figure 30-2:** Isolating a public server from your network can improve security.

# Summary

✦ The Internet uses an entire family of protocols, the most well-known of which are IP, TCP, HTTP, FTP, SMTP, and PPP.

✦ Internet connections are between a client program, which makes requests, and a server, which carries them out.

✦ The Internet is not reliable, and it's not inherently secure. You have to take steps to deal with these issues yourself.

✦ It can take a lot of computing power to support a large, popular Web site.

✦        ✦        ✦

# Putting It Together

# Growth and Combining Components

**W**e covered a lot of different components in Parts III and IV, from cases and motherboards through modems and networks. Not all combinations of things make sense, though, so in this chapter we'll recap some of the most important issues for those components and lay out a strategy of how to plan new machines and upgrades.

## Choke Points and Wide Loads — the Motherboard

Everything that happens in your computer involves moving numbers from one point to another. Instructions are numbers, keystrokes are numbers, display pixels are numbers, sounds are numbers — it's all the same. Because of that, the performance you get comes down to how many numbers you have to push around, where they have to go, and how fast you can push them. Choke points occur when the volume of numbers exceeds what the hardware can handle.

Cross-Reference    See Chapter 4 for more information on finding and eliminating computer choke points.

## Where are the choke points?

We can start to isolate choke points by looking at where the high-rate points are in your computer. The places where performance bogs down if there's not enough capacity include:

✦ *Processor.* The highest data rates in your computer are inside the processor, between the Level 1 (L1) cache and the computational circuits. There are multiple data paths in the processor, each of which is typically 4 bytes (32 bits) wide with a clock rate of up to 600 MHz or more. That means that each data path is capable of moving data at 2.4 GBps. This is an astonishingly high number, but it has to be because your processor has to move a lot of numbers around (at least 4 to 8 bytes per instruction).

✦ *Memory (or host) bus.* The processor cache filters out much of the memory traffic, but the second highest data rates in your computer are still between the processor and memory. The size of the cache determines the percentage of the memory references handled in the cache (the hit rate), with a bigger cache providing higher hit rates and lower memory access rates.

Choosing a higher-performance host bus and memory subsystem means you'll be able to use a faster processor before you run out of memory. That's why the latest, fastest processors are using Rambus, which is less of a choke point than even PC133 synchronous DRAM. Independent of the memory architecture, though, remember that configuring a computer with too little memory is one of the worst things you can do.

✦ *Display bus.* The bus in your display card that transfers data from video memory to the digital to analog converter may run at over 700 MBps, depending on the video resolution and color depth you select. The current-version PCI bus can burst at 133 MBps but does not sustain that rate. AGP at 2X can sustain 528 MBps; 4X AGP will be shipping before the end of 1999.

✦ *Local bus.* In a trilevel bus architecture (for example, host, PCI, and ISA buses), all the I/O and display traffic goes from the host bus to the PCI bus. Some of that traffic may be diverted onto PCI adapters (such as disk host adapters or display cards), while the rest of it will be transferred onto the ISA bus. The local bus therefore transfers data more slowly than the host bus, but faster than the ISA bus.

✦ *I/O bus.* If it's attached to the local bus, the I/O bus (IDE or SCSI) may be faster than the ISA bus, transferring data to and from your disk, CD-ROM, and other I/O devices.

✦ *ISA bus.* The ISA bus (or EISA bus) handles all the traffic not handled by the host and local bus. It's typically the slowest bus in the computer, limited to a few megabytes per second.

Table 31-1 summarizes the situation. Choke points occur when there's a disconnect between two components. For example, if you put a display card on an ISA bus, it's going to be starved for data because it could want hundreds of megabytes per second for high resolution and high frame rates, while the ISA bus creeps along at a few megabytes per second. The same thing happens with a fast disk on an ISA bus.

The information in the table suggests that the likely choke points are the memory, local bus, and disk host adapter interface. Make sure you have enough cache to control the memory load, and that your display and host adapter cards are on the local bus (as is the case with PCI).

### Table 31-1
### Approximate Data Rates Show Performance at Different Points on Your Motherboard

| Component | Approximate Data Rates |
|-----------|------------------------|
| Processor | Can be over 2GB per second |
| Video A/D converter bus | From 17 to 800 MBps |
| Memory | 100 to 1,600 MBps |
| Local bus | 133 MBps (PCI burst) |
| I/O bus | 5 to 40 MBps |
| ISA bus | 2 to 4 MBps |
| Hard disk | 3 to 25 MBps (sustained) |

## Where are the motherboard upgrade points?

You have a range of options when you pick a motherboard or go to upgrade one:

✦ *Processor and processor speed.* You have two ways to upgrade your processor: speed and type. If you can simply plug in a faster processor (swapping in a 550 MHz Pentium III processor for a 350 MHz Pentium II version, for example), your costs are lower than if you have to buy an entire new motherboard. Strategically, this means you want to look at the range of chips a motherboard can accept, not just the chip that you buy with the board.

✦ *Processor socket type.* Intel has defined several standard processor socket designs. The *Socket 5* specification was good for a Pentium processor up to 133 MHz; the *Socket 7* specification would run up to 200 or 233 MHz. The Pentium Pro used the *Socket 8* specification. The Slot 1 socket handled Pentium II and Pentium III processors up to 600 MHz, plus some Celeron processors. The 370-pin Plastic Pin Grid Array (PPGA) handled Celeron processors as fast as 466 MHz and beyond.

✦ *L2 cache size.* You'll get many varying opinions about the size of L2 cache, but on Intel processors you're limited to what's built into the processor. AMD offers some other choices, including a third level of cache in some designs.

✦ *Memory size and type.* Whatever amount of memory you put in your computer, choose dense memory — modules that pack as many bytes as possible on each strip — to minimize the number of memory sockets you use up. If you populate your machine with 128MB of DIMMs, for instance, you're better off using one 128MB strip, leaving at least one other socket unused and available for upgrades.

DIMM-based motherboards typically have only two memory sockets. If a motherboard has more than two sockets, it gives you more flexibility for memory upgrades.

As of the second quarter of 1999, DIMM memory is standard, with PC100 memory the most common. PC133 memory is starting to ship and will work in PC100 systems. Once PC133 memory drops the cost premium, it will make sense to buy the more capable memory to expand the number of systems you can use the module in.

✦ *Local bus type and number of slots.* Computers are no longer available with any bus but PCI. If video performance matters to you, get a 2X (or 4X when it's available) AGP slot. You have to choose the bus when you pick the motherboard; get one with four or more PCI slots if you can. A disk host adapter, display adapter, and network adapter fill three of them in a heartbeat. If you decide later to add FireWire (or some other new, fast interface), you'll want that fourth PCI slot.

✦ *I/O bus type and motherboard connection.* You need to consider price, capacity, expansion, and performance when you choose between IDE and SCSI I/O buses. IDE is less expensive (especially if it's built into your motherboard on a PCI interface) but can't be expanded as much. SCSI can handle larger maximum-size drives and handles multiple drives better. Whichever way you go, don't scrimp on disk space — you'll use it.

Fortunately, you don't have to choose exclusively between IDE and SCSI. You can attach an IDE drive to a motherboard now and later upgrade with a SCSI host adapter and peripherals — the IDE drive will continue to work.

If you plan to use IDE, however, make sure that your motherboard provides at least one PCI IDE port. Most do, and it's a simpler, less expensive solution than a separate PCI IDE adapter card. ISA IDE adapters (with serial ports, a parallel port, and a game port) are common but are nowhere near as fast as a PCI interface.

✦ *Peripherals.* You should look for a motherboard with a floppy disk controller, two serial ports, a mouse port, a parallel port, and two USB ports. It's relatively inexpensive to put them on the motherboard; doing so saves card slots, and the mouse port saves a serial port. If you run out of serial or parallel ports, get one of the new USB devices that add serial and parallel ports.

The display bus type, its number of slots, and the built-in peripherals are fundamental decisions about your motherboard — you can't get a different bus or more slots unless you replace the motherboard.

Table 31-2 shows the limits most computers put on how many of each kind of port you can have. You can exceed these limits in some situations, but you'll need unusual hardware at increased cost. Try to count up the devices you want to connect and see whether the total exceeds these limits.

## Table 31-2
## Adding More Than the Usual Number of Ports Can Be Difficult and Expensive

| Port Type | Usual Limit |
|---|---|
| Floppy | 1 (for two drives) |
| IDE | 2 (for four drives) |
| Joystick (game port) | 1 |
| Local Area Network | 1 (per adapter) |
| Mouse | 1 |
| Parallel | 3 |
| SCSI (usually requires adapter card) | 7 (narrow), 15 (wide) |
| Serial | 2 simultaneous; 4 independently |
| Sound | 1 or 2 input 1 or 2 output |
| USB | 2 (127 devices per port using powered hubs) |
| Video | 1 (use multiple cards for multiple displays under Windows 98 and Windows 2000) |

# Other Trends and Issues

It's nothing mystical to predict that the most dramatic improvements in the hardware technology you can buy will continue to be in processors and memory, followed closely by disks. Everything about hardware is ultimately fueled by the engineering improvements that make better processors, memories, and disks possible; over time you'll see ripple effects in the capabilities of new displays, monitors, printers, scanners, networks, and all other components.

As dramatic as hardware improvements can be, the most interesting trend is the changes happening in software. Hardware is continuing to outstrip what common applications require. The operating system platforms—Windows, OS/2, and UNIX— are all (finally!) 32-bit versions capable of exploiting the capabilities of that hardware. That means software designers can turn to helping you work more effectively, stepping off the treadmill of ever-increasing feature lists.

**Cross-Reference**

That software designers can turn to helping you work more effectively is much of what Dr. Ted Selker of IBM had to say about software—you might want to go back and reread the sidebar in Chapter 5. He illustrated his comments with some specific examples, but it's a good bet that none of us can really predict what software developers will invent over the next five or ten years. In the same way the word processors and spreadsheets changed the way we do office work, and the Web opened up the Internet to anyone with an interest, spare computational capacity is going to once again change how and when we use our computers.

It's easy to bash software developers as always consuming every available bit of memory and processing power, and certainly some of what goes into program revisions is suspect, but there is a core of useful, improved function. Programmers are an inventive lot, and they can be quick to jump on new opportunities. Once the wave of "Internet-aware" applications rolls past, look for new thinking and new software that starts to tread new ground. We've already seen some examples, such as the spelling autocorrect and on-the-fly checking functions in Microsoft Word for Windows (see the sidebar "Do what I mean")—this is a trend that can only increase.

The trend toward using the excess capabilities in computers suggests that you'll at least want to be able to upgrade to some of that excess capability (if you don't build it in to start with). The increased use of sound and video in software (and in the work people do) can only increase your requirements for computer power. (It's no accident that Intel says desktop video recording and editing—a real challenge today—will be common in a few years.)

## Do what I mean

Barry did some programming on large Digital Equipment Corporation computers in the mid-seventies using an interesting programming environment called InterLISP. Among the features of InterLISP was a facility called Do What I Mean, or DWIM.

Most of the time, InterLISP chugged along doing what it was told. At times, though, it would encounter a mistake in the program and give control to DWIM. DWIM could do a number of things; one of the most common was to suggest that something was misspelled. For example, it might suggest that a word it didn't recognize—say, "oen"—should really be some other word it did know ("one" in this case).

DWIM was stunning the first time people saw it in action, because it was so unexpected. It consumed scarce machine resources, however, only really dealt well with a very restricted set of issues, and was hard to extend to more general circumstances. Worse, LISP has never been common outside computer-science circles (a notable exception is that it's in AutoCAD and some games). The result was that DWIM never evolved, although its legacy is there in the WinWord autocorrect. It's a good example of what computers can do beyond direct response to your commands—what's lacking at this time is only the application of creativity and time to the idea of having computers do work on your behalf, even if you didn't ask.

# Should you wait six months to buy or upgrade?

No.

It has turned out that circuit density on a given amount of silicon has roughly doubled every year since the technology was invented (1962). This observation is commonly called Moore's Law after Gordon E. Moore, the chairman emeritus of Intel, even though Moore actually said every 18 months to 2 years. Stated much less precisely (because not all of what's in your computer is chips), every year computer prices drop by half. Every two decades, the price of computer power drops by a factor of a thousand.

This trend might change eventually—Moore's current estimate is that it may only continue through 2017 or so. Because of that trend, what you can get in a computer for a given price will expand and the price will continue to drop—you'll never catch up with the market by waiting.

Instead, what you want to do is figure out what a computer or upgrade will cost you, and compare it against the value of the things it lets you do. It doesn't take very many hours of wasted labor waiting for your word processor to repaginate, your presentation graphics program to redraw, or your spreadsheet to recalculate to equal the cost of more memory or a faster processor. When the pain of waiting exceeds the pain of what the upgrade costs, it's time to act.

The key is to plan ahead. When you buy a computer, assume you'll want to upgrade it, and be sure to make the decisions that reduce the cost of upgrades. We noted bunches of these earlier —for example, choosing a motherboard that can directly accommodate a faster processor, leaving available memory sockets, and starting with spare disk space.

# Buying a complete system

Don't make the mistake of thinking that all these details and analyses only apply if you're building a system from components. Even if you're buying a complete system, you can ask the manufacturer for the details of what's in it; you may have alternatives. For example, as of May 1999, Micron PC would let you make these choices even on a low-end system:

- ✦ *Processor type and speed.* Choices include a 400 to 466 MHz Celeron, or a 400 MHz Pentium II

- ✦ *Memory.* From 32 to 256MB of PC100 SDRAM memory in 1 or 2 slots

- ✦ *Keyboard.* Standard or Microsoft Natural

- ✦ *Mouse.* Microsoft Intellimouse or Logitech 3-button

✦ *Operating System.* Windows 98 or NT 4

✦ *CD-ROM or DVD.* 40X CD-ROM, 5X DVD, or CD-RW

✦ *Disk size and interface.* 8.4 to 22GB IDE

✦ *Backup/removable.* Seagate 4GB (uncompressed tape) and Iomega ZIP

✦ *Sound.* Conventional or 3D audio, with or without speakers, and with optional upgraded speakers

✦ *Display adapter.* (no options)

✦ *Monitor.* 15 to 21 inches; size, dot pitch, maximum resolution, and manufacturer

✦ *Network.* 10 or 10/100 Mbps operation

✦ *Software.* Antivirus, speech recognition, training, and other options available

✦ *Peripherals.* Printers, scanners, photo card readers, and UPS

You can get the details and choose the system you want. There are enough quality system vendors that if one won't give you what you want, you can go talk to another and still get a great system.

## Sizing what you buy

You want to look at both better and lesser options when you configure a machine (or an upgrade) to see what the best value is. For example:

✦ *Getting enough disk space.* Not having enough disk space seems to be a constant state of affairs if you use your computer for very many things. With the price of disk capacity continuing to drop like a stone, you might be surprised how little a bigger disk costs.

✦ *Check the number of drive bays.* If you don't have a place to mount another disk, a tape, or a CD-ROM, all the ports in the world won't do you any good. Count up what you need and check it against what you'll get. Leave room for upgrades.

✦ *DVD.* We expect software to start to be published widely on DVD within a year or so. Getting a DVD now, paying the $50 or so price premium, ensures you'll be ready.

✦ *Printer memory and other proprietary traps.* Be sure to ask about whether the memory in your computer, printer, or any other upgradable component is standard or is proprietary. Both prepackaged systems and printers are notorious for this gambit, greatly increasing your costs. You don't have to accept either.

# Hands-On Upgrades

In many ways, returning an obsolete computer to useful service is the ultimate upgrade problem. Obsolete implies that you can't run current-generation applications at reasonable speed, or can't load them at all. To make the upgrade worth the cost, you'll have to balance the result you get against the cost of parts and the time the work takes.

## Resurrecting an old 486 computer

Despite the best of plans, you're as likely as not to end up with an old 486-based computer on your hands. It will probably have two to eight megabytes of memory, VGA video, and a few hundred megabytes of disk. You might have only a 200-Watt power supply, and the memory and disk may be proprietary.

You've got a few options:

✦ *Leave it on a doorstop*. In a random, unscientific poll, this was the unsolicited answer we received most on what to do with an old, slow computer. We'll not relate the suggestions we received for 386 and older processors other than to say that many of them involved precise application of high explosives.

✦ *Donate it*. You may find people or organizations that can make use of the computer as-is, using the software it's capable of running. This may be harder than you expect, because many organizations you'd expect to have use for donated computers won't take computers this limited. We ran a search on the query "+computer +donate +charity" (no quotes) with AltaVista (`http://www.altavista.digital.com`) and came up with some candidates, so you might try that if you don't have some preferred choices.

✦ *Use what you can and send the rest for recycling*. If all else fails, you might find some parts in the machine that you could use for emergency spares, such as keyboards, mice, network and video cards, floppy disk drives, the power supply, and CD-ROMs. The case and power supply might be useful if you're building up a machine from scratch, but if it's an AT case, you might find it useless. Be sure to recycle the rest of the machine properly, because some of what's inside a computer isn't environmentally wonderful.

✦ *Build a print or fax server*. You can install FreeBSD, Linux, or Windows 9x on a 486. If you add some memory (up to at least 16MB), compress the disk under Windows 9x, and add a network interface card, you could put the machine on your network as a shared print server. If you add a fax modem (a 14.4 Kbps or better unit you've upgraded out of something else should do), you can use the same machine as a fax server and share it across your network.

This is actually a pretty good idea, because it need not cost much, and it can have a nice payoff. Many printers slow the machine noticeably, so moving the load to a dedicated machine eliminates that annoyance and lets you turn conventional printers into network printers. Better yet, moving the printer and fax responsibilities to a dedicated machine means that people retrieving printouts and faxes don't interrupt the person using the machine.

Not all combinations of slow computers and printers work well as simultaneous print and fax servers. Ink jet printers, for example, are notorious for the processor load they create, enough of a load that the machine is likely to fail to receive an incoming fax while printing.

✦ *Rip and shred.* The most drastic option is to upgrade the machine. If you're really aiming for a useful machine, you're likely to save little but the case and power supply, floppy disk drive, network card, CD-ROM, keyboard, and mouse. The value of those components bought new is $300, tops, and with the recycled parts you'll have to live with the issues of partly expended service life and lesser performance. You'll definitely end up replacing the motherboard, processor, and memory. It's likely you'll want to replace the disk and video card; if the machine has an eight-bit network card you'll probably want to replace that too.

Using an old case limits your choice of motherboard — you won't be using the new ATX form factor products. That severely limits your choice of motherboard vendor (Intel no longer manufactures AT boards, for example), and means you lose the benefits of supplying 3.3 Volts directly from the power supply and having a prebuilt I/O panel integrated onto the motherboard.

**Tip**

Overall, a massive upgrade to an obsolete machine is a great training exercise for teaching PC technology. Doing this to a large number of computers is likely to leave you with a fleet of machines that are all different, though, each with its own problems and each with its own required spares. Be sure to think through the cost of maintaining a hodgepodge like that — ask whether the cost will outweigh the one-time savings from reusing the existing components.

If you're dealing with very old memory and motherboards, resist the temptation to move 30-pin SIMM memory forward into 72-pin SIMM motherboards using converter modules. Converters can add delay to the memory access and may introduce noise and other degradations into the signal path. The end result is that memory in converters isn't likely to be as reliable as the sort directly intended for the motherboard. Because the 72-pin motherboard is likely to be a higher-performance unit to begin with, creating those problems for yourself isn't a good idea.

# Summary

✦ Available computer power grows relentlessly. It takes awhile for programmers to exploit it, but they do.

✦ Picking the right motherboard can dramatically reduce your system upgrade costs.

✦ Get some spare computer power and capacity when you buy.

✦ It's pointless to wait longer than the time when the value of a new computer or an upgrade is as much as its cost. You're not going to catch up with the market by waiting.

✦     ✦     ✦

# Making Choices That Fit the Road Warrior

**D**espite the seemingly reasonable goal of integrating desktop and laptop computers, laptops remain a breed apart. The added constraints of minimum size and extended battery operation change the design decisions laptop engineers make and raise the cost. The convenience of using the same computer for both desktop and portable situations may save you some time, but it's not clear if it will save money, or if it will even really save you time.

The problem is that when you're traveling, you typically want very different capabilities from those you prefer in your home or office.

Table 32-1 shows the problem — weight and size matter most in a laptop. The farther you carry your laptop, the closer its weight approaches 20 tons. It's reasonable to make compromises in your laptop's features and performance to get the size and weight down because most people don't do things with a laptop that are as complex as they might do with a desktop computer, and they don't do as many things at once.

| Table 32-1 Contrary to What You May Have Been Told, Size Counts — So Does Weight | | |
|---|---|---|
| *Requirement* | *Traveling* | *Desktop* |
| Workload proposals. | Notes, electronic mail, small proposals. | Reports, electronic mail, major proposals. |
| Interruptions | You're relatively isolated, so you are interrupted less often (takeoffs and landings notwithstanding). | You're a sitting duck. |
| Weight and Size | Every ounce and cubic inch matters after you've carried your laptop from one end to the other of the Delta Airlines terminal in the Dallas–Fort Worth airport. | Size may matter, but only in terms of fitting in your office (not your briefcase or pack). Weight is less of a concern. |
| Power | You'll carry it with you, so in addition to needing enough batteries to keep running on transcontinental or transoceanic flights, all those batteries are weight you have to carry. | It comes from the wall. |

Because your laptop's portability is paramount, the compromises you're likely to make may limit its suitability as a desktop machine — it may be short on memory or disk, have a limited display, and have a lesser processor than you might want.

In the following sections, we'll look at the specific compromises you might end up making in a laptop. The section after that covers docking stations, which are hardware you can leave on your desk to make up for shortcomings in the laptop itself.

# What's in Your Laptop?

Like any other personal computer, your laptop has the usual processor, disk, memory, display, keyboard, and communications. Where laptops differ from desktop machines is in the specifications for these components to cope with limited size, weight, and power. Reducing the power requirement is not only a way to extend battery life, but also a way to limit the heat generated inside the laptop case. This is a vital need because protecting the computer from shock and damage requires that the electronics be tightly enclosed, which limits how much heat can be dissipated.

## Processor, memory, and bus

It's difficult to blow air through a laptop to cool it, which further limits heat dissipation. This restricts how much heat any one device in a laptop can generate because if the rate at which heat builds up exceeds how fast it dissipates, the device temperature will increase until the laptop fails. Because the heat a processor generates is directly proportional to its clock speed, designers commonly limit processor speed to control heat generated in the chip.

You can expect the processor in your laptop to be a Pentium II or Celeron processor at speeds up to 366 MHz, or a Pentium III at up to 500 MHz. The speed limit will increase over time. You can expect laptop speed ratings to be roughly similar to those for the desktop computers that preceded them by about a year.

The memory and buses in laptop computers are likely to be somewhat different from those in desktop machines; the highly constrained space in a laptop doesn't leave room for conventional packaging. The resulting proprietary designs inevitably don't conform to any widespread industry standard, so you can expect upgrades to be expensive. If you're willing to pay the price, however, you can get more memory than you'll need for virtually anything you would do (laptops that can handle up to 384 megabytes of memory are available). Similarly, you can get laptops with a PCI bus. Don't expect PCI cards designed for a desktop machine to plug right in, though, because there isn't room.

## PC Card and PC CardBus

The exception to proprietary components in laptop computers is a standard created specifically to allow modules to plug into laptops — the PC CardBus and PC Cards. This standard was formerly known as PCMCIA (Personal Computer Memory Card International Association). As we saw in Chapter 9, PC Cards support read/write and read-only memory, hard disk drives, modems, network adapters, SCSI adapters, and sound adapters.

PC CardBus isn't a cure-all. It's limited to two megabytes per second, which is acceptable for all these applications, although it's not what you'd really want for memory. The success of the PC Card is reflected in the variety of devices you can buy. The most popular are communications interfaces and disks. Manufacturers have recognized that your communications needs are different at your desk from those you have when you're mobile; they've built products combining a modem with an Ethernet interface. This device is likely to take up residence in your laptop because it works no matter where you are.

Table 32-2 shows what you can expect to get in PC Card functions. The cards have most of the features you'd expect in full-size units — the most likely reason to compromise is that they're expensive.

**Table 32-2**
**The Exceptions to Proprietary Components in Laptops Are the PC CardBus and PC Cards**

| Function | Typical Characteristics |
| --- | --- |
| Drives | Hundreds of megabytes |
| Memory | Megabytes |
| Modem | 33.6 and 56 Kbps fax modems<br>Combined fax modem, cellular modem, and Ethernet |
| I/O bus | SCSI2, some combined with sound |
| Sound | Including 16-bit |

Be careful about cables or connectors for PC Cards. Because the card is thin, the connectors can be fragile. (So can the card — more than one has been destroyed when someone left it in their wallet and sat on it.) Check with the manufacturer before you buy — we've seen situations in which replacement cables either were not available or were so expensive that it was cheaper to buy another card.

## Laptop displays

Of the flat-panel display technologies mentioned in Chapter 19, nearly all laptops use liquid crystal displays (LCDs). Plasma panels competed in the market for a while, but the much lower power consumption of LCD doomed plasma. The best color laptops use active-matrix Thin Film Transistor (TFT) or passive-matrix Dual-Scan Twisted Nematic (DSTN). Active matrix is more expensive but is also brighter, sharper, and viewable at almost any angle. Passive matrix essentially requires that you look straight at the screen.

The newer, high-performance LCDs are as large as 15 inches diagonal, 1,024 × 768 resolution (1,280 × 1,024 is available), and 18-bit or 24-bit color TFT LCDs. Support chips for LCD panels are starting to incorporate acceleration functions, bringing the performance of your desktop display to your laptop.

## Disk

Laptop disk drives, like desktop drives, have increased in size. You no longer have to struggle to make all of your applications fit — you can get 3 to 14GB drives.

The two biggest differences (besides size) between laptop disk drives and desktop disk drives are transfer rates and power management. Laptop disks are typically slow compared to desktop drives and get powered down after a short period of inactivity. The motors in the disks consume a significant amount of power, so this is an important measure. When your laptop wants access to the disk, you'll wait while the disk spins up to operating speed.

There's an important tradeoff between memory and disk in a laptop computer. If you have too little memory, your computer will go to the disk relatively often for fragments of programs, requiring the disk keep running (or spin up) to satisfy the request. That activity keeps the disk running, drawing power, and slows down operation. If you have enough memory in the laptop (say, at least 64 megabytes if you'll be running only one program at a time), Windows will use the extra memory as a large cache, reducing disk access and letting the disk stay powered down. Your laptop runs faster and longer on each battery.

Nearly all laptops now include CD-ROM drives, so you can load software and run multimedia applications. This capability is particularly useful if you take along programs such as Microsoft Automap Streets or Automap Road Atlas. We print maps for the destination before flying on business, but with a CD-ROM in your laptop, you can take the full electronic map with you and know you can find your way.

## Communications and ports

Laptop computers commonly come with a serial port, parallel port, video port, and docking-station port. Many now provide USB ports. If your laptop doesn't include a built-in pointing device (like a trackball), you'll have to use an external mouse, which is not permitted in flight by some airlines.

The ports you'll care the most about are the ones for a modem or network interface. You care about both because communications requirements with your laptop depend on where you are. If you're in your office, you may want to tie the computer in to your network. If you're on the road, you'll probably want a modem to dial in to your home system, private network, or the Internet. You'll typically have to use a PC Card or docking station for the network interface. Modems are sometimes built into laptops; otherwise, you'll need a PC Card or USB modem.

**Tip**   Think a little about built-in modems. It's more common than you might think to plug a modem into a jack in a hotel room, only to find out that the hotel's telephone system is digital (or otherwise incompatible). You can easily burn out the interface circuits in a modem this way. If the entire computer has to go in for repair, you're out of business. If you can replace the internal modem yourself (or a PC Card modem), you can keep on going. Be sure you check the replacement price of the internal modem before you buy the computer because you might be better off with a PC Card modem to begin with. You'll also want to check that the modem can be disabled so that it's not consuming power when you're nowhere near a telephone line.

# Batteries

We looked at power management, which is the technology evolved in laptops to extend their battery life, in Chapter 9 Power management only transferred into desktop machines when people noticed that reducing the power consumption of hundreds of millions of desktop computers could significantly reduce worldwide power consumption.

Beyond power management (and low power consumption), the key power issue for laptop computers is the battery. There has been tremendous progress in battery technology in order to power camcorders, laptops, and other portable electronics, resulting in several competing battery technologies:

✦ *Nickel-cadmium.* Nickel-cadmium (NiCd) batteries are being phased out because of memory problems. The batteries "remember" when they're only partially discharged and don't recharge to full capacity. Recharging a nickel-cadmium battery that's not fully discharged can keep the battery from ever being fully charged again unless you go through a special discharge/recharge cycle.

✦ *Nickel–metal hydride.* Nickel–metal hydride (NiMH) batteries have an advantage over NiCd because they are not subject to the memory effect when being recharged. The newest versions of nickel–metal hydride batteries are claimed to have higher energy-density levels than lithium-ion batteries, and at less cost. Nickel–metal hydride batteries have a short shelf-life (they discharge in a few days), so be sure to recharge them completely before you go traveling.

✦ *Lithium-ion.* Lithium-ion batteries are a recent development but are now widely available. You can expect 20 to 30 percent longer performance than with the older versions of nickel–metal hydride (possibly as long as seven hours' operation) with a good shelf-life. A lithium-ion battery provides three times the voltage of a nickel-cadmium, which lets designers reduce the number of batteries required. There is no memory effect, and the battery has a life cycle of 1,200 charge/discharge cycles. Lithium-ion batteries don't require environmentally polluting material (such as cadmium, mercury, or PVC).

✦ *Zinc-air.* Rechargeable zinc-air batteries can last up to 15 hours. The battery is large (nearly the size of the laptop itself), heavy, and expensive.

✦ *Lithium-polymer.* Lithium-polymer batteries are still in development. The battery looks like a sheet of plastic about the size of a playing card and can be wrapped around other components. Projections are that the technology will weigh 75 percent less and run four times longer on a single charge than a nickel-cadmium battery of similar weight. Lithium-polymer batteries can be molded into any shape. The batteries support high energy densities, do not have memory-drain problems, and use environmentally safe materials. However, lithium-polymer batteries currently have a limited life cycle (about 175 hours) and may not be viable for several years.

Whichever battery technology you have in your laptop, be sure to recycle any battery at the end of its useful life. Some battery components are explosive in fires, whereas others are toxic and difficult to remove from the environment. Check with your local recycling company to find out about safe battery disposal.

# Laptop Docking Stations

You may find it unacceptable to have two computers (one for travel and one for your desk). For example, if you use your laptop with a cellular modem to work on the move in a warehouse, having to switch constantly between a laptop and desktop machine is really an inconvenience.

If so, you may want to look at what are called docking stations — boxes that sit on your desk and into which you can plug your laptop. The docking station provides additional resources, such as power, a monitor, a full-sized keyboard, a network interface, a floppy disk, a hard disk, or a CD-ROM. The idea is that you don't need those extras while you're mobile, but the docking station makes them available when you're at your desk. The added resources could be enough to let the one computer meet your fixed and mobile requirements.

Don't assume you'll save money with a docking station, however. The electrical interface between laptop and docking station will be a proprietary connector; the physical fit of the laptop into the docking station will be unique to the specific model. That means that you're likely to have only one source for the docking station, which boosts cost.

# Handheld PCs

Not everyone needs a computer of heroic proportion to carry around with him or her — it may well be you only need something that tracks your address and telephone book, reminds you of appointments, or lets you check e-mail, fax, or other limited tasks.

If that lesser list matches your needs, you may find that a handheld PC — a unit literally about the size of your hand running Windows CE or other specialized operating system — may be sufficient. In return for limited capability, you get the advantages of a small, lightweight machine (also called a PDA, or Personal Digital Assistant) that runs for tens of hours on AA- or AAA-class batteries. Windows CE software isn't quite the same as conventional Windows software — it runs on a different processor and uses a (much) smaller version of Windows that Microsoft tailored to fit in a very limited amount of memory. You'll also get a relatively small keyboard, or no keyboard — you won't do high-speed touch typing on the tiny keyboard or its on-screen equivalent unless you have *really* small hands. Nevertheless, you can get versions of software you're probably used to that cooperate with software on your Windows PC.

An alternative to PDA-class machines is the mininotebook such as the Toshiba Libretto. These machines are about the size of a VHS video cassette and could be confused with a Windows CE machine. Don't. You can get one with processors as fast as a Pentium 233, an active matrix color screen, up to 32MB of memory, and over 4GB of disk. It runs full-up Windows 9*x* or NT, not Windows CE. The Libretto is expensive by comparison with Windows CE or the 3Com Palm machines — you should evaluate the broader capabilities and decide if they're worth the cost.

A capable handheld unit can connect to a modem, letting you send and receive faxes and connect to the Internet. With a Web browser and the capabilities available through Web pages, you can get at an enormous range of information, including news, stock quotes, and street maps. With e-mail software, you can connect to your Internet service provider and both send and receive messages. With the Ricochet modem in a PC Card slot, you can connect to CPDP networks and be completely mobile while on the Internet.

Be careful about the power consumption of devices you plug into the PC Card slot. There's not a lot of power in the batteries in a handheld computer, and they can be quickly drained by power-hungry devices like modems.

# Products

Picking the features you want in a laptop is more than simply choosing everything you can afford because everything you choose adds weight, takes up space, and consumes power. Add enough to your laptop and you might as well carry around a desktop computer (and a long power cord).

Having said that, we should note that the laptop computers from several manufacturers include both models with exceptional features and ones that are exceptionally small and light.

## Toshiba Tecra 8000 Series

The Toshiba laptops are very highly regarded in the industry; their Tecra series is representative of what you can expect in a full-featured machine. Figure 32-1 shows the Tecra 8000 Series, which, although it includes a 233 to 366 MHz Intel Pentium II processor, up to 256MB of memory, and as much as 8GB of disk, is nevertheless highly mobile, weighing in at no more than 6.35 pounds. Despite being only 1.69 inches high, it is a highly capable computer.

Table 32-3 shows the range specifications you can get with various options for the Tecra 8000. You can get all the options you'd put in a capable desktop machine — less than the fastest processor, less than the disk and memory you'd put in a server, but nevertheless a very capable machine. The fact that you can carry it around in a small, lightweight package is remarkable.

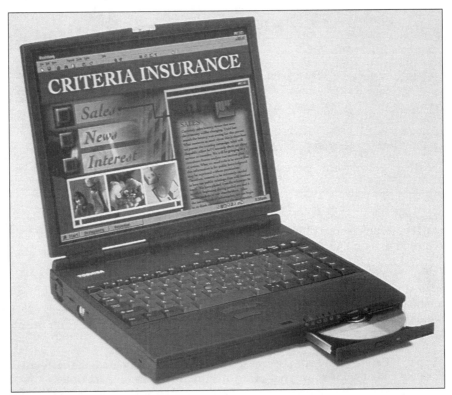

**Figure 32-1:** The Toshiba Tecra 8000 series carries a long list of features. (Photo courtesy Toshiba America, Inc.)

| Table 32-3 You Can Pack a Lot into the Tecra 8000, but You Pay in Battery Life | |
|---|---|
| *Characteristic* | *Specification* |
| Processor | 233 to 366 MHz Intel Pentium II |
| Memory | Synchronous DRAM, up to 256MB |
| Display | 12.1-inch TFT active matrix color; 800 × 600 resolution up to 14.1 inch at 1,024 × 768 resolution. DVD decoder with S-video output available |
| Disk | 4 to 8.1GB hard disk; 24X CD-ROM or 2X DVD; 3.5 inch floppy |
| Ports | Infrared, PC Card/CardBus, Serial, Enhanced Parallel, Floppy Disk (detachable drive), Universal Serial Bus, Video, Docking Station |
| Keyboard | Full-size 84-key, with AccuPoint pointing device set into keyboard |

*continued*

| Table 32-3 *(continued)* | |
|---|---|
| **Characteristic** | **Specification** |
| Audio | SoundBlaster Pro compatible, including Yamaha OPL3-SA3 with Dolby Digital and 3D sound support. Internal stereo speakers and microphone |
| Modem | Built-in 56 Kbps V.90 voice/data/fax |
| Dimensions and Weight | 12.24" × 10" × 1.66", 6.36 pounds with CD-ROM installed |
| Battery | Lithium-ion, estimated three-hour life |

The Tecra 8000 provides a bay on the right side (Toshiba calls it a "Selectbay") into which you can insert a CD-ROM, a DVD drive, a floppy disk drive, another battery, or a second hard disk of up to 8GB capacity.

The Tecra offers two Type I/II PC Card slots, opening up the possibilities for expansion. You can load separate modem and network cards (if you don't have a combo card), a network card and SCSI card to interface a scanner, or a modem card and digital camera memory card. If you need to share a disk with another laptop, you can plug in a Type III card containing a small hard disk (which consumes both slots).

You pay for all that power in decreased battery life — fully loaded, the Tecra 8000 will run only for somewhat over three hours. Less compact or less powerful machines that deliver longer run times are available. Installing a second battery (instead of the CD-ROM) extends battery life to over six hours, though, enough for all but the transoceanic airline flights.

## Eiger PC Card network adapters, modems, and desktop adapters

At the point you go to connect your laptop to a network, you'll be looking for either a network adapter or a modem. Assuming your laptop doesn't have those built-in, you're likely to want a PC Card adapter. The PC Card cards from Eiger offer a lot of flexibility for connecting to combinations of systems. Figure 32-2 shows the EigerNet 10Base-T and 100Base-TX Ethernet Adapter. Table 32-4 shows the range of adapters you can get, including 56 Kbps modems, analog and cellular modems, combined modems and Ethernet adapters, and multiple-speed or interface Ethernet adapters.

**Figure 32-2:** The EigerNet 10Base-T and 100Base-TX Ethernet Adapter lets you connect to legacy or newer, faster networks. (Photo courtesy Eiger Labs, Incorporated.)

| Table 32-4 | |
| --- | --- |
| **The Eiger PC Card Adapters Offer Versatile Connections to Networks** | |

| Adapter | Capabilities |
| --- | --- |
| EigerCom 56K fax modem | Data: K56Flex (Rockwell/Lucent), V.34, others<br>Fax: Class 1 and 2 operation, speeds to 14.4 Kbps<br>Type II PC Card |
| EigerCombo 33.6 Kbps v.34 + 10BaseT/2 Ethernet combination | Data Modem: V.34 to 33.6 Kbps, with cellular support<br>Fax modem: Class 1 and 2 operation, speeds to 14.4 Kbps<br>Ethernet: 10Base-T and 10Base-2Type II PC Card |
| EigerNet 10Base-T or 10Base-2 Ethernet adapter | Ethernet: 10Base-T or 10Base-T + 10Base-2, depending on model<br>Type I PC Card |
| EigerNet 10Base-T and 100Base-TX Ethernet adapter | Ethernet: Full duplex 10Base-T and 100Base-TX (autosense) Type I PC Card |

Eiger offers another interesting device—the CardPort (Figure 32-3)—which is an adapter for your desktop computer that provides two PC Card slots. The CardPort handles two Type I cards, two Type II cards, or one each Type I and Type III cards. It includes the required drivers and supports hot swapping cards in and out with the power on. You can use the CardPort to share PC Card devices between your laptop and desktop, or to quickly read image files off a PC Card used in a digital camera.

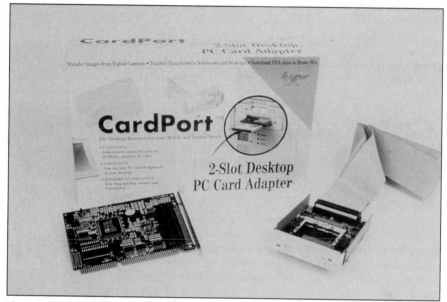

**Figure 32-3:** The Eiger CardPort lets you use PC Cards in your desktop computer. (Photo courtesy Eiger Labs, Incorporated.)

If you're reading the smaller CompactFlash cards, though, look for the reader marketed by Kodak and others that directly accepts the CompactFlash. That way, you won't have to keep track of the adapter bracket that makes a CompactFlash card fit a PC Card reader.

## Casio Cassiopeia

The Casio Cassiopeia (the model E-15 is shown in Figure 32-4) is a typical Windows CE–based handheld computer. It includes reduced versions of Microsoft Word, Excel, and Inbox, along with applets for your calendar, contacts, and tasks (much as in Microsoft Outlook). Accessory programs include a terminal emulator; you can download versions of Internet Explorer, Microsoft Automap Streets, and the Power Toy accessories from the Microsoft Web site.

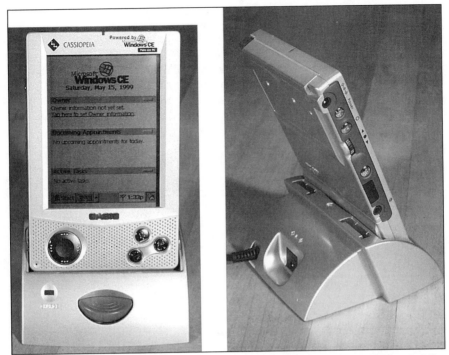

**Figure 32-4:** The Casio Cassiopeia (E-15 shown) provides a Windows-like capability in a small, highly portable package. The included stand provides communication to your desktop PC.

Don't overlook the Internet as a source of software and updates for a handheld computer. Not only will you find updates and fixes from both the manufacturer and (in the case of Windows CE) Microsoft, you'll find trial or free versions of a range of software from fax handling to desktop accessories.

**Tip** You can connect a Windows CE version 2 computer to the Internet through your desktop machine or through a modem. The modem can be either a PC Card modem inserted into the machine or an external modem connected via the serial port you'd otherwise connect to your desktop machine. You're not going to slip the machine and PC Card modem in your pocket and be ready to go, though, because a PC Card modem needs more power than two small batteries are going to provide. If you're going to be mobile with a modem, plan on carting around the (relatively small) power module for your handheld too.

The latest palm-sized computers provide an on-screen keyboard and a window into which you can write (called the "Jot" window on the Cassiopeia). Written characters are recognized and translated to typed ones; we found that once we got used to how the computer wants characters written, the recognition was usable. The on-screen keyboard, as well as the real keyboard on models that have them, is too small for touch typing, but it's in a standard layout and usable for light duty.

There are two varieties of user interface, one in handheld PCs, and one in palm PCs. Both work very much like Windows 95 and Windows NT 4, Start button and all, so if you're comfortable with those systems, the interface will be familiar. The screen shot of a typical handheld PC desktop in Figure 32-5 shows a desktop with shortcuts to icons and files, just as in conventional versions of Windows, along with a Start button, taskbar, and the area for icons and the clock. Just as you can change "My Computer" on your Windows computer to personalize your computer, so can you change the corresponding icon on a Windows CE computer.

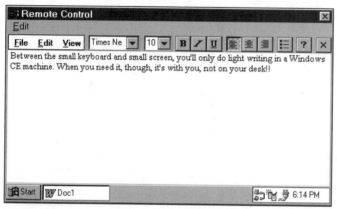

**Figure 32-5:** The Cassiopeia desktop looks like Windows 95 or Windows NT, reflecting its Windows CE heritage

Palm PCs, such as the Cassiopeia E-15, don't use the desktop in Figure 32-5. Instead, you switch from one application to another with the Start button or (in the case of the E-15) with one of the three application select buttons you can see in the bottom right of the unit in Figure 32-4. The applications standard in the E-15 are similar to what Microsoft Outlook provides — calendar, contacts, inbox, and tasks — plus a note taker and a voice recorder. The voice recorder is particularly useful for quick notes when you don't want to take the time to use the keyboard or written interface. The note taker lets you write or draw directly, type on the keyboard, or write into the character recognition window. You can switch among the three input modes in the same note.

Figure 32-6 shows the desktop (or home) screen on an E-15. You can choose what reminders appear on screen (we've chosen appointments and unread messages). The usual Windows Start button is at the lower left in the taskbar. The button to the right of the Start button turns on and off the handwriting recognizer or typewriter windows; the little up arrow lets you select between the two. The Home button at the far lower right brings up the home screen.

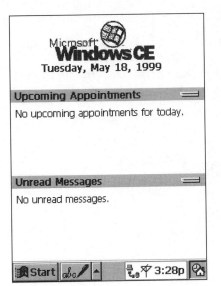

**Figure 32-6:** The Cassiopeia palm PC desktop also looks like Windows 95 or Windows NT.

You can have only one program visible on the screen at once, selected with the Start button or physical buttons on the front of the unit, but all the programs stay running. You can be writing a note, go look at e-mail, and then come back to writing the note to have it still there. Figure 32-7 shows what the screen looks like while you're writing a note with the handwriting recognizer (called the Jot window). An automatic completion function guesses at what word you're really writing; if it guesses right you can just select the word and have the machine type out the remaining characters.

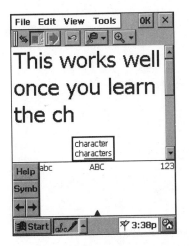

**Figure 32-7:** The Jot window (at bottom) sees lowercase on the left, uppercase in the middle, and numbers at the right.

If you turn off both the Jot window and the keyboard window, you can simply draw directly into your note, as shown in Figure 32-8.

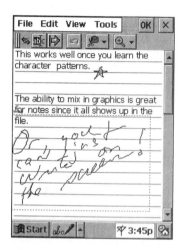

**Figure 32-8:** You can draw directly into a note for graphics or direct handwritten input.

Other programs in the palm PC provide calendar, reminder, and contact list functions very similar to Microsoft Outlook. Figure 32-9 shows the year calendar view; Figure 32-10 shows one day's appointments (including one at 4 P.M.).

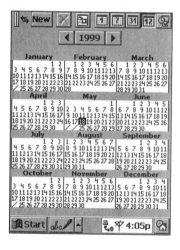

**Figure 32-9:** The palm PC calendar is similar to the calendar you are used to on your desktop PC.

**Figure 32-10:** Reminders can be synchronized with your desktop PC to keep your calendar current.

You can download add-on programs to these machines, including the pocket version of Automap Streets (part of West Los Angeles is shown in Figure 32-11). When you load programs into your Windows CE machine, though, remember that all storage in a handheld computer (16MB on the Cassiopeia E-15) is really RAM chips with a battery backup, not a disk. That memory gets split between programs and other storage, with the boundary something you can set and move. Just as with larger computers, memory goes fast — don't plan on keeping very many street maps or old e-mail files on your handheld.

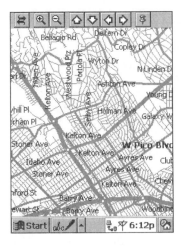

**Figure 32-11:** Additional programs available for a palm PC include street maps, Web browsers, and more.

Versions of Word and Excel come with some handheld PCs but use their own file formats (one that's translated to and from normal Word and Excel formats when you transfer files to and from your desktop computer). They don't include all the features of the desktop versions, but the basic functions are there. In Figure 32-12 (a screen shot from a Cassiopeia A-11), you see not only the usual Word editing area, but the usual combo boxes for font name and size, boldface, italics, underline, paragraph left-center-right justification, bulleting, and help. The "X" to the right of the help button is the standard Windows icon to close the application.

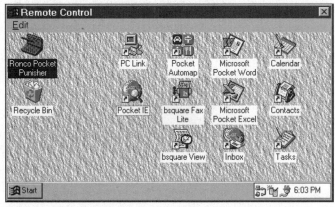

**Figure 32-12:** Don't plan on writing a novel with the version of Word in a handheld PC, but it's quite capable of creating faxes and small documents.

Software supplied with the handheld computer lets you manage the files on your handheld and take care of automatic synchronization of your calendar and contacts list between the two machines against the Windows Inbox (Exchange) and Schedule+, or against Microsoft Outlook. Software on your desktop PC also provides the capability to back up your machine onto your desktop computer — protection against the day when the batteries go out.

The capability to automatically synchronize key files between your two machines solves a key problem that's faced people with pocket and desktop systems, be the pocket system paper or electronic. The two systems always get out of date with respect to each other, and without strong personal discipline you'll eventually get to the point where one or both systems are so out of date that you give up. Because a Windows CE machine handles this automatically (you'll need third-party software if you're not using the Microsoft e-mail and organizer products), you're likely to be able to use both systems on a continuing basis.

# Hands-On Upgrades

You need to recognize that there are upgrades you can reasonably do to a laptop, and upgrades you can't. You can add memory, storage, and anything hooked to a PC Card. You can add batteries (at least as spares you carry, if not in the machine). You're not going to change the processor speed or make the bus faster, and you're not likely to change the display (although we've seen manufacturers offer trade-in programs to improve the overall machine).

Assuming the upgrade you need falls in the doable category, you've got two options. You can upgrade with a PC Card, which means you can buy in a competitive market with multiple manufacturers, or you can buy specialized devices designed for your specific laptop. The latter are likely to be more expensive with fewer options available, but in the case of internal large disks or CD-ROMs, high-speed memory, or internal batteries, they may be your only choice. They may be your best choice too, because the software in the laptop will be tailored to know how to adapt to the new devices.

The Toshiba Tecra 8000 is not only a typical example of an upgradable laptop, it's a good argument for proprietary devices in laptops. The Tecra 8000 has a bay on the side into which you can plug a second battery, a floppy disk drive, a CD-ROM, or a 2GB hard disk. There's almost no chance of installing one wrong—just power down the machine, take out one module, and plug in the next. Done. Power up the computer and it recognizes the new configuration. (Not to say you can't louse it up—if you installed software onto the second hard disk that's required during boot, removing the disk makes booting an adventure.)

# Summary

- ✦ You'll get fewer features in exchange for the reduced size and weight of a laptop.

- ✦ Limited battery power and the limitations of rugged, small packaging constrain how fast your laptop can be and how much it can store.

- ✦ Battery technology will continue to improve.

✦     ✦     ✦

# System Management

If you have more than a few computers, someone's going to get the (often thankless) job of keeping them up and running. We'll talk about how to repair a broken computer in Chapter 36 ; in this chapter, we'll look at how to keep the support workload manageable.

## Turning an Oil Tanker

We almost called this section "10,000 Lemmings Sit Anywhere They Want To" for the first edition of this book. The point we wanted to make is that any time you get a lot of computers together, all your problems get worse. You can cope when installing new software crashes one computer; it's very different when all 10,000 (or even all four) are down, and different yet when those 10,000 computers are in four countries.

Supporting a set of computers — and their users — is hard. You'll have users who know more than you do (and won't let you forget it for a minute), users who haven't a clue, and users who simply don't care. If you have enough computers to require a support staff, you'll probably have staff in all three categories as well.

The more computers (and users) you have, the harder this job is. It's like turning an oil tanker, because you have no choice but to do it, it's hard to do, it takes a long time, and it helps if you plan ahead and know what you're doing. You're not done when you power up a new computer; on the contrary, you're tied to it forever. Here are some of the more visible issues in personal computer support:

✦ *Nonstandard configurations.* Unless you have rigid, tight-fisted control that would make a schoolmaster proud, the computers you support are not going to be the same. The hardware configurations will change over time because users' needs are different and (probably) because you won't buy them all at the same time. The software configurations will change over time because these are *personal* computers, and it's not practical to lock down every possible change to the computers.

Because the configurations are not all the same, they'll have different problems. As much as we would wish it were otherwise, not all combinations of hardware and software work together. Your support problems may be worse than broken or misconfigured hardware and software; they may be due to bad combinations as well.

✦ *Different revision levels.* Hardware and software manufacturers don't always clearly identify the versions of their products. Instead, it's a common industry practice to "slipstream" a modified version of a product into production with no notice. This reduces the demand by users for free updates to the latest version but boosts your requirement for serious pain reliever, because even if two machines seem to be running the same hardware or software, they might actually be different.

✦ *The cost of downtime.* If you goof, the results can be highly visible and very expensive. (The AOL router disaster of 1996 comes to mind, in which an innocuous router software configuration change took millions of people offline for 19 hours.) You may have fewer users, but the cost of taking them down may be higher.

✦ *User training (or, where's the "any" key?).* Don't underestimate how confused people can be about computers. Some very smart people are completely uninformed about what's in a computer, how it works, and how to use it. (Nevertheless, the resulting problems can be pretty funny if you're not on the confused end. Take a look at `http://www.auricular.com/TST`.)

✦ *Obsolete machines.* You may not have the capital to upgrade and replace computers regularly. If so, you can end up with a mix of machines, some of which may not run your preferred software. (True story: Barry used to work for a computer manufacturer that — in 1992 — was still putting 8088-based machines capable of running nothing but DOS and DOS applications on people's desks. No matter that Windows was the industry standard; there were a lot of those 8088 machines available in the company.)

Any one of these is a hard problem. Collectively, they're the stuff of nightmares unless you're prepared. Here are some of the strategies you can use to simplify the problems:

✦ *Make as many things the same on each computer (and network device) as you can.* The fewer combinations of things you have to deal with, the fewer problems there are likely to be. You'll have things that are nonstandard to adapt to users' requirements, but if you can keep the core configurations down to a reasonable few, you're better off.

✦ *Arrange as much visibility as you can.* By the time things go wrong, the clock is running on downtime. Preparing for trouble in advance by keeping logs and having the right tools in place helps you respond on the fly.

✦ *Counter ignorance with information.* The more information you make available to users about how their machines work and about why you've set things up as they are, the fewer problems they'll create due to operator error and the more likely they will be to understand what's happening when something goes wrong.

✦ *Don't go it alone.* You don't have to be Wyatt Earp (the lone gunslinger who rides into town and takes out the bad guy). Lining up support resources in advance means you have help when you need it (and it might help you avoid trouble to begin with too).

Let's look at some specific approaches to implementing these strategies.

## Create baseline hardware configurations

If you buy computers in relatively large lots, you can ensure that groups of machines have the same configuration. You can extend this strategy by upgrading older machines too. You can frequently buy the same motherboard and adapter cards on the open market as you find in complete computer systems, so when you upgrade an older machine, you can make it more similar to one of your baseline configurations by using the same components. In addition, if you maintain your own machines, using standard components in many machines means you don't need to keep as many different spares on hand. That reduces your costs.

Be careful to document the configuration for every system. You can do this with the Windows Device Manager, printing out the device configuration (or saving it to a file you can keep in a database).

## Use managed hardware whenever possible

You can't be everywhere, so you need tools to help you watch for trouble. The technologies for that are called systems management (for computers) and network management (for networks). You can do systems management using the results of the Desktop Management Initiative (DMI), and network management using the Simple Network Management Protocol (SNMP). Not all products natively support either DMI or SNMP, so you'll want to make that an important factor in product selection.

You can do three basic things with managed equipment:

✦ *Performance monitoring.* You can log the long-term performance of elements of your systems. The data you collect is a good basis for finding network choke points and for historical studies after you identify a problem (or security threat).

✦ *Exception reporting through alarms.* The management software that collects data from all your managed devices (often called *enterprise management software*) should let you set thresholds that, when crossed, indicate there's a problem. You can trigger an automatic response from an alarm, alert a monitoring center, or simply log the alarm.

✦ *Diagnosis and reconfiguration.* The management agents in your computers and network devices let you examine and modify the state of the units. You can use this to help troubleshoot problems and take corrective action, and you can do that without going to the equipment location.

The end result is that you can find out about problems and start troubleshooting before users call. When you do have to go to the remote site, you'll go with better information, so you'll be more likely to take the right tools and repair parts with you.

## Create a baseline software configuration

You'll want to define a baseline configuration for commonly used software (such as word processors, spreadsheets, and web browsers). This can be difficult to do to everyone's satisfaction. Some users will want to use their favorite package, and unless you have a very small number of users, the chances everyone will agree on one are very small.

The benefits of a standard software suite go beyond simplifying support; you get a better price on the copies you need to license, and you eliminate problems of file exchange among users. Despite the fact that all the major word processors read each other's files, they don't do it perfectly; differences crop up when importing foreign file formats.

You can take standardization too far, though. Even though software such as Microsoft Word is capable of doing page layout, it may not meet the needs of your publication department. The simple drawings you might do in Microsoft PowerPoint might not meet the needs of graphic artists. You're better off working to implement flexibility in your system, ensuring you have better information about what's going on, than to have to fight a constant guerrilla war you're not likely to win.

## Run all standard software from a server

If you can standardize on a baseline software configuration, software upgrades will be simpler. With few exceptions, you can make all the standard software available from a network file server. Because all users are then loading from one place, you have a lot less effort to go through when you want to update to new versions.

The liabilities of running all software from a server are that you increase the required network capacity (compared to loading the software off a local hard disk), and that the impact of the network or server going down is far worse. If you have few enough users (or enough partitioning in the network and horsepower in the servers), performance won't be a problem. Redundancy and fault tolerance in the servers can help eliminate problems with reliability. Otherwise, you might want to compare the costs of upgrading the network and servers to the costs of installing software upgrades on users' machines.

## Train users (and the support staff) aggressively

Not all of your users will be highly competent power users. It's likely that not all your support staff will be, either. Because a large proportion of service calls are due to user error, training can reduce your support costs. In-depth training for your support staff can improve their effectiveness and reduce the time each case takes; training for users can help reduce the load on the support staff.

## Do Windows housecleaning periodically

Many programs dump files into the directories occupied by Windows. The setup program guidelines Microsoft promotes for Windows 95 and Windows NT include requirements to allow the user to uninstall the program, but even then it's difficult or impossible to do this for shared files (which is much of what goes into the Windows directories).

Because of this, garbage starts to build up in your Windows directories as you acquire and discard programs. There's no dependable way to remove the garbage, because there's no good way to be completely certain what programs need a given file. The only completely reliable way to get rid of the buildup is to save everything somewhere else, reformat the drive, and rebuild from the ground up.

The advantage of doing this every few years is that you'll get rid of duplicate and unused files, and prune the Registry. The Registry, where Windows keeps program settings, has largely replaced .ini files in the Windows directory. That housekeeping tends to eliminate conflicts that were caused by the older components and reduce the size of the Windows directory tree. The end result can be fewer system crashes.

## Have diagnostics and procedures in place

You know with complete certainty that computers (and networks) will break, crash, or otherwise malfunction. If you have diagnostic tools and procedures in place—plus the training in their use—then you're closer to a solution than if you have to reason forward from zero. That means less downtime for your users.

**Tip** You'll find a demonstration version of AMI's AMIDiag, a system diagnostic and information tool, at `ftp://ftp.megatrends.com/download/amidemo.exe`.

## Use the technical resources available to you

Technical support to end users is a major cost for computer hardware and software manufacturers. Trying to avoid some of that cost has many of them seeking ways to get support information into your hands without involving a support representative on the telephone. Two of your best sources for support information are the manufacturer's Web pages, online bulletin boards, and Microsoft TechNet:

✦ *Web pages.* Appendix B includes an extensive index of hardware and software manufacturers, with addresses, telephone numbers, Web sites, and electronic mail addresses.

Manufacturer Web sites generally contain product data, technical support information, and links to the latest drivers and software updates for their products.

✦ *Microsoft TechNet.* TechNet is a CD-ROM publication from Microsoft containing technical information on Microsoft products. It includes the Microsoft Knowledge Base (their technical support information database, which is also available on the Microsoft Web site), resource kits for different products, and a variety of technical white papers. For Windows-based systems, TechNet is the most comprehensive support tool Microsoft offers.

# Simple Network Management Protocol

As we said above, managed hardware is the key to knowing when things go wrong in your network, and the Simple Network Management Protocol (SNMP) is the key to managing your hardware. SNMP operates between a management station and an agent in a managed device, using TCP/IP for the underlying communications. The management stations collect data over time and use graphical user inter faces to draw network maps annotated with network status.

SNMP activities center around a Management Information Block (MIB), information kept by the agent in the managed device. The management station requests some or all of the data in the MIB; the agent responds to the request by sending the data. The management station then analyzes the return, looking for anomalies. When some returned data violates parameters you specify, the management station sends out an alarm.

For example, suppose you use SNMP managed hubs in your 10Base-T network. The MIB in the hub will contain information on the status of the hub, its attached lines, and perhaps on the volume of traffic in that portion of your network. You could program your network management station to periodically sample the MIB, raising an alarm if any of the devices attached to the hub go offline or if network utilization consistently goes above 30 percent. Depending on your management software, you may be able to set warning thresholds outside the fault thresholds, allowing you some advance warning before actual failure occurs.

In addition to MIBs, there are three essential components to SNMP:

✦ *Managers*. SNMP managers collect status and traps from managed devices. If the manager detects that a device is operating outside normal parameters (which you define), it sets an alarm. Capable managers support alarms on-screen, through e-mail, and to pagers.

Enterprise-scale managers do more than query devices — they provide the tools to map and organize your view of your network. Using TCP/IP to reach out over a wide area network, an enterprise-scale network manager can let you control a world-wide network from a single control center. In addition to the well-known network managers, including Hewlett-Packard OpenView and Sun Net Manager, Web browser–based tools such as Asanté IntraSpection are starting to penetrate the market.

✦ *Agents*. An SNMP agent is software resident in a managed device responsible for reporting status into the MIB, for responding to commands from the manager, and for issuing traps to the manager when unexpected events occur. The agent's essential function is to mediate between the variables and commands used by the software that runs the device and the (somewhat different) variables and commands implemented in the MIB.

Although agents implementing standardized MIBs are valuable because they can work with a wide variety of managers, you can implement SNMP management for virtually anything by building the corresponding MIB and agent. We've used SNMP to monitor and control mission critical processes on remote computers; in the same way, you can install an SNMP agent into Windows 95 and Windows NT to do limited observations.

Figure 33-1 shows the relationship among agents, managers, MIBs, and the other elements implementing an SNMP management system. As with all IP-based protocols, SNMP implements communications between logical peers. In Figure 33-1, you see the SNMP layers communicating with each other logically, using TCP/IP to accomplish the physical communications. The agent and manager in turn sit on SNMP, using it to do the physical communication implementing their logical conversation.

✦ *Proxies*. Some devices (for example, a UPS with only a serial port interface) lack the resources to directly implement an SNMP agent. The lack may be that the device isn't directly connected to the network, or that the device lacks the internal computing resources to support an agent. If the device can be attached to and controlled by a computer, the agent can reside in the computer. This arrangement, shown in Figure 33-2, permits nearly any device capable of communicating with another computer to be observed and controlled using SNMP. In cases where the communication is only from the managed device to the proxy agent computer, the agent can only support observation, and not control.

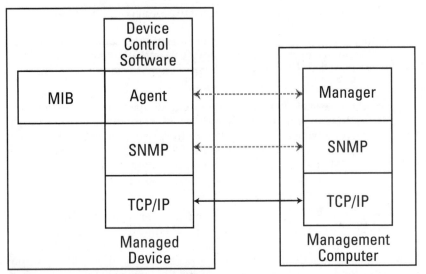

**Figure 33-1:** Agent software on a managed device communicates with a manager to implement SNMP systems management.

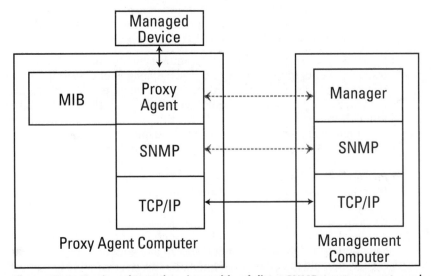

**Figure 33-2:** Devices themselves incapable of direct SNMP agent support can be managed through a proxy agent.

# Desktop Management Initiative

A Gartner Group study estimates that as many as one half of all support calls to vendors are related to device installation and configuration. Client/server costs over networks are dominated (70 percent) by the cost to manage the system accounts. As many as 70 percent of PC vendor support calls come from computer novices.

In response to the inability to monitor and diagnose remote personal computers, the Desktop Management Initiative (DMI) lets you manage desktop computers, hardware and software products, and peripherals as intelligent devices on a network. The infrastructure for that capability is the DMI Service Layer, a program on your personal computer to collect information from products, store that information in the Management Information Format (MIF) database, and communicate with DMI management applications.

Many personal computers and devices support DMI. Looking for DMI capability in systems you buy will slowly bring more of your equipment inventory online with management capability, simplifying your support problems. DMI supports SNMP, allowing you to integrate it into your enterprise network management.

# Making Choices

Ultimately, systems management comes down to a set of choices and priorities. You'll care more about systems management when you have hundreds or thousands of computers than when you have one or two. The kind of work your users do will affect your decisions; service representatives in a mail-order teleprocessing center have far less need for variations in their configurations than engineers doing research and development, but the costs of downtime in the teleprocessing center may be thousands of times greater.

One of the decisions that is sometimes ignored (except during the media frenzy that accompanies a new release of Windows) is that the operating system you choose affects the stability and dependability of your computers. Windows NT is more reliable than Windows 95, for example, because it makes fewer compromises to achieve compatibility with older hardware and software. You'll therefore have fewer problems with hardware and software interactions under Windows NT once you get it running, but you'll be able to use a wider range of hardware and software under Windows 95.

# Summary

✦ All your problems get worse as you have more computers and networks to support.

✦ You must plan ahead to avoid being overwhelmed by support.

✦ There are systems management technologies to help you be prepared and to respond to problems, but you have to deploy them widely to get much value.

✦        ✦        ✦

# You're Going to Put That Where?

**W**e've limited the personal computer applications in this book primarily to home, home office/small office, Internet and telecommuting, multimedia/gaming, technical writing and editing, and programming, because that's by far how most personal computers are used. You can do an unlimited number of other things with a PC, though, ending up with PCs in the oddest places. This chapter covers a sample of applications, including what you need to do with the hardware to make the application work.

## Mapping, Surveying, and Position Location

Some of the most interesting applications of a PC are to create maps, survey property, and locate things like pipes, roads, buildings, and other objects. These applications are made possible by an inexpensive portable receiver for the Global Positioning System (GPS). Using several in tandem, you can achieve sub-meter measurement accuracy.

GPS works by measuring the distance from you to a constellation of satellites. Figure 34-1 shows the idea. Your GPS receiver can accurately measure the time it takes for a radio signal to travel from each of the satellites to you (which, as a side benefit, means that a GPS receiver always knows the current time accurately). It uses that time — and an accurate knowledge of the satellite's position — to compute the distance you are from the satellite. After doing those computations for the signals from a number of satellites, it can compute the point that is simultaneously the right distance from all the satellites, and that's where you are.

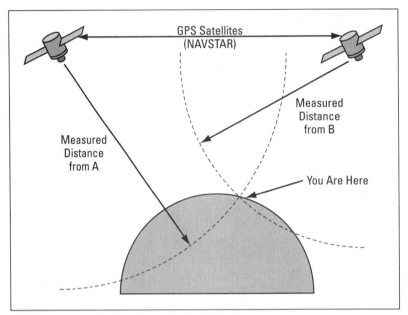

**Figure 34-1:** GPS works by finding the location that puts you at the right distance from all the satellites your receiver can see.

In Figure 34-1, the dashed-line arcs are (in two dimensions) the places at the right distance from each satellite. The point labeled "You Are Here" is the point at the right distance from both satellites. (Actually, there's a point above the top of the figure where the two arcs meet again. Factoring in measurements from more satellites lets your receiver decide which of the two points is your location.)

Three spread-spectrum signals are transmitted from every GPS satellite — the C/A code signal (for civilian users), the P code signal (much more accurate, but is restricted to military users), and the Y code signal (restricted to military users with the right decryption key). Typical position accuracy in three dimensions for the C/A code signal is 93 meters.

Because mapping and other applications need accuracy better than that, though, people have devised ways to get around the errors introduced into the civilian C/A signal. The key is to have two receivers, one stationary (and very accurately surveyed for position), and the other moving around but in the same vicinity as the stationary one. The stationary receiver (the "reference receiver") continually calculates the error in the signal and retransmits that value to the moving one, which in turn combines its received signals with the error measurement to derive a very accurate position. It's becoming common for the U.S. Coast Guard and other international agencies to post reference receivers around harbors, waterways, and other locations.

A GPS receiver, such as the Trimble ASPEN Card or Mobile GPS Gold Card (http://www.trimble.com), can fit into your laptop computer. With an internal GPS receiver, your notebook computer, and GPS-aware street map software, you have a portable mapping and navigation system. If your mapping software lets you record positions, you can create your own maps. The low-cost DeLorme EarthMate GPS receiver connects to a serial port and is integrated with their mapping software to let you track position on roads in North America. A version of the software on a handheld computer makes an ideal walk-around solution.

For example, suppose you need to survey the track a herd of deer take from their feeding grounds to a nearby river. You start at one end of the track, recording positions every few meters as you walk the track (or continuously, depending on your software). When you're done, you have an accurate map of the track you can superimpose on a topographic map to display the information you collected.

Expect more inventive GPS applications as the technology becomes less expensive and handheld digital devices become more capable. In mid-1999, for example, Kodak started shipping a version of the DCS265 digital camera bundled with a Garmin GPS receiver, giving you all the tools you need to stamp digital photos with the precise time and location of the picture.

# Factory Process Control and Inspection

Personal computers can be programmed to do data acquisition and factory process control, using I/O ports connected to the factory equipment through cards containing switches, digital-to-analog converters, and analog-to-digital converters. It's more common to use dedicated process control computers for this purpose, but we've seen some complex light manufacturing lines built this way.

For example, Barry once worked for a company that built the sensors used to fire off automobile air bags during a collision. The production line was completely automated, using a series of personal computers to control and monitor the machinery. The basis of the line was a conveyor belt that moved forward until the computer sensed that the assemblies had reached the next station. The computer then triggered robot arms, welders, and other devices at each station to perform the next operation in sequence. As the operation progressed, the computer sampled information (such as the amount of power fed to the spot welders) to verify that the operations had been performed correctly.

# Remote Instrumentation Control

You can use personal computers to control instruments in remote, inaccessible locations. For example, you might put a radio transmitter on top of a mountain as a relay. During the winter, the transmitter may be impossible to reach except by helicopter (which is expensive and inconvenient). If you run a telephone line up to the relay site, you can network a computer up there to another one down at your business location. Together, the two computers can send commands you issue to the transmitters or switching equipment. The same two computers can monitor received signal quality, sense alarm conditions (like power failure), and provide site security monitoring:

✦ *Commands.* Many instruments connect to the IEEE 488 standard instrumentation bus (once known by the name its inventor — Hewlett-Packard — gave it, General Purpose Interface Bus, or GPIB). A PC with an IEEE 488 interface card can connect to a number of instruments, sending commands and receiving back status and data.

✦ *Monitoring.* You don't have to send all the data you monitor and collect down the mountain from the control computer. Software you run in the control computer can filter the data (much like the management station does for SNMP; see Chapter 33, "System Management"). When some of the data falls outside the thresholds you set, the control computer sends a warning message to your local machine.

✦ *Site security.* You can use videoconferencing hardware and software to provide site security. In this application, you mount cameras around the site and run their outputs to a switch controlled by the computer. (You can use the IEEE 488 bus to control the switch.) The switch output goes into a video compression card and, through videoconferencing software, down to your local computer. If you see something of concern, you can set the switch to specific locations; otherwise, the computer can sequence the switch from one camera to another in order or in random sequence.

It's important to make the remote computer as reliable and dependable as you can. We would choose Windows NT or FreeBSD over Windows 9x for its operating system, and we would consider the APC CallUPS product on the UPS to allow you to reset the power from a telephone call in case the system does lock up.

# Point of Sale and Signature Verification

You can get inexpensive cash register drawers that plug into a computer using either a serial or parallel port. With the right software, a personal computer then becomes an intelligent point of sale terminal. With a network, you can collect data back into a server to keep track of inventory, sales, and other store management data. There is no shortage of companies willing to sell you the software you'll need (which is far more important a choice than the cash register drawer). If you search the Web for "cash register drawer computer," you'll find several of them.

Computers can do signature verification as well. We've seen systems like this at department stores like Sears. They put a digitizing tablet (see Chapter 22, "Mouse/Trackball/Joystick/Tablet") under a form you sign. The tablet feeds the "drawing" of your signature into the computer, which compares it to a record of your signature. It takes well-written software to distinguish normal signature variations from forgeries, though, so there's always the issue of false rejections and unwarranted acceptances.

Worse yet, keeping a record of your signature on file can be a security risk. If the computer stores its comparison version of your signature as a drawing, it's possible to reverse the process, printing the drawing and producing a perfect forgery. To be secure, the software should only store characteristics computed from the signature (and characteristics from which the original signature can't be computed). You can't tell by looking if the software is secure or not — we won't sign on signature verification readers for that reason. If the store won't accept our signatures without electronic scanning, we'll go somewhere else.

# Information Kiosks

Walk-up stands offering information are seemingly everywhere, from hotels and airports to malls and truck stops. They usually have a personal computer inside, using data on a CD-ROM for the information you see on-screen.

Aside from interesting content and a self-evident user interface, the keys to a workable kiosk are reliability and protection from people. Reliability in a kiosk means that the hardware keeps working, the software never crashes, and the entire system restarts properly after disruptions in power. None of this is hard to achieve.

Protection from people is a lot harder, because people attack. (It's the same sort of things that happen to soft drink machines.) Whether the attacks are accidental (like a drink spilled into the machine) or intentional, a kiosk out of operation is useless. One of the most vulnerable points in a computer is the keyboard. The keys are subject to destruction (or having the caps removed), while the spaces between the keys allow easy entry of coffee, ice cream, paper clips, and battery acid.

The best approach to protecting the keyboard is to not use it. Many kiosks use touch-sensitive panels over the display screen (Figure 34-2).

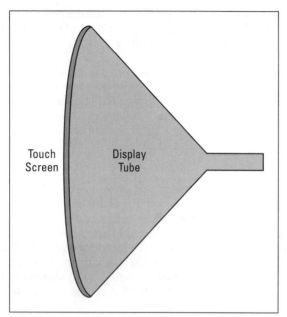

**Figure 34-2:** A touch screen covers the front of the display tube, offering protection as well as a user input mechanism.

Unlike a keyboard, a touch screen lets you wipe off peanut butter. When the user touches the screen, the computer gets an input (often as a mouse click) and sequences to the next display. The touch screen hardware usually connects through a serial port and includes a glass surface that fits over the actual display tube. Touch screens use a variety of technologies to sense where you point, generally with better resolution than your finger has. Some touch screens can report pressure as well as location.

## Tour Guides

If you combine GPS, mapping, and CD-ROM multimedia presentations in a laptop computer, you can build a self-contained tour guide. For instance:

✦ *Navigation.* The GPS-directed map can tell the presentation software where you are, letting it identify the nearby points of interest for you. When you choose one, the software can use the map to derive directions to get there.

✦ *Points of interest.* As you approach a landmark, the software can calculate what's visible and show you a picture, helping you identify where to go.

✦ *Description.* Once you get to where you're going, the computer can tell you about what's there, walk you through the area, and provide background and analysis.

Of course, there's still the issue of a heads-up display you can see without taking your eyes off where you're going. Fighter planes have them, but they're expensive. PCs with tour guide–like features are starting to show up in cars for navigation and route planning, but they're typically on the console readable in a "heads down" position.

# Reading Papers and Books

Although speech recognition is still not ready for everyday use, text-to-speech technology works reasonably well. It's not the same as listening to James Earl Jones (few things are), but if you're blind and can't read, it's a way to hear the full text of books instead of the abbreviated versions on the popular audio tapes. A limited number of books is currently available in full text form for reading—mainly older works no longer under copyright—but the number is growing. The complete works of Shakespeare are available on CD-ROM (and on the Internet). Many newspapers are also on the Web, with more adding electronic editions regularly.

You don't need highly specialized hardware to have your computer read to you. You merely need the source of material (such as a CD-ROM or a modem), a sound card, and speakers.

Electronic books are coming to market, too. Using an electronic book, you buy the text in electronic form rather than paper, and download the text to an electronic reader about the size and shape of a book. It's still unclear how the business will work—if you'll buy or rent the text, for instance—and it's unclear if people will want to pay the costs for the as-yet expensive readers.

# Mobile Music

The MP3 compressed audio format (based on MPEG compression) swept the Internet in a matter of a few years to become a strong, worldwide standard for near CD-quality compressed music. The widespread availability of music on the Web in MP3 format, requiring about a megabyte of storage per minute, created demand so strong that at one point almost any commercial title at all (copyrights notwithstanding) could be found on the Net.

Aggressive intervention by music companies made it harder to find free copyrighted music on the Net but hasn't reduced the value of the MP3 format. Portable, personal MP3 players (including ones from Eiger Labs and Diamond Multimedia) make it possible for you to carry an hour or more of music with you in a compact, all-digital player having no moving parts. You can read song tracks from CD on your PC (called *ripping*), compress to MP3 format with one of several MP3 compression tools, and then download the compressed track to the player. As of mid-1999, the Recording Industry Association of America lost a court challenge to the Diamond Multimedia MP3 player, suggesting the legal future of the MP3 format is quite secure.

There's another way to use a mobile MP3 player — if you have an audio tape of a book you want to hear, you can record the tape digitally (using GoldWave from the CD-ROM with this book) and then compress the recording to a very low data rate — it's just spoken voice. The resulting compressed format should fit into many of the higher-capacity MP3 players. If that's too much work, look at the Web site of Audible, Inc. — http://www.audible.com — where you can get books and other prerecorded material for MP3 players.

# Sports Training

A number of sporting goods stores and sports facilities have started to offer computer-based skill training. Their equipment typically includes video projectors to create a simulated environment and electronic sensors to measure what you do. Programs in the computer take the measurements, analyze what happened, and project an appropriate image in response.

Golf is one of the most common and most effective of these. The projector shows a view of the course and the flight of the ball. Sensors track your swing and let the computer project the flight path. The result is a highly realistic experience.

Flight simulators (and entertainment-level air combat simulation) are other popular applications of the same technology. Some offer realistic mockups of aircraft cockpits, with the sky and land projected on a screen outside the cockpit. You fly with the usual stick and pedals. More realistic versions are being built with highly realistic virtual reality technology.

# Internet Phone

You can use the Internet and your computer for long-distance voice connections. This is a simpler version of Internet-based video conferencing, requiring only a microphone, sound card, speakers, and an Internet connection. Software to support Internet voice connections is bundled with Web browsers or available as a separate product. In the United States, the Federal Communications Commission has decided to permit continued use of the Internet for voice connections, so you can expect to see the market grow. The advantage of Internet telephone, of course, is that you pay only for the local call to your Internet service provider, not a long-distance call to the person you're calling.

The compression formats and network protocols used in Internet phone programs are not standardized, so you can't be assured that software from two different vendors will communicate properly. You also don't know that the person you want to call will be connected to the Internet when you want to call, so you may have to precede your Internet conversation with a short telephone call. Most Internet phone software will run on fairly modest machines and can give you reasonable voice quality with a 14.4 Kbps connection. You can't currently call a conventional telephone from an Internet phone, but it's technically possible, so if there's a market for the service, you can expect to see it happen.

# Identification and Access Control

You can read bar codes and magnetic stripes on cards with a personal computer using bar code and magnetic stripe readers. Bar code readers scan the bars with a bright light, sensing the bars with a photocell. Your computer decodes the varying width of the stripes into data.

Magnetic stripe readers depend on a strip of magnetic material on paper or plastic. The strip is composed of magnetic particles in paint or a binder that get exposed to a magnetic field before the paint dries. The field causes the particles to line up magnetically, which allows the stripe to be magnetized in one or the other direction. From that point on, the read and write heads are similar to those in tape or disk drives, modified for slower (and less constant) speeds past the head (and for better error correction). An ISO standard card can hold up to 226 characters, although the most commonly used part of the stripe holds only 107.

A reader station can scan the information stored in the stripe, feeding it into a personal computer. The PC then looks in a database to see who the bearer of the card is supposed to be and whether the bearer is authorized. Security and forgery are significant problems for bar code and magnetic stripe cards because of the simplicity of making new ones. Technologies are under development, but none have proved to be superior yet. Most of the new technologies use unique biometric characteristics, such as fingerprints, voiceprints, and retina prints. You'll need to match the strengths and weaknesses of individual technologies to your requirements, because no one biometric system works well in all applications.

# The Internet Refrigerator

As has been true for every other successful technology in history, people spend a lot of time thinking about how to do more and reach further with the Internet. Some of the ideas are almost plausible, such as a refrigerator that knows to order more milk when you're nearly out, but others (such as a toaster you can signal when you leave work) are merely silly.

No matter what the details are, though, it seems like a good bet that there are going to be a lot more devices hooked up to LANs and to the Internet, that those devices will be far simpler than a PC, and that they will need to hook up and run without TCP/IP or other network setup by users.

The no-setup requirement is a stiff one — it implies there needs to be a way for devices to find out what services are available on the network, automatically get network addresses, register with the appropriate services, and agree on communication protocols. Several industry players are working on the problem; the most notable are JINI (being developed and promoted by Sun Microsystems) and Universal Plug and Play (being developed and promoted by Microsoft). As of the second quarter of 1999, neither approach has developed an overwhelming following, and neither is guaranteed of market success. It's inevitable that some automatic connection technology will succeed, though, and the fierce competition between those two companies should provide interesting theatrics for some time to come.

## Summary

✦ A personal computer is a completely general machine, capable of nearly anything.

✦ Many new applications for personal computers are created by building new devices that can be queried and controlled by the computer. New developments in other electronic fields often couple well with personal computers.

✦     ✦     ✦

# Benchmarking

Throughout this book, we've tried to stress the importance of measurement as a way to compare systems and to isolate choke points in individual systems. Manufacturers' claims often reflect tests different from the situation you'll experience, as do informal observations of performance. If you're going to get a valid measurement, you must measure under controlled conditions, and the results must reflect your situation.

In this chapter, we'll look at how to make those measurements.

## Who Needs Data When You Can Guess?

The most obvious choice for evaluating how a computer performs, or how a change to a computer performs, is to use it. Run your standard applications, doing your usual work, and see what happens. This isn't your best choice, though, for the following reasons:

+ *Imprecision.* What you do, what you measure, and how you measure aren't well controlled by simply using the machine. It would be very hard or impossible to run a duplicate test.

+ *Poor isolation.* It's hard to tell why you get the results you do. You don't have good isolation from one part of the computer to the next. Consequently, you don't have information that lets you judge what to do next if you don't like the results, or to figure out why things are good if you do like them.

+ *Indeterminate coverage.* You don't know how thoroughly you've stressed your system when you tested it, so you don't know what the likely result will be when you do something new and different.

Comparing products isn't unique to personal computers, of course. The usual way to develop sound comparisons is to create an artificial test designed specifically to examine systems and components. These tests are commonly called *benchmarks*.

# Lies and Benchmarks

Benchmarks have their own problems; the most important is that a benchmark is an artificial construction. For that reason, it may be difficult to understand how the benchmark results relate to the results you'll get in real life. For example, you can run a cache memory benchmark that tells you the speed of the cache, but it's very difficult to make conclusions on the basis of that number about the performance you can expect.

Overall, here's what you should look for when you choose or create a benchmark.

✦ *Clearly defined coverage.* The benchmark should isolate the elements of the computer it covers, remaining free of effects from other components.

✦ *Explicitly reported test conditions.* The benchmark should report the machine configuration and test conditions relevant to the test. It's acceptable for that reporting to be manual — with you writing the data down — as long as you keep careful records.

✦ *Stability.* Running the benchmark multiple times on the same equipment, including after having done other things with the computer in between, should produce the same results (or, at least, results with differences that are not statistically significant).

✦ *Comparability.* You should be able to compare the results of the benchmark run on one system with the results on another. That means that the benchmark results have to be quantitative, and that the benchmark itself shouldn't depend on unique properties of the system (unless that's what you're evaluating).

✦ *Widespread acceptance.* It's best (but not mandatory) for the benchmark to be distributed and used widely so that you can find data from other people's measurements to compare to yours.

Benchmarks don't have to be complex, professionally developed products (although there are some very good ones available). You can create your own benchmarks with some careful thought and work. In a sense, creating and running a good benchmark is no different from doing a good scientific experiment. You want to have a clear hypothesis you're testing, a well-defined test method, careful data collection, and sound data analysis.

✦ *Hypothesis.* It's easy to ignore setting a hypothesis and leap straight into the tests. You'll be better off if you do some thinking up front, however, because it will help you focus on what the benchmark test needs to do. For example, suppose we're interested in comparing the performance of two SCSI drives.

If my hypothesis is that one has a faster rotation rate than the other, we'll devise a different test than if my hypothesis is that one has a faster sustained transfer rate than the other.

✦ *Test method.* You have to design your test to isolate the effects you're interested in from all other interactions. For example, if you want to test a system's speed writing out a file and reading it back in sequentially, you can't simply write out the file and read it back. If you do, you're likely to get unrealistically fast performance measurements because of interference from the disk cache. There are ways to avoid this interference, but you have to know it can happen and design your test method to avoid it.

✦ *Data collection.* You'll want to make sure that the benchmark reports enough data, both configuration and test results. You need to have enough data from the test to be able to figure out what happened after you're done.

✦ *Data analysis.* Ultimately, you'll want to boil your raw data down to summary numbers you can use for comparisons. You'll either need to get that data directly or be able to compute them from the data you collect.

# Techniques

The details are crucial for good benchmarks. Unless you work the details carefully, you won't get sound measurements. The following sections cover some of the issues involved.

## Processor

You have to define whether you want to measure the processor's performance with or without a cache. You might choose to include the cache in the measurement on the basis that real-world performance includes the effect of the cache, or you might decide that you want to isolate your measurements down to the computational engine itself.

Both are valid decisions. Which you should choose depends on the hypothesis you're testing. If you're comparing processor performance between different speed chips — holding the motherboard and cache configuration the same — then it's reasonable to include the effect of the cache. If you're a programmer looking at processor performance on a particular algorithm, then you probably want to divorce the operation of the cache from that of the processor.

Let's look at the issue of isolating processor operation down to a small section of code. The details involved help highlight the difficulty of constructing a good benchmark.

✦ *Isolate cache effects.* Isolating out the cache effects doesn't necessarily mean you have to disable the cache (which you can do in software). If the program segment you're testing is small enough to run entirely out of the cache, then you're better off letting that happen because that better reflects what happens in real life. You'll have to ensure that no other programs get in and dump your code out of the cache, though (see the next point).

✦ *Be sure what you measure.* Measuring the performance of one piece of code means that you have excluded any other code that's running from your measurement. Windows does things in the background (as do most other operating systems), such as keeping track of time, tracking mouse movement, and tracking keyboard input. If you're going to keep the measurement focused on just your code, you have to either prevent these other events from happening or know what they contribute to the total measurement. A common approach is to measure the time it takes to run many iterations of a loop that does nothing, and then repeat the same loop with your code in it. The difference between the two measurements is (presumably) the time your code actually added to the process.

✦ *Time the operation.* The usual timer in a PC has a resolution of about 55ms. If you're timing a small stretch of code, it's going to finish before even one timer tick occurs. You'll probably want to use the high-resolution timers Windows has, and run your code in a loop to increase the time interval you measure.

You have to consider what aspect of processor performance you're interested in when you choose a benchmark. For example:

✦ *Class of code.* Older 16-bit code uses the processor differently than does newer 32-bit code. Because processors (such as the Pentium Pro) may be sensitive to those differences, you'll want to be sure to benchmark using the class of code you'll be running when you use the system. Keep the benchmark as close to real life as you can.

✦ *Type of application.* Your processor handles four kinds of operations: floating-point mathematics, integer mathematics, decision making, and system operations (such as switching between programs, handling interrupts, and I/O). Scientific programs, spreadsheets, and 3D graphics commonly use floating-point mathematics; most programs (including image-processing programs) do integer mathematics and decision making; and the operating system itself does system operations. You can't assume that processor performance is uniformly better or worse among these categories when making comparisons. You have to run programs that focus on each kind of operation.

The class of code issue is why the Ziff-Davis WinBench and Winstone benchmarks (covered later in this chapter) were rewritten some years ago to 32-bit code; 16-bit code doesn't effectively measure what you can expect from current revisions of your programs. The type-of-application issue is why the same benchmarks include a wide range of tests, and why Intel uses a mix of benchmarks in its iCOMP and iCOMP Index 2.0 or 3.0 ratings (see Chapter 8, "Processors"). The approach they use is to make specific measurements by application type and then compute a weighted average reflecting the proportion each type contributes to performance in a typical situation.

Many processor benchmarks in wide circulation don't use a broad-based set of tests to come up with their results. The method for processor speed evaluation in the System Information (SI) program of the Norton Utilities isn't officially documented, but at one time it was known to be little more than a small code loop. It's dangerous to compare processor performance based on simple measures like that because they inevitably fail to model accurately over a realistic range of application.

## Cache and memory

Checking how your cache performs and how it integrates into the rest of your system is difficult, partly because there are no standard ways for the benchmark to discover what the cache structures in the machine are. The program, CACHECHK by Ray Van Tassle (found at http://www.softseek.com/Utilities/Benchmarking_and_Tune _Up/Review_2226_index.html), lets you do this testing. The history of the PC industry makes cache testing more than an interesting exercise: Some small motherboard vendors have been found to ship systems without a cache or with less of a cache than advertised. The BIOS in these systems is modified to report incorrect cache sizes when the system boots, so you can't simply trust what you see on the screen.

The output that follows is for a 450 MHz Pentium III system using an Intel SE440BX2 motherboard and 128MB of PC100 SDRAM. The processor is reported as a Pentium Pro by CACHECHK because the Pentium Pro, Pentium II, Celeron, and Pentium III are all Type 6 Intel processors. We measured performance with the command

```
cachechk > foo.txt
```

The > foo.txt part of the command line sent the results to a file so that we could bring them directly into the book. We ran the test after booting the computers directly to a DOS command line (part of Windows 9x, but with Windows not running) with no other software loaded, skipping both the CONFIG.SYS and AUTOEXEC.BAT files. Here are the results:

```
CACHECHK V7 11/23/98  Copyright (c) 1995-98 by Ray Van Tassle.
(-h for help)
 CMOS reports: conv_mem= 640K, ext_mem= 65,535K, Total RAM=
66,175K
 BIOS reports:                  ext_mem= 129,984K  Total mem:
127 MB
 "GenuineIntel"  Pentium Pro Clocked at 449.6 MHz
```

```
Reading from memory.
MegaByte#:       --------- Memory Access Block sizes (KB)-----
         1    2    4    8   16   32   64  128  256  512 1024 2048
4096 <-- KB
  0:   2    2    2    2    2    3    3    3    3    3    -    -    -
us/KB
  1:   2    2    2    2    2    3    3    3    3    3    7    7
7    us/KB
  2:   2    2    2    2    2    3    3    3    3    3    7    7
7    us/KB
  3:   2    2    2    2    2    3    3    3    3    3    7    7
7    us/KB
 4  5  6  7  8  9  <--- same as above.
 10:   2    2    2    2    2    3    3    3    3    3    7    7
7    us/KB
 11:   2    2    2    2    2    3    3    3    3    3    7    7
7    us/KB
12 13 14 15 16 17  <--- same as above.
 18:   2    2    2    2    2    3    3    3    3    3    7    7
7    us/KB
 19:   2    2    2    2    2    3    3    3    3    3    7    7
7    us/KB
20  <--- same as above.
 21:   2    2    2    2    2    3    3    3    3    3    7    7
7    us/KB
 22:   2    2    2    2    2    3    3    3    3    3    7    7
7    us/KB
23 24 25 26 27 28  <--- same as above.
 29:   2    2    2    2    2    3    3    3    3    3    7    7
7    us/KB
 30:   2    2    2    2    2    3    3    3    3    3    7    7
7    us/KB
31  <--- same as above.
 32:   2    2    2    2    2    3    3    3    3    3    7    7
7    us/KB
 33:   2    2    2    2    2    3    3    3    3    3    7    7
7    us/KB
34 35 36 37 38 39  <--- same as above.
 40:   2    2    2    2    2    3    3    3    3    3    7    7
7    us/KB
 41:   2    2    2    2    2    3    3    3    3    3    7    7
7    us/KB
42  <--- same as above.
 43:   2    2    2    2    2    3    3    3    3    3    7    7
7    us/KB
 44:   2    2    2    2    2    3    3    3    3    3    7    7
7    us/KB
45 46 47  <--- same as above.
 48:   2    2    2    2    2    3    3    3    3    3    7    7
7    us/KB
```

```
49:    2    2    2    2    2    3    3    3    3    3    7    7
7    us/KB
50  <--- same as above.
51:    2    2    2    2    2    3    3    3    3    3    7    7
7    us/KB
52:    2    2    2    2    2    3    3    3    3    3    7    7
7    us/KB
53 54 55 56 57 58 59 60 61 62 63 64   <--- same as above.

 Extra tests----
 Wrt    1    1    1    0    0    3    3    3    3    3    5
6    6<-Writing
 This machine seems to have both L1 and L2 cache. [reading]
     L1 cache is    16KB-- 546.4 MB/s   1.9 ns/byte (330%) (124%)
3.3 clks
     L2 cache is   512KB-- 439.6 MB/s   2.4 ns/byte (266%) (100%)
4.1 clks
     Main memory speed—165.2 MB/s    6.3 ns/byte (100%) [reading]
10.9 clks
     Effective RAM access time (read ) is  50ns (a RAM bank is 8
bytes wide).
     Effective RAM access time (write) is  37ns (a RAM bank is 8
bytes wide).
     "GenuineIntel"  Pentium Pro Clocked at 449.6 MHz.   Cache
ENABLED.
 Options: -t0
```

For comparison, here are test results from three older systems (we've also used an older version of CACHECHK, but there seem to be no important differences in the results). System A, a 50 MHz Intel 486DX2 with 64K cache, proprietary memory and ISA buses, and 70ns Fast Page Mode memory, gives these results:

```
CACHECHK v4 2/7/96 Copyright (c) 1995 by Ray Van Tassle. (-h
for help)
 CMOS reports: conv_mem= 640K, ext_mem= 15,232K, Total RAM=
15,872K
 Clocked at 486 50.0 MHz
 Reading from memory.
 MegaByte#: -------- Memory Access Block sizes (KB)----
 1 2 4 8 16 32 64 128 256 512 1024 2048 4096 <-- KB
 0: 21 21 21 21 32 32 32 95 95 95—----æs/KB
 1: 21 21 21 21 32 32 32 95 95 95 95 95 95 æs/KB
 2 3 4 5 6 7 8 9 10 11 12 13 14 15 <-- same as above.

 Extra tests----
 Wrt 66 66 66 66 66 66 66 66 66 66 66 66 66<-Write mem
 This machine seems to have both L1 and L2 cache. [read]
 L1 cache is 8KB—51.7 MB/s 20.3 ns/byte (449%) (150%) 3.9 clks
 L2 cache is 64KB—34.4 MB/s 30.5 ns/byte (299%) (100%) 5.8 clks
```

```
  Main memory speed—11.5 MB/s 91.0 ns/byte (100%) [read] 17.4
clks
  Effective RAM access time (read ) is 364 ns (a RAM bank is 4
bytes wide).
  Effective RAM access time (write) is 252 ns (a RAM bank is 4
bytes wide).
  Clocked at 486 50.0 MHz. Cache ENABLED.
  Options: -t0
```

**System B, using a 133 MHz Pentium processor, an Intel Advanced/EV motherboard, a 512K pipeline burst cache, a PCI bus, and 60ns EDO memory, reports these numbers:**

```
CACHECHK v4 2/7/96 Copyright (c) 1995 by Ray Van Tassle. (-h
for help)
  CMOS reports: conv_mem= 640K, ext_mem= 31,744K, Total RAM=
32,384K
  "GenuineIntel" Pentium Clocked at 132.9 MHz
  Reading from memory.
  MegaByte#: ------- Memory Access Block sizes (KB)----
  1 2 4 8 16 32 64 128 256 512 1024 2048 4096 <-- KB
  0: 6 6 6 6 9 9 9 9 9 9----ýs/KB
  1: 6 6 6 6 9 9 9 9 9 9 14 14 14 ýs/KB
  2 3 4 5 6 7 8 9 10 11 12 13 14 15 16 17 18 <-- same as above.
  19 20 21 22 23 24 25 26 27 28 29 30 31 <-- same as above.

     Extra tests----
  Wrt 12 12 12 12 12 12 12 12 12 12 12 12 12<-Write mem
  This machine seems to have both L1 and L2 cache. [read]
  L1 cache is 8KB—182.5 MB/s 5.7 ns/byte (237%) (155%) 2.9 clks
  L2 cache is 512KB—117.3 MB/s 8.9 ns/byte (152%) (100%) 4.5
clks
  Main memory speed—76.9 MB/s 13.6 ns/byte (100%) [read] 6.9
clks
  Effective RAM access time (read ) is 108 ns (a RAM bank is 8
bytes wide).
  Effective RAM access time (write) is 92 ns (a RAM bank is 8
bytes wide).
  "GenuineIntel" Pentium Clocked at 132.9 MHz. Cache ENABLED.
  Options: -t0
```

**System C, running a 166 MHz Pentium on an AMI Atlas PCI II motherboard, a 512K pipeline burst cache, a PCI bus, and 60ns Fast Page Mode memory, gives these results:**

```
CACHECHK v4 2/7/96 Copyright (c) 1995 by Ray Van Tassle. (-h
for help)
  CMOS reports: conv_mem= 640K, ext_mem= 64,512K, Total RAM=
65,152K
  "GenuineIntel" Pentium Clocked at 166.5 MHz
  Reading from memory.
  MegaByte#: ------- Memory Access Block sizes (KB)----
```

```
 1 2 4 8 16 32 64 128 256 512 1024 2048 4096 <-- KB
 0: 5 5 5 5 9 9 9 9 9 9 9----ýs/KB
 1: 5 5 5 5 9 9 9 9 9 9 9 13 13 13 ýs/KB
 2 3 4 5 6 7 8 9 10 11 12 13 14 15 16 17 18 <-- same as above.
19 20 21 22 23 24 25 26 27 28 29 30 31 32 33 34 35 <-- same as
above.
36 37 38 39 40 41 42 43 44 45 46 47 48 49 50 51 52 <-- same as
above.
53 54 55 56 57 58 59 60 61 62 63 <-- same as above.

 Extra tests----
 Wrt 24 24 24 24 24 24 24 24 24 24 24 24 24<-Write mem
 This machine seems to have both L1 and L2 cache. [read]
 L1 cache is 8KB-226.5 MB/s 4.6 ns/byte (265%) (182%) 2.9 clks
 L2 cache is 512KB-123.9 MB/s 8.5 ns/byte (145%) (100%) 5.4
clks
 Main memory speed-85.3 MB/s 12.3 ns/byte (100%) [read] 7.8
clks
 Effective RAM access time (read ) is 98 ns (a RAM bank is 8
bytes wide).
 Effective RAM access time (write) is 182 ns (a RAM bank is 8
bytes wide).
 "GenuineIntel" Pentium Clocked at 166.5 MHz. Cache ENABLED.
 Options: -t0
```

Let's look first at what CACHECHK reports, and then at the comparisons we can draw among systems. We'll examine excerpts from the Pentium III output to show what CACHECHK reports.

The first part of the CACHECHK output is an identification of the version of the program and the configuration data it has discovered by looking at the computer:

```
CACHECHKV711/23/98Copyright(c)1995-98 by Ray Van Tassle.(-h for
help)
 CMOS reports:conv_mem= 640K,ext_mem=65,535K,Total RAM= 66,175K
 BIOS reports:        ext_mem= 129,984K  Total mem: 127 MB
 "GenuineIntel"  Pentium Pro Clocked at 449.6 MHz
```

Reporting this data contributes to making CACHECHK a good benchmark because it lets you ensure you're looking at comparable data. Different versions of benchmark programs might produce different results, so you're better off comparing from the identical version. Labeling the output with the hardware configuration helps ensure that you know what the test conditions are.

You'll also note in the output that the BIOS reports more memory than the CMOS (because CMOS is limited to 65MB) and that (as we mentioned previously), the processor reports as a Pentium Pro rather than the Pentium III we actually ran.

The first part of the test reads the memory. CACHECHK tests each 1MB section of memory independently and does the reads over a range of sizes to check how the cache interacts with the read process. You can't read or write the cache explicitly, so CACHECHK measures the effect of the cache by accessing memory repetitively in blocks that bracket likely cache sizes. As the block size grows to exceed the cache size, the memory references are forced out to the next level cache or to memory, slowing the reference down and revealing the boundary of the cache.

```
Reading from memory.
 MegaByte#:         --------- Memory Access Block sizes (KB)-----
 1    2    4    8   16   32   64  128  256  512 1024 2048 4096<-- KB
 0:   2    2    2    2    2    3    3    3    3    3    -    -    -  us/KB
 1:   2    2    2    2    2    3    3    3    3    3    7    7    7  us/KB
 2:   2    2    2    2    2    3    3    3    3    3    7    7    7  us/KB
 3:   2    2    2    2    2    3    3    3.   3    3    7    7    7  us/KB
 4  5  6  7  8  9 10 11 12 13 14 15 16 17 18 19 20<--same as above.
21 22 23 24 25 26 27 28 29 30 31 32 33 34 35 36 37<---same as
above.
38 39 40 41 42 43 44 45 46 47 48 49 50 51 52 53 54<---same as
above.
55 56 57 58 59 60 61 62 63 64<---same as above.
```

We've condensed this output from what CACHECHK really output to save space; the actual output was as shown at the beginning of this section.

The first row of numbers shows the size of the blocks CACHECHK is using to reference memory, running from 1K to 4MB. The second line of numbers starts with a label (0:) that shows which megabyte of memory the program is working on. The combination of the block sizes and the megabyte labels forms a matrix that gets filled in with the time per kilobyte it takes to read the block. (The first line of measurements stops at 256K blocks because there is only 640K actually there in the first megabyte. Programs like EMM386 and Windows move other memory into the upper address region between 640K and 1MB, but because we explicitly didn't load those programs so that there'd be no contamination of the results, that mapping hasn't happened.)

Look at the first line of measurements in the data. It's apparent that there's a break in performance when we jump from 16KB to 32KB blocks. The next line reveals another break when we jump to 1,024KB blocks. That's all the raw data shows, remaining consistent through all 64MB.

Suppose you have a motherboard with no cache outside the processor. You'd see only one speed transition—from the Level 1 cache in the processor to main memory—because there is no intervening L2 cache. If the motherboard had less cache than you thought, the transition from Level 2 to main memory would be to the left of where you'd expect. (CACHECHK calculates the apparent cache sizes a little later in its output.)

Suppose you had a computer that failed to properly cache memory above 8MB. (There have been a lot of them shipped; other computers fail to cache above 64MB.) In that case, the CACHECHK results would start to show different performance breaks as the memory references started to reach the area above 8MB. A typical pattern would be that the first break (between 2 and 3 microseconds in the preceding data) would lead directly to the slower speed (7 microseconds in that case) characteristic of a main memory reference. The transition would show up first in the 4MB block size, moving downward as the rows moved to higher memory addresses until there was finally a direct transition from the fastest value to the slowest.

```
Extra tests----
  Wrt   1   1   1   0   0   3   3   3   3   3   5   6   6<-
Writing
```

CACHECHK also measures the speed your computer achieves when writing to memory. The Pentium III we tested uses a write-back cache, meaning the processor writes only to the cache and the cache writes to memory when it can. (Refer to Chapter 9, "Cache, Memory, and Bus," for more details on cache types.) The effect of that isn't obvious from the results just shown — there's no difference in write speed as the block size gets larger.

After the raw data, CACHECHK does some data analysis for you, computing how much cache it thinks is in your machine and how fast the processor is able to access memory:

```
This machine seems to have both L1 and L2 cache. [reading]
L1 cache is 16KB--546.4MB/s 1.9ns/byte(330%)(124%) 3.3 clks
L2 cache is 512KB--439.6MB/s 2.4ns/byte(266%)(100%) 4.1 clks
Main memory speed--165.2MB/s 6.3ns/byte(100%)[reading]10.9 clks
Effective RAM access time (read) is 50ns (a RAM bank is 8 bytes
wide).
Effective RAM access time (write)is 37ns (a RAM bank is 8 bytes
wide).
"GenuineIntel" Pentium Pro Clocked at 449.6 MHz. Cache ENABLED.
Options: -t0
```

The comparisons among the four systems are dramatic. Table 35-1 provides a summary.

Table 35-1
## Comparison of CACHECHK Results

| System | L1 / L2 Cache Size (KB) | L1 Speed (ns) | L2 Speed (ns) | Main Memory Speed (ns) |
|---|---|---|---|---|
| A (50 MHz 486) | 8 / 64 | 20.3 | 30.5 | 91.0 |
| B (133 MHz Pentium) | 8 / 512 | 5.7 | 8.9 | 13.6 |
| C (166 MHz Pentium) | 8 / 512 | 4.6 | 8.5 | 12.3 |
| Pentium III (450 MHz) | 16 / 512 | 1.9 | 2.4 | 6.3 |

Here's what the computed results mean:

✦ *Sizes and speeds.* The L1 and L2 cache sizes are reported as calculated from the raw data. In System C, you can see that the L1 cache is nearly twice as fast as L2, and over two and one half times as fast as main memory. The Pentium III L1 cache is over 3.3 times faster than memory, even though the memory itself is much faster than in the other systems.

✦ *Access time.* A 64-bit wide bus lets the processor access eight bytes of memory at once. The main memory speed reported (6.3 nanoseconds per byte for the Pentium III) is an average of one cycle of actual access and seven of cached access. The actual memory cycle (the time to read in all eight) is eight bytes times the average time per byte, which works out to 50 nanoseconds per byte. The same process shows that memory write cycles take 37 nanoseconds.

It's interesting to note that, unlike the older processors, the Pentium III is *faster* writing to memory than reading. That's because the memory cycle can itself cache the eight bytes being written, letting the processor move on.

System A clearly suffers in this comparison. Its cache and memory access times are terrible. It's too simplistic an analysis simply to observe that those results map well to the fact that System A is slow, however. Take a look at the comparisons in Table 35-2, in which we've shown the ratios of speeds for each system as compared to the L1 cache speed. The main memory speed in System A shows up as the real problem; it's much slower when compared to the cache speeds than the memory in the other two systems. You'll also note that the main memory speed ratios climb to 3.3 with the Pentium III, reflecting the fact that PC100 memory is running out of speed with a processor as fast as 450 MHz. The benchmark suggests that you should expect the faster systems (above 600 MHz) to need PC133 or Rambus memory for top performance.

| Table 35-2 Main Memory Speed Compared to Cache Speed | | | |
|---|---|---|---|
| System | L1 : L1 | L2: L1 | Main : L1 |
| A (50 MHz 486) | 1.00 | 1.52 | 4.52 |
| B (133 MHz Pentium) | 1.00 | 1.50 | 2.33 |
| C (166 MHz Pentium) | 1.00 | 1.80 | 2.60 |
| Pentium III (450 MHz) | 1.00 | 1.26 | 3.32 |

# Video

We saw in Chapter 18, "Video Adapters," that video accelerators take over much of the processing to draw images on your screen, reducing the load on the processor and the amount of data that has to be sent from processor to video card. It's an accurate conclusion from that analysis that the key issues for video benchmarking are these:

✦ *Control the amount of data.* You move far more data using higher resolutions and more colors. Benchmarks at different resolutions and colors therefore don't compare directly because the changes in volume of data may not affect performance in direct proportion. You should run video benchmarks at the resolution and color depth you expect to run the system in during normal operation.

✦ *Control the software.* Video drivers are a critical aspect of video performance, so it's pointless to try to separate measurement of the hardware from measurement of the combined hardware and driver set. You can't assume that drivers are the same under different operating systems, so in the end you want to run video benchmarks under the operating system you'll be using.

✦ *Control the load on the processor.* You want to ensure that as little interferes with the measurement as possible. In Windows, mouse movement and windows that overlap on top of the window in which the tests are run can severely change the result. (See the sidebar "Follow that mouse," which follows this list.)

✦ *Measure separate characteristics, not a composite.* We saw in Chapter 18 that the Windows Graphics Device Interface has a number of separate primitive operations, including drawing lines, moving and drawing rectangles, and others. If you measure the performance of each of these and compare different video products (keeping everything else constant, of course), you'll discover that the different products are optimized in different ways, resulting in different mixes of performance among the primitive operations. If you don't make the measurements separately, you won't be able to make those kinds of comparisons.

## Follow that mouse

Moving the mouse around creates more of a load on your processor than you might expect. To see how bad it can get, start System Monitor on your Windows computer (or the equivalent program for CPU load monitoring if you have X Window up and running on your UNIX machine) and set it up to show the processor utilization. Unless you have some program running that uses the processor in the background, you'll see a display like the one shown in the following figure, in which there's little or no processor utilization.

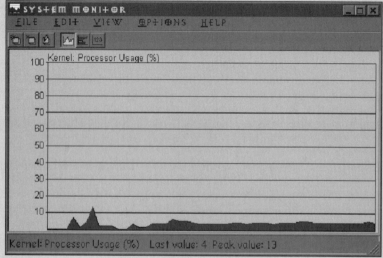

An idle Windows system makes little or no use of processor resources.

When you have established your measurement baseline, start moving the mouse around vigorously and watch what happens. When we did this, we got the result shown in the following figure. You'll get a different result because you'll move the mouse in different patterns and at different speeds than we did. Moreover, you may have a different version of Windows 9x, a different processor or motherboard, or a different video board.

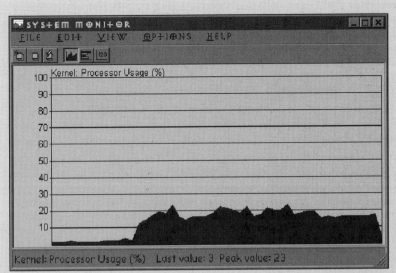

Moving the mouse can use nearly one quarter of the available processor performance.

The point isn't to duplicate our result, of course; it's to discover how much load the mouse can really generate. The conclusion you should draw from this experiment is that things that seem simple can drastically affect the results you measure, so you have to control your experimental conditions carefully.

The WinBench benchmark has a comprehensive set of video performance benchmarks, which you can supplement for 3D accelerated video boards with the 3Dbench tool. You can create your own benchmark (such as by scrolling a large document from top to bottom in a word processor one page at a time), but it will be difficult to be sure what you're measuring. In the case of the word processor–based test, you won't know how much of what you measure is due to characteristics of the word processor versus those of the video hardware and drivers. You also won't know the upper limits of what the video subsystem is capable of, and you won't know the interaction among the test and other components of your computer.

This isn't to say that WinBench or another explicit video benchmark is the only way to test video performance, however. For example, video-intensive games sometimes include video performance measures, letting you directly measure the performance you're getting under realistic game conditions. For example, if you start Quake, Quake 2, or Quake 3: Arena running and type the sequence

```
~host_speeds 1
```

and then press Enter, Quake will give you a display at the top of the screen telling you how fast it's running (the TOT number is the time per frame). The screen shown in Figure 35-1 shows the sort of results you get running the command in Quake.

**Figure 35-1:** Quake will show you total game performance, server load, graphics load, and sound load as it runs.

The image in Figure 35-1 is rendered entirely in software, not using 3D hardware acceleration. The frame time numbers for a 450 MHz Pentium III we measured were almost 4.7 times as fast as those for a 166 MHz Pentium. There's more detail on using the host_speeds command, and others, in the TECHINFO.TXT file that comes with Quake.)

Even host_speeds has its drawbacks as a benchmark because the conditions aren't well controlled. Other tools in Quake provide that capability using a scripted sequence through the game. The commands vary depending on which version (1, 2, or 3) you have; information on running Quake benchmarks is available on the Web at http://eel.bradley.edu/~ironmike/Benchmarks/Benchmark.html; commands for using other games for benchmarks are shown at http://www.3dgaming.com/games/framerates.html.

## Disk

Disk performance is very much dependent on the access patterns programs carry out. We saw in the section on seek and rotational latency in Chapter 13, "Hard Disks and Disk Arrays," that single-sector transfers on a reasonably fast disk could reduce the sustained transfer down to tens of kilobytes per second. In Chapter 12, "I/O Buses," we saw that if the data you want is already in the disk's onboard cache, you can have it at rates upward of tens of megabytes per second.

Beyond the usual procedure of eliminating things that divert the processor or consume resources, you need to control two things while doing a disk benchmark:

✦ *Access pattern.* Programs usually do either sequential access, as when you save a presentation in Microsoft PowerPoint, or random access, as when you query a database in Microsoft Access. You should conduct benchmark tests on both patterns.

✦ *Disk cache.* You may or may not want to have the disk cache active when you run tests. If you're trying to measure raw disk performance, the cache interferes with what you're doing. If you're trying to evaluate likely application performance, however, the cache is mandatory. You'll have to control the amount of memory in the machine and what other programs are loaded because they affect how Windows uses memory for a disk cache.

You can do a simple disk performance test by copying a large file from one place to another, but it's hard doing that to control the state of the cache. One approach that works well is to make sure the file you copy is at least twice the maximum size of the disk cache, and to do the test several times in succession. There are some sequential disk access benchmarks that do this and similar things; many of them (for UNIX, MS-DOS, and Windows) can be found at Advanced Computer and Network Corporation's Web page (http://www.acnc.com/benchmarks.html). Reasonably comprehensive disk benchmarks are included in WinBench and Winstone.

If you have a SCSI system, Adaptec's EZ-SCSI includes SCSIBench, a tool to analyze low-level SCSI device performance. SCSIBench lets you look at single transfer sizes from 2K to 64K per block; at random, sequential, and same-sector I/O; and at devices singly or in combination. (One interesting thing to do with SCSIBench is to look at same-sector performance differences between 2K and 64K. On one system using an Adaptec AHA-3940UW host adapter, we get over 23MB per second same-sector transfer rate at a 64K block size. If we drop the block size down to 2K, we get a rate no better than 2.5MB per second. There's not enough information to know if the limit at the smaller size is processor related, but the increased number of block transactions that have to start and stop is a good bet that it is.)

# Printers

Printer performance is relatively easy to benchmark because the printer is an independent device with fewer issues involved in controlling the benchmark.

The key to printer benchmarking is to create the printer output as a file once, before you start the benchmark. Use a standard document as the source for printing, letting the application program print through each printer's driver. You make the printer output file by using a print driver entry that has FILE: as its output destination rather than LPT1:, some other local printer port, or a network printer. Once you have the print file, you run the benchmark by simply copying the file to the printer using the DOS `copy /b` command. Make sure the file you print is large enough to generate enough pages to time the printer activity accurately, and be sure you include elements such as graphics and color in the document that contribute to a diverse printer workload.

Doing the benchmark this way enables you to differentiate the performance of your computer itself, the print drivers, and the application software from the rate at which the printer can print. It's an equally valid benchmark to print directly from the application to the printer, as long as you realize that you're measuring a more complex set of interactions that you might not be able to sort apart.

## Complete systems

We tend to chuckle somewhat when personal computer magazines rate the top 1, 10, or 20 computer systems. It's not that they don't use good tools to rate the machines (some of them do), nor that there aren't some really lousy machines out there (there are), and it's not that people aren't looking for an easy answer what to buy (many are). The problem is that, in the space of a magazine article, it's not likely that you'll find more than a summary of a few composite benchmark numbers, which isn't enough to figure out whether the machine meets your needs or not.

In practice, you have two choices. You can take the ratings the magazines publish, recognize that they're targeted at the mythical average user, and hope for the best. If that seems like a poor plan, your alternative is to do the testing yourself (or find out whether the vendor has complete benchmark data they'll send you). It takes more work to do the latter, but you'll have a better chance of getting the machine you want.

The most common benchmarks for personal computers are the WinBench and Winstone evaluations. There's a fairly comprehensive disclosure that manufacturers and other users of those benchmarks are required to do to publish the results, so you have a good chance of finding out about the machine used to run the test. The commonality of those two benchmarks improves the chances you'll get comparable data on machines from different vendors.

## Networks

Benchmarking a network is difficult because of all the things you need to control in many different places and because the differences in network topology and user activity mean that no two networks are the same. You can run programs that generate network traffic (such as using a disk file access benchmark over the network to a drive on another machine) to create a load on the network, but you'll need to synchronize events on several machines to create a repeatable, defined load. (Note that the Ziff-Davis NetBench benchmark measures file server performance and is not isolated down to network performance.)

For this reason, you may find that it's better to simply gather statistics about the load on your network as it runs in real life. Routers and some bridges commonly gather statistics; for example, the Compatible Systems MicroRouter 900i we looked at in Chapter 28, "Peripheral Network Equipment," maintains counters and variables to collect these statistics (and some others).

✦ *Ethernet.* Packets in, packets out, CRC errors (corrupt packets), frame errors, missed packets, receive errors, transmit errors

✦ *Wide area network (WAN).* Connection state, PPP state, IP state, inactivity timeout left, current connection duration, average connection duration, total connection duration, dial tries, dial connections

✦ *Serial port.* Received packets, output packets, discarded packets, CRC errors, overrun errors, framing errors, oversize errors

What the router statistics don't show you is average and peak loads on the network media. Devices called *network sniffers* can do this; they contain Ethernet interfaces programmed to receive all packets (regardless of address), and they use the information in them plus times of arrival to create a map of network activity.

Sniffers and router statistics may not get you what you want to understand the performance of a wide area network, however. For example, few people have authorization to wire a sniffer onto parts of the MCI high-speed backbone in the Internet, so the sniffer approach is not an option for finding out how heavily loaded the MCI backbone is.

There are tools that look at wide area network performance, but they're not terribly powerful. Most of them depend on the Ping function built into the Internet Protocol, on the assumption that the round trip times are representative of the network loading at the time of the measurement. The Ping program itself is too crude for this purpose, though, because it ignores the fact that there are many hops between computers and routers between you and your destination—all you get from Ping is the end-to-end round-trip time. A better approach is a program called *traceroute* (or tracert on Windows systems). Here's a trace from one Internet service provider to the Microsoft Web site:

```
Tracing route to www.microsoft.com [207.68.137.41]
over a maximum of 30 hops:

1 6 ms 6 ms 20 ms []
2 * * * Request timed out.
3 151 ms 143 ms 144 ms 205.164.111.1
4 248 ms 183 ms 171 ms 207.49.20.65
5 228 ms 174 ms 138 ms 207.0.56.17
6 330 ms 241 ms 237 ms border2-hssi2-0.Denver.mci.net
[204.70.29.9]
```

```
7 159 ms 155 ms 161 ms core1-fddi-1.Denver.mci.net
[204.70.3.113]
8 262 ms 268 ms 235 ms borderx1-fddi-1.Seattle.mci.net
[204.70.203.52]
9 268 ms 233 ms 264 ms borderx1-fddi-1.Seattle.mci.net
[204.70.203.52]
10 200 ms 239 ms 220 ms microsoft.Seattle.mci.net
[204.70.203.106]
11 203 ms 196 ms 201 ms msft1-f0.moswest.msn.net
[207.68.145.46]
12 199 ms 198 ms 224 ms www.microsoft.com [207.68.137.41]

Trace complete.
```

Each entry shows the times for three attempts to reach the destination. You can see from the names of the devices the trace runs through that traffic to the Microsoft site runs to Denver, and from Denver to Seattle. Such rerouting is common; backbone connections don't exist between all cities, so your messages might get routed places you don't expect before they get where they're going. (This can get ridiculous. To get from our computers to a site about 20 miles from us, messages go in turn to Denver, Chicago, Kansas City, and back to here. That sort of silliness happens when the two sites are on different backbones and the junction between the two backbone networks is at a distant location.)

# Hands-On Upgrades

Despite having the goal of creating objective, quantitative measures you can use to evaluate and compare computers, benchmarking is something of an art. The decisions you'll make to decide what to measure, how to measure, and how to use the results are not simple—you need to think the issues through carefully.

You can avoid some of the difficulty of deciding how to measure performance by using benchmarks developed and validated by competent, independent sources. The WinBench and Winstone benchmarks (for overall evaluation), and the Adaptec EZ-SCSI and ThreadMark benchmarks (for I/O performance) are examples of quality third-party benchmarks.

## The WinBench and Winstone benchmarks

The standard for Windows personal computer benchmarking is the series of benchmarks developed by the Ziff-Davis Benchmark Operation (a division of the Ziff-Davis Publishing Company). Overall, they offer these PC-related benchmarks:

✦ *Winstone* measures a PC's overall Windows performance by running Windows-based applications. Winstone 32 is a newer, 32-bit version that measures a PC's overall Windows 95 or Windows NT performance.

✦ *WinBench* benchmarks the major PC subsystems: processor, memory, video, disk, full-motion video, and CD-ROM.

✦ *3D Winbench* measures the performance of the video subsystem in machines equipped with 3D video hardware.

✦ *NetBench* evaluates the performance of a file server by supplying file I/O requests. (Client types can include systems running DOS, 32-bit Windows, 16-bit Windows, and/or Mac OS systems.)

✦ *ServerBench* measures the performance of application servers in a client/server environment.

✦ *BatteryMark* measures the battery life of notebook computers.

You can download most of these benchmarks from their Web site (`http://www.zdnet.com/zdbop/`), or you can order them on CD-ROM. (The cost is only to cover shipping and handling.) The benchmarks are licensed software, but there's no charge to download them. The Winstone benchmark is not available on the Web site, nor are the CD-ROM and full-motion video test in WinBench (due to size constraints). Scores from different versions of the benchmarks are not comparable, but the benchmark installation includes sample results from a number of different machines that you can use for comparison. Each benchmark includes a manual describing how to use it.

As of the second quarter of 1999, the current versions of these programs were Winstone 99, WinBench 99 (including CPUmark 99), 3D WinBench 99, NetBench 5.01, ServerBench 4.02, and BatteryMark 2.0.

Here's how to use Winstone and WinBench to analyze a computer:

1. Run a complete Winstone evaluation. Compare your computer's scores in the application categories that pertain to your workload with those from the samples provided.

2. Run a complete WinBench evaluation. Compare your computer's scores for the subsystems with the samples provided.

3. Look for relationships in the data. For instance, if your computer is slower doing database work than a similar machine in the sample database (or another machine you've measured the same way), look at the subsystem measures for the same two machines to see what's slower on your machine. That's the likely set of choke points, although you'll want to consider the possibility that your machine doesn't have enough memory.

The last step—analyzing what's causing the differences you see—is the real art to benchmarking. The measurements give you only the data. You need to combine that data with some insight into what the applications and hardware components do to draw good conclusions.

You need to do four things to be able to draw sound conclusions from your benchmarks:

✦ *Keep accurate records.* Two months (or maybe two minutes) after you run a test, you won't remember what the precise hardware configuration was you tested. The database in the ZD benchmarks lets you keep relatively detailed records of the configuration—use them carefully. Don't miss the small details. For example, having the cache enabled in the disk drive itself for one test but not another will give radically different results—differences you'd mistakenly ascribe to other factors if you didn't check.

✦ *Change one thing at a time.* If you really intend to compare benchmark results at the component level, be careful to make only minimal changes in the system configuration between test runs. If you change too many things, you won't be able to figure out what performance changes were caused by what system changes.

✦ *Make multiple, quantitative comparisons.* Save the results of each benchmark run in the database so that you can retrieve the numbers later. When you do compare sets of data, be sure to look not only at the summary tests but the detailed ones—try to understand if the detailed quantitative behavior matches what you expected when you changed the system configuration.

✦ *Isolate software and hardware changes.* Changes you make in your software configuration can radically affect the performance you get from your system. For example:

  • *Video performance.* Newer device drivers (such as Microsoft's DirectX 6.1) may give you better Windows video performance than the older ones originally shipped with Windows 95 and Windows NT 4.0. Some systems may benefit from PCI BIOS performance settings, too.

  • *Disk performance.* If you have multiple disks, you can create RAID arrays in software in Windows NT.

  • *Caching and buffering.* FreeBSD and Windows both let you configure the buffering, caching, and swap file sizes. Subject to disk and memory limits, you can drastically affect performance by properly (or improperly) setting those configurations.

## Adaptec disk benchmarks (EZ-SCSI and ThreadMark)

Adaptec has developed a pair of tools useful for benchmarking disk performance under Windows. The SCSIBench program included in EZ-SCSI 4.0 measures performance on SCSI drives, whereas the ThreadMark benchmark examines any drive accessible under Windows, including both SCSI and IDE.

We ran both benchmarks against the Seagate ST15150W (a 4GB Barracuda) in a Pentium system. The drive is a fast wide SCSI unit interfaced through an Adaptec AHA-3940UW controller. The processor is an Intel 166 MHz Pentium backed by 64MB of 60ns EDO memory. Results are in Table 35-3 (we've not focused on overall system performance here because we're out to highlight a specific disk issue).

### Table 35-3
### Sequential I/O Benchmark Results on System C / Seagate ST15150W

| Benchmark | Estimated Throughput | Comments |
|---|---|---|
| Adaptec EZ-SCSI SCSIBench | 2.8 MBps | 2KB blocks |
| Adaptec EZ-SCSI SCSIBench | 5.4 MBps | 4KB blocks |
| Adaptec EZ-SCSI SCSIBench | 6.9 MBps | 8–64KB blocks |
| Adaptec ThreadMark | 3.16 MBps | Aggregate score |

More than anything, the table says you can get nearly any result from a benchmark you want. Let's dig a little into why such a wide range of values appears in the table.

## SCSIBench

SCSIBench measures performance at a physical I/O level. The benchmark program communicates directly with the Advanced SCSI Programming Interface (ASPI) layer in Windows. This means that the overhead of the software implementing the FAT or NTFS file system is skipped, which at least in part accounts for the higher throughput estimates for SCSIBench we've shown in Table 35-3.

SCSIBench can monitor the throughput of multiple devices on the bus at one time. We have an Iomega ZIP drive, a Seagate ST15150W, a Micropolis 4110, and a Seagate ST32155W in the test computer; exercising all of them at the same time in SCSIBench with 64KB blocks and the sequential I/O test, we measured an aggregate throughput of 13.5 MBps. This configuration uses both channels of the AHA-3940UW plus an AHA-1542CP for the Zip drive. We measured about 70 percent processor utilization at the same time, which implies that the processor isn't the choke point.

## Never take no for an answer

We were initially prompted to measure the processor utilization for the SCSIBench tests so that we'd have data to compare against the results we measured with ThreadMark. We opened the Windows 9x System Monitor to look at processor usage while the benchmark ran, and we were dismayed to see that SCSIBench seems to be one of those programs that use all the available processor capacity — even when it's doing nothing.

We had the Windows Plus Pack installed, however, and it turns out that the software that's responsible for full-window drag is within Windows itself. That means that when we're moving a window, the normal message processing in the application is suspended. As long as the measurement part of the benchmark kept running, we'd be in business.

That approach turns out to work, although not completely reliably — there are instances where the processor usage jumps back to 100 percent. For purposes of the measurements we were doing, we assumed that as long as the percentage was below 100 percent, we were seeing actual utilization.

The sum of the sustained transfer rates of each device is 13.9 MBps, which is very close to the measured aggregate. From the collection of data points, it's reasonable to assume that the I/O system is capable of performing near to the capacity of the devices.

### Adaptec ThreadMark

ThreadMark is a different class of disk benchmark from SCSIBench. Rather than operate at the ASPI level, underneath the file system, ThreadMark uses standard Windows function calls to read and write files in whatever file system is operating on the drive. For that reason, ThreadMark incurs more overhead than SCSIBench and so reports lower performance. Because it uses the same software as do applications, though, ThreadMark offers a better representation of the performance applications can achieve.

ThreadMark varies several parameters as it measures disk performance, including block size (512 bytes to 64KB), read/write, and number of parallel operations (1 to 4). It measures throughput and processor utilization for each combination, producing a set of two values for each of 64 tests. Once it's completed the test sequence, it combines the values using a set of weightings intended to help reflect the characteristics of real-world systems to develop a single performance estimate. The combinations are done first by block size, then by read versus write, then by number of threads, using the factors in Table 35-4.

<table>
<tr><td colspan="9">Table 35-4<br>**Adaptec ThreadMark Weighting Factors**</td></tr>
</table>

*I/O Transaction Size*

| Block size | 512 | 1KB | 2KB | 4KB | 8KB | 16KB | 32KB | 64KB |
|---|---|---|---|---|---|---|---|---|
| Weighting | 10% | 2% | 2% | 40% | 2% | 4% | 10% | 30% |

**I/O Direction**

| Direction | Read | Write |
|---|---|---|
| Weighting | 80% | 20% |

**Parallel Threads**

| Threads | 1 | 2 | 3 | 4 |
|---|---|---|---|---|
| Weighting | 50% | 35% | 10% | 5% |

The weightings reflect Adaptec's estimates of what happens in real systems — that the most common I/O block size is 4KB, that there are four times as many reads as writes, and that most I/O occurs in isolation.

Don't be misled by the name ThreadMark into thinking that parallel I/O in your computer requires multithreaded applications. The "thread" in ThreadMark is internal to the benchmark. I/O parallelism in your computer can be due to multithreaded programs, but is also quite likely due to operations by other programs you're running, or due to actions of the operating system itself (such as paging).

Given this background into ThreadMark, it's easier to see why it reports lower values than SCSIBench — it's using a range of block sizes, doing writes as well as reads, and using the full file system rather than low-level I/O.

# Summary

✦ Benchmarks can provide precise, repeatable, comparable measurements not possible simply by doing your usual work.

✦ You have to construct benchmarks carefully and be sure the benchmarks you use reflect how you use your computer.

✦ A number of well-built, well-characterized benchmarks are available at low cost. You don't have to build your own unless you have unique requirements.

✦    ✦    ✦

# Diagnosis and Repair

This may well be the chapter you turned to first because one of the most common reasons people want computer hardware help is to fix problems. There's certainly no shortage of people with broken or unreliable computers. There's no magic prescription for fixing broken computers, though — just plodding, methodical analysis to eliminate what is working right until what's left is the problem. Nor are all the methods we'll look at painless. Some involve stripping all of your data and programs off the disk and starting over from scratch; others involve substituting components (which gets expensive if you're wrong about what the trouble is). If you don't have good backups plus the master copies of your software, you could be in trouble when — not if — your computer goes down.

Repair isn't a very pleasant subject. Unless the problem is as simple as cleaning dust out of the machine (fairly common, actually) or reseating cards and cables, you're going to be swapping components and working with low-level software.

Don't be misled by the term *repair*, either. Actually repairing a broken motherboard, adapter card, or drive in a personal computer is beyond the tools and skills of most people. If there's really been a hardware failure, repairing a personal computer requires that you *replace* the broken part. You can sometimes test your diagnosis by swapping in replacement parts from another computer, but if you have only one computer, swapping components means buying components.

The good news, if you can call it that, is that most problems in running computers are due to software problems. Once you get things set up properly and are past the first few months of operation, personal computers are quite reliable. Failures happen, but nowhere nearly as often as software conflicts and crashes. We'll focus on hardware problems, but the isolation techniques we'll cover can help you with software problems as well.

There's a lesson in that last observation—the most reliable personal computers are ones that people *use*, not ones that people fiddle with. Once you get a computer to where it's stable, it's likely to stay that way unless you install new software or hardware, or change settings on software you already have installed. We're not saying you should never install new things or make system changes—we simply want to warn you that it's those things that are most likely to create problems.

# Basic Techniques

There are three things you have to do if you're going to work on computer hardware without doing more damage than good. Here they are:

✦ *Control static electricity.* You absolutely must eliminate static electricity— electrostatic discharge (ESD). Voltages you can't see or feel can kill the chips in your computer.

✦ *Follow careful, well-defined procedures.* You get nowhere ripping hardware (or software) apart, making random changes in the hope something will work. You must have a carefully thought-through sequence of tests and changes in mind. You'll want to change only one thing at a time so that you can isolate what causes different results.

✦ *Use the proper tools.* We're as guilty as anyone of using a Vise Grip as the universal tool, but that's not the right way to go about working on computer hardware (we usually reserve the Vise Grip for plumbing). The parts are relatively small and fragile, so you must have tools appropriate to the job.

We discussed both static electricity and tools in Chapter 1 because they're terribly important—we wanted to make sure you didn't miss them. If you *did* skip that part, please go back and read them now.

# Mechanical Procedures

With the exception of blowing dust out of floppy disk drives and tape drives, hardware work involves taking the case of your computer apart. We don't recommend taking apart monitors (because of the severe high-voltage safety hazards and because there aren't any parts inside replaceable without specialized training, parts, and tools) or other external devices (because there usually aren't any user-replaceable parts inside). You may want to avoid taking apart a laptop computer, too (again because of lack of replaceable parts inside).

You have to judge for yourself whether or not you think you can take apart and reassemble your computer. If you're reasonably skilled at delicate mechanical disassembly and reassembly, you have a good chance of being able to put the machine back together no worse than when you started even if you've never taken one apart before. Here are some guidelines to consider:

✦ *Power supplies.* There are no repairs you can do inside a power supply without a good understanding of power conversion electronics. You can create a safety hazard by doing the wrong thing inside a power supply, so unless you're trained to do electronics repair, don't disassemble or stick anything inside the power supply. The same caution applies to the wiring between the power supply and the on/off switch on AT cases.

If you're careful, though, it's reasonable to consider replacing a power supply.

✦ *Disk drives.* Don't ever take a disk drive apart (floppy disk, hard disk, CD-ROM, DVD, or any other kind). Removing one from a computer (or adding one in) is a possibility, but you can damage a disk drive irreparably by taking it apart. (Not even the manufacturers repair disks. For example, both Seagate and Quantum test failed disks to see what happened, record the results for future quality control analysis, and then scrap them.)

✦ *Processor.* It's quite straightforward to remove and replace a processor that's in a zero-insertion-force (ZIF) or Slot 1 socket. (ZIF sockets have a lever on the side that releases the pressure on the processor's pins when raised.) Most motherboards use these sockets. If the processor should happen to be soldered down (very rare now), you need to be experienced in large chip removal and replacement to do the job without risking damage to the chip and the motherboard.

✦ *Memory and cache.* Most memory is on plug-in modules and is straightforward to insert or remove. If the memory is soldered to the motherboard, forget it. If the chips are plugged directly into sockets, as on some very old motherboards, you can remove them, but it's unlikely that you'll find something better to plug in. (If you do remove chips from sockets, try hard not to bend the pins. They're likely to break off.)

✦ *Adapter boards.* Boards that plug into your motherboard are straightforward to remove and replace. Some may have configuration issues, and you may have problems getting the right cables, but board insertion and removal are easy.

✦ *Motherboards.* Physically replacing a motherboard is a completely mechanical job. The hard part is figuring out how to reconnect all the cables that used to go on the old board onto the new board, and how to set up the new board to work with your adapter cards and with your software. Have a motherboard replacement done for you unless you understand why these points are issues and know how to go about solving them.

## Disassembly tips

In all cases, be sure to follow good ESD protection practice, and make a drawing of the assembly as you disassemble. The drawing has to be good enough to enable you to put the machine back together exactly as you found it. The following sections cover some details you'll want to be careful to note.

## Which slot is the board in?

Not all slots are equivalent. Some older ISA machines had one slot at the end near the power supply that was unique. Some old PCI motherboards require you to designate which PCI slots are bus masters, which ends up differentiating one slot from another. The sequence of boards in slots can matter for PCI cards. (For example, if we plug multiple PCI SCSI host adapters into a system, one of them gets looked at first, so drive ID 0 on that board will be the boot drive, and all drives on that board will be assigned drive letters before the second card is processed.)

Cable lengths may restrict the slots a card can go in. Cables may run from card to device or card to card.

## What cables connect to the card?

You can't depend on cables inside a computer being capable of plugging into only one place because cables for different purposes sometimes have the same connectors. If you plug a cable into a socket other than where it came from (and is designed to go), the best you can hope for is that things won't work right. If you're unlucky, you can destroy a drive, adapter card, or motherboard.

Some cables connect to more than one device. The cable from the floppy disk controller can connect to two floppy disks. A cable from an IDE host adapter can connect to two disks, a disk and a CD-ROM, a CD-ROM and a tape drive, or other combinations of two devices. Make sure you know which connector goes to which device.

It doesn't generally matter which power cable connects to which drive, as long as you're careful not to stretch them beyond their length. Cables shouldn't be under tension.

## Where is pin number one?

The orientation of connections is important. Not all connectors have notches or irregular shapes to prevent incorrect insertion, so things can plug in either of two (or more) ways. The same results are likely if you orient something the wrong way as if you plug something into the wrong place: Either it won't work or you'll destroy something.

**Caution**    Be especially careful to get orientation right if you have a motherboard that uses an internal cable from the motherboard to USB connectors mounted on the back of the case. If you get the orientation of the connector on the motherboard wrong, you can destroy the motherboard the first time you connect a USB device.

Problems like these are why everything that disconnects inside your computer is marked or keyed. Data cables (usually flat, wide ribbons of wires) have the wire at one edge marked with a stripe, a different color (usually red), or some other distinguishing feature. The marked wire goes to pin one. The printed circuit card should have numbering on the face near the connector. Sometimes only pin one is numbered, sometimes pins at both ends are numbered, and sometimes all pins are numbered. Don't take the connection apart without being sure you can identify how to put it back together.

Power supply cable orientation matters, too. The connections from the power supply to the motherboard have to be precisely correct and are not always keyed on AT systems. Connections to disk drives use a standard four-wire connection that is keyed and sometimes difficult to make fit. Connections to 3.5-inch floppy drives are smaller, keyed by skirts that descend from the side of the power cable connector. (The skirts on the smaller connectors are easy to defeat if you happen to insert the connector upside down.)

Processor chips designed for ZIF sockets have a unique mark in one corner, and usually one pin that's different in the array of pins. Processors should go in only one way, and you'll bend pins trying to force one in another way. Processor, memory, and cache module orientation in their sockets is keyed by clips and/or keys on the socket.

A number of twisted pairs of wires connect to the motherboard or to an adapter card. These wires connect to the speaker, keylock, reset button, turbo switch and indicator, disk activity indicator, ATX power switch, and other controls on the front panel. The twisted pairs will have one color that's common to all of them, and another color that's unique. Some (but not all) of the pairs have to be oriented the right way when plugged in; these include the pairs that connect to indicator LEDs and that supply power to the front panel. There are a lot of different schemes for marking the connectors that the wires plug into, so you'll need to make a very careful drawing (and check it twice before you unplug anything).

## Top-level disassembly

Be sure to disconnect your computer from the wall outlet before you start taking it apart. Power line voltages are dangerous, and you don't want to risk coming in contact with them. You may see other sources (including some versions of the A+ Certification exams) recommend you turn the power off but leave the cord connected to maintain a ground path. We disagree for two reasons:

✦ *High voltage.* Many AT-style cases have the high voltage power switch on the front of the case, not inside the power supply. There's 120 or 240 V present on the terminals of that switch, and if someone working on the machine before you damaged or removed the safety covers, you could be at risk.

✦ *ATX 5 V supply.* ATX power supplies provide a low-power 5 V supply to the motherboard even when the system is turned off. You don't want to be working on the system with any power present because you could damage components when you connect or disconnect them. The best way to shut down that 5V supply is to disconnect the power cord.

Opening the case typically requires that you remove four to six screws and take off the cover. Be sure to remove the cover screws and not those holding in the power supply — they're easy to confuse. Be careful while removing the cover that you don't catch it on cables or other components inside the case. (For that matter, be equally careful putting the case back on when you're done. Crimped wires can result in damaged insulation and shorted connections.) When you're working inside the computer, be careful not to dislodge connectors by accidentally pushing or pulling on cables.

Familiarize yourself with what's inside once you open the case; take detailed, close-up photos of all the connections if you want a good, permanent record. (You might want to look at the photograph in Figure 10-1 for some examples of what you're looking at.) You can identify most of the adapter cards from what plugs into them. For example, the monitor plugs into the video card, your disk drives plug into either the motherboard or a host adapter, external speakers usually plug into the sound card, and the telephone line plugs into a modem. A CD-ROM can plug into the motherboard, a host adapter, or the sound card. Cards that don't connect to anything (inside or outside) are probably memory cards.

There's no completely general procedure for disassembly. Adapter cards usually have one screw at the top of the bracket, and you'll need to disconnect the internal and external cables. Disk drives typically have screws at the side. (Be very careful to use the same screws when you reassemble the machine, without mixing them up. Disk drives in particular often have limitations on how long the screws into the side of the drive can be. If you use a longer one, you risk cracking a printed circuit board, damaging a component, or shorting out wires inside the drive. Don't expect that to be covered by warranty.)

Be sure to put circuit boards and disk drives in antistatic bags after you remove them. It's a good idea to keep the bags the boards were shipped in for this purpose.

As a matter of practice, use a minimalist approach to taking things apart. Disassemble what you must, but leave everything else alone.

# Isolation Procedures

The most irritating thing we ever hear from a technical support representative is when we're told — without having explained the problem and the steps we've taken to isolate it — to remove the autoexec.bat and config.sys files, remove and reinstall Windows, and see if the problem's still there. (The most annoying case of this we had was when we'd called merely to ask if the company's Web server had moved to another address. The representative had to work from a preset script and couldn't believe that it wasn't our computer's problem.) Nevertheless, there's an important concept behind that standard silliness, which is that most problems are caused by bad interactions, and that whatever the problem, you're closer to a solution by simplifying the situation as far as possible. Removing those files and reverting to a brand-new Windows installation accomplishes that.

We're going to restrict the isolation and diagnosis procedures in this book to hardware-related issues, simply because adding in software problems would expand what we need to look at to another complete book.

## Rules of thumb

Let's summarize the rules of thumb—the concepts that will guide your work—you want to remember working on computer hardware:

✦ Keep what's called *Occam's Razor* in mind when you think through problems. Named after the fourteenth-century English philosopher William of Occam, Occam's Razor says "Do not proliferate theoretical entities unnecessarily." In our context, that means the simplest explanation that accounts for all the evidence is the one to try first.

✦ Be observant and precise. Make sure you look carefully to see what's going on, and don't jump to assumptions or generalizations that aren't warranted by what you observe. Know the details of the error messages you see, and look around the point of failure for other indications.

✦ Have specific failures in mind. When you go to explain the problems you see, remember that usually only one piece of hardware will fail at a time. If your analysis requires two failures, you're likely to have violated Occam's Razor.

## Observation and low-level isolation

The first thing to do is to simply step back and look at what's going on. Does the computer light up as if it has power into it? What about the monitor? Personal computers have a typical set of sounds they make as they start to boot, including the memory test count up, noises from the floppy disk, and a beep right before the operating system starts. Different or missing sounds can be a clue to what's malfunctioning.

If the computer or monitor seems completely dead, check to make sure that it's plugged in, that it's turned on, and that there's really power at the outlet. We've fixed more than a few "broken" computers that way. Remember that the outlet may have a wall-mounted switch, there may be a power strip between the wall and the computer, extension cords can be disconnected, and power strip switches can be turned off or circuit breakers popped.

While you're at it, check that the computer cables themselves are all plugged into the right places and are seated securely. We've seen computer systems that color-coded the cables and sockets. You can write on the back of the computer with a fine-point Sanford Sharpie marker to label what goes where, or you can use masking tape to write on (so you can change things when you upgrade the computer).

The first thing you see on the monitor as the system boots may be the version and copyright of the video card Basic Input/Output System (BIOS), or it may be the initial display from the motherboard BIOS. Two other alternatives are:

✦ *Error codes.* You may see an error code on the screen. A common one is the number 103, which usually means a keyboard problem. (You can get this just by pressing a key before the computer finishes resetting.) Check with your system (or motherboard or BIOS) vendor for the meaning of the error codes.

✦ *Beeps.* If not enough of the computer is working to allow a screen display (such as a memory failure in the first bank) or if the video card isn't working, you'll get a series of long and short beeps. The meaning of the beep sequence is specific to the system, motherboard, or BIOS vendor. Some motherboard manuals include the explanation of beep codes in an appendix; if yours doesn't, you'll have to call the manufacturer's technical support line and tell them the pattern of long and short beeps.

There's a database of beep codes in the shareware section of the CD-ROM with this book (courtesy of Microsystems Development) covering most of the BIOSes you're likely to find. The same database includes POST (Power On Self Test) codes for those BIOSes, which you can see as the BIOS brings up the machine using a POST code card.

## BIOS beep codes

The beep codes we described earlier in this chapter as the BIOS mechanism to notify you of problems early in the boot sequence aren't, unfortunately, common across all BIOS manufacturers. Worse, some motherboard manufacturers change the codes from those developed by the BIOS manufacturer. Table 36-1 and 36-2 list the generic AMI BIOS beep codes and the Phoenix BIOS beep codes, respectively.

### Table 36-1
### Generic AMI BIOS Beep Codes

| Number of Beeps | Problem |
| --- | --- |
| 1 | DRAM refresh failure |
| 2 | Parity failure |
| 3 | Base (64KB) RAM failure |
| 4 | System timer failure |
| 5 | Processor failure |
| 6 | Keyboard controller / gate A20 failure |
| 7 | Virtual mode exception |
| 8 | Display memory read/write failure |
| 9 | ROM BIOS checksum failure |
| 10 | CMOS shutdown register read/write error |

## Table 36-2
## Phoenix BIOS Beep Codes

| Beep Sequence | Problem |
|---|---|
| 1-1-3 | CMOS read/write failure |
| 1-1-4 | ROM BIOS checksum failure |
| 1-2-1 | Programmable interval timer failure |
| 1-2-2 | DMA initialization failure |
| 1-2-3 | DMA page register read/write failure |
| 1-3-1 | RAM refresh verification error |
| 1-3-3 | First 64K RAM chip/data line failure |
| 1-4-2 | Parity failure first 64K RAM |
| 1-4-3 | Fail safe timer feature (EISA only) |
| 1-4-4 | Software NMI port failure (EISA only) |
| 2-1-1 through 2-1-4, 2-2-1 through 2-2-4, 2-3-1 through 2-3-4, 2-4-1 through 2-4-4 | First 64K RAM chip/data line failure |
| 3-1-1 | Slave DMA register test failure |
| 3-1-2 | Master DMA register test failure |
| 3-1-3 | Master interrupt mask register failure |
| 3-1-4 | Slave interrupt mask register failure |
| 3-2-4 | Keyboard controller failure |
| 3-3-4 | Screen memory failure |
| 3-4-2 | Screen retrace failure |
| 4-2-1 | Timer tick failure |
| 4-2-2 | Shutdown failure |
| 4-2-3 | Gate A20 failure |
| 4-2-4 | Unexpected interrupt in protected mode |
| 4-3-1 | RAM test of memory above 64K failed |
| 4-3-2 | Programmable interval timer channel 2 failure |
| 4-3-4 | Realtime clock test failure |
| 4-4-1 | Serial port test failure |
| 4-4-2 | Parallel port test failure |
| 4-4-3 | Math coprocessor test failure |

The heavy-duty version of beep codes is the Power On Self Test (POST) code, a number from 0 to 255 output to I/O port 80 as the BIOS sequences through startup. You can get a small ISA card that goes in any eight-bit slot and reports POST codes as they are output during boot. An typical card is the *Post Code Master* from Microsystems Development, (408) 296-4000.

### System unresponsive

If there's no video and no beep from the system during boot (and you're sure the speaker is plugged into the motherboard), check to see if there's power from the power supply. If you can hear the disk drives and fans start to spin, and if you can see LEDs on the front panel, it's likely that the power supply is working. If you're skilled with a multimeter, you can check this at the connectors where the power cables come into the motherboard. Relative to any of the black wires, the red wire should be at 5 volts, the yellow at 12, the blue at –12, and the white at –5. You can do a simpler check on a disk drive connector; the yellow wire should be +12, the red one +5, and the two middle ones ground.

You have to do these measurements with the power supply connected to the motherboard or a hard disk; the power supply needs the load to work properly.

If the power supply appears to have failed and you know the power line is feeding power to the system, check these items:

✦ *Fuse.* Some power supplies have externally replaceable fuses accessible from the back of the computer. After unplugging the computer, check if the fuse has blown, and replace it if so. If the replacement fuse blows, something's drawing much too much power inside the computer. You might need to replace the power supply, but you equally well might have a short circuit in the power wiring within the computer.

✦ *Power switch.* Check the connection to the power switch (assuming it's outside the power supply). Some switches attach with a connector, which might have pulled loose. Check for additional power switches, too — some systems have a power switch on the back of the case in addition to the one on the front. ATX systems have a low-voltage connection on the motherboard to the power switch; if disconnected, it prevents the system from starting up.

If the power supply appears operational, try removing all the adapter cards from the motherboard, disconnecting power from all the drives, and removing the memory modules. This should leave only the motherboard connected to the power supply. If the system is still unresponsive, either you have a failed motherboard (or processor) or there's a more subtle problem in the power supply. At this point, you can check the power supply with a multimeter (as described previously) and can check the processor by putting it in another known-good motherboard. Make sure the motherboard speed and voltage settings are right if you try this last check. Put the processor in a known-good motherboard rather than a known-good processor in the questionable motherboard — it's less likely that a failed processor will damage a motherboard than that a failed motherboard will damage a processor.

The point of removing all the adapter cards, disconnecting the drive power connectors, and removing the memory is to simplify the test. In that configuration, there are only three replaceable components that could have failed: power supply and power switch, motherboard, and processor. Although you remove the memory for this test, you should leave any plug-in cache modules in place because some machines can't run with the cache removed unless you disable the cache first in the BIOS. If you could get into the BIOS to disable the cache, we wouldn't be doing this test in the first place.

If the motherboard now responds with beeps from the speaker, the problem is in one of the components you disconnected. You can isolate which one by adding them back one by one. The last one you added at the point things stop responding again is the culprit. Remember to turn off the power before removing or adding cards. We've assumed that the problem here isn't a conflict between two cards; such conflicts rarely cause the system to be completely unresponsive. Once you find the failed component, replace it.

### Monitor unresponsive

If the system seems to be responding properly (such as the right sounds as it boots, disk activity, and the Windows startup sound) but there's no video, look at the screen closely with the brightness and contrast turned up all the way. A completely dark screen could indicate no power to the monitor or a failure within the monitor. A scrambled image on the screen (or no image but a visible background raster present) could indicate a damaged cable or connector or a failure in either the monitor or the display card. In either case, you can isolate the problem between the monitor and the computer by trying another monitor. If that fixes the problem, you'll need to either replace the monitor or have it fixed. Check the cost of fixing the monitor before you decide to have the repair done; the cost of monitors is low enough (we've seen very good 17-inch monitors for under $400; 14- and 15-inch monitors are under $200) that the repair cost may not be much different from the replacement cost (if you can find someone to do the repair at all), and replacement will give you a monitor with fewer hours of service on it.

## Video operational during boot

If you can get video during boot, the system can help you figure out what's wrong. If you get an error message before the actual operating system startup sequence starts (such as "Starting Windows 98" or "Starting MS-DOS"), then you need to identify what component the message refers to. You figure that out by seeing where in the boot sequence the message occurs in addition to reading the text of the message. The typical boot sequence goes like this:

✦ *Video BIOS startup.* Even though the motherboard BIOS is active before video BIOS startup, nothing can show up on the screen until the video adapter BIOS initializes the card. A message from the BIOS may identify the card and date of the video BIOS.

✦ *Motherboard BIOS sign-on.* The motherboard BIOS identifies itself, including version, and may provide some configuration information about the system.

✦ *Peripheral device initialization.* The BIOS initializes the devices it controls. This includes the IDE disks and CD-ROM, keyboard and mouse, and the floppy disk.

✦ *Adapter card initialization.* There's a BIOS on some other adapter cards (such as SCSI disk host adapters). The motherboard BIOS calls the adapter BIOS for each card in sequence (typically ISA cards followed by PCI cards). Each adapter BIOS displays a message identifying the product and the BIOS version. Some, such as SCSI host adapters, search for and identify devices attached to the card, too.

✦ *Operating system start.* This is signaled by the initial message from the operating system such as "Starting Windows 98."

✦ *Hardware configuration check and device driver load.* As the operating system loads, it checks the hardware configuration to see if it matches what's expected, and loads drivers to control the hardware. Drivers (and other programs) are loaded in the config.sys and autoexec.bat files for Windows 9*x*; both Windows 9*x* and Windows NT load drivers as the 32-bit part of the operating system loads. UNIX systems typically output a long report of attempts to load drivers and of configuration settings as the system starts.

**Tip**    You can get an idea of where the problem lies from what's going on in the boot sequence when the problem happens. For example, if the BIOS expects to find an IDE disk but the disk is not responding, the boot may hang (or stop for a long time) after the motherboard sign-on message. Some versions of the AMI BIOS display a "WAIT..." message at that point; your BIOS may be different. Similarly, if an adapter card sign-on message is followed by an error code, you know that the problem lies with that adapter or something else in the boot sequence prior to the next message you normally see. It really helps in troubleshooting to know precisely what normal behavior should be!

If the machine initializes normally but won't boot, saying that it found no operating system and you should insert a bootable floppy, you have one of three problems:

✦ *Failed disk or host adapter.* On some systems, the boot sequence continues even if the disk drive is inoperative. At the point when the BIOS tries to find an operating system, you get the message that no operating system was found because the BIOS can't read the disk. Problems with the power supply or data cables to the disk could cause this, too.

✦ *Corrupted disk.* If the contents of the disk have been scrambled, the BIOS might not be able to find what looks like an operating system. This is one of the situations in which you'll either be thankful for good backups or wish you had them. (Before you panic, though, try a reset or power off/on cycle — we've seen a number of cases where the hardware simply was in a bad state easily cured this way.)

✦ *No active partition.* Among the information that the disk partition table keeps are an indicator of what type of file system each partition contains and an indicator of whether or not a partition is active (that is, bootable). A common mistake when you initially partition a disk is to forget to mark the first partition as bootable. After you format the disk and try to make it boot, you get the "No operating system" error, even though you just put it there.

If you can boot from a floppy, you can start trying to find out why the hard disk won't boot. Check if you can hear the drive spinning and if there's an activity light on the disk. Be sure to check the activity light directly on the disk if there is one, and not the one on the machine front panel because the light on the front panel sees status from the host adapter, not individual disks. If the front panel light isn't working, you know the disk isn't seeing commands. If the disk is broken or the cable damaged, though, the front panel light can be on and nothing happening at the disk. If the disk is operational, look for software-related problems such as a scrambled file system.

## Memory failures

Another possibility is that either the power-on self test, the parity testing hardware, or the memory test in the Windows 9*x* himem.sys driver detects a bad memory location. You enable memory testing in the himem.sys driver by putting this as the first DEVICE line in your config.sys file:

```
DEVICE=C:\WINDOWS\HIMEM.SYS /TESTMEM:ON
```

The difference from the usual himem.sys invocation is the "/TESTMEM:ON" parameter, which enables memory testing when the driver loads. The test isn't as comprehensive as what you get from a memory diagnostic, but it's better than what's in most BIOS power-on tests.

If you have more than one memory bank (there are typically two modules per bank on a Pentium SIMM-based motherboard, and one module per bank for motherboards using DIMMs), you have some options.

✦ *Failed bank zero.* The computer won't boot if the first bank of memory (that's either bank zero or one, depending on how your motherboard is numbered) is bad. If you have two banks, you can swap bank zero and bank one (or bank one and bank two if your numbering starts at one). If the memory was in fact the problem, swapping the two banks should move the problem to a higher address (corresponding to the higher-numbered bank) and allow the computer to boot.

You won't want to do this if you have different memory types or speeds set up in your BIOS. If you can't boot into the BIOS, you can't tell it you moved the memory around. This is a really good reason to have all the memory in a computer the same. If you use standard memory everywhere at your site, you can reduce the amount of spare memory you have to keep on hand.

✦ *Failed other bank*. If other than the first bank of memory has failed, you may have two choices: Leave it in or take it out. Many systems detect the failed memory, complain (and possibly require you to go into setup and confirm the new limit), and run. If yours is one of those, you can leave the failed memory in; otherwise, take it out and reconfigure the setting in the BIOS to let you run with reduced memory. If your computer has more than two banks of memory, you can relocate the removed bank to the end, making the most of the memory you have left.

## Diagnostics

Observation and replacement only go so far (unless you have a really well-stocked parts bin). Ultimately, you'll want the ability to run a comprehensive set of diagnostics to help isolate what's wrong. We prefer to run diagnostics from DOS—without the interference of the device drivers and other software in Windows—and to run DOS without any device drivers loaded. You'll want to make sure you have an emergency boot floppy disk (see Chapter 38, "Building a Clone—Software Installation," and Chapter 40, "Building a Server—Software Installation") so that you can start the machine without a hard disk running.

The industrial-strength diagnostics we use are AMIDiag by AMI and QAPlus/FE by DiagSoft. Both tools will locate and diagnose most problems associated with the major components of your PC. You can run individual tests or groups of tests in a batch, specify parameters to use for each test, and save test settings as a script for future use. Hard drive tests handle both SCSI and IDE drives. System information includes a map of how the first megabyte of system memory is used, how interrupt levels and direct memory access channels are assigned, and what device drivers are loaded. Hardware configuration reporting includes detailed information on drive types, number of heads, cylinders and sectors, interleave factor, and rotation speed.

Specific test modules cover the motherboard and processor, memory, video adapter, hard disk, floppy disk, CD-ROM, serial port, parallel port, printer, keyboard, mouse, USB, and speaker. Utilities include a CMOS editor (to check and set BIOS configuration parameters), a memory chip locator (to identify which memory strip has failed using the address of the failure), a serial port debugger, and hard disk utilities for locating bad tracks and low-level disk formatting. A database supports recording and reporting test results and configuration information over your entire configuration. When a problem comes up, you can compare the current configuration to the previously recorded configuration to help troubleshoot the problem.

# Problems in Functioning Machines

It's much harder to fix problems in machines that mostly work because in many ways a dead machine is the easiest to troubleshoot. The range of things that can have failed in a dead machine is limited, it's easy to replicate the problem, and it's easy to tell when you've fixed it.

Ignoring software-related problems, there are three other kinds of problems you'll face in partly functional machines, all of which can be much harder to solve:

✦ *Configuration.* You may encounter conflicts among devices for resources (interrupts, direct memory access channels, memory addresses, or bus slots).

✦ *Incompatibilities.* Some hardware simply doesn't work properly with other hardware, even if both parts are installed correctly and there are no resource conflicts. Incompatibilities can lead to instability and crashes.

✦ *Something doesn't work right.* Even if the machine is stable, sometimes the hardware doesn't work the way it should.

The next sections discuss each of these problem types and suggest how to approach repairs.

## Configuration problems

Much of what goes wrong in hardware is the result of two or more devices wanting the same resources. The conflict can be over an interrupt, a direct memory access channel, a reserved memory address, or a physical bus slot (or combinations of these). IBM added automatic configuration to the Micro Channel Architecture bus; Intel put autoconfiguration into the PCI bus; and Microsoft introduced Plug and Play in Windows 9x to help solve configuration problems. (Windows NT won't have Plug and Play until Windows 2000 is released.) None are perfect, and none completely solve the problems introduced by older ISA bus cards built without benefit of these technologies.

In practice, your best tool for finding conflicts (assuming you can get Windows to come up) is the Windows 9x Device Manager. (Start the System applet in the Control Panel to get to Device Manager.) Unlike the 16-bit device drivers in Windows 3.1, the 32-bit device drivers in Windows 9x and Windows NT 4.0 report the resources they have assigned. Cross-checking the assigned resources lets Windows find out about conflicts, reporting the results in the Device Manager. Old drivers are a weakness in Windows 9x's detection of hardware conflicts because Windows doesn't get resource usage reports for any device using a DOS driver or an old 16-bit Windows driver. (Another weakness is buggy drivers — we've seen a few that reported resource usage incorrectly, masking actual problems.)

When the Device Manager finds a conflict, it flags the device with a yellow or red warning symbol. You'll want to check what problem Windows is reporting (it might be something besides a conflict) and resolve it if you can. You resolve conflicts by changing the resources assigned to devices. Non–Plug and Play cards may require that you change switch or jumper settings on the card, or that you rerun the card setup software. Service Release 2 of Windows 95 improved the interrupt conflict situation by improving support for sharing interrupts on capable hardware. For example, a network card, a video card, and a SCSI host adapter can all share an interrupt.

The reverse of the conflict problem is the case where a card doesn't have the resources it needs. For example, without realizing what we had done, we once installed a PCI network card into an older motherboard that was incapable of assigning interrupts automatically to the PCI bus. Until we realized that the card didn't have an interrupt, we had the odd situation where Windows automatically recognized the card and installed the necessary software, but the network wouldn't work. The card worked in another machine (one with a BIOS that assigned PCI interrupts automatically). We discovered the problem by noticing that the Device Manager had no interrupt assigned to the card; after we assigned an interrupt to the right PCI slot, everything worked properly.

Some other configuration problems and troubleshooting assets are reported under the Windows 9x Performance tab (to the right of that for the Device Manager):

✦ *Virtual memory.* You don't want to disable virtual memory in Windows. You don't even want to run out of space for the swap file Windows uses to implement virtual memory. We once accidentally disabled virtual memory on one of our systems, and even though the system had 64MB of memory at the time, it would crash regularly. We've also had bad experiences when we've run out of disk space to hold the swap file — you should assume that the swap file can get to be two or three times the size of memory on your machine, and you should make sure you have at least that much space.

✦ *Graphics.* The accelerators (or their drivers) on some graphics cards are simply trouble. You can progressively disable more and more of the accelerator functionality using the dialog box behind the Graphics button on the Performance tab of the System Properties sheet. If this fixes an unreliable system, see if the card manufacturer can help. If not, consider another manufacturer.

✦ *File system.* The dialog box accessed from the File System button (on the Performance tab of the System Properties sheet) has a tab labeled Troubleshooting. Two of the settings there are useful for troubleshooting hardware problems — if you're seeing the machine lock up or crash, try the one labeled "Disable protected-mode hard disk interrupt handling" and the one labeled "Disable all 32-bit protected-mode disk drivers." If either one solves the instability, you either have an incompatibility or conflict in the hardware or have problems with device drivers.

A more powerful tool yet in Windows 98 Second Edition is the MSCONFIG program, shown in Figure 36-1. MSCONFIG gives you very fine-grained control over the Windows 98 startup sequence, including what drivers are loaded and what configuration files are processed. You can select elements wholesale on the General tab or choose individual elements using the tabs to the right of General.

The Advanced button on the General tab gives you access to driver startup configuration controls (see Figure 36-2). One of the options we mentioned earlier, "Disable protected-mode hard disk interrupt handling," is equivalent to "Disable Virtual HD IRQ" on this dialog. "Force Compatibility mode disk access" will eliminate the 32-bit disk drivers.

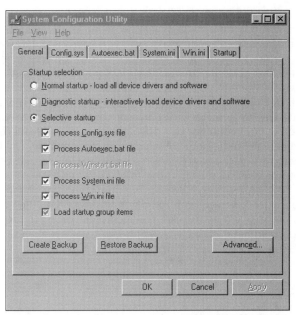

**Figure 36-1:** The Windows 98 Second Edition MSCONFIG utility gives you extensive control over the boot and runtime configuration of your system.

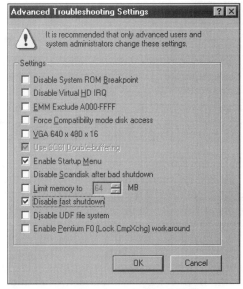

**Figure 36-2:** Use this advanced dialog to restrict low-level operation of disk and video drivers, and to alter startup settings.

The ultimate simplification of your Windows installation is to format the disk and reinstall Windows from scratch. As obnoxious as that is, an unstable system is really a prime target for such drastic treatment. Make sure you have complete backups — and test the backup — before you reformat, and make sure you have the installation master disks and installation keys (if required) for all of your software. At the point you've rebuilt Windows (but before you start reloading software), you're assured you won't have software-related problems due to conflicts among third-party programs or due to incorrect old settings for hardware. If the system becomes stable at that point, you can reinstall the rest of your software (not from the backup — from the original versions) and reload your data from tape. Try to exercise the system carefully after adding back each application so that you'll be able to identify a problem as soon as it happens.

It's difficult to carry out a from-scratch rebuild if you intermix data files with application programs because it's hard to know which files belong to the program and which to you. We recommend trying to keep the files you create and work with in a place separate from programs for just that reason.

## Incompatibilities

Although most hardware works as advertised, more components have incompatibilities with one another than anyone would like. It's not a problem that's likely to go away, either, because with so many companies building personal computer hardware, it's not possible to test all combinations. When you find one of those situations, your only recourse may be to replace one of the incompatible components with another one that works.

Here's an example. We had a machine that was stable and had been working well for about eight months when we installed a 3D-accelerated video adapter into it. The install went well, the diagnostics said things were working, and we put the machine back in service. Within about a day, though, the machine started to crash unpredictably. Some experimentation showed that if we replaced the video card (or switched to a vanilla VGA driver rather than the one specialized to the card) the crashes stopped. Oddly, though, moving the slider to disable the accelerator (Control Panel ➪ System ➪ Performance ➪ Graphics) had no effect.

On the assumption the problem is in the hardware, one of the things you'll want to try in similar situations is to go into the BIOS and disable the more advanced PCI bus settings, the memory shadowing, and the L2 cache. (Check the motherboard manual on how to do this; some BIOSs have a command that loads a complete set of conservative settings. Be sure to write down all the current settings before making changes. You may have to disable the cache and shadowing separately from the command for conservative — "fail safe" — settings.) In the case of this machine, turning off some of the more aggressive bus settings solved the problem. The machine slowed down, however, so we then reenabled things one by one until we discovered which setting had been the problem.

You should draw several lessons from the example:

✦ Problems don't always show up immediately.

✦ Whether the problems are with hardware or with drivers doesn't matter unless you can get updated drivers that fix the problem.

✦ Limit how many changes you make to a machine until you're convinced it's working so that you know what to do to revert to the prior stable configuration.

✦ You often have several ways to fix (or mask) a problem.

## It doesn't work right

Most often, a malfunctioning machine won't have the grace to simply fail outright. Instead, just certain things won't work, and they either won't work at all or will work randomly or erratically. This category is an enormous catchall, of course, but in a lot of cases what seem to be hardware problems are really issues with device drivers. There's a great article by Microsoft on what to do to help solve this kind of problem with Windows 9x—the article "Troubleshooting Windows 95 Using Safe Mode," to which Microsoft has assigned ID Q156126. You can find the article on Microsoft TechNet or on the Microsoft Web site. Other useful Microsoft articles can be found by searching on the keywords "Troubleshooting Win95."

The inverse of the device driver problem is that there are times when you don't want certain device drivers. In particular, we've seen a number of computers that—even though the CD-ROM was recognized in Windows 9x and supported by 32-bit drivers—were still configured to load the DOS CD-ROM device driver in config.sys and the MSCDEX file system extensions in autoexec.bat. In some cases, the CD-ROM on these computers had odd problems, such as not playing audio CDs or locking up at odd times. Windows doesn't need a mouse driver loaded in config.sys or autoexec.bat either. The lesson is that you want to eliminate everything you can from those files—many computers will work fine under Windows without a config.sys and autoexec.bat at all.

Another oddity is the phantom PS/2 mouse port problem. On many machines, Windows 9x detects a PS/2 mouse port even if there isn't one, and persists in redetecting it if you remove the entry from the Device Manager. The problem is typically a configuration that's not reported properly from the BIOS to Windows. You can work around the problem by disabling the device in the hardware configuration (do this through the properties for the PS/2 mouse port in Device Manager), after which the only liability is a warning in the Device Manager. Worrying about the problem beyond that is not worth anyone's time and effort.

Another of the most important lessons in trying to troubleshoot complex malfunctions is to get the people using the computer to be as precise as possible when describing the problem. A complaint of "the modem's broken" might more precisely be described as "I can't get e-mail, and when I try I don't hear the modem dial." That more precise description should lead you to initially check the phone line, cable, and modem.

# Loading Software onto a New Machine

If you build a computer from components, or if you replace the boot drive in a computer, you have to face the problem of getting software onto an empty drive that's incapable of booting.

In reality, the disk drive isn't the problem — the CD-ROM is. You can't get to the CD-ROM without drivers, and in many cases the drivers (or Windows itself) are on a CD-ROM. Catch 22. Here are your options:

✦ *Plan ahead.* To begin with, you'll need a floppy disk to boot from. If you've prepared a Windows emergency boot disk and added the DOS CD-ROM drivers to it, you're ready to go. Emergency boot disks created by Windows 98 inherently include CD-ROM drivers suitable for most machines, along with a set of tools useful in emergencies. Test the disk before you need it if you can, and make sure the FORMAT and FDISK programs are present.

Versions of FreeBSD and Linux either come with boot floppies that can handle most CD-ROM setups or come with files on the CD-ROM to make a boot floppy.

✦ *Install Windows completely from floppies.* Most people won't have a copy of Windows on floppy, and even if you do, this is a painful option. If you do have the floppy disk distribution of Windows, you can use your startup disk to partition and format the drive, and then load Windows.

✦ *Get CD-ROM drivers from floppies.* Many CD-ROMs come with a disk containing DOS drivers. You can build a CD-ROM-capable boot disk from that. If you have a SCSI CD-ROM, the Adaptec EZ-SCSI software includes a CD-ROM plus a floppy that lets you install the CD-ROM software. Once the CD-ROM is operational, you're set to install directly.

✦ *Copy to hard disk, and then install.* If you can temporarily put the hard disk in another machine as a second drive, you may be able to format the disk, install the system boot files, and copy the operating system distribution CD-ROM to the disk. Once you reinstall in the new computer, the hard disk should boot and let you do the operating system installation from the files you placed on disk.

# Network Diagnosis

Just as your computers will fail periodically, you can expect your network to fail, too. Many network problems are due to misconfiguration of the protocols, routing tables, or other configuration data. Although TCP/IP configuration and troubleshooting is a book entirely to itself, troubleshooting your network hardware is fairly simple (although potentially tedious if you have a large network). If you have a small network, the manual procedures we'll look at in this section are sufficient. For larger and more complex networks, for geographically distributed networks, and for networks you can't afford to have down for very long, you'll want to take advantage of the automation that the Simple Network Management Protocol (SNMP) offers (see Chapter 33, "System Management").

**Caution**     Don't overlook the fact that network problems can cause machines to seem to malfunction, and machine failures can take down a network.

The fundamental problem with broken network hardware is that some sections of your network become inoperative or unreachable. The strategy for finding the failure is to identify the point in the network that can cause the symptoms you see. If necessary, you can isolate down to finer-grained symptoms by partitioning the network in half, dividing the broken half into smaller and smaller halves until you isolate the failed component. You may have to disconnect parts of the network physically to isolate halves, or you may be able to get the insight you need by using the ping and traceroute programs (see Chapter 30, "Accessing and Serving the Internet"). The Ipswitch What'sUp Gold program can give you similar information and, because it can survey the entire list of computers on your net at once, may save you a lot of time finding the problem.

By far the majority of network failures are due to cabling problems — bad connectors, broken terminators, and shorted or open cable. One failed machine on a 10Base-2 network can cause other machines to hang during boot and can cause the entire network to malfunction.

✦ *10Base-2.* The terminators and tee connectors in a 10Base-2 network are particularly vulnerable to damage. A cracked, shorted, or open resistor inside a terminator is rarely visible but can be caused by things like whacking the terminator against a wall while you're pulling cable. Cracked insulation in tee connectors can be equally bad and may not be apparent even if you remove and inspect the connector. It's easy to destroy a tee just by pushing the computer back into a wall. The only certain way to check a tee or connector is to replace it with a known good one and see if that fixes the problem you're having.

✦ *10Base-T and other hub-based wiring.* The hubs and switches in your network usually provide indicators on their front panels to indicate operational and faulted status of connections. Between those indicators and selective disconnection to isolate suspect subnetworks, you shouldn't have much problem isolating what's wrong. That's really the big advantage of 10Base-T and 100Base-T.

Poor modem performance caused by a noisy telephone line can cause your network to appear to have failed. If you can hear the noise (pick up the receiver and dial one number — other than zero — to stop the dial tone), so can your modem. Your Internet service provider may be able to tell you how many retransmissions you're getting, and if the number is higher than usual for your area. As with all other problems, the troubleshooting approach is to think through how the components related to the problem work, list the ways in which their operation could fail, and test those ways one by one.

# Hands-On Upgrades

This section tells you where to look for more information on how to diagnose and repair your computer and provides a description of how we approached troubleshooting and repair of one specific broken machine. There are too many different ways computers can fail for a cookbook or checklist to ever give you useful guidance—our objective here and throughout this book is to give you the insight to think through what you're seeing and why the computer might behave in that manner.

## Tools

Although most PC maintenance and repair can be carried out with little more than a couple of screwdrivers, you'll find a well planned toolkit can save you time and frustration. You can accumulate a tool kit yourself; we suggest these items in a minimal toolkit:

✦ Phillips and slotted screwdrivers in a range of sizes from very small to medium

✦ Socket wrenches, including at least the $\frac{3}{16}$-, $\frac{7}{32}$-, and $\frac{1}{4}$-inch sizes (we've seen very few metric heads in computers)

✦ Flashlight and spare batteries

✦ Antistatic strap

✦ Small needle or thin-nose pliers

✦ Knife or other cutter

A vacuum cleaner is useful, too (be careful to keep it away from components because moving air can build up static electricity), but we've not seen toolkit-sized ones that moved enough air to be useful. You'll probably want a can of compressed air too; if you work at different places and not at a bench, you can use the compressed air as a substitute for a vacuum. Look at what's in the compressed air can before you buy it—we've come across ones filled with material that was flammable or gave off fumes we didn't want to breathe.

If you don't have the tools you need handy, you can buy a preassembled toolkit. Figure 36-3 shows a 55-piece kit by Belkin containing all the essential items except an antistatic strap—you'll have to buy that separately. The kit adds a few wonderful items, including a tool to reach small things that have fallen in awkward places and a clamp to hold things in position before you secure them fully.

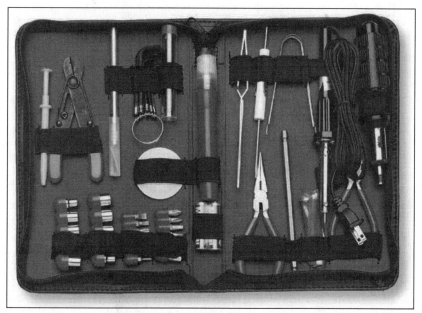

**Figure 36-3:** This Belkin 55-piece toolkit has most of the essential items and a few very handy additions.

Another useful item to add to your toolkit is a small plastic pillbox—get one with several compartments—in which you can keep an assortment of screws, jumpers, motherboard mounting standoffs, and other loose parts. You'll want some cleaning supplies in your kit, too. You can get a canister of antistatic cleaning wipes from Belkin that are good because they contain nothing but water and isopropyl alcohol—they should leave no residue.

We don't think most computer repair technicians need soldering tools. You can use them to repair some serial data cables, and to work on power wiring, but they're useless for repairs on ribbon cables, and few people have the skills or required spare parts to troubleshoot and repair printed wiring boards.

## The Micro House Technical Library and Support Source

If you're saddled with maintaining or supporting equipment from multiple vendors, or equipment for which you don't have documentation, you might want to consider the Micro House Technical Library, and the more general Micro House Support Source (http://www.microhouse.com/). The Technical Library is an information subscription service covering jumper settings, diagrams, configuration details, and other information on tens of thousands of products — both new and outdated — from hundreds of PC hardware manufacturers. Other Micro House information modules provide tools for support desks covering hardware, applications, and networks and do background Web searches of hardware vendor Web sites for new and updated information.

One of the problems you face looking for the information you want is having too much data to wade through — you know that what you want ought to be in there somewhere, but it's not where you looked. Support Source is Micro House's response to this problem. They've combined a search engine similar to that used in good Web searchers with a large information base (including the modules described previously). You can do text and database searches across multiple sources, knowing that you'll not have to paw through endless pages of search results irrelevant to what you need.

## Case study: a dead machine

At one point, an older machine of ours failed. We've described the sequence of events leading up to the failure in this section, along with the steps for troubleshooting and recovery. Every failure is different in some way, so it's not our intent to define a cookbook troubleshooting sequence here. Instead, this section is here to provide some insight into the thought processes that can help you repair machines.

Well before the time of the failure we'd upgraded the system to use an Intel Advanced/EV Pentium motherboard in a generic minitower chassis (see Chapter 6, "Cases, Power Supplies, and Uninterruptible Power Supplies" for photos). The machine had 32MB of memory, a pair of IDE disks (540MB and 1.2GB), an ATI Video Expression PCI video card (and the ATI TV tuner), a 3Com 3C509B network card, and a Microsoft bus mouse. Windows 95 (OEM SR2) was the operating system; no disks were compressed. The system had been in operation for about a year following upgrade to the Intel motherboard and a 133 MHz Pentium processor, and it was very stable. Backups of the machine existed on tape, but because little changed on the machine that couldn't be reconstructed, we did backups only every four weeks or so. (Infrequent backups on the machine were a conscious decision we made, and the effort to reconstruct did in fact turn out to be minimal. Nevertheless, that's a decision you shouldn't make without careful thought.)

The first indication that something was wrong was that the machine started to lock up randomly, with the lockups happening infrequently at first, but then more often. We made copies of critical files at that point – we weren't convinced that the machine was stable enough to back it up entirely, but we wanted to make sure that the most volatile files were safe. We didn't overwrite the existing tape backup when we did that because we didn't know if the problem we had might cause random, undetected corruption in the files. Instead, we copied them to another computer on the network.

One of the first things we tried to isolate the problem between hardware and software was to reinstall Windows on top of itself. That kind of reinstallation (as opposed to an install on a reformatted disk) is a pretty benign operation; it doesn't take too long, little gets changed, and in many cases the operation restores altered or corrupted Dynamic Link Library (DLL) files and fixes problems in the Registry. It's a reasonable thing to try when you can't pin down a problem to any set of programs or operations before you progress to more drastic measures.

It's not an easy analysis whether lockups are due to hardware or software problems — particularly with Windows — but because we knew that the software on the machine hadn't changed, it was worth looking into hardware issues when the problem persisted through a reinstall of Windows. One of the first hardware issues we look for when a computer starts to act up randomly is excessive heat. Fans that stop working or blocked airflow can raise the temperature inside chips to beyond their rated limits. When that happens, the least that's likely to happen is that the chip will operate incorrectly – signals take longer to propagate through hot chips, so critical timing is more likely to be missed.

The first hardware check we did was to check the power supply air outlet temperature. Do this with the back of your hand close to the air outlet for the fan in the power supply. Use the back of your hand simply because it's more sensitive to temperature and air movement than the skin on your fingers. We noticed that there was relatively little airflow, and that the air was warmer than we expected. Looking at the fan showed it was running, so we went looking for clogged air vents.

We'd never looked closely at the air inlets in that chassis. We knew the machine had no air filters, and because of that we had concluded it needed no periodic cleaning. What we found was both surprising and disturbing – the *only* air inlet was a single very narrow slit across the front of the case. That meant that under the best of circumstances only a restricted amount of air could get through the case. What was worse was that the slit was almost completely blocked with dust, so there was almost no air at all moving.

Vacuuming the slit clean restored reasonably cool airflow. We started the system running a looping series of diagnostics to exercise it, and after it remained stable for a day we put it back in operation.

After two weeks of stable behavior, the system failed to boot one morning. We were making coffee as it started, but when we returned to the machine Windows had started partially and then hung. We couldn't see anything else remarkable, so we reset the machine and let it reboot. Operation resumed normally, but we again copied volatile files across the network to another machine and left a note for people to watch the machine more carefully again. Nothing out of the ordinary happened for a few days, but then the machine failed completely. Powering on the system resulted in the usual disk spin-up noises, the fan ran in the power supply, and with one exception, the lights on the front panel looked normal. Nevertheless, the machine did not even start to boot — no video, no beep codes, no nothing.

The one exception to the front panel lights looking normal is that the power light blinked rather than remaining on steady, with the blink at a reasonably constant rate. Nothing in the documentation for the motherboard described this behavior, so beyond noting the difference, there was no diagnostic information to be had. (In retrospect, we suspect that the blink is indeed a diagnostic indication Intel's built into the motherboard logic.)

Using the approach we described earlier under "System unresponsive," we concluded that at some level the power supply was working because we had lights on the front panel and could hear the disks spin. We removed all adapter cards and memory from the motherboard, disconnected the disks, and tried the system. We received the same response—lights, but nothing else. Given that, the problem had to be the power supply, the motherboard, or the processor.

We had a spare power supply in stock, but not a spare processor or motherboard. We therefore temporarily replaced the power supply and tested the system. Nothing changed—the system continued to be inoperative.

That test showed the problem was either the motherboard or the processor—it's unlikely both would have failed. We had to make some choices about how to proceed – we could either start exchanging parts with another machine, taking it down for the duration of the test, or else take our best guess as to which had failed and order a replacement part. Here are some of the considerations we made:

✦ The simplest test would be to swap the processor, a 133 MHz Intel Pentium, with one known to be working. We had a machine available with the same processor in it, but physical location and the structure of its case made it difficult to remove the processor.

✦ At the time of the failure, a replacement processor cost $135, whereas a replacement motherboard cost $250. The motherboard was still under warranty, but the chip was not.

✦ One or two weeks after the upgrade to the Advanced/EV motherboard, its onboard sound chip failed. There was no objective reason to think the two failures were related, but the suspicion is hard to ignore.

In practice, we chose to disassemble the other, working machine and swap processors. The machine wasn't busy at the time, so we didn't inconvenience anyone, and making the test allowed us to be sure which component had failed. The processor from the failed machine did not work in the good machine; the processor from the good machine brought the failed machine to life. That was conclusive evidence that the processor itself had failed. In the process, we had the opportunity to power up the failed machine with no processor whatsoever, and we noticed that the front panel power light continued to flash. With a working processor, the light remains on steadily.

Once we'd proved that the processor was bad, the only remaining decision was how to replace it. We looked at prices for Pentium processors at 133, 150, and 166 MHz (this was before Intel released the MMX technology) and found them to be $135, $150, and $250, respectively. We decided that the improvement from 133 to 150 MHz was worth $15, but that the gain from 133 to 166 MHz wasn't worth $115.

Processors that have been in operation for as long as this one had are very reliable, so we thought some about why the chip had failed before we reassembled the system (including changing the processor speed setup on the motherboard). The most likely causes of computer failure are static electricity, overvoltage, overclocking, and heat. Because we hadn't disassembled the machine, we could most likely rule out static electricity. We run computers on a UPS and within clock specifications, so we could rule out overvoltage and overclocking. That left only heat as a likely suspect, and we knew that the machine had cooling problems sufficient to cause random lockups only a few weeks before the failure. We couldn't prove the cause of failure without sophisticated analysis of the chip we're unequipped to carry out, but we believe there's sufficient evidence to draw a conclusion safely.

An implication of the argument that heat killed the old processor is that there might have been enough heat buildup to damage other components. For that reason, we didn't return the machine to service immediately – we set it running an endless series of motherboard tests with DiagSoft's QAFE, logging the results, and left the machine alone for a period of a week. When it completed that time with no failures, we checked the file system for corruption, reloaded the one bad file we found from backup, and returned the machine to service. It's operated properly for years since then.

# Summary

- ✦ Your best troubleshooting tool is a planned, methodical approach and careful observation.
- ✦ You'll want a good (small) set of tools, including protection from static electricity.
- ✦ You shouldn't have to force anything. The bigger hammer approach doesn't apply to computer disassembly and reassembly.

✦     ✦     ✦

# Just Do It

✦ ✦ ✦ ✦

✦ ✦ ✦ ✦

# Building a Desktop – Hardware

**CHAPTER**

**37**

◆ ◆ ◆ ◆

**In This Chapter**

Mechanical assembly

Motherboard configuration and installation

Processor installation

Final assembly

◆ ◆ ◆ ◆

**B**uilding a computer from components — building a desktop computer — works in three phases. You need to plan what you'll put in the machine, assemble these components, and then install software. We'll show you how to plan and assemble the machine in this chapter, while software installation is covered in Chapter 38.

## Planning

Planning which components you'll use in your computer lets you develop a parts list. You'll choose each of the components based on what you'll use the machine for, what you want to pay for the components, how long you expect the machine to be in service, and how the components relate to other machines you service and support.

The machine we'll describe building in this chapter has the parts list shown in Table 37-1.

Our goal when choosing components for the machine were to provide a high-quality machine with the best possible performance — including 3D gaming and Internet applications — while keeping cost down. We chose the components listed for very specific reasons:

## Table 37-1
## The Desktop Parts List

| Component | Manufacturer | Model |
|---|---|---|
| Chassis | In Win | A660 mid-tower with 235 W power supply and auxiliary fan |
| Disk | Seagate | Medalist Pro ST36451A 6.4GB |
| DVD | Toshiba | SD-M1212 |
| Floppy | Teac | 3½ inch |
| Keyboard | Microsoft | Natural Elite Keyboard |
| Memory | Crucial (Micron) | 64MB PC100 SDRAM |
| Modem | U.S. Robotics | 56K Faxmodem External |
| Monitor | Hitachi | SuperScan Elite 641 |
| Motherboard | Intel | SR440BX microATX motherboard, including nVidia Riva TNT 2X AGP graphics with 16MB SDRAM video memory and Creative Labs SoundBlaster AudioPCI 64V sound |
| Mouse | Logitech | USB Wheel Mouse |
| Network | 3Com | 3C509B-TPO |
| Processor | Intel | 550 MHz Pentium III Processor with attached heat sink |
| Speakers | Microsoft | Digital Sound System 80 |
| Uninterruptible | APC | Back-UPS Pro 650 power supply |
| Video camera | Kodak | DVC 323 |

✦ *Chassis and motherboard form factor.* There are no useful alternatives to ATX for new machines — the industry has all but abandoned the AT form factor. The ATX form factor simplifies assembly and improves reliability. Because the cabling for the external I/O connections is mechanically integrated into the motherboard, there's no need for most of the internal cables and connectors you find in AT form factor computers.

✦ *Processor.* This machine is a desktop system useful for Internet applications (including videophone and e-mail), gaming, image processing and graphics, and word processing. The 550 MHz Pentium III is an obvious choice because it's the fastest Intel processor (as of late second quarter of 1999) and delivers the performance benefits of the Streaming SIMD Extension instructions. The processor price was expensive when initially introduced; you might choose to save money by picking a processor a notch or two slower than the fastest available.

✦ *Memory.* We consider 64MB of memory a floor for new machines and make sure to use a single 64MB memory module in machines with only two DIMM slots. Game and Internet performance isn't likely to benefit from an increase to 128MB, but image processing would. (For comparison, the machine we use for Photoshop work on the photographs for this book has 192MB and often runs out of memory, at which time it becomes unusably slow. People doing extensive image processing, particularly on entire groups of images, should seriously consider 256MB or more of memory.)

We used PC100 SDRAM to match the requirements of the motherboard. At the time we bought the memory, ECC modules were actually less expensive, so we bought those. Non-ECC memory should be fine in a desktop if it's less expensive. The SR440BX motherboard handles up to 512MB and supports ECC.

✦ *Disk and host adapter.* Although our preference is to use the SCSI bus, we built this machine using the IDE ports on the SR440BX motherboard to reduce cost. The DVD drive is available only in IDE, and there's little or no performance advantage to using SCSI with a single disk.

✦ *Video.* The SR440BX includes the nVidia TNT video chip onboard, providing high-performance 2D and 3D graphics in 32-bit color. Chipsets, including the TNT2 and 3dfx Voodoo3, can outperform the TNT by 10 or 20 percent, but the combination of TNT video and onboard PCI sound at less than US $200 is a great cost savings.

We chose the manufacturers and models for all these components based on reliable past experience. There's no question it's possible to assemble a machine with equivalent specifications at lower cost using other components; we'll simply note that in our experience, quality components pay off in better reliability and fewer problems.

# Preliminary Mechanical Assembly

The first step in assembling the computer was to perform the gross mechanical assembly, mounting the disk drives into the chassis. You would also mount the power supply at this time if you received it separately from the chassis.

## Chassis layout

Figure 37-1 shows a back view of the inside of the In Win ATX chassis. The chassis uses a separate removable tray to mount the motherboard (see Figure 37-2); the left face of the chassis in Figure 37-1 includes slide rails for the tray. The power supply in the upper-right corner of the back panel pulls in outside air and blows it out inside the chassis. In a conventional ATX layout, the processor is located right under the fan, ensuring a good air stream over the processor and supporting chips. The chassis cover, secured by four screws at the back, slides over the sides and top of the chassis when it's fully assembled. Clips on the cover engage the bottom edge of the chassis, ensuring a good fit.

Don't plan on using an AT form factor motherboard in an ATX — it won't fit.

5.25 inch drive bays      Power supply fan      Master power switch

Motherboard tray mounting rail      3.5 inch drive bays      Power supply air inlet

**Figure 37-1:** The In Win A660 ATX mid-tower chassis provides open access throughout, speeding assembly and maintenance.

**Figure 37-2:** A slide-out motherboard mounting tray in the In Win A660 chassis lets the motherboard and all adapter cards be removed at once without extensive disassembly.

You can mount an auxiliary fan in the plastic module that holds the speaker, as shown in Figure 37-3. The module mounts in the open perforated space at the bottom front of the chassis visible in Figure 37-1. We tend to use auxiliary fans to increase total airflow through the chassis in all the computers we build, reducing heat in the chassis and improving component reliability. You'll probably want the optional fan if you're mounting several hard disks in the chassis, or if you're using higher-performance disks with higher power dissipation requirements (such as the Seagate Cheetah).

Figure 37-4 shows the front and back of the removable chassis front panel. You can see the openings for the external 5¼- and 3½-inch drive bays at the top, with the control LEDs and switches below. There are three 5¼-inch external bays immediately above the two 3½-inch bays. The controls, top to bottom, are power on/off, power LED, drive activity LED, and reset. The cable visible in the right side of the figure connects the controls to pins on the motherboard.

**Figure 37-3:** The plastic speaker mounting module can hold an auxiliary fan to increase airflow through the chassis.

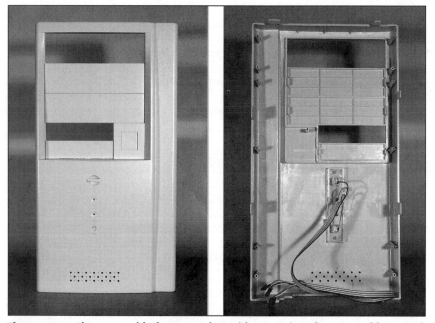

**Figure 37-4:** The removable front panel provides openings for external bays and controls for the computer.

## Mounting the drives

The first assembly step is to mount the floppy and hard disk drives. Figure 37-5 shows the layout of the front of the case, including bays for 3½-and 5¼-drives. You mount drives in either size bay directly with screws through the surrounding metal frame.

We're going to remind you again about the importance of an antistatic wrist strap — *any* time you touch a board with electronic devices on it, you need to use effective antistatic protection. If you don't, you could end up with some very useless equipment.

**Figure 37-5:** The front of the chassis provides 5¼drive bays at the top and 3½bays in the middle. The small oval opening to the right of the 3½bays is for the cable from the front panel.

The close up in Figure 37-6 shows that one of the 3½-inch bays is for an internal drive only, while the other two 3½-inch bays and all three 5¼-inch bays can handle internal or external drives.

**Figure 37-6:** Look closely at the panels in front of the drive bays. One of the 3½-inch panels and all the 5¼-inch panels can be removed to permit installation of an externally accessible drive.

You'll mount drives in the chassis using screws directly through the bay walls into the drive. Be sure to use the right size and length screws — too long a screw can damage components inside the drive.

We install the floppy drive before the hard drive because it's smaller and harder to reach, and to help prevent banging around the hard drive while we work. Position the floppy drive in the chassis as shown in Figure 37-7. The mounting holes in the bracket are positioned to line up with the screw holes in the drive, leaving enough of the drive protruding from the front of the chassis to line up flush with the front of the front panel. Check the positioning against the chassis and front panel before you tighten everything up.

**Figure 37-7:** Mount the floppy drive in the chassis so that it protrudes enough to line up flush with the front of the front panel.

Once you have the floppy drive secure, configure and mount the hard disk. Be sure to configure jumpers on the drive before you mount it. If you're mounting an IDE drive, you'll want to set it for master or slave (typically, master if it's the only drive). If you have a SCSI drive, you'll need to set the SCSI ID and termination. If this is the only SCSI device in the system, use SCSI ID 0 and enable the terminators. If you have Ultra2 SCSI, be sure you have the required terminator at the end of the cable—the drives themselves don't provide termination.

Termination requires a little thought if you have more than one device, especially if you're mixing narrow and wide SCSI devices. Here are some suggestions:

✦ *All devices the same (either narrow or wide SCSI).* Use the terminators on whichever device offers active termination, if any. If both or neither has active terminators, simply pick one.

✦ *Mixed narrow and wide SCSI devices on the same cable.* If you have a cable that supports both narrow and wide devices, let one of the wide devices provide termination so that all lines are properly terminated. If you have more than one wide device, choose one (if you can) that provides active termination.

✦ *Mixed narrow and wide SCSI devices on narrow and wide cables, respectively.* Some adapters, such as the Adaptec AHA-2940UW SCSI host adapter, have three connectors (68-pin internal, 50-pin internal, and 68-pin external), of which you can use any two. If you forego the external connector, you can use the two internal connectors to attach both narrow and wide cables. If you do that, both cables must have the last device away from the host adapter terminated, using active terminators if you can.

Remember that the device with termination enabled must be at the physical end of the cable away from the host adapter. You'll typically configure all devices to *not* supply termination power to the SCSI bus (it's generally best to let the host adapter do that).

Figure 37-8 shows the Seagate drive we used in the desktop system, an IDE 6.4GB Seagate Medalist Pro. Don't overlook the label on the top of the drive — it's likely to have all the information you need to configure jumpers and figure out which end of the data connector has pin 1 (it's often the one closest to the power connector).

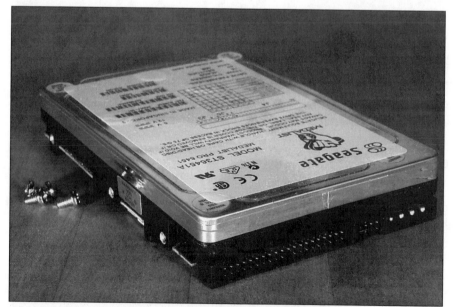

**Figure 37-8:** Threaded holes on the side of the hard disk line up with slots on the chassis. Mount the drive connectors facing into the chassis.

Mount the hard disk in the lower, internal bay of the chassis, as shown in Figure 37-9. (the floppy drive and speaker/fan module are also visible in the figure.) The drive extends out from the back of the bracket, creating clearance between the front of the drive and the front plate of the chassis. Two mounting screws (short!) on either side secure the drive.

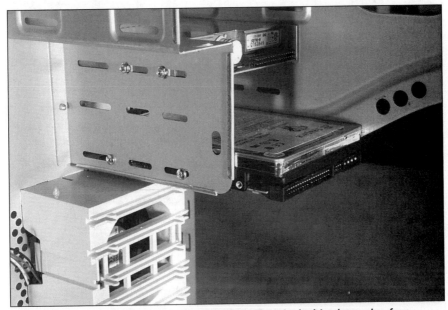

**Figure 37-9:** Secure the hard disk in the internal 3½-inch drive bay using four mounting screws.

Figure 37-10 shows a top view of the floppy and hard disk mounted in the chassis. You can see in the figure how the chassis brackets are straight on the left side but indented in on the right from the 5¼-inch width bays above these drives to form the 3½-inch bays. Positioning the hard disk as shown ensures it's far enough out to both clear the chassis front metal surface and reach the connectors. You don't have that option with the floppy drive because it has to be positioned so that it ends up flush with the front panel opening.

## Installing the DVD drive

The next step is to install the DVD drive. We put it in the topmost external 5¼-inch bay, but you can use any of the three available bays in the chassis. Figure 37-11 is a closeup of one side of the 5¼-inch bay opening. If you look at the side wall of the bay, you'll see two horizontal tabs sticking out. Other cases use slide rails that mount on the drive and engage slots in the chassis brackets; the In Win case uses these tabs (there's another pair on the left side) to support the drive until you affix it in place with mounting screws through the oval openings in the bracket.

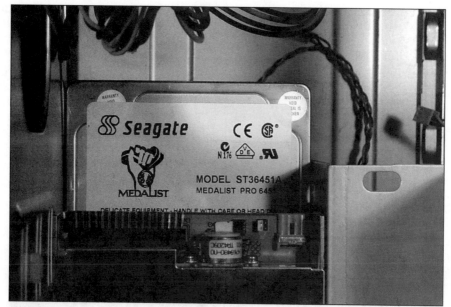

**Figure 37-10:** Position the hard disk so that it's easy to work with. You have to position the floppy to fit into the front panel opening.

**Figure 37-11:** Tabs on the In Win chassis support the DVD drive until you anchor it with screws.

The drive slides into the chassis from the front. Figure 37-12 shows the details of how the DVD drive is positioned in the chassis before lining it up with the front panel. The easiest way to install the drive is to put the mounting screws in loosely with the drive in approximately the right place, then position the drive exactly and tighten the screws.

**Figure 37-12:** Slide the DVD drive in from the front, then put the front panel in place and line the drive up precisely.

# Motherboard Configuration and Installation

Now that you have the drives installed, it's time to turn to the motherboard. Figure 37-13 is an outline drawing of the Intel SR440BX motherboard, typical of drawings you'll find in manufacturer's manuals. Typically, you'll not need to set any jumpers on the SR440BX because the board detects and sets processor speed and voltage automatically. As it is, there is only one jumper on the board to cause the BIOS to boot into a special configuration mode, from which you can set any of the BIOS parameters and (if necessary) set the processor speed.

There's one ISA slot (V in the drawing) and four PCI slots (U in the drawing). There's no AGP slot on the motherboard because the nVidia TNT video chip (the white square under N in the drawing) uses the AGP connection. We connected the DVD audio to the port at (C); the floppy and both IDE drives connect at (O) and (P and Q), respectively. The controls on the front panel connect at (M) and (J). The power supply connects at (I).

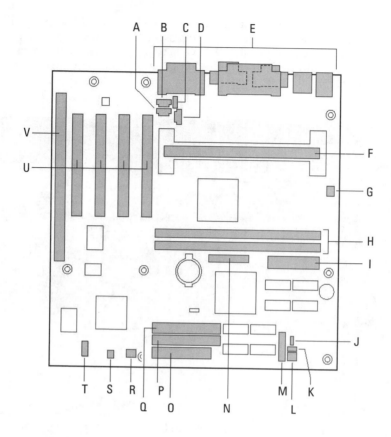

| | | | | |
|---|---|---|---|---|
| A | ATAPI-style auxiliary line in connector | L | Fan 1 (power supply fan) connector |
| B | ATAPI-style telephony connector | M | Front panel connector |
| C | Legacy 2 mm CD-ROM connector | N | VIP video connector |
| D | ATAPI-style CD-ROM connector | O | Diskette drive connector |
| E | Back panel I/O connectors | P | Primary IDE connector |
| F | 242-contact slot connector | Q | Secondary IDE connector |
| G | Fan 3 (processor fan) connector | R | Fan 2 (system fan) connector |
| H | DIMM sockets | S | Wake on ring connector |
| I | Power supply connector | T | Serial port B header |
| J | Front panel LED connector | V | ISA slot |
| K | Wake on LAN technology connector | | |

**Figure 37-13:** You won't need to touch a single jumper to set up the SR440BX for processor voltage and speed. (Drawing courtesy Intel.)

The connectors for the ATX I/O panel are at the upper left of the drawing and are detailed in Figure 37-14. The VGA port at (G) is positioned where you'll find the second serial port on most motherboards; if you need that port, you'll have to cable it in to a connector elsewhere on the motherboard.

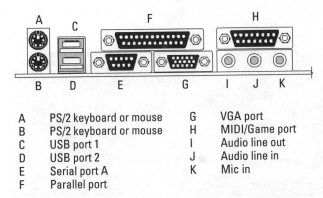

| | | | |
|---|---|---|---|
| A | PS/2 keyboard or mouse | G | VGA port |
| B | PS/2 keyboard or mouse | H | MIDI/Game port |
| C | USB port 1 | I | Audio line out |
| D | USB port 2 | J | Audio line in |
| E | Serial port A | K | Mic in |
| F | Parallel port | | |

**Figure 37-14:** Connectors on the ATX I/O panel give access to everything but serial port B. (Drawing courtesy Intel.)

## Mounting the motherboard on the tray

The next step is to mount the motherboard on the chassis tray. The removable motherboard tray is unusual in the In Win chassis, but it really simplifies assembling and maintaining the system because you can get to the mounting positions and insert adapter cards without having the chassis box in the way. ATX chassis use threaded metal clips or solid metal standoffs to mount the motherboard; these attach to holes in the tray. You want to use a standoff in each hole in the tray that lines up with one of the metal-rimmed holes in the motherboard. There's a view of a motherboard mounting clip typical of most chassis in Figure 37-15; the In Win tray is similar. The clip pushes into the chassis from the reverse side. Set the motherboard onto the tray, being careful to align the I/O connectors into the I/O panel.

Loosely secure the motherboard to the chassis clips with matching screws. Fit an adapter card into the motherboard as a pathfinder, and screw it to the card bracket panel—the card helps set the fine position of the motherboard before you tighten the motherboard mounting screws. You can see the SR440BX motherboard in the tray in Figure 37-16 with the 3Com network card installed as a pathfinder. We typically mount two cards, one at either end of the slots, to avoid misalignment due to pivoting around a single card. Once you've inserted the adapter cards and tightened up the card brackets, gently tighten all the motherboard mounting screws.

## Installing the processor

We recommend installing the processor on the motherboard after mounting the motherboard in the chassis. In the case of the In Win case, that recommendation translates to mounting the processor after attaching the motherboard to the tray, but before sliding the tray into the chassis.

Card Bracket    Motherboard    ATX I/O    Optional
Panel    Mounting Clip    Panel    Fan Mount    Power Supply

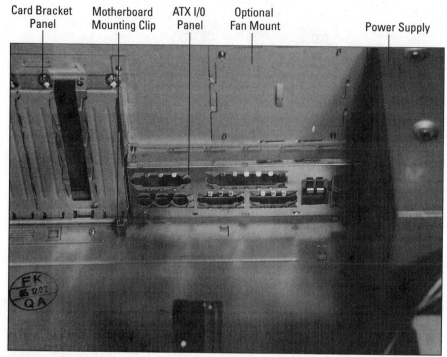

**Figure 37-15:** The last part of chassis assembly before you mount the motherboard is to fit the mounting clips or standoffs into the chassis holes matching the mounting holes in the motherboard.

There are several forms of bracket used to attach Slot 1–based Pentium II, Celeron, and Pentium III processors to motherboards (Celerons also come in a flat package using a flat socket). Figure 37-17 shows one end of a Pentium III processor; Figure 37-18 shows one of a pair of mounting brackets in place on the SR440BX motherboard. The other common form of Slot 1 processor package is a completely enclosed cartridge (usually with attached fan); Figure 37-19 shows the single bracket that attaches to the motherboard for those processors.

A Slot 1 processor should snap down into the connector on the motherboard. We've had the retention mechanism in Figure 37-18 make a very tight fit when secured to the motherboard, so we generally wait to push down the white anchor pins until the chip is completely in place in the socket.

Figure 37-20 shows the processor in place on the motherboard. Be careful that the processor is completely seated in the socket, and that the retention mechanism clips are securely anchored to the motherboard. None of these operations should require significant force; if you push too hard on the motherboard, you're likely to cause microscopic cracks in the wiring and destroy it.

**Figure 37-16:** Mount pathfinder cards in the motherboard before you tighten its mounting screws. (Copyright 1999 Barry and Marcia Press. Used with permission.)

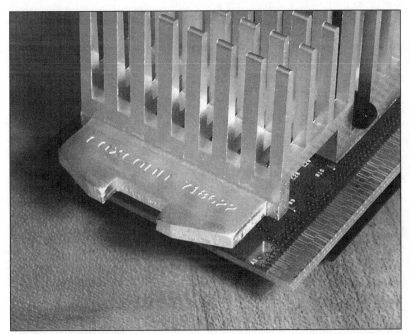

**Figure 37-17:** The end of the heat sink and Slot 1 processor module card edge fit into the retention mechanism on the motherboard. (Copyright 1999 Barry and Marcia Press. Used with permission.)

**Figure 37-18:** The retention mechanism for the processor in Figure 37-17 is a small clip at either end of the Slot 1 connector. You might want to delay pushing in the white anchor pins until after you insert the processor.

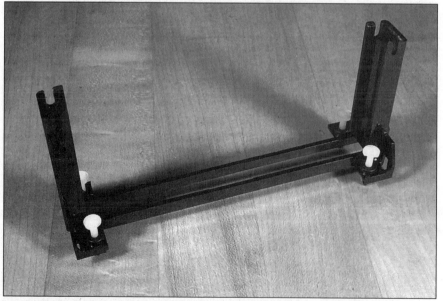

**Figure 37-19:** This one-piece retention mechanism fits Slot 1 processors with a completely enclosed cartridge.

**Figure 37-20:** This Pentium III is evenly and completely seated in the SR440BX motherboard. (Copyright 1999 Barry and Marcia Press. Used with permission.)

Figure 37-21 shows a motherboard with a Zero Insertion Force (ZIF) socket similar to those used with newer Celeron processors. Figure 37-22 shows the processor in the socket with a PC Power and Cooling CPU-Cool fan mounted on the chip. Follow the directions carefully for mounting the fan onto the chip. If your fan includes thermal grease (as does the CPU-Cool), be sure to use only a thin layer that completely covers the contact area between processor and fan without gaps. A thin layer helps pull heat from the chip; too thick a layer actually degrades thermal conduction.

You install a socketed processor by lifting the release arm on the ZIF socket and inserting the chip/fan assembly in the socket. Line up pin 1 on the chip and socket — if everything's lined up properly, the chip should drop into complete contact with the socket without force that would bend pins. After you've checked that the processor is seated, clamp it into the socket by moving the lever to its down and latched position.

## Inserting the memory

Your next step is to insert the memory strips. Read the motherboard documentation to see if there are restrictions on the order in which you populate memory sockets; some boards require you use specific banks if you don't put memory in every socket.

**Figure 37-21:** The Zero Insertion Force socket makes processor insertion and removal safe and reliable.

**Figure 37-22:** Route the power wire for the processor cooling fan so it doesn't interfere with the operation of the fan.

Figure 37-23 shows one end of the DIMM sockets on the SR440BX. The white latches are in the open position, ready for us to insert memory. The sockets themselves are keyed, so you can insert the memory only one way.

**Figure 37-23:** Open the latches fully before inserting DIMM strips into the memory socket. (Copyright 1999 Barry and Marcia Press. Used with permission.)

Once you insert the DIMM into the socket, you'll be able to close the latches completely as shown in Figure 37-24. If you don't get the memory in the socket properly, the BIOS won't see it when you boot the computer. The latches should fit all the way into the notches on the DIMM strips.

## Cabling in the power supply

Installing the processor and memory on the motherboard finishes the motherboard preparation, so the next step is to insert the motherboard tray into the chassis and wire the power supply to the connectors on the motherboard. Figure 37-25 shows the result after you plug in the power supply cable.

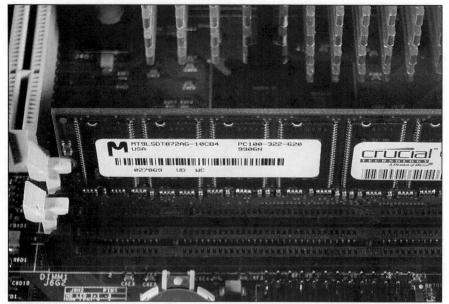

**Figure 37-24:** Latches on the DIMM socket fit completely into the notches on the DIMM strip. (Copyright 1999 Barry and Marcia Press. Used with permission.)

The ATX form factor makes the power supply cabling itself trivial—plug the cable from the power supply with the long rectangular multipin connector into the matching pins at the top of the motherboard. You have to orient the connector properly, but ATX eliminates issues of high-voltage wiring to a switch and orientation of multiple power connections. Keying on the connector should make it impossible to install the connector backward.

## Wiring the chassis to the motherboard connectors

The next step is to wire the chassis to the motherboard connectors. Figure 37-26 shows part of the motherboard, with callouts showing the front panel connectors. For the In Win chassis, you'll wire up the power switch, reset switch, hard disk activity LED, and power LED. You won't hook up the speaker because there's a speakerlike device mounted on the motherboard—there's no speaker connection available.

Figure 37-27 shows the motherboard installed in the chassis with the power supply and chassis wiring complete. The fan power connector next to the front panel connection isn't used here (it would normally connect to a fan on the processor), but you can see in the background that we've wired the auxiliary chassis fan to a similar fan power connector further back on the motherboard. The orientation doesn't matter for the switches on the front panel, but you need to get it right for the front panel power and LEDs. The white wire will usually be ground; check the motherboard documentation to see which pin on the board is ground and put the white wire there.

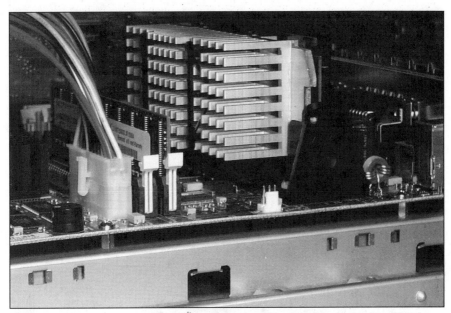

**Figure 37-25:** Keying on the ATX power supply cable should prevent installing it backward. (Copyright 1999 Barry and Marcia Press. Used with permission.)

**Figure 37-26:** The front panel connectors of the motherboard.

**Figure 37-27:** Connector orientation doesn't matter for front panel switches but is important for power and LED.

## Final Cabling

At this point, you've built up the chassis and drives, installed the processor and memory, mounted the motherboard in the chassis, and cabled the chassis to the motherboard. All that's left is to hook up all the ribbon cables and power connections. (This is also a good time to check that you provided power to the processor and auxiliary fans if you have them.)

Figure 37-28 is a closeup of the floppy disk and IDE connectors on the SR440BX motherboard. The shorter one on the bottom is the floppy disk connector; if you look to the left of the connectors you can see the labels on the motherboard, including indications of which are the primary and secondary IDE ports. Look below the floppy disk connector under the leftmost pin — you'll see a small number 1, which is the marker that tells you which end of the connector is pin 1. All three connectors will be turned the same way, with pin 1 on the left. (The jumper above the top IDE connector is the configuration jumper to put the BIOS in configuration mode on boot.)

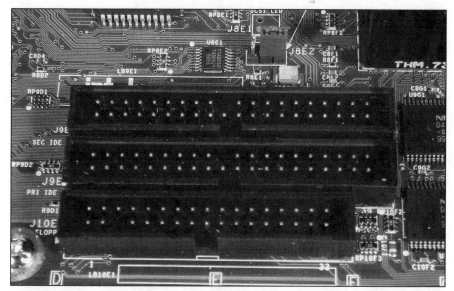

**Figure 37-28:** Look for a group of three ribbon cable connectors to support the floppy and IDE drives.

Figure 37-29 shows the completed power and data cable wiring. In the figure are three ribbon cables, two IDE cables, and the floppy drive cable. We used the primary IDE port for the hard disk and the secondary port for the DVD drive. That approach prevents the slower DVD drive from slowing down the relatively fast hard disk. Check to make sure you line up pin 1 of the ribbon cables everywhere, and that you orient the power connectors according to the keyed edges of the connectors.

If you run out of power connectors, use a "Y" connector to split one. Try to avoid long chains of splitters.

Check that the machine will boot into the BIOS and recognize the disk drives before putting on the cover. Once you complete these tasks, the rear of the computer looks like Figure 37-30.

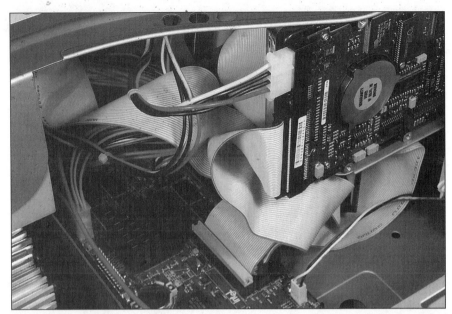

**Figure 37-29:** Installing the ribbon cables and power connections is the last internal assembly step in your computer.

## All those cable pinout tables are a waste of space

If you were keeping score, you noticed that every cable you needed to assemble the computer came with the components. The Intel SR440BX motherboard includes floppy drive and IDE cables; if you use a SCSI host adapter, it's going to come with cables, too. The power supply in the chassis includes enough power connections for the devices we installed.

If you *do* need additional cables, such as for a network adapter, you're most likely to be better off buying them either locally or from a company like Inmac. Purchased cables should be pretested and should include a strong backshell or molded boot on the connectors.

Making good, reliable cables is difficult. A lot of companies choose to subcontract cable manufacture for their own products rather than tool up to do them well. Unless you're making a lot of cables or have such unique requirements you can't order cables, you're probably much better off buying them.

So, you're not going to find endless pages of connector and cable pinout definitions in this book. There's much more valuable information we want to give you in these pages.

**Figure 37-30:** You have a full set of I/O connections and capabilities on the rear panel of the finished computer.

# Summary

✦ Assembling a computer in the right order makes things simpler and avoids damage to more fragile components. Assemble the chassis, drives, motherboard, processor, memory, and internal cables in that order.

✦ Depart from most computer users' standard practice — read the documentation for your hardware components carefully, looking for detailed steps you need to accomplish and for limitations on what you can do.

✦ Assembling a computer isn't really that hard — planning what you're going to build, a basic understanding of the components, and a careful approach to component selection are the keys to success.

✦    ✦    ✦

# Building a Desktop — Software Installation

✦ ✦ ✦ ✦

**In This Chapter**

Configuring the
BIOS, disk, and
DOS-level devices

Installing Windows
9x and applications

Tuning

✦ ✦ ✦ ✦

**Y**ou have seven steps to accomplish to install software on your desktop computer once it's built. You might use Windows 9x, Windows NT, or some variant of UNIX on a desktop machine. Here are the steps:

1. *BIOS configuration.* You need to set up the BIOS to reflect your hardware and how you've set it up.

2. *Disk partitioning and formatting.* You'll then decide how you want your available disk space divided and format it for the operating systems you'll use.

3. *Device drivers.* You'll probably be installing software from CD-ROM. If you're using UNIX or Windows NT, the installation boot floppies contain the CD-ROM drivers you need. If you're installing Windows 9x, you'll need to boot a version of DOS and install CD-ROM device drivers.

4. *OS installation.* After all those preliminaries, you can install the operating system.

5. *Application installation.* Once you have a working operating system and file system, you can install your applications.

6. *Tuning.* Once everything is installed and working, you can tweak settings to optimize performance and set up the computer the way you want it.

7. *Backup.* This should go without saying but rarely does. Once you have it right, make a backup as a snapshot of your initial configuration.

Let's look at these steps individually.

# BIOS Configuration

Assuming you're continuing on from the assembly steps in the last chapter, take a last look at all the adapters and cables in the computer, making sure everything is wired to the right point and oriented properly. Once you're convinced things are seated tightly, nothing's missing, and everything's aligned, hook up a keyboard, mouse, and display; plug in the computer and display; and power them on. We suggest you power the display on a minute before the computer so you'll see everything on the display output by the computer.

Listen carefully to the computer as it powers up. Normal sounds include the power supply and other fans, disks spinning up, and the starting beep from the speaker. Abnormal behavior includes the absence of those sounds or the presence of beep codes from the speaker. Follow the instructions in Chapter 36, "Diagnosis and Repair," if you don't get the normal sounds, or if you don't get a normal BIOS startup display on the monitor.

Once the BIOS shows on-screen, push the key that gets you into the BIOS setup screen. This is F2 for the Intel BIOS on the SR440BX motherboard we used in the last chapter, and it often is Del (Delete) for the AMI BIOS. We've seen systems where the BIOS entry keystroke was Control+Alt+S or some other combination. The documentation that came with the computer or motherboard should tell you the combination if it's not apparent on-screen.

The Intel SR440BX BIOS does more automatically than many BIOSes, leaving fewer manual settings. Once you enter the BIOS, the top-level menu has choices for Main, Advanced, Security, Power, Boot, and Exit. We'll describe the key BIOS settings using a notation like *Main ⇨ ECC Configuration* to indicate the path through the menus to the setting we're describing. Here are the most important settings:

✦ *Main ⇨ ECC Configuration*. You can tell the BIOS if it should configure the memory controller to expect ECC memory or not with this setting. Don't bother if you don't have ECC memory installed, although nothing bad should happen.

✦ *Main ⇨ L2 Cache ECC Support*. Independent of whether or not you have ECC memory, you can turn on error correcting codes for the data path between the L2 cache (which is inside the processor module for the Intel processors) and the processor itself.

✦ *Main ⇨ Processor Serial Number*. Intel programs a unique processor serial number (PSN) into every Pentium III processor. This BIOS option, which only shows up if a Pentium III processor is installed, lets you choose whether or not to enable access to the PSN. If you choose to disable the PSN, be sure to do so in the BIOS using this option. All other methods are less secure.

✦ *Advanced ➪ Plug & Play O/S.* Turn this on if you're running Windows 9*x* or Windows 2000. Turn it off for Windows NT 4, FreeBSD, or Linux. Eventually you can expect the UNIX systems to gain Plug and Play support, at which time (if you still have ISA cards) you could enable the option. The difference the option makes is to control whether the BIOS sets up resources for PnP cards or leaves the work for the operating system.

✦ *Advanced ➪ Peripheral Configuration.* Several items below this menu let you set up characteristics for the onboard serial and parallel ports. Also under here is *Legacy USB Support;* be sure to enable that option if you have a USB mouse or keyboard so that they'll work if you boot into the BIOS, an emergency recovery disk, or an operating system without USB support.

✦ *Advanced ➪ IDE Configuration.* Normally, you'll use the default, automatic settings to configure IDE drives. Use this menu to limit what the machine does in abnormal cases (such as if you're not using the secondary IDE port and need another device to be able to use IRQ 15).

✦ *Advanced ➪ Video Configuration ➪ AGP Aperture Size.* AGP video boards get an address space allocated to them; you can choose a 64MB or 256MB address space independent of the actual memory on the board. Some boards give better performance with one setting than another. You can run 3D video benchmarks to test; from other boards our experience has been that the TNT chip on the SR440BX works better with a 256MB aperture.

✦ *Power ➪ Power Management.* Mysterious instabilities in systems sometimes have problems with power management at their core. When you're trying to troubleshoot an instability and have run out of options, try turning off power management with this BIOS setting.

✦ *Boot ➪ Boot-time Diagnostic Screen.* By default, the SR440BX BIOS displays a graphic logo instead of the more useful BIOS startup messages, even though the F2 key still works to enter BIOS setup. Change this setting to *Enabled* to see the boot messages.

✦ *Boot ➪ First/Second/Third/Fourth Boot Device.* It's reasonably common for viruses to be passed from one machine to another by accidentally booting off an infected floppy disk. If you change the order of the boot devices, you can set up the machine to first try to boot off the hard disk, which eliminates the possibility of accidentally booting a floppy disk.

Removing the floppy disk from the boot sequence ensures that an infected floppy can't pass the virus to your machine by being booted, but it avoids issues created by turning on virus protection in the BIOS, which can interfere with proper operation of Windows setup. If you ever do have to boot from a floppy, just go into the BIOS and reenable the floppy into the boot sequence.

# Disk Partitioning and Formatting

You'll need to partition and format the hard disk before installing software. Some drives come already partitioned and formatted, but even in those cases it's likely you'll want to examine and reconsider the partition and format that came with the drive.

Disks have what are called low-level and high-level formats. All drives come with at least a low-level format in place, and you'll almost never need to replace the low-level format. Partitions divide the space on the drive into areas where you can place file systems. A partition corresponds to a drive letter for Windows 9*x* and, usually, Windows NT. UNIX doesn't use drive letters, because it collects file systems on various partitions into named branches rooted into a tree.

You're going to want multiple partitions if you're going to run multiple operating systems, because only one file system type can reside in a single partition. Partitioning has the disadvantage that it may isolate part of the disk from other operating systems that can't read the file system in the partition. Each operating system has a native file system — Windows 9*x* uses FAT (File Allocation Table) or FAT32; Windows NT prefers NTFS (NT File System) but can use FAT or (in Windows 2000) FAT32; and UNIX uses a file system dependent on whether it's based on Linux, on the Berkeley UNIX distribution, or on UNIX System V. UNIX systems can typically read FAT file systems, and depending on the version, they can read FAT32. You're typically better off running an operating system from its native file system format, and you may have to do so.

You have three ways to partition your disk: You can use the FDISK program that comes with DOS, Windows, or UNIX; you can use a third-party utility such as Partition Magic, or you can use partitioning tools unique to your operating system. Windows NT and UNIX, for instance, can create native partitions in empty space on your drive. To install Windows NT or UNIX onto an empty, unpartitioned disk, for example, it's sufficient to create standard boot floppies and run the standard installation process. The same is true for some OEM versions of Windows 9*x*. If you have the retail version of Windows 9*x* (but not the upgrade-only version), you'll need to run FDISK and FORMAT to partition and format the disk.

Let's look more closely at the file system options you have, because the file system you choose determines what kind of partition you need.

✦ *FAT* is the native file system format for DOS and all versions of Windows 9*x*, and it is used almost exclusively on floppy disks. There are versions of FAT using 12 and 16 bits per entry in the table; FAT is limited to 2GB in a partition. Essentially any Intel-architecture operating system should be able to read file systems in one of the FAT formats. FAT is relatively simple, but that simplicity carries the price that a FAT file system implements no on-the-fly protection against damage or corruption.

✦ *FAT32* is a newer version of FAT that expands the table entry size to 32 bits. FAT32 is supported by later versions of Windows 95 (service release 2, generally only available with complete machines), by Windows 98, and by Windows 2000. UNIX support for FAT32 is not universally available. FAT32 implements long, case-sensitive filenames, and partition sizes up to several terabytes. Unless you need the file system to be read by multiple operating systems, or you need to maintain compatibility with old versions of low-level disk utilities that haven't been upgraded to FAT32, FAT32 is superior in almost all ways to FAT. The only exception to that recommendation is that FAT32 file systems don't support compressing the entire contents of the drive.

✦ *HPFS* is a file system implemented in OS/2 and Windows NT designed to replace FAT. HPFS has been supplanted by NTFS as the Windows NT file system, so it should only be of interest if you're running OS/2.

✦ *NTFS* is the next generation past HPFS. Unlike FAT and FAT32, NTFS offers security through access lists and other features, file properties, and improved space allocation. Many of the features of Windows NT, and even more so of Windows 2000, are only available through NTFS.

✦ *UNIX* implements several file system versions depending on the UNIX base your system is derived from. All UNIX systems share characteristics of access control based on groupings into the file owner, the group the owner is part of, and the rest of the users.

When you are installing Windows 95 OEM SR2 or Windows 98, we recommend using FAT32 and a single partition unless you have specific requirements that make other layouts necessary. If you're building a new machine and aren't constrained by requirements from an Information Technology department, there's no reason to use any version of Windows 9*x* besides Windows 98 Second Edition.

# Device Drivers

Current-generation operating systems do a lot more than early versions of DOS or CP/M, but with this improved functionality comes the cost of many large files. Floppies are now impractical for installing operating systems — the installation media are now more than likely to be CD-ROM.

If you have only a CD-ROM in your hand, starting up a new machine can range from simple to complex.

✦ *Windows 9x.* You have to be able to access the file system on the CD-ROM to start the setup program. To do that, you have to load device drivers and other programs.

✦ *Windows NT.* Although the Windows NT 4.0 CD-ROM looks bootable to capable host adapters (such as the Adaptec AHA-2940UW, or most IDE motherboards), the boot doesn't work. In order to load Windows NT 4.0, you need to make a set of boot floppies. We'll show you how in the next few pages.

✦ *FreeBSD.* The FreeBSD CD-ROM included with this book is bootable into the installation process. You can also make a boot floppy by accessing the CD-ROM on any CD-ROM-capable computer and running the command *makeflp.*

We started the Windows 98 software installation process for the desktop machine by creating a boot disk on another machine itself running Windows 98. Use the Add/Remove Programs ➪ Startup Disk ➪ Create Disk function, because under Windows 98 the resulting floppy has most of the tools you'll need plus CD-ROM drivers for most systems.

## Windows NT boot floppies

If you're going to use Windows NT on your desktop machine and you received only a CD-ROM with Windows NT, you'll need to make bootable floppies. If you have another Windows-based computer with a working CD-ROM, you can use it to make the floppies; otherwise, you can use a Windows 98 startup disk to bring the computer up first under DOS.

The program you'll want to run to make boot floppies is winnt.exe, which is in the \I386 directory on the CD-ROM. Running it with the "/?" parameter tells you the options it takes:

```
I:>winnt /?
Installs Windows NT.

WINNT [/S[:]sourcepath] [/T[:]tempdrive] [/I[:]inffile]
      [/O[X]] [/X | [/F] [/C]] [/B] [/U[:scriptfile]]
      [/R[X]:directory] [/E:command]

/S[:]sourcepath
        Specifies the source location of Windows NT files.
        Must be a full path of the form x:\[path] or
        \\server\share[\path].
        The default is the current directory.
/T[:]tempdrive
        Specifies a drive to contain temporary setup files.
        If not specified, Setup will attempt to locate a drive
for you.
/I[:]inffile
        Specifies the filename (no path) of the setup
information file.
        The default is DOSNET.INF.
/OX     Create boot floppies for CD-ROM installation.
/X      Do not create the Setup boot floppies.
```

```
/F      Do not verify files as they are copied to the Setup boot
floppies.
/C      Skip free-space check on the Setup boot floppies you
provide.
/B      Floppyless operation (requires /s).
/U      Unattended operation and optional script file (requires
/s).
/R      Specifies optional directory to be installed.
/RX     Specifies optional directory to be copied.
/E      Specifies command to be executed at the end of GUI
setup.

To get help one screen at a time, use WINNT /? | MORE
```

The option you want is "/OX" to create boot floppies. Use this option rather than
the "/B" option, because the boot floppies are also part of what you'll need for
emergency recovery of a failed Windows NT system. You'll need three formatted,
blank, high-density floppy disks to create the boot floppies, and a fourth later on for
the emergency recovery disk. The command to create boot floppies is therefore:

```
winnt /OX
```

The program writes the necessary files onto the boot floppies, starting with disk
number three and working backward to disk number one. The Windows NT setup
program on the floppies contains the drivers needed to access your CD-ROM.

This process applies to both Windows NT Workstation and Windows NT Server.
We'll look at the details of installing Windows NT Server later when we install
software on the server computer in Chapter 40, "Building a Server—Software
Installation. Installing a Windows NT workstation is very similar, so we haven't
covered it further in this chapter.

## FreeBSD

Systems that support bootable ("El Torito") format CD-ROMs should require no
boot floppy for the FreeBSD CD-ROM included with this book, although you may
have to enable boot from the CD-ROM in a SCSI adapter BIOS. For the Intel SR440BX
motherboard, the default boot device order (floppy, hard disk, CD-ROM) should
cause a CD-ROM boot if the hard disk has no partition or format applied and there's
nothing in the floppy drive.

If you do need a bootable floppy, make one on any DOS or Windows machine—put
a formatted, blank, high-density floppy disk in the floppy drive and run the
makeflp.bat file in the root of the CD-ROM. While you have the CD-ROM handy, be
sure to run the view.exe program and take a look at the information in the different
text files on the disk.

The details for installing FreeBSD UNIX are also covered in Chapter 40, "Building a
Server—Software Installation."

# OS Installation

At this point, your computer should be capable of booting to DOS, either from a floppy disk or the hard disk, and should be able to access the CD-ROM. If you're running Windows 9x, you should install any required DOS-level software for your video card at this point. The newest cards don't require this with Windows 98, but some cards still in widespread use require that you configure the refresh rates versus screen resolution using a file on disk and a command in the autoexec.bat file. Installing the video card software and configuring the card to match the monitor helps avoid issues during Windows installation. See Chapter 18, "Video Adapters," for how to do the software configuration.

Those capabilities are enough to prepare for installing Windows 98. Now all you need to do is to put the CD-ROM in the drive, switch to that drive letter, and run setup.exe. Windows 98 installation is nearly automatic — just follow the prompts. We choose the Custom installation type so we can explicitly choose which components we want installed, but you can equally well choose a Typical installation and change what's installed after setup completes.

The Windows setup software will reboot the computer one or more times; once setup is completely done, reboot the computer again. That step ensures that your computer is in its permanent configuration, with no leftovers from setup running.

**Tip**    If you have an IDE CD-ROM, be careful to disable the CD-ROM device drivers in the config.sys file after Windows installation completes. We've seen machines where the CD-ROM was unstable unless we disabled the DOS-level device driver, and the driver shouldn't be necessary once Windows is running. You can disable the driver by putting REM in front of the line in the config.sys file. For example, this line loads the device driver for an IDE CD-ROM on one of the machines we use:

```
DEVICEHIGH=C:\CDROM\GSCDROM.SYS /D:MSCD000 /v
```

Adding REM at the front (case doesn't matter here) disables the line:

```
rem DEVICEHIGH=C:\CDROM\GSCDROM.SYS /D:MSCD000 /v
```

Now go ahead and install into Windows any required manufacturer's drivers. For the desktop machine we built in the previous chapter, the drivers list includes ones on a CD-ROM Intel supplies with the SR440BX motherboard for the nVidia TNT video adapter and Creative Labs sound, along with the Kodak DVC 323 USB drivers and the monitoring software for the APC UPS.

# Application Installation

Once Windows is up and stable, you can go ahead and install applications, the first of which should be a good antivirus program. We use VirusScan from Network Associates (née McAfee). The complete default installation of VirusScan is what you want, because it will scan the drive for boot-sector viruses when the machine starts and install a virus shield that watches for infections and suspicious activity while the computer runs. By disabling floppy disk boots in the BIOS, using the McAfee software, and enabling the macro virus protection in the Microsoft Office programs, we've been able to avoid all virus infections on any of our machines to this point.

We usually let programs install to their default directories unless that's \windows, in which case we force the installation elsewhere. We strongly recommend that you set up your applications (or discipline yourself while you work) so that your data files are *not* in the same directory as the application, because when you go to upgrade or uninstall a program, you may find that having the files intermixed with the application makes it hard to figure out which files are yours and which are part of the program.

Instead, we organize folders by project and intermix data files of all types in the folder for the project they're part of. We put programs and data on the same disk drive, and we use the selection features of backup programs when we want to exclude certain items (such as the cache for World Wide Web browsers).

# Tuning

The first thing to do once you have the bulk of your software installed is to defragment the disk. You can access this function as Start ➪ Programs ➪ Accessories ➪ System Tools ➪ Disk Defragmenter. Windows will likely complain that the disk doesn't need to be defragmented, but force it to run anyway. If you look at the detailed display from the disk defragmenter program while it runs, you'll see that there's a lot of empty space interspersed with your files. Although Windows is telling you that the files themselves are not fragmented, which is probably true, it isn't looking at how fragmented free disk space is. By running the defragmenter now, you close up that empty space and help keep the work you do later from fragmenting.

## BIOS-level tuning

For most purposes, setting your BIOS to the "optimal" setting (if there is one) is all you need to do for good performance. We described some specific BIOS settings for the SR440BX earlier in this chapter, and we'll cover some others in Chapter 401, "Building a Server—Software Installation." If you have problems with the optimal configuration, revert to a more conservative one (sometimes called "fail safe") and one by one make the changes between that and optimal. When you find one that causes problems, leave it in the fail-safe setting.

## DOS-level tuning

The next step is to tune the boot-time configuration of the machine. Although most computers can do without this, you can gain more memory in DOS windows and the ability to personalize some aspects of the machine. Let's start with the config.sys file. Here's a tuned version usable on nearly all systems:

### config.sys

```
files = 99
dos=high,umb

device=C:\WINDOWS\himem.sys /testmem:on
device=C:\WINDOWS\emm386.exe noems
```

There are three effects of including these lines in config.sys:

✦ *(Slightly) improved memory self testing.* The memory check in himem.sys is somewhat better than that in the BIOS Power On Self Test. It delays the boot somewhat, and if you're in a hurry it may not be worthwhile.

✦ *More memory in DOS windows.* Loading himem.sys and emm386.exe together adds software to control the allocation of memory between 640KB and 1MB. Once you have those memory managers, you can load DOS components high (dos=high,umb for example), saving DOS memory in the region from 0 to 640KB. More commands that can load things high can be found in the Windows 9*x* Resource Kits.

The *noems* parameter on the line that loads emm386.exe says that we're not going to run programs using the old Expanded Memory Specification, so Windows doesn't need to reserve addresses in the area from 640KB to 1MB. Those addresses can therefore be used for other purposes, increasing the benefit of loading DOS components high.

✦ *More files accessible from DOS programs.* The default limits in Windows for the number of files that can be open at once might be too small. The line

```
files = 99
```

increases that number.

If you're not short of memory for large DOS applications, you can probably dispense with all of this and have no config.sys file whatsoever. Windows loads himem.sys whether you say to or not; the real change is the loading of emm386.exe.

The autoexec.bat file is next, but most of what you'll put in there is for customization and not configuration purposes.

### autoexec.bat

Of the lines in the autoexec.bat file that follows, none actually change the configuration of the system. The commands in the file are for virus protection or for

setting up environment variables used by programs. Here's a complete
autoexec.bat for the desktop system we built in the previous chapter:

```
@echo off

C:\PROGRA~1\NETWOR~1\MCAFEE~1\SCAN.EXE C:\
@IF ERRORLEVEL 1 PAUSE

path C:\WINDOWS;C:\WINDOWS\COMMAND;c:\bin
SET BLASTER=A220 I7 D1 T2
set dircmd=/o:gen /l /p
SET SNDSCAPE=C:\WINDOWS
set TEMP=C:\TEMP
set tmp=%temp%
set tz=MST7MDT
set winpmt=[Windows 98] $d $t $p$_$n:$z$g
prompt $d $t $p$_$n:$z$g
```

Here's what the lines in the file do:

✦ *Run silently.* It's difficult to separate legitimate program messages and
   errors from the text of the commands as they scroll by. We use the @echo
   off command to suppress the useless command text. You can remark that
   line out if you need to see where an error is happening.

✦ *Run antivirus checks.* The next two lines run the Network Associates (McAfee)
   DOS-level antivirus checks and pause the boot sequence if a problem shows
   up. The installation program puts these lines in front of the @echo off line;
   you can move them safely to the position shown.

✦ *Set environment variables.* The rest of the file initializes environment variables
   that personalize the system.

   • path — This controls where Windows will look for programs. We've
     added a directory (c:\bin) in which we keep some DOS utilities to the
     two defaults Windows sets up.

   • BLASTER — This sets up the parameters for the Creative Labs audio on
     the SR440BX motherboard. The audio driver installation program
     added this and the SNDSCAPE lines automatically. If you need this
     added by hand for some reason, you can open a DOS window, run the
     set command with no parameters, and get the necessary BLASTER
     settings from there.

   • dircmd — You can set default parameters for the dir DOS command by
     setting them into the dircmd environment variable. The value we've set
     here sorts the listing by directory, file type, and filename; forces all
     output to lowercase; and pauses when the screen is full.

- TEMP and TMP — The *temp* directory is where Windows and applications put temporary files. By default, Windows will make the temporary directory \windows\temp; we typically move it to a root-level directory to make it easier to get to. We also tend to keep it on the disk with the most free space if the machine has more than one disk.

  The tmp variable defines the temporary file directory for some programs that don't happen to use the temp variable. The form of the command you see in the example causes tmp to be the same as whatever we set up for temp.

- tz — the tz variable defines the time zone and how some programs display the time zone abbreviation. The first three letters are the abbreviation without daylight saving; the last three are with daylight saving. The number seems to be ignored by Windows in favor of the setting you make through the control panel. The three-letter strings preserve the case you use.

- prompt and winpmt — The prompt variable, as with DOS, controls the prompt you get at the DOS command line. It can be confusing to work in a DOS window that you've made full-screen (as opposed to booting to DOS outside of Windows), because there are no indications that Windows is active behind the screen. If you set a different prompt string into the winpmt variable (as in this example), it gets used in DOS windows, providing the visual cue you need.

# Windows 9*x* tuning

The last step is to tune settings in Windows 9*x* itself. Everything you need to do is in the System applet within the control panel.

## Device Manager tab

Select the Device Manager tab in the System applet, and look for yellow or red icons that indicate problems. If you find problems, check under the properties of that device for clues as to what the problem is and what corrective action you need to take. Devices you find shown as unknown indicate that you probably need to install a manufacturer-supplied driver.

Check any SCSI devices, and if necessary enable synchronous operation and disconnection. You may have to force the drive letter for your CD-ROM if it didn't come up on the letter you want.

For each of your devices, check the manufacturer's Web site (look in the contact list — Appendix B or the CD-ROM with the book) for more current drivers for your operating system. You'll want to do that periodically, but be sure to evaluate new drivers before putting them on machines used for productive work.

### Performance tab

Your last tuning stop is the Performance tab in the System applet. The last entry under *Performance status* should say your system is configured for optimal performance; most specifically, the display should show the right amount of memory, and 32-bit operation for the file system and virtual memory. If you have PC Card or Disk Compression drivers installed, they should show 32-bit operation too. Check in Windows Help or the Windows 9x Resource Kit for help if these characteristics aren't right.

Next, check the File System option. You can set the machine as a desktop computer, mobile or docking system, or network server, which affects how the disk cache is used by Windows. You can also use the read-ahead slider to tune how aggressively you want Windows to anticipate further sequential file reads.

Select the CD-ROM tab, and set the access pattern to correspond to your CD-ROM speed. If you have a relatively large amount of memory, push the supplemental cache size slider to the right to make the cache as big as possible.

Select the Graphics option next, and be sure the hardware acceleration slider is all the way to the right. You would only move it to the left if you're having video or mouse problems.

The Virtual Memory tab lets you exercise some finer control over the location and size of the swap file than what Windows does automatically. Unless you want to move the location, you're best off leaving the settings alone.

## Backup

Once the machine is up, running, and tuned, back it up. Completely. Brand new machines aren't always as stable as you'd like — having a complete backup can make life simpler if you need to retrieve a corrupted file or return to the starting configuration.

Backup — just do it.

# Summary

✦ As with all other computer-related work, a planned methodical approach works best.

✦ Remember to install manufacturer's DOS drivers before Windows, and their Windows drivers afterward. Check the Internet to be sure the ones delivered with the device are the latest ones.

✦ When things go wrong, use the basic troubleshooting pattern — simplify and isolate.

✦      ✦      ✦

# Building a Server – Hardware

◆ ◆ ◆ ◆

**In This Chapter**

Analyzing what
you need

Designing for data
availability

Mechanical and
electrical assembly

◆ ◆ ◆ ◆

**A**s we said in Chapter 37, "Building a Clone—Hardware,"
the first step in building a computer from components—
this time a server—is planning what you'll put in the machine.
In this chapter, we'll analyze the entire process, building two
machines—one using a single Pentium III processor on a
conventional motherboard, and the other using two Pentium II
Xeon processors on an Intel C440GX+ server board. In the
process, you'll see how to assemble the components for both
machines. We'll install Windows 2000 Server and FreeBSD
software on the C440GX+ system in the next chapter.

## Analysis

Your server configuration analysis starts with requirements,
from which you can move to component and system-level
decisions. We targeted the machine as a network and Internet
server that would provide file archives for a local area
network and Web and FTP services to the Internet. More
specifically, the machine had to meet these requirements:

    ◆ *File storage and archives.* The workgroup we designed
      the machine to support has a near-term requirement for
      an additional 8GB of storage, with growth likely on a
      continuing basis. The projects stored on the server
      require online access—even for completed projects—
      so tape archive wasn't an option.

    ◆ *High-capacity removable storage for backup and data
      transfer.* The projects developed on the machine have to
      be shipped to customers when complete. Files for the
      typical project are 200 to 500MB, typically shipped
      on CD-ROM.

✦ *Twenty-four hour operation and high data availability.* The work the machine supports (and access from the Internet) happens on a 24-hour basis. It's only practical to back up the machine late at night, so measures to ensure high data availability were desirable.

✦ *Room for expansion.* The peripherals on the machine from the beginning had to include tape, CD-ROM or DVD, CD-ROM writer, and a lot of disk. Together, those requirements imply room in the case for a lot of equipment and for a large motherboard.

✦ *Network access.* We planned to connect the machine to a 100 Mbps LAN. Internet access would be across the LAN to a router.

✦ *Dial-up access.* The workgroup typically has someone traveling once or twice a month. We wanted to provide dial-up access to files, printers, and e-mail, but the load is light enough that a single analog modem line tied directly to the server is adequate.

At a high level, these requirements are typical of a midrange server used to run processing applications as well as provide file access. The machines we're going to build meeting these requirements have the parts lists shown in Table 39-1.

## Table 39-1
## The Server Parts Lists

| Component | Pentium III System Manufacturer and Model | Dual Xeon System Manufacturer and Model |
|---|---|---|
| CD-ROM / DVD | Toshiba SD-M1201 4.8X SCSI | Toshiba XM-6401B 40X SCSI |
| CD-RW recorder | Yamaha CRW4416S SCSI | |
| Chassis | YY YY-0210B Cube Mini-Server (ATX, 300 W Power Supply) | YY YY-0420 Server Cube (ATX, Dual 300 W Power Supplies) |
| Disk | Seagate ST118273LW (18.2GB Ultra2 Wide SCSI) | Seagate ST118273LW (18.2GB Ultra2 Wide SCSI) |
| Floppy | Teac 3 ½ inch | Teac 3 ½ inch |
| Keyboard | Microsoft Natural Keyboard | Microsoft Natural Keyboard |
| Memory | Crucial 128MB ECC PC100 (CT16M72S4D8E) | Crucial 128MB ECC PC100 (CT16M72S4D8E) |
| Modem | U.S. Robotics Courier V. Everything External | U.S. Robotics Courier V.Everything External |
| Monitor | Hitachi SuperScan Elite 641 | Hitachi SuperScan Elite 641 |
| Motherboard | Intel SE440BX-2 1 AGP, 3 PCI, 1 PCI/ISA slots | Intel C440GX + 6 PCI (2 66 MHz, 1 64 bit) |
| Mouse | Microsoft Intellimouse | Microsoft Intellimouse |

| Component | Pentium III System Manufacturer and Model | Dual Xeon System Manufacturer and Model |
|---|---|---|
| Network | 3Com Fast EtherLink XL 10/100 PCI | (on motherboard) |
| Processors | Intel 600 MHz Pentium III | Two 400 MHz Pentium II Xeon 1,024KB L2 Cache |
| Processor fans | (included with processor) | PC Power and Cooling Dual CPU-Cool X2 |
| SCSI cables | (supplied with host adapter) | Granite Digital SCSI Vue Gold Olefin |
| SCSI host adapter (boot) | Adaptec AHA-2940U2W (Ultra2 Wide) | (on motherboard) |
| Tape | Seagate Scorpion 24 DAT | Seagate Scorpion 24 DAT |
| Uninterruptible power supply | APC SmartUPS 1400 | APC SmartUPS 1400 |
| Video adapter | ATI Rage Fury | (on motherboard) |

We had slightly different objectives for the two columns in Table 39-1. For the Pentium III-based system, we compromised reliability somewhat but included high-performance multimedia components. For the dual Xeon system, we focused on high reliability using dual power supplies and a server board designed with added features for reliability. Based on those objectives and the overall system requirements, here's why we chose the components in Table 39-1:

✦ *Power supply, chassis, and motherboard.* In the smaller server, we chose a single 300 W supply to reduce cost. We specified dual redundant 300 W power supplies as the foundation for reliable operation, part of a strategy to meet the data availability requirement. Because the total power requirement of the machine will be well under 300 watts, we're assured that even if one supply of the dual pair fails, the machine can run without interruption.

Both boards use the now-universal ATX form factor. The YY cases are not desktop sized, but their cube shapes tend to put a lot of working space in a small package.

✦ *Motherboard.* The motherboard choices are really driven by reliability and expansion capabilities. The C440GX+ has ports for emergency remote server management and a wealth of other features that make it suitable for 24-hour-a-day, 7-day-a-week operation with fast, efficient system recovery. The SE440BX-2 has (with the Pentium III) better multimedia and compression performance. You might choose the Pentium III over the Pentium II Xeon processor if you were running a site serving real time streaming audio or video and had software optimized to exploit the Pentium III Streaming Software Extensions (as does RealNetworks RealPlayer). Both boards support ECC memory and USB.

The SE440BX-2 motherboard is a little skimpy on PCI slots — for the best expansion options we'd recommend the C440GX+ board.

✦ *Memory*. We wanted both performance and reliable operation from memory, so we picked 128MB ECC SDRAMs. The choice of 128MB as the memory size was something of a compromise we made, assuming the server would not be hosting a large-scale Web site nor a database driving the Internet server. If the Internet server load on the machine were to go up, we'd want at least 256MB, and maybe up toward 1GB if the Web or database load went high enough.

✦ *Disks and host adapters*. Network server performance benefits from high disk transfer rates and low access times. We achieved that plus high capacity with the 18.2GB Seagate drive. The requirement for a relatively large, expandable file system led us to choose SCSI disks and host adapters. An Adaptec AHA-2940U2W was a straightforward choice for the Pentium II system's host adapter; the Xeon system provides the SCSI adapter on the motherboard.

✦ *Video*. Servers deployed as hands-off systems can make do with most any reliable PCI video card, as on the C440GX+. For the Pentium III system, though, we chose the high-performance ATI Rage Fury to provide good video performance and DVD decode in a single slot.

✦ *CD-ROM writer*. There's typically little or no time to spare when disks have to be burned, so it's very inconvenient to have to defragment the disk, make a master image, and write. We picked the Yamaha CRW4416S because it's a packet CD-RW writer, not subject to buffer underruns.

✦ *Tape*. Backup tapes are the last line of defense in the data availability strategy for this machine (overall, that strategy includes a UPS, redundant power supply, RAID disk, and tape). Because of the relatively large file systems we expected on the computer, the on-the-fly verification a DAT drive gives was important — it eliminates the second pass over the tape that doubles the backup time. We didn't think the cost of DLT or AIT tape was warranted, but a 24GB (12GB native) drive should let us do backups on a single tape.

As with the desktop machine in the previous chapter, we chose the manufacturers and models for all the components based on reliable past experience and (in the case of the mouse and keyboard) personal preference of the machine's user.

# Preliminary Mechanical Assembly

Assembling the server is more complex than assembling the desktop machine, but only because there's more to do. None of the individual steps are more difficult. As with the desktop, the first step is to do the gross mechanical assembly, mounting the disk drives into the chassis.

# Mounting internal disk drives

The YY server cubes provide a place for drive mounting well inside the case in addition to the external drive bays. We put the hard drive in one of the bays at the back where the chassis can accommodate eight drives (see Figure 39-1). Installing drives in these bays requires taking out the individual mounting brackets. The modules come installed in the case, but with them in place you can't reach to screw the far side of the drive bay frame.

**Figure 39-1:** Installing drives into the internal drive bays requires removing the brackets, so try to get the drive configuration right before installing.

The relative difficulty of installing and removing drives from the internal bays makes it all the more important that you configure the drives properly before you install them. The Seagate drive, because it uses LVD signaling, requires separate termination at the end of the LVD cable, so the only critical configuration item on the drive was the SCSI ID.

Figure 39-2 shows the drive installed into one of the mounting brackets. You want to preserve room to work in the chassis, so mount the drive as far toward the back of the bracket as possible.

**Figure 39-2:** Mount drives toward the back of the brackets so they protrude as little as possible into the chassis.

Figure 39-3 shows the drive/bracket assembly mounted back into the chassis. The drive extends only a little past the edge of the power supply above it, minimizing the space required in the chassis. We mounted the drive one drive space away from the power supply to reduce the heat concentrated in one place; we'd similarly space drives away from each other until we had so many that closer positioning became mandatory.

## Mounting external peripherals

The next steps in assembling the server are to mount the drives in the external bays at the front of the chassis. All the external bays are 5¼-inch spaces; there are six half-height horizontal bays on the right side of the chassis.

The case requires the floppy drive go on the top; you'll want to determine the top-to-bottom ordering of devices in the external bays based on wiring and usage. You want to keep drives on the same SCSI or IDE cable together in a block to avoid tangling the cables up, and you have to position the block to ensure the cable can reach to the connector on the motherboard. Those considerations led us to an ordering in which we put the floppy on top, then the DVD drive, then the SCSI CD-RW drive and DAT drive together as a group.

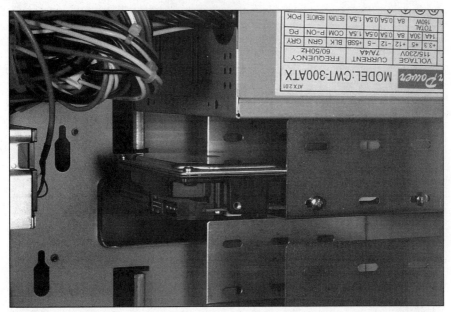

**Figure 39-3:** Stack drives with clearance away from other heat-generating items if you can.

The worst offenders for cable length problems are the cables from IDE drives to the PCI IDE port on the motherboard. You can't have more than 18 inches (sometimes less), so you may have a restricted set of choices for where to put the disks.

We installed the floppy drive first and then worked on down. We worked top to bottom so that if we dropped parts they'd fall to the bottom of the chassis instead of falling into another drive.

Putting the 3½-inch drive into one of the 5¼-inch bays requires an adapter bracket different from that for hard disks because the bracket has to provide an expansion of the floppy drive's front bezel. Figure 39-4 shows the components of the assembly — the floppy itself is centered in the outer bezel, which in turn screws to the rails that affix the assembly to the chassis itself. We used a black bracket and floppy bezel to match the black server case.

Assemble the drive and bracket by snapping the bezel into the bracket, and then mounting the drive into the bracket. Once you've completed the subassembly, install it into the chassis as shown in Figure 39-5. The slide rails are offset back from the front of the floppy a short distance to accommodate the space needed for the chassis front panel.

**Figure 39-4:** You wrap a mounting bracket around a 3½-inch floppy to install it into a 5¼-inch bay.

**Figure 39-5:** The completed drive and bracket assembly mounts to the chassis with an offset to fit the front panel.

Figure 39-6 shows the Toshiba DVD drive being mounted below the floppy drive. You use the same mounting scheme—screw slide rails to the side of the drive and then affix the assembly to the chassis. As with the floppy drive, you need to leave an offset to space the front of the drive out to the chassis front panel.

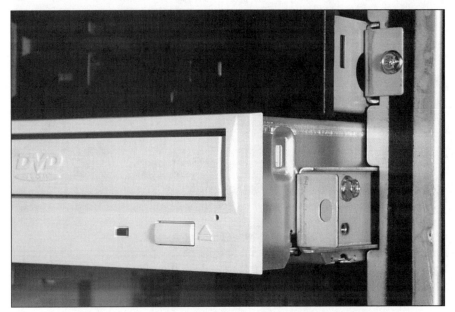

**Figure 39-6:** Slide rails let you mount drives in the case from the front.

Mounting the rest of the drives at the front of the chassis is a repeat of the floppy drive and DVD process. Some drives, such as the Seagate DAT drive we used, come with 5¼-inch mounting brackets installed and need only the mounting rails screwed on. Some (such as the CD-RW) are already 5¼ inches wide. Others are 3-inch devices like the floppy drive and need mounting brackets.

There are no configuration settings on the floppy drive, but the other devices are all likely to require setup before mounting. Figure 39-7 shows the configuration switches for the Seagate DAT drive, which are located on the bottom of the unit. Seagate pastes a label on the bottom that tells you the function of each switch, so even if you've misplaced the documentation that came with the drive you can still do what you need to. (Alternatively, manufacturers commonly put switch and jumper settings on their Web sites—it really cuts down on support calls.)

DIP Switch                    Configuration
Settings Key                  DIP Switches

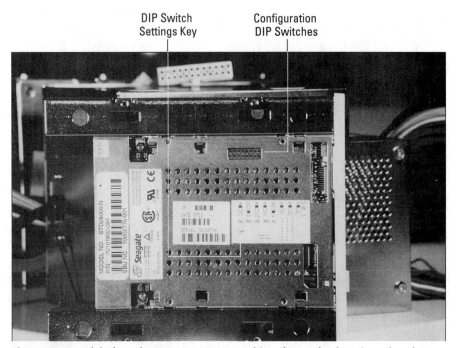

**Figure 39-7:** A label on the Seagate DAT tape drive shows the function of each configuration switch.

We let the tape drive be the narrow SCSI cable terminator, using its active termination, and set the drive for SCSI ID 4. The choice of ID was arbitrary, with the proviso that we needed to reserve ID 0 for the hard disk that's the boot drive for the system. We set the CD-RW for ID 5.

When you're done mounting drives, fill the remaining space on the front of the chassis with covers or fans. Figure 39-8 shows an auxiliary fan to cover two external drive bays on the YY chassis.

## Assigning front panel indicators

Figure 39-9 shows the front panel indicators and controls for the server cube. Listed left to right, the manufacturer's suggestions for the four LEDs on top are as indicators for tape, COM1:, turbo, and power. The four LEDs on the bottom are recommended for disks 1 through 4. These recommendations don't make a lot of sense in practice because few systems provide activity circuits for tape or serial ports, current generation motherboards don't indicate high or low processor speed (many don't even support switching), and few systems have four separate disk I/O channels. Fortunately, you can use all the LEDs for any purpose you want, although we do recommend using the power LED for that purpose so you'll know when the system is on.

**Figure 39-8:** Be sure to get enough air flow through your chassis to guarantee good component cooling.

**Figure 39-9:** The front panel indicators and controls for the server cube.

In the system we built, we used the turbo LED for the IDE DVD drive and the COM1: LED for the SCSI disk interface. Those choices grouped all the active LEDs in one place.

The switches at the right of Figure 39-9 are (left to right) labeled keyboard lock, reset, and standby. Because ATX motherboards require a momentary contact to turn power on or off, and because we'd not want to put a server into standby, we used the standby switch for system power.

## Installing the motherboard

The next step is to mount the motherboard. Figure 39-10 shows the key structures on the C440GX+ server board. Unlike the other motherboards shown in this book, the C440GX+ uses socketed voltage regulator modules (VRMs) in addition to voltage regulators mounted directly on the motherboard.

**Figure 39-10:** The C440GX+ motherboard uses a full-size ATX form factor to hold dual Pentium II or III Xeon processors, four banks of memory, six PCI slots, and one ISA slot. (Copyright 1999 Barry and Marcia Press. Used with permission.)

Attach the processor mounting brackets before you install the motherboard. Figure 39-11 shows where the brackets go on the SE440BX-2 motherboard, using the shorter brackets appropriate for the Pentium III. The top image shows the mount point on the motherboard; the bottom shows one of the two brackets in place. We'll show how the Xeon processors mount later in this chapter. The Xeon processors are significantly larger than conventional Pentium II and III processors, with a more complex mounting scheme.

**Figure 39-11:** Processor mounting brackets clip or screw onto the motherboard to anchor the processor.

The motherboard installs in the left cavity of the YY cube chassis. Figure 39-12 shows the interior of the chassis with two of the motherboard mounting studs in place. There are two kinds of mounting holes on the motherboard, ones with a metal ring on the circuit board, and ones without. You can use either nylon standoffs or metal standoffs and screws on the ones with the metal ring, but you can use only nylon standoffs on the others. Use metal studs everywhere you can instead of plastic standoffs, but above all make sure that all parts of the board are well supported.

**Figure 39-12:** Use metal mounting studs for the motherboard everywhere you can to improve signal grounding.

You might want to use a drop of Loctite or cyanoacrylate-type glue on the metal standoffs once they're gently tightened in place to keep them from ever coming out. The threaded stem on the standoffs isn't so strong that it will withstand great force, which means that you can't tighten them so much that they'll never unscrew. That limitation can lead to the standoff coming out rather than the screw through the motherboard when you're trying to remove the motherboard. The glue prevents this problem.

Nylon standoffs sit in the bottom of elongated holes as you position the motherboard. Snap the standoffs through the motherboard, and then gently slide the motherboard upward until it's secured by the top edge retainers. You may have to wiggle the standoffs slightly to maneuver them upward in their holes. When the motherboard is fully engaged into the retainers, you should be able to see the metal standoffs through the corresponding holes in the motherboard. Hold the motherboard in place with screws put loosely into the standoffs, and then (as we did for the desktop motherboard assembly) use a pair of pathfinder adapter cards to determine the final position. Tighten the screws, although not so tight as to crack the motherboard, and mounting is complete.

## Wiring the chassis to the motherboard

The next step is to plug in the power connections, and then attach the external chassis connections. Follow the instructions in Chapter 37 to do this—it's essentially the same as for the desktop machine. In addition to the power connectors for disk drives, there is a 20-pin ATX power connector coming out of the power supply. The connector is polarized, so you can insert it in the motherboard only one way.

## Installing the processors, processor fans, and memory

If your processor(s) came without cooling fans or heat sinks attached, the next step is to assemble those pieces together. Figure 39-13 shows the Pentium III processor we used, which came with a large heat sink attached.

**Figure 39-13:** The large heat sink on this Pentium III processor came as part of an integrated processor assembly.

Once the processor and cooling fan or heat sink are together, snap the assembly into the motherboard. Figure 39-14 shows the Pentium III processor in place on the SE440BX-2.

**Figure 39-14:** The Pentium III processor snaps into the retaining brackets on the SE440BX-2 motherboard. (Copyright 1999 Barry and Marcia Press. Used with permission.)

Processor assembly and installation are more complex for the Pentium II Xeon processors we used with the C440GX+ server board. Assembly starts by mounting the cooling fans on the processors. The PC Power and Cooling fans we used are a dual ball bearing fan assembly in a large heat sink, as shown mounted on the processor in Figure 39-15. You use a thin layer of thermal grease on the machined area of the fan/heat sink that contacts the processor, leaving no gaps and no blobs. PC Power and Cooling specifies using 6-32 × 3/8-inch screws to attach the cooling assembly to the processor module.

The C440GX+ server board can mount two Xeon processors, using brackets at either end of the processor pair to lock the processor modules in position. The brackets (supplied in the Intel chassis integrators' kit) bolt through the motherboard to mounts on the chassis because the motherboard itself isn't strong enough to carry the structural load without cracking. Because of that, you'll install the brackets after the motherboard is mounted in the chassis, not before as with the Pentium III.

**Figure 39-15:** The combined fan/heat sink assembly bolts to the Pentium II Xeon processor modules. (Copyright 1999 Barry and Marcia Press. Used with permission.)

Figure 39-16 shows the first part of the buildup, with the two end brackets in place and one processor in position. We've shown the processor without fan and heat sink in the photograph so that the bracket details would be apparent. Be careful to install the end bracket with the fans at the end of the processor modules — the cooling fans and heat sinks have a preferred direction of air flow (toward the left in Figure 39-15) that you must establish with the end bracket fans.

The processor nearest the edge of the motherboard is the primary system processor. If you're building a uniprocessor system (you'd do this if you expected to upgrade later), install the terminator board from the Intel chassis integrators' kit in the other processor slot, as shown in Figure 39-17. If you install two processors, as we did, you'll get the result shown in Figure 39-18 (fans and heat sinks still omitted). Clips and screws anchor the processors to the top of the end brackets.

**Figure 39-16:** Be sure the end bracket cooling fans create airflow in the direction required by the processor module cooling fans.

**Figure 39-17:** A terminator card in the secondary processor slot is required for proper operation of the multiprocessor bus.

**Figure 39-18:** Be sure to follow the chassis integrator's kit directions for fan installation if you use a processor heat sink instead of the combined fan/heat sinks we used to make sure the motherboard chip set (below the processor) stays cool.

That's about all there is to it. Install Voltage Regulator Modules from the chassis integrator's kit, memory, and the adapter cards, then cable up the floppy and SCSI devices, and assembly is complete. For the Pentium III system, top to bottom, we installed the cards in the order AGP video adapter, NIC, SCSI host adapter, and sound card. Not only are there *no* ISA cards in this configuration, because we omitted a sound card from the Xeon server, there are no *adapter* cards in the C440GX+ machine!

Check your work (especially wiring and pin 1 issues) and power on the machine. You should see the BIOS sign-on. When you do, go into the BIOS setup and turn to the next chapter.

# Summary

✦ Servers span an enormous range of capability and requirements, so it's worth the time to analyze what you need and design a machine to meet those requirements.

✦ You can do a lot for data availability with the simple combination of a UPS, redundant power supplies, and (for the best protection) RAID level 5 storage.

✦ The mechanics of server assembly are essentially the same as what you do to assemble a desktop computer.

✦    ✦    ✦

# Building a Server – Software Installation

✦  ✦  ✦  ✦

## In This Chapter

Configuring the BIOS

Installing Windows 2000 Server

Installing FreeBSD UNIX and XFree86

✦  ✦  ✦  ✦

**Y**our newly built machine doesn't really come to life until you get its software set up. In this chapter, we'll look at BIOS and operating system–level setup, including both Windows 2000 Server and FreeBSD 3.2.

The very first question you need to think through is whether you're going to dual-boot your machine between operating systems (such as Windows 2000 and FreeBSD). If you'll be using only one operating system, you can simply dedicate the entire disk drive to a single partition, but if you're using two or more operating systems, you'll probably want to create unique partitions for each one. If you were booting to Windows 9*x*, Windows 2000, and FreeBSD, you might choose to divide the boot drive into three partitions. Here's how you might choose to do it from the perspective of each operating system.

✦ *Windows 98.* If you want to have the Windows 9*x* file system visible from both Windows NT or 2000, or from FreeBSD, you'll have some constraints on the file systems you can use. Windows NT can handle the FAT file system, but not FAT32. Windows 2000 adds FAT32 compatibility. Recent enough versions of FreeBSD (such as 3.2 or later) can read both too. If you are forced to use FAT, you'll have to limit the partition to no more than 2GB, and because the cluster size gets large as a FAT file system gets big, you'll probably want to limit the file system partition to 1GB.

✦ *Windows NT or Windows 2000.* You'll want Windows NT Server or Windows 2000 Server to run on an NTFS partition to take advantages of the performance, reliability, and security of NTFS. Some features (such as Active Directory in Windows 2000) can run only from an NTFS partition. Neither Windows 98 nor FreeBSD support reading the NTFS file system, although there is a utility on the Internet (NTFSDOS) that lets the file system be seen from DOS and Windows 9*x*. We recommend using NTFSDOS only in an emergency.

Because Windows NT and 2000 require NTFS for many of their advanced features, you're probably going to have to resort to two Windows partitions if you're going to have a multiboot system. You'd put NTFS on the Windows NT or Windows 2000 boot partition and create a second partition with FAT or FAT32 to be a shared area across operating systems.

We generally leave servers alone once they're running and stable, so for Windows 2000, we'd partition the entire disk into a single NTFS partition.

✦ *FreeBSD.* FreeBSD runs the Fast File System (FFS). Tools in the FreeBSD install will automatically set up the disk configuration with a reasonable default. FreeBSD can mount a FAT or FAT32 file system and may handle NTFS, but in general it's easier to exchange files over the LAN.

# BIOS Setup and Configuration

Once you build a machine (or get one in to repair or rework), your first step after powering up the machine successfully is to set up and configure the BIOS. We'll use the version P01 BIOS for the Intel C440GX+ motherboard in the examples — it's an Intel version of the Phoenix BIOS core. The BIOS doesn't offer the options to configure chipset settings present in other products — it sets up the chipset in the way defined by Intel.

As the BIOS starts up and counts memory, you'll see a message to push F2 to run SETUP. Do that; after the BIOS SETUP starts, you'll see a screen with menu bar at the top and information/setup fields in the main area. The BIOS on the C440GX+ motherboard also includes the BIOS for the onboard Adaptec SCSI controller, which is essentially the same as for standard Adaptec board-level products

The elements on the top menu bar are Main, Advanced, Security, Server, Boot, and Exit. The Main menu lets you set up the IDE disk I/O, keyboard settings, and processor settings. (We discourage using IDE devices on servers with the exception that you may want to use an IDE DVD drive.) The Advanced menu lets you control how the BIOS handles Plug and Play (Windows 98, Windows 2000, and FreeBSD 3.2 all handle PnP in the operating system); set up mastering for the PCI slots; configure the onboard serial ports, parallel ports, and floppy disk controller; and configure some specific characteristics of the motherboard chip set.

The Security menu lets you configure passwords for access to the machine ("User") and to the BIOS ("Supervisor"), and to enable disk boot sector write protection to help defeat viruses. You have to explicitly enable password protection in the Security menu — it's not enough to just enter passwords. You can also use the Security menu to activate "Secure Mode" on the C440GX+, which (after an interval elapses) locks down the keyboard, video, and chassis front panel.

BIOS antivirus protection issues a warning when any program (legitimate or virus) tries to format or write to the boot sector of the hard drive. The antivirus detection doesn't apply to SCSI disks and may interact badly with operating system installation. Overall, you're better off not using it — use a good antivirus package (such as Network Associates NetShield for Windows NT and Windows 2000 servers) instead.

The Server menu gives you low-level control over the unique server features of the C440GX+ — System Management, Console Redirection, and hardware fault detection.

The Boot menu controls the order in which the system looks at storage and network devices to find an operating system and start running.

The Exit menu lets you control saving or rejecting changes you've made and lets you reset the BIOS defaults. Be sure to reset the defaults if you upgrade the BIOS to ensure the CMOS data configuration is properly initialized for the new version.

**Tip**  If you ever have a CMOS battery fail, or upgrade a BIOS, you're going to lose your current BIOS settings. In some machines, recreating what's required to make the system work properly can be hard. Rather than fight that battle, write down (or print with PrintScrn) all the settings on all the BIOS screens. When you have to reload, just pull out your record, load the generic defaults, and proceed from one BIOS screen to the next.

You have to get the BIOS set up right, so let's look in more detail at each top-level menu.

## Main menu

The main menu in the Intel version of the Phoenix BIOS lets you configure the system CMOS date and time, the two floppy drives, the four possible IDE drives, the keyboard, and the processors.

The date and time setup is completely straightforward. You normally set the time for your local time zone (although some operating systems have an option with which you can indicate that the motherboard clock is set for Greenwich Mean Time).

Floppy disk configuration choices are equally straightforward — for both A: and B: you get the full range from a 360KB 5¼-inch drive to a 2.88MB 3½-inch drive. Set the BIOS for *not installed* if the drive is in fact not there.

> **Tip**
>
> In practice, you may not need a floppy disk drive on your server. As we'll describe in this chapter, you can install both Windows 2000 Server and FreeBSD from the CD-ROM. The operating system has been the last holdout requiring floppy disk support for the past few years; with the OS manufacturers now shipping working bootable CD-ROMs, there's really little reason for a floppy drive. (If you do choose this approach, though, make sure the OS lets you recover a damaged system without a floppy drive and disk.)

For each of the IDE drives, you can choose that the drive isn't installed; is to be automatically detected; is to use a geometry you specify; is a CD-ROM; or is an ATAPI removable drive (such as an LS-120 floppy drive). More and more BIOS versions are eliminating the old, predefined disk geometries because no one has disks any longer that match the old definitions.

You're better off specifying *not installed* instead of automatic detection for drives that aren't there because the boot sequence won't have to pause looking for the drive. All recent-manufacture IDE drives you're likely to encounter support the commands required to let the BIOS automatically detect their size and transfer rate, so use automatic detection unless there's a specific reason not to.

> **Tip**
>
> We intend you to take our recommendation to use automatic IDE detection strongly. We've seen combinations of disks and BIOS that could access the full capacity of the drive only if you use automatic detection — manual setup limited the capacity of the drive you could access.

The keyboard settings are what you'd expect — you can set the boot-time NumLock status, enable or disable keyclick, and set up autorepeat rate and delay.

Processor settings are only slightly more complex than for keyboard — you can view the processor speed setting, stepping (revision) ID, and cache size, and you can enable or disable the cache. There's one other important setting — you can tell the BIOS to clear the historical processor status and test both processors on the next boot. This is part of the system management and reliability built into the C440GX+ — if a processor fails, the motherboard remembers and does not enable it. Once you fix the problem, you need to tell the BIOS to clear the logs and retest, or the second processor won't be used.

The BIOS in the C440GX+ lets you select the language for the BIOS menus and messages, choosing from English, French, Spanish, German, Italian, and Japanese. (We'll see later that you can redirect the BIOS console from the monitor to a serial port; if you do that, the BIOS disables Japanese as a language option.)

## Advanced menu

You configure BIOS features in advanced setup. Here's what each option does, along with why you'd choose among the alternatives you get.

✦ *Installed OS.* Your choices are Other and Plug-n-Play. If you choose Other, you're telling the BIOS that the operating system doesn't have the capability to do PnP resource assignments, the BIOS completes resource assignment to Plug and Play cards before the operating system starts running. If you choose Plug-n-Play, the BIOS initializes the cards but leaves resource decisions to the operating system. You'd use the Plug-n-Play choice for Windows 9*x,* Windows 2000, and FreeBSD version 3.2 and later. Choose Other for Windows NT 3.51, NT 4.0, and Linux (unless you have the experimental Linux kernel patch to handle Plug and Play).

✦ *Reset Configuration Data.* The Extended System Configuration Data (ESCD) is information related to Plug and Play maintained by the BIOS. According to the Microsoft/Intel PC 99 specification, ESCD is not supported by Windows 98 or Windows 2000. Permitted settings are Yes and No; if you change the setting to Yes, the ESCD area will be cleared on the next boot.

✦ *Use Multiprocessor Specification.* The BIOS sets up tables to communicate information to the operating system defining the multiprocessor configuration of the system. Options for this setting are 1.1 and 1.4; the 1.4 specification added extensions to the 1.1 version for multiple PCI bus configurations. Unless you have a good reason to use the 1.1 specification, use 1.4.

✦ *Large Disk Access Mode.* You can choose between CHS (Cylinder, Head, Sector) and LBA (Large Block Addressing), controlling how the BIOS handles IDE disks. Unless your operating system requires CHS, use LBA.

✦ *Delay on Option ROMs.* The default is Disabled; if you change the setting to Enabled, the BIOS will force a short delay at the end of each Option ROM scan. An option ROM is a BIOS fragment that can be included with adapter cards that's called by the main BIOS to initialize the card. Including the delay has the effect of allowing some time for the hardware on the card to settle after being initialized. The delay slows bootup a little; try turning this on if you get erratic hardware initialization results when you boot.

The first submenu under the Advanced menu is for PCI configuration. There's a third-level menu available here for each PCI device, including the onboard SCSI controller and the 6 PCI slots. The options on the third-level menus are these:

✦ *Option ROM SCAN.* The option ROM scan applies only to the SCSI controller; it enables or disables processing initializations by the ROM. Those initializations include scanning the SCSI bus for devices; generally you'd leave this enabled.

✦ *Enable Master.* Turning on this setting (the choices are Enabled and Disabled) sets up for the card in the slot to function as a PCI bus master. There's no common reason to ever disable this setting.

✦ *Latency Timer.* The latency timer sets the minimum guaranteed time (in units of PCI bus clocks) a device is guaranteed to be able to conduct a PCI bus master transaction. Values are Default and (in base 16) 20, 40, 60, 80, A0, C0, and E0. The latency timer interacts with the priority of the device on the bus and with the characteristics of the transactions themselves. In general, you'll leave this setting at 40. (It takes only 1.2 microseconds for 40 PCI bus clocks. Very fast for you, but slow to a 400 or 600 MHz processor.)

The Integrated Peripheral Configuration submenu lets you set up the two serial ports, one parallel port, and floppy disk controller. You can choose to enable or disable the serial ports; if you enable them, you can choose from addresses corresponding to COM1: through COM4: and from interrupt requests (IRQs) 3 and 4. You can set up the parallel port to be disabled, to be enabled with a specified configuration, to operate with an automatically determined configuration (determined by the BIOS or OW), or to be controlled by the operating system. The same setup options (disabled through operating system controlled) apply to the floppy disk controller.

The Advanced Chipset Control submenu has only three settings:

✦ *640-768K Memory Region.* You can enable or disable this; if enabled, ISA Master and DMA cycles are forwarded to the PCI bus. If disabled, those cycles are forwarded to memory. Only specific system configurations are going to work if you disable this setting, so unless you know that you have no ISA devices handling addresses in this range, you should leave the setting enabled.

✦ *Delayed Transaction.* The C440GX+ uses an Intel PIIX4E IDE controller. Enabling this setting turns on the delayed PCI transaction mechanism in the PIIX4E. In general, you'd leave this on unless specific devices have conflicts with that mechanism.

✦ *Passive Release.* The PIIX4E provides another mechanism, called passive release, that alters operations on the PCI bus. Leave this option enabled unless you see devices that conflict.

## Security menu

Security in the C440GX+ BIOS is more than passwords for boot and BIOS setup — there's a BIOS-level capability to lock down the entire machine with passwords after a period of inactivity elapses, after which you'll have to enter a password to restore normal operation. The secure mode password is the same as the one to boot the machine in the first place, distinct from the one to enter BIOS setup.

Secure mode is both comprehensive and simple to set up. You have to enter a user password and then choose the timer interval and a hot key to initiate secure mode. You control booting in secure mode with an enable/disable setting; separate enable/disable controls define whether or not secure mode causes the monitor to blank, the floppy to become read-only, and front panel switches to be ignored.

# Server menu

The server you'd run your business on requires a greater degree of control and identification than the average desktop computer. Servers are often kept away from people or racked in groups, connected to common keyboards and displays. Either way, it's important to be able to positively identify the physical hardware and to monitor and reboot the server when required. The C440GX+ supports these requirements with a variety of features:

✦ *Server Management Info.* The C440GX+ reports the motherboard part number and serial number through this submenu. Fields are also available to report the system part and serial number and chassis part and serial number that can be programmed by the system integrator.

✦ *System Event Logging.* A variety of critical system events, such as memory errors corrected by ECC, can be logged by the motherboard. Use this setting to enable or disable logging. You view the log through the System Setup Utility (SSU) supplied by Intel with the motherboard. The Clear Event Log lets you erase all prior log entries.

✦ *EMP Password.* The C440GX+ includes a feature called the Emergency Management Port, which is a serial port through which an operator can power the server on and off, reset the server, and (from the local server monitor and keyboard) connect to remote servers. You connect to the EMP directly, via another computer's serial port, or through a modem for dial-up access.

The EMP Password setting lets you secure access to the EMP console— unless an operator enters the correct password, access will be denied.

✦ *EMP Escape Sequence.* If you're communicating with the EMP via modem, the system needs a way to force the attached modem to its command mode. Most modems use a special string to signal a request to go into command mode; if you're using a modem compatible with the Hayes AT command set (as most modems are), that string, called an *escape sequence*, will be the three characters "+++." Whatever escape sequence your modem needs, you enter it here in the BIOS.

✦ *EMP Hangup Line Sequence.* The system also needs to be able to force the modem to hang up an ongoing call. AT command set modems use the escape sequence to force command mode and then send the command "ATH." The C440GX+ lets you program the specific string required with the EMP Hangup Line Sequence.

✦ *Modem Init String and High Modem Init String.* Modems have a large number of programmable options to configure data rates, compression, flow control, call reception, and other characteristics. Enter the required string in this setting (use the high string if the overall sequence is longer than 16 characters).

✦ *EMP Access Mode.* You have several options you can configure here for when the EMP is accessible, including Pre-boot Only (allowing access until the power-on self test sequence completes), Always Active (which dedicates the COM2: port for the EMP), and Disabled.

✦ *EMP Restricted Mode Access.* This setting is disabled by default; if it is enabled, you cannot cycle power on the server and cannot reset the hardware. Without those capabilities, you're looking at a trip to the server if it locks up.

✦ *EMP Direct Connect / Modem Mode.* The default is Modem Mode, which instructs the BIOS to use the escape sequence, hangup line sequence, and init string. Direct Connect Mode suppresses those sequences on the assumption that another computer is wired serial port to serial port.

The final submenu under the Server menu is that for console redirection, which works only in the BIOS or under DOS. More sophisticated operating environments may not respond to these settings. Your options are these:

✦ *COM Port Address.* You can disable this setting or choose addresses corresponding to COM1: through COM3:. Be sure the address here matches that for COM2: in the Advanced menu.

✦ *Baud Rate.* This setting controls the data rate through the console port. 19.2 Kbps is the default; you can also pick 9.6, 38.4, and 115.2 Kbps.

✦ *Flow Control.* Flow control is a term for the mechanism used to make sure characters are sent no faster than they can be accepted. This is important, for instance, when sending characters to a modem — you want to send faster than the phone line transmission rate so that you can take advantage of compression (which should be fairly effective for the text the console sends), but you have to ensure you don't send faster than the modem can accept. Your options are No Flow Control, CTS/RTS (which uses the Clear to Send / Request to Send modem hardware), XON/XOFF (which uses special characters monitored in software), and CTS/RTS+CD (which combines standard hardware flow control with detection of successful modem connection using the Carrier Detect signal).

## Boot menu

Reflecting the need to carefully direct how servers start operation, the C440GX+ BIOS gives you close control over how the system boots. In addition to being able to choose if the BIOS startup messages are displayed (using the Boot-time Diagnostic Screen setting), you can choose the order in which devices are searched for a bootable operating system image. The Boot Device Priority submenu lets you choose the order of boot device category among removable devices (such as floppies), hard drives, ATAPI CD-ROM drives, and your LAN. The Hard Drive submenu lets you order devices within the hard drive category, including IDE drives, SCSI drives, and removable devices of both types.

## Exit menu

The Exit menu gives you the options you'd expect — Exit Saving Changes and Exit Discarding Changes — plus some conveniences. You can reinitialize the BIOS to the defaults, save a custom set of defaults, reload the custom defaults, save your work in progress, and discard your work in progress.

# Low-level BIOS controls

The Intel/Phoenix BIOS offers relatively high-level choices and doesn't give you the fine-grained control typical in other systems. The next three sections describe settings from an AMI BIOS more representative of what you'll find in a BIOS offering more detailed control.

## Chipset setup

The very low-level machine characteristics are controlled in the AMI BIOS by the options in the Chipset setup window. BIOS chipset settings are often poorly documented, but if you search the manufacturer's Web site for documentation and specifications for the chipset (commonly made by Intel, Via, and a few others), you can often dig out much more specific information. Here's what each option does:

✦ *DRAM Speed (ns).* SIMM-based motherboards accept memory at speeds of 50, 60, and 70ns; current generation motherboards most often want PC100. If the BIOS lets you set memory speed, you should match the BIOS setting to the speed of the slowest memory you have installed. You run the risk of erratic operation or failure using a setting faster than the installed memory.

✦ *DRAM Integrity Mode (ECC).* You can enable ECC processing by the processor using parity memory. Enable parity checking too.

✦ *DRAM Fast Leadoff.* This option alters the memory access timing. The Intel chipset documentation suggests that most systems will work with the faster setting. If you enable the option, you might want to run an extensive set of memory diagnostics to verify reliability before you depend on the system.

✦ *DRAM Refresh Type.* This option selects the signal sequence used to refresh memory. The options are *RAS Only* and *RAS/CAS*. RAS (Row Address Strobe) and CAS (Column Address Strobe) are the signals used to clock addresses into the memory array; the RAS only option varies only the row addresses, whereas RAS/CAS varies both. Performance gains by changing this option are likely to be minimal, assuming the machine remains reliable.

✦ *DRAM Refresh Queue.* Some chipsets are capable of stacking up multiple DRAM refresh requests until the bus is available to perform the operation. The queue is typically four requests deep. This option should work on all systems.

✦ *VGA Frame Buffer USWC, PCI Frame Buffer USWC,* and *USWC Write Posting.* USWC is Uncached Speculative Write Combining, a technique for increasing the bandwidth to video memory. In the Intel line, the option only exists on Pentium Pro and later processors. On some systems, enabling USWC can increase video performance by as much as 65 percent when used in combination with USWC write posting, so this is probably the most important BIOS optimization you'll find. There's not much risk in turning the options on, so it's definitely worth trying.

✦ *Fixed Memory Hole.* You can create a hole in DRAM space with this option. If you do, both processor and PCI cycles in the hole are ignored by the chipset. You might use this when a PCI board requires isolated control of the addresses, a feature not required in most systems.

✦ *CPU To IDE Posting.* Posting is a general technique that lets the chipset temporarily buffer processor operations. It generally works, and in this case, it improves the transfer rate to disk using the onboard PCI IDE controller.

✦ *CPU To PCI Posting.* This is the same idea, but for more general operations than CPU to IDE posting. It should work for most systems.

✦ *PCI To DRAM Pipeline.* You permit the chipset to run multiple cycles back to back when accessing DRAM, which improves memory access performance. The setting should work for most systems.

✦ *PCI Burst Write Combine.* The PCI bus is eight bytes wide, so it's more efficient to transfer two four-byte words in one operation. PCI burst write combine permits the chipset to do that optimization. It should work on most systems.

✦ *Read Around Write.* Enabling this option allows memory reads to be processed even though there are writes outstanding in the chipset. Because the processor typically does work after reads and before writes, being able to read around outstanding writes boosts performance. This should work on most systems.

✦ *Deturbo Mode.* Believe it or not, the chipset allows you to intentionally slow down the processor by disabling the cache in the processor and periodically stalling the processor pipeline.

✦ *TypeF DMA Buffer Control1 and Control2.* Whereas normal DMA cycles consume eight bus cycles, type F DMA uses only three (so it's much faster). You need to coordinate setting these options with the devices using the DMA channels you intend to speed up to make sure the device can handle the accelerated timing. The two controls let you specify two DMA channels to accelerate. There's not much use for the option because it tends to affect only floppy drives.

✦ *USB Function Enable.* You can enable or disable the onboard USB ports with this control.

✦ *USB Keyboard Support.* If you use a USB keyboard, you need the BIOS to handle the interface until your operating system installs its own drivers. This option enables that function.

✦ *USB Passive Release Enable.* Normal PCI cycles require eight clocks. The USB bus interface can support faster timing, releasing the bus in the middle of a normal cycle (which lets other devices on the bus sooner).

## Power management setup

The AMI BIOS supports a range of power management features. It's not likely you'd want to power down a server if it's intended for 24-hour access, although the instant-on option is worth experimenting with. If you're using the machine as a workstation, several of these settings might be useful. Here's what you can set:

✦ *Power Management/APM.* This option is the master enable for the rest of the power management features. You can set it to *disabled, enabled,* or *instant-on.* If disabled, no power management features are available. The instant-on choice enables two other options, *Instant-On Timeout* and *Green PC Monitor Power State.* The enabled choice enables all the other options except *Instant-On Timeout.* Optimal: Enabled.

✦ *Instant-On Timeout (Minute).* You can set the timer to expire after intervals in the range of 1 to 15 minutes. If the system remains inactive for that long in the full power state, the BIOS will switch over to a lower power state. Detected activity returns to full power (and therefore full speed) operation immediately.

✦ *Green PC Monitor Power State.* If you have a motherboard with connectors to route the VGA signals through circuitry on the motherboard, the BIOS can force standby and power-down modes onto the monitor. You can set the option to *off, standby,* or *suspend,* each of which have different times required for the monitor to resume operation.

✦ *Video Power Down Mode.* If you have a video subsystem on the motherboard, the BIOS can force it to a lower power state after a period of inactivity. You can set the option to *disabled, standby,* or *suspend,* which in order consume decreasing power and take more time to return to normal operation. You're much better off if you have monitor and video power saving controls in your operating system so that their operation can be more effectively coordinated with the rest of system operation.

✦ *Hard Disk Power Down Mode.* The BIOS can spin down cooperating IDE hard disks after a specified period of inactivity (see Hard Disk Timeout) elapses. The motherboard BIOS has no control over SCSI drives. Your choices are *disabled, standby,* and *suspend.* The operating system frequently provides similar controls.

✦ *Hard Disk Time Out (Minute).* You specify the timeout in conjunction with the mode in the prior option. The range of intervals is 1 to 15 minutes.

✦ *Standby Time Out (Minute).* The first stage of system power down is the transition from full power to standby state. This option specifies the inactivity interval after which the BIOS switches over to standby operation. The interval can range from 1 to 15 minutes.

✦ *Suspend Time Out (Minute).* If the system remains inactive for the interval specified by this option while in standby state, the BIOS will enter suspend state, in which the computer uses yet less power but takes longer to recover to full speed operation. The interval can range from 1 to 15 minutes.

✦ *Slow Clock Ratio.* Much of the difference among full power and reduced power states is the speed of the processor clock. (Slowing the processor effectively slows the memory access rate; slowing the processor and memory collectively therefore reduces the power consumption of most of the devices on the motherboard.) When the BIOS enters a lower power state, it divides the processor clock by the ratio specified in this option. For a 400 MHz clock system, setting the ratio to 1:8 means that the low power clock runs at 50 MHz.

✦ *Display Activity.* The remaining power management options control what elements of the computer the BIOS monitors looking for indications of activity. The display activity option looks for changes in the display, signaled by operations on the display subsystem. Your choices are *monitor* and *ignore*.

✦ *IRQ 3, 4, 5, 7, 9, 10, 11, 12, 13, 14, and 15.* Interrupts from external devices typically signal that there's work for the computer to do. IRQ 3 and 4, for example, signal that the serial ports need attention. You'd usually want to go to full power operation when an interrupt happens; these options let you tailor the computer's response to the specific devices connected to each interrupt.

## PCI/PnP setup

The PCI/PnP section of BIOS setup lets you configure BIOS operation relative to those devices, and to control certain aspects of PCI bus operation.

✦ *PCI Latency Timer.* The PCI bus specification includes provisions to ensure that that one device can't block out others. Central to this idea is the latency timer, a counter that limits how long a PCI device can continue to hold the bus after another device makes a request. The BIOS option lets you set the timer in bus clocks; larger values make it more likely that the active device finishes its transfer; they reduce the overhead of switching between devices but also increase the delay before other devices can be serviced — there's less interleaving. Unless your system includes PCI bus master devices capable of very long transfers (I've seen some ATM devices programmed this way to meet stringent performance requirements), increasing this setting won't matter much.

✦ *PCI VGA Palette Snoop.* VGA video cards use a palette in 256-color mode to define which colors are available for display. A set of registers, the palette registers, sit at specific addresses on the bus and are written by the processor to define the current color set. Because normal PCI/ISA bridge operation routes I/O and memory operations to only one of the two buses, writes to the VGA palette registers will typically stop at the PCI video card if you have one.

This scheme runs into trouble in the case of two VGA cards — one ISA and one PCI — in a system, as is supported by Windows 98. Both cards typically need to see the palette information, but without special attention, only the PCI board sees the data. Turning on PCI VGA Palette Snoop causes the bus to route the data to ISA as well as PCI. (Some video boards require this option under other circumstances — check the documentation.)

✦ *PCI IDE Bus Master.* Implementations of IDE disk channels initially used only Programmed I/O (PIO), meaning that all the data had to go through the processor on its way to and from the disk — the processor had to explicitly execute I/O instructions to transfer the data. Direct Memory Access (DMA) implemented by a bus master controller on the PCI bus places significantly less load on the processor (although it may not speed up the I/O operations themselves). If you enable this option, IDE drives connected to the motherboard PCI IDE ports can be driven by an onboard bus master (you'll also need to enable support in the operating system). Be wary of older IDE drives that don't support DMA modes, as well as some of the older ones claiming to — not all meet the specification. If there's any doubt, check with the drive manufacturer.

✦ *Offboard PCI IDE Card, Offboard PCI IDE Primary IRQ, and Offboard PCI IDE Secondary IRQ.* The motherboard typically reserves the resources for its onboard PCI IDE controller. Should you install IDE controller cards into slots on the motherboard, the BIOS tries to detect and adapt to those devices. If the BIOS doesn't get the setup right, you can use these three options to do the configuration yourself.

✦ *PCI Slot 1, 2, 3, and 4 IRQ Priority.* Normally, the BIOS allocates resources (including interrupts) automatically to PCI slots according to the resources the boards state they need. You can override that process, forcing each of four slots to one of eight interrupts (3, 4, 5, 7, 9, 10, 11, or 12). There are only four options, even though the P6DNF (for example) has five PCI slots.

✦ *DMA Channel 0, 1, 3, 5, 6, and 7.* DMA channel allocation is typically handled by Plug and Play. If you force an ISA card to non-PnP mode that requires a DMA channel, or if you use a legacy non-PnP card, you'll want to take the channel out of the PnP allocation pool and force it to be allocated to the ISA or EISA buses.

✦ *IRQ3, 4, 5, 7, 9, 10, 11, 14, 15.* In the same way that a forced or legacy ISA card can require a DMA channel to be forcibly allocated to the ISA/EISA bus, you may have to reserve an interrupt for the same purpose. Note that not all IRQs are available for forced assignment.

✦ *Reserved Memory Size and Reserved Memory Address.* Some legacy ISA cards may have onboard ROMs that don't show up until enabled by a software driver. Because the ROM isn't visible to the BIOS, it's possible for the BIOS to give the ROM address to PCI or other ISA cards. Use these two options to block off memory for cards with this problem.

# Windows 2000 Server Setup and Configuration

If your system supports bootable CD-ROMs, you can install Windows 2000 Server without ever making or using boot floppies. It doesn't matter what order you install Windows 2000 Server or FreeBSD if you're installing both — they don't interfere with each other's boot managers.

We'll assume here that you're installing directly from CD-ROM to a new, unpartitioned disk. Be sure to set up the BIOS to support booting from CD-ROM, and to configure for a Plug and Play operating system.

The Windows 2000 setup program begins by loading drivers and some other components. The first interaction you'll have is to get the hard disk ready—the setup program will warn you that the disk is either new, erased, or configured for a completely incompatible OS. If you tell it to go ahead, setup will partition the disk, losing any information on the disk. We let setup do that; the program found the entire 18GB drive and created a single partition filling it. We then chose to use the NTFS file system, after which setup formatted the drive.

Setup will then copy a lot of files from CD-ROM to disk. Copying files takes a while, even on a fast machine. Once the text-based file copy is done, the setup program restarts your computer and begins running the graphical Setup Wizard.

The first act by the wizard is to scan for and install drivers for all the devices in the computer. The screen will blank for a few seconds at times as setup probes to discover what graphics adapter is installed. The device detection process is very different from that for Windows NT 4, during which you were prompted to explicitly choose the type of computer, graphics card, keyboard, and mouse.

Once device installation completes, the Setup Wizard will ask you to confirm your regional settings and keyboard layout. The regional settings, also called the *locale* in Windows, define the format for items such as numbers, currency, and dates. The keyboard layout defines what unique characters appear on your keyboard and where they are found.

After asking you about what licensing terms you have for the server, setup lets you define the password for the system administrator. *Don't forget the password you choose.* You'll then pick the specific software components to be loaded onto the system. The choice of what components to load isn't fixed—you can use Start ⇨ Settings ⇨ Control Panel ⇨ Add/Remove Programs ⇨ Add/Remove Windows Components to reconfigure the system later.

Network configuration is next; a server isn't worth much without a network connection. Depending on how your LAN is set up, you may have some work to do here. The default configuration installs the TCP/IP protocol but assumes all the details (IP address, netmask, domain name server address, and Internet gateway address) will be provided by a DHCP (Dynamic Host Configuration Protocol) server elsewhere on the LAN. DHCP is an excellent tool to simplify the work you have to do when you move a computer from one place in a large network to another, but it requires good planning to coordinate properly. On a relatively small network, you might want to simply assign static IP addresses. If you do that, you'll have to choose the custom network settings so that you can enter the required addresses and other settings manually. You'll also want to choose custom network settings if you have other protocols on your network, such as IPX/SPX or ATM, or if you want to install the driver for the network monitoring tools.

## When all else fails . . .

Somehow, while working with another operating system, we managed to corrupt the Windows NTFS file system to the point that it would not boot and all attempts to repair it through boot floppies and the emergency repair disk failed. Booting DOS and mounting the file system with NTFSDOS showed there were severe problems—the file listing for the root directory cycled over and over, repeating directories and files endlessly. Both of the other operating systems on the machine (Windows 9x and FreeBSD) verified that their native file systems were in good shape, so we were confident that the problem was restricted to the NTFS file system itself.

As a last resort before we deleted and recreated the NTFS partition, we tried reinstalling Windows NT over itself, selecting the complete examination of the disk before installation. That worked, repairing the damage to the file system and preserving the data in the file systems. We lost the existing Windows NT users and settings for installed programs but retained everything else.

The point is that reinstallation can cure a multitude of software problems—particularly for Windows NT, Windows 2000, and Windows 9x—and may be worth a try when nothing else works.

Upon completion of the network setup dialogs, setup will copy files to the disk and install the components you've selected. Final tasks, including setup of the Start menu and Registry, plus some cleanup, finish the setup process. You'll then be prompted to remove the CD-ROM and press the Finish button, after which the system reboots into Windows 2000 Server. You'll be prompted to configure the server after the reboot; that's your opportunity to set up file and printer sharing, directory services, network management services, Web services, and more. We recommend you adjust the screen resolution upward before you start detailed server configuration so that you can see more on the screen (use Start ➪ Settings ➪ Control Panel ➪ Display, or right-click the desktop background and choose Properties).

Windows 2000 setup lets you pick the individual components you want to install. Here are your choices:

✦ *Accessories and Utilities*. You can select or deselect the Accessibility Wizard, a tool to help configure Windows for specific vision, hearing, and mobility needs, accessories, communications, games, and multimedia.

✦ *Certificate Services*. This is an authority service you use along with applications using public key cryptographic security.

✦ *Indexing Service*. A generalization of the older Microsoft Office Find Fast, the indexing service enables fast, full-text searches of files.

✦ *Internet Information Services (IIS)*. IIS is the built-in Windows 2000 capability to work as a Web and FTP server, including extensions for the FrontPage HTML editor, database interaction, and other features. IIS is relatively simple to set up, far less complex than the Apache Web server commonly used on UNIX systems.

✦ *Management and Monitoring Tools*. This category includes tools you can use to monitor and improve network performance.

✦ *Message Queuing Service (MQS)*. Microsoft has developed a software architecture to improve applications running across several computers. The Message Queuing Service is one component of that architecture. If you're not running software built to use MQS, there's no advantage to installing it.

✦ *Networking Services* and *Other Network File and Print Services*. This is a large collection of specialized services for advanced network operations. Components in the category include the DNS and DHCP servers, along with UNIX print support services, so don't assume you can ignore what's here.

✦ *Remote Installation Services*. If you have hundreds or thousands of computers on a LAN, upgrading to a new operating system is a monumental job. If the network interface cards on those computers support remote booting, the Remote Installation Services can let you install Windows 2000 without traveling to the computer itself.

✦ *Remote Storage*. Windows 2000 incorporates a new set of tools to help you migrate seldom-used file to and from tape, reducing the total amount of storage you need to have on disk.

✦ *Script Debugger*. Web developers commonly include scripts in Web pages to enhance the functionality and appeal of those pages. Scripts are programs, though, so just like all other programmers, script developers need debugging tools.

✦ *Terminal Services (and Licensing)*. Windows 2000 supports a variant of the Network Computer idea, with which remote terminal computers can run Windows programs. Those programs actually run on the server, transmitting only display information back to the terminal. Choose these components if you're going to run Windows terminals.

# FreeBSD Setup and Configuration

Instead of Windows 2000 Server, you might choose to install FreeBSD. You can install and configure both FreeBSD and X11R6 (the X Window system) from the FreeBSD CD-ROM included with this book, but for more in-depth information than we can include here we strongly recommend that you order a copy of *The Complete FreeBSD* by Greg Lehey, published by Walnut Creek CDROM Books, ISBN 1-57176-159-4. (You can call Walnut Creek CDROM at 1-800-786-9907 or 1-510-674-0783.) There's far more detail on installing and configuring FreeBSD than there's space for in this book, and while we expect that you'll be up and running with what's here, the added detail is very useful.

## Why FreeBSD?

Linux is the version of UNIX that gets the most recognition, so it's a worthwhile question why we chose FreeBSD for this book. The short answer is that, in practice, our experience and the experience of ISPs we consulted suggest that FreeBSD is more stable than Linux. Both are fine products, but because the reason most people will run UNIX is to support a server, stability is an overwhelming consideration.

The first step is to make sure you've enabled CD-ROM boot support on the IDE or SCSI disk controller. The FreeBSD CD-ROM included with this book is bootable, and installation from CD-ROM is the most painless approach you have for a bare machine. Once you've confirmed CD-ROM booting is enabled, insert the FreeBSD CD-ROM in the drive and reboot. The system will detect the bootable CD-ROM and start the installation operating system kernel.

A basic FreeBSD installation goes in four phases:

✦ *Initial kernel boot and file system installation.* You'll start a generic FreeBSD kernel, create a FreeBSD partition on a disk, and copy in the distribution files. FreeBSD will not run in a partition shared with Windows – you'll have to make a new one. (You can use tools that come with FreeBSD to make room if there's no unallocated partition space on your disk.)

✦ *Reboot and generic kernel configuration.* Once you have FreeBSD on your disk, you'll boot into the on-disk kernel (you can install the BootEasy boot manager to be able to multiboot over several operating systems). You'll then want to edit the kernel configuration to eliminate device drivers you don't need, add ones you do, and generally tune the basic setup.

✦ *X Window configuration.* You'll likely want to run the X Window system, giving you the multitasking options of a graphical user interface. FreeBSD includes X11R6, the current version, with a simplified graphical setup program. The latest versions of FreeBSD include new, sophisticated options for the graphical desktop, KDE and Gnome, that approach Windows in power and usability.

✦ *Backup.* It's particularly important to back up your tailored kernel to make sure you always have an easily bootable system.

## Picking hardware

FreeBSD includes drivers for a wide range of popular hardware, but it's not universal—it's not guaranteed that your Whizbang 47338 UltraScreamer IDE controller and toaster will be supported. Drivers for FreeBSD are generally ones that the FreeBSD community has written, not ones written by manufacturers, so until someone in the community decides to develop one, it won't exist.

We chose the hardware for the server we looked at building in the last chapter with this issue in mind. The Intel C440GX+ motherboard, including the Cirrus Logic video adapter, Adaptec SCSI controller, and Intel NIC, are all supported. You can always find the current list of supported hardware for FreeBSD at `http://www.freebsd.org/handbook/hw.html`.

Picking a motherboard for FreeBSD is worth some care. If you look at the information on the FreeBSD Web page just cited, for instance, you'll see that there are some issues with older Intel Pentium and Pentium Pro support chipsets. The C440GX+ we used in the server is built around the Intel 82443GX+ chipset and supported FreeBSD without problems.

The FreeBSD Web site states that the system will run in as little as 4 to 5MB of memory. Don't bother — you won't be able to do anything useful.

The FreeBSD NIC drivers typically don't support autodetection of media type on combo cards — for example, they won't select between 10Base-2 and 10Base-T. You can use the utility programs that come with most combo NICs to force one or the other interface.

## Initial kernel boot and file system installation

Put the FreeBSD CD-ROM in the drive and boot the system (don't forget to enable bootable CD-ROM detection!). The first thing you'll see once the boot software starts is a screen labeled the kernel configuration menu that offers you three choices:

✦ Skip kernel configuration and continue with installation.

✦ Start kernel configuration in visual mode.

✦ Start kernel configuration in CLI mode (experts only).

It's unlikely that the generic kernel (which is what you'll be booting) will run without configuration because there are so many devices compiled into it that conflicts are unavoidable. That means you probably won't want the first option. The second one is your best choice because the visual editor is a fast, simple way to edit devices into and out of the configuration. Pick the visual configuration editor with the down-arrow key, then push Enter.

Once you do, you'll see the visual kernel configuration editor, which is a screen like this:

```
---Active-Drivers-----------23 conflicts-----Dev---IRQ--Port--
   Storage :              (Collapsed)
   Network :              (Collapsed)
   Communications :       (Collapsed)
   Input :                (Collapsed)
   Multimedia :
   PCI :                  (Collapsed)
```

```
Miscellaneous :

---Inactive-Drivers------------------------------Dev-------------
Storage :
Network :
Communications :        (Collapsed)
Input :                 (Collapsed)
Multimedia :
PCI :
Miscellaneous :         (Collapsed)
------------------------------------------------------------------




------------------------------------------------------------------
[Enter] Expand device list      [X]   Expand all lists
[TAB]   Change fields           [Q]   Save and Exit    [?] Help
```

There are four sections to the display. Top to bottom, they are active drivers, inactive drivers, device details and configuration (the blank area in the preceding example), and usage directions.

Your goal with the configuration editor is to eliminate most, if not all, of the conflicts reported on the top line by slimming the configuration down to just the devices in your computer. Conflicts in the configuration editor result from active devices being configured to use the same IRQ or I/O port, so what you have to do is to either remove devices from the active configuration or change the resources they're configured to use.

Move the cursor to the "Storage" line in the active devices section and press Enter to expand that category. When you do, you'll see a display like this:

```
---Active-Drivers------------23 conflicts-----Dev---IRQ--Port--
Storage :
 Adaptec 154x SCSI controller                CONF aha0        0x330
 Adaptec 152x SCSI and compatible sound cards aic0     11 0x340
 Buslogic SCSI controller                     CONF bt0         0x330
 Floppy disk controller                            fdc0     6 0x3f0
 Matsushita/Panasonic/Creative CDROM          CONF matcdc0     0x230
 Mitsumi CD-ROM                               CONF mcd0     10 0x300
 ProAudio Spectrum SCSI and compatibles  CONF nca0     10 0x1f88
---Inactive-Drivers-----------------------------Dev-------------
Storage :
Network :
Communications :        (Collapsed)
Input :                 (Collapsed)
Multimedia :
PCI :
Miscellaneous :         (Collapsed)
------------------------------------------------------------------
```

```
----------------------------------------------------------
[Enter] Expand device list     [X]   Expand all lists
[TAB]   Change fields          [Q]   Save and Exit    [?] Help
```

The lines you now see under Storage are the drivers that would be active in the kernel were you to boot the system with this configuration. The lines that show "CONF" have conflicts with other devices. For example, in this display you can see that the Adaptec 154x SCSI controller driver needs port 0x330, but so does the Buslogic SCSI controller. The problem with the Matsushita/Panasonic/Creative CD-ROM (a proprietary interface) isn't apparent from what's on the screen, but if you were to scroll down (use the down arrow key), you'd see by comparing IRQ and Port addresses that it conflicts with the Sony CD-ROM (another proprietary interface). (You'd also see that the Ultrastor 14F/24F/34F SCSI controller conflicts on port 0x330 — it's not the case that only two devices can be conflicting.)

In these cases, you can eliminate the conflicts by deleting the devices — move the cursor to the line you want to make inactive, and push the Del key. The device will move from active to inactive, and the conflict count on the top line will drop. A server that is exclusively PCI helps here — you can delete everything under Storage except the floppy disk controller.

Continue the configuration process by expanding the Network category. You can delete everything there too if you used the C440GX+ because the onboard NIC is a PCI device and therefore in the PCI category rather than the Network category.

Once you remove all the remaining conflicts, you'll see this display:

```
---Active-Drivers----------------------------Dev---IRQ--Port--
Storage :
 Floppy disk controller                       fdc0    6  0x3f0
Network :
Communications :      (Collapsed)
Input :               (Collapsed)
Multimedia :
PCI :                 (Collapsed)
Miscellaneous :
---Inactive-Drivers----------------------------Dev-------------
Storage :
Network :
Communications :      (Collapsed)
Input :               (Collapsed)
Multimedia :
PCI :
Miscellaneous :       (Collapsed)
----------------------------------------------------------


----------------------------------------------------------
[Enter] Expand device list     [X]   Expand all lists
[TAB]   Change fields          [Q]   Save and Exit    [?] Help
```

## When all else fails and there *are* no directions . . .

It's no accident that we cautioned you not to delete the Syscons console driver to solve the conflict with the PS/2 mouse driver. We unwittingly made just this mistake, and struggled for some time to figure out why the system did nothing (or rebooted) after we quit out of the configuration editor.

There was nothing in the documentation about this issue, so here's how we worked our way past the problem. It's worth noting that this is the standard troubleshooting procedure we've recommended throughout the book:

✦ *Strip down the machine.* The first step was to remove everything from the machine we didn't need on the assumption that automatic detection of some hardware was hanging. That meant we removed the NIC and most other cards, leaving only the video card and the SCSI host adapter with the boot disk.

Unfortunately, that didn't help. Configuring the kernel as before (without the console driver and with the PS/2 mouse) still hung.

✦ *Strip down the software.* The next step was to include as little in the kernel as possible. We knew we could always add the mouse driver back later, so we deleted everything we didn't explicitly need, left in the console driver, and proceeded.

That worked.

It wasn't obvious exactly what had been the problem after the system continued the kernel boot properly, so we retraced our steps to find out. Adding in the PS/2 mouse still worked; deleting the console driver failed reliably.

There's more to do, even though there are no remaining conflicts. Looking at the remaining active collapsed categories, we find these items:

✦ *LPT2.* By default, the kernel will look for a second parallel port. There isn't one in our server, but the kernel won't care as it boots. You can either leave it in or take it out.

✦ *Microsoft Bus Mouse.* The generic kernel includes a driver for the Microsoft bus mouse as an active device (reflecting that serial ports are valuable for other things on a server, such as modems and UPS interfaces). Delete it from the configuration if your motherboard supports a PS/2 mouse.

You can expand the PCI category, and if you do you'll find a raft of devices you don't have. You can't make any of them inactive, though — the kernel can probe for PCI devices accurately (well, . . .), so it's built to test for them all.

Now, press the Tab key to move to the inactive drivers, and expand the Input category. In there, you'll find the PS/2 mouse driver, which we want. Select it and press Enter to activate it. When you do, you'll find that it conflicts with the Syscons console driver, leading to two conflicts. Whatever you do, don't follow your instinct and delete the console driver because the system will malfunction once you leave the configuration editor — it will have no way to output messages.

In practice, this is a harmless conflict — the kernel drivers have been programmed to know about the conflict and work around it. The configuration editor gives you a subtle clue about this, noting down in the device details section for the PS/2 mouse that the conflict is allowed. You'll see this only if you select the PS/2 mouse — the entry for the Syscons console driver has no such indicator.

There are some other features in the configuration editor. For example, if you select a device in the active section and press Enter, you drop into the device configuration section, where you can change the default port address and IRQ. There are also "flags" you can change, but you'll need to look in the obscure, hard or impossible to find documentation for the device driver to know what values have any meaning.

At this point, you're ready to go — you've done what's required to eliminate conflicts. Press the Q key (save and exit), and answer Yes to the question "Save these parameters before exiting?" At that point, you'll immediately see lines show up on the screen starting with one that reports available memory. This is the generic kernel booting according to the configuration you set. You may see error messages scroll by, and as it is you can't pause the process to look at them. That's okay because later in the configuration process you can look at a record of those messages kept in a file (use the *dmesg* utility once the system comes up and you log in).

Here's what scrolls by as we boot the generic FreeBSD version 3.2 kernel on the C440GX+ server.

```
Copyright (c) 1992-1999 FreeBSD Inc.
Copyright (c) 1982, 1986, 1989, 1991, 1993
   The Regents of the University of California. All rights
reserved.
FreeBSD 3.2-RELEASE #0: Tue May 18 04:05:08 GMT 1999
    jkh@cathair:/usr/src/sys/compile/GENERIC
Timecounter "i8254"  frequency 1193182 Hz
Timecounter "TSC"  frequency 398271204 Hz
CPU: Pentium II/Xeon/Celeron (398.27-MHz 686-class CPU)
   Origin = "GenuineIntel"  Id = 0x653  Stepping=3

Features=0x183fbff<FPU,VME,DE,PSE,TSC,MSR,PAE,MCE,CX8,APIC,SEP,
MTRR,PGE,MCA,CMOV,PAT,
         PSE36,MMX,<b24>
real memory  = 134217728 (131072K bytes)
avail memory = 127070208 (124092K bytes)
Preloaded elf kernel "kernel.GENERIC" at 0xc0358000.
```

The server actually has 128MB of memory (131,072KB, which you see in the *real memory* line in the log). Earlier versions of the kernel could see only the maximum of 64MB reported by the CMOS and had to be edited to work around the problem.

```
Probing for devices on PCI bus 0:
chip0: <Intel 82443GX host to PCI bridge> rev 0x00 on pci0.0.0
chip1: <Intel 82443GX host to AGP bridge> rev 0x00 on pci0.1.0
ahc0: <Adaptec aic7896/97 Ultra2 SCSI adapter> rev 0x00 int a
irq 11 on pci0.12.0
ahc0: aic7896/97 Wide Channel A, SCSI Id=7, 16/255 SCBs
ahc1: <Adaptec aic7896/97 Ultra2 SCSI adapter> rev 0x00 int a
irq 11 on pci0.12.1
ahc1: aic7896/97 Wide Channel B, SCSI Id=7, 16/255 SCBs
fxp0: <Intel EtherExpress Pro 10/100B Ethernet> rev 0x08 int a
irq 10 on pci0.14.0
fxp0: Ethernet address 00:a0:c9:ec:d1:9b
chip2: <Intel 82371AB PCI to ISA bridge> rev 0x02 on pci0.18.0
ide_pci0: <Intel PIIX4 Bus-master IDE controller> rev 0x01 on
pci0.18.1
chip3: <Intel 82371AB Power management controller> rev 0x02 on
pci0.18.3
vga0: <Cirrus Logic model 00bc VGA-compatible display device>
rev 0x23 on pci0.20.0
Probing for devices on PCI bus 1:
chip4: <PCI to PCI bridge (vendor=1011 device=0023)> rev 0x05
on pci1.15.0
Probing for devices on PCI bus 2:
```

You can see from this part of the log that all the devices on the C440GX+ motherboard are recognized and supported by FreeBSD version 3.2, a process that's made far simpler and more reliable by the fact that they're all PCI devices. The identifiers on the left are the UNIX device IDs assigned by the kernel; they are tied to specific device drivers:

✦ *ahc0: and ahc1:* are the two Adaptec SCSI channels.

✦ *fxp0:* is the Intel network interface adapter.

✦ *vga0:* is the Cirrus Logic graphics adapter.

The kernel then looks for the remainder of the devices, searching the ISA resources on the board:

```
Probing for PnP devices:
Probing for devices on the ISA bus:
sc0 on isa
sc0: VGA color <16 virtual consoles, flags=0x0>
ed0 not found at 0x280
fe0 not found at 0x300
atkbdc0 at 0x60-0x6f on motherboard
```

```
atkbd0 irq 1 on isa
psm0 irq 12 on isa
psm0: model IntelliMouse, device ID 3
sio0 at 0x3f8-0x3ff irq 4 flags 0x10 on isa
sio0: type 16550A
sio1 at 0x2f8-0x2ff irq 3 on isa
sio1: type 16550A
```

The device sc0: is the system console; psm0: is the PS/2 mouse port; sio0: and sio1: are the serial ports. In the fragment that follows, fdc0: is the floppy disk controller; wdc0: the primary IDE controller; wdc1: the secondary IDE controller; acd0: the ATAPI CD-ROM. The other devices are as noted in the log.

```
fdc0 at 0x3f0-0x3f7 irq 6 drq 2 on isa
wdc0 at 0x1f0-0x1f7 irq 14 on isa
wdc0: unit 0 (atapi): <ATAPI CDROM/V1.70>, removable, dma,
iordy
acd0: drive speed 4153KB/sec, 120KB cache
acd0: supported read types: CD-R, CD-RW, CD-DA
acd0: Audio: play, 255 volume levels
acd0: Mechanism: ejectable tray
acd0: Medium: no/blank disc inside, unlocked
wdc1 not found at 0x170
wt0 not found at 0x300
mcd0 not found at 0x300
matcdc0 not found at 0x230
scd0 not found at 0x230
ppc0 at 0x378 irq 7 flags 0x40 on isa
ppc0: Generic chipset (ECP/PS2/NIBBLE) in COMPATIBLE mode
ppc0: FIFO with 16/16/8 bytes threshold
lpt0: <generic printer> on ppbus 0
lpt0: Interrupt-driven port
ppi0: <generic parallel i/o> on ppbus 0
plip0: <PLIP network interface> on ppbus 0
lpt0: <generic printer> on ppbus 0
lpt0: Interrupt-driven port
```

We've omitted a number of lines for devices known to the kernel but not found on this system (see the sidebar FreeBSD ISA device names), then picked up the log again as detection continues:

## FreeBSD ISA device names

The following table shows the correspondence between FreeBSD ISA device names and the actual hardware. We've annotated the right column to show what each one is, including the DOS name for differences like *lpt0* (FreeBSD) versus *LPT1* (DOS). Devices with names *ed0* and *ed1* are different instances of the same device type.

| *FreeBSD Device* | *DOS or Other Device* |
| --- | --- |
| aha0: | Adaptec SCSI host adapter |
| aic0: | Adaptec SCSI host adapter |
| apm0: | Advanced power management |
| bt0: | Buslogic SCSI host adapter |
| ed0: and ed1: | NE2000 or compatible NIC |
| ep0: | 3Com 3C509 NIC |
| ex0: | Intel EtherExpress Pro NIC |
| fdc0: | Floppy disk controller |
| fe0: | Fujitsu MB86960A/MB86965 NIC |
| ie0: and ie1: | AT&T StarLAN 10 NIC |
| le0: | Digital EtherWorks 2 & 3 NIC |
| lnc0: | Lance/PCnet NIC |
| lpt0: to lpt1: | LPT1: to LPT2: |
| matcdc0: | Matsushita/Panasonic CD-ROM |
| mcd0: | Mitsumi CD-ROM |
| mse0: | Logitech/ATI bus mouse |
| nca0: and nca1: | ProAudioSpectrum SCSI host adapter |
| npx0: | Floating-point math coprocessor |
| psm0: | PS/2 mouse |
| sc0: | System console |
| scd0: | Sony CD-ROM |
| sea0: | Seagate SCSI host adapter |
| sio0: to sio3: | COM1: to COM4 |
| uha0: | Ultrastore SCSI host adapter |
| wdc0: and wdc1: | Primary and secondary IDE controllers |
| wt0: | Wangtek/Archive tape drives |
| ze0: | IBM PC Card NIC |
| zp0: | 3Com PC Card Etherlink III NIC |

```
vga0 at 0x3b0-0x3df maddr 0xa0000 msize 131072 on isa
npx0 on motherboard
npx0: INT 16 interface
Waiting 15 seconds for SCSI devices to settle
```

There's a fair amount of conservatism built into the generic kernel, including a delay of 15 seconds after any SCSI controller is recognized to allow connected devices to finish resetting. We'll reduce this delay when we customize the kernel to speed the boot.

```
changing root device to da0s1a
da0 at ahc0 bus 0 target 0 lun 0
da0: <SEAGATE ST118273LW 6246> Fixed Direct Access SCSI-2
device
da0: 80.000MB/s transfers (40.000MHz, offset 15, 16bit), Tagged
Queueing Enabled
da0: 17366MB (35566480 512 byte sectors: 255H 63S/T 2213C)
```

The kernel discovers attached SCSI devices as it boots, so you don't have to build them into the kernel itself. In this case, it's found the 18GB drive.

That's the end of the hardware boot. You'll then see the menu from *sysinstall*, the utility that you'll use to configure system options. The initial sysinstall menu is in Figure 40-1.

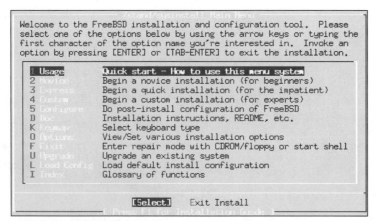

**Figure 40-1:** The sysinstall program is where you'll work to set up your initial FreeBSD configuration once you've booted the generic kernel.

Choose "Novice" installation. (I don't care if you *do* have 45 years experience with every computer ever built. Unless you know FreeBSD installation backward and forward, which means you're reading this section for sport, Novice is what you want!)

Novice installation will first take you to a screen with which you set up the partitions you're going to use. If you have more than one drive, you'll be asked to pick which one you want. The C440GX+ server has one drive called *da0*. Once you pick a drive, you'll have to create the FreeBSD partition. The screen for that looks like Figure 40-2 after creation of the FreeBSD partition using all the space on the drive.

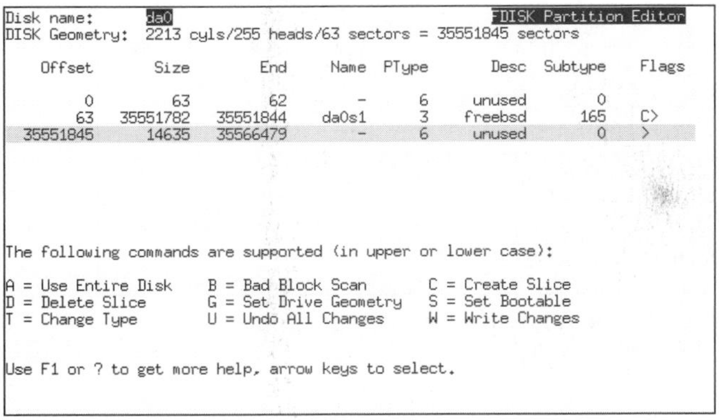

Disk name: da0
FDISK Partition Editor
DISK Geometry: 2213 cyls/255 heads/63 sectors = 35551845 sectors
Offset Size End Name PType Desc Subtype Flags
0 63 62 - 6 unused 0
63 35551782 35551844 da0s1 3 freebsd 165 C>
35551845 14635 35566479 - 6 unused 0 >
The following commands are supported (in upper or lower case):
A = Use Entire Disk B = Bad Block Scan C = Create Slice
D = Delete Slice G = Set Drive Geometry S = Set Bootable
T = Change Type U = Undo All Changes W = Write Changes
Use F1 or ? to get more help, arrow keys to select.

**Figure 40-2:** Pay careful attention to the names each partition gets in the partition.

Once you tell the partition editor you're finished, it will ask if you want to install Booteasy, the FreeBSD boot manager. This is a good idea because it's the first step in creating choices for booting to whichever operating system you've installed. (See Figure 40-3.) (Look in the FreeBSD file system for documents on Booteasy — they'll tell you how to configure it to boot directly into any of the operating systems you've loaded.)

FreeBSD comes with a boot selector that allows you to easily
select between FreeBSD and any other operating systems on your machine
at boot time. If you have more than one drive and want to boot
from the second one, the boot selector will also make it possible
to do so (limitations in the PC BIOS usually prevent this otherwise).
If you do not want a boot selector, or wish to replace an existing
one, select "standard". If you would prefer your Master Boot
Record to remain untouched then select "None".
NOTE: PC-DOS users will almost certainly require "None"!
(*) BootMgr Install the FreeBSD Boot Manager
( ) Standard Install a standard MBR (no boot manager)
( ) None Leave the Master Boot Record untouched
[ OK ] Cancel

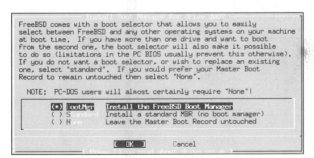

**Figure 40-3:** You can configure Booteasy to know about all the operating systems you've installed.

Next, you have to label the FreeBSD partition. The label editor does this; as long as you have more than a few hundred megabytes in the FreeBSD partition, go ahead and let it do the job using the "Auto Defaults" option the label editor offers you. The result should be as in Figure 40-4.

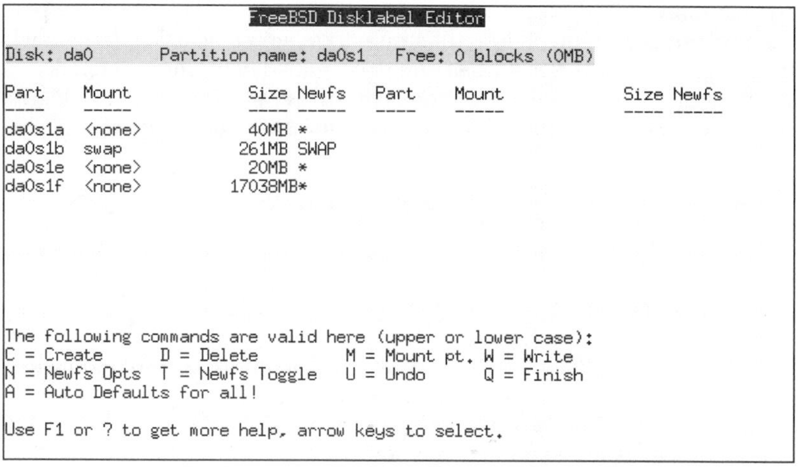

```
                    ┌──FreeBSD Disklabel Editor──┐

Disk: da0       Partition name: da0s1   Free: 0 blocks (0MB)

Part    Mount            Size Newfs   Part    Mount           Size Newfs
----    -----            ---- -----   ----    -----           ---- -----
da0s1a  <none>           40MB *
da0s1b  swap            261MB SWAP
da0s1e  <none>           20MB *
da0s1f  <none>         17038MB*




The following commands are valid here (upper or lower case):
C = Create      D = Delete       M = Mount pt. W = Write
N = Newfs Opts  T = Newfs Toggle  U = Undo      Q = Finish
A = Auto Defaults for all!

Use F1 or ? to get more help, arrow keys to select.
```

**Figure 40-4:** The FreeBSD label editor defines the components of the file systems, including the swap space.

By now, you've told sysinstall how to lay out the disks completely, and it's time to choose what you want to install. Sysinstall sequences you to the screen in Figure 40-5 to do that. As long as you have the disk space, I'd recommend installing everything to make sure you can do whatever configuration you need to. If you don't want games (company policy, for example), choose *X-Developer*, otherwise choose *All*. You'll need about 400MB to install everything; if you choose X-Developer, you should need about 200MB.

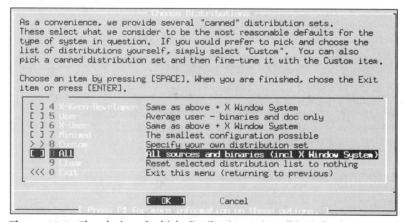

**Figure 40-5:** The choice of which distribution to install isn't final—you can install others later after the system is up and running.

You may get submenus to configure the distributions you choose. When you're done, choose OK to exit the top-level menu. You'll then see a screen letting you choose the installation medium; choose CD-ROM. You'll have other options to install from a DOS file system, from a mounted FreeBSD file system, from a set of floppy disks (!!!), from an FTP server, from a Network File System (NFS), and from tape.

That's all there is to initial installation. Confirm to the installer to go ahead and do the work, at which time sysinstall will create partitions, mount swap space, create file systems, and read in files. After that completes, the Novice install will want to configure your network interface. You'll have to postpone that until later if the generic kernel doesn't have a driver for your network card; otherwise, you'll get a screen to pick the interface. Following that screen, you'll see another screen to set the host name, domain name, gateway, name server, IP address, and netmask—the usual IP configuration data.

Once you're done, the system will reboot. If you booted from CD-ROM to begin with, be sure to interrupt the boot cycle and disable bootable CD-ROM support. Make sure no floppy is in the drive, and reboot. When you do that, the sequence of messages will look much like before, but rather than jumping into sysinstall, you'll receive a "login:" prompt. Type **root** (it won't ask for a password yet) and you're running.

## Generic kernel configuration

What you have now is a generic FreeBSD kernel installed and running on your server, a step somewhat harder than installing Windows. What you want to do next is to configure and build a kernel specific to your hardware. You'll execute these steps to accomplish that task:

✦ Create and customize a configuration definition file.

✦ Compile the configuration definition file.

✦ Install and test the configuration definition file.

A configuration definition file is a set of directives that the FreeBSD config program uses to set up the source code files you'll then compile to form the new kernel. Here's the GENERIC configuration file (/usr/src/sys/i386/conf/GENERIC — don't change it directly) along with the changes we need to make for the example server:

```
#
# ARIES—Intel C440GX+ SMP Dual Xeon Motherboard with SCSI disk
#        Modified 7/10/99 by Barry Press
#
# For more information read the handbook part System
Administration ->
# Configuring the FreeBSD Kernel -> The Configuration File.
# The handbook is available in /usr/share/doc/handbook or
online as
# latest version from the FreeBSD World Wide Web server
# <URL:http://www.FreeBSD.ORG/>
```

```
#
# An exhaustive list of options and more detailed explanations of the
# device lines is present in the ./LINT configuration file. If you are
# in doubt as to the purpose or necessity of a line, check first in LINT.
#
# $Id: GENERIC,v 1.143.2.12 1999/05/14 15:12:26 jkh Exp $

machine         "i386"
#cpu            "I386_CPU"
#cpu            "I486_CPU"
#cpu            "I586_CPU"
cpu             "I686_CPU"
```

The example server has a pair of Pentium II Xeon processors, so we can eliminate the support targeted at any other processors. Rather than delete the lines, it's a good idea to comment them out with a pound sign (#) character at the front of the line. These lines also show how to put anything with numbers, spaces, or special characters in quotes in a configuration file. You'll notice at the top that we've named the server ARIES and use this throughout. The configuration filename is ARIES too, making it easier to keep things straight if you maintain kernels for multiple machines.

```
ident           ARIES
```

The ident string is part of what prints out as the kernel boots. It's a good idea to keep the ident string the same as the name of the kernel configuration file so that you can figure out what kernel came from what configuration file.

```
maxusers 32
```

The term *maxusers* is a misleading name — it has no direct relationship to how many users can log into the server. What maxusers really does is to set the size of some kernel tables that control how many processes (and other things) there can be. Launching some programs (as required for a new user) can require many processes, which is where the relationship comes in. Unless you're running on a machine with highly limited memory, there's no liability from having a larger number.

```
#options       , MATH_EMULATE    #Support for x87 emulation
options         INET            #InterNETworking
options         FFS             #Berkeley Fast Filesystem
options         FFS_ROOT        #FFS usable as root device
[keep this!]
options         MFS             #Memory Filesystem
```

```
options          MFS_ROOT              #MFS usable as root device,
"MFS" req'ed
options          NFS                   #Network Filesystem
options          NFS_ROOT              #NFS usable as root device,
"NFS" req'ed
options          MSDOSFS                    #MSDOS Filesystem
options          "CD9660"              #ISO 9660 Filesystem
options          "CD9660_ROOT"         #CD-ROM usable as root.
"CD9660" req'ed
options          PROCFS                #Process filesystem
options          "COMPAT_43"           #Compatible with BSD 4.3
[KEEP THIS!]
```

These options control whether some features are compiled into the kernel. We've removed floating-point coprocessor emulation because the Pentium II Xeon processors have built-in coprocessors. *INET* is support for internetworking; don't take it out because if you do things won't work—UNIX is simply too dependent on having networking built in. *FFS and MFS* are the standard FreeBSD file system and a memory file system, and both are required. *NFS* is the network file system (used for remote TCP/IP file access) and is optional. *MSDOSFS* is support for FAT file system access. *CD9660* is support for CD-ROMs. *PROCFS* and *COMPAT_43* are internals of FreeBSD and are required.

```
#options         SCSI_DELAY=15000      #Be pessimistic about Joe
SCSI device
options          SCSI_DELAY=2000       #Be less pessimistic about
Joe SCSI device
```

As shipped, the generic kernel waits a long time for SCSI devices to settle after a bus reset, which is tedious (and probably unnecessary) if you're booting often (such as while you're testing). We changed the delay to 2 seconds with no ill effects.

```
options          UCONSOLE              #Allow users to grab the
console
options          FAILSAFE              #Be conservative
options          USERCONFIG            #boot -c editor
options          VISUAL_USERCONFIG     #visual boot -c editor
```

These are relatively standard options you'd not want to change except under odd circumstances. *FAILSAFE* eliminates some higher-performance options.

```
options          PQ_HUGECACHE          # color for 1024k/16k cache
```

The Pentium II Xeon processors we used had a 1MB L2 cache, so we added this option to improve performance. (You can find all the options for kernel configuration in the file /usr/src/sys/i386/conf/LINT.)

```
config           kernel root on da0
```

The *config* statement controls the name and location of the kernel. You shouldn't change the name (kernel) because some programs rely on it. We've changed the location from *wd0* (as in the generic kernel) to *da0* because this is a SCSI-based machine. You can add other parameters to control the location for crash dumps, but typically you'd want to manage that using UNIX tools and not build it into the kernel.

```
# To make an SMP kernel, the next two are needed
options  SMP                     # Symmetric MultiProcessor Kernel
options  APIC_IO                      # Symmetric (APIC) I/O
# Optionally these may need tweaked, (defaults shown):
#options NCPU=2                  # number of CPUs
#options NBUS=4                  # number of busses
#options NAPIC=1                     # number of IO APICs
#options NINTR=24                # number of INTs
```

The FreeBSD kernel incorporates support for symmetric multiprocessor (SMP) systems, but it's not enabled by default. You have to uncomment the SMP and APIC_IO option lines (remove the leading # character) to build SMP support into the kernel.

```
controller      isa0
controller      pnp0
#controller     eisa0
controller      pci0
```

These statements determine the buses for which the kernel will include drivers. We commented out the EISA driver since there are only PCI and ISA buses in the machine. The current FreeBSD kernel includes built-in support for Plug and Play, included through the option statement here.

```
controller      fdc0    at isa? port "IO_FD1" bio irq 6 drq 2
disk            fd0     at fdc0 drive 0
#disk           fd1     at fdc0 drive 1

#options        "CMD640"        # work around CMD640 chip
deficiency
controller      wdc0    at isa? port "IO_WD1" bio irq 14
disk            wd0     at wdc0 drive 0
disk            wd1     at wdc0 drive 1

#controller     wdc1    at isa? port "IO_WD2" bio irq 15
#disk           wd2     at wdc1 drive 0
#disk           wd3     at wdc1 drive 1

options         ATAPI           #Enable ATAPI support for IDE bus
options         ATAPI_STATIC    #Don't do it as an LKM
device          acd0            #IDE CD-ROM
#device         wfd0            #IDE Floppy (e.g. LS-120)
```

## Debugging kernel configuration mistakes

One of the programs we'll run in the steps to build a kernel, called *config*, checks for syntax errors in your configuration file, reporting the line number of the ill-formed line. What it can't do, though, is find logical problems that will keep the kernel from working. There's no straightforward approach to solving those problems — you either have to reason forward from symptoms or resort to brute force.

Here's an example. When we initially built the kernel for the server, we commented out the line for the EISA controller. One of the steps in the build failed (*make*), saying that there were unresolved externals for the EISA controller, which means that one part of the software couldn't find another part it knew it needed. That seemed odd, but lacking more information we took the brute-force approach and added back in the EISA controller. The resulting configuration built correctly, but when I went to boot it, the boot failed with a UNIX failure called a *panic*.

Panic is a wonderfully anthropomorphic term for what the kernel does when it can't figure out any other way out of a deadly problem. In more mundane terms, the system crashes, which is exactly what our broken kernel did — it would get through the boot to where it needed to mount the root file system, find it couldn't, and panic. A few seconds later, it would reboot and try again. Not too useful, but all it could figure out to do.

Looking at the boot messages as they scrolled by on the way to failure, we noticed that we didn't see the usual messages as the kernel discovered SCSI devices. We booted back into the generic kernel (by typing any character but Enter at the boot prompt, then the commands `unload` and `boot kernel.GENERIC` at the prompt) and went sleuthing in the configuration file. What we found was that we'd accidentally left the driver for the Adaptec AHA-174x (EISA) series of controllers enabled, removing the one for the PCI controller. That explained the whole sequence of issues — we had unresolved externals for the EISA controller because we'd left the EISA SCSI driver in; we had a panic at boot time because we had no driver for the only disk controllers in the system. The kernel couldn't mount the root file system because it couldn't find any disks.

Once we'd realized what was wrong, the fix was easy — remove the EISA controller, remove the EISA SCSI adapter, and put back the PCI SCSI adapter. The resulting kernel worked perfectly.

Our visit to floppy and IDE-land will be mercifully short. We removed support for a second floppy, for IDE floppies, and for the secondary IDE controller (we wanted to hook a CD-ROM to the primary port). We also removed support for the CMD640 chip — this is an old, relatively broken IDE controller that has problems with independent operations on the two IDE ports.

```
# A single entry for any of these controllers (ncr, ahb, ahc)
is
```

```
# sufficient for any number of installed devices.
#controller     ncr0
#controller     ahb0
controller      ahc0
#controller     isp0

# This controller offers a number of configuration options, too
many to
# document here  - see the LINT file in this directory and look
up the
# dpt0 entry there for much fuller documentation on this.
#controller     dpt0

#controller     adv0    at isa? port ? cam irq ?
#controller     adw0
#controller     bt0     at isa? port ? cam irq ?
#controller     aha0    at isa? port ? cam irq ?
```

These are the SCSI controllers and devices. Most Adaptec PCI controllers are handled as *ahc* devices. (The mistake we made in the preceding sidebar was to include the *ahb* driver rather than the *ahc*.) None of the rest are in the machine, so by eliminating them we can eliminate the probing for their existence at boot time (speeding the boot) and the memory they use. This means we can't freely add one of the omitted devices — for example, if we wanted to install an Adaptec ISA controller (the AHA-1542CP, for example), we'd have to rebuild a new kernel with the support added in.

```
controller      scbus0

device          da0

device          sa0

device          pass0

device          cd0     #Only need one of these, the code
dynamically grows
```

These are the SCSI devices: disks, optical disks, tapes, and CD-ROMs, respectively.

```
#device         wt0     at isa? port 0x300 bio irq 5 drq 1
#device         mcd0    at isa? port 0x300 bio irq 10

#controller     matcd0 at isa? port 0x230 bio

#device         scd0    at isa? port 0x230 bio
```

These are all proprietary devices (non-SCSI) that will never be on this machine, so we took them out.

```
# atkbdc0 controls both the keyboard and the PS/2 mouse
controller      atkbdc0         at isa? port IO_KBD tty
```

```
device          atkbd0 at isa? tty irq 1   # keyboard controller
device          psm0   at isa? tty irq 12  # ps/2 mouse

device          vga0   at isa? port ? conflicts

# splash screen/screen saver
pseudo-device   splash

# syscons is the default console driver, resembling an SCO
console
device          sc0    at isa? tty
# Enable this and PCVT_FREEBSD for pcvt vt220 compatible
console driver
#device         vt0    at isa? tty
options         XSERVER                     # support for X
server
#options        FAT_CURSOR          # start with block cursor
# If you have a ThinkPAD, uncomment this along with the rest of
the PCVT lines
#options        PCVT_SCANSET=2              # IBM keyboards are
non-std
```

The important lines here are those for *sc0* and *XSERVER*. The default console driver is *sc0*, but you'll have to uncomment the line for *XSERVER*. The rest of the options here are for specialized requirements; read the online documents if they look like something you need.

```
# Mandatory, don't remove
device          npx0   at isa? port IO_NPX irq 13

#
# Laptop support (see LINT for more options)
#
device          apm0   at isa?     disable      flags 0x31 #
Advanced Power Management

# PCCARD (PCMCIA) support
#controller     card0
#device         pcic0  at card?
#device         pcic1  at card?
```

These are pretty self-explanatory. Uncomment the lines at the bottom to enable PC Card support if you put FreeBSD on your laptop. It's OK to leave the APM device in so that it can take advantage of power management on your server, but be careful what you finally enable.

```
device          sio0   at isa? port "IO_COM1" flags 0x10 tty irq
4
device          sio1   at isa? port "IO_COM2" tty irq 3
device          sio2   at isa? disable port "IO_COM3" tty irq 5
device          sio3   at isa? disable port "IO_COM4" tty irq 9
```

The example server has only two serial ports, but there's no need to comment out the lines — the disable keyword lets you put the driver in, but (unless you use the boot configuration editor) the driver will remain inactive.

```
# Parallel port
device          ppc0    at isa? port? flags 0x40 net irq 7
controller      ppbus0
device          lpt0    at ppbus?
device          plip0   at ppbus?
device          ppi0    at ppbus?
#controller     vpo0    at ppbus?
```

Parallel ports. The example server has only one.

```
#
# The following Ethernet NICs are all PCI devices.
#
#device ax0                  # ASIX AX88140A
#device de0                  # DEC/Intel DC21x4x (``Tulip'')
device fxp0                  # Intel EtherExpress PRO/100B (82557,
82558)
#device mx0                  # Macronix 98713/98715/98725 (``PMAC'')
#device pn0                  # Lite-On 82c168/82c169 (``PNIC'')
#device rl0                  # RealTek 8129/8139
#device tl0                  # Texas Instruments ThunderLAN
#device tx0                  # SMC 9432TX (83c170 ``EPIC'')
#device vr0                  # VIA Rhine, Rhine II
#device vx0                  # 3Com 3c590, 3c595 (``Vortex'')
#device wb0                  # Winbond W89C840F
#device xl0                  # 3Com 3c90x (``Boomerang'', ``Cyclone'')

# Order is important here due to intrusive probes, do *not*
alphabetize
# this list of network interfaces until the probes have been
fixed.
# Right now it appears that the ie0 must be probed before ep0.
See
# revision 1.20 of this file.

#device ed0 at isa? port 0x280 net irq 10 iomem 0xd8000
#device ie0 at isa? port 0x300 net irq 10 iomem 0xd0000
#device ep0 at isa? port 0x300 net irq 10
#device ex0 at isa? port? net irq?
#device fe0 at isa? port 0x300 net irq ?
#device le0 at isa? port 0x300 net irq 5 iomem 0xd0000
#device lnc0 at isa? port 0x280 net irq 10 drq 0
#device ze0 at isa? port 0x300 net irq 10 iomem 0xd8000
#device zp0 at isa? port 0x300 net irq 10 iomem 0xd8000
#device cs0 at isa? port 0x300 net irq ?
```

These are the NICs. We required only the onboard PCI interface — *fxp0* — so we took the rest out.

```
pseudo-device   loop
pseudo-device   ether
pseudo-device   sl      1
pseudo-device   ppp     1
pseudo-device   tun     1
pseudo-device   pty     16
pseudo-device   gzip            # Exec gzipped a.out's
```

These are standard networking capabilities—loopback, mandatory Ethernet support, logging, SLIP, PPP, and some others.

```
# KTRACE enables the system-call tracing facility ktrace(2).
# This adds 4 KB bloat to your kernel, and slightly increases
# the costs of each syscall.
options         KTRACE          #kernel tracing

# This provides support for System V shared memory and message
queues.
#
options         SYSVSHM
options         SYSVMSG
options         SYSVSEM
```

*KTRACE* is useful for debugging problems, so leave it in. The others support compatibility with other forms of UNIX.

```
#  The `bpfilter' pseudo-device enables the Berkeley Packet
Filter.  Be
#  aware of the legal and administrative consequences of
enabling this
#  option.  The number of devices determines the maximum number
of
#  simultaneous BPF clients programs runnable.
#pseudo-device bpfilter 4    #Berkeley packet filter
```

That's the end of it. The Berkeley packet filters let you access network packets at a very low level, useful for network sniffing and packet-level firewall protection.

## Building and installing the new kernel

Here are the steps to actually configure, build, and install your customized kernel. Remember that you *never* want to edit the GENERIC configuration file—it's your baseline. You'll need to be logged in as the root user to follow these steps.

1. *Create a new configuration file if you haven't done so yet.* The configuration files are in /usr/src/sys/i386/conf. Use the `cd` command to move there, and run the configuration program on your kernel configuration file. Continuing the ARIES kernel from the preceding example, you'd have done this to initially create the configuration file:

```
cd /usr/src/sys/i386/conf
cp GENERIC ARIES
```

The `cd` command is the UNIX command to change directories; `cp` is the command to copy files. With these two lines, you've created a new file, ARIES, that is an identical copy of the file GENERIC. (Note: UNIX filenames are case sensitive.)

2. *Edit the file into the configuration you want.* The `ee` editor supplied with FreeBSD is pretty simple to work with if you don't have another preference:

```
ee ARIES
```

Press Esc (Escape) to get the menu when you're done; then press Enter to select "leave the editor." Choose "save file" and you're back to the command prompt.

3. *Create the kernel build environment.* You'll be compiling some programs written in the C language in the next step; in this step, a program (*config*) sets up the files to be compiled. This pretty much falls in the mystic incantation category—run this command:

```
/usr/sbin/config ARIES
```

where if your kernel configuration file is named something different from ARIES, you use what ever that name is. If you've run `config` on this kernel configuration file previously, you'll get a line of output saying it removed the old directory; in all cases, you'll get another line identifying the kernel build directory (in this case, that directory is ../../compile/**ARIES**).

You may receive error messages from `config` reporting errors like mistyped keywords or otherwise bad syntax. Load the file back up into the editor, go to the indicated line, and stare at it until you figure out what's wrong.

4. *Build the kernel.* Switch to the build directory, compile the software, and link it together. This is simpler than it sounds:

```
cd ../../compile/ ARIES
make depend
make
```

5. *Install the kernel and reboot.* If the kernel build worked (no error messages at the end), install it with the command

```
make install
```

All that's left is to reboot, which you do with the command

```
shutdown -r now
```

which means to halt the system and reboot with no delay. Your new kernel should boot to the usual login prompt. If not, reboot again, press any key but Enter to get to a prompt, then type in the commands **unload** and **boot kernel.old** (or **boot kernel.GENERIC** to get back to the installation kernel; the kernel.old file is where your previously running kernel has been saved). The kernel.old file is replaced on each "make install"—once you have a copy of a good kernel, you might want to save a copy as kernel.save.

**6.** *Check the boot log for errors.* Run the command

```
dmesg | more
```

to be able to scroll through the boot log. (Press the Spacebar to sequence to the next page; type **h** for help.) Verify the devices you expect were found and that they initialized properly. If not, check over your kernel configuration and rebuild as necessary.

## X Window configuration

Once you've built a working kernel specific to your hardware, you'll probably want to set up the X Window graphical multitasking environment. There are two ways to do this—the hard way is with the `xf86config` utility, a command line tool, whereas the easy way is with XF86Setup, a graphics-based tool. (You'll need to have installed XFree86 for this to work, as well as to have configured your kernel for X Window support.)

You need to know at least these things to configure XFree86:

✦ Your mouse type, which includes manufacturer, number of buttons, interface (serial, PS/2, or bus), and the device it's hooked to (the configuration programs are often wrong—expect the device to be */dev/ttyd0* or */dev/ttyd1* for serial mice on COM1 or COM2, respectively; */dev/mse0* for a bus mouse; or */dev/psm0* for a PS/2 mouse). The mouse will probably be configured during installation; if so, you'll have seen a message that you can use */dev/sysmouse* and the *SysMouse* mouse protocol.

✦ The type of video board, and (if possible) the chip type and amount of video memory.

✦ The minimum and maximum values for the vertical and horizontal scan frequencies of your monitor.

The first thing XF86Setup will want to do is to set up the mouse interface. This is a really good idea because navigating around with the keyboard is a pain.

When XF86Setup starts, you'll see a screen with some general instructions. After reading them, press Enter to go to the Mouse configuration screen (the Mouse button you'll see at the top-left corner of the window will have been highlighted, which is why Enter does this — it's taking the default action). You'll get the mouse configuration screen (Figure 40-6) in response, but over that will be a help screen to guide you through the mouse configuration process. Dismiss the help box by pressing Enter, and then do these steps. *Avoid moving the mouse before the step where you test it because otherwise the initialization might not work right.*

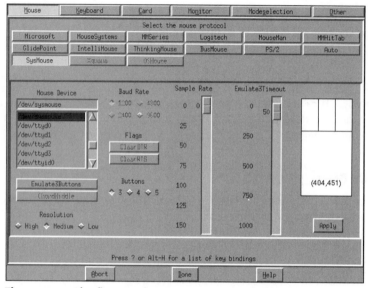

**Figure 40-6:** The first step in XF86Setup is to configure the mouse so that you can use it for the remaining steps.

1. *Choose the mouse protocol.* You can sequence among the protocol buttons by repeatedly pressing the P key. Our server had a PS/2 mouse, so the *SysMouse* protocol choice was defined. Press the A key to apply the change.

   Most current non-PS/2 mice use either the *Microsoft* or *MouseMan* protocols. The *Logitech* protocol is really only for older mice.

2. *Choose the mouse device.* If possible, use */dev/sysmouse*; otherwise, use */dev/ttyd0* or */dev/ttyd1* for serial mice on COM1 or COM2, respectively; */dev/mse0* for a bus mouse; or */dev/psm0* for a PS/2 mouse. You can step to the mouse device choices by repeatedly pressing the Tab key, and then use the up and down arrow keys in the list box of choices. Press the A key once you've picked the right device to apply your choice.

3. *Test the mouse.* Once you pick the protocol and device (and maybe the baud rate), move the mouse around. If the mouse pointer moves properly, you're in good shape. If not, try other devices if nothing happens; try other protocols or speeds if the mouse moves improperly.

4. *Set up three-button emulation.* X Window uses the middle button for copy and paste. If you have a two-button mouse, you'll want to emulate the third button as a simultaneous click of both the left and right buttons (Note: The Microsoft Intellimouse we used in the example server worked as a three-button mouse for this purpose; test your wheel using the image on the right of the screen.). You can turn on emulation by clicking the "Emulate3Buttons" button (don't forget to click Apply!). Test the mouse buttons by clicking them—the small rectangles at the top of the mouse drawing should turn black appropriately as you click and release the buttons, while the numbers in the body of the mouse drawing should track the mouse cursor position.

Once the mouse is working properly, move on to the keyboard configuration by selecting the Keyboard tab at the top of the window (don't click Done at the bottom of the screen yet). The keyboard configuration screen looks like Figure 40-7; the important work for initial setup is to select the keyboard model and layout (and language variant for non-US keyboards). The three controls work much like Windows drop-down lists—click the down arrow and pick the line you want. Click Apply when you have the right choices.

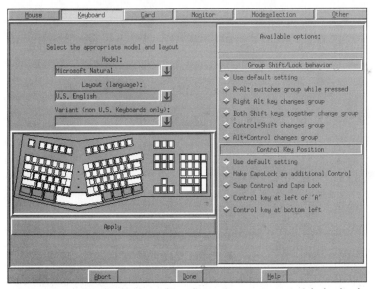

**Figure 40-7:** Use the keyboard configuration screen to pick the keyboard model, layout, and variant.

Things may get a little more complex at this point — it's time to pick and configure your video card. Select the Card tab at the top of the window, and then the Card List button at the bottom right. If your card shows up in the list, pick it and return to the Detailed Setup screen; otherwise, just return to detailed setup. (If your card is too new to be listed, check http://www.xfree86.org for a newer version of XFree86 — it might have the newer driver you need.) Figure 40-8 shows the Card screen after I'd selected the ATI Video Expression card. XFree86 will probe the card at X Window startup time for information it needs you don't specify, including chipset, RAMDAC (the D/A converter) type, clock chip type, RAMDAC maximum speed, and size of video memory. If things don't turn out to work right, you may have to force some of these settings.

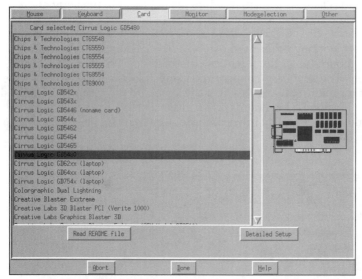

**Figure 40-8:** Use the detailed settings if XFree86 doesn't provide settings for your video board.

If your board isn't directly supported, you can try setting the parameters directly. The SVGA "Server" (an X Window video server is the video card driver) should handle most boards, although without acceleration.

Finally, select the Monitor tab. What you have to do with this screen (Figure 40-9) is to fill in the two lines at the top — the horizontal and vertical monitor sync rates. Your best option is to fill them in directly from the manufacturer's specifications, separating the minimum and maximum values with a dash. If you can't get the specifications, you can try one of the choices in the middle of the screen.

IMPORTANT: The vertical frequencies are doubled if your monitor will be running interlaced. In Figure 40-8, for instance, the monitor (not the Sylvania I used with the example server) only does 45 Hz at 1,024 × 768, but because it's interlaced I had to use 90 Hz for the upper limit.

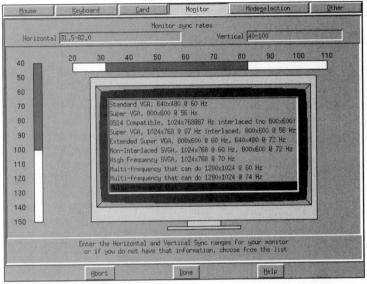

**Figure 40-9:** Be careful about interlace settings when specifying monitor capabilities.

You're done with basic X Window setup. Click Done and the succeeding buttons to write out the configuration file. Once you're back at the command line prompt, run the command

```
startx
```

to start the X Window system. If everything worked properly, you'll see a gray background painted on the screen, then three other windows (*login* and two *xterm* windows). If it doesn't work, you can abort X Window with the Ctrl+Alt+Backspace key combination, reconfigure, and try again. You can exit X Window normally by putting the mouse over the login window and pressing Ctrl+D.

Recent versions of FreeBSD come with the KDE and Gnome desktop environments, software that alters the appearance and operation of the X Window system to look and operate similar to Windows 9*x*. Unless you're familiar with X Window, we recommend you use one of these environments. If you're going to do that, start /stand/sysinstall and choose post-install configuration. When you do, you'll see the screen in Figure 40-10. Choose to configure the Xfree86 desktop.

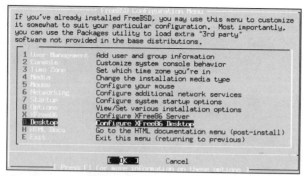

**Figure 40-10:** Use /stand/sysinstall to install and configure
the KDE or Gnome desktop.

You'll go from Figure 40-10 to a screen that lets you choose from KDE, Gnome, and
some other desktops. We installed KDE; the screenshot in Figure 40-11 shows KDE
in operation while we were downloading and getting ready to install Netscape
Communicator.

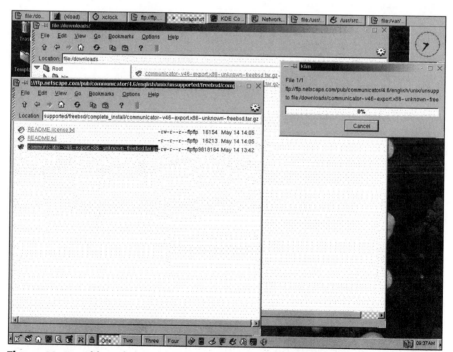

**Figure 40-11:** Although KDE includes a simple Web capability in its Windows
Explorer-like windows, you'll want a fully capable browser like Netscape Communicator.

# Summary

✦ The biggest issues in setting up a server are a careful plan of attack, training, and methodically checking documentation when your course of action is unclear.

✦ Exactly the same issues confront the system administrator—a server affects the work of many people, so you want to be sure what you're doing.

✦    ✦    ✦

# Certification

I t's hard to know if people are good at what they do, harder if they do complex things. Although it's not a guarantee of competence, the difficulty of making that determination is why doctors, lawyers, and accountants are certified by governments and by professional organizations.

Engineering disciplines make use of certification, too. Some engineers attain the status of Professional Engineer, awarded by one or another state; in the computer-related fields companies have made a range of certification programs available to recognize specific competencies.

## Why Be Certified?

For lack of a better term, let's call people who build, upgrade, and repair personal computers *technicians*. As technician, it's worth asking if you should be certified. In this chapter, we'll look at that question from the perspective of people building, upgrading, and repairing PCs.

From the point of view of the individual, certification will take time and cost money even if you're highly experienced. The experienced person may not have to study as much as a rookie, but you'd still want to study to be familiar with the format of the exam and current on the areas to be covered. You can expect exam fees to be in the range of a few hundred dollars — possibly more — plus the cost of your time. The time and cost suggest you'd only want to become certified if there's really a payoff from certification. Certification isn't currently required in most situations — it's mostly a requirement imposed by specific employers.

From the point of view of a company or organization that hires technicians, or that makes use of their services in some way, you may benefit from certified technicians. Here's why:

✦ *Competency.* Although certification is no guarantee that a technician will do what you want when you want it, it is an assurance that the individual meets a certain minimum standard.

✦ *Defined coverage.* Whether the detailed subject is hardware, networks, operating systems, or application programs, there's no one standard for what a technician needs to know. If you choose the certification and sponsor carefully, you gain some assurance that the scope of what's covered in the exam is relevant to the topic, is important, and has no significant gaps.

✦ *Objective measure.* Because certification is (almost always) granted based on a written examination scored either by machine or by qualified examiner, you get some assurance that every certified technician meets the minimum standard for the certificate.

The easiest mistake to make is to expect too much from certification. A self-study course and a one- or two-hour examination isn't a substitute for four or more years of university education in electrical engineering — a certified technician may well not be the person you want designing a high-speed motherboard.

Relative to PC upgrade and repair, there are three key areas for certification — computer hardware, operating systems, and networks. There's no widely accepted standard for UNIX-related certification, so in this chapter we'll examine hardware certification and the certifications Microsoft offers related to versions of Windows.

# A+

The most widely accepted certification for hardware technicians is the A+ certification, a program managed by the Computing Technology Industry Association (CompTIA). CompTIA suggests that the A+ certification provides proof of professional achievement, job opportunities, potential career advancement, opportunity to skip entry-level training by completing tests, customer satisfaction, and more successful hiring.

From a company point of view, keep in mind that if other companies and the general public come to agree that certification ensures better performance, operations that are based on certified technicians can use that fact to competitive advantage. CompTIA, for example, states that more than 1,400 companies have 50 percent or more of their computer service technicians A+ certified and so have earned the designation of A+ Authorized Service Center.

## Content

The A+ examination has four content areas — configuring, installing and upgrading, diagnosis, and repair. The examination has three parts: a core examination and two specialized modules — one for Windows and DOS, and one for the Macintosh. To achieve certification, a technician has to pass the core examination and one specialized module.

Let's look at what CompTIA states an A+ certified technician can be expected to do.

## Configuring personal computers

As a certified technician, you should be able to identify the hardware components in a computer, and you should know how to set them up. That means you need to understand not only what the display, system unit, keyboard, printer, and other box-level units are, you need to understand the serviceable components inside such as disk drives, host and video adapters, and memory modules. Here's some more details:

✦ You should be able to identify what components are replaceable in the field. For each of those components, you should know what they do and what likely results are if they fail.

✦ For each of the key components of a computer, such as the motherboard, display, video adapter, modem, disk, or CD-ROM, you should be able to identify the key elements of the component and explain what the element does.

✦ You should be able to identify the connectors throughout the system, including knowing what the function is of the interface at the connector, what type of devices can be connected at the interface, and what the characteristics of the interface are.

✦ You should know a plan of attack to identify and isolate faults within a computer system, including knowing what is correct behavior and what is faulty.

✦ You should know the tools and procedures required to work on personal computers, including antistatic protection, visual inspection, and documentation.

✦ You should be able to initialize components in the system, including partitioning and formatting disks, and setting resolution and frequencies for displays and video cards.

✦ You should know how to install operating systems on the computer, and how to configure them for operation.

✦ You should be familiar with the I/O port, interrupt request, and DMA requirements for common ISA devices such as serial and parallel ports, sound cards, and network cards. Common usage for the blocks in the memory area from 640KB to 1MB is worthwhile as well. PCI devices usually assign resources at boot time, so it's less important what resources they use.

## Installing and upgrading personal computers

Because the computer industry is continuously creating new, higher-performance systems, a technician is often faced with the requirement to evaluate how to improve the capabilities of a computer or of a number of computers in an organization. A certified technician should be competent to

✦ Analyze the resources and capabilities of a computer, evaluating them against the requirements of the work being done on the computer.

✦ Develop options for upgrading a computer to relieve choke points, increasing the performance and capabilities for the machine's workload.

✦ Replace system components (including motherboards, memory, and disk), removing old ones if necessary, configuring and installing new ones, and reconfiguring system software as necessary.

✦ Identify drivers used in the system, and determine what needs to be changed as the system is upgraded.

## Diagnosing problems in personal computers

Software problems and operator error aside, my experience is that a personal computer in constant use will have a failure of some sort every one to two years. The problems you'll see will include defective floppy disks, failed monitors and power supplies, blocked or failed cooling fans, dirty mice, bad telephone lines or network connections, and more. A hardware technician sees all these issues, leading to concentration on the following issues in the examination:

✦ Be able to effectively gather information from the computer's user to establish a sound basis for diagnosis.

✦ Be able to identify common hardware and software failures from information provided.

✦ Be able to create efficient hypotheses and conduct experiments to resolve among several possible failures.

✦ Be able to identify the stages in the computer boot sequence, and determine problems that could cause anomalous behavior at each stage.

✦ Be able to separate environmental problems, such as poor quality power or high ambient temperature, from hardware failures.

## Repairing personal computers

The pressures in the personal computer industry to increase performance, reduce cost, and reduce size have created innovative technology and packaging, but in the process they have changed the repair operations required of service technicians. At one time, technicians could be expected to isolate failures down to individual chips, replacing failed components to return a board to service. The relatively high cost of the boards made such repairs economically feasible. Today, the high levels of integration needed for high-performance, low-cost systems have all but eliminated the option of board-level repairs. The information to verify that a specific chip has failed isn't widely available, the fine pitch of leads on components and surface mount soldering technology has raised the cost of doing the chip-level repair, and the proprietary chips involved may well not be available.

For those reasons, personal computer repairs mostly consist of identifying the failed large-scale component (for instance, a board or a disk) and making the necessary replacement. Those changes determine the skills a repair technician needs:

✦ Know proper handling and disassembly procedures (including antistatic protection) to be able to reassemble the machine retaining all the mechanical, safety, and electromagnetic shielding protections designed into the equipment.

✦ Know how to remove and replace hardware components.

The increased complexity of the software in personal computers means that many of the problems and failures people encounter aren't hardware problems; they're software or interactions between software and hardware. This change adds another requirement to the necessary set of skills:

✦ Be able to identify, isolate, and solve software problems.

The requirement to deal with software issues is one of the great weaknesses of the industry. Far too many companies leave users with impractical answers to problems, pawning off the interaction between their products and those of another company as not their problem. Although comprehensive answers are expensive, no one is well served by the current practice—not users, who at best get less than full operation from their systems; and not manufacturers, who get little sympathy from users and often lose dissatisfied customers.

Many times, the service technician is in the middle of the issue. An independent service technician rarely has a "hot line" into the engineering staff in the manufacturer's plant but is still expected to solve the problem encountered by the customer. The technician may have no recourse but to reconfigure the system (a potentially expensive operation) to eliminate the conflicting components.

## Training courses

Beyond the fact that a thorough understanding of the material in this book is a good foundation for taking the A+ certification exam, many people will want training courses specifically targeted at A+ certification. There's no shortage of sources for that training—we did a search on the Internet using Digital Equipment Corporation's AltaVista search engine (`http://www.altavista.digital.com`) using the search terms

```
+"A+ certification" +training
```

The plus sign in front of each of the three terms means that each one must appear in a page returned from the search; the quotes around "A+ certification" ensures that the phrase is seen properly as a search term.

The results of the search were surprising, in that over 700 pages met the search criteria. Some were irrelevant, but most were companies and schools either offering training or noting that they offer certified service. Don't overlook colleges and other local schools for training—not just companies offering training.

Don't overbalance the importance of training when you compare it to what you know and the experience you have. While searching the Internet, we found training courses for A+ certification with tuition costs in the $5,000 to $10,000 range. Because the cost of a core exam plus one specialty module is about US $250 (as of June 1999), it might be a good investment to simply take the test if you have good experience.

Self-study isn't for everyone, but it's usually a lower-cost option than courses taught by an instructor. For example, as of June 1999, Heathkit Educational Systems (http://www.heathkit.com) offered an A+ certification individual learning package, including software, reference library, study guide/workbook, and case for $399. A package including the software and study guide alone was available for $179.

CompTIA lists A+ training sources on their Web site (http://www.comptia.com) at http://www.comptia.com/index.asp?ContentPage=certification/certific ation.htm; click on the "Training Resources" link in the upper right.

# Achieving certification

Once you've mastered the A+ certification material, you have two more steps to become certified: sign up for the exam and pass it.

## How to sign up for the A+ examination

Within North America, A+ certification tests are given at Sylvan Authorized Test Centers (there are hundreds of them worldwide). Call Sylvan at 1-800-776-4276 to register. Outside North America, contact AFSMI through their Web site.

Regardless of whether you're in North America or not, you'll need this information to register for the exam:

✦ Sylvan identification number (you can get this when you register)

✦ Telephone number

✦ Mailing address

✦ Billing address, if applicable

✦ Exam number and title

✦ Method of payment (credit card or check)

✦ Date to take the test

Expect to pay the test fees when you register. You can pay either by credit card, by prepaid voucher, or, under some circumstances, by requesting an invoice be sent to you or your employer. Checks are sometimes accepted.

If you don't pass the exam, you can retake it as often as you want (although not several times on the same day!). You have to pass the core and one specialty module within 90 days of each other to become certified. Test centers require scheduling exams two (US and Canada) or three (International) days in advance.

## What the examination is like

The A+ certification exam is a timed, multiple-choice test taken on a computer and scored by computer. You get your results immediately after completing the test. Don't bother to bring books, calculators, laptop computers, or other reference materials — you can't use them during the test. Nor will you need pens, pencils, or paper during the test.

You *will* require two forms of identification, at least one of which must include a picture.

You'll encounter three kinds of questions, all of which require you to choose from a list of choices. Questions may have one correct answer or several; when there are several correct answers, you have to identify them all.

✦ *Situational questions.* You'll be presented with problems cast as a scenario you might find yourself in. The situation description ends with a question.

✦ *Conventional.* You'll be asked a short, direct question.

✦ *Identification.* You'll be shown a diagram, flowchart, or illustration with items called out. You have to choose the answer that correctly identifies the items called out.

There's no penalty for incorrect answers, and unanswered questions count as wrong. That means that even if you're unsure of the answer, you should guess. You don't have to answer all the questions in sequence, so you can go through the exam picking off the easy questions, and then return to the beginning and work on the harder ones. You have 75 minutes to complete the core exam (about 70 questions) and 60 minutes for a specialty module (about 50 questions). All questions have at least one correct answer in the choices you'll see.

The Sylvan test computers include programming for an online tutorial you can use to become familiar with how to answer the different question types. The tutorial should take about 15 minutes.

# Microsoft Certifications

Beyond the A+ certification, a key skill set is the ability to install, configure, and troubleshoot the Microsoft operating systems. Microsoft offers training and certification in Windows 9*x*, Windows NT Workstation and Server, and its BackOffice Internet products.

## What's offered?

Microsoft has established a range of examinations for its products. Passing a defined set of examinations qualifies you for one of the levels of Microsoft Certified Professional (MCP), which include Microsoft Certified Systems Engineer, Microsoft Certified Solution Developer, Microsoft Certified Product Specialist, and Microsoft Certified Trainer.

Qualifying as a Microsoft Certified Systems Engineer, for example, requires that you pass four operating system exams and two elective exams. (More details are at `http://www.microsoft.com/mcp/certstep/mcse.htm`). Table 41-1 is an overview of the examinations Microsoft has defined for the Windows NT 4.0 study track. You must pass an exam in each of the required groups, plus two exams from the elective groups.

| Table 41-1 | |
| :--- | :--- |
| **Microsoft Examinations for Windows NT 4.0 Study Track** | |
| **Examinations** | **Notes** |
| 70-067: Implementing and Supporting Microsoft® Windows NT® Server 4.0 | Required |
| 70-068: Implementing and Supporting Microsoft® Windows NT® Server 4.0 in the Enterprise | Required |
| 70-064: Implementing and Supporting Microsoft® Windows® 95 or 70-073: Microsoft® Windows NT® Workstation 4.0 or 70-098: Implementing and Supporting Microsoft® Windows® 98 | Required |
| 70-058: Networking Essentials | Required |
| 70-013: Implementing and Supporting Microsoft® SNA Server 3.0 or 70-085: Implementing and Supporting Microsoft® SNA Server 4.0 | Elective |

| Examinations | Notes |
|---|---|
| 70-018: Implementing and Supporting Microsoft® Systems Management Server 1.2 or 70-086: Implementing and Supporting Microsoft® Systems Management Server 2.0 | Elective |
| 70-019: Designing and Implementing Data Warehouses with Microsoft® SQL Server(tm) 7.0 | Elective |
| 70-027: Implementing a Database Design on Microsoft® SQL Server(tm) 6.5 or 70-029: Designing and Implementing Databases with Microsoft® SQL Server(tm) 7.0 | Elective |
| 70-026: System Administration for Microsoft® SQL Server(tm) 6.5 or 70-028: Administering Microsoft® SQL Server(tm) 7.0 | Elective |
| 70-059: Internetworking with Microsoft® TCP/IP on Microsoft® Windows NT® 4.0 | Elective |
| 70-056: Implementing and Supporting Web Sites Using Microsoft® Site Server 3.0 | Elective |
| 70-076: Implementing and Supporting Microsoft® Exchange Server 5 or 70-081: Implementing and Supporting Microsoft® Exchange Server 5.5 | Elective |
| 70-077: Implementing and Supporting Microsoft® Internet Information Server 3.0 and Microsoft® Index Server 1.1 or 70-087: Implementing and Supporting Microsoft® Internet Information Server 4.0 | Elective |
| 70-078: Implementing and Supporting Microsoft® Proxy Server 1.0 or 70-088: Implementing and Supporting Microsoft® Proxy Server 2.0 | Elective |
| 70-079: Implementing and Supporting Microsoft® Internet Explorer 4.0 by Using the Internet Explorer Administration Kit | Elective |

The format of the exams is quite similar to the A+ certification exam — the software for the assessment exams is the Sylvan test driver.

## Training courses

You have lots of choices for training before taking the Microsoft exams, including classroom training, online training, and self-study. Microsoft has authorized both companies and schools to conduct classroom training. You can get full information on the Microsoft Official Curriculum and the corresponding training options at http://www.microsoft.com/Train_Cert/train/moc.htm. You can also get self-paced training through a number of books, approved study guides, and videotapes.

## Achieving certification

You have several steps to become Microsoft-certified.

1. Choose a certification you're going after, and decide which exams you'll take to achieve certification.

2. Get the exam's preparation guide and determine what skills you need to master.

3. If you don't already have all the required skills mastered, get the training you need.

4. Work with the product — book learning isn't enough. You'll want to understand how the software works on real machines, what can go wrong, and what to do about it.

5. Take a practice test. You can download practice tests for most certification exams from the Microsoft Web site.

6. Take the test. Like the A+ certification exam, the Microsoft certification exams are administered by Sylvan Prometric. Call 1-800-755-3926 to find a testing center near you (there's more information in the section on the A+ certification). Bring one photo ID and one other ID to the testing center.

Evaluate Microsoft certification as you would any other certification program — decide if the qualification will improve your skills (or those of your employees) in a way that benefits your career or business, and decide if the improvements are worth the time and expense. The prevalence of Microsoft operating systems and products on personal computers makes it likely some of their courses will be of benefit, but you should still work through the cost/benefit analysis.

# Summary

✦ Certification is, in essence, quality assurance for complex skills.

✦ Certification may or may not be right for everyone. Evaluate it from a skills and competitive viewpoint.

✦ You register with Sylvan Prometric (1-800-755-3926) for the A+ and Microsoft certifications.

✦          ✦          ✦

# Appendixes

# On the CD-ROM

Included on the CD-ROM that accompanies this book is the FreeBSD UNIX operating system application packages. As discussed in Chapter 40, "Building a Server — Software Installation," you may choose to install FreeBSD instead of Windows 2000 Server. From this CD-ROM you can install and configure both FreeBSD and X11R6 (the X Window system).

## FreeBSD

FreeBSD is a UNIX operating system for PC-compatible computers from the Regents of the University of California. It offers advanced networking, performance, and security features and makes a powerful Internet or intranet server.

All of the documentation and software included in the 4.4BSD and 4.4BSD-Lite Releases is copyrighted by The Regents of the University of California.

### Installation Instructions

To install FreeBSD, insert the CD-ROM into your CD-ROM drive and double-click the file named ABOUT.TXT for more information. See also Chapter 40, for additional information on setup and configuration.

◆    ◆    ◆

# Vendor List

**H**ere's what you need to know before using this vendor list:

+ No pay or premium service telephone numbers are included.

+ Where vendors provide bulletin board services (BBS), the list assumes 14.4 Kbps service at eight bits, no parity, and one stop bit. Vendors using setups different than this are noted.

+ Don't be terribly surprised if things in the list change. Web addresses are especially subject to change. If you find one that doesn't work, try just the computer address. For example, it used to be that the main page for Seagate Software was `http://www.smg.seagatesoftware.com/index.htm`. At the time this list was frozen, though, that address was invalid, with the server saying the page couldn't be found. Trying `http://www.smg.seagatesoftware.com` instead works. Telephone numbers and addresses are also subject to change, particularly at the rate mergers and acquisitions happen in this industry.

+ We've tried to be comprehensive in this list. You shouldn't assume, simply because a company is included here, that we're suggesting you buy their products. The industry has some real dogs, and you'll need the support telephone numbers for them, too (maybe more).

+ We've noted when tech support is available 24 hours per day, 7 days per week using the code "24/7." This may or may not mean they are open on holidays.

@Home Network
425 Broadway Street
Redwood City, CA  94063
(650) 569-5000
Fax: (650) 569-5100
Web Site: `http://www.home.net`

3Com Corporation
5400 Bayfront Plaza
P.O. Box 58145
Santa Clara, CA 95052-8145
Corporate: (408) 326-5000
Sales: (800) NET3COM (638-3266)
Fax: (408) 326-5001
Support: (800) 876-3266
Fax Back: (408) 727-7021
BBS: (408) 980-8204
Support Web Site:
`http://infodeli.3com.com`
Knowledgebase Web Site:
`http://knowledgebase.3com.com`
Anonymous FTP Site:
`ftp://ftp.3com.com`
Web Site: `http://www.3com.com`

3dfx Interactive, Inc.
4435 Fortran Drive
San Jose, CA 95134
(408) 935-4400
Web Site: `http://www.3dfx.com`

The 3DO Company
600 Galveston Drive
Redwood City, CA 94063
(650) 261-3000
Customer Support: (650) 261-3454
M–F 9 a.m.–noon, 2 p.m.–5 p.m. PST
Customer Support Fax: (650) 261-3419
E-mail: customer-service@3do.com
Web Site: `http://www.3do.com`

3D Realms Entertainment
Division of Apogee
3960 Broadway Boulevard, Suite 235
P.O. Box 4496419
Garland, TX 75043
Sales: (800) 3DREALMS (337-3256)
Fax: (972) 278-4670
Web Site: `http://www.3drealms.com`

3M Data Storage Products
Now Imation Corporation
1 Imation Place
Oakdale, MN 55128-3414
(888) 466-3456
Sales: (800) 328-9438
Technical Support M–F
7 a.m.–6 p.m. CSTT
SuperDisk Products: (800) 888-2700
Other Data Storage: (800) 854-0033
Data Recovery Services: (888) 704-7799
Printing and Proofing Products:
(800) 328-1303
Document Imaging Products:
(800) 328-2910
Photo Color Products: (800) 695-3456
Fax Back: (888) 466-3456 or
(651) 704-4000
Web Site: `http://www.imation.com`

4Home Productions
Acquired by Simply Media
(781) 642-1776
7th Level, Inc.
1200 Richardson Drive
Richardson, TX 75080
(972) 498-8100
Fax: (972) 498-0111
Support Line: (972) 498-8004 M–F 8
a.m.–9 p.m., Sat 8 a.m.–7 p.m. CDT
E-mail Technical Support:
support@7thlevel.com
Web Site: `http://www.7thlevel.com`

Abacus Accounting Systems, Inc.
Now Exchequer Software, Inc.
Suite 1800, Canadian Western Bank Place
10303 Jasper Avenue
Edmonton, Alberta
Canada T5J 3N6
Canada: (800) 665-6657
U.S.: (800) 992-0616
International: (403) 488-8100
Fax — Canada: (403) 488-8150
BBS: (403) 488-3426
Technical Support, M–F, 8:00 a.m.–
4:30 p.m. MST
Canada: (800) 665-6657
U.S.: (780) 424-8100

Fax: (780) 423-4949
E-mail: sales@abacus-group.com
E-mail: tech@abacus-group.com
Anonymous FTP Site: `ftp://ftp.`
`abacus-group.com`
Web Site:
`http://www.abacus-group. com`

Abacus Concepts, Inc.
Statview acquired by SAS Institute
Web Site: `http://www.statview.com`

ABIT Computer Corporation
46808 Lakeview Boulevard
Fremont, CA 94538
(510) 623-0500
Fax: (650) 623-1092
Taiwanese Headquarters:
886-2-2698-1888
Taiwanese Headquarters Fax:
886-2-2698-1811
English FAQ Web Site: `http://www.`
`abit-usa.com/html/ faq.htm`
Web Site: `http://www.abit-usa.com`

Acceleration Software International
Corporation
1223 Finn Hill Road
Poulsbo, WA 98370
(360) 697-9260
Fax: (360) 598-2450
Technical Support: (360) 598-2456
Fax: (360) 598-2453
Web Site:
`http://www.ballardsynergy.com`
Web Site:
`http://www.accelerationsw.com`

Accent Software International, Ltd.
2864 South Circle Drive, Suite 340
Colorado Springs, CO 80906
(800) 694-4050 or (719) 955-3400
Fax: (719) 955-0282
28 Pierre Koenig Street
POB 53063
Jerusalem 91530, Israel
972-2-6793-723
Fax: 972-2-6793-731

Web Site:
`http://www.accentsoft.com`

Access Software Incorporated
4750 West Wiley Post Way
Salt Lake City, UT 84116
(800) 793-8324 or (801) 359-2900
Acclaim Communications
Acquired by Level One
Communications, Inc.
9750 Goethe Road
Sacramento, CA 95827
(916) 855-5000
Fax: (916) 854-1102
Web Site: `http://www.level1.com`

Acclaim Entertainment
One Acclaim Plaza
Glen Cove, NY 11542
(516) 656-5000
Fax: (516) 656-2030
Technical Support: (516) 759-7800,
M–F 9 a.m.–7 p.m. EST
Web Site: `http://www.aklm.com`

Accolade, Inc.
5300 Stevens Creek Boulevard, Suite 500
San Jose, CA 95129
(408) 985-1700
Fax: (408) 246-0246
Sales: (800) 245-7744
Technical Support: (408) 246-8400
E-mail: techelp@accolade.com.
Web Site: `http://www.accolade.com`

Accton Technology Corporation
6 Hughes
Irvine, CA 92618
(949) 707-2300 or (800) 926-9288
Fax: (949) 707-2460
Technical Support: (888) 398-4101 or
(949) 707-4847
E-mail Technical Support:
tech.support@accton-irv.com
FTP Site: `ftp://ftp.accton.com`
Web Site: `http://www.accton.com`

Acer America Corporation
2641 Orchard Parkway
San Jose, CA 95134
(408) 432-6200 or (800) SEE-ACER
(733-2237)
Fax: (408) 922-2933
Taiwanese Headquarters:
886-2-2696-1234
Fax: 886-2-2696-1777
Fax Back: (800) 554-2494
BBS: (408) 428-0140, 28.8 Kbps
Acer Aspire Support: (800) 938-2237
AcerPower or AcerEntra Support:
(800) 445-6495
Laptop Support: (800) 816-2237
Server Support: (800) 873-7255
Anonymous FTP Site:
ftp://ftp.acer.com
Web Site: http://www.acer.com

ACI US, Inc.
3031 Tisch Way
San Jose, CA 95128
(408) 557-4600 or (800) 881-3466
Fax: (408) 557-4625
Web Site: http://www.aci-4D.com
Web Site: http://www.acius.com

Active Voice Corp.
2901 Third Avenue
Seattle, WA 98121
(206) 441-4700
Web Site: http://activevoice.com

Activision Customer Support
3100 Ocean Park Boulevard
Santa Monica, CA 90405
(310) 255-2000
Fax: (310) 255-2151
BBS: (310) 255-2146, 28.8 Kbps
Fax Back: (310) 255-2153
Customer Support, Voice Mail, and FAQ:
(310) 255-2050
E-mail: support@activision.com
Web Site:
http://www.activision.com

Actix Systems, Inc.
3350 Scott Boulevard, Bldg. 9

Santa Clara, CA 95054
Sales: (800) 927-5557
Service: (408) 986-1625
Fax: (408) 986-1646
BBS: (408) 970-3719
A.D.A.M. Software, Inc.
1600 RiverEdge Parkway, Suite 800
Atlanta, GA 30328
(800) 273-ADAM (2326) or
(770) 980-0888
Fax: (770) 955-3088
E-mail Technical Support:
techsupport@adam.com
Fax: (770) 955-3088
Web Site: http://www.adam.com

Adante, Inc.
2141 Palomar Airport Road, Suite 100
Carlsabad, CA 92009
(760) 431-6480 or (888) 827-5557
Fax: (760) 431-6423
Technical Support (760) 431-6425
Web Site: http://www.adante.com

Adaptec, Inc.
691 South Milpitas Boulevard
Milpitas, CA 95035
(408) 945-8600
Fax: (408) 262-2533
Sales (800) 442-SCSI
Customer Service: (800) 959-7274
Fax Back: (303) 684-3400
Automated Support: (800) 959-7274,
Option 1
Technical Support: (408) 934-7274,
M–F 6 a.m.–5 p.m. PST
Technical Support Fax: (408) 957-6776
Software Products Technical Support:
(408) 934-7283, M–F 6 a.m.–5 p.m. PST
Software Products Technical Support Fax:
(408) 957-6776
Automated Technical Support:
(800) 959-7274
Literature Hotline: (800) 934-2766
Webmail Support: http://www.adaptec.
com/support/webmail.html
Anonymous FTP Site:
ftp://ftp.adaptec.com/pub/BBS
Web Site: http://www.adaptec.com

Adaptiv Software Corporation
2130 Main Street, Suite 200
Huntington Beach, CA 92648
(714) 960-2211
Fax: (714) 960-9511
Sales Department: (800) 598-1222
Technical Support: (714) 960-2211,
M–F 7 a.m.–5 p.m. PT
Web Site: http://www.adaptiv.com

Adesso
100 Corporate Pointe, Suite 230
Culver City, CA 90230
(310) 216-7777
Fax: (310) 216-7898
Technical Support: (310) 216-7777, x109
E-mail: support@adessoinc.com
Web Site: http://www.adessoinc.com

ADI Systems, Inc.
2115 Ringwood Avenue
San Jose, CA 95131
(408) 944-0100
Fax: (408) 944-0300
E-mail: techsupport@adiusa.com
Web Site: http://www.adiusa.com

Adobe Systems Incorporated
345 Park Avenue
San Jose, CA 95110-2704
(408) 536-6000
Fax: (408) 537-6000
Customer Service: (800) 833-6687,
24/7Fax: (408) 644-2004
Fax Back: (650) 556-8481
BBS: (206) 623-6984
Technical Support for Windows
Registered Products Only:
Acrobat: (206) 675-6304
FrameMaker: (206) 675-6312
Frame Viewer: (206) 675-6315
Gallery Effects: (206) 675-6358
Illustrator: (206) 675-6307
ImageReady: (206) 675-6370
ImageStyler (206) 675-6373
PageMaker: (206) 675-6301
PageMill (206) 675-6313
PhotoDeluxe (206) 675-6309
Photoshop: (206) 675-6303

PostScript Drivers: (206) 675-6314
Premiere: (206) 675-6305
Streamline: (206) 675-6317
Type Manager/Type Products:
(206) 675-6306
Type Twister: (206) 675-6367
E-mail: techdocs@adobe.com
Anonymous FTP Site:
ftp://ftp.adobe.com/pub/adobe
Web Site: http://www.adobe.com

Adrenaline Vault
Web Site: http://www.avault.com

Advanced Digital Information Corporation
11431 Willows Road NE
Redmond, WA 98052
(800) 336-1233 or (425) 881-8004
Fax: (425) 881-2296
Technical Support Fax: (425) 885-9356
E-mail Technical Support:
support@adic.com
Web Site: http://www.adic.com

Advanced Digital Systems
355 Sinclair Frontage Road
Milpitas, CA 95035
(888) 873-9553 Western Region or
(800) 873-9553 Eastern Region
BBS: (408) 956-8918
Technical Support: (408) 956-0800
Fax: (408) 956-8668
E-mail: adswest@adspc.com
Anonymous FTP Site:
ftp://ftp.adspc.com
Web Site: http://www.adspc.com

Advanced Gravis Computer Technology, Ltd.
Part of Kensington Technology Group
2855 Campus Drive
San Mateo, CA 94403
(605) 572-2700
Customer Service: (800) 535-4242
Technical Support: (610) 266-9505
M–F 9 a.m.–6 p.m. ET
Fax: (610) 231-1022
Technical Support E-mail:
pcstick@gravis.com or sound@gravis.com
Web Site: http://www.gravis.com

Advanced Logic Research
Acquired by Gateway
9401 Jeronimo
Irvine, CA 92618
Sales: (800) 444-4ALR (4257) or
(949) 581-6770
Fax: (949) 581-9240
Automated Technical Support:
(800) 846-2118
General Technical Support: (800) 846-2301
TDD Technical Support: (800) 846-1778
Technical Support E-mail: tech@alr.com
Web Site: http://www.alr.com

Advanced Micro Devices, Inc. (AMD)
One AMD Place
P.O. Box 3453
Sunnyvale, CA 94088-3453
(800) 538-8450 or (408) 732-2400
PC CPU Support: (408) 749-3060
Other Product Support: (800) 222-9323 or
(408) 749-5703
Fax on Demand: (800) 222-9323 — Option 2
E-mail Technical Support:
HW.support@amd.com
Anonymous FTP Site: ftp://ftp.amd.com
Web Site: http://www.amd.com

AEC Software, Inc.
22611-113 Markey Court
Sterling, VA 20166
(703) 450-1980
Fax: (703) 450-9786
Technical Support: (703) 450-2318
E-mail Technical Support:
support@aecsoft.com
Web Site: http://www.aecsoft.com

Agfa Division,
Bayer Corp
100 Challenger Road
Ridgefield Park, NJ 07660
(201) 440-2500
Fax: (201) 440-5733
Agfa Newsgroups accessed through:
http://www.agfa.com/newsgroups
Chromapres Technical Support:
(800) 879-2432

Imaging Technical Support:
(800) TRY-AGFA
ePhoto Technical Support:
(970) 522-1380
Anonymous FTP Site:
ftp://ftp.agfa.com/pub
Support Web Site:
http://support.agfa.com
Photography Web Site:
http://www.agfaphoto.com
Web Site: http://www.agfahome.com
Web Site: http://www.agfa.com

The AG Group, Inc
2540 Camino Diablo, Suite 200
Walnut Creek, CA 94596
(800) 466-2447 or (925) 937-7900
Fax: (925) 937-2479
E-mail: info@aggroup.com
Technical Support: (925) 937-7900
Fax: (510) 937-2479
E-mail: techsupport@aggroup.com
Anonymous FTP Site:
ftp://ftp.aggroup.com/public/support
Web Site: http://www.aggroup.com

AITech International
47987 Fremont Boulevard
Fremont, CA 94538
(510) 226-8960
Sales: (800) 882-8184
BBS: (510) 226-8267, 28.8 Kbps
Fax: (510) 226-8996
Technical Support: (510) 226-9246,
M–F 8 a.m.–5 p.m.
Product Support:
tech_support@aitech.com
Web Site: http://www.aitech.com

AIWA America, Inc.
U.S.A Headquarters
800 Corporate Drive
Mahwah, NJ 07430
(201) 512-3600
Fax: (201) 512-3704
(800) BUY-AIWA (289-2492)
Product Literature Information:
(800) 920-2673
Dealer Nearest You: (201) 512-3606

RAID Technical Support: (800) 274-7425
Tape Technical Support: (888) 297-3004
Web Site: http://www.aiwa.com

AIWA Data Products Services, Inc.
6500 East Rogers Circle
Boca Raton, FL 33487
(561) 989-3440
Fax: (561) 997-6291
BBS: (561) 241-2929
Technical Support: (800), 24/7
Aladdin Systems
165 Westridge Drive
Watsonville, CA 95076
(831) 761-6200
Fax: (831) 761-6206
E-mail: win.support@aladdinsys.com
Anonymous FTP Site:
ftp://ftp.aladdinsys.com/pub
Web Site: http://www.aladdinsys.com

Allegro New Media
Now Software Publishing Corporation
3A Oak Road
Fairfield, NJ 07004
(973) 808-1992
Fax: (973) 808-2645
Customer Service: (800) 489-6720
Harvard Graphics Technical Support:
(603) 886-6642
Fax: (603) 889-6642
Fax: (603) 889-1127
E-mail: support@harvardgraphics.com
Serif, Inc products Customer Support:
(603) 886-6642, M–F 9 a.m.–5 p.m. EST
Fax: (603) 889-1127
E-mail: support@serif.com
Web Site: http://www.
harvardgraphics.com/index.htm
Web Site: http://www.serif.com/
index.htm
Web Site: http://www.spco.com

Allied Telesyn International Corp.
960 Stewart Drive
Sunnyvale, CA 94086
U.S.: (800) 424-4284 or (408) 730-0950
Canada: (905) 709-7444
Fax: (408) 736-0100

Pre-Sales and Product Information:
(800) 424-4284
Fax: (425) 489-9191
BBS: (425) 483-7979
Technical Support: (800) 428-4835,
5 a.m.–5 p.m. PST
Fax: (918) 628-3222
E-mail: TS1@alliedtelesyn.com
Technical Support Web Site:
http://support.alphasoftware.com
Web Site:
http://www.alliedtelesyn.com

Alpha Software Corporation
Acquired by SoftQuad International,
Inc., now NewKidCo International, Inc.
131 Middlesex Turnpike
Burlington, MA 01803
(800) 451-1018 or (781) 229-2924
Customer Service: (800) 451-1018 x117
BBS: (781) 272-4876
Technical Support Alpha Four or Five:
(800) 229-3460
Technical Support all other products:
(781) 229-9497
Fax Installation Support: (617) 272-8222
Automated Support: (800) 225-3766
Web Site:
http://www.alphasoftware.com

Alps Electric (North America), Inc.
3553 North First Street
San Jose, CA 95134
(408) 432-6000
Fax: (408) 432-6035
Alps Electric (U.S.A.), Inc.
3553 North First Street
San Jose, CA 95134
(408) 432-6000 or
(800) 825-ALPS (825-2577)
Fax: (408) 432-6035
Direct Connect: (800) 950-2577
BBS: (408) 432-6424
Technical Support: (800) 449-2577
Technical Support Form:
http://www.alpsusa.com/tsuppt.cgi
Web Site:
http://www.alps.co.jp/index-e.htm
Web Site: http://www.alpsusa.com

Altec Lansing Technologies, Inc.
RTS 6 & 209
Milford, PA 18337-0277
(800) 648-6663 or (717) 296-4434
Fax: (717) 296-1222
Consumer Support:
(800) Altec-88 (258-3288)
Web Site: http://www.altecmm.com

Amdahl Corporation,
Subsidiary of Fujitsu Ltd.
1250 East Arques Avenue
Sunnyvale, CA 94088
(408) 746-6000
Fax: (408) 746-3243
Web Site: http://www.Amdahl.com

Amdek Corporation
*See Wyse Technology*
American Business Information, Inc.,
now infoUSA, Inc.
5711 South 86th Circle
P.O. Box 27347
Omaha, NE 68127
(800) 321-0869 or (402) 593-4500
Fax: (402) 537-6065
Help: (800) 321-0869
E-mail: help@infousa.com
Web Site: http://www.abii.com
http://www.infousa.com

American Lasergames, Inc.
4801 Lincoln Road Northeast
Albuquerque, NM 87109
(800) 863-4263
Fax: (505) 880-1557
Web Site: http://www.algames.com

American Megatrends, Inc. (AMI)
6145-F Northbelt Parkway
Norcross, GA 30071
(770) 246-8600
Sales: (800) 828-9264
Fax: (770) 246-8791
Support: (770) 246-8645
FTP Site: ftp://ftp.megatrends.com
Web Site: http://www.ami.com

American Power Conversion
Corporation (APC)
132 Fairgrounds Road
West Kingston, RI 02892
U.S. and Canada: (800) 788-2208 or
(401) 789-5735
Fax: (401) 789-3710
Customer Service and Technical
Support: (800) 800-4272
Customer Service E-mail:
apcinfo@apcc.com
Technical Support E-mail:
apctech@apcc.com
Technical Support Search:
http://www.apcc.com/english/
svice/index.cfm
Web Site: http://www.apcc.com

America Online (AOL)
2200 AOL Way
Dulles, VA 20166
(703) 448-8700
Billing Services: (800) 827-6364
Customer Service and Technical
Support:
(800) 827-3338, 8 a.m.–2 a.m.,
7 days a week EST
Web Site: http://www.aol.com

AMP Incorporated
P.O. Box 3608
Harrisburg, PA 17105-3608
(717) 564-0100
Product Information: (800) 522-6752
Fax: (717) 986-7575
Fax Back U.S.: (800) 522-6752
Fax Back Canada: (800) 245-4356
Fax Back International: (717) 986-3500
Product Quality Hotline:
U.S.A.: (800) 526-0721,
International: (717) 986-7771
Customer Support: U.S.A. only
(800) 522-6752 or (717) 986-7777
Fax: (717) 986-7575
E-mail: product.info@amp.com
Web Site: http://www.amp.com

Antec, Inc.
47900 Fremont Boulevard

Fremont, CA 94538
(510) 770-1200
Fax: (510) 770-1288
Customer Service (888) 542-6832
Technical Support:
(800) 22ANTEC (222-6832)
(510) 770-1200 x322, 9 a.m.–6 p.m. PST
Fax: (510) 770-1288, Attn.: Tech. Support
Technical Support Call-Back:
(800) 222-6832
FTP Site: ftp://ftp.antec-inc.com/
pub/antec-inc
Web Site: http://www.antec-inc.com

Antec Network Technologies
5720 Peachtree Parkway NW
Norcross, GA 30092
(770) 441-0007
Fax: (770) 441-8388
Web Site: http://www.antec.com

Apex Data, Inc., subsidiary of Smart
Modular Technologies, Inc.
4305 Cushing Parkway
Fremont, CA 94538
(510) 623-1231
Fax: (510) 623-1434
Sales: (510) 624-8180
BBS: (510) 249-1601
Technical Support: (510) 249-1605
Fax: (510) 249-1604
E-mail:
support@smartm.com
sales@smartm.com
service@artecon.com
Driver Downloads:
http://www.smartm.com/support/
html/drivers.html#apex
Web Site: http://www.smartm.com

Apogee Software, Ltd.
P.O. Box 496389
Garland, TX 75047
(972) 278-5655
Fax: (972) 278-4670
Sales: (800) APOGEE1 or
(800) 3DREALMS
Customer Service: (972) 278-5655
Web Site: http://www.apogee1.com

Arcada Software Incorporated
See Veritas Software Corporation
Web Site: http://www.veritas.com

Artecon, Inc.
6305 El Camino Real
Carlsbad, CA 92009
(800) USA-ARTE (872-2783)
(760) 931-5500
Fax: (760) 931-5527
Technical Support: (800) 833-2783 or
(760) 931-5500, M–F 7 a.m.–5 p.m. PST
Support E-mail: support@artecon.com
Web Site: http://www.artecon.com

Artisoft
5 Cambridge Center
Cambridge, MA 02142
(617) 354-0600
Fax: (617) 354-7744
Sales: (800) 914-9985
Networking and Communications
One South Church Avenue, Suite 2200
Tucson, AZ 85701
(520) 670-7100
Fax: (520) 670-7101
Sales and Customer Service:
(800) 846-9726
BBS: (520) 884-8648
Automated Technical Support:
(520) 670-7000
On-Line Technical Support:
http://support.artisoft.com
FTP Site: ftp://ftp.artisoft.com
Web Site: http://www.artisoft.com

Asante Technologies
821 Fox Lane
San Jose, CA 95131
(408) 435-8388
Fax Back: (800) 741-8607,
(408) 954-8607 or (408) 432-9547
BBS: (408) 432-1416
Technical Support: (800) 622-7464
or (801) 566-8991
Technical Support Fax: (801) 566-3787
Technical Support E-mail:
support@asante.com
Web Site: http://www.asante.com

Ascend Communications, Inc.
One Ascend Plaza
1701 Harbor Bay Parkway
Alameda, CA 94502
(800) 621-6578 or (510) 769-6001
Fax: (510) 814-2300
Fax on Demand: (415) 688-4343
Online Fax: http://napa.boomerang.
com/webfax/ascendfax
Product and pricing (800) 621-9578
BBS: (510) 814-2302
Technical Support: (800) 272-3634,
6 a.m.–6 p.m. PST
Technical Support International:
(510) 814-2333 6 a.m.–6 p.m. PST
Technical Support Fax: (510) 814-2312
Technical Support E-mail:
support@ascend.com
Technical Form http://www.ascend.
com/forms/techsupportna.htmy
Anonymous FTP Site:
ftp://ftp.ascend.com/pub
Web Site: http://www.ascend.com

AST Research, Inc.
Subsidiary of Samsung Electronics Co., Ltd.
16215 Alton Parkway
Irvine, CA 92618-3618
(714) 727-4141
Fax: (714) 727-9355
Customer Service and Sales
(877) 278-2661
End User Technical Support:
For Systems manufactured after
January 12, 1999, (877) 278-2661
E-mail: web.support@ast.com
For systems manufactured prior to
January 12, 1999, U.S. and Canada
(800) 727-1278
E-mail: Customer.support@ari-service.com
Technical Support: http://www.ast.
com/support/support.htm
Tech Form: http://www.ast.com/
support/techasst.htm
Web Site: http://www.ast.com

Astound, Inc.
5155 Spectrum Way Unit 5
Mississauga, Ontario

Canada L4W 5A1
(905) 602-4000
Customer Service: (877) ASTOUND
(278-6863) M–F, 9 a.m.–5 p.m. EST
Fax: (905) 602-4001
Customer Service: (800) 982-9888
Technical Support: (905) 602-5292,
M–F 10 a.m.–6 p.m. EST
Technical Support Fax: (905) 602-0393
E-mail: tech@astound.com
Web Site: http://www.astound.com

ASUS Computer International
(ASUSTEK Computer, Inc., Worldwide)
6737 Mowry Avenue
Newark, CA 94560
(510) 739-3777
Fax: (510) 608-4555
RMA Fax: (510) 608-4511
BBS: (510) 739-3774
Technical Support E-mail:
tsd-usa@asus.com.tw
ASUS Newsgroup:
news:alt.comp.periphs.mainboard.asus.
Web Site: http://www.asus.com.tw
Web Site: http://www.asus.com

Asymetrix Learning Systems, Inc.
110 110th Avenue NE, Suite 700
Bellevue, WA 98004
(425) 462-0501 or (800) 448-6543
Fax: (425) 637-1504
Fax Back: (800) 770-5444 or
(206) 637-5833
Technical Support: (425) 637-1600,
M–Th 6 a.m.–6 p.m., F 6 a.m.–3 p.m. PST
Fax: (425) 455-3701
E-mail: support@asymetrix.com
Anonymous FTP Site:
ftp://ftp.asymetrix.com/pub
Web Site: http://www.asymetrix.com

AT&T
32 Avenue of the Americas
New York, NY 10013-2412
(212) 387-5400
Telephone Lookup Web Site:
http://www.anywho.com
Web Site: http://www.att.com

AT&T (Personal Computers)
Now NCR Corporation
1700 South Patterson Boulevard
Dayton, OH 45479
(937) 445-5000
Sales: (800) CALL-NCR (225-5627)
Sales Support: (800) 746-4722
Customer Support: (800) 774-7406, 24/7
Fax: (803) 939-7824
Web Site: http://www.ncr.com

AT&T Business Services
Technical Information: http://www.att.
com/business/solutions.html
T1 Services: http://www.att.com/t1
AT&T Wireless Data Services:
http://www.attws.com
Business Home Page:
http://www.att.com/business
AT&T Paradyne
See Paradyne
AT&T WorldNet
(800) WORLDNET (967-5363)
Technical Support: (800) 400-1447
Web Site: http://www.att.net

ATI Technologies Incorporated
33 Commerce Valley Drive East
Thornhill, Ontario
Canada L3T 7N6
Head Office, Sales, and Marketing:
(905) 882-2600
Corporate Fax: (905) 882-2620
BBS: (905) 764-9404
Fax Back: (905) 882-2600
Technical Support: (905) 882-2626,
M–F 9 a.m.–7 p.m. EST
Technical Support Fax: (905) 882-0546
FTP Site: ftp://ftp.atitech.ca/pub
Technical Support Web Site:
http://support.atitech.ca
Web Site: http://www.atitech.ca

Attachmate Corporation
3617 131st Avenue SE
Bellevue, WA 98006
(800) 426-6283 or (425) 644-4010
Fax: (425) 747-9924

Product Information: (800) 426-6283
Technical Support: (425) 957-4607,
M–F 6 a.m.–5 p.m. PST
Technical Support Web Site:
http://supportweb.attachmate.com
Web Site: http://www.attachmate.com

Autodesk Incorporated
111 McInnis Parkway
San Rafael, CA 94903
(415) 507-5000
Fax: (415) 507-5100
Customer Satisfaction Center:
(800) 538-6401
Product Literature: (800) 964-6432,
International: (415) 507-5000
Fax Back: (415) 507-5595
Web Site: http://www.autodesk.com

Avalon Hill Game Company, acquired by
Hasbro Interactive
50 Dunham Road
Beverly, MA 01915-1844
(978) 921-3700
Sales: (800) 400-1352
Support Web Site: http://support.
hasbro.com/avalon.asp
CD-ROM Patches: http://www.
avalonhill.com/patches.html
Web Site: http://www.hasbro.com

Avery Dennison Corporation
Consumer Service Center
50 Pointe Drive
Brea, CA 92821
(800) 252-8379, M–F 6 a.m.–4 p.m. PST
Fax: (800) 831-2496
Technical Support: (972) 389-3699,
M–F 7 a.m.–7 p.m. CST
Fax: (972) 446-2717
Web Site:
http://www.avery.com/kids
Web Site:
http://www.avery.com/index_
norm.html
Web Site:
http://www.averydennison.com/
index.html

Avid Technology, Inc.
Metropolitan Technology Park,
One Park West
Tewksbury, MA 01876
(800) 949-AVID or (978) 640-6789
Support: (800) 800-AVID
Web Site: http://www.avid.com

Award Software International, Inc.,
merged with Phoenix Technologies, Ltd.
411 East Plumeria Drive
San Jose, CA 95134
(408) 570-1000
Fax: (408) 570-1001
Web Site: http://www.phoenix.com

Axis Communications, Inc.
4 Constitution Way, Suite G
Woburn, MA 01801-1030
(800) 444-AXIS or (781) 938-1188
Fax: (781) 938-6161
BBS: (781) 932-3363
Technical Support: (781) 938-1188
Technical Support Fax: (781) 938-0774
Technical Support Web Site:
http://www.axis.se/techsup
Self Help Knowledge Base:
http://www.rightnowtech.com/
cgi-bin/axis/
Anonymous FTP Site:
ftp://ftp.axis.com/pub/axis
Web Site: http://www.axis.com

Aztech Labs, Inc.
45645 Northport Loop East
Fremont, CA 94538
(510) 623-8988
Fax: (510) 623-8989
Technical Support: (510) 623-9037
Fax: (510) 353-4327
E-mail: support@aztechca.com
Support Web Page:
http://www.aztech.com.sg/C&T/
index.htm
Web Site: http://www.aztech.com.sg
Web Site: http://www.aztechca.com
Web Site: http://www.aztechlabs.com

Ballard Synergy
Now Acceleration Software
International Corporation
1223 Finn Hill Road
Poulsbo, WA 98370
(360) 697-9260
Fax: (360) 598-2450
Technical Support: (360) 598-2456
Fax: (360) 598-2453
Web Site:
http://www.ballardsynergy.com
Web Site:
http://www.accelerationsw.com

Banner Blue Software, Division of
Broderbund Software, Inc.
39500 Stevenson Place, Suite 204
Fremont, CA 94539
Customer Support: (617) 761-3000
M–F 8 a.m.–8 p.m. EST
Automated Technical Support:
(800) 409-1497
Technical Support: (319) 247-3333,
M–F 9 a.m.–9 p.m., EST
Technical Support Fax: (319) 395-9600
E-mail Technical Support:
help@tlcsupport.com
FTP Site: ftp://ftp.learningco.com/
support/tlcfiles.html
Web Site:
http://www.familytreemaker.com

Battery Technology, Inc.
16500 E. Gale Avenue
City of Industry, CA 91745
(213) 728-7874
Fax: (213) 728-7996
Technical Support: (800) 982-8284,
M–F 8:30 a.m.–5:00 p.m. PST
E-mail: support@batterytech.com
Web Site:
http://www.batterytech.com

Bay Networks, Inc.,
now Nortel Networks
4401 Great American Parkway
Santa Clara, CA 95052
General Information: (800) 4NORTEL
(466-7835)

Pre-Sale Support and Product
Questions: (800) 231-4213,
M–F 6 a.m.–5 p.m. PST
Post Sales Support: (800) 2LANWAN
(252-6926)
Product Literature: (800) 8BAYNET
Web Site:
http://www.nortelnetworks.com

Belkin Components
501 West Walnut Street
Compton, CA 90220
(800) 223-5546 or (310) 898-1100
Fax: (310) 898-1111
Technical Support: (800) 223-5546 x2263
or (310) 604-2265, M–F 8 a.m.–5 p.m.
Fax: (310) 631-3629
E-mail: support@belkin.com
Web Site: http://www.belkin.com

Berkeley Systems, Inc., Division of
Sierra On-Line
2095 Rose Street
Berkeley, CA 94709
Customer Service: (425) 746-5771
Technical Support: (425) 644-4343,
M–F 8:00 a.m.–4:45 p.m. PST
E-mail: support@sierra.com
FTP Site: ftp://ftp.berksys.com
Web Site: http://www.berksys.com

Best Data Products, Inc.
19748 Dearborn Street
Chatsworth, CA 91311
(818) 773-9600
Fax: (818) 773-9619
Customer Service: (818) 773-9600
Technical Support: (818) 773-9600,
M–F 8 a.m.–5 p.m. PST
FTP Site:
ftp://ftp.bestdata.com/pub
Web Site: http://www.bestdata.com

Best Power
Unit of General Signal
Power Systems, Inc.
Corporate Headquarters
P.O. Box 280
Necedah, WI 54646

(800) 356-5794 or (608) 565-7200
Fax: (608) 565-2221,
International Fax: (608) 565-7675
Fax Back: (800) 487-6813
E-mail: service@bestpower.com
Web Site: http://www.bestpower.com

Best!Ware
300 Roundhill Drive
Rockaway, NJ 07866
(973) 586-2200
Fax: (973) 586-8885
Sales and Customer Service:
(800) 322-MYOB (332-6962)
Technical Support: (973) 586-2325,
M–F 9 a.m.–6 p.m. EST
Web Site: http://www.bestware.com

Bethesda Softworks, Division of
Media Technology Limited
1370 Piccard Drive, Suite 120
Rockville, MD 20850
(301) 926-8300
Fax: (301) 926-8010
Sales: (800) 677-0700
Customer Service: (301) 963-2000
Technical Support: (301) 963-2002
Fax: (301) 926-8010
E-mail: tech@bethsoft.com
Web Site: http://www.bethsoft.com

Biblesoft
22014 7th Avenue South
Seattle, WA 98198-6235
(206) 824-0547
Fax: (206) 824-1828
Customer Service: (206) 824-8360
Technical Support: (206) 870-1463
E-mail: techsupp@biblesoft.com
Web Site: http://www.biblesoft.com

Bitstream
215 First Street
Cambridge, MA 02142
(800) 522-3668 or (617) 497-6222
Fax: (617) 868-0784
Web Site: http://www.bitstream.com

Black Box Corporation
1000 Park Drive
Lawrence, PA 15055-1018
(877) 877-2269
Fax: (800) 321-0746
E-mail: info@blackbox.com
Web Site: http://www.blackbox.com

Blizzerd Entertainment
P O Box 18979
Irvine, CA 92623
Sales: (800) 953-0283
Automated Technical Support:
(949) 955-1382, #1
Technical Support: (949) 955-1382,
M–F 9 a.m.–6 p.m. PST
Fax: (949) 955-0157
E-mail: support@blizzard.com
Web Site: http://www.blizzerd.com

Block Financial Corporation
4435 Main Street
Kansas City, MO 64111
(816) 753-6900
Sales: (800) 457-9525
Customer Service: (617) 428-1119
Technical Support: (913) 599-2885,
M–F 9 a.m.–6 p.m. CST.
Extended Hours Feb. 1–April 15,
M–F 9 a.m.–10 p.m., weekends,
9 a.m.–3 p.m. CST
Fax: (913) 438-3749
Web Site: http://www.taxcut.com
Web Site: http://www.net-wealth.com
Web Site: http://www.blocksoft.com

Blue Mountain Arts, Inc.
P O Box 4549
Boulder, CO 80306
(303) 449-0536
Web Site:
http://www.bluemountain.com

Boca Research Incorporated
1377 Clint Moore Road
Boca Raton, FL 33487
(561) 997-6227
Fax Back: (561) 995-9456

BBS: (561) 241-1601
Boca Research Technical Support:
(561) 241-8088,
M–F 8:00 a.m.–6:30 p.m. EST
Technical Support Fax: (561) 997-2163
Global Village Technical Support
(408) 523-1050
Technical Support E-mail:
support@bocaresearch.com
FTP Site:
ftp://ftp.bocaresearch.com
Web Site:
http://www.bocaresearch.com

Books That Work, Inc.,
acquired by Sierra
3380 146th Place SE, Suite 300
Bellevue, WA 98007
(425) 649-9800
Customer Service: (425) 562-4223
Technical Support: (425) 644-4343
Web Site: http://www.sierra.com

Borland International, Inc.,
now Inprise Corporation
100 Enterprise Way
Scotts Valley, CA 95066
(408) 431-1000
Sales: (800) 632-2864
Customer Service: (800) 932-9994
Product Registration: (800) 932-9994
Pre-Sales Support: (800) 523-7070
Paradox for DOS and Paradox for
Windows: See Corel Corporation,
(800) 772-6735
Technical Support: (800) 523-7070 or
(831) 461-9144, M–F 7 a.m.–4 p.m. PST
Online newsgroups: http://www.
borland.com/newsgroups
Anonymous FTP Web Site:
ftp://ftp.borland.com/pub/
Web Site: http://www.borland.com

Bose Corporation
The Mountain
Framingham, MA 01701
(508) 879-7330
Fax: (508) 872-6645

Sales: (800) 999-2673,
M–F 8:30 a.m.–9:00 p.m.,
Sat 9 a.m.–5 p.m. EST
Fax (508) 820-3465
E-mail: support@bose.com
Web Site: http://www.bose.com

Brighter Child Interactive
4079 Executive Parkway, Suite 303
Columbus, OH 43081
Fax: (614) 818-7035
Sales: (888) 2TEACH ME (283-2246)
Web Site:
http://www.brighterchild.com

Broderbund Software, Inc.,
acquired by The Learning Company
500 Redwood Boulevard
Novato, CA 94947
Corporate: (415) 382-4400
Sales: (800) 973-5111
Customer Assistance: (319) 395-0115,
M–F 8 a.m.–6 p.m.
Customer Service: (617) 761-3000
M–F 8 a.m.–8 p.m. EST
Download Help: (319) 393-1425,
M–F 8 a.m.–5 p.m. CST
Automated Technical Support:
(800) 409-1497
Technical Support: (319) 247-3333,
M–F 9 a.m.–9 p.m., EST
Technical Support Fax: (319) 395-9600
E-mail Technical Support:
help@tlcsupport.com
FTP Site: ftp://ftp.learningco.com/
support/tlcfiles.html
Web Site: http://www.broderbund.com

Brother Industries, Ltd.
15-1, Naeshiro-cho,
Mizuho-ku, Nagoya
467-8561 Japan
052-824-2511
Japanese Web Site:
http://www.brother.co.jp

Brother International Corporation
Vantage Court, 200 Cottontail Lane
Somerset, NJ 08875-6714
(908) 356-8880
Fax: (908) 469-5338
Customer Service: (949) 859-9700
BBS (888) 298-3616
Printers and Scanners:
Fax Back: (800) 521-2846
Technical Support: (800) 276-7746,
M–F 8 a.m.–6 p.m. CST
Support Fax: (949) 859-2272
Fax Support: (800) 284-4329
Multifunction and Facsimile:
Technical Support (800) 284-4329
Fax: (908) 575-8790
FTP link: http://www.brother.com/pub
Web Site: http://www.brother.com

BSDI World Headquarters
(Berkeley Software Design, Inc.)
5575 Tech Center Drive, #110
Colorado Springs, CO 80919
(719) 593-9445
Fax: (719) 598-4238
Sales: (800) 776-BSDI (776-2734)
Information: (800) 800-4BSD (800-4273)
Support: (800) ITS-BSD8 (487-2738),
M–F 9 a.m.–5 p.m. MST
Technical Support Form: http://www.
bsdi.com/support/request
Map of FTP Web Site:
http://www.bsdi.com/ftpdir
Anonymous FTP Site:
ftp://ftp.bsdi.com
Web Site: http://www.bsdi.com

Bungie Software
350 West Ontario Street
Chicago, IL 60610
Mailing address:
P.O. Box 7877
Chicago, IL 60680-7877
(312) 397-0500
Sales: (800) 295-0060
Technical Support: (312) 255-9600
Web Site: http://www.bungie.com

BusinessVision Management Systems
Airport Square
2600 Skymark Avenue, Building 3
Mississauga, Ontario
Canada L4W 5B2
(905) 629-3233, U.S. (800) 537-4296
Fax: (905) 629-3208
Technical Support: (905) 629-1406
Fax: (905) 629-8854
E-mail: sales@businessvision.com
Web Site:
http://www.businessvision. com

Buslogic, Inc.
Acquired by Mylex Corporation
34551 Ardenwood Boulevard
Fremont, CA 94555
(510) 796-6100 or (800) 77MYLEX
(776-9539)
Fax: (510) 797-7983
BBS: (510) 793-3491
Technical Support: (510) 608-2400,
M–F 6 a.m.–6 p.m. PST
Technical Support Fax: (510) 745-7715
Technical Support E-mail:
techsup@mylex.com
FTP Site: ftp://ftp.mylex.com/pub/
Web Site: http://www.mylex.com

Cabletron Systems, Inc.
35 Industrial Way
Rochester, NH 03867
(603) 332-9400
Fax: (603) 337-2211
BBS: (603) 335-3358
Technical Support: (603) 332-9400,
M–F 8 a.m.–12 a.m.
Fax: (603) 337-3075
E-mail: support@cabletron.com
Anonymous FTP Site:
ftp://ftp.cabletron.com/pub
Web Site: http://www.cabletron.com

Caere Corp.
100 Cooper Court
Los Gatos, CA 95032
(408) 395-7000
Fax: (408) 354-2743
Sales: (800) 535-7226

Customer Service: (800) 654-1187
Fax Back: (408) 354-8471
BBS: (408) 395-1631
Technical Support: (408) 395-8319,
M–F 7 a.m.–5 p.m. PST
Web Site: http://www.caere.com

Cakewalk Music Software
5 Cambridge Center
Cambridge, MA 02142
(617) 441-7870
Sales: (888) CAKEWALK (225-3925)
Fax: (617) 441-7887
E-mail Technical Support:
support@cakewalk.com
FTP Site: ftp://ftp.cakewalk.com/pub
Web Site: http://www.cakewalk.com

CalComp Technology, Inc.
2411 West La Palma Avenue
Anaheim, CA 92801-2689
(714) 821-2000
Fax: (714) 821-2832
Sales: (800) 225-2667
Printer Technical Help: (800) 225-2667
Scanner and Digitizer Technical Help:
(800) 458-5888
E-mail Information: info@calcomp.com
FTP Site: ftp://ftp.calcomp.com/
pub/drivers
Web Site: http://www.calcomp.com

Calera Recognition Systems
Acquired by Caere Corp.
California PC Products
205 Apollo Way
Hollister, CA 95023
(831) 637-2250
Fax: (831) 637-7473
Sales: (800) 394-4122
Web Site: http://www.calpc.com

Cambridge SoundWorks, Inc.
Subsidiary of Creative Labs, Inc.
311 Needham Street
Newton Upper Falls, MA 02464
(617) 332-5936
Fax: (617) 367-9229
Technical Support: (800) 367-4434

Fax: (617) 527-3194
Web Site:: http://www.hifi.com

Campbell Services, Inc., see Open Text, Inc.,
OnTime Group
38777 West Six Mile Road, Suite 101
Livonia, MI 48152
(810) 559-5955
Sales: (800) 559-5955
Fax: (734) 542-1805
Fax Back: (800) 559-5955
E-mail: support@ontime.com
FTP Site: ftp://ftp.ontime.com
Web Site: http://www.ontime.com

Canon Computer Systems Incorporated
2995 Redhill Avenue
Costa Mesa, CA 92626
Product Literature (800) 848-4123
Customer Care (800) 423-2366, 24/7
Fax Back: (800) 526-4345
Canon Accessories Technical
(800) 671-1090
Technical Support: (757) 413-2848,
M–F 8 a.m.–10 p.m., Sat 12 p.m.–6 p.m. EST
Technical Support Web Site:
http://www.ccsi.canon.com/care/
inquiries/index.html
Web Site: http://www.ccsi.canon.com

Canon U.S.A, Inc.
One Canon Plaza
Lake Success, NY 11042
(516) 488-6700
Product Information: (800) OK-CANON
(652-2666)
Web Site: http://www.powershot.com
Web Site: http://www.usa.canon.com

Capstone
7200 NW 19th Street, Suite 500
Miami, FL 33126
(305) 373-7700
Fax: (305) 577-9875
Technical Support: (305) 373-7700
Cardexpert Technology, Inc.
47881 Fremont Boulevard
Fremont, CA 94538
(510) 252-1118

Fax: (510) 252-9889
E-mail: cardex@compuserve.com
Web Site:
http://www.gainward.com/us.htm

Cardinal Technologies, Incorporated
(Acquired by Hayes Microcomputer
Products, Inc.)
5854 Peachtree Corners East
Norcross, GA 30092
(770) 840-2157
Fax: (770) 729-6513
BBS: (770) 840-7586
Fax Back: (800) 947-0808
Automated Technical Support:
(800) 947-0808
Technical Support: (770) 840-2157,
8 a.m.–8 p.m. EST M–F
Technical Support Fax: (770) 729-6513
Web Site: http://www.cardtech.com

Casady & Greene, Inc.
22734 Portola Drive
Salinas, CA 93908-1119
(831) 484-9228
Fax: (831) 484-9218
Sales: (800) 359-4920
Technical Support: (831) 484-9228
E-mail Technical Support:
tech@casadyg.com
FTP Site: ftp://ftp.casadyg.com
Web Site: http://www.casadyg.com

Case Logic, Inc.
6303 Dry Creek Parkway
Longmont, CO 80503
(800) 925-8111 or (303) 530-3800
Fax: (303) 652-1094
E-mail: customer.service@caselogic.com
Web Site: http://www.caselogic.com

Casio, Inc.
571 Mount Pleasant Drive
Dover, NJ 07801
Automated Information: (800) 962-2746
Customer Service: (973) 442-5707
Catalogs and Manuals: (973) 328-1670,
M–F 9 a.m.–5 p.m. EST

Cassiopeia HPC: (888) 204-7765,
Live Support M–F 9 a.m.–8 p.m. EST
Digital Cameras, Image Printers:
(800) 435-77332,
Live Support M–F 9 a.m.–10 p.m.,
Sat-Sun 9 a.m.–5 p.m. EST
Fax Support: (973) 361-3819
Web Site: http://www.casio.com

CE Software, Inc.
P.O. Box 65580
1801 Industrial Circle
West Des Moines, IA 50265
(515) 221-1801
Fax: (515) 221-1806
Sales: (800) 523-7638
Sales Fax: (515) 221-2258
Fax Back: (800) 579-9733 or (515) 221-2168
Technical Support: (515) 221-1803
Technical Support Fax: (515) 221-2169
Newsgroups: http://help.cesoft.com/
tech/newsgroups.html
FTP Site: ftp://ftp.cesoft.com/pub
Web Site: http://www.cesoft.com

Cendant Software, acquired by Havas
Interactive, a subsidiary of Vivendi
Vivendi America
800 Third Avenue
New York, NY 10012
(212) 753-2000
Fax: (212) 753-9301
Central Point Software
See Symantec Corporation
Centura Software Corporation
975 Island Drive
Redwood Shores, CA 94065
(650) 596-3400
Fax: (650) 596-4900
InfoLine Hotline: (800) 444-8782
Customer Service (888) 523-6887
Web Site: http://www.centurasoft.com

Century Software
5284 South Commerce Drive, Suite C-134
Salt Lake City, UT 84107
(800) 877-3088 or (801) 268-3088
(800) 268-2772

FTP Site: ftp://ftp.censoft.com/pub
Web Site: http://www.censoft.com

Cheyenne
A Division of Computer Associates
International, Inc.
One Computer Associates Plaza
Islandia, New York 11788
(516) 342-5224, (800) 225-5224
Sales: (800) 243-9462
ARCserve Technical Support:
(516) 342-5880, 8 a.m.–8 p.m. EST
ARCserveIT Technical Support:
(516) 342-5885, 8 a.m.–8 p.m. EST
ARCsolo Technical Support:
(516) 342-5896, 8 a.m.–8 p.m. EST
Backup Technical Support:
(516) 342-5896, 8 a.m.–8 p.m. EST
Other Technical Support: (800) 654-3042
FTP Site: ftp://ftp.cai.com
Tech Support Web Site:
http://support.cai.com
Web Site: http://www.cai.com

Chips and Technologies, Inc., part of
the Graphics Component Division
(GCD) of Intel Corporation
2950 Zanker Road
San Jose, CA 95134
(408) 434-0600
Fax: (408) 894-2082
Web Site: http://www.chips.com

CH Products
970 Park Center Drive
Vista, CA 92083
(760) 598-2518
Fax: (760) 598-2524
Technical Support: (760) 598-7833
E-mail Technical Support Group:
tech@chproducts.com
Web Site: http://www.chproducts.com

Cirque Corporation
433 West Lawndale Drive
Salt Lake City, UT 84115
(801) 467-1100 or (800) 454-3375
Fax: (801) 467-0208

Technical Support: (800) 454-3375,
M–F 8 a.m.–5 p.m. MST
Web Site: http://www.cirque.com

Cirrus Logic, Inc.
3100 West Warren Avenue
Fremont, CA 94538
(510) 623-8300
Fax: (510) 252-6020
Fax Back: (800) 359-6414, or
International (510) 249-4200
Web Site: http://www.cirrus.com

Cisco Systems, Inc.
170 West Tasman Drive
San Jose, CA 95134-1706
(800) 326-1941 or (408) 526-4000
Fax: (408) 526-4100
Customer Service U.S.: (800) 553-NETS
(553-6387) or (408) 526-7208
Customer Service Fax International:
(408) 526-7000
Sales: (800) 859-6387
E-mail Customer Service: cs-rep@cisco.com
Technical Support: (800) 553-2447 or
(408) 526-7209
Technical Assistance Center E-mail:
tac@cisco.com
Technical Support Europe: 32-2-778-4242
E-mail: euro-tac@cisco.com
Web Site: http://cco.cisco.com
Web Site: http://www.cisco.com

Citadel Technology
3811 Turtle Creek Boulevard, Suite 600
Dallas, TX 75219-4421
U.S.A. and Canada Sales: (800) 962-0701
Technical Support and International
Sales: (214) 520-9292
Fax: (214) 520-9293
Web Site: http://www.citadel.com

Citizen America Corporation
831 South Douglas Street, Suite 121
PO Box 1021
El Segundo, CA 90245-1021
(310) 643-9825
Fax: (310) 725-0969
Customer Service and Technical Support

Desktop or Portable Printers:
(310) 643-9825, M–F 8 a.m.–Noon,
1 p.m.–4 p.m. PST
IDP Printer: (201) 944-1313 or
(800) 421-6516
Fax: (201) 944-6669
Web Site:
http://www.citizen-america.com

Claris Corporation, now FileMaker, Inc.
5201 Patrick Henry Drive
Box 58168
Santa Clara, CA 95052-8168
(408) 987-7000
General Services: (800) 544-8554
Customer Relations Fax: (408) 987-3932
Fax Back: (800) 800-8954
Automated Support: (800) 735-7393
Technical Support: (512) 873-4300
Web Site: http://www.apple.com

CLEAR Software
Acquired by SPSS, Inc.
233 South Wacker Drive, 11th Floor
Chicago, IL 60606-6307
(312) 651-3000
Sales and Information: (800) 543-2185
Customer Service: (800) 521-1337
Fax: (800) 841-0064
Technical Support: (312) 651-3410,
9 a.m.–5 p.m. CST
Bay Area Technical Support:
(510) 412-2900, 8 a.m.–5 p.m. PST
Technical Support Form:
http://www.spss.com/tech/
MailForm. html
Online Listserves:
http://www.spss.com/tech/
listserves.html
Web Site: http://www.spss.com

Cliffs Notes, Inc.
1610 South 70th Street, Suite 102
Lincoln, NE 68506
(402) 423-5050
Fax: (402) 327-9912
Sales: (800) 228-4078
Web Site: http://www.cliffs.com

CMD Technology, Inc.
19 Morgan
Irvine, CA 92618
(949) 454-0800
Fax: (949) 455-1656
Sales: (800) 426-3832
Sales Fax: (949) 454-1181
BBS: (949) 454-0795
Technical Support: (949) 454-0800
Technical Support Fax: (949) 454-8314
FTP Site: ftp://ftp.cmd.com/pub
Web Site: http://www.cmd.com

CNET, Inc.
150 Chestnut Street
San Francisco, CA 94111
(415) 395-7800
Web Site: http://www.news.com
Web Site: http://www.computers.com
Web Site: http://www.builder.com
Web Site: http://www.gamecenter.com
Web Site: http://www.download.com
Web Site: http://www.shareware.com
Web Site: http://www.search.com
Web Site: http://www.shopper.com
Web Site: http://www.cnet.com

Cogent Data Technologies, Inc.,
acquired by Adaptec, Inc.
691 South Milpitas Blvd.
Milpitas, CA 95035
(408) 945-8600
Fax: (408) 262-2533
Technical Support: (408) 934-7274
Support Fax: (408) 957-6776
Technical Support E-mail:
support@adaptec.com
Web Site: http://www.adaptec.com

Colorado Memory Systems
See Hewlett-Packard Company
Compaq Computer Corporation
20555 State Hwy 249
Houston, TX 77070-2698
Mailing Address:
P.O. Box 692000
Houston, TX 77269-2000
(281) 370-0670
Fax: (281) 514-1740

Product Information: U.S. (800)
345-1518, Canada (800) 567-1616, 24/7
Fax Back: (800) 345-1518, option 1
BBS: (281) 518-1418
Windows 95 Upgrade Support:
(800) WIN95-45 (946-9545)
Technical Support: (800) OKCOMPAQ
(652-6672), 24/7
Server Technical Support:
(800) 386-2172
E-mail: support@compaq.com
FTP Site: ftp://ftp.compaq.com/pub
Web Site: http://www.compaq.com

Compatible Systems
4730 Walnut Street, Suite 102
P.O. Box 17220
Boulder, CO 80308
(800) 356-0283 or (303) 444-9532
Fax: (303) 444-9595
Technical Support: (800) 356-0283,
M–F 8 a.m.–6 p.m. MST
E-mail: support@compatible.com
Web Site:
http://www.compatible.com

Comptons New Media, acquired by
The Learning Company
One Athenaeum Street
Cambridge, MA 02142
(617) 494-1200
Customer Support: (617) 761-3000
M–F 8 a.m.–8 p.m. EST
Fax: (617) 494-1219
Automated Technical Support:
(800) 409-1497
Technical Support: (319) 247-3333,
M–F 9 a.m.–9 p.m., EST
Technical Support Fax: (319) 395-9600
FTP Site: ftp://ftp.learningco.com/
support/tlcfiles.html
E-mail: help@tlcsupport.com
Web Site: http://www.learningco.com

Compuserve Interactive Services, Inc.,
Acquired by AOL
5000 Arlington Centre Boulevard
P.O. Box 20212
Columbus, OH 43220

(614) 457-8600
Customer Service: (800) 609-1674,
(800) 843-8990
Access Number Lookup:
http://www.compuserve.com/content/
phone/phone.asp
Web Site: http://www.compuserve.com

Computer Associates International, Inc.
One Computer Associates Plaza
Islandia, NY 11788-7000
Corporate: (516) DIAL CAI (342-5224)
Client Care: (800) 225-5224
Fax: (516) 342-5734
Fax Back: (800) 225-5224
ACCPAC Technical Support:
(604) 207-9481
ARCserve Technical Support:
(516) 342-5880
InocuLAN for Windows Technical
Support: (516) 342-5896
InocuLAN for NT Technical Support:
(516) 342-5880
If product number not found:
(800) 645-3042
Technical Support Web Site:
http://www.cai.com/casuppt.htm
Anonymous FTP Site: ftp://mf.cai.com
Web Site: http://www.cai.com

Computing Technology Industry
Association (CompTIA)
450 East 22nd Street, Suite 230
Lombard, IL 60418-6158
(630) 268-1818
Fax (630) 268-1384
Web Site: http://www.comptia.org

Concentric Data Systems
Subsidiary of Wall Data Incorporated
110 Turnpike Road
Westborough, MA 01581
(508) 366-1122 or (800) 325-9035
Web Site: http://www.walldata.com

Connectix Corporation
2955 Campus Drive
San Mateo, CA 94403
(650) 571-5100

Customer Service: (800) 950-5880,
M–F 8 a.m.–5 p.m. PST
Fax: (650) 571-0850
Technical Support: (970) 304-9533,
M–F 8 a.m.–8 p.m. PST
Technical Support Fax: (650) 571-5195
E-mail: support@connectix.com
Web Site: http://www.connectix.com

Conner Peripherals
Now Seagate Technology
Conner Storage Systems
Now Seagate Technology
1650 Sunflower Avenue
Costa Mesa, CA 92626
Sales: (800) 626-6637 or (714) 641-1230
Fax: (714) 966-5573
Fax Back and Automated Technical
Support: (800) SEAGATE (732-4283) or
(405) 936-1220
Technical Support: (405) 936-1400,
M–F 8:00 a.m.–12:15 p.m., 1:30 p.m.–6:00 p.m.
Fax: (408) 936-1683
TDD: (405) 936-1687
Web Site: http://www.seagate.com/
tape/tapetop.shtml

Core Design
See Eidos Interactive
Corel CD Creator
See Adaptec, Inc.
Corel Corporation
1600 Carling Avenue
Ottawa, Ontario
Canada K1Z 8R7
(613) 728-3733
Fax: (613) 761-9176
Fax Back: (613) 728-0826
BBS: (613) 728-4752
Customer Service U.S. and Canada:
(800) 772-6735
Fax Back: (801) 765-4037
Technical Support:
WordPerfect Suite 8: U.S. (716) 871-2325,
Canada (613) 728-5324
WordPerfect Suite 7: U.S. (716) 871-2316,
Canada (613) 728-2702

*Continued*

*(continued)*
Office Professional 7: U.S. (716)
871-2317, Canada (613) 728-2822
Paradox for DOS or Windows:
(613) 728-5258
Paradox 7, Corel Paradox 8:
(613): 728-4657
CorelDRAW 5: (613) 728-6641
CorelDRAW 6, 7, 8: (613) 728-7070
Corel Print: (613) 728-6891
FTP Site: ftp://ftp.corel.com/pub
Newsgroups: http://www.corel.com/
support/newsgroup.htm
Web Site: http://www.corel.com

CoStar Corporation
599 West Putnam Avenue
Greenwich, CT 06830
Customer Service: (800) 426-7827 or
(203) 661-9700, 9:00 a.m.–5:30 p.m. EST
Technical Support: (203) 661-9700,
M–F 9 a.m.–5 p.m. EST
Fax: (203) 661-1540 or (203) 661-6534
E-mail: support@costar.com
Web Site: http://www.costar.com

Cray Communications, Inc.
Acquired by Osicom Technologies
International
9020 Junction Drive
Annapolis Junction, MD 20701
(800) 359-7710
Sales: (301) 317-7710
Fax: (301) 317-7220
Technical Support: (800) 674-2668
FTP Site:
ftp://craygate.craycom.com/pub
Web Site: http://www.craycom.com

Cray Research, Inc
Subsidiary of Silicon Graphics, Inc. (SGI)
655 Lone Oak Drive
Eagan, MN 55121
(612) 452-6650
Fax: (612) 683-7199
Support: (800) 950-CRAY (800 950-2729)
Web Site: http://www.cray.com

Creative Labs Incorporated
1901 McCarthy Boulevard
Milpitas, CA 95035
Sales Customer Service: (800) 998-1000,
M–F 8 a.m.–7 p.m. CST
Customer Assistance: (800) 998-5227,
M-Sat 8 a.m.–10 p.m., Sun 12 p.m.–8 p.m.
CST
TDD: (405) 372-7341
Fax Back: (405) 372-5227
BBS: (405) 742-6660
Technical Support: (405) 742-6622,
M-Sat 8 a.m.–10 p.m., Sun 12 p.m.–8 p.m.
CST
Technical Support Fax: (405) 742-6633
Technical Support Web Site:
http://support.soundblaster.com
FTP Site: ftp://ftp.creaf.com/pub
Web Site: http://www.sblive.com
Web Site: http://www.soundblaster.
com/live
Web Site: http://www.creaf.com
Web Site: http://www.creaf.com/
welcome.html
Web Site: http://www.creaf.com

Crucial Technology
3475 E. Commercial Ct.
Meridian, ID 83642
Customer Service: (800) 336-8915
Technical Support: (800) 336-8916
Web Site: http://www.micron.com

Crystal Services
See Seagate Software
CTX International, Inc.
748 Epperson Dr.
City of Industry, CA 91748
(626) 839-0500 or (800) 888-9052
Fax: (626) 810-1957
Monitor:
Customer Services (800) 888-2012
Technical Support: (800) 888-2120,
M–F 6 a.m.–6 p.m. PST
Fax: (909) 598-8294
Desktop:
Customer Service: (800) 742-5289,
M–F 6 a.m.–6 p.m. PST
Technical Support: (800) 285-1889, 24/7

Fax: (800) 863-8463
BBS: (909) 595-3870
Notebook:
Customer Service: (800) 281-1052,
M–F 6 a.m.–6 p.m. PST
Parts: (800) 289-8808, M–F 6 a.m.–6 p.m.
PST
Technical Support: (800) 888-2017, 24/7
Fax: (909) 595-6293
BBS: (909) 595-6096
Web Site: http://www.ctxintl.com

CUC International, acquired by Havas
International
Web Site: http://www.cucsoftware.com

Curtis Computer Products, acquired by
Esselte
2210 Second Avenue
Muscatine, IA 52761
(800) 272-2366
Fax: (800) 272-2382
Curtis Connections (800) 877-8262
Web Site:
http://www.curtisconnections.com
Web Site:
http://www.curtis.com/curtis

Cybermedia, part of the McAfee
Software Division of Network Associates
3000 Ocean Park Boulevard, Suite 2001
Santa Monica, CA 90405
(310) 581-4700
Customer Care: (408) 988-3832
Technical Support: (801) 492-2700,
M–F 7 a.m.–6 p.m. Central
Web Site: http://www.mcafee.com

Cybex Computer Products Corporation
4991 Corporate Drive
Huntsville, AL 35805
(800) 462-9239 or (256) 430-4000
Fax: (256) 430-4030
Fax on Demand: (800) GO-CYBEX
Technical Support: (256) 430-4000,
M–F 8 a.m.–6 p.m. CST
Technical Support Fax: (256) 430-4031
Web Site: http://www.cybex.com

Cyrix Corporation, a subsidiary of
National Semiconductor Corporation
2703 N. Central Expressway
Richardson, TX 75080
(972) 968-8388
Fax: (972) 699-9857
Processor Technical Support and Sales:
(800) 462-9749
E-mail: tech_support@cyrix.com
E-mail: games@cyrix.com
Web Site: http://www.cyrix.com

DacEasy, Inc., subsidiary of The Sage
Group
17950 Preston Road, Suite 50
Dallas, TX 75252
(800) DAC EASY (322-3279)
(972) 732-7500
Fax: (972) 713-6331
FTP Index: http://www.daceasy.com/
support/ftplist.htm
Web Site: http://www.daceasy.com

Data Fellows, Inc.
675 N. First Street, 8th Floor
San Jose, CA 95112
(408) 938 6700
Fax: (408) 938 6701
E-mail: info@DataFellows.com
E-mail:
Anti-virus-Support@DataFellows.com
Anonymous FTP Site:
ftp://ftp.datafellows.com
Also see Web Site:
http://www.f-prot.com
Computer Virus Information Web
Site: http://www.datafellows.
com/vir-info
Web Site:
http://www.datafellows.com

Dataproducts Corporation, Group
Hitachi Koki, now Hitachi Koki Imaging
Solutions
1757 Tapo Canyon Road
Simi Valley, CA 93063
(805) 578-4000

*Continued*

*(continued)*
Fax: (805) 578-4001
Customer Services: (800) 887-8848 or
(805) 578 4455
Fax Back: (805) 578-9255
Technical Support: (800) 887-8848 or
(805) 578-4455, M–F 6 a.m.–5 p.m. PST
FTP Site: ftp://ftp.dpc.com
Web Site: http://www.dpc.com

Datastor
12601 Monarch Street
Garden Grove, CA 92841
(800) 777-6621
Fax: (949) 833-9600
Web Site: http://www.dstor.com

Datastorm Technologies, acquired by
Symantec Corporation
175 West Broadway
Eugene, OR 97401
(541) 334-6054
Fax: (541) 984-8020
Customer Service: (800) 441-7234 or
(541) 334-6054
Technical Support: (541) 984-7830,
M–F 7 a.m.–4 p.m. PST
Web Site: http://www.datastorm.com

Datatech Enterprises, Inc.
10 Clipper Road
West Conshohocken, PA 19428
(800) 523-0320
Fax: (610) 825-1397
Web Site: http://www.datatechusa.com

DataViz, Inc.
55 Corporate Drive
Trumbull, CT 06611
(203) 268-0030
Fax: (203) 268-4345
Sales and Upgrade Information:
(800) 733-0030
Technical Support: (203) 268-0030
Web Site: http://www.dataviz.com

Davidson & Associates, acquired by
Knowledge Adventure, Inc.
19840 Pioneer Avenue
Torrance, CA 90503

(310) 793-0600
Fax: (310) 793-0601
Sales and Customer Service:
(800) 545-7677
E-mail: sales@davd.com
Fax Back: (800) 556-6141
Learning Center Series Technical
Support: (612) 884-7935
9:00 a.m.–4:30 p.m. CST
Learning Center Series Technical
Support:
http://lcs.havasinteractive.com
Other Technical Support:
(800) 556-6141, M–F 7 a.m.–5 p.m. PST
Web Site: http://www.
knowledgeadventure.com

Da Vinci Systems
See ON Technology
Dayna Communications, Inc., acquired
by Intel Corporation
849 West Levoy Drive, Sorenson
Research Park
Salt Lake City, UT 84123
(801) 269-7200
Fax: (801) 269-7363
E-mail: support@dayna.com
Web Site: http://www.dayna.com

DEC
See Digital Equipment Corporation
Dell Computer Corporation
One Dell Way
Round Rock, TX 78682-2244
(512) 338-4400
Fax: (512) 728-3653
Product Information: (800) 289-3355
Customer Service: (800) 624-9897
Dell Service Parts: (800) 372-3355
Fax Back (888) 560-8324
Technical Support: (888) 560-8324, 24/7
TTY Technical Support: (877) 335-5889,
M–F 8 a.m.–5 p.m. S–S 10 a.m.–2 p.m. CST
Support Web Site: http://www.dell.com/
support/index.htm
E-mail: support@dell.com
Web Site: http://support.dell.
com/support
Web Site: http://www.dell.com

DeLorme Mapping
Two DeLorme Drive
P.O. Box 298
Yarmouth, ME 04096
(207) 864-7000
Sales: (800) 452-5931
Fax: (800) 575-2244
Customer Service: (800) 511-2459
Automated Information Library:
(207) 846-7058
Technical Support: (207) 846-8900,
MTWF 8:30 a.m.–5:00 p.m.,
Th 9 a.m.–5 p.m. ET
Fax: (207) 846-7051
Web Site: http://www.delorme.com

Delrina Technology Incorporated
See Symantec Corporation
Deltec Electronics, now Powerware
2727 Kurtz Street
San Diego, CA 92110
(619) 291-4211 or (800) 854-2658
Technical Support: (800) 848-4734, 24/7
Fax: (619) 692-6592
Web Site: http://www.powerware.com

Deneba Software
7400 S.W. 87th Avenue
Miami, FL 33173
(305) 596-5644
Fax: (305) 273-9069
Sales: (305) 596-5644
Customer Support: (305) 596-5644
Web Site: http://www.deneba.com

DFI-USA
Diamond Flower Electric Instrument Co.,
(U.S.A.) Inc.
135 Main Avenue
Sacramento, CA 95838
(916) 568-1234
Fax: (916) 568-1233
Technical Support: (732) 651-8890,
9:00 a.m.–5:30 p.m., M–F EST
Fax: (732) 390-2817
Technical Support (916) 568-1234,
8 a.m.–5 p.m., M–F, PST
Fax: (916) 568-1216
FTP Site: ftp://ftp.dfine.com
FTP Site: ftp://ftp.dfiusa.com

East Coast Web Site:
http://www.itox.com
West Coast Web Site:
http://www.dfiusa.com

Diagsoft Incorporated, subsidiary of
Sykes Enterprises, Inc.
100 North Tampa Street
Tampa, FL, 33602
(813) 274-1000
Fax: (813) 209-4445
E-mail: support@diagsoft.com
Web Site: http://www.diagsoft.com

Diamond Multimedia Systems
Incorporated
2880 Junction Avenue
San Jose, CA 95134-1922
(408) 325-7000 or (800) 468-5846
Fax: (408) 325-7070
Customer Service: (800) 468-5846,
M–F 6 a.m.–7 p.m. PST
Fax: (408) 325-7408
Fax Back: (800) 380-0030 or
(541) 967-2424
BBS: (408) 325-7080 or (408) 325-7175,
28.8 Kbps
Technical Support: (541) 967-2450,
M–F 5 a.m.–7 p.m. Sat 8 a.m.–4 p.m. PST
Fax: (541) 967-2401
TTY/TDD (541) 967-2451
FTP Site: ftp://ftp.diamondmm.com
Web Site: http://www.diamondmm.com

Digi International
Corporate Headquarters
11001 Bren Road East
Minnetonka, MN 55343
(800) 344-4273 or (612) 912-3444
Fax: (612) 912-4952
Customer Service: (612) 912-3456
Customer Service Fax: (612) 912-4959
Fax Back: (612) 912-4990
Technical Support: (612) 912-3456
Technical Support Fax: (612) 912-4958
Technical Support E-mail:
support@dgii.com
FTP Site: ftp://ftp.dgii.com/support
Web Site: http://www.dgii.com

Digital Directory Assistance, Inc.,
acquired by infoUSA, Inc.
Digital Equipment Corporation,
acquired by Compaq Corporation
146 Main Street
Maynard, MA 01754
(800) 344-4825, 8 a.m.–8 p.m. ET
Fax: (800) 676-7517
Information: (800) 722-9332, 8:30
a.m.–8:00 p.m. ET
Sales: (800) 344-4825
Fax Back: (800) 344-4825
Automated Technical Support:
(800) 354-9000
Customer Support Center,
M–F 8 a.m.–8 p.m. EST and Desktop
Support, 8 a.m.–1 a.m. M–F EST
U.S.: (800) 354-9000
Canada: English (800) 267-5251, French
(800) 267-2603
Web Site: http://www.digital.com

Digital Products, Inc., now NETsilicon
Subsidiary of Osicom Technologies
411 Waverly Oaks Road, Suite 227
Waltham, MA 02154
U.S. and Canada: (800) 243-2333,
International: (781) 647-1234
Fax: (781) 647-4474
Fax Back: (781) 398-4950
Technical Support: (800) 984-9004 or
(781) 647-1234, M–F 8:30 a.m.–8:30 p.m. EST
E-mail: techsup@digprod.com
FTP Site: ftp://ftp.digprod.com
Web Site: http://www.digprod.com

Discovery Channel Multimedia
7700 Wisconsin Avenue
Bethesda, MD 20814
(301) 986-1999
Sales: (800) 889-9950
Customer Service: (800) 627-9399,
8 a.m.–9 p.m. EST M–F
Web Site:
http://multimedia.discovery.com

Disney Interactive
500 South Buena Vista Street
Burbank, CA 91521-6385

(800) 228-0988
Sales: (800) 688-1520
Technical Support: (800) 228-0988,
M–F 7 a.m.–6 p.m. PST
Web Site: http://disney.go.com/
DisneyInteractive/index.html

Ditek International
60 West Wilmot Street
Richmond Hill, Ontario
Canada, L4B 1M6
(905) 771-8000
Technical Support: (905) 771-8000
PhotoWorks 4.1 acquired by MGI
Software Corp
Web Site: http://www.ditek.com

D-Link Systems, Inc.
53 Discovery Drive
Irvine, CA 92618
(949) 788-0805
Sales: (800) 326-1688
Technical Support: (949) 788-0805
Web Site: http://www.dlink.com

Domark
See Eidos Interactive
DSP Group, Inc.
3120 Scott Boulevard
Santa Clara, CA 95054
(408) 986-4300
Fax: (408) 986-4323
Web Site: http://www.dspg.com

DTC Data Technology Corporation
1515 Centre Pointe Drive
Milpitas, CA 95035
(408) 942-4000
Fax: (408) 942-4027
BBS: (408) 942-4010
Fax Back: (408) 942-4005
Technical Support: (408) 262-7700
Web Site:
http://www.datatechnology.com

Edmark Corporation
P.O. Box 97021
Redmond, WA 98073-9721
(425) 556-8400

Fax: (425) 556-8998
Sales: (800) 691-2986
Customer Service: (800) 691-2986 or
(425) 556-8400, M–F 6:30 a.m.–5:00 p.m. PST
Automated Support and Fax Back:
(800) 320-8381
Technical Support: (425) 556-8480,
M–F 8 a.m.–8 p.m. PST
Fax: (425) 556-8940
Web Site: http://www.edmark.com

Eidos Interactive
Formerly Domark, US Gold, and
Core Design
651 Brannan Street, 4th Floor
San Francisco, CA 94107
(415) 547-1200
Fax: (415) 547-1201
Technical Support: (415) 547-1244
Technical Support E-mail:
techsupp@eidos.com
Web Site:
http://www.eidosinteractive.com

Eiger Labs, Inc
37800 Central Court
Newark, CA 94560
(510) 739-0900
Fax: (510) 739-0749
Technical Support: (510) 739-2626
Web Site: http://www.eigerlabs.com

Electronic Arts
209 Redwood Shores Parkway
Redwood City, CA 94065
(650) 628-1500
Technical Support: (650) 628-4311
Technical Support Fax: (650) 628-5999
Web Site: http://www.ea.com

ELSA, Inc.
2231 Calle de Luna
Santa Clara, CA 95054
(800) 272-ELSA or (408) 919-9100
Fax: (408) 919-2120
Technical Support: (800) 272-ELSA or
(408) 919-9100, M–F 8 a.m.–5 p.m.
Fax: (408) 919-2120

E-mail: sup-us@elsa.com
Web Site: http://www.elsa.com

Emulex Corporation
3535 Harbor Boulevard
Costa Mesa, CA 92626
U.S.: (800) 854-7112, International:
(714) 662-5600
Pre-Sales Product Support:
(800) EMULEX1 (368-5391)
BBS: (714) 662-1445
Fax Back: (800) 854-7112 x8277 and
(714) 513-8277
Technical Support: (800) 854-7112 x8270
or (714) 513-8270, 24/7
E-mail:
Questions on your order:
orderadmin@emulex.com
Product Warranty Registrations:
register@emulex.com
Technical Support:
techsupport@emulex.com
Anonymous FTP Site:
ftp://ftp.emulex.com
Web Site: http://www.emulex.com

E-mu Systems, Inc.,
Subsidiary of Creative Labs, Inc.
1600 Green Hills Road
P.O. Box 660015
Scotts Valley, CA 95067-0015
(408) 438-1921
Fax: (408) 438-8612
Technical Support: (408) 438-1921,
8 a.m.–5 p.m. PST
Web Site: http://www.emu.com

Encore Real Time Computing, Inc.
1700 NW 66th Avenue
Fort Lauderdale, FL 33313
(954) 377-1100
Web Site: http://www.encore.com

Ensoniq Corp., subsidiary of Creative
Labs, Inc.
155 Great Valley Parkway
Malvern, PA 19355

*Continued*

*(continued)*
(610) 647-3930
Fax: (610) 647-8908
Information: (800) 553-5151,
M–F 8:30 a.m.–5 p.m. EST
BBS: Multimedia products (610) 647-3195
Fax Back: (800) 257-1439 or (610) 408-0741
Customer Service and Technical
Support: (610) 647-3930, (Ensoniq PCI
soundcards are supported by Creative
Labs, Inc. Technical Support.)
Web Site: http://www.ensoniq.com

Enteractive, Inc.
110 W. 40th Street, Suite 2100
New York, NY 10018
Sales: (800) 433-4464
Support: (860) 236-8600,
M–F 9:30 a.m.–6:00 p.m. EST
Web Site: http://www.enteractive.com

Enterprise Corporation International
(ECI)
2600 Grand Avenue, Suite 302
Des Moines, IA 50312
(800) 842-5788 or (515) 282-4490
Fax: (515) 282-4689
Mitsumi CD Phone Support: (800) 801-7927
Online Customer Support: http://www.
eciusa.com/tempform.html
Web Site: http://www.eciusa.com

Epic MegaGames, Inc.
3204 Tower Oaks Boulevard, #410
Rockville, MD 20850
Web Site: http://www.epicgames.com

Epson America, Inc.
20770 Madrona Avenue
Torrance, CA 90503
(310) 782-0770
Fax: (310) 782-5220
Pre-Sales Support: (800) 463-7766
Fax Back: (800) 442-2110
Automated Support: (800) 922-8911
Technical Support, (310) 782-2600,
M–F 9 a.m.–9 p.m. PST.
FTP Site: ftp://ftp.epson.com
Web Site: http://www.epson.com

Equilibrium
3 Harbor Drive, Suite 111
Sausalito, CA 94965
(415) 332-4343
Fax: (415) 332-4433
Technical Support: (415) 332-4343
Fax: (415) 332-4433
FTP Site:
ftp://ftp.equilibrium.com/pub
Web Site:
http://www.equilibrium.com

ESC Technologies
4412 NorthStar Way
Modesto, CA 95356
(800) 427-3726 or (209) 550-4999
Fax: (209) 550-4998
Technical Support: (209) 550-4999,
M–F 9:00 a.m.–5:30 p.m. PST
Web Site: http://www.whatisnew.
com/today.cfm
Web Site: http://www.esc-tech.com

ESRI, Inc.
(Environmental Systems Research
Institute, Inc.)
380 New York Street
Redlands, CA 92373
(909) 793-2853
Fax: (909) 307-3025
Information and Sales: (800) GIS-XPRT
(447-9778)
Customer Service: (909) 793-2853
Technical Support: (909) 793-3774,
M–F 6 a.m.–6 p.m. PST
Fax: (909) 792-0960
Web Site: http://www.esri.com

Everex Systems Incorporated
5020 Brandin Court
Fremont, CA 94538
(510) 498-1111
Sales Information: (800) 383-7391
Fax: (510) 683-2186
Fax Back: (510) 683-2800
Freestyle Technical Support:
(888) 383-7399
Fax: (510) 683-2280, M–F 8 a.m.–6 P.M.
PST

PC Technical Support: (800) 262-3312 or
(510) 498-4411, M–F 7 a.m.–6 p.m. PST
Technical Support: Fax (510) 683-2044
Web Site: http://www.everex.com

Evergreen Technologies, Inc
808 NW Buchanan Ave.
Corvallis, OR 97330-6218
Sales: (541) 757-0934
Fax: (541) 757-7350
Customer Service: (541) 757-0934,
M–F 7 a.m.–5 p.m. PST
Technical Support: (541) 757-7341,
M–F 8 a.m.–5 p.m. PST
Fax: (541) 752-9851
E-mail: techsupport@evertech.com
Web Site: http://www.evertech.com

Exabyte Corporation
1685 38th Street
Boulder, CO 80301
(303) 442-4333
BBS: (303) 417-7100
Fax Back: (800) 445-7736 or
(303) 417-7792
Automated Technical Support:
(800) 442-3923 or (800) 445-7736
Technical Support: (800) 445-7736 or
(303) 417-7792, 6 a.m.–6 p.m. MST
Technical Support Fax: (303) 417-7160
E-mail Technical Support:
support@exabyte.com
Web Site: http://www.exabyte.com

Exide Electronics Corporation, now
Powerware
Forum III
8609 Six Forks Road
Raleigh, NC 27615
(800) 554-3448 or (919) 872-3020
Fax: (800) 753-9433
6kVA or less UPS Technical Support:
(800) 365-4892, M–F 8 a.m.–8 p.m. EST
Greater than 6kVA Technical Support:
(800) 843-9433 or (919) 871-1800, 24/7
Fax: (919) 871-1822
Web Site: http://www.powerware.com

ExperTelligence, Inc.
203 Chapala Street
Santa Barbara CA 93101
(805) 962-2558 or (800) 888-8670
Fax: (805) 962-5188
Web Site: http://www.webbase.com

Expert Graphics
1908 Cliff Valley Way, Suite 2010
Atlanta, GA 30329
(404) 320-0800 or (800) 648-7249
Fax: (404) 315-7645
Technical Support: (404) 315-7644
FTP Site: ftp://ftp.expertg.com
Web Site: http://www.expertg.com

Expert Software, Inc.
800 Douglas Road
North Tower, Suite 600
Coral Gables, FL 33134
(305) 567-9990
Fax: (305) 569-1111
Technical Support: (305) 567-9996,
M–F 9 a.m.–5 p.m. EST
Technical Support Web Site: http://www.
expertsoftware.com/support.htm
Web Site:
http://www.expertsoftware.com

Extended Systems, Incorporated
5777 N. Meeker Avenue
Boise, ID 83713
(800) 235-7576, International
(208) 322-7800
Fax: (208) 377-1906
Fax Back: (800) 251-2612
Automated Support: (800) 251-2612
Technical Support: (800) 235-7576
Fax: (406) 587-9170
E-mail: Support: info@extendsys.com
FTP Site:
ftp://ftp.extendsys.com/pub
Web Site: http://www.extendsys.com

Extensis Corporation
1800 SW 1st Avenue, Suite 500
Portland, OR 97201
(503) 274-2020 or (800) 796-9798

*Continued*

*(continued)*
Fax: (503) 274-0530
Customer Service: (800) 796-9798,
M–F 8 a.m.–5 p.m. PST
Technical Support: (503) 274-7030,
M–F 8 a.m.–5 p.m. PST
Fax: (503) 274-0530
E-mail: support@extensis.com
Web Site: http://www.extensis.com

Farallon Communications, Inc.
3089 Teagarden Street
San Leandro, CA 94577
(510) 346-8000
Fax: (510) 346-8119
Customer Service and Technical
Support: (510) 346-8001,
M–F 7:00 a.m.–4:30 p.m. PST
Fax: (510) 346-8117
Sales: sales@farallon.com
Customer Service and Technical
Support: ask_farallon@farallon.com
Web Site: http://www.farallon.com

FARGO Electronics, Incorporated
6533 Flying Cloud Drive
Eden Prairie, MN 55344
(800) 327-4622, or (612) 941-9470
Fax: (612) 941-7836
Technical Support: (612) 941-0050,
M–F 7:30 a.m.–5:30 p.m. CST
Technical Support Fax: (612) 941-1852
Web Site: http://www.fargo.com

FileMaker, Inc., was Claris Corporation
5201 Patrick Henry Drive
Box 58168
Santa Clara, CA 95052-8168
(408) 987-7000
General Services: (800) 544-8554
Customer Relations Fax: (408) 987-3932
Fax Back: (800) 800-8954
Automated Support: (800) 735-7393
Technical Support: (512) 873-4300
Web Site: http://www.apple.com

FORE Systems, Inc.
1000 FORE Drive
Warrendale, PA 15086-7502

(724) 742-4444
Product Information: (888) 404-0444
Product Fax: (724) 635-3695
Web Site: http://www.fore.com

FormGen, Inc.
Acquired by GT Interactive
Technical Support Web Page:
http://www.gtisonline.com
Web Site:
http://www.gtinteractive.com

Forté, Inc., acquired by Genesis
Telecommunications Laboratories, Inc.
2141 Palomar Airport Road, Suite 200
Carlsbad, CA 92009
(760) 431-6460
Fax: (760) 431-6465
Sales: (760) 431-6496, M–F 8 a.m.–5 p.m.
PST
Support: http://www.forteinc.com/
agsup/index.htm
Adante Web Site:
http://www.adante.com
Web Site: http://www.forteinc.com

Forte Software, Inc.
1800 Harrison Street
Oakland, CA 94612
(510) 869-3400
Fax: (510) 869-3480
Web Site: http://www.forte.com

Forte Technologies, Inc., now Interactive
Imaging Systems, Inc.
2616 Brighton-Henrietta TL Road, Suite B
Rochester, NY 14623
(716) 240-8000
Fax: (716) 240-8003
Technical Support: (716) 427-8604,
8 a.m.–6 p.m. EST
Fax: (716) 427-8003
FTP Site:
ftp://ftp.fortevr.com/pub/forte
Web Site: http://www.fortevr.com
Web Site: http://www.iisvr.com

Fox Interactive
2121 Avenue of the Stars

25th Floor
Los Angeles, CA 90067
Web Site:
http://www.foxinteractive.com

Fractal Design Corporation, now
MetaCreations
6303 Carpinteria Avenue
Carpinteria, CA 93013
(805) 566-6200
Fax: (805) 566-6385
Sales: (800) 846-0111
Customer Service: (888) 707-6382 or
(831) 430-4100
Fax: (831) 438-9670
Web Site: http://www.fractal.com
Web Site:
http://www.metacreations.com

Franklin Covey
2200 West Parkway Boulevard
West Valley City, UT 84119
(801) 975-1776
Sales: (800) 654-1776 or (801) 817-1776
Customer Service: (800) 655-1492
TDD: (800) 729-1492 or (801) 817-1492
Technical Support: (801) 975-9999
Web Site:
http://www.franklinquest.com

Frontier Software Development, Inc.,
now NetScout Systems, Inc.
4 Technology Park Drive
Westford, MA 01886
(978) 614-4000
Fax: (978) 614-4004
Sales: (800) 357-7666
Customer Support: (888) 357-7666
Web Site: http://www.netscout.com

Frontier Technologies
12121 N. Corporate Parkway
Mequon, WI 53092
(414) 243-4141
Fax: (414) 243-4135
Technical Support: (414) 243-4128,
M–F 8 a.m.–5 p.m. CST
Fax: (414) 243-4135 ATTN: Tech Support
Support: support@frontiertech.com

Web Site:
http://www.frontiertech.com

FTP Software, Inc., acquired by
NetManage, Inc.
2 High Street
Andover, MA 01845
(978) 685-4000 or (800) 282-4387
Fax: (978) 794-4488
Sales: (800) 282-4387 or (978) 685-4000
Technical Support: (978) 684-6705,
8 a.m.–4 p.m. EST
Web Site: http://www.ftp.com

Fujitsu America, Inc. (FAI)
3055 Orchard Drive
San Jose, CA 95134
(408) 432-1300
Fax: (408) 432-1318 or 1319
Web Site:
http://www.fujitsu.com/FAI

Fujitsu Compound Semiconductor, Inc.
(FCSI)
2355 Zanker Road
San Jose, CA 95131
(408) 232-9500
Fax: (408) 428-9111
Web Site:
http://www.fcsi.fujitsu.com

Fujitsu Computer Packaging
Technologies, Inc. (FCPT)
3811 Zanker Road
San Jose, CA 95131
(408) 943-7700
Fax: (408) 943-7790
Web Site: http://www.fcpt.com

Fujitsu Computer Products of America
(FCPA)
Corporate Headquarters
2904 Orchard Parkway
San Jose, CA 95134-2009
(800) 626-4686 or (408) 432-6333
Fax: (408) 432-9044
Sales: (800) 626-4686

*Continued*

*(continued)*
Customer Information Center:
(800) 626-4686
Fax Back: (408) 428-0456
Technical Support: (800) 626-4686,
M–F 5 a.m.–p.m., Sat 7 a.m.–3 p.m. PST
E-mail: Info@fcpa.fujitsu.com
Web Site: http://www.fcpa.com

Fujitsu Limited
4-1-1 Kamikodanaka, Nakahara-ku
Kawasaki, Kanagawa
211-8588 Japan
81 0 44-777-1111
Web Site: http://www.fujitsu.co.
jp/index-e.html

Fujitsu Microelectronics, Inc. (FMI)
3545 North First Street
San Jose, CA 95134-1804
(408) 922-9000
Fax: (408) 432-9044
Consumer Response Center:
(800) 866-8608, M–F 7 a.m.–5 p.m. PST
Web Site:
http://www.fujitsumicro.com

Fujitsu Network Communications, Inc.
(FNC)
2801 Telecom Parkway
Richardson, TX 75082
(972) 690-6000
Fax: (972) 479-6900
Web Site: http://www.fnc.fujitsu.com

Fujitsu Nexion, Inc.
289 Great Road
Acton, MA 01720-4739
(978) 266-4500
Fax: (978) 266-2300
Web Site: http://www.nexen.com

Fujitsu PC Corporation (FPC)
598 Gibraltar Drive
Milpitas, CA 95035
(408) 935-8800
Fax: (408) 935-1591
Service and Support: (800) 8-FUJITSU, 24/7

International Support (408) 935-1698,
M–F 7 a.m.–7 p.m. CST
E-mail: 8fujitsu@fpc.fujitsu.com
Web Site:
http://www.fujitsu-pc.com

Fujitsu Personal Systems, Inc. (FPSI)
5200 Patrick Henry Drive
Santa Clara, CA 95054
(800) 831-3183 or (408) 982-9500
Fax: (408) 496-0180
Support: (408) 764-9388,
M–F 7:30 a.m.–5 p.m. PST
Fax: (408) 764-9418
Web Site:
http://www.fpsi.fujitsu.com

Fujitsu Software Corporation (FSC)
3055 Orchard Drive
San Jose, CA 95134-2017
(408) 432-1300
Fax: (408) 456-7050
Web Site: http://www.fsc.fujitsu.com

FutureSoft
12012 Wickchester, Suite 600
Houston, TX 77079
(281) 496-9400
Fax: (281) 496-1090
Sales: (800) 989-8908
BBS: (281) 588-6870, to 28.8 Kbps
Telnet: bbs.fse.com
Technical Support: (281) 588-6868,
M–F 8 a.m.–5 p.m. CST
Fax: (281) 496-1090
E-mail: support@futuresoft.com
Web Site: http://www.futuresoft.com

Gainward Co., LTD.
12F #996 Hsin Tai Wu Road  Sec 1
His-chih, Taipei Hsien, Taiwan
886-2-2696-6777, 886-2-2696-6577
Fax: 886-2-2696-6599
E-mail: elvisc@gainward.com.tw
Web Site: http://www.gainward.com

GammaLink
Division of Dialogic
3120 Scott Boulevard

Santa Clara, CA 95054
(408) 969-5200
Fax: (408) 969-0999
Sales: (800) FAX-4-PCs
Technical Support: (973) 993-1443,
8 a.m.–8 p.m. EST
Technical Support Fax: (973) 993-8387
Web Site: http://www.gammalink.com

Gandalf Technologies, Inc., a Division of
Mitel
350 Legget Drive
Kanata, Ontario
Canada K2K 2W7
(800) 426-3253
Service: (800) GANDALF (426-3253)
Web Site: http://www.gandalf.ca

Gateway 2000
610 Gateway Drive
P.O. Box 2000
North Sioux City, SD 57049
(800) 846-2000 or (605) 232-2000
General Fax: (605) 232-2023
Sales: (800) 846-4208
Add On Sales: (800) 846-2080
Customer Service: (800) 846-2000
Customer Service Canada:
(800) 846-3609
Customer Service TDD: (800) 855-2881
Fax Back U.S.A. and Canada: (800)
846-4526, International: (605) 232-2561
Automated Troubleshooting System:
(800) 846-2118
Technical Support, 24/7:
General: (800) 846-2301
Windows 95: (800) 846-5259
Windows NT: (800) 270-5731
International: (605) 232-2191
Portable: (800) 846-2302
TDD: (800) 846-1778
International Technical Support:
(605) 232-2191
Technical Support Fax: (605) 232-2182
Automated Technical Support:
(800) 846-2118
Web Site:
http://www.gateway.com/home

Gathering of Developers, LLP
2700 Fairmount
Dallas, TX
(214) 880-0001
Technical Support (214) 303-1202
Support@godgames.com
Web Site: http://www.godgames.com

GCC Technologies, Inc.
209 Burlington Road
Bedford, MA 01730-9143
(781) 275-5800
Fax: (781) 275-1115
Sales: (800) 422-7777 or (781) 275-5800
E-mail: sales@gcctech.com
Information: (800) 422-7777
Technical Support: (781) 276-8620,
International (617) 275-5800
Fax: (781) 275-1115
E-mail: support@gcctech.com
Web Site: http://www.gcctech.com

GDT Softworks Incorporated, merged
with Infowave Wireless Messaging, Inc.
4664 Lougheed Highway, Suite 188
Burnaby, British Columbia
Canada V5C 6B7
(604) 473-3600 or (800) 663-6222
Fax: (604) 473-3699
Customer Service: (800) 663-6222 or
(604) 473-3600, M–F 9 a.m.–4 p.m. PST
Fax: (604) 473-3699
Customer Support: (604) 473-3678,
M–F 8 a.m.–4 p.m. PST
Fax: (604) 473-3636
Web Site: http://www.infowave.com

Genesys Telecommunications
Laboratories, Inc.
1155 Market Street, 11th Floor
San Francisco, CA 94103
(888) 436-3797 or U.S. (415) 437-1100,
Canada (506) 658-1080
Fax: U.S. (415) 437-1260,
Canada (506) 694-2478
Technical Support: (888) 369-5555,
M–F 5 a.m.–5 p.m. PST
Fax: (506) 694-2478
Web Site: http://www.genesyslab.com

GENICOM Corporation
14800 Conference Center Drive, Suite 400
Chantilly, VA 20151-3820
(703) 802-9200
Fax: (703) 802-9039
Technical Support: (540) 949-1031
Fax: (540) 949-1505
E-mail: techsupport@genicom.com
Web Site: http://www.genicom.com

Globalink, Inc., acquired by Lernout &
Hauspie
9302 Lee Highway
Fairfax, VA 22031
(800) 255-5660 or (703) 273-5600
Fax: (703) 273-3866
Customer Service: (800) 255-5660
Technical Support: (781) 203-5055
Web Site: http://www.lhsl.com

Global Village Communication
1380 Bordeaux Drive
Sunnyvale, CA 94089
(408) 548-2000
Fax: (408) 523-2407
Sales: (800) 336-2009
Personal/single-user products:
BBS: (800) 335-6003 or (408) 523-2403
Fax Back: (800) 890-4562 or
(408) 548-2402
Technical Support: (561) 241-8088
Fax Support: (800) 607-4562 or
(408) 548-2664
FTP Site: ftp://ftp.globalvillage.
com/pub/software
Web Site:
http://www.globalvillage.com

Gold Disk Incorporated
See Astound, Inc.
For VideoDirector products see Pinnacle
Systems, Inc.
Goldstar Technology, Inc.
LG Electronics USA, Inc.
1000 Sylvan Avenue
Englewood Cliff, NJ 07632
Sales: (201) 816-2000
Fax: (201) 816-0636

Customer Information Center:
(800) 243-0000, M–F 7 a.m.–7 p.m. CST
Canada: (905) 795-6223, M–F 8 a.m.–5 p.m.
Fax: (205) 772-8987
Technical Support: (800) 243-0000
M–F 8 a.m.–5 p.m.
Technical Support Fax: (205) 772-8987
Web Site: http://www.lgeus.com

Granite Digital
3101 Whipple Road
Union City, CA 94587
(510) 471-6442
Fax: (510) 471-6267
Web Site: http://www.scsipro.com

Great Plains Software
1701 SW 38th Street
Fargo, ND 58103
(800) 456-0025 or (701) 281-0550
Fax: (701) 281-6868
Technical Support: (800) 456-0025 or
(701) 281-0550
Web Site: http://www.gps.com

Grolier Interactive
90 Sherman Turnpike
Danbury, CT 06816
(203) 797-3530
Fax: (203) 797-3197
Sales: (800) 285-4534
Registration: (800) 619-9515
Customer Service: (203) 797-3530,
M–F 8:30 a.m.–4:30 p.m. EST
Fax: (203) 797-3130
Automated System: (800) 285-4534 or
(203) 797-3530
Technical Support: (203) 796-2536,
M–F 9 a.m.–5 p.m. EST
Fax: (203) 797-3110
E-mail: techsup@grolier.com
Web Site: http://www.grolier.com

Group 1 Software
4200 Parliament Place, Suite 600
Lanham, MD 20706-1844
(800) 368-5806 or (301) 731-2300
Fax: (301) 731-0360
Fax Back: (301) 918-0781

PC Support: purchased by Datatech Enterprises
Large System Support Hotline: (800) 367-6950
Web Site: http://www.gl.com

Gryphon Software Corporation, acquired by Knowledge Adventure, Inc.
Technical Support: (800) 556-6141, M–F 7 a.m.–5 p.m. PST
Web Site: http://www. knowledgeadventure.com

GVC
See MaxTech, Inc.
HAL Computer Systems, Inc. (HAL)
A Fujitsu Company
1315 Dell Avenue
Campbell, CA 95008
(408) 379-7000
Fax: (408) 341-5401
Customer Service: (800) 425-9111
Web Site: http://www.hal.com

Harpercollins Interactive
10 East 53rd Street
New York, NY 10022
(212) 207-7000
Fax: (212) 207-7433
Web Site: http://www.harpercollins.com

Hasbro Interactive
50 Dunham Lane
Beverly, MA 01915
(978) 921-3700
Sales: (800) 638-6927
Technical Support: (410) 568-2377, M–F 8 a.m.–12 a.m., S–S 8 a.m. 8 p.m. EST
Web Site: http://www.hasbro.com

Havas
31 Rue du Colisee
75383 Paris, Cedex 08
France
33 1 53 53 30 33
Fax: 33 1 47 16 91 02
Web Site: http://www.havas.fr

Hayes Microcomputer Products, Inc.
5835 Peachtree Corners East
Norcross, GA 30092
(770) 840-9200
Fax: (770) 441-1213
Customer Service: (770) 441-1617, M–F 8 a.m.–6 p.m. EST
BBS: (770) 446-6336
BBS ISDN: (770) 729-6525
Hayes Fax Response: 800-HAYESFX
Technical Support: (770) 441-1617, M–F 8 a.m.–6 p.m. EST
Fax: (770) 449-0087
E-mail: support@os.hayes.com
FTP Site: ftp://ftp.hayes.com
Web Site: http://www.hayes.com

Helix Software Company, acquired by Network Associates
Technical Support: (801) 492-2700, 7 a.m.–6 p.m. CST
Web Site: http://www.helixsoftware.com

Hercules Computer Technology, Inc.
3839 Spinnaker Court
Fremont, CA 94538
(510) 623-6030 or (800) 323-0601
Fax: (510) 623-1112
Fax Back: (800) 711-HERC (711-4372)
BBS: (510) 623-7449
Technical Support: (800) 323-0601 or (510) 623-6050, M–F 6 a.m.–6 p.m. PST
Technical Support Fax: (510) 623-4215
E-mail: support@hercules.com
FTP Site: ftp://ftp.hercules.com
Web Site: http://www.hercules.com

HerInteractive.com
11808 Northrup Way, Suite W-160
Bellview, WA 98005
(425) 889-2900
Fax: (425) 822-6121
Technical Support: (425) 889-2900 Ext. 30, M–F 1 p.m.–6 p.m. PST
Web Site: http://www.herinteractive.com

Hewlett-Packard Company
3000 Hanover Street
Palo Alto, CA 94304
(650) 875-1501
Fax: (650) 852-8342
Computer Products Information:
(800) 752-0900
Sales: (800) 637-7740
Fax: (208) 323-4004
BBS: (208) 344 1691
Fax Back: (800) 333-1917, International:
(208) 344-4809
Customer Support: (800) 858-8867, 24/7
Handheld Devices Technical Support:
(970) 392-1001, M–F 5 a.m.–5 p.m. MST
Computer Products Technical Support:
(208) 323-2551, M–F 6 a.m.–10 p.m.,
Sat 8 a.m.–3 p.m. MST
HP Colorado:
BBS: (970) 635-0650, 28.8 Kbps
Fax Back: (800) 333-1917 or
(970) 635-1510
Technical Support: (970) 635-1500,
M–F 7 a.m.–5 p.m. MST
Fax: (970) 667-0997
Electronic Support Center: http://
us-support.external.hp.com:80/
FTP Site: ftp://ftp.hp.com/pub/
information_storage/hp-colorado
FTP Site: ftp://ftp.hp.com
Web Site: http://www.hp.com

Hilgraeve, Inc.
111 Conant Avenue, Suite A
Monroe, MI 48161
(734) 243-0576
Sales: (800) 826-2760
Fax: (734) 243-0645
BBS: (734) 243-5915
E-mail: support@hilgraeve.com
Tech Form: http://www.hilgraeve.
com/dzsupport.html
Web Site: http://www.hilgraeve.com

Hitachi, Ltd.
Head Office
6 Kanda Surugadai 4-chome
Chiyoda-ku, Tokyo, 101-10 Japan
81 (3) 3258-1111

Hitachi America, Ltd.
50 Prospect Avenue
Tarrytown, NY 10591
(914) 332-5800
Fax: (914) 332-5555
Web Site: http://www.hitachi.com

Hitachi America, Ltd.
Computer Division
2000 Sierra Point Parkway
Brisbane, CA 94005
(800) HITACHI (448-2244)
Multimedia Recorder Technical Support:
(800) 981-2588 Ext 3756
Web Site: http://www.mpegcam.com

Hitachi America, Ltd.
Computer Division — Storage
2000 Sierra Point Parkway, MS #500
Brisbane, CA 94005-1835
(800) 448-2244
BBS: (619) 661-0245
Fax Back: (800) HIT-FAX1 (448-3291) or
(415) 589-7648
CD and DVD Technical Support:
(800) 545-8317, M–F 8 a.m.–5 p.m. PST
Hard Disk Drive Technical Support Fax:
(408) 235-8942
Hard Disk Drive Technical Support
E-mail: drivesupport@hal.Hitachi.com
Web Site:
http://www.hitachi.com/storage

Hitachi America, Ltd.
Computer Division
Office Automation Systems
110 Summit Avenue
Montvale, NJ 07645
(201) 573-0774
Fax: (201) 573-7660
Office Automation Systems
47427 Fremont Boulevard
Fremont, CA 94538
(510) 661-0777
Fax: (510) 661-6300
CD-ROM BBS: (619) 661-0245
CD-ROM Technical Support:
(619) 661-3444, 8 a.m.–5 p.m. PST
E-mail: cdromsupport@halsp.hitachi.com

Hitachi America, Ltd.
Flat Panel Displays Division
Hitachi Plaza
2000 Sierra Point Parkway
Brisbane, CA 94005-1835
(800) 241-6558, International (415) 589-8300
Fax: (415) 583-4207
Technical Support: (800) 555-6820
Technical Support Fax: (800) 555-4625
Web Site: `http://www.hitachi.com`

Hitachi America, Ltd.
Monitor Division
200 Lowder Brook Drive, Suite 2200
Westwood, MA 02092
(781) 461-8300
Customer Relations: (800) 441-4832
Fax Back (800) 555-8552
Customer Service and Technical
Support: (800) 536-6721
Web Site:
`http://www.hitachidisplays.com`

Hitachi Computer Products (America), Inc.
(800) HITACHI (448-2244) or (408) 986-9770
Web Site:
`http://www.hicam.hitachi.com`

Hitachi Data Systems Corporation
750 Central Expressway
Santa Clara, CA 95056
(408) 970-1000
Fax: (408) 727-8036
Web Site: `http://www.hdshq.com`

Hitachi Digital Graphics (USA), Inc.
815 Hermosa Drive
Sunnyvale, CA 94086
(408) 735-0577
Fax: (408) 739-3425
Web Site:
`http://www.hitachidigital.com`

Hitachi Internetworking
3101 Tasman Drive
Santa Clara, CA 95054
(408) 986-9770
Fax: (408) 988-0778
Information: (888) 484-4773

HiSpeed Switch Technical Support:
(800) 611-4551 or (408) 588-3119
All other Product Technical Support:
(800) 448-2244
Web Site: `http://www.`
`internetworking.hitachi.com`

Hitachi Koki Imaging Solutions
1757 Tapo Canyon Road
Simi Valley, CA 93063
(805) 578-4000
Fax: (805) 578-4001
Customer Services: (800) 887-8848 or
(805) 578-4455
Fax Back: (805) 578-9255
Technical Support: (800) 887-8848 or
(805) 578-4455, M–F 6 a.m.–5 p.m. PST
FTP Site: `ftp://ftp.dpc.com`
Web Site: `http://www.dpc.com`

Hitachi Micro Systems, Inc.
179 E. Tasman Drive
San Jose, CA 95134
(408) 433-1990
How To Read Part Numbers Web Site:
`http://www.hmsi.com/`
`partnumbers.pdf`
Web Site: `http://www.hmsi.com`

Hitachi PC
1565 Barber Lane
Milpitas, CA (408) 546-8000
BBS: (408) 546-8173
Fax Back: (800) 555-9621 or
(408) 546-8217
Technical Support: (800) HITACHI
(448-2244) or (800) 555-6820,
International (408) 546-8216, 24/7
Fax: (800) 555-4625, or (408) 546-8218
FTP Site: `ftp://ftp.hitachipc.com`
Web Site: `http://www.hitachipc.com`

Hitachi Software Engineering America, Inc.
601 Gateway Boulevard, Suite 500
South San Francisco, CA 94080
(800) 624-6176 or (650) 615-9600
Fax: (650) 615-7699
Web Site:
`http://www.hitachi-soft.com/`

Hopkins Technology, LLC
421 Hazel Lane
Hopkins, MN 55343-7116
(612) 931-9376
Fax: (612) 931-9377
Web Site: http://www.hoptechno.com

Horizons Technology, Inc.
700 Technology Park Drive
Billerica, MA 01821
(978) 663-6600
Fax: (978) 663-8357
Web Site: http://www.horizons.com

Houghton Mifflin Interactive
120 Beacon Street
Somerville, MA 02143
(617) 503-4800
Fax: (617) 503-4900
Technical Support: (800) 210-0241
Web Site: http://www.hminet.com

Humongous Entertainment
Acquired by GT Interactive Software Corp.
13110 NE 177th Place, Suite 180
Woodinville, WA 98034
(425) 486-9258
Direct Sales: (800) 499-8386 or
(425) 867-2596
Customer Service: (800) 791-7128
Technical Support: (425) 485-1212
E-mail: support@humongous.com
Web Site: http://www.humongous.com

Hyperglot Software Company, Inc.
See The Learning Company
Hyundai Electronics America (HEA)
America Head Office
3101 North First Street
San Jose, CA 95134
(408) 232-8000
Monitor Information: (800) 568-0060
Camera Issues: (714) 899-4033
Web Site: http://www.hea.com

IBM (International Business Machines
Corporation)
Old Orchard Road
Armonk, NY 10504

(914) 499-1900
General Information: (800) IBM-4YOU
(426-4968), 8 a.m.–7 p.m. CST
International: (770) 863-1234
Special Needs Information:
(800) 426-4832, TDD (800) 426-4833
IBM PC HelpCenter: U.S. (800) 772-2227,
Canada (800) 565-3344 24/7
Personal Systems HelpCenter: (TDD)
(800) IBM-4238, or (214) 280-3387
7 a.m.–7 p.m. CST
PC Fax Back: (800) IBM-3395 or
(919) 517-0011
Software Support: (800) 237-5511, 24/7
Parts Order and Maintenance Center:
(800) 388-7080 24/7
Manuals (to order): (800) 879-2755,
8:30 a.m.–7:00 p.m. EST
PC Company BBS: (919) 517-0001
Personal Computing Fax Back
Information Service: (800) IBM-4FAX
(426-4329)
IBM Hursley Labs FTP Site:
ftp://ftp.hursley.ibm.com
IBM PC Company FTP Site:
ftp://ftp.pc.ibm.com
IBM Software FTP Site:
ftp://ftp.software.ibm.com
Lotus FTP Site:
ftp://ftp.support.lotus.com
IBM Main Web Site:
http://www.ibm.com
IBM Gopher Servers:
gopher://index.almaden.ibm.com
IBM Hursley Labs Web Site:
http://ncc.hursley.ibm.com
IBM Internet Connection Services
Web Site: http://www.ibm.net
IBM K-12 Education Web Site:
http://www.solutions.ibm.com/
k12/welcome.html

IBM Networking Web Site:
http://www.networking.ibm.com
IBM Personal Computing Web Site:
http://www.pc.ibm.com
IBM Printing Systems:
http://www.printers.ibm.com

IBM Almaden Research Center:
http://www.almaden.ibm.com/almaden
IBM Research Web Site:
http://www.research.ibm.com
IBM T J Watson Research Web Site:
http://www.watson.ibm.com
IBM Servers:
http://www.ibm.com/Servers
IBM Software Web Site:
http://www.software.ibm.com
IBM Software Technical Support
Web Site:
http://service.boulder.ibm.com
IBM Special Needs Solutions
Web Site: http://www.austin.ibm.
com/sns/index.html
IBM Storage Systems Web Site:
http://www.storage.ibm.com
IBM Support Home Page:
http://www.ibm.com/Support
IBM Technical Journals Web Site:
http://www.almaden.ibm.com/
journal

IDG Books Worldwide
919 East Hillsdale Boulevard, Suite 400
Foster City, CA 94404
(415) 655-3000
Customer Service: (800) 762-2974,
Canada: (800) 667-1115
Web Site: http://www.idgbooks.com

id Software
18601 LBJ Freeway, Suite 666
Town East Tower
Mesquite, TX 75150
(972) 613-3589
Sales: (800) id-Games (434-2637)
Web Site: http://www.idsoftware.com

Imation Corp.
(Previously 3M Data Storage Products)
1 Imation Place
Oakdale, MN 55128-3414
(651) 704-4000 or (888) 466-3456
Fax: (800) 537-4675
Sales: (800) 328-9438
Customer Care Center (888) 466-3456 or
(651) 704-4000, M–F 7 a.m.–6 p.m. CST

Technical Support M–F 7 a.m.–6 p.m. CST
SuperDisk Products: (800) 888-2700
Data Storage Products: (800) 328-9438
Printing and Proofing Products:
(800) 328-1303
Photo Color Products: (800) 695-3456
Web Site: http://www.imation.com

IMC Networks Corporation
19772 Pauling
Foothill Ranch, CA 92610
(949) 465-3000
Fax: (949) 465-3020
Technical Support: (800) 624-1070,
M–F 6 a.m.–5 p.m. PST
Web Site: http://www.imcnetworks.com

Incat Systems
See Adaptec, Inc.
In Focus Systems
27700B SW Parkway Avenue
Wilsonville, OR 97070-9215
(800) 294-6400 or (503) 685-8888
Fax: (503) 685-8887
Sales: (800) 294-6400
Customer Support: (800) 799-9911 or
(503) 685-7244, M–F 6 a.m.–6 pm. PST
Fax: (503) 685-8888
Web Site: http://www.infs.com

Informix Software, Inc.
4100 Bohannon Drive
Menlo Park, CA 94025
(650) 926-6300
Telemarketing Hotline: (800) 331-1763
Web Site: http://www.informix.com

infoUSA, Inc.
5711 South 86th Circle
Omaha, NB 68127
(402) 593-4500
Web Site: http://www.infousa.com

Infowave Wireless Messaging, Inc.
4664 Lougheed Highway, Suite 188
Burnaby, British Columbia
Canada V5C 6B7
(604) 473-3600 or (800) 663-6222

*Continued*

*(continued)*
Fax: (604) 473-3699
Customer Service: (800) 663-6222 or
(604) 473-3600, M–F 9 a.m.–4 p.m. PST
Fax: (604) 473-3699
Customer Support: (604) 473-3678,
M–F 8 a.m.–4 p.m. PST
Fax: (604) 473-3636
Web Site: http://www.infowave.com

Inset Systems
See Quarterdeck Corporation
Insignia Solutions, Inc.
41300 Christy Street
Fremont, CA 94538-3115
(510) 360-3700 or (800) 848-7677
Fax: (510) 360-3701
Sales and Customer Service: (800) 848-7677
Fax Back: (800) 876-3872
E-mail Technical Support:
support@isltd.insignia.com
Web Site: http://www.insignia.com

Inso Corporation
31 St. James Avenue
Boston, MA 02116
(617) 753-6500 or (800) 733-5799
Fax: (617) 753-6666
Technical Support: (800) 333-1395
(U.S. only)
Fax: (312) 670-0820
Web Site: http://www.inso.com

Intel Corporation
2200 Mission College Boulevard
P.O. Box 58119
Santa Clara, CA 95052-8119
(800) 628-8686 or (408) 765-8080
Fax: (408) 765-9904
BBS North America: (503) 264-7999
BBS UK: 44-1 793 432955
Fax Back U.S.: (800) 525-3019,
(503) 264-6835
Fax Back UK: +44-1 793 432 509
Literature: (800) 879-4683,
M–F 8 a.m.–6 p.m. MST
Technical Support:
CPU and Processors: (800) 321-4044,
M–F 5 a.m.–5 p.m. PST

Network, ProShare Conferencing/Video
Products: (916) 377-7000,
M–F 7 a.m.–5 p.m. PST
Technical Support UK: +44-0-870 607
2439, 08:30-16:00 GMT M–F
FTP Site: ftp://ftp.intel.com
FTP Customer Support Files:
ftp://ftp.intel.com/pub/support
FAQS Web Site: http://www.intel.
com/procs/support/faqs
Customer Support Web Site: http://
support.intel.com/sites/support
Online Newsgroups:
http://newsgroups.intel.com and
http://support.intel.com/
newsgroups/
Processor Web Sites of Interest:
Performance:
http://www.intel.com/procs/perf
How to Identify a Pentium II:
http://support.intel.com/
support/processors/pentiumII/
identify.htm
Pentium III Technical Issues:
http://support.intel.com/
support/processors/pentiumiii
Celeron Technical Issues:
http://support.intel.com/
support/processors/celeron
Pentium II Technical Issues:
http://support.intel.com/
support/processors/pentiumii
Motherboards Web Site:
http://support.intel.com/
support/motherboards
Web Site: http://www.intel.com

Interactive Imaging Systems, Inc., was
Forte Technologies, Inc.
2616 Brighton-Henrietta TL Road, Suite B
Rochester, NY 14623
(716) 240-8000
Fax: (716) 240-8003
Technical Support: (716) 427-8604,
8 a.m.–6 p.m. EST
Fax: (716) 427-8003
Web Site: http://www.fortevr.com
Web Site: http://www.iisvr.com

Interactive Magic, Incorporated
P.O. Box 13491
Research Triangle Park, NC 27709
(919) 461-0722
Fax: (919) 461-0723
Sales: (800) 789-1534
Technical Support: (919) 461-0883,
M–F 9 a.m.–12 A.M. EST
E-mail: techsupport@imagicgames.com
FTP Site:
ftp://ftp.imagicgames.com/pub
Web Site: http://www.imagicgames.com

Interplay Productions, Inc.
16815 Von Karman Avenue
Irvine, CA 92606
(949) 553-6655
Fax: (949) 252-2820
Customer Service: (949) 553-6678
Product Information: (800) 969-GAME
Technical Support: (949) 553-6678,
M–F 8:00 a.m.–5:45 p.m. PST
Automated Help: (949) 553-6678
Fax: (714) 252-2820, Attn: Customer Service
E-mail: support@interplay.com
FTP Site: ftp://ftp1.interplay.com
Web Site: http://www.interplay.com

Intuit
2535 Garcia Avenue
Mountain Valley, CA 94039
(800) 446-8848 or (650) 944-6000
Support Web Site: http://www.intuit.
com/support/index.html
Web Site: http://www.intuit.com

Iomega Corporation
1821 West Iomega Way
Roy, UT 84067
(800) 697-8833 or (801) 778-1000
Fax: (801) 778-3748
BBS: (801) 778-5888
Fax Back: (801) 778-5763
Automated Technical Support:
(800) 879-7660
30 day warranty period Technical Support:
(888) 4-IOMEGA (446-6342), M–F 6 a.m.–9
p.m., Sat 7 a..m.–2 p.m. MST

E-mail: support@iomega.com
Technical Support Web Site:
http://www.iomega.com/
support/index.html
Web Site: http://www.iomega.com

Ionstorm
2200 Ross Avenue, Suite 3050
Dallas, TX 75201
(214) 953-0101
Web Site: http://www.ionstorm.com

Ipswitch, Inc.
81 Hartwell Avenue
Lexington, MA 02421
(718) 676-5700
Fax: (718) 676-5710
Sales: (718) 676-5700
WS_FTP Pro and What's Up Sales:
(800) 793-4825
Purchased Product Technical Support:
(718) 676-5784, M–F 9 a.m.–6 p.m. EST
E-mail: info@ipswitch.com
Web Site: Support:
http://www.ipswitch.com/Suppor
t/index.html
Web Site: http://www.ipswitch.com

Janna Systems, Inc.
3080 Younge Street, Suite 6020
Toronto, Ontario
Canada M4N 3N1
(416) 483-7711
Fax: (416) 483-3220
Customer Support: (416) 483-1451,
M–F 10 a.m.–8 p.m. EST
Web Site: http://www.janna.com

JP Software, Inc.
P.O. Box 1470
East Arlington, MA 02474
(781) 646-3975
Fax: (617) 646-0904
Sales: (800) 368-8777
U.S. and Canada Support: (781) 646-0798
Fax: (781) 646-0904
Web Site: http://www.jpsoft.com

Kaetron Software Corporation
26119 Oak Ridge Drive, Suite 1024
Spring, TX 77380
(800) 938-8900 or (281) 298-1500
Fax: (281) 298-2520
Technical Support: (281) 298-1547,
M–F 8:30 a.m.–5:30 p.m. CST
Fax: (713) 298-2520
Web Site: http://www.kaetron.com

KDS USA
12300 Edison Way
Garden Grove, CA 92841
(714) 379-5599 or (800) 237-9988
Fax: (714) 379-5591
Customer Support: (800) 283-1311
Web Site: http://www.kdsusa.com

Kensington Technology Group,
a Division of ACCO Brands
2855 Campus Drive
San Mateo, CA 94403
(800) 535-4242 or (650) 572-2700
Fax: (415) 572-9675
Fax Back: (800) 280-8318
Customer Service: (800) 280-8318
Customer Relations: 9800) 235-6708
Technical Support: (800) 535-4242,
M–F 10 a.m.–7 p.m. EST
Fax: (610) 231-1022
Web Site: http://www.kensington.com

Kent*Marsh Ltd.
Merged with Citadel Technology
3811 Turtle Creek Boulevard, Suite 600
Dallas, TX 75219
U.S.A. and Canada Sales: (800) 962-0701
Tech. Support and International Sales:
(214) 520-9292
Fax: (214) 520-9293
Web Site: http://www.citadel.com

Key Tronic Corp.
North 4424 Sullivan
Spokane, WA 99216
(509) 928-8000 or (509) 927-5273
Accessory Sales: (800) 262-6006
Technical Support: (800) 262-6006

Fax: (509) 927-5252
Web Site: http://www.keytronic.com

Kingston Technology Company
17600 Newhope Street
Fountain Valley, CA 92708
(800) 337-8410 or (714) 435-2600
Fax: (714) 435-1820
Fax Back: (800) 435-0056
Technical Support: (800) 435-0640 or
(714) 435-2639
Technical Fax: (714) 437-3939
Web Site: http://www.kingston.com

Knowledge Adventure, Inc., acquired by
Havas International
1311 Grand Central Avenue
Glendale, CA, 91201
(818) 246-4400
Customer Service and Sales:
(800) 542-7677, M–F 8 a.m.–7 p.m.,
Sat 9 a.m.–2 p.m. PST
Fax: (310) 793-4307
Automated Technical Support
(800) 556-6141
Technical Support: (800) 556-6141,
M–F 7 a.m.–5 p.m. PST
Fax: (818) 246-5604
E-mail: support@adventure.com
Web Site: http://www.cuc.com
Web Site: http://www.adventure.com

Kodak
Eastman Kodak Company
343 State Street
Rochester, NY 14650
(716) 724-4000
Fax: (716) 724-9261
KODAK Service:
Business Imaging Systems:
(800) 22KODAK (225-6325)
For All Services in Canada:
(800) GOKODAK (465-6325)
Service: (800) 23-KODAK (235-6325)
General and Technical Support:
Digital Imaging Support Center:
(800) 235-6325, International
(716) 726-7260, M–F 9 a.m.–8 p.m.

Copiers, Duplicators, Copier Printers:
(800) 255-3434, International:
(716) 784-0982, M–F 8 a.m.–8 p.m.
Web Site: http://www.kodak.com/
go/birdcam
Web Site: http://www.kodak.com

Kurzweil Educational Systems Group,
acquired by Lernout & Hauspie
52 Third Avenue
Burlington, MA 01803
(781) 203-5000
Fax: (781) 238-0986
Sales: (800) 634-8723
Customer Support: (781) 203-5000 or
(800) 894-5374
Fax: (781) 203-5033
Web Site: http://www.kurzweil.com

Labtec Enterprises, Inc.
3801 109th Avenue, Suite J
Vancouver, WA 98682
(360) 896-2000
Fax: (360) 896-2020
Web Site: http://www.labtec.com

Lantronix
15353 Barranca Parkway
Irvine, CA 92618
(800) 422-7055
Fax: (714) 453-3995
E-mail: sales@lantronix.com
BBS: (714) 367-1051 to 28.8 Kbps
Technical Support: (800) 422-7044,
International: (714) 453-3990,
7 a.m.–5 p.m. PST
Technical Support Fax: (714) 450-7226
E-mail Technical Support:
support@lantronix.com.
FTP Site: ftp://ftp.lantronix.com
Web Site: http://www.lantronix.com

The Learning Company
One Athenaeum Street
Cambridge, MA 02142
(617) 494-1200
Fax: (617) 494-1219
Customer Service: (617) 494-5700

Customer Support: (617) 761-3000
M–F 8 a.m.–8 p.m. EST
Automated Technical Support:
(800) 409-1497
Technical Support: (319) 247-3333,
M–F 9 a.m.–9 p.m., EST
Technical Support Fax: (319) 395-9600
E-mail: help@tlcsupport.com
FTP Site: ftp://ftp.learningco.
com/support/tlcfiles.html
Web Site: http://www.learningco.com

Legato Systems, Inc.
3210 Porter Drive
Palo Alto, CA 94304
(650) 812-6000
Fax: (650) 812-6032
Technical Support: (650) 812-6100
Fax: (650) 842-9344
E-mail: service@legato.com
E-mail: support@legato.com
Web Site: http://www.legato.com

Lernout & Hauspie Speech Products
U.S.A., Inc.
52 Third Avenue
Burlington, MA 01803
(781) 203-5000
Fax: (781) 238-0986
Techncial Suppport: (781) 203-5000,
M–F 8 a.m.–8 p.m. EST
Fax: (781) 238-0986
Lexmark International Group, Inc.
740 New Circle Road, NW
Lexington, KY 40550
(606) 232-3000
Fax: (606) 232-2380
Information: (800) 539-6275
BBS: (606) 232-5238
Autofax System: (606) 232-2380
Automated Technical Support:
(800) 553-9457
Printer Technical Support:
(888) LEXMARK (539-6275),
M–F 9 a.m.–9 p.m., S–S 12 p.m.–6 p.m. EST
Medley Warranty and Setup Assistance:
(800) 236-1751, M–F 10 a.m.–7 p.m. EST

*Continued*

*(continued)*
Laptop Technical Support:
(800) 554-3202, M–F 10 a.m.–5 p.m. EST
Medley Technical Support:
(800) 236-1751, M–F 9 a.m.—6 p.m.
FTP Site:
ftp://ftp.lexmark.com/pub/driver
Web Site: http://www.lexmark.com

Lifestyle Software Group
Concept Development Associates, Inc.
2155 Old Moultrie Road
St. Augustine, FL 32086
(904) 794-7070
Fax: (904) 794-4888
E-mail: support@lifeware.com
Web Site: http://www.lifeware.com

Lind Electronics, Inc.
6414 Cambridge Street
Minneapolis, MN 55426
(612) 927-6303 or (800) 697-3702
Fax: (612) 927-7740
Web Site:
http://www.lindelectronics.com

Linksys
16811 Millikan Avenue
Irvine, CA 92714-5011
(949) 261-1288
BBS: (949) 261-2888
Technical Support: (949) 261-1288,
M–F 8 a.m.–5 p.m. PST
Fax: (949) 261-8868
E-mail: info@linksys.com
Web Site: http://www.linksys.com

Locutus Codeware
PO Box 53587
984 W. Broadway
Vancouver, BC
Canada V5Z 1K0
E-mail: locutus@locutuscodeware.com
Web Site: http://locutuscodeware.com

Logitech, Inc.
6505 Kaiser Drive
Fremont, CA 94555
(800) 231-7717 or (510) 795-8500
Fax: (510) 792-8901

Automated Support: (800) 231-7717
Customer Support: (702) 269-3457,
M–F 7:00 a.m.–3:30 p.m. PST
FTP Site: ftp://ftp.logitech.com
Web Site: http://www.logitech.com

Lotus Development Corporation
Acquired by IBM
55 Cambridge Parkway
Cambridge, MA 02142
(617) 577-8500
Pre-Sales Questions: (800) 343-5414,
M–F 8:30 a.m.–7:00 p.m. EST
Technical Support: (978) 988-2800
Technical Support:
http://www.support.lotus.com
FTP Site:
ftp://ftp.support.lotus.com/pub
Web Site: http://www.lotus.com

Lucas Arts Entertainment Company LLC
P.O. Box 10307
San Rafael, CA 94912
Sales: (800) 98-LUCAS (985-8227)
Fax: (415) 444-8488
Technical Support Hotline:
(415) 507-4545, M–Th 8:45 a.m.–11:45 a.m.,
1:00 p.m.–5:30 p.m., F 8:45 a.m.–11:45 a.m.
1 p.m.–4:30 p.m. PST
Fax: (415) 507-0300
Yoda's Help Desk: http://www.
lucasarts.com/support/default2.htm
Web Site: http://www.lucasarts.com

Lucent Technologies
Corporate Headquarters
600 Mountain Avenue
Murray Hill, NJ 07974
(888) 4LUCENT (458-2368) or
(908) 582-8500
Information: (888) 584-6366 or
(317) 322-6848
Business Large Systems Support:
(800) 242-2121, 24/7
Business Small Systems Support:
(800) 628-2888, 24/7
Self-Service Center: http://www.lucent.
com/enterprise/selfservice
Web Site: http://www.lucent.com

Macromedia, Incorporated
600 Townsend Street
San Francisco, CA 94103
(415) 252-2000
Fax: (415) 626-0554
Customer Service: (800) 470-7211
Product Literature: (800) 326-2128
Product Upgrades: (800) 457-1774
Technical Support: (415) 252-9080,
M–F 6 a.m.–5 p.m. PST
Fax: (415) 703-0924
FreeHand/Fontographer Fax Support:
(972) 680-0535
Technical Support Web Site: http://www.
macromedia.com/support
Web Site: http://www.macromedia.com

Madge Networks
2310 North First Street
San Jose, CA 95131-1011
(408) 955-0700
Fax: (408) 955-0970
Fax Back: (408) 383-1002
BBS: (408) 955-0262
Technical Support: (800) 876-2343
Fax: (408) 955-0970
Web Site: http://www.madge.com

MAG Innovision
MAG Technology USA, Inc.
20 Goodyear
Irvine, CA 92618
(800) 827-3998 or (949) 855-4930
Fax: (949) 855-4535
Fax Back: (714) 751-0166
Technical Support:
Fax: (949) 598-4920
Web Site:
http://www.maginnovision.com

Magitronic Technology, Inc.
6585 Crescent Drive
Norcross, GA 30071
(770) 849-0667
Fax: (770) 441-2874
E-mail: techsupt@magitronic.com
FTP Site: ftp://ftp.magitronic.com
Web Site: http://www.magitronic.com

Magnavox
See Philips Consumer Electronics North
America
Customer Support: (800) 531-0039
Web Site: http://www.magnavox.com

Manugistic, Inc.
2115 East Jefferson Street
Rockville, MD 20852-4999
(301) 984-5000
Fax: (301) 984-5370
Web Site: http://www.manugistics.com

Marimba, Inc.
440 Clyde Avenue
Mountain View, CA 94043
(650) 930-5282
Fax: (650) 930-5600
E-mail: info@marimba.com
Web Site: http://www.marimba.com

Mathematica
See V_Graph, Inc.
MathSoft, Inc.
101 Main Street
Cambridge, MA 02142-1521
(617) 577-1017
Fax: (617) 577-8829
Mathcad/Axum Sales and Pricing:
(800) 628-4223
Mathcad and Axum Technical Support:
(617) 577-1778, 9:00 a.m.–5:30 p.m. EST
7 days
Fax: (617) 577-8829
Automated Solution Center:
(617) 621-1140
S-PLUS Support: (206) 283-8802,
M–F 7:30 a.m.–5:00 p.m. PST
Fax: (206) 283-6310
E-mail: support@mathsoft.com
Web Site: http://www.mathsoft.com

Matrox Graphics, Inc.
1055 St. Regis Boulevard
Dorval, Quebec
Canada H9P 2T4
(514) 685-7230

*Continued*

*(continued)*
Fax: (514) 685-2853
(800) 361-1408
BBS: (514) 685-6008
Fax Back: (514) 685-0174
Technical Support: (514) 685-0270,
M–F 8 a.m.–6 p.m. EST
Fax: (514) 822-6363
E-mail: graphics.techsupport@matrox.com
FTP Site:
ftp://ftp.matrox.com/pub/mga
Web Site: http://www.matrox.com

Maxell Corporation of America
22-08 Route 208
Fair Lawn, NJ 07410
(201) 794-5900 or (800) 533-2836
Fax: (201) 796-8790
Fax Back: (888) 629-5329
Data Storage Customer Service:
U.S. (800) 525-2797, Canada (905) 669-8107
Technical Support: (800) 377-5887
E-mail: techsupp@maxell.com
Web Site: http://www.maxell.com

Maxis, Inc., division of Electronic Arts.
2121 North California Boulevard, Suite 600
Walnut Creek, CA 94596-3572
(925) 933-5630
Fax: (925) 927-3736
Sales: (800) 336-2947 or (800) 245-4525
BBS: (510) 927-3910, 28.8 Kbps
Technical Support: (650) 628-4311
Web Site: http://www.ea.com

Maxi Switch
2901 East Elvira Road
Tucson, AZ 85706
(520) 294-5450
Fax: (520) 294-6890
E-mail: maxiswitch@maxiswitch.com
Web Site: http://www.maxiswitch.com

MaxTech, Inc.
13915 Cerritos Corporate Drive
Cerritos, CA 90703
(562) 921-1698
Fax: (562) 802-9605
Technical Support: (562) 921-4438

Tech Fax: (562) 921-4439
FTP Site: ftp://ftp.maxcorp.com/pub
Web Site: http://www.maxcorp.com

Maxtor Corporation
Subsidiary of Hyundai Electronics
America (HEA)
510 Cottonwood Drive
Milpitas, CA 95035
(408) 432-1700
Fax: (408) 432-4210
Customer Service: (800) 2-MAXTOR
(262-9867) — Option 2, M–F 6 a.m.–6 p.m.
MST
Fax: (408) 922-2085
International: (408) 432-1700 or
(303) 678-2015
BBS: (303) 678-2222
Online BBS: http://www.maxtor.
com:80/bbsindex.html
Fax Back: (800) 2-MAXTOR (262-9867) —
Option 3
Technical Assistance: (800) 2-MAXTOR
(262-9867) — Option 1, M–F 6 a.m.–6 p.m.
MST
Technical Assistance Fax: (303) 260-2260
Web Site: http://www.maxtor.com

McAfee Associates, now Network
Associates, Inc.
3695 Freedom Circle
Santa Clara, CA 95054
(408) 988-3832
Fax: (408) 970-9727
Sales Support: (408) 988-3832
Customer Care: (408) 988-3832
Fax: (408) 970-9727
Automated Voice and Fax System
(408) 988-3034
Corporate Technical Support:
(408) 988-9832, 8 a.m.–8 p.m. CST M–F
Retail Technical Support: (801)
492-2700, 8 a.m.–8 p.m. CST M–F
FTP Site: ftp://ftp.mcafee.com
Web Site: http://www.mcafee.com
Web Site: http://www.nai.com

MECA Software, L.L.C.
115 Corporate Drive

Trumbull, CT 06611
(203) 452-2600
Fax: (203) 452-5257
Sales: (203) 452-2623
Technical Support: (203) 452-2736
Fax: (203) 452-8706
Web Site: http://www.mymnet.com

MECC
(Minneapolis Educational Computing
Corporation)
Division of The Learning Company
6160 Summit Drive North
Minneapolis, MN 55430
(612) 569-1500
Customer Support: (617) 761-3000,
M–F 8 a.m.–8 p.m. EST
Automated Technical Support:
(800) 409-1497
Technical Support: (319) 247-3333,
M–F, 9 a.m.–9 p.m. EST
Fax: (319) 395-9600
Technical Support Web Site:
http://support.learningco.com
Web Site: http://www.mecc.com

Megahertz Corporation
Acquired by 3Com Corporation
605 North Eddie Rickenbacker Drive
Salt Lake City, UT 84116
(801) 320-7000
Technical Support: (800) 638-3266
FTP Site: ftp://ftp.megahertz.com
Technical Support Web Site:
http://www.mhz.com/support
Web Site: http://www.megahertz.com
Web Site: http://www.3com.com

Meridian Data
5615 Scotts Valley Drive
Scotts Valley, CA 95066
(831) 438-3100 or (800) 342-1129
Fax: (831) 438-6816
Technical Support: (800) 755-8324 or
(831) 461-5128
Fax: (831) 438-8001
E-mail: support@meridian-data.com
FTP Site:
ftp://ftp.meridian-data.com

Web Site:
http://www.meridian-data.com

Metatools, now MetaCreations
6303 Carpinteria Avenue
Carpinteria, CA 93013
(805) 566-6200
Fax: (805) 566-6385
Sales: (800) 846-0111
Customer Service: (888) 707-6382 or
(831) 430-4100
Fax: (831) 438-9670
Web Site: http://www.metatools.com
Web Site: http://www.metacreations.
com

Metrowerks, Inc.
9801 Metric Bldg 100
Austin, TX 78758
(800) 377-5416 or (512) 873-4700
Fax: (512) 873-4900
Tech Form:
http://www.metrowerks.com/
feedback/mailforms/cw_support.html
Web Site: http://www.metrowerks.com

MGI Software Corp.
40 West Wilmot Street
Richmond Hill, Ontario
Canada L4B 1H8
(905) 764-7000
Fax: (905) 764-7110
Web Site: http://www.mgisoft.com

MGM-UA Interactive
Web Site: http://www.mgmua.com/
interactive2

Microcom, Inc., acquired by
Compaq Corporation
Web Site: http://www.compaq.com/
products/networking

Micro Computer Systems, Inc.
2300 Valley View, Suite 800
Irving, TX 75062
(972) 659-1514
Fax: (972) 659-1624
Web Site: http://www.mcsdallas.com

Microcom Corporation
8333 A Green Meadows Drive North
Westerville, OH 43081
(740) 548-6262 or (800) MICROCOM
(642-7626)
Fax: (740) 548-6556
Tech Form: http://www.microcomcorp.com/support.html
Web Site:
http://www.microcomcorp.com

Micro Design International, Inc.
6985 University Boulevard
Winter Park, FL 32792
(800) 920-8205 or (407) 677-8333
Fax: (407) 677-8365
BBS: (407) 677-4854
Technical Support: (407) 677-8333 x149,
M–F 8 a.m.–6 p.m. EST
Fax: (407) 677-0221
E-mail: support@mdi.com
Web Site: http://www.mdi.com

Microdyne
3601 Eisenhower Avenue
Alexandria, VA 22304
(800) 255-3967
(703) 329-3700 or International
(703) 960-9661
Web Site: http://www.microdyne.com

Micrografx, Inc.
1303 E. Arapaho Road
Richardson, TX 75081
(972) 994-6525 or (972) 234-1769
Fax: (972) 234-2410
Sales: (800) 733-3729
Technical Support: (972) 234-2694
Web Site: http://www.micrografx.com

Micro House International
2477 N. 55th Street #101
Boulder, CO 80301
Corporate Office: 303-443-3388
Sales: (800) 926-8299
Fax: (303) 443-3323
BBS: (303) 443-9957
Support Source Support: (800) 222-5916
or (303) 443-3388

Utility Products Support: (303) 443-3389
FTP Site: ftp://ftp.microhouse.com
Web Site: http://www.microhouse.com

Micro Logic Corp.
89 Leuning Street
South Hackensack, NJ 07606
(201) 342-6518
Sales: (800) 342-5930 or (201) 342-6518
Fax: (201) 342-0370
Web Site: http://www.miclog.com

Micron PC, Inc.
900 East Karcher Road
Nampa, ID 83687
(208) 893-3900
Fax on Demand: (877) MICRON4
Sales: (888) 224-4247
BBS: (208) 893-8982
BBS (download only): (800) 270-1207
Customer Service: (877) 894-5693 or
(208) 893-7390, M–F 6 a.m.–8 p.m.,
Sat 7 a.m.–5 p.m. MST
Fax: (208) 893-7985
Technical Support: (888) 652-7252,
(877) 894-5693 or (208) 893-7390, 24/7
Fax: (208) 893-7390
TDD: (800) 528-1672
Micron Vetix Server Support:
(800) 249-1178 or (208) 893-4502
Web Site: http://www.micronpc.com

Micron Technology, Inc.
8000 S. Federal Way
P.O. Box 6
Boise, ID 83707-0006
(208) 368-3900
Fax: (208) 368-4431
Web Site: http://www.micron.com

Micron Technology, Inc.
Crucial Technology
3475 E. Commercial Ct.
Meridian, ID 83642
Customer Service: (800) 336-8915
Technical Support: (800) 336-8916
Web Site: http://www.micron.com

Micropolis Corporation, acquired by Singapore Technologies and filed bankruptcy
Web Site: http://www.st.com.sg

Microsoft Corporation
One Microsoft Way
Redmond, WA 98052
Redmond Campus (425) 882-8080
Corporate Fax-Redmond: (425) 936-7329
Sales and Information—Products and Services: (800) 426-9400
Microsoft Corporation TT/TDD Number (425) 936-5066
Microsoft Press (800) MSPRESS (677-7377)
MSN:
Sales and Service: (800) 386-5550, TDD (800) 840-9890
MSN Internet Access Support: (425) 635-7019, TDD (425) 635-4948
FastTips (Fax Back), U.S. and Canada:
Desktop Applications: (800) 936-4100
Home Products: (800) 936-4100
Hardware and Desktop Systems: (800) 936-4200
Development (800): 936-4300
Advanced Systems: (800) 936-4400
TT/TDD (Text Telephone):
U.S.: (425) 635-4948, Canada: (905) 568-9641
Desktop Applications–M–F 6 a.m.–6 p.m. PST:
Microsoft Excel, U.S.: (425) 635-7070, Canada: (905) 568-2294
Internet Explorer, U.S.: (425) 635-7123, Canada: (905) 568-3503
Outlook, U.S.: (425) 635-7031, Canada: (905) 568-4494
Office, U.S.: (425) 635-7056, Canada: (905) 568-2294
PowerPoint, U.S.: (425) 635-7145, Canada: (905) 568-3503
Project, U.S.: (425) 635-7155, Canada: (905) 568-3503
Word, U.S.: (425) 462-9673, Canada: (905) 568-2294
Works, U.S.: (425) 635-7130, Canada: (905) 568-3503

Windows 95: (425) 635-7000, Canada: (905) 568-4494
Windows 98: (425) 635-7222, Canada: (905) 568-4494
Windows NT: (425) 635-7018; Canada,: (905) 568-4494
Development Tools:
Canada: (905) 568-3503
U.S.:
C++, Visual Basic, and Visual J++: (425) 635-7012
Fortran: (425) 635-7015
Microsoft Mouse, Microsoft Ballpoint, Windows Digital Sound System and Other Microsoft Hardware, U.S. (425) 635-7040, Canada: (905) 568-4494
Microsoft Support: http://support.microsoft.com/support
Web Site: http://www.microsoft.com

Micro Solutions Incorporated
132 West Lincoln Highway
DeKalb, IL 60115
Sales: (800) 890-7227 or (815) 756-3411
Fax: (815) 756-2928
BBS: (815) 756-9100
Fax Back: (815) 754-4600
Technical Support: (815) 754-4500, M–F 8 a.m.–5 p.m. CST
Fax: (815) 756-4986
Web Site: http://www.micro-solutions.com

MicroSpeed
2495 Industrial Parkway West
Hayward, CA 94545
(510) 259-1270
Fax: (510) 259-1291
Technical Support: 9510) 259-1270
E-mail Technical Support: support@microspeed.com
Web Site: http://www.microspeed.com

MicroSystems Development Technologies, Inc.
4100 Moorpark Avenue, #104
San Jose, CA 95117

*Continued*

*(continued)*
(408) 296-4000
Fax: (408) 296-5877
Technical Support: (408) 296-4000
Web Site: http://www.msd.com

Microtest
4747 North 22nd Street
Phoenix, AZ 85016-4708
(602) 952-6400
Sales: (800) 526-9675
Fax: (602) 952-6401
BBS: (602) 957-7716
Fax Back: (602) 952-6450
Technical Support: (800) 638-3497 or
(602) 952-6483
Fax: (800) 419-8991 or (602) 952-6494
E-mail: support@microtest.com
FTP Site: ftp://ftp.microtest.com/pub
Web Site: http://www.microtest.com

Midisoft Corporation
1605 N. W. Sammamish Road, Suite 205
Issaquah, WA. 98027
(800) 776-6434 or (425) 391-3610
Fax: 9425) 391-3422
Sales: (800) 776-6434
BBS: (425) 391-7966
Technical Support: (425) 391-3610
Web Site: http://www.midisoft.com

Mindscape, division of The Learning
Company
88 Rowland Way
Novato, CA 94945
(415) 895-2000
Fax: (415) 895-2102
Technical Support Fax: (617) 494-5898
Web Site: http://www.mindscape.com

Minolta Corporation
101 Williams Drive
Ramsey, NJ 07446
(800) 964-6658 or (201) 825-4000
Minolta Business Systems:
(201) 825-8600
Laser Printer Support: (800) 459-3250
Web Site: http://www.minolta.com

MIRAGE Multi Media Systems, Inc.
9750 South La Cienega
Inglewood, CA 90301
Sales: (800) 228-3349 or International
Sales: (310) 258-1202, M–F 9 a.m.–5 p.m.
Customer Service and Technical
Support: (310) 258-1205,
M–F 9 a.m.–4 p.m. PST
Sales or Technical Support by Fax:
(310) 258-1210
Technical Support E-mail:
tech@mirage-mmc.com
Web Site: http://www.mirage-mmc.com

mIRC
Khaled Mardam-Bey
56 Gloucester Road, #347
London, SW7 4UB
United Kingdom
E-mail: khaled@mardam.demon.co.uk
Web Site: http://www.mirc.co.uk

miro Computer Products, Inc., acquired
by Pinnacle Systems
280 North Bernardo Avenue
Mountain View, CA 94043
(650) 526-1600
Fax: (650) 526-1601
Fax Back: (650) 237 1973
Support Hotline: (650) 237 1800,
M–F 9 a.m.@@5 p.m.
Web Site: http://www.pinnaclesys.com

Mitsubishi Display Products:
Imaging Products Division
5665 Plaza Drive
Cypress, CA 90630
(714) 220-2500 or (800) 843-2516
Fax: (714) 236-6339
Fax Back: (714) 236-6453
Technical Support: (800) 344-6352,
M–F 5 a.m.–5 p.m., Sat-Sun 9 a.m.–5 p.m.
PST
Web Site:
http://www.mitsubishi-display.com

Mitsubishi Electric Corporation
2-3 Marunouchi 2-chome
Chiyoda-ku, Tokyo 100, Japan
81-3-3218-2111
Fax: 81-3-3218-2431
E-mail: mpac@tk.mitsubishi.co.jp
Web Site: http://www.melco.co.jp

Mitsubishi Electronics America, Inc.
Americas Corporate Office
5665 Plaza Drive
Cypress, CA 90630
(714) 220-2500
Fax: (714) 229-3898
Web Site: http://www.
mitsubishielectric-usa.com

Mitsubishi Electronics America, Inc.
Telecommunications and Network
System Division
12007 Sunrise Valley Drive, Suite 220
Reston, VA 22091
(703) 758-7811
Web Site: http://www.melamsat.com

Mitsubishi Wireless Communications, Inc.
3805 Crestwood Parkway,
Duluth, GA 30096
(770) 638-2100
Fax: (770) 921-4522
Customer Service: (800) 888-9879,
M–F 8 a.m.–8 p.m. EST
Fax: (480) 753-4848
Fax Back: (408) 753-4838
Web Site:
http://www.mitsubishiwireless.com

Mitsubishi Wireless Communications,
Inc. (MWCI)
Personal Mobile Communications
Division
1050 East Arques Avenue
Sunnyvale, CA 94086
(408) 703-5900
Fax: (408) 736-5912
Web Site:
http://www.mobileaccessphone.com

Mitsumi Electronics Corporation
Sales:
5808 West Campus Circle Drive
Irving, TX 75063
(972) 550-7300
Fax: (972) 550-7424
Technical Support for End Users of
Mitsumi CD-ROM Drives, see Enterprise
Corporation International
Technical Support: (800) 801-7927 or
(800) MITSUMI (648-7864)
Fax: (214) 550-7300
BBS: (408) 970-0700
Web Site: http://www.mitsumi.com

Moon Valley Software, Inc.
1880 Santa Barbara Street
San Luis Obispo, CA 93401
(805) 781-3890
Fax: (805) 781-3898
Online Forums: http://www.moonvalley.
com/wwwboard/forum.htm
Web Site: http://www.moonvalley.com

Mortice Kern Systems, Inc.
185 Columbia Street West
Waterloo, Ontario
Canada, N2L 5Z5
(519) 884-2251
Sales: (800) 265-2797
Technical Support: (519) 884-2270,
8:30 a.m.–6:00 p.m. EST
Fax: (519) 884-8861
Web Site: http://www.mks.com

Motorola, Inc.
Corporate Offices
1303 East Algonquin Road
Schaumburg, IL 60196
(847) 576-5000
Web Site: http://www.mot.com

Motorola, Inc. — General Systems Sector
Motorola Computer Group (MCG)
2900 South Diablo Way
Tempe, AZ 85282
Sales: (800) 759-1107 Ext. SC2 or
(512) 434-1526 Ext. SC2

*Continued*

*(continued)*
Fax on Demand: (800) 682-6128
Technical Support and Service:
(800) 551-1016 U.S., (800) 387-2416
Canada
Web Site: `http://www.mcg.mot.com`

Motorola, Inc. — General Systems Sector
Motorola Computer Group
Motorola PowerPC Information Line
(800) 845-MOTO, International
(512) 434-1502
Fax: (512) 244-9222
E-mail: motorola@selectnet.com
Fax Back: `http://www.sps-mot.com/`
`home/fax_rqst.html`
FTP Site: `ftp://www.mot.com/pub/`
`SPS/PowerPC/support`
Web Site:
`http://www.mot.com/SPS/PowerPC`

Motorola, Inc. — Messaging, Information
and Media Sector
Information Systems Group (ISG)
Technical Support Center
Mansfield, MA
(508) 261-0366
(800) 544-0062
Motorola, Inc. — Messaging, Information
and Media Sector
Information Systems Group (ISG)
Technical Support Center
Huntsville, AL
(205) 726-0798
or
Technical Support Center
Mansfield, MA
(508) 261-0366
(800) 544-0062 U.S. and Canada
Fax Back: (800) 221-4380
FTP Site:
`ftp://www.mot.com/pub/MIMS/ISG`
Web Site:
`http://www.mot.com/MIMS/ISG`

Mouse Systems Corporation
41660 Boscell Road
Fremont, CA 94538
(510) 656-1117

Fax: (510) 656-4409
Technical Support: (510) 656-1117
Fax: (510) 656-4409
E-mail: support@mousesystems.com
Web Site:
`http://www.mousesystems.com`

MTX, Inc.
3301 Terminal Drive
Raleigh, NC 27604
(919) 250-6100
Web Site: `http://www.mtc.com`

Multicom Publishing, Inc.
2017 Eighth Avenue, 3rd Floor
Seattle, WA 98101
(800) 850-7272 or (206) 622-5530
Fax: (206) 622-4380
Customer Service and Orders:
(800) 850-7272 or (206) 622-5530,
8:30 a.m.–5:00 p.m. M–F PST
E-mail: info@multicom.com
Technical Support: (206) 343-5934,
M–F 9 a.m.–5 p.m. PST
Fax: (206) 622-4380
E-mail: techsupport@multicom.com
Web Site: `http://www.multicom.com`

Multi-Tech Systems
2205 Woodale Drive
Mounds View, MN 55112
(612) 785-3500 or (800) 328-9717
Fax: (612) 785-9874
Fax Back: System (612) 717-5888
BBS: (612) 785-3702 or (800) 392-2432
Technical Support: (800) 972-2439
FTP Site: `ftp://ftp.multitech.com`
Web Site: `http://www.multitech.com`

Musicware, Inc.
8654 154th Avenue NE
Redmond, WA 98052
(206) 881-9797
Fax: (206) 881-9664
Sales: (800) 99-PIANO
Technical Support: (206) 881-1419
Web Site:
`http://www.musicwareinc.com`

Mustang Software, Incorporated
6200 Lake Ming Road
Bakersfield, CA 93306
(661) 873-2500
Fax: (805) 873-2599
Technical Support: (805) 873-2550,
M–F 9 a.m.–5 p.m. PST
E-mail Technical Support:
support@mustang.com
Web Site: http://www.mustang.com

Mustek, Inc.
121 Waterworks Way, #100
Irvine, CA 92618
(949) 788-3600
Fax: (949) 788-3670
Fax Back: (949) 788-3600
Web Site: http://www.mustek.com

Mylex Corporation
34551 Ardenwood Boulevard
Fremont, CA 94555
(510) 796-6100 or (800) 77MYLEX
(776-9539)
Fax: (510) 797-7983
BBS: (510) 793-3491
Technical Support: (510) 608-2400,
M–F 6 a.m.–6 p.m. PST
Technical Support Fax: (510) 745-7715
Technical Support E-mail:
support@mylex.com
FTP Site: ftp://ftp.mylex.com/pub/
Web Site: http://www.mylex.com

Mysoftware Company Incorporated
2197 East Bayshore Road
Palo Alto, CA 94303
Fax: (650) 325-0873
Sales: (800) 325-3508
Customer Service: (650) 473-3620
Web Site: http://www.mysoftware.com

Nanao USA Corporation
Now EIZO Nanao Technologies, Inc.
5710 Warland Drive
Cypress, CA 90630
(562) 431-5011 or (800) 800-5202
Fax: (562) 431-4811
E-mail Support: support@eizo.com

Web Site:
http://www.eizo.com/index.htm

National Geographic Society
1145 17th Street N.W.
Washington DC 20090-8199
Information (800) 647-5463
TDD Information: (800) 548-9797
Web Site:
http://www.nationalgeographic.com

National Semiconductor Corporation
2900 Semiconductor Drive
P.O. Box 58090
Santa Clara, CA 95050
(408) 721-5000
Fax: (408) 721-3238
Customer Support Center:
(800) 272-9959
Fax: (800) 737-7018
Web Site: http://www.national.com

Nbase Communications
Division of MRV Communications, Inc.
8943 Fullbright Avenue
Chatsworth, CA 91311
(818) 773-0900
Fax: (818) 773-0906
Technical Support: (800) 435-7997
FTP Site: ftp://ftp.xyplex.com/pub
Web Site: http://www.nbase.com

NEBS (New England Business Services,
Inc.)
500 Main Street
Groton, MA 01471
(508) 448-6111
Sales: (800) 225-6380
Customer Service: (888) 823-6327,
M–F 7 a.m.–1 a.m., Sat 7 a.m.–7 p.m.,
Sun 1 p.m.–7 p.m. EST
Web Site: http://www.nebs.com

NEC Technologies, Inc.
1250 North Arlington Heights Road,
Suite 500 Avenue
Itasca, IL 60143-1248

*Continued*

*(continued)*
(630) 467-5000
Fax: (630) 467-5010
General Information: (800) 338-9549
Product Information: (800) NEC-INFO
(632-4636)
Server Products: (800) 325-5500
Fax Back: (800) 366-0476
BBS: (916) 379-4499
Customer Service:
Customer Service Center: (800) 388-8888
Onsite and Depot Repairs (U.S.)
Customer Service Center: (800) 268-4191
Onsite and Depot Repairs
(Canada)Versa UltraCare Service:
(800) 332-8004
Spare Parts Sales: (800) 233-6321,
Canada: (800) 727-2787
Technical Support:
NEC CD-ROM Products: (800) 632-4667
NEC PowerMate Products:
(800) 632-4525
NEC Ready Products Office:
(801) 578-5104
NEC Versa Products: (800) 632-4525
NEC MultiSync Monitors: (800) 632-4662
NEC Printer Products: (800) 632-4650
NEC Server Products: (800) 325-5500
NEC ATM Switching: (214) 518-5111
Broadband Access, Digital Loop, and
Fiber Optic/SONET: (800) 367-6321
Semiconductors and Electronic
Component Support: (800) 366-9782
FTP Site: ftp://ftp.nectech.com/pub
Web Site: http://www.nec.com

NetCarta Corporation
Acquired by Microsoft Corporation
NETCOM On-line Communications, Inc.,
acquired by MindSpring
2 North Second Street, Plaza A
San Jose, CA 95113
Customer Service: (800) 815-9111,
M–F 8 a.m.–12 a.m. EST
Technical Support: (800) 719-4660, 24/7
TDD Service and Support: (888) 566-6774
Web Site: http://www.netcom.com

NetGuard, Inc.
2445 Midway Road
Carrollton, TX 75006
(972) 738-6900
Fax: (214) 738-6999
Web Site: http://www.netguard.com

NetManage
10725 North De Anza Boulevard
Cupertino, CA 95014
(408) 973-7171
Fax: (408) 257-6405
Web Site: http://www.netmanage.com

Net Nanny, Ltd.
525 Seymour Street, Suite 108
Vancouver, B.C.
Canada V6B 3H7
Fax: (604) 662-8525
Technical Support Fax: (604) 662-8525
E-mail Technical Support:
NNSupport@netnanny.com
Web Site: http://www.netnanny.com

Netscape Communications Corporation,
acquired by AOL
501 E. Middlefield Road
Mountain View, CA 94043
Executive Offices: (650) 254-1900
Fax: (650) 528-4124
Product and Sales Information:
Individuals:(650) 937-3777, 7 a.m.–5 p.m.
PST
Corporate: (650) 937-2555, 7 a.m.–5 p.m.
PST
Installation Assistance: (800) 639-0939
Web Site: http://www.netscape.com

Network Associates, Inc.
3695 Freedom Circle
Santa Clara, CA 95054
(408) 988-3832
Fax: (408) 970-9727
Sales Support: (408) 988-3832
Customer Care: (408) 988-3832
Fax: (408) 970-9727
Automated Voice and Fax System
(408) 988-3034

Corporate Technical Support: (408)
988-9832, 8 a.m.–8 p.m. CST M–F
Retail Technical Support: (801)
492-2700, 8 a.m.–8 p.m. CST M–F
FTP Site: ftp://ftp.mcafee.com
Web Site: http://www.mcafee.com
Web Site: http://www.nai.com

Network Computing Devices, Inc. (NCD)
350 North Bernardo Avenue
Mountain View, CA 94043-5207
(650) 694-0650 or (800) 800-9599
Fax: (650) 961-7711
E-mail: info@ncd.com
NCD Technical Support Hotline:
(503) 641-2200
NCD Technical Support Fax: (503) 641-2959
E-mail: support@ncd.com
Web Site: http://www.ncd.com

Networth Incorporated
Acquired by Compaq Computer
Corporation
a.m.p.m.p.m.Newbridge Networks
Corporation
Corporate Headquarters
600 March Road
Kanata, Ontario
Canada K2K 2E6
(613) 591-3600
Fax: (613) 591-3680
Technical Support: (703) 834-5300
Web Site: http://www.newbridge.com

New World Computing, Inc.
Acquired by The 3DO Company
600 Galveston Drive
Redwood City, CA 94063
Sales: (800) 325-8898
BBS: (818) 889-5684
Technical and Customer Support:
(650) 261-3454, M–F 9 a.m.–noon,
2 p.m.–5 p.m. PST
Fax: (650) 261-3419
Web Site: http://www.nwcomputing.com

NexGen, acquired by Advanced Micro
Devices, Inc. (AMD)
Nico Mak Computing, Inc.

P.O. Box 540
Mansfield, CT 06268-0540
Office and Administrative: (860) 429-3539
Sales, Credit Cards: (800) 242-4775
Tech Form:
http://www.winzip.com/xtech.htm
Web Site: http://www.winzip.com

Nikon, Inc.
1300 Walt Whitman Road
Melville, NY 11747-3064
(516) 547-4200
Fax: (516) 547-0299
Information — Electronic Imaging:
(800) 526-4566
Web Site: http://www.nikonusa.com

Nikon Corporation
Fuji Building
2-3, 3-chome
Marunouchi, Chiyoda-ku,
Tokyo 100, Japan
011 81-03-3214-5311
Fax: 011 81-03-3201-5856
Worldwide Site: http://www.nikon.com
Web Site: http://www.klt.co.
jp/main/index_e.htm

Nikon Electronic Imaging Department
1300 Walt Whitman Road
Melville, NY 11747
(800) 52-NIKON or (516) 547-4355
Fax: (516) 547-0299
Repair Service: (800) 645-6678
Web Site: http://www.klt.co.
jp/Nikon/EID/index.html

Nissei Sangyo America, Ltd. (NSA)
2850 Golf Road, Suite 200
Rolling Meadows, IL 60008
(847) 981-8989
Fax: (847) 364-9052
General Information: (800) 441-4832
Technical Support: (800) 536-6721, M–F
8:30 a.m.–8:00 p.m. EST
Web Site:
http://www.hitachidisplays.com
Web Site: http://www.nissei.com

NMB Technologies Incorporated
9730 Independence Avenue
Chatsworth, CA 91311
(818) 341-3355
Fax: (818) 341-8207
Web Site: http://www.nmbtech.com

Nokia Corporate Communications
(Americas)
6000 Connection Drive
Irving, TX 75039
(972) 854-5000
Fax: (972) 854-5050
Nokia Display Products, Inc.
123 Second Street
Sausalito, CA 94965
(415) 331-4244
Fax: (415) 331-6211
Information: (800) BY-NOKIA (296-6542),
International: (415) 331-4244
Customer Service: (800) 483-7952
Technical Support: (800) 483-7952,
M–F 8 a.m.–8 p.m. EST
Nokia Group
Corporate Communications
Keilalahdentie 4, FIN-02150 Espoo
P.O. Box 226, FIN-00045 NOKIA GROUP
358 9 180 71
Fax: 358 9 656 388
Web Site: http://www.nokia.com
Web Site:
http://www.nokia-americas.com

Nokia Mobile Phones
Customer Service: (888) 665-4228
Nokia Telecommunications, Inc.
7 Village Circle, Suite 100
Westlake, TX 76262
(817) 491-5800
Fax: (817) 491-5888
Nolo Press
950 Parker Street
Berkeley, CA 94710
Customer Service: (800) 728-3555,
M–F 9 a.m.–5 p.m. PST
Fax: (800) 645-0895, (510) 548-5902
Software Technical Support:
(510) 549-4660, M–F 9 a.m.–5 p.m. PST
Web Site: http://www.nolo.com

Nortel Networks
8200 Dixie Road
Brampton, Ontario
Canada L6T 5P6
(905) 863-0000
Sales and Information: (800) 4-NORTEL
Web Site:
http://www.nortelnetworks.com

Norton-Lambert
P.O. Box 4085
Santa Barbara, CA 93140
(805) 964-6767
Fax: (805) 683-5679
BBS: (805) 683-2249
Technical Support: (805) 964-6767,
M–F 7:00 a.m.–4:45 p.m. PST
Fax: (805) 683-5679
Web Site:
http://www.nortonlambert.com

NovaStor Corporation
80-B W. Cochran
Simi Valley, CA 93065
(805) 579-6700
Fax: (805) 579-6710
BBS: (805) 579-6720
Technical Support: (805) 579-6700,
M–F 6 a.m.–7 p.m. PST
FTP Site: ftp://ftp.novastor.com
Web Site: http://www.novastor.com

Novell, Inc.
122 East 1700 South
Provo, UT 84606
(801) 861-7000 or (800) 638-9273
Technical Support: (800) 858-4000,
International (801) 861-4000
Fax: (801) 429-5040
Web Site: http://www.novell.com

Novell — Wordperfect
See Corel Corporation
Number Nine Visual Technology Corp.
18 Hartwell Avenue
Lexington, MA 02173-3103
(781) 674-0009 or (781) 869-7230
Sales and Information: 800-GET-NINE
(438-6463)

Fax Back: (800) 438-6463 or
(617) 869-7214
BBS: (617) 862-7502
Technical Support: (781) 869-7214,
M–Th 8:30 a.m.–6:00 p.m.,
F 8:30–5:00 p.m. EST
Fax: (781) 869-7222
FTP Site: ftp://ftp.nine.com
Web Site: http://www.nine.com

The Numerical Algorithms Group Ltd.
(NAG Ltd.)
Wilkinson House
Jordan Hill Road
OXFORD, OX2 8DR
England UK
44 1865 511245
Fax: 44 1865 310139
Web Site: http://www.nag.co.uk

Numerical Algorithms Group (NAG, Inc.)
1400 Opus Place, Suite 200
Downers Grove, IL 60515-5702
(630) 971-2337
Fax: (630) 971-2706
Web Site: http://www.nag.com

NVIDIA Corp.
3535 Monroe Street
Santa Clara, CA 95051
(408) 615-2500
Fax: (408) 615-2800
Web Site: http://www.nvidia.com

Oak Technology, USA
139 Kifer Court
Sunnyvale, CA 94086
(408) 737-0888
Fax: (408) 737-3838
Fax Back: (800) 239-0319
Web Site: http://www.oaktech.com

Oki America, Inc.
Three University Plaza
Hackensack, NJ 07601
(201) 646-0011, (800) 654-3282
Fax: (201) 646-9229
Web Site: http://www.oki.com

Okidata
Subsidiary of Oki America, Inc.
532 Fellowship Road
Mount Laurel, NJ 08054
(609) 235-2600
Fax: (609) 778-4184
Customer Support and Information:
(800) OKIDATA (654-3282), 24/7
Fax Back: (800) 654-6651
Information System Automated
Attendant: (800) 654-3282
Okidata Regional Service Depots
(800) 809-4948
BBS: (609) 234-5344
(800) OKIDATA for the Location of the
Nearest Authorized Okidata Service
Dealer
Web Site: http://www.okidata.com

Olicom USA, Inc.
Marlborough Facility
450 Donald Lynch Boulevard
Marlborough, MA 01742
(508) 481-4060
Fax: (508) 229-5535
BBS: (972) 422-9835
Hotline Support: 800-OLICOM-1 or
(972) 907-4200, 24/7
Fax: (972) 671-7524
FTP Site: ftp://ftp.olicom.com
Web Site FTP:
http://www.olicom.com/software
Web Site: http://www.olicom.com

ON Technology
One Cambridge Center
Cambridge, MA 02142
(617) 374-1400
Fax: (617) 374-1433
Web Site: http://www.on.com

Ontrack Data International, Inc.
6321 Bury Drive
Eden Prairie, MN 55346
(800) 872-2599 or (612) 937-5161
Fax: (612) 937-5750
Product Registration: (800) 778-7357
BBS: (612) 937-0860

*Continued*

*(continued)*
Technical Support: (612) 937-2121
8 a.m.–7 p.m. CST
Web Site: http://www.ontrack.com

OPTi, Inc.
1440 McCarthy Boulevard
Milpitas, CA 95035
(408) 486-8000
Fax: (408) 486-8001
FTP Site: ftp://ftp.opti.com/pub
Web Site: http://www.opti.com

Oracle Corporation
500 Oracle Parkway
Redwood City, CA 94065-1600
(650) 506-7000
Support Sales: (415) 506-5577,
M–F 7 a.m.–5 p.m. PST
Web Site: http://www.oracle.com

Orchestra Multisystems, Incorporated,
acquired by KDS USA
12300 Edison Way
Garden Grove, CA 92841
(714) 891-3861 or (800) 237-9988
Fax: (714) 891-2661
Sales: (800) 237-9988
Customer Service and Technical
Support: (800) 283-0543
Web Site: http://www.orchestra.com

Orchid Technology, acquired by
Diamond Multimedia Systems, Inc.
O'Reilly & Associates
101 Morris Street
Sebastopol, CA 95472
(800) 998-9938 or (707) 829-0515
Fax: (707) 829-0104
General and Information: E-mail:
nuts@ora.com
Web Site: http://www.ora.com

Osicom Technologies, Inc.
2800 28th Street, Suite 100
Santa Monica, CA 90405
(310) 581-4030
Fax: (310) 581-4032
(888) 674-2668

FTP Site: ftp://ftp.osicom.com
Web Site: http://www.osicom.com

Packard Bell NECComputer Systems
Division
339 North Bernardo Avenue
Mountain View, CA 94043
(650) 528-6000
Sales and Information: (800) 733-5858
Fax Back: (888) 329-0088
Ready Technical Support: U.S.
(800) 632-4554 or (801) 578-5108,
Canada (905) 564-1925
Versa and PowerMate Technical
Support: (800) 632-4525
Fax: (801) 579-0092, Canada
(905) 564-3699
FTP Site:
ftp://ftp.packardbell.com/pub
Web Site:
http://www.packardbell.com
Palindrome Corporation acquired by
Veritas
Web Site: http://www.veritas.com

Panasonic
Part of Matsushita Electric Corporation
of America
One Panasonic Way
Secaucus, NJ 07094
Information: (201) 348-9090
Parts and Service Locations:
(800) 545-2672
Customer Care: (800) 973-4326,
M–F 9 a.m.–8 p.m. EST:
East: (215) 741-0676
Midwest: (847) 468-5530
South: (770) 338-6860
West: (714) 373-7132
Product Literature: (800) 344-2112,
Ext. 200
Bread Bakery Products Help Line:
(800) 211-7262 M–F 9 a.m.–9 p.m.,
S–S 9 a.m.–7 p.m. EST
Fax Products Help Line: (800) 435-7329
M–F 9 a.m.–8 p.m. EST
Panasonic DSS: (888) 726-2377,
M–F 8 a.m.–10 p.m.,
Sat–Sun 10 a.m.–10 p.m. EST

Digital Camera and Photo Printer Support
(800) 272-7033, M–F 9 a.m.–8 p.m. EST
Monitor Support: (800) 726-2797, 24/7
Panasonic Software Customer Support:
(408) 653-1898, M–F 9 a.m.–5 p.m. PST
Laptop Computers: (800) 527-8675, 24/7
Color Laser Technical Support:
(888) 744-2424,, M–F 9 a.m.–7 p.m. EST
Other Printer Support: (800) 222-0584
M–F 9 a.m.–7 p.m. EST
CD-ROM, Scanners, and Imaging Support:
(800) 726-2797, M–F 9 a.m.–7 p.m. EST
Video Teleconferencing Support: (800)
211-7262, M–F 9 a.m.–9 p.m.,
Sat-Sun 9 a.m.–7 p.m., open holidays
Wireless Products: 9800) 414-9408,
M–F 9 a.m.–5 p.m. EST
FTP Site: ftp://ftp.panasonic.com/pub
Web Site: http://www.mei.co.jp
Web Site: http://www.panasonic.com

Panasonic Interactive Media.com
4701 Patrick Henry Drive, Suite 1101
Santa Clara, CA 95054
(408) 653-1888
Fax: (408) 653-1899
Technical Support: (425) 889-7095
Digital Imaging Support: (888) 726-2746
Web Site: http://www.pimcom.com

Pantone, Inc.
590 Commerce Boulevard
Carlstadt, NJ 07072-3098
(201) 935-5500 or (800) 726-8663
Fax: (201) 896-0242
E-mail: support@pantone.com
Web Site: http://www.pantone.com

Paradise
Acquired by Relialogic Technology
Corporation
48507 Milmont Drive
Fremont, CA 95438
(800) 444-3617 or (510) 770-3990
BBS: (510) 668-1135
Fax: (510) 770-3994
Web Site: http://www.paradisemmp.com

Paradyne
8545 126th Avenue North
Largo, FL 33773
(813) 530-2000 or (800) 727-2396
Fax: (813) 530-8216
Technical Support: (800) 870-2221
Web Site: http://www.paradyne.com

ParcPlace Digitalk, Inc., now
ObjectShare, Inc.
16811 Hale Avenue, Suite A
Irvine, CA 92060
(949) 833-1122
Fax: (949) 833-0209
Web Site:
http://www.objectshare.com

Parsons Technology, Division of The
Learning Company
One Parsons Drive
P.O. Box 100
Hiawatha, IA 52233
(319) 395-0102
Sales: (800) 973-5111
Customer Assistance: (319) 395-0115,
M–F 8 a.m.–6 p.m. CST
Fax: (319) 395-0466
Download Help: (319) 393-1425
M–F 8 a.m.–5 p.m. CST
Technical Support: (319) 247-3333,
MTThF 8 a.m.–7 p.m., W 9:30 a.m.–7:00 p.m.
EST
Automated Support: (888) 830-HELP (4357)
Web Site: http://www.parsonstech.com

PC Power & Cooling, Inc.
5995 Avenida Encinas
Carlsbad, CA 92008
(619) 931-5700, or (800) 722-6555,
M–F 7 a.m.–6 p.m. PST
Fax: (619) 931-6988
Web Site:
http://www.pcpowercooling.com

PC-Xdivision
Division of Network Computing Devices,
Inc.
9590 SW Gemini Drive
Beaverton, OR 97005
(503) 641-2200 or (800) 800-9599
BBS: (503) 646-1743
Fax: (503) 643-8642
Technical Support: (503) 641-2200,
8 a.m.–5 p.m. PST, M–F
Fax: (503) 641-2959
FTP Site:
ftp://ftp.ncd.com/pub/pcx/Archive
Web Site: http://www.ncd.com
Web Site:
http://www.ncd.com/ppcx/ppcx.html

Peachtree Software, Inc.
1505 Pavilion Place
Norcross, GA 30093
(770) 724-4000
Fax: (770) 564-5888
Information: (800) 247-3224
Web Site: http://www.peachtree.com

PerfectData Corporation
110 West Easy Street
Simi Valley, CA 93065
Sales and Information: (800) 9PERFECT
(973-7332)
Web Site: http://www.perfectdata.com

Persoft, Inc.
465 Science Drive
P.O. Box 44953
Madison, WI 53744-4953
(608) 273-6000 or (800) 368-5283
Fax: (608) 273-8227
BBS: (608) 273-6595
Technical Support: (608) 273-4357,
M–F 8:30 a.m.–5:00 p.m. CST
Anonymous FTP Server:
ftp://ftp.persoft.com
Web Site: http://www.persoft.com

Personal Training Systems, Inc.
1005 Hamilton Court
Menlo Park, CA 94025
(800) 832-2499 or (415) 614-5950

Fax: (415) 463-2522
Web Site: http://www.ptst.com

Philips Computer Monitors
64 Perimeter Center East
Atlanta, GA 30346
(770) 821-2400
Customer Service: (800) 531-0039
Web Site: http://www.magnavox.com

Philips Consumer Electronics Company
64 Perimeter Center East
Atlanta, GA 30046-6400
(770) 821-2400
Customer Support: (800) 531-0039,
M–SAT 8 a.m.–11 p.m. EST,
Sun 8 a.m..–9 p.m.
Philips LMS Legacy Products:
(714) 259-7602
Norelco Consumer Support:
(800) 243-7884
Web Site:
http://www.philipsmagnavox.com

Philips Digital Video Systems
2300 South Decker Lake Boulevard
Salt Lake City, UT 84119
(810) 972-8000
Philips Electronics North America
Corporation
North American Headquarters
100 East 42nd Street
New York, NY 10017-5699
(800) 223-1828
Fax: (212) 850-5362
Web Site: http://www.philips.com

Philips Media
10960 Wilshire Boulevard
Los Angeles, CA 90024
(800) 340-7888
Web Site:
http://www.media.philips.com

Philips Paradise
Acquired by Relialogic Technology
Corporation
2925 Bayview Drive
Fremont, CA 95438

(800) 444-3617 or (510) 770-3990
Fax: (510) 770-3994
Web Site: http://www.paradisemmp.com

Philips Research
345 Scarborough Road
Briarcliff Manor, NY 10510
(914) 945-6000
Fax: (914) 945-6375
Philips Research Silicon Valley
1000 West Maude Avenue
Sunnyvale, CA
(650) 846-4300
Fax: (650) 846-4309
Philips Speech Processing
64 Perimeter Center East
Atlanta, GA 30046-6400
(770) 821-3678
Phoenix Technologies Ltd.
411 East Plumeria Drive
San Jose, CA 95134
(408) 570-1000
Fax: (408) 570-1001
Web Site: http://www.phoenix.com

PhotoDisc, Inc.
2013 4th Avenue, 4th Floor
Seattle, WA 98121
(206) 441-9355 or (800) 979-4413
Fax: (206) 441-4961
Customer Service: (800) 528-3472
Web Site: http://www.photodisc.com

PictureTel Corporation
100 Minuteman Road
Andover, MA 01810
(978) 292-5000 or (800) 716-6000
Fax: (508) 292-3300
Technical Support: (800) 874-2835 or
(978) 292-3567
Fax: (978) 292-3333
Web Site: http://www.pictel.com

Pinnacle Micro, Inc.
140 Technology, Suite 500
Irvine, CA 92618
(949) 789-3000 or (800) 553-7070
Fax: (949) 789-3150

Technical Support: (888) 805-3588 or
(949) 595-2185
Web Site:
http://www.pinnaclemicro.com

Pinnacle Systems, Inc.
280 N. Bernardo Avenue
Mountain View, CA 94043
(650) 237-1600 or (650) 526-1600
Fax: (650) 526-1601
BBS: (408) 933-8630
Fax Back: (650) 237-1973
Technical Support: (650) 237-1800
Web Site:
http://www.pinnaclesys.com

Pioneer New Media Technologies
2265 East 220th Street
Long Beach, CA 90810
(310) 952-2111 or (800) 444-6784
Fax: (310) 952-2990
BBS: (310) 835-7980
Support: (800) 872-4159
Fax: (310) 952-2309
Web Site: http://www.pioneerusa.com

PKWARE, Inc.
9025 N. Deerwood Drive
Brown Deer, WI 53223-2480
(414) 354-8699
Fax: (414) 354-8559
BBS: (414) 354-8670
E-mail: info@pkware.com
Customer Response Form: http://www.
pkware.com/response.html
Web Site: http://www.pkware.com

Plaintree Systems
44 Iber Road
Stittsville, Ontario
Canada K2S 1E7
(800) 370-2724 or (613) 831-8300
Fax: (613) 831-3283
Technical Support: (800) 831-1095 or
(613) 831-8883, M–F 8 a.m.–8 p.m. EST
Fax: (613) 831-6120
E-mail: support@plaintree.com
Web Site: http://www.plaintree.com

Plantronics, Inc.
337 Encinal Street
Santa Cruz, CA 95061
(800) 544-4660, International (831)
426-5858
Fax Back: (800) 544-4660
Support: (800) 544-4660, M–F 7 a.m.–5 p.m.
PST
Web Site: http://www.plantronics.com

Play Incorporated
2890 Kilgore Road
Rancho Cordova, CA 95670
(916) 851-0800
Fax: (916) 851-0801
Technical Support: (916) 851-0900,
M–F 7:00 a.m.–5:30 p.m. PST
Fax: (916) 853-9831
Web Site: http://www.play.com

Plextor
4255 Burton Drive
Santa Clara, CA 95054
(408) 980-1838 or (800) 866-3935
Fax: (408) 986-1010
BBS: (408) 986-1569 or 986-1474
Technical Support: (800) 475-3986,
M–F 6:30 a.m.–5:30 p.m. PST
Technical Support Fax: (408) 986-1010
E-mail: support@plextor.com
Web Site: http://www.plextor.com

Plustek USA
169 Pullman Street
Livermore, CA 94550
(925) 453-8888
Fax: (925) 453-8899
Technical Support: (925) 453-8888
Web Site: http://www.plustek.com
Web Site: http://www.plustekusa.com

PNY Technologies, Inc.
299 Webro Road
Parsippany, NJ 07054
(973) 515-9700
Fax: (973) 560-5590
Fax Back: (800) 234-4597
Technical Support: (800) 234-4597
Web Site: http://www.pny.com

PointCast, Inc.
501 Macara Avenue
Sunnyvale, CA 94086
(408) 990-7000
Fax: (408) 990-0080
PCN StatusLine: (800) 586-4733
Tech Form: http://pioneer.
pointcast.com/support/pcn/
forms/ask-question.html
Web Site: http://www.pointcast.com

Polaris Software
PO Box 462886
Escondido, CA 92046-2886
(760) 433-8927
Technical Support: (760) 433-8927,
M–F 8:00 a.m.–4:30 p.m. PST
Web Site:
http://www.polarissoftware.com

Polaroid Corporation
784 Memorial Drive
Cambridge, MA 02139
(781) 386-2000
Product Information: (800) 816-2611
Digital Products Support: (800) 432-5355
For All Other Products: Customer Care
Center: (800) 343-5000, Canada:
(800) 268-6970 M–F 8 a.m.–8 p.m. EST
Digital Product Support Form:
http://www.polaroid.com/cgi-bin/
mailto-eis.cgi
All Other Products Support Form:
http://www.polaroid.com/cgi-bin/
mailto-support.cgi
Web Site: http://www.polaroid.com

Portable Software Corporation, now
Concur Technologies
6222 185th Avenue NE
Redmond, WA 98052
(800) 478-7411 or (425) 702-8808
Fax: (425) 702-8828
Web Site: http://www.concur.com

Portrait Displays, Inc.
5117 Johnson Drive
Pleasanton, CA 94588
(925) 227-2700 or (800) 858-7744

Fax: (925) 227-2705
Technical Support: (925) 227-2716,
M–F, 8 a.m.-5 P.M. PST
Fax: (925) 227-2705
Web Site: http://www.portrait.com

PowerQuest Corporation
1359 North Research Way, Building K
Orem, UT 84097
(800) 379-2566, (801) 437-8900, or
(801) 226-8977
Fax: (801) 226-8941
Fax Back: (800) 720-0391 or (801) 437-7921
Technical Support: (801) 226-6834
FTP Site:
ftp://ftp.powerquest.com/pub
Web Site: http://www.powerquest.com

Powersoft, acquired by Sybase, Inc.
6475 Christie Avenue
Emeryville, CA 94608
(510) 922-3500
Technical Support: (800) 8SYBASE,
 a.m.–6 p.m.
Web Site: http://www.sybase.com

Powerware, previously Exide
Electronics Corporation
Forum III
8609 Six Forks Road
Raleigh, NC 27615
(800) 554-3448 or (919) 872-3020
Fax: (800) 753-9433
6kVA or less UPS Technical Support:
(800) 365-4892, M–F 8 a.m.–8 p.m. EST
Greater than 6kVA Technical Support:
(800) 843-9433 or (919) 871-1800, 24/7
Fax: (919) 871-1822
Web Site: http://www.powerware.com

PraeoTek, Inc., formerly VidTech
(612) 785-9717
Fax: (612) 780-2040
BBS: (612) 780-8033
Prairie Group
P.O. Box 65820
West Des Moines, IA 50265
(515) 225-3720
Fax: (515) 225-2422

Sales: (800) 346-5392
Technical Support: (515) 225-4122
FTP Site: ftp://ftp.prgrsoft.com/
prairieftp
Web Site: http://www.prgrsoft.com
Pretty Good Privacy, Inc. acquired by
Network Associates, Inc.
Web Site: http://www.nai.com

Primavera Systems, Inc.
Two Bala Plaza
Bala Cynwyd, PA 19004
(610) 667-8600 or (800) 423-0245
Fax: (610) 667-7894
BBS: (610) 660-5833
Web Site: http://www.primavera.com

Primax Electronic Incorporated
521 Alamanor Avenue
Sunnyvale, CA
(408) 522-1200
Web Site: http://www.primaxelec.com

Princeton Graphic Systems
2801 South Yale Street, Suite 110
Santa Ana, CA 92704
(714) 751-8405
Fax: (714) 751-5736
Sales: (800) 747-6249
Web Site: http://www.prgr.com
Princeton Review
Web Site: http://www.review.com
Prodigy Services Company
Customer Service: (800) 284-5933
Web Site: http://www.prodigy.com

Promise Technology
1460 Koll Circle
San Jose, CA 95112
(408) 452-0948
Fax: (408) 452-1534
Sales: (800) 888-0245
Fax Back: (408) 452-9160
BBS: (408) 452-1267
Technical Support: (408) 452-1180
Fax: (408) 452-9163
Web Site: http://www.promise.com

Proteon Incorporated
Nine Technology Drive
Westboro, MA 01581
(508) 898-2800
Sales: (800) 545-7464
FTP Site:
ftp://ftp.proteon.com/pub/bbs
Web Site: http://www.proteon.com

Proxim
295 N. Bernardo Avenue
Mountain View, CA 94043
(415) 960-1630
Fax: (415) 960-1984
Sales: (800) 229-1630
BBS: (415) 960-2419
Technical Support: (415) 526-3640 or (800)
477-6946, M–F 6:00 a.m.–5:30 p.m. PST
Fax: (415) 960-1106
Web Site: http://www.proxim.com

Pure Data, Incorporated
Acquired by Banksoft Canada, Ltd.
9225 Leslie Street
Richmond Hill, Ontario
Canada L4B 3H6
(905) 731-6444
Fax: (905) 731-7017
Fax Back: (800) 801-4549
Technical Support: (877) 226-5738,
M–F 9 a.m.–5 p.m. EST
Web Site: http://www.puredata.com

S3 Incorporated
2841 Mission College Boulevard
Santa Clara, CA 95054
(408) 588-8000
Fax: (408) 980-5444
BBS: (408) 654-5676
Web Site: http://www.s3.com

Samsung Electronics, Ltd.
Customer Support Web Site:
http://www.sec.samsung.co.kr/
Customer/Customer.Services.html
Web Site:
http://www.sec.samsung.co.kr

Samsung Electronics America, Inc.
One Samsung Place
Ledgewood, New Jersey 07852
(800) 767-4657 or (201) 347-8004
BBS: (201) 691-6238 to 28.8 Kbps
Information Systems Technical Support:
(800) SAMSUNG (726-7864) or
(201) 691-6200, 24/7
Fax: (201) 347-8650
Customer Service and Technical Support:
(201) 229-4000, M–F 9 a.m.–5 p.m. EST
Fax: (201) 229-4029
Samsung North America, Inc.
105 Challenger Park
Ridgefield, NJ 07660
(201) 229-7000
Fax: (201) 229-7030
Web Site: http://www.samsung.com

Samtron Displays, Inc.
Samsung Electronics Group
Los Angeles, CA
(310) 537-7000
Fax: (310) 537-1033
Savin Corporation
See Ricoh Corporation
SciTech Software
505 Wall Street
Chico, CA 95928
(916) 894-8400
Fax: (916) 894-9069
BBS: (916) 894-9047
Technical Support: (916) 894-8400,
M–F 9 a.m.–6 p.m. PST
Technical Support Fax: (916) 894-9069
Technical Support Form: http://www.
scitechsoft.com/t_reqsdd.html
E-mail: support@scitechsoft.com
FTP Site: ftp://ftp.scitechsoft.com
Web Site:
http://www.scitechsoft.com

Seagate Software (IMG)
1095 West Pender Street
Vancouver, BC
Canada V6E 2M6
(800) 877-2340 or (604) 681-3435
Fax: (604) 681-2934
Fax Back: (604) 681-3450

Technical Support: (604) 669-8379,
MTuTh 8 a.m.–5 p.m., WF 8 a.m.–4 p.m.
(PST)
Fax: (604) 681-7163
FTP Site: ftp://ftp.img.
seagatesoftware.com/pub/crystal
Web Site:
http://www.seagatesoftware.com

Seagate Software, Network and Storage
Management Group (SMG)
Acquired by Veritas Corporation
Web Site: http://www.veritas.com

Seagate Technology (Disc)
920 Disc Drive
Scotts Valley, CA 95066
(800) 468-3472, or (831) 438-8111
BBS: (405) 936-1600
Fax Back and Automated Technical
Support: (800) SEAGATE (732-4283) or
(405) 936-1234
Service Centers: (800) 468-DISC
(468-3475)
Technical Support: (405) 936-1200, ,
M–F 8:00 a.m.–12:15 p.m.,
1:30 p.m.–6:00 p.m. CST
TechFax: (405) 936-1685
TDD Support: (405) 936-1687
FTP Site: ftp://ftp.seagate.com
Web Site: http://www.seagate.com

Seagate Technology (Tape)
1650 Sunflower Avenue
Costa Mesa, CA 92626
Sales: (800) 626-6637 or (714) 641-1230
Fax: (714) 944-5573
BBS: (405) 936-1630
Fax Back and Automated Technical
Support: (800) SEAGATE (732-4283) or
(405) 936-1234
Technical Support: (405) 936-1400,
M–F 8:00 a.m.–12:15 p.m.,
1:30 p.m.–6:00 p.m. CST
Fax: (408) 936-1683
TDD: (405) 936-1687
Web Site: http://www.seagate.com/
tape/tapetop.shtml

Sega Of America, Inc.
150 Shoreline Drive
Redwood City, CA 94065
Customer Service and Technical Support:
(800) USA SEGA (872-7342), Canada:
(800) 872-7342, M–F 8 a.m.–9 p.m.
Sat–Sun 8 a.m.–5 p.m. PST
Web Site: http://www.sega.com

Seiko Epson Corporation
3-3-5, Owa, Suwa-si
Nagano-ken, 392 Japan
(81) 266-52-3131
Fax: (81) 266-53-4844
Web Site: http://www.epson.co.jp/
epson/weleng.htm

Seiko Instruments USA, Inc.
1130 Ringwood Court
San Jose, CA 95131
(408) 922-5806
Fax: (408) 922-5808
and
2990 West Lomita Boulevard
Torrance, CA 90505
(310) 517-7700
Fax: (310) 517-7709
Web Site: http://www.
seiko-instruments-usa.com

Seiko Instruments USA, Inc.
Compact Convenience Products Division
1130 Ringwood Court
San Jose, CA 95131
(408) 922-5900
Fax: (408) 433-3261
Product Information: (800) 688-0817 or
(716) 871-6711
Fax: (716) 873-0906
BBS: (408) 383-9474
Service and Support: (800) 757-1011,
6 a.m.–8 p.m. PST
Web Site: http://www.seikosmart.com

Seiko Instruments USA, Inc.
Consumer Products Division
2990 West Lomita Boulevard
Torrance, CA 90505

*Continued*

*(continued)*
Sales: (310) 517-7810
Fax: (310) 517-7793
E-mail: cpd.info@seiko-la.com
Support and Service: (800) 873-4508 or
(310) 517-8121
Fax: (310) 517-7793
Web Site: http://www.seiko-usa-cpd.com/cpd
Web Site:
http://www.theriver.com/cpd

Seiko Instruments USA, Inc.
Digital Imaging Division
1130 Ringwood Court
San Jose, CA 95131
Information: (800) 888-0817
Customer Service: (800) 553-5312
Fax: (409) 922-5838
Technical Support: (800) 553-5312
Fax: (408) 922-5867
Web Site: http://www.did.seiko.com

Seiko Instruments USA, Inc.
Electronic Components Division
2990 West Lomita Boulevard
Torrance, CA 90505
Components (310) 517-7822
Fax: (310) 517-8131
Fiber Optics (310) 517-8113
Fax: (310) 517-7792
Web Site: http://www.seiko-usa-ecd.com

Seiko Instruments USA, Inc.
Micro Printer Division
2990 West Lomita Boulevard
Torrance, CA 90505
Sales and Support: (310) 517-7778
Fax: (310) 517-8154
Sharp Corporation
22-22 Nagaike-cho Abeno-ku
Osaka 545, Japan
81-6-621-1221
Web Site: http://www.sharp.co.jp/index-e.html

Sharp Digital Information Products (SDI)
Division of SMT
5901 Bolsa Avenue
Huntington Beach, CA 92648
(714) 903-5000
Fax: (714) 901-2243
Web Site: http://www.sharpsdi.com

Sharp Electronics Corporation (SEC)
Sharp Plaza
Mahwah, NJ 07430
(201) 529-8200
Fax: (210) 529-8425
Information, or the nearest Authorized
Service: (800) BE SHARP (237-4277)
Frequently Asked Questions:
(708) 378-9987
Fax: (708) 378-9853
Web Site: http://www.sharp-usa.com

Sharp Flat Display Manufacturing
Company (SFDM)
5700 Northwest Pacific Rim Boulevard
Camas, WA 98607
(360) 834-2500
Fax: (360) 834-8903
Sharp Laboratories of America, Inc. (SLA)
5750 Northwest Pacific Rim Boulevard
Suite 20,
Camas, WA 98607
(360) 817-8400
Fax: (360) 817-8436
Web Site: http://www.sharplabs.com

Sharp Manufacturing Company of
America (SMCA)
Manufacturing Division of SEC
Sharp Plaza Boulevard
Memphis, TN 38193
(901) 795-6510
Fax: (901) 367-5493
Web Site: http://www.smcausa.com

Sharp Microelectronics Technology, Inc.
(SMT)
Sharp Microelectronics Corporation —
Microelectronics Group
5700 Northwest Pacific Rim Boulevard
Camas, WA 98607

(360) 834-8700
Fax: (360) 834-8611
Web Site: http://www.sharpsma.com

Shiva Corporation, acquired by Intel
Corporation
28 Crosby Drive
Bedford, MA 01730
(781) 687-1400
Fax: (781) 687-1337
Web Site: http://www.shiva.com

Sierra On-Line, Inc.
3380 — 146th Place SE, Suite 300
Bellevue, WA, 98007
(415) 649-9800, M–F 8 a.m.–5 p.m.
Sales Hotline: (800), 24 hours per day
Customer Service: (425) 426-5771,
M–F 8 a.m.–5 p.m.
Fax: (425) 562-4223
Fax Back: (425) 644-4343
Technical Support: (425) 644-4343,
M–F 8:00 a.m.–4:45 p.m. PST
Fax: (425) 644-7697
FTP Site: ftp://ftp.sierra.com
Web Site: http://www.sierra.com

Sigma Designs, Inc.
355 Fairview Way
Milpitas, CA 95035-3024
(510) 770-0100
Fax: (510) 770-2640
Sales: (800) 845-8086
Fax Back: (510) 770-2904
BBS: (510) 770-0111
Technical Support: (970) 339-7120
Online Newsgroups:
news://news.sigma-designs.com
FTP Site:
ftp://ftp.SigmaDesigns.com/pub
Web Site: http://www.REALmagic.com
Web Site:
http://www.sigmadesigns.com

SIIG, Inc.
6078 Stewart Drive
Fremont, CA 94538
(510) 657-8688
Sales: (510) 353-7542

Fax: (510) 657-5962
Technical Support: (510) 353-7542
Web Site: http://www.siig.com

Silicon Engineering, Inc., subsidiary of
Creative Labs, Inc.
269 Mt. Hermon Road, Suite 207
Scotts Valley, CA 95066
(408) 438-5330
Fax: (408) 438-8509
Web Site: http://www.sei.com

Silicon Graphics, Inc., now SGI
1600 Amphitheatre Parkway
Mountain View, CA 94043
(650) 960-1980 or (800) 800-7441
Fax: (650) 960-0197
Technical Support: (800) 800-4SGI
(800-4744), 8 a.m.–5 p.m.
Fax: (415) 960-3393
Web Site: http://www.sgi.com

Simon & Schuster Interactive
1230 Avenue of the Americas, 11th Floor
New York, NY 10020
(212) 698-7000
Customer Service: (800) 223-2348
Fax: (310) 214-7937
Web Site: http://www.simonsays.com

Simple Technology, Inc.
3001 Daimler Street
Santa Ana, CA 92705
Information: (800) 4-SIMPLE (474-6753),
International: (714) 476-1180
Sales: (800) 367-7330, International:
(714) 476-1180
General Assistance: (714) 476-1180
Fax: (714) 476-1209
BBS: (714) 476-9034
Technical Support: (800) 367-7330,
M–F 6 a.m.–6 p.m. PST
Web Site: http://www.simpletech.com

Sirius Publishing
7320 East Butherus Drive
Scottsdale, AZ 85260
(602) 951-3288

*Continued*

*(continued)*
Customer Service: (800) 247-0307
Technical Support: (602) 951-8405
Web Site: http://www.siriuspub.com/

Smart and Friendly
20520 Nordhoff Street
Chatsworth, CA 91311
(818) 772-8001 or (800) 959-7001
Fax: (818) 772-2888
Technical Support Form:
http://www.smartandfriendly.com/
techsup.html
Web Site:
http://www.smartandfriendly.com

SMC Networks, Inc.
6 Hughes
Irvine, CA 92618
Sales: (800) 553-7731
(949) 707-2400
Fax: (949) 707-2460
Technical Support: (800) SMC-4-YOU
(762-4968), International (516) 435-6250
FTP Site: ftp://ftp.smc.com/pub
Web Site: http://www.smc.com

Smith Micro Software, Inc.
51 Columbia
Aliso Viejo, CA 92656
(714) 362-5800
Fax: (714) 362-2300
Web Site: http://www.smithmicro.com

Softimage, Inc.
Microsoft Subsidiary
3510 St-Laurent, Suite 400
Montréal, Québec
Canada H2X 2V2
(800) 576-3846 or (514) 845-1636
Fax: (514) 845-5676
Support: (514) 845-2199, M–F, 9 a.m.–9 p.m.
EST
Fax: (514) 845-8252
E-mail: support@softimage.com
FTP Site: ftp://ftp.softimage.com
Web Site: http://www.softimage.com

SoftKey International
One Athenaeum Street
Cambridge, MA 02142
(617) 494-1200
Customer Service: (617) 761-3000,
M–F 8 a.m.–8 p.m. EST
Fax: (617) 494-5895
Automated Support: (800) 409-1497
Technical Support: (319) 247-3333,
M–F 9 a.m.–9 p.m. EST
Fax: (319) 395-9600
E-mail: tech_support@learningco.com
FTP Site: ftp://ftp.learningco.com/
support/tlcfiles.html
Web Site: http://www.learningco.com

SoftQuad International, Inc., now
NewKidCO International, Inc.
168 Middlesex Turnpike
Burlington, MA 01803
(781) 229-2924
Fax: (781) 272-4876
Web Site: http://www.newkidco.com

SoftQuad Software, Inc.
161 Eglinton Avenue East, Suite 400
Toronto, Ontario
Canada M4P 1J5
(416) 544-9000
Fax (416) 544-0300
Technical Support: (416) 544-8879
Fax: (416) 544-0300
E-mail: support@softquad.com
HoTMetaL E-mail: hotmetal-
support@softquad.com
HoTMetaL Application E-mail:
hmapps-support@softquad.com
Web Site: http://www.softquad.com

Softsource
301 West Holly
Bellingham, WA 98225
(360) 676-0999
Fax: (360) 671-1131
FTP Site: ftp://ftp.softsource.com
Anti-Piracy Home Page: http://www.
spa.org/piracy/homepage.htm
Web Site: http://www.softsource.com

Software Publishers Association
Now SIIA
Software Publishing Corporation
111 North Market Street
San Jose, CA 95113
(408) 537-3000 or (800) 336-8360
Fax: (408) 537-3500
Web Site: http://www.spco.com

Solectek
6370 Nancy Ridge Drive, Suite 109
San Diego, CA 92121
(800) 437-1518 or (619) 450-1220
Fax: (619) 457-2681
Technical Support: (619) 450-1220
Fax: (619) 457-2681
Web Site: http://www.solectek.com

SONERA Technologies
P.O. Box 565
Rumson, NJ 07760
(732) 747-6886
Fax: (732) 747-4523
Orders: (800) 932-6323 or (732) 747-6886
Customer Support and Technical Service:
(732) 747-6886, M–F 9 a.m.–5 p.m. EST
E-mail: support@displaymate.com
Web Site: http://www.sonera.com
Web Site: http://www.displaymate.com

Sonic Systems, Inc.
575 North Pastoria Avenue
Sunnyvale, CA 94086
(408) 736-1900
Fax: (408) 736-7228
Customer Service and Sales: (888) 222-6563
Technical Support: (408) 736-1900
E-mail Technical Support:
tech@sonicsys.com
FTP Site: ftp://ftp.sonicsys.com
Web Site: http://www.sonicsys.com

Sony Electronics
3300 Zanker Road
San Jose, CA 95134
(408) 432-1600
Fax: (408) 943-0740
BBS Computer Products: (408) 955-5107

Dealer Locations and Data Sheets, U.S.:
(800) 352-7669
Fax Retrieval System (Techfax), U.S.:
(800) 883-7669, Canada: (800) 961-7669
BBS: (408) 955-5107
Technical Support, U.S.: (800) 326-9551,
Canada: (416) 499-1414
Personal Computer Technical Support:
(800) 476-6972
Service Center Locations Computer and
Consumer Products: (800) 282-2848
Service Parts Computer Monitors and
Consumer Products: (800) 488-7669
Service Parts Computer Storage Devices:
(408) 922-0699
FTP Site: ftp://ftp.sony.com
E-mail: contact@sel.sony.com
Web Site: http://www.sel.sony.com
Sony Online
Web Site: http://www.sony.com

Sound Source Interactive
26115 Mureau Road, Suite B
Calabasas, CA 91302-3126
(818) 878-0505
Sales: (800) 877-4778
Fax: (818) 878-0007
Web Site: http://www.
soundsourceinteractive.com

Spacetec IMC Corporation
100 Foot of John Street
Lowell, MA 01852
(508) 275-6100
Fax: (508) 275-6200
Technical Support: (508) 970-0440
Web Site: http://www.spacetec.com

Spectrum Holobyte, Inc., now
MicroProse USA
2490 Mariner Square Loop, Suite 100
Alameda, CA
(510) 864-4550
Customer Support: (510) 864-4550
M–F 9 a.m.–5 p.m. PST
Fax: (510) 864-4602
FTP Site:
ftp://ftp.microprose.com/pub
Web Site: http://www.microprose.com

SPRY, Inc., acquired by CompuServe
Internet Division now part of MindSpring
3535 128th Avenue SE
Bellevue, WA 98006
(425) 957-8000
Fax: (425) 957-6000
Customer Service: (800) 719-4660
E-mail: service@sprynet.com
Technical Support: (800) 557-9614
Web Site: http://www.spry.com

SPSS, Inc.
233 South Wacker Drive, 11th Floor
Chicago, IL 60606-6307
(312) 651-3000
Sales and Information: (800) 543-2185
Customer Service: (800) 521-1337
Fax: (800) 841-0064
Technical Support: (312) 651-3410,
9 a.m.–5 p.m. CST
Bay Area Technical Support:
(510) 412-2900, 8 a.m.–5 p.m. PST
Technical Support Form: http://www.
spss.com/tech/MailForm.html
Online List Serves: http://www.spss.
com/tech/listserves.html
Web Site: http://www.spss.com

Spyglass, Inc.
1240 E. Diehl Road
Naperville, IL 60563
(630) 505-1010
Fax: (630) 505-4944
Web Site: http://www.spyglass.com

STAC Electronics
12636 High Bluff Drive
San Diego, CA 92130-2093
(619) 794-3741 or (800) 522-7822
Fax: (619) 794-4575
BBS: (619) 794-3711
Technical Support: (619) 794-3700,
M–F 8 a.m.–5 p.m. PST
Web Site: http://www.stac.com

Starfish Software
1700 Green Hills Road
Scotts Valley, CA, 95066
(408) 461-5800

Fax: (408) 461-5900
Sales: (888) STARFISH (782-7347)
Fax Back: (800) 503-3847
BBS: (408) 461-5930
Technical Support: Installation and Initial
Configuration Only: (970) 522-4610
Web Site:
http://www.starfishsoftware.com

STB Systems, Inc., acquired by 3dfx
4435 Fortran Drive
San Jose, CA 95134
(888) 367-3339
BBS: (972) 437-9615 to 28.8Kbps
Fax Back: (972) 234-8750
Technical Support: (800) 234-4334,
M–Th 8 a.m.–8 p.m., F 8 a.m.–6 p.m.,
Sat 10 a.m.–6 p.m. CST
Fax: (972) 669-1873
FTP Site: ftp://ftp.stb.com
Web Site: http://www.stb.com

Storage Dimensions, merged into
Artecon, Inc.
6305 El Camino Real
Carlsbad, CA 92009
(760) 931-5500 or (800) 870-2783
Fax: (760) 931-5527
Technical Support: (760) 931-5500,
7 a.m.–5 p.m. PST
Web Site: http://www.artecon.com

Summagraphics Corporation, GTCO
CalComp, Inc.
14555 N. 82nd Street
Scottsdale, AZ 85260
(480) 948-6540 or (800) 458-5888
Fax: (480) 948-5508
Technical Support: (480) 443-2214
Web Site:
http://www.gtcocalcomp.com

Supra Corporation, acquired by
Diamond Multimedia Communications
BBS: (541) 967-2444
Fax Back: (541) 967-2424 or
(800) 380-0030
Technical Support: (541) 967-2450,
M–F 5 a.m.–7 p.m., Sat 8 a.m.–4 p.m. PST

Fax: (541) 967-2401
Web Site: http://www.diamondmm.com

Swan Technologies Corporation
6682 N.W. 16th Terrace
Fort Lauderdale, FL 33309
(954) 975-2205
Fax: (954) 975-2112
Web Site: http://www.swantech.com

Sybase, Inc.
6475 Christie Avenue
Emeryville, CA 94608
(510) 922-3500
Fax: (510) 922-3210
Technical Support: (800) 8-SYBASE or
(510) 922-3555
Fax: (617) 564-6148 or (510) 922-3911
Web Site: http://www.sybase.com

Sykes Enterprises, Incorporated
100 North Tampa Street, Suite 3900
Tampa, FL 33602
(800) 867-9537 or (813) 274-1000
Web Site: http://www.sykes.com

Symantec Corporation
10201 Torre Avenue
Cupertino, CA 95014-2132
(408) 253-9600
Marketing Fax: (408) 253-3968
Customer Service Headquarters
Symantec Corporation
175 West Broadway
Eugene, OR 97401
(541) 334-6054 or (800) 441-7234
Technical Support: M–F 7 a.m.–4 p.m. PST
ACT!: (541) 465-8645
Norton Antivirus: (541) 465-8420
Norton Backup: (541) 334-6054
Norton Utilities: (541) 465-8440
pcAnywhere: (541) 465-8430
Q&A, Q&A Writer, TimeLine:
(541) 465-8600
WinFax PRO: (716) 843-1060
Other products, see Web Site
Web Site: http://www.symantec.com

SyQuest Technology, Inc.
46939 Bayside Parkway
Fremont, CA 94538
Sales Fax: (510) 226-2770
Web Site: http://www.syquest.com

Syracuse Language Systems
Syracuse, NY
Customer Service: (800) 797-5264,
M–F 9 a.m.–8 p.m. EST
E-mail: customer_service@syrlang.com
Technical Support: (800) 797-5264,
M–F 9 a.m.–7 p.m. EST
E-mail: tech_support@syrlang.com
Web Site: http://www.syrlang.com

Targus
6180 Valley View
Buena Park, CA 90620
(714) 523-5429
Fax: (714) 523-0153
Web Site: http://www.targus.com

TDK Corporation
Corporate Headquarters
1-13-1, Nihonbashi, Chuo-ku
Tokyo 103, Japan
03-3278-5111
Fax: 03-5201-7135
Web Site: http://www.tdk.co.jp

TDK Electronics Corporation
12 Harbor Park Drive
Port Washington, NY 11050
(516) 625-0100, or (800) 835-8273
Fax: (516) 625-0651
Web Site: http://www.tdk.com

TDK Systems
136 New Mohawk Road
Nevada City, CA 95959
(530) 478-8421
Fax: (530) 478-8290
Marketing Hotline: (530) 478-8421
TDK Systems Fax: (530) 478-8290
BBS: (530) 265-8271
UK and Europe: 44-0-1737-77-8130

*Continued*

*(continued)*
Technical Support Hotline: (800) 999-4TDK
(999-4835), 8:00 a.m.–4:30 p.m. PST
Fax: (916) 265-8290
Technical Support Form:
http://www.tdksystems.com/TECHSPT/
tsemail.htm
Web Site: http://www.tdksystems.com

TDK U.S.A. Corporation
12 Harbor Park Drive
Port Washington, NY 11050
(516) 625-0100
Fax: (516) 625-2923
Web Site: http://www.tdk.com

Teac America, Inc.
7733 Telegraph Road
Montebello, CA 90640
(323) 726-0303
Fax: (323) 727-7656
Web Site: http://www.teac.com

TechWorks
4030 West Braker Lane
Austin, TX, 78759
(512) 794-8533
Technical Support: (800) 933-6113
M–F 8:30 a.m.–6:30 p.m. CST
Web Site: http://www.techworks.com

Tecmar Technologies Incorporated
1900 Pike Road, Building E
Longmont, CO, 80501
(303) 682-3700 or (800) 422-2587
Fax: (303) 776-7706
Fax Back: (303) 776-1085
Technical Support: (800) 922-9916
Web Site: http://www.tecmar.com

Tektronix
P. O. Box 1000
Wilsonville, OR 97070-1000
(800) 835-9433
Fax: (503) 685-2980
BBS: (503) 685-4504
Measurement Technical Support:
(800) 935-9433, 6 a.m.–5 p.m. PST

Color Printer Support: (800) 835-6100
x1152, 6 a.m.–5 p.m. PST
Web Site: http://www.tek.com

Televideo, Inc.
2345 Harris Way
San Jose, CA 95131
(408) 954-8333
Fax: (408) 954-0931
BBS: (408) 954-8231
Technical Support: (408) 955-7711
Fax: (408) 951-0623 Attn: Technical
Support
Web Site:
http://www.televideoinc.com

Texas Imperial Software
1602 Harvest Moon Place
Cedar Park, TX 78613-1419
(512) 378-3246
Fax: (512) 378-3246
E-mail: alun@texis.com
Web Site: http://www.wftpd.com

Texas Instruments Incorporated
8505 Forest Lane
P.O. Box 660199
Dallas, TX 75266
(972) 995-2011
Fax: (972) 995-3773
(800) TI-TEXAS (848-3927)
Printer Technical Support: Contact
Genicom Corporation
See Web Site:
http://www.genicom.com/techsupp

Laptop Technical Support : Contact
Acer America Corporation
See Web Site: http://www.acer.com/
aac/ti_index.htm
Web Site: http://www.ti.com

ThrustMaster, Inc.
7175 NW Evergreen Parkway, #400
Hillsboro, OR 97124
(503) 615-3200
Fax: (503) 615-3300
Technical Support: (503) 615-3200,
M-TH 7 a.m.–6 p.m., F 9 a.m.–6 p.m. PST

E-mail: techsupp@thrustmaster.com
Web Site:
http://www.thrustmaster.com

Timeslips Corporation
17950 Preston Road, Suite 800
Dallas, TX 75252
(972) 248-3900 or (800) 285-999
Fax: (972) 248-9245
Fax Back: (508) 768-6100
Technical Support Fax: (508) 768-7532
Web Site: http://www.timeslips.com

Time Warner Electronic Publishing
1271 Avenue of the Americas
New York, NY 10020
Web Site:
http://www.pathfinder.com/twep

Toshiba America, Inc. (TAI)
Holding Company
1251 Avenue of the Americas, 41st Floor
New York, NY 10020
(212) 596-0600
Fax: (212) 593-3875
Web Site: http://www.toshiba.com

Toshiba America Consumer Products,
Inc. (TACP)
82 Totowa Road
Wayne, NJ 07470
(201) 628-8000
Fax: (201) 628-1875
Customer Support: (800) 631-3811
Web Site:
http://www.toshiba.com/tacp

Toshiba America Electronic
Components, Inc. (TAEC)
9775 Toledo Way
Irvine, CA 92718
(949) 455-2000
Fax: (949) 859-3963
Literature: (800) 879-4963
Disk Products Technical Support:
(949) 754-5456
E-mail: toshibapd@cerplex.com
Web Site:
http://www.toshiba.com/taec

Toshiba America Information Systems,
Inc. (TAIS)
9740 Irvine Boulevard
Irvine, CA 92718
(949) 583-3000
Fax Back: (888) 598-7802
Customer/Product Support:
(800) TOSHIBA
Technical Support: (888) 824-8674
Techncial Support Web Site:
http://www.csd.toshiba.com/
tais/csd/support
Web Site: http://www.toshiba.com

Toshiba Display Devices, Inc. (TDD)
Westinghouse Circle
Horseheads, NY 14845
(607) 796-3500
Fax: (607) 796-3605
Toshiba International Corporation (TIC)
Industrial Division and Instrumentation
13131 West Little York Road
Houston, TX 77041
(713) 466-0277 or (800) 231-1412
Fax: (713) 466-8773
Web Site: http://www.toshiba.com/
tic/ticind

Toshiba of Canada Limited (TCL)
191 McNabb Street
Markham, Ontario
Canada, L3R 8H2
(905) 470-3500
Fax: (905) 470-3509
TouchStone Software Corporation
1538 Turnpike St.
North Andover, MA 01845
(978) 686-6468 — Phone
(978) 683-1630 — Fax
Web Site: http://www.checkit.com

Traveling Software, Inc.
18702 North Creek Parkway
Bothell, WA, U.S.A. 98011
Phone: (800) 343-8080
Fax: (425) 487-1284
Sales: (425) 483-8088

*Continued*

*(continued)*
BBS: (425) 485-1736
Technical Support: (425) 487-8803,
M–F 8 a.m.–5 p.m. PST
Fax: (425) 487-5440
Technical Support Web Site:
`http://webserv1.travsoft.com/`
`techkb.nsf`
Web Site: `http://www.travsoft.com`

Trio Information Systems,
U.S. Headquarters
6404 Falls of the Neuse
Suite 201
Raleigh, NC 27615
(919) 376-4100
Fax: (919) 376-4125
Web Site: `http://www.trio.com`

Tripp Lite
500 North Orleans
Chicago, IL 60610
(312) 755-5400
Fax: (312) 644-6505
Sales: (312) 755-5408
Fax Back: (312) 755-5420
Customer Support: (312) 755-5401,
International (312) 755-5402
Web Site: `http://tripplite.com`

Truevision
Now Pinnacle Systems
Trusted Information Systems, Inc.
Now Network Associates
Tseng Labs
Now Cell Pathways, Inc.
Turtle Beach Systems
Division of Voyetra Technologies, Inc.
5 Odell Plaza
Yonkers, NY 10701-1406
(510) 624-6200
Fax: (510) 624-6291
Fax Back: (914) 966-0600
BBS: (914) 966-1216 to 28.8 Kbps
Support: (914) 966-2150, M–F 9 a.m.–6 p.m.
EST
Support Fax: (914) 966-1102
FTP Site: `ftp://ftp.tbeach.com`
Web Site: `http://www.tbeach.com`

Tut Systems, Inc.
2495 Estand Way
Pleasant Hill, CA 94523
(925) 682-6510
Fax: (925) 682-4125
Web Site: `http://www.tutsys.com`

TYAN Computer Corporation
2495 Estand Way
Pleasant Hill
CA 94523-3911
(408) 956-8000
Fax: (408) 956-8044
BBS: (408) 956-8171 to 9600 baud
Technical Support: (408) 935-7884,
8 a.m.–5 p.m. PST
RMA Department: (408) 935-7893
FTP Web Site: `ftp://ftp.tyan.com`
Web Site: `http://www.tyan.com`

Ulead Systems
970 West 190th Street, Suite 520
Torrance, CA 90502
(310) 523-9393
Sales: (800) 858-5323
Fax: (310) 523-9399
BBS: (310) 523-9389
Technical Support: (310) 523-9391
Web Site: `http://www.ulead.com`

UMAX Technologies
3561 Gateway Boulevard
Fremont, CA 94538
(800) 562-0311 or (510) 651-4000
Fax: (510) 651-8834
BBS: (510) 651-2550
Fax Back: (800) 286-6186
Technical Support: (510) 651-8883
Fax: (510) 561-2610
Web Site: `http://www.umax.com`

US Gold
See Eidos Interactive
U.S. Robotics Incorporated
Acquired by 3Com Corporation
7700 North Frontage Road
Skokie, IL 60077-2690
Personal Communications Division:
Sales: (800) 342-5877

Fax: (847) 676-7320
Support: (847) 982-5151
Fax: (847) 676-7314
Network Systems Division:
Sales: (800) 877-2677
Fax: (847) 933-5800
Courier Support: (800) 550-7800
Total Control and Allegra Support:
(800) 231-8770
Fax: (847) 222-0823
Mobile Communications Division:
Questions (800) 527-8677 or (801) 320-7000
Fax Back: (800) 527-8677, Ext. 6220
Megahertz, AllPoints, and Sportster
Model 1626 PC Cards Support:
(847) 982-5151
Courier PC Card Support: (800) 550-7800
Support: (801) 320-7777
Palm Computing Division:
Fax Back: (800) 762-6163 or (847) 676-8536
Palm: (847) 676-1441
Telephony: (800) 949-6757
FTP Site: ftp://ftp.usr.com
Web Site: http://www.usr.com
Web Site: http://www.3com.com

Van Tassle, Ray
Cachechk
1020 Fox Run Lane
Algonquin, IL 60102
Verbatim Corp.
Subsidiary of Mitsubishi Chemical
Corporation
1200 W.T. Harris Boulevard
Charlotte, NC 28262
(704) 547-6500
Fax: (704) 547-6609
Web Site:
http://www.verbatimcorp.com

Veritas Software Corporation
1600 Plymouth Street
Mountain View, CA 94043
(650) 335-8000
Fax: (650) 335-8050
Customer Support: (800) 342-0652 or
(650) 335-8555
Fax: (650) 335-8428
Web Site: http://www.veritas.com

Vertisoft Systems, Inc.
Acquired by Quarterdeck Corporation
V_Graph, Inc.
P.O. Box 105
1276 Westtown Thronton Road
Westtown, PA
(610) 399-1521
Fax: (610) 399-0566
E-mail: v_graph@zola.trend1.com
Web Site: http://www.v-graph.com

VideoLogic, Inc.
1001 Bayhill Drive, Suite 310
San Bruno, CA 94066
(800) 578-5644
Fax: (650) 875-4167
BBS: (650) 875-7748
Fax Back: (800) 928-8295
Technical Support Form:
http://www.videologic.com/support/
techreqUSA.htm
Web Site:
http://www.videologic.com

VidTech
Now PraeoTek, Inc.
ViewSonic Corporation
381 Brea Canyon Road
Walnut, CA 91789
(800) 888-8583 or (909) 869-7976
Fax: (909) 869-7958
BBS: (909) 468-1241
Fax Back: (909) 869-7318
Sales and Customer Support:
(800) 888-8583 or (909) 869-7976
Web Site: http://www.viewsonic.com

Virgin Interactive Entertainment, Inc.
Now Irvine Games, Inc.
Virtual Entertainment, Inc.
200 Highland Avenue
Needham, MA 02194
(617) 449-7567 or (800) 301-9545
Fax: (617) 449-4887
E-mail: support@virtent.com
Web Site: http://www.virtent.com

Virtus Corporation
114 MacKenan Drive, Suite 100
Cary, NC 27511
(919) 467-9700
Fax: (919) 460-4530
Sales and Information: (888) 847-8871
Technical Support: (919) 467-9599,
M–F 9 a.m.–6 p.m. EST
Fax: (919) 460-4530
Web Site: http://www.virtus.com

Visio Corporation
520 Pike Street, Suite 1800
Seattle, WA 98101
(206) 521-4500
Fax: (206) 521-4501
Customer Service: (800) 24-VISIO
(248-4746) or (716) 586-0030,
M–F 5 a.m.–6 p.m. PST
Customer Service Fax: (716) 586-0820
Fax on Demand: (206) 521-4550
Technical Support: (206) 882-8687,
M–F 6 a.m.–5 p.m. PST
Fax: (541) 882-8446
Web Site: http://www.visio.com

VocalTec, Incorporated
35 Industrial Parkway
Northvale, NJ 07647
(201) 768-9400
Fax: (201) 768-8893
Technical Support: (201) 768-9400,
M–F 9:30 a.m.–5:30 p.m. EST
E-mail: info@vocaltec.com
E-mail Technical Support:
support@vocaltec.com
Web Site: http://www.vocaltec.com

Voyetra Technologies
5 Odell Plaza
Yonkers, NY 10701-1406
Sales and Information: (800) 233-9377
Fax: (914) 966-1102
BBS: (914) 966-1216 to 28.8Kbps
Fax Back: (914) 966-0600
Technical Support: (914) 966-0600
Support Fax: (914) 966-1102
Web Site: http://www.voyetra.com

WACOM Technology Corporation
501 S.E. Columbia Shores Boulevard,
Suite 300
Vancouver, WA 98661
(800) 922-9348
International: (360) 750-8882
Fax: (360) 750-8924
BBS: (360) 750-0638
E-mail:
Sales: sales@wacom.com
Technical Support:
support@wacom.com
Web Site: http://www.wacom.com

Wall Data Incorporated
11332 N.E. 122nd Way
Kirkland, WA 98034-6931
(800) 755-9225 or (425) 814-9255
Fax: (425) 856-9265
Fax on Demand: (425) 814-4362
Technical Support: (425) 814-3403,
M–F 6 a.m.–6 p.m. PST
FTP Site: ftp://ftp.walldata.com
Web Site: http://www.walldata.com

Walnut Creek CD-ROM
4041 Pike Lane, Suite E
Concord, CA 94520
Sales: (800) 786-9907, (510) 674-0783
Fax: (510) 674-0821
Technical Support: (510) 603-1234,
M–F 9 a.m.–5 p.m. PST
Fax: (510) 674-0821
E-mail: support@cdrom.com
FTP Site: ftp://ftp.cdrom.com
Technical Support Web Site: http://www.
cdrom.com/techsupp/index.htm
Web Site: http://www.cdrom.com

Western Digital Corporation
8105 Irvine Center Drive
Irvine, CA 92618
(714) 932-5000
Fax: (714) 932-6294
Fax Back: (714) 932-4300
BBS: (714) 753-1234 to 28.8Kbps
Automated Technical Support:
(714) 932-4900

Technical Support: (714) 932-4900,
M–Th 8 a.m.–5 p.m., F 8 a.m.–3 p.m. PST
Technical Support: (507) 286-7900,
M–Th 9 a.m.–6 p.m. CST, F 9 a.m.–4 p.m.
CST, Saturday 8 a.m.–5 p.m. CST
Enterprise SCSI Hard Drive Support:
(507) 286-7972
FTP Site: ftp://ftp.wdc.com
Web Site: http://www.wdc.com

White Pine Software, Inc.
542 Amherst Street
Nashua, NH 03063
(603) 886-9050
Fax: (603) 886-9051
Sales Hotline: (800) 241-PINE (241-7463)
Web Site: http://www.wpine.com

WildCard Technologies, Inc., now
Puredata
Acquired by Banksoft Canada, Ltd.
9225 Leslie Street
Richmond Hill, Ontario
Canada L4B 3H6
(905) 731-6444
Fax: (905) 731-7017
Fax Back: (800) 801-4549
Technical Support: (877) 226-5738,
M–F 9 a.m.–5 p.m. EST
Web Site: http://www.puredata.com

Willow Peripherals
190 Willow Avenue
Bronx, NY 10454
(800) 444-1585 or (516) 329-4222
Fax: (718) 402-9603
BBS: (718) 993-2066
E-mail: peripherals@willow.com
Web Site: http://www.willow.com

Wyse Technology
3471 North First Street
San Jose, CA 95134
(408) 473-1200
Fax: (408) 473-2401
Customer Service: (800) 800-WYSE
(800 -973)
BBS: (408) 922-4400
Fax Back: (800) 800-9973

Technical Support: (800) 800-9973
Wyse PC Techncial Support: (888)
997-3435 or (770) 638-6984
Web Site: http://www.wyse.com

Xerox Corporation
800 Long Ridge Road
P.O. Box 1600
Stamford, CT 06904
(203) 968-3000
Xerox Corporation — U.S. Customer
Operations
Xerox Square
100 Clinton Avenue South
Rochester, NY 14644
(716) 423-5090
9 Centennial Drive
Peabody, MA 01960
Information: (800) ASK-XEROX
(275-9376)
Product Information: (800) 334-6200
Xerox Documentation and Software
Services (XDSS): (800) 327-9753
Fax: (310) 333-7982
FTP Site:
ftp://ftp.spectrum.xerox.com
Web Site: http://www.xerox.com

Xircom, Inc.
2300 Corporate Center Drive
Thousand Oaks, CA 91320-1420
(805) 376-9300
Fax: (805) 376-9311
Sales Support: (800) 438-4526
Fax: (805) 376-9220
BBS: (805) 376-9130 to 33.6 Kbps
BBS: (805) 375-5280 K56flex only
Technical Support: (805) 376-9200
Fax: (805) 376-9100
Fax Back: (800) 775-0400
FTP Site: ftp://ftp.xircom.com/pub
Web Site: http://www.xircom.com

Yamaha Corporation Of America
6600 Orangethorpe Avenue
Buena Park, CA 90620
(714) 522-9011 or (800) 88-YAMAHA

*Continued*

*(continued)*
Fax: (714) 522-9961
Preferred Customer Service Center:
(800) 4 YAMAHA (492-6242)
Order Owner or Service Manuals, Parts,
and Literature: (714) 522-9011
Web Site: http://www.yamaha.com

Yamaha Systems Technology, Inc.
100 Century Center Court
San Jose, CA 95112
(408) 467-2300 or (800) 543-7457
Fax: (408) 437-8791
Automated Technical Support:
(408) 467-2330
Web Site: http://www.yamahayst.com

Zenith Data Systems
2455 Horse Pen Road, #100
Herndon, VA 22071
(800) 654-1394 or (703) 713-3020
Fax: (703) 713-3001
Fax Back: (800) 582-8194
BBS: (916) 386-9899
Technical Support: (800) 227-3360
Web Site: http://www.zds.com

Zenographics
111 Innovation Drive, Suite 200
Irvine, CA 92612
(949) 737-4500
Fax: (949) 737-4501
Web Site: http://www.zeno.com

ZEOS PC Products
Now Micron Electronics
BBS: (208) 893-4481
Fax Back: (877) 642-7664
Technical Support: (800) 228-5390, 24/7
TDD (800) 892-4480
Fax: (208) 893-4482
Technical Support E-mail: zeosupport@micronpc.com
Zoom Telephonics Incorporated
207 South Street
Boston, MA 02111-2723
(617) 423-1072
Tech Form: http://www.zoomtel.com/techsprt/askzoom.shtml
Web Site: http://www.zoomtel.com

ZyXEL Communications, Inc.
1650 Miraloma Ave.
Placentia, CA 92870
(714) 693-0804
Sales: (800) 255-4101
Fax: (714) 632-0858
BBS: (714) 693-0762
Technical Support: (714) 632-0882
E-mail: support@zyxel.com
FTP Site: ftp://ftp.zyxel.com
Web Site: http://www.zyxel.com

# Glossary

**µM** Micron (or micrometer). A unit of length equal to one millionth of a meter.

**µS** Microsecond. one millionth of a second.

**100Base-FX** Proposed IEEE 802.3 physical layer specification for 100 Mbps Ethernet over two strands of optical fiber.

**100Base-T** The group of proposed IEEE 802.3 physical layer specifications for 100 Mbps over various wiring specifications.

**100Base-T4** Proposed IEEE 802.3 physical layer specification for 100 Mbps Ethernet over four pairs of Category 3, 4, or 5 unshielded twisted-pair wire.

**100Base-TX** Proposed IEEE physical layer specification for 100 Mbps Ethernet over two pairs of Category 5 unshielded twisted-pair or shielded twisted-pair wire.

**100VG-AnyLAN** A 100 Mbps technology developed by Hewlett-Packard that uses a demand priority network access method.

**10Base-2** Also known as "cheapernet" and "thinnet." Another name for Ethernet using thin (0.2-inch) coaxial cable and BNC connectors.

**10Base-5** Original Ethernet using 0.4-inch coaxial cable and screw-together connectors.

**10Base-T** IEEE 802.3 physical layer specification for 10 Mbps Ethernet over two pairs of Category 3, 4, or 5 unshielded twisted-pair wire. 10Base-T is recognizable by its characteristic RJ-45 connectors.

**1TR6** A widely deployed, German-specific ISDN switch standard that existed prior to the ETSI NET3 standard.

**24-Bit** The number of bits that represent each pixel, or point on the screen, in "True Color" video. An 8-bit-per-pixel card can generate 256 colors; 24 bits per pixel yields 16.8 million colors.

**3270** A terminal emulation standard for connecting to mainframe computers.

**802** A set of IEEE standards for local area networks (LANs) and metropolitan area networks (MANs).

**802.1** A set of IEEE standards for general management and internetwork operations such as bridging.

**802.2** A set of IEEE standards at the logical link control sublayer of the data link layer.

**802.3** IEEE standards for the CSMA/CD (Carrier Sense Multiple Access/Collision Detect) network access method used by Ethernet networks. These standards apply at the physical layer and the media access control (MAC) sublayer.

**802.4** IEEE standards for a token passing bus.

**802.5** IEEE standards for a token ring network.

**802.6** IEEE Metropolitan Area Network standards.

**8514** An IBM color monitor (and associated video display card) capable of resolutions of 720 × 400 noninterlaced with a refresh rate of 70 MHz; 640 × 480 noninterlaced at 60 MHz; or 1,024 × 768 interlaced at 43.58 MHz. All of these resolutions are in 256 colors.

**AAL** ATM adaptation layer. One of three layers of the ATM protocol reference model. The AAL translates incoming data into ATM cell payloads and translates outgoing cells into format readable by the higher layers. Five AALs have been defined: AAL1 and AAL2 handle isochronous (constant bit rate) traffic, such as voice and video, whereas AAL3/4 and AAL5 apply to data communications through the segmentation and reassembly of packets.

**AAL3/4** An ATM adaptation layer for connection-oriented transfer of connectionless data.

**AAL5** A low-overhead ATM adaptation layer for protocols such as Frame Relay and multiprotocol LAN packets.

**aberration** Variations in focus of a laser beam spot, resulting in the beam of light being diffused at different points. Aberrations can create focusing errors in the laser pick-up. The thinner 0.6mm base utilized on DVD discs significantly reduces aberrations of the laser spot pick-up, improving accuracy in a high-density environment.

**ABM (Asynchronous Balanced Mode)** A communication mode used in HDLC that allows either of two workstations in a peer-oriented point-to-point configuration to initiate a data transfer.

**ABR (average bit rate or available bit rate)** Bit rate refers to the speed at which the processor can read and process data from the disc or from a communications line. DVD utilizes a variable bit rate to better allocate storage capacity on a disc; average bit rate is the measure of transfer rate across the entire disk. Communications circuits (particularly ATM) may provide available bit rate service to enable a transmission to use all the circuit capacity not otherwise allocated.

**AC-3** The audio standard for DVDs distributed in North America. Dolby Laboratory's AC-3 is an audio format that uses five independent sound channels (left front, right front, center front, right rear, and left rear) plus a nondirectional subwoofer. Due to the use of five channels plus a subwoofer, this system is often referred to as a Dolby 5.1 system. In Europe, DVDs use the MPEG-2 audio format as a standard.

**Acceptable Use Policy (AUP)** A policy that defines allowable conduct using network resources. You'll usually see an acceptable use policy defined by Internet service providers and other entities providing net access.

**access method** The method by which networked stations determine when they can transmit data on a shared transmission medium such as a local area network.

**access time** The average time interval between a storage peripheral (usually a disk drive or semiconductor memory) receiving a request to read or write a certain location and returning the value read or completing the write.

**ACK** An ASCII character typically used to confirm message reception. Also, a packet used for the same purpose.

**ACS** Access Control System.

**active hub** A multiport device that amplifies LAN transmission signals.

**adapter** A board installed in a computer system, usually a PC. Adapters provide a variety of functions, including disk interface, video, sound, and network communications.

**ADSL** Asymmetric Digital Subscriber Line. An xDSL technology that allows more bandwidth from the network to you than from you to the network.

**Advanced Research Projects Agency Network (ARPANET)** The network (funded by what's now the Defense Advanced Research Projects Agency) that evolved into the Internet.

**agent** Software that receives queries and returns replies on behalf of an application. In network management systems, agents reside in all managed devices and report the values of specified variables to management stations. Also, software that operates somewhat autonomously on behalf of a user.

**AGP** Accelerated Graphics Port is a new bus interface for graphics accelerators providing fast, high-throughput direct access to system memory. As PC applications become more graphics intensive (as with multiplayer 3D games and advanced CAD programs), the bandwidth required to display each screen rises dramatically. AGP graphics addresses this bandwidth bottleneck with a high-bandwidth pipeline between the graphics accelerator and system memory.

**algorithm** A formula or procedure that states the various methods defining how data is to be used to give a prescribed result.

**amplitude** The magnitude of a signal. Amplitudes are often compared in decibels (dB).

**analog signals** Signals that can vary over a continuous range (for instance, the human voice over conventional telephone lines). Analog circuitry is more subject to distortion and noise but can often more easily handle complex signals than can digital signals, which can have only discrete values.

**analog sound** Recorded sound depicted by fluctuations in amplitude.

**anonymous FTP** The facility that lets you log into an FTP server without having your own account on that server. You login with "anonymous" as your user ID and your e-mail address as the password.

**ANSI** American National Standards Institute.

**aperture** The opening or width of a lens. Also, the part of memory space allocated to an AGP video card.

**API (application program interface)** A means of interface between programs to give one program access to another. APIs provide a method of allowing programs to work with one another without requiring the programmers to know all the details of all the programs, and they provide a means for programs to operate on a standard platform (such as Windows).

**AppleTalk** An Apple networking system that operates over shielded twisted-pair wire at 230 Kbps.

**Application layer** Layer 7 of the OSI Reference Model; implemented by various network applications including electronic mail, file transfer, and terminal emulation.

**ARAP** AppleTalk Remote Access Protocol.

**Archie** An Internet service that catalogs files available on the Internet via anonymous FTP. An Archie server gathers and indexes files, interrogating FTP servers to discover what files they archive.

**ARP (Address Resolution Protocol)** An Internet protocol for dynamically mapping Internet addresses to physical hardware addresses on LANs. Limited to LANs that support hardware broadcast. Required to permit computers to discover the physical addresses of other computers on the same network.

**ARQ** Automatic request for retransmission. A type of communications link where the receiver asks the transmitter to resend a block of data when errors are detected.

**array** The part of a RAM that stores the bits. The array consists of rows and columns, with a cell at each intersection that can store a bit. The large rectangular section in the center of the die where the memory is stored.

**ASCII** American Standard Code for Information Interchange. A method of encoding text as binary values. The standard ASCII character set consists of 128 decimal numbers (0–127) for letters of the alphabet, numerals, punctuation marks, and common special characters. The extended ASCII character set extends to 255 characters and contains special mathematical, graphics, and foreign characters. A subset of the Windows NT UNICODE character sets.

**ASIC (application-specific integrated circuit)** A highly integrated logic chip designed for specific applications to work alongside a microprocessor (for instance, a math coprocessor, graphics processor, artificial intelligence processor, LAN processor, digital signal processor). These chips offload some of the specialized work from the main processor.

**aspect ratio** The relationship between width and height of a computer monitor or television set. Current television products feature a 4:3 aspect ratio. DVD supports 4:3, letterbox, and 16:9 aspect ratios.

**ASPI** Advanced SCSI Programming Interface. A standard SCSI software interface that acts as a liaison between host adapters and SCSI device drivers. ASPI enables host adapters and device drivers to provide a standard SCSI software interface, enabling the development of SCSI-aware applications that are independent of the specific host adapter.

**async (asynchronous)** Of a form of communication in which the absolute timing of the data transmission is variable. Asynchronous data transmission typically frames the bits in each byte with start and stop bits.

**asynchronous** Literally, actions that proceed without time synchronization. An asynchronous process in a multitasking system is one whose execution can proceed independently, "in the background." Other processes may be started before the asynchronous process has finished. In logic design, asynchronous logic is a design technique in which a device responds to input signals whenever they occur rather than at specific points in time designated by a clock signal.

**asynchronous data transfer** A method of SCSI data transfer. This is the type of transfer rate originally introduced with SCSI 1, and it requires a complete handshake between the sending and receiving devices. With asynchronous data transfer, transfer rates of 2 MBps are common.

**asynchronous transmission** Data transmission one character at a time, with intervals of varying lengths between characters. Overhead in the form of start and stop bits framing each character control the transmission. See also synchronous transmission.

**async-sync PPP conversion** A method by which asynchronous PPP data sent between a computer's serial port and an ISDN device is converted by the terminal adapter to synchronous traffic required on the network.

**AT command set** The name of the commands used to control most personal computer modems, taken from the characters AT that precede most commands. Originally developed by Hayes.

**ATM** Asynchronous Transfer Mode. A form of data transmission based on fixed-length packets, called cells, that can carry data, voice, and video at high speeds. This technology is designed to combine the benefits of switching technology with those of packet switching. ATM is defined by ITU-T and ATM Forum specifications.

**ATM Forum** A 700-member vendor and end-user consortium created to promote standards and interoperability for ATM products.

**ATM switch** A hardware device that takes an incoming ATM cell and directs it to one or more output interfaces based on routing information in the cell.

**attenuation** The decrease in magnitude of the power of a signal transmitted over a wire, measured in decibels. As attenuation increases, signal power decreases.

**AUI** Attachment Unit Interface.

**AUI cable** An IEEE 802.3 cable connecting the MAU (Media Access Unit) to a networked device such as a computer.

**AUI connector** Attachment Unit Interface; a 15-pin "D" connector for use with external transceivers, such as 10 Base-5 or fiber optics.

**authentication**  An exchange to ensure that users are who they say they are and are authorized to access remote resources. A common example is the sequence requiring you to enter a user name and password to access the Internet through your Internet service provider.

**auto precharge**  A Synchronous DRAM feature that allows the memory chip's circuitry to close a page automatically at the end of a burst.

**autonomous system (AS)**  In Internet (TCP/IP) terminology, a series of gateways or routers that fall under a single administrative entity and cooperate using the same Interior Gateway Protocol (IGP).

**autopartitioning**  A function of repeaters, whereby a faulty segment is automatically isolated to prevent the fault from affecting the entire network. The segment is automatically reconnected by the repeater when the fault condition is rectified.

**backbone**  A LAN or WAN that interconnects intermediate systems (bridges and/or routers).

**back door**  A preprogrammed hole in an otherwise secure system that compromises its defenses, allowing intruders access.

**backplane**  The main bus that carries data within a device, often synonymous with motherboard.

**backup**  Copying information from a hard disk onto another data storage medium (for instance, Travan minicartridges).

**balun (balanced-unbalanced)**  An impedance-matching device that connects a balanced line (such as a twisted-pair line) with an unbalanced line (such as a coaxial cable).

**bandwidth**  Measure of the information capacity of a transmission channel. Strictly speaking, bandwidth is the difference, expressed in hertz (Hz), between the highest and lowest frequencies of the channel. For a given modulation and power level, the data rate you can transmit down the channel is proportional to the bandwidth.

**bandwidth-on-demand**  See Dynamic bandwidth allocation.

**bank**  A slot or group of slots that must be populated with memory modules of like capacity and fulfill the data width requirement of the CPU.

**bank schema**  A method of diagramming memory configurations. The bank schema system consists of rows and columns that represent memory sockets on a system: Rows indicate independent sockets, and columns represent banks of sockets.

**bare board** A printed circuit board (PCB) that does not have any components on it.

**baseband** A transmission scheme in which the entire bandwidth, or data-carrying capacity, of a medium (such as coaxial cable) is used to carry a single digital pulse, or signal, between multiple users. Because digital signals are not modulated, only one kind of data can be transmitted at a time.

**Basic Rate Interface (BRI)** An international standard switched digital interface (a form of ISDN) offering two 64 Kbps B, or bearer, channels and a 16 Kbps D, or signaling, channel to carry voice, data, or video signals.

**bastion gateway** A machine placed on the perimeter network to defend the inner network hosts from attack. Although secured against attack, it is assumed to be compromised because it is directly exposed to the Internet.

**bastion host** A machine placed on the perimeter network to provide publicly available services. Although secured against attack, it is assumed to be compromised because it is exposed to the Internet.

**bay** The brackets in a chassis that hold disk and tape drives. External bays have an opening to the outside; internal bays do not.

**B channel** In ISDN, a full-duplex, 64 Kbps channel for sending data.

**beacon** Token ring frame signaling that the ring is inoperative because of a serious hardware error. Defective cable or faulty nodes are possible causes.

**BECN** Backward Explicit Congestion Notification.

**BEDO** Burst EDO. A variant on EDO DRAM in which read or write cycles are batched in bursts of four. Burst EDO bus speeds range from 40 MHz to 66 MHz, well above the 33 MHz bus speeds of Fast Page Mode or EDO DRAM.

**Bell standards** Refers to the U.S. modulation protocol standards developed by the former AT&T Bell Systems such as Bell 103 (300 bps transmission) and Bell 212A (1,200 bps transmission).

**BER** Bit error rate. Measures the rate of errors in bits transmitted on a communications channel as the number of incorrect bits per bit transmitted.

**B-frame** MPEG-2 bidirectional frames use both a past and subsequent frames as a reference to calculate compressed frame data.

**BGP (Border Gateway Protocol)** A protocol for communications between a router in one autonomous system and routers in other ASs.

**binary** A method of encoding numbers as a series of bits. The binary number system, also referred to as base 2, uses combinations of only two digits: 0 and 1.

**binary synchronous communication, or bisync** A character-oriented data link protocol for half-duplex applications. Typically used in mainframe applications.

**BIOS** Basic Input Output System. Provides fundamental services required for the operation of a computer. Permanently present in the machine, these routines are generally stored in ROM (read-only memory) or flash memory. The motherboard contains a BIOS to support all of its standard functions. Adapter cards can carry additions to the BIOS for their own unique functions.

**BISDN (Broadband Integrated Services Digital Network)** A communications standard designed to handle high-bandwidth applications such as video over broadband. Typically based on ATM.

**bit** The smallest unit of information a computer processes. A bit can have a value of either 1 or 0.

**bit block transfer** A method of quickly implementing graphics operations as rectangular memory-to-memory operations.

**bit error rate** The percentage of bits in a transmittal received in error. See BER.

**bitmapped register** A value held in a digital device in which each bit or group of bits has a specific, independent function. In the case of AT-compatible modems, control functions are driven by values stored in locations called S-registers.

**blind dialing** An automated process whereby the modem goes off-hook and dials without waiting for a dial tone. This is prohibited in many countries.

**block** A physical unit of information. Block size is usually expressed in bytes.

**block diagram** A circuit or system drawing concerned with major functions and interconnections between functions.

**Block Transfer Control** Determines whether or not the modem uses block or stream mode during an MNP connection. In stream mode, MNP sends data frames in varying length. Block mode sends fixed data frames of 256 characters.

**BNC connector** BNC jacks and plugs connect network hardware via thin Ethernet cable (10Base-2). A BNC barrel connector joins two lengths of thin Ethernet cable. A BNC tee connector joins two lengths of thin Ethernet cable to the back of a device. A BNC terminator closes off an unused end of a BNC tee.

**BOC** Bell Operating Company. See also RBOC.

**bonded disc**  DVD video discs are 1.2mm thick and consist of two 0.6mm layers permanently bonded together. This procedure produces a disc that is more resistant to warpage and offers improved tilt margins, making it possible to use both sides of the DVD disc.

**bonding**  An international standard for aggregating multiple data channels into a single logical connection. Very popular in videoconferencing applications. Commonly applied to ISDN.

**boot drive**  The drive from which the operating system loads (usually A or C).

**boot PROM**  Boot programmable read-only memory. A ROM chip that enables a personal computer to load the operating system from a storage device or the network.

**booting**  Booting is a process by which a computer starts and loads the operating system.

**BOOTP**  A protocol that a network workstation uses on bootup to determine the IP address of its Ethernet interfaces.

**BOT**  Beginning of tape.

**bottlenecks**  Traffic slowdowns that result when too many network nodes try to access a single node, often a server node, at once.

**Boundary Routing System Architecture**  Software algorithms and methodology that enable a router at a central node of a wide area network to perform protocol-specific routing and bridging path table management on behalf of a router at a peripheral (leaf) node, greatly simplifying the router at the leaf node.

**BPDU (Bridge Protocol Data Units)**  A packet to initiate communications between devices under a spanning-tree protocol. Compare PDU.

**bps**  Bits per second.

**Bps**  Bytes per second.

**break handling**  Determines how the modem responds when a break signal is received from either the DTE (Data Terminal Equipment or computer/terminal) or the remote modem. This is controlled by the MNP-based AT extended commands. A break signal is represented on the communications line by a steady space signal for a significant length of time.

**BRI**  Basic Rate Interface.

**bridge** A device that interconnects local or remote networks no matter what higher-level protocols (such as IPX, NetBEUI, or TCP/IP) are involved. Bridges form a single logical network, centralizing network administration. They operate at the physical and link layers of the Open Systems Interconnect (OSI) reference model. See also SRT (source routing transparent) bridge and STA (Spanning Tree Algorithm). Contrast with router and gateway.

**bridge/router** A device that can provide the functions of a bridge, router, or both concurrently. A bridge/router can route one or more protocols, such as TCP/IP and/or IPX, and bridge all other traffic.

**broadband** A data-transmission scheme in which multiple signals share the bandwidth of a medium. This allows the transmission of voice, data, and video signals over a single medium. Cable television uses broadband techniques to deliver dozens of channels over one cable. Contrast with baseband.

**broadcast** A message forwarded to all network destinations.

**broadcast storm** Multiple simultaneous broadcasts that typically absorb available network bandwidth and can cause network time-outs.

**buffer** An area in a device for temporary storage of data in transit; can accommodate differences in processing speeds between devices by storing data blocks until they are ready to be processed by a slower device.

**buffering** Adding logic to provide compatibility between two signals, for instance, changing voltage levels or current capability. Buffering is used to overcome signal variations caused by loading. (Commonly found in SDRAM memory.)

**burn-in** The process of exercising an integrated circuit at elevated voltage and temperature. This process accelerates failure normally seen as "infant mortality" in a chip. (Those chips that would fail early during actual usage will fail during burn-in. Those that pass have a life expectancy much greater than that required for normal usage.) Also refers to the process of running a complete system (sometimes at elevated temperature) with the intent of screening out infant mortality failures.

**bus** A pathway for data in a computer system. All PCs have a bus, which is able to host add-on (expansion) devices, such as modems, adapter boards, and video adapters. Expansion devices use the bus to send data to and receive data from the PC's CPU or memory. PCI, VL, ISA, EISA, and Micro Channel are the major bus standards used in PCs.

**bus cycle** A single transaction between two devices connected to the bus.

**bus mastering** A high-performance method of data transfer in which the host adapter's onboard processor handles the transfer of data directly to and from a computer's memory without intervention from the computer's processor. This is the fastest method of data transfer available for multitasking operating systems.

**bus topology** A network topology in which nodes are connected to a single cable with terminators at each end.

**bypass mode** An operating mode on ring networks such as FDDI and token ring in which an interface has dropped from the ring.

**byte** A unit of information made up of eight bits. The byte is a fundamental unit of computer processing; almost all aspects of a computer's performance and specifications are measured in bytes or multiples thereof (such as kilobytes or megabytes).

**cache memory** A small, fast memory holding recently accessed data, designed to speed up subsequent access to the same data. Most commonly refers to high-speed memory located between the CPU and the main memory. Cache is designed to supply the processor with the most frequently requested instructions and data. Cache memory can be three to five times faster than main memory. Two levels of cache are typical: Level 1 cache (usually inside the processor), and Level 2 cache, which sits between Level 1 cache and main memory.

**caching** The process by which data requested by the operating system is retrieved from RAM instead of from a hard disk (or some other mass storage medium). Caching algorithms will check if the requested data is in its "cache" (or RAM). RAM access is much faster than access to mass storage devices, so the more hits in the cache, the faster overall system performance will be. Cache can be on the host adapter, on the motherboard (controlled by the operating system), and on the device (storage or network).

**camera angles** Scenes that make up a movie may be shot from multiple camera angles, each providing a unique perspective of the program. DVD allows up to nine different camera angles to be recorded on a disc.

**capacitance** The property of a circuit element that allows it to store an electrical charge.

**CAPI** In Europe, CAPI (Common Application Interface) provides a common ISDN software platform for communication applications.

**CAS** Column address strobe. The signal that tells the DRAM to accept the given address as a column address. Used with RAS and a row address to select a bit within the DRAM.

**catastrophic failure** When a device that was initially good now fails to function under any condition.

**CAU (controller access unit)** A managed concentrator on a token ring network; essentially, an intelligent version of an MAU. Handles the ring in/ring out function.

**CBR (CAS before RAS; also constant bit rate)** Column address strobe before row address strobe. A fast refresh technique in which the DRAM keeps track of the next row it needs to refresh, thus simplifying what a system would have to do to refresh the part. In communications, constant bit rate defines a circuit that receives a fixed, guaranteed level of service.

**CCITT (Consultative Committee for International Telegraph and Telephone)** An international organization that develops communications standards known as "Recommendations" for all internally controlled forms of analog and digital communication (Recommendation X.25 is an example). Now superseded by the ITU-T.

**CCS** Common Channel Signaling.

**CD quality** Recording quality similar to that of a compact disc player. This means that 16 bits of information are recorded for every sample taken, and that each channel is sampled 44,100 times per second.

**CDDI (Copper Distributed Data Interface)** A standard for FDDI over UTP or STP wiring (unshielded or shielded twisted-pair copper media). Supports data rates of 100 Mbps over transmission distances of about 100 meters. Uses a dual-ring architecture to provide redundancy.

**cell relay** A network transmission format that uses small packets of uniform size, called *cells*. The fixed-length cells can be processed and transmitted by hardware at very high speeds. Acts as a basis for SMDS Interface Protocol and ATM.

**Centronics Interface** A 36-pin connection that became the standard way to attach printers to a PC parallel data port.

**CERT (Computer Emergency Response Team)** An organization tasked to facilitate response to Internet computer security events. The CERT security issue archive is at ftp.cert.org and includes information about how to defeat attacks. Their e-mail address is cert@cert.org. The 24-hour telephone hotline is (412) 268-7090.

**CGA** Color Graphics Adapter. A medium-resolution IBM graphics standard capable of displaying 640 × 200 pixels in two colors, or 320 × 200 pixels in four colors.

**Challenge-Handshake Authentication Protocol (CHAP)** An authentication method used in connecting to some Internet service providers.

**channel aggregation** Channel aggregation combines multiple physical channels into one logical channel of greater bandwidth. With BRI ISDN connections, channel aggregation would combine the two 64 Kbps B channels into a single, logical 128 Kbps channel. Also termed *bonding*.

**CHAP**  Challenge Handshake Authentication Protocol.

**Cheapernet**  The IEEE 802.3 10Base-2 standard (or cable used in such installations). Thinnet, another term for the standard, specifies a less expensive, thinner version of traditional Ethernet cable.

**check bits**  Extra data bits provided by a module to support ECC parity.

**Chicago**  In addition to being the Windy City in Illinois, the development code name for Windows 95.

**CHMOS**  High-density Complementary Metal Oxide Semiconductor.

**CICS (Customer Information Control System)**  An IBM application subsystem that permits transactions entered at remote terminals to be processed concurrently by user applications.

**CIR (committed information rate)**  The transport speed the frame relay network will maintain between service locations.

**circuit-switched network**  A network that establishes a physical circuit temporarily, until it receives a disconnect signal.

**CISC**  Complex Instruction Set Computing. This design logic is usually associated with microprocessors. CISC chips use instructions, or commands, that involve several steps in one. Contrast with RISC.

**client**  The user-end software supporting specific functions, such as Telnet or FTP. The other end of the connection is the server.

**client/server**  A distributed system model of computing that brings computing power to the desktop, where users (clients) access resources from servers.

**CLNP (Connectionless Network Protocol)**  See Connectionless Network Service.

**clock**  A source of digital timing signals.

**clock rate**  The number of pulses emitted by a computer's clock in one second; it determines the rate at which logical or arithmetic gating is performed in a synchronous computer.

**CMIP (Common Management Information Protocol)**  A protocol to manage large networks. Includes fault management, performance management, security, and accounting. ISO 9596.

**CMIP/CMIS (Common Management Information Protocol/Services)** An OSI-based protocol that provides standard ways to manage large multivendor networks.

**CMOL** CMIP Over LLC.

**CMOS** Complementary metal-oxide semiconductor. Outside of digital design, a term used to refer to the device in personal computers that holds configuration data while power is turned off. In digital design, CMOS is a semiconductor manufacturing process that uses both N- and P-channel devices in a complementary fashion to achieve small geometries and low power consumption.

**CMOT (CMIP over TCP/IP)** An Internet standard defining the use of CMIP (an OSI-based protocol) over TCP for managing TCP/IP networks.

**CMT (Connection Management)** A process in FDDI for controlling the transition of the ring through its various operating states (off, connect, active, and so on) under the X3T9.5 specification.

**CO (Central Office)** A local telephone company office that connects to all local loops (subscriber lines) in a given area and where circuit switching of customer lines occurs.

**coaxial cable** A data transmission medium with a single-wire conductor insulated by an outer shield from electromagnetic and radio frequency interference.

**COB** Chip On Board. A system in which semiconductor dice are mounted directly on a PC board and connected with bonded wires or solder bumps. The dice are usually mechanically protected with epoxy.

**CO-IPX** Connection-Oriented IPX. A native ATM protocol based on IPX under development by Novell.

**cold boot** Starting a computer by applying power.

**collapsed backbone** Network architecture under which the backplane of a device such as a hub performs the function of a network backbone; the backplane routes traffic between desktop nodes and between other hubs serving multiple LANs.

**column** Part of the memory array. A bit can be stored where a column and a row intersect.

**COM port** The DOS and Windows name for a serial port.

**command.com** The command processor for MS-DOS-based systems. It provides the C> prompt.

**command mode** The state of a modem when it is listening to the serial port for "AT" commands. Command mode occurs when the modem is turned on or reset, when it loses its connection to a remote modem, or when escape characters (+++) are typed. To transmit data, the modem must be in data mode. The modem does not transmit data when in command mode.

**command swapping** A SCSI host adapter feature that allows the host adapter to support up to 255 simultaneous commands.

**committed information rate** The transport speed a Frame Relay network guarantees between service locations under normal conditions.

**common carrier** A licensed utility that provides communications services at government-regulated rates.

**communications protocol** A set of procedures that controls how a data communications link or network operates.

**component video** The elements that make up a video signal, consisting of luminance, which represents brightness in the video image, and separate Red and Blue (Y R-Y B-Y) signals. DVD is mastered as component video. Component video is preferred because it provides improved color purity and superior color detail, as well as a reduction in color noise and NTSC artifacts.

**compression** Reversibly reducing the size of data in order to lower the bandwidth or space required for transmission or storage.

**concentrator** A device that serves as a wiring hub in a star-topology network. Sometimes refers to a device containing multiple modules of network equipment. More generally, a device that connects multiple network ports into a single (and usually faster) port.

**conditioned analog line** An analog line to which devices have been added to improve the electrical signal. Conditioned lines typically have lower noise levels but may have restricted frequency response (which is undesirable for high-speed modems).

**config.sys** The low-level file on a PC that tells DOS how to configure itself prior to starting the command interpreter.

**congestion** A condition of excessive network traffic resulting in reduced performance.

**congestion control** In a frame relay network, the mechanisms (see also BECN and FECN) designed to limit excessive traffic and provide network switches with a means of alerting the access node (for instance, a router) to slow its transmission. Frame relay congestion control is an instance of the more general idea of flow control.

**connectionless communications** A form of packet-switching that relies on global addresses in each packet rather than on predefined virtual circuits. Connectionless transmission is characterized by unsolicited and unacknowledged transmissions from one point to another. Because it does not require circuit setup or teardown and does not require confirmation that messages were received correctly, it has less overhead than connection-oriented transmission.

**Connectionless Network Service (CLNS)** A packet-switched network based on connectionless communications.

**connection-oriented communications** A form of packet-switching that requires a circuit from source to destination to be established before data can be transferred.

**connection (or call) spoofing** The technique of mimicking correct responses to keep level requests alive at the local end of a temporarily broken connection is called connection (or call) spoofing. Call spoofing saves connect time charges by allowing the call to be disconnected without causing the NOS to time-out the client/host connection. It also enhances data throughput by keeping the line clear of these network administration packets. It is useful when the connection needs to be torn down and rebuilt to meet short-term needs of the network.

**connectivity system** A collection of network devices that are logically related and managed as a single entity.

**CONS (Connection-Oriented Network Service)** An OSI protocol for packet-switched networks that exchange information over a virtual circuit (a logical circuit where connection methods and protocols are preestablished). Compare to connectionless communications.

**contention** A network access method where devices compete for the right to access the physical medium.

**COS** Class of Service.

**COSP** Connection-Oriented Session Protocol.

**CPCS** Common Part Convergence Sublayer.

**CPE (customer premises equipment)** Terminating equipment, such as terminals, phones, and modems, supplied by the telecommunications company, installed at customer sites, and connected to the company network.

**CPN** Customer Premises Network.

**CPU (central processing unit)** The chip in a computer that has primary responsibility for executing program instructions. The basic components of a computer are the processor, memory, display, storage, and input/output devices.

**CRC** Cyclic redundancy check. A mathematical method (related to checksums) used to check that data is error-free.

**credit card memory** A type of memory typically used in laptop and notebook computers. Credit card memory features a small form factor and is named for its similarity to the size of a credit card. See also PCMCIA.

**CSMA/CD** Carrier-Sense Multiple Access with Collision Detection. Channel access method used by Ethernet and IEEE 802.3 in which devices transmit only after finding the data channel clear for some period of time. When two devices transmit simultaneously, a collision occurs and the colliding devices delay their retransmissions for a random length of time.

**CSU/DSU** Channel Service Unit/Data Service Unit. Digital interface equipment that connects end-user equipment to the local digital telephone loop. The CSU/DSU recovers the data from the transmission medium and isolates the user from the communications network.

**CTS (Clear to Send)** An RS-232 signal that indicates transmission can proceed from terminal to modem.

**custom signaling** ISDN signaling protocols used in AT&T and Northern Telecom switches prior to the advent of the National ISDN 1 standard.

**cylinder** The set of tracks spanning multiple platters and platter sides on a disk.

**DAC** Dual-attached concentrator. A device that is attached to and allows access to both rings in an FDDI network. Also, digital-to-analog converter, a device that transforms a number into a voltage proportional to the value of the number.

**DAS** Dual-attached station. A station with two connections to an FDDI network, one to each logical ring. If one of the rings should fail, the network automatically reconfigures to continue normal operation.

**DASD** Direct access storage device.

**data compression** For lossless compression, a technique that examines transmitted data for redundancy and replaces strings (groups) of characters with special codes that the receiving modem interprets and restores to its original form. Transmission of compressed data results in shorter connect times and, hence, cost savings for connect charges. Data compression is sometimes called "source encoding." More generally, it is a reversible data transformation that exploits statistical characteristics of the data to produce a more compact representation.

Data compression may be lossless, in which case the exact original data can be reconstructed from the compressed form, or lossy, in which case an approximation that contains some differences is reconstructed. For sound, images, and other data sampled from the real world, the errors in lossy compression may be imperceptible.

**Data Encryption Standard (DES)** A standardized encryption method widely used by banks.

**datagram** A logical block of data sent as a unit without prior establishment of a network connection. Contains source and destination address information as well as the data itself.

**data mode** The modem is in data mode when a connection has been established with a remote modem. User data may then be transmitted or received. See also Command mode.

**data out** The signal line that carries the data read from the RAM (random access memory).

**data reduction** In video, the process of compressing raw digitized video. Digital video that has not been compressed carries more picture information than is necessary to produce a quality image. Digitized video identifies the precise brightness and color of each pixel. It is not necessary to assign this large amount of storage space to each pixel, because common picture elements can be grouped together and represented by smaller segments of code. This is the basis of MPEG-2. For example, the picture elements of a static image do not need to be stored as new information over and over to create successive frames. Through the use of I-frames (a reference frame that appears once every 15 frames), bi-directional B-frames, and P-frames ( predictive frames that fill in the information between the I-frames), the amount of data storage necessary to reproduce high-quality moving images is greatly reduced.

**date code** On boards: the date of preliminary release (the date that printed circuit boards are approved for fabrication). On components: the date of manufacture. In the test area: the code (on the part) showing the year and work week the part was marked.

**DCD** Data Carrier Detect. A modem signal in an RS-232C interface that indicates to the computer that the modem is receiving a valid carrier signal from a remote modem (and therefore has a live connection).

**DCE** Data communications equipment. A communications device that can establish, maintain, and terminate a connection (for example, a modem). A DCE may also provide signal conversion between the data terminal equipment (DTE) and the common carrier's channel. Contrast DTE.

**D channel** The D channel is the full-duplex 16 Kbps (basic rate interface) or 64 Kbps (primary rate interface) ISDN signaling channel that carries control messages between the customer equipment and the public switch. The control messages communicate things like call request information (phone numbers) and incoming call information.

**DDS** Digital Data Service.

**decibel (dB)** A means of measuring amplitude.

**DECNet** Digital Equipment Corporation's proprietary network architecture.

**decoder** A circuit that determines the content of a DVD data stream and performs digital-to-analog conversion of picture and sound elements.

**decoding** The process that decompresses encoded video and audio information for playback.

**dedicated line** A transmission circuit installed between two sites of a private network and "open" or available at all times. Also termed a "nailed-up connection."

**default route** Entry in a routing table used to redirect all frames for which the table has no explicit listing for the next hop.

**demodulation** Opposite of modulation; the process of retrieving data from a modulated carrier wave.

**DES** Data Encryption Standard.

**designated router** In OSPF, each multiaccess network with at least two attached routers has a designated router. The designated router has special duties in the running of the protocol, such as generating a link state advertisement for the multiaccess network. This concept helps reduce the number of adjacencies required on a multiaccess network, which cuts routing protocol traffic and the size of the topological database.

**Desktop ATM25 Alliance** An ATM Forum subgroup formed to promote international standards for 25 Mbps ATM products.

**device driver** A software module that enables other software in a computer to communicate with hardware devices such as disk drives, sound cards, video cards, or mice. Each kind of device typically requires a different driver.

**dial modifier** Special characters appended to the AT D command that instruct the modem how to place a call. Examples include T (ATDT) for tone dialing or P (ATDP) for pulse dialing.

**dialup** A type of communication that is established by a switched-circuit connection using the telephone network. The term comes from the fact that one of the connections dials up the telephone at the other end. Also, a widely used method of accessing the Internet. A dialup connection uses regular phone lines to connect one computer to another via modem.

**die** An individual cell on a semiconductor wafer that contains the complete circuitry to perform a specific function. The internal circuitry is made of thousands of tiny electronic parts. 'Die' refers to a semiconductor component or part that has not yet been packaged (also known as "IC" [Integrated Circuit] or "chip").

**dielectric** A material that conducts no current when it has voltage applied to it. Two dielectrics used in semiconductor processing are silicon dioxide and silicon nitride.

**dielectric deposition** A layer of deposited oxide used to isolate metal 1 from metal 2 on double-level metal processes.

**die pick-up tool** The bondhead tool on the machine that picks up the die from the precisor and places it on the leadframe.

**die size** The physical measurements of the die.

**differential** A term referring to the electrical characteristics of signals. Differential signals occupy two conductors, with a positive (+) and negative (–) polarity component of the signal on either conductor. This minimizes the effect of common mode signal noise and allows the signal to be transmitted reliably over greater distances at a higher speed. Differential signals are used in specialized versions of SCSI, in twisted-pair local area networks, and other high-speed applications.

**diffusion** The intermingling of molecules of two or more substances. When high-temperature processes are done in diffusion tubes, the high temperature accelerates diffusion. Typical diffusion furnace temperature is 950 degrees Centigrade, or 1,742 degrees Fahrenheit.

**digital modem** A digital modem accepts the bit stream corresponding to an analog call over a 64 Kbps ISDN channel. The modem interprets the bit stream as a call originated by an analog modem, applying signal processing equations to demodulate the signal. This action generally requires the use of a digital signal processor or other specialized modem chip.

**digital recording** A recording technique in which sounds and/or images are converted into groups of electronic bits for storage. The groups of bits are retrieved electronically, by a laser, as a series of ones and zeros. This binary code is converted into the audio and video images to be displayed.

**digital signal** A discrete signal that can take on only one of several (usually only two) discrete levels. In contrast, analog signals can take a continuous range of levels.

**digital sound** Recorded and stored sound as a series of numerical values rather than fluctuations in amplitude. Also called wave audio.

**DIMM (dual in-line memory module)** A printed circuit board with gold or tin/lead contacts and memory devices. A DIMM is similar to a SIMM, but with this primary difference: Unlike the metal leads on either side of a SIMM, which are "tied together" electrically, the leads on either side of a DIMM are electrically independent. Decoupling the leads on either side creates more signals, allowing more address lines and a wider bus interface, but makes it more critical that every signal line seat precisely in the socket.

**DIN connector** A German connector standard. DIN connectors are commonly used for keyboards, PS/2 style mice, and audio/video interfaces.

**DIP (dual in-line package)** A form of integrated circuit (chip) packaging. DIPs can be either installed in sockets or permanently soldered into holes extending into the surface of the printed circuit board. The DIP package has largely been superseded by surface mount devices, which allow components to be packaged closer together on the board.

**DIP switch** A switch mounted on PC board for configuration options.

**direct address** A computer memory address that is included as part of the instruction.

**DirectX** A group of technologies designed by Microsoft to let Windows-based computers run applications with multimedia elements such as full-color graphics, video, 3D animation, and surround sound.

**distributed processing** Systems using multiple computers, processors, intelligent input/output controllers, or DMA control to increase performance.

**DLCI (data link connection identifier)** A value in Frame Relay that identifies a logical connection.

**DLCX** Data Link Control Exchange.

**DLL** Dynamic link library, a Windows software module typically shared among multiple programs.

**DLUR/DLUS** Dependent LU Requester/Dependent LU Server.

**DMA (direct memory access)** DMA provides peripheral devices direct access to system memory without adding to CPU overhead. DMA allows hardware control of the transfer of streams of data to or from the main memory of a computing system. The mechanism may require setup by the host software. After initialization, it automatically sequences the required data transfer and provides the necessary address information.

**DMTF** Desktop Management Task Force.

**Dolby Digital Sound (AC-3)** AC-3 provides six separate discrete audio channels: left, right, and center front; right and left surround; and a low-frequency woofer as a listener option.

**Domain Name System (DNS)** A distributed Internet-wide database used with TCP/IP to associate host names and IP addresses. DNS lets you specify computers by name rather than numerical IP addresses, simplifying access and making changes of IP address relatively transparent.

**dongle** An electronic "key" typically attached to a parallel port to verify access to protected software.

**doping** The introduction of an element that alters the conductivity of a semiconductor. Adding boron to silicon will create a P-type (more positive) material, while adding phosphorus or arsenic to silicon will create N-type (more negative) material.

**DOS partition** A section of a disk storage device, created by the DOS FDISK program, in which data and/or software programs are stored. Computers have a primary DOS partition that contains the special files needed to boot the computer. A computer's disk devices may also have extended DOS partitions. Each DOS partition is assigned a unique drive letter, such as C or D. A single disk device can have multiple partitions. *See also* NTFS.

**DPA** Demand Protocol Architecture.

**DPAM** Demand Priority Access Method.

**DQDB (Distributed Queue Dual Bus)** A communications protocol proposed by the IEEE 802.6 committee for use in Metropolitan Area Networks. *See also* SMDS.

**DRA** Distributed Repeater Architecture.

**DRAM** Dynamic random access memory. The most common system memory technology, DRAM can hold a charge (that is, data) for only a short period of time. Therefore, to retain the data, it must be refreshed periodically. If the cell is not refreshed, the data is lost (see also RAM and SRAM).

**DRI** Distributed recovery intelligence. The ability to track down a network problem and automatically isolate the malfunctioning node.

**drop cable** A cable that connects a network device such as a computer to a physical medium such as an Ethernet network. Drop cable is also called transceiver cable because it runs from the network node to a transceiver (a transmit/receiver) attached to the trunk cable (see also AUI cable). Alternatively, the coaxial cable from a cable operator's splitter to the customer premises.

**DS (Digital Signal)** A standard for the electrical characteristics of data transmissions sent over telephone carriers. DS1 is 1.544 Mbps; DS3 is 44.736 Mbps.

**DSP** Digital signal processor. A specialized microprocessor designed for high performance while computing the complex mathematical functions used to manipulate waveforms. Useful in processing audio and video signals.

**DSR (Data Set Ready)** An RS-232 signal indicating that a modem is ready to send and receive data.

**DSU/CSU** Data service unit/channel service unit. The device that connects an external digital circuit to a digital circuit on the customer's premises. The DSU converts data into the correct format, and the CSU terminates the communications line, conditions the signal, and participates in remote testing of the connection.

**DS*x*** Digital Signal. A standard specifying the electrical characteristics for data transmission over four-wire telephone circuits. DS1 is 1.544 Mbps, and DS3 is 44.736 Mbps. These two are commonly referred to as T1 and T3, respectively.

**DTE** Data terminal equipment. The computer or terminal, either local (yours), or the remote (the one you're communicating with). A DTE is usually connected to a DCE.

**DTR** Data Terminal Ready. One of the control lines in the RS-232C specification. The computer issues this signal to the attached modem indicating that it is ready to receive data.

**Dual-attached servers** Servers attached to both paths of an FDDI ring for load balancing and redundancy.

**Dual homing** The technique of attaching a router or other network device to two independent points in the backbone network. Used when network availability is critical.

**DVD** A high-density digital format consisting of a 5-inch disc, 1.2mm in thickness, featuring two bonded layers, each measuring 0.6mm. This storage system can hold up to 133 minutes of high-quality moving pictures on one side. The DVD disc can also provide up to eight audio streams in addition to supporting subtitles in a maximum of 32 languages. DVD-ROM drives substantially improve upon the storage capability of conventional CD-ROM drives, providing 7 to 13 times the current storage capability on a single side of the disc.

**DVD-10** Double-sided/single-layer type DVD with 9.4GB storage capability.

**DVD-18** Double-sided/dual-layer type DVD with 17GB storage capability.

**DVD-5** Single-sided/single-layer type DVD with 4.7GB storage capability.

**DVD-9** Single-sided/dual-layer type DVD with 8.5GB storage capability.

**DVD-R** Write-once type DVD-recordable discs with 3.8GB storage capacity per side.

**DVD-RAM** A rewritable DVD disc, also as referred to as "erasable"; a medium that allows rewriting many times. It offers more than 2.6GB storage capacity per side.

**DVD-ROM** A DVD disc for data storage in computers.

**DVD-Video** A DVD disc intended for playback on a consumer DVD player or PC.

**DXI** Data Exchange Interface. A communications protocol between devices such as routers and CSU/DSUs. In the case of ATM, for example, the ATM DXI protocol allows a DTE (such as a router) and a DCE (such as an ATM DSU) to provide an ATM User Network Interface (UNI) for networks.

**dynamic bandwidth allocation** The capability to add and drop ISDN B channels based on the sending of threshold data levels. Specifically, the capability to raise a call over a second B channel when the first B channel becomes saturated and to drop the call when data rates decline.

**dynamic routing** Routing that adjusts automatically to changes in network topology or traffic.

**E.164** Specifies the ISDN numbers, including telephone numbers up to 15 digits long.

**E-1** European equivalent of T-1. The transmission rate is higher than for the North American T-1 standard.

**E2PROM** Electrically Erasable PROM.

**E-3** European designation for T-3. The transmission rate is higher than for the North American T-3 standard.

**EAROM** Electrically Alterable Read-Only Memory.

**ECC** Error correction code. A mathematical extension of the checksum idea. ECC is used to check (and recover) data integrity in memory, on disk, and over communications links. ECC is a more elaborate error detection method than parity; the sort used with memory can detect multiple-bit errors and can locate and fix single-bit errors.

**ECD** Enhanced Color Display. An EGA specification. A TTL monitor capable of displaying video signals with horizontal scan frequencies of 15.750 kHz (CGA) or 21.850 kHz (EGA) only.

**edge device** A device, such as a router or Ethernet-to-ATM switch, that is directly connected to an ATM network. The UNI defines the connection between the edge device and the ATM network switch. It is the first device a user sees when sending traffic to the ATM network. Also called an *end device*.

**EDI** Electronic Data Interchange. A method for passing orders, invoices, and other transactions electronically between locations or organizations.

**EDL** Ethernet Data Link.

**EDO** Extended Data Out. A form of DRAM technology that shortens the read cycle between memory and CPU by holding the data on the bus longer, which allows overlapped operation. On computer systems designed to support it, EDO memory allows a CPU to access memory 10 to 15 percent faster than comparable fast page mode chips.

**EEPLD** Electrically Erasable Programmable Logic Device. A CMOS programmable logic device (PLD) made by using EEPROM technology. It can be erased and reprogrammed.

**EEPROM** Electrically Erasable Programmable Read Only Memory. These are normally read-only chips (holding their contents when the power goes off) that can be erased on command.

**EGA** Enhanced Graphics Adapter. An IBM graphics standard capable of displaying 640 × 350 pixels in 16 colors out of a palette of 64 colors.

**EGP** Exterior Gateway Protocol (TCP/IP). The service by which gateways exchange information about what systems they can reach; generally, an exterior gateway protocol is any internetworking protocol for passing routing information between autonomous systems.

**EIA/TIA** Electronic Industries Association/Telecommunications Industries Association.

**EISA** Extended Industry Standard Architecture. A computer bus standard upward-compatible with ISA having a 32-bit data path.

**electronic mail (e-mail)** Messages sent electronically from one user to another over a network. Internet e-mail is based on the SMTP protocol.

**electrostatic discharge (esd)** The dissipation of electricity. ESD can easily destroy the semiconductor product.

**ELM** Ethernet LAN module.

**embedded** With reference to computer systems, an embedded system is one that is contained within a larger system and not used as an individual entity. For example, there is a processor embedded in a laser printer.

**encapsulation** Wrapping a data set in a protocol header. For example, Ethernet data is wrapped in a specific Ethernet header before network transit. Also, a method of bridging dissimilar networks where the entire frame from one network is simply enclosed in the header used by the link-layer protocol of the other network. Also, the process of applying a cured-plastic protective housing to components.

**encoder** The real-time MPEG-2 processor that converts digital studio masters into a digital tape formatted for DVD replication.

**encoding** A process by which redundant video information, elements that are the same or nearly so, are identified and removed. Encoding can remove over 97 percent of the data required to represent the video without affecting image quality. DVD uses the MPEG-2 digital video encoding standard.

**encryption** Applying a specific algorithm to data so as to alter the data's appearance and prevent other devices from reading the information without the appropriate knowledge. Decryption applies the algorithm in reverse to restore the data to its original form.

**enterprise network** Larger network connecting most major points in a company. Differs from a WAN in that it is typically private and contained within a single organization.

**EOS** ECC on SIMM. A data-integrity-checking technology that features ECC data-integrity checking built onto a SIMM.

**EPROM** Erasable Programmable Read Only Memory. These devices can be erased by placing them under an ultraviolet light for several minutes. They can then be reused.

**error detection and correction** The transmitting modem attaches a special pattern (called a frame check sequence) calculated according to a prescribed algorithm from user-defined data to the end of a block of data. The receiving modem performs the same algorithm and compares it to the one with the transmitted data. If these match, then the block of data has been received correctly. If not, the block of data is retransmitted until no errors are detected.

**escape sequence**  Generally, a sequence of characters in a data stream that indicates that the following characters are to receive unique interpretation. When sending data to an AT command set modem, the escape sequence of three plus symbols (+++) places the modem in command mode and interrupts user data transmission but does not terminate the data connection. This allows the entering of commands while the connection is maintained.

**ESF**  Extended Super Frame.

**ESM**  Ethernet switching module.

**etch**  A process using a chemical bath (wet etch) or a plasma (dry etch) that removes unwanted substances from the wafer surface.

**Ethernet**  A 10 Mbps baseband, CSMA/CD network originally designed by the Xerox Corporation. Ethernet is now an industry standard (Project 802.3 of the IEEE) that specifies protocols for connection and transmission in local area networks. Ethernet operates at 10 Mbps and now 100 Mbps. Also, the IEEE standard network media and physical layer protocols for transmission on a network medium. See also CSMA/CD.

**ETSI**  European Telecommunications Standards Institute.

**even parity**  A type of data-integrity checking where the parity bit checks for an even number of ones.

**Explorer Super Frame**  A frame sent out by a networked device in a source route bridging environment to determine the optimal route to another networked device.

**Extended AT command**  Extended commands were developed to provide greater functionality and control over modem operations than is available from the basic AT command set. Sadly, they're usually nonstandard.

**failure rate**  Description of the rate at which parts fail, usually expressed as percent per 1,000,000.

**FAQ**  Frequently Asked Questions. Files kept on the Internet on a variety of topics to make answers to common, widely asked questions available.

**Fast Ethernet**  A 100 Mbps technology based on the 10Base-T Ethernet CSMA/CD network access method.

**Fast Page Mode**  A common DRAM data-access scheme. Accessing DRAM is similar to finding information in a book. First, you turn to a particular page; then you select information from the page. Fast Page Mode enables the CPU to access new data in half the normal access time, as long as it is on the same page as the previous request.

**Fast SCSI** Provides for performance and compatibility enhancements to SCSI-1 by increasing the maximum synchronous data transfer rate on the SCSI bus from 5 Mbps to 10 Mbps.

**FAT** File Allocation Table. A DOS data structure, kept on the disk, that shows which clusters are in use for files, and which are available for use.

**fault tolerance** Generally, the capability to prevent a problem on a device from affecting other devices on the same port.

**fax mode** The modem is in fax mode when, through use of fax communications software, it can send and receive faxes, print and display fax files, convert files to fax files, and set certain fax-related features. Note: The modulation protocol used by the modem in fax mode is also different from the usual data mode modulation.

**FCM** FDDI concentrator module.

**FCS** First customer ship. The date the released final product is shipped to the sales channel.

**FCS** Frame check sequence. Extra characters added to a frame for error control purposes; an HDLC term adopted for subsequent link layer protocols.

**FDDI** Fiber Distributed Data Interface. An American National Standards Institute (ANSI) standard for a 100 Mbps token-passing ring based on fiber-optic transmission media.

**FEA** Fast Ethernet Alliance.

**FEAM** FDDI Enterprise Access Module.

**feature connector** A connector provided on graphics adapters to allow attaching other video-related devices (such as TV tuners).

**FECN** Forward Explicit Congestion Notification.

**FEP** Front-end processor. Device or board that provides a network interface for networked devices. In SNA, typically an IBM 3745 device.

**fiber-optic cable** A transmission medium that uses glass or plastic fibers, rather than copper wire, to transport data or voice signals. The signal is imposed on the fibers via modulated light from a laser or a light-emitting diode (LED). Because of its high bandwidth and lack of susceptibility to interference, fiber-optic cable is used in long-haul or noisy applications.

**file server** A device on a LAN that provides mass storage of files. A file server can be dedicated (only performs network service functions) or nondedicated (where user applications can coexist while the network is available).

**firewall** A router, workstation, or other computer with multiple network interfaces and software that controls and limits specific protocols, types of traffic within each protocol, types of services, and direction of the flow of information. Used to improve the security of a network.

**flag** A status bit that causes some indication of the state or condition of the processing unit.

**flash EPROM** PROM (Programmable read-only memory) technology providing nonvolatile storage that can be electrically erased in the circuit and reprogrammed; developed by Intel and licensed to other semiconductor companies.

**flash memory** A nonvolatile memory device that retains its data when the power is removed. The device is similar to EPROM with the exception that it can be electrically erased, whereas an EPROM must be exposed to ultraviolet light to erase.

**flatpack** A flat, rectangular IC package type with leads sticking out from the sides of the package.

**flat panel display** A computer display using plasma or LCD technology to produce an image.

**flip-flop** A circuit with two stable states that can be changed from one to the other. Flip-flops are the storage element in most SRAMs.

**floating** Pertaining to the condition of a device or circuit that is neither grounded nor connected to any potential. (Potential is voltage course or current course).

**floating gate** In Silicon Gate MOS technology: a gate that is not directly connected to the rest of the circuit. Used in EEPROMs.

**flooding** A technique where routing information received by a routing device is sent out through every interface on that device except the one on which the information was received.

**flow control** A computer interaction technique that compensates for the difference between the rate at which data reaches a device and the rate at which the device processes and transmits. The two common types of flow control used with modems are RTS/CTS signaling (a hardware-based method, employing an electrical signal) and XON/XOFF (a software-based method using standard ASCII control characters to pause or resume transmission).

**FLP** Fast Link Pulse.

**FOIRL** Fiber optic inter-repeater link. A fiber-optic signaling methodology based on the IEEE 802.3 fiber-optic specification.

**FPM** Fast Page Mode. A feature used to support faster sequential access to DRAM by allowing any number of accesses to the currently open row to be made after supplying the row address just once.

**Fractional T-1** A WAN communications service that provides the user with some portion of a T1 circuit that has been divided into 24 separate 64 Kbps channels; Fractional E-1 in Europe.

**fragment** A piece of a larger packet that has been broken down into smaller units.

**fragmentation** Breaking a packet into smaller units when transmitting over a network medium that cannot support the original size of the packet. Also, disjoint storage of files on a disk, which degrades performance.

**frame** Set of bits that form an elementary block of data to be sent over a communications channel. Usually, a frame contains its own control information, including the transmission address and data for error detection.

**Frame Relay** A packet-switching wide-area technology for interconnecting LANs at high speeds. Frame Relay defines the interface between user equipment and a WAN; it does not define internal operation of the network or the interfaces or protocols used within the WAN itself. For this reason, the term "Frame-Relay cloud" is often used to describe the internal operation of a WAN that has a Frame-Relay interface.

**frequency converter** A device or system that can change the frequency of an alternating current, whether or not it changes the voltage or phase.

**FSP** File Service Protocol.

**FTP** File Transfer Protocol (TCP/IP). The Internet application and protocol used to send complete files over TCP/IP services.

**full duplex** The capability of a device or line to transmit data simultaneously in both directions.

**functional grouping** Placing all users performing the same function, and the servers they require, on the same ring. A means to reduce network traffic outside the related group of computers.

**FUNI** Frame-based UNI.

**gateway** A device that can interconnect networks using different communications protocols. The gateway performs a protocol conversion to translate one set of protocols to another (for example, from TCP/IP to SNA or from TCP/IP to X.25). Contrast bridge and router.

**Gbps** Gigabits per second.

**General MIDI** A table of 128 standard sounds or instruments for MIDI cards and synthesizers.

**GGP** Gateway-to-Gateway Protocol. A MILNET protocol that uses a distributed shortest path algorithm to control how core gateways (or routers) should exchange access and routing information.

**gigabit** Approximately 1 billion bits: 1 bit × $1,024^3$ (that is, 1,073,741,824 bits).

**Gigabit Ethernet** A proposed IEEE standard for 1,000 Mbps Ethernet.

**gigabyte** Approximately 1 billion bytes: 1 byte × $1024^3$ (that is, 1,073,741,824 bytes).

**GND** Ground.

**gold wire** The wire used to make a physical connection from an integrated circuit device to the leadframe.

**GPF** A trap within the processor when a program performs an illegal operation (such as accessing restricted spaces in memory).

**guardbands** The high and low temperature limits used to make sure parts are being tested within an acceptable temperature range. On a hot test, the guardbands are normally set at +/–3 degrees Centigrade. At a room temperature test, they are normally set at +4/–9 degrees Centigrade.

**guard tone** Guard tones are used in the United Kingdom and other countries. This requires that the modem transmit an 1,800 Hz tone after it sends an answer tone. Guard tones are not used in the United States.

**GUI** Graphical user interface.

**half duplex** Data transmission that can occur in two directions over a single line, but only one direction at a time. Contrast full duplex.

**hard failure** Parts that fail functionality testing. In integrated circuits, hard failures have a visual defect 99 percent of the time, such as poly or metal bridging, missing geometries or layers, particles, or contaminants.

**hardware graphics cursor** Provides a faster method of displaying/moving a cursor (GUI arrow) on the screen. The video adapter's main chipset controls this function, which resides in system memory, as opposed to slower handling by the application software. Also called a sprite.

**Hayes-compatible** Hayes Microcomputer Products, Inc. developed the AT command set, now a de facto industry standard. Hayes commands are always initiated with an AT (attention code) prefix.

**HDLC** High-Speed Data Link Control. A protocol defined by the International Standards Organization and used in X.25 communications; specifies an encapsulation method for data on synchronous serial data links. Various manufacturers have proprietary versions of HDLC, including IBM's SDLC.

**heat sink** A structure attached to or part of a semiconductor device that serves the purpose of dissipating heat to the surrounding environment. Some packages serve as heat sinks.

**HGC** Hercules Graphics Card. Compatible with MDA, but also capable of displaying 720 × 348 pixels in a four-bank graphics mode.

**hierarchical routing** Routing based on a hierarchical addressing system. IP routing algorithms use IP addresses, for example, which contain network numbers, host numbers, and, frequently, subnet numbers.

**hi-res** Short for "high resolution," at one time meaning 640 × 350 resolution and above. Hi-res is a moving target, and currently means (at least) "higher than 640 × 480 resolution."

**HLM** Heterogeneous LAN Management. Management of LANs that contain dissimilar devices running different protocols and different applications.

**hook flash** The dial modifier "!" causes the modem to go on-hook (hang up) for one-half second. Also controlled by the ATH command.

**hop** A unit that equates to the passage of a packet through one router.

**hop count** A routing metric used to measure the distance between a source and a destination.

**horizontal scan rate** The frequency in kHz (kilohertz) at which the monitor is scanned in a horizontal direction; high horizontal scan rates produce higher resolution. The EGA horizontal scan rate is 21.8 kHz, while the extended EGA horizontal scan rate is 30.1 kHz.

**host** A computer in which a host adapter is installed; the computer housing the host adapter. The host uses software to request the services of the host adapter in transferring information to and from peripheral devices attached to the SCSI bus connector of the host adapter.

**host adapter** A printed circuit board that installs in a standard microcomputer and provides an I/O bus connection so that devices can be connected to the microcomputer.

**HSSI** High-Speed Serial Interface. A de facto standard for high-speed serial communications at up to 52 Mbps over WAN links. Used for the physical connection between a router and a DSU.

**HTML** Hypertext Markup Language.

**HTTP** The Hypertext Transfer Protocol.

**hub** A concentrator or repeater in a star topology at which node connections meet.

**IBM PC AT compatible** Typically, any computer system that uses an ISA backplane bus and follows the usual BIOS conventions.

**IC** Integrated circuit. An electronic circuit consisting of components and connectors contained on a semiconductor chip. Usually packaged in a plastic or ceramic case with external connector pins.

**ICMP** Internet Control Message Protocol (TCP/IP). The collection of messages exchanged by IP modules in both hosts and gateways to report errors, problems, and operating information. You interact through ICMP when you use the Ping command.

**ID** Identification Detect. Pins present on DIMMs to provide information to the system using the module.

**IEEE** Institute of Electrical and Electronics Engineers. A professional organization that, among other things, defines network standards, such as Ethernet. IEEE committees develop and propose computer standards. Members represent an international cross section of users, vendors, and engineering professionals.

**IEEE-488** One of several standards set by IEEE (Institute of Electrical and Electronics Engineers) for communication between pieces of electronic apparatus. Based on GPIB (General Purpose Interface Bus) technology developed by Hewlett-Packard.

**IETF** Internet Engineering Task Force. The technical body that oversees the development of the Internet suite of protocols.

**I-frame** Frames that generally occur twice during every 30 frames of digital video, depending on the complexity of the picture. I-frames work to reduce data by providing a full frame reference of the video image. The I-frames identify the entire background and are the initial reference frames for bidirectional and P-frames.

**IGP** Interior Gateway Protocol. The protocol used to exchange routing information between collaborating routers in the Internet. RIP and OSPF are examples of IGPs.

**ILMI** Interim Local Management Interface. An interim requirements definition in ATM Forum Specification UNI 3.1. It supports bidirectional exchange of management information between UNI Management Entities related to the ATM layer and physical layer parameters.

**impedance** The resistance and reactance a wire offers to a change in current as the current runs down the length of the wire, measured in ohms.

**Industry Standard Architecture (ISA)** The IBM PC-AT functions have been duplicated by a number of manufacturers. All the IBM PC-AT compatible machines use a backplane bus that very closely emulates the function of the backplane bus of the PC-AT. Because of the broad usage of this bus structure, it has become known as the Industry Standard Architecture bus, even though there is no currently accepted standard for the bus.

**infant mortality failure** A part that fails early in its lifetime due to manufacturing defects.

**input packet filtering** Security filtering applied to packets immediately upon reaching the router, before they reach the router's internal forwarding processing. Because the packets never enter the router, the router itself is protected against an external attack.

**interlaced** A screen scanned by a method that results in alternate lines being drawn with each full pass of the electron beam. The resulting display is less stable than a flicker-free noninterlaced display.

**InterLata** InterLata are connections between local access companies, that is, long-distance connections.

**Internet** The worldwide internetwork, incorporating large backbone nets (MILNET, NSFNET, and CREN, for example) and an array of regional and local campus networks worldwide. Uses the Internet protocol suite.

**Internet address** A 32-bit address assigned to hosts using TCP/IP.

**Internet Assigned Numbers Authority (IANA)** The central registry for various Internet protocol parameters, such as port, protocol, and enterprise numbers.

**Internet Relay Chat (IRC)**  An Internet service that allows multiple users to converse in real time on different subjects (each subject is called a channel).

**Internet service provider (ISP)**  A company that sells dial-up (or other) access to the Internet.

**Internetwork**  A series of networks interconnected by routers or other devices that functions as a single network. Sometimes called an internet, which is not synonymous with the Internet.

**Interrupt 13**  This is the software interrupt for disk I/O used by DOS. DOS does "Interrupt 13 calls" to read or write from a floppy disk. A SCSI host adapter translates these Interrupt 13 commands into SCSI commands for SCSI disk drives.

**Interrupt 19**  This is the software interrupt that handles the boot function. The boot code is typically handled by the motherboard BIOS.

**inverse multiplexing**  The logical aggregation of multiple switched circuits to achieve a higher effective transmission speed.

**I/O**  Refers to an operation, program, or device whose purpose is to enter data into or to extract data from a computer.

**I/O port**  A connection to a CPU that is configured or programmed to provide a data path between the CPU and external devices such as a keyboard, display, or reader; it may be an input port or an output port, or it may be bidirectional.

**IOPS**  Input/output (operations or requests) per second.

**IP**  Internet Protocol. Associated with TCP and UDP, IP is a set of communications protocols developed to internetwork dissimilar systems.

**IP address**  The sequence of four numbers that identify your computer on the Internet.

**IP address mask**  A sequence of numbers (for instance, 255.255.255.0) that divides your IP address into the network portion (for instance, 255.255.255) and the host number portion (for instance, 0).

**IP spoofing**  The use of a forged IP source address to circumvent a firewall. The packet appears to have come from inside the protected network and to be eligible for forwarding into the network.

**IP switching**  A hardware-based technology to speed the operation of router functions.

**IP/RIP** Internet Protocol/Routing Internet Protocol.

**IPX** Internetwork Packet Exchange. A Novell NetWare communications protocol used to route messages from one node to another. Novell's version of IP (not directly interoperable with IP).

**IR** An abbreviation for infrared.

**IRQ** Interrupt request. The identifier of a signal that a device can send to the processor to indicate it needs service.

**IS** Intermediate system. A bridge, router, gateway, or hub that interconnects network segments.

**ISA** Industry Standard Architecture. A type of computer bus used in most PCs. ISA enables expansion devices such as network cards, video adapters, and modems to send data to and receive data from the PC's CPU and memory 16 bits at a time. Expansion devices are plugged into sockets in the PC's motherboard. ISA is sometimes called the AT bus, because it was originally introduced with the IBM PC-AT in 1983.

**ISDN** Integrated Services Digital Network. The recommendation published by CCITT for private or public digital telephone networks where binary data, such as graphics and digitized voice and data transmission, pass over the same digital network that carries most telephone transmissions today. Further definition within the United States can be found in the National ISDN Standard.

**ISO/OSI** International Standards Organization/Open Systems Interconnection.

**ITU** International Telecommunication Union.

**ITU-TSS** International Telecommunication Union Telecommunications Standardization Sector.

**IXC** Interexchange Carrier. A long-distance telephone company offering circuit-switched, leased-line, or packet-switched service or some combination.

**jabber** The uncontrolled transmission of oversized frames to the network by a faulty device. This occurs when there are excessively long data packets being transmitted from the node (workstation or server). At that point, the hub, or concentrator, partitions (isolates) the node from the network until the condition is corrected.

**JEDEC** Joint Electron Device Engineering Council, the group that establishes the industry standards for memory operation, features, and packaging.

**jitter**  Variance in the timing of arrival of signals or packets. Jitter causes degradation of the signal as it traverses the cable or the network interface cards (NICs). Common in token ring environments and causes errors in accuracy of signal.

**Kbps**  Kilobits per second (multiples of one thousand and twenty-four bits per second).

**keys**  Notches on a memory module or other connector that prevent it from being installed incorrectly or into an incompatible system.

**kilobit**  Approximately one thousand bits: 1 bit × $2^{10}$ (that is, 1,024 bits).

**kilobyte**  Approximately one thousand bytes: 1 byte × $2^{10}$ (that is, 1,024 bytes).

**Kpps**  Kilo packets per second (one thousand packets per second).

**LAN**  Local area network. A data communications network confined to a limited geographic area, with moderate to high data rates (100 Kbps to 100 Mbps, for example). The area served may consist of a single building or a campus-type arrangement. A LAN is typically owned by its users, includes some type of switching technology, and does not use common carrier circuits (although it may have gateways or bridges to other public or private networks).

**LANE (LAN Emulation)**  As specified by the ATM Forum, a standard implementation for making edge devices appear as though they were attached to a LAN. An emulated LAN has all of the benefits (and weaknesses) of the traditional LANs they are emulating. Currently only Ethernet and Token Ring LAN Emulation are specified. Most vendors are implementing Ethernet LAN Emulation first.

**LAN segmentation**  Dividing LAN bandwidth into multiple independent LANs to improve performance.

**LAPM**  Link Access Protocol Modem. A V.42 type of error correction protocol. LAPM may be activated with or without V.42bis data compression.

**laser scribe**  A process using a laser to melt the silicon in a dot matrix to form wafer scribe numbers.

**LAT**  Local Area Transport. A protocol developed by Digital Equipment Corporation.

**LATA**  Local access transport area. A telephone company term that defines a geographic area; sometimes corresponds to an area code.

**Latch**  A circuit element that stores a given value on its output until told to store a different value.

**latch up** An undesired phenomenon in an integrated circuit whereby a circuit locks in a certain state and will not change.

**latch voltage** The effective input voltage at which a flip-flop changes states.

**latency** Delay between two events, such as the time delay between when the first bit of a packet is received and the last bit is forwarded.

**layer** A level of the OSI Reference Model. Each layer performs certain tasks to move the information from sender to receiver. Protocols within the layers define the tasks for networks, but not how the software accomplishes the tasks. Interfaces pass information between the layers they connect.

**lead** One of the metal extensions from an IC package or discrete component that connects the component to the PCB. The leg or contact point of the component that is either physically soldered to a PC board or placed within a socket for connection.

**leadframe** A metal structure that is part of an integrated circuit device. The die is attached to the leadframe.

**leads** Also "legs": The official name for the metal "feet" on an IC. Also called "pins." The part of the lead assembly that is formed after a portion of the lead frame is cut away. The part's connection to the outside world.

**leakage** Undesirable conductive paths in components, subsystems, and systems; also the current through such paths.

**leased line** Also referred to as a private line. A leased line is obtained from a communications company (carrier) to provide a transmission medium between two points. The line consists of a permanent dedicated circuit between two points, or to a set of previously arranged points. The cost of the line is usually based on the distance between locations. This is in contrast to switched or dial-up lines, which can be connected to any point on the network.

**LEC** Local exchange carrier. Jargon for your local telephone company.

**LEC** LAN emulation client. An edge device, directly attached to the ATM Network, operating in an ATM Emulated LAN. This can be, for example, a PC, a router, or an Ethernet-to-ATM switch directly connected to the ATM switch running LAN Emulation Client software.

**LECS** LAN emulation configuration server.

**LED** Light-emitting diode.

**LEN** Low-Entry Networking.

**LES** LAN emulation server.

**life testing** Accelerated testing of electronic components to establish their field reliability.

**linear circuit** A circuit that produces a voltage output approximately proportional to the input voltage, generally over a limited range of voltage and frequency.

**linear regulator** A power supply design in which the voltage is held constant by dissipating much of the total power as a margin.

**Line In** A connector on audio equipment to which a device such as a CD player or tape cassette player may be attached. See also Line-Out.

**line modulation** The means by which a carrier is varied to represent a signal carrying information. In a modem, the user's digital data is used to modulate the modem's transmitter's carrier to allow the digital signal to be carried over analog facilities.

**Line Out** A connector on audio equipment to which audio components can be attached such as stereo speakers. See also Line In.

**link** A physical connection between two nodes in a network. It can consist of a data communication circuit or a direct channel (cable) connection.

**Listserv** An automated mailing list distribution system. Listservs are organized by topic of interest and maintained on an ad hoc basis.

**LMI** Local Management Interface.

**load balancing** In routing, the capability of the router to distribute traffic over all its network ports that are the same distance from the destination address. It increases the use of network segments, which increases effective network bandwidth.

**local loop** The line from a telephone customer's premises to the telephone company CO (central office).

**logical ring** A network that is treated logically as a ring even though it may be cabled as a physical star topology.

**logic board** See Motherboard.

**logic circuit** An integrated circuit that provides a fixed set of output signals according to the signals present at the input.

**logic gate** Several individual device functions on an integrated circuit chip.

**long space disconnect** Determines whether or not a modem disconnects when it receives a continuous break from a remote modem.

**loopback tests** Means to verify correct operation of circuits. In modem practice, there are four types of loopback tests: (1) the local digital loopback tests the operation of the DTE, including whether or not data is leaving the terminal or computer port; (2) the local analog loopback tests the digital and analog circuits of the modem; (3) the remote digital loopback checks the operating condition of the line and remote modem; (4) the remote analog loopback tests the line to the remote modem.

**LSA** LAN Security Architecture.

**LSL** Link support layer.

**LUNI** LAN emulation user network interface.

**MAC** Media Access Control. A method of controlling access to a transmission medium. For example, token ring, Ethernet, or FDDI.

**make/break ratio** The ratio of the off-hook (make) to on-hook (break) interval used by the modem when it pulse dials.

**MAN** Metropolitan area network. A data communication network covering the geographic area of a city (generally, larger than a LAN but smaller than a WAN). FDDI can provide a private MAN, whereas IEEE 802.6 can provide a public MAN.

**management information base** Data from a device that can be accessed via a network management protocol.

**MAU** Medium attachment unit, or multistation access unit. A hub in a token ring network; each MAU supports up to eight nodes and servers and can be connected to other units to create large networks.

**Mb** Megabit.

**MB** Megabyte.

**MBONE (multicast backbone)** An interconnected set of Internet subnetworks and routers that support the delivery of IP multicast traffic. The MBONE is a virtual network that is layered on top of sections of the physical Internet.

**Mbps** Megabits per second (one million bits per second).

**MBps** Megabytes per second (one million bytes per second).

**MCA** Micro Channel Architecture. IBM PS/2 (models 50–95) and compatible computers had an MCA computer bus inside. Can be driven by multiple independent bus master processors.

**MCS** MultiCast Server.

**MDA** Monochrome Display Adapter. Early IBM Video display board designed for use with IBM monochrome text standard.

**megabit** Approximately one million bits: 1 bit × 1,024² (that is, 1,048,576 bits).

**megabits per second** A megabit contains one million bits. Megabits per second is a measurement of processing speed broken down to the smallest binary digit, a bit.

**megabyte** Approximately one million bytes: 1 byte × 1,024² (that is, 1,048,576 bytes).

**memory** The term commonly used to refer to a computer system's random access memory (see also RAM). The term "memory" has also been used to refer to all types of electronic data storage (see also Storage). A computer system's memory is crucial to its operation; without memory, a computer could not read programs or retain data. Memory stores data electronically in memory cells contained in chips. The two most common types of memory chips are DRAM and SRAM.

**memory bank** A logical unit of memory in a computer, the size of which is determined by the computer's CPU. For example, a 32-bit CPU calls for memory banks that provide 32 bits of information at a time.

**memory controller** The interface between system memory and the central processing unit. The memory controller consists of special circuitry — usually a microprocessor — within a computer system that interprets requests from the central processing unit in order to locate data locations, or addresses, in memory.

**memory cycle** The minimum amount of time required for a memory to complete a cycle such as read, write, read/write, or read/modify/write.

**memory types** Cache Data SRAM: a quick-access chip. DRAM: dynamic random access memory. EPROM: erasable, programmable, read-only memory. PROM: programmable read-only memory. RAM: random access memory. ROM: read-only memory (permanent memory that cannot be changed). SRAM: static random access memory.

**MIB** Management information base. A collection of objects that can be accessed via a network management protocol.

**micron** A unit of measure equivalent to one-millionth of a meter; synonymous with micrometer.

**MIDI** Musical Instrument Digital Interface. A standard that allows for the exchange of data between two music synthesizers or a synthesizer and a computer. Sound data may be communicated from the synthesizer to the computer and stored as a MIDI file. Or a MIDI file can be transmitted to the synthesizer for playback.

**MIPS** Millions of instructions per second. This measurement is generally used when describing the speed of computer systems.

**MLID** Multiple link interface drive.

**MNP** Microcom Networking Protocol. A series of data communications protocols developed by Microcom for full-duplex, error-free communications.

**modulation** A process by which signal characteristics are transformed to represent information. In DVD, signal modulation refers to the process by which the bits representing user data are converted to the modulation code bits recorded on the disc. This process increases reading accuracy and reduces crosstalk between primary signal information and tracking servo mechanism pits on the disc. DVD utilizes an eight-to-sixteen modulation system that creates a slightly larger buffer between streams of digital information, ensuring a high measure of accuracy in signal processing.

**monolithic** Contained on one chip or substrate, as a microprocessor system including not only the logic but also memory or input/output circuits.

**MOS** Metal oxide semiconductor. Layers used to create a semiconductor circuit. A thin insulating layer of oxide is deposited on the surface of the wafer. Then a highly conductive layer of tungsten silicide is placed over the top of the oxide dielectric.

**MOS device** A device in which current flow occurs in a single channel of P- or N-type material and is controlled by an insulated electrode on the surface of the channel region.

**MOS process** The set of chemical and metallurgical steps used to make MOS large scale integration.

**motherboard** Also known as logic board, main board, or system board; your computer's main electronics board, which in most cases either contains all CPU, memory, and I/O functions or has expansion slots that support them.

**MPC** Multimedia PC. A computer configured to store and retrieve large multimedia files according to one of several industry specifications.

**MPEG** Motion Picture Expert Group. A type of lossy data compression for storage and playback of video and audio data.

**MPEG-1** A form of digital signal compression developed by the Moving Pictures Expert Group, a division of ISO (International Standards Organization). MPEG-1 is a small-picture format mode offering a resolution of 352 X 240 pixels and operating at a rate of 30 frames per second with CD-quality audio. This system achieves more than a 6:1 compression ratio.

**MPEG-2** The standard used to compress DVD video in North America. In Europe, both video and audio are compressed using the MPEG-2 compression standards. MPEG-2 operates at a resolution of 720 × 480 pixels and delivers 30 frames of video playback per second with a variable compression ration as high as 200:1. Broadcast-quality video can be achieved with a 30:1 compression ratio. MPEG-2 supports MPEG-1 playback.

**MPOA** MultiProtocol over ATM.

**MPR** Multiprotocol router.

**MSCDEX** Microsoft CD-Extensions. A DOS-resident program that interprets a CD-ROM file system.

**MTBF** Mean time between failures.

**MTTF** Mean time to failure.

**MTTR** Mean Time to repair.

**MTU** Maximum transmission unit. The largest possible unit of data that can be sent on a given physical medium.

**multicast** A special form of broadcast where copies of the packet are delivered only to a subset of all possible destinations.

**Multi-Language** A DVD feature that allows up to eight different audio tracks to be mastered on a single Digital Video Disc. Users can then select the language track that suits their preferences.

**multilink ppp** Multilink PPP is a variant of PPP that addresses the additional features of compression and channel aggregation. PPP-ML, as it is known, is outlined in IETF RFC 1717.

**multimedia** A combination of media used for entertainment, education, and communication.

**multiple-frequency monitor** A monitor capable of displaying video signals over a wide range of horizontal scan frequencies. This may include a horizontal capture range from 5.5 kHz to 35 kHz or wider. Examples of monitors in this class are the NEC MultiSync and the Sony Multiscan. The Multiscan has a wide horizontal scan capture range that enables it to display monochrome signals.

**multiplexer** A telecommunications device that funnels multiple signals onto a single channel.

**multiplexing** A technique that enables several data streams to be sent over a single physical link. Also, MUX.

**Multipurpose Internet Mail Extensions (MIME)** An Internet standard for converting multiple file formats to ASCII text prior to transmission in e-mail.

**multitasking** The execution of commands in such a way that more than one command is in progress at the same time.

**nano** Literally, one-billionth ($10^{-9}$).

**nanometer** A measurement equal to one-billionth of a meter. The shorter-wavelength thinner-beam red laser incorporated in DVD players measures 650 nanometers compared to 780 nanometers for a conventional CD player laser.

**nanosecond** One billionth of a second. Light travels approximately eight inches in one nanosecond.

**nanosecond (ns)** One billionth of a second. Memory data access times are measured in nanoseconds. For example, memory access times for typical 30- and 72-pin SIMM modules range from 60 to 100 nanoseconds.

**Narrow SCSI** A term for 8-bit standard SCSI devices. This term is necessary to distinguish 8-bit SCSI devices from 16-bit Wide SCSI devices.

**National ISDN1** NI-1 is the ISDN standard in the United States. It is the first successful attempt to standardize at a level allowing the same end-user equipment to connect transparently to different switch vendor's equipment. Prior to this standard, all end-user equipment needed to understand the particulars of the switch to which it was connected.

**NC** Not connected.

**NCP** Network Control Protocol (or Program).

**NDIS** Network Driver Interface Specification. Produced by Microsoft, a specification for a generic, hardware- and protocol-independent device driver for NICs.

**negotiation fallback** Setting this register in a modem indicates what action to take when a desired connection cannot be made (for instance, hang-up, direct mode connect, normal mode connect).

**NET3** Norme Europenne de Telecommunications 3 is the European-wide standard for ISDN. The trade name for the standard is EuroISDN.

**NetBIOS** Network Basic Input/Output System. Standard interface to networks on IBM PC and compatible systems. Rarely used any longer.

**NetID** Network Identifier.

**Network Driver Interface Specification** Microsoft/3Com specification for a generic, hardware- and protocol-independent device driver for network interface cards.

**Network layer** The protocol layer that is responsible for routing, switching, and subnetwork access.

**Network News Transfer Protocol (NNTP)** The Internet protocol supporting Usenet newsgroups.

**network topology** The arrangement of nodes usually forming a star, ring, tree, or bus pattern.

**NFS** Network File System.

**nibble** Usually four bits or half a byte.

**NIC** Network interface card. See also adapter.

**N-ISDN** Narrowband ISDN.

**NLM** NetWare loadable module.

**NLPID** Network layer protocol identifier.

**NLSP** NetWare Link Services Protocol (Novell).

**NMOS** N-channel metal oxide semiconductor. This pertains to MOS devices constructed on a P-type substrate in which electrons flow between N-type source and drain contacts. NMOS devices are typically two to three times faster than PMOS devices.

**NNI** Network-to-network interface.

**node** Any device including servers and workstations connected to a network; also the point where devices are connected.

**nonvolatile memory** A memory that retains information if power is removed and then reapplied.

**nonvolatile RAM** Also NVRAM. Random access memory whose data is retained when power is turned off. This is especially useful for modems to store user-defined default configuration settings and frequently used telephone numbers. This information would be loaded into modem RAM at power-up.

**NOS** Network operating system.

**NS** nanosecond (ns). One billionth of a second; used to measure the speed of digital parts.

**NT1** NT1 is the equipment required to convert from the two-wire U interface to the four-wire S/T interface. This equipment is *not required* outside North America.

**NT2** Network Termination, type 2.

**NTFS** NT File System. This alternative to the DOS FAT file system is used by Windows NT to provide increased performance and enhanced security.

**NTSA** Network Technical Support Alliance.

**NTSC** National Television System Committee, which devised the NTSC television broadcast system in 1953. The NTSC standard has a fixed vertical resolution of 525 horizontal lines stacked on top of each other, with varying numbers of "lines" making up the horizontal resolution, depending on the electronics and formats involved. There are 59.94 fields displayed per second. A field is a set of even lines, or odd lines. The odd and even fields are displayed sequentially, thus, interlacing the full frame. One full frame, therefore, is made of two interlaced fields and is displayed about every 1/30 of a second.

**numerical aperture** The number representing the lens aperture of a laser pick-up device. An increased numerical aperture, 0.6 on a DVD player, allows for the finer track pitch, pit length, and pitch width necessary for the increased storage capacity of a DVD. Thinner substrates that diffuse less light allow a laser with an increased aperture to be utilized while still maintaining high reading accuracy.

**NVRAM** Nonvolatile Random Access Memory.

**OC-*n*** Optical Carrier *n*. Optical signal standards. The "n" indicates the level where the respective data rate is exactly "n" times the first level, OC-1. OC-1 has a data rate of 51.84 Mbps. OC-3 is thus three times OC-1, or 155.52 Mbps. A c following an OC level identifies concatenation of payload (for instance, OC-3c).

**odd parity** A type of data-integrity checking where the parity bit checks for an odd number of ones.

**ODI** Open Data-link Interface. A Novell specification providing standardized access to networks.

**ohm** A unit of measure of electrical resistance.

**online state** Same as data mode. To transmit or receive data, the modem must be in the online state. When placing a call, the modem is put online with the dial command.

**open**  A circuit interruption that results in an incomplete path for the current flow. (for instance, an open wire or switch that opens the path of the current).

**open source**  Computer software for which the source code is made available for public examination and modification.

**operating system**  Software controlling the overall operation of a multipurpose computer system, including such tasks as memory allocation, input and output distribution, interrupt processing, and job scheduling.

**operational amplifier**  An electronic circuit that amplifies "linear" (also called analog) signals.

**Optic-RAM**  A 64K or 256K DRAM in a package with a clear glass top. The DRAM has a natural sensitivity to light that can be exploited to send a "picture" to a computer.

**OSF**  Open Software Foundation.

**OSI**  Open Systems Interconnection. The goal for internetworking computers from different vendors, to be achieved by full adherence to international standards.

**OSI reference model**  A seven-layer network architecture model of data communication protocols developed by ISO and CCITT. Each layer specifies particular network functions such as addressing, flow control, error control, encapsulation, and reliable message transfer.

**OSPF**  Open Shortest Path First. A routing protocol for TCP/IP networks.

**output packet filtering**  Filtering applied to packets after they have been through the router's internal forward processing.

**packet**  A collection of bits comprising data and control information formatted for transmission from one node to another.

**packet filtering**  Examination of en-route packets by a router to decide whether or not to allow transmission of each packet.

**packetization**  Information that, instead of being transported as a constant stream of information, is transported as blocks.

**packet-switched network**  A network in which data is transmitted in units called *packets*. The packets can be routed individually over the best available network connection and reassembled to form a complete message at the destination.

**packet switching**  A type of data transfer that occupies a communication link only during the time of actual data transmission. Messages are split into packets and reassembled at the receiving end of the communication link.

**PAD** Packet assembler-dissembler. The mechanism for disassembling packets at the sending end and assembling them to form the complete message at the receiving end; traditionally used in X.25 networks.

**pad** A conductive bonding island located on circuit chips for interconnecting circuit elements or for bringing connections from circuit leads to the outside.

**page** The bits that can be accessed from one memory row address.

**page mode** A mode in which if RAS is kept low and the DRAM is given a column address without being given a new row address, the chip will remember which row it was on the last time and automatically stay on that row.

**PAL** PAL stands for Phase Alternation by Line and refers to a standard that was adopted in Europe for television signals in 1967. It has 625 horizontal lines making up the vertical resolution. 50 fields are displayed and interlaced per second, making for a 25-frame-per-second system. Also Programmable Array Logic, a device that can be programmed to do certain logic functions. Then a fuse inside of the device can be blown so the programmed information can never be changed. Sometimes called a PLD (Programmable Logic Device) Language.

**palette** The range of colors from which you can select the actual colors that the video adapter will display simultaneously. Also, the hardware in a video board that stores the available colors.

**PAP** Password Authentication Protocol.

**PAR** Positive Acknowledgment with Retransmission.

**parametrics** A series of voltage and current tests that checks for variations in the fabrication process. Test results are used by engineers to modify or correct processes.

**parametric test** A test of a chip that checks for pin leakage, the amount of current it draws, opens, and shorts.

**parity** A method of data-integrity checking that adds a single bit to each byte of data. The parity bit is responsible for checking for errors in the other 8 bits.

**parity bit** A bit added to a group of bits to detect the presence of an error.

**passive device** A circuit element without an energy source such as a capacitor or resistor.

**PBX** Private branch exchange. A telephone switch at a customer site.

**PCB**  Printed circuit board. A component made up of layers of copper and fiberglass; the surface of a PCB features a pattern of copper lines, or "traces," that provide electrical connections for chips and other components that mount on the surface of the PCB. Examples: motherboard, SIMM, credit card memory, and so on.

**PCI**  Peripheral Component Interconnect. A type of high-speed computer bus.

**PCM**  Physical Connection Management (FDDI).

**PCM**  Linear audio pulse code modulation.

**PCMCIA**  Personal Computer Memory Card International Association. Now called PC Card. A standard that allows interchangeability of various computing components on the same connector. The PCMCIA standard is designed to support input/output devices, including memory, fax/modem, SCSI, and networking products.

**PD**  Presence Detect. Indicator pins on SIMMs and DIMMs that provide information to the system using the module.

**PDN**  Public data network.

**PDS**  Packet-Driver Specification.

**PDU**  Protocol data unit. OSI terminology for "packet." A PDU is a data object exchanged by protocol machines within a given layer of the OSI Reference Model containing both Protocol Control Information and user data.

**peer-to-peer communications**  A type of communications and data exchange between peer entities on two or more networks.

**PEP**  Packet Exchange Protocol.

**perimeter network**  A small, single-segment network between a firewall and the Internet for services that the organization wants to make publicly accessible to the Internet without exposing the network as a whole.

**peripheral**  A device installed on a computer system.

**P-frame**  As a part of MPEG-2 decoding, P-frames are constructed by analyzing previous frames and estimating where objects will be in the next frame. The capability to predict where static and moving objects will appear in successive frames provides superior adaptivity to motion in the picture. P-frames take up the least possible amount of bandwidth in transmission.

**PGA**  Pin Grid Array.

**PHY** Short for physical layer. The network protocol layer that passes data from the media to the ATM layer, and vice versa. Also, the physical layer of FDDI; also, a term for FDDI fiber-optic cable. In the layer structure, PHY is positioned between the MAC and the PMD.

**pin** The metal extensions from an IC package or discrete component that connect the component to the PCB.

**Ping** A program used to test reachability of destinations by sending them an ICMP echo request and waiting for a reply. Ping is used as a verb: "Ping the host to see if it is available."

**pin-one hole** The hole located on the "pin one" side of the leadframe.

**pin-one indicator** An indentation or mark on the top of the part that indicates where the first lead of the die inside is located.

**PIO** Programmed input/output. A method of data transfer in which the host microprocessor transfers data to and from memory via the computer's I/O ports. PIO enables very fast data transfer rates, especially in single-tasking operating systems like DOS.

**pitch** A sound's tone, usually determined by the sound's frequency.

**pits and lands** The recording surface of a CD-ROM or DVD disc is made up of a series of impressions (pits) and flat surfaces (lands) that are read by a laser as the series of ones and zeros (Binary code) comprising audio, video and tracking information.

**pixel** A single dot on the CRT display. This word is derived from the words "picture" and "element."

**PLA** Programmable logic array. An array of logic elements that can be programmed to perform a specific logic function. It can be as simple as a gate or as complex as a ROM and can be programmed (often by mask programming) so that a given input combination produces a known output function.

**PLL** Phase-locked loop. A function that ensures accurate signal timing in a token ring network automatically, as opposed to Tank circuits, which must be adjusted manually.

**Plug and Play** A standard, pioneered by Microsoft and endorsed by industry leaders. This standard hopes to address the problems of adding I/O adapters to a PC computer system. Adapters designed to the Plug and Play standard will self-configure and will automatically resolve system resources such as interrupts (IRQ), DMA, port addresses, and BIOS addresses.

**PMD**  Physical (layer) Media Dependent. Refers to the part of a network interface card's design that must interface with (and is therefore dependent on) the chosen transmission medium (for instance, Unshielded Twisted Pair or Multi Mode Fiber).

**PMOS**  P-channel metal oxide semiconductor. This pertains to MOS devices constructed on an N-type silicon substrate in which holes flow between source and drain contacts.

**PNNI**  Private Network-Node Interface. Allows multivendor switch interoperability for SVC setup. It will eventually allow dynamic ATM networks to be constructed with heterogeneous (multivendor) components.

**polling**  A method of controlling the sequence of transmission by devices on a multipoint line by requiring each device to wait until the controlling processor requests it to transmit.

**POP**  Point of presence.

**populated board**  A PCB with components.

**port density**  The number of ports, physical or logical, per network device.

**port I/O address**  A window through which software programs communicate commands to an installed host adapter board.

**POST**  Power-On Self-Test, a set of diagnostic routines that run when a computer is first turned on.

**Post Office Protocol (POP)**  An Internet standard protocol for reading mail from a server. The commonly used version is POP3.

**POTS**  Plain old telephone service. Really. POTS is the existing analog telephone lines and is the universal term in the telecommunications industry.

**power down**  To turn the system's power OFF.

**power up**  To turn the system's power ON.

**PPP**  Point-to-Point Protocol. Successor to SLIP; provides router-to-router and host-to-network connections over both synchronous and asynchronous circuits.

**PPS**  Packets per second.

**PQFP**  Plastic quad flat pack. A square, flat package with 18–52 gullwing leads located around all four sides of the package.

**PRI** Primary Rate Interface. In the U.S., PRI is split into 23 B channels and one 64 Kbps D channel. PRI is delivered over the same physical link as a T1, or 1.544 Mbps link. In Europe, PRI is split into 30 B channels and one 64 Kbps D channel and is delivered over a single E1 link (2.048 Mbps).

**PROM** Programmable read only memory. This is a version of a ROM that is programmable once using special devices.

**proprietary memory** Memory that is custom-designed for a specific computer.

**protocol** A standardized set of rules that specify the format, timing, sequencing, and/or error checking for data transmissions.

**protocol converter** A device for translating the data transmission code and/or protocol of one network or device to the corresponding code or protocol of another network or device, enabling equipment with different conventions to communicate with one another.

**protocol islands** Network topologies confined to a single leaf network that have no interconnection needs with other leaf networks or the central node.

**protocol stack** Related layers of protocol software that function together to implement a particular communications architecture.

**PSDN** Packet switching data network.

**PTT** PTT, or Public Telephone and Telegraph, is a generic term for European telephone companies. Most are (currently) state owned and operated. The Deutsche Bundespost is one example of a PTT.

**pulse dialing** Also referred to as rotary dialing, that is, dialing with the older-style rotary dial wheel. The dial modifier ATDP sets the modem to pulse dialing, which is the default method as opposed to tone dialing (push-button touch-tone), which is enabled with ATDT. All telephone exchanges will accept older-style pulse dialing, and most exchanges will accept modern tone dialing. Tone dialing is faster and more reliable because mechanical relays and their inherent failure mechanisms are avoided.

**PVC (permanent virtual circuit)** Generally, a virtual circuit that is permanently established. PVCs save bandwidth associated with circuit establishment and tear down in situations where certain virtual circuits exist all the time. See also SVC.

**Q.921** This is the link layer protocol for ISDN.

**Q.931** This is the network layer protocol for ISDN. Q.931 was developed for out-of-band call control.

**QIC** Quarter-Inch Cartridge; also Quarter-Inch Cartridge Drive Standards, Inc. A standard for 1/4-inch data cartridge drives, cartridges, and interfaces.

**QoS** Quality of Service. Term to describe delay, throughput, bandwidth, and so on, of a circuit.

**quad flat pack** QFP. A flat, rectangular, integrated circuit with its leads projecting from all four sides of the package without radius.

**RAM** Random access memory. A configuration of memory cells that hold data for processing by a computer's central processing unit, or CPU (see also Memory). The term "random" derives from the fact that the CPU can retrieve data from any individual location, or address, within RAM, at any time.

**RAMDAC** RAM digital to analog converter.

**random failure region** The portion of the bathtub-shaped failure rate curve that represents the useful portion of device life.

**range** The difference between the smallest and largest values in a set of data. This is the simplest measure of variation.

**RAS** Row address strobe: the signal that tells the DRAM to accept the given address as a row address. Used with CAS and a column address to select a bit within the DRAM.

**rate adaptation** The conversion of non-ISDN data traffic to a format compatible with ISDN 64 Kbps transmission.

**RBCS** Remote Boot and Configuration Service.

**RBOC** Regional Bell Operating Company. The companies (the Baby Bells) are the seven regional telephone companies that were spun off as part of the AT&T divestiture in 1984. The seven RBOCs are Ameritech, Bell Atlantic, Bell South, Nynex, Pacific Bell, Southwestern Bell, and US West.

**Read the manual (RTFM)** Acronym suggesting a response to an easily answered question.

**read time** The amount of time required for the output data to become valid once the read and address inputs have been enabled; generally called access time.

**read/write memory** A generic term for random access memory.

**redirector** Software that intercepts requests for resources within a computer and analyzes them for remote access requirements.

**refresh** An electrical process used to maintain data stored in DRAM. The process of refreshing electrical cells on a DRAM component is similar to that of recharging batteries. Different DRAM components call for different refresh methods.

**refresh rate** Also called vertical scan rate, the speed at which the screen is repainted. Typically, color displays must be refreshed at 60 times per second to avoid flicker. Also, a specification determined by the number of rows on a DRAM component that must be refreshed. Two common refresh rates are 2KB and 4KB.

**register-level compatibility** Complete compatibility to the hardware level.

**relative address** An identifier that indicates the position of a memory location in a computer routine relative to the base address as opposed to the memory location's absolute address.

**release time** The amount of time data must remain stable after a device or circuit has been clocked; also called "hold time."

**remote bridge** A bridge that connects physically dissimilar network segments across WAN links.

**remote networking** Extending the logical boundaries of a corporate LAN over wide area links to give remote offices, telecommuters, and mobile users access to critical information and resources.

**remote user** A telecommuter, individual contractor, business traveler, or nomadic user who needs client access to a corporate enterprise LAN over dial-up WAN links.

**removability** A feature where the media in a removable media disk drive can be removed and then replaced with the same or different media without causing problems to the operating system. If removability was not supported, media in a removable media drive could not be removed without potential loss of data unless the computer was turned off.

**repeater** Used to extend the topology, allowing two or more cable segments to be joined. In a 10Base-T network, the repeater provides the central connection point where the gathering of statistics and network management functions take place. See also Hub.

**resist** A material that prevents etching or plating of the area it covers; also called photoresist.

**result code** A response sent by the modem after executing a command. The response reports the modem's status or the progress of a call and can take the form of either digits (numeric) or words (verbose). Issuing a V1 command enables word responses. A V0 (V-zero) command enables numeric responses. The Q1 command disables their use entirely. Example: "OK" (word), or 0 (numeric) indicates that the modem successfully executed a command.

**retrain** An adjustment process performed when one of the modems detects signal distortion or line noise that threatens data integrity.

**Reverse ARP** Reverse Address Resolution Protocol.

**RFC** Request for Comments from the IETF.

**RGB** Red/green/blue.

**RIF** Routing information field.

**ring latency** The time required for a signal to propagate once around a ring in a token ring or IEEE 802.5 network.

**ring topology** A network topology in which nodes are connected in a closed loop; no terminators are required because there are no unconnected ends.

**RIP** Routing Information Protocol. A routing protocol for TCP/IP networks. Also, Rest In Peace (really!!), a verb describing the act of a Windows program issuing a fatal error.

**RISC** Reduced instruction set computing. The design methodology is usually associated with microprocessors. RISC chips use simpler instructions, or commands, than CISC chips. However, they need to use more steps to perform many functions that CISC chips perform in one step. SPARC and MIPS chips are based on RISC.

**rise time** The amount of time required for a signal level change to increase from ten percent to ninety percent of its final specified value.

**RMA** Returned Material Authorization; required if a customer desires to return products. Also refers to parts that have been returned from a customer.

**RMON (Remote Monitoring)** A subset of SNMP MIB II that allows flexible and comprehensive monitoring and management capabilities by addressing up to 10 different groups of information.

**ROM** Read only memory. This is generally a chip on a computer or I/O card with software programmed inside of it that controls some function or functions.

**root bridge** Appointed by the spanning tree and used to determine which managed bridges to block in the spanning tree topology.

**router** A protocol-dependent device that connects subnetworks together. It is useful in breaking down a very large network into smaller subnetworks. Routers introduce longer delays and typically have much lower throughput rates than bridges.

**routing bridge** A MAC-layer bridge that uses network layer methods to determine a network's topology.

**routing protocol** A protocol that accomplishes routing through the implementation of a specific routing algorithm.

**routing table** A table stored in a router or some other internetworking device that keeps track of routes (and, in some cases, metrics associated with those routes) to particular network destinations.

**routing update** A message sent from a router to indicate network reachability and associated cost information. Routing updates are typically sent at regular intervals and after a change in network topology.

**row** Part of the RAM array; a bit can be stored where a column and a row intersect.

**row address** The number of the row where a particular bit is stored.

**RPC** Remote Procedure Call.

**RPL** Remote Program Load.

**RS-232** A serial data transmission interface specification.

**RSPC-Reed Soloman Product Code** An error correction method used in DVD system. This process, developed by MIT mathematicians in 1960, compensates for gaps in digital information that can be caused by imperfections or scratches in the substrate of the DVD, maintaining picture and sound quality. This type of system is used in magnetic and optical storage systems and allows for more flexibility as the DVD system develops. The advanced RSPC error correction system utilized in DVD is six times as robust as that of a conventional compact disc.

**RTS/CTS** Request to Send/Clear to Send. RTS and CTS are two control signal lines between the modem (DCE) and terminal (DTE) that allow the terminal to control the flow of information. See also flow control.

**SAAL** Signaling AAL.

**SAM** Serial asynchronous module.

**Sample** A measurement of sound taken during a certain duration. In digital recording, sampling means recording voltages that make a sound as a sequence of numerical values representing the sound's amplitude.

**SAP** Service Advertisement Protocol, or Service Access Point.

**SAR** Segmentation and Reassembly. Converts between the adaptation layer and the ATM layer (for instance, AAL5 frame to ATM cells).

**SCAM** SCSI Configured Auto Magically. Really. This is also known as Plug and Play for SCSI. Using this specification, the SCSI host adapter is able to automatically select the SCSI ID of itself and attached SCSI devices. It can also enable/disable termination as required to properly terminate the SCSI bus.

**scan rate** The frequency in Hertz (Hz) at which the monitor is scanned horizontally. Generally, the higher the scan rate, the higher the resolution.

**scribe** A marking on a wafer that identifies the wafer and the lot it came from. The scribe is located on the front of the wafer, opposite the major flat.

**SCSI** Small Computer Systems Interface. A bus interface standard that defines standard physical and electrical connections for devices. SCSI provides a standard interface that enables many different kinds of devices, such as disk drives, magneto-optical disks, CD-ROM drives, and tape drives to interface with the host computer.

**SCSI device** A device such as a host adapter board, fixed disk drive, or CD-ROM drive that conforms to the SCSI interface standard and is attached to a SCSI bus cable. The device may be an initiator, a target, or capable of both types of operation.

**SCSI overhead** This is the time it takes for the host adapter to internally process a SCSI command.

**SDDI** Shielded Data Distributed Interface (FDDI over STP).

**SDH** Synchronous Digital Hierarchy, the ITU-T version of SONET. The basic SDH rate (STM-1) is 155.52 Mbps (mostly equivalent to SONETs STS-3/OC-3).

**SDLC** Synchronous Data Link Control. An IBM communications line discipline or protocol, a version of HDLC. SDLC provides for control of a single communications line or link, accommodates a number of network arrangements, and operates in half or full duplex over private or switched facilities.

**SDRAM** Synchronous dynamic random-access memory. Delivers bursts of data at very high speeds using a synchronous interface.

**SDU** Service Data Unit.

**sector** The smallest storage access unit on a hard drive.

**secure logging** A method whereby an audit trail of system activity is received from a bastion host and placed in a secure location.

**seek time** The average time it takes for a hard drive to position its heads to a specific sector.

**segmentation** Splitting an overloaded ring into two or more separate rings, linked by a bridge/router or multipurpose hub.

**self-refresh** A memory technology that enables DRAM to refresh on its own, independent of the CPU or external refresh circuitry. This technology is built into the DRAM chip itself and reduces power consumption dramatically. It is commonly used in notebook and laptop computers.

**semiconductor** An element, such as silicon, that has intermediate electrical conductivity between conductors and insulators, and in which conduction takes place by means of holes and electrons.

**SER** Soft error rate. An error caused by temporary disruption of memory cell.

**serial interface** An interface that requires serial transmission, or the transfer of information in which the bits composing a character are sent sequentially. Implies only a single transmission channel.

**serial port** A connection for a serial device like a mouse or a modem.

**serial presence detect** An enhanced presence detect that uses an EEPROM to store manufacturer data.

**server** A computer that provides shared resources, such as files and printers, to the network.

**server clustering** Placing all the servers on one or more rings in a central location.

**server farm** A cluster of servers in a centralized location serving a wide user population.

**Session layer** The OSI layer that provides means for dialogue control between end systems.

**SGRAM** Synchronous graphics RAM. A single-port DRAM designed for graphics hardware that require high speed throughput such as 3D rendering and full-motion video.

**shared Ethernet** A conventional CSMA/CD Ethernet configuration, where all stations are attached to a hub sharing 10 Mbps of bandwidth; only one station can transmit at a time.

**shrink** A reduction in die (chip) size. A reduction in the size of the circuit design resulting in smaller die sizes that increases the number of possible die per wafer.

**SIMM** Single in-line memory module. A printed circuit board with gold or tin/lead contacts and memory devices. A SIMM plugs into a computer's memory expansion socket. SIMMs offer two main advantages: ease of installation and minimal consumption of horizontal surface area. A vertically mounted SIMM requires only a fraction of the space required by horizontally mounted DRAM. A SIMM may have as few as 30 or as many as 200 pins. On a SIMM, the metal leads on either side of the board are electrically "tied together."

**SIMM socket** A component mounted on the system board, or motherboard, designed to hold a single SIMM.

**simplex transmission** Data transmission that can occur in only one direction on a given line. Compare half duplex and full duplex.

**single-mode fiber** Fiber with a relatively narrow diameter, through which only one mode will propagate. Carries higher bandwidth than multimode fiber, but requires a light source with a narrow spectral width.

**SIP** Single in line package. A component or module that has one row of leads along one side. Many resistors come in SIP form. SIP was also a memory module form factor (now obsolete).

**sleep inactivity timer** Determines the length of time the modem operates in normal mode with no activity before entering low-power "sleep" mode.

**SLIP** Serial Line Interface Protocol. Internet protocol used to run IP over serial lines such as telephone circuits or RS-232 cables interconnecting two systems. SLIP has largely been replaced by PPP.

**SMDS** Switched Multimegabit Data Service.

**SMI** Structure of Management Information.

**SMM** System Management Module.

**SMS** Specific Multicast Server.

**SMT** Station Management. That part of the FDDI specification that manages stations on the ring, as defined by the X3T9.5 specification.

**SMTP** Simple Mail Transfer Protocol. A protocol governing mail transmissions; defined in RFC 821, with associated message format descriptions in RFC 822.

**SNAP** Sub Network Access Protocol. An Internet protocol that operates between a network entity in the subnetwork and a network entity in the end system and specifies a standard method of encapsulating IP datagrams and ARP messages on IEEE networks.

**SNMP** Simple Network Management Protocol. The preferred network management system for TCP/IP-based internets.

**SNP** Subnetwork Protocol (TCP/IP). A protocol residing in the subnetwork layer below IP that provides data transfer through the local subnet. In some systems, an adapter module must be inserted between IP and the Subnetwork Protocol to reconcile their dissimilar interfaces.

**SODIMM** Small Outline Dual In-line Memory Module. A smaller and thinner version of a standard DIMM. The small outline DIMM is about half the length of a typical 72-pin SIMM. SODIMMs are typically used in laptop computers.

**soft error** In memory components, a correctable data error made by a device not having anything wrong with it.

**SOJ** Small outline J-lead package. A common form of surface-mount DRAM packaging. A rectangular package with leads sticking out of the side of the package. The leads are formed in a J-bend profile, bending underneath and toward the bottom of the package. Lead counts range from 20 to 44 leads.

**SONET** Synchronous optical network. A U.S. standard for optical digital transmission at hierarchical rates from 51.84 Mbps to 2.5 Gbps and beyond.

**sound file** Any file that holds sound data. Examples: files with .mid filename extensions are compatible with the MIDI standard; a file with a .wav filename extension contains data in the standard Microsoft file format for storing waveform audio data.

**spanning tree** A technique that detects loops in a network and logically blocks the redundant paths, ensuring that only one route exists between any two LANs; used in an IEEE 802.1d bridged network.

**SPC** Statistical Process Control. The use of statistical measures to determine trends and establish uniformity around a target value.

**speed** The time it takes the RAM to put information into its memory or get information out of its memory. It is measured from the time that an address and proper control signals are given, until the information is stored or placed in the device's output(s).

**speed grade** Coding for the speed that the stored information in the part can be retrieved by a computer. For DRAMs, a –5 may be 50 nanoseconds, a –6 may be 60 nanoseconds, a –7 may be 70 nanoseconds, and so on. For SRAMs, a –10 may be 10 nanoseconds, and so on.

**SPID** A Service Profile ID, which uniquely identifies a B channel on the ISDN network. The SPID must be stored in any device accessing the ISDN.

**spike** The sudden drastic portion of a pulse that significantly exceeds its average amplitude.

**split horizon** A routing technique where information about routes is prevented from exiting router interfaces through which that information was received. Useful in preventing routing loops.

**spoofing** The use of a forged IP source address to circumvent a firewall. The packet appears to have come from inside the protected network, and to be eligible for forwarding into the network.

**SQE** Signal quality error. A transmission sent by a transceiver back to the controller to let the controller know whether the collision circuitry is functional.

**SR** Source Routing.

**SRAM (static random access memory)** An integrated circuit similar to a DRAM (dynamic random access memory) with the exception that the memory does not need to be refreshed.

**SRT (Source Routing Transparent) bridge** A proposed IEEE 802.1 bridge to combine source routing (in which the source end system provides routing information) with transparent bridging (in which the bridge makes independent message handling choices and, therefore, is transparent to the message source and destination).

**SS7** Signaling System number 7. A protocol used in the public networks to establish connections between switches. ISDN connections to switches that support SS7 have access to true 64 Kbps connections between public switches. ISDN connections to switches that do not support SS7 are limited to 56 Kbps on each B channel as the switch signaling must be accommodated in-band.

**SSCOP** Service-Specific Connection-Oriented Protocol.

**SSCS** Service-Specific Convergence Sublayer.

**STA** Spanning Tree Algorithm. A function of managed bridges that allows redundant bridges to be used for network resilience, without the broadcast storms associated with looping. If a bridge fails, a new path to a redundant bridge is opened.

**stack** A group of network devices that are logically integrated into a single system star topology. A network configuration where all the nodes are connected to a central point via individual cables. Also, short for Protocol Stack.

**standard deviation** A measure of variation for a particular process or product characteristic. This is often abbreviated as "STD DEV" or "STD."

**star topology** A network topology in which nodes are connected to a common device such as a hub or concentrator.

**starting address** The smallest or lowest address that a memory system will respond to.

**static RAM** Unlike volatile memory, static memory retains its contents even when the main current is turned off. The trickle of electricity from a battery is enough to refresh it.

**static routing** A system in which routing information is manually entered into the routing table.

**STE** Spanning Tree Explorer.

**S/T interface** An S/T interface is a four-wire BRI interface presented to the customer by the PTTs in non-U.S. markets. It is the customer side of the NT1 device.

**STM** Synchronous Transport Module. Specifies the electrical and optical transmission over SDH. Transmission rates are based on 155.52 Mbps (STM-1, equivalent to SONETs OC-3).

**storage** A medium designed to hold data, such as a hard disk or CD-ROM.

**storage capacity** The limit to the amount of information that can be recorded on any recording medium. In DVD, this varies from 4.7GB on a DVD-5 disc to 17GB on a DVD-18 disc.

**STP** Shielded Twisted Pair. A common transmission medium that consists of a Receive (RX) and a Transmit (TX) wire twisted together to reduce crosstalk. The twisted pair is shielded by a braided outer sheath.

**strobe** An input that allows parallel data to be entered asynchronously.

**STS** Synchronous Transport Signal. The logical signal specification for SONET frame structure.

**subnetwork** A collection of end systems and intermediate systems under the control of one administrative domain and using a single network access protocol. For example, private X.25 networks, a series of bridged LANs. Compare Autonomous System.

**substrate (DVD)** Polycarbonate material that encases and protects the stamped information on a disc. On a DVD, the utilization of two bonded substrates, measuring 0.6mm each, significantly reduces the distance between the surface of the disc and the pits on the disc that hold information when compared to that of conventional CD/CD-ROM media. Reduction in the thickness of the disc substrate is an important component in achieving the increased storage capacity and improved tilt margins of DVDs.

**substrate (integrated circuits)** The actual structural material on which semiconductor devices are fabricated, whether passive or active. The term applies to any supportive material, such as the materials used in the fabrication of printed circuits.

**surface-mount package** A package that can be mounted directly on the surface of printed wiring boards (as opposed to through-hole packages).

**surround sound** A multiple-channel sound system to produce an audio ambience similar to the cinema sound experience.

**SVC** Switched virtual circuit. A logical (not physical) connection between end points established by the ATM network on demand after receiving a connection request from the source, which it transmits using the UNI signaling protocol. See also PVC.

**S-video** A connector between the video source and the television providing higher-quality signal transmission than the more common RCA video connector.

**Switched 56** A switched data transmission service at 56 Kbps (as opposed to service on dedicated leased lines).

**Switched Ethernet** An Ethernet hub with integrated MAC layer bridging or switching capability to provide each port with 10 Mbps of bandwidth; separate transmissions can occur on each port of the switching hub, and the switch filters traffic according to the destination MAC address.

**switched virtual LAN** A logical network consisting of several different LAN emulation domains controlled through an intelligent network management application.

**switching hubs** Hubs that use intelligent Ethernet switching technology to interconnect multiple Ethernet LANs and higher-speed LANs such as FDDI. See also Switched Ethernet.

**synchronous communications** A method of transmission in which data bits are sent continuously at the same rate under the control of a fixed-frequency clock signal.

**synchronous DRAM** A DRAM technology that uses a clock to synchronize signal input and output on a memory chip. The clock is coordinated with the CPU clock so the timing of the memory chips and the timing of the CPU are "in synch." Synchronous DRAM saves time in executing commands and transmitting data, thereby increasing the overall performance of the computer.

**synchronous transfer** A method of SCSI data transfer. With this type of data transfer, the SCSI host adapter and the SCSI device agree to a transfer rate that both support (this is known as synchronous negotiation). With this type of data transfer method, transfer rates of 5 MBps or 10 MBps (for FAST SCSI) are common.

**synchronous transmission** A form of usually high-speed data communication that uses synchronization bytes instead of start or stop bits to tell the receiving device about the coming transmission. More complex than asynchronous.

**system board** See motherboard.

**T1** A communications circuit provided by long-distance carriers for voice and data transmission. Runs at 1.544 Mbps in the United States and Canada. Similar to E1 transmission at 2.054 Mbps in Europe.

**T3** Digital communications circuit standard created by AT&T that operates at 45 Mbps.

**TA** Terminal adapter.

**tagged queuing** A SCSI-2 feature that increases performance on SCSI disk drives. With tagged queuing, the host adapter, the host adapter driver, and the hard disk drive work together to increase performance by reordering the requests from the host adapter to minimize head switching and seeking. For example, the host adapter may ask for the following data in the following order: LBA 0, 1, 101, 102, 5, 6 (LBA = logical block address, or a byte of data). Without tagged queuing, the drive would seek to LBA 0; transfer bytes 0 and then 1; then seek to 101; transfer 101 and 102; then seek back to LBA 5, transfer 5 and then 6. This involves three seeks (initial seek to 0, seek to 101, then seek back to 5). If tagged queuing was enabled, the drive would seek to LBA 0, transfer bytes 0, then 1, 5, and 6, then seek to 101, transferring 101 and 102. At this point all the data would be transferred. This involves two seeks (the initial seek to 0, then the seek to 101). Seeking on a disk drive takes a relatively long time, so saving seeks and head switches really speeds up performance.

**tank circuit** Ensures accurate signal tracking in token ring networks and prevents degradation of the signal; must be adjusted manually.

**TB** Transparent Bridging.

**TBD** To Be Determined.

**T-connector** A T-shaped device with two female and one male BNC connectors.

**TCP** Transmission Control Protocol. See also IP.

**TCP/IP** Transmission Control Protocol/Internet Protocol. A set of protocols developed by the U.S. Defense Department's Advanced Research Projects Agency (ARPA) during the early 1970s. Its intent was to develop ways to connect different kinds of networks and computers.

**TDM** Time Division Multiplexing. A technique where information from multiple channels may be allocated bandwidth on a single wire based on time slot assignment.

**TDU** Topology Database Update.

**TE** Terminal equipment.

**telco** Abbreviation for "telephone company." The RBOCs are a subset of all telcos.

**Telnet** The Internet standard protocol to connect to a computer as a remote terminal.

**terminal server** Communications processor that connects asynchronous devices to a LAN or WAN through network and terminal emulation software.

**termination** A controlled impedance at either end of a transmission line used to prevent signal reflections. A physical requirement of the SCSI bus. The first and last devices on the SCSI bus must have terminating resistors installed, and the devices in the middle of the bus must have terminating resistors removed. A 50-ohm coaxial plug used to attach to one end of a BNC T-connector when the associated station is first or last in the group.

**TFTP** Trivial File Transfer Protocol.

**Thinnet** See Cheapernet.

**TIC** Token-ring interface coupler.

**tilt margin** The amount of variation in the laser focus, caused by the physical characteristics of a disc, that can be accommodated while maintaining signal integrity. The 0.6mm substrate of a DVD diffuses less of the laser's focus than does a conventional CD's 1.2 mm substrate, resulting in a more accurate beam spot. The bonded substrates of a DVD reduces warpage and further improves tilt margins.

**timbre** How the ear identifies and classifies sound. Example: The timbre of the same note played by two different instruments (flute and tuba) will not be the same.

**TN3270** Terminal emulation software that allows a terminal to appear to an IBM host as a 3270 model 2 terminal.

**token** Control information frame, possession of which grants a network device the right to transmit.

**token ring** An industry standard (Project 802.5 of the IEEE) that specifies protocols for connection and transmission in local area networks. Token ring transmits at 4 Mbps or 16 Mbps.

**topology** The physical layout of a network. The principal LAN topologies are bus, ring, and star.

**touch-tone dialing** Push-button tone dialing as used on contemporary phone sets. The dial modifier ATDT sets the modem to "tone" mode. Tone dialing is faster and more reliable than older-style pulse dialing.

**TP** Twisted pair. Cable consisting of two 18 to 24 AWG (American Wire Gauge) solid copper strands twisted around each other. The twisting provides a measure of protection from electromagnetic and radio-frequency interference. Twisted-pair cable typically contains multiple sets of paired wires.

**TP-PMD** Twisted Pair/Physical Medium Dependent.

**tracking** Tracking is important for the most accurate reading of the information being retrieved from a disc. Located on a DVD disc are tracking and A/V data. The laser reads the primary information that represents the audio and video signals to be displayed, as well as pits on either side of the main track that serve to provide tracking information. The information they return to the pick-up keeps the main beam spot aimed at the correct track on the disc, resulting in accurate retrieval of digital information.

**transceiver** An AUI (Attachment Unit Interface) device for receiving and transmitting data that often provides collision detection as well.

**transistor** A semiconductor device that uses a stream of charge carriers to produce active electronic effects.

**translation bridging** Bridging between networks with dissimilar MAC sublayer protocols.

**transparent bridging** A bridging scheme preferred by Ethernet and IEEE 802.3 networks in which bridges pass frames along one hop at a time according to tables associating end nodes with bridge ports.

**Transport layer** The OSI layer that is responsible for reliable end-to-end data transfer between end systems.

**Travan** A high-capacity minicartridge technology developed by Imation Corporation (formerly a division of 3M Company).

**trellis coding** A method of modulation that targets specific modulation points. Signals falling outside these points are treated as line noise, thus ensuring greater noise immunity over a given line. QAM (quadrature amplitude modulation) functions similarly but has a broader tolerance and results in lesser noise immunity than trellis coding.

**True Color** Video cards that can show 24-bit color (up to 16.7 million colors).

**TSOP** Thin small outline package. A type of DRAM package that uses gull-wing-shaped leads on both sides. TSOP DRAM mounts directly on the surface of the printed circuit board. The advantage of the TSOP package is that it is one-third the thickness of an SOJ package. TSOP components are commonly used in small outline DIMM and credit card memory applications. Height distinguishes the TSOP from the SSOP. Lead counts range from 20 to 40 leads.

**TSR** Terminate and stay resident. A DOS program that remains in memory after it has been loaded.

**TTL** Transistor-transistor logic; a fast, reasonable-cost type of integrated circuit used extensively in computers before other lower-power logic types became prevalent.

**TTL monitor** Video and synchronization signals (all digital) are on separate lines and have TTL-compatible voltage levels.

**TWAIN** A programming interface for scanners.

**twisted-pair cable** A wiring scheme with one or more pairs of 18- to 24-gauge copper strands.

**UART** Universal asynchronous receiver/transmitter chip, used as communications (COM) port in personal computers. Maximum data rates vary with model; the National Semiconductor 16550A.

**UDLC** Universal Data Link Control.

**UDP** User Datagram Protocol. An Internet standard protocol that allows an application on one machine to send a datagram to an application program on another machine. No confirmation of arrival is supplied, and order of arrival is not guaranteed, so UDP is faster than TCP.

**U interface** A two-wire interface presented to the customer by the telco in the U.S. market. The customer is responsible for converting this signal to the four-wire S/T interface in order to make a connection.

**UltraSCSI** A method that enables very fast data transfer rate on the SCSI bus. The maximum UltraSCSI data transfer rates are 20 MBps (40 MBps for Wide SCSI host adapters).

**UNI** User-to-network interface. The interface between a user's device and an ATM switch, defined as the physical, ATM, and higher layer (for instance, signaling).

**Universal Disk Format** The Universal Disk Format, or UDF, specification defines data structures such as volumes, files, blocks, sectors, CRCs, paths, records, allocation tables, partitions, character sets, time stamps, and so forth; and methods for reading, writing, and other operations. It is a very flexible, multiplatform, multiapplication, multilanguage, multiuser oriented format that has been adapted for DVD.

**Universal Resource Locator (URL)** A form of Internet address used by World Wide Web browsers. Each browser-accessible resource on the Internet has a unique URL (for instance, `http://www.idgbooks.com`).

**USB** Universal Serial Bus. A high-speed serial interface expected to connect keyboard, mouse, speakers, monitor, and other devices to your computer.

**Usenet** More commonly known as newsgroups, Usenet is a world-wide bulletin board system incorporating tens of thousands of groups on thousands of servers around the world.

**UTP** Unshielded Twisted Pair. See also STP.

**V.17** A CCITT facsimile analog modem signaling standard providing up to 14,400 Kbps data rates and backward compatible to the V.29 standard, which supports speeds up to 9,600 Kbps.

**V.32bis** CCITT analog modem signaling standard providing up to 14.4 Kbps data rates.

**V.35** The CCITT recommendation governing data transmission at 48 Kbps using 60–108 kHz band circuits.

**V.42bis** The CCITT analog modem data compression standard. Provides a theoretical maximum of 4:1 compression, although 2:1 or less is more commonly experienced.

**variable** A condition, transaction, or event that changes or may be changed as a result of processing additional data through a system.

**variable bit rate**  The flow of data, or bit rate, of a DVD is variable depending on the complexity of the signal being processed. A detailed, rapidly moving scene with multiple picture elements would require a high bit rate, while a static image with little detail would receive far fewer bits. This advance in processing, a part of the MPEG-2 system, uses bits more efficiently, allocating storage capacity according to the requirement of the signal.

**VC**  Virtual channel. A point-to-point or point-to-multipoint connection between ATM end-stations. Can either be switched or permanent. It is identified by the combination of the VCI and VPI.

**VCC**  Virtual channel connection. Defined by a series of VCs logically assigned to make an end-to-end link.

**VCI**  Virtual connection identifier. A 16-bit identifier having only local significance on the link between ATM nodes. See also VC.

**VDS**  Virtual DMA Services. A software standard developed by Microsoft so that bus master host adapters could work efficiently under DOS protected mode and virtual 86 mode programs.

**Veronica**  A search engine built into Gopher. It allows searches of all Gopher sites for files, directories, and other resources.

**VESA**  Video Electronics Standards Association. Sponsors efforts to set standards in all areas of graphics and video technology.

**VGA**  Video Graphics Array. An analog graphics standard introduced with the IBM PS/2 series. Backward compatible with EGA at the BIOS level but provides higher resolutions. Supports a maximum resolution of 640 × 480 pixels in 16 colors out of a palette of 262,144 colors.

**virtual channel identifier (VCI)**  A unique numerical tag for every virtual channel across an ATM interface.

**Virtual circuit**  Circuit-like service provided by the software protocols of a network, enabling two end points to communicate as though connected by a physical circuit. Network nodes provide the addressing information needed in the packets that carry the source data to the destination.

**VL-bus**  A specification for a local bus developed by the VESA local bus committee.

**VLSI**  Very large scale integration.

**VN3/VN4**  VN3 and VN4 are the French ISDN standards.

**voice annotation** Embedding of a voice message into a document for later playback.

**VPC** Virtual path connection.

**VPI** Virtual path identifier. An eight-bit identifier identifying semipermanent connections between ATM endpoints. See also VC.

**VRAM** Video RAM. DRAM with an on-board serial register/serial access memory designed for video applications.

**WAN** Wide area network. A network that uses common carrier–provided lines; contrast with LAN.

**warm boot** Rebooting a computer without turning the power off (for instance, Ctrl+Alt+Del).

**wave file** A standard Microsoft file format for storing waveform audio data.

**waveform** A graph showing the amplitude of a sound over a particular interval of time. Any portion of that interval is a sample.

**Wide SCSI** Provides for performance and compatibility enhancements to SCSI-1 by adding a 16- or 32-bit data path. Combined with Fast SCSI, this can result in SCSI bus data transfer rates of 20 MBps (with a 16-bit bus) or 40 MBps (with a 32-bit bus).

**write-back cache** Cache memory that holds data written by the processor until the bus and main memory have time to perform the write.

**write-through cache** Cache memory that executes processor writes to main memory immediately, requiring the processor to wait until the operation is complete.

**write time** Time expended from the moment data is entered for storage to the time it is actually stored.

**WWW** World Wide Web. The Internet-based hypertext system.

**X.21** Recommendations developed by CCITT that define a protocol for communication between user devices and a circuit-switched network.

**X.25** Recommendations developed by CCITT that define a protocol for communication between packet-switched public data networks and user devices in the packet-switched mode.

**X.400** An international standard for a store-and-forward message handling system in a multivendor environment.

**XID** Exchange identifier.

**XNS** Xerox Network Systems. A peer-to-peer protocol involving layered data communications protocols developed by Xerox and incorporated into Ethernet local area networks.

**XON/XOFF** XON and XOFF are the names of two different flow control characters. See also flow control.

**ZDL** Zero delay lockout. Technology designed to prevent beaconing stations on a token ring from inserting into the ring and causing faults.

**ZIF socket** Zero insertion force socket. A mechanism for a processor socket supporting simple replacement of chips.

✦     ✦     ✦

# CompTIA A+ Certification Exam Objectives

**T**he material in this appendix, provided by the Computing Technology Industry Association (CompTIA), defines the objectives for the A+ certification examination. We've provided both the core objectives and the DOS/Windows ones; you'll want to be comfortable with the concepts and information required to respond to each of the points before you apply to take the A+ exam.

## Core Objectives

### FINAL REVISION (as of July 17, 1998)

### A+ Core Service Technician Examination Blueprint

NOTE: This is the FINAL revision of the A+ Core Service Technician exam blueprint. This document was produced after the final technical and psychometric review of the item pool following the beta-testing period. This document is reflective of the topics and technologies that appear as part of the A+ Core Service Technician exam.

#### Introduction

For A+ Certification, the examinee must pass both this examination and the A+ DOS/Windows Service Technician examination. This examination measures essential competencies for a break/fix microcomputer hardware service technician with six months of on-the-job experience. The examinee must demonstrate knowledge to properly install, configure, upgrade, troubleshoot, and repair microcomputer hardware. This includes basic knowledge of desktop and portable systems, basic networking concepts, and printers. The examinee must also demonstrate knowledge of safety and common preventive maintenance procedures.

Since customer satisfaction is a key aspect of providing microcomputer hardware service, this examination will include questions that measure the examinee's knowledge of effective behaviors that contribute to customer satisfaction. The customer satisfaction questions will be scored but will not impact final pass/fail score on this examination.

The skills and knowledge measured by this examination are derived from an industry-wide job task analysis and validated through a worldwide survey of 5,000 A+ Certified professionals. The results of the worldwide survey were used in weighting the domains and ensuring that the weighting is representative of the relative importance of that content to the job requirements of a service technician with six months on-the-job experience. The results of the job task analysis and survey can be found in the following reports:

✦ *CompTIA A+ Certification Technical and Customer Satisfaction Job Task Analysis: Phase 1 Report (June 27, 1997)*

✦ *CompTIA A+ Certification Technical and Customer Satisfaction Job Task Analysis: Phase 2 Report Survey Results (November 10, 1997)*

This examination blueprint includes weighting, test objectives, and example content. Example topics and concepts are included to clarify the test objectives; they should not be construed as a comprehensive listing of the content of this examination.

The table below lists the domains measured by this examination and the approximate extent to which they are represented.

| *Domain*<br>*% of Examination (approximately)* |
| --- |
| 1.0 Installation, Configuration, and Upgrading |
| 30% |
| 2.0 Diagnosing and Troubleshooting |
| 20% |
| 3.0 Safety and Preventive Maintenance |
| 10% |

| **Domain**<br>**% of Examination (approximately)** |
| --- |
| 4.0 Motherboard/Processors/Memory |
| 10% |
| 5.0 Printers |
| 10% |
| 6.0 Portable Systems |
| 5% |
| 7.0 Basic Networking |
| 5% |
| 8.0 Customer Satisfaction |
| 10%[1] |
| **Total** |
| 100.00% |

[1] Note: The Customer Satisfaction domain will be scored but will not impact final pass/fail score on the A+ Core examination.

# Domain 1.0 Installation, Configuration, and Upgrading

This domain requires the knowledge and skills to identify, install, configure, and upgrade microcomputer modules and peripherals, following established basic procedures for system assembly and disassembly of field replaceable modules. Elements include ability to identify and configure IRQs, DMAs, I/O addresses, and set switches and jumpers.

## Content Limits

**1.1 Identify basic terms, concepts, and functions of system modules, including how each module should work during normal operation.**

**Examples of concepts and modules:**

✦ System board

✦ Power supply

✦ Processor /CPU

✦ Memory

✦ Storage devices

✦ Monitor

✦ Modem

✦ Firmware

✦ Boot process

✦ BIOS

✦ CMOS

**1.2 Identify basic procedures for adding and removing field replaceable modules.**

**Examples of modules:**

✦ System board

✦ Storage device

✦ Power supply

✦ Processor /CPU

✦ Memory

✦ Input devices

**1.3 Identify available IRQs, DMAs, and I/O addresses and procedures for configuring them for device installation.**

**Content may include the following:**

✦ Standard IRQ settings

✦ Modems

✦ Floppy drives

✦ Hard drive

**1.4 Identify common peripheral ports, associated cabling, and their connectors.**

**Content may include the following:**

✦ Cable types

✦ Cable orientation

✦ Serial versus parallel

✦ Pin connections

**Examples of types of connectors:**

✦ DB-9

✦ DB-25

✦ RJ-11

✦ RJ-45

✦ BNC

✦ PS2/MINI-DIN

**1.5 Identify proper procedures for installing and configuring IDE/EIDE devices.**

**Content may include the following:**

✦ Master/slave

✦ Devices per channel

**1.6 Identify proper procedures for installing and configuring SCSI devices.**

**Content may include the following:**

✦ Address/Termination conflicts

✦ Cabling

✦ Types (example: regular, wide, ultra-wide)

✦ Internal versus external

✦ Switch and jumper settings

**1.7 Identify proper procedures for installing and configuring peripheral devices.**

**Content may include the following:**

✦ Monitor/Video Card

✦ Modem

✦ Storage devices

**1.8 Identify concepts and procedures relating to BIOS.**

✦ Methods for upgrading

✦ When to upgrade

**1.9 Identify hardware methods of system optimization and when to use them.**

**Content may include the following:**

- ✦ Memory
- ✦ Hard Drives
- ✦ CPU
- ✦ Cache memory

**Response Limits:**

The examinee selects, from four (4) response options, the one option that best completes the statement or answers the question. Distracters or wrong answers are response options that examinees with incomplete knowledge or skill would likely choose, but are generally plausible responses fitting into the content area.

**Sample Directions:**

Read the statement or question and, from the response options, select only one letter that represents the most correct or best answer.

**Sample Test Items**

1. Which statement is true regarding SCSI termination?

A. Only drives must be terminated.

B. Only adapters must be terminated.

C. No termination is necessary.

D. Both ends of the chain must be terminated.

Correct answer: D

2. External modems are usually connected to a(n)

A. SCSI port

B. LPT port

C. serial port

D. parallel port

Correct answer: C

3. The major advantage of using Flash ROM is

A. you can upgrade BIOS without replacing the chip

B. you do not have to re-load the operating system

C. hard drives are protected

D. memory capacity is increased

Correct answer: A

# Domain 2.0 Diagnosing and Troubleshooting

This domain requires the ability to apply knowledge relating to diagnosing and troubleshooting common module problems and system malfunctions. This includes knowledge of the symptoms relating to common problems.

## Content Limits

**2.1 Identify common symptoms and problems associated with each module and how to troubleshoot and isolate the problems.**

**Content may include the following:**

- ✦ Processor/Memory symptoms
- ✦ Mouse
- ✦ Floppy drive failures
- ✦ Parallel ports
- ✦ Hard Drives
- ✦ Sound Card/Audio
- ✦ Monitor/Video
- ✦ Motherboards
- ✦ Modems
- ✦ BIOS
- ✦ CMOS
- ✦ Power supply
- ✦ Slot covers
- ✦ POST audible/visual error codes
- ✦ Troubleshooting tools; for example, multimeter

**2.2 Identify basic troubleshooting procedures and good practices for eliciting problem symptoms from customers.**

**Content may include the following:**

✦ Troubleshooting/isolation/problem determination procedures

✦ Determine whether hardware or software problem

✦ Gather information from user regarding, for example, multimeter

- Customer environment
- Symptoms/error codes
- Situation when the problem occurred

## Response Limits:

The examinee selects, from four (4) response options, the one option that best completes the statement or answers the question. Distracters or wrong answers are response options that examinees with incomplete knowledge or skill would likely choose, but are generally plausible responses fitting into the content area.

## Sample Directions:

Read the statement or question and, from the response options, select only one letter that represents the most correct or best answer.

## Sample Test Items:

1. Installing a floppy cable backwards will

A. destroy the floppy drive

B. cause the controller card to fail and require replacement

C. cause the system to lock up

D. render the drive inoperable but cause no damage

Correct answer: D

2. You have a system with one EIDE drive. You connect a second EIDE drive to the same cable as the first drive, set it to slave, and apply power. The original drive auto-detects, but not the new one. What could be the problem?

A. The CMOS is loose.

B. The LBA or E-CHS is not active.

C. The master drive has a separate "single drive" setting.

D. There is no power to the master drive.

Correct answer: C

3. When an I/O device such as a serial port or modem is not enabled during startup, what is the cause?

A. corrupted memory

B. failed BIOS

C. lost clusters

D. monitor burnout

Correct answer: B

# Domain 3.0 Safety and Preventive Maintenance

This domain requires the knowledge of safety and preventive maintenance. With regard to safety, it includes the potential hazards to personnel and equipment when working with lasers, high voltage equipment, ESD, and items that require special disposal procedures that comply with environmental guidelines. With regard to preventive maintenance, this includes knowledge of preventive maintenance products, procedures, environmental hazards, and precautions when working on microcomputer systems.

## Content Limits

**3.1 Identify the purpose of various types of preventive maintenance products and procedures and when to use/perform them.**

**Content may include the following:**

- ✦ Liquid cleaning compounds
- ✦ Types of materials to clean contacts and connections
- ✦ Vacuum out systems, power supplies, fans

**3.2 Identify procedures and devices for protecting against environmental hazards.**

**Content may include the following:**

- ✦ UPS (uninterruptible power supply) and suppressors
- ✦ Determining the signs of power issues
- ✦ Proper methods of storage of components for future use

**3.3 Identify the potential hazards and proper safety procedures relating to lasers and high-voltage equipment.**

- ✦ Lasers
- ✦ High-voltage equipment
- ✦ Power supply
- ✦ CRT

**3.4 Identify items that require special disposal procedures that comply with environmental guidelines.**

**Content may include the following:**

- ✦ Batteries
- ✦ CRTs
- ✦ Toner kits/cartridges
- ✦ Chemical solvents and cans
- ✦ MSDS (Material Safety Data Sheet)

**3.5 Identify ESD (Electrostatic Discharge) precautions and procedures, including the use of ESD protection devices.**

**Content may include the following:**

- ✦ What ESD can do, how it may be apparent, or hidden
- ✦ Common ESD protection devices
- ✦ Situations that could present a danger or hazard

## Response Limits:

The examinee selects, from four (4) response options, the one option that best completes the statement or answers the question. Distracters or wrong answers are response options that examinees with incomplete knowledge or skill would likely choose, but are generally plausible responses fitting into the content area.

## Sample Directions:

Read the statement or question and, from the response options, select only one letter that represents the most correct or best answer.

## Sample Test Items:

1. When power is restored after a power outage, what should you do to protect your system?

A. Disconnect the CRT.

B. Close all programs.

C. Turn off the power.

D. Unplug all power cords.

Correct answer: D

2. What is the first step to safely service a laser unit?

A. Unplug the unit.

B. Check the paper feed.

C. Inspect the mechanism.

D. Check for power.

Correct answer: A

3. Electrostatic discharge occurs when objects

A. are ungrounded

B. have dissimilar electric potential

C. are in a humid environment

D. are removed from their protective bags

Correct answer: B

# Domain 4.0 Motherboard/Processors/Memory

This domain requires knowledge of specific terminology, facts, ways, and means of dealing with classifications, categories, and principles of motherboards, processors, and memory in microcomputer systems.

## Content Limits

**4.1 Distinguish between the popular CPU chips in terms of their basic characteristics.**

**Content may include the following:**

+ Popular CPU chips
+ Characteristics:
+ Physical size
+ Voltage
+ Speeds
+ On board cache or not
+ Sockets
+ Number of pins

**4.2 Identify the categories of RAM (Random Access Memory) terminology, their locations, and physical characteristics.**

**Content may include the following:**

+ Terminology:
  • EDO RAM (Extended Data Output RAM) DRAM
  • (Dynamic Random Access Memory)
  • SRAM (Static RAM)
  • VRAM (Video RAM)
  • WRAM (Windows Accelerator Card RAM)
+ Locations and physical characteristics:
  • Memory bank
  • Memory chips (8-bit, 16-bit, and 32-bit)
  • SIMMS (Single In-line Memory Module)
  • DIMMS (Dual In-line Memory Module)
  • Parity chips versus non-parity chips

**4.3 Identify the most popular type of motherboards, their components, and their architecture (for example, bus structures and power supplies).**

**Content may include the following:**

✦ Types of motherboards:
  - AT (Full and Baby)
  - ATX

✦ Components:
  - Communication ports
  - SIMM AND DIMM
  - Processor sockets
  - External cache memory (Level 2)

✦ Bus Architecture
  - ISA
  - EISA
  - PCI
  - USB (Universal Serial Bus)
  - VESA local bus (VL-Bus)
  - PC Card (PCMCIA)

✦ Basic compatibility guidelines

**4.4 Identify the purpose of CMOS (Complementary Metal-Oxide Semiconductor), what it contains and how to change its basic parameters.**

**Example Basic CMOS Settings:**

✦ Printer parallel portUni., bi-directional, disable/enable, ECP, EPP

✦ COM/serial portmemory address, interrupt request, disable

✦ Floppy driveenable/disable drive or boot, speed, density

✦ Hard drivesize and drive type

✦ Memoryparity, non-parity

✦ Boot sequence

✦ Date/Time

✦ Passwords

## Response Limits:

The examinee selects, from four (4) response options, the one option that best completes the statement or answers the question. Distracters or wrong answers are response options that examinees with incomplete knowledge or skill would likely choose, but are generally plausible responses fitting into the content area.

## Sample Directions:

Read the statement or question and, from the response options, select only one letter that represents the most correct or best answer.

## Sample Test Items:

1. MMX capability enhances

A. caching speed

B. floppy disk transfer

C. multimedia

D. media mix execution

Correct answer: C

2. One reason for an incorrect time/date setting could be

A. low power supply voltage

B. low CMOS battery

C. low disk space

D. a bad UPS

Correct answer: B

3. The following drive type parameters can be configured in CMOS EXCEPT

A. tracks

B. cylinders

C. seek time

D. number of heads

Correct answer: C

# Domain 5.0 Printers

This domain requires knowledge of basic types of printers, basic concepts, printer components, how they work, how they print onto a page, paper path, care and service techniques, and common problems.

## Content Limits

**5.1 Identify basic concepts, printer operations and printer components.**

**Content may include the following:**

- ✦ Types of Printers
  - Laser
  - Inkjet
  - Dot Matrix
- ✦ Paper feeder mechanisms

**5.2 Identify care and service techniques and common problems with primary printer types.**

**Content may include the following:**

- ✦ Feed and output
- ✦ Errors
- ✦ Paper jam
- ✦ Print quality
- ✦ Safety precautions
- ✦ Preventive maintenance

**5.3 Identify the types of printer connections and configurations.**

**Content may include the following:**

- ✦ Parallel
- ✦ Serial
- ✦ Network

## Response Limits:

The examinee selects, from four (4) response options, the one option that best completes the statement or answers the question. Distracters or wrong answers are response options that examinees with incomplete knowledge or skill would likely choose, but are generally plausible responses fitting into the content area.

## Sample Directions:

Read the statement or question and, from the response options, select only one letter that represents the most correct or best answer.

## Sample Test Items:

1. On a laser printer, the laser beam

A. burns the toner to the paper

B. fuses the image to the transfer corona

C. changes the charge on the photosensitive drum

D. provides the main power to the primary corona

Correct answer: C

2. A laser printer keeps getting a "MEM Overflow" error. Which of the following is NOT a possible fix?

A. Reduce RET.

B. Replace the printer's RAM.

C. Add more RAM to the printer.

D. Reduce the print resolution.

Correct answer: B

3. Which type of connector is used for a parallel connection on a printer?

A. Centronics (36-pin) D-Shell

B. 25-pin (DB-25) male

C. 25-pin (DB-25) female

D. 9-pin (DB-9) male

Correct answer: A

# Domain 6.0 Portable Systems

This domain requires knowledge of portable computers and their unique components and problems.

## Content Limits

**6.1 Identify the unique components of portable systems and their unique problems.**

**Content may include the following:**

- ✦ Battery
- ✦ LCD
- ✦ AC adapter
- ✦ Docking stations
- ✦ Hard Drive
- ✦ Types I, II, III cards
- ✦ Network cards
- ✦ Memory

## Response Limits:

The examinee selects, from four (4) response options, the one option that best completes the statement or answers the question. Distracters or wrong answers are response options that examinees with incomplete knowledge or skill would likely choose, but are generally plausible responses fitting into the content area.

## Sample Directions:

Read the statement or question and, from the response options, select only one letter that represents the most correct or best answer.

## Sample Test Item:

1. Type I PC Card (PCMCIA) is

A. the thinnest and measures 3.5mm in thickness

B. the thickest and measures 10.5mm in thickness

C. the same size as other cards but configured differently

D. not compatible with new laptops

Correct answer: A

2. A laptop has a black border on the screen and the screen does not fill the entire LCD. This could indicate

A. a bad battery

B. incorrect BIOS

C. incorrect display settings

D. insufficient system RAM

Correct answer: C

3. Which term refers to a PC Card (PCMCIA) you can remove and replace without powering off?

A. card services

B. hot-swappable

C. socket services

D. Plug and Play

Correct answer: B

# Domain 7.0 Basic Networking

This domain requires knowledge of basic network concepts and terminology, ability to determine whether a computer is networked, knowledge of procedures for swapping and configuring network interface cards, and knowledge of the ramifications of repairs when a computer is networked.

## Content Limits

**7.1 Identify basic networking concepts, including how a network works.**

**Content may include the following:**

- ✦ Network access
- ✦ Protocol
- ✦ Network Interface Cards
- ✦ Full-duplex
- ✦ CablingTwisted Pair, Coaxial, Fiber Optic
- ✦ Ways to network a PC

**7.2 Identify procedures for swapping and configuring network interface cards.**

**7.3 Identify the ramifications of repairs on the network.**

**Content may include the following:**

- ✦ Reduced bandwidth
- ✦ Loss of data
- ✦ Network slowdown

## Response Limits:

The examinee selects, from four (4) response options, the one option that best completes the statement or answers the question. Distracters or wrong answers are response options that examinees with incomplete knowledge or skill would likely choose, but are generally plausible responses fitting into the content area.

## Sample Directions:

Read the statement or question and, from the response options, select only one letter that represents the most correct or best answer.

## Sample Test Items:

1. A 10BaseT cable is normally connected to a computer with a(n)

A. BNC connector

B. TX connector

C. RJ-11 connector

D. RJ-45 connector

Correct answer: D

2. An improperly configured network interface card could

A. prohibit the PC from powering up

B. prohibit network access

C. damage a sound card

D. cause screen flicker

Correct answer: B

3. The IRQ for a PCI network interface card is NOT configured with

A. CMOS

B. BIOS

C. jumpers

D. the operating system

Correct answer: C

# Domain 8.0 Customer Satisfaction

This domain requires knowledge of — and sensitivity around — those behaviors that contribute to satisfying customers. More specifically, these behaviors include such things as: the quality of technician-customer personal interactions; the way a technician conducts him or herself professionally within the customer's business setting; the credibility and confidence projected by the technician that, in turn, engenders customer confidence; the resilience, friendliness, and efficiency that can unexpectedly delight the customer above and beyond the solving of a technical problem. This domain is NOT a test of specific company policies or procedures.

## Content Limits

**8.1 Differentiate effective from ineffective behaviors as these contribute to the maintenance or achievement of customer satisfaction.**

**Content may include the following:**

- ✦ Communicating and listening (face-to-face or over the phone)
- ✦ Interpreting verbal and nonverbal cues
- ✦ Responding appropriately to the customer's technical level
- ✦ Establishing personal rapport with the customer
- ✦ Professional conduct; for example, punctuality, accountability
- ✦ Helping and guiding a customer with problem descriptions
- ✦ Responding to and closing a service call
- ✦ Handling complaints and upset customers, conflict avoidance, and resolution
- ✦ Showing empathy and flexibility
- ✦ Sharing the customer's sense of urgency

## Response Limits:

The examinee selects, from four (4) response options, the one option that best completes the statement or answers the question. Distracters or wrong answers are response options that examinees with incomplete knowledge would likely choose, but are generally plausible responses fitting into the content area.

## Sample Directions:

For each item below, choose the one BEST answer. The overriding objective of this test is to test your knowledge of and sensitivity to behaviors that promote customer satisfaction. Base your choices solely on what would "please the customer" and NOT on any particular company or service organization's policy.

## Sample Test Items:

### Item 1.

*Technician:* "Please take a moment and tell me in your own words what happened. What's the problem?"

*Customer:* "Thanks, I'd welcome the opportunity. Well, I reached over to turn the PC on and it just wouldn't start. It seemed like..."

*Technician:* "Wait! Back up just a minute! Did you have to stand up or move your chair when you reached over to power up the PC? Is it possible that your electrical cord was exposed and that you may have accidentally unplugged it with your foot? Where was your foot in relation to the power strip? This problem is common among inexperienced users. You folks haven't had time yet to learn to be comfortable with the equipment. As a rule, inexperienced customers tend to be overly clumsy or timid. Why don't we check the cord"

*Customer:* "As I was saying, it seemed like the power supply was acting up again. You should probably know that I'm an electrical engineer with a bit more experience in these matters than you seem to indicate. Now, with your permission, I'll continue..."

1. From the options listed below, select the one answer that BEST exemplifies how the technician should have handled this situation to increase customer satisfaction.

A. Allowed the customer to explain the problem fully before exploring specific causes.

B. Not assumed that the cord was unplugged since the symptom could be caused by other problems.

C. Asked the customer to review the troubleshooting guide for common problems before calling for help.

D. Avoided abrupt orders like "back up!" in favor of more polite expressions such as "may I interrupt?"

Correct answer: A

2. The BEST way for a technician to communicate with a customer is to speak

A. rapidly without interruption so that the customer's time is not wasted

B. very slowly, focusing on the message so that the discussion does not get off-track

C. excitedly with dramatic hand gestures in order to keep the customer's attention

D. clearly and at a pace that accommodates the customers ability to understand

Correct answer: D

# DOS/Windows Objectives

## FINAL REVISION (as of July 17, 1998)

## A+ DOS/Windows Service Technician Examination Blueprint

**NOTE:** This is the FINAL revision of the A+ DOS/Windows Service Technician exam blueprint. This document was produced after the final technical and psychometric review of the item pool following the beta-testing period. This document is reflective of the topics and technologies which appear as part of the A+ DOS/Windows Service Technician exam.

### Introduction

For A+ Certification, the examinee must pass both this examination and the A+ Core Service Technician examination. This examination measures essential operating system competencies for a break/fix microcomputer hardware service technician with six months of on-the-job experience. The examinee must demonstrate basic knowledge of DOS, Windows 3.x, and Windows 95 for installing, configuring, upgrading, troubleshooting, and repairing microcomputer systems.

The skills and knowledge measured by this examination are derived from an industry-wide job task analysis and validated through a worldwide survey of 5,000 A+ Certified professionals. The results of the worldwide survey were used in weighting the domains and ensuring that the weighting is representative of the relative importance of that content to the job requirements of a service technician with six months on-the-job experience. The results of the job task analysis and survey can be found in the following reports:

✦ *CompTIA A+ Certification Technical and Customer Satisfaction Job Task Analysis: Phase 1 Report (June 27, 1997)*

✦ *CompTIA A+ Certification Technical and Customer Satisfaction Job Task Analysis: Phase 2 Report Survey Results (November 10, 1997)*

This examination blueprint includes weighting, test objectives, and example content. Example topics and concepts are included to clarify the test objectives; they should not be construed as a comprehensive listing of the content of this examination.

The table below lists the domains measured by this examination and the approximate extent to which they are represented.

| *Domain*<br>*% of Examination (approximately)* |
| --- |
| 1.0 Function, Structure, Operation, and File Management |
| 30% |
| 2.0 Memory Management |
| 10% |
| 3.0 Installation, Configuration and Upgrading |
| 30% |
| 4.0 Diagnosing and Troubleshooting |
| 20% |
| 5.0 Networks |
| 10% |
| Total |
| 100.00% |

Approximately 75% of the test items will relate to Windows 95 and the remaining 25% will relate to DOS and Windows 3.x.

# Domain 1.0 Function, Structure Operation, and File Management

This domain requires knowledge of DOS, Windows 3.x, and Windows 95 operating systems in terms of its functions and structure, for managing files and directories, and running programs. It also includes navigating through the operating system from DOS command line prompts and Windows procedures for accessing and retrieving information.

## Content Limits
### 1.1 Identify the operating system's functions, structure, and major system files.

**Content may include the following:**

✦ Functions of DOS, Windows 3.x and Windows 95

✦ Major components of DOS, Windows 3.x and Windows 95

✦ Contrasts between Windows 3.x and Windows 95

✦ Major system files: what they are, where they are located, how they are used and what they contain:

✦ System, Configuration, and User Interface files

✦ DOS

- Autoexec.bat
- Config.sys
- Io.sys
- Ansi.sys
- Msdos.sys
- Emm386.exe
- HIMEM.SYS
- Command.com (internal DOS commands)

✦ Windows 3.x

- Win.ini
- System.ini
- User.exe
- Gdi.exe
- win.ini
- Win.com
- Progman.ini
- progMAN.exe
- Krnlxxx.exe

✦ Windows 95

- Io.sys
- Msdos.sys

- Command.com
- regedit.exe
- System.dat
- User.dat

**1.2 Identify ways to navigate the operating system and how to get to needed technical information.**

**Content may include the following:**

- ✦ Procedures (e.g., menu or icon-driven) for navigating through DOS to perform such things as locating, accessing, and retrieving information
- ✦ Procedures for navigating through the Windows 3.x/Windows 95 operating system, accessing, and retrieving information

**1.3 Identify basic concepts and procedures for creating, viewing, and managing files and directories, including procedures for changing file attributes and the ramifications of those changes (for example, security issues).**

**Content may include the following:**

- ✦ File attributes
- ✦ File naming conventions
- ✦ Command syntax
- ✦ Read Only, Hidden, System, and Archive attributes

**1.4 Identify the procedures for basic disk management.**

**Content may include the following:**

- ✦ Using disk management utilities
- ✦ Backing up
- ✦ Formatting
- ✦ Partitioning
- ✦ Defragmenting
- ✦ ScanDisk
- ✦ FAT32
- ✦ File allocation tables (FAT)
- ✦ Virtual file allocation tables (VFAT)

## Response Limits:

The examinee selects, from four (4) response options, the one option that best completes the statement or answers the question. Distracters or wrong answers are response options that examinees with incomplete knowledge or skill would likely choose, but are generally plausible responses fitting into the content area.

## Sample Directions:

Read the statement or question and, from the response options, select only one letter that represents the most correct or best answer.

## Sample Test Items:

1. Which two files make up the Registry in Windows 95?

A. CONFIG.SYS and AUTOEXEC.BAT

B. COMMAND.COM and CONFIG.SYS

C. MSDOS.SYS and IO.SYS

D. USER.DAT and SYSTEM.DAT

Correct answer: D

2. Which file starts programs automatically when Windows 3.1 starts?

A. WIN.INI

B. SETUP.INI

C. SYSTEM.INI

D. SYSTEM.DA0

Correct answer: A

3. The .PIF files are used by Windows to support _____ programs.

A. Windows

B. DOS

C. protected-mode

D. multitasking

Correct answer: B

# Domain 2.0 Memory Management

This domain requires knowledge of the types of memory used by DOS and Windows, and the potential for memory address conflicts.

## Content Limits

**2.1 Differentiate between types of memory.**

**Content may include the following:**

- ✦ Conventional
- ✦ Extended/upper memory
- ✦ High memory
- ✦ Expanded memory
- ✦ Virtual memory

**2.2 Identify typical memory conflict problems and how to optimize memory use.**

**Content may include the following:**

- ✦ What a memory conflict is
- ✦ How it happens
- ✦ When to employ utilities
- ✦ System Monitor
- ✦ General Protection Fault
- ✦ Illegal operations occurrences
- ✦ MemMaker or other optimization utilities
- ✦ Himem.sys
- ✦ SMARTDRV
- ✦ Use of expanded memory blocks (using Emm386.exe)

## Response Limits:

The examinee selects, from four (4) response options, the one option that best completes the statement or answers the question. Distracters or wrong answers are response options that examinees with incomplete knowledge or skill would likely choose, but are generally plausible responses fitting into the content area.

## Sample Directions:

Read the statement or question and, from the response options, select only one letter that represents the most correct or best answer.

## Sample Test Items:

1. The memory addresses from 0 to 640KB are known as

A. common memory

B. high memory

C. expanded memory

D. conventional memory

Correct answer: D

2. Your customer's computer has two hard drives. Drive 1 is the C: drive; drive 2 is the D: drive. Windows 95 and all applications are installed on the C: drive. Drive D: is mostly free space. The virtual memory settings are set to the default. How can you optimize your customer's computer via virtual memory?

A. Virtual memory settings are best kept as default.

B. Move the virtual memory swap file to the D: drive.

C. Move the virtual memory to the D: drive by copying the virtual memory swap file

D. Remove the virtual memory swap file, reboot, and let Windows 95 add the swap file automatically.

Correct answer: B

3. Your customer has a laptop computer with an 8-speed CD-ROM and 24MB of RAM. The optimize access pattern for CD-ROM is currently set to "Quad-Speed or Higher." How can you make sure the CD-ROM file system performance is optimized?

A. Leave the setting as it is.

B. Change the setting to "No read ahead."

C. Change the setting to "Full read ahead."

D. Change the setting to "16MB of RAM or higher."

Correct answer: A

# Domain 3.0 Installation, Configuration, and Upgrading

This domain requires knowledge of installing, configuring and upgrading DOS, Windows 3.x, and Windows 95. This includes knowledge of system boot sequences.

## Content Limits

**3.1 Identify the procedures for installing DOS, Windows 3.x, and Windows 95, and for bringing the software to a basic operational level.**

Content may include the following:

+ Partition

+ Format drive

+ Run appropriate set up utility

+ Loading drivers

**3.2 Identify steps to perform an operating system upgrade.**

Content may include the following:

+ Upgrading from DOS to Windows 95

+ Upgrading from Windows 3.x to Windows 95

**3.3 Identify the basic system boot sequences, and alternative ways to boot the system software, including the steps to create an emergency boot disk with utilities installed.**

Content may include the following:

+ Files required to boot

+ Creating emergency boot disk

+ Startup disk

+ Safe Mode

+ DOS mode

**3.4 Identify procedures for loading/adding device drivers and the necessary software for certain devices.**

**Content may include the following:**

✦ Windows 3.x procedures

✦ Windows 95 Plug and Play

**3.5 Identify the procedures for changing options, configuring, and using the Windows printing subsystem.**

**3.6 Identify the procedures for installing and launching typical Windows and non-Windows applications.**

## Response Limits:

The examinee selects, from four (4) response options, the one option that best completes the statement or answers the question. Distracters or wrong answers are response options that examinees with incomplete knowledge or skill would likely choose, but are generally plausible responses fitting into the content area.

## Sample Directions:

Read the statement or question and, from the response options, select only one letter that represents the most correct or best answer.

## Sample Test Items:

1. A(n) _____ partition must exist on the hard drive in order to install Windows 95.

A. CDFS

B. HPFS

C. FAT

D. NTFS

Correct answer: C

2. COMMAND.COM contains which type of DOS commands?

A. internal

B. external

C. real mode

D. standard mode

Correct answer: A

3. In Windows 95, Plug and Play must use _____ virtual device drivers called VxDs.

A. 8-bit

B. 16-bit

C. 32-bit

D. 64-bit

Correct answer: C

# Domain 4.0 Diagnosing and Troubleshooting

This domain requires the ability to apply knowledge to diagnose and troubleshoot common problems relating to DOS, Windows 3.x, and Windows 95. This includes understanding normal operation and symptoms relating to common problems.

## Content Limits

**4.1 Recognize and interpret the meaning of common error codes and startup messages from the boot sequence, and identify steps to correct the problems.**

**Content may include the following:**

- ✦ Safe Mode
- ✦ Incorrect DOS version
- ✦ No operating system found
- ✦ Error in CONFIG.SYS line XX
- ✦ Bad or missing Command.com
- ✦ Himem.sys not loaded
- ✦ Missing or corrupt Himem.sys
- ✦ Swap file
- ✦ A device referenced in SYSTEM.INI could not be found

**4.2 Recognize Windows-specific printing problems and identify the procedures for correcting them.**

**Content may include the following:**

- ✦ Print spool is stalled
- ✦ Incorrect/incompatible driver for print

**4.3 Recognize common problems and determine how to resolve them.**

**Content may include the following:**

- ✦ Common problems
  - • General Protection Faults
  - • Illegal operation
  - • Invalid working directory
  - • System lock up
  - • Option will not function
  - • Application will not start or load
  - • Cannot log on to network
- ✦ DOS and Windows-based utilities
  - • ScanDisk
  - • Device manager
  - • ATTRIB.EXE
  - • EXTRACT.EXE
  - • Defrag.exe
  - • Edit.com
  - • Fdisk.exe
  - • MSD.EXE
  - • Mem.exe
  - • SYSEDIT.EXE

**4.4 Identify concepts relating to viruses and virus types their danger, their symptoms, sources of viruses, how they infect, how to protect against them, and how to identify and remove them.**

**Content may include the following:**

- ✦ What they are
- ✦ Sources
- ✦ How to determine presence

## Response Limits:

The examinee selects, from four (4) response options, the one option that best completes the statement or answers the question. Distracters or wrong answers are response options that examinees with incomplete knowledge or skill would likely choose, but are generally plausible responses fitting into the content area.

## Sample Directions:

Read the statement or question and, from the response options, select only one letter that represents the most correct or best answer.

## Sample Test Items:

1. What is one way to recover from the error message "No operating system found" when starting Windows 95?

A. Insert a CD-ROM with the system files and run the SYS command.

B. Reboot on a floppy with system files and use the FORMAT C: /F command.

C. Insert the Windows 95 CD-ROM and use the FORMAT C: /F command.

D. Reboot on a floppy with system files and use the SYS C: command.

Correct answer: D

2. During a Windows 3.x boot process, the error "Bad or Missing HIMEM.SYS" is displayed. This means HIMEM.SYS is not loaded in

A. WIN.INI

B. CONFIG.SYS

C. SYSTEM.INI

D. AUTOEXEC.BAT

Correct answer: B

3. In order to modify the Registry, which tool must first be used?

A. DEFRAG

B. REGMOD

C. FDISK

D. REGEDIT

Correct answer: D

# Domain 5.0 Networks

This domain requires knowledge of network capabilities of DOS and Windows, and how to connect to networks, including what the Internet is about, its capabilities, basic concepts relating to Internet access, and generic procedures for system setup.

## Content Limits

**5.1 Identify the networking capabilities of DOS and Windows including procedures for connecting to the network.**

Content may include the following:

- ✦ Sharing disk drives
- ✦ Sharing print and file services
- ✦ Network type and network card

**5.2 Identify concepts and capabilities relating to the Internet and basic procedures for setting up a system for Internet access.**

Content may include the following:

- ✦ TCP/IP
- ✦ E-mail
- ✦ HTML
- ✦ HTTP://
- ✦ FTP
- ✦ Domain Names (Web sites)
- ✦ ISP
- ✦ Dial-up access

## Response Limits:

The examinee selects, from four (4) response options, the one option that best completes the statement or answers the question. Distracters or wrong answers are response options that examinees with incomplete knowledge or skill would likely choose, but are generally plausible responses fitting into the content area.

## Sample Directions:

Read the statement or question and, from the response options, select only one letter that represents the most correct or best answer.

## Sample Test Items:

1. How do you connect to a shared printer?

A. From Control Panel select Add New Hardware and choose Network Printer.

B. From the Printer folder double-click Add Printer and choose Network Printer.

C. From Explorer choose Connect to Network Printer.

D. From Control Panel choose Connect to Network Printer.

Correct answer: B

2. In a Windows 95 system, which tool will display the type of network card that is installed?

A. Device Manager

B. Internet

C. Explorer

D. File Manager

Correct answer: A

3. Which protocol does the Internet use?

A. DLC

B. IPX/SPX

C. TCP/IP

D. NetBEUI

Correct answer: C

✦     ✦     ✦

# Index